Pitreavie Primary School

Presented to

Andrew Forrester

*as a memento of the years
spent in Primary Education.
Best wishes for the future.*

June 2000

CHAMBERS

School
DICTIONARY

CHAMBERS

School DICTIONARY

edited by
Imogen Kerr
and
Megan Thomson

CHAMBERS

CHAMBERS
An imprint of Chambers Harrap Publishers Ltd
7 Hopetoun Crescent
Edinburgh, EH7 4AY

Reprinted 1998 (Twice), 1999

A CIP catalogue record for this book is
available from the British Library.

ISBN 0-550-10716-9

Typeset by Selwood Systems, Midsomer Norton
Printed and bound in Great Britain by
Caledonian International Book Manufacturing Ltd, Glasgow

Contents

Teacher's preface

We have written this entirely new *Chambers School Dictionary* for use by school pupils aged 11 to 14. It contains all the essential elements of an adult dictionary, whilst giving priority to a clear layout and avoiding all but the most familiar abbreviations in the editorial explanations.

The dictionary will provide your pupils with more than just definitions. Where a word is likely to be mispronounced, straightforward pronunciation help is given, showing clearly where to place the main stress and how to pronounce the syllables. This is particularly useful in words like *impotent* and *lamentable* where the stress has shifted from its place in the base-word. At selected entries, pupils will find banks containing synonyms or near-synonyms, intended to provide them with a source of possible alternatives to words which they might be tempted to over-use. Examples of entries with these 'word-banks' are *clean, dangerous, walk...* and, of course, *nice*! We have included usage notes at various entries to help with confusables, spelling and grammar – taking care to provide not only warnings but also, wherever possible, some way of remembering the correct usage. Word histories (etymologies) have been shown at certain entries, following the rationale that they should be either interesting (that is, provoking interest in the way words enter the language, or how their forms and meanings can develop over the centuries), or that they should be useful (providing some extra information to clarify the way words are linked, or to aid differentiation between words).

At the end of the book, you will find a guide to the main parts of speech. We hope that this will provide pupils with a useful reference tool, whilst giving you a structure which you can work with in the classroom.

The *Chambers School Dictionary* is full of ideas for language exploration and study. Wherever you see the 🖉 icon, you will find suggestions for activities which will encourage pupils to develop their general awareness of language, to write, or to use their dictionary for a specific task.

We would urge you to first of all take some time to cover the *Using Your Dictionary* section in class. This section guides pupils round the structure of an entry, showing them where to find the information they need, and enabling them to use their dictionary with confidence. It is followed by a short quiz to give them a chance to practise their dictionary skills.

The Editors

Using your dictionary

• Finding what you're looking for

Guide-words
The entries in this dictionary are in alphabetical order. At the top of each page, you will see two 'guide-words':

The word on the left is the headword for the first entry you will find on this page

The word on the right is the headword for the last entry you will find on this page

Sense numbers
If a word has more than one meaning, each new definition is marked by a sense (or meaning) number:

blood *noun* 1 the red liquid which flows in the bodies of human beings and animals 2 someone's descent or parentage: *royal blood*

Phrasal verbs and idioms
Phrasal verbs and idioms come at the end of the main entry:

care *noun* 1 close attention 2 worry, anxiety 3 protection, keeping: *in my care* □ *verb* to be concerned or worried: *I don't care what happens now* □ **care for 1** to look after 2 to feel affection or liking for □ **care of** at the house of (often written as **c/o**)□ **take care** to be careful; watch out

Related words
Most words in this dictionary have a separate entry to themselves. However, some words that are derived from other words can be easily understood from their form, and don't need definitions. In such cases, they may be included at the end of the entry with their part of speech but no separate definition:

banish *verb* 1 to order to leave (a country) 2 to drive away (doubts, fears *etc*) □ **banishment** *noun*

• Grammar

Parts of speech
The part of speech (eg noun, verb, adjective) is given in *italic* print after the headword:

axiom *noun* a truth, an accepted principle

If the headword can be used as more than one part of speech, the entry is divided up to show this:

doze *verb* to sleep lightly □ *noun* a light, short sleep

Singular nouns/plural nouns
Some nouns occur only in a singular form, and always take a singular verb. These nouns are labelled *noun singular*:

Some nouns occur only in a plural form, and always take a plural verb. These nouns are labelled *noun plural*:

civics *noun singular* the study of people's duties as citizens

catacombs *noun plural* an underground burial place

Plurals
The plurals of nouns are occasionally given – sometimes with pronunciation – if there is a possibility that they might be formed incorrectly:

deer *noun (plural* **deer***)* an animal with antlers in the male, such as the reindeer

Main forms of verbs
The main forms of a verb are given if the verb does not follow the normal pattern, look*s*, look*ing*, look*ed* OR search*es*, search*ing*, search*ed*. When the forms are given, they appear in the following order: present tense 3rd person (he/she/it); present participle ('-*ing*' form); past tense 3rd person (he/she/it); past participle (if different from the past tense):

arise ⇨ arise*s*, aris*ing*, ar*ose*, aris*en*

If the past tense is the same as the past participle, it is not repeated:

catch *verb* ⇨ catch*es*, catch*ing*, caught

Comparatives and superlatives of adjectives and adverbs
If the comparative or superlative is formed in an unusual way OR if you need to double the final consonant etc, these forms are given in a shaded box:

far *adjective* ⇨ farth*er*, farth*est*

hot ⇨ hott*er*, hott*est*

• Extra help and information

Pronunciation
Where pronunciation help is given, it comes in brackets at the start of an entry or section:

dilatory *(pronounced* **dil***-at-o-*ri*)* *adjective* slow to act, inclined to delay

Examples
Examples of the word in use are often given in *italic* print after the definition:

comparative *adjective* **1** judged by comparing with something else; relative: *comparative improvement* **2** near to being: *a comparative stranger* **3** *grammar* the degree of an adjective or adverb between positive and superlative, *eg* black*er*, *better*, *more* courageous

Register
Differences in style of language, eg formal language, poetic language or slang, are called differences in register.

The register labels used in this dictionary are *formal*, *informal* and *slang*. These tell you whether it is appropriate to use the word or phrase in a particular situation. Register, where marked, is given in *italics* at the start of an entry or section:

ablutions *noun plural*, formal washing of the body

ex *noun*, informal a former husband, wife or lover

chick *noun* **1** a chicken **2** slang a girl, a young woman

forward *adjective* **1** advancing: *a forward movement* **2** near or at the front **3** of fruit: ripe earlier than usual **4** too quick to speak or act, pert □ *verb* **1** to help towards success: *forwarded his plans* **2** to send on (letters) □ *adverb* forwards

Usage notes
These are to help you use English more effectively, and to warn you against making common mistakes:

Do not confuse with: foreword. It is helpful to remember that forWARD is an indication of direction, similar to backWARDs and homeWARDs

Word origins and language notes
Straightforward word origins are signalled by a clock ☉:

techno- or **techn-** *prefix* **1** forms words relating to the art or craft involved in doing something: *technical* **2** of or relating to technology

☉ Comes from Greek *techne* meaning 'skill'

Word histories which tell a story appear in a tinted box:

aftermath *noun* the bad results of something: *the aftermath of the election*

Originally a second crop coming after the main harvest

Alternative words
These are intended to give you ideas for words which you might consider using in place of the headword of this entry. In this way, you can add variety to your writing. Never use a word which is unfamiliar to you without first looking it up at its entry in the dictionary!:

correct *verb* **1** to remove errors from **2** to set right **3** to punish □ *adjective* **1** having no errors **2** true **3** suitable and acceptable

▤ **Alternative words**: (verb, meaning 1) emend; (verb, meaning 2) rectify, remedy, redress, amend

Opposites
Direct opposites of words are occasionally included:

convict *verb* to declare or prove that someone is guilty □ *noun* someone found guilty of a crime and sent to prison

▤ **Opposite**: (verb) acquit

• Suggestions for language activities

These are signalled by a pen ✎. You will find them at some entries in the dictionary. If you finish a class activity before the others, look for the symbol ✎, and get your thinking-cap on! (To start you off, you'll find two activities in letter P).

Dictionary Quiz

Finding what you're looking for

1 Without looking at your dictionary, name three other words which
you would expect to find on the pages with guide-words **abhorrence**
to **abridgement**, **EEC** to **eject** and **sensibility** to **seraphic**.

2 As well as being a small animal, **mouse** has a special meaning in
computing. Find this special meaning in the entry for **mouse**. What is
its sense number?

3 What are the adjectives from the nouns (a) **anomaly**, (b) **elephant**, and
(c) **climate**?

Meanings

4 What would (a) a **psephologist**, (b) a **numismatist** and (c) an **entomologist**
be interested in?

5 What would (a) an **agoraphobic** person and (b) a **hydrophobic** person
suffer from?

6 If you describe someone as **pulchritudinous**, what do you think of their
appearance? What sort of language would you be using with this
word in it?

Grammar

7 (a) Give each of the following words its part of speech: **pint**, **costly**,
AZT, **me**, **for**, **although**, **enjoy**, **soon**. Now check in the dictionary
to see if you were right.

  (b) How many parts of speech do you think the following words have:
master, **ship**, **quick**, **glimmer**, **over**, **contact**? Now check in the
dictionary to see if you were right.

8 What is the plural of the following nouns: **criterion**, **court-martial**,
bacillus, **corpus**, **calypso**?

9 Insert the correct prepositions in the following phrases:
the elegant simplicity peculiar _____ *Rennie Mackintosh's work*
His behaviour is suggestive _____ *mental illness*
She is prone _____ *tantrums*

Spelling

10 Correct the spelling mistakes in this passage:

> *I am, of course, refering to the suggestion you made earlier. With plenty of practise, you're playing could be grately improved. Would you consider traveling to Edinburgh for lessons?*

11 Give the superlative form of the adjective **busy** and make up a sentence using it.

12 Choose the correct spelling of the word in brackets:
> *I enclose two (complementary/complimentary) tickets for the show.*
> *My secretary won't ask awkward questions; she's very (discreet/ discrete).*
> *It's impossible to get a (straight/ strait) answer from him.*
> *Her plan was quite (ingenuous/ ingenious).*
> *He was (born/ borne) in India.*

Pronunciation

13 Which is the stressed syllable in the words **irrevocable, impotent** and **lamentable**?

14 Which is the silent letter in **fracas**?

Register

15 Which of the words in the following sentences would you *not* use in a formal situation? What word might you use instead?
> *Do you suppose she's brainy enough to pass the exam?*
> *His doctor's advised him to see a shrink.*
> *They're too chicken to swim in the river.*
> *The steak was served with broccoli, carrots and spuds.*
> *Chuck the ball over here, would you!*

Other information

16 **Polyandry** is made up of two Greek word-parts, **poly-** and **andr-**. It is related to the word **polygamy**. Can you work out what it means?

17 What is the opposite of a **chronic** illness?

Answers

1 Check pages 2, 162 and 475 in your dictionary to see if your words are there. **2** sense number 3 **3** (a) anomalous, (b) elephantine, (c) climatic **4** (a) elections and voting trends, (b) coins, (c) insects **5** (a) a fear of open spaces, (b) a fear of water **6** beautiful; formal language **8** criteria, courts-martial, bacilli, corpora, calypsos **9** to, of, to **10** referring, practice, your, greatly, travelling **11** busiest **12** complimentary, discreet, straight, ingenious, born **13** '-rev-', 'im-', 'lam-' **14** s **15** brainy (intelligent/clever), shrink (psychiatrist), chicken (cowardly), spuds (potatoes), chuck (throw) **16** the practice of having several husbands or male mates at the same time **17** an acute illness

Pronunciation

This dictionary provides help in cases where the pronunciation of a word may not be obvious. Pronunciations are shown in a way which is designed to be immediately understandable. The syllables are separated by hyphens, and the stressed syllable (the syllable pronounced with most emphasis) is shown in thick black type. Any vowel or group of vowels which is pronounced as a neutral 'uh' (or *schwa*) sound is shown in italic type. Pronunciations are given in brackets, signalled by the word *pronounced*, for example:

obligatory (*pronounced* *o*b-**lig**-*a*t-*o*-ri)

A few sounds are difficult to show in normal English letters. The following list is a guide to the way these sounds are shown in pronunciation sections:

Consonants

'ng' shows the sound as in ri**ng**
'ngg' shows the sound as in fi**ng**er
'th' shows the sound as in **th**in
'dh' shows the sound as in **th**is
'sz' shows the sound as in deci**s**ion, mea**s**ure
'kh' shows the sound as in lo**ch**

Vowels

'uw' shows the sound as in b**oo**k, p**u**t
'oo' shows the sound as in m**oo**n, l**o**se
'ah' shows the sound as in **ar**m, d**a**nce
'aw' shows the sound as in s**aw**, ign**o**re
'er' shows the sound as in f**er**n, b**ir**d, h**ear**d
'ei' shows the sound as in d**ay**, s**a**me
'ai' shows the sound as in m**y**, p**i**ne
'oi' shows the sound as in b**oy**, s**oi**l
'oh' shows the sound as in b**o**ne, n**o**, th**ough**
'ow' shows the sound as in n**ow**, b**ough**

Sound-combinations

'eer' shows the sound as in n**ear**, b**eer**, t**ier**
'eir" shows the sound as in h**air**, c**are**, th**ere**
'oor' shows the sound as in p**oor**, s**ure**
'air' shows the sound as in f**ire**, h**igher**

Abbreviations used in the dictionary

Austral	Australian	*N*	North
cap	capital letter	*orig*	originally
comp	comparative	*S*	South
E	East	*superl*	superlative
eg	for example	*TV*	television
etc	and so on, and other things	*UK*	United Kingdom
		US(A)	United States (of America)
ie	that is	*W*	West

Labels used in the dictionary

All abbreviated labels used in the dictionary are given below; others are used in full (eg *architecture*, *golf* or *music*):

Austral	used in Australian English
Brit	used generally in British English, not in US or Australian *etc*
euphem	euphemism
formal	used mainly in formal English
informal	common and generally acceptable in spoken or informal English
Irish	used in Irish English
maths	mathematics
med	medicine
offensive	a word which is offensive to the person addressed or to someone referred to
old	no longer commonly used in modern English
photog	photography
S African	used in South African English
Scot	used in Scottish English
slang	less generally acceptable, even in informal English, than informal
taboo	not generally acceptable, even in informal use
trademark	a word which is registered as a trademark
US	used in US (and often Canadian) English

Aa

a or **an** *adjective* **1** one: *a knock at the door* **2** any: *an ant has six legs* **3** in, to or for each: *four times a day*

> The form *a* is used before words beginning with a consonant, *eg* knock; *an* is used before words beginning with a vowel, *eg* ant

aback *adverb*: **taken aback** surprised

abacus (*pronounced* **ab**-*a*-k*u*s) *noun* (*plural* **abacuses**) a frame with columns of beads for counting

abandon *verb* **1** to leave, without meaning to return to **2** to give up (an idea *etc*)
□ *noun* lack of inhibition: *dancing with gay abandon*

> **abandon** *verb* ⇨ abandon**s**, abandon**ing**, abandon**ed**

■ **Alternative words**: (verb) give up, drop, forget, quit, let go, part with, sacrifice

abandonment *noun* the action of abandoning something such as an out-of-date piece of equipment

abase *verb*, *formal* to make humble: *abase yourself before God*

abasement *noun* **1** being humbled or degraded **2** humiliation

abashed *adjective* embarrassed, confused

abate *verb* to make or grow less: *wait for the storm to abate*

abatement *noun* a lessening or stopping

abattoir (*pronounced* **ab**-*a*-twahr) *noun* a (public) slaughter-house

abbess *noun* (plural **abbesses**) the female head of an abbey or a convent

abbey *noun* (*plural* **abbeys**) **1** a monastery or convent ruled by an abbot or an abbess **2** the church now or formerly attached to such a monastery or convent

abbot *noun* the male head of an abbey

abbreviate *verb* to shorten (a word, phrase *etc*)
🕓 Comes from Latin *brevis* meaning 'short'

abbreviation *noun* a shortened form of a word or group of words, either with some letters missing, eg *maths* for *mathematics*, or with each word represented by its first letter, eg *BBC* for *British Broadcasting Corporation*

abdicate (*pronounced* **ab**-di-kayt) *verb* to give up (a position, especially that of king or queen)

abdication *noun* the act of giving up an office, especially the throne

abdomen (*pronounced* **ab**-dom-*e*n) *noun* the part of the human body between the chest and the hips

abdominal (*pronounced* ab-**dom**-in-*a*l) *adjective* relating to or concerning the abdomen

abduct *verb* to take away by force or fraud

abduction *noun* kidnapping

abet *verb* to help or encourage to do wrong: *He was aided and abetted by his partner in crime*

> **abet** ⇨ abet**s**, abet**ting**, abet**ted**

abeyance *noun*: **in abeyance** undecided; not to be dealt with for the time being

abhor *verb* to hate, or look upon with horror

abhor ⇨ abhors, abhorring, abhorred

abhorrence *noun* horror and hatred

abhorrent *adjective* hateful

abide *verb* to put up with, tolerate □ **abide by** to keep, act according to

abiding *adjective* lasting

ability *noun* (*plural* **abilities**) 1 power or means to do something 2 talent
ⓘ Comes from Latin *habilitas* meaning 'skill'

abject (*pronounced* **ab**-jekt) *adjective* miserable, degraded

ablaze *adjective* 1 burning fiercely 2 gleaming like fire

able *adjective* 1 having the power or means (to do something) 2 clever

ablutions *noun plural*, *formal* washing of the body

ably *adverb* in an efficient or competent way

abnormal *adjective* 1 not normal (in behaviour *etc*) 2 unusual

abnormality *noun* (*plural* **abnormalities**) 1 something which is abnormal 2 the condition of being abnormal

abnormally *adverb* unusually; unnaturally

aboard *adverb* & *preposition* on (to) or in(to) (a ship or aeroplane)

abode *noun* a formal word for a dwelling place

abolish *verb* to put an official end to (*eg* a custom)

abolition *noun* the act of abolishing something or the state of being abolished

abolitionist *noun* someone who tries to do away with anything, especially slavery

abominable *adjective* 1 hateful 2 very bad, terrible □ **the Abominable Snowman** (*also called* **Yeti**) a large animal believed to exist in the Himalayas □ **abominably** *adverb* (meaning 2): *behave abominably*

abominate *verb* to hate very much

abomination *noun* 1 great hatred 2 anything hateful

Aboriginal (*pronounced* a-bor-**ij**-i-nal) or **Aborigine** (*pronounced* a-bor-**ij**-i-nee) *noun* a member of the original or native people of Australia □ **Aboriginal** *adjective*
ⓘ Comes from Latin *ab* meaning 'from', and *origo* meaning 'beginning'

abort *verb* 1 of a plan *etc*: to come to nothing, stay undeveloped 2 to end a pregnancy deliberately by having an abortion

abortion *noun* an operation to end an unwanted or dangerous pregnancy

abortive *adjective* coming to nothing, useless: *an abortive attempt*

abound *verb* to be very plentiful □ **abounding in** full of, having many

about *preposition* 1 around: *look about you* 2 near (in time, size *etc*): *about ten o'clock* 3 here and there in: *scattered about the room* □ *adverb* 1 around: *stood about waiting* 2 in motion or in action: *running about* 3 in the opposite direction: *turned about and walked away* □ **about to** on the point of (doing something)

above *preposition* 1 over, in a higher position than: *above your head* 2 greater than: *above average* 3 too good for: *above jealousy* □ *adverb* 1 overhead, on high 2 earlier on (in a letter *etc*): *See above for details*
ⓘ Comes from Old English *bufan* meaning 'above'

above board *adjective* open □ *adverb* openly

abrasion *noun* 1 the action of rubbing off 2 a graze on the body

abrasive *adjective* 1 rough and scratchy 2 having a hurtful manner □ *noun* something used for rubbing or polishing □ **abrasively** *adverb* (meaning 2): *There's no need to criticize her so abrasively*

abreast *adverb* side by side □ **abreast of** up to date with: *abreast of current affairs*

abridge *verb* to shorten (a book, story *etc*)

abridgement or **abridgment** *noun* a shorter form of a work, especially a book

abroad *adverb* 1 in another country 2 *formal* outside: *witches go abroad after dark*

abrupt *adjective* 1 sudden, without warning 2 of speech or behaviour: bad-tempered or snappy □ **abruptly** *adverb*

ABS *abbreviation* anti-lock braking system

abscess (*pronounced* **ab**-ses) *noun* (*plural* **abscesses**) a boil or other inflammation filled with pus

abscond *verb* to run away secretly: *absconded with the money*

abseil (*pronounced* **ab**-sayl) *verb* to let yourself down a rock face using a double rope
① Comes from German *ab* meaning 'down', and *Seil* meaning 'rope'

absence *noun* the state of being away

absent *adjective* (*pronounced* **ab**-sent) away, not present □ *verb* (*pronounced* *a*b-**sent**): **absent yourself** to keep away

absentee *noun* someone who is absent

absently *adverb* in a dreamy way: *'I suppose so,' he replied absently*

absent-minded *adjective* forgetful

absolute *adjective* complete, not limited by anything: *absolute power*

■ **Alternative words**: supreme, total, utter, complete

absolutely *adverb* 1 completely, certainly 2 (as an informal enthusiastic reply) yes, I agree

absolution *noun* forgiveness, pardon

absolve *verb*, *formal* to pardon: *absolve me of my sins*

absorb *verb* 1 to soak up (liquid) 2 to take up the whole attention of: *He's totally absorbed in what he's doing*

absorbent *adjective* able to soak up liquid

absorption *noun* 1 the act of absorbing 2 complete mental concentration

abstain *verb* 1 to refuse to cast a vote for or against 2 **abstain from something** or **from doing something** to hold yourself back from it or from doing it

abstemious (*pronounced* ab-**steem**-i-us) *adjective* not greedy, sparing in food, drink *etc*

abstention *noun* 1 the act of choosing not to do something, especially not to take food or alcohol 2 a refusal to vote; a person who has abstained from voting

abstinence (*pronounced* **ab**-stin-ens) *noun* abstaining from alcohol *etc*

abstinent *adjective* keeping oneself from indulgence, especially in alcohol

abstract *adjective* existing only as an idea, not as a real thing □ *noun* a summary

abstraction *noun* 1 a thing existing only as an idea: *No-one really has 1.7 children. It's a statistical abstraction* 2 the quality of being based on an idea rather than reality: *the increasing abstraction of his arguments* 3 absent-mindedness: *an air of abstraction* 4 the industrial process of drawing out some material from a source: *abstraction of water from rivers*

abstruse (*pronounced* ab-**stroos**) *adjective* difficult to understand

absurd *adjective* clearly wrong; ridiculous

absurdity *noun* (*plural* **absurdities**) 1 being absurd: *the utter absurdity of this accusation* 2 something that is absurd: *the absurdities of the court martial system*

abundance *noun* a plentiful supply

abundant *adjective* plentiful
□ **abundantly** *adverb* to a great degree, extremely: *'Why are you angry?' — 'I think it's abundantly obvious.'*

abuse *verb* (*pronounced* a-**byooz**) 1 to use wrongly 2 to insult or speak unkindly to; treat badly □ *noun* (*pronounced* a-**byoos**) 1 wrongful use 2 insulting language or behaviour

abusive *adjective* insulting or rude

abysmal (*pronounced* a-**biz**-mal) *adjective* 1 very bad; terrible 2 bottomless □ **abysmally** *adverb* (meaning 1): *He performed abysmally*

abyss (*pronounced* a-**bis**) *noun* (*plural* **abysses**) a bottomless depth

AC *abbreviation* alternating current (*compare with*: **DC**)

a/c *abbreviation* account

acacia (*pronounced* a-**kay**-sha) *noun* a family of thorny shrubs and trees

academic *adjective* **1** concerned with theoretical education or complicated ideas: *academic qualifications* **2** not practical: *purely of academic interest* **3** of a university *etc* □ *noun* a university or college teacher □ **academically** *adverb* (meaning 1): *He's not academically bright, but he's got a lot of common sense*

academy *noun* (*plural* **academies**) **1** a college for special study or training **2** a society for encouraging science or art **3** in Scotland, a senior school

> Comes from Greek *Akademeia*, which was Plato's school of philosophy, named after the garden outside Athens where Plato taught

acanthus *noun* a Mediterranean ornamental shrub

accede (*pronounced* ak-**seed**) *verb*: **accede to** *formal* to agree to

accelerate *verb* to increase in speed ◑ Comes from Latin *celer* meaning 'swift'

acceleration *noun* **1** an increasing of speed; the rate of increase of speed **2** the power of a vehicle to increase speed quickly

accelerator *noun* a lever or pedal used to increase the speed of a car *etc*

accent *noun* **1** (a mark indicating) stress on a syllable or word **2** a mark used in writing to show the quality of a vowel **3** emphasis: *the accent must be on hard work* **4** the way in which words are pronounced in a particular area *etc*: *a Scottish accent*

accentuate (*pronounced* ak-**sen**-choo-ayt) *verb* to make more obvious; emphasize

accept *verb* **1** to take something offered **2** to agree or submit to

❡ Do not confuse with: **except**

acceptable *adjective* satisfactory; pleasing

acceptably *adverb* suitably, properly, appropriately for the circumstances: *acceptably few errors/ How long could he acceptably wait before paying the bill?*

acceptance *noun* **1** the act of accepting: *total acceptance of the situation* **2** an official statement that someone or something has been accepted: *an acceptance from Stirling University*

access (*pronounced* **ak**-ses) *noun* right or means of approach or entry

accessibility *noun* being accessible

accessible (*pronounced* ak-**ses**-i-bl) *adjective* easily approached or reached

accession (*pronounced* ak-se-shun) *noun* a coming to: *accession to the throne*

accessory (*pronounced* ak-**ses**-or-i) *noun* (*plural* **accessories**) **1** an item chosen to match or complement a piece of clothing or an outfit, *eg* a piece of jewellery, a handbag *etc* **2** a helper, especially in crime

accident *noun* **1** an unexpected event causing injury **2** a mishap: *I had a little accident with the cream* **3** chance: *I came upon the book by accident*

accidental *adjective* happening by chance □ **accidentally** *adverb*

acclaim *verb* to welcome enthusiastically □ *noun* enthusiastic reception: *met with critical acclaim*

acclamation *noun* noisy sign of approval

acclimatization *noun* becoming accustomed to a new climate or environment

acclimatize *verb* to accustom to another climate or situation

accommodate *verb* **1** to find room for: *A few families are being accommodated in hotels* **2** to make suitable **3** to be helpful to; supply (with): *We hope to accommodate all our customers as best we can*

accommodating *adjective* making an effort to be helpful

accommodation *noun* a place to live or to stay, lodgings: *student accommodation*

accompaniment *noun* **1** something that accompanies **2** the music played while a singer sings *etc*

accompanist *noun* someone who plays an accompaniment

accompany *verb* **1** to go or be with **2** to play an instrument (*eg* a piano) while a singer sings *etc*

> **accompany** ⇨ accompani*es*, accompany*ing*, accompani*ed*

accomplice *noun* someone who helps another person, especially to commit a crime

accomplish *verb* **1** to complete **2** to manage to do

accomplished *adjective* **1** completed **2** skilled, talented

accomplishment *noun* **1** completion **2** a personal talent or skill

accord *verb* **1** to agree (with): *These results do not accord with our previous data* **2** to give, grant: *His employer accorded him one more day of leave* □ *noun* an official agreement: *an international accord on nuclear disarmament* □ **of your own accord** of your own free will

accordance *noun* agreement: *I am acting in accordance with his wishes*

according: **according to 1** as told by **2** in relation to: *paid according to your work*

accordingly *adverb* **1** in a way which is in agreement with something already mentioned: *You know your duty, and I expect you to act accordingly* **2** therefore: *She won her case, and accordingly received full compensation*

accordion *noun* a musical instrument with bellows, a keyboard and metal reeds

accordionist *noun* an accordion player

accost *verb* to approach and speak to in a forceful or threatening way

account *verb*: **account for 1** to give a reason (for): *He's had bad news? That would account for his silence* **2** to make up: *Tax accounts for most of the price of a bottle of whisky* □ *noun* **1** a bill **2** a record of finances **3** a description of events *etc*; an explanation □ **on account of** because of

accountable *adjective* answerable, responsible: *learn to be accountable for your actions*

accountant *noun* a keeper or inspector of accounts

accoutrements (*pronounced* a-**koo**-tre-ments) *noun plural* dress and equipment, especially military

accredited *adjective* having official status, or the official power to act: *language schools accredited by the British Council*

accrue (*pronounced* a-**kroo**) *verb* to accumulate, collect: *the account accrued no interest* □ **accrue to** to be given or added to: *the benefits that could accrue to the town* □ **accrued** *adjective*

accumulate *verb* **1** to collect: *accumulate a large sum of money* **2** to increase: *toxins which accumulate in the water supply*

accumulation *noun* **1** a collection **2** a mass or pile

accumulator *noun* a type of battery used in a car *etc*

accuracy *noun* exactness

accurate *adjective* correct, exact □ **accurately** *adverb*

accursed *adjective* **1** *formal* under a curse **2** hateful

accusation *noun* **1** the act of accusing **2** a statement accusing someone of something

accuse *verb*: **accuse someone of something** or **of doing something** to claim that someone has done something wrong □ **the accused** *noun* (*plural* **the accused**) the person charged with a crime *etc*

accuser *noun* a person who accuses or blames

accustomed *adjective* **1** used to: *accustomed to travel* **2** usual: *Is this your accustomed way of dealing with the public?*

ace *noun* **1** the one on playing-cards **2** an expert: *a computer ace* **3** *tennis* an unreturned first serve □ *adjective, informal* excellent
  ⊕ The adjective is a new sense of 'ace', first used in the mid 20th century

acetylene (*pronounced* a-**set**-il-een) *noun* a gas used for giving light and heat

ache *noun* a continuous pain □ *verb* to be in continuous pain

achieve *verb* **1** to get (something) done, accomplish **2** to win

achievement *noun* **1** the gaining of something, usually after working hard for it **2** something that has been done or gained by effort

acid *adjective* **1** of taste: sharp **2** sarcastic □ *noun* **1** a substance containing hydrogen which will dissolve metals (*contrasted with*: **alkali**) **2** *slang* the drug LSD

acidify *verb* to make or become acid

> **acidify** ⇨ acidifies, acidifying, acidified

acidity *noun* the state of being acid

acid rain rain containing sulphur and nitrogen compounds and other pollutants

acknowledge *verb* **1** to admit the truth of something **2** to admit that you know or are aware of something **3** to (write to) say you have received something **4** to express gratitude or thanks

acknowledgement or **acknowledgment** *noun* **1** the act of acknowledging someone or something **2** something done, given or said to acknowledge something

acme (*pronounced* **ak**-mi) *noun, formal* the highest point, perfection

acne (*pronounced* **ak**-ni) *noun* a common skin disease with pimples

acorn *noun* the fruit of the oak tree

acoustic (*pronounced* a-**koo**-stik) *adjective* of hearing or sound

acoustics (*pronounced* a-**koo**-stiks) *noun* **1** *singular* the study of sound **2** *plural* the characteristics of a room *etc* which affect the hearing of sound in it

acquaint *verb*: **acquaint someone with** to make someone familiar with: *Are you acquainted with the facts?*

acquaintance *noun* **1** knowledge **2** someone whom you know slightly

acquiesce (*pronounced* ak-wi-**es**) *verb*: **acquiesce to** or **in something** to agree to it: *acquiesce to their demands/ acquiesce in the terms of this agreement*

acquiescence *noun* quiet agreement or acceptance

acquiescent *adjective* quietly accepting or agreeing

acquire *verb* to obtain, get □ **acquired** *adjective* gained; not something you were born with or have inherited

acquisition *noun* **1** the act of getting **2** something got: *This painting is the art gallery's most recent acquisition*

acquisitive *adjective* eager to get things, especially desirable items to add to your property

acquit *verb* to declare (someone) innocent of a crime: *the decision to acquit him of the crime* □ **acquit yourself well** to do well, be successful □ **acquit yourself badly** to do badly, be unsuccessful

> **acquit** ⇨ acquits, acquitting, acquitted

acquittal *noun* a legal judgement of 'not guilty'

acre *noun* a land measure containing 4840 square yards or about 4000 square metres

acreage *noun* the number of acres in a piece of land

acrid (*pronounced* **ak**-rid) *adjective* harsh, bitter

acrimonious (*pronounced* ak-rim-**oh**-ni-*us*) *adjective* bitter; accusing

acrimony (*pronounced* **ak**-rim-*on*-i) *noun* bitterness of feeling or speech

acrobat *noun* someone who performs gymnastic tricks, tightrope-walking *etc*

acrobatic *adjective* able to perform gymnastic tricks; agile

acronym (*pronounced* **ak**-ron-im) *noun* a word formed from the initial letters of other words, *eg radar* for *ra*dio *de*tecting *a*nd *ra*nging
ⓘ A word invented in the mid 20th century, and formed from the prefix *acro-*, and Greek *onyma* meaning 'name'

across *adverb* & *preposition* to or at the other side (of): *swam across the river/ winked at him across the table*

▫ **across the board** involving everyone or everything; sweeping

acrostic (*pronounced* a-**kros**-tik) *noun* a poem *etc* in which the first or last letters of each line, taken in order, spell a word or words

acrylic (*pronounced* a-**kril**-ik) *noun* a synthetically produced fibre ▫ *adjective* made with this material

act *verb* **1** to do something **2** to behave in a particular way: *act foolishly* **3** to play a dramatic role on stage, film *etc* ▫ *noun* **1** something done **2** a government law **3** a section of a play ▫ **act up** *informal* to behave or act wrongly or badly
🕐 Comes from Latin *actum* meaning 'a thing which has been done'

■ **Alternative words**: (verb: meaning 1) serve, function; (noun: meaning 1) action

action *noun* **1** a deed, an act **2** a law case **3** dramatic events portrayed in a film, play *etc*

actionable *adjective* likely to cause a law case: *actionable statement*

activate *verb* to start (something) working

active *adjective* **1** busy; lively **2** able to perform physical tasks **3** *grammar* describing the form of a verb in which the subject performs the action of the verb, eg 'the dog bit the postman' ▫ **actively** *adverb* in a way which involves doing things: *actively involved in nature conservation*

activity *noun* (*plural* **activities**) **1** the state of being active: *The office was a hive of activity* **2** anything that you do, either for pleasure or as part of an organized programme: *outdoor activities/ the gang's criminal activities*

actor *noun* someone who acts a part in a play or film

actress *noun* (*plural* **actresses**) a female actor

actual *adjective* real, existing in fact

actuality *noun* fact; reality

actually *adverb* really, in fact, as a matter of fact

actuarial (*pronounced* ak-choo-**air**-i-al) *adjective* relating to actuaries or their work

actuary (*pronounced* **ak**-choo-ar-i) *noun* (*plural* **actuaries**) someone who works out the price of insurance

actuate *verb* **1** to put into action: *a radar detector, actuated by certain frequencies of radio waves* **2** to drive or urge on

acumen (*pronounced* **ak**-yoo-men) *noun* quickness of understanding: *He owes his success to his keen business acumen*

acupressure (*pronounced* **ak**-yoo-pre-sher) *noun* a method of treating illness by applying pressure to certain key points on the body

acupuncture (*pronounced* **ak**-yoo-punk-cher) *noun* a method of treating illness by piercing the skin with needles
🕐 Comes from Latin *acu* meaning 'needle'

acute *adjective* **1** quick at understanding **2** severe and causing great discomfort: *acute back pain/ acute difficulties/ acute appendicitis* **3** of an angle: less than a right angle (contrasted with: **obtuse**) ▫ **acute accent** a forward-leaning stroke (′) placed over letters in some languages to show their pronunciation ▫ **acutely** *adverb* extremely, painfully: *an acutely embarrassing situation/ He was acutely aware that he was being observed* ▫ **acuteness** *noun* the quality of being acute, used especially of mental perception

AD *abbreviation* in the year of our Lord (from Latin *anno Domini*). Used with a date, eg AD1900, to show that it refers to the time after, and not before, the birth of Christ

▨ **Opposite**: BC

ad *noun, informal* an advertisement

adage (*pronounced* **a**-dij) *noun* an old saying, a proverb

adagio (*pronounced* a-**dah**-jee-oh) *noun* a slow-paced piece of music
🕐 In Italian *ad agio* means 'at ease'

adamant (*pronounced* **ad**-am-ant) *adjective* unwilling to give way

Adam's apple the natural lump which sticks out from a man's throat

From the story that the lump was part of the forbidden apple stuck in Adam's throat

adapt *verb*: **adapt to** to make suitable for; alter so as to fit

adaptable *adjective* easily altered to suit new conditions

adaptation *noun* a change in the form of something to make it suitable for another situation or purpose: *a popular television adaptation of this classic novel*

adaptor *noun* a device allowing an electrical plug to be used in a socket for which it was not designed, or several plugs to be used on the same socket

add *verb* **1** to make one thing join another to give a sum total or whole **2** to mix in: *add water to the dough* **3** to say further □ **add up 1** to combine, grow to a large quantity: *add up the different quantities/ All these expenses soon add up* **2** to make sense, seem logical: *His story just doesn't add up*

addendum (*pronounced* a-**den**-dum) *noun* (*plural* **addenda**) something added

adder *noun* the common name of the viper, a poisonous snake

addict (*pronounced* **a**-dikt) *noun* someone who cannot stop using something, often a drug or alcohol, because they are either physically or mentally dependent on it

addicted (*pronounced* a-**dik**-tid) *adjective*: **addicted to** unable to do without

addictive (*pronounced* a-**dikt**-iv) *adjective* more and more difficult to do without, the more often it is used

addition *noun* **1** the act of adding **2** something added

additional *adjective* extra; more than usual

additionally *adverb* as well as that: *He had a family history of heart disease. Additionally, he was obese*

additive *noun* a chemical *etc* added to another substance

address *verb* **1** to speak to **2** to write the address on (a letter *etc*) □ *noun* (*plural* **addresses**) **1** the name of the

house, street, and town where someone lives *etc* **2** a speech

adenoids (*pronounced* **a**-de-noydz) *noun plural* tissue at the back of the nose which can swell and make it difficult to breathe

adept (*pronounced* a-**dept**) *adjective* very skilful

adequacy *noun* being adequate; sufficiency

adequate *adjective* sufficient, enough □ **adequately** *adverb*

adhere *verb* **1** to stick (to): *adhere to a clean, dry surface* **2** to give support (to), be loyal (to): *adhere to a strict dress code*

adherence *noun* **1** the act of adhering **2** loyalty

adherent *adjective* sticking (to) □ *noun* a follower or supporter of a cause *etc*

adhesion *noun* the act of sticking (to)

adhesive *adjective* sticky, gummed □ *noun* something which makes things stick to each other

ad hoc *adjective* set up for a particular purpose only

ad infinitum (*pronounced* ad in-fi-**nai**-tum) *adverb* for ever

adjacent (*pronounced* a-**jei**-sent) *adjective* (**adjacent to**) lying next to

adjective *noun* a word which tells something about a noun, *eg* 'the *black* cat,' 'times are *hard*' □ **adjectival** *adjective*

adjoin *verb* to be joined to: *A large shed adjoins the house* □ **adjoining** *adjective*

adjourn *verb* **1** to stop (a meeting *etc*) with the intention of continuing it at another time or place: *adjourn the meeting till this afternoon* **2** **adjourn to** somewhere to go to another place: *adjourn to the lounge* □ **adjournment** *noun*

adjudicate *verb* **1** to give a judgement on (a dispute *etc*): *It is my duty to adjudicate on such matters/ adjudicate disputes between employers and employees* **2** to act as a judge at a competition □ **adjudication** *noun*

adjudicator *noun* someone who adjudicates

adjunct (*pronounced* **aj**-unkt) *noun* something joined or added

adjust *verb* to rearrange or alter to suit the circumstances □ **adjustable** *adjective* □ **adjustment** *noun*

■ **Alternative words**: adapt, acclimatize

ad-lib *verb* to speak without plan or preparation □ *adjective* without preparation

ad-lib *verb* ⇨ ad-libs, ad-libbing, ad-libbed

administer *verb* **1** to manage or govern: *South Pacific islands administered by France* **2** to carry out (the law *etc*) **3** to give (help, medicine *etc*): *A qualified doctor must administer the drug to patients*

administrate *verb* to manage or govern

administration *noun* **1** management **2** (the body that carries on) the government of a country *etc*

administrative *adjective* having to do with management or government

administrator *noun* someone involved in the administration of a country *etc*

admirable *adjective* worthy of being admired □ **admirably** *adverb*

admiral *noun* the commander of a navy

admiralty *noun* the government office which manages naval affairs

admire *verb* **1** to think very highly of **2** to look at with pleasure □ **admiration** *noun* □ **admirer** *noun*

admissible *adjective* allowable

admission *noun* **1** (the price of) being let in **2** anything admitted

■ **Alternative words**: (meaning 1) entrance fee

admit *verb* **1** to let in **2** to acknowledge the truth of, confess **3 admit of something** to leave room for, allow: *admits of no other explanation*

admit ⇨ admits, admitting, admitted

■ **Alternative words**: (meaning 2) allow, concede, confess, own

admittance *noun* the right or permission to enter

admonish *verb* **1** to warn **2** to rebuke, scold

admonition *noun* a warning □ **admonitory** *adjective*

ad nauseam (*pronounced* ad **naw**-zi-am) *adverb* to a tiresome degree

ado (*pronounced* a-**doo**) *noun* trouble, fuss

adolescent *noun* someone between a child and an adult in age □ *adjective* of this age □ **adolescence** *noun*

adopt *verb* **1** to take as your own (especially a child of other parents) **2** to take (eg precautions), choose formally: *adopt certain new measures in the fight against crime* □ **adoption** *noun*

adoptive *adjective* adopted, taken as your own: *her adoptive country*

adorable *adjective* very loveable

adoration *noun* **1** worship **2** great love

adore *verb* **1** to love very much **2** to worship

adorn *verb* to decorate (with ornaments *etc*): *Her head was adorned with flowers*

adornment *noun* ornament

adrenaline (*pronounced* a-**dren**-a-lin) *noun* a hormone produced in response to fear, anger *etc*, preparing the body for quick action

adrift *adverb* drifting, floating

adroit (*pronounced* a-**droit**) *adjective* skilful

adulation (*pronounced* ad-yoo-**lei**-shun) *noun* great flattery □ **adulatory** *adjective*

adult *adjective* grown up □ *noun* a grown-up person

■ **Alternative words**: mature, full-grown, developed

adulterate *verb* to make impure by adding something else □ **adulteration** *noun*

adultery *noun* unfaithfulness to a husband or wife □ **adulterer** or **adulteress** *noun*

advance *verb* **1** to go forward **2** to put forward (a plan *etc*): *He advanced a* *number of proposals* **3** to help the progress of: *research which has advanced our understanding of HIV* **4** to pay before the usual or agreed time: *Could you advance me £50 and take it off my next pay cheque?* □ *noun* **1** movement forward **2** improvement **3** a loan of money □ **in advance** beforehand

advanced *adjective* well forward in progress

advancement *noun* progress

advantage *noun* **1** a better position, superiority **2** gain or benefit □ *verb* to help, benefit □ **take advantage of** to make use of (a situation, person *etc*) in such a way as to benefit yourself

advantageous *adjective* profitable; helpful

advent (*pronounced* ad-vent) *noun* **1** coming, arrival: *before the advent of television* **2 Advent** in the Christian church, the four weeks before Christmas

adventure *noun* a bold or exciting undertaking or experience

adventurer *noun* **1** someone who takes risks, especially in the hope of making a lot of money **2** a mercenary soldier

adventurous *adjective* taking risks, liking adventure

adverb *noun* a word which gives a more definite meaning to a verb, adjective, or other adverb, *eg* 'eat *slowly*,' '*extremely* hard,' '*very* carefully'

adverbial *adjective* of or like an adverb

adversary (*pronounced* ad-ve-sar-i) *noun* (*plural* **adversaries**) an enemy; an opponent

adverse (*pronounced* ad-vers) *adjective* unfavourable: *adverse criticism*

adversity *noun* (*plural* **adversities**) misfortune

advert *noun, informal* an advertisement

advertise *verb* **1** to make known to the public **2** to stress the good points of (a product for sale)

advertisement *noun* a photograph, short film *etc* intended to persuade the public to buy a particular product

advice *noun* **1** something said as a help

to someone trying to make a decision *etc* **2** a formal notice

☛ Do not confuse with: **advise**. To help you remember – 'ice' is a noun, 'ise' is not!

advisable *adjective* wise, sensible □ **advisability** *noun*

advise *verb* **1** to give advice to **2** to recommend (an action *etc*) □ **adviser** *noun*

☛ Do not confuse with: **advice**. To help you remember – 'ice' is a noun...so 'ise' must be the verb!

advisory *adjective* advice-giving: *advisory body*

advocate *noun* (*pronounced* ad-vo-kat) **1** someone who pleads for another **2** in Scotland, a court lawyer □ *verb* (*pronounced* ad-vo-keit) **1** to plead or argue for **2** to recommend: *Would you advocate the legalization of cannabis?*

aegis (*pronounced* ee-jis) *noun* protection; patronage

aeon or **eon** (*pronounced* ee-on) *noun* a very long period of time, an age

aerate (*pronounced* eir-**reit**) *verb* to put air or another gas into (a liquid)

aerial *adjective* **1** of, in or from the air: *aerial photography* **2** placed high up or overhead: *aerial railway* □ *noun* a wire or rod (or a set of these) by means of which radio or television signals are received or sent

aero- *prefix* of air or aircraft
⏱ Comes from Greek *aer* meaning 'air'

aerobatics *noun plural* stunts performed by an aircraft

aerobics *noun singular* a system of rhythmic physical exercise which aims to strengthen the heart and lungs by increasing the body's oxygen consumption

aerodrome *noun* a landing and maintenance station for aircraft

aeronautics *noun singular* the science or art of navigation in the air

aeroplane or *US* **airplane** *noun* an engine-powered flying machine with fixed wings

aerosol *noun* a container of liquid and

gas under pressure, from which the liquid is squirted as a mist

aesthetic (*pronounced* ees-**thet**-ik) *adjective* **1** of beauty or its appreciation **2** artistic, pleasing to the eye
□ **aesthetically** *adverb*: *aesthetically pleasing*

affable *adjective* pleasant, easy to speak to □ **affability** *noun*

affair *noun* **1** events *etc* connected with one person or thing: *the Watergate affair* **2 affairs** personal concerns, transactions *etc*: *his affairs seemed to be in order* **3** business, concern: *that's not your affair* **4** a love affair

affect *verb* **1** to act upon **2** to have an effect on; move the feelings of **3** to pretend to feel *etc*: *affect an air of indifference*
ⓞ Meanings 1 and 2: come from Latin *afficere* meaning 'to do something to'; meaning 3: comes from Latin *affectare* meaning 'to strive after'

🖝 Do not confuse with: **effect**. **Affect** is usually a verb. **Effect** is usually a noun. 'To AFFECT' means 'to have an EFFECT on'

affectation *noun* pretence

affected *adjective* **1** moved in your feelings **2** not natural, sham

affecting *adjective* moving the feelings

affection *noun* a strong liking

affectionate *adjective* loving

affidavit (*pronounced* af-i-**dei**-vit) *noun*, *law* a written statement made on oath

affiliated: *adjective* **affiliated with** or **affiliated to** connected with or attached to □ **affiliation** *noun*

affinity *noun* (*plural* **affinities**) a close likeness or agreement

affirm *verb* to state firmly: *He affirmed that they had an excellent safety record/ a chance to affirm his religious beliefs*

affirmation *noun* a firm statement

affirmative *adjective* saying 'yes'

affix *verb* to attach to

afflict *verb* to give continued pain or distress to: *What sadness afflicts him?*

afflicted *adjective* suffering: *She has been afflicted by this disease since her childhood*

affliction *noun* great suffering, misery

affluence (*pronounced* **af**-loo-ens) *noun* wealth

affluent (*pronounced* **af**-loo-ent) *adjective* wealthy □ *noun* a stream flowing into a river or lake

afford *verb* **1** to be able to pay for **2** *formal* to give, provide with: *I hoped the situation would afford me a chance to speak to him*

afforest *verb* to cover land with forest □ **afforestation** *noun*

affray *noun* a fight, a brawl

affront *verb* to insult openly □ *noun* an insult

afloat *adverb* & *adjective* floating

afoot *adverb* happening or about to happen: *I could tell something was afoot*

aforesaid (*pronounced* a-**faw**-sed) *adjective* said or named before: *the aforesaid person*

afraid *adjective* **1** struck with fear **2** *informal* sorry to have to admit that: *I'm afraid there are no tickets left*

📖 **Alternative words**: (meaning 1) frightened, terrified, timorous, fearful, cowardly

afresh *adverb* once again, anew

aft (*pronounced* ahft) *adverb* near or towards the stern of a vessel

after *preposition* **1** later in time than: *after dinner* **2** following: *arrived one after another/ day after day* **3** in memory or honour of: *named after his father* **4** in pursuit of: *run after the bus* **5** about: *asked after her health* **6** despite: *after all my efforts, it still didn't work* **7** in the style of: *after Rubens* □ *adverb* later in time or place: *we left soon after* □ *conjunction* later than the time when: *after she arrived, things improved* □ **after all 1** all things considered: *after all, he's still young* **2** despite everything said or done before: *I went after all*

after- *prefix* later in time or place: *aftertaste/ afterthought*

afterbirth *noun* the placenta and membranes expelled from the uterus after giving birth

aftermath *noun* the bad results of something: *the aftermath of the election*

  Originally a second crop coming after the main harvest

afternoon *noun* the time between noon and evening □ *adjective* taking place in the afternoon

aftershave *noun* a lotion used on the face after shaving

afterthought *noun* a later thought

afterwards *adverb* later

again *adverb* **1** once more: *say that again* **2** in or into the original state, place *etc*: *there and back again* **3** on the other hand: *again, I might be wrong* **4** *informal* at another later time: *see you again*

against *preposition* **1** in opposition to: *against the law/ fight against injustice* **2** in the opposite direction to: *against the wind* **3** on a background of: *against the sky* **4** close to, touching: *lean against the wall* **5** as protection from: *guard against infection*

age *noun* **1** a long period of time **2** the time someone or something has lived or existed □ *verb* to grow or make visibly older: *He has aged ten years (= seems to have grown ten years older) in the past six months/ That hat ages her (= makes her look older)* □ **of age** legally an adult

  age *verb* ⇨ ages, ageing or aging, aged

aged *adjective* **1** (*pronounced* **eij**-id) old **2** (*pronounced* eijd) of the age of: *aged five*

ageism *noun* discrimination on grounds of age

ageist *adjective* discriminating on grounds of age

agency *noun* (*plural* **agencies**) **1** the office or business of an agent **2** action, means by which something is done

agenda *noun* a list of things to be done, especially at a meeting

agent *noun* **1** someone or something that acts **2** someone who acts for another **3** a spy

aggrandize *verb* to make greater

aggrandizement (*pronounced* a-**gran**-diz-ment) *noun* the process of making (yourself) seem greater or more powerful: *You should not enter politics for self-aggrandizement*

aggravate *verb* **1** to make worse **2** *informal* to annoy □ **aggravating** *adjective* □ **aggravation** *noun*

  ≢ **Opposite**: (meaning 1) alleviate

aggregate (*pronounced* **ag**-ri-gat) *noun* a total

aggressive *adjective* **1** ready to attack first **2** quarrelsome □ **aggression** *noun* □ **aggressor** *noun*

aggrieved (*pronounced* a-**greevd**) *adjective* hurt, upset

aghast (*pronounced* a-**gahst**) *adjective* struck with horror

agile *adjective* active, nimble □ **agility** *noun*

  ■ **Alternative words**: athletic

agitate *verb* **1** to stir up **2** to excite, disturb □ **agitation** *noun*

agitator *noun* someone who stirs up others

agnostic (*pronounced* ag-**nos**-tik) *noun* someone who believes it is impossible to know whether God exists or not □ **agnosticism** *noun*

ago *adverb* in the past: *that happened five years ago*

agog (*pronounced* a-**gog**) *adjective* eager, excited

agonized *adjective* showing great pain

agonizing *adjective* causing great pain

agony *noun* (*plural* **agonies**) great pain

agony aunt someone who gives advice in an agony column

agony column a regular column in a newspaper or magazine in which readers submit and receive advice about personal problems

agoraphobia (*pronounced* ag-ra-**foh**-bi-a) *noun* great fear of open spaces

agoraphobic (*pronounced* ag-ra-**foh**-bik) *noun & adjective* (someone) suffering from agoraphobia

agrarian *adjective* of farmland or farming

agree verb 1 to be alike in opinions, decisions etc 2 to say that you will do something: Toby has agreed to play us a tune 3 **agree with** to suit 4 **agree with** to cause no problems in digestion: the fish didn't agree with me 5 to be the same or consistent, fit together: I'd like to believe them both, but their stories don't agree

■ **Alternative words**: (meaning 2) consent, assent; (meaning 5) tally, accord

agreeable adjective 1 pleasant 2 ready to agree

agreement noun 1 likeness (especially of opinions) 2 a written statement making a bargain

agri- prefix of fields, land use, or farming
◷ Comes from Latin ager meaning 'field'

agriculture noun the cultivation of the land, farming □ **agricultural** adjective

agro- prefix of fields, land use, or farming: agrobiology (= the study of plant nutrition)/ agrochemical (a chemical used in farming the land)
◷ Comes from Greek agros meaning 'field'

aground adjective & adverb stuck on the bottom of the sea or a river: run aground

ahead adverb in front; in advance: finishing ahead of time

aid verb to help, assist □ noun help

AIDS or **Aids** abbreviation Acquired Immune Deficiency Syndrome

aikido (pronounced ai-**kee**-doh) noun a Japanese martial art using pressure against the joints

ail verb, old to be or make ill: My poor father is ailing/ What ails thee?

ailing adjective 1 troubled, in a bad state: the ailing steel industry 2 ill

ailment noun a trouble, disease

aim verb 1 to point at (especially with a gun) 2 to intend to do 3 to have as your purpose □ noun 1 the act of, or skill in, aiming 2 the point aimed at, goal, intention

aimless adjective without aim or

purpose □ **aimlessly** adverb: drifting aimlessly through life

air noun 1 the mixture of gases (mainly oxygen and nitrogen) which we breathe, the atmosphere 2 a light breeze 3 fresh air 4 space overhead 5 a tune 6 the look or manner (of a person) □ verb 1 to expose to the air 2 to make known (an opinion etc) □ **on the air** broadcasting

airbag noun a bag which automatically inflates inside a car on impact to protect the driver from injury

airbed noun a mattress which can be inflated

airborne adjective in the air, flying

air-conditioned adjective equipped with a system for filtering and controlling the temperature of the air

aircraft noun (plural **aircraft**) a flying machine

air force the branch of the armed forces using aircraft

air-gun noun a gun worked by means of compressed air

airily adverb in a light and not very serious way

airing noun 1 the act of exposing to the air: give the room an airing 2 the act of talking about something openly: give your views an airing

airless adjective stuffy, with no circulation of fresh air

airlock noun 1 a bubble in a pipe obstructing the flow of a liquid 2 a compartment with two doors for entering and leaving an airtight spaceship etc

airplane US for **aeroplane**

airport noun a place where aircraft land and take off, with buildings for customs, waiting-rooms etc

air-raid noun an attack by aeroplanes

airship noun a large balloon which can be steered and driven

airstream noun a flow of air

airtight adjective made so that air cannot pass in or out

airy adjective 1 of or like the air 2 well supplied with fresh air 3 light-hearted

aisle (*pronounced* ail) *noun* **1** the side part of a church **2** a passage between seats in a theatre *etc*

ajar *adverb* partly open: *leave the door ajar*

aka (*pronounced* ei-kei-**ei**) *abbreviation* also known as: *Stevens, aka The Fly*

akimbo *adverb* with hand on hip and elbow bent outward

From an Old Norse term meaning 'bowed' or 'curved'

akin *adjective* similar

à la carte *adjective* & *adverb* **1** according to the menu **2** each dish chosen and priced separately

alack! *exclamation, old* alas

alacrity *noun* briskness, cheerful readiness

à la mode (*pronounced* a la **mod**) *adjective* & *adverb* **1** fashionable **2** *US* served with ice-cream: *apple pie à la mode*

alarm *noun* **1** sudden fear **2** something which rouses to action or gives warning of danger □ *verb* to frighten □ **alarming** *adjective*

alarmist *noun* someone who frightens others needlessly

alas! *exclamation* a cry showing grief

albatross *noun* (*plural* **albatrosses**) a type of large sea-bird

albino *noun* (*plural* **albinos**) someone or an animal with no natural colour in their skin, hair and eye irises

album *noun* **1** a book with blank pages for holding photographs, stamps *etc* **2** a long-playing record **3** recordings issued under one title

albumen (*pronounced* **al**-byu-men) *noun* the white of eggs

alchemist *noun* someone who practised alchemy

alchemy *noun* an early form of chemistry aimed at changing other metals into gold

alcohol *noun* **1** the colourless, flammable liquid which you get when you ferment sugar, and which is present in all drinks which can make people drunk **2** any drink which can make people drunk

alcoholic *adjective* of or containing alcohol □ *noun* someone addicted to alcohol

alcoholism *noun* addiction to alcohol

alcove *noun* a recess in a room's wall

alder *noun* a type of tree which grows beside ponds and rivers

alderman *noun* **1** *historical* a councillor next in rank to the mayor of a town *etc* **2** *US* a member of the governing body of a city

ale *noun* a drink made from malt, hops *etc*

alert *noun* signal to be ready for action □ *verb* to make alert, warn: *alert them to the dangers of the job* □ *adjective* **1** watchful **2** quick-thinking □ **on the alert** on the watch (for)

algae (*pronounced* **al**-gi or **al**-ji) *noun* a group of simple plants which includes seaweed

algebra *noun* a part of mathematics in which letters and signs are used to represent numbers

alias *adverb* also known as: *Mitchell alias Grassic Gibbon* □ *noun* (*plural* **aliases**) a false name

alibi *noun* **1** the plea that someone charged with a crime was elsewhere when it was done **2** the state or fact of being elsewhere when a crime was committed

alien *adjective* foreign □ *noun* a foreigner □ **alien to** not in keeping with: *alien to her nature*

alienate *verb* to make someone unfriendly, probably by causing them to feel unwanted or rejected: *We must be careful not to alienate our old supporters*

alight *verb* **1** to climb *etc* down: *alight from the train* **2** to settle, land □ *adjective* & *adverb* on fire, burning

alight *verb* ⇨ alights, alight*ing*, alight*ed*

align (*pronounced* a-**lain**) *verb* **1** to set in line: *align the row of holes with the row of plastic teeth* **2** to take sides in an argument *etc*: *align yourself with environmentalists on this issue*

alignment *noun* arrangement in a line

alike *adjective* like one another, similar □ *adverb* in the same way, similarly

alimentary *adjective* of food □ **alimentary canal** the passage through the body which begins at the mouth

alimony *noun* an allowance paid by a husband to his wife, or a wife to her husband, to provide support when they are legally separated

alive *adjective* **1** living **2** full of activity □ **alive to** aware of

■ **Alternative words:** (meaning 2) animated, vivacious

alkali *noun* a substance such as soda or potash (*contrasted with*: **acid**) □ **alkaline** *adjective*

all *adjective* & *pronoun* **1** every one (of): *we are all invited/ all letters will be answered* **2** the whole (of): *painted all the house* □ *adverb* wholly, completely: *dressed all in red* □ **all in 1** with everything included: *all-in price* **2** *informal* exhausted □ **all over 1** over the whole of **2** everywhere **3** finished, ended

all ready totally ready

◆ Do not use this as an alternative spelling for 'already'

all right in a normal state; not hurt, unhappy, or feeling strange

◆ It is best to avoid the spelling 'alright', since some people say it is incorrect

all together together as a group

◆ Do not use this as an alternative spelling for 'altogether'

all ways in every way possible

◆ Do not use this as an alternative spelling for 'always'

Allah *noun* in Islam, God

allay *verb* **1** to make less, relieve: *tried to allay my fears* **2** to calm

allege *verb* to say without proof: *allege that this man was involved in the crime* □ **allegation** *noun*

allegiance *noun* loyalty

allegory *noun* (*plural* **allegories**) a story or fable which deals with a subject in a way which is meant to suggest a deeper, more serious subject □ **allegorical** *adjective*

allergy *noun* (*plural* **allergies**) abnormal sensitiveness of the body to something □ **allergic** *adjective*

alleviate *verb* to make lighter, lessen: *try to alleviate their suffering* □ **alleviation** *noun*

■ **Opposite:** aggravate

alley *noun* (*plural* **alleys**) **1** a narrow passage or lane **2** an enclosure for bowls or skittles

alliance *noun* a joining together of two people, nations *etc,* for a common cause

allied *adjective* joined by an alliance

alligator *noun* a large reptile like a crocodile

alliteration *noun* the repetition of the same sound at the beginning of two or more words close together, *eg* 'round and round the rugged rock' or 'sing a song of sixpence' □ **alliterative** *adjective*

✎ Can you think of some short phrases containing alliteration?

allo- *prefix* other, different, from outside
① Comes from Greek *allos* meaning 'other'

allocate *verb* to allot, share out, reserve for a particular purpose: *The task of collecting the data has been allocated to you* □ **allocation** *noun*

allopathic *adjective* of medicine: conventional, treating disease with drugs which have an effect on the body which is opposite to that of the disease (*contrasted with*: **homeopathic**)

allot *verb* to give each person a share of, distribute, reserve: *A ten-minute slot will be allotted to each candidate/ fail to finish the task in the allotted time*

allot ⇨ allot*s*, allott*ing*, allott*ed*

allotment *noun* **1** the act of distributing **2** a small plot of ground for growing vegetables *etc*

allow *verb* **1** to let (someone do something) **2** **allow for** to take into consideration (in sums, plans *etc*) **3** to admit, confess: *I do allow that we could have handled the situation better* **4** to give, especially at regular intervals: *she allows him £40 a week* □ **allowable** *adjective*

■ **Alternative words:** (meaning 1) enable

allowance *noun* a fixed sum or amount given regularly □ **make allowances for** to treat differently because of taking into consideration special circumstances *etc*

alloy *noun* a mixture of two or more metals

all-rounder *noun* someone skilled in many kinds of work, sport *etc*

allude *verb*: **allude to** to mention in passing
① Comes from Latin *adludere* meaning 'to play with'

☛ Do not confuse with: **elude**

allure *verb* to tempt, draw on by promises *etc* □ **allurement** *noun* □ **alluring** *adjective*

allusion *noun* an indirect reference

☛ Do not confuse with: **delusion** and **illusion**. An **allusion** is a comment which **alludes to** something

allusive *adjective* referring indirectly, hinting

☛ Do not confuse with: **elusive** and **illusive**. **Allusive** is related to the verb **allude** and the noun **allusion**

alluvium *noun* (*plural* **alluvia**) earth, sand *etc* brought down and left by rivers in flood □ **alluvial** *adjective*

ally *verb* to join yourself to by treaty *etc*: *a small organization seeking to ally itself with larger ones* □ *noun* (*plural* **allies**) someone in alliance with another; a friend

ally *verb* ⇨ all*ies*, all*ying*, all*ied*

almanac *noun* a calendar for any year, with information about the phases of the moon *etc*

almighty *adjective* having much power □ **the Almighty** God

almond *noun* the kernel of the fruit of the almond-tree

almost *adverb* very nearly but not quite: *almost five years old/ almost home*

alms (*pronounced* ahmz) *noun* gifts to the poor

aloft *adverb* **1** on high **2** upward

alone *adjective* not accompanied by others, solitary: *alone in the house* □ *adverb* **1** only, without anything else: *that alone is bad enough* **2** not accompanied by others: *do you live alone?* □ **leave alone** to let be, leave undisturbed

along *preposition* over the length of: *walk along the road* □ *adverb* onward: *come along!* □ **along with** together with

alongside *preposition* beside □ *adverb* near a ship's side

aloof *adjective* & *adverb* **1** at a distance, apart **2** showing no interest in others

aloud *adverb* so as to be heard

alpha *noun* the first letter of the Greek alphabet

alphabet *noun* letters of a language given in a fixed order

alphabetic or **alphabetical** *adjective* in the order of the letters of the alphabet

alpine *adjective* of the Alps or other high mountains

already *adverb* **1** before this or that time: *I've already done that* **2** now, before the expected time: *you can't have finished already*

☛ If you write 'all ready' as two words, it has the very different meaning of 'totally ready': *Are you all ready for the big day?*

alright

☛ It is best to spell this as two words: 'all right'. Some people consider the spelling 'alright' to be incorrect

alsatian *noun* a German shepherd dog

also *adverb* in addition, besides, too: *I also need to buy milk*

also-ran *noun* someone or something that competed (as in a race) but was not among the winners

altar *noun* **1** a raised place for offerings to a god **2** in Christian churches, the communion table

alter *verb* to change □ **alteration** *noun*

altercation *noun* an argument or quarrel

alter ego 1 a second self **2** a trusted friend, a confidant(e)

alternate *verb* (*pronounced* **ol**-te-neit) of two things: to do or happen in turn: *Meetings alternate between my house and hers* □ *adjective* (*pronounced* ol-**tern**-at) happening *etc* in turns: *A grocery van serves the village on alternate days* (= every other day) □ **alternation** *noun*

☞ Do not confuse: **alternate** and **alternative**. 'To ALTERNATE' is to move between two possibilities. **Alternate** is the adjective from this verb

alternative *adjective* offering a second possibility: *an alternative solution* □ *noun* a second possibility, a different course of action: *I had no alternative but to agree*

although *conjunction* though, in spite of the fact that

altimeter *noun* an instrument for measuring height above sea level

altitude *noun* height above sea level

alto *noun* (*plural* **altos**), *music* **1** the male voice of the highest pitch **2** the female voice of lowest pitch

An alternative term for the female *alto* voice is **contralto**

altogether *adverb* **1** considering everything, in all: *there were 20 of us altogether* **2** completely: *not altogether satisfied*

☞ If you write 'all together' as two words, it has the very different meaning of 'together in a group': *It's great to be all together for Christmas*

altruism *noun* unselfish concern for the good of others □ **altruistic** *adjective*

aluminium (*pronounced* al-yuw-**min**-i-um) or *US* **aluminum** (*pronounced* a-**loo**-min-um) *noun* an element, a very light metal

always *adverb* **1** for ever: *he'll always remember this day* **2** every time: *she always gets it wrong*

☞ If you write 'all ways' as two words, it has the very different meaning of 'in every way possible': *I've tried all ways to tell her, but she just won't listen*

Alzheimer's (*pronounced* **alts**-hai-mez) **disease** an illness affecting the brain and causing dementia in middle-aged and elderly people

AM *abbreviation* amplitude modulation (*compare with:* **FM**)

am *abbreviation* before noon (from Latin *ante meridiem*)

am *see* **be**

amalgam *noun* a mixture (especially of metals)

amalgamate *verb* **1** to join together, combine: *The company recently amalgamated with a large French firm* **2** to mix □ **amalgamation** *noun*

amass *verb* to collect in large quantity: *amass a lot of furniture over the years*

amateur *noun* someone who takes part in a thing for the love of it, not for money (*contrasted with:* **professional**)

amateurish *adjective* not done properly; not skilful

amaze *verb* to surprise greatly □ **amazement** *noun* □ **amazing** *adjective* □ **amazingly** *adverb*

■ **Alternative words:** astonish

Amazon *noun* **1** one of a nation of mythological warrior women **2** a very strong or manlike woman

ambassador *noun* **1** a government minister sent to look after the interests of one country in another country **2** a representative

amber *noun* a hard yellowish fossil resin used in making jewellery □ *adjective* **1** made of amber **2** of the colour of amber

ambi- *prefix* **1** both, on both sides **2** round
🕔 Comes from Latin *ambo* meaning 'both'

ambidextrous *adjective* able to use both hands with equal skill □ **ambidexterity** *noun*

ambience *noun* environment, atmosphere

ambient *adjective*: **ambient temperature** the temperature of the air in an enclosed space, *eg* a room

ambiguity *noun* (*plural* **ambiguities**) uncertainty in meaning

ambiguous *adjective* 1 having two possible meanings 2 not clear
ⓘ Comes from Latin *ambiguus* meaning 'changing from one to another'

   🖝 Do not confuse with: **ambivalent**

ambition *noun* the desire for success, power, fame *etc* □ **ambitious** *adjective* □ **ambitiously** *adverb*

ambivalent *adjective* having two contrasting attitudes towards something □ **ambivalence** *noun*
ⓘ Comes from the prefix *ambi-*, and Latin *valens* meaning 'strong'

   🖝 Do not confuse with: **ambiguous**

amble *verb* to walk without hurrying □ *noun* an unhurried walk

ambrosia *noun* the mythological food of the gods, which gave eternal youth and beauty

ambulance *noun* a vehicle for carrying the sick or injured

ambush *noun* (*plural* **ambushes**) 1 the act of lying hidden in order to make a surprise attack 2 the people hidden in this way 3 their place of hiding □ *verb* to attack suddenly from a position of hiding

amenable *adjective* open to advice or suggestion

amend *verb* 1 to correct, improve (a text or statement) by making small additions 2 to alter (a text or statement) slightly by making small additions □ **make amends** to make up for having done wrong

   🖝 Do not confuse with: **emend**. **Amending** involves making changes or improvements. **Emending** consists simply of getting rid of errors

   ▣ Alternative words: **make amends** atone

amendment *noun* a change, often in something written

amenity *noun* (*plural* **amenities**) a

pleasant or convenient feature of a place *etc*

amethyst *noun* a precious stone of a bluish-violet colour

amiable *adjective* likeable; friendly □ **amiability** *noun* □ **amiably** *adverb*

amicable *adjective* friendly

amid or **amidst** *preposition* in the middle of, surrounded by: *staying calm amidst all the confusion*
ⓘ Comes from Old English *on middan* meaning 'in middle'

   🖝 Use 'amid' or 'amidst' when the thing or things doing the surrounding cannot be counted: *amidst the confusion/ sitting amidst the wild poppies.* Use 'among' or 'amongst' when the thing or things can be counted: *celebrate your birthday among friends*

amiss *adverb* wrongly; badly

amity *noun, formal* friendship

ammonia *noun* a strong-smelling gas made of hydrogen and nitrogen

ammunition *noun* gunpowder, shot, bullets, bombs *etc*

amnesia *noun* loss of memory

amnesiac *noun & adjective* (someone) suffering from amnesia

amnesty *noun* (*plural* **amnesties**) a general pardon of wrongdoers

amoeba (*pronounced* a-mee-ba) *noun* (*plural* **amoebas** or **amoebae** – *pronounced* a-mee-bi or a-mee-bai) a very simple form of animal life found in ponds *etc*

amok or **amuck** *adverb*: **run amok** to go mad and do a lot of damage, run riot

   From a Malay word meaning 'fighting frenziedly'

among or **amongst** *preposition* 1 surrounded by or in the middle of: *among friends* 2 in shares, in parts: *divide amongst yourselves* 3 in the group of: *among all her novels, this is the best*
ⓘ Comes from Old English *on-gemang* meaning 'in mixture or crowd'

● Use 'among' or 'amongst' when the thing or things doing the surrounding can be counted. Use 'amid' or 'amidst' when the thing or things cannot be counted

amoral *adjective* incapable of distinguishing between right and wrong □ **amorality** *noun*

⏰ Comes from Greek prefix *a-* meaning 'the opposite of', and Latin *moralis* meaning 'moral'

● Do not confuse with: **immoral**. An **amoral** person behaves badly because they do not understand the difference between right and wrong. An **immoral** person behaves badly in the full knowledge that what they are doing is wrong

amorous *adjective* loving; ready or inclined to love

amount *noun* 1 total, sum 2 a quantity □ **amount to** to add up to

amp *noun* 1 an ampère 2 *informal* an amplifier

ampère *noun* the standard unit of electric current

ampersand *noun* the character (&) representing *and*

From phrase *and per se and*, 'and by itself and'

amphetamine (*pronounced* am-**fet**-*a*-meen) *noun* a type of drug used as a stimulant

amphi- *prefix* 1 both, on both sides or ends 2 around

⏰ Comes from Greek *amphi* meaning 'on both sides' or 'around'

amphibian *noun* 1 an animal that lives on land and in water 2 a vehicle for use on land and in water □ *adjective* living on land and water

amphibious *adjective* amphibian

amphitheatre *noun* a theatre with seats surrounding a central arena

ample *adjective* 1 plenty of 2 large enough

amplification *noun* 1 the process or product of making something louder, larger, or more detailed

amplifier *noun* an electrical device for increasing loudness

amplify *verb* 1 to make louder 2 to make more pronounced

amplify ⇨ amplifies, amplifying, amplified

amplitude *noun* 1 largeness 2 size

amputate *verb* to cut off (especially a human limb) □ **amputation** *noun*

amputee *noun* someone who has had a limb amputated

amuck *another spelling of* **amok**

amuse *verb* 1 to make to laugh 2 to give pleasure to □ **amusement** *noun*

amusing *adjective* 1 funny 2 giving pleasure

an *see* **a**

an- or **a-** *prefix* without, not, opposite to: *anaerobic/ anodyne* (= without pain)

⏰ Comes from Greek *a-* meaning 'without' or 'not'

ana- or **an-** *prefix* up, back, again: *anabolic/ aneurism*

⏰ Comes from Greek prefix *ana-* with the same meaning

anabolic steroids steroids used to increase the build-up of body tissue, especially muscle

anachronism (*pronounced* a-**nak**-ro-nizm) *noun* the mention of something which did not exist or was not yet invented at the time spoken about □ **anachronistic** *adjective*

anaconda *noun* a large South American water snake

anaemia or *US* **anemia** (*both pronounced* a-**nee**-mi-*a*) *noun* a shortage of red cells in the blood

anaemic (*pronounced* a-**nee**-mik) *adjective* 1 suffering from anaemia 2 pale or ill-looking

anaerobic *adjective* not requiring oxygen to live

anaesthesia or *US* **anesthesia** (*both pronounced* an-es-**thee**-zi-*a*) *noun* loss of feeling or sensation

anaesthetic or *US* **anesthetic** (*both pronounced* an-es-**thet**-ik) *noun* a substance which produces lack of feeling for a time in a part of the body, or which makes someone unconscious

anaesthetist (*pronounced* an-**ees**-the-tist) *noun* a doctor trained to administer anaesthetics

anagram *noun* a word or sentence formed by reordering the letters of another word or sentence, *eg* veil is an anagram of *evil*

 MAKE THE REAL SHAPES is an anagram of a famous playwright and one of his best-known plays. Can you solve it?
Now have a go at inventing some anagrams of your own.

anal *adjective* of the anus

analgesic *adjective* causing insensibility to pain

analogous *adjective* similar, alike in some way

analogy *noun* (*plural* **analogies**) a likeness, resemblance in certain ways

analyse or *US* **analyze** *verb* 1 to break down, separate into parts 2 to examine in detail

analysis *noun* (*plural* **analyses**) 1 a breaking up of a thing into its parts 2 a detailed examination (of something)

analyst *noun* 1 someone who analyses 2 a psychiatrist or psychologist

analyze *US spelling* of **analyse**

anarchic or **anarchical** *adjective* 1 refusing to obey any rules 2 in a state of disorder or confusion

anarchist *noun* someone who believes in anarchy

anarchy *noun* 1 lack or absence of government 2 disorder or confusion

anathema (*pronounced* a-**nath**-e-ma) *noun* 1 a curse 2 a hated person or thing: *opera is anathema to him*

anatomist *noun* a person who specializes in the study of the human body

anatomy *noun* 1 the study of the parts of the body 2 the body

ancestor *noun* a person from whom someone is descended by birth; a forefather □ **ancestral** *adjective*

■ Alternative words: antecedent

ancestry *noun* line of ancestors

anchor *noun* a heavy piece of iron, with hooked ends, for holding a ship fast to the bed of the sea *etc* □ *verb* 1 to fix by anchor 2 to let down the anchor □ **cast anchor** to let down the anchor □ **weigh anchor** to pull up the anchor

anchorage *noun* a place where a ship can anchor

anchorman, anchorwoman *noun* the main presenter of a television news programme *etc*

anchovy *noun* (*plural* **anchovies**) a type of small fish of the herring family

ancient *adjective* 1 very old 2 of times long past

ancient monument a building, grave *etc* remaining from ancient times

ancillary *adjective* serving or supporting something more important

and *conjunction* 1 joining two statements, pieces of information *etc*: *black and white film/ add milk and stir* 2 in addition to: *2 and 2 make 4*

andro- or **andr-** *prefix* having to do with men, male
Ⓛ Comes from Greek *aner, andros* meaning 'man' or 'male'

android *noun* a robot in human form

anecdote *noun* a short, interesting or amusing story, usually true □ **anecdotal** *adjective*

anemo- *prefix* of the wind
Ⓛ Comes from Greek *anemos* meaning 'wind'

anemometer *noun* an instrument for measuring the speed of the wind

anemone (*pronounced* a-**nem**-o-ni) *noun* a type of woodland or garden flower

aneroid barometer a barometer which measures air pressure without the use of mercury

aneurism (*pronounced* **an**-yoo-ri-zm) *noun* 1 dilatation of an artery 2 abnormal enlargement

angel 1 *noun* a messenger or attendant of God 2 a very good or beautiful person **angelic** *adjective* as perfectly sweet and good as an angel

angelica *noun* a plant whose candied leaf-stalks are used as cake decoration

angelically *adverb* in a perfectly sweet and virtuous way: *'Of course,' she replied angelically*

anger *noun* a bitter feeling against someone, annoyance, rage □ *verb* to make angry

angina *noun* a form of heart disease causing acute pains

angle *noun* **1** the V-shape made by two lines meeting at a point **2** a corner **3** a point of view □ *verb* to try to get by hints *etc*: *angling for a job*

angler *noun* someone who fishes with rod and line

Anglican *adjective* of the Church of England □ *noun* a member of the Church of England

anglicize *verb* **1** to turn into the English language **2** to make English in character □ **anglicization** *noun*

angling *noun* the sport of fishing with a rod and line

Anglo-Saxon *adjective* & *noun* **1** (of) the people of England before the Norman Conquest **2** (of) their language

angry *adjective* feeling or showing anger □ **angrily** *adverb*

■ **Alternative words**: cross, irate, incensed, enraged, furious

anguish *noun* very great pain or distress

angular *adjective* **1** having angles **2** thin, bony □ **angularity** *noun*

animal *noun* **1** a living being which can feel and move of its own accord **2** an animal other than a human □ *adjective* of or like an animal

animate *verb* (*pronounced* **an**-im-eit) **1** to give life to **2** to make lively □ *adjective* (*pronounced* **an**-im-at) living

■ **Opposite**: (adjective) inanimate

animated *adjective* **1** lively **2** made to move as if alive

animation *noun* **1** liveliness **2** a film made from a series of drawings that

give the illusion of movement when shown in sequence

animator *noun* an artist who works in animation

animosity *noun* bitter hatred, enmity

aniseed *noun* a seed with a flavour like that of liquorice

ankle *noun* the joint connecting the foot and leg

annals *noun plural* yearly historical accounts of events

annex *verb* **1** to take possession of **2** to add, attach □ *noun* (*also spelled* **annexe**) a building added to another □ **annexation** *noun*

annihilate (*pronounced* a-**nai**-*i*-leit) *verb* to destroy completely □ **annihilation** *noun*

anniversary *noun* (*plural* **anniversaries**) the day of each year when a particular event is remembered

annotate *verb* **1** to make notes upon **2** to add notes or explanation to □ **annotation** *noun*

announce *verb* to make publicly known □ **announcement** *noun*

announcer *noun* someone who announces programmes on TV *etc*, or reads the news

annoy *verb* to make rather angry; irritate □ **annoyance** *noun*

■ **Alternative words**: aggravate, irritate, pester, rile, vex, irk

annual *adjective* yearly □ *noun* **1** a plant that lives only one year **2** a book published yearly

annually *adverb* every year

annuity *noun* (*plural* **annuities**) a yearly payment made for a certain time or for life

annul *verb* **1** to put an end to **2** to declare no longer valid □ **annulment** *noun*

annul ➪ annul**s**, annull**ing**, annull**ed**

anodyne *adjective* **1** soothing, relieving pain **2** bland and harmless: *a fairly anodyne comment* □ *noun* something that soothes pain

anoint *verb* to smear with ointment or oil

anomaly *noun* (*plural* **anomalies**) something unusual, not according to rule □ **anomalous** *adjective*

anon *abbreviation* anonymous

anonymous *adjective* without the name of the author, giver *etc* being known or given □ **anonymously** *adverb*: *He sent the letter anonymously*

anorak *noun* a hooded waterproof jacket

anorexia *noun* 1 (*also called* **anorexia nervosa**) an emotional illness causing the sufferer to refuse food and become sometimes dangerously thin 2 lack of appetite

anorexic *adjective* of or suffering from anorexia □ *noun* someone suffering from anorexia

another *adjective* 1 a different (thing or person): *moving to another job* 2 one more of the same kind: *have another biscuit* □ *pronoun* an additional thing of the same kind: *do you want another?*

answer *verb* 1 to speak, write *etc* in return or reply 2 to find the result or solution (of a sum, problem *etc*) □ *noun* something said, written *etc* in return or reply; a solution □ **answer back** to give a cheeky or aggressive answer to someone in authority □ **answer for** 1 to be responsible for 2 to suffer for, be punished for

answerable *adjective* 1 able to be answered 2 responsible: *answerable for her actions*

ant *noun* a very small insect which lives in organized colonies □ **have ants in your pants** to be impatient or restless

antagonism *noun* hostility, opposition, enmity

antagonist *noun* 1 an enemy 2 an opponent

antagonistic *adjective* opposed (to), unfriendly, hostile

antagonize *verb* to make an enemy of, cause dislike

Antarctic *adjective* of the South Pole or regions round it

ante- *prefix* before

⏱ Comes from Latin *ante* meaning 'before'

anteater *noun* an American animal with a long snout which feeds on ants and termites

ante-bellum *adjective* of the period before a particular war

antecedent (*pronounced* ant-i-**see**-dent) *adjective* going before in time □ *noun* 1 someone who lived at an earlier time; an ancestor 2 **antecedents** previous conduct, history *etc*

antedate *verb* 1 to backdate (= put a date on a document which is earlier than the day you are actually writing it) 2 to be earlier in date than

antediluvian *adjective* very old or old-fashioned

Literally 'before the flood', in allusion to the Biblical story of Noah

antelope *noun* a graceful, swift-running animal like a deer

antenatal *adjective* 1 before birth 2 relating to pregnancy: *antenatal clinic*

antenna *noun* 1 (*plural* **antennae** – *pronounced* an-**ten**-ee) an insect's feeler 2 (*plural* **antennas**) an aerial

anteroom *noun* a room leading into a large room

anthem *noun* 1 a piece of music for a church choir 2 any song of praise

ant-hill *noun* an earth mound built by ants as a nest

antho- *prefix* of or relating to flowers: *anthology/ anthomania* (= a craze for flowers)

⏱ Comes from Greek *anthos* meaning 'flower'

anthology *noun* (*plural* **anthologies**) a collection of specially chosen poems, stories *etc*

⏱ Comes from Greek *anthos* meaning 'flower', and *logia* meaning 'collection'

anthracite *noun* coal that burns with a hot, smokeless flame

anthrax *noun* an infectious disease of cattle, sheep *etc*, sometimes transferred to humans

anthropo- or **anthrop-** *prefix* of or relating to humans

🕐 Comes from Greek *anthropos* meaning 'human being'

anthropoid *adjective* of apes: resembling humans

anthropology *noun* the study of mankind □ **anthropological** *adjective* □ **anthropologist** *noun*

anti- *prefix* against, opposite: *anti-terrorist*

🕐 Comes from Greek *anti* meaning 'against'

antibiotic *noun* a medicine taken to kill disease-causing bacteria

antibody *noun* (*plural* **antibodies**) a substance produced in the human body to fight bacteria *etc*

anticipate *verb* 1 to look forward to, expect 2 to see or know in advance 3 to act before (someone or something)

anticipation *noun* 1 expectation 2 excitement

anticipatory *adjective* full of anticipation

anticlimax *noun* a dull or disappointing ending

anticlockwise *adjective & adverb* in the opposite direction to the hands of a clock

antics *noun plural* tricks, odd or amusing actions

anticyclone *noun* a circling movement of air round an area of high air pressure, causing calm weather

antidote *noun* something given to act against the effect of poison

antifreeze *noun* a chemical with a low freezing-point, added to a car radiator to prevent freezing

antihistamine *noun* a medicine used to treat an allergy

antipathy *noun* extreme dislike

antiperspirant *noun* a substance applied to the body to reduce sweating

antipodes (*pronounced* an-**tip**-*o*d-eez) *noun plural* places on the earth's surface exactly opposite each other, especially Australia and New Zealand in relation to Europe □ **antipodean** *adjective*

antiquarian *noun* a dealer in antiques

antiquated *adjective* grown old, or out of fashion

antique *noun* an old, interesting or valuable object from earlier times □ *adjective* 1 old, from earlier times 2 old-fashioned

antiquity *noun* (*plural* **antiquities**) 1 ancient times, especially those of the Greeks and Romans 2 great age 3 **antiquities** objects from earlier times

antiseptic *adjective* germ-destroying □ *noun* a chemical *etc* which destroys germs

antisocial *adjective* 1 not fitting in with, harmful to other people 2 disliking the company of other people

antithesis *noun* (*plural* **antitheses**) the exact opposite: *the antithesis of good taste* □ **antithetical** *adjective*

antler *noun* the horn of a deer

anus (*pronounced* ei-n*u*s) *noun* the lower opening of the bowel through which faeces pass

anvil *noun* a metal block on which blacksmiths hammer metal into shape

anxiety *noun* (*plural* **anxieties**) worry about what may happen, apprehensiveness

anxious *adjective* 1 worried, apprehensive 2 full of worry or uncertainty 3 eager, keen: *anxious to please*

■ **Alternative words**: (meaning 1) apprehensive, jittery; (meaning 2) tense, uneasy

any *adjective* 1 some: *is there any milk?* 2 every, no matter which: *any day will suit me* □ *pronoun* some: *there aren't any left* □ *adverb* at all: *I can't work any faster* □ **at any rate** in any case, whatever happens

anybody *pronoun* any person

anyhow *adverb* 1 in any case: *I think I'll go anyhow* 2 carelessly: *scattered anyhow over the floor*

anyone *pronoun* any person

anything *pronoun* something of any kind

anyway *adverb* at any rate

anywhere *adverb* in any place

apart adverb **1** aside **2** in or into pieces: came apart in my hands **3** in opposite directions □ **apart from 1** separate, or separately, from **2** except for: who else knows apart from us?

apartheid noun the political policy of keeping people of different races apart

apartment noun **1** a room in a house **2** US a flat

apathy noun lack of feeling or interest □ **apathetic** adjective

ape noun a member of a group of animals related to monkeys, but larger, tailless and walking upright □ verb to imitate

aperitif (pronounced a-pe-ri-**teef**) noun a drink taken before a meal

aperture noun an opening, a hole

apex noun (plural **apexes** or **apices** – pronounced **ei**-pi-seez) the highest point of anything

aphid (pronounced **ei**-fid) noun a small insect which feeds on plants

aphrodisiac noun a drug, food etc that increases sexual desire □ adjective causing increased sexual desire

apiarist (pronounced **ei**-pi-a-rist) noun someone who keeps an apiary or studies bees

apiary (pronounced **ei**-pi-a-ri) noun (plural **apiaries**) a place where bees are kept

apiece adverb to or for each one: three chocolates apiece

aplomb noun self-confidence

apo- or **ap-** prefix from, off, away, quite
⏲ Comes from Greek prefix apo- with the same meaning

apocalypse noun the destruction of the world □ **apocalyptic** adjective

apocryphal (pronounced a-**pok**-rif-al) adjective unlikely to be true

apogee (pronounced **ap**-o-jee) noun **1** a culmination, a climax **2** the point of an orbit furthest from the earth

apologetic adjective expressing regret

apologize verb to express regret, say you are sorry

apology noun (plural **apologies**) an

expression of regret for having done wrong

apoplexy noun sudden loss of ability to feel, move etc, a stroke □ **apoplectic** adjective

apoptosis noun, biochemistry cell death

apostle noun **1** a religious preacher, especially one of the disciples of Christ **2** an advocate for a cause

apostrophe noun **1** a mark (') indicating possession: the minister's cat **2** a similar mark indicating that a letter etc has been missed out, eg isn't for is not

apothecary noun (plural **apothecaries**) old a chemist or druggist

appal verb to horrify, shock

appal ⇨ appals, appalling, appalled

appalling adjective shocking

apparatus noun **1** an instrument or machine **2** instruments, tools or material required for a piece of work

apparel noun a formal or literary word for clothing

apparent adjective easily seen, evident □ **apparently** adverb: 'But I thought they were going out together.' 'Apparently not.'

apparition noun **1** something remarkable which appears suddenly **2** a ghost

appeal verb **1** to ask earnestly (for help etc): appeal to the public for information **2** law to take a case that has been lost to a higher court **3** appeal to someone to be pleasing to someone □ noun **1** a request for help **2** law the taking of a case to a higher court

appealing adjective **1** arousing liking or sympathy **2** asking earnestly

appear verb **1** to come into view **2** to arrive **3** to seem □ **appearance** noun

appease verb to soothe or satisfy, especially by giving what was asked for: Nothing would appease his anger

appendectomy noun, medical surgical removal of the appendix

appendicitis noun, medical inflammation of the appendix

appendix noun (plural **appendices** or

appendixes) 1 a part added at the end of a book **2** a small worm-shaped part of the bowels

appertain to *verb, formal* **1** to belong to: *duties appertaining to senior officers* **2** to be relevant to: *This section appertains most particularly to your situation*

appetite *noun* **1** desire for food **2** taste or enthusiasm (for): *no appetite for violence*

appetizer *noun* a snack taken before a main meal

appetizing *adjective* tempting to the appetite

applaud *verb* **1** to show approval of by clapping the hands **2** to express strong approval of and admiration for: *I applaud the Prime Minister's decision*

applause *noun* a show of approval by clapping

apple *noun* a round firm fruit, usually red or green □ **the apple of someone's eye** a person or thing that is greatly loved by someone

appliance *noun* a tool, instrument, machine *etc*

applicable *adjective* **1** able to be applied **2** suitable, relevant

applicant *noun* someone who applies or asks

application *noun* **1** the act of applying **2** something applied, *eg* an ointment **3** a formal request, usually on paper **4** hard work, close attention

appliqué (*pronounced* ap-**leek**-ei) *noun* needlework in which cut pieces of fabric are sewn on to a background to form patterns

apply *verb* **1** to put on (an ointment *etc*) **2** to use: *apply these rules in each case* **3** to ask formally (for) **4** to be suitable or relevant **5** **apply to** to affect □ **apply yourself** to work hard

apply ⇨ applies, applying, applied

appoint *verb* **1** to fix (a date *etc*) **2** to place in a job: *she was appointed manager* □ **appointed** *adjective* (meaning 1): *fail to arrive at the appointed time*

appointment *noun* **1** the act of

appointing **2** a job, a post **3** an arrangement to meet someone

apportion *verb* to divide in fair shares: *The blame must be apportioned among several different people*

apposite (*pronounced* **ap**-*o*-zit) *adjective* suitable, appropriate

appraise *verb* to estimate the value or quality of: *appraise someone's work* □ **appraisal** *noun*

appraising *adjective* quickly summing up

appreciable *adjective* noticeable, considerable

appreciate *verb* **1** to see or understand the good points, beauties *etc* of: *appreciate art* **2** to understand: *I appreciate your point* **3** to rise in value □ **appreciation** *noun*

⬛ **Opposite**: (meaning 3) depreciate

apprehend *verb* **1** to arrest: *The escaped prisoner was apprehended early today* **2** *formal* to understand

apprehension *noun* **1** arrest **2** fear or nervousness **3** *formal* understanding

apprehensive *adjective* afraid

apprentice *noun* someone who is learning a trade

apprenticeship *noun* the time during which someone is an apprentice

approach *verb* **1** to come near **2** to be nearly equal to **3** to speak to in order to ask for something □ *noun* (*plural* **approaches**) **1** a coming near to **2** a way leading to a place

approachable *adjective* **1** able to be reached **2** easy to speak to, friendly

approbation *noun* good opinion, approval

appropriate *adjective* (*pronounced* a-**proh**-pri-*a*t) suitable, fitting □ *verb* (*pronounced* a-**proh**-pri-eit) **1** to take possession of: *She seems to have appropriated certain items of my clothing* **2** to set (money *etc*) apart for a purpose: *Funds must be appropriated for this work* □ **appropriately** *adverb*: *the appropriately-named 'Wall of Death'* □ **appropriation** *noun*

'to appropriate' (meaning 1) is often used as a euphemism for 'to steal'

■ **Alternative words**: (adjective) apt

---

approval noun 1 permission 2 satisfaction, favourable judgement □ **on approval** on trial, for return to a shop if not bought

approve verb 1 to agree to, permit 2 to think well (of): did he approve of the new curtains?

approximate adjective (pronounced ap-**rok**-sim-at) more or less accurate □ verb (pronounced ap-**rok**-sim-eit): **approximate to** to be or come near to: The money set aside doesn't approximate to the amount needed □ **approximately** adverb: at approximately half past two

approximation noun a rough estimate

apricot noun an orange-coloured fruit like a small peach

April noun the fourth month of the year

a priori (pronounced ei prai-**aw**-ri or ah pri-**aw**-ri) adjective based on accepted principles or arguments

apron noun 1 a garment worn to protect the front of the clothes 2 a hard surface for aircraft to stand on

apron stage the part of the stage in front of the curtains in a theatre

apropos (pronounced a-pro-**poh**) adverb: **apropos of** in connection with, concerning

apse noun a rounded domed section, especially at the east end of a church

apt adjective 1 likely (to): apt to change his mind 2 suitable, fitting

aptitude noun talent, ability

aptness noun suitability

aqua- prefix of or relating to water
🕐 Comes from Latin aqua meaning 'water'

aqualung noun a breathing apparatus worn by divers

aquamarine noun 1 a type of bluish-green precious stone 2 a bluish-green colour □ adjective bluish-green

aquarium noun (plural **aquaria** or **aquariums**) a tank or tanks for keeping fish or water animals

aquatic adjective living, growing or taking place in water

aqueduct noun a bridge for taking a canal etc across a valley

aquiline adjective 1 like an eagle 2 of a nose: curved or hooked

arable adjective of land: used for growing crops

arbiter noun 1 a judge, an umpire, someone chosen by opposing parties to decide between them 2 someone who sets a standard or has influence: arbiter of good taste

arbitrage noun the practice of buying goods etc in one market and selling in another to make a profit

arbitrary adjective 1 fixed according to opinion, not objective rules 2 occurring haphazardly □ **arbitrarily** adverb

arbitrate verb to act as a judge between people or their claims etc: arbitrate between the different parties/ It falls to me to arbitrate this case

arbitration noun 1 the act of judging between claims etc 2 the settlement of a dispute by an arbiter

arbitrator noun someone who arbitrates

arboreal (pronounced ah-**baw**-ri-al) adjective of trees, living in trees

arbour noun a seat in a garden shaded by tree-branches etc

arc noun part of the circumference of a circle, a curve

arcade noun a covered walk, especially one with shops on both sides

arch noun (plural **arches**) the curved part above people's heads in a gateway or the curved support for a bridge, roof etc □ adjective mischievous, roguish □ verb to raise or curve in the shape of an arch

arch- prefix chief, main: arch-enemy
🕐 Comes from Greek archos meaning 'chief'

Arch- is usually pronounced ahch (as in 'March'), but in archangel it is pronounced ahk (like 'ark')

archaeo- prefix of or relating to ancient or primitive things
🕐 Comes from Greek archaios meaning 'ancient'

archaeology noun the study of the

people of earlier times from the remains of their buildings *etc* □ **archaeological** *adjective* □ **archaeologist** *noun*

archaic (*pronounced* ahk-**ei**-ik) *adjective* no longer used, old-fashioned

archaism (*pronounced* **ahk**-ei-i-sm) *noun* an old-fashioned word *etc*

archangel *noun* a chief angel

archbishop *noun* a chief bishop

archdeacon *noun* a clergyman next in rank below a bishop

archduke *noun, historical* the title of the ruling princes of Austria

archer *noun* someone who shoots arrows from a bow

archery *noun* the sport of shooting with a bow and arrows

archetype (*pronounced* **ahk**-i-taip) *noun* the original pattern or model from which copies are made □ **archetypal** *adjective*

archipelago *noun* (*plural* **archipelagoes** or **archipelagos**) a group of small islands

> From an ancient Greek term for the Aegean Sea, which translates as 'chief sea'

architect *noun* someone who plans and designs buildings

architecture *noun* **1** the study of building **2** the style of a building

archives *noun plural* **1** historical papers, written records *etc* **2** a building *etc* in which these are kept

archway *noun* a passage or road beneath an arch

arc-lamp or **arc-light** *noun* a bright lamp lit by a special kind of electric current

Arctic or **arctic** *adjective* **1** (usually **Arctic**) of the district round the North Pole **2** (usually **arctic**) very cold

ardent *adjective* eager, passionate □ **ardently** *adverb* □ **ardour** *noun*

arduous *adjective* difficult

are *see* **be**

area *noun* **1** the extent of a surface measured in square metres *etc* **2** a region, a piece of land or ground

arena *noun* **1** any place for a public contest, show *etc* **2** *historical* the centre of an amphitheatre *etc* where gladiators fought

argosy *noun* (*plural* **argosies**) a literary word meaning a large trading-ship with a valuable cargo

arguable *adjective* that can be argued as being true

arguably *adverb* in certain people's opinion (although this opinion could be disagreed with): *This is arguably the best Scottish film of the decade*

argue *verb* **1** to quarrel in words **2** to try to prove by giving reasons (that) **3** **argue for** or **against something** to give reasons for or against something as a way of persuading people **4** **argue someone into** or **out of something** to persuade someone, by arguing with them, to do or not to do something

> **argue** ⇨ argu*es*, argu*ing*, argu*ed*

■ **Alternative words**: (meaning 1) wrangle, remonstrate, dispute, debate; (meaning 2) reason, contend, hold, maintain

argument *noun* **1** a heated discussion, quarrel **2** reasoning (for or against something)

■ **Alternative words**: (meaning 1) dispute

argumentative *adjective* fond of arguing

■ **Alternative words**: quarrelsome

aria *noun* a song for solo voice in an opera

arid *adjective* dry □ **aridity** or **aridness** *noun*

arise *verb* **1** to rise up **2** to come into being

> **arise** ⇨ aris*es*, aris*ing*, a*rose*, aris*en*

aristocracy *noun* those of the nobility and upper class

aristocrat *noun* a member of the aristocracy

aristocratic *adjective* of the aristocracy

arithmetic *noun* a way of counting and calculating by using numbers □ **arithmetical** *adjective*

ark *noun* the covered boat used by Noah in the Biblical story of the Flood

arm *noun* **1** the part of the body between the shoulder and the hand **2** anything jutting out like this **3 arms** weapons □ *verb* to equip with weapons □ **the long arm of the law** the power or authority of the police force □ **chance your arm** to say or do something which, though a bit risky, could possibly get you what you want

armada *noun* a fleet of armed ships

armadillo *noun* (*plural* **armadillos**) a small American animal whose body is protected by bony plates

armageddon *noun* a final battle or devastation, an apocalypse

armaments *noun plural* equipment for war, especially the guns of a ship, tank *etc*

armchair *noun* a chair with arms at each side

armed *adjective* carrying a weapon, now especially a gun

armistice *noun* a halt in fighting during war, a truce

armour *noun, historical* a protective suit of metal worn by knights

armoured *adjective* of a vehicle: protected by metal plates

armoury *noun* (*plural* **armouries**) an arms store

arm-pit *noun* the hollow under the arm at the shoulder

army *noun* (*plural* **armies**) **1** a large number of soldiers armed for war **2** a great number of anything

aroma *noun* a sweet smell

aromatherapy *noun* a healing therapy involving massage with plant oils

arose *past form* of **arise**

around *preposition* **1** in a circle about **2** on all sides of, surrounding **3** all over, at several places in: *papers scattered around the room* **4** somewhere near in time, place, amount: *I left him around here/ come back around three o'clock* □ *adverb* all about, in various places: *people stood around watching* □ **get around 1** of a story: to become known to everyone **2** to be active

arousal *noun* **1** the state of being stimulated or excited, especially sexually **2** awakening (of feelings)

arouse *verb* **1** to awaken **2** to stir, move (a feeling or person)

arpeggio *noun, music* a chord with the notes played in rapid succession, not at the same time

arrange *verb* **1** to put in some order **2** to plan, settle

arrangement *noun* **1** a pattern or particular order **2** an agreed plan

array *noun* order, arrangement; clothing □ *verb* **1** to put in order: *a huge collection of insects, carefully arrayed in glass cases* **2** to dress, adorn: *arraying themselves in brightly-coloured garments*

arrears *noun plural*: **in arrears** not up to date; behind with payments

arrest *verb* **1** to seize, capture, especially by power of the law **2** to stop **3** to catch (the attention *etc*) □ *noun* **1** capture by the police **2** stopping

arresting *adjective* striking, capturing the attention

arrival *noun* **1** the act of arriving **2** someone or something that arrives

arrive *verb* to reach a place □ **arrive at** to reach, come to (a decision *etc*)

arrogant *adjective* proud, haughty, self-important □ **arrogance** *noun* □ **arrogantly** *adverb*: *arrogantly tossing her head*

arrow *noun* **1** a straight, pointed weapon shot from a bow **2** an arrow-shape, *eg* on a road-sign, showing direction

arsenal *noun* a factory or store for weapons, ammunition *etc*

arsenic *noun* an element that, combined with oxygen, makes a strong poison

arson *noun* the crime of setting fire to a house *etc* on purpose □ **arsonist** *noun*

art *noun* **1** drawing, painting, sculpture *etc* **2** cleverness, skill; cunning **3 arts** non-scientific school or university subjects

artefact or **artifact** *noun* a human-made object

arterial *adjective* of or like arteries

arterial road a main traffic road

artery *noun* (*plural* **arteries**) a tube which carries blood from the heart to pass through the body

artesian well a well in which water rises to the surface by natural pressure

artful *adjective* wily, cunning

artichoke *noun* a thistle-like plant with an edible flower-head

article *noun* **1** a thing, object **2** a composition in a newspaper, journal *etc* **3** a section of a document **4 articles** an agreement made up of clauses: *articles of apprenticeship* **5** *grammar* the name of the words *the, a, an* □ *verb* to bind (an apprentice *etc*) by articles

articulate *adjective* (*pronounced* ah-**tik**-yu-la*t*) expressing thoughts or words clearly □ *verb* (*pronounced* ah-**tik**-yu-leit) to express clearly □ **articulation** *noun*

articulated lorry a lorry with a cab which can turn at an angle to the main part of the lorry, making cornering easier

artifact *another spelling of* **artefact**

artificial *adjective* not natural; human-made □ **artificiality** *noun*

■ **Alternative words**: synthetic, man-made, affected, assumed, spurious

artificial insemination the insertion of sperm into the uterus by means other than sexual intercourse

artillery *noun* **1** big guns **2** an army division that uses these

artisan *noun* a skilled worker

artist *noun* **1** someone who paints pictures **2** someone skilled in anything **3** an artiste

artiste (*pronounced* ah-**teest**) *noun* a performer in a theatre, circus *etc*

artistic *adjective* **1** of artists: *the artistic community* **2** having a talent for art

artistry *noun* skill as an artist

artless *adjective* simple, frank

as *adverb* & *conjunction* in phrases expressing comparison or similarity: *as good as his brother/ the same as this one*

□ *conjunction* **1** while, when: *happened as I was walking past* **2** because, since: *we stayed at home as it was raining* **3** in the same way that: *he thinks as I do* □ *adverb* for instance □ **as for** concerning, regarding □ **as if** or **as though** as it would be if □ **as to** regarding □ **as well (as)** too, in addition (to)

asbestos *noun* a thread-like mineral which can be woven and which will not burn

asbestosis *noun* a lung disease caused by inhaling asbestos dust

ascend *verb* **1** to climb, go up **2** to rise or slope upwards □ **ascend the throne** to be crowned king or queen

ascendancy or **ascendency** *noun* control (over)

ascendant or **ascendent** *adjective* rising

ascent *noun* **1** an upward move or climb **2** a slope upwards; a rise

ascertain *verb* **1** to find out **2** to make certain

ascetic *noun* someone who keeps away from all kinds of pleasure

ascribe *verb*: **ascribe something to someone** or **something** to think of as belonging to or due to that person or thing: *ascribing the blame to the Secretary General*

ash *noun* (*plural* **ashes**) **1** a type of hard-wood tree with silvery bark **2 ashes** what is left after anything is burnt □ **rise from the ashes** to develop and flourish after experiencing ruin or disaster

This phrase comes from the image of the phoenix, a mythical bird which destroyed itself in fire and was reborn again from the ashes

ashamed *adjective* feeling shame

ashen *adjective* very pale

ashore *adverb* on or on to the shore

aside *adverb* on or to one side; apart □ *noun* words spoken which those nearby are not supposed to hear

asinine *adjective* **1** of an ass **2** stupid

ask *verb* **1** to request information about: *asked for my address* **2** to invite:

we've asked over twenty people to come
□ **ask after someone** to make enquiries about someone's health and well-being

askance *adverb* off the straight □ **look askance at** to look at with suspicion

askew *adverb* off the straight, to one side

asleep *adjective* **1** sleeping **2** of limbs: numbed

ASLEF *abbreviation* Associated Society of Locomotive Engineers and Firemen

asp *noun* a small poisonous snake

asparagus *noun* a plant whose young shoots are eaten as a vegetable

aspect *noun* **1** look, appearance **2** view, point of view **3** side of a building *etc* or the direction it faces in

aspen *noun* a kind of poplar tree

asperity *noun* **1** harshness, sharpness of temper **2** bitter coldness

asphalt *noun* a tarry mixture used to make pavements, paths *etc*

asphyxia (*pronounced* as-**fik**-si-a) *noun* suffocation by smoke or other fumes

asphyxiate *verb* to suffocate
□ **asphyxiation** *noun*

aspidistra *noun* a kind of pot-plant with large leaves

aspiration *noun* a goal which you hope to achieve

aspire *verb*: **aspire to something** or **after something** to try to achieve or reach something difficult, ambitious *etc*

aspirin *noun* a pain-killing drug

aspiring *adjective* trying or wishing to be: *an aspiring director*

ass *noun* (*plural* **asses**) **1** a donkey **2** a stupid person

assail *verb* to attack

assailant *noun* an attacker

assassin *noun* someone who assassinates, a murderer

> Literally 'hashish eater', after an Islamic sect during the Crusades who consumed the drug before assassinating Christians

assassinate *verb* to murder (especially a politically important person)
□ **assassination** *noun*

assault *noun* an attack, especially a sudden one □ *verb* to attack

assegai (*pronounced* as-eg-ai) *noun* a South African spear, tipped with metal

assemblage *noun* a collection, a gathering

assemble *verb* **1** to bring (people) together **2** to put together (a machine *etc*) **3** to meet together

assembly *noun* (*plural* **assemblies**) **1** a putting together **2** a gathering of people, especially for a special purpose

assembly line series of machines and workers necessary for the manufacture of an article

assent *verb* to agree: *The committee assents to your request* □ *noun* agreement

assert *verb* **1** to state firmly: *She asserts that she did not take the money* **2** to insist on (a right *etc*): *women asserting their right to equal pay with men*
□ **assert yourself** to make yourself noticed, heard *etc* □ **assertion** *noun*

assertive *adjective* not shy, inclined to assert yourself

assess *verb* **1** to estimate the value, power of *etc* **2** to fix an amount (to be paid in tax *etc*) □ **assessment** *noun*

assessor *noun* someone who assesses

asset *noun* **1** an advantage, a help **2** **assets** the property of a person, company *etc*

■ **Alternative words**: (meaning 1) boon

assiduous *adjective* persevering; hard-working

assign (*pronounced* a-**sain**) *verb* **1** to give to someone as a share or task: *I've assigned these tasks to you* **2** to fix (a time or place): *assign a date for the meeting*

assignation (*pronounced* as-ig-**nei**-shun) *noun* an appointment to meet

assignment *noun* **1** an act of assigning **2** a task given

assimilation *noun* the taking in and successful digesting of (food or information)

assimilate *verb* to take in: *assimilate all the information*

assist *verb* to help □ **assistance** *noun*

assistant *noun* **1** a helper, *eg* to a senior worker **2** someone who serves in a shop *etc*

assizes *noun plural* the name of certain law courts in England

associate *verb* **1 associate with** to keep company with **2 associate yourself with** to join with in partnership or friendship: *He has never associated himself with environmental pressure groups* **3** to connect in thought: *I don't associate him with hard work* □ *adjective* joined or connected (with) □ *noun* a friend, partner, companion

association *noun* **1** a club, society, union *etc* **2** a partnership, friendship **3** a connection made in the mind

assorted *adjective* various, mixed

assortment *noun* a variety, a mixture

assuage *verb* to soothe, ease (pain, hunger *etc*)

assume *verb* **1** to take upon yourself: *assume responsibility for the errors which have been made* **2** to take as true without further proof, take for granted **3** to put on (a disguise *etc*)

assumed *adjective* false or pretended: *an assumed air of confidence/ an assumed name*

assumption *noun* **1** the act of assuming **2** something taken for granted

assurance *noun* **1** a feeling of certainty; confidence **2** a promise **3** insurance

assure *verb* **1** to make (someone) sure: *I assured him of my intention to return home* **2** to state positively (that)

assured *adjective* certain; confident

asterisk *noun* a star (*) used in printing for various purposes, especially to point out a footnote or insertion

astern *adverb* at or towards the back of a ship

asthma (*pronounced* **as**-ma) *noun* an illness causing difficulty in breathing, coughing *etc*

asthmatic (*pronounced* as-**mat**-ik) *adjective* suffering from asthma □ *noun* someone with asthma

astonish *verb* to surprise greatly □ **astonishing** *adjective*

■ **Alternative words**: amaze

astonishment *noun* amazement, wonder

astound *verb* to surprise greatly, amaze □ **astounding** *adjective*

astral *adjective* of the stars

astray *adverb* out of the right way, straying

astride *adverb* with legs apart □ *preposition* with legs on each side of

astringent *noun* a lotion *etc* used for closing up the skin's pores □ *adjective* **1** used for closing the pores **2** of manner: sharp, sarcastic

astro- or **astr-** *prefix* of or relating to stars or outer space
① Comes from Greek *astron* meaning 'a star'

astrology *noun* the study of the stars and their supposed power over the lives of humans □ **astrologer** *noun*

astronaut *noun* someone who travels in space

astronomer *noun* someone who studies astronomy

astronomical *adjective* **1** of astronomy **2** of a number: very large

astronomy *noun* the study of the stars and their movements

astute *adjective* cunning, clever □ **astutely** *adverb*

asunder *adverb* a literary word meaning 'apart' or 'into pieces'

asylum *noun* **1** a place of refuge or safety **2** *old* a home for the mentally ill

at *preposition* **1** showing position, time *etc*: *I'll be at home/ come at 7 o'clock* **2** costing: *cakes at 25 pence each* □ **at all** in any way: *not worried at all*

ate *past form of* **eat**

atheism *noun* belief that there is no God

atheist *noun* someone who does not believe in a God □ **atheistic** *adjective*

athlete *noun* someone good at sport, especially running, gymnastics *etc*

athlete's foot a fungal condition which affects the feet, making them sore and itchy

athletic *adjective* **1** of athletics **2** good at sports; strong, powerful

■ **Alternative words**: (meaning 2) agile

athletics *noun plural* running, jumping *etc* or competitions in these

atlas *noun* (*plural* **atlases**) a book of maps

After the mythological *Atlas*, punished by the Greek gods by having to carry the heavens on his shoulders

atmosphere *noun* **1** the air round the earth **2** any surrounding feeling: *friendly atmosphere*

■ **Alternative words**: (meaning 2) ambience

atmospheric *adjective* **1** of the atmosphere **2** with a noticeable atmosphere

atmospheric pressure the pressure exerted by the atmosphere at the earth's surface, due to the weight of the air

atmospherics *noun plural* air disturbances causing crackling noises on the radio *etc*

atoll *noun* a coral island or reef

atom *noun* **1** the smallest part of an element **2** anything very small

atom bomb or **atomic bomb** a bomb in which the explosion is caused by nuclear energy

atomic *adjective* nuclear

atomic energy nuclear energy

atomizer or **atomiser** *noun* an instrument for discharging liquids in a fine spray

atone *verb* to make up for wrong-doing: *atone for your sins* □ **atonement** *noun*

atrocious *adjective* **1** cruel or wicked **2** *informal* very bad

atrocity *noun* (*plural* **atrocities**) **1** a terrible crime **2** *informal* something very ugly

attach *verb* **1** to fasten or join (to) **2** to think of (something) as having: *don't atttach any importance to it*

attaché (*pronounced* a-**tash**-ei) *noun* a junior member of an embassy staff

attaché-case *noun* small case for papers *etc*

attached *adjective* **1** fastened **2** **attached to** fond of

attachment *noun* **1** something attached **2** a joining by love or friendship

attack *verb* **1** to fall upon suddenly or violently **2** to speak or write against □ *noun* **1** an act of attacking **2** a fit (of an illness *etc*)

attain *verb* to reach; gain

attainable *adjective* able to be attained

■ **Opposite**: unattainable

attainment *noun* act of attaining; the thing attained, an achievement or accomplishment

attempt *verb* to try □ *noun* **1** a try or effort: *first attempt* **2** an attack: *an attempt on the president's life*

■ **Alternative words**: (verb) endeavour; (noun, meaning 1) endeavour

attend *verb* **1** to be present at **2** **attend to something** to pay attention to something **3** to wait on, look after **4** to accompany

attendance *noun* **1** the fact of being present: *my attendance was expected* **2** the number of people present: *good attendance at the first night*

attendant *noun* someone employed to look after a public place, shop *etc*: *cloakroom attendant* □ *adjective* accompanying, related: *stress and its attendant health problems*

attention *noun* **1** careful notice: *pay attention* **2** concentration **3** care **4** *military* a stiffly straight standing position: *stand to attention*

attentive *adjective* **1** giving or showing attention **2** polite □ **attentively** *adverb*: *listening attentively*

attic *noun* a room just under the roof of a house

From *Attica* in ancient Greece, famous for a type of square architectural column used in upper storeys of classical buildings

attire *verb* to dress □ *noun* clothing

attitude *noun* **1** a way of thinking or

feeling: *positive attitude* **2** a position of the body

attorney *noun* (*plural* **attorneys**) **1** someone with legal power to act for another **2** *US* a lawyer

attract *verb* **1** to draw to or towards **2** to arouse liking or interest

attraction *noun* **1** the power of attracting **2** something which attracts visitors *etc*: *tourist attraction*

attractive *adjective* **1** good-looking, likeable **2** pleasing: *attractive price*

attribute *verb* (*pronounced* a-**trib**-yoot) **1** to state or consider as the source or cause of: *attribute the accident to human error* **2** to state as the author or originator of: *attributed to Rembrandt* □ *noun* (*pronounced* **a**-trib-yoot) an attendant characteristic: *attributes of power* □ **attributable** *adjective*

attributive *adjective* **1** expressing an attribute **2** of an adjective: placed immediately before or immediately after the noun it describes *eg* 'pretty' ('the pretty girl')

Most adjectives can be used in this 'attributive' way. The opposite of attributive (meaning 2) is 'predicative'. An example of an adjective which is only ever used in a predicative way is 'asleep', because you cannot use it to make phrases like 'the asleep girl'

aubergine (*pronounced* **oh**-be-zeen) *noun* an oval dark purple fruit, eaten as a vegetable

auburn *adjective* of hair: reddish-brown in colour

auction *noun* a public sale in which articles are sold to the highest bidder □ *verb* to sell by auction

auctioneer *noun* someone who sells by auction

audacious *adjective* daring, bold □ **audacity** *noun*

audible *adjective* able to be heard □ **audibility** *noun*

audience *noun* **1** a number of people gathered to watch or hear a performance *etc* **2** a formal interview with someone important: *an audience with the Pope*

audio *noun* the reproduction of recorded or radio sound □ *adjective* relating to such sound: *an audio tape*

audio- *prefix* of or relating to sounds which can be heard
① Comes from Latin *audio* meaning 'I hear'

audio-typist *noun* a typist able to type from a recording on a tape-recorder

audio-visual *adjective* concerned with hearing and seeing at the same time □ **audio-visual aids** films, recordings *etc* used in teaching

audit *verb* to examine accounts officially □ *noun* an official examination of a company's accounts

audition *noun* a hearing to test an actor, singer *etc*

auditor *noun* someone who audits accounts

auditorium *noun* (*plural* **auditoria** or **auditoriums**) the part of a theatre *etc* where the audience sits

auditory *adjective* of hearing

augment *verb* to increase in size, number or amount □ **augmentation** *noun*

augmentative *adjective* having the quality or power of increasing in size, number or amount

augur *verb*: **augur well** to be a good sign for the future □ **augur ill** to be a bad sign for the future

August *noun* the eighth month of the year

august (*pronounced* aw-**gust**) *adjective* full of dignity, stately

au naturel (*pronounced* oh nat-yu-**rel**) *adverb* with no additions; plain, natural

aunt *noun* a father's or a mother's sister, or an uncle's wife

au pair a foreign person, usually a girl, who does domestic duties in return for board, lodging and pocket money

aural *adjective* relating to the ear
① Comes from Latin *auris* meaning 'ear'

☞ Do not confuse with: **oral**. Oral means 'relating to the mouth'. It may help to think of the 'O' as looking like an open mouth; and to remember that many words related to listening start with 'AU', like 'audition' and 'auditorium'

aurora borealis the Northern lights

auspices *noun plural*: **under the auspices of** under the control or supervision of

auspicious *adjective* favourable; promising luck

austere *adjective* 1 severe 2 without luxury; simple, sparse □ **austerity** *noun*

authentic *adjective* true, real, genuine □ **authenticity** *noun*

authenticate *verb* to show to be true or real □ **authentication** *noun*

author *noun* the writer of a book, poem, play *etc*

authoress *noun, old* a female author

authoritative *adjective* stated by an expert or someone in authority

authority *noun* (*plural* **authorities**) 1 power or right 2 someone whose opinion is reliable, an expert 3 someone or a body of people having control (over something) 4 **authorities** people in power

authorize *verb* 1 to give (a person) the power or the right to do something: *I have authorized him to carry out these tasks* 2 to give permission (for something to be done): *The proposed renovation work has been authorized* □ **authorization** *noun*

autism *noun* a disability affecting a person's ability to relate to and communicate with other people

autistic *adjective* affected with autism

auto- or **aut-** *prefix* 1 self: *autobiography/ autism* (= a mental condition in which a person is absorbed in his or her own mental activity) 2 same 3 self-caused or automatic 4 of or relating to cars
Ⓞ Comes from Greek *autos* meaning 'self' or 'same'

autobiographer *noun* the writer of an autobiography

autobiography *noun* (*plural* **autobiographies**) the story of someone's life, written or told by themself □ **autobiographical** *adjective*

autocracy *noun* government by an autocrat

autocrat *noun* a ruler who has complete power

autocratic *adjective* expecting complete obedience

autograph *noun* 1 someone's own signature 2 someone's own handwriting □ *verb* to write your own name on: *autograph the book*

automate *verb* to make automatic by introducing machines *etc*

automatic *adjective* 1 of a machine *etc* self-working 2 of an action: unconscious, without thinking □ *noun* 1 something automatic (*eg* an automatic washing-machine) 2 a kind of self-loading gun □ **automatically** *adverb*: *Second-time offenders will automatically lose their licence*

automatic pilot 1 a device which can be set to control an aircraft on a course 2 the doing of anything unthinkingly or abstractedly

automation *noun* the use of machines for controlling other machines in factories *etc*

automaton *noun* (*plural* **automata**) 1 a mechanical toy or machine made to look and move like a human 2 someone who acts mindlessly, like a machine

automobile *noun, US* a car

autonomy *noun* the power or right of a country to govern itself □ **autonomous** *adjective*

autopsy *noun* (*plural* **autopsies**) an examination of a body after death

auto-reverse *noun* a feature on a cassette player *etc* allowing it to play the second side of a tape without being changed manually

autostereogram *noun* a computer-generated picture which combines two separate images of the same subject, creating a 3-D effect when viewed

autoteller *noun* an automatic teller machine

autumn *noun* the season of the year following summer, when leaves change colour and fruits are ripe

autumnal *adjective* **1** relating to autumn **2** like those of autumn: *autumnal colours*

auxiliary *adjective* supplementary, additional □ *noun* (*plural* **auxiliaries**) a helper, an assistant

avail *verb*: **avail yourself of** to make use of: *You must make every effort to avail yourself of this opportunity* □ *noun*: **to no avail** without any effect, of no use

available *adjective* able or ready to be made use of □ **availability** *noun*

avalanche *noun* **1** a mass of snow and ice sliding down from a mountain **2** a great amount: *an avalanche of work*

avant-garde *adjective* ahead of fashion, very modern: *an avant-garde writer*

avarice *noun* greed, especially for riches

avaricious *adjective* greedy

avenge *verb* to take revenge for (a wrong): *avenge his sister's death/ determined to avenge herself*

avenge ⇨ avenge*s*, aveng*ing*, avenge*d*

avenue *noun* **1** a tree-lined street or approach to a house **2** a means, a way: *avenue of escape*

average *noun* the result obtained by adding several amounts and dividing the total by this number, eg the average of 3, 7, 9, 13 is 8 (32÷4) □ *adjective* **1** ordinary, usual; of medium size *etc* **2** obtained by working out an average: *the average cost will be £10 each* □ *verb* **1** to form an average **2** to find the average of

■ **Alternative words**: (adjective, meaning 1) mediocre

averse *adjective* not fond of, opposed (to)

aversion *noun* **1** extreme dislike or distaste: *an aversion to sprouts* **2** something that is hated

avert *verb*, *formal* **1** to turn away or aside: *avert your eyes* **2** to prevent from happening: *avert the danger*

aviary *noun* (*plural* **aviaries**) a place for keeping birds

aviation *noun* the practice of flying or piloting aircraft

aviator *noun* an aircraft pilot

avid *adjective* eager, greedy: *an avid reader* □ **avidity** *noun*

avocado *noun* **1** a pear-shaped fruit with a rough peel and rich, creamy flesh **2** a light, yellowish-green colour

avoid *verb* to escape, keep clear of □ **avoidable** *adjective* □ **avoidance** *noun*

avoirdupois (*pronounced* av-wah-dyoo-**pwah**) *noun* the system of measuring weights in pounds and ounces (*compare with*: **metric**)

avow *verb*, *formal* to declare openly: *She will be forced to avow her guilt/ The Party's avowed aim is to reduce Government spending* □ **avowal** *noun*

avowed *adjective* openly stated and determinedly sought after

await *verb* to wait for: *await the arrival of the Queen/ this long-awaited moment*

awake *verb* **1** to rouse from sleep **2** to stop sleeping □ *adjective* not asleep

awaken *verb* **1** to awake **2** to arouse (interest *etc*)

awakening *noun* the act or process of waking up or coming into existence: *the awakening of unfamiliar feelings/ a rude awakening* (= an event which brings someone sharply out of a dreamlike state and into the world of harsh reality)

award *verb* **1** to give, grant (a prize *etc*) **2** to grant legally □ *noun* something that is awarded, a prize *etc*

aware *adjective* **1** having knowledge (of), conscious (of): *aware of the dangers* **2** alert

away *adverb* **1** to a distance from the speaker or person spoken to: *throw that ball away* **2** not here; not at home or work: *she is away all this week* **3** in the opposite direction: *he turned away and left* **4** into nothing: *the sound died away* **5** constantly; diligently: *working away* □ **do away with** to abolish, get rid of □ **get away with** to do (something) without being punished □ **make away with** to steal and escape with □ **right away** immediately

awe *noun* wonder or admiration mixed with fear □ *verb* to affect with awe: *awed by the occasion*

awesome *adjective* 1 causing fear 2 *informal* remarkable, admirable

awestruck *adjective* full of awe

awful *adjective* 1 *informal* bad: *an awful headache* 2 *informal* very great: *an awful lot* 3 terrible: *I feel awful about what happened*

awfully *adverb, informal* very, extremely: *awfully good of you*

awkward *adjective* 1 clumsy, not graceful 2 difficult to deal with: *awkward customer*

awl *noun* a pointed tool for boring small holes

awning *noun* a covering of canvas *etc* providing shelter

awry (*pronounced* a-**rai**) *adjective* & *adverb* 1 not according to plan, wrong 2 crooked

axe *noun* (*plural* **axes**) a tool for

chopping □ *verb* 1 to cancel (a plan *etc*) 2 to reduce greatly (costs, services *etc*) □ **have an axe to grind** to have a strong point of view or resentful feelings which you tend to express at any opportunity

■ **Alternative words**: (verb, meaning 1) abort

axiom *noun* a truth, an accepted principle

axis *noun* (*plural* **axes**) 1 the line, real or imaginary, on which a thing turns 2 the axis of the earth, from North to South Pole, around which the earth turns 3 a fixed line taken as a reference, as in a graph

axle *noun* the rod on which a wheel turns

ayatollah *noun* a religious leader of the Shiah sect of Islam

azalea *noun* a flowering plant related to the rhododendron

AZT *abbreviation* azidothymidine, a drug used in the treatment of AIDS

azure *adjective* sky-coloured, clear blue

Bb

BA *abbreviation* **1** British Airways **2** Bachelor of Arts

babble *verb* to talk indistinctly or foolishly □ *noun* indistinct or foolish talk

babe *noun* **1** a baby **2** *informal* a girl or young woman

baboon *noun* a large monkey with a dog-like snout

baby *noun* (*plural* **babies**) a very young child, an infant □ *verb* to treat like a baby

baby *verb* ⇨ bab*ies*, bab*ying*, bab*ied*

babyhood *noun* the time when someone is a baby

babysitter *noun* someone who stays in the house with a child while its parents are out

bachelor *noun* an unmarried man □ **Bachelor of Arts**, **Bachelor of Science** *etc* someone who has passed examinations at a certain level in subjects at a university

bacillus (*pronounced* ba-**sil**-*us*) *noun* (*plural* **bacilli** - *pronounced* ba-**sil**-ai) a rod-shaped germ

back *noun* **1** the part of the human body from the neck to the base of the spine **2** the upper part of an animal's body **3** the part of anything situated behind: *sitting at the back of the bus* **4** *football etc* a player positioned behind the forwards □ *adjective* of or at the back □ *adverb* **1** to or in the place from which someone or something came: *back at the house/ walked back home* **2** to or in a former time or condition: *thinking back to their youth* □ *verb* **1** to move backwards **2** to bet on (a horse *etc*) **3** (often **back up**) to help or support □ **back down** to change your opinion *etc* □ **back out 1** to move out backwards **2** to excuse yourself from keeping to an agreement □ **put your back into** to work hard at □ **put someone's back up** to irritate someone □ **with your back to the wall** in desperate difficulties
① Comes from Old English *bæc*

backbone *noun* **1** the spine **2** the main support of something **3** firmness, resolve

backfire *verb* **1** of a vehicle: to make an explosive noise in the exhaust pipe **2** of a plan: to go wrong

backgammon *noun* a game similar to draughts, played with dice

background *noun* **1** the space behind the principal figures of a picture **2** details that explain something **3** someone's family and upbringing

backhand *noun*, *tennis* a stroke played with the back of the hand facing the ball □ **backhanded compliment** a compliment with a double, unflattering meaning

backing *noun* **1** support **2** material used on the back of a picture *etc* **3** a musical accompaniment on a recording

backlash *noun* a violent reaction against something

backstroke *noun* a stroke used in swimming on the back

backward *adjective* **1** to or towards the back: *backward glance* **2** slow in learning or development

backwards *adverb* **1** towards the back: *walked backwards out of the room* **2** in a reverse direction; back to front:

written backwards **3** towards the past

backwash *noun* a backward current, such as that caused by an outgoing wave

backwater *noun* **1** a river pool separate from the main stream **2** a place not affected by what is happening in the outside world

bacon *noun* pig's flesh salted and dried, used as food

bacteria (*pronounced* bak-**tee**-ri-*a*) *noun plural* germs found in air, water, living and dead bodies, and especially decaying matter □ **bacterial** *adjective*

bad *adjective* **1** not good; wicked **2** not of a good standard: *bad workmanship/ bad at maths* **3** (often **bad for**) harmful: *smoking is bad for you* **4** of food: rotten, decaying **5** severe, serious: *bad dose of flu* **6** unwell □ **badly** *adverb* **1** not well **2** seriously **3** very much

Alternative words: (meaning 1) unpleasant, evil, naughty, disobedient; (meaning 2) poor, inferior, deficient, useless; (meaning 3) detrimental, adverse; (meaning 4) putrid, rancid

badge *noun* a mark or sign or brooch-like ornament giving some information about the wearer

badger *noun* a burrowing animal of the weasel family which comes out at night □ *verb* to pester or annoy

badminton *noun* a game resembling tennis, played with shuttlecocks

Although based on a 16th-century game, this was first played in its modern form in *Badminton* House in Avon

baffle *verb* **1** to be too difficult for; puzzle, confound **2** to prevent from being carried out; hinder □ **baffling** *adjective* (meaning 1)

bag *noun* **1** a holder or container, often of a soft material **2** a quantity of fish or game caught □ *verb* **1** to put in a bag **2** to secure possession of, claim: *bag a seat* **3** to kill (game) in a hunt

bag *verb* ▷ bag*s*, bagg*ing*, bagg*ed*

bagatelle *noun* a board game, in which balls are struck into numbered holes

baggage *noun* luggage

baggy *adjective* of clothes: large and loose □ *noun* (**baggies**) *informal* wide, knee-length shorts

bag lady a homeless woman who carries her belongings with her in shopping bags

bagpipes *noun plural* a wind instrument made up of a bag and several pipes

bail¹ *noun* money given to bail out a prisoner □ **bail out** *verb* to obtain temporary release of (an untried prisoner) by giving money which will be forfeited if they do not return for trial ⓛ Comes from Old French *bail* meaning 'custody'

⚔ Do not confuse with: **bale**

bail² *verb*: **bail out** to bale out

bail³ *noun, cricket* one of the crosspieces on the top of the wickets ⓛ Probably comes from Old French *baillier* meaning 'to enclose', or from Latin *baculum* meaning 'stick'

⚔ Do not confuse with: **bale**

bailiff *noun* **1** an officer who works for a sheriff **2** a landowner's agent

bain-marie (*pronounced* ban-ma-**ree**) *noun* a double-boiler for cooking

Originally an alchemist's pot, named after the Biblical Mary, sister of Moses

bairn *noun, Scottish* a child

bait *noun* **1** food put on a hook to make fish bite, or in a trap to attract animals **2** something tempting or alluring □ *verb* **1** to put bait on a hook *etc* **2** to worry, annoy

baize (*pronounced* beiz) *noun* a coarse woollen cloth

bake *verb* **1** to cook in an oven **2** to dry or harden in the sun or in an oven

baker *noun* someone who bakes or sells bread *etc* □ **bakery** or **bakehouse** *noun* a place used for baking in

balaklava *noun* a knitted covering for the head and neck

balance *noun* **1** steadiness: *lost my balance and fell over* **2** the money needed to make the two sides of an

account equal **3** a weighing machine
□ *verb* **1** to be the same in weight **2** to
make both sides of an account the same
3 to make or keep steady: *balanced it
on her head*

balcony *noun* (*plural* **balconies**) **1** a
platform built out from the wall of a
building **2** an upper floor or gallery in
a theatre *etc*

bald *adjective* **1** without hair **2** plain,
frank: *a bald statement*

bale[1] *noun* a large tight bundle of
cotton, hay *etc*
🕔 Perhaps comes from Old High German
balla, palla meaning 'ball'

♠ Do not confuse with: **bail**

bale[2] *verb*: **bale out 1** to escape by
parachute from an aircraft in an
emergency **2** to scoop water out of a
boat (also **bail out**)

baleful *adjective* harmful, malevolent:
baleful influence

balk *verb* **1** to hinder, baffle **2 balk at
something** to refuse to do it

ball[1] *noun* **1** anything round: *ball of
wool* **2** the round or roundish object
used in playing many games □ **on the
ball** *informal* in touch with a situation,
alert □ **play ball** *informal* to play along,
cooperate

ball[2] *noun* a formal party at which
dancing takes place □ **have a ball**
informal to have a great time, enjoy
yourself

ballad *noun* **1** a narrative poem with a
simple rhyme scheme, usually in verses
of four lines **2** a simple song

ballast *noun* sand, gravel *etc* put into
a ship to steady it

ball-bearings *noun plural* small steel
balls that sit loosely in grooves and
ease the revolving of one machinery
part over another

ballerina *noun* a female ballet dancer

ballet *noun* a form of stylized dancing
which tells a story by mime

ballistic missile a self-guided missile
which falls on to its target

balloon *noun* a bag filled with gas to
make it float in the air, especially one

made of thin rubber used as a toy *etc*
□ *verb* to puff or swell out

ballot *noun* a way of voting in secret
by marking a paper and putting it into
a special box □ *verb* to collect votes
from by ballot

ballpark *noun, US* a sports field for
ball-games □ *adjective* rough,
estimated: *ballpark figure*

ballpoint *noun* a pen with a tiny ball as
the writing point

ballroom *noun* a large room used for
public dances *etc*

balm *noun* **1** something soothing **2** a
sweet-smelling healing ointment

balmy *adjective* **1** mild, gentle;
soothing: *balmy air* **2** sweet-smelling

balsam *noun* an oily sweet-smelling
substance obtained from certain trees

balsawood *noun* a lightweight wood
obtained from a tropical American tree

balustrade *noun* a row of pillars on a
balcony *etc*, joined by a rail

bamboo *noun* the woody, jointed stem
of a very tall Indian grass

bamboozle *verb* to trick, puzzle
□ **bamboozling** *adjective*

ban *noun* an order forbidding
something □ *verb* to forbid officially
(the publication of a book *etc*)

ban *verb* ⇨ **bans, banning, banned**

banal *adjective* lacking originality or
wit, commonplace □ **banality** *noun*

banana *noun* the long yellow fruit of a
type of tropical tree

band *noun* **1** a group of people **2** a
group of musicians playing together **3**
a strip of some material to put round
something **4** a stripe (of colour *etc*) **5** a
group of wavelengths for radio
broadcasts □ *verb* to join together

bandage *noun* a strip of cloth *etc* or
special dressing for a wound

bandit *noun* an outlaw, robber,
especially a member of a gang of
robbers

bandy *adjective* of legs: bent outward
at the knee □ **bandy words** to argue

bane *noun* a cause of ruin or trouble:
the bane of my life

bang noun 1 a sudden, loud noise 2 a heavy blow □ verb 1 to close with a bang, slam 2 to hit, strike: *banged his head on the door*

bangle noun a large ring worn on an arm or leg

banish verb 1 to order to leave (a country) 2 to drive away (doubts, fear etc) □ **banishment** noun

banister noun the posts and handrail of a staircase

banjo noun (plural **banjoes** or **banjos**) a stringed musical instrument like a guitar, with a long neck and a round body

bank noun 1 a mound or ridge of earth etc 2 the edge of a river 3 a place where money is lent, put for safety etc 4 a place where blood etc is stored till needed 5 a public bin for collecting items for recycling: *bottle bank* □ **bank on** to depend on, count on

banker noun someone who manages a bank

bank holiday a day on which all banks and many shops etc are closed

banknote noun a piece of paper money issued by a bank

bankrupt noun someone who has no money to pay their debts □ adjective 1 unable to pay debts 2 utterly lacking in: *bankrupt of ideas* □ **bankruptcy** noun (plural **bankruptcies**)

banner noun 1 a large flag carried in processions etc, often hung between two poles 2 any flag

banns noun plural a public announcement of a forthcoming marriage

banquet noun a ceremonial dinner

bantam noun a small kind of hen

banter verb to tease in fun □ noun light teasing

baptize verb 1 to dip in, or sprinkle with, water as a sign of admission into the Christian church 2 to christen, give a name to □ **baptism** noun □ **baptismal** adjective

bar noun 1 a rod of solid material 2 a broad line or band 3 a piece, a cake: *bar of soap* 4 a hindrance, a block 5 a bank of sand etc at the mouth of a river 6 a room, or counter, where drinks are served in a public house, hotel etc 7 a public house 8 the rail at which prisoners stand for trial 9 the lawyers who plead in a court 10 a time division in music □ preposition except: *all the runners, bar Ian, finished the race* □ verb 1 to fasten with a bar 2 to exclude, shut out: *barred from the competition*

bar verb ⇨ bars, barring, barred

barb noun the backward-pointing spike on an arrow, fish-hook etc

barbarian noun an uncivilized person □ adjective uncivilized

barbaric adjective 1 uncivilized 2 extremely cruel □ **barbarity** noun

barbecue noun 1 a frame on which to grill food over an open fire 2 an outdoor party providing food from a barbecue □ verb to cook (food) on a barbecue

From a Haitian creole term for a wooden grid or frame

barbed adjective having a barb or barbs □ **barbed wire** wire with regular clusters of sharp points, used for fencing etc

barber noun a men's hairdresser

barbiturate noun a type of sedative drug

bard noun, formal a poet

bare adjective 1 uncovered, naked 2 plain, simple 3 empty □ verb to uncover, expose □ **barely** adverb hardly, scarcely

barefaced adjective impudent, unashamed: *barefaced lie*

bargain noun 1 an agreement, especially about buying or selling 2 something bought cheaply □ verb to argue about a price etc □ **bargain for** to expect: *more than he bargained for* □ **into the bargain** in addition, besides

barge noun a flat-bottomed boat used on rivers and canals □ verb 1 to rush clumsily 2 to push or bump (into) 3 to push your way (into) rudely

baritone noun 1 a male singing voice between tenor and bass 2 a singer with this voice

bark[1] noun the noise made by a dog etc

□ *verb* **1** to give a bark **2** to speak sharply or angrily

bark² *noun* the rough outer covering of a tree's trunk and branches

barley *noun* a grain used for food and for making malt liquors and spirits

barley sugar sugar candied by melting and cooling to make a sweet

bar mitzvah a Jewish ceremony to mark a boy's coming of age

barn *noun* a building in which grain, hay *etc* is stored

barnacle *noun* a type of shellfish which sticks to rocks, ships' hulls *etc*

barometer *noun* an instrument which measures the weight or pressure of the air and shows changes in the weather

baron *noun* **1** a nobleman, the lowest in the British peerage **2** a powerful person, especially in a business: *drug baron* **baronial** *adjective* (meaning 1)

baroness *noun* (*plural* **baronesses**) a baron's wife or a female baron

baronet *noun* the lowest title that can be passed on to an heir □ **baronetcy** *noun* the rank of baronet

baroque *adjective* extravagantly ornamented

barracks *noun plural* a place for housing soldiers

barracuda *noun* a voracious West Indian fish

barrage *noun* **1** heavy gunfire against an enemy **2** an overwhelming number: *barrage of questions* **3** a bar across a river to make the water deeper

barrel *noun* **1** a wooden cask with curved sides **2** the metal tube of a gun through which the shot is fired

barren *adjective* not able to reproduce, infertile

barricade *noun* a barrier put up to block a street *etc* □ *verb* **1** to block or strengthen against attack **2** to shut behind a barrier

barrier *noun* **1** a strong fence *etc* used for enclosing or keeping out **2** an obstacle

barrister *noun* a lawyer who pleads cases in English or in Irish courts

barrow *noun* **1** a small hand-cart **2** a mound built over an ancient grave

barter *verb* to give one thing in exchange for another □ *noun* trading by exchanging goods without using money

basalt *noun* a hard, dark-coloured rock thrown up as lava from volcanoes

base *noun* **1** something on which a thing stands or rests **2** the lowest part **3** a place from where an expedition, military action *etc* is carried out □ *verb* to use as a foundation: *based on the facts* □ *adjective* worthless, cowardly

baseball *noun* a North American ball-game in which players make a circuit of four bases on a field

base jumping *noun* the sport of parachuting from low-level objects and structures *eg* buildings

baseless *adjective* without foundation; untrue

basement *noun* a storey below ground level in a building

bash *verb* to hit hard □ *noun* a heavy blow □ **have a bash** *informal* to make an attempt

basic *adjective* **1** of or forming a base **2** necessary, fundamental □ **basically** *adverb* fundamentally, essentially

basil *noun* an aromatic herb used in cooking

basilica *noun* a church with a large central hall

basilisk *noun* **1** a mythological reptile with a deadly look and poisonous breath **2** a type of American lizard

basin *noun* **1** a wide, open dish **2** a washhand basin **3** a large hollow holding water **4** the land drained by a river and its tributaries

basis *noun* (*plural* **bases**) **1** something on which a thing rests, a foundation: *the basis of their friendship* **2** the main ingredient

bask *verb* **1** to lie in warmth **2** to enjoy, feel great pleasure (in): *basking in glory*

basket *noun* **1** a container made of strips of wood, rushes *etc* woven together **2** a related group or collection: *basket of currencies*

basketball *noun* a team game in which goals are scored by throwing a ball into a raised net

bass¹ (*pronounced* beis) *noun* (*plural* **basses**) **1** the low part in music **2** a deep male singing voice **3** a singer with this voice □ *adjective* low or deep in tone

bass² (*pronounced* bas) *noun* (*plural* **bass** or **basses**) a kind of fish of the perch family

bass clef *noun* a musical sign (𝄢), placed on a stave to fix the pitch of the notes

bassoon *noun* a musical wind instrument with low notes

bastard *noun* **1** a child born to parents who are not married to each other **2** *informal* a general term of abuse

baste¹ *verb* to spoon fat over (meat) while roasting to keep (it) from drying out

baste² *verb* to sew loosely together with big stitches; tack

bastion *noun* **1** a defensive position, a preserve: *the last bastions of male power* **2** a tower on a castle *etc*

bat¹ *noun* a shaped piece of wood *etc* for striking a ball in some games □ *verb* to use the bat in cricket *etc*

> **bat** *verb* ⇨ **bats**, **batting**, **batted**

bat² *noun* a mouse-like flying animal

bat³ *verb* to flutter (eyelids *etc*)

> **bat** *verb* ⇨ **bats**, **batting**, **batted**

batch *noun* (*plural* **batches**) a quantity of things made *etc* at one time

bated *adjective*: **with bated breath** anxiously

bath *noun* **1** a vessel which holds water in which to wash the body **2** the water in which to wash **3** a washing of the body in water **4** **baths** a public building with an artificial pool for swimming □ *verb* to wash (oneself or another person) in a bath

bathchair *noun* an old-fashioned wheelchair

bathe *verb* **1** to swim in water **2** to wash gently: *bathe your eyes* **3** to take

a bath □ *noun*: *go for a bathe* □ **bathed in** covered with

baton *noun* **1** a small wooden stick **2** a light stick used by a conductor of music

batsman *noun* a man who bats in cricket *etc*

batswoman *noun* a woman who bats in cricket *etc*

battalion *noun* a part of a regiment of foot soldiers

batten *noun* **1** a piece of sawn timber **2** a strip of wood used to fasten down a ship's hatches during a storm □ *verb*: **batten down** to fasten down firmly

batter *verb* to hit repeatedly □ *noun* a beaten mixture of flour, milk and eggs, for cooking □ **battered** *adjective* **1** beaten, ill-treated **2** worn out by use **3** dipped in batter and fried

battering-ram *noun, historical* a heavy beam used as a weapon for breaking through walls *etc*

battery *noun* (*plural* **batteries**) **1** a number of large guns **2** a device for storing and transmitting electricity **3** a series of cages *etc* in which hens are kept for egg-laying

battle *noun* a fight, especially between armies □ *verb* to fight

battlefield *noun* the site of a battle

battlement *noun* a wall on the top of a building, with openings or notches for firing

battleship *noun* a heavily armed and armoured warship

bauble *noun* a brightly-coloured ornament of little value

bawl *verb* to shout or cry out loudly □ *noun* a loud cry

bay *noun* **1** a wide inlet of the sea in a coastline **2** a space in a room *etc* set back, a recess **3** a compartment in an aircraft **4** the laurel tree □ *verb* of dogs: to bark □ **hold at bay** to fight off □ **stand at bay** to stand and face attackers *etc*

bayonet *noun* a steel stabbing blade that can be fixed to the muzzle of a rifle □ *verb* to stab with this

bay window a window that forms a recess

bazaar *noun* **1** a sale of goods for

charity *etc* **2** an Eastern market-place **3** a shop

BBC *abbreviation* British Broadcasting Corporation

BC *abbreviation* before Christ: *55BC*

■ **Opposite**: AD

be *verb* **1** to live, exist: *there may be some milk left* **2** to have a position, quality *etc*: *she wants to be a dentist/ if only you could be happy*

> **be** ⇨ *present form* **am, are, is**, *past form* **was, were**, *past participle* **been** □ **be** is also used to form tenses of other verbs, *eg* I *was* running for the bus/ when *will* you *be* arriving?

⏲ Present tense: comes from Anglo-Saxon *beon*, to live or exist; past tense: comes from Anglo-Saxon *weran*, to be

be- *prefix* used **1** to add to words the sense of: around, in all directions, thoroughly: *besiege* **2** to form verbs from adjectives and nouns: *befriend/ belittle* **3** to make intransitive verbs (*eg fall*) into transitive verbs (*befall someone*)

beach *noun* (*plural* **beaches**) the shore of the sea *etc*, especially when sandy or pebbly □ *verb* to drive or haul a boat up on the beach

beachcomber *noun* someone who searches beaches for useful or saleable articles

beacon *noun* **1** a flashing light or other warning signal **2** *historical* a fire on a hill used as a signal of danger

bead *noun* **1** a small pierced ball of glass, plastic *etc*, used in needlework or jewellery-making **2** a drop of liquid: *beads of sweat*

beadle *noun* an officer of a church or college

beagle *noun* a small hound used in hunting hares

beak *noun* **1** the hard, horny part of a bird's mouth with which it gathers food **2** a point, a projection

beaker *noun* a tall cup or glass, usually without a handle

beam *noun* **1** a long straight piece of wood or metal **2** a shaft of light **3** a radio signal **4** the greatest breadth of a ship □ *verb* **1** to shine **2** to smile broadly **3** to divert by radio wave

bean *noun* **1** a pod-bearing plant **2** the seed of this used as food

bear¹ *noun* a heavy animal with shaggy fur and hooked claws

bear² *verb* **1** *formal* to carry **2** to endure, put up with **3** to produce (fruit, children *etc*) □ **bear in mind** to remember, take into account □ **bear out** to confirm: *this bears out my suspicions* □ **bear with** to be patient with □ **bring to bear** to bring into use

> **bear** *verb* ⇨ bear*s*, bear*ing*, bore, borne or born □ **born** is used for the past participle when referring to the birth of a child, idea *etc*: *when were you born?*; otherwise the form is **borne**: *I couldn't have borne it any longer*

■ **Alternative words**: (meaning 2) abide

bearable *adjective* able to be borne or endured

beard *noun* the hair that grows on a man's chin and cheeks □ *verb* to face up to, defy

bearer *noun* a carrier or messenger

bearing *noun* **1** behaviour **2** direction **3** connection: *it has no bearing on the issue* **4** part of a machine supporting a moving part

beast *noun* **1** a four-footed animal **2** a brutal person □ **beastly** *adjective* **1** behaving like an animal **2** horrible **3** unpleasant

beat *verb* **1** to hit repeatedly **2** to overcome, defeat **3** of a pulse: to move or throb in the normal way **4** to mark (time) in music **5** to stir (a mixture *etc*) with quick movements **6** to strike bushes *etc* to rouse birds □ *noun* **1** a stroke **2** the regular round of a police officer *etc* □ **beaten** *adjective* **1** of metal: shaped **2** of earth: worn smooth by treading **3** defeated □ **beat up** to injure by repeated hitting, kicking *etc*

> **beat** *verb* ⇨ beat*s*, beat*ing*, beat, beat*en*

beatific (*pronounced* bei-*a*-**tif**-ik) *adjective* of, or showing, great happiness

beautiful *adjective* very attractive or pleasing in appearance, sound *etc* □ **beautifully** *adverb* **1** in a way which is pleasing to the eye, ear *etc*: *sing beautifully* **2** with much skill and sensitivity: *She acted the part of Juliet beautifully*

■ **Alternative words**: attractive, fair, pretty, lovely, good-looking, handsome, gorgeous, ravishing, stunning, pleasing, appealing, alluring, charming, exquisite, pulchritudinous
☒ **Opposite**: ugly

beautify *verb* to make beautiful

beautify ➪ beauti*fies*, beautify*ing*, beautif*ied*

beauty *noun* (*plural* **beauties**) **1** very attractive or pleasing appearance, sound *etc* **2** a very attractive person, especially a woman

beaver *noun* **1** a gnawing animal that can dam streams **2** a member of the most junior branch of the Scout Association

becalmed *adjective* of a sailing ship: unable to move for lack of wind

because *conjunction* for the reason that: *we didn't go because it was raining* □ *adverb* **because of** on account of: *because of the holiday, the bank will be shut*

beck *noun*: **at someone's beck and call** obeying all their orders or requests

beckon *verb* to make a sign (with the finger) to summon someone

become *verb* **1** to come to be: *she became angry* **2** to suit: *that tie becomes you* □ **becoming** *adjective* **1** suiting well **2** of behaviour: appropriate, suitable

bed *noun* **1** a place on which to rest or sleep **2** a plot for flowers *etc* in a garden **3** the bottom of a river *etc* □ *verb* **1** to plant in soil *etc* **2** to provide a bed for **3** *informal* to have sexual intercourse with

bed *verb* ➪ bed*s*, bed*ding*, bed*ded*

bedclothes *noun plural* bedcovers

bedding *noun* **1** mattress, bedcovers *etc* **2** straw *etc* for cattle to lie on

bedlam *noun* a place full of uproar and confusion

After St Mary of *Bethlehem* Hospital, a former mental asylum in London

bedraggled *adjective* wet and untidy

bedridden *adjective* kept in bed by weakness, illness *etc*

bedrock *noun* the solid rock under the soil

bedroom *noun* a room for sleeping

bedspread *noun* a top cover for a bed

bedstead *noun* a frame supporting a bed

bee *noun* **1** a winged insect that makes honey in wax cells **2** a group of people who gather together for some activity

beech *noun* (*plural* **beeches**) a forest tree with grey smooth bark

beef *noun* the flesh of an ox or cow, used as food

beefeater *noun* **1** a guardian of the Tower of London **2** a member of the Queen's or King's Guard

beefy *adjective* stout, muscular

beehive *noun* a dome or box in which bees are kept

beeline *noun*: **make a beeline for** to go directly towards

Beelzebub (*pronounced* bi-**el**-zib-ub) *noun, old* the Devil, Satan

been *see* be

beer *noun* an alcoholic drink flavoured with hops

beet *noun* a plant with a carrot-like root, one type (**sugar beet**) used as a source of sugar, the other (**beetroot**) used as a vegetable

beetle *noun* an insect with four wings, the front pair forming hard covers for the back pair

beetling *adjective* **1** of cliffs *etc*: overhanging **2** of eyebrows: heavy, frowning

befall *verb, formal* to happen to, strike: *a disaster befell them*

befall ➪ befall*s*, befall*ing*, be*fell*

before *preposition* **1** in front of: *before the entrance to the tunnel* **2** earlier than: *before three o'clock* **3** rather than, in

preference to: *I'd die before telling him*
□ *adverb* **1** in front **2** earlier
□ *conjunction* earlier than the time that:
before he was born

beforehand *adverb* previously, before
the time when something else is done

befriend *verb* to act as a friend to, help

beg *verb* **1** to ask for money *etc* from
others **2** to ask earnestly: *he begged her
to stay* □ **beg the question** to take as
being proved the very point that needs
to be proved

> **beg** ⇨ begs, begging, begged

began *past form of* **begin**

beget *verb, formal* **1** to be the father
of **2** to cause

> **beget** ⇨ begets, begetting, begat,
> begotten

beggar *noun* **1** someone who begs for
money **2** a very poor person □ *verb* to
make poor □ **beggarly** *adjective* poor;
worthless □ **beggar belief** to be beyond
belief, be incredible

begin *verb* to make a start on
□ **beginning** *noun*

> **begin** ⇨ begins, beginning, began,
> begun

begone *exclamation, formal* be off, go
away!

begrudge *verb* to grudge, envy: *he
begrudged me my success*

beguile *verb* **1** to cheat **2** to pass (time)
pleasantly; amuse, entertain

begun *past participle of* **begin**

behalf *noun:* **on behalf of 1** as the
representative of: *on behalf of my client*
2 in aid of: *collecting on behalf of the
homeless*

behave *verb* **1** to act (in a certain way):
he always behaves badly at parties **2** to
conduct yourself well: *can't you behave
for just a minute?* □ **behaviour** *noun*

behead *verb* to cut off the head of

behest *noun, formal* command

behind *preposition* **1** at or towards the
back of: *behind the door* **2** after **3** in
support of, encouraging: *behind him in
his struggle* □ *adverb* **1** at the back **2**
not up to date: *behind with his work*

behold *verb, formal* to look (at), see

beholden to *adjective* grateful to
because of a good turn

behove *verb:* **it behoves you to** you
ought to

being *noun* **1** existence **2** a living person
or thing

belated *adjective* arriving late

belch *verb* **1** bring up wind from the
stomach through the mouth **2** of a fire
etc: send up (smoke *etc*) violently

beleaguer (*pronounced* be-**leeg**-er) *verb*
to besiege

belfry *noun* (*plural* **belfries**) the part of
a steeple or tower in which the bells
are hung

belief *noun* **1** what someone thinks to
be true **2** faith

believe *verb* **1** to think of as true or as
existing **2** to trust (in) **3** to think or
suppose □ **make believe** to pretend

Belisha beacon *Brit* a pole with an
orange globe on top, marking a
pedestrian crossing

belittle *verb* to make to seem small or
unimportant

bell *noun* a hollow metal object which
gives a ringing sound when struck by
the tongue or clapper inside

bellicose *adjective* inclined to fight,
quarrelsome □ **bellicosity** *noun*

belligerent *adjective* quarrelsome,
aggressive □ **belligerence** or
belligerency *noun*

bellow *verb* to roar like a bull □ *noun*
a deep roar

bellows *noun plural* an instrument for
making a blast of air, *eg* to increase a
fire

belly *noun* (*plural* **bellies**) **1** the
abdomen **2** the underpart of an
animal's body **3** the bulging part of
anything □ *verb* to swell or bulge out

> **belly** *verb* ⇨ bellies, bellying, bellied

belly-button *noun, informal* the navel

belly-dance *noun* a sensuous dance
performed by women with circling
movements of the stomach and hips

belly-flop *noun* an inexpert dive
landing face down on the water

belong *verb* **1** to be someone's property: *this book belongs to me* **2** to be a member of (a club *etc*) **3** to be born in or live in: *I belong to Glasgow* **4** of an object: to have its place in: *those glasses belong in the kitchen* □ **belongings** *noun plural* what someone possesses

beloved *adjective* much loved, very dear □ *noun* someone much loved

below *preposition* lower in position than: *her skirt reached below her knees/ a captain ranks below a major* □ *adverb* in a lower position: *looking down at the street below*

■ **Opposite**: above

belt *noun* **1** a strip of leather, cloth *etc* worn around the waist **2** a continuous band on a machine for conveying objects in a factory *etc* **3** a broad strip, *eg* of land □ *verb* **1** to put a belt round **2** to beat with a belt **3** *informal* to beat, hit

bemoan *verb* to weep about, mourn

bench *noun* (*plural* **benches**) **1** a long seat **2** a work-table **3** **the bench** the judges of a court

bend *verb* **1** to curve **2** to stoop □ *noun* **1** a curve **2** a turn in a road

   bend *verb* ⇨ bend**s**, bend**ing**, bent

■ **Alternative words**: (meaning 1) deflect, veer, diverge, contort, buckle; (meaning 2) lean, crouch

beneath *preposition* **1** under, in a lower position than: *sitting beneath the tree reading a book* **2** covered by: *wearing a black dress beneath her coat* **3** considered too low a task *etc* for: *sweeping floors was beneath him* □ *adverb* below

benediction *noun* a blessing

benefactor *noun* someone who does good to others

beneficial *adjective* bringing gain or advantage (to)

beneficiary *noun* (*plural* **beneficiaries**) someone who receives a gift, an advantage *etc*

benefit *noun* **1** something good to receive or have done to you **2** money received from social security or insurance schemes: *unemployment*

benefit □ *verb* **1** to do good to **2** to gain advantage: *benefited from the cut in interest rates*

   benefit *verb* ⇨ benefit**s**, benefit**ing**, benefit**ed**

benevolence *noun* **1** tendency to do good; kindliness **2** a kind act □ **benevolent** *adjective* kindly

benign (*pronounced* bi-**nain**) *adjective* **1** gentle, kindly **2** of disease: not causing death (*contrasted with*: **malignant**)

bent *noun* a natural liking or aptitude (for something) □ *adjective* **1** curved, crooked **2** *informal* dishonest □ **be bent on** to be determined to □ *past form* of **bend**

bequeath *verb* to leave by will

bequest *noun* money, property *etc* left in a will

bereaved *adjective* suffering from the recent death of a relative or friend □ **bereavement** *noun*

bereft *adjective* lacking, deprived (of)

beret (*pronounced* **be**-rei) *noun* a flat, round hat

berry *noun* (*plural* **berries**) a small juicy fruit enclosing seeds

berserk *adverb* in a frenzy, mad

berth *noun* **1** a room for sleeping in a ship *etc* **2** the place where a ship is tied up in a dock □ *verb* to moor (a ship) □ **give a wide berth to** to keep well away from

beryl *noun* a type of precious stone such as an emerald or aquamarine

beseech *verb* to ask earnestly

beset *verb* to attack from all sides; surround

   beset ⇨ beset**s**, beset**ting**, beset

beside *preposition* **1** by the side of, near: *the building beside the station* **2** compared with: *beside her sister she seems quite shy* **3** away from, wide of: *beside the point* □ **be beside yourself** to lose self-control □ **beside the point** irrelevant

besides *preposition* **1** in addition to: *he has other friends, besides me* **2** other than, except: *nothing in the fridge besides some cheese* □ *adverb* **1** also, moreover: *besides, it was your idea* **2** in addition: *plenty more besides*

besiege *verb* **1** to surround (a town *etc*) with an army **2** to crowd round; overwhelm: *besieged with letters*

besiege ⇨ besieges, besieging, besieged

besotted *adjective*: **besotted with** foolishly fond of

bespoke *adjective* of clothes: ordered to be made

best *adjective* good in the most excellent way □ *adverb* in the most excellent way □ *verb* to defeat □ **at best** under the most favourable circumstances □ **do your best** to try as hard as you can □ **make the best of** to do as well as possible with
ⓘ Comes from Old English *betst/ betest*

bestial *adjective* like a beast, beastly

best man someone who attends a man who is being married

bestow *verb* to give

best part the largest or greatest part

bestseller *noun* a book *etc* which sells exceedingly well

bet *noun* money put down to be lost or kept depending on the outcome of a race *etc* □ *verb* to place a bet

bet *verb* ⇨ bets, betting, bet or betted

bête noir (*pronounced* bet **nwahr**) a particular dislike

betray *verb* **1** to give up (secrets, friends *etc*) to an enemy **2** to show signs of: *his face betrayed no emotion* □ **betrayal** *noun*

betroth *verb*, *formal* to promise in marriage □ **betrothal** *noun* □ **betrothed to** engaged to be married to

better *adjective* **1** good to a greater degree, of a more excellent kind **2** healthier **3** completely recovered from illness: *don't go back to work until you're better* □ *adverb* in a more excellent way □ *verb* to improve □ **better off** in a better position, wealthier □ **get the better of** to defeat, overcome □ **had better** ought to, must □ **think better of** to change your mind about
ⓘ Comes from Old English *betera*

between *preposition* **1** in or through the space dividing two people or things: *there was an empty seat between us/ between 3 o'clock and 6 o'clock* **2** in parts, in shares to: *divide the chocolates between you* **3** from one thing to another: *the road between Edinburgh and Glasgow* **4** comparing one to the other: *the only difference between them is the price*

bevel *noun* a slanting edge □ *verb* to give a slanting edge to □ **bevelled** *adjective*

bevel *verb* ⇨ bevels, bevelling, bevelled

beverage *noun* a drink

bevy[1] *noun* (*plural* **bevies**) **1** a group of women or girls **2** a flock of quails

bevy[2] or **bevvy** *noun* (*plural* **bevies** or **bevvies**) *Brit informal* **1** an alcoholic drink **2** a drinking session

bewail *verb* to mourn loudly over

beware *verb* to watch out for (something dangerous)

bewilder *verb* to puzzle, confuse □ **bewildering** *adjective* □ **bewilderment** *noun* confusion

bewitch *verb* to put under a spell; charm □ **bewitching** *adjective* charming; very beautiful

beyond *preposition* **1** on the far side of: *beyond the next set of traffic-lights* **2** later than: *beyond January* **3** more than: *beyond the call of duty* **4** too far gone for: *beyond repair* **5** too difficult or confusing for: *it's beyond me!* □ *adverb* on or to the far side, further away

bi- *prefix* **1** having two: *biped/ bipolar* (having two poles or extremities)/ *bicycle* **2** occurring twice in a certain period, or once in every two periods: *bi-monthly*
ⓘ Comes from Latin *bis* meaning 'twice' or 'two'

biannual *adjective* happening twice a year
ⓘ Comes from Latin *bi-* meaning 'two' or 'twice', and *annus* meaning 'year'

⚡ Do not confuse with: **biennial**

bias *noun* **1** the favouring of one person or point of view over any others **2** a tendency to move in a particular direction **3** a weight on or in an object making it move in a particular direction □ *verb* to give a bias to

bias *verb* ⇨ bias*es*, bias*ing* or biass*ing*, bias*ed* or biass*ed*

bib *noun* **1** a piece of cloth put under a child's chin to protect their clothes from food stains *etc* **2** a part of an apron, overalls *etc* above the waist, covering the chest

Bible *noun* the holy book of the Christian Church □ **Biblical** *adjective*

biblio- *prefix* of or relating to books ① Comes from Greek *biblion* meaning 'book'

bibliographer *noun* someone who compiles bibliographies, or who studies book classification

bibliography *noun* (*plural* **bibliographies**) **1** a list of books (about a subject) **2** the art of classifying books

bibliophile *noun* a lover of books

bicentenary *noun* (*plural* **bicentenaries**) the two-hundredth year after an event *eg* someone's birth

biceps *noun singular* the muscle in front of the upper part of the arm

bicker *verb* to quarrel over small matters

bicycle *noun* a vehicle with two wheels, driven by foot-pedals

bid *verb* **1** to offer a price (for) **2** to tell, say: *bidding her farewell* **3** to command; invite □ *noun* an offer of a price; a bold attempt: *a bid for freedom*

bid *verb* ⇨ bid*s*, bid*ding*, bade or bid, bid*den* or bid

bidet (*pronounced* **beed**-ei) *noun* a low wash-basin for washing the genital area and feet

bier (*pronounced* beer) *noun* a carriage or frame for carrying a dead body

big *adjective* **1** large in size, amount, extent *etc* **2** important **3** boastful

big ⇨ bigg*er*, bigg*est*

■ **Alternative words**: (meaning 1) large, great, sizable, considerable, immense, substantial, huge, enormous, massive, colossal, gigantic, mammoth, burly, bulky, extensive, spacious, vast, voluminous

bigamy *noun* the crime or fact of having two wives or two husbands at once □ **bigamist** *noun* □ **bigamous** *adjective*

bight *noun* a small bay

bigot *noun* someone with narrow-minded, prejudiced beliefs □ **bigoted** *adjective* prejudiced □ **bigotry** *noun*

bike *noun, informal* a bicycle

bikini *noun* (*plural* **bikinis**) a woman's brief two-piece bathing suit

Named after *Bikini* Atoll atomic test site, because of its supposedly 'explosive' effect on men

bilateral *adjective* **1** having two sides **2** affecting two sides, parties *etc*: *bilateral agreement* □ **bilaterally** *adverb*

bilberry *noun* a type of plant with an edible dark-blue berry

bile *noun* a fluid coming from the liver

bilge *noun* **1** the broadest part of a ship's bottom **2** bilgewater **3** *informal* nonsense □ **bilgewater** *noun* water which lies in the ship's bottom

bilingual *adjective* using or fluent in two languages

bilious *adjective* **1** ill with too much bile; nauseated **2** greenish-yellow in colour

bill *noun* **1** a bird's beak **2** an account for money **3** an early version of a law before it has been passed by parliament **4** a printed sheet of information

billet *noun* a lodging, especially for soldiers □ *verb* to lodge (soldiers) in private houses

billiards *noun* a game played with a cue and balls on a table

billion *noun* **1** a million millions (1 000 000 000 000) **2** *US* (now often in Britain) a thousand millions (1 000 000 000)

billow *noun* **1** a great wave **2** a mass of

something such as smoke rising on or being swept along by the wind □ *verb* to be filled and swelled with, or moved along by, the wind: *sheets on a washing-line billowing in the wind/ a billowing sail/ billowing smoke* □ **billowy** *adjective* giving the impression of billowing: *billowy clouds*

billy *noun* (*plural* **billies**) or **billycan** a container for cooking, making tea *etc* outdoors

billy-goat *noun* a male goat

bin *noun a container for storing goods or rubbish* □ *verb* **1** to put in a bin **2** to throw away

> **bin** *verb* ⇨ bins, binning, binned

binary *adjective* made up of two

binary system a mathematical system in which numbers are expressed by two digits only, 1 and 0

bind *verb* **1** to tie with a band **2** to fasten together **3** to make to promise

> **bind** ⇨ binds, binding, bound

binding *noun* **1** anything that binds **2** the cover, stitching *etc* which holds a book together

binge *verb* eat and drink too much □ *noun* a spell of over-eating or drinking too much

bingo *noun* a popular gambling game using numbers

binoculars *noun plural* a small double telescope

bio- *prefix* of or relating to life or living organisms
ⓘ Comes from Greek *bios* meaning 'life'

biodegradable *adjective* able to be broken down into parts by bacteria

biographer *noun* someone who writes a biography

biography *noun* (*plural* **biographies**) a written account of someone's life □ **biographical** *adjective*

biological *adjective* **1** relating to the way that living organisms grow and behave: *What is the biological explanation for the aging process?/ biological washing powder* (containing enzymes which break down certain types of dirt) **2** relating to biology □ **biological warfare** war using as

weapons germs which can cause disease

biology *noun* the study of living things □ **biologist** *noun*

biped *noun* an animal with two feet, *eg* a bird

birch *noun* (*plural* **birches**) **1** a type of hardwood tree **2** a bundle of birch twigs, used for beating □ *verb* to beat with a birch

bird *noun* a feathered, egg-laying creature □ **bird of prey** a bird (*eg* a hawk) which kills and eats small animals or birds □ **bird's-eye view** a wide view, as would be seen from above □ **get the bird** *slang* to be booed or hissed at; be dismissed

birdwatching *noun* the study of birds in their natural surroundings

birl *verb*, *Scottish* to spin round, whirl

Biro *noun*, *trademark* a type of ballpoint pen

birth *noun* the very beginning of someone's life

birthday *noun* **1** the day on which someone is born **2** the date of this day each year

birthmark *noun* a mark on the body from birth

birthright *noun* the right which someone may claim because of their parentage

biscuit *noun* dough baked hard in a small cake

bisect *verb* to cut in two equal parts

bishop *noun* a high-ranking member of the clergy (next below an archbishop) in the Roman Catholic Church and the Church of England □ **bishopric** *noun* the district ruled by a bishop

bison *noun* (*plural* **bison**) a large wild ox with shaggy hair and a fat hump

bistro (*pronounced* **beest**-roh) *noun* (*plural* **bistros**) a small bar or restaurant

bit¹ *noun* **1** a small piece **2** a small tool for boring **3** the part of the bridle which the horse holds in its mouth **4** *computing* the smallest unit of information □ **do your bit** to do your required share □ **bit by bit** gradually □ **to bits** apart, in pieces

bit² *past form* of **bite**

bitch noun (plural **bitches**) 1 a female dog, wolf etc 2 slang an unpleasant woman

bitchy adjective catty, malicious

bite verb to grip, cut or tear with the teeth □ noun 1 a grip with the teeth 2 the part bitten off 3 a nibble at a fishing bait 4 a wound caused by an animal's or insect's bite

bite verb ⇨ bites, biting, bit, bitten

bitmap noun, computing a method of screen display where each small element (**pixel**) is assigned on one or more bits of memory □ verb display something using this method □ **bitmapped** adjective □ **bitmapping** noun

bitmap verb ⇨ bitmaps, bitmapping, bitmapped

bitten past participle of **bite**

bitter adjective 1 unpleasant to the taste; sour 2 harsh: bitter cold 3 resentful, angry through disappointment

bittern noun a bird resembling a heron

bitterness noun 1 the quality of being bitter: the bitterness of the drink 2 bitter feelings: the bitterness I used to feel towards him

bitty (from **bit**[1]) adjective piecemeal, scrappy

bivouac noun an overnight camp outdoors without a tent □ verb to sleep outdoors without a tent

bivouac verb ⇨ bivouacs, bivouacking, bivouacked

bi-weekly adjective happening twice a week or once every two weeks

bizarre adjective odd, strange

blab verb 1 to talk a lot 2 to let out a secret

blab ⇨ blabs, blabbing, blabbed

black adjective dark and colourless □ noun black colour □ **black out** to become unconscious

black-and-blue adjective badly bruised

blackball verb to ostracize, exclude from (a club etc)

black belt an award for skill in judo or karate

blackberry noun (plural **blackberries**) a blackish-purple soft fruit growing on a prickly stem

blackbird noun a type of black, thrush-like bird

blackboard noun a dark-coloured board for writing on in chalk

blacken verb 1 to make black or dark 2 to dishonour, defame: blackening his name

black eye a bruised area round the eye as the result of a blow

blackguard noun, old a wicked person

black ice a thin transparent layer of ice on a road etc

blackleg noun someone who works when other workers are on strike

blacklist noun a list of people to be refused credit, jobs etc □ verb to put on a blacklist

black magic magic performed for an evil purpose; witchcraft

blackmail noun the crime of threatening to reveal secrets unless money is paid □ verb to threaten by blackmail □ **blackmailer** noun

black market illegal or dishonest buying and selling

blackout noun 1 total darkness caused by putting out or covering all lights 2 a temporary loss of consciousness

black-pudding noun blood sausage

black sheep someone who is considered a failure or outsider in a group

blacksmith noun someone who makes or repairs iron goods, especially horseshoes

black tie formal evening dress

black widow a very poisonous American spider, the female of which often eats her mate

bladder noun 1 the organ in which urine collects in the body 2 a bag with thin, membrane-like walls

bladderwrack noun a common seaweed with air bladders on its strands

blade noun 1 the cutting part of a knife, sword etc 2 a leaf of grass or wheat

blame *verb* to find fault with; consider responsible for □ *noun* fault; responsibility for something bad □ **blameless** *adjective*

blameworthy *adjective* deserving blame

blancmange (*pronounced* bla-**monsz**) *noun* a jelly-like pudding made with milk

bland *adjective* 1 mild, not strong or irritating: *bland taste* 2 dull, insipid

blandishments *noun plural* acts or words meant to flatter

blank *adjective* 1 clear, unmarked: *blank sheet of paper* 2 expressionless: *a blank look* □ *noun* 1 an empty space 2 a cartridge without a bullet

blanket *noun* 1 a bedcovering of wool *etc* 2 a widespread, soft covering: *blanket of snow* □ *adjective* covering a group of things: *blanket agreement* □ *verb* to cover widely or thickly

blanket bombing bombing from the air over a widespread area

blank verse non-rhyming poetry in a metre of 5 feet per line

blare *verb* to sound loudly □ *noun* a loud sound, *eg* on a trumpet

blasé (*pronounced* blah-**zei**) *adjective* indifferent, unconcerned, especially because of being already familiar with something

blaspheme *verb* 1 to speak irreverently of a god 2 to swear, curse □ **blasphemer** *noun* □ **blasphemous** *adjective* □ **blasphemy** *noun* (*plural* **blasphemies**) 1 the act of speaking irreverently of a god 2 a swear-word: *uttering foul blasphemies*

blast *noun* 1 a blowing or gust of wind 2 a loud note, *eg* on a trumpet 3 an explosion □ *verb* 1 to break (stones, a bridge *etc*) by explosion 2 to produce a loud noise 3 *formal* to wither, destroy □ *exclamation* damn! □ **at full blast** as quickly, strongly *etc* as possible

blast furnace a furnace used in iron-smelting into which hot air is blown

blast-off *noun* the moment of the launching of a rocket

blatant *adjective* very obvious; shameless: *blatant lie*

blaze *noun* a rush of light or flame □ *verb* 1 to burn with a strong flame 2 to throw out a strong light

blazer *noun* a light jacket often worn as part of a uniform

bleach *verb* to whiten, remove the colour from □ *noun* (*plural* **bleaches**) a substance which bleaches, used for cleaning, whitening clothes *etc*

bleak *adjective* dull and cheerless; cold, unsheltered □ **bleakly** *adverb* sadly, wistfully

bleary *adjective* of eyes: tired and inflamed □ **blearily** *adverb* with tired-looking, watery eyes: *He opened his eyes and looked at me blearily*

bleat *verb* 1 to cry like a sheep 2 to complain in an irritating or whining way □ *noun* 1 a sheep's cry 2 an irritating whine

bleed *verb* 1 to lose blood 2 to draw blood from

> **bleed** ⇨ bleed**s**, bleed**ing**, bled

bleeding *noun* a flow of blood

bleep *noun* a high-pitched intermittent sound □ *verb* to give out such a sound

blemish *noun* (*plural* **blemishes**) a stain; a fault or flaw □ *verb* to stain, spoil

blend *verb* to mix together □ *noun* a mixture

blender *noun* an electric machine which mixes thoroughly and liquidizes food

bless *verb* 1 to wish happiness to 2 to make happy 3 to make holy □ **blessed** or (in poetry *etc*) **blest** *adjective* 1 happy; fortunate 2 made holy, consecrated

blessing *noun* 1 wish or prayer for happiness 2 a source of happiness or relief: *the extra money was a blessing to them* □ **blessing in disguise** something unexpectedly useful or beneficial

blether *verb*, *Scottish* to chatter; talk nonsense

blight *noun* 1 a disease which makes plants wither 2 a cause of destruction □ *verb* to destroy

blind *adjective* unable to see □ *noun* 1 a window screen 2 a deception, a trick

□ *verb* **1** to make blind **2** to dazzle
□ **blindness** *noun*

blind alley a street open only at one end; anything which leads nowhere

blindfold *noun* a bandage or cover which is put over a person's eyes to prevent them from seeing □ *adjective* with the eyes bandaged or covered, so as not to see □ *verb* to apply a blindfold to

blindman's buff a game in which a blindfold person tries to catch others

blink *verb* to close the eyes for a moment; shine unsteadily □ *noun*

blinkers *noun plural* pieces of leather over a horse's eyes to prevent it seeing in any direction except in front

bliss *noun* very great happiness □ **blissful** *adjective* bringing feelings of great happiness, lovely: *a blissful holiday*

blister *noun* a thin bubble on the skin full of watery matter □ *verb* to rise up in a blister

blithe *adjective* happy, merry □ **blithely** *adverb*: *He blithely imagines he'll pass his exams without studying*

blitz *noun* (*plural* **blitzes**) **1** an air attack **2** a sudden violent attack

blizzard *noun* a fierce storm of wind and snow

bloated *adjective* swollen, puffed out

bloater *noun* a type of smoked herring

blob *noun* **1** a drop of liquid **2** a round spot

block *noun* **1** a lump of wood, stone *etc* **2** a connected group of buildings **3** an obstruction: *road block* **4** an engraved piece of wood or metal for printing **5** *historical* the wood on which people were beheaded □ *verb* to hinder, prevent from progess □ **block letters** capital letters

blockade *verb* to surround a fort or country so that food *etc* cannot reach it □ *noun* the surrounding of a place in this way

blond *adjective* **1** light-coloured **2** fair-haired

blonde *adjective* having fair skin and

light-coloured hair □ *noun* a woman with this colouring

blood *noun* **1** the red liquid which flows in the bodies of human beings and animals **2** someone's descent or parentage: *royal blood*

blood donor someone who gives blood which is stored and given to others in transfusions *etc*

blood group any one of the types into which human blood is divided

bloodhound *noun* a breed of large dog with a good sense of smell

bloodless *adjective* without bloodshed: *bloodless revolution*

bloodshed *noun* violent loss of lfe, slaughter

bloodshot *adjective* of eyes: inflamed with blood

bloodthirsty *adjective* cruel, eager to kill

blood-vessel *noun* a vein or artery in which the blood circulates

bloody *adjective* **1** covered with blood **2** extremely violent, gory **3** *informal* terrible, awful □ **bloodily** *adverb* in a violent way involving lots of blood

bloom *verb* **1** of a plant: to flower **2** to be in good health □ *noun* **1** a flower **2** rosy colour **3** freshness, perfection **4** a powder on the skin of fresh fruits

bloomers *noun plural* **1** loose underpants with legs gathered above the knee **2** *historical* a woman's outfit of a jacket, skirt and baggy knee-length trousers

After Amelia *Bloomer*, 19th-century US feminist who promoted the use of the outfit for women

blossom *noun* **1** a flower **2** the flowers on a fruit-tree □ *verb* **1** to produce flowers **2** to open out, develop, flourish

blot *noun* **1** a spot of ink **2** a stain □ *verb* **1** to spot, stain **2** to dry writing with blotting paper □ **blot out** to remove from sight or memory

blot *verb* ⇨ blots, blot*ting*, blot*ted*

■ **Alternative words: blot out**
obliterate

blotch *noun* (*plural* **blotches**) a spot or

patch of colour *etc* □ *verb* to mark with blotches □ **blotched** *adjective* □ **blotchy** *adjective* with skin or another surface which is temporarily an uneven colour: *Her face was blotchy from crying*

blotting paper thick paper for absorbing spilled or excess ink

blouse *noun* a loose piece of clothing for the upper body

blow *noun* 1 a hard stroke or knock, *eg* with the fist 2 *informal* a sudden piece of bad luck □ *verb* 1 of wind: to move around 2 to drive air upon or into 3 to sound (a wind instrument) 4 to breathe hard or with difficulty □ **blow over** to pass and be forgotten □ **blow up** to destroy by explosion

blow *verb* ➭ blow**s**, blow**ing**, **blew**, **blown**

blowlamp or **blowtorch** *noun* a tool for aiming a very hot flame at a particular spot

blowy *adjective* windy

blubber *noun* the fat of whales and other sea animals

bludgeon *noun* a short stick with a heavy end

blue *noun* the colour of a clear sky □ *adjective* 1 of this colour 2 *informal* unhappy, depressed 3 containing sexual material: *blue film* □ **the blues** *noun plural* 1 a slow, sad song 2 low spirits, depression □ **out of the blue** unexpectedly

bluebell *noun* 1 the wild hyacinth 2 in Scotland, the harebell

blue blood royal or aristocratic blood

bluebottle *noun* a large fly with a blue abdomen

blue-chip *adjective* of a business company: reliable for investment; prestigious

Blue Peter a blue flag with white centre, raised when a ship is about to sail

blueprint *noun* a plan of work to be done

bluff *adjective* 1 rough and cheerful in manner 2 frank, outspoken □ *verb* to try to deceive by pretending self-confidence □ *noun* 1 a steep bank

overlooking the sea or a river 2 deception, trickery

blunder *verb* to make a bad mistake □ *noun* a bad mistake

blunderbuss *noun* (*plural* **blunderbusses**) a short hand-gun with a wide mouth

blunt *adjective* 1 having an edge or point that is not sharp 2 rough in manner □ *verb* to make less sharp or less painful □ **bluntly** *adverb* frankly, straightforwardly

blur *noun* an indistinct area of something; a smudge, a smear □ *verb* to make indistinct, smudge □ **blurred** *adjective*

blur *verb* ➭ blur**s**, blur**ring**, blur**red**

blurt *verb*: **blurt out** to speak suddenly and without thinking

blush *noun* (*plural* **blushes**) 1 a red glow on the face caused by embarrassment *etc* 2 a reddish glow □ *verb* to go red in the face

bluster *verb* 1 to blow strongly 2 to boast loudly □ *noun* 1 a blasting wind 2 empty boasting

BMA *abbreviation* British Medical Association

boa *noun* a long scarf of fur or feathers

boa constrictor a large snake which kills its prey by winding itself round it and crushing it

boar *noun* 1 a male pig 2 a wild pig

board *noun* 1 a sheet of wood 2 a group of people who run a business: *board of directors* 3 stiff card used to bind books 4 food: *bed and board* □ *verb* 1 to cover with boards 2 to supply with food at fixed terms 3 to enter (a ship, aeroplane *etc*) □ **boarder** *noun* someone who receives food and lodging

boarding-house *noun* a house where paying guests receive meals at a fixed price

boarding-school *noun* a school in which food and lodging is given

boat *noun* 1 a vessel for sailing or rowing; a ship 2 a boat-shaped dish: *sauceboat* □ *verb* to sail about in a boat

boater *noun* a straw hat with a brim

boatswain or **bosun** (*both pronounced*

boh-sun) *noun* an officer who looks after a ship's boats, rigging *etc*

bob¹ *verb* 1 to move up and down rapidly 2 to cut (hair) to about neck level □ *noun* a bobbed haircut

bob *verb* ⇨ bobs, bobb*ing*, bobb*ed*

bob² *noun* a bobsleigh

bobbin *noun* a reel or spool on which thread is wound

bobby *noun*, *Brit informal* a police officer

After *Robert* Peel, who introduced the Metropolitan Police Force when Home Secretary in 1828

bobsleigh *noun* a long sledge or two short sledges joined together with one long seat

bode *verb*: **bode well** or **bode ill** to be a good or bad sign

bodice *noun* the close-fitting part of a woman's or a child's dress above the waist

bodily *adjective* of the body

bodkin *noun*, *old* a large blunt needle

body *noun* (*plural* **bodies**) 1 the whole or main part of a human being or animal 2 a corpse 3 the main part of anything 4 a mass of people 5 *informal* a bodystocking

bodyguard *noun* someone or a group of people whose job is to protect another person from harm or attack

body language communication by means of conscious or unconscious gestures, attitudes, facial expressions *etc*

bodystocking *noun* a one-piece woman's under-garment

bodywarmer *noun* a padded sleeveless jacket

boffin *noun*, *informal* a research scientist

Said to come from a scientist who gave his colleagues nicknames from Dickens, Mr Boffin being a character in *Our Mutual Friend*

bog *noun* 1 a marsh 2 *slang* a toilet □ **boggy** *adjective* marshy □ **bog down** to prevent from making progress

bogey *noun* something greatly feared

boggle *verb* to be astonished at

bogus *adjective* false

bohemian *noun* someone who lives outside social conventions, especially an artist or writer □ *adjective* of the lifestyle of a bohemian

boil *verb* 1 of a liquid: to reach the temperature at which it turns to vapour 2 to bubble up owing to heat 3 *informal* to be hot 4 *informal* to be angry □ *noun* a kind of inflamed swelling

boiler *noun* a container in which water is heated or steam is produced

boiling-point *noun* the temperature at which a liquid turns to vapour (*eg* for water, 100°C)

boisterous *adjective* 1 wild, noisy 2 of weather: stormy

bold *adjective* 1 daring, full of courage 2 cheeky 3 striking, well-marked: *bold colours* 4 of printing type: thick and clear □ **boldly** *adjective* (meanings 1, 2 and 3)

bollard *noun* 1 a post to which ropes are fastened on a ship or quay 2 a short post on a street used for traffic control

Bolshevik *noun* 1 *historical* a member of the Extreme Socialist Party in revolutionary Russia 2 *derogatory* a communist

A Russian word based on *bolshe* 'greater', because of the majority held by the Bolsheviks in the Social Democratic Congress of 1903

bolshy *adjective*, *informal* awkward, uncooperative

Originally a shortening of **Bolshevik**

bolster *noun* a long cylindrical pillow or cushion □ **bolster up** to support

bolt *noun* 1 a small metal sliding bar used to fasten a door *etc* 2 a large screw or pin 3 a roll of cloth □ *verb* 1 to fasten with a bolt 2 to swallow (food) hurriedly 3 to rush away, escape □ **bolt upright** sitting with a very straight back

bomb *noun* 1 a case containing explosive or other harmful material thrown, dropped, timed to go off automatically *etc* 2 **the bomb** the nuclear bomb □ *verb* to drop bombs on

bombard verb 1 to attack with artillery 2 to overwhelm (with): *bombarded with letters* □ **bombardment** noun

bombast noun pompous language □ **bombastic** adjective using pompous language

bomber noun 1 an aeroplane built for bombing 2 someone who throws or plants bombs

bombshell noun 1 a startling piece of news 2 a stunningly attractive woman

bona fide (*pronounced* bohn-*a* **fai**-dei) adjective real, genuine: *bona fide excuse*

In Latin, *bona fide* translates as 'in good faith'

bond noun 1 something which binds, eg a rope 2 something which brings people together: *music was a bond between them* 3 a promise to pay or do something □ **in bond** in a bonded warehouse

bondage noun slavery

bonded warehouse a warehouse where goods are kept until taxes have been paid on them

bone noun 1 a hard material forming the skeleton of animals 2 one of the connected pieces of a skeleton: *the hip bone* □ verb to take the bones out of (meat *etc*)

bony adjective 1 full of bones 2 not fleshy, thin 3 made of bone or bone-like substance

bonfire noun a large fire in the open air

bonk noun the sound of a blow

bonnet noun 1 a decorative woman's hat, fastened under the chin 2 the covering over a car engine

bonny adjective good-looking; pretty

bonsai (*pronounced* **bon**-sai) noun a miniature or dwarf tree created by special pruning

bonus noun (*plural* **bonuses**) 1 an extra payment in addition to wages 2 something extra

boo verb to make a sound of disapproval □ noun a sound of disapproval

boob noun, *informal* a mistake

booby noun (*plural* **boobies**) an idiot □ **booby prize** a prize for the person who is last in a competition □ **booby trap** a device hidden or disguised as something harmless, intended to injure the first person to come near it

book noun 1 a number of pages bound together 2 a written work which has appeared, or is intended to appear, in the form of a book □ verb to order (places *etc*) beforehand

book-keeping noun the keeping of accounts

booklet noun a small paperback book

bookmaker noun someone who takes bets and pays winnings

bookworm noun 1 an avid reader 2 a grub that eats holes in books

boom verb 1 to make a hollow sound or roar 2 to increase in prosperity, success *etc* □ noun 1 a loud, hollow sound 2 a rush or increase of trade, prosperity *etc*: *oil boom/ property boom* 3 a pole along which a sail is stretched

boomerang noun a curved piece of wood which when thrown returns to the thrower, a traditional hunting weapon of Australian Aboriginals

boon noun something to be grateful for, a blessing □ **boon companion** a close friend who is good company

boor noun a rough or rude person □ **boorish** adjective

boost verb to push up, raise, increase: *boost the sales figures* □ noun an increase, a rise

booster noun 1 a device for increasing the power of a machine *etc* 2 the first of several stages of a rocket

boot noun 1 a heavy shoe covering the foot and lower part of the leg 2 *Brit* a place for stowing luggage in a car 3 the starting of a computer from its start-up programs 4 a kick □ verb to kick □ **boot up** to start (a computer) by running its start-up programs □ **to boot** in addition, as well

bootee noun a knitted boot for a baby

booth noun 1 a covered stall, eg at a market 2 a small compartment for telephoning, voting *etc*

booty noun plunder, gains taken in war etc

border noun 1 the edge or side of anything 2 the boundary of a country 3 a flowerbed in a garden □ verb **border on** to be near to: bordering on the absurd

bore[1] verb 1 to make a hole by piercing 2 to weary, be tiresome to: this book bores me □ noun 1 a pierced hole 2 the size across the tube of a gun 3 a tiresome person or thing 4 a wave that rushes up a river mouth at high tide

bore[2] past form of **bear**

boredom noun lack of interest, weariness

boring adjective not at all interesting

■ **Alternative words**: tedious, monotonous, repetitious, humdrum, trite, insipid

born adjective by birth, natural: a born actor □ **be born 1** of a baby: to come out of the mother's womb 2 to come into existence

   ◆ Do not confuse: **born** and **borne**. **Born** is used for the past participle of **bear** when referring to the birth of a child, idea etc; otherwise the form is **borne**: I couldn't have borne it any longer

borne past participle of **bear**
   ◆ Do not confuse: **borne** and **born**

borough noun 1 historical a town with special privileges granted by royal charter 2 a town that elects Members of Parliament

borrow verb to get on loan

bosom noun the breast; midst, centre: bosom of her family □ adjective of a friend: close, intimate

boss noun (plural **bosses**) a manager, a chief □ verb to order about in a high-handed way

bossy adjective tending to boss others, domineering

bosun see **boatswain**

botanic garden a large public garden containing plants and trees from different countries

botanist noun someone who studies botany

botany noun the study of plants □ **botanic** or **botanical** adjective

botch verb to mend clumsily; do badly □ noun a badly done piece of work

both adjective & pronoun the two, the one and the other: we're both going to Paris/ both the men are dead □ adverb equally, together: both willing and able

bother verb 1 to be a nuisance to: stop bothering me! 2 to take time or trouble over something: don't bother with the dishes □ noun trouble, inconvenience

bothy noun (plural **bothies**) 1 in Scotland, a hut to give shelter to hillwalkers 2 a simply furnished hut for farm workers

bottle noun a hollow narrow-necked vessel for holding liquids □ verb to put in a bottle □ **bottle up** to keep in, hold back (feelings)

bottleneck noun 1 a narrow part of a road likely to become crowded with traffic 2 a stage in a process where progress is held up

bottom noun 1 the lowest part or underside of anything 2 the buttocks

bottomless adjective extremely deep

boudoir (pronounced **bood**-wahr) noun a lady's private room

bough noun a branch of a tree

bought past form of **buy**

boulder noun a large stone

bounce verb 1 to jump up after striking the ground etc 2 to make (a ball etc) do this □ noun a jumping back up □ **bounce back** to recover after a setback or trouble

bouncer noun someone employed to force troublemakers to leave a club etc

bouncing adjective full of life, lively

bound[1] noun 1 a leap, a jump 2 **bounds** borders, limits □ verb 1 to jump, leap 2 to enclose, surround □ **bound for** ready to go to, on the way to □ **bound to** certain to □ **out of bounds** beyond the permitted limits

bound[2] past form of **bind**

boundary noun (plural **boundaries**) 1 an edge, a limit 2 a line etc marking an edge

boundless *adjective* having no limit, vast

bounteous or **bountiful** *adjective* generous; plentiful

bounty *noun* (*plural* **bounties**) **1** a gift; generosity **2** money given as a help □ **bounty hunter** someone who tracks down people wanted by the authorities to collect the rewards offered

bouquet (*pronounced* boo-**kei**) *noun* **1** a bunch of flowers **2** a scent, *eg* of wine

bourgeois (*pronounced* **boorsz**-wah) *adjective* of the middle class □ **the bourgeoisie** *noun* a rather insulting name for the kind of middle-class people who have a comfortable but unimaginative lifestyle

bout *noun* **1** a round in a contest **2** a spell, a fit: *bout of flu*

boutique *noun* a small shop selling fashionable clothes *etc*

bovine *adjective* **1** of or like cattle **2** stupid

bow[1] (*pronounced* bow) *verb* **1** to bend **2** to nod the head or bend the body in greeting **3** to give in: *bow to pressure* **4** to weigh down, crush □ *noun* **1** a bending of the head or body **2** the front part of a ship

bow[2] (*pronounced* boh) *noun* **1** anything in the shape of a curve or arch **2** a weapon for shooting arrows, made of a stick of springy wood bent by a string **3** a looped knot **4** a wooden rod with horsehair stretched along it, by which the strings of a violin *etc* are played □ **bow-legged** *adjective* having legs curving outwards □ **bow window** a window built in a curve

bowdlerize *verb* to censor heavily

After Thomas *Bowdler*, who produced a heavily censored edition of Shakespeare in the 19th century

bowels *noun plural* **1** the large and small intestines **2** the innermost or deepest parts of anything: *in the bowels of the earth*

bower (*pronounced* **bow**-er) *noun* a shady spot in a garden

bowl *noun* **1** a basin for holding liquids **2** a basin-shaped hollow **3** a heavy wooden ball, used in skittles *etc* **4** **bowls** a game played on a green with specially weighted bowls □ *verb* **1** to play at bowls **2** to move speedily like a bowl **3** *cricket* to send the ball at the wicket **4** *cricket* to put out by knocking the wicket with the ball □ **bowl over 1** to knock down **2** to surprise greatly □ **bowler** *noun* **1** someone who plays bowls **2** someone who bowls in cricket **3** a hat with a rounded top

box *noun* (*plural* **boxes**) **1** a case for holding anything **2** a hardwood tree **3** an evergreen shrub **4** an enclosure of private seats in a theatre □ *verb* **1** to put in a box **2** to confine in a small space **3** to punch **4** to engage in the sport of boxing

boxer *noun* **1** someone who boxes as a sport **2** a breed of large smooth-haired dog with a head like a bulldog's

boxer shorts loose-fitting men's underpants

boxing *noun* the sport of fighting with the fists wearing padded gloves

Boxing Day the first weekday after Christmas Day

box office an office where theatre tickets *etc* may be bought

boy *noun* **1** a male child **2** a male servant

boycott *verb* to refuse to do business or trade with □ *noun* a refusal to trade or do business

After Charles *Boycott*, British estate manager ostracized by the Irish Land League in the 19th century

boyhood *noun* the time of being a boy

boyish *adjective* **1** of a girl: having an appearance or behaviour which gives an impression of masculinity **2** of a man: having an appearance or behaviour which gives an impression of youthfulness

bra *noun*, *informal* a brassière

brace *noun* **1** an instrument which draws things together and holds them firmly **2** a piece of wire fitted over teeth to straighten them **3** a pair of pheasant, grouse *etc* when shot **4** a carpenter's tool for boring **5** **braces** shoulder-straps for holding up trousers □ *verb* to strengthen, give firmness to

bracelet *noun* **1** a circular ornament placed around the wrist **2** *slang* a handcuff

bracing *adjective* giving strength

bracken *noun* a coarse kind of fern

bracket *noun* **1** a support for something fastened to a wall **2** each of a pair of written or printed marks, *eg* ( ), [ ], used to group together several words **3** a grouping, category: *in the same age bracket* □ *verb* **1** to enclose in brackets **2** to group together

brackish *adjective* of water: rather salty

brag *verb* to boast □ *noun* a boast

brag *verb* ⇨ brag**s**, brag**ging**, brag**ged**

braggart *noun* someone vain and boastful

braid *verb* to plait (the hair) □ *noun* **1** a plait of hair **2** decorative ribbon used as trimming

braille *noun* a system of raised marks on paper which blind people can read by feeling

Named after its inventor, French teacher Louis *Braille*

brain *noun* the part of the body inside the skull, the centre of feeling and thinking □ *verb* to knock out the brains of; hit hard on the head

brainwashing *noun* forcing (a person) to change their views

brainwave *noun* a good idea

brainy *adjective, informal* clever

braise *verb* to stew (meat) in a small amount of liquid

brake *noun* a part of a vehicle used for stopping or slowing down □ *verb* to slow down by using the brake(s)

bramble *noun* **1** the blackberry bush **2** its fruit

bran *noun* the inner husks of wheat *etc*, separated from flour after grinding

branch *noun* (*plural* **branches**) **1** an arm-like limb of a tree **2** a small shop, bank *etc* belonging to a bigger one □ *verb* to spread out like branches

brand *noun* **1** a make of goods with a special trademark **2** a burning piece of wood **3** a permanent mark made by a red-hot iron □ *verb* **1** to mark with a brand **2** to mark permanently; impress deeply **3** to mark with disgrace: *branded as a thief*

brandish *verb* to wave (a weapon *etc*) about

brand-new *adjective* absolutely new

brandy *noun* (*plural* **brandies**) an alcoholic spirit made from wine

brass *noun* (*plural* **brasses**) **1** metal made by mixing copper and zinc **2** *music* brass wind instruments □ *adjective* **1** made of brass **2** playing brass musical instruments: *brass band*

brassière *noun* an article of women's underwear for supporting the breasts

brassy *adjective* **1** like brass **2** of a voice: harsh

brat *noun* a disapproving name for a child

bravado *noun* a show of bravery, bold pretence

brave *adjective* ready to meet danger, pain *etc* without showing fear; courageous, noble □ *verb* to face or meet boldly and without fear □ *noun* a Native American warrior

bravery *noun* the quality of being brave and acting with courage

bravo *exclamation* well done!

brawl *noun* a noisy quarrel; a fight □ *verb* to quarrel or fight noisily

brawn *noun* muscle power □ **brawny** *adjective* big and strong

bray *noun* **1** a cry like that of an ass **2** a pin pressing against a string on a harp to produce a buzzing effect □ *verb* to cry like an ass

brazen *adjective* **1** impudent, shameless: *brazen hussy* **2** of or like brass □ **brazen it out** to face a difficult situation with bold impudence

brazier *noun* an iron basket for holding burning coals

breach *noun* (*plural* **breaches**) **1** a break, a gap **2** a breaking of a law, a promise *etc* **3** a quarrel □ *verb* to make a gap or opening in □ **breach of the peace** a breach of the law by noisy, offensive behaviour

bread *noun* food made of flour or meal and baked

breadth noun 1 distance from side to side, width 2 extent: *breadth of knowledge*

breadwinner noun someone who earns a living for a family

break verb 1 to (cause to) fall to pieces or apart 2 to act against (a law, promise etc) 3 to interrupt (a silence) 4 to tell (news) 5 to check, soften the effect of (a fall) 6 to cure (a habit) 7 of a boy's voice: to drop to a deep male tone □ noun 1 an opening 2 a pause 3 *informal* a lucky chance □ **break down** 1 to divide into parts 2 of an engine: to fail 3 to be overcome with weeping or nervous exhaustion □ **break in** to tame, train (a wild horse etc) □ **break into** to enter by force □ **break out** 1 to appear suddenly 2 to escape 3 **break out in something** to become covered (with a rash etc) □ **break up** 1 to (cause to) fall to pieces or apart 2 to separate, leave one another □ **breakable** adjective

> **break** verb ⇨ break*s*, break*ing*, broke, broken

breakage noun 1 the act of breaking 2 something broken

breakdown noun 1 a division into parts 2 a collapse from nervous exhaustion etc

breaker noun a large wave

breakfast noun the first meal of the day □ verb to eat this meal

break-in noun illegal forced entry of a house etc with intent to steal

break-through noun a sudden success after some effort

breakwater noun a barrier to break the force of waves

breast noun 1 either of the milk-producing glands on a woman's body 2 the front part of a human or animal body between neck and belly 3 a part of a jacket or coat which covers the breast □ **make a clean breast** to make a full confession

breastbone noun the bone running down the middle of the breast; the sternum

breastplate noun a piece of armour for the breast

breath (*pronounced* breth) noun 1 the air drawn into and then sent out from the lungs 2 an instance of breathing 3 a very slight breeze

> ☞ Do not confuse: **breath** and **breathe**

Breathalyser noun, *trademark* a device into which someone breathes to indicate the amount of alcohol in their blood

breathe (*pronounced* breedh) verb 1 to draw in and send out air from the lungs 2 to whisper

> **breathe** ⇨ breath*es*, breath*ing*, breath*ed*

> ☞ Do not confuse: **breathe** and **breath**

breather noun a rest or pause

breathless adjective 1 breathing very fast, panting 2 excited

bred past form of **breed**

breech noun the back part, especially of a gun

breeches (*pronounced* brich-iz) noun plural trousers reaching to just below the knee

breed verb 1 to produce (children or a family) 2 to mate and rear (animals) 3 to cause: *dirt breeds disease* □ noun 1 a group of animals etc descended from the same ancestor 2 type, sort: *a new breed of salesmen*

> **breed** verb ⇨ breed*s*, breed*ing*, bred

breeding noun 1 act of producing or rearing 2 good manners; education and training

breeze noun a gentle wind

breeze block a type of large, grey brick used in building

breezy adjective 1 windy, gusty 2 bright, lively □ **breezily** adverb (meaning 2)

brethren noun plural, old brothers

breve (*pronounced* breev) noun a long musical note (◦) which is 8 beats in length

brevity noun shortness, conciseness

brew verb 1 to make beer 2 to make (tea etc) 3 to be gathering or forming: *there's trouble brewing* 4 to plot, plan:

brewing mischief □ **brewer** *noun* someone who brews beer *etc*

brewery *noun* (*plural* **breweries**) a place where beer is made

briar or **brier** *noun* **1** the wild rose **2** a heather plant whose wood is used for making tobacco pipes

bribe *noun* a gift of money *etc* given to persuade someone to do something □ *verb* to give a bribe to

bribe *verb* ⟹ brib*es*, brib*ing*, brib*ed*

bribery *noun* the act of bribing someone to do something

bric-à-brac *noun* small odds and ends

brick *noun* **1** a block of baked clay for building **2** a toy building-block of wood *etc*

bridal *adjective* of a bride or a wedding

bride *noun* a woman about to be married, or newly married

bridegroom *noun* a man about to be married, or newly married

bridesmaid *noun* an unmarried woman who attends the bride at a wedding

bridge¹ *noun* **1** a structure built to carry a track or road across a river *etc* **2** the captain's platform on a ship **3** the bony part of the nose **4** a thin piece of wood holding up the strings of a violin *etc* □ *verb* **1** to be a bridge over; span **2** to build a bridge over **3** to get over (a difficulty)

bridge *verb* ⟹ bridg*es*, bridg*ing*, bridg*ed*

bridge² *noun* a card game for two pairs of players

bridle *noun* the harness on a horse's head to which the reins are attached □ *verb* **1** to put on a bridle **2** to toss the head indignantly □ **bridle path** *noun* a path for horseriders

brief *adjective* short; taking a short time □ *noun* a set of notes giving information or instructions, especially to a lawyer about a law case □ *verb* to instruct or inform □ **in brief** in a few words □ **briefly** *adverb*

briefs *noun plural* close-fitting underpants

brier *another spelling of* **briar**

brigade *noun* a body of soldiers, usually two battalions

brigadier *noun* a senior army officer

brigand *noun*, *old* a robber, a bandit

bright *adjective* **1** shining; full of light **2** clever **3** cheerful

brighten *verb* to make or grow bright

brilliant *adjective* **1** very clever **2** sparkling **3** *informal* very good, excellent □ **brilliance** *noun* □ **brilliantly** *adverb*: *brilliantly intelligent/ the edges of the diamond gleamed brilliantly/ He did brilliantly in his exams*

brim *noun* **1** the edge of a cup *etc*: *filled to the brim* **2** the protruding lower edge of a hat or cap □ *verb* to be full □ **brimful** *adjective* full to the brim

brim *verb* ⟹ brim*s*, brimm*ing*, brimm*ed*

brimstone *noun* sulphur

brine *noun* salt water □ **briny** *adjective*

bring *verb* **1** to fetch, lead or carry (to a place) **2** to cause to come: *the medicine brings him relief* □ **bring about** to cause □ **bring home to** to make (someone) realize (something) □ **bring off** to do (something) successfully □ **bring to** to revive □ **bring up 1** to rear, feed and educate: *brought up three children single-handed* **2** to mention: *I'll bring it up at the meeting* **3** *informal* to vomit

bring ⟹ bring*s*, bring*ing*, brought

⊙ Comes from Old English *bringan* meaning 'to carry' or 'to bring'

brink *noun* the edge of a cliff *etc* □ **on the brink of** almost at the point of, on the verge of: *on the brink of tears*

brisk *adjective* **1** moving quickly: *a brisk walk* **2** lively and efficient: *a brisk manner* □ **briskly** *adverb*

bristle *noun* a short, stiff hair on an animal, a brush *etc* □ *verb* **1** of hair *etc*: to stand on end **2** to show anger and indignation: *he bristled at my remark* □ **bristly** *adjective* having bristles; rough

brittle *adjective* hard but easily broken

broach *verb* **1** to begin to talk about: *broached the subject* **2** to open, begin using (*eg* a cask of wine)

broad *adjective* **1** wide, extensive **2** of an accent *etc*: strong, obvious □ **broadly**

adverb **1** widely: *smile broadly* **2** generally: *Broadly speaking, we're all afraid of the same things*

broadcast *verb* to transmit (a programme *etc*) on radio or television □ *noun* a programme transmitted on radio or television

broaden *verb* to make or grow broader

broad-gauge *adjective* of a railway: having the distance between rails greater than the *standard gauge* (4ft 8in or 1.435 metre)

broadsheet *noun* a large-format quality newspaper (*compare with*: **tabloid**)

broadside *noun* **1** a strong attack in an argument *etc* **2** a shot by all the guns on one side of a ship

brocade *noun* a silk cloth on which fine patterns are sewn

broccoli *noun* a hardy variety of cauliflower with small green or purple flower-heads

brochure (*pronounced* broh-**shoor** or broh-**sh**ur) *noun* a booklet, a pamphlet: *holiday brochure*

brogue[1] (*pronounced* brohg) *noun* a strong shoe

brogue[2] (*pronounced* brohg) *noun* a broad accent in speaking: *Irish brogue*

broil *verb* **1** to make or be very hot **2** *US* to grill

broke *past form of* **break** □ *adjective*, *informal* having no money

broken *past participle of* **break**

■ **Alternative words**: fractured, faulty, defective, disjointed

broker *noun* someone who buys and sells stocks and shares for others □ *verb* **1** to act as a broker **2** to negotiate on behalf of others: *broker a deal*

bromide *noun* **1** a chemical used as a sedative **2** a dull person **3** a platitude **4** a monochrome photographic print

bronchial (*pronounced* **brong**-ki-*a*l) *adjective* having to do with the windpipe

bronchitis (*pronounced* brong-**kait**-*is*) *noun* an illness affecting the windpipe, causing difficulty in breathing

bronco *noun* (*plural* **broncos**) *US* a half-tamed horse

brontosaurus *noun* a large dinosaur

bronze *noun* a golden-brown mixture of copper and tin □ *adjective* of this colour □ **bronzed** *adjective* suntanned

brooch (*pronounced* brohch) *noun* (*plural* **brooches**) an ornament pinned to the clothing

brood *verb* **1** of a hen *etc*: to sit on eggs **2** to think anxiously for some time □ *noun* **1** a number of young birds hatched at one time **2** young animals or children of the same family

brook *noun* a small stream □ *verb* to put up with, endure

broom *noun* **1** a type of shrub with yellow flowers **2** a brush for sweeping

broomstick *noun* the handle of a broom

brose *noun, Scottish* a liquid food of boiling water poured on oatmeal *etc*

broth *noun* soup, especially one made with vegetables

brothel *noun* a house where prostitution is practised

Originally *brothel-house*, *brothel* being a general term of abuse that was later applied specifically to prostitutes

brother *noun* **1** a male born of the same parents as yourself **2** a companion, a fellow-worker

brotherhood *noun* **1** comradeship between men **2** a men's association

brother-in-law *noun* **1** the brother of your husband or wife **2** the husband of your sister or sister-in-law

brotherly *adjective* like a brother; affectionate

brought *past form of* **bring**

brow *noun* **1** a forehead **2** an eyebrow **3** the edge of a hill

browbeat *verb* to bully

brown *noun* a dark colour made by mixing red, yellow, black *etc* □ *adjective* **1** of this colour **2** *informal* suntanned

brownie *noun* **1** a helpful fairy or goblin **2** a Brownie Guide □ **Brownie Guide** a junior Guide

browse *verb* **1** to glance through a range of books, shop merchandise *etc* **2** to feed on the shoots or leaves of plants

bruise *noun* a discoloured area on the skin, the surface of fruit *etc*, where it has been struck □ *verb* to cause bruises (to)

brunette *noun* a woman with dark brown hair

brunt *noun*: **bear** or **take the brunt** to take the chief strain

brush *noun* (*plural* **brushes**) **1** an instrument with tufts of bristles, hair *etc* for smoothing the hair, cleaning, painting *etc* **2** a disagreement, a brief quarrel **3** the tail of a fox **4** undergrowth □ *verb* **1** to pass a brush over **2** to remove by sweeping **3** to touch lightly in passing

brushwood *noun* **1** broken branches, twigs *etc* **2** undergrowth

Brussels sprouts a type of vegetable with sprouts like small cabbages on the stem

brute *noun* **1** an animal **2** a cruel person

brutish *adjective* like a brute, savage, coarse

BSE *abbreviation* bovine spongiform encephalopathy, a brain disease of cattle

Bt *abbreviation* baronet

bubble *noun* **1** a thin ball of liquid blown out with air **2** a small ball of air in anything □ *verb* to rise in bubbles

bubbly *adjective* **1** full of bubbles **2** lively, vivacious □ *noun, informal* champagne; sparkling wine

buccaneer *noun, old* a pirate □ **buccaneering** *adjective* like a pirate

buck *noun* **1** the male of the deer, goat, hare and rabbit **2** *US informal* a dollar □ *verb* of a horse *etc*: to attempt to throw a rider by rapid jumps into the air

bucket *noun* a container for water *etc*

buckle *noun* a clip for fastening straps or belts □ *verb* to fasten with a buckle

buckler *noun* a small shield

bucolic *adjective* of the countryside; pastoral, rural

bud *noun* the first shoot of a tree or plant □ *verb* to produce buds
     bud *verb* ⇨ bud*s*, bud*ding*, bud*ded*

Buddhism *noun* a religion whose followers worship Buddha □ **Buddhist** *noun & adjective*

budding *adjective* showing signs of becoming: *budding author*

budge *verb* to move slightly, stir
     budge ⇨ budge*s*, budg*ing*, budg*ed*

budgerigar *noun* a kind of small parrot often kept as a pet

budget *noun* **1** a government plan for the year's spending **2** any plan of their future spending □ *verb* to allow for in a budget: *the project has been budgeted for*

> Originally a small bag; the parliamentary sense of *budget* stems from a political insult directed at Robert Walpole implying that he was a quack or pedlar

budgie *noun, informal* a budgerigar

buff *noun* **1** a light yellowish brown colour **2** an enthusiast, a fan: *film buff* □ *verb* to polish

> The later meaning of 'enthusiast' derives from the *buff*-coloured uniforms once used by volunteer firefighters in New York

buffalo *noun* (*plural* **buffaloes**) **1** a large Asian ox, used to draw loads **2** the North American bison

buffer *noun* something which lessens the force of a blow or collision

buffet[1] *noun* (*pronounced* **buf**-it) *verb* to strike, knock about □ *noun* a slap or a blow

buffet[2] *noun* (*pronounced* **buwf**-ei) **1** a counter or café serving food and drink **2** a range of dishes set out at a party, *etc* for people to serve themselves

buffoon *noun* a clown, fool □ **buffoonery** *noun* silly behaviour, clowning around

bug *noun* **1** a small, especially irritating, insect **2** a disease germ: *a tummy bug* **3** a tiny hidden microphone for recording conversations **4** a problem in a computer program causing errors in its execution □ *verb* **1** to conceal a microphone in (a room *etc*) **2** to record with a hidden microphone **3** *informal* to annoy, harass

bug *verb* ⇨ bug*s*, bug*ging*, bug*ged*

bugbear *noun* something that frightens or annoys

buggy *noun* (*plural* **buggies**) a child's push-chair

bugle *noun* a small military trumpet □ **bugler** *noun* someone who plays the bugle

build *verb* to put together the parts of anything □ *noun* physique, physical character: *a man of heavy build* □ **builder** *noun*

build *verb* ⇨ build*s*, build*ing*, built

building *noun* **1** the act or trade of building (houses *etc*) **2** a house or other built dwelling

building society an institution like a bank which accepts investments and whose main business is to lend people money to buy a house

built-up *adjective* of an area: containing houses and other buildings

bulb *noun* **1** the rounded part of the stem of an onion, tulip *etc*, in which they store their food **2** a glass globe surrounding the element of an electric light □ **bulbous** *adjective* bulb-shaped

bulge *noun* **1** a swelling **2** a noticeable increase □ *verb* to swell out

bulge *verb* ⇨ bulge*s*, bulg*ing*, bulg*ed*

bulimia *noun* an eating disorder in which bingeing is followed by self-induced vomiting or purging □ **bulimic** *adjective* suffering from bulimia

bulk *noun* **1** large size **2** the greater part: *the bulk of the population*

bulkhead *noun* a wall in the inside of a ship, meant to keep out water in a collision

bulky *adjective* taking up a lot of room □ **bulkily** *adverb*

bull *noun* the male of animals of the ox family, also of the whale, elephant *etc*

bulldog *noun* a breed of strong, fierce-looking dog

bulldoze *verb* **1** to use a bulldozer on

2 to force: *bulldozed his way into the room*

bulldozer *noun* a machine for levelling land and clearing away obstacles

bullet *noun* the piece of metal fired from a gun

bulletin *noun* a report of current news, someone's health *etc*

bullet-proof *adjective* not able to be pierced by bullets

bullfight *noun* a public entertainment in Spain *etc*, in which a bull is angered and usually killed

bullfinch *noun* a small pink-breasted bird

bullion *noun* gold or silver in the form of bars *etc*

bullock *noun* a young bull

bull's-eye *noun* **1** the mark in the middle of a target **2** a striped sweet

bully *noun* (*plural* **bullies**) someone who unfairly uses their size and strength to hurt or frighten others □ *verb* to act like a bully

Originally a term of affection that developed to mean 'pimp' and so to someone who harasses others

bulrush *noun* (*plural* **bulrushes**) a large strong reed which grows on wet land or in water

bulwark (*pronounced* **buwl**-wak) *noun* **1** a strong defensive wall **2** a prop, a defence

bum[1] *noun*, *Brit slang* the buttocks

bum[2] *noun*, *US slang* a tramp □ *adjective* useless, dud □ **give someone the bum's rush** to get rid of them quickly

bumbag *noun* a carrying pouch strapped round the waist

bumble-bee *noun* a type of large bee

bumf *another spelling of* **bumph**

bump *verb* **1** to strike heavily **2** to knock by accident □ *noun* **1** the sound of a heavy blow **2** an accidental knock **3** a raised lump

bumper *noun* a bar round the front and back of a car's body to protect it from damage □ *adjective* large: *bumper crop*

bumph or **bumf** *noun, Brit informal* miscellaneous, uninteresting papers, leaflets *etc*

Originally short for 'bum-fodder', *ie* toilet paper

bumpkin *noun* a clumsy, awkward, country person

bumptious *adjective* self-important

bun *noun* **1** a sweet roll made of egg dough **2** hair wound into a rounded mass

bunch *noun (plural* **bunches)** a number of things tied together or growing together □ *verb* to crowd together

bundle *noun* a number of things loosely bound together □ *verb* **1** to tie in a bundle **2** to push roughly: *bundled the children into the car*

bung *noun* the stopper of the hole in a barrel, bottle *etc* □ *verb* to stop up with a bung

bungalow *noun* a one-storey detached house

bungee jumping the sport of jumping from a height with strong rubber ropes attached to the ankles so that the jumper bounces up before reaching the ground

bungle *verb* **1** to do badly or clumsily **2** to mishandle, mismanage □ *noun* a clumsy or mishandled action

bunion *noun* a lump or swelling on the joint of the big toe

bunk *noun* a narrow bed, *eg* in a ship's cabin

bunkbed *noun* one of a pair of narrow beds one above the other

bunker *noun* **1** a sandpit on a golf course **2** an underground shelter **3** a large box for keeping coal

bunkum *noun* nonsense

From *Buncombe* county in N Carolina, whose representative once gave a rambling speech in Congress

bunny *noun (plural* **bunnies)** a child's name for a rabbit

Bunsen burner a gas-burner used in laboratories

bunting¹ *noun* **1** a thin cloth used for making flags **2** flags

bunting² *noun* a bird of the finch family

buoy *(pronounced* boi) *noun* **1** a floating mark acting as a guide or warning for ships **2** a float, *eg* a lifebuoy

buoyant *adjective* **1** able to float **2** cheerful, bouncy □ **buoyancy** *noun*

bur *another spelling of* **burr**

burden *noun* **1** a load **2** something difficult to bear, *eg* poverty or sorrow **3** *old* the chorus of a song □ **burdensome** *adjective*

bureau *(pronounced* **byoo**-roh) *noun (plural* **bureaux** or **bureaus** – *both pronounced* **byoo**-rohz) **1** a writing table **2** an office

Bureau is a French word, and comes from the name of a type of course cloth *(burel)* which was used as a cover for writing tables

bureaucracy *(pronounced* byoo-**rok**-ra-si) *noun* government by officials

bureaucrat *noun* an administrative official

bureaucratic *adjective* **1** involving bureaucracy **2** full of complicated and irritating official procedures

burgh *noun* in Scotland, a borough

burglar *noun* someone who breaks into a house to steal

burglary *noun (plural* **burglaries)** a break-in into a house by a person who wants to steal things

burgle *verb* to commit burglary

burial *noun* the placing of a body under the ground after death

burlesque *noun* a piece of writing, acting *etc*, making fun of somebody

burly *adjective* broad and strong

burn¹ *verb* **1** to set fire to **2** to be on fire, or scorching **3** to injure by burning □ *noun* an injury or mark caused by fire

burn *verb* ⇨ burn*s*, burn*ing*, burn*t* or burn*ed*

burn² *noun, Scottish* a small stream

burner *noun* the part of a lamp or gas-jet from which the flame rises

burnish *verb* to polish □ *noun* polish

burnt *past form of* **burn**

burr or **bur** *noun* the prickly seedcase or head of certain plants

burrow *noun* a hole or passage in the ground dug by certain animals for shelter □ *verb* to make a passage beneath the ground

burst *verb* **1** to break suddenly (after increased pressure) **2** to move, speak *etc* suddenly or violently

bury *verb* **1** to place (a dead body *etc*) under the ground **2** to cover, hide

bury ⇨ bur**ies**, bury**ing**, bur**ied**

bus *noun* (*plural* **buses**) a large road vehicle, often used for public transport

busby *noun* (*plural* **busbies**) a tall fur hat worn by certain soldiers

bush *noun* (*plural* **bushes**) **1** a growing thing with a plant and a tree in size **2** wild, unfarmed country in Africa *etc* □ **bush telegraph** the quick passing-on of news from person to person

bushy *adjective* **1** growing thickly: *bushy eyebrows* **2** full of bushes □ **bushily** *adverb* in a tangled, dense way: *His eyebrows sprouted bushily over his glasses*

business *noun* (*plural* **businesses**) **1** someone's work or job **2** trade, commerce: *business is booming* **3** a matter of personal interest or concern: *none of your business*

businesslike *adjective* practical, methodical, alert and prompt

businessman *noun* a man who works in commerce

businesswoman *noun* a woman who works in commerce

busk *verb* to play or sing in the street for money □ **busker** *noun*

bus stop an official stopping place for buses

bust *noun* **1** a woman's breasts **2** a sculpture of someone's head and shoulders

bustard *noun* a large, fast-running bird similar to a turkey

bustle *verb* to busy oneself noisily □ *noun* **1** noisy activity, fuss **2** *historical* a stuffed pad worn under a woman's full skirt

busy *adjective* having a lot to do □ **busy yourself with** to occupy yourself with □ **busily** *adverb*

busy *adjective* ⇨ busi**er**, busi**est**

busybody *noun* someone nosey about others

but *conjunction* **1** showing a contrast between two ideas *etc*: *my brother can swim but I can't/ that paint isn't black but brown* **2** except that, without that: *it never rains but it pours* □ *preposition* except, with the exception of: *no one but Tom had any money/ take the next road but one (ie the second road)* □ *adverb* only: *we can but hope* □ **but for** were it not for: *but for your car, we would have been late*

butch *adjective* of a woman: looking or behaving in a masculine way

butcher *noun* someone whose work is to carve up meat and sell it □ *verb* **1** to kill and carve up (an animal) for food **2** to kill cruelly

butchery *noun* great or cruel slaughter

butler *noun* the chief manservant in a household who looks after and serves wines *etc*

butt *noun* **1** a large cask, a barrel **2** someone of whom others make fun **3** the thick heavy end of a rifle *etc* **4** the end of a finished cigarette or cigar **5** a push with the head **6** *US slang* the buttocks □ *verb* to strike with the head □ **butt in** to interrupt, interfere □ **butt out** *slang* to stop interfering

butter *noun* a fatty food made by churning cream □ *verb* to spread over with butter □ **butter up** to flatter, soften up

buttercup *noun* a plant with a cup-like yellow flower

butterfly *noun* (*plural* **butterflies**) a kind of insect with large, often patterned wings

buttermilk *noun* the milk that is left after butter has been made

butterscotch *noun* a hard toffee made with butter

buttocks *noun plural* the two fleshy

parts of the body on which you sit; the rump

button *noun* **1** a knob or disc of metal, plastic *etc* used to fasten clothing **2** a knob pressed to work an electrical device □ *verb* to fasten by means of buttons □ **button up** to be quiet; shut up

buttonhole *noun* a hole through which a button is passed □ *verb* to catch the attention of (someone) and force them to listen

buttress *noun* (*plural* **buttresses**) a support on the outside of a wall □ *verb* to support, prop up

buxom *adjective* plump and pretty

buy *verb* to get in exchange for money □ *noun* a purchase: *a good buy* □ **buyer** *noun*

buy *verb* ⇨ buys, buying, bought

buzz *verb* **1** to make a humming noise like bees **2** *informal* to call, telephone **3** of aircraft: to fly close to □ *noun* **1** a humming sound **2** *informal* a phonecall

buzzard *noun* a large bird of prey

buzzer *noun* a signalling device which makes a buzzing noise

buzzword *noun* a word well-established in a particular jargon, its use suggesting up-to-date specialized knowledge

by *adverb* **1** near: *a crowd stood by, watching* **2** past: *people strolled by* **3** aside: *money put by for an emergency* □ *preposition* **1** next to, near: *standing by the door* **2** past: *going by the house* **3**

through, along, across: *we came by the main road* **4** indicating the person who does something: *written by Burns/ played by a young actor* **5** of time: not after: *it'll be ready by four o'clock* **6** during the time of: *working by night* **7** by means of: *by train* **8** to the extent of: *taller by a head* **9** used to express measurements, compass directions *etc*: *6 metres by 4 metres/ north by northwest* **10** in the quantity of: *sold by the pound/ paid by the week*

bye *noun, cricket* **1** a ball bowled past the wicket **2** a run made from this

by-election *noun* an election for parliament during a parliamentary session

bygone *adjective* past □ **bygones** *noun plural* old grievances or events that have been, or should be, forgotten

by-law or **bye-law** *noun* a local (not a national) law

bypass *noun* a road built round a town *etc* so that traffic need not pass through it

by-product *noun* something useful obtained during the manufacture of something else

byroad or **byway** *noun* a side road

bystander *noun* someone who stands watching an event or accident

byte (*pronounced* bait) *noun, computing* a unit used to measure data or memory

byword *noun* someone or something well-known for a particular quality

Cc

°C *abbreviation* degree(s) Celsius or centigrade

CAB *abbreviation* Citizens Advice Bureau

cab *noun* **1** a taxi **2** *historical* a hired carriage

cabaret (*pronounced* **kab**-*a*-rei) *noun* **1** an entertainment consisting of variety acts **2** a restaurant with a cabaret

cabbage *noun* a type of vegetable with edible leaves

caber (*pronounced* **kei**-ber) *noun* a heavy pole tossed in competition at Highland games

cabin *noun* **1** a wooden hut **2** a small room used for living quarters in a ship **3** the part of a commercial aircraft containing passenger seating

cabin crew the flight attendants on a commercial airline

cabinet *noun* **1** a cupboard which has shelves and doors **2** a similar container for storage *etc* **3** a wooden case with drawers **4** a selected number of government ministers who decide on policy

cabinet-maker *noun* a maker of fine furniture

cable *noun* **1** a strong rope or thick metal line **2** a line of covered telegraph wires laid under the sea or underground **3** a telegram sent by such a line **4** an underground wire **5** *informal* cable television □ *verb* to telegraph by cable

cable television a service transmitting television programmes to individual subscribers by underground cable

cacao *noun* a tree from whose seeds cocoa and chocolate are made

cache (*pronounced* kash) *noun* **1** a store or hiding place for ammunition, treasure *etc* **2** things hidden
ⓘ Comes from French *cacher* meaning 'to hide'

cachet (*pronounced* ka-**shei**) *noun* **1** prestige, credit **2** an official stamp or seal

cackle *noun* **1** the sound made by a hen or goose **2** a laugh which sounds like this

caco- *prefix* bad, incorrect
ⓘ Comes from Greek *kakos* meaning 'bad'

cacophonous *adjective* noisy and unpleasant-sounding: *a cacophonous wailing*

cacophony *noun* (*plural* **cacophonies**) an unpleasant noise

cactus *noun* (*plural* **cactuses** or **cacti**) a type of prickly plant

CAD *abbreviation* computer-aided design

cad *noun, old* a mean, despicable person

cadaver (*pronounced* ka-**dav**-er) *noun* a human corpse

cadaverous *adjective* corpse-like, very pale and thin

caddie *noun* an assistant who carries a golfer's clubs

caddy *noun* (*plural* **caddies**) a box for keeping tea fresh

cadence *noun* **1** a fall of the voice, *eg* at the end of a sentence **2** a group of chords ending a piece of music

cadenza *noun* a musical passage at the end of a movement, concerto *etc*

cadet (*pronounced* ka-**det**) *noun* **1** an officer trainee in the armed forces or police service **2** a school pupil who takes military training

cadge *verb* to beg □ **cadger** *noun*

> cadge ⇨ cadges, cadging, cadged

Caesarean (*pronounced* se-**zeir**-ri-an) *adjective* of a birth: delivered by cutting through the walls of the mother's abdomen □ *noun* a Caesarian birth or operation

caesura (*pronounced* se-**zyoo**-ra) *noun* a pause, a breathing space

café *noun* a small restaurant serving coffee, tea, snacks *etc*

cafeteria *noun* a self-service restaurant

caffeine *noun* a stimulating drug found in coffee and tea

caftan *noun* a long-sleeved, ankle-length Middle-Eastern garment

cage *noun* **1** a barred enclosure for birds or animals **2** a lift used by miners □ *verb* to close up in a cage

> cage ⇨ cages, caging, caged

cagey or **cagy** *adjective* unwilling to speak freely; wary □ **caginess** *noun*

cagoule *noun* a lightweight anorak

cahoots *noun plural*: **in cahoots with** in collusion with

cairn *noun* **1** a heap of stones marking a grave, or on top of a mountain **2** a breed of small terrier

cairngorm *noun* a brown or yellow variety of quartz, used for brooches *etc*

cajole *verb* to coax by flattery □ **cajolery** *noun*

cake *noun* **1** a baked piece of dough made from flour, eggs, sugar *etc* **2** something pressed into a lump: *cake of soap* □ *verb* to become dry and hard □ **have your cake and eat it** to enjoy both of two alternative things

calamine *noun* a pink powder containing a zinc salt, used to make a skin-soothing lotion

calamitous *adjective* extremely unfortunate, disastrous

calamity *noun* (*plural* **calamities**) a great disaster, a misfortune

calcium *noun* a metal which forms the chief part of lime

calculable *adjective* able to be counted or measured

calculate *verb* **1** to count, work out by mathematics **2** to think out in an exact way

calculating *adjective* thinking selfishly

calculation *noun* a mathematical reckoning, a sum

calculator *noun* a machine which makes mathematical calculations

calculus *noun* a mathematical system of calculation

calendar *noun* a table or list showing the year divided into months, weeks and days

calf[1] *noun* (*plural* **calves**) **1** the young of a cow or ox **2** the young of certain other mammals, *eg* an elephant or whale **3** calf's skin cured as leather

calf[2] *noun* (*plural* **calves**) the back of the lower part of the leg

calibrate *verb* **1** to mark the scale on (a measuring instrument) **2** to check or adjust the scale of (a measuring instrument)

calibre or *US* **caliber** *noun* **1** measurement across the opening of a tube or gun **2** of a person: quality of character, ability

> ✎ This is one of a large number of words which are spelled with an **-re** ending in British English, but with an **-er** in American English, *eg* centre/center, metre/meter, lustre/luster

calico *noun* a patterned kind of cotton cloth

> Originally *Calicut cloth*, after the port in SW India from where it was exported

call *verb* **1** to cry aloud **2** to name: *what is your cat called?* **3** to summon **4** to make a short visit **5** to telephone □ *noun* **1** a loud cry **2** a short visit **3** a telephone conversation □ **call off** to cancel

> ≣ Alternative words: **call off** abort

calligraphy *noun* the art of handwriting

calling *noun* a vocation, a job

callipers or **calipers** *noun* **1** *plural* an instrument like compasses, used to measure thickness **2** *singular* a splint to support the leg, made of two metal rods

callous *adjective* cruel, hardhearted □ **callously** *adverb*
Ⓛ Comes from Latin *callosus* meaning 'thick-skinned'

☞ Do not confuse with: **callus**

callow *adjective* not mature; inexperienced, naive □ **callowly** *adverb*

callus *noun* (*plural* **calluses**) an area of thickened or hardened skin
Ⓛ Comes from Latin *callus* meaning 'hardened skin'

☞ Do not confuse with: **callous**

calm *adjective* **1** still or quiet **2** not anxious or flustered □ *noun* **1** absence of wind **2** quietness, peacefulness □ *verb* to make peaceful □ **calmly** *adverb*

calorie *noun* **1** a measure of heat **2** a measure of the energy-giving value of food

calumny *noun* (*plural* **calumnies**) a false accusation or lie about a person

calve *verb* to give birth to a calf

calypso *noun* (*plural* **calypsos**) a West Indian improvised song

calyx (*pronounced* **kal**-iks) *noun* (*plural* **calyces** – *pronounced* **kal**-i-seez – or **calyxes**) the outer covering or cup of a flower

CAM *abbreviation* computer-aided manufacturing

camaraderie *noun* comradeship, fellowship

camber *noun* a slight curve on a road *etc* making the middle higher than the sides

camcorder *noun* a hand-held device combining a video camera and video recorder

came past form of **come**

camel *noun* an animal native to Asia and Africa, with a humped back, used for transport

cameo *noun* (*plural* **cameos**) a gem or stone with a figure carved in relief

camera[1] *noun* an instrument for taking photographs

camera[2] *noun*: **in camera** in private

Literally 'in a room', from Latin word 'room' or 'chamber'

camisole (*pronounced* **kam**-i-sohl) *noun* a woman's undervest with thin shoulder straps

camomile *noun* a plant with pale yellow flowers, used as a medicinal herb

camouflage (*pronounced* **kam**-ouf-lahsz) *noun* **1** the disguising of the appearance of something to blend in with its background **2** natural protective colouring in animals □ *verb* to disguise by camouflage

camp *noun* **1** a group of tents, caravans *etc* forming a temporary settlement **2** fixed military quarters □ *verb* **1** to pitch tents **2** to set up a temporary home

campaign *noun* **1** organized action in support of a cause or movement **2** a planned series of battles or movements during a war □ *verb* **1** to organize support: *campaigning against the poll tax* **2** to serve in a military campaign

camp bed a small portable folding bed

camphor *noun* a pungent solid oil obtained from a cinnamon tree, or a synthetic substitute for it, used to repel insects *etc*

campion *noun* a plant with pink or white star-shaped flowers

campsite *noun* an area set aside for pitching tents

campus *noun* (*plural* **campuses**) the grounds and buildings of a university or college

can[1] *verb* **1** to be able to (do something): *can anybody here play the piano?* **2** to have permission to (do something): *asked if I could have the day off* □ **can but** can only: *we can but hope*

can[1] *verb* ⇨ *present form* **can**, *past form* **could**
Ⓛ Comes from Old English *cunnan* meaning 'to know how to' or 'to be able'

can[2] *noun* a sealed tin container for preserving food or liquids □ *verb* to put into a sealed tin to preserve

can[2] *verb* ⇨ **can**s, **can**ning, **can**ned

canal *noun* an artificial waterway for boats

canary *noun* (*plural* **canaries**) a songbird with yellow plumage, kept as a pet

canasta *noun* a card-game similar to rummy

cancan *noun* a high-kicking dance performed by women

cancel *verb* 1 to put off permanently, call off: *cancel all engagements for the week* 2 to mark for deletion by crossing with lines □ **cancel out** to make ineffective by balancing each other

> **cancel** ⇨ cancels, cancelling, cancelled

cancer *noun* a serious disease in which cells in the body grow rapidly into lumps which can spread and may cause death □ **cancerous** *adjective*

candid *adjective* frank, open, honest □ **candidly** *adverb*

candida (*pronounced* **kan**-did-*a*) *noun* an infection caused by a yeastlike fungus

candidacy or **candidature** *noun* the state of being a candidate for something

candidate *noun* 1 an entrant for an examination, or competition for a job, prize *etc* 2 an entrant in a political election

> From a Latin word meaning 'dressed in white', because of the white togas worn by electoral candidates in ancient Rome

candied *adjective* cooked or coated in sugar

candle *noun* a stick of wax containing a wick, used for giving light □ **not worth the candle** not worth the effort or expense needed

candlestick *noun* a holder for a candle

candour or *US* **candor** *noun* frankness, honesty

candy *noun* 1 sugar crystallized by boiling 2 *US* (*plural* **candies**) sweets, chocolate

cane *noun* 1 the woody stem of bamboo, sugar cane *etc* 2 a walking stick □ *verb* to beat with a cane

cane sugar sugar extracted from sugar cane

canine *adjective* of dogs

canine tooth a sharp-pointed tooth found on each side of the upper and lower jaw

canister *noun* a tin or other container for tea *etc*

canker *noun* 1 a spreading sore 2 a disease in trees, plants *etc*

> ☛ Do not confuse with: **chancre**

cannabis *noun* a narcotic drug obtained from the hemp plant

canned music pre-recorded bland music

cannibal *noun* 1 someone who eats human flesh 2 an animal that eats its own kind □ **cannibalism** *noun* □ **cannibalistic** *adjective*

cannon *noun* a large gun mounted on a wheel-carriage

> ◷ Comes from Italian *canna* meaning 'reed' or 'tube'

> ☛ Do not confuse with: **canon**

cannonball *noun* a solid metal ball shot from a cannon

cannot *verb* 1 used with another verb to express inability to do something: *I cannot understand this* 2 used to refuse permission: *he cannot see me today*

canny *adjective* wise, shrewd, cautious □ **cannily** *adverb*

canoe *noun* a light narrow boat driven by paddles

canon *noun* 1 a rule used as a standard to judge by 2 a member of the Anglican clergy connected with a cathedral 3 a list of saints 4 an accepted or established list: *not in the literary canon* 5 a piece of music in which parts follow each other repeating the melody

> ◷ Comes from Greek *kanon* meaning 'a straight rod'

> ☛ Do not confuse with: **cannon**

cañon *noun* another spelling of **canyon**

canonical *adjective* part of an accepted canon: *canonical text*

canonization *noun* the process of making someone a saint

canonize *verb* to put on the list of saints

canopy *noun* (*plural* **canopies**) a canvas or cloth covering suspended over a bed *etc*

cant[1] *noun* **1** the slang or vocabulary of a particular group: *thieves' cant* **2** insincere talk

cant[2] *noun* a slope, an incline □ *verb* to tilt from a level position

can't *short form* of **cannot**

cantankerous *adjective* crotchety, bad-tempered, quarrelsome

cantata *noun* a short piece of music for a choir

canteen *noun* **1** a place serving food and drink in a workplace *etc* **2** a water-flask **3** a case for storing cutlery

canter *verb* to move at an easy gallop □ *noun* an easy gallop

Originally *Canterbury gallop*, referring to the pace at which pilgrims rode to the town

cantilever *noun* a large projecting bracket used to support a balcony or staircase

cantilever bridge a bridge consisting of upright piers with cantilevers extending to meet one another

canton *noun* a federal state in Switzerland

canvas *noun* (*plural* **canvases**) **1** coarse, strong cloth used for sails, tents *etc* **2** a piece of this stretched and used for painting on

canvass *verb* to go round asking for votes, money *etc* □ **canvasser** *noun*

canyon or **cañon** *noun* a deep, steep-sided river valley

cap *noun* **1** a peaked soft hat **2** a lid, a top **3** a contraceptive diaphragm □ *verb* **1** to put a cap on **2** to set a limit to (a budget *etc*) **3** to do better than, improve on: *no-one can cap this story* **4** to select for a national sports team **5** to confer a university degree on

cap *verb* ⇨ **caps, capping, cap**p**ed**

capability *noun* (*plural* **capabilities**) the ability, potential or skill to do something: *He has the capability to do*

it, but does he have the commitment?

capable *adjective* able to cope with difficulties without help □ **capable of** able or likely to achieve, produce *etc*: *capable of a better performance*

■ **Alternative words**: able

capably *adverb* in an efficient and confident way

capacious *adjective* roomy, wide □ **capaciously** *adverb* □ **capaciousness** *noun*

capacitor *noun* a device for collecting and storing electricity

capacity *noun* (*plural* **capacities**) **1** power of understanding **2** ability to do something: *capacity for growth* **3** the amount that something can hold **4** post, position: *capacity as leader* □ **to capacity** to the greatest extent possible: *filled to capacity*

cape[1] *noun* a thick shawl or covering for the shoulders

cape[2] *noun* a point of land running into the sea

caper[1] *verb* to leap, dance about □ *noun* **1** a leap **2** *informal* a prank, an adventure

caper[2] *noun* the flower-bud of a shrub, pickled or salted for eating

capercaillie or **capercailzie** (*pronounced* kap-*e*-**kei**-li or **keip**-*e*-kei-li) *noun* a kind of large grouse

capillary *noun* (*plural* **capillaries**) **1** a tiny blood vessel **2** a very fine tube □ *adjective* very fine, like a hair

capital *adjective* **1** chief, most important **2** punishable by death: *capital offence* **3** *informal* excellent **4** of a letter: written or printed in upper case, eg A, B or C □ *noun* **1** the chief city of a country: *Paris is the capital of France* **2** an upper-case letter **3** money for running a business **4** money invested, accumulated wealth □ **make capital out of** to turn to your advantage

capitalism *noun* a system in which a country's wealth is owned by individuals, not by the State

capitalist *noun* someone who supports or practises capitalism □ **capitalistic** *adjective*

capitalize verb 1 to write in capital letters 2 to turn to your advantage □ **capitalization** noun

capital punishment punishment by death

capitulate verb to give in to an enemy

capitulation noun the act of giving in to an enemy

capon noun a young castrated cock, fattened for eating

caprice (pronounced ka-**rees**) noun a sudden, impulsive change of mind or mood

> Originally meaning 'horror', from an Italian word which translates as 'hedgehog head'

capricious adjective full of caprice; impulsive, fickle □ **capriciously** adverb in a way which is characterized by mood swings or unpredictable behaviour: The car has been behaving a bit capriciously

capsize verb to upset, overturn

capstan noun a device used for winding in heavy ropes on a ship or quay

capsule noun 1 a small gelatine case containing a dose of medicine etc 2 a dry seed-pod on a plant 3 a self-contained, detachable part of a spacecraft

captain noun 1 the commander of a company of soldiers, a ship or an aircraft 2 the leader of a sports team, club etc □ verb to lead

captaincy noun (plural **captaincies**) the rank of captain

caption noun a heading for a newspaper article, photograph etc

captious adjective quick to find fault; judgemental

captivate verb to charm, fascinate

captive noun a prisoner □ adjective 1 taken or kept prisoner 2 not able to get away: captive audience

captivity noun 1 the state of being a prisoner 2 the enclosure of an animal in a zoo etc, not in the wild

captor noun someone who takes a prisoner

capture verb 1 to take by force 2 to get hold of; seize: capture the

imagination □ noun 1 the act of capturing 2 something captured

car noun 1 a small enclosed motor vehicle 2 US a train carriage

carafe (pronounced ka-**raf**) noun a bottle for serving wine, water etc

caramel noun 1 sugar melted and browned 2 a sweet made with sugar and butter

carat noun 1 a measure of purity for gold 2 a measure of weight for gemstones
① Perhaps from Greek keration meaning 'a carob-seed, used as a weight'
◆ Do not confuse with: **carrot**

caravan noun 1 a covered vehicle with living accommodation drawn behind a car 2 a number of travellers etc crossing the desert together

caraway noun a plant with spicy seeds used in cooking

carbohydrate noun a compound of carbon, hydrogen and oxygen, eg sugar or starch

carbon noun an element of which charcoal is one form

carbon copy 1 a copy of a document made by using carbon paper 2 an exact copy

carbon dioxide a gas present in the air and breathed out by humans and animals

carboniferous adjective producing or containing coal or carbon

carbon monoxide a poisonous gas with no smell

carbon paper paper coated with black ink, interleaved between ordinary paper when typing to produce exact copies

carbuncle noun 1 a fiery-red precious stone 2 an inflamed swelling under the skin

carburettor or **carburetter** or US **carburetor** noun the part of a car engine which changes the petrol into vapour

carcass or **carcase** noun the dead body (of an animal)

carcinogen noun a substance that

encourages the growth of cancer

carcinogenic *adjective* causing cancer

carcinoma (*pronounced* kah-si-**noh**-ma) *noun* (*plural* **carcinomas** or **carcinomata**) a cancerous growth

card *noun* **1** pasteboard or very thick paper **2** an illustrated, folded square of paper sent in greeting *etc* **3** tool for combing wool *etc* **4 cards** any of the many types of games played with a pack of special cards □ *verb* to comb (wool *etc*)

cardboard *noun* stiff pasteboard

cardiac *adjective* of the heart: *cardiac failure*
Ⓒ Comes from Greek *kardia* meaning 'heart'

cardigan *noun* a knitted woollen jacket
Named after the 19th-century Earl of *Cardigan* who advocated the use of buttonable woollen jackets

cardinal *adjective* principal, important □ *noun* the highest rank of priest in the Roman Catholic Church

cardinal number a number which expresses quantity, *eg* 1,2,3 (*contrasted with*: **ordinal number**)

care *noun* **1** close attention **2** worry, anxiety **3** protection, keeping: *in my care* □ *verb* to be concerned or worried: *I don't care what happens now* □ **care for 1** to look after **2** to feel affection or liking for □ **care of** at the house of (often written as **c/o**) □ **take care** to be careful; watch out

career *noun* **1** life work; trade, profession **2** course, progress through life **3** headlong rush □ *verb* to run rapidly and wildly: *careering along the road*

carefree *adjective* having no worries

careful *adjective* attentive, taking care □ **carefully** *adverb*

■ **Alternative words**: cautious, circumspect, chary, vigilant, meticulous, punctilious

careless *adjective* paying little attention; not taking care □ **carelessly** *adverb*

■ **Alternative words**: neglectful, slipshod, slapdash, cursory, unthinking

caress *verb* to touch gently and lovingly □ *noun* (*plural* **caresses**) a gentle touch

caretaker *noun* someone who looks after a building □ *adjective* in charge temporarily; interim: *caretaker government*

careworn *adjective* worn out by anxiety

carfuffle (*pronounced* ka-**fu**-fl) *noun* commotion, fuss

cargo *noun* (*plural* **cargoes**) a ship's load

caribou *noun* the North American reindeer

caricature *noun* a picture of someone which exaggerates certain of their features □ *verb* to draw a caricature of □ **caricaturist** *noun*

caries (*pronounced* **kei**-ri-eez) *noun* decay, especially of the teeth

carmine *noun* a bright red colour □ *adjective* of this colour

carnage *noun* slaughter, killing

carnation *noun* a type of garden flower, often pink, red or white

carni- or **carn-** *prefix* of or relating to meat or flesh: *carnivore/ carnage*

carnival *noun* a celebration with merriment, feasting *etc*

carnivore *noun* a flesh-eating animal

carnivorous *adjective* eating meat or flesh

carol *noun* a hymn or song sung at Christmas

caroller *noun* a person who sings carols

carolling *noun* the singing of carols

carousal (*pronounced* ka-**row**-zal) *noun* drinking and having a merry time

carouse *verb* to take part in a drinking bout

carousel (*pronounced* ka-rou-**sel**) *noun* **1** *US* a merry-go-round **2** a rotating conveyor belt for luggage at an airport *etc*

carp[1] *noun* a freshwater fish found in ponds

carp[2] *verb* to find fault with small errors; complain about nothing

car park a place where cars *etc* may be left for a time

carpe diem seize the day; make the most of the present

carpenter *noun* a worker in wood, *eg* for building

carpentry *noun* the trade of a carpenter

carpet *noun* the woven covering of floors, stairs *etc* □ *verb* to cover with a carpet

car pool 1 a number of cars owned by a business for use by employees **2** an arrangement between car owners to take turns at driving each other to work *etc*

carriage *noun* **1** a vehicle for carrying people **2** the act or cost of carrying **3** a way of walking; bearing

carrier *noun* **1** someone who carries goods **2** a machine or container for carrying **3** someone who passes on a disease

carrier pigeon a pigeon used to carry messages

carrion *noun* rotting animal flesh

carrot *noun* a vegetable with an edible orange-coloured root
ⓘ Comes from French *carotte*

  ● Do not confuse with: **carat**

carry *verb* **1** to pick up and take to another place **2** to contain and take to a destination: *cables carrying electricity* **3** to bear, have as a mark: *carry a scar* **4** of a voice: to be able to be heard at a distance **5** to win, succeed: *carry the day* **6** to keep for sale: *we don't carry cigarettes* □ **carried away** overcome by emotion; overexcited □ **carry on** to continue (doing) □ **carry out** to accomplish; succeed in doing □ **carry the can** to accept responsibility for an error □ **carry weight** to have force or authority

  carry ⇨ car**ri**es, car**ry**ing, car**ri**ed

carry-on *noun* a fuss, a to-do

carry-out *noun* a take-away meal or alcoholic drink

cart *noun* **1** a horse-drawn vehicle used for carrying loads **2** a small wheeled vehicle pushed by hand □ *verb* **1** to carry by cart **2** to drag, haul: *carted off the stage*

carte blanche (*pronounced* kaht **blonsh**) freedom of action; a free hand

In French, **carte blanche** means 'white card', and the expression refers to a blank piece of paper which a person has signed and given to you, thus giving you their official advance permission for whatever you wish to write on the paper

cart-horse *noun* a large, heavy work-horse

cartilage *noun* a strong elastic material in the bodies of humans and animals; gristle

cartography *noun* the science of map-making □ **cartographer** *noun*

carton *noun* a small container made of cardboard, plastic *etc*

cartoon *noun* **1** a comic drawing, or strip of drawings, often with a caption **2** an animated film **3** a drawing used as the basis for a large painting *etc*

cartoonist *noun* someone who draws cartoons

cartridge *noun* **1** a case holding the powder and bullet fired by a gun **2** a spool of film or tape enclosed in a case **3** a tube of ink for loading a pen **4** the part of a record-player which holds the stylus

cartwheel *noun* **1** the wheel of a cart **2** a sideways somersault with hands touching the ground

cartwright *noun* someone who makes carts

carve *verb* **1** to make or shape by cutting **2** to cut up (meat) into slices

cascade *noun* **1** a waterfall **2** an abundant hanging display: *cascade of curls* □ *verb* to fall like or in a waterfall

case *noun* **1** a container or outer covering **2** that which happens, an occurrence **3** a statement of facts, an argument **4** state of affairs, what is true: *if that is the case* **5** a trial in a law-court: *murder case*
ⓘ meaning 1: comes from Latin *capsa*

meaning 'a holder' or 'a box'; meanings 2,3,4 and 5: come from Latin *casus* meaning 'a falling'

casement *noun* 1 a window-frame 2 a window that swings on hinges

cash *noun* money in the form of coins and notes □ *verb* to turn into, or change for, money □ **cash in on** to profit from

cash card a card issued by a bank *etc* that allows the holder to use a cash dispenser

cash dispenser an automatic teller machine

cashew *noun* a kidney-shaped nut produced by a tropical tree

cashier *noun* someone who looks after the receiving and paying of money □ *verb, military* to dismiss in disgrace

cashmere *noun* fine soft goat's wool

cash register a machine for holding money that records the amount put in

casino (*pronounced* ka-**see**-noh) *noun* (*plural* **casinos**) a building in which gambling takes place

cask *noun* a barrel containing wine *etc*

casket *noun* 1 a small box for holding jewels *etc* 2 *US* a coffin

cassava *noun* a tropical plant with roots from which tapioca is obtained

casserole *noun* 1 a covered ovenproof dish for cooking and serving food 2 food cooked in a casserole

cassette *noun* 1 a small case for film, magnetic recording tape *etc* 2 the magnetic tape itself

cassock *noun* a long robe worn by priests

cast *verb* 1 to throw, fling 2 to throw off; drop, shed 3 to shape in a mould 4 to choose (actors) for a play or film 5 to give a part to (an actor *etc*) □ *noun* 1 something shaped in a mould 2 plaster encasing a broken limb 3 the actors in a play 4 a small heap of earth thrown up by a worm 5 a type: *cast of mind* 6 an eye squint □ **cast down** *adjective* depressed □ **cast off** *adjective* used by someone else, second-hand

cast *verb* ⇨ casts, cast*ing*, cast

castanets *noun plural* hollow shells of ivory or hard wood, clicked together to accompany a dance

From a Spanish word for 'chestnuts', because of their shape

castaway *noun* a deserted or shipwrecked person

caste *noun* a class or rank of people, especially in the Indian subcontinent

caster *another spelling of* **castor**

caster oil a kind of palm oil used medicinally

castigate *verb* to scold, punish □ **castigation** *noun*

castle *noun* a fortified house or fortress

castor or **caster** *noun* a small wheel, *eg* on the legs of furniture

castor sugar or **caster sugar** very fine granulated sugar

castrate *verb* to remove the testicles of

casual *adjective* 1 happening by chance: *casual encounter* 2 not regular, temporary: *casual labour* 3 informal: *casual clothes* 4 not careful, unconcerned: *casual attitude to work*

casualty *noun* (*plural* **casualties**) 1 someone who is killed or wounded 2 a casualty department

casualty department a hospital department for treating accidental injuries *etc*

cat *noun* 1 a sharp-clawed furry animal kept as a pet 2 an animal of a family which includes lions, tigers *etc*

cata- or **cath-** *prefix* down: *catastrophe* (= a turning down)/ *cathode* (= a going down)

Comes from Greek *kata* meaning 'down'

cataclysm *noun* 1 a violent change; an upheaval 2 a great flood of water

catacombs *noun plural* an underground burial place

catalogue *noun* an ordered list of names, books, objects for sale *etc* □ *verb* 1 to list in order 2 to compile details of (a book) for a library catalogue

catalyst *noun* 1 a substance which helps or prevents a chemical reaction without itself changing 2 something that brings about a change

catamaran *noun* a boat with two parallel hulls

catapult *noun* **1** a small forked stick with a piece of elastic attached, used for firing small stones **2** *historical* a weapon for throwing heavy stones in warfare

cataract *noun* **1** a waterfall **2** a disease of the outer eye

catarrh *noun* inflammation of the lining of the nose and throat causing a discharge

catastrophe (*pronounced* kat-**as**-tro-fi) *noun* a sudden disaster

catastrophic (*pronounced* kat-*a*s-**trof**-ik) *adjective* disastrous, absolutely terrible

cat burglar a burglar who breaks into houses by climbing walls *etc*

catch *verb* **1** to take hold of, capture **2** to take (a disease): *catch a cold* **3** to be in time for: *catch the last train* **4** to surprise (in an act): *caught him stealing* □ *noun* **1** a haul of fish *etc* **2** something you are lucky to have got or won **3** a hidden flaw or disadvantage: *where's the catch?* **4** a fastening: *window catch* □ **catch on** to become popular □ **catch-22** *noun* an absurd situation with no way out □ **catchy** *adjective* of a tune: easily remembered □ **catch up on 1** to draw level with, overtake **2** to get up-to-date with (work *etc*)

catch *verb* ⇨ catch*es*, catch*ing*, caught

catching *adjective* infectious

catchment area 1 an area from which a river or reservoir draws its water supply **2** an area from which the pupils in a school are drawn

catch-phrase *noun* a phrase which is popular for a while

catchword *noun* a word which is popular for a while

catechize (*pronounced* **kat**-e-kaiz) *verb* to ask many questions

categorical *adjective* allowing no doubt or argument: *categorical denial*

categorically *adverb* in such a sure way that there can be no discussion or argument: *he has stated quite categorically that he is not interested*

categorize *verb* to divide into categories

category *noun* (*plural* **categories**) a class or group of similar people or things

cater *verb* **1** to provide food **2** to supply what is required: *cater for all tastes*

caterer *noun* someone whose job is to provide ready-prepared food and drinks for people

caterpillar *noun* the larva of an insect that feeds on plant leaves □ *adjective* moving on rotating metal belts: *caterpillar tractor*

Based on a Latin phrase which translates as 'hairy cat'

caterwaul *verb* to howl or yell like a cat

cat flap a small door set in a larger door to allow a cat entry and exit

catgut *noun* cord made from sheep's stomachs, used to make strings for violins, harps *etc*

cathedral *noun* **1** the church of a bishop **2** the chief church in a bishop's district

catherine-wheel *noun* a firework which rotates as it burns

cathode ray tube a device in a television set *etc*, which causes a narrow beam of electrons to strike against a screen

Catholic *adjective* of the Roman Catholic Church

catholic *adjective* wide, comprehensive: *a catholic taste in literature*

catkin *noun* a tuft of small flowers on certain trees, *eg* the willow and hazel

cat-o'-nine-tails *noun* a whip with nine lashes

cat's cradle a children's game of creating patterns by winding string around the fingers

cat's-eye *noun*, *trademark* a small mirror fixed in a road surface to reflect light at night

cattle *noun plural* oxen, bulls and cows, and other grass-eating animals of this family

caucus (*pronounced* **kaw**-kus) *noun*, *US*

a meeting of members of a political party to nominate candidates for election *etc*

caught *past form of* **catch**

cauldron *noun* a large pan

cauliflower *noun* a kind of cabbage with an edible white flower-head

cause *noun* **1** that which makes something happen **2** a reason for action: *cause for complaint* **3** an aim for which a group or person works: *the cause of peace* □ *verb* to make happen

causeway *noun* a raised road over wet ground or shallow water

caustic *adjective* **1** burning, corroding **2** bitter, severe: *caustic wit* □ **caustically** *adverb*

■ **Alternative words**: (meaning 2) abrasive

cauterize *verb* to burn away flesh with a hot iron *etc* in order to make a wound heal cleanly

caution *noun* **1** carefulness because of potential danger: *approach with caution* **2** a warning □ *verb* to warn

cautionary *adjective* giving a warning

cautious *adjective* careful, showing caution

cavalcade *noun* a procession on horseback, in cars *etc*

cavalier *noun, historical* a supporter of the king in the English Civil War of the 17th century □ *adjective* offhand, careless: *cavalier fashion*

cavalry *noun* soldiers mounted on horses

cave *noun* a hollow place in the earth or in rock □ **cave in** to fall or collapse inwards

caveat (*pronounced* **kav**-i-at) *noun* a warning

caveman *noun* a prehistoric cave-dweller

cavern *noun* a deep hollow place in the earth

cavernous *adjective* **1** huge and hollow **2** full of caverns

cavewoman *noun* a female prehistoric cave-dweller

caviare or **caviar** *noun* the pickled eggs of the sturgeon

cavil *verb* to make objections over small, unimportant details

cavil ⇨ cavi**ls**, cavi**lling**, cavi**lled**

cavity *noun* (*plural* **cavities**) **1** a hollow place, a hole **2** a decayed hollow in a tooth

cavort *verb* to dance or leap around

caw *verb* to call like a crow □ *noun* a crow's call

cc *abbreviation* cubic centimetre(s)

CD *abbreviation* compact disc

CD-I *abbreviation* compact disc interactive

CD-R *abbreviation* compact disc recordable

CD-ROM *abbreviation* compact disc read-only memory

cease *verb* to come or bring to an end

ceasefire *noun* **1** an order to stop firing weapons **2** an agreed, although maybe temporary, end to active hostilities

ceaseless *adjective* without stopping

cedar *noun* a large evergreen tree with a hard sweet-smelling wood

cede *verb* to yield, give up

ceilidh (*pronounced* **kei**-li) *noun* an event involving traditional Scottish dancing, sometimes combined with musical performances

ceiling *noun* **1** the inner roof of a room **2** an upper limit

celandine *noun* a small yellow wild-flower

celebrate *verb* to commemorate an event (*eg* a birthday or marriage) by going out, having a party *etc* □ **celebration** *noun*

celebrated *adjective* famous

celebrity *noun* (*plural* **celebrities**) **1** a famous person, a star **2** fame

celery *noun* a type of vegetable with edible fibrous stalks

celestial *adjective* **1** of the sky: *celestial bodies* (= stars and planets) **2** heavenly

celibacy *noun* a lifestyle without sexual intercourse

celibate *adjective* abstaining from sexual intercourse

cell *noun* **1** a small room in a prison, monastery *etc* **2** the smallest, fundamental part of living things **3** the part of an electric battery containing electrodes

cellar *noun* an underground room used for storing coal, wine *etc*

cellist (*pronounced* **chel**-ist) *noun* someone who plays the cello

cello (*pronounced* **chel**-oh) *noun* (*short for* **violoncello**) a large stringed musical instrument, similar in shape to a violin

cellophane *noun, trademark* a thin transparent wrapping material

cellphone *noun* a pocket telephone for use in a cellular radio system based on a network of transmitters

cellular *adjective* made of or having cells

celluloid *noun* a very hard elastic substance used for making photographic film *etc*

cellulose *noun* a substance found in plants and wood used to make paper, textiles *etc*

Celsius (*pronounced* **sel**-si-*u*s) *adjective* **1** of a temperature scale: consisting of a hundred degrees, on which water freezes at 0° and boils at 100° **2** of a degree: measured on this scale: *10° Celsius*

cement *noun* **1** the mixture of clay and lime used to secure bricks in a wall **2** something used to make two things stick together □ *verb* **1** to put together with cement **2** to join firmly, fix: *cemented their friendship*

cemetery *noun* (*plural* **cemeteries**) a place where the dead are buried

cenotaph *noun* a monument to someone or a group buried elsewhere

censer *noun* a container for burning incense in a church
Ⓞ Comes from Latin *incens-*, a form of *incendere* meaning 'to burn'

　🖝 Do not confuse: **censer, censor** and **censure**

censor *noun* someone whose job is to examine books, films *etc* with power to delete any of the contents □ *verb* to examine (books *etc*) in this way
Ⓞ Comes from Latin *censor*

　🖝 Do not confuse: **censor, censer** and **censure**

censorious *adjective* fault-finding; judgemental

censure *noun* blame, expression of disapproval □ *verb* to blame, criticize
Ⓞ Comes from Latin *censura* meaning 'censorship'

　🖝 Do not confuse: **censure, censer** and **censor**

census *noun* (*plural* **censuses**) a periodical official count of the people who live in a country
Ⓞ Comes from Latin *census* meaning 'a register'

　🖝 Do not confuse with: **consensus**

cent *noun* a coin which is the hundredth part of a larger coin, *eg* of a US dollar
Ⓞ Comes from Latin *centum* meaning 'a hundred'

centaur *noun* a mythological creature, half man and half horse

centenarian *noun* someone a hundred or more years old

centenary *noun* (*plural* **centenaries**) a hundredth anniversary; the hundredth year since an event took place

centennial *adjective* **1** having lasted a hundred years **2** happening every hundred years □ *noun* a centenary

centi- or **cent-** *prefix* hundred; a hundredth part of
Ⓞ Comes from Latin *centum* meaning 'a hundred'

centigrade *adjective* **1** of a temperature scale: consisting of a hundred degrees **2** measured on this scale: *5° centigrade* **3** Celsius

centigramme *noun* a hundredth part of a gramme

centilitre *noun* a hundredth part of a litre

centimetre *noun* a hundredth part of a metre

centipede *noun* a small crawling insect with many legs

central *adjective* **1** belonging to the

centre **2** chief, main: *central point of the argument*

central heating heating of a building by water, steam or air from a central point

centralization *noun* the process of moving power and decision-making away from small local groups into a single large governing body, probably located in a city

centralize *verb* **1** to group in a single place **2** to bring (government authority) under one central control

central locking a system whereby all the doors of a vehicle are locked by the locking of the driver's door

centre or *US* **center** *noun* **1** the middle point or part **2** a building used for some special activity: *sports centre/ shopping centre* □ *verb* to put in the centre

> **centre** *verb* ⇨ centre*s*, centr*ing*, centr*ed*

> ⬥ This is one of a large number of words which are spelled with an **-re** ending in British English, but with an **-er** in American English *eg* metre/meter, calibre/caliber, lustre/luster

centrifugal *adjective* moving away from the centre

centripetal *adjective* moving towards the centre

centurion *historical* a commander of 100 Roman soldiers

century *noun* (*plural* **centuries**) **1** a hundred years **2** *cricket* a hundred runs

ceramic *adjective* **1** made of pottery **2** of pottery-making □ *noun* **1** something made of pottery **2 ceramics** the art of pottery

cereal *noun* **1** grain used as food **2** a breakfast food prepared from grain

cerebral *adjective* of the brain

ceremonial *adjective* with or of ceremony

ceremonially *adverb* for a ceremony: *ceremonially clad in long, flowing robes*

ceremonious *adjective* full of ceremony

ceremoniously *adverb* in a grand, important way: *the pudding was placed ceremoniously on the table*

ceremony *noun* (*plural* **ceremonies**) the formal acts that accompany an important event: *marriage ceremony*

certain *adjective* **1** sure; not to be doubted **2** fixed, settled **3** particular but unnamed: *stopping at certain places/ a certain look*

certainly *adverb* **1** definitely, without any doubt **2** of course

certainty *noun* **1** a sure thing: *it's almost a certainty that he will be re-elected* **2** the quality of being certain: *I can tell you this with absolute certainty*

certificate *noun* a written or printed statement giving details of a birth, passed examination *etc*

certify *verb* to put down in writing as an official promise or statement *etc*

> **certify** ⇨ certif*ies*, certify*ing*, certif*ied*

cervical *adjective* of the cervix

cervical smear a collection of a sample of cells from the cervix for examination under a microscope

cervigram *noun* a photograph of the cervix used to detect early signs of cancer

cervix *noun* the neck of the womb

cessation *noun* a ceasing or stopping; an ending

cesspool *noun* a pool or tank for storing liquid waste or sewage

cf *abbreviation* compare (from Latin *confer*)

CFC *abbreviation* chlorofluorocarbon

chafe *verb* **1** to make hot or sore by rubbing **2** to wear away by rubbing **3** to become annoyed

chaff *noun* **1** husks of corn left after threshing **2** something of little value **3** good-natured teasing □ *verb* to tease jokingly

chaffinch *noun* (*plural* **chaffinches**) a small songbird of the finch family

chagrin (*pronounced* sha-grin or sha-green) *noun* annoyance, irritation

chagrined *adjective* annoyed and disappointed

chain *noun* 1 a number of metal links or rings passing through one another 2 **chains** these used to tie a prisoner's limbs; fetters 3 a number of connected things: *mountain chain* 4 a group of shops owned by one person or company 5 a number of atoms of an element joined together □ *verb* to fasten or imprison with a chain

chain letter a letter containing promises or threats, requesting the recipient to send a similar letter to several other people

chain mail armour made of iron links

chain reaction a chemical process in which each reaction in turn causes a similar reaction

chain saw a power-driven saw with teeth on a rotating chain

chain-smoker *noun* someone who smokes continuously

chain-store *noun* one of several shops under the same ownership

chair *noun* 1 a seat for one person with a back to it 2 a university professorship: *the chair of French literature* 3 a chairman or chairwoman

chairlift *noun* a row of chairs on a rotating cable for carrying people up mountains *etc*

chairman *noun* someone who presides at or is in charge of a meeting

It is possible to use **chairman** when referring to a woman (*eg Madam Chairman*). However, it is more 'politically correct' to use **chairman** for a man and **chairwoman** for a woman.

chairperson *noun* a chairman or chairwoman

chairwoman *noun* a woman who presides at or is in charge of a meeting

chalet (*pronounced* **shal**-ei) *noun* 1 a small wooden house used by holiday-makers 2 a summer hut used by Swiss herdsmen in the Alps

chalice *noun* a cup for wine, used *eg* in church services

chalk *noun* 1 a type of limestone 2 a compressed stick of coloured powder used for writing or drawing □ *verb* to mark with chalk

chalky *adjective* 1 of chalk 2 white, pale

challenge *verb* 1 to question another's right to do something 2 to ask (someone) to take part in a contest, *eg* to settle a quarrel □ *noun* 1 a questioning of another's right 2 a call to a contest

challenger *noun* someone who challenges a person such as a champion or holder of an important position to a competition for their status

challenging *adjective* interesting but difficult

chamber *noun* 1 a room 2 a place where a parliament meets 3 a room where legal cases are heard by a judge 4 an enclosed space or cavity 5 the part of a gun that holds the cartridges

chamberlain *noun* an officer appointed by the crown or a local authority to carry out certain duties

chamber music music for a small group of players, suitable for performance in a room rather than a large hall

chamberpot *noun* a receptacle for urine *etc*, used in the bedroom

chameleon (*pronounced* ka-**meel**-yon) *noun* a small lizard able to change its colour to match its surroundings

chamois *noun* 1 (*pronounced* **sham**-wah) a goat-like deer living in mountainous country 2 (*pronounced* **sham**-i) (*also spelt* **shammy**) a soft kind of leather made from its skin

champ *verb* to chew noisily □ **champing at the bit** impatient to act

champagne (*pronounced* sham-**pein**) *noun* a type of white sparkling wine

champion *noun* 1 someone who has beaten all others in a competition 2 a strong supporter of a cause: *champion of free speech* □ *verb* to support the cause of

championship *noun* 1 the act of championing 2 a contest to find a champion 3 the title of champion

chance *noun* 1 a risk, a possibility 2 something unexpected or unplanned 3 an opportunity □ *verb* 1 to risk 2 to happen by accident □ *adjective* happening by accident □ **by chance** not by arrangement, unexpectedly □ **chance upon** to meet or find unexpectedly

chancel *noun* the part of a church near the altar

chancellor *noun* **1** a high-ranking government minister **2** the head of a university

Chancellor of the Exchequer the minister in the British cabinet in charge of government spending

chancre (*pronounced* **shang**-ker) *noun* a small lump occurring in the early stages of syphilis

☛ Do not confuse with: **canker**

chancy *adjective* risky

chandelier (*pronounced* shan-de-**leer**) *noun* a fixture hanging from the ceiling with branches for holding lights

change *verb* **1** to make or become different **2** to give up or leave (a job, house *etc*) for another **3** to put on different clothes **4** to give (money of one kind) in exchange for (money of another kind) □ *noun* **1** the act of making or becoming different **2** another set of clothing **3** money in the form of coins **4** money returned when a buyer gives more than the price of an article □ **change of life** the menopause

change *verb* ⇨ changes, changing, changed

changeable *adjective* likely to change; often changing

changeling *noun* in stories: a fairy child secretly left in place of a human one

channel *noun* **1** the bed of a stream **2** a passage for ships **3** a narrow sea **4** a groove; a gutter **5** a band of frequencies for radio or television signals □ *verb* to direct into a particular course

channel *verb* ⇨ channels, channelling, channelled

chant *verb* to recite in a singing manner □ *noun* a singing recitation

chaos (*pronounced* **kei**-os) *noun* disorder, confusion

chaotic *adjective* disordered, confused □ **chaotically** *adverb*

chap *noun*, *informal* a man

chapati *noun* a round of unleavened Indian bread

chapel *noun* **1** a small church **2** a small part of a larger church

chaperone *noun* a woman who attends a younger one when she goes out in public □ *verb* to act as a chaperone to

chaplain *noun* a member of the clergy accompanying an army, navy *etc*

chapped *adjective* of skin: cracked by cold or wet weather

chapter *noun* **1** a division of a book **2** a branch of a society or organization □ **chapter of accidents** a series of accidents

char[1] *verb* to burn until black

char *verb* ⇨ chars, charring, charred

char[2] *verb* to do odd jobs of housework, cleaning *etc* □ *noun*, *informal* a charwoman

character *noun* **1** the nature and qualities of someone **2** the good and bad points which make up a person's nature **3** self-control, firmness **4** someone noted for eccentric behaviour **5** someone in a play, story or film

characteristic *noun* a typical and noticeable feature of someone or something □ *adjective* typical

characteristically *adverb* typically, as always: *his suggestions were characteristically tactful*

characterization *noun* the creation and development of the different characters in a book, story or piece of drama: *Jane Austen's power of characterization*

characterize *verb* **1** to be typical of **2** to describe (as)

charade (*pronounced* sha-**rahd** or sha-**reid**) *noun* **1** a ridiculous pretence **2 charades** a game in which players have to guess a word from gestures representing its sound or meaning

charcoal *noun* wood burnt black, used for fuel or sketching

charge *verb* **1** to accuse: *charged with murder* **2** to ask (a price) **3** to ask to do; give responsibility for **4** to load (a gun) **5** to attack in a rush □ *noun* **1** accusation for a crime **2** a price, a fee

3 an attack **4** the gunpowder in a shell or bullet **5** care, responsibility **6** someone looked after by another person ▫ **in charge** in command or control ▫ **take charge of** to take command of

charge *verb* ⇨ charges, charging, charged

charger *noun* a horse used in battle

chariot *noun*, *historical* a wheeled carriage used in battle

charioteer *noun* a chariot-driver

charisma (*pronounced* ka-**riz**-ma) *noun* a personal quality that impresses others

charismatic *adjective* full of charisma or charm

charitable *adjective* **1** giving to the poor; kindly **2** of a charity: *charitable status*

charitably *adverb* in a kind or generous way: *he said charitably that the fault was all his*

charity *noun* (*plural* **charities**) **1** donation of money to the poor *etc* **2** an organization which collects money and gives it to those in need **3** kindness, humanity

charlatan (*pronounced* **shah**-lat-an) *noun* someone who claims greater powers or abilities than they really have

charm *noun* **1** something thought to have magical powers **2** a magical spell **3** personal power to attract ▫ *verb* **1** to please greatly, delight **2** to put under a spell

charming *adjective* lovely, delightful

chart *noun* **1** a table or diagram giving particular information: *temperature chart* **2** a geographical map of the sea **3** a rough map ▫ *verb* to make into a chart; plot

charter *noun* a written paper showing the official granting of rights, lands *etc* ▫ *verb* to hire (a boat, aeroplane *etc*) ▫ *adjective* hired for a special purpose: *charter flight*

chartered *adjective* **1** qualified under the regulations of a professional body: *chartered surveyor* **2** hired for a purpose

charwoman *noun* a woman hired to do domestic cleaning *etc*

chary *adjective* cautious, careful (of)

chase *verb* **1** to run after, pursue **2** to hunt ▫ *noun* a pursuit, a hunt

chasm (*pronounced* ka-zm) *noun* **1** a steep drop between high rocks *etc* **2** a wide difference; a gulf

chassis (*pronounced* **shas**-i) *noun* (*plural* **chassis** – *pronounced* **shas**-iz) **1** the frame, wheels and machinery of a car **2** an aeroplane's landing carriage

chaste *adjective* **1** pure, virtuous **2** virgin

chastely *adverb* in a pure, virtuous way

chasten *verb* **1** to make humble **2** to scold

chastened *adjective* humble or sorry, as a result of receiving a scolding

chastise *verb* to punish, especially by beating ▫ **chastisement** *noun*

chastity *noun* virginity: *a chastity belt* (= an item of clothing which women were sometimes forced to wear in the past to prevent them from having sex)

chat *verb* talk in an easy, friendly way ▫ *noun* a friendly conversation

chat *verb* ⇨ chats, chatting, chatted

chateau (*pronounced* **shat**-oh) *noun* (*plural* **chateaux** – *pronounced* **shat**-ohz) a French castle or country house

chat-show *noun* a radio or TV programme in which personalities talk informally with their host

chattels *noun plural* movable possessions ▫ **goods and chattels** personal possessions

chatter *verb* **1** to talk idly or rapidly; gossip **2** of teeth: to rattle together because of cold

chatterbox *noun* someone who talks a great deal

chattily *adverb* of speaking: in an informal way intended to put someone at their ease and start a conversation: *'So, how's things?' she asked chattily*

chatty *adjective* willing to talk, talkative

chauffeur (*pronounced* **shoh**-fer) *noun* someone employed to drive a car

chauvinism *noun* extreme nationalism or patriotism

After Nicholas *Chauvin*, Napoleonic French soldier and keen patriot

chauvinist *noun* **1** a man who practises sexism towards women □ **chauvinistic** *adjective*

cheap *adjective* **1** low in price, inexpensive **2** of little value, worthless

■ **Alternative words:** (meaning 1) reasonable, bargain, economical; (meaning 2) tawdry, shoddy, inferior

cheapen *verb* to make cheap

cheaply *adverb* for a low price: *you can see that this skirt was cheaply made*

cheat *verb* **1** to deceive **2** to act dishonestly to gain an advantage □ *noun* **1** someone who cheats **2** a dishonest trick

■ **Alternative words:** (verb, meaning 1) defraud, swindle, fleece, hoodwink, bamboozle, beguile

check *verb* **1** to bring to a stop **2** to hold back, restrain **3** to see if (a total *etc*) is correct or accurate **4** to see if (a machine *etc*) is in good condition or working properly □ *noun* **1** a sudden stop **2** a restraint **3** a test of correctness or accuracy **4** a square, *eg* on a draughtboard **5** a pattern of squares □ **check in** or **check out** to record your arrival at or departure from (a hotel *etc*)

☞ Do not confuse with: **cheque**

■ **Alternative words:** (verb, meaning 3) verify; (verb, meanings 3 and 4) examine, scrutinize, monitor

checked *adjective* patterned with squares

checkered *another spelling of* **chequered**

checkers *another spelling of* **chequers**

checkmate *noun, chess* a position from which the king cannot escape

checkout *noun* a place where payment is made in a supermarket

cheek *noun* **1** the side of the face below the eye **2** a buttock **3** insolence, disrespectful behaviour

cheeky *adjective* impudent, insolent □ **cheekily** *adverb*

cheep *verb* to make a faint sound like a small bird □ *noun* the sound of a small bird

cheer *noun* a shout of approval or welcome □ *verb* **1** to shout approval **2** to encourage, urge on **3** to comfort, gladden □ **cheer up** to make or become less gloomy

cheerful *adjective* happy, in good spirits □ **cheerfully** *adverb*

cheerio *exclamation* goodbye!

cheerless *adjective* sad, gloomy

cheers *exclamation* **1** good health! **2** regards, best wishes

cheery *adjective* lively and merry □ **cheerily** *adverb*

cheese *noun* a solid food made from milk

cheesecloth *noun* loosely-woven cotton cloth

cheesy 1 tasting of cheese **2** of a smile: broad

cheetah *noun* a fast-running animal similar to a leopard

chef *noun* a head cook in a restaurant

chef d'oeuvre a masterpiece; a life's work

chemical *adjective* relating to the reactions between elements *etc* □ *noun* a substance formed by or used in a chemical process

chemist *noun* **1** someone who studies chemistry **2** someone who makes up and sells medicines; a pharmacist

chemistry *noun* the study of the elements and the ways they combine or react with each other

chemotherapy (*pronounced* keem-oh-the-rap-i) *noun* treatment of infectious diseases or cancer using chemical compounds

cheque or *US* **check** *noun* a written order to a banker to pay money from a bank account to another person

☞ Do not confuse with: **check**

cheque book a book containing cheques

chequered or **checkered** adjective **1** marked like a chessboard **2** partly good, partly bad: a chequered career

chequers or **checkers** noun plural **1** a pattern of squares, eg on a chessboard **2** the game of draughts

cherish verb **1** to protect and treat with fondness or kindness **2** to keep in your mind or heart: cherish a hope

cherry noun (plural **cherries**) **1** a small bright-red fruit with a stone **2** the tree that produces this fruit

cherub noun (plural **cherubs** or **cherubim**) **1** an angel with a plump, childish face and body **2** a beautiful child

chess noun a game for two players in which pieces are moved in turn on a board marked in alternate black and white squares

chessboard noun the board which you play chess on

chessman or **chesspiece** noun one of the little figures which you move on a chessboard when playing chess

chest noun **1** a large strong box **2** the part of the body between the neck and the stomach □ **chest of drawers** a piece of furniture fitted with a set of drawers

chesterfield noun a kind of sofa

chestnut noun **1** a reddish-brown edible nut (= **sweet chestnut**), or the tree that produces it **2** a reddish-brown inedible nut (= **horse-chestnut**), or the tree that produces it **3** a reddish-brown horse **4** an old joke

chevron noun a V-shape, eg on a badge or road-sign

chew verb **1** to break up (food) with the teeth before swallowing **2** to reflect or ponder (on)

chic (pronounced sheek) adjective smart and fashionable □ noun style, fashionable elegance

chicanery (pronounced shik-**ein**-e-ri) noun dishonest cleverness

chick noun **1** a chicken **2** slang a girl, a young woman

chicken noun **1** the young of birds, especially of domestic poultry **2**

informal a coward □ adjective, informal cowardly

chicken-feed noun **1** food for poultry **2** something paltry or worthless

chicken-hearted adjective cowardly

chickenpox noun an infectious disease which causes red, itchy spots

chickpea noun a plant of the pea family with a brown edible seed

chicory noun **1** a plant with sharp-tasting leaves eaten in salads **2** its root, roasted and ground to mix with coffee

chide verb to scold with words

chief adjective **1** main, most important **2** largest □ noun **1** a leader or ruler **2** the head of a department, organization etc

chiefly adverb mainly, for the most part

chieftain noun the head of a clan or tribe

chiffon noun a thin flimsy material made of silk or nylon

chihuahua (pronounced chi-**wah**-wah) noun a breed of very small dog, originally from Mexico

chilblain noun a painful swelling on hands and feet, caused by cold weather

child noun (plural **children**) **1** a young human being **2** a son or daughter: is that your child?
Ⓞ Comes from Old English cild

childhood noun the time of being a child

childish adjective **1** of or like a child **2** silly, immature □ **childishly** adverb

childlike adjective innocent

chile noun another spelling of **chilli**

chill noun **1** coldness **2** an illness that causes fever and shivering **3** lack of warmth or enthusiasm □ adjective cold □ verb **1** to make cold **2** to refrigerate

chilli or **chile** noun **1** the hot-tasting pod of a kind of pepper, sometimes dried for cooking **2** a dish or sauce made with this

chilly adjective cold

chime noun **1** the sound of bells ringing **2 chimes** a set of bells, eg in a clock □ verb **1** to ring **2** of a clock: to strike

chimney noun (plural **chimneys**) a passage allowing smoke or heated air to escape from a fire

chimneypot noun a metal or earthenware pipe placed at the top of a chimney

chimneystack noun **1** a tall chimney, eg in a factory **2** a number of chimneys built up together

chimneysweep noun someone employed to clean chimneys

chimpanzee noun a type of African ape

chin noun the part of the face below the mouth

china noun **1** fine kind of earthenware; porcelain **2** articles made of this

chink noun **1** a narrow opening **2** the sound of coins etc striking together

chintz noun (plural **chintzes**) a cotton cloth with brightly coloured patterning

From a Hindi word for painted or multicoloured cotton

chip verb to break or cut small pieces (from or off) □ noun **1** a small piece chipped off **2** a part damaged by chipping **3** a long thin piece of potato fried **4** US a potato or corn crisp

chip verb ⇨ chips, chipping, chipped

chipmunk noun a kind of N American squirrel

chipolata noun a type of small sausage

chiropodist noun someone who treats minor disorders and diseases of the feet

chiropody noun the discipline of caring for people's feet and treating minor foot problems such as verrucas and corns

chirp or **chirrup** verb of a bird: make a sharp, shrill sound

chirpy adjective merry, cheerful

chisel noun a metal tool to cut or hollow out wood, stone etc □ verb to cut with a chisel

chisel verb ⇨ chisels, chiselling, chiselled

chit noun **1** a short note **2** a child, a young woman: chit of a girl

chit-chat noun gossip, talk □ verb to gossip, talk

chivalrous (pronounced **shiv**-al-rus) adjective gallant, showing traditional good manners especially to women

chivalry (pronounced **shiv**-al-ri) noun **1** kindness, especially towards women or the weak **2** historical the standard of behaviour expected of knights in medieval times

chives noun an onion-like herb used in cooking

chlamydia noun a sexually transmitted disease that can cause infertility in women

chlorinated adjective mixed with chlorine or a substance containing chlorine

chlorine noun a yellowish-green gas with a sharp smell, used as a bleach and disinfectant

chloroform noun a liquid whose vapour causes unconsciousness if inhaled

chock-a-block adjective completely full or congested

chockfull adjective completely full

chocolate noun **1** a sweet made from the seeds of the cacao tree **2** a drink made from these seeds (also called **cocoa**) □ adjective dark brown in colour

chocolatey adjective tasting of chocolate

choice noun **1** the act or power of choosing **2** something chosen □ adjective of a high quality: choice vegetables

choir noun **1** a group or society of singers **2** a part of a church where a choir sits
① Comes from Latin chorus meaning 'a band of singers and dancers'

✎ Do not confuse with: **quire**

choke verb **1** to stop or partly stop the breathing of **2** to block or clog (a pipe etc) **3** to have your breathing stopped or interrupted, eg by smoke □ noun a valve in a petrol engine which controls the inflow of air

■ **Alternative words**: (verb, meanings 1 and 3) asphyxiate

cholera (*pronounced* **kol**-*e*-*ra*) *noun* an infectious intestinal disease, causing severe vomiting and diarrhoea

cholesterol *noun* a substance found in body cells which carries fats through the bloodstream

chomp *verb, informal* to munch noisily

choose *verb* 1 to select and take from two or several things: *choose whichever book you like* 2 to decide, prefer to: *we chose to leave before the film began*

choose ⇨ chooses, choosing, chose, chosen

■ **Alternative words**: (meaning 1) select, designate, adopt; (meaning 2) opt, elect

chop *verb* 1 to cut into small pieces 2 to cut with a sudden blow □ *noun* 1 a chopping blow 2 a slice of meat containing a bone: *mutton chop* □ **chop and change** to keep changing

chop *verb* ⇨ chops, chopping, chopped

chopper *noun* 1 a knife or axe for chopping 2 *informal* a helicopter

choppy *adjective* of the sea: not calm, having small waves

chopsticks *noun plural* a pair of small sticks of wood, ivory *etc* used instead of a knife and fork for eating Chinese food

Literally 'quick sticks', from Pidgin English *chop* for 'quick'

choral *adjective* sung by or written for a choir

chord *noun* 1 a musical sound made by playing several notes together 2 a straight line joining any two points on a curve

Meaning 1 of **chord** comes from the word 'accord', while meaning 2 comes from the Greek *chorde* meaning 'a string'. From this you might expect meaning 1 to be spelt without an 'h', but through the influence of meaning 2 their spelling has become identical

🖝 Do not confuse with: **cord**

chore *noun* 1 a dull, boring job 2 **chores** housework

choreographer *noun* a person who designs dances and dance steps, usually for a team of dancers *eg* in a dancing display or a musical

choreography *noun* the arrangement of dancing and dance steps

chorister *noun* a member of a choir

chortle *verb* to laugh, chuckle

chorus *noun* (*plural* **choruses**) 1 a band of singers and dancers 2 a choir or choral group 3 a part of a song repeated after each verse

chose *past form of* **choose**

chosen *past participle of* **choose**

christen *verb* to baptize and give a name to

christening *noun* the ceremony of baptism

Christian *noun* a believer in Christianity □ *adjective* of Christianity

Christianity *noun* the religion which follows the teachings of Christ

Christian name a first or personal name

Christmas *noun* an annual Christian holiday or festival, in memory of the birth of Christ, held on 25 December

Christmas Eve 24 December

Christmassy *adjective* typical of, or suitable for Christmas

Christmas tree an evergreen tree hung with lights, decorations and gifts at Christmas

chromatic *adjective* 1 of colours 2 coloured 3 *music* of or written in a scale in which each note is separated from the next by a semitone

chromium *noun* a metal which does not rust

chromosome *noun* a rod-like part of a body cell that determines the characteristics of an individual

chronic *adjective* 1 of a disease: long-term and progressing slowly 2 *informal* very bad □ **chronically** *adverb*: *chronically ill/ chronically short of supplies*

Opposite: (meaning 1) acute

chronicle *noun* a record of events in order of time □ *verb* to write down events in order □ **chronicler** *noun*

chrono- or **chron-** of or relating to time: *chronological/ synchronize/ anachronism*

🕐 Comes from Greek *chronos* meaning 'time'

chronological *adjective* arranged in the order of the time of happening □ **chronologically** *adverb*

chronometer *noun* an instrument for measuring time

chrysalis *noun* an insect (especially a butterfly or moth) in its early stage of life, with no wings and encased in a soft cocoon

chrysanthemum *noun* a type of garden flower with a large bushy head

chubby *adjective* plump

chubby ⟹ chubb*ier*, chubb*iest*

chuck *verb* **1** to throw, toss **2** to pat gently under the chin □ **chuck out** *informal* **1** to throw away, get rid of **2** to expel

chuckle *noun* a quiet laugh □ *verb* to laugh quietly

chuffed *adjective*, *informal* very pleased

chum *informal* a close friend

chummy *adjective* very friendly

chump *noun*: **off your chump** *informal* off your head; mad

chunk *noun* a thick piece

chunky *adjective* heavy, thick

church *noun* (*plural* **churches**) **1** a building for public, especially Christian, worship **2** any group of people who meet together for worship

churchyard *noun* a burial ground next to a church

churlish *adjective* bad-mannered, rude

churn *noun* a machine for making butter from milk □ *verb* **1** to make (butter) in a churn **2** to shake or stir about violently

chute (*pronounced* shoot) *noun* **1** a sloping trough for sending water, parcels *etc* to a lower level **2** a sloping structure for children to slide down, with steps for climbing back up

chutney *noun* (*plural* **chutneys**) a sauce made with vegetables or fruits and vinegar

CIA *abbreviation* Central Intelligence Agency (in the USA)

CID *abbreviation* Criminal Investigation Department

cider *noun* an alcoholic drink made from fermented apple-juice

cigar *noun* a roll of tobacco leaves for smoking

cigarette *noun* a tube of fine tobacco enclosed in thin paper

cinder *noun* a burnt-out piece of coal

cinema *noun* **1** a place where films are shown **2** films as an art form or industry

cinnamon *noun* a yellowish-brown spice obtained from tree bark

cipher *noun* **1** a secret writing, a code **2** nought, zero **3** someone of no importance

Originally meaning 'zero' and later 'number', because of the early use of numbers in encoded documents

circa *preposition* about (in dates): *circa 300*BC

circle *noun* **1** a figure formed from an endless curved line **2** something in the form of a circle; a ring **3** a society or group of people **4** a tier of seats in a theatre *etc* □ *verb* **1** to enclose in a circle **2** to move round in a circle

circuit *noun* **1** a movement in a circle **2** a connected group of places, events *etc*: *the American tennis circuit* **3** the path of an electric current

circuitous *adjective* not direct, roundabout: *by a circuitous route*

circular *adjective* round, like a circle □ *noun* a letter sent round to a number of people

circulate *verb* **1** to move round **2** to send round: *circulate a memo*

circulation *noun* **1** the act of circulating **2** the movement of the blood **3** the total sales of a newspaper or magazine

circum- or **circu-** *prefix* round: *circumnavigate/ circuit*
ⓘ Comes from Latin *circum* meaning 'all around'

circumference *noun* **1** the outside line of a circle **2** the length of this line

circumlocution *noun* a roundabout way of saying something

circumnavigate *verb* to sail or fly right round something □ **circumnavigator** *noun*

circumscribe *verb* **1** to draw a line round **2** to put limits on, restrict

circumscription *noun* **1** a limitation **2** an inscription or line running round something

circumspect *adjective* wary, cautious

circumspection *noun* caution

circumstance *noun* **1** a condition of time, place *etc* which affects someone, an action or an event **2 circumstances** the state of someone's financial affairs

circumstantial *adjective* of evidence: pointing to a conclusion without giving absolute proof

circumstantiate *verb* to prove by giving details

circumvent *verb* **1** to get round (a difficulty) **2** to outwit □ **circumvention** *noun*

circus *noun* (*plural* **circuses**) **1** a travelling company of acrobats, clowns *etc* **2** a large sports arena

cirrhosis *noun* a disease of the liver

cirrus *noun* a fleecy kind of cloud

cissy *noun, informal* an effeminate person

cistern *noun* a tank for storing water

citadel *noun* a fortress within a city

citation *noun* **1** something quoted **2** a summons to appear in court **3** official recognition of an achievement or action

cite *verb* **1** to quote as an example or as proof **2** to summon to appear in court
ⓘ Comes from Latin *citare* meaning 'to call'

🖝 Do not confuse with: **sight** and **site**

citizen *noun* someone who lives in a city or state

citizenry *noun plural* the inhabitants of a city or state

citizenship *noun* the rights or state of being a citizen

citric acid a sharp-tasting acid found in citrus fruits

citron *noun* a type of fruit similar to a lemon

citrus fruit one of a group of fruits including the orange, lemon and lime

city *noun* (*plural* **cities**) **1** a large town **2** a town with a cathedral □ **the City** *Brit* the part of London regarded as the centre of business

civic *adjective* relating to a city or citizens

civics *noun singular* the study of people's duties as citizens

civil *adjective* **1** relating to a community **2** non-military, civilian **3** polite

civil engineer an engineer who plans bridges, roads *etc*

civilian *noun* someone who is not in the armed forces □ *adjective* non-military

civility *noun* politeness, good manners

civilization *noun* **1** making or becoming civilized **2** life under a civilized system **3** a particular culture: *a prehistoric civilization*

civilize *verb* to bring (a people) under a regular system of laws, education *etc*

civilized *adjective* living under a system of laws, education *etc*; not savage

civil law law concerned with citizens' rights, not criminal acts

civil list the expenses of the royal household

civil marriage a marriage which does not take place in church

civil rights the rights of a citizen

civil service the paid administrative officials of the country, excluding the armed forces

civil war war between citizens of the same country

clachan (*pronounced* **kla**-khan) *noun, Scottish* a small village

clad *adjective, formal* clothed: *clad in leather from head to toe*

claim *verb* **1** to demand as a right **2** to state as a truth; assert (that) □ *noun* an act of claiming

■ **Alternative words**: (verb, meaning 2) allege

claimant *noun* someone who makes a claim

clairvoyant *adjective* able to see into the future, or to contact the spirit world □ *noun* someone with clairvoyant powers □ **clairvoyance** *noun*

clam *noun* a large shellfish with two shells hinged together

clamber *verb* to climb awkwardly or with difficulty

clammy *adjective* moist and sticky

clamorous *adjective* noisy

clamour *noun* a loud, continuous noise or outcry □ *verb* **1** to cry aloud **2** to make a loud demand (for)

clamp *noun* a piece of metal, wood *etc* used to fasten things together □ *verb* to bind with a clamp □ **clamp down on** to suppress firmly

clan *noun* **1** a number of families with the same surname, traditionally under a single chieftain **2** a sect, a clique

From Scottish Gaelic *clann* meaning 'children'

clandestine *adjective* hidden, secret, underhand

clang *verb* to make a loud, deep ringing sound □ *noun* a loud, deep ring

clank *noun* a sound like that made by metal hitting metal □ *verb* to make this sound

clansman *noun* a male member of a clan

clanswoman *noun* a female member of a clan

clap *noun* **1** the noise made by striking together two things, especially the hands **2** a burst of sound, especially thunder **3** (or **the clap**) *slang* gonorrhoea □ *verb* **1** to strike noisily together **2** to strike the hands together to show approval **3** *informal* to put suddenly, throw: *clap in jail*

clap *verb* ⇨ clap**s**, clap**ping**, clap**ped**

clapper *noun* the tongue of a bell

claptrap *noun* meaningless words, nonsense

claret *noun* a type of red wine

clarify *verb* **1** to make clear and understandable **2** to make (a liquid) clear and pure

clarify ⇨ clarif**ies**, clarif**ying**, clarif**ied**

clarinet *noun* a musical wind instrument, usually made of wood

clarinettist *noun* someone who plays the clarinet

clarion *noun, old* **1** a kind of trumpet **2** a shrill, rousing noise

clarion call a clear call to action

clarity *noun* clearness

clash *noun* (*plural* **clashes**) **1** a loud noise made by striking swords *etc* **2** a disagreement, a fight □ *verb* **1** to bang noisily together **2** to disagree **3** of events: to take place at the same time **4** of two colours *etc*: not to look well together

clasp *noun* **1** a hook or pin for fastening: *hair clasp* **2** a handshake **3** an embrace □ *verb* **1** to hold closely; grasp **2** to fasten

class *noun* (*plural* **classes**) **1** a rank or order of people or things **2** a group of schoolchildren or students taught together **3** a group of plants or animals with something in common □ *verb* **1** to place in a class **2** to arrange in some order

classification *noun* **1** the activity of arranging things into classes or categories **2** the label or name that you give something in order to indicate its class or category

classify *verb* **1** arrange in classes **2** put into a class or category

classify ⇨ classif**ies**, classif**ying**, classif**ied**

classic *noun* **1** a great book or other work of art **2** something typical and influential of its kind **3 classics** the study of ancient Greek and Latin literature □ *adjective* **1** excellent **2** standard, typical of its kind: *a classic* *example* **3** simple and elegant in style: *a classic black dress*

classical *adjective* **1** of a classic or the classics **2** of music: serious, not light

classy *adjective* elegant, stylish

clatter *noun* a noise of plates *etc* banged together

clause *noun* **1** a part of a sentence containing a finite verb **2** a part of a will, act of parliament *etc*

claustrophobia (*pronounced* klos-tro-**foh**-bi-*a*) *noun* an abnormal fear of enclosed spaces

claustrophobic *adjective* **1** suffering from or affected by claustrophobia: *she can't go in because she'll get claustrophobic* **2** causing feelings of anxiety related to being in an enclosed space or to feeling trapped or enclosed in some other way: *a claustrophobic little room/ a claustrophobic relationship*

claw *noun* **1** an animal's or bird's foot with hooked nails **2** a hooked nail on one of these feet □ *verb* to scratch or tear

clay *noun* soft, sticky earth, often used to make pottery, bricks *etc* □ **clayey** *adjective*

clean *adjective* **1** free from dirt; pure **2** neat, complete: *a clean break* □ *adverb* completely: *got clean away* □ *verb* to make clean; free from dirt □ **cleanly** *adverb* (meaning 2): *a single blow with the axe split the wood cleanly along its grain*

■ **Alternative words**: (adjective, meaning 1) washed, aseptic, immaculate, unsullied; (verb) wash, cleanse, purge, decontaminate

cleaner *noun* **1** someone employed to clean a building *etc* **2** a substance which cleans

cleanliness (*pronounced* **klen**-li-nes) *noun* the quality of being free from dirt

cleanse (*pronounced* klenz) *verb* to make clean

clear *adjective* **1** bright, undimmed **2** free from mist or cloud: *clear sky* **3** transparent **4** free from difficulty or obstructions **5** easy to see, hear or understand **6** after deductions and

charges have been made: *clear profit* **7** without a stain **8** without touching: *clear of the rocks* □ *verb* **1** to make clear **2** to empty **3** to free from blame **4** to leap over without touching **5** of the sky: to become bright □ **clear out** or **clear off** to go away □ **clearness** *noun* (adjective, meanings 1, 2, 3, 4 and 5)

■ **Alternative words**: (verb, meaning 3) absolve, exonerate, acquit

clearance *noun* **1** the activity of getting rid of all the things which are in a certain place so that a new start can be made: *a clearance sale* (= a cut-price sale in a shop to get rid of all the old stock)/ *woodland clearance* (= cutting down and removal of all the trees and plants in a piece of forest)/ *the Highland Clearances* (= the removal of tenant farmers from the Scottish Highlands by landowners in the 19th century) **2** permission to do something: *receive official clearance for the project*

clear-cut *adjective* distinct, obvious

clearing *noun* land free of trees

clearly *adverb* **1** obviously **2** in a clear way

cleavage *noun* **1** splitting **2** the way in which two things are split or divided **3** the hollow between a woman's breasts

cleave *verb* **1** to divide, split **2** to crack **3** to stick (to)

> **cleave** ⇨ cleaves, cleaving, clove or cleft or cleaved, cloven or cleft or cleaved

cleaver *noun* a heavy knife for splitting meat carcases *etc*

clef *noun* a musical sign, (𝄞 **treble clef**) or (𝄢 **bass clef**), placed on a stave to fix the pitch of the notes

cleft *noun* an opening made by splitting; a crack □ *past form* of **cleave**

cleft palate a deformity in the roof of the mouth, present in some people at birth

clemency *noun* readiness to forgive; mercy

clement *adjective* mild; merciful

clench *verb* to press firmly together: *clenching his teeth*

clergy *noun plural* the ministers of the Christian church

clergyman *noun* a male Christian minister

clergywoman *noun* a female Christian minister

cleric *noun* a member of the clergy

clerical *adjective* 1 relating to office work 2 of the clergy

clerk *noun* an office worker who writes letters, keeps accounts *etc* □ *verb* to act as clerk

clever *adjective* 1 quick in learning and understanding 2 intelligent, skilful: *a clever answer* □ **cleverly** *adverb*

cliché (*pronounced* **klee**-shei) *noun* an idea, phrase *etc* that has been used too much and has little meaning

From a French word for 'stereotype', in the sense of a fixed printing plate

click *noun* a short sharp sound like a clock's tick □ *verb* make this sound

client *noun* 1 a customer of a shop *etc* 2 someone who goes to a lawyer *etc* for advice

clientele (*pronounced* klee-en-**tel** or klai-en-**tel**) *noun* the customers of a lawyer, shopkeeper *etc*

cliff *noun* a very steep, rocky slope, especially by the sea

climactic *adjective* most important or intense, of the climax: *the climactic moment of the play*

climate *noun* 1 the weather conditions of a particular area 2 general condition or situation: *in the present cultural climate* □ **climatic** *adjective* (meaning 1)

climax *noun* (*plural* **climaxes**) the point of greatest interest or importance in a situation

climb *verb* 1 to go to the top of 2 to go up using hands and feet 3 to slope upward □ *noun* an act of climbing

■ **Alternative words**: (verb, meaning 1) ascend, mount, top; (verb, meaning 2) scale, clamber, shin up; (verb, meaning 3) rise, soar

climber *noun* 1 someone who climbs 2 a plant which climbs up walls *etc*

clinch *verb* 1 to grasp tightly 2 to settle (an argument, bargain *etc*) □ *noun* (*plural* **clinches**) 1 *boxing* a position in which the boxers hold each other with their arms 2 a passionate embrace

clincher *noun* the thing which settles (an argument, bargain *etc*): *I had more experience than him. That was the clincher in the end*

cling *verb* to stick or hang on (to) □ **clingy** *adjective*

cling ⇨ cling*s*, cling*ing*, clung

clingfilm *noun* thin transparent plastic material used to wrap food

clinic *noun* a place or part of a hospital where a particular kind of treatment is given

clinical *adjective* 1 of a clinic 2 based on observation: *clinical medicine* 3 objective, cool and unemotional: *clinical approach*

clinically *adverb* 1 according to medical diagnosis: *clinically depressed* 2 as an object of medical observation: *his skin condition is clinically interesting*

clink *noun* a ringing sound of knocked glasses *etc* □ *verb*

clip *verb* 1 to cut (off) 2 to fasten with a clip □ *noun* 1 something clipped off 2 a small fastener 3 *informal* a smart blow

clip *verb* ⇨ clip*s*, clip*ping*, clip*ped*

clipper *noun* 1 a fast-sailing ship 2 **clippers** large scissors for clipping

clique (*pronounced* kleek) *noun* a small group of people who help each other but keep others at a distance

clitoris (*pronounced* **klit**-or-is) *noun* a small structure at the front of the external female sex organs □ **clitoral** *adjective*

cloak *noun* 1 a loose outer garment 2 something which hides: *cloak of darkness* □ *verb* 1 to cover as with a cloak 2 to hide

cloakroom a place where coats, hats *etc* may be left for a time

cloche (*pronounced* klosh) *noun* (*plural* **cloches**) a transparent frame for protecting plants

clock *noun* a machine for measuring time □ **clock in** or **clock out** to record your time of arrival at, or departure from, work

clockwise *adjective* turning or moving in the same direction as the hands of a clock

clockwork *adjective* worked by machinery such as that of a clock □ **like clockwork** smoothly, without difficulties

clod *noun* **1** a thick lump of turf **2** a stupid man

clodhopper *noun* a stupid clumsy person □ **clodhopping** *adjective*

clog *noun* a shoe with a wooden sole □ *verb* to block (pipes *etc*)

clog *verb* ⇨ clogs, clogging, clogged

cloister *noun* **1** a covered-in walk in a monastery or convent **2** a monastery or convent

cloistered *adjective* **1** shut up in a monastery *etc* **2** sheltered

close[1] (*pronounced* klohs) *adjective* **1** near in time, place *etc* **2** shut up, with no opening **3** without fresh air, stuffy **4** narrow, confined **5** mean **6** secretive **7** beloved, very dear: *a close friend* **8** decided by a small amount: *a close contest* □ *noun* **1** a narrow passage off a street **2** the gardens, walks *etc* near a cathedral

close[2] (*pronounced* klohz) *verb* **1** to shut **2** to finish **3** to come closer to and fight (with) □ *noun* the end

closed-circuit television a system of television cameras and receivers for use in shops *etc*

closely *adverb* **1** carefully: *observe something closely/ listen closely* **2** strongly, intimately: *he was closely involved in these activities* **3** in a way that brings things close together: *objects packed closely together in a box*

closet *noun*, *US* a cupboard □ *verb* to take into a room for a private conference □ **closeted with** in private conference with

close-up *noun* a film or photograph taken very near the subject

closure *noun* the act of closing

clot *noun* **1** a lump that forms in blood, cream *etc* **2** *informal* an idiot □ *verb* to form into clots

clot *verb* ⇨ clots, clotting, clotted

cloth *noun* **1** woven material of cotton, wool, silk *etc* **2** a piece of this **3** a table-cover

clothe *verb* **1** to put clothes on **2** to provide with clothes **3** to cover

clothes *noun plural* **1** things worn to cover the body and limbs, *eg* shirt, trousers, skirt **2** sheets and coverings for a bed

clothing *noun* clothes

cloud *noun* **1** a mass of tiny drops of water or ice floating in the sky **2** a mass of anything: *cloud of bees* □ *verb* to become dim or blurred □ **clouded** *adjective* □ **cloudless** *adjective* (noun, meaning 1)

cloudburst *noun* a sudden heavy fall of rain

cloudy *adjective* **1** darkened with clouds **2** not clear or transparent

clout *noun*, *informal* **1** a blow **2** influence, power □ *verb*, *informal* to hit

clove[1] *noun* **1** a flower bud of the clove tree, used as a spice **2** a small section of a bulb of garlic

The spice gets its name from French *clou* meaning 'nail' because of its shape

clove[2] *past form* of **cleave**

cloven-hoofed *adjective* having a divided hoof like an ox, sheep *etc*

clover *noun* a field plant with leaves usually in three parts □ **in clover** in luxury

clown *noun* **1** a comedian with a painted face and comical clothes in a circus **2** a fool

clowning *noun* silly or comical behaviour

clownish *adjective* like a clown; awkward

cloy *verb* of something sweet: to become unpleasant when too much is taken

cloying *adjective* over-sweet, sickly

club *noun* **1** a heavy stick **2** a stick used

to hit the ball in golf **3** a group of people who meet for social events *etc* **4** the place where these people meet **5 clubs** one of the four suits in playing-cards □ *verb* to beat with a club □ **club together** to put money into a joint fund for some purpose

club *verb* ⇨ clubs, clubb*ing*, clubb*ed*

cluck *noun* a sound like that made by a hen □ *verb* to make this sound

clue *noun* a sign or piece of evidence that helps to solve a mystery

clump *noun* a cluster of trees or shrubs □ *verb* to walk heavily

clumsy *adjective* **1** awkward in movement or actions **2** tactless, thoughtless: *clumsy apology* □ **clumsily** *adverb*

clumsy ⇨ clums*ier*, clums*iest*

clung *past form of* **cling**

cluster *noun* **1** a bunch of fruit *etc* **2** a crowd □ *verb* to group together in clusters

clutch *verb* **1** to hold firmly **2** to seize, grasp □ *noun* (*plural* **clutches**) **1** a grasp **2** part of a car engine used for changing gears **3** a brood of chickens

clutter *noun* **1** a muddled or disordered collection of things **2** disorder, confusion, untidiness □ *verb* **1** to crowd together untidily **2 clutter up** to fill or cover in an untidy, disordered way

CND *abbreviation* Campaign for Nuclear Disarmament

CO *abbreviation* **1** carbon monoxide **2** Commanding Officer

Co *abbreviation* **1** Company **2** County

c/o *abbreviation* care of

co- *also* **col-, con-, com-, cor-** *prefix* **1** joint, working with, together with: *co-author/ co-driver/ connect/ compound/ collision/ correspond* **2** sometimes just gives extra emphasis to a word: *corroborate/ commemorate* ℚ Comes from Latin *cum* meaning 'with'

coach *noun* (*plural* **coaches**) **1** a bus for long-distance travel **2** a closed, four-wheeled horse carriage **3** a railway carriage **4** a private trainer for sportspeople □ *verb* to train or help to

prepare for an examination, sports contest *etc*

coagulate *verb* to thicken; clot

coal *noun* a black substance dug out of the earth and used for burning, making gas *etc*

coalesce (*pronounced* koh-*a*-**les**) *verb* to come together and unite

coalfield *noun* an area where there is coal to be mined

coal gas the mixture of gases obtained from coal, used for lighting and heating

coalition *noun* a joining together of different parts or groups

coalmine *noun* a mine from which coal is dug

coarse *adjective* **1** not fine in texture; rough, harsh **2** vulgar

coarsen *verb* to make coarse

coast *noun* the border of land next to the sea □ *verb* **1** to sail along or near a coast **2** to move without the use of power on a bike, in a car *etc*

coastal *adjective* of or on the coast

coastguard *noun* someone who acts as a guard along the coast to help those in danger in boats *etc*

coat *noun* **1** an outer garment with sleeves **2** an animal's covering of hair or wool **3** a layer of paint □ *verb* to cover with a coat or layer □ **coat of arms** the badge or crest of a family

coating *noun* a covering

coax *verb* to persuade to do what is wanted without using force

cob *noun* **1** a head of corn, wheat *etc* **2** a male swan

cobalt *noun* **1** a silvery metal **2** a blue colouring obtained from this

cobble *noun* **1** a rounded stone used in paving roads (*also called* **cobblestone**) □ *verb* **1** to mend (shoes) **2** to repair roughly or hurriedly

cobbled *adjective* of streets: paved with cobbles

cobbler *noun* someone who mends shoes

cobra *noun* a poisonous snake found in India and Africa

cobweb *noun* a spider's web

cocaine *noun* a narcotic drug

cock *noun* 1 the male of most kinds of bird, especially of the farmyard hen 2 a tap or valve for controlling the flow of liquid 3 a hammer-like part of a gun which fires the shot 4 a small heap of hay □ *verb* 1 to draw back the cock of a gun 2 to set (the ears) upright to listen 3 to tilt (the head) to one side

cockatoo *noun* a kind of parrot

cockerel *noun* a young cock

cocker spaniel a breed of small spaniel

cockle *noun* a type of shellfish □ **cockles of the heart** someone's inmost heart

cockleshell *noun* the shell of a cockle

cockney *noun* (*plural* **cockneys**) 1 someone born in the East End of London 2 the speech characteristic of this area

Literally 'cock's egg', an old word for a misshapen egg which was later applied to an effeminate person, and so to a soft-living city-dweller

cockpit *noun* 1 the space for the pilot or driver in an aeroplane or small boat 2 a pit where game cocks fight

cockroach *noun* (*plural* **cockroaches**) a type of crawling insect

cocksure *adjective* very confident, often without cause

cocktail *noun* a mixed alcoholic drink

cocky *adjective* conceited, self-confident

cocoa *noun* a drink made from the ground seeds of the cacao tree

coconut *noun* the large, hard-shelled nut of a type of palm tree

Based on a Portuguese word meaning 'grimace', because of the resemblance of the three holes on the base of the fruit to a human face

cocoon *noun* a protective covering of silk spun by the larva of a butterfly, moth *etc*

cod *noun* (*plural* **cod**) a fish much used as food, found in the northern seas

coddle *verb* 1 to pamper, over-protect 2 to cook (an egg) gently over hot water

code *noun* 1 a way of signalling or sending secret messages, using letters *etc* agreed beforehand 2 a book or collection of laws, rules *etc*

codger (*pronounced* **koj**-er) *noun* an old, eccentric man

codicil *noun* a note added to a will or treaty

codify *verb* to arrange in an orderly way, classify

codify ⇨ codif*ies*, codify*ing*, codif*ied*

coed (*pronounced* koh-**ed**) *adjective, informal* coeducational

coeducation *noun* the education of boys and girls together □ **coeducational** *adjective*

coerce *verb* to make to do; force, compel □ **coercion** *noun*

coercive *adjective* using force

coeval (*pronounced* koh-**ee**-v*al*) *adjective* of the same age or time

coexist *verb* to exist at the same time □ **coexistence** *noun* □ **coexistent** *adjective*

coffee *noun* 1 a drink made from the roasted, ground beans of the coffee shrub 2 a pale brown colour

coffer *noun* a chest for holding money, gold *etc*

coffer-dam *noun* a watertight dam enclosing the foundations of a bridge

coffin *noun* a box in which a dead body is buried or cremated

cog *noun* a tooth on a wheel

cogent *adjective* convincing, believable □ **cogency** *noun*

cogitate *verb* to think carefully □ **cogitation** *noun*

cognac *noun* a kind of French brandy

cogwheel *noun* a toothed wheel

cohere *verb* to stick together

coherence *noun* connection between thoughts, ideas *etc*

coherent *adjective* **1** sticking together **2** clear and logical in thought or speech

cohesion *noun* the act of sticking together

cohesive *adjective* of a group: consisting of members who are closely linked together or associated with each other: *act together as a cohesive unit*

cohort *noun, historical* a tenth part of a Roman legion

coil *verb* to wind in rings; twist □ *noun* **1** a wound arrangement of hair, rope *etc* **2** a contraceptive device fitted in the uterus

coin *noun* a piece of stamped metal used as money □ *verb* **1** to make metal into money **2** to make up (a new word *etc*)

coinage *noun* **1** the system of coins used in a country **2** a newly-made word

coincide *verb* **1** (often **coincide with**) to be the same as: *their interests coincide/ his story coincides with mine* **2** (often **coincide with**) to happen at the same time as: *coincided with his departure*

coincidence *noun* the occurrence of two things simultaneously without planning

coincidental *adjective* happening by chance, the result of a coincidence: *Any resemblance to real people is purely coincidental* □ **coincidentally** *adverb* by chance, as the result of a coincidence: *Coincidentally, both our new jobs started on the same day*

coke *noun* **1** a type of fuel made by heating coal till the gas is driven out **2** *informal* cocaine

col- *see* **co-**

colander *noun* a bowl with small holes in it for straining vegetables *etc*

cold *adjective* **1** low in temperature **2** lower in temperature than is comfortable **3** unfriendly □ *noun* **1** the state of being cold **2** an infectious disease causing shivering, running nose *etc* □ **coldly** *adverb* (adjective, meanings 2 and 3) □ **coldness** *noun*

■ **Alternative words**: (adjective, meaning 1) unheated, cool, chilled; (adjective, meaning 2) raw, biting, wintry, glacial, chill

cold-blooded *adjective* **1** of fishes *etc*: having cold blood **2** cruel; lacking in feelings

cold-calling *noun* the contacting of potential business contacts *etc* without appointment

cold feet lack of courage

cold sore a blister on or near the mouth, caused by a contagious virus similar to that which causes genital herpes

cold war a power struggle between nations without open warfare

coleslaw *noun* a salad made from raw cabbage

colic *noun* a severe stomach pain

collaborate *verb* **1** to work together (with) **2** to work with (an enemy) to betray your country □ **collaboration** *noun* □ **collaborator** *noun*
○ Comes from Latin *col-* meaning 'together with', and *laborare* meaning 'to work'

🖝 Do not confuse with: **corroborate**

collage (*pronounced* ko-lahsz) *noun* a design made of scraps of paper pasted on wood, card *etc*

collapse *verb* **1** to fall or break down **2** to cave or fall in **3** to become unable to continue □ *noun* a falling down or caving in

collapsible *adjective* of a chair *etc*: able to be folded up

collar *noun* **1** a band, strip *etc* worn round the neck **2** part of a garment that fits round the neck □ *verb, informal* to seize

collarbone *noun* either of two bones joining the breast bone and shoulderblade

collate *verb* **1** to examine and compare **2** to gather together and arrange in order: *collate the pages for the book*

collateral *noun* an additional security for repayment of a debt

collation *noun* **1** a light, often cold meal **2** a comparison

colleague *noun* someone who works in the same company *etc* as yourself

collect *verb* **1** to bring together **2** to gather together

collected *adjective* **1** gathered together **2** calm, composed

collection *noun* **1** the act of collecting **2** a number of objects or people **3** money gathered at a meeting, *eg* a church service

collective *adjective* **1** acting together **2** of several things or people, not of one: *collective decision* □ *noun* a business *etc* owned and managed by the workers

collector *noun* someone who collects a particular group of things: *stamp collector*

colleen *noun*, *Irish* a young woman, a girl

college *noun* **1** a building housing students, forming part of a university **2** a higher-education institute

collegiate *adjective* of a university: divided into colleges

collide *verb* to come together with great force; clash

collision *noun* **1** a crash between two moving vehicles *etc* **2** a disagreement, a clash of interests *etc*

collie *noun* a breed of long-haired dog with a pointed nose

collier *noun* **1** a coal-miner **2** a coal ship

colliery *noun* (*plural* **collieries**) a coalmine

colloquial *adjective* used in everyday speech but not in formal writing or speaking □ **colloquially** *adverb*

colloquialism *noun* an example of colloquial speech

collusion *noun* a secret or clandestine agreement

cologne *noun* light perfume made with plant oils and alcohol

colon[1] *noun* a punctuation mark (:) used *eg* to introduce a list of examples

colon[2] *noun* a part of the bowel

colonel (*pronounced* **ker**-nel) *noun* a senior army officer fulfilling a staff appointment

colonial *adjective* of colonies abroad

colonialism *noun* the policy of setting up colonies abroad

colonialist *noun* someone who supports the policy of setting up and maintaining colonies abroad □ *adjective* related to colonialism

colonist *noun* a settler

colonize *verb* to set up a colony in

colonnade *noun* a row of columns or pillars

colony *noun* (*plural* **colonies**) **1** a group of settlers or the settlement they make in another country **2** a group of people, animals *etc* of the same type living together

colossal *adjective* huge, enormous

colossus *noun* an enormous statue

colour or *US* **color** *noun* **1** a quality that an object shows in the light, *eg* redness, blueness *etc* **2** a shade or tint **3** vividness, brightness **4 colours** a flag or standard □ *verb* **1** to put colour on **2** to blush **3** to influence: *coloured my attitude to life* □ **off colour** unwell

colour-blind *adjective* unable to distinguish certain colours, *eg* red and green

coloured *adjective* **1** having colour **2** an old-fashioned and possibly offensive adjective meaning 'not white-skinned'

It is generally considered more 'politically correct' to say 'black' for sense 2

colourful *adjective* **1** brightly coloured **2** vivid, interesting

colouring *noun* **1** shade or combination of colours **2** complexion

colourless *adjective* **1** without colour **2** dull, bland

colt *noun* a young horse

column *noun* **1** an upright stone or wooden pillar **2** something of a long or tall, narrow shape **3** a vertical line of print, figures *etc* on a page **4** a regular feature in a newspaper **5** an arrangement of troops *etc* one behind the other

columnist *noun* someone who writes a regular newspaper column

com- *see* **co-**

coma *noun* unconsciousness lasting a long time

comatose *adjective* **1** in or of a coma **2** drowsy, sluggish

comb *noun* **1** a toothed instrument for separating or smoothing hair, wool *etc* **2** the crest of certain birds **3** a collection of cells for honey □ *verb* **1** to arrange or smooth with a comb **2** to search through thoroughly

combat *verb* to fight or struggle against □ *noun* a fight or struggle

combatant *noun* someone who is fighting □ *adjective* fighting

combative *adjective* quarrelsome; fighting

combination *noun* **1** a joining together of things or people **2** a set of things or people combined **3** a series of letters or figures dialled to open a safe **4 combinations** *old* underwear for the body and legs

combine *verb* to join together □ *noun* a number of traders *etc* who join together

combine harvester a machine that both cuts and threshes crops

combustible *adjective* liable to catch fire and burn □ *noun* anything that will catch fire

combustion *noun* burning

come *verb* **1** to move towards this place (*opposite* of **go**): *come here!* **2** to draw near: *Christmas is coming* **3** to arrive: *we'll have tea when you come* **4** to happen, occur: *the index comes at the end* □ **come about** to happen □ **come across** or **come upon** to meet or find accidentally □ **come by** to obtain □ **come into** to inherit □ **come of age** to reach the age at which you become an adult for legal purposes □ **come round** or **come to** to recover from a faint *etc* □ **come upon** to come across □ **to come** in the future

come ⇨ come*s*, com*ing*, came, come

🕔 Comes from Old English *cuman*

comedian *noun* a performer who tells jokes, acts in comedy *etc*

comedy *noun* (*plural* **comedies**) a light-hearted or amusing play (*contrasted with:* **tragedy**)

comely *adjective* good-looking, pleasing □ **comeliness** *noun*

comet *noun* a kind of star which has a tail of light

comfort *verb* to help, soothe (someone in pain or distress) □ *noun* **1** ease; quiet enjoyment **2** something that brings ease and happiness

comfortable *adjective* **1** at ease; free from trouble, pain *etc* **2** giving comfort **3** having enough money for a pleasant lifestyle

comfortably *adverb* **1** easily, happily, or without any problems: *He can comfortably talk for hours without a break* **2** in a way which involves no pain or physical irritation: *Are you sitting comfortably?* **3** financially well: *comfortably-off*

comfrey *noun* a plant with hairy leaves, used in herbal medicine

comic *adjective* **1** of comedy **2** amusing, funny □ *noun* **1** a professional comedian **2** a children's magazine with illustrated stories *etc*

comical *adjective* funny, amusing □ **comically** *adverb*

comic strip a strip of small pictures outlining a story

comma *noun* a punctuation mark (,) indicating a pause in a sentence

command *verb* **1** to give an order **2** to be in charge of **3** to look over or down upon: *commanding a view* □ *noun* **1** an order **2** control: *in command of the situation*

commandant *noun* an officer in command of a place or of troops

commandeer *verb* to seize (something) especially for the use of an army

commander *noun* **1** someone who commands **2** a naval officer next in rank below captain

commandment *noun* an order or command

commando *noun* (*plural* **commandoes**) a soldier in an army unit trained for special tasks

commemorate verb 1 to bring to memory by some solemn act 2 to serve as a memorial of

commemoration noun 1 the official act of remembering something, especially something sad 2 a ceremony to honour the memory of something

commence verb to begin

commencement noun the start or beginning

commend verb 1 to praise 2 to give into the care of

commendable adjective praiseworthy

commendation noun praise

commendatory adjective praising

comment noun 1 a remark 2 a criticism □ verb to remark on; criticize

commentary noun (plural **commentaries**) 1 a description of an event etc by someone who is watching it 2 a set of explanatory notes for a book etc

commentator noun someone who gives or writes a commentary

commerce noun the buying and selling of goods between people or nations; trade, dealings

commercial adjective 1 of commerce 2 paid for by advertisements: commercial radio □ noun an advertisement on radio, TV etc

commercially adverb 1 in a way which can make money: a commercially attractive proposal 2 as a large-scale industrial process: A home-made gift is more personal than a commercially-produced one 3 on the open market: It will be a while before these gadgets are commercially available.

commiserate verb to sympathize (with)

commiseration noun pity

commiserations noun plural an expression of sympathy when someone has failed to do or achieve something

commission noun 1 the act of committing 2 a document giving authority to an officer in the armed forces 3 an order for a work of art 4 a fee for doing business on another's behalf 5 a group of people appointed to investigate something □ verb to give a commission or power to □ **in** or **out of commission** in or not in use

commissionaire noun a uniformed doorkeeper

commissioner noun 1 someone with high authority in a district 2 a member of a commission

commit verb 1 to give or hand over; entrust 2 to make a promise to do: committed to finishing this book 3 to do, bring about: commit a crime

commit ⇨ commits, committing, committed

commitment noun 1 a promise 2 a task that must be done

committal noun the act of committing

committed adjective strong in belief or support: a committed socialist

committee noun a number of people chosen from a larger body to attend to special business

commodious adjective roomy, spacious

commodity noun (plural **commodities**) 1 an article to be bought or sold 2 **commodities** goods, produce

commodore noun an officer next above a captain in the navy

common adjective 1 shared by all or many: common belief 2 seen or happening often: common occurrence 3 ordinary, normal □ noun land belonging to the people of a town, parish etc

commoner noun someone who is not a noble

common law unwritten law based on custom

Common Market the European Community, the EC

common noun a name for any one of a class of things (contrasted with: **proper noun**)

commonplace adjective ordinary

common room noun a sitting-room for the use of a group in a school etc

Commons or **House of Commons** the lower House of Parliament

common sense practical good sense

commonwealth *noun* an association of self-governing states

commotion *noun* a disturbance among several people

communal *adjective* common, shared **communally** *adverb*

commune *noun* a group of people living together, sharing work *etc* □ *verb* to talk together

communicable *adjective* able to be passed on to others: *communicable disease*

communicate *verb* 1 to make known, tell 2 to pass on 3 to get in touch (with) 4 to have a connecting door

communication *noun* 1 a means of conveying information 2 a message 3 a way of passing from place to place

communicative *adjective* willing to give information, talkative

communion *noun* 1 the act of sharing thoughts, feelings *etc*; fellowship 2 **Communion** in the Christian Church, the celebration of the Lord's supper

communiqué (*pronounced* kom-**yoon**-ik-ei) *noun* an official announcement

communism *noun* a form of socialism where industry is controlled by the state

communist *adjective* of communism □ *noun* someone who believes in communism

community *noun* (*plural* **communities**) 1 a group of people living in one place 2 the public in general

community charge a local tax in the UK to pay for public services, charged according to property values

commute *verb* 1 to travel regularly between two places, *eg* between home and work 2 to change (a punishment) for one less severe

commuter *noun* someone who travels regularly some distance to work from their home

compact *adjective* fitted or packed closely together □ *noun* a bargain or agreement

compact disc a small disc on which digitally recorded sound is registered as a series of pits to be read by a laser beam

companion *noun* someone or something that accompanies; a friend

companionable *adjective* friendly

companionship *noun* friendship; the act of accompanying

company *noun* (*plural* **companies**) 1 a gathering of people 2 a business firm 3 a part of a regiment 4 a ship's crew 5 companionship
○ Comes from French *compagnie* meaning 'company' or 'a gathering of people'

comparable *adjective* roughly similar or equal in some way: *The two films are comparable in terms of quality*

comparative *adjective* 1 judged by comparing with something else; relative: *comparative improvement* 2 near to being: *a comparative stranger* 3 *grammar* the degree of an adjective or adverb between positive and superlative, *eg* blacker, *better*, *more courageous*

compare *verb* 1 to set things together to see how similar or different they are 2 to liken □ **beyond compare** much better than all rivals

comparison *noun* the act of comparing

compartment *noun* a separate part or division, *eg* of a railway carriage

compass *noun* (*plural* **compasses**) 1 an instrument with a magnetized needle for showing direction 2 **compasses** an instrument with one fixed and one movable leg for drawing circles

compassion *noun* pity for another's suffering; mercy

compassionate *adjective* pitying, merciful □ **compassionately** *adverb*

compatibility *noun* the natural tendency for two or more people or groups to get on well together

compatible *adjective* 1 able to live with, agree with *etc* 2 of pieces of electronic equipment: able to be connected and used together □ **compatibly** *adverb*

compatriot *noun* a fellow-countryman or -countrywoman

compel *verb* force to do something

compel ⇨ compel*s*, compel*ling*, compel*led*

compensate *verb* to make up for wrong or damage done, especially by giving money

compensation *noun* something given to make up for wrong or damage

compère *noun* someone who introduces acts as part of an entertainment □ *verb* to act as compère

compete *verb* to try to beat others in a race *etc*

competent *adjective* 1 capable, efficient 2 skilled; properly trained or qualified □ **competence** *noun*

competently *adverb* in a satisfactory or successful way

competition *noun* 1 a contest between rivals 2 rivalry

competitive *adjective* 1 of sport: based on competitions 2 fond of competing with others

competitor *noun* someone who competes; a rival

compilation *noun* 1 a collection of several short, related pieces of writing, music or information: *I've made you a compilation of my favourite songs* 2 the activity of compiling something

compile *verb* to make (a book *etc*) from information that has been collected

compiler *noun* a person whose job consists of compiling: *a quiz-game compiler*

complacence or **complacency** *noun* a lazy attitude resulting from an exaggerated belief in your own security

complacent *adjective* self-satisfied and with a tendency to be lazy □ **complacently** *adverb*

complain *verb* 1 to express dissatisfaction about something 2 to grumble

■ **Alternative words**: (meaning 1) protest, bemoan, bewail; (meaning 2) grouse, gripe, carp

complaint *noun* 1 a statement of dissatisfaction 2 an illness

complement *noun* 1 something which completes or fills up 2 the full number or quantity needed to fill something 3 the angle that must be added to a given angle to make up a right angle

◆ Do not confuse with: **compliment**. Remember – **COMPLE**ment and **COMPLE**te are related in meaning, and the first six letters of both words are the same

complementary *adjective* 1 together making up a whole 2 making up a right angle

◆ Do not confuse with: **complimentary**. **Complementary** is related to the noun **complement**

complete *adjective* 1 having nothing missing; whole 2 finished □ *verb* 1 to finish 2 to make whole □ **completion** *noun*

completely *adverb* totally, absolutely

complex *adjective* 1 made up of many parts 2 complicated, difficult □ *noun* (*plural* **complexes**) 1 a set of repressed emotions and ideas which affect someone's behaviour 2 an exaggerated reaction, an obsession: *has a complex about her height* 3 a group of related buildings: *sports complex*

complexion *noun* 1 the colour or look of the skin of the face 2 appearance

complexity *noun* (*plural* **complexities**) the quality of being complicated or difficult: *the complexity of this problem*

compliance *noun* the act of complying; agreement with another's wishes

compliant *adjective* yielding, giving agreement

complicate *verb* to make difficult

complicated *adjective* difficult to understand; detailed

complication *noun* 1 a difficulty 2 a development in an illness which makes things worse

complicity *noun* (*plural* **complicities**) a share in a crime or other misdeed

compliment *noun* 1 an expression of praise or flattery 2 **compliments** good wishes □ *verb* to praise, congratulate: *complimented me on my cooking*

🖝 Do not confuse with: **complement**. Remember, if you make a **compLIment**, you are being **poLIte**, and an 'I' comes after the 'L' in both words

complimentary *adjective* **1** flattering, praising **2** given free: *complimentary ticket*

🖝 Do not confuse with: **complementary**. **Complimentary** is related to the noun **compliment**

comply *verb* to agree to do something that someone else orders or wishes

comply ⇨ complies, complying, complied

component *adjective* forming one of the parts of a whole □ *noun* one of several parts, *eg* of a machine

compose *verb* **1** to put together or in order; arrange **2** to create (a piece of music, a poem *etc*)

composed *adjective* quiet, calm

composer *noun* someone who writes music

composite *adjective* made up of parts

composition *noun* **1** the act of composing **2** a created piece of writing or music **3** a mixture of things

compos mentis sane, rational

compost *noun* a mixture of natural manures for spreading on soil

composure *noun* calmness, self-possession

compound *adjective* **1** made up of a number of different parts **2** not simple □ *noun* **1** *chemistry* a substance formed from two or more elements **2** an enclosure round a building

comprehend *verb* **1** to understand **2** to include □ **comprehension** *noun* (meaning 1)

comprehensible *adjective* able to be understood

comprehensive *adjective* taking in or including much or all

comprehensive school a state-funded school providing all types of secondary education

compress *verb* (*pronounced* kom-**pres**)

1 to press together **2** to force into a narrower or smaller space □ *noun* (*pronounced* kom-pres) a pad used to create pressure on a part of the body or to reduce inflammation □ **compression** *noun*

comprise *verb* **1** to include, contain **2** to consist of

🖝 Do not confuse with: **consist**. Remember, you do not need the word 'of' after **comprise**. You say *the exam comprises three parts*, but *the exam consists of three parts*

compromise *noun* an agreement reached by both sides giving up something □ *verb* **1** to make a compromise **2** to put in a difficult or embarrassing position

compulsion *noun* a force driving someone to do something

compulsive *adjective* unable to stop yourself, obsessional: *compulsive liar*

🖝 Do not confuse: **compulsive** and **compulsory**

compulsory *adjective* **1** requiring to be done **2** forced upon someone

🖝 Do not confuse: **compulsory** and **compulsive**

■ **Alternative words**: (meaning 1) obligatory
▨ **Opposite**: (meaning 1) optional

compunction *noun* regret

computation *noun* counting, calculation

compute *verb* to count, calculate

computer *noun* an electronic machine that stores and sorts information of various kinds

comrade *noun* a companion, a friend

con *verb* to trick, play a confidence trick on □ *noun* a trick, a deceit

con *verb* ⇨ cons, conning, conned

con- see **co-**

concave *adjective* hollow or curved inwards (*contrasted with*: **convex**)

concavity *noun* (*plural* **concavities**) a hollow

conceal *verb* to hide, keep secret □ **concealment** *noun*

concede verb 1 to give up, yield 2 to admit the truth of something: *I concede that you may be right*

conceit noun a too high opinion of yourself; vanity

conceited adjective full of conceit; vain

conceivable adjective able to be imagined

conceivably adverb possibly: *He can't conceivably expect you to finish all the work by Monday*

conceive verb 1 to form in the mind, imagine 2 to become pregnant

concentrate verb 1 to direct all your attention or effort towards something 2 to bring together to one place

concentrated adjective made stronger or less dilute □ **concentration** noun

concentric adjective of circles: placed one inside the other with the same centre point (*contrasted with*: **eccentric**)

concept noun a general idea about something

conception noun 1 the act of conceiving 2 an idea

concern verb 1 to have to do with 2 to make uneasy 3 to interest, affect □ noun 1 anxiety 2 a cause of anxiety, a worry 3 a business □ **concern yourself with** to be worried about

concerning preposition about: *concerning your application*

concert noun a musical performance □ **in concert** together

🖋 Do not confuse with: **consort**

concerted adjective planned or performed together

concertina noun a type of musical wind instrument, with bellows and keys

concerto noun (*plural* **concertos**) a long piece of music for a solo instrument with orchestral accompaniment

concession noun 1 a granting or allowing of something: *a concession for oil exploration* 2 something granted or allowed 3 a reduction in the price of something for children, the unemployed, senior citizens *etc*

conciliate verb to win over (someone previously unfriendly or angry)

conciliation noun the act or process of making peace with a person or group

conciliatory adjective having the aim of making peace: *a conciliatory gesture*

concise adjective brief, using few words

🕓 Comes from Latin *concisus* meaning 'cut up'

🖋 Do not confuse with: **precise**

conclude verb 1 to end 2 to reach a decision or judgement; settle

concluding adjective last, final

conclusion noun 1 end 2 decision, judgement

conclusive adjective settling, deciding: *conclusive proof*

conclusively adverb in a way which leaves no doubt: *prove conclusively that there is no other life in the solar system*

concoct verb 1 to mix together (a dish or drink) 2 to make up, invent: *concoct a story* □ **concoction** noun

concord noun agreement

concourse noun 1 a crowd 2 a large open space in a building *etc*

concrete adjective 1 solid, real 2 made of concrete □ noun a mixture of gravel, cement *etc* used in building

📖 **Opposite**: (adjective, meaning 1) abstract

concur verb to agree

concur ⇨ concur**s**, concur**ring**, concur**red**

concurrence noun agreement

concurrent adjective 1 happening together 2 agreeing □ **concurrently** adverb (meaning 1)

concussion noun temporary harm done to the brain from a knock on the head

condemn verb 1 to blame 2 to sentence to (a certain punishment) 3 to declare (a building) unfit for use □ **condemnation** noun (meaning 1)

condemned cell a cell for a prisoner condemned to death

condensation noun 1 the act of

condensing **2** drops of liquid formed from vapour

condense *verb* **1** to make to go into a smaller space **2** of steam: to turn to liquid

condescend *verb* to act towards someone as if you are better than them
□ **condescending** *adjective*
□ **condescension** *noun*

condiment *noun* a seasoning for food, especially salt or pepper

condition *noun* **1** the state in which anything is: *in poor condition* **2** something that must happen before some other thing happens **3** a point in a bargain, treaty *etc*

conditional *adjective* depending on certain things happening
□ **conditionally** *adverb*

condolence *noun* sharing in another's sorrow; sympathy

condom *noun* a contraceptive rubber sheath

condone *verb* to allow (an offence) to pass unchecked

conducive *adjective* helping, favourable (to): *conducive to peace*

conduct *verb* (*pronounced* kon-**dukt**) **1** to lead, guide **2** to control, be in charge of **3** to direct (an orchestra) **4** to transmit (electricity *etc*) **5** to behave: *conducted himself correctly* □ *noun* (*pronounced* **kon**-dukt) behaviour

conduction *noun* transmission of heat, electricity *etc*

conductor *noun* **1** someone who directs an orchestra **2** someone who collects fares on a bus *etc* **3** something that transmits heat, electricity *etc*

conduit (*pronounced* **kon**-dit) *noun* a channel or pipe to carry water, electric wires *etc*

cone *noun* **1** a shape that is round at the bottom and comes to a point **2** the fruit of a pine or fir-tree *etc* an ice-cream cornet

confectioner *noun* someone who makes or sells sweets, cakes *etc*

confectionery *noun* **1** sweets, cakes *etc* **2** the shop or business of a confectioner

confederacy *noun* (*plural*

confederacies) **1** a league, an alliance **2 Confederacy** *US, historical* the union of Southern states in the American Civil War

confederate *adjective* **1** joined together by treaty **2** *US, historical* supporting the Confederacy □ *noun* someone acting in an alliance with others

confederation *noun* a union, a league

confer *verb* **1** to talk together **2** to give, grant: *confer a degree*

> **confer** ⇨ confers, conferring, conferred

conference *noun* a meeting for discussion

confess *verb* to own up, admit to (wrong)

confessed *adjective* admitted, not secret

confession *noun* an admission of wrong-doing

confetti *noun plural* small pieces of coloured paper thrown at weddings or other celebrations

confidant (*pronounced* con-fi-**dont**) *noun* someone trusted with a secret

  ✸ Do not confuse with: **confident**

confidante (*pronounced* con-fi-**dont**) *noun* a female confidant

confide *verb*: **confide in 1** to tell secrets to **2** to hand over to someone's care

confidence *noun* **1** trust, belief **2** self-assurance, boldness **3** something told privately

confidence trick a trick to get money *etc* from someone by first gaining their trust

confident *adjective* **1** very self-assured **2** certain of an outcome: *confident that they would win* □ **confidently** *adverb*

  ✸ Do not confuse with: **confidant** and **confidante**

confidential *adjective* **1** to be kept as a secret: *confidential information* **2** entrusted with secrets

confidentially *adverb* as a secret, privately, in a secretive way

confiding *adjective* trusting

confine *verb* 1 to shut up, imprison 2 to keep within limits

confinement *noun* 1 the state of being confined 2 imprisonment 3 the time of a woman's labour and childbirth

confines (*pronounced* **kon**-fainz) *noun plural* limits

confirm *verb* 1 to make firm, strengthen 2 to make sure 3 to show to be true 4 to admit into full membership of a church

confirmation *noun* 1 a making sure 2 proof 3 the ceremony by which someone is made a full member of a church

confirmed *adjective* settled in a habit *etc*: *a confirmed bachelor*

confiscate *verb* to take away, as a punishment □ **confiscation** *noun*

conflagration *noun* a large, widespread fire

conflict *noun* 1 a struggle, a contest 2 a battle 3 disagreement □ *verb* of statements *etc*: to contradict each other □ **conflicting** *adjective*

confluence *noun* a place where rivers join

conform *verb* to follow the example of most other people in behaviour, dress *etc*

conformation *noun* the way something is made up from different parts; structure: *a horse with excellent conformation* (= physically well-built)

conformity *noun* (*plural* **conformities**) 1 likeness 2 the act of conforming

confound *verb* to puzzle, confuse

confront *verb* 1 to face, meet: *confronted the difficulty* 2 to bring face to face (with): *confronted with the evidence*

confrontation *noun* a situation in which two people or groups are challenging each other openly

confuse *verb* 1 to mix up, disorder 2 to puzzle, bewilder □ **confusion** *noun*

■ **Alternative words**: (meaning 1) muddle, disarrange; (meaning 2) baffle, perplex, confound, disorient, disconcert, discompose

confusing *adjective* puzzling, bewildering

congeal *verb* 1 to become solid, especially by cooling 2 to freeze

congenial *adjective* agreeable, pleasant □ **congenially** *adverb*

congenital *adjective* of a disease: present in someone from birth

conger (*pronounced* **kong**-ger) *noun* a kind of large sea-eel

congested *adjective* 1 overcrowded, especially with traffic 2 clogged 3 of part of the body: too full of blood □ **congestion** *noun*

conglomeration *noun* a heap or collection

congratulate *verb* to express joy to (someone) at their success

congratulations *noun plural* an expression of joy at someone's success

congratulatory *adjective* expressing congratulations

congregate *verb* to come together in a crowd

congregation *noun* a gathering, especially of people in a church

congress *noun* (*plural* **congresses**) 1 a large meeting of people from different countries *etc* for discussion 2 **Congress** the parliament of the United States, consisting of the Senate and the House of Representatives

congruent *adjective* of triangles: exactly matching

conical *adjective* cone-shaped

conifer *noun* a cone-bearing tree □ **coniferous** *adjective*

conjecture *noun* a guess □ *verb* to guess □ **conjectural** *adjective*

conjugal *adjective* of marriage

conjugate *verb* to give the different grammatical parts of (a verb)

conjugation *noun* the different grammatical parts of (a verb)

conjunction *noun* 1 *grammar* a word that joins sentences or phrases, *eg* and, but 2 a union, a combination □ **in conjunction with** together with, acting with

conjure *verb* to perform tricks that seem magical

conjuror or **conjurer** *noun* someone who performs conjuring tricks

conker *noun* 1 a horse-chestnut 2 **conkers** a game in which players try to hit and destroy each other's chestnut, held on the end of a string

con-man *noun* someone who regularly plays confidence tricks on people in order to cheat them out of money

connect *verb* to join or fasten together

connection *noun* 1 something that connects 2 a state of being connected 3 a train, aeroplane *etc* which takes you to the next part of a journey 4 an acquaintance, a friend □ **in connection with** concerning

conning-tower *noun* the place on a warship or submarine from which orders for steering are given

connive *verb*: **connive at** to disregard (a misdeed) □ **connivance** *noun*

connoisseur (*pronounced* kon-*o*-**ser**) *noun* someone with an expert knowledge of a subject: *wine connoisseur*

connotation *noun* 1 a meaning 2 what is suggested by a word in addition to its simple meaning

conquer *verb* 1 to gain by force 2 to overcome: *conquered his fear of heights*

conqueror *noun* someone who conquers

conquest *noun* 1 something won by force 2 an act of conquering

conscience *noun* an inner sense of what is right and wrong

conscientious *adjective* careful and diligent in work *etc* □ **conscientiously** *adverb*

conscious *adjective* 1 aware of yourself and your surroundings; awake 2 aware, knowing 3 deliberate, intentional: *conscious decision* □ **consciously** *adverb*: *If I suggested that, I certainly didn't do it consciously* □ **consciousness** *noun*: *lose consciousness*

conscript *noun* (*pronounced* **kon**-skript) someone obliged by law to serve in the armed forces □ *verb* (*pronounced* kon-**skript**) to compel to serve in the armed forces □ **conscription** *noun*

consecrate *verb* to set apart for sacred use □ **consecration** *noun*

consecutive *adjective* coming in order, one after the other

consensus *noun* an agreement of opinion

Ⓛ Comes from Latin *consensus* meaning 'agreement'

🖝 Do not confuse with: **census**

consent *verb* to agree (to) □ *noun* 1 agreement 2 permission □ **age of consent** the age at which someone is legally able to consent to sexual intercourse

consequence *noun* 1 something that follows as a result 2 importance

consequent *adjective* following as a result □ **consequently** *adverb*: *I am his deputy and consequently shall stand in for him during his absence*

consequential *adjective* 1 following as a result 2 important

conservation *noun* the maintaining of old buildings, the countryside *etc* in an undamaged state

conservationist *noun* someone who encourages and practises conservation

conservative *adjective* 1 resistant to change 2 moderate, not extreme: *conservative estimate* □ *noun* 1 someone of conservative views 2 **Conservative** a supporter of the Conservative Party

Conservative Party a right-wing political party in the UK

conservatory (*pronounced* kon-**ser**-vat-ri) *noun* (*plural* **conservatories**) a glass-house for plants, or a similar room used as a lounge, attached to and entered from, the house

conserve *verb* to keep from being wasted or lost; preserve

consider *verb* 1 to think about carefully 2 to think of as, regard as 3 to pay attention to the wishes of (someone)

considerable *adjective* fairly large, substantial

considerably *adverb* substantially,

quite a lot: *He received considerably more money than was previously thought*

considerate *adjective* taking others' wishes into account; thoughtful

consideration *noun* **1** serious thought **2** thoughtfulness for others **3** a small payment

considering *preposition* taking into account: *considering your age*

consign (*pronounced* kon-**sain**) *verb* to give into the care of

consignment (*pronounced* kon-**sain**-ment) *noun* a load, *eg* of goods

consist *verb* to be made up (of)

☛ Do not confuse with: **comprise**. You need the word 'of' after **consist**, but not after **comprise**. You say *the exam **consists of** three parts*, but *the exam **comprises** three parts*

consistency *noun* (*plural* **consistencies**) **1** thickness, firmness **2** the quality of always being the same

consistent *adjective* **1** not changing, regular **2** of statements *etc*: not contradicting each other □ **consistently** *adverb*

consolation *noun* something that makes trouble *etc* more easy to bear

console *verb* to comfort, cheer up

consolidate *verb* **1** to make or become strong **2** to unite □ **consolidation** *noun*

consonant *noun* a letter of the alphabet that is not a vowel, *eg* b, c, d

consort *noun* (*pronounced* **kon**-sawt)**1** a husband or wife **2** a companion □ *verb* (*pronounced* kon-**sawt**): **consort with** to keep company with

☛ Do not confuse with: **concert**

conspicuous *adjective* clearly seen, noticeable □ **conspicuously** *adverb*

conspiracy *noun* (*plural* **conspiracies**) a plot by a group of people

conspirator *noun* someone who takes part in a conspiracy

conspire *verb* to plan or plot together

constable *noun* **1** a policeman **2** *historical* a high officer of state

constabulary *noun* the police force

constant *adjective* **1** never stopping **2** never changing **3** faithful □ **constancy** *noun*

constantly *adverb* always

constellation *noun* a group of stars

consternation *noun* dismay, astonishment

constipate *verb* to cause constipation in

constipation *noun* sluggish working of the bowels

constituency *noun* (*plural* **constituencies**) **1** a district which has a member of parliament **2** the voters in such a district

constituent *adjective* making or forming □ *noun* **1** a necessary part **2** a voter in a constituency

constitute *verb* **1** to step up, establish **2** to form, make up **3** to be the equivalent of: *this action constitutes a crime*

constitution *noun* **1** the way in which something is made up **2** the natural condition of a body in terms of health *etc*: *a weak constitution* **3** a set of laws or rules governing a country or organization

constitutional *adjective* of a constitution □ *noun* a short walk for the sake of your health

constrain *verb* to force to act in a certain way

constraint *noun* **1** compulsion, force **2** restraint, repression

constrict *verb* **1** to press together tightly **2** to surround and squeeze

construct *verb* to build, make

construction *noun* **1** the act of constructing **2** something built **3** the arrangement of words in a sentence **4** meaning

constructive *adjective* **1** of construction **2** helping to improve: *constructive criticism* □ **constructively** *adverb* (meaning 2)

consul *noun* **1** someone who looks after their country's affairs in a foreign country **2** *historical* a chief ruler in ancient Rome □ **consular** *adjective*

consulate *noun* **1** the official residence

consult *verb* to seek advice or information from

consultant *noun* **1** someone who gives professional or expert advice **2** the senior grade of hospital doctor

consultation *noun* **1** the activity of looking in *eg* reference books for information **2** a meeting with someone to exchange ideas and opinions **3** discussion

consulting room a room where a doctor sees patients

consume *verb* **1** to eat up **2** to use (up) **3** to destroy

consumer *noun* someone who buys, eats or uses goods

consummate *verb* (*pronounced* kon-sum-eit or **kon**-syoo-meit) **1** to complete **2** to make (marriage) legally complete by sexual intercourse □ *adjective* (*pronounced* **kon**-syoo-mat or kon-**sum**-at) complete, perfect

consumption *noun* **1** the act of consuming **2** an amount consumed **3** *old* tuberculosis

cont or **contd** *abbreviation* continued

contact *noun* **1** touch **2** meeting, communication **3** an acquaintance; someone who can be of help: *business contact* **4** someone who has been with someone suffering from an infectious disease □ *verb* to get into contact with

contact lens a plastic lens worn in contact with the eyeball instead of spectacles

contagious *adjective* of disease: spreading from person to person, especially by touch

contain *verb* **1** to hold or have inside **2** to hold back: *couldn't contain her anger*

container *noun* a box, tin, jar *etc* for holding anything

contaminate *verb* to make impure or dirty □ **contamination** *noun*

contd *another spelling of* **cont**

contemplate (*pronounced* **kon**-temp-leit) *verb* **1** to look at or think about attentively **2** to intend: *contemplating suicide* □ **contemplation** *noun*

contemplative (*pronounced* kon-temp-lat-iv) *adjective* quiet and absorbed in thought: *in contemplative mood*

contemporary *adjective* belonging to the same time □ *noun* someone of roughly the same age as yourself

contempt *noun* complete lack of respect; scorn □ **contempt of court** deliberate disobedience to and disrespect for the law and those who carry it out

contemptible *adjective* deserving scorn, worthless

> 🖋 Do not confuse: **contemptible** and **contemptuous**.
> **Contemptible** is formed from **contempt** + **-ible** ⇨ able to be scorned, worthy of scorn. Use it in phrases like *a contemptible little tell-tale*

contemptuous *adjective* scornful

> **Contemptuous** means 'full of contempt' (for something or someone). Use it in phrases like *a contemptuous laugh* or *he was contemptuous of my achievement*

contend *verb* **1** to struggle against **2** to hold firmly to a belief; maintain (that)

content (*pronounced* kon-**tent**) *adjective* happy, satisfied □ *noun* happiness, satisfaction □ *verb* to make happy, satisfy □ *noun* **contents** (*pronounced* **kon**-tents) that which is contained in anything

contented *adjective* happy, content

contention *noun* **1** an opinion strongly held **2** a quarrel, a dispute

contentious *adjective* quarrelsome

contentment *noun* happiness, content

contest *verb* to fight for, argue against □ *noun* a fight, a competition

contestant *noun* a participant in a contest

context *noun* **1** the place in a book *etc* to which a certain part belongs **2** the background of an event, remark *etc*

contiguous *adjective* touching, close □ **contiguity** *noun*

continent *noun* one of the five large divisions of the earth's land surface (Europe, Asia, Africa, Australia, America) □ **the Continent** *Brit* the mainland of Europe

continental *adjective* 1 of a continent 2 *Brit* European

contingency *noun* (*plural* **contingencies**) a chance happening

contingency plan a plan of action in case something does not happen as expected

contingent *adjective* depending (on) □ *noun* a group, especially of soldiers

continual *adjective* happening again and again at close intervals

> ✎ Do not confuse with:
> **continuous**. Something which is **continual** happens often, but there are short breaks when it is not happening. Something which is **continuous** happens all the time without stopping. So you could talk about, for example, *continual interruptions*, but *the continuous lapping of waves on a beach*

continually *adverb* all the time, repeatedly

continuation *noun* 1 the act of continuing 2 a part that continues, an extension

continue *verb* to keep on, go on (doing something)

continuity *noun* the state of having no gaps or breaks

continuous *adjective* coming one after the other or in a steady stream without any gap or break □ **continuously** *adverb*

> ✎ Do not confuse with: **continual**

■ **Alternative words**: consecutive, constant, unceasing, unremitting

contort *verb* to twist or turn violently

contortion *noun* a violent twisting

contortionist *noun* someone who can twist their body into strange shapes

contour *noun* (often **contours**) outline, shape

contour line a line drawn on a map

through points all at the same height above sea-level

contra- *see* **counter-**

contraband *noun* 1 goods legally forbidden to be brought into a country 2 smuggled goods

contraception *noun* the prevention of conceiving children

contraceptive *adjective* used to prevent the conceiving of children □ *noun* a contraceptive device or drug

contract *verb* (*pronounced* kon-**trakt**) 1 to become or make smaller 2 to bargain for 3 to promise in writing □ *noun* (*pronounced* **kon**-trakt) a written agreement

contraction *noun* 1 a shortening 2 a shortened form of a word 3 a muscle spasm, *eg* during childbirth

contractor *noun* someone who promises to do work, or supply goods, at an arranged price

contradict *verb* to say the opposite of; deny □ **contradiction** *noun*

contradictory *adjective* 1 contradicting something 2 of two pieces of information: contradicting each other: *receive contradictory advice from two doctors*

contralto *noun* (*plural* **contraltos**) the lowest singing voice in women

contraption *noun* a machine, a device

contrapuntal (from **counterpoint**) *adjective, music* involving the combination of two or more melodies to make a piece of music: *Bach's music tends to be contrapuntal*

contrary[1] (*pronounced* **kon**-tra-ri) *adjective* opposite □ *noun* the opposite □ **on the contrary** just the opposite

contrary[2] (*pronounced* kon-**treir**-ri) *adjective* always doing or saying the opposite, perverse

contrast *verb* 1 to compare so as to show differences 2 to show a marked difference from □ *noun* a difference between (two) things

contravene *verb* to break (a law *etc*) □ **contravention** *noun*

contretemps (*pronounced* kon-tre-tom) *noun* a mishap at an awkward moment

contribute *verb* **1** to give (money, help *etc*) along with others **2** to supply (articles *etc*) for a publication **3** to help to cause: *contributed to a nervous breakdown*

contribution *noun* something given or supplied □ **make a contribution** to give or supply something, play a part

contributor *noun* a person or thing that contributes

contributory *adjective* contributing to, or playing a part in some result: *Overwork was not the sole cause of her breakdown, but it was a contributory factor*

con-trick *noun* a confidence trick

contrite *adjective* very sorry for having done wrong □ **contrition** *noun*

contrivance *noun* an act of contriving; an invention

contrive *verb* **1** to plan **2** to bring about, manage: *contrived to be out of the office*

contro- *see* **counter-**

control *noun* **1** authority to rule, manage, restrain *etc* **2** (often **controls**) means by which a driver keeps a machine powered or guided □ *verb* **1** to exercise control over **2** to have power over □ **controlled** *adjective* □ **controller** *noun*

control tower an airport building from which landing and take-off instructions are given

controversial *adjective* likely to cause argument

controversy *noun* (*plural* **controversies**) an argument, a disagreement

conundrum *noun* a riddle, a question

conurbation *noun* a group of towns forming a single built-up area

convalesce *verb* to recover health gradually after being ill

convalescence *noun* a gradual return to health and strength

convalescent *noun* someone convalescing from illness

convection *noun* the spreading of heat by movement of heated air or water

convector *noun* a heater which works by convection

convene *verb* to call or come together

convener *noun* **1** someone who calls a meeting **2** the chairman or chairwoman of a committee

convenience *noun* **1** suitableness, handiness **2** a means of giving ease or comfort **3** *informal* a public lavatory □ **at your convenience** when it suits you best

convenient *adjective* easy to reach or use, handy □ **conveniently** *adverb*

■ **Alternative words**: accessible, commodious, beneficial, opportune, timely

convent *noun* a building accommodating an order of nuns

convention *noun* **1** a way of behaving that has become usual, a custom **2** a large meeting, an assembly **3** a treaty or agreement

conventional *adjective* **1** done by habit or custom **2** having traditional attitudes and behaviour □ **conventionally** *adverb*

converge *verb* to come together, meet at a point □ **convergence** *noun* □ **convergent** *adjective*

conversation *noun* talk, exchange of ideas, news *etc*

conversational *adjective* **1** of conversation **2** talkative

converse¹ (*pronounced* kon-**vers**) *verb* to talk □ *noun* conversation

converse² (*pronounced* **kon**-vers) *noun* the opposite □ *adjective* opposite

convert *verb* (*pronounced* kon-**vert**) **1** to change (from one thing into another) **2** to turn from one religion to another □ *noun* (*pronounced* **kon**-vert) someone who has been converted □ **conversion** *noun*

convertible *adjective* able to be changed from one thing to another □ *noun* a car with a folding roof

convex *adjective* curved on the outside (*contrasted with*: **concave**) □ **convexity** *noun* (*plural* **convexities**)

convey *verb* **1** to carry, transport **2** to send **3** *law* to hand over: *convey property*

conveyance *noun* **1** the act of conveying **2** a vehicle

conveyancing *noun*, *law* the process of handing over from one party to another the legal ownership of property

conveyor or **conveyor belt** *noun* an endless moving mechanism for conveying articles, especially in a factory

convict *verb* (*pronounced* kon-**vikt**) to declare or prove that someone is guilty □ *noun* (*pronounced* **kon**-vikt) someone found guilty of a crime and sent to prison

⇥ Opposite: (verb) acquit

conviction *noun* **1** the passing of a guilty sentence on someone in court **2** a strong belief

⇥ Opposite: (meaning 1) acquittal

convince *verb* **1** to make (someone) believe that something is true **2** to persuade (someone) by showing

convivial *adjective* jolly, festive □ **conviviality** *noun*

convoy *verb* to go along with and protect □ *noun* **1** merchant ships protected by warships **2** a line of army lorries with armed guard

convulse *verb* to cause to shake violently: *convulsed with laughter*

convulsion *noun* **1** a sudden stiffening or jerking of the muscles **2** a violent disturbance □ **convulsive** *adjective*

coo *noun* a sound like that of a dove □ *verb* make this sound

cook *verb* **1** to prepare (food) by heating **2** *informal* to alter (accounts *etc*) dishonestly □ *noun* someone who cooks and prepares food

cooker *noun* **1** a stove for cooking **2** an apple *etc* used in cooking, not for eating raw

cookery *noun* the art of cooking

cool *adjective* **1** slightly cold **2** calm, not excited **3** *informal* acceptable **4** *informal* good, fashionable □ *verb* make

or grow cool; calm □ **coolness** *noun* (adjective, meanings 1 and 2)

coolly *adjective* **1** in a calm way **2** in a slightly unfriendly way

coop *noun* a box or cage for hens *etc* □ *verb* to shut (up) as in a coop

co-op *see* **cooperative society**

cooper *noun* someone who makes barrels

cooperate *verb* to work or act together

cooperation *noun* **1** a working together **2** willingness to act together

cooperative *noun* a business or farm *etc* owned by the workers

cooperative society or **co-op** a trading organization in which the profits are shared among members

co-opt *verb* to choose (someone) to join a committee or other body

co-ordinate *verb* to make things fit in or work smoothly together

co-ordination *noun* **1** the activity or skill of co-ordinating things **2** the ability to move and use the different parts of your body smoothly together: *You must have good co-ordination if you want to be a dancer*

coot *noun* a water-bird with a white spot on the forehead

cop *noun*, *slang* a police officer □ *verb* catch, seize □ **cop it** to land in trouble □ **cop out** to avoid responsibility

cop *verb* ⇨ cop**s**, cop**ping**, cop**ped**

cope *verb* to struggle or deal successfully (with), manage

coping *noun* the top layer of stone in a wall

coping-stone *noun* the top stone of a wall

copious *adjective* plentiful □ **copiously** *adjective*

copper *noun* **1** a hard reddish-brown metal **2** a reddish-brown colour **3** a coin made from copper **4** a large vessel made of copper, for boiling water

copperplate *noun* a style of very fine and regular handwriting

copra *noun* the dried kernel of the coconut, yielding coconut oil

copse or **coppice** *noun* a wood of low-growing trees

copy *noun* (*plural* **copies**) **1** an imitation **2** a print or reproduction of a picture *etc* **3** an individual example of a certain book *etc* □ *verb* **1** to make a copy of **2** to imitate

copyright *noun* the right of one person or body to publish a book, perform a play, print music *etc* □ *adjective* of or protected by the law of copyright

coquette *noun* a flirtatious woman

coquettish *adjective* flirtatious

cor- *see* **co-**

coral *noun* a hard substance made from the skeletons of a tiny animal

coral reef a rock-like mass of coral built up gradually from the sea-bed

cord *noun* **1** thin rope or strong string **2** a thick strand of anything
① Comes from French *corde* meaning 'a rope'

 Do not confuse with: **chord**

cordial *adjective* cheery, friendly □ *noun* a refreshing drink □ **cordiality** *noun*

cordon *noun* a line of guards, police *etc* to keep people back

cordon bleu *adjective* of a cook or cooking: first-class, excellent

Literally 'blue ribbon' in French, after the ribbon worn by the Knights of the Holy Ghost

corduroy *noun* a ribbed cotton cloth resembling velvet

core *noun* the inner part of anything, especially fruit □ *verb* to take out the core of (fruit)

corespondent (*pronounced* coh-res-pon-dent) *noun* a man or woman charged with having committed adultery with a wife or husband (the **respondent**)
① Comes from prefix *co-*, and *respondent*

 Do not confuse with: **correspondent**

corgi *noun* a breed of short-legged dog

cork *noun* **1** the outer bark of a type of oak found in southern Europe *etc* **2** a stopper for a bottle *etc* made of cork □ *adjective* made of cork □ *verb* to plug or stop up with a cork

corkscrew *noun* a tool with a screw-like spike for taking out corks □ *adjective* shaped like a corkscrew

corm *noun* the bulb-like underground stem of certain plants

cormorant *noun* a type of big sea-bird

corn *noun* **1** wheat, oats or maize **2** a small lump of hard skin, especially on a toe

cornea *noun* the transparent covering of the eyeball

corned beef salted tinned beef

corner *noun* **1** the point where two walls, roads *etc* meet **2** a small secluded place **3** *informal* a difficult situation □ *verb* to force into a position from which there is no escape

cornerstone *noun* **1** the stone at the corner of a building's foundations **2** something upon which much depends

cornet *noun* **1** a musical instrument like a small trumpet **2** an ice-cream in a cone-shaped wafer

cornflour *noun* finely ground maize flour

cornflower *noun* a type of plant, with a blue flower

cornice *noun* an ornamental border round a ceiling

coronary *noun* (*plural* **coronaries**) (*short for* **coronary thrombosis**) a heart disease caused by blockage of one of the arteries supplying the heart

coronation *noun* the crowning of a king or queen

coroner *noun* a government officer who holds inquiries into the causes of sudden or accidental deaths

coronet *noun* **1** a small crown **2** a crown-like head-dress

corporal[1] *noun* the rank next below sergeant in the British army

corporal[2] *adjective* of the body

corporal punishment physical punishment by beating

corporate *adjective* of or forming a whole, united

corporation *noun* a body of people acting as one for administrative or business purposes

corps (*pronounced* kawr) *noun* (*plural* **corps** - *pronounced* kawz) **1** a division of an army **2** an organized group

☛ Do not confuse: **corps** and **corpse**

corpse *noun* a dead body

corpulence *noun* obesity, fatness

corpulent *adjective* fat

corpus *noun* (*plural* **corpora**) a collection of writing *etc*

corpuscle *noun* **1** a very small particle **2** a blood cell, red or white □ **corpuscular** *adjective*

corral *noun*, *US* a fenced enclosure for animals □ *verb* enclose, pen

corral *verb* ⇨ corral**s**, corral**ling**, corral**led**

correct *verb* **1** to remove errors from **2** to set right **3** to punish □ *adjective* **1** having no errors **2** true **3** suitable and acceptable

■ **Alternative words**: (verb, meaning 1) emend; (verb, meaning 2) rectify, remedy, redress, amend

correction *noun* **1** the putting right of a mistake **2** punishment

corrective *adjective* with the purpose of putting right some fault or of punishing someone

correspond *verb* **1** to write letters to **2** to be similar (to), match

correspondence *noun* **1** letters **2** likeness, similarity

correspondent *noun* **1** someone who writes letters **2** someone who contributes reports to a newspaper *etc*
① Comes from Latin *cor* meaning 'with', and *respondere* meaning 'to answer'

☛ Do not confuse with: **corespondent**

corridor *noun* a passageway

corroborate *verb* to give evidence which strengthens evidence already given □ **corroboration** *noun*
□ **corroborative** *adjective*
① Comes from Latin *cor-* giving emphasis, and *roborare* meaning 'to make strong'

☛ Do not confuse with: **collaborate**

corrode *verb* **1** to rust **2** to eat away at, erode □ **corrosion** *noun*

corrosive *adjective* **1** able to destroy or wear away materials such as metal by reacting chemically with them: *Nitric acid is highly corrosive* **2** having the effect of gradually wearing down or destroying something

corrugated *adjective* folded or shaped into ridges: *corrugated iron*

corrupt *verb* **1** to make evil or rotten **2** to make dishonest, bribe □ *adjective* **1** dishonest, taking bribes **2** bad, rotten

corruptible *adjective* able to be corrupted, usually because of being innocent or naive

corruption *noun* **1** dishonesty, often involving the taking of bribes **2** the process of taking away someone's innocence or goodness: *corruption of the mind* **3** the unconscious changing of a word in speech or text, or a word which has changed in this way: *'Yeah' is a corruption of the word 'yes'*

corsair *noun*, *old* **1** a pirate **2** a pirate-ship

corset *noun* a tight-fitting under-garment to support the body

cortège (*pronounced* kaw-**tesz**) *noun* a funeral procession

cosh *noun* (*plural* **coshes**) a short heavy stick □ *verb* to hit with a cosh

cosmetic *noun* something designed to improve the appearance, especially of the face □ *adjective* **1** applied as a cosmetic **2** superficial, for appearances only

cosmic *adjective* **1** of the universe or outer space **2** *informal* excellent

cosmonaut *noun*, *historical* an astronaut of the former USSR

cosmopolitan *adjective* **1** including people from many countries **2** familiar with, or comfortable in, many different countries

cosmos noun the universe

cosset verb to treat with too much kindness, pamper

cost verb 1 to be priced at 2 to cause the loss of: *the war cost many lives* □ noun what must be spent or suffered in order to get something

cost verb ⇨ costs, costing, cost

costly adjective high-priced, valuable □ **costliness** noun

costume noun 1 a set of clothes 2 clothes to wear in a play 3 fancy dress 4 a swim-suit

costume jewellery inexpensive, imitation jewellery

cosy adjective warm and comfortable □ noun (plural **cosies**) a covering to keep a teapot etc warm

cot noun 1 a small high-sided bed for children 2 US a small collapsible bed; a camp bed

cot death the sudden unexplained death in sleep of an apparently healthy baby

cottage noun a small house, especially in the countryside or a village

cottage cheese a soft, white cheese made from skimmed milk

cottager noun someone who lives in a cottage

cotton noun 1 a soft fluffy substance obtained from the seeds of the cotton plant 2 cloth made of cotton □ adjective made of cotton

cottonwool noun cotton in a fluffy state, used for wiping or absorbing

couch noun (plural **couches**) a sofa □ verb to express verbally: *couched in archaic language*

couch grass a kind of grass, a troublesome weed

couch potato someone who spends their free time watching TV etc

cougar noun, US the puma

cough noun a noisy effort of the lungs to throw out air and harmful matter from the throat □ verb to make this effort

could verb 1 the form of the verb **can** used to express a condition: *he could afford it if he tried/ I could understand a small mistake, but this is ridiculous* 2 past form of the verb **can**
ⓘ Comes from Old English *cuthe* meaning 'was able'

council noun a group of people elected to discuss or give advice about policy, government etc
ⓘ Comes from Latin *concilium* meaning 'a calling together'
☛ Do not confuse with: **counsel**

councillor noun a member of a council

counsel noun 1 advice 2 US someone who gives legal advice; a lawyer □ verb to give advice to

counsel verb ⇨ counsels, counselling, counselled
ⓘ Comes from Latin *consilium* meaning 'advice'
☛ Do not confuse with: **council**

counsellor noun someone who gives advice, or who is involved in counselling

count¹ verb 1 to find the total number of, add up 2 to say numbers in order (1, 2, 3 etc) 3 to think, consider: *count yourself lucky!* □ noun 1 the act of counting 2 the number counted, eg of votes at an election 3 a charge, an accusation 4 a point being considered □ **count on** to rely on, depend on

count² noun a nobleman in certain countries

countenance noun 1 the face 2 the expression on someone's face □ verb to allow, encourage

counter¹ verb to answer or oppose (a move, act etc) by another □ adverb in the opposite direction □ adjective opposed; opposite

counter² noun 1 a token used in counting 2 a small plastic disc used in ludo etc 3 a table across which payments are made in a shop

counter- also contra-, contro- prefix 1 against, opposing: *counter-argument* 2 opposite
ⓘ Comes from Latin *contra* meaning 'against'

counteract verb to block or defeat (an action) by doing the opposite

counterattack *noun* an attack made by the defenders upon an attacking enemy □ *verb* to launch a counterattack

counterattraction *noun* something which draws away the attention from something else

countercharge *noun* a charge against someone who has accused you □ *verb* to make a countercharge against

counterfeit *adjective* **1** not genuine, not real **2** made in imitation for criminal purposes: *counterfeit money* □ *verb* to make a copy of

counterfoil *noun* a part of a cheque, postal order *etc* kept by the payer or sender

countermand *verb* to give an order which goes against one already given

counterpane *noun* a top cover for a bed

counterpart *noun* someone or something which is just like or which corresponds to another person or thing

counterpoint *noun* the combining of two or more melodies to make a piece of music

counterpoise *noun* a weight which balances another weight

countersign *verb* to sign your name after someone else's signature to show that a document is genuine

counter-tenor *noun* the highest alto male voice

countess *noun* **1** a woman of the same rank as a count or earl **2** the wife or widow of a count or earl

countless *adjective* too many to be counted, very many

country *noun* (*plural* **countries**) **1** a nation **2** a land under one government **3** the land in which someone lives **4** a district which is not in a town or city **5** an area or stretch of land □ *adjective* belonging to the country
ⓘ Comes from Old French *contrée* meaning 'a stretch of land'

countryside *noun* the parts of a country other than towns and cities

county *noun* (*plural* **counties**) a division of a country

coup (*pronounced* koo) *noun* **1** a sudden outstandingly successful move or act **2** a coup d'état

coup d'état (*pronounced* koo dei-**tah**) a sudden and violent change in government

couple *noun* **1** a pair, two of a kind together **2** a husband and wife □ *verb* to join together

couplet *noun* two lines of rhyming verse

coupling *noun* a link for joining railway carriages *etc*

coupon *noun* a piece of paper which may be exchanged for goods or money

courage *noun* bravery, lack of fear

courageous *adjective* brave, fearless

courgette *noun* a type of small marrow

courier *noun* **1** someone who acts as guide for tourists **2** a messenger

course *noun* **1** a path in which anything moves **2** movement from point to point **3** a track along which athletes *etc* run **4** a direction to be followed: *the ship held its course* **5** line of action: *the best course to follow* **6** a part of a meal **7** a number of things following each other: *a course of twelve lectures* **8** one of the rows of bricks in a wall □ *verb* **1** to move quickly **2** to hunt □ **in due course** after a while, in its proper time □ **in the course of** during
ⓘ Comes from French *cours* meaning 'course', 'lesson' or 'currency'

coursing *noun* the hunting of hares with greyhounds

court *noun* **1** an open space surrounded by houses **2** an area marked out for playing tennis *etc* **3** the people who attend a monarch *etc* **4** a royal residence **5** a room or building where legal cases are heard or tried □ *verb* **1** to woo as a potential lover **2** to try to gain: *courting her affections* **3** to come near to achieving: *courting disaster*

courteous *adjective* polite; obliging □ **courteously** *adverb*

courtesy *noun* politeness

courtier *noun* a member of a royal court

courtly *adjective* having fine manners

court-martial noun (plural **courts-martial**) an internal court held to try those who break navy or army laws □ verb to try in a court-martial

courtship noun the act or time of courting or wooing

courtyard noun a court or enclosed space beside a house

cousin noun the son or daughter of an uncle or aunt

cove noun a small inlet on the sea coast; a bay

coven noun a gathering of witches

covenant noun an important agreement between people to do or not to do something

cover verb 1 to put or spread something on or over 2 to hide 3 to stretch over: *the hills were covered with heather/ my diary covers three years* 4 to include, deal with: *covering the news story* 5 to be enough for: *five pounds should cover the cost* 6 to travel over: *covering 3 kilometres a day* 7 to point a weapon at: *had the gangster covered* □ noun something that covers, hides or protects □ **cover up 1** to cover completely **2** to conceal deliberately

coverage noun 1 an area covered 2 the extent of news covered by a newspaper *etc* 3 the amount of protection given by an insurance policy

coverlet noun a bed cover
🕑 Comes from French *couvrir* meaning 'to cover', and *lit* meaning 'bed'

covert adjective secret, not done openly □ noun a hiding place for animals or birds when hunted

cover-up noun a deliberate concealment, especially by people in authority

covet verb to desire eagerly, especially something belonging to another person

covetous adjective having a tendency to desire things, especially things which belong to other people □ **covetously** adverb

covey noun (plural **coveys**) a flock of birds, especially partridges

cow noun 1 the female of various types of ox, bred by humans for giving milk

2 the female of an elephant, whale *etc* □ verb to frighten, subdue

coward noun someone who has no courage and shows fear easily □ **cowardly** adjective

cowardice noun lack of courage

cowboy noun a man who works with cattle on a ranch

cowed adjective frightened, subdued

cower verb to crouch down or shrink back through fear

cowgirl noun a woman who works with cattle on a ranch

cowherd noun someone who looks after cows

cowl noun 1 a hood, especially that of a monk 2 a cover for a chimney

cowslip noun a yellow wild flower

cox noun (pl **coxes**) the person who steers a racing crew

coxcomb noun 1 historical a head-covering notched like a cock's comb, worn by a jester 2 a vain or conceited person

coxswain noun 1 someone who steers a boat 2 an officer in charge of a boat and crew

coy adjective too modest or shy

coyote (pronounced kai-oh-ti) noun (plural **coyote** or **coyotes**) a type of small North American wolf

coypu (pronounced **koi**-poo) noun a large, beaverlike animal living in rivers and marshes

crab noun 1 a sea creature with a shell and five pairs of legs, the first pair of which have large claws 2 informal **crabs** pubic lice

crab apple a type of small, bitter apple

crabbed (pronounced **krab**-id) adjective bad-tempered

crabwise adverb sideways like a crab

crack verb 1 to (cause to) make a sharp, sudden sound 2 to break partly without falling to pieces 3 to break into (a safe) 4 to decipher (a code) 5 to break open (a nut) 6 to make (a joke) □ noun 1 a sharp sound 2 a split, a break 3 a narrow opening 4 informal a sharp, witty remark 5 informal a pure form of cocaine □ *adjective* excellent: *a crack tennis player* □ **crack up** to go to pieces, collapse

cracked 1 split, damaged 2 mad, crazy

cracker *noun* 1 a hollow paper tube containing a small gift, which breaks with a bang when the ends are pulled 2 a thin, crisp biscuit 3 *informal* something excellent: *a cracker of a story*

crackle *verb* to make a continuous cracking noise

crackling *noun* 1 a cracking sound 2 the rind or outer skin of roast pork

cradle *noun* 1 a baby's bed, especially one which can be rocked 2 a frame under a ship that is being built

craft *noun* 1 a trade, a skill 2 a boat, a small ship 3 slyness, cunning

craftsman *noun* a man who works at a trade, especially with his hands

craftswoman *noun* a woman who works at a trade, especially with her hands

craftworker *noun* a craftsman or craftswoman

crafty *adjective* cunning, sly □ **craftily** *adverb*

crag *noun* a rough steep rock

craggy *adjective* 1 rocky 2 of a face: well-marked, lined

cram *verb* 1 to fill full, stuff 2 to learn up facts for an examination in a short time

cram ⇨ cram*s*, cram*ming*, cram*med*

cramp *noun* 1 a painful stiffening of the muscles 2 **cramps** an acute stomach pain □ *verb* 1 to confine in too small a space 2 to hinder, restrict

cramped *adjective* 1 without enough room 2 of handwriting: small and closely-written

cranberry *noun* (*plural* **cranberries**) a type of red, sour berry

crane *noun* 1 a large wading bird with long legs, neck and bill 2 a machine for lifting heavy weights □ *verb* to stretch out (the neck) to see round or over something

cranium *noun* (*plural* **crania** or **craniums**) the skull

crank *noun* 1 a handle for turning an axle 2 a lever which converts a horizontal movement into a rotating one 3 an eccentric □ *verb* to start (an engine) with a crank

cranky *adjective* 1 odd, eccentric 2 cross, irritable

cranny *noun* (*plural* **crannies**) a small opening or crack

crape *another spelling of* **crêpe**

crash *noun* (*plural* **crashes**) 1 a noise of heavy things breaking or banging together 2 a collision causing damage, *eg* between vehicles 3 the failure of a business □ *adjective* short but intensive: *crash course in French* □ *verb* 1 to be involved in a crash 2 of a business: to fail 3 of a computer program: to break down, fail 4 *informal* to attend (a party) uninvited (*also called* **gatecrash**)

crash-helmet *noun* a protective covering for the head worn by motor-cyclists *etc*

crash-land *verb* to land (an aircraft) in an emergency, causing some structural damage □ **crash-landing** *noun*

crass *adjective* stupid □ **crassly** *adverb*

crate *noun* a container for carrying goods, often made of wooden slats

crater *noun* 1 the bowl-shaped mouth of a volcano 2 a hole made by an explosion

cravat (*pronounced* kra-**vat**) *noun* a scarf worn in place of a tie

From a French word for 'Croat', because of the linen neckbands worn by 17th-century Croatian soldiers

craven *adjective, old* cowardly

crawl *verb* 1 to move on hands and knees 2 to move slowly 3 to be covered (with): *crawling with wasps* 4 to be obsequious, fawn □ *noun* 1 the act of crawling 2 a swimming stroke of kicking the feet and alternating the arms

crawler *noun, informal* an obsequious, fawning person

crayon *noun* a coloured pencil or stick for drawing

craze noun a temporary fashion or enthusiasm

crazy adjective mad, unreasonable □ **crazily** adverb

■ **Alternative words**: mad, deranged, crazed, silly, preposterous, impracticable, wild

crazy patchwork patchwork made with irregular shapes of fabric

crazy paving paving with stones of irregular shape

creak verb to make a sharp, grating sound like a hinge in need of oiling

cream noun 1 the fatty substance which forms on milk 2 something like this in texture: *cleansing cream/ shaving cream* 3 the best part: *cream of society* □ verb 1 to take the cream from 2 to take away (the best part)

creamy adjective full of or like cream

crease noun 1 a mark made by folding 2 *cricket* a line showing the position of a batsman and bowler □ verb 1 to make creases in 2 to become creased

create verb 1 to bring into being; make 2 *informal* to make a fuss

creation noun 1 the act of creating 2 something created

creative adjective having the ability to create, artistic □ **creativity** noun

creator noun the person who has created something □ **the Creator** God

creature noun an animal or person

crèche noun a nursery for children

credentials noun plural documents carried as proof of identity, character etc

credible adjective able to be believed □ **credibility** noun

👉 Do not confuse with: **credulous**

credit noun 1 recognition of good qualities, achievements *etc*: *give him credit for some common sense* 2 good qualities 3 a source of honour: *a credit to the family* 4 trustworthiness in ability to pay for goods 5 the sale of goods to be paid for later 6 the side of an account on which payments received are entered 7 a sum of money in a bank account 8 belief, trust 9 **credits** the naming of people who have helped in a film *etc* □ verb 1 to believe 2 to enter on the credit side of an account 3 **credit someone with** to believe them to have: *I credited him with more sense*

creditable adjective bringing honour or good reputation to

creditably adverb in a way which can be approved of or admired

credit card a card allowing the holder to pay for purchased articles at a later date

creditor noun someone to whom money is due

credulity noun willingness to believe things which may be untrue: *They took advantage of your credulity*

credulous adjective believing too easily

👉 Do not confuse with: **credible**

creed noun a belief, especially a religious one

creek noun 1 a small inlet or bay on the sea coast 2 a short river

creep verb 1 to move slowly and silently 2 to move with the body close to the ground 3 to shiver with fear or disgust: *makes your flesh creep* 4 of a plant: to grow along the ground or up a wall □ noun 1 a move in a creeping way 2 *informal* an unpleasant person □ **the creeps** *informal* a feeling of disgust or fear □ **creep up on** to approach silently from behind

creep verb ⇨ creeps, creeping, crept

creeper noun a plant growing along the ground or up a wall

creepy adjective unsettlingly sinister

cremate verb to burn (a dead body) □ **cremation** noun

crematorium noun a place where dead bodies are burnt

creosote noun an oily liquid made from wood tar, used to keep wood from rotting

crêpe noun 1 a type of fine, crinkly material 2 a thin pancake

crêpe paper paper with a crinkled appearance

crept past form of **creep**

crescendo *noun* **1** a musical passage of increasing loudness **2** a climax

crescent *adjective* shaped like the new or old moon; curved □ *noun* **1** something in a curved shape **2** a curved road or street

cress *noun* a plant with small, slightly bitter-tasting leaves, used in salads

crest *noun* **1** a tuft on the head of a cock or other bird **2** the top of a hill, wave *etc* **3** feathers on top of a helmet **4** a badge

crestfallen *adjective* down-hearted, discouraged

cretin *noun, informal* an idiot, a fool

crevasse (*pronounced* kre-**vas**) *noun* a deep split in snow or ice

☛ Do not confuse: **crevasse** and **crevice**

crevice (*pronounced* **krev**-is) *noun* a crack, a narrow opening

crew[1] *noun* **1** the people who man a ship, aircraft *etc* **2** a gang, a mob □ *verb* to act as a member of a crew

crew[2] *past form of* **crow**

crewcut *noun* an extremely short hairstyle

crib *noun* **1** a manger **2** a child's bed **3** a ready-made translation of a school text *etc* □ *verb* to copy someone else's work

crib *verb* ⇨ crib**s**, crib**b**ing, crib**b**ed

cribbage *noun* a type of card game in which the score is kept with a pegged board

crick *noun* a sharp pain, especially in the neck □ *verb* to produce a crick in

cricket *noun* **1** a game played with bats, ball and wickets, between two sides of 11 each **2** an insect similar to a grasshopper

cricketer *noun* someone who plays cricket

cried *past form of* **cry**

crime *noun* an act or deed which is against the law

criminal *adjective* **1** forbidden by law **2** very wrong □ *noun* someone guilty of a crime

crimson *noun* a deep red colour □ *adjective* of this colour

cringe *verb* **1** to crouch or shrink back in fear **2** to behave in too humble a way

crinkle *verb* **1** to wrinkle, crease **2** to make a crackling sound

crinkly *adjective* wrinkled

crinoline *noun* a wide petticoat or skirt shaped by concentric hoops

cripple *noun* a disabled person □ *verb* **1** to make lame **2** to make less strong, less efficient *etc*: *their policies crippled the economy*

crisis *noun* (*plural* **crises**) **1** a deciding moment, a turning point **2** a time of great danger or suspense

crisp *adjective* **1** stiff and dry; brittle **2** cool and fresh: *crisp air* **3** firm and fresh: *crisp lettuce* **4** sharp □ *noun* a thin crisp piece of fried potato eaten cold □ **crispy** *adjective*

criss-cross *adjective* having a pattern of crossing lines □ *verb* to move across and back: *railway lines criss-cross the landscape*

Based on the phrase *Christ's cross*

criterion *noun* (*plural* **criteria**) a means or rule by which something can be judged; a standard

critic *noun* **1** someone who judges the merits or faults of a book, film *etc* **2** someone who finds faults in a thing or person

critical *adjective* **1** fault-finding **2** of criticism: *critical commentary* **3** of or at a crisis **4** very ill **5** serious, very important

criticism *noun* **1** a judgement or opinion on (something), especially one showing up faults **2** the act of criticizing

criticize *verb* **1** to find fault with **2** to give an opinion or judgement on

croak *verb* to make a low, hoarse sound □ *noun* a low, hoarse sound

croaky *adjective* of sounds: low and hoarse

crochet (*pronounced* **kroh**-shei) *noun* a form of knitting done with one hooked needle □ *verb* to work in crochet

crock *noun* **1** an earthenware pot or jar **2** a worthless, old and decrepit person or thing

crockery *noun* china or earthenware dishes

crocodile *noun* **1** a large reptile found in rivers in Asia, Africa *etc* **2** a procession of children walking two by two

crocodile tears pretended tears

crocus *noun* (*plural* **crocuses**) a yellow, purple or white flower which grows from a bulb

croft *noun* a small farm with a cottage, especially in the Scottish Highlands

crofter *noun* someone who farms on a croft

crofting *noun* farming on a croft

croissant *noun* a curved roll of rich bread dough

crone *noun* an ugly old woman

crony *noun* (*plural* **cronies**) *informal* a close friend

crook *noun* **1** a shepherd's or bishop's stick bent at the end **2** a criminal □ *verb* to bend or form into a hook

crooked (*pronounced* **kruwk**-id) *adjective* **1** bent, hooked **2** dishonest, criminal

croon *verb* to sing or hum in a low voice □ **crooning** *noun*

crop *noun* **1** natural produce gathered for food from fields, trees or bushes **2** a part of a bird's stomach **3** a riding whip **4** the hair on the head **5** a short haircut □ *verb* **1** to cut short **2** to gather a crop (of wheat *etc*) □ **crop up** to happen unexpectedly

crop *verb* ⇨ crops, cropping, cropped

cropper *noun*: **come a cropper 1** to fail badly **2** to have a bad fall

croquet (*pronounced* **kroh**-kei) *noun* a game in which players use long-handled mallets to drive wooden balls through hoops in the ground

cross *noun* **1** a shape (×) or (+) formed of two lines intersecting in the middle **2** a crucifix **3** a street monument marking the site of a market *etc* **4** the result of breeding an animal or plant with one of another kind: *a cross*

between a horse and a donkey **5** a trouble that must be endured □ *verb* **1** to mark with a cross **2** to go to the other side of (a room, road *etc*) **3** to lie or pass across **4** to meet and pass **5** to go against the wishes of **6** to draw two lines across to validate (a cheque) **7** to breed (one kind) with (another) □ *adjective* bad-tempered, angry

crossbow *noun* a bow fixed crosswise to a wooden stand with a device for pulling back the bowstring

cross-country *adjective* of a race: across fields *etc*, not on roads

cross-examine *verb* question closely in court to test accuracy of a statement *etc*

cross-eyed *adjective* having a squint

crossing *noun* **1** a place where a street, river *etc* may be crossed **2** a journey over the sea

crossly *adverb* angrily

crossness *noun* bad temper, sulkiness

cross-reference *noun* a statement in a reference book directing the reader to further information in another section

crossroads *noun singular* a place where roads cross each other

cross-section *noun* **1** a section made by cutting across something **2** a sample taken as representative of the whole: *a cross-section of voters*

crossword *noun* a puzzle in which letters are written into blank squares to form words

crotch *noun* the area between the tops of the legs

crotchet *noun* a musical note (♩) equivalent to a quarter of a whole note or semibreve

crotchety *adjective* bad-tempered

crouch *verb* **1** to stand with the knees well bent **2** of an animal: to lie close to the ground

croup[1] (*pronounced* kroop) *noun* a children's disease causing difficulty in breathing and a harsh cough

croup[2] (*pronounced* kroop) *noun* the hindquarters of a horse

crow *noun* **1** a large bird, generally black **2** the cry of a cock **3** the happy sounds made by a baby □ *verb* **1** to cry like a cock **2** to boast **3** of a baby: to make happy noises □ **as the crow flies** in a straight line

> **crow** *verb* ⇨ crows, crowing, crew or crowed □ **crew** is used as the past form for meaning 1 only: *the cock crew*; otherwise the form is **crowed**: *crowed about his exam results*

crowbar *noun* a large iron bar used as a lever

crowd *noun* a number of people or things together □ *verb* **1** to gather into a crowd **2** to fill too full **3** to keep too close to, impede

crown *noun* **1** a jewelled head-dress worn by monarchs on ceremonial occasions **2** the top of the head **3** the highest part of something **4** *Brit, historical* a coin worth five shillings *verb* **1** to put a crown on **2** to make a monarch **3** *informal* to hit on the head **4** to reward, finish happily: *crowned with success*

crow's-nest *noun* a sheltered and enclosed platform near the mast-head of a ship from which a lookout is kept

crucial *adjective* extremely important, critical: *crucial question* □ **crucially** *adverb*

crucible *noun* a small container for melting metals *etc*

crucifix *noun* (*plural* **crucifixes**) a figure or picture of Christ fixed to the cross

crucifixion *noun* **1** the act of crucifying **2** death on the cross, especially that of Christ

crucify *verb* to put to death by fixing the hands and feet to a cross

> **crucify** ⇨ crucifies, crucifying, crucified

crude *adjective* **1** not purified or refined: *crude oil* **2** roughly made or done **3** rude, blunt, tactless □ **crudely** *adverb* □ **crudity** *noun*

cruel *adjective* **1** causing pain or distress **2** having no pity for others' sufferings □ **cruelly** *adverb* □ **cruelty** *noun* (*plural* **cruelties**)

■ **Alternative words**: (meaning 2) barbarous, sadistic, malevolent, callous, ruthless, inexorable

cruet (*pronounced* **kroo**-it) *noun* **1** a small jar for salt, pepper, mustard *etc* **2** two or more such jars on a stand

cruise *verb* to travel by car, ship *etc* at a steady speed □ *noun* a journey by ship made for pleasure

cruiser *noun* a middle-sized warship

crumb *noun* a small bit of anything, especially bread

crumble *verb* **1** to break into crumbs or small pieces **2** to fall to pieces □ *noun* a dish of stewed fruit *etc* topped with crumbs

crumbly *adjective* having a tendency to fall to pieces

crumpet *noun* a soft cake, baked on a griddle and eaten with butter

crumple *verb* **1** to crush into creases or wrinkles **2** to become creased **3** to collapse

crumple zone a buffer area in a car *etc* to absorb the impact of a crash

crunch *verb* **1** to chew hard so as to make a noise **2** to crush □ *noun* **1** a noise of crunching **2** *informal* a testing moment, a turning-point

crusade *noun* **1** a movement undertaken for some good cause **2** *historical* a Christian expedition to regain the Holy Land from the Turks

crusader *noun* someone who goes on a crusade

crush *verb* **1** to squeeze together **2** to beat down, overcome **3** to crease, crumple □ *noun* **1** a violent squeezing **2** a pressing crowd of people **3** a drink made by squeezing fruit

crushed *adjective* **1** squeezed, squashed **2** completely defeated or miserable

crust *noun* a hard outside coating, *eg* on bread, a pie, a planet

crustacean (*pronounced* krus-**tei**-shun) *noun* one of a large group of animals with a hard shell, including crabs, lobsters, shrimps *etc*

crusty *adjective* **1** having a crust **2** cross, irritable

crutch *noun* (*plural* **crutches**) **1** a stick held under the armpit or elbow, used for support in walking **2** a support, a prop

crux *noun* the most important or difficult part of a problem

cry *verb* **1** to make a loud sound in pain or sorrow **2** to weep **3** to call loudly □ *noun* (*plural* **cries**) a loud call □ **cry off** to cancel □ **cry over spilt milk** to be worried about a misfortune that is past

cry ⇨ cries, crying, cried

■ **Alternative words:** (verb, meaning 2) sob, blubber, wail, bawl, whimper, snivel

crying *adjective* **1** weeping **2** calling loudly **3** requiring notice or attention: *a crying need*

crypt *noun* an underground cell or chapel, especially one used for burial

cryptic *adjective* mysterious, difficult to understand: *cryptic remark* □ **cryptically** *adverb*

crypto- or **crypt-** *prefix* hidden: *cryptic*
🕐 Comes from Greek *kryptos* meaning 'hidden'

cryptography *noun* the art of coding and reading codes

crystal *noun* **1** very clear glass often used for making drinking glasses *etc* **2** the regular shape taken by each small part of certain substances, *eg* salt or sugar

crystalline *adjective* made up of crystals

crystallize *verb* **1** to form into the shape of a crystal **2** to take a form or shape, become clear □ **crystallization** *noun*

CSA *abbreviation* Child Support Agency

cub *noun* **1** the young of certain animals, *eg* foxes **2** a Cub Scout

cube *noun* **1** a solid body having six equal square sides **2** the answer to a sum in which a number is multiplied by itself twice: *8 is the cube of 2*

cubic *adjective* **1** of cubes **2** in the shape of a cube

cubicle *noun* a small room closed off in some way from a larger one

Cub Scout a junior Scout

cuckoo *noun* a bird which visits Britain in summer and lays its eggs in the nests of other birds

cucumber *noun* a creeping plant with a long green fruit used in salads

cud *noun* food regurgitated by certain animals, *eg* sheep and cows

cuddle *verb* to put your arms round, hug □ *noun* a hug, an embrace

cudgel *noun* a heavy stick, a club □ *verb* to beat with a cudgel

cudgel *verb* ⇨ cudgels, cudgelling, cudgelled

cue[1] *noun* **1** a sign to tell an actor when to speak *etc* **2** a hint, an indication

cue[2] *noun* the stick used to hit a ball in billiards and snooker

cuff *noun* **1** the end of a sleeve near the wrist **2** the turned-back hem of a trouser leg **3** a blow with the open hand □ *verb* to hit with the hand □ **off the cuff** without planning or rehearsal

cufflinks *noun plural* a pair of ornamental buttons *etc* used to fasten a shirt cuff

cuisine (*pronounced* kwi-**zeen**) *noun* **1** the art of cookery **2** a style of cooking: *Mexican cuisine*

cul-de-sac (*pronounced* **kul**-de-sak) *noun* a street closed at one end

culinary *adjective* of or used for cookery

cull *verb* **1** to gather **2** to choose from a group **3** to pick out (seals, deer *etc*) from a herd and kill for the good of the herd □ *noun* such a killing

culminate *verb* **1** to reach the highest point **2** to reach the most important or greatest point, end (in): *culminated in divorce* □ **culmination** *noun*

culpable *adjective* guilty, blameworthy

culprit *noun* **1** someone who is to blame for something **2** *English* and *US law* a prisoner accused but not yet tried

cult *noun* **1** a religious sect **2** a general strong enthusiasm for something: *the cult of physical fitness*

cultivate *verb* **1** to grow (vegetables *etc*) **2** to plough, sow **3** to try to develop and improve: *cultivated my friendship*

cultivated *adjective* 1 farmed, ploughed 2 educated, informed □ **cultivation** *noun*

cultivator *noun* 1 a person who cultivates the land 2 a machine or tool that you use for cultivating

culture *noun* 1 a type of civilization with its associated customs: *Mediterranean culture* 2 development of the mind by education 3 educated tastes in art, music *etc* 4 cultivation of plants

cultured *adjective* well-educated in literature, art *etc*

culvert *noun* an arched drain for carrying water under a road or railway

cum *preposition* used for both of two stated purposes: *a newsagent-cum-grocer*

cumbersome *adjective* awkward to handle

cummerbund *noun* a sash worn around the waist

cumulative *adjective* increasing with additions: *cumulative effect*

cumulus *noun* a kind of cloud common in summer, made up of rounded heaps

cunning *adjective* 1 sly, clever in a deceitful way 2 skilful, clever □ *noun* 1 slyness 2 skill, knowledge

cup *noun* 1 a hollow container holding liquid for drinking 2 an ornamental vessel given as a prize in sports events □ *verb* to make (hands *etc*) into the shape of a cup

cup *verb* ⇨ cups, cupp*ing*, cupp*ed*

cupboard *noun* a shelved recess, or a box with drawers, used for storage

cupful *noun* (*plural* **cupfuls**) as much as fills a cup

Cupid (*pronounced* **kyoop**-id) *noun* the Roman god of sexual love

cupidity (*pronounced* kyoo-**pid**-*i*t-i) *noun* greed

cupola (*pronounced* **kyoop**-ol-*a*) *noun* a curved ceiling or dome on the top of a building

cup-tie *noun* a game in a sports competition for which the prize is a cup

cur *noun* 1 a dog of mixed breed 2 a cowardly person

curable *adjective* able to be treated and cured

curate *noun* a member of the Church of England clergy assisting a rector or vicar

curative *adjective* likely to cure

curator *noun* someone who has charge of a museum, art gallery *etc*

curb *verb* to hold back, restrain □ *noun* a restraint

🖋 Do not confuse with: **kerb**

curd *noun* 1 milk thickened by acid 2 the cheese part of milk, as opposed to the **whey**

curdle *verb* to turn into curd □ **curdle someone's blood** to shock or terrify them

cure *noun* 1 freeing from disease, healing 2 something which frees from disease □ *verb* 1 to heal 2 to get rid of (a bad habit *etc*) 3 to preserve by drying, salting *etc*

■ **Alternative words**: (noun, meaning 2) antidote

curfew *noun* an order forbidding people to be out of their houses after a certain hour

curio *noun* (*plural* **curios**) an article valued for its oddness or rarity

curiosity *noun* (*plural* **curiosities**) 1 strong desire to find something out 2 something unusual, an oddity

curious *adjective* 1 anxious to find out 2 unusual, odd □ **curiously** *adverb*

curl *verb* 1 to twist (hair) into small coils 2 of hair: to grow naturally in small coils 3 of smoke: to move in a spiral 4 to twist, form a curved shape 5 to play at the game of curling □ *noun* a small coil or roll, *eg* of hair

curlew *noun* a wading bird with very long slender bill and legs

curler *noun* 1 something used to make curls 2 someone who plays the game of curling

curliness *noun* the quality of being curled or of having lots of curls

curling *noun* a game played by

throwing round, flat stones along a sheet of ice

curly *adjective* having curls

curmudgeon *noun* a miser

currant *noun* 1 a small black raisin 2 a berry of various kinds of soft fruit: *redcurrant*

♦ Do not confuse: **currant** and **current**

currency *noun* (*plural* **currencies**) 1 the money used in a particular country 2 the state of being generally known: *the story gained currency*

current *adjective* 1 belonging to the present time: *the current year* 2 generally known and talked about: *that story is current* □ *noun* a stream of water, air or electrical power moving in one direction

current account a bank account from which money may be withdrawn by cheque

curriculum *noun* the course of study at a university, school *etc*

curriculum vitae a brief account of the main events of a person's life

curry[1] *noun* (*plural* **curries**) a dish containing a mixture of spices with a strong, peppery flavour □ *verb* to make into a curry by adding spices

curry *verb* ⇨ **curries, currying, curried**

curry[2] *verb* rub down (a horse) □ **curry favour** to try hard to be someone's favourite

curry powder a selection of ground spices used in making curry

curse *verb* 1 to use swear words 2 to wish evil towards □ *noun* 1 a wish for evil or a magic spell 2 an evil or a great misfortune or the cause of this

cursed *adjective* under a curse; hateful

cursor *noun* a flashing device that appears on a VDU screen to show the position for entering data

cursorily *adverb* briefly, hurriedly, without taking a lot of care

cursory *adjective* hurried

curt *adjective* of someone's way of speaking: clipped and unfriendly □ **curtly** *adverb*

■ **Alternative words:** abrupt

curtail *verb* to make less, reduce □ **curtailment** *noun*

curtain *noun* a piece of material hung to cover a window, stage *etc*

curtsy or **curtsey** *noun* (*plural* **curtsies**) a bow made by bending the knees

curvature *noun* 1 a curving or bending 2 a curved piece 3 an abnormal curving of the spine

curve *noun* 1 a rounded line, like part of the edge of a circle 2 a bend: *a curve in the road*

cushion *noun* 1 a fabric casing stuffed with feathers, foam *etc*, for resting on 2 a soft pad

cushy *adjective, informal* easy and comfortable: *a cushy job*

cusp *noun* 1 a point 2 a division between signs of the zodiac

custard *noun* a sweet sauce made from eggs, milk and sugar

custodian *noun* 1 a keeper 2 a caretaker, *eg* of a museum

custody *noun* 1 care, guardianship 2 imprisonment

custom *noun* 1 something done by habit 2 the regular or frequent doing of something; habit 3 the buying of goods at a shop 4 **customs** taxes on goods coming into a country 5 **customs** the government department that collects these

customary *adjective* usual

custom-built *adjective* built to suit a particular purpose

customer *noun* 1 someone who buys from a shop 2 *informal* a person: *an awkward customer*

cut *verb* 1 to make a slit in, or divide, with a blade: *cut a hole/ cut a slice of bread* 2 to wound 3 to trim with a blade *etc*: *cut the grass/ my hair needs cutting* 4 to reduce in amount 5 to shorten (a play, book *etc*) by removing parts 6 to refuse to acknowledge (someone you know) 7 to divide (a pack of cards) in two 8 to stop filming 9 *informal* to play truant from (school) □ *noun* 1 a slit made by cutting 2 a wound made with something sharp **3** a stroke, a blow **4** a thrust with a sword **5** the way something is cut **6** the shape and style of clothes **7** a piece of meat □ **cut down 1** to take down by cutting **2** to reduce □ **cut down on** to reduce the intake of □ **cut in** to interrupt □ **cut off 1** to separate, isolate: *cut off from the mainland* **2** to stop: *cut off supplies* □ **cut out 1** to shape (a dress *etc*) by cutting **2** *informal* to stop **3** of an engine: to fail

cut *verb* ⇨ cuts, cutting, cut

cut-and-dried *adjective* arranged carefully and exactly

cute *adjective* **1** smart, clever **2** pretty and pleasing

cut glass glass with ornamental patterns cut on the surface

cuticle *noun* the skin at the bottom and edges of finger and toe nails

cutlass *noun* (*plural* **cutlasses**) a short broad sword

cutlery *noun* knives, forks, spoons *etc*

cutlet *noun* a slice of meat with the bone attached

cut-price *adjective* sold at a price lower than usual

cut-throat *noun* a ruffian □ *adjective* fiercely competitive: *cut-throat business*

cutting *noun* **1** a piece cut from a newspaper **2** a trench cut in the earth or rock for a road *etc* **3** a shoot of a tree or plant □ *adjective* wounding, hurtful: *cutting remark*

cuttlefish *noun* a type of sea creature like a squid

cut-up *adjective* distressed

cyanide *noun* a kind of poison

cyber- (*pronounced* **saib**-er) *prefix* relating to computers or electronic media: *cyberspace/ cyber-selling*

This prefix was taken from the word *cybernetics*, meaning 'the study of communication or control systems'.

Its origin is the Greek word *kybernetes*, meaning 'the person who steers a boat or ship'

cycle *noun* **1** a bicycle **2** a round of events following on from one another repeatedly: *the cycle of the seasons* **3** a series of poems, stories *etc* written about a single person or event □ *verb* **1** to ride a bicycle **2** to move in a cycle; rotate

cyclist *noun* someone who rides a bicycle

cyclone *noun* **1** a whirling windstorm **2** a system of winds blowing in a spiral □ **cyclonic** *adjective*

cygnet (*pronounced* **sig**-net) *noun* a young swan
🕐 Comes from Latin *cygnus* meaning 'swan'

◆ Do not confuse with: **signet**

cylinder *noun* a solid or hollow tube-shaped object; in machines, car engines *etc*, the hollow tube in which a piston works

cylindrical *adjective* shaped like a cylinder

cymbals (*pronounced* **sim**-balz) *noun plural* brass, plate-like musical instruments, beaten together in pairs

cynic (*pronounced* **sin**-ik) *noun* someone who believes the worst about people □ **cynicism** *noun*

cynical (*pronounced* **sin**-i-kal) *adjective* sneering; believing the worst of people □ **cynically** *adverb*

cypress *noun* a type of evergreen tree

cyst (*pronounced* sist) *noun* a liquid-filled blister within the body or just under the skin

cystic fibrosis a hereditary disease which is present at birth or appears in early childhood

cystitis *noun* inflammation of the bladder, often caused by infection

czar *another spelling of* **tsar**

czarina *another spelling of* **tsarina**

Dd

dab *verb* to touch gently with a pad *etc* to soak up moisture □ *noun* **1** the act of dabbing **2** a small lump of something soft **3** a gentle blow, a pat **4** a small kind of flounder

dab *verb* ⇨ dab**s**, dab**bing**, dab**bed**

dabble *verb* **1** to play in water with hands or feet **2** to do in a half-serious way or as a hobby: *he dabbles in computers*

dab-hand *noun, informal* an expert

dachshund (*pronounced* **daks**-huwnt or **daks**-huwnd) *noun* a breed of dog with short legs and a long body
⊙ Comes from German *Dachs* meaning 'badger', and *Hund* meaning 'dog'

dad or **daddy** *noun, informal* father

daffodil *noun* a type of yellow flower which grows from a bulb

daft *adjective* silly

dagger *noun* a short sword for stabbing

dahlia *noun* a type of garden plant with large flowers

Named after Anders *Dahl*, 18th-century Swiss botanist

daily *adjective & adverb* every day □ *noun* (*plural* **dailies**) **1** a paper published every day **2** someone employed to clean a house regularly

daily bread necessary food, means of living

dainty *adjective* **1** small and neat **2** pleasant-tasting □ *noun* (*plural* **dainties**) a tasty morsel of food □ **daintily** *adverb* (adjective, meaning 1)

dairy *noun* (*plural* **dairies**) **1** a building for storing milk and making butter and cheese **2** a shop which sells milk, butter, cheese *etc*

dairy cattle cows kept for their milk, not their meat

dairy farm a farm concerned with the production of milk, butter *etc*

dairymaid *noun* an old-fashioned name for a woman working in a dairy

dairyman *noun* an old-fashioned name for a man working in a dairy

dairy products food made of milk, butter or cheese

dais *noun* (*plural* **daises**) a raised floor at the upper end of a hall

daisy *noun* (*plural* **daisies**) a small common flower with white petals

Literally 'day's eye', so called because of its opening during the day

daisy-chain *noun* a string of daisies threaded through each other's stems

daisy-wheel *noun* a flat printing wheel with characters at the end of spokes

dalai lama the spiritual leader of Tibetan Buddhism

dale *noun* low ground between hills

dally *verb* **1** to waste time idling or playing **2** to play (with) □ **dalliance** *noun*

dally ⇨ dall**ies**, dally**ing**, dall**ied**

Dalmatian *noun* a breed of large spotted dog

dam *noun* **1** a wall of earth, concrete *etc* to keep back water **2** water kept in like this □ *verb* **1** to keep back by a dam **2** to hold back, restrain (tears *etc*)

dam ⇨ dam**s**, dam**ming**, dam**med**

125

damage *noun* 1 hurt, injury 2 **damages** money paid by one person to another to make up for injury, insults *etc* □ *verb* to spoil, make less effective or unusable

■ **Alternative words**: (verb) harm, impair, mar, incapacitate

damask *noun* silk, linen or cotton cloth, with figures and designs in the weave

After *Damascus* in Syria, from where it was exported in the Middle Ages

dame *noun* 1 a comic woman in a pantomime, played by a man in drag 2 **Dame** the title of a woman of the same rank as a knight

damn *verb* 1 to sentence to unending punishment in hell 2 to condemn as wrong, bad *etc* □ *exclamation* an expression of annoyance

damnable *adjective* 1 deserving to be condemned 2 hateful

damnably *adverb* extremely

damnation *noun* 1 unending punishment in hell 2 condemnation

damning *adjective* leading to conviction or ruin: *damning evidence*

damp *noun* 1 moist air 2 wetness, moistness □ *verb* 1 to wet slightly 2 to make less fierce or intense □ *adjective* moist, slightly wet

damp-course *noun* a layer of damp-proof material inside a wall or under a floor

dampen *verb* 1 to make or become damp; moisten 2 to lessen (enthusiasm *etc*)

damper *noun, music* a pad which touches the strings inside a piano, silencing each note after it has been played □ **put a damper on something** to make it less cheerful

dampness *noun* the quality of being damp

damp-proof course a damp-course

damsel *noun, old* an unmarried girl

damson *noun* a type of small dark-red plum

dance *verb* to move in time to music □ *noun* 1 a sequence of steps in time to music 2 a social event with dancing □ **dancer** *noun*

dandelion *noun* a type of common plant with a yellow flower

From the French phrase *dent de lion*, meaning 'lion's tooth'

dandruff *noun* dead skin which collects under the hair and falls off in flakes

dandy *noun* (*plural* **dandies**) a man who pays great attention to his dress and looks

danger *noun* 1 something potentially harmful: *the canal is a danger to children* 2 potential harm: *unaware of the danger*

dangerous *adjective* 1 unsafe, likely to cause harm 2 full of risks

■ **Alternative words**: threatening, menacing, reckless, risky, hazardous, perilous, treacherous

dangerously *adverb* 1 in a dangerous way, or a way that threatens danger 2 to such a great degree that danger is involved: *come dangerously close to being expelled*

dangle *verb* to hang loosely

dank *adjective* moist, wet and cold

dapper *adjective* small and neat

dappled *adjective* marked with spots or splashes of colour

dare *verb* 1 to be brave or bold enough (to): *I didn't dare tell him* 2 to lay yourself open to, risk 3 to challenge: *dared him to cross the railway line* □ **I dare say** I suppose: *I dare say you're right*

dare-devil *noun* a rash person fond of taking risks □ *adjective* rash, risky

daring *adjective* bold, fearless □ *noun* boldness □ **daringly** *adverb*

dark *adjective* 1 without light 2 black or near to black 3 gloomy 4 evil: *dark deeds* □ *noun* absence of light, nightfall □ **in the dark** knowing nothing about something □ **keep dark** to keep (something) secret □ **darkness** *noun*

■ **Alternative words**: (meaning 1) unlit, overcast, dim, unilluminated, shadowy; (meanings 1 and 2) murky, cloudy, dusky, dingy

darken *verb* to make or grow dark or darker

dark horse someone about whom little is known

darling *noun* **1** a word showing affection **2** someone dearly loved; a favourite

darn *verb* to mend (clothes) with crossing rows of stitches □ *noun* a patch mended in this way

dart *noun* **1** a pointed weapon for throwing or shooting **2** something which pierces □ *verb* to move quickly and suddenly

dartboard *noun* the board used in playing the game of darts

darts *noun singular* a game in which small darts are aimed at a board marked off in circles and numbered sections

dash *verb* **1** to throw or knock violently, especially so as to break **2** to ruin (hopes) **3** to depress, sadden (spirits) **4** to rush with speed or violence □ *noun* (*plural* **dashes**) **1** a rush **2** a short race **3** a small amount of a drink *etc* **4** liveliness **5** a short line (-) to show a break in a sentence *etc*

dashing *adjective* **1** hasty **2** smart, elegant

dastardly *adjective, formal* cowardly

data *noun plural* (*singular* **datum**) **1** available facts from which conclusions may be drawn **2** facts stored in a computer

database *noun, computing* a collection of systematically stored files that are often connected with each other

date[1] *noun* **1** a statement of time in terms of the day, month and year, *eg* 23 December 1995 **2** the time at which an event occurs **3** the period of time to which something belongs **4** an appointment □ *verb* **1** to give a date to **2** to belong to a certain time: *dates from the 12th century* **3** to become old-fashioned: *that dress will date quickly*

date[2] *noun* **1** a type of palm tree **2** its blackish, shiny fruit with a hard stone

datum *singular* of **data**

daub *verb* **1** to smear **2** to paint roughly

daughter *noun* a female child

daughter-in-law *noun* a son's wife

daunt *verb* **1** to frighten **2** to be discouraging

dauntless *adjective* unable to be frightened

Davy-lamp *noun* an early kind of safety lamp for coalminers

dawdle *verb* to move slowly □ **dawdler** *noun*

dawn *noun* **1** daybreak **2** a beginning: *dawn of a new era* □ *verb* **1** to become day **2** to begin to appear □ **dawn on** to become suddenly clear to (someone)

dawn chorus the singing of birds at dawn

dawning *noun* a rather poetic way of saying 'dawn'

day *noun* **1** the time of light, from sunrise to sunset **2** twenty-four hours, from one midnight to the next **3** the time or hours spent at work **4** (often **days**) a particular time or period: *in the days of steam* □ **day in, day out** on and on, continuously □ **the other day** recently: *saw her just the other day* ① Comes from Old English *dæg*

daydream *noun* an imagining of pleasant events while awake □ *verb* to imagine in this way

dayglo *noun, trademark* a luminously bright colour

daylight *noun* **1** the light of day, sunlight **2** a clear space

day-release *noun* time off from work for training or education

daze *verb* **1** to stun with a blow **2** to confuse, bewilder

dazzle *verb* **1** to shine on so as to prevent from seeing clearly **2** to shine brilliantly **3** to fascinate, impress deeply

DC *abbreviation* **1** District of Columbia (US) **2** detective constable **3** direct current (*compare with*: **AC**)

deacon *noun* **1** the lowest rank of clergy in the Church of England **2** a church official in other churches

deaconess *noun* a woman deacon

dead *adjective* **1** not living, without life **2** cold and cheerless **3** numb **4** not working; no longer in use **5** complete, utter: *dead silence* **6** exact: *dead centre* **7** certain: *a dead shot* □ *adverb* **1** completely: *dead certain* **2** suddenly and completely: *stop dead* □ *noun* **1** those who have died: *speak well of the dead* **2** the time of greatest stillness *etc*: *the dead of night* □ **dead-and-alive** *adjective* dull, having little life □ **dead-beat** *adjective* having no strength left □ **dead end 1** a road *etc* closed at one end **2** a job *etc* not leading to promotion □ **dead heat** a race in which two or more runners finish equal □ **dead ringer** *informal* someone looking exactly like someone else

deaden *verb* to lessen (pain *etc*)

deadline *noun* a date by which something must be done

> Originally a line in a military prison, the penalty for crossing which was death

deadlock *noun* a standstill resulting from a complete failure to agree

deadly *adjective* **1** likely to cause death, fatal **2** intense, very great: *deadly hush* □ *adverb* intensely, extremely □ **deadliness** *noun*

deadpan *adjective* without expression on the face

deaf *adjective* **1** unable to hear **2** refusing to listen

deafen *verb* **1** to make deaf **2** to be unpleasantly loud **3** to make (walls *etc*) soundproof

deafening *adjective* extremely loud

deaf-mute *noun* someone who is both deaf and dumb

deal *noun* **1** an agreement, especially in business **2** an amount or quantity: *a good deal of paper* **3** the dividing out of playing-cards in a game **4** a kind of softwood □ *verb* **1** to divide, give out **2** to trade (in) **3** to do business (with) □ **deal with** to take action concerning, cope with

dealer *noun* **1** someone who deals out cards at a game **2** a trader **3** a stock-broker

dean *noun* **1** the chief religious officer in a cathedral church **2** the head of a faculty in a university

dear *adjective* **1** high in price **2** highly valued; much loved □ *noun* **1** someone who is loved **2** someone who is lovable or charming □ *adverb* at a high price

dearly *adverb* **1** very much, sincerely: *love someone dearly* **2** involving a great cost, either financially or in some other way: *His freedom was dearly bought*

dearth (*pronounced* derth) *noun* a scarcity, shortage

death *noun* **1** the state of being dead, the end of life **2** the end of something: *the death of steam railways*

death-blow *noun* **1** a blow that causes death **2** an event that causes something to end

death-knell *noun* **1** a bell announcing a death **2** something indicating the end of a scheme, hope *etc*

deathly *adjective* **1** very pale or ill-looking **2** deadly

death-mask *noun* a plastercast taken of a dead person's face

death rattle a rattling in the throat sometimes heard before someone dies

death wish a conscious or unconscious desire to die

debar *verb* to keep from, prevent

> **debar** ⇨ debars, debarring, debarred

debase *verb* **1** to lessen in value **2** to make bad, wicked *etc* □ **debased** *adjective* □ **debasement** *noun*

debatable *adjective* arguable, doubtful: *a debatable point*

debatably *adverb* in the opinion of some people, although this opinion may be challenged or disagreed with: *debatably the world's most urgent environmental problem*

debate *noun* **1** a discussion, especially a formal one before an audience **2** an argument □ *verb* to engage in debate, discuss

debauched *adjective* inclined to debauchery

debauchery *noun* excessive indulgence in drunkenness, lewdness *etc*

debilitate *verb* to make weak

debility *noun* weakness of the body

debit

debit *noun* a debt □ *verb* to mark down as a debt

debonair *adjective* of pleasant and cheerful appearance and behaviour

debrief *verb* to gather information from an astronaut, spy *etc* after a mission

debriefing *noun* the process of debriefing someone, or the meeting at which this is done

debris (*pronounced* **deb**-ree) *noun* 1 the remains of something broken, destroyed *etc* 2 rubbish

debt (*pronounced* det) *noun* what one person owes to another □ **in debt** owing money □ **in someone's debt** under an obligation to them

debtor (*pronounced* **det**-or) *noun* someone who owes a debt

début (*pronounced* **dei**-byoo) *noun* the first public appearance, *eg* of an actor □ *adjective* first before the public: *début concert*

deca- or **dec-** *prefix* ten, multiplied by ten: *decathlon*
Ⓛ Comes from Greek *deka* meaning 'ten'

decade *noun* 1 a period of ten years 2 a set or series of ten

decadence *noun* a falling from high to low standards in morals, the arts *etc*

decadent *adjective* wicked, throwing away moral standards for the sake of pleasure

decaff *adjective, informal* decaffeinated

decaffeinated *adjective* with the caffeine removed

decamp *verb* to run away

decant *verb* to pour (wine *etc*) from a bottle into a decanter

decanter *noun* an ornamental bottle with a glass stopper for wine, whisky *etc*

decapitate *verb* to cut the head from **decapitation** *noun*

decathlon *noun* an athletics competition combining contests in ten separate disciplines

decay *verb* to become bad, worse or rotten □ *noun* the process of rotting or worsening □ **decayed** *adjective*

decease *noun, formal* death

deceased *adjective, formal* dead □ *noun* (**the deceased**) a dead person

deceit *noun* the act of deceiving

deceitful *adjective* inclined to deceive; lying □ **deceitfully** *adverb*

deceive *verb* to tell lies to so as to mislead □ **deceiver** *noun*

decelerate *verb* to slow down □ **deceleration** *noun*

December *noun* the twelfth month of the year

decent *adjective* 1 respectable 2 good enough, adequate: *decent salary* 3 kind: *decent of you to help* □ **decency** *noun* (meanings 1 and 3) □ **decently** *adverb*

deception *noun* 1 the act of deceiving 2 something that deceives or is intended to deceive

deceptive *adjective* misleading: *appearances may be deceptive* □ **deceptively** *adverb*

deci- *prefix* one-tenth: *decimal/decimate*
Ⓛ Comes from Latin *decimus* meaning 'tenth'

decibel *noun* a unit of loudness of sound

decide *verb* 1 to make up your mind to do something: *I've decided to take your advice* 2 to settle (an argument *etc*)

decided *adjective* 1 clear: *decided difference* 2 with mind made up: *he was decided on the issue*

decidedly *adverb* definitely

deciduous *adjective* of a tree: having leaves that fall in autumn

decimal *adjective* 1 numbered by tens 2 of ten parts or the number 10 □ *noun* a decimal fraction

decimal currency a system of money in which each coin or note is either a tenth of another or ten times another in value

decimal fraction a fraction expressed in tenths, hundredths, thousandths *etc*, separated by a decimal point

decimalize *verb* to convert (figures or currency) to decimal form □ **decimalization** *noun*

decimal point a dot used to separate units from decimal fractions, *eg* 0.1 = 1/10, 2.33 = 233/100

decimate *verb* to make much smaller in numbers by destruction

Literally 'reduce by a tenth'

decipher *verb* **1** to translate (a code) into ordinary, understandable language **2** to make out the meaning of: *can't decipher his handwriting*

decision *noun* **1** the act of deciding **2** clear judgement, firmness: *acting with decision*

decisive *adjective* **1** final, putting an end to a contest *etc*: *a decisive defeat* **2** showing decision and firmness: *a decisive manner* □ **decisively** *adverb*

deck *noun* **1** a platform forming the floor of a ship, bus *etc* **2** a pack of playing-cards **3** the turntable of a record-player □ *verb* to decorate, adorn □ **clear the decks** to get rid of old papers, work *etc* before starting something fresh

deckchair *noun* a collapsible chair of wood and canvas *etc*

declaim *verb* **1** to make a speech in impressive dramatic language **2** to speak violently (against) □ **declamation** *noun*

declamatory *adjective* of a speech or announcement: impressive and dramatic

declare *verb* **1** to make known (goods or income on which tax is payable) **2** to announce formally or publicly: *declare war* **3** to say firmly **4** *cricket* to end an innings before ten wickets have fallen □ **declaration** *noun*

decline *verb* **1** to say 'no' to, refuse: *I had to decline his offer* **2** to weaken, become worse **3** to slope down □ *noun* **1** a downward slope **2** a gradual worsening of health *etc*

decode *verb* to translate (a coded message) into ordinary, understandable language

decommission *verb* to take out of operation (*eg* a warship, atomic reactor, or weapons used in a war)

decompose *verb* **1** to rot, decay **2** to

separate in parts or elements
□ **decomposition** *noun*

décor (*pronounced* **dei**-kawr) *noun* the decoration of, and arrangement of objects in, a room *etc*

decorate *verb* **1** to add ornament to **2** to paint or paper the walls of (a room *etc*) **3** to pin a badge or medal on (someone) as a mark of honour
□ **decoration** *noun*

decorative *adjective* **1** ornamental **2** pretty

decorator *noun* someone who decorates houses, rooms *etc*

decorous *adjective* behaving in an acceptable or dignified way

decorum *noun* good behaviour

decoy *verb* to lead into a trap or into evil □ *noun* something or someone intended to lead another into a trap

decrease *verb* to make or become less in number □ *noun* a growing less

decree *noun* **1** an order, a law **2** a judge's decision □ *verb* to give an order

decree *verb* ⇨ decrees, decreeing, decreed

decrepit *adjective* **1** weak and infirm because of old age **2** in ruins or disrepair □ **decrepitude** *noun*

dedicate *verb* **1** to devote yourself (to): *dedicated to his music* **2** to set apart for a sacred purpose **3** to inscribe or publish (a book *etc*) in tribute to someone or something: *I dedicate this book to my father* □ **dedication** *noun*

deduce *verb* to find out something by putting together all that is known

✐ Do not confuse: **deduce** and **deduct**

deduct *verb* to subtract, take away (from)

deduction *noun* **1** a subtraction **2** finding something out using logic, or a thing which has been found out in this way

deed *noun* **1** something done, an act **2** *law* a signed statement or bargain

deed poll a document by which someone legally changes their name

From an old meaning of *poll* as 'cut' or 'trimmed', because these were written on paper with cut edges

deep *adjective* **1** being or going far down **2** hard to understand; cunning **3** involved to a great extent: *deep in debt/ deep in thought* **4** intense, strong: *a deep red colour/ deep affection* **5** low in pitch □ *noun* (**the deep**) the sea □ **in deep water** in serious trouble

■ **Alternative words**: (meaning 1) profound, yawning; (meaning 5) low, bass, resonant, booming

deepen *verb* to make or become deep

deep freeze a low-temperature refrigerator that can freeze and preserve food frozen for a long time

deep-seated *adjective* firmly fixed, not easily removed

deer *noun* (*plural* **deer**) an animal with antlers in the male, such as the reindeer

deface *verb* to spoil the appearance of, disfigure □ **defacement** *noun*

defamatory *adjective* intended to harm, or having the effect of harming, someone's reputation

defame *verb* to try to harm the reputation of □ **defamation** *noun*

default *verb* to fail to do something you ought to do, *eg* to pay a debt □ **by default** because of a failure to do something

defaulter *noun* a person who has defaulted

defeat *verb* to beat, win a victory over □ *noun* a win, a victory

defect *noun* (*pronounced* **dee**-fekt) a lack of something needed for completeness or perfection; a flaw □ *verb* (*pronounced* di-**fekt**) to desert a country, political party *etc* to join or go to another

defection *noun* **1** failure in duty **2** desertion

defective *adjective* **1** faulty; incomplete **2** not having normal mental or physical ability

☞ Do not confuse with: **deficient**

defence or *US* **defense** *noun* **1** the act of defending against attack **2** a means

or method of protection **3** *law* the argument defending the accused person in a case (*contrasted with*: **prosecution**) **4** *law* the lawyer(s) putting forward this argument

defenceless *adjective* without defence

defend *verb* **1** to guard or protect against attack **2** *law* to conduct the defence of **3** to support against criticism

defendant *noun* **1** someone who resists attack **2** *law* the accused person in a law case

defensible *adjective* able to be defended

defensive *adjective* **1** used for defence **2** expecting criticism, ready to justify actions □ **on the defensive** prepared to defend yourself against attack or criticism

defer *verb* **1** to put off to another time **2** to give way (to): *he deferred to my wishes*

defer ⇨ defer**s**, defer**ring**, defer**red**

deference *noun* **1** willingness to consider the wishes *etc* of others **2** the act of giving way to another

deferential *adjective* showing deference, respectful

defiance *noun* open disobedience or opposition □ **defiant** *adjective* □ **defiantly** *adverb*

deficiency *noun* (*plural* **deficiencies**) **1** lack, want **2** an amount lacking

deficient *adjective* lacking in what is needed

☞ Do not confuse with: **defective**

deficit *noun* an amount by which a sum of money *etc* is too little

defile *verb* **1** to make dirty, soil **2** to corrupt, make bad □ **defilement** *noun*

define *verb* **1** to fix the bounds or limits of **2** to outline or show clearly **3** to state the exact meaning of

definite *adjective* **1** having clear limits, fixed **2** exact **3** certain, sure

definite article the name given to the adjective *the*

definitely *adverb* certainly, without doubt

definition *noun* **1** an explanation of the

exact meaning of a word or phrase **2** sharpness or clearness of outline

definitive *adjective* **1** fixed, final **2** not able to be bettered: *definitive biography* □ **definitively** *adverb* (meaning 1)

deflate *verb* **1** to let the air out of (a tyre *etc*) **2** to reduce in self-importance or self-confidence

deflation *noun* **1** an economic term describing a situation where a country experiences a reduction of the amount of money in circulation, resulting in a lower level of industrial activity, industrial output and employment, and a lower rate of increase in wages and prices **2** the letting out of air (from *eg* a tyre) **3** the feeling of sadness or disappointment which you get *eg* when your hopes have been dashed

deflationary *adjective* having the purpose of creating economic deflation

deflect *verb* to turn aside (from a fixed course) □ **deflection** *noun*

deform *verb* **1** to spoil the shape of **2** to make ugly

deformed *adjective* badly or abnormally formed

deformity *noun* (*plural* **deformities**) **1** something abnormal in shape **2** the fact of being badly shaped

defraud *verb* **1** to cheat **2 defraud someone of something** to take or keep it from them by cheating or fraud

defray *verb* to pay for (expenses)

defrost *verb* to remove frost or ice (from); thaw

deft *adjective* clever with the hands, handy □ **deftly** *adverb*

defunct *adjective* no longer active or in use

defy *verb* **1** to dare to do something, challenge **2** to resist openly **3** to make impossible: *its beauty defies description*
  defy ⇨ defies, defying, defied

degenerate *adjective* (*pronounced* di-**jen**-e-rat) having become immoral or very bad □ *verb* (*pronounced* di-**jen**-e-reit) to become or grow bad or worse □ **degeneration** *noun*

degradation *noun* humiliation, loss of dignity

degrade *verb* **1** to lower in grade or rank **2** to disgrace

degrading *adjective* humiliating and embarrassing

degree 1 a step or stage in a process **2** rank or grade **3** amount, extent: *a degree of certainty* **4** a unit of temperature **5** a unit by which angles are measured, one 360th part of the circumference of a circle **6** a certificate given by a university, gained by examination or given as an honour

dehydrate *verb* **1** to remove water from (food *etc*) **2** to lose excessive water from the body

dehydrated *adjective* **1** weak and exhausted as a result of losing too much water from your body **2** dried (food *etc*)

dehydration *noun* a lack of sufficient water in the body

deign *verb* to act as if doing a favour: *she deigned to answer us*

deity (*pronounced* **dei**-it-i) *noun* (*plural* **deities**) a god or goddess

déjà vu (*pronounced* dei-szah **voo**) the feeling of having experienced something before

dejected *adjective* gloomy, dispirited □ **dejection** *noun*

delay *verb* **1** to put off, postpone **2** to keep back, hinder □ *noun* **1** a postponement **2** a hindrance

delectable *adjective* delightful, pleasing □ **delectably** *adverb*

delectation *noun* delight, enjoyment

delegate *verb* (*pronounced* **del**-ig-eit) to give (a task) to someone else to do □ *noun* (*pronounced* **del**-ig-at) someone acting on behalf of another; a representative

delegation *noun* a group of delegates

delete *verb* to rub or strike out (*eg* a piece of writing) □ **deletion** *noun*

deli (*pronounced* **del**-i) *noun*, *informal* a delicatessen

deliberate *verb* (*pronounced* di-**lib**-e-reit) to think carefully or seriously (about) □ *adjective* (*pronounced* di-**lib**-e-rat) **1** intentional, not accidental **2** slow in deciding **3** not hurried □ **deliberately** *adverb*

deliberation *noun* **1** careful thought **2** calmness, coolness **3 deliberations** *formal* discussions

delicacy *noun* (*plural* **delicacies**) **1** tact **2** something delicious to eat

delicate *adjective* **1** not strong, frail **2** easily damaged **3** fine, dainty: *delicate features* **4** pleasant to taste **5** tactful **6** requiring skill or care: *delicate operation*

delicatessen *noun* a shop selling food cooked or prepared ready for eating

delicious *adjective* **1** very pleasant to taste **2** giving pleasure

■ **Alternative words:** (meaning 1) appetizing, tasty, delectable, scrumptious, mouth-watering, succulent, savoury

deliciously *adverb* to just the right degree for maximum pleasure: *The breeze was deliciously cool*

delight *verb* **1** to please greatly **2** to take great pleasure (in) □ *noun* great pleasure

delighted *adjective* very pleased

delightful *adjective* very pleasing □ **delightfully** *adverb*

delinquency *noun* **1** wrongdoing, misdeeds **2** failure in duty

delinquent *adjective* **1** guilty of an offence or misdeed **2** not carrying out your duties □ *noun* **1** someone guilty of an offence **2** someone who fails in their duty

delirious *adjective* **1** raving, wandering in the mind **2** wildly excited □ **deliriously** *adverb*

delirium *noun* **1** a delirious state, especially caused by fever **2** wild excitement

delirium tremens a delirious disorder of the brain caused by excessive alcohol

deliver *verb* **1** to hand over **2** to give out (*eg* a speech, a blow) **3** to set free, rescue **4** to assist at the birth of (a child) □ **deliverance** *noun* (meaning 3)

delivery *noun* (*plural* **deliveries**) **1** a handing over, *eg* of letters **2** the birth of a child **3** a style of speaking

delphinium *noun* a branching garden plant with blue flowers

> From a Greek word translating as 'little dolphin', because of the shape of the flowerheads

delta *noun* the triangular stretch of land at the mouth of a river

> Originally from a Hebrew word meaning 'tent door'

delude *verb* to deceive
> Comes from Latin *deludere* meaning 'to play false'

deluge *noun* **1** a great flood of water **2** an overwhelming amount: *deluge of work* □ *verb* **1** to flood, drench **2** to overwhelm

delusion *noun* a false belief, especially as a symptom of mental illness

> ◆ Do not confuse with: **allusion** and **illusion**. Delusion comes from the verb **delude**

delve *verb* **1** to dig **2** to rummage, search through: *delved in her bag for her keys*

demagogue *noun* a popular leader

demand *verb* **1** to ask, or ask for, firmly **2** to insist: *I demand that you listen* **3** to require, call for: *demanding attention* □ *noun* **1** a forceful request **2** an urgent claim: *many demands on his time* **3** a need for certain goods *etc*

demean *verb* to lower, degrade

demeanour *noun* behaviour, conduct

demented *adjective* mad, insane

demise *noun*, *formal* death

demobilize *verb* **1** to break up an army after a war is over **2** to free (a soldier) from army service □ **demobilization** *noun*

democracy *noun* government of the people by the people through their elected representatives

democrat *noun* **1** someone who believes in democracy **2 Democrat** *US* a member of the American Democratic Party

democratic *adjective* **1** of or governed by democracy **2 Democratic** *US* belonging to one of the two chief political parties in the USA

□ **democratically** *adverb* (meaning 1)

demolish *verb* **1** to destroy completely **2** to pull down (a building *etc*) □ **demolition** *noun*

demon *noun* an evil spirit, a devil □ **demonic** *adjective*

demonstrable *adjective* able to be shown clearly

demonstrate *verb* **1** to show clearly; prove **2** to show (a machine *etc*) in action **3** to express an opinion by marching, showing placards *etc* in public

demonstration *noun* **1** a showing, a display **2** a public expression of opinion by a procession, mass-meeting *etc*

demonstrative *adjective* **1** pointing out; proving **2** inclined to show feelings openly

demonstrator *noun* **1** a person who takes part in a public demonstration to express their opinion about something **2** a person who explains how something works, or shows you how to do something

demoralize *verb* to take away the confidence of □ **demoralization** *noun*

demote *verb* to reduce to a lower rank or grade □ **demotion** *noun*

demur *verb* to object, say 'no'

> **demur** ⇨ demur**s**, demurr**ing**, demurr**ed**

demure *adjective* shy and modest □ **demurely** *adverb*

den *noun* **1** the lair of a wild animal **2** a small private room for working *etc*

denial *noun* the act of denying □ **in denial** doggedly refusing to accept something

denier (*pronounced* den-i-er) *noun* a unit of weight of nylon, silk *etc*

denigrate *verb* to attack the reputation of, defame

denim *noun* a hard-wearing cotton cloth used for jeans, overalls *etc*

> **Denim** was first manufactured in the town of Nîmes in the south of France, and this is how it got its name (*de Nîmes* means 'from Nîmes')

denizen *noun* a dweller, an inhabitant

denomination *noun* **1** name, title **2** a value of a coin, stamp *etc* **3** a religious sect □ **denominational** *adjective*

denominator *noun* the lower number in a vulgar fraction by which the upper number is divided, *eg* the 3 in $\frac{2}{3}$ (*compare with*: **numerator**)

denote *verb* to mean, signify

dénouement (*pronounced* dei-**noo**-mon) *noun* the ending of a story where mysteries *etc* are explained

> Literally 'untying' or 'unravelling', from French

denounce *verb* **1** to accuse publicly of a crime **2** to inform against: *denounced him to the enemy*

dense *adjective* **1** closely packed together; thick **2** very stupid □ **densely** *adverb* (meaning 1)

density *noun* (*plural* **densities**) **1** thickness **2** weight (of water) in proportion to volume **3** *computing* the extent to which data can be held on a floppy disk

dent *noun* a hollow made by a blow or pressure □ *verb* to make a dent in

dental *adjective* of or for a tooth or teeth

dentist *noun* a doctor who examines teeth and treats dental problems

dentistry *noun* the work of a dentist

dentures *noun plural* a set of false teeth

denude *verb* to make bare, strip: *denuded of leaves* □ **denudation** *noun*

denunciation (from **denounce**) *noun* a strongly expressed public criticism or condemnation

deny *verb* **1** to declare to be untrue: *he denied that he did it* **2** to refuse, forbid: *denied the right to appeal* □ **deny yourself** to do without things you want or need

> **deny** ⇨ den**ies**, deny**ing**, den**ied**

deodorant *noun* something that hides unpleasant smells

depart *verb* **1** to go away **2** to turn aside from: *departing from the plan*

department *noun* a self-contained section within a shop, university, government *etc*

departure *noun* 1 the act of leaving or going away 2 a break with something expected or traditional □ **a new departure** a new course of action

depend *verb*: **depend on** 1 to rely on 2 to receive necessary financial support from 3 to be controlled or decided by: *it all depends on the weather*

■ **Alternative words**: (meaning 1) count on, calculate on, trust in, expect

dependable *adjective* to be trusted

dependant *noun* someone who is kept or supported by another

● Do not confuse: **dependant** and **dependent**

dependence *noun* the state of being dependent

dependent *adjective* relying or depending (on)

depict *verb* 1 to draw, paint *etc* 2 to describe

deplete *verb* to make smaller in amount or number □ **depletion** *noun*

deplorable *adjective* regrettable; very bad

deplore *verb* to disapprove of, regret: *deplored his use of language*

deploy *verb* to place in position ready for action

depopulate *verb* to reduce greatly in population □ **depopulated** *adjective*

deport *verb* to send (someone) out of a country □ **deportation** *noun*

deportment *noun* behaviour, bearing

depose *verb* to remove from a high position, especially a monarch from a throne □ **deposition** *noun*

deposit *verb* 1 to put or set down 2 to put in for safe keeping, *eg* money in a bank □ *noun* 1 money paid in part payment of something 2 money put in a bank account 3 a solid that has settled at the bottom of a liquid 4 a layer of coal, iron *etc* occurring naturally in rock

deposit account a bank account from which money must be withdrawn in person, not by cheque

deposition *noun* 1 the removal of

someone from a high position, especially a monarch from a throne 2 a written piece of evidence

depository *noun* (*plural* **depositories**) a place where anything is deposited

depot (*pronounced* dep-oh) *noun* 1 a storehouse 2 a building where railway engines, buses *etc* are kept and repaired

deprave *verb* to make wicked

depraved *adjective* wicked

depravity (*pronounced* dip-**rav**-it-i) *noun* wickedness

deprecate (*pronounced* **dep**-rik-eit) *verb* to show disapproval of, condemn
① Comes from Latin *de* meaning 'away', and *precari* meaning 'to pray'

● Do not confuse: **deprecate** and **depreciate**

deprecating or **deprecatory** *adjective* disapproving, extremely critical

deprecation *noun* the act or process of disapproving of, devaluing or condemning something: *self-deprecation* (= bringing yourself down, being too self-critical)

depreciate (*pronounced* dip-ree-shi-eit) *verb* 1 to lessen the value of 2 to fall in value □ **depreciation** *noun*
① Comes from Latin *de* meaning 'down', and *pretium* meaning 'price'

● Be careful. **Depreciate** is most frequently used to refer to a fall or a bringing down in FINANCIAL value. Don't use it when you really mean **deprecate**

depredations *noun plural* plundering

depress *verb* 1 to make gloomy or unhappy 2 to press down 3 to make lower in value or intensity

depressed *adjective* gloomy, in low spirits

depressing *adjective* having the effect of making you gloomy or unhappy

depression *noun* 1 low spirits, gloominess 2 a hollow 3 a lowering in value 4 a low period in a country's economy with unemployment, lack of trade *etc* 5 a region of low atmospheric pressure

deprivation *noun* great hardship; lack

of the basic necessities in life, *eg* food or human contact

deprive *verb*: **deprive of** to take away from

deprived *adjective* suffering from hardship; disadvantaged

Dept *abbreviation* department

depth *noun* 1 deepness 2 a deep place 3 the deepest part: *from the depth of her soul* 4 the middle: *depth of winter* 5 intensity, strength: *depth of colour* □ **in depth** thoroughly, carefully □ **out of your depth** concerned in problems too difficult to understand

deputation *noun* a group of people chosen and sent as representatives

deputize *verb* to take another's place, act as substitute

deputy *noun* (*plural* **deputies**) 1 a delegate, a representative 2 a second-in-command

derail *verb* to cause to leave the rails □ **derailment** *noun*

derange *verb* to put out of place, or out of working order

deranged *adjective* mad, insane

derangement *noun* an old-fashioned word meaning 'madness' or 'insanity'

derelict *adjective* broken-down, abandoned

dereliction *noun* neglect of what should be attended to: *dereliction of duty*

deride *verb* to laugh at, mock

de rigueur *adjective* required by custom or fashion

derision *noun* mockery

derisive *adjective* mocking

derisory *adjective* so small or inadequate as to be not worth taking seriously, laughable: *He offered me a derisory (= ridiculously small) sum for the work I'd done*

derivative *adjective* not original □ *noun* 1 a word formed on the base of another word, *eg fabulous* from *fable* 2 **derivatives** stock market trading in futures and options

derive *verb* 1 to be descended or formed (from) 2 to trace (a word) back to the beginning of its existence 3 to receive, obtain: *derive satisfaction* □ **derivation** *noun*

dermatitis *noun* inflammation of the skin

dermato- also **dermat-**, **-derm-** of or relating to the skin: *dermatology/ dermatitis/ hypodermic/ pachyderm/ taxidermist*

dermatology *noun* the study and treatment of skin diseases □ **dermatologist** *noun*

derogatory *adjective* 1 harmful to reputation, dignity *etc* 2 scornful, belittling, disparaging

derrick *noun* 1 a crane for lifting weights 2 a framework over an oil well that holds the drilling machinery

Named after *Derrick*, a famous 17th-century hangman in Tyburn, England

derring-do *noun* daring action, boldness

Based on a misprint of a medieval English phrase *dorring do*, meaning 'daring to do'

dervish *noun* a member of an austere Islamic sect

descant *noun*, *music* a tune played or sung above the main tune

descend *verb* 1 to go or climb down 2 to slope downwards 3 **descend from** to have as an ancestor: *claims he's descended from Napoleon* 4 to go from a better to a worse state

descendant *noun* someone descended from another

descent *noun* 1 an act of descending 2 a downward slope

describe *verb* 1 to give an account of in words 2 to draw the outline of, trace

description *noun* 1 the act of describing 2 an account in words 3 sort, kind: *people of all descriptions* □ **descriptive** *adjective* (meaning 1)

desecrate *verb* 1 to spoil (something sacred) 2 to treat without respect □ **desecration** *noun*

Desecrate was formed by taking the word 'consecrate' and replacing the 'con-' with the Latin prefix 'de-' (= from)

💣 Do not confuse with: **desiccate**.
Remember that **desecRate** and
sacRed are related, and they both
contain an **R**

desert¹ *verb* **1** to run away from (the
army) **2** to leave, abandon: *deserted his
wife/ his courage deserted him* □ **deserter**
noun (meaning 1) □ **desertion** *noun*

desert² *noun* a stretch of barren
country with very little water
⊕ Comes from Latin *desertum* meaning
'deserted'

💣 Do not confuse with: **dessert**

desert island an uninhabited island in
a tropical area

deserve *verb* to have earned as a right,
be worthy of: *you deserve a holiday*

deservedly *adverb* justly

deserving *adjective* **1** worthy of being
rewarded or helped **2 be deserving of
something** to deserve it

desiccate *verb* **1** to dry up **2** to
preserve by drying: *desiccated coconut*
⊕ Comes from Latin *desiccare* meaning
'to dry up'

💣 Do not confuse with: **desecrate**.
Remember that **desecRate** and
sacRed are related, and they both
contain an **R**

design *verb* **1** to make a plan of (eg a
building) before it is made **2** to intend
□ *noun* **1** a plan, a sketch **2** a painted
picture, pattern *etc* **3** an intention
□ **have designs on** to plan to get for
yourself

designate (*pronounced* **dez**-ig-neit)
verb **1** to point out, indicate **2** to name
3 to appoint, select □ *adjective*
appointed to a post but not yet
occupying it: *director designate*

designation (*pronounced* dez-ig-**nei**-
sh*u*n) *noun* a name, a title

designing *adjective* crafty, cunning

desirable *adjective* pleasing; worth
having □ **desirability** *noun*

desire *verb* to wish for greatly □ *noun*
1 a longing for **2** a wish

desist *verb, formal* to stop (doing
something)

desk *noun* a table for writing, reading
etc

desolate *adjective* **1** deeply unhappy **2**
empty of people, deserted **3** barren

desolated *adjective* overcome by grief

desolation *noun* **1** deep sorrow **2**
barren land **3** ruin

despair *verb* to give up hope □ *noun* **1**
lack of hope **2** a cause of despair: *she
was the despair of her mother*

despairing *adjective* in despair

despatch *another spelling of* **dispatch**

desperado *noun* (*plural* **desperadoes**
or **desperados**) a violent criminal

desperate *adjective* **1** without hope,
despairing **2** very bad, awful **3** reckless;
violent

desperately *adverb* very much, very
intensely: *desperately proud of his baby
daughter/ missing you desperately*

desperation *noun* the feeling you have
when your situation is so bad that you
are prepared to do anything for the
chance to get out of it

despicable *adjective* contemptible,
hateful

despise *verb* to look on with contempt

despite *preposition* in spite of: *we had
a picnic despite the weather*

despoil *verb* to rob, plunder
□ **despoliation** *noun*

despondent *adjective* downhearted,
dejected □ **despondency** *noun*

despot (*pronounced* **des**-pot) *noun* a
ruler with unlimited power, a tyrant
□ **despotic** *adjective* □ **despotism**
(*pronounced* **des**-pot-i-zm) *noun*

dessert *noun* fruits, sweets *etc* served
at the end of a meal
⊕ Comes from Old French *dessert*
meaning 'the clearing of the table'

💣 Do not confuse with: **desert**

destination *noun* the place to which
someone or something is going

destine *verb* to set apart for a certain
use

destined *adjective* **1** bound (for) **2**
intended (for) by fate: *destined to
succeed*

destiny noun (plural **destinies**) what is destined to happen; fate

destitute adjective **1** in need of food, shelter etc **2 destitute of** completely lacking in: destitute of wit

destitution noun the state of having nothing, not even food and shelter

destroy verb **1** to pull down, knock to pieces **2** to ruin **3** to kill

destroyer noun **1** someone who destroys **2** a type of fast warship

destructible adjective able to be destroyed

destruction noun **1** the act of destroying or being destroyed **2** ruin **3** death

destructive adjective **1** doing great damage **2** of criticism: pointing out faults without suggesting improvements

desultory (pronounced **dez-u**l-tri) adjective **1** moving from one thing to another without a fixed plan **2** changing from subject to subject, rambling

detach verb to unfasten, remove (from)

detachable adjective able to be taken off: detachable lining

detached adjective **1** standing apart, by itself: detached house **2** not personally involved, showing no emotion

detachment noun **1** the state of being detached **2** a body or group (eg of troops on special service)

detail noun a small part, fact, item etc □ verb **1** to describe fully, give particulars of **2** to set to do a special job or task: detailed to keep watch □ **in detail** giving attention to details, item by item

detailed adjective with nothing left out

detain verb **1** to hold back **2** to keep late **3** to keep under guard

detect verb **1** to discover **2** to notice □ **detection** noun

detective noun someone who tries to find criminals or watches suspects

detention noun **1** imprisonment **2** a forced stay after school as punishment

deter verb to discourage or prevent through fear

> **deter** ⇨ deters, deterring, deterred

detergent noun a soapless substance used with water for washing dishes etc

deteriorate verb to grow worse: her health is deteriorating rapidly □ **deterioration** noun

determination noun **1** the fact of being determined **2** stubbornness, firmness of purpose

determine verb **1** to decide (on) **2** to fix, settle: determined his course of action

determined adjective **1** firmly decided; having a strong intention: determined to succeed **2** fixed, settled

deterrent (from **deter**) noun something, especially a threat of some kind, which deters or discourages people from a particular course of action

detest verb to hate greatly

detestable adjective very hateful

detestation noun great hatred

detonate verb to (cause to) explode

detonation noun an explosion

detonator noun something which sets off an explosive

detour noun a circuitous route

detract verb to take away (from), lessen □ **detraction** noun

detriment noun harm, damage, disadvantage

detrimental adjective disadvantageous (to), causing harm or damage

de trop (pronounced de **troh**) adjective in the way, unwelcome

deuce (pronounced dyoos) noun **1** a playing-card with two pips **2** tennis a score of forty points each

deus ex machina (pronounced dei-uws eks **mak**-in-a) a contrived solution or way out

> Literally a 'god from a machine' referring to the pulley device used in ancient Greek theatres to lower the character of a god on to the stage

devastate *verb* **1** to lay in ruins **2** to overwhelm with grief *etc* □ **devastation** *noun*

develop *verb* **1** to (make to) grow bigger or more advanced **2** to acquire gradually: *developed a taste for opera* **3** to become active or visible **4** to unfold gradually **5** to use chemicals to make (a photograph) appear

developer *noun* a chemical mixture used to make an image appear from a photograph

development *noun* **1** growth in size or sophistication **2** work done on studying and improving on previous or basic models, designs or techniques **3** improvement of land so as to make it more fertile, useful or profitable **4** an area of housing built by a developer **5** an occurrence that affects or influences a situation **6** the gradual unfolding of something *eg* a story **7** the process of using chemicals to make a photograph appear

deviate *verb* to turn aside, especially from a standard course

deviation *noun* **1** something which is different, or which departs from the normal course **2** *statistics* the amount of difference between the average of a group of numbers and one of the numbers in that group

device *noun* **1** a tool, an instrument **2** a plan **3** a design on a coat of arms

❡ Do not confuse with: **devise**. To help you remember – 'ice' is a noun, 'ise' is not!

devil *noun* **1** an evil spirit **2** Satan **3** a wicked person

devilish *adjective* very wicked

devil-may-care *adjective* not caring what happens

devilment or **devilry** *noun* mischief

devil's advocate someone who argues against a proposal

devious *adjective* **1** not direct, roundabout **2** not straightforward

devise *verb* **1** to make up, put together **2** to plan, plot

❡ Do not confuse with: **device**. To help you remember – 'ice' is a noun…so 'ise' must be the verb!

devoid *adjective*: **devoid of** empty of, free from: *devoid of curiosity*

devolution *noun* the delegation of certain legislative powers to regional or national assemblies

devolutionist *noun* a supporter of devolution

devolve *verb* **1** to fall as a duty (on) **2** to delegate (power) to a regional or national assembly

devote *verb* to give up wholly (to)

devoted *adjective* **1** loving and loyal **2** given up (to): *devoted to her work*

devotee *noun* a keen follower

devotion *noun* great love

devour *verb* **1** to eat up greedily **2** to destroy

devout *adjective* **1** earnest, sincere **2** religious □ **devoutly** *adverb*

dew *noun* tiny drops of water which form from the air as it cools at night

dewy *adjective* covered in dew; moist

dexterity *noun* skill, quickness □ **dexterous** or **dextrous** *adjective*

di- *prefix* two, twice or double: *carbon dioxide* (= having molecules containing two oxygen atoms)
◑ Comes from Greek *dis* meaning 'two', 'twice' or 'double'

diabetes *noun* a disease in which there is too much sugar in the blood

diabetic *noun* & *adjective* (someone) suffering from diabetes

diabolic or **diabolical** *adjective* devilish, very wicked

diabolically *adverb* **1** extremely: *a diabolically strong cocktail* **2** in a devilish or wicked way: *cackling diabolically*

diadem *noun* a kind of crown

diagnose *verb* to identify (a cause of illness) after making an examination

diagnosis *noun* (*plural* **diagnoses**) the identification (of the cause of illness) in a patient

diagnostic *adjective* having the purpose of identifying the cause of illness in a patient

diagonal *adjective* going from one

diagram 140 **differentiate**

corner to the opposite corner □ *noun* a line from one corner to the opposite corner □ **diagonally** *adverb*

diagram *noun* a drawing to explain something

diagrammatic or **diagrammatical** *adjective* in the form of a diagram

dial *noun* **1** the face of a clock or watch **2** a rotating disc over the numbers on some telephones □ *verb* to call (a number) on a telephone using a dial or buttons

dial *verb* ⇨ dials, dial*ling*, dial*led*

dialect *noun* a way of speaking found only in a certain area or among a certain group of people

dialogue *noun* a talk between two or more people

dialysis *noun* removal of impurities from the blood by a kidney machine

diameter *noun* a line which dissects a circle, passing through its centre

diamond *noun* **1** a very hard, precious stone **2** an elongated, four-cornered shape (♦) **3** a playing-card with red diamond pips

diaper *noun, US* a baby's nappy

Originally a kind of decorated white silk. The current US meaning was used in British English in the 16th century

diaphragm *noun* **1** a layer of muscle separating the lower part of the body from the chest **2** a thin dividing layer **3** a contraceptive device that fits over the cervix

diarrhoea *noun* frequent emptying of the bowels, with too much liquid in the faeces

diary *noun* (*plural* **diaries**) **1** a record of daily happenings **2** a book detailing these

diatribe *noun* an angry attack in words

dice or **die** *noun* (*plural* **dice**) a small cube with numbered sides or faces, used in certain games □ *verb* (**dice**) to cut (food) into small cubes

dictate *verb* **1** to speak the text of (a letter *etc*) for someone else to write down **2** to give firm commands □ *noun* an order, a command

dictation *noun* the act of dictating

dictator *noun* an all-powerful ruler

dictatorial *adjective* like a dictator; domineering

diction *noun* **1** manner of speaking **2** choice of words

dictionary *noun* (*plural* **dictionaries**) **1** a book giving the words of a language in alphabetical order, together with their meanings **2** any alphabetically ordered reference book

did *see* **do**

die[1] *verb* **1** to lose life **2** to wither □ **die down** to become less intense

die *verb* ⇨ dies, dy*ing*, di*ed*

■ **Alternative words**: (meaning 1) decease, perish, expire □ **die down** subside, abate

die[2] *noun* **1** a stamp or punch for making raised designs on money *etc* **2** *singular* form of **dice**

diehard *noun* an obstinate or determined person

diesel *noun* an internal combustion engine in which heavy oil is ignited by heat generated by compression

diet[1] *noun* **1** food **2** a course of recommended foods, *eg* to lose weight □ *verb* to eat certain kinds of food only, especially to lose weight □ **dietetic** *adjective*

diet[2] *noun* **1** a council, an assembly **2** **Diet** the national legislature of Japan

differ *verb* **1** differ from to be unlike **2** to disagree

differ ⇨ differs, differ*ing*, differ*ed*

difference *noun* **1** a point in which things differ **2** the amount by which one number is greater than another **3** a disagreement

different *adjective*: **1** different from unlike **2** varying, not the same **3** unusual

■ **Alternative words**: (meaning 1) dissimilar; (meaning 2) varied, various, diverse, assorted, disparate, many, several, sundry

differentiate *verb* to make a difference or distinction between

difficult *adjective* **1** not easy, hard to do, understand or deal with **2** hard to please

difficulty *noun* (*plural* **difficulties**) **1** lack of easiness, hardness **2** anything difficult **3** anything which makes something difficult; an obstacle, hindrance *etc* **4 difficulties** troubles

diffident *adjective* shy, not confident □ **diffidence** *noun*

diffuse *verb* (*pronounced* dif-**yooz**) to spread in all directions □ *adjective* (*pronounced* dif-**yoos**) widely spread

dig *verb* **1** to turn up (earth) with a spade *etc* **2** to make (a hole) by this means **3** to poke or push (something) into □ *noun* **1** a poke, a thrust **2** an archaeological excavation

> **dig** *verb* ⇨ dig**s**, dig**ging**, **dug**

digest *verb* (*pronounced* dai-**jest**) **1** to break down (food) in the stomach into a form that the body can make use of **2** to think over □ *noun* (*pronounced* **dai**-jest) **1** a summing-up **2** a collection of written material

digestible *adjective* able to be digested

digestion *noun* the act or power of digesting

digestive *adjective* aiding digestion

digger *noun* a machine for digging

digit *noun* **1** a finger or toe **2** any of the numbers 0–9

digital *adjective* of a clock *etc*: using the numbers 0–9

digital audio tape a magnetic audio tape on which sound has been recorded digitally

digital recording the recording of sound by storing electrical pulses representing the audio signal on compact disc, digital audio tape *etc*

dignified *adjective* stately, serious

dignitary *noun* (*plural* **dignitaries**) someone of high rank or office

dignity *noun* **1** manner showing a sense of your own worth or the seriousness of the occasion **2** high rank

digress *verb* to wander from the point in speaking or writing □ **digression** *noun*

dike or **dyke** *noun* **1** a wall; an embankment **2** a ditch

dilapidated *adjective* falling to pieces, needing repair

dilate *verb* to make or grow larger, swell out □ **dilatation** or **dilation** *noun*

dilatory (*pronounced* **dil**-*a*-t-*o*-ri) *adjective* slow to act, inclined to delay

dilemma *noun* a situation offering a difficult choice between two options

diligent *adjective* hard-working, industrious □ **diligence** *noun* □ **diligently** *adverb*

■ **Alternative words**: assiduous

dilly-dally *verb* to loiter, waste time

> **dilly-dally** ⇨ dilly-dall**ies**, dilly-dally**ing**, dilly-dall**ied**

dilute *verb* to lessen the strength of a liquid *etc,* especially by adding water □ *adjective*: *a dilute form of the same substance* □ **diluted** *adjective* □ **dilution** *noun*

dim *adjective* **1** not bright or clear **2** not understanding clearly, stupid □ *verb* to make or become dim

> **dim** *verb* ⇨ dim**s**, dim**ming**, dim**med**

dime *noun* a tenth of a US or Canadian dollar, ten cents

dimension *noun* **1** a measurement of length, width or thickness **2** (**dimensions**) size, measurements

diminish *verb* to make or grow less

diminuendo *noun* a fading or falling sound

diminution *noun* a lessening

diminutive *adjective* very small

dimly *adverb* vaguely, not brightly or clearly

dimness *noun* haziness, half-light, lack of clarity

dimple *noun* a small hollow, especially on the cheek or chin

din *noun* a loud, lasting noise □ *verb* to put (into) someone's mind by constant repetition

> **din** *verb* ⇨ din**s**, din**ning**, din**ned**

dine *verb* to eat dinner

dinghy noun (plural **dinghies**) a small rowing boat

dingy adjective dull, faded or dirty-looking □ **dinginess** noun

dinner noun 1 a main evening meal 2 a midday meal, lunch

dinosaur noun any of various types of extinct giant reptile

> Coined in the 19th century, from Greek words which translate as 'terrible lizard'

dint noun a hollow made by a blow, a dent □ **by dint of** by means of

diocese noun a bishop's district

dip verb 1 to plunge into a liquid quickly 2 to lower (eg a flag) and raise again 3 to slope down 4 to look briefly into (a book etc) □ noun 1 a liquid in which anything is dipped 2 a creamy sauce into which biscuits etc are dipped 3 a downward slope 4 a hollow 5 a short bathe or swim

> **dip** verb ⇨ dips, dipping, dipped

diphtheria (pronounced dif-**theer**-i-a) noun an infectious throat disease

diphthong noun two vowel-sounds pronounced as one syllable (for example the ow sound in out)

diploma noun a written statement conferring a degree, confirming a pass in an examination etc

> From a Greek word meaning a letter folded double

diplomacy noun 1 the business of making agreements, treaties etc between countries 2 skill in making people agree, tact

diplomat noun someone engaged in diplomacy

diplomatic adjective 1 of diplomacy 2 tactful

dire adjective dreadful: in dire need

direct adjective 1 straight, not roundabout 2 frank, outspoken □ verb 1 to point or aim at 2 to show the way 3 to order, instruct 4 to control, organize 5 to put a name and address on (a letter)

direction noun 1 the act of directing 2 the place or point to which someone moves, looks etc 3 an order 4 guidance 5 **directions** instructions on how to get somewhere

directly adverb 1 straight away, immediately: I shall do it directly 2 straight: I looked directly at him 3 just, exactly: directly opposite

directness noun frankness, with no effort to be tactful

director noun 1 a manager of a business etc 2 the person who controls the shooting of a film etc

directory noun (plural **directories**) 1 a book of names and addresses etc 2 a named group of files on a computer disk

direct speech speech reported in the speaker's exact words

dirge noun a lament; a funeral hymn

dirk noun a kind of dagger

dirt noun any unclean substance, such as mud, dust, dung etc

dirt track an earth track for motor-cycle racing

dirty adjective 1 not clean, soiled 2 obscene, lewd □ verb to soil with dirt □ **dirtily** adverb

> **dirty** ⇨ dirties, dirtying, dirtied

■ **Alternative words**: (adjective, meaning 1) filthy, squalid, miry, sullied; (adjective, meaning 2) indecent, sordid, salacious

dis- also **dif-**, **di-** prefix 1 apart: disjointed/ divide 2 not: dislike
ⓛ Comes from Latin prefix dis-, di- with the same meaning

disability noun (plural **disabilities**) something which disables

disable verb to take away power or strength from, cripple

disabled adjective having a severely restricted lifestyle as the result of an injury, or a physical or mental illness or handicap

disablement noun the state of being, or the process of becoming, disabled

disadvantage noun an unfavourable circumstance, a drawback

disadvantaged adjective suffering a

disadvantage, especially poverty or homelessness

disadvantageous *adjective* not advantageous

disagree *verb* 1 (often **disagree with**) to hold different opinions (from) 2 to quarrel 3 **disagree with** of food: to make feel ill

■ **Alternative words**: (meaning 1) dissent, oppose, contend, dispute, contest

disagreeable *adjective* unpleasant

disagreement *noun* a difference of opinion or quarrel

disallow *verb* not to allow

disappear *verb* to go out of sight, vanish □ **disappearance** *noun*

■ **Alternative words**: wane, recede, ebb, evaporate

disappoint *verb* 1 to fail to come up to the hopes or expectations (of) 2 to fail to fulfil

disappointed *adjective* sad because your hopes or expectations have not been fulfilled

disappointment *noun* something which disappoints you, or the feeling of being disappointed

disapprove *verb* to have an unfavourable opinion (of) □ **disapproval** *noun*

disarm *verb* 1 to take (a weapon) away from 2 to get rid of war weapons 3 to make less angry, charm

disarmament *noun* the removal or disabling of war weapons

disarming *adjective* gaining friendliness, charming: *disarming smile*

disarray *noun* disorder

disaster *noun* an extremely unfortunate happening, often causing great damage or loss □ **disastrous** *adjective* □ **disastrously** *adverb*

disband *verb* to break up, separate: *the gang disbanded* □ **disbandment** *noun*

disbelief *noun* inability to believe something

disbelieve *verb* not to believe □ **disbeliever** *noun*

disburse *verb* to pay out □ **disbursement** *noun*

disc *noun* 1 a flat, round shape 2 a pad of cartilage between vertebrae 3 a gramophone record

discard *verb* to throw away as useless

disc brakes vehicle brakes which use pads that are hydraulically forced against discs on the wheels

discern *verb* to see, realize

discernible *adjective* noticeable: *discernible difference*

discerning *adjective* quick at noticing; discriminating: *a discerning eye*

discernment *noun* good taste, ability to judge between good and bad things

discharge *verb* 1 to unload (cargo) 2 to set free 3 to dismiss 4 to fire (a gun) 5 to perform (duties) 6 to pay (a debt) 7 to give off (*eg* smoke) 8 to let out (pus) □ *noun* 1 a discharging 2 dismissal 3 pus *etc* discharged from the body 4 performance (of duties) 5 payment

disciple *noun* 1 someone who believes in another's teaching 2 *historical* one of the followers of Christ

disciplinarian *noun* someone who insists on strict discipline

disciplinary *adjective* relating to the enforcement of rules and discipline, and the punishment of disobedience and other offences

discipline *noun* 1 training in an orderly way of life 2 order kept by means of control 3 punishment 4 a subject of study or training □ *verb* 1 to bring to order 2 to punish

disc jockey someone who introduces and plays recorded music on radio *etc*

disclaim *verb* to refuse to have anything to do with, deny

disclaimer *noun* a denial

disclose *verb* to uncover, reveal, make known

disclosure *noun* 1 the act of disclosing 2 something disclosed

disco *noun* (*plural* **discos**) an event or place where recorded music is played for dancing

discolour or *US* **discolor** *verb* to spoil

the colour of; stain □ **discoloration** *noun*

discomfit *verb* 1 to disconcert 2 to thwart, defeat

discomfiture *noun* feeling of slight embarrassment

discomfort *noun* lack of comfort, uneasiness

disconcert *verb* to upset, confuse

disconnect *verb* to separate, break the connection between

disconnected *adjective* 1 separated, no longer connected 2 of thoughts *etc*: not following logically, rambling

disconsolate *adjective* sad, disappointed

discontent *noun* dissatisfaction

discontented *adjective* dissatisfied, cross

discontentment *noun* dissatisfaction

discontinue *verb* to stop, cease to continue

discord *noun* 1 disagreement, quarrelling 2 *music* a jarring of notes

discordant *adjective* 1 *music* made up of notes which do not make pleasant harmonies, creating a strange or unpleasant effect 2 strange or unpleasant because not made up of parts which fit well together

discotheque *noun* a disco

discount *noun* a small sum taken off the price of something: *10% discount* □ *verb* 1 to leave out, not consider: *completely discounted my ideas* 2 to allow for exaggeration in (*eg* a story)

discourage *verb* 1 to take away the confidence, hope *etc* of 2 to try to prevent by showing dislike or disapproval: *discouraged his advances*

discouragement *noun* 1 loss of confidence, hope *etc* 2 an attempt at preventing something by showing dislike or disapproval

discouraging *adjective* giving little hope or encouragement

discourse *noun* 1 a speech, a lecture 2 an essay 3 a conversation □ *verb* to talk, especially at some length

discourteous *adjective* not polite, rude

□ **discourteously** *adverb* □ **discourtesy** *noun*

discover *verb* 1 to find out 2 to find by chance, especially for the first time □ **discoverer** *noun*

discovery *noun* (*plural* **discoveries**) 1 the act of finding or finding out 2 something discovered

discredit *verb* 1 to refuse to believe 2 to cause to doubt 3 to disgrace □ *noun* 1 disgrace 2 disbelief

discreditable *adjective* disgraceful

discreet *adjective* wisely cautious, tactful □ **discreetly** *adverb*

> ☛ Do not confuse with: **discrete**

discrepancy *noun* (*plural* **discrepancies**) a difference or disagreement between two things: *some discrepancy in the figures*

discrete *adjective* separate, distinct

> ☛ Do not confuse with: **discreet**. It may help you to think of **Crete**, which is an island separate from the rest of Greece

discretion (from **discreet**) *noun* wise caution, tact □ **at someone's discretion** according to that person's own judgement

discriminate *verb* 1 to make differences (between), distinguish 2 to treat (people) differently because of their gender, race *etc*

discriminating *adjective* showing good judgement

discrimination *noun* 1 ability to discriminate 2 adverse treatment on grounds of gender, race *etc*

discus *noun* a heavy disc thrown in an athletic competition

discuss *verb* to talk about □ **discussion** *noun*

disdain *verb* 1 to look down on, scorn 2 to be too proud to do □ *noun* scorn □ **disdainful** *adjective*

disease *noun* illness

diseased *adjective* affected by disease

disembark *verb* to put or go ashore □ **disembarkation** *noun*

disembodied *adjective* of a soul *etc*: separated from the body

disengage *verb* to separate, free □ **disengaged** *adjective*

disentangle *verb* to free from entanglement, unravel

disfavour or *US* **disfavor** *noun* dislike, disapproval

disfigure *verb* to spoil the beauty or appearance of □ **disfigurement** *noun*

disgorge *verb* 1 to throw out 2 to give up (something previously taken)

disgrace *noun* the state of being out of favour; shame □ *verb* to bring shame on

disgraceful *adjective* shameful; very bad □ **disgracefully** *adverb*

disgruntled *adjective* sulky, discontented

disguise *verb* 1 to change the appearance of 2 to hide (feelings *etc*) □ *noun* 1 a disguised state 2 a costume *etc* which disguises

disgust *noun* 1 strong dislike, loathing 2 indignation □ *verb* 1 to cause loathing, revolt 2 to make indignant

disgusting *adjective* sickening; causing disgust

dish *noun* (*plural* **dishes**) 1 a plate or bowl for food 2 food prepared for eating 3 a saucer-shaped aerial for receiving information from a satellite □ *verb* 1 to serve (food) 2 to deal (out), distribute

dishearten *verb* to take away courage or hope from □ **disheartened** *adjective* □ **disheartening** *adjective*

dishevelled *adjective* untidy, with hair *etc* disordered

dishonest *adjective* not honest, deceitful □ **dishonesty** *noun*

dishonour *noun* disgrace, shame □ *verb* to cause shame to

dishonourable *adjective* disgraceful

disillusion *verb* to take away a false belief from

disillusioned *adjective* unhappy and disappointed after your happy impressions of something have been destroyed

disillusionment *noun* the feeling of being disillusioned

disinclined *adjective* unwilling

disinfect *verb* to destroy disease-causing germs in

disinfectant *noun* a substance that kills germs

disinherit *verb* to take away the rights of an heir □ **disinheritance** *noun*

disinherited *adjective* in the position of having lost your rights as an heir

disintegrate *verb* to fall into pieces; break down □ **disintegration** *noun*

disinterested *adjective* unbiased, not influenced by personal feelings

> ♣ Do not confuse with: **uninterested**. It is generally a positive thing to be **disinterested** (= fair), especially if you are trying to make an unbiased decision. It is generally a negative thing to be **uninterested** (= bored)

disjointed *adjective* of speech *etc*: not well connected together

disk *noun* 1 *US spelling* of **disc** 2 *computing* a flat round magnetic plate used for storing data

disk drive *computing* part of a computer that records data on to and retrieves data from disks

dislike *verb* not to like, disapprove of □ *noun* disapproval

dislocate *verb* 1 to put (a bone) out of joint 2 to upset, disorder □ **dislocation** *noun*

dislodge *verb* 1 to drive from a place of rest, hiding or defence 2 to knock out of place accidentally

disloyal *adjective* not loyal, unfaithful □ **disloyalty** *noun*

dismal *adjective* gloomy; sorrowful, sad

> Based on a Latin phrase *dies mali* 'evil days', referring to two days each month which were believed to be unusually unlucky

dismantle *verb* 1 to remove fittings, furniture *etc* from 2 to take to pieces

dismay *verb* to make to feel hopeless, upset □ *noun: watching in dismay*

dismember *verb* 1 to tear to pieces 2 to cut the limbs from

dismiss *verb* 1 to send or put away 2

to remove (someone) from a job, sack
3 to close (a law case) □ **dismissal** *noun*

dismount *verb* to come down off a horse, bicycle *etc*

disobedient *adjective* refusing or failing to obey

disobey *verb* to fail or refuse to do what is commanded □ **disobedience** *noun*

disorder *noun* **1** lack of order, confusion **2** a disease □ *verb* to throw out of order

disorderly *adjective* **1** out of order **2** behaving in a lawless (noisy) manner □ **disorderliness** *noun*

disown *verb* to refuse or cease to recognize as your own

disparage *verb* to speak of as being of little worth or importance, belittle □ **disparagement** *noun* □ **disparaging** *adjective*

disparity *noun* (*plural* **disparities**) great difference, inequality

dispassionate *adjective* **1** favouring no one, unbiased **2** calm, cool □ **dispassionately** *adverb*

dispatch or **despatch** *verb* **1** to send off (a letter *etc*) **2** to kill, finish off **3** to do or deal with quickly □ *noun* (*plural* **dispatches** or **despatches**) **1** the act of sending off **2** a report to a newspaper **3** speed in doing something **4** killing **5** **dispatches** official papers (especially military or diplomatic)

dispatch box 1 a case for official papers **2** the box beside which members of parliament stand to make speeches in the House of Commons

dispatch rider a courier who delivers military dispatches by motor-cycle

dispel *verb* to drive away, make disappear

dispel ⇨ dispel*s*, dispel*ling*, dispel*led*

dispensable *adjective* able to be done without

dispensary *noun* (*plural* **dispensaries**) a place where medicines are given out

dispensation *noun* special leave to break a rule *etc*

dispense *verb* **1** to give out **2** to prepare (medicines) for giving out

dispense with something to do without it

dispenser *noun* **1** a machine that issues something to you **2** a holder or container from which you can get something one at a time or in measured quantities

dispersal *noun* a scattering

disperse *verb* **1** to scatter; spread **2** to (cause to) vanish

dispersion *noun* a scattering

dispirited *adjective* sad, discouraged

displace *verb* **1** to put out of place **2** to disorder, disarrange **3** to put (someone) out of office □ **displacement** *noun*

displaced person someone forced to leave his or her own country because of war, political reasons *etc*

display *verb* to set out for show □ *noun* a show, exhibition

displease *verb* not to please; to offend, annoy

displeasure *noun* annoyance, disapproval

disposable *adjective* intended to be thrown away

disposal *noun* the act or process of getting rid of something □ **at your disposal** available for your use

dispose *verb* **1** to arrange, settle **2** to get rid (of): *they disposed of the body* **3** to make inclined

disposed *adjective* inclined, willing □ **be well disposed towards someone** to favour them and be inclined to treat them well

disposition *noun* **1** arrangement **2** nature, personality **3** *law* the handing over of property *etc* to another

disproportionate *adjective* too big or too little, not in proportion

disprove *verb* to prove to be false

disputable *adjective* not certain, able to be argued about

disputation *noun* an argument

dispute *verb* to argue about □ *noun* an argument, quarrel

disqualification *noun* the act of

disqualifying someone or the state of being disqualified

disqualify *verb* 1 to put out of a competition for breaking rules 2 to take away a qualification or right

disqualify ⇨ disqualif*ies*, disqualify*ing*, disqualif*ied*

disquiet *noun* uneasiness, anxiety

disregard *verb* to pay no attention to, ignore □ *noun* neglect

disrepair *noun* a state of bad repair

disreputable *adjective* having a bad reputation, not respectable

disrepute *noun* bad reputation

disrespect *noun* rudeness, lack of politeness □ **disrespectful** *adjective*

disrupt *verb* 1 to break up 2 to throw (a meeting *etc*) into disorder

disruption *noun* an obstacle or disturbance

disruptive *adjective* causing disorder

dissatisfaction *noun* displeasure, annoyance

dissatisfy *verb* to bring no satisfaction, displease □ **dissatisfied** *adjective*

dissatisfy ⇨ dissatisf*ies*, dissatisfy*ing*, dissatisf*ied*

dissect *verb* 1 to cut into parts for examination 2 to study and criticize □ **dissection** *noun*

dissemble *verb* to hide, disguise (intentions *etc*)

disseminate *verb* to scatter, spread □ **dissemination** *noun*

dissent *verb* 1 to have a different opinion 2 to refuse to agree □ *noun* disagreement

dissertation *noun* a long piece of writing or talk on a particular (often academic) subject

disservice *noun* harm, a bad turn

dissident *noun* someone who disagrees, especially with a political regime

dissimilar *adjective* not the same □ **dissimilarity** *noun* (*plural* **dissimilarities**)

dissipate *verb* 1 to (cause to) disappear 2 to waste, squander □ **dissipation** *noun*

dissipated *adjective* worn out by indulging in pleasures; dissolute

dissociate *verb* to separate □ **dissociate yourself from** to refuse to be associated with

dissolute *adjective* having loose morals; debauched

dissolve *verb* 1 to melt 2 to break up 3 to put an end to □ **dissolution** *noun* (meanings 2 and 3)

dissonance *noun* 1 discord, especially used deliberately for musical effect 2 disagreement □ **dissonant** *adjective*

dissuade *verb* to persuade not to do something □ **dissuasion** *noun*

distaff *noun* a stick used to hold flax or wool being spun

distance *noun* 1 the space between things 2 a far-off place or point: *in the distance* 3 coldness of manner

distant *adjective* 1 far off or far apart in place or time: *distant era/ distant land* 2 not close: *distant cousin* 3 cold in manner

distantly *adverb* 1 with a dreamy or cold manner 2 not closely: *distantly related*

distaste *noun* dislike

distasteful *adjective* disagreeable, unpleasant

distemper *noun* 1 a kind of paint used chiefly for walls 2 a viral disease of dogs, foxes *etc* □ *verb* to paint with distemper

distend *verb* to swell; stretch outwards □ **distension** *noun*

distil *verb* 1 to purify (liquid) by heating to a vapour and cooling 2 to extract the spirit or essence from 3 to (cause to) fall in drops □ **distillation** *noun* □ **distiller** *noun*

distil ⇨ distil*s*, distil*ling*, distil*led*

distillery *noun* (*plural* **distilleries**) a place where whisky, brandy *etc* is distilled

distinct *adjective* 1 clear; easily seen or noticed: *a distinct improvement* 2 different: *the two languages are quite distinct*

❡ Do not confuse: **distinct** and **distinctive**

distinction *noun* **1** a difference **2** outstanding worth or merit

distinctive *adjective* different, special, easily recognizable: *That singer has a very distinctive voice* □ **distinctively** *adverb*

distinguish *verb* **1** to recognize a difference (between) **2** to mark off as different **3** to recognize **4** to give distinction to

distinguished *adjective* **1** outstanding, famous **2** dignified

distort *verb* **1** to twist out of shape **2** to turn or twist (a statement *etc*) from its true meaning **3** to make (a sound) unclear and harsh □ **distortion** *noun*

distract *verb* **1** to divert (the attention) **2** to trouble, confuse **3** to make mad

distracted *adjective* mad with pain, grief *etc*

distraction *noun* **1** something which diverts your attention **2** anxiety, confusion **3** amusement **4** madness

distraught *adjective* extremely agitated or anxious

distress *noun* **1** pain, trouble, sorrow **2** a cause of suffering □ *verb* to cause pain or sorrow to □ **distressed** *adjective* □ **distressing** *adjective*

distribute *verb* **1** to divide among several **2** to spread out widely □ **distribution** *noun*

district *noun* a region of a country or town

distrust *noun* lack of trust, suspicion □ *verb* to have no trust in □ **distrustful** *adjective*

disturb *verb* **1** to confuse, worry, upset **2** to interrupt

disturbance *noun* **1** an outbreak of violent behaviour, especially in public **2** an act of disturbing, agitating or disorganizing **3** psychological damage or illness

disturbed *adjective* **1** *psychology* mentally or emotionally ill or damaged **2** **disturbed about something** very anxious about it **3** full of trouble and anxiety

disuse *noun* the state of being no longer used

disused *adjective* no longer used

ditch *noun* (*plural* **ditches**) a long narrow hollow trench dug in the ground, especially to carry water

dither *verb* **1** to hesitate, be undecided **2** to act in a nervous, uncertain manner □ *noun* a state of indecision

ditto *noun* (often written as **do**) the same as already written or said

ditto marks a character (") written below a word in a text, meaning it is to be understood as repeated

ditty *noun* (*plural* **ditties**) a simple, short song

divan *noun* **1** a long, low couch without a back **2** a bed without a headboard

dive *verb* **1** to plunge headfirst into water **2** to swoop through the air **3** to go down steeply and quickly □ *noun* an act of diving

dive *verb* ⇨ dives, diving, dived or *US* dove

dive-bomb *verb* to bomb from an aircraft in a steep downward dive □ **dive-bomber** *noun*

diver *noun* **1** someone who works under water using special breathing equipment **2** a type of diving bird

diverge *verb* to separate and go in different directions; differ □ **divergence** *noun* □ **divergent** *adjective*

diverse *adjective* different, various

diversify *verb* to make or become different or varied

diversify ⇨ diversifies, diversifying, diversified

diversion *noun* **1** turning aside **2** an alteration to a traffic route **3** an amusement

diversity *noun* difference; variety

divert *verb* **1** to turn aside, change the direction of **2** to entertain, amuse

diverting *adjective* entertaining, amusing

divest *verb* to strip or deprive of: *divested him of his authority*

divide *verb* **1** to separate into parts **2**

to share (among) **3** to (cause to) go into separate groups **4** *maths* to find out how many times one number contains another

dividend *noun* **1** an amount to be divided (*compare with*: **divisor**) **2** a share of profits from a business

dividers *noun plural* measuring compasses

divine *adjective* **1** of a god; holy **2** *informal* splendid, wonderful □ *verb* **1** to guess **2** to foretell, predict

diviner *noun* someone who claims special powers in finding hidden water or metals

divinity *noun* (*plural* **divinities**) **1** a god **2** the nature of a god **3** religious studies

divisible *adjective* able to be divided □ **divisibility** *noun*

division *noun* **1** the act of dividing **2** a barrier, a separator **3** a section, especially of an army **4** separation **5** disagreement

divisional *adjective* of a division

divisor *noun* the number by which another number (the **dividend**) is divided

divorce *noun* **1** the legal ending of a marriage **2** a complete separation □ *verb* **1** to end a marriage with **2** to separate (from)

divulge *verb* to let out, make known (a secret *etc*)

Diwali or **Dewali** *noun* the Hindu and Sikh festival of lamps, celebrated in October or November

DIY *abbreviation* do-it-yourself

dizzy *adjective* **1** giddy, confused **2** causing giddiness: *from a dizzy height* □ **dizzily** *adverb*

DJ *abbreviation* disc jockey

djinn (*pronounced* jeen or jin) *noun plural* **djinni** -*pronounced* jeen-i or jin-ee) a group of spirits in Islamic folklore

DNA *abbreviation* deoxyribonucleic acid, a compound carrying genetic instructions for passing on hereditary characteristics

do *verb* **1** to carry out, perform (a job *etc*) **2** to perform an action on, *eg* clean (dishes), arrange (hair) *etc* **3** *slang* to swindle **4** to act: *do as you please* **5** to get on: *I hear she's doing very well/ how are you doing?* **6** to be enough: *a pound will do* **7** used to avoid repeating a verb: *I seldom see him now, and when I do, he ignores me* **8** used with a more important verb (1) in questions: *do you see what I mean?* (2) in sentences with **not**: *I don't know;* or (3) for emphasis: *I do hope she'll be there* □ *noun* (*plural* **dos**) *informal* a social event, a party □ **do away with** to put an end to, destroy □ **do down** *informal* to get the better of □ **do in** *informal* **1** to exhaust, wear out **2** to murder □ **done to death** too often repeated □ **do or die** a desperate final attempt at something whatever the consequences □ **do out of** to swindle out of □ **do someone proud** *see* **proud** □ **do up 1** to fasten **2** to renovate

do *verb* ⇨ does, doing, did, done

🕐 Comes from Old English *don*

do *abbreviation* ditto

docile *adjective* tame, easy to manage □ **docilely** *adverb* □ **docility** *noun*

dock *noun* **1** (often **docks**) a deepened part of a harbour where ships go for loading, repair *etc* **2** the box in a law court where the accused person stands **3** a weed with large leaves □ *verb* **1** to put in or enter a dock **2** to clip or cut short **3** of a spacecraft: to join on to another craft in space

docker *noun* someone who works in the docks

docket *noun* a label listing the contents of something

dockyard *noun* a naval harbour with docks, stores *etc*

doctor *noun* **1** someone trained in and licensed to practise medicine **2** someone with the highest university degree in any subject □ *verb* **1** to treat as a patient **2** to tamper with, alter

doctrine *noun* a belief that is taught □ **doctrinal** *adjective*

document *noun* a written statement giving proof, information *etc*

documentary *noun* (*plural* **documentaries**) a film giving information about real people or events □ *adjective* **1** of or in documents:

documentary evidence **2** of a documentary

dodder *verb* to shake, tremble, especially as a result of old age

doddery *adjective* shaky or slow because of old age

doddle *noun, informal* an easy task

dodge *verb* to avoid by a sudden or clever movement □ *noun* a trick

dodo *noun* (*plural* **dodoes** or **dodos**) a type of large extinct bird

doe *noun* the female of certain animals, *eg* a deer, rabbit or hare

doer (from **do**) *noun* an active person who does a lot of things

doff *verb* to take off (a hat) in greeting

dog *noun* **1** a four-footed animal often kept as a pet **2** one of the dog family which includes wolves, foxes *etc* □ *adjective* of certain animals: male □ *verb* **1** to follow and watch constantly **2** to hamper, plague: *dogged by ill health* □ **dog in the manger** someone who stands in the way of a plan or proposal □ **go to the dogs** to be ruined

dog *verb* ⇨ **dogs, dogging, dogged**

dog-collar *noun* **1** a collar for dogs **2** the stiff white collar of a vicar

dog-eared *adjective* of a page: turned down at the corner

dog-eat-dog *adjective* viciously competitive

dog-fight *noun* a fight between aeroplanes at close quarters

dogfish *noun* a kind of small shark

dogged (*pronounced* **dog**-id) *adjective* determined, stubborn: *dogged refusal* □ **doggedly** *adverb*

doggerel *noun* badly-written poetry

doggy *adjective* of or for dogs □ *noun, informal* a child's name for a dog

doggy-bag *noun* a bag used to take away left-over food from a restaurant meal

doggy-paddle *noun* a simple style of swimming

dog-leg *noun* a sharp bend

dogma *noun* an opinion, especially

religious, accepted or fixed by an authority

dogmatic *adjective* **1** of dogma **2** stubbornly forcing your opinions on others □ **dogmatically** *adverb*

do-gooder *noun* someone who tries to help others in a self-righteous way

dogsbody *noun, informal* someone who is given unpleasant or dreary tasks to do

dog's breakfast or **dog's dinner** a complete mess

dog's life a life of misery

dog-tag *noun* **1** a dog's identity disc **2** an identity disc worn by soldiers *etc*

dog-tired *adjective* completely worn out

doily or **doyley** *noun* (*plural* **doilies** or **doyleys**) a perforated paper napkin put underneath cakes *etc*

Originally a light summer fabric, named after *Doily*'s drapery shop in 17th-century London

doings *noun plural* actions

Dolby *noun, trademark* a system for reducing background noise, used in recording music or soundtracks

doldrums *noun plural* low spirits: *in the doldrums*

The *doldrums* take their name from an area of the ocean about the equator famous for calms and variable winds

dole *verb* to deal (out) in small amounts □ *noun, informal* unemployment benefit

doleful *adjective* sad, unhappy □ **dolefully** *adverb*

doll *noun* a toy in the shape of a small human being

dollar *noun* the main unit of currency in several countries, *eg* the USA, Canada, Australia and New Zealand

dolmen *noun* an ancient tomb in the shape of a stone table

dolphin *noun* a type of sea animal like a porpoise

dolt *noun* a stupid person □ **doltish** *adjective*

domain *noun* **1** a kingdom **2** a country

estate **3** an area of interest or knowledge

dome *noun* **1** the shape of a half sphere or ball **2** the roof of a building *etc* in this shape □ **domed** *adjective*

domestic *adjective* **1** of the home or house **2** of an animal: tame, domesticated **3** not foreign, of your own country: *domestic products* □ *noun* a live-in maid *etc*

domesticated *adjective* **1** of an animal: tame, used for farming *etc* **2** fond of doing housework, cooking *etc*

domesticity *noun* home life

domestic science *old* cookery, needlework *etc*, taught as a subject

domicile *noun* the country *etc* in which someone lives permanently

dominant *adjective* ruling; most powerful or important □ **dominance** *noun*

dominate *verb* **1** to have command or influence over **2** to be most strong, or most noticeable: *the castle dominates the skyline* **3** to tower above, overlook □ **domination** *noun*

domineering *adjective* overbearing, like a tyrant

dominion *noun* **1** rule, authority **2** an area with one ruler or government

domino *noun* (*plural* **dominoes**) **1** a piece used in the game of dominoes **2** *historical* a long silk cloak worn at masked balls

dominoes *noun singular* a game played on a table with pieces marked with dots, each side of which must match a piece placed next to it

don *noun* a college or university lecturer □ *verb* to put on (a coat *etc*)

   don *verb* ⇨ **don**s, **don**n*ing*, **don**n*ed*

donate *verb* to present a gift

donation *noun* a gift of money or goods

done *past participle* of **do** □ *adjective* finished

donkey *noun* (*plural* **donkeys**) (*also called* **ass**) a type of animal with long ears, related to the horse

donor *noun* **1** a giver of a gift **2** someone

who agrees to let their body organs be used for transplant operations

don't *short for* do not

doom *noun* **1** judgement; fate **2** ruin

doomed *adjective* **1** destined, condemned **2** bound to fail or be destroyed

door *noun* **1** a hinged barrier which closes the entrance to a room or building **2** the entrance itself

doorstep *noun* the step in front of the door of a house

doorway *noun* the space filled by a door, the entrance

dope *noun, informal* **1** the drug cannabis **2** an idiot □ *verb* to drug

dormant *adjective* sleeping, inactive: *a dormant volcano*

   Opposite: active

dormitory *noun* (*plural* **dormitories**) a room with beds for several people

dormouse *noun* (*plural* **dormice**) a small animal which hibernates
   ⓘ Probably from Latin *dormire* meaning 'to sleep', and English *mouse*

dorsal *adjective* of the back: *dorsal fin*

DOS (*pronounced* dos) *abbreviation, computing* disk operating system

dose *noun* **1** a quantity of medicine to be taken at one time **2** a bout of something unpleasant: *dose of flu* □ *verb* to give medicine to

doss *verb, informal* to lie down to sleep somewhere temporary

doss-house *noun, informal* a cheap lodging-house

dossier (*pronounced* dos-i-eh) *noun* a set of papers containing information about a certain person or subject

dot *noun* a small, round mark □ *verb* **1** to mark with a dot **2** to scatter □ **on the dot** exactly on time

   dot *verb* ⇨ **dot**s, **dot**t*ing*, **dot**t*ed*

dotage *noun* the foolishness and childishness of old age

dote *verb*: **dote on** to be foolishly fond of

double *verb* **1** to multiply by two **2** to

fold □ *noun* **1** twice as much: *he ate double the amount* **2** someone so like another as to be mistaken for them □ *adjective* **1** containing twice as much: *a double dose* **2** made up of two of the same sort **3** folded over **4** deceitful □ **at the double** very quickly □ **double back** to turn sharply and go back the way you have come □ **double up 1** to writhe in pain **2** to share accommodation (with)

double agent a spy paid by each of two rival countries, but loyal to only one of them

double bass a type of large stringed musical instrument

double-breasted *adjective* of a coat: with one half of the front overlapping the other

double-cross *verb* to cheat

double-dealer *noun* a deceitful, cheating person □ **double-dealing** *noun*

double-decker *noun* a bus with two floors

double-Dutch *noun* incomprehensible talk, gibberish

double entendre (*pronounced* doob-lon-**ton**-dre) a word or phrase with two meanings, one of them usually sexual

double glazing two sheets of glass in a window to keep in the heat or keep out noise

doublet *noun, historical* a man's close-fitting jacket

double-take *noun* a second look at something surprising or confusing

double-think *noun* the holding of two contradictory opinions or ideas

double-time *noun* payment for overtime work *etc* at twice the usual rate

doubly *adverb* **1** extra, especially: *check the door to make doubly sure you have locked it* **2** in two ways: *He's doubly responsible for the mess we're in*

doubt *verb* **1** to be unsure or undecided about **2** to think unlikely: *I doubt that we'll be able to go* □ *noun* a lack of certainty or trust; suspicion □ **no doubt** probably

doubtful *adjective* **1** doubtful about

something unsure about it **2** unlikely, uncertain or unreliable **3** strange, raising suspicion

doubtless *adverb* probably

dough *noun* **1** a mass of flour, moistened and kneaded **2** *informal* money

doughnut *noun* a ring-shaped cake fried in fat

doughty (*pronounced* **dowt**-i) *adjective* strong; brave

dour (*pronounced* door) *adjective* dull, humourless

dove[1] (*pronounced* duv) *noun* a pigeon

dove[2] (*pronounced* dohv) *US past form of* **dive**

dovecote *noun* a pigeon-house

dovetail *verb* to fit one thing exactly into another

dowdy *adjective* not smart, badly dressed

down[1] *adverb* **1** towards or in a lower position: *fell down/ sitting down* **2** to a smaller size: *grind down* **3** to a later generation: *handed down from mother to daughter* **4** on the spot, in cash: *£10 down* □ *preposition* **1** towards or in the lower part of: *rolled back down the hill* **2** along: *strolling down the road* □ *adjective* going downwards: *the down escalator* □ **go down with** or **be down with** to become or be ill with

down[2] *noun* light, soft feathers

down-at-heel *adjective* worn down, shabby

downcast *adjective* sad

downers *noun plural, slang* the drug barbiturate

downfall *noun* ruin, defeat

downhearted *adjective* discouraged

downpour *noun* a heavy fall of rain

downs *noun plural* low, grassy hills

downstairs *adjective* on a lower floor of a building □ *adverb* to a lower floor

downstream *adverb* further down a river, in the direction of its flow

downtrodden *adjective* kept in a lowly, inferior position

downwards *adverb* moving or leading down

downy *adjective* soft, feathery

dowry *noun* (*plural* **dowries**) money and property brought by a woman to her husband on their marriage

doyley *noun* another spelling of **doily**

doze *verb* to sleep lightly □ *noun* a light, short sleep

dozen *noun* twelve

drab *adjective* dull, monotonous

draft *noun* 1 a rough outline, a sketch 2 a group of people selected for a special purpose 3 *US* conscription into the army 4 an order for payment of money 5 *US* spelling of **draught** □ *verb* 1 to make a rough plan 2 to select for a purpose 3 *US* to conscript

   ✒ Do not confuse with: **draught**

draftsman, draftswoman *US spellings* of **draughtsman, draughtswoman**

drag *verb* 1 to pull roughly 2 to move slowly and heavily 3 to trail along the ground 4 to search (a river-bed *etc*) with a net or hook □ *noun, informal* 1 a dreary task 2 a tedious person 3 clothes for one sex worn by the other □ **drag your feet** or **drag your heels** to be slow to do something

dragon *noun* 1 an imaginary fire-breathing, winged reptile 2 a fierce, intimidating person

dragonfly *noun* a winged insect with a long body and double wings

dragoon *noun* a heavily-armed horse soldier □ *verb* to force or bully (into)

drain *verb* 1 to clear (land) of water by trenches or pipes 2 to drink the contents of (a glass *etc*) 3 to use up completely □ *noun* a channel or pipe used to carry off water

drainage *noun* the drawing-off of water by rivers, pipes *etc*

drained *adjective* 1 emptied of liquid 2 sapped of strength

drake *noun* a male duck

drama *noun* 1 a play for acting in the theatre 2 exciting or tense action

dramatic *adjective* 1 relating to plays 2 exciting, thrilling 3 unexpected, sudden □ **dramatically** *adverb*

dramatis personae the characters in a play

dramatist *noun* a playwright

dramatize *verb* 1 to turn into a play for the theatre 2 to make vivid or sensational □ **dramatization** *noun*

drank *past form of* **drink**

drape *verb* to arrange (cloth) to hang gracefully □ *noun* (**drapes**) *US* curtains

draper *noun* a dealer in cloth

drapery *noun* 1 cloth goods 2 a draper's shop

drastic *adjective* severe, extreme □ **drastically** *adverb*

draught (*pronounced* drahft) *noun* 1 a current of air 2 the act of drawing or pulling 3 something drawn out 4 a drink taken all at once 5 **draughts** a game for two, played by moving pieces on a squared board

   ✒ Do not confuse with: **draft**

draughtsman, draughtswoman *noun* 1 someone employed to draw plans 2 someone skilled in drawing

draughty *adjective* full of air currents, chilly

draw *verb* 1 to make a picture with pencil, crayons *etc* 2 to pull after or along 3 to attract: *drew a large crowd* 4 to obtain money from a fund: *drawing a pension* 5 to require (a depth) for floating: *this ship draws 20 feet* 6 to approach, come: *night is drawing near* 7 to score equal points in a game □ *noun* 1 an equal score 2 a lottery □ **draw a blank** to get no result □ **draw a conclusion** to form an opinion from evidence heard □ **drawn and quartered** *historical* disembowelled and cut in pieces after being hanged □ **draw on** 1 to approach 2 to use as a resource: *drawing on experience* □ **draw out** 1 to lengthen 2 to persuade (someone) to talk and be at ease □ **draw the line at** to refuse to allow or accept □ **draw up** 1 to come to a stop 2 to move closer 3 to plan, write out (a contract *etc*)

   draw *verb* ⇨ draw*s*, draw*ing*, drew, drawn

drawback *noun* a disadvantage

drawbridge *noun* a bridge at the entrance to a castle which can be drawn up or let down

drawer *noun* 1 someone who draws 2 (*pronounced* drawr) a sliding box fitting into a chest, table *etc*

drawing *noun* a picture made by pencil, crayon *etc*

drawing-pin *noun* a pin with a large flat head for fastening paper on a board *etc*

drawing-room *noun* a sitting-room

drawl *verb* to speak in a slow, lazy manner □ *noun* a drawling voice

drawn *past participle* of **draw**

dread *noun* great fear □ *adjective* terrifying □ *verb* to be greatly afraid of □ **dreaded** *adjective*

dreadful *adjective* 1 terrible 2 *informal* very bad □ **dreadfully** *adverb*

■ **Alternative words**: appalling

dreadlock *noun* a thick, twisted strand of hair

dreadnought *noun*, *historical* a kind of battleship

dream *noun* 1 a series of images and sounds in the mind during sleep 2 something imagined, not real 3 something very beautiful 4 a hope, an ambition: *her dream was to go to Mexico* □ *verb* to have a dream □ **dream up** to invent

dream *verb* ⇨ dream*s*, dream*ing*, dream*t* or dream*ed*

dreamy *adjective* 1 sleepy, half-awake 2 vague, dim 3 *informal* beautiful □ **dreamily** *adverb*

dreary *adjective* gloomy, cheerless □ **drearily** *adverb*

dredge *verb* 1 to drag a net or bucket along a river-or sea-bed to bring up fish, mud *etc* 2 to sprinkle with (sugar or flour) □ *noun* an instrument for dredging a river *etc*

dredger *noun* 1 a ship which digs a channel by lifting mud from the bottom 2 a perforated jar for sprinkling sugar or flour

dregs *noun plural* 1 sediment on the bottom of a liquid: *dregs of wine* 2 last remnants 3 a worthless or useless part

dreich (*pronounced* dreekh) *adjective*, *Scottish* dreary, miserable

drench *verb* to soak

dress *verb* 1 to put on clothes or a covering 2 to prepare (food *etc*) for use 3 to arrange (hair) 4 to treat and bandage (wounds) □ *noun* (*plural* **dresses**) 1 clothes 2 a one-piece woman's garment combining skirt and top 3 a style of clothing: *formal dress* □ *adjective* of clothes: for formal use: *a dress shirt*

dresser *noun* a kitchen sideboard for dishes

dressing *noun* 1 a covering 2 a seasoned sauce poured over salads *etc* 3 a bandage

dressing-gown *noun* a loose, light coat worn indoors over pyjamas *etc*

dress rehearsal the final rehearsal of a play, in which the actors wear their costumes

dressy *adjective* stylish, smart

drew *past form* of **draw**

drey *noun* (*plural* **dreys**) a squirrel's nest

dribble *verb* 1 to (cause to) fall in small drops 2 to let saliva run down the chin 3 *football* to move the ball forward by short kicks

dried *see* **dry**

drift *noun* 1 snow, sand *etc* driven by the wind 2 the direction in which something is driven 3 the general meaning of someone's words □ *verb* 1 to go with the tide or current 2 to be driven into heaps by the wind 3 to wander about 4 to live aimlessly

drifter *noun* 1 someone who drifts 2 a fishing boat that uses drift-nets

drift-net *noun* a fishing net which stays near the surface of the water

driftwood *noun* wood driven on to the seashore by winds or tides

drill *verb* 1 to make a hole in 2 to make with a drill 3 to exercise (soldiers) 4 to sow (seeds) in rows □ *noun* 1 a tool for making holes in wood *etc* 2 military exercise 3 a row of seeds or plants

drily *another spelling* of **dryly**

drink verb 1 to swallow (a liquid) 2 to take alcoholic drink, especially excessively □ noun 1 liquid to be drunk 2 alcoholic liquids □ **drink in** to listen to eagerly □ **drink to** to drink a toast to □ **drink up** to finish a drink

> **drink** verb ⇨ drinks, drinking, drank, drunk

drip verb 1 to fall in drops 2 to let (water etc) fall in drops □ noun 1 a drop 2 a continual dropping, eg of water 3 a device for adding liquid slowly to a vein etc

> **drip** verb ⇨ drips, dripping, dripped

drip-dry verb to dry (a garment) by hanging it up to dry without wringing it first

dripping noun fat from roasting meat

drive verb 1 to control or guide (a car etc) 2 to go in a vehicle: driving to work 3 to force or urge along 4 to hurry on 5 to hit hard (a ball, nail etc) 6 to bring about: drive a bargain □ noun 1 a journey in a car 2 a private road to a house 3 an avenue or road 4 energy, enthusiasm 5 a campaign: a drive to save the local school 6 a games tournament: whist drive 7 a hard stroke with a club or bat □ **what are you driving at?** what are you suggesting or implying?

> **drive** ⇨ drives, driving, drove, driven

drive-in noun, US a cinema where the audience watches the screen while staying in their cars

drivel noun, informal nonsense □ verb to talk nonsense

> **drivel** verb ⇨ drivels, drivelling, drivelled

driven past participle of **drive**

driver noun 1 someone who drives a car etc 2 a wooden-headed golf club

drizzle noun light rain □ verb to rain lightly □ **drizzly** adjective

droll adjective 1 funny, amusing 2 odd

dromedary noun (plural **dromedaries**) an Arabian camel with one hump

drone verb 1 to make a low humming sound 2 to speak in a dull boring voice □ noun 1 a low humming sound 2 a dull boring voice 3 the low-sounding pipe of

a bagpipe 4 a male bee 5 a lazy, idle person

drool verb 1 to produce saliva 2 to anticipate something in an obvious way

droop verb 1 to hang down: your hem is drooping 2 to grow weak or discouraged

drop noun 1 a small round or pear-shaped blob of liquid 2 a small quantity: a drop of whisky 3 a fall from a height: a drop of six feet 4 a small flavoured sweet: pear drop □ verb 1 to fall suddenly 2 to let fall 3 to fall in drops 4 to set down from a car etc: drop me at the corner 5 to give up, abandon (a friend, habit etc) □ **drop off** to fall asleep □ **drop out** to withdraw from a class, the rat-race etc

> **drop** ⇨ drops, dropping, dropped

droplet noun a tiny drop

droppings noun plural animal or bird dung

dross noun 1 scum produced by melting metal 2 waste material, impurities 3 coal dust 4 anything worthless

drought noun a period of time when no rain falls

drove noun 1 a number of moving cattle or other animals 2 **droves** a great number of people □ past form of **drive**

drover noun someone who drives cattle

drown verb 1 to die by suffocating in water 2 to kill (someone) in this way 3 to flood or soak completely 4 to block out (a sound) with a louder one

drowsy adjective sleepy □ **drowsily** adverb

drubbing noun a thrashing

drudge verb to do very humble or boring work □ noun someone who does such work

drudgery noun hard, uninteresting work

drug noun 1 a substance used in medicine to treat illness, kill pain etc 2 a stimulant or narcotic substance taken habitually for its effects □ verb 1 to administer drugs to 2 to make to lose consciousness by drugs

> **drug** ⇨ drugs, drugging, drugged

druggist *noun* a chemist

drugstore *noun*, *US* a shop selling newspapers, soft drinks *etc* as well as medicines

drum *noun* 1 a musical instrument of skin *etc* stretched on a round frame and beaten with sticks 2 a cylindrical container: *oil drum/ biscuit drum* □ *verb* 1 to beat a drum 2 to tap continuously with the fingers □ **drummer** *noun*

> **drum** ⇨ drum*s*, drum*ming*, drum*med*

drumstick *noun* 1 a stick for beating a drum 2 the lower part of the leg of a cooked chicken *etc*

drunk *adjective* showing the effects (giddiness, unsteadiness *etc*) of drinking too much alcohol □ *noun* someone who is drunk, or habitually drunk □ *past participle* of **drink**

> ■ **Alternative words**: (adjective) inebriated, intoxicated, drunken

drunkard *noun* a drunk

drunken *adjective* 1 habitually drunk 2 caused by too much alcohol: *drunken stupor* 3 involving much alcohol: *drunken orgy* □ **drunkenness** *noun*

dry *adjective* 1 not moist or wet 2 thirsty 3 uninteresting: *makes very dry reading* 4 reserved, matter-of-fact 5 of wine: not sweet 6 of a sense of humour: funny in a quiet, subtle way □ *verb* to make or become dry

> **dry** *verb* ⇨ drie*s*, dry*ing*, drie*d*

dryad (*pronounced* **drai**-ad) *noun* a mythological wood nymph

dry-clean *verb* to clean (clothes *etc*) with chemicals, not with water

dryly or **drily** *adverb* 1 in a reserved, matter-of-fact, emotionless way 2 with quiet, subtle humour

dryness *noun* the quality of being dry

dry-rot *noun* a disease causing wood to become dry and crumbly

dry-stane *Scottish* or **dry-stone** *adjective* built of stone without cement or mortar

DSS *abbreviation* Department of Social Services (previously **DHSS** Department of Health and Social Security)

DTI *abbreviation* Department of Trade and Industry

DTP *abbreviation* desktop publishing

dual *adjective* double; made up of two
> ☛ Do not confuse with: **duel**

dual carriageway a road divided by a central barrier or boundary, with each side used by traffic moving in one direction

dual-purpose *adjective* able to be used for two purposes

dub *verb* 1 to declare (a knight) by touching each shoulder with a sword 2 to name or nickname 3 to add sound effects to a film 4 to give (a film) a new sound-track in a different language

> **dub** ⇨ dub*s*, dub*bing*, dub*bed*

dubbin or **dubbing** *noun* a grease for softening or waterproofing leather

dubiety *noun* doubt

dubious *adjective* 1 doubtful, uncertain 2 probably dishonest: *dubious dealings*

ducal *adjective* of a duke

ducat *noun*, *historical* an old European gold coin

duchess *noun* (*plural* **duchesses**) 1 a woman of the same rank as a duke 2 the wife or widow of a duke

duchy *noun* (*plural* **duchies**) the land owned by a duke or duchess

duck *noun* 1 a web-footed bird, with a broad flat beak 2 *cricket* a score of no runs □ *verb* 1 to lower the head quickly as if to avoid a blow 2 to push (someone's head) under water □ **duck out (of)** to avoid responsibility (for)
> The meaning in cricket comes from the use of 'duck's egg' to mean a nought on a scoring sheet

duck-billed platypus *see* **platypus**

duckling *noun* a baby duck

duct *noun* a pipe for carrying liquids, electric cables *etc*

ductile *adjective* easily led, yielding

dud *adjective*, *informal* useless, broken

dudgeon *noun*: **in high dudgeon** very angry, indignant

due *adjective* 1 owed, needing to be

paid: *the rent is due next week* **2** expected to arrive etc: *they're due here at six* **3** proper, appropriate: *due care* □ *adverb* directly: *due south* □ *noun* **1** something you have a right to: *give him his due* **2** **dues** the amount of money charged for belonging to a club *etc* □ **due to** brought about by, caused by

duel *noun, historical* a formalized fight with pistols or swords between two people □ *verb* to fight in a duel

🖝 Do not confuse with: **dual**

duellist *noun* someone who fights in a duel

duet (*pronounced* dyoo-et) *noun* a piece of music for two singers or players

duff *adjective, informal* useless, broken

duffel bag a cylindrical canvas bag tied with a drawstring

duffel coat a heavy woollen coat, fastened with toggles

After *Duffel*, a town in Belgium where the fabric was first made

duffer *noun, informal* a stupid or incompetent person

dug *past form of* **dig**

dugout *noun* **1** a boat made by hollowing out the trunk of a tree **2** a rough shelter dug out of a slope or bank or in a trench **3** *football* a bench beside the pitch for team managers, trainers, and extra players

duke *noun* a nobleman next in rank below a prince

dukedom *noun* the title, rank or lands of a duke

dulcet *adjective, formal* pleasant-sounding, melodious

dulcimer *noun* a musical instrument with stretched wires which are struck with small hammers

dull *adjective* **1** not lively **2** slow to understand or learn **3** not exciting or interesting **4** of weather: cloudy, not bright or clear **5** not bright in colour **6** of sounds: not clear or ringing **7** blunt, not sharp **8** of pain: present in the background, but not acute □ *verb* to make dull □ **dullness** *noun* □ **dully** *adverb* (adjective, meanings 1, 5, 6 and 8)

duly *adverb* at the proper or expected time; as expected: *he duly arrived*

dumb *adjective* **1** without the power of speech **2** silent **3** *informal* stupid

dumbfound *verb* to astonish

dumbly *adverb* in silence

dumb show acting without words

dummy *noun* (*plural* **dummies**) **1** a mock-up of something used for display **2** a model used for displaying clothes *etc* **3** an artificial teat used to comfort a baby **4** *slang* a stupid person

dummy run a try-out, a practice

dump *verb* **1** to throw down heavily **2** to unload and leave (rubbish *etc*) **3** to sell at a low price □ *noun* a place for leaving rubbish □ **in the dumps** feeling low or depressed

dumpling *noun* a cooked ball of dough

dumpy *adjective* short and thick or fat

dun *adjective* greyish-brown, mouse-coloured □ *verb* to demand payment

dun *verb* ⇨ duns, dun**n**ing, dun**n**ed

dunce *noun* a stupid or slow-learning person

Originally a term of abuse applied to followers of the medieval Scottish philosopher, John *Duns Scotus*

dunderhead *noun, informal* a stupid person

dune *noun* a low hill of sand

dung *noun* animal faeces, manure

dungarees *noun plural* trousers made of coarse, hard-wearing material with a bib

dungeon *noun* a dark underground prison

dunt *noun, Scottish* a thump, a knock

duodenum *noun* the first part of the small intestine

dupe *noun* someone easily cheated □ *verb* to deceive, trick

duplicate *adjective* exactly the same □ *noun* an exact copy □ *verb* to make a copy or copies of □ **duplication** *noun*

duplicity *noun* deceit, double-dealing □ **duplicitous** *adjective*

durable *adjective* lasting, able to last; wearing well □ **durability** *noun*

duration *noun* the time a thing lasts □ **for the duration** *informal* for a long time, for ages

duress (*pronounced* dyoo-**res**) *noun* illegal force used to make someone do something □ **under duress** under the influence of force, threats *etc*

during *preposition* **1** throughout all or part of: *we lived here during the war* **2** at a particular point within: *she died during the night*

dusk *noun* twilight, partial dark

dusky *adjective* dark-coloured □ **duskiness** *noun*

dust *noun* **1** fine grains or specks of earth, sand *etc* **2** fine powder □ *verb* **1** to free from dust: *dusted the table* **2** to sprinkle lightly with powder

dustbin *noun* a container for household rubbish

duster *noun* a cloth for removing dust

dust jacket a paper cover on a book

dustman *noun* someone employed to collect household rubbish

dusty *adjective* covered with dust

dutiful *adjective* obedient □ **dutifully** *adverb*

duty *noun* (*plural* **duties**) **1** something a person ought to do **2** an action required to be done **3** a tax **4 duties** the various tasks involved in a job

duty-free *adjective* not taxed

duvet (*pronounced* **doo**-vei) *noun* a quilt stuffed with feathers or synthetic material, used instead of blankets

dux (*pronounced* duks) *noun* (*plural* **duxes**) the top boy or girl in some Scottish schools
🕐 Comes from Latin *dux* meaning 'a leader'

dwarf *noun* (*plural* **dwarfs** or **dwarves**) an undersized person, animal or plant □ *verb* to make to appear small by comparison □ *adjective* not growing to full or usual height: *dwarf cherry-tree*

dwell *verb* **1** to live, inhabit, stay **2 dwell on** to think habitually about something: *dwelling on the past*

dwindle *verb* to grow less, waste away

dye *verb* to give a colour to (fabric *etc*) □ *noun* a powder or liquid for colouring

dyeing *noun* the putting of colour into cloth

dying *present participle* of **die**

dyke *another spelling of* **dike**

dynamic *adjective* forceful, energetic □ **dynamically** *adverb*

dynamics *noun singular* the scientific study of movement and force

dynamite *noun* a type of powerful explosive

dynamo *noun* (*plural* **dynamos**) a machine for turning the energy produced by movement into electricity

dynasty (*pronounced* **din**-as-ti) *noun* (*plural* **dynasties**) a succession of monarchs, leaders *etc* of the same family □ **dynastic** *adjective*

dys- (*pronounced* dis) *prefix* forms words which describe disorders of some part of the body or of the mind: *dyslexia/ dyspepsia/ dysentery* (= an infectious disease of the intestine)
🕐 Comes from Greek prefix *dys-* meaning 'badly'

dysentery *noun* an infectious disease causing fever, pain and diarrhoea

dyslexia *noun* difficulty in learning to read and in spelling

dyslexic *noun & adjective* (someone) suffering from dyslexia

dyspepsia *noun* indigestion □ **dyspeptic** *adjective*

Ee

If the word you're looking for sounds like it begins **EE** but you can't find it there, try looking under **AE** for words like *aesthetic*, and **OE** for words like *oestrus*.

E *abbreviation* **1** east; eastern **2** the drug Ecstasy

each *adjective* of two or more things: every one taken individually: *there is a postbox on each side of the road/ she was late on each occasion* □ *pronoun* every one individually: *each of them won a prize* □ **each other** used when an action takes place between two people: *we don't see each other very often*

eager *adjective* keen, anxious to do or get (something) □ **eagerly** *adverb*

■ Alternative words: anxious

eagle *noun* a kind of large bird of prey

eaglet *noun* a young eagle

ear *noun* **1** the part of the body through which you hear sounds **2** a head (of corn *etc*) □ **a good ear** the ability to tell one sound from another □ **lend an ear** to listen

eardrum *noun* the membrane in the middle of the ear

earl *noun* a member of the British aristocracy between a marquis and a viscount

earldom *noun* the lands or title of an earl

ear-lobe *noun* the soft fleshy part at the bottom of the human ear

early *adjective* **1** in good time **2** at or near the beginning: *in an earlier chapter* **3** sooner than expected: *you're early!* □ *adverb*: *the bus left early* □ **earliness** *noun*

early ⇨ earlier, earliest

early bird 1 an early riser **2** someone who gains an advantage by acting more quickly than rivals

earmark *verb* to mark or set aside for a special purpose

ear-muffs *noun plural* two pads of warm material joined by a band across the head, which you use to cover your ears to stop them getting cold

earn *verb* **1** to receive (money) for work **2** to deserve

earnest *adjective* serious, serious-minded □ *noun* **1** seriousness **2** money *etc* given to make sure that a bargain will be kept □ **in earnest** meaning what you say or do □ **earnestly** *adverb*

earnings *noun plural* pay for work done

earphones *noun plural* a pair of tiny speakers fitting in or against the ear for listening to a radio *etc*

ear-piercing *adjective* very loud or shrill

earplugs *noun plural* a pair of plugs placed in the ears to block off outside noise

earshot *noun* the distance at which a sound can be heard

earth *noun* **1** the third planet from the sun; our world **2** its surface **3** soil **4** the hole of a fox, badger *etc* **5** an electrical connection with the ground □ *verb* to connect electrically with the ground

earthenware *noun* pottery, dishes made of clay

earthily *adverb* in a coarse, natural, unrefined way

earthiness *noun* coarseness, naturalness, lack of refinement

earthly *adjective* of the earth as opposed to heaven

earthquake *noun* a shaking of the earth's crust

earthshattering *adjective* of great importance

earthworm *noun* the common worm

earthy *adjective* **1** like soil **2** covered in soil **3** coarse and natural, not refined

earwig *noun* a type of insect with pincers at its tail

ease *noun* **1** freedom from difficulty: *finished the race with ease* **2** freedom from pain, worry or embarrassment **3** rest from work □ *verb* **1** to make or become less painful or difficult **2** to move carefully and gradually: *ease the stone into position* □ **at ease** comfortable, relaxed □ **stand at ease** to stand with your legs apart and arms behind your back

■ **Alternative words**: (verb, meaning 1) alleviate

easel *noun* a stand for an artist's canvas while painting *etc*

easily *adverb* **1** without difficulty **2** without pain, worry or discomfort **3** obviously, clearly, beyond doubt or by a long way: *He's easily the most accomplished actor in Britain today* **4** more quickly or more readily than most people **5** very possibly: *He could easily be out for a couple of hours*

easiness *noun* the quality of being or feeling easy

east *noun* one of the four chief directions, that in which the sun rises □ *adjective* in or from the east: *an east wind*

Easter *noun* **1** the Christian celebration of Christ's rising from the dead **2** the weekend when this is celebrated each year, sometime in spring

easterly *adjective* coming from or facing the east

eastern *adjective* of the east

eastward or **eastwards** *adjective & adverb* towards the east

easy *adjective* **1** not hard to do **2** free from pain, worry or discomfort

easy ⇨ easi*er*, easi*est*

■ **Alternative words**: (adjective, meaning 1) effortless, simple, undemanding; (adjective, meaning 2) relaxed, leisurely

eat *verb* **1** to chew and swallow (food) **2** to destroy gradually, waste away

eat ⇨ eats, eat*ing*, ate, eate*n*

eatable *adjective* fit to eat, edible

eaves *noun plural* the edge of a roof overhanging the walls

eavesdrop *verb* to listen secretly to a private conversation □ **eavesdropper** *noun*

ebb *noun* **1** the flowing away of the tide after high tide **2** a lessening, a worsening □ *verb* **1** to flow away **2** to grow less or worse

ebony *noun* a type of black, hard wood □ *adjective* **1** made of ebony **2** black

EC *abbreviation* European Community

eccentric *adjective* **1** odd, acting strangely **2** of circles: not having the same centre (*contrasted with*: **concentric**)

eccentricity *noun* (*plural* **eccentricities**) oddness of manner or conduct

ecclesiastic or **ecclesiastical** *adjective* of the church or clergy

echo *noun* (*plural* **echoes**) **1** the repetition of a sound by its striking a surface and coming back **2** something that evokes a memory: *echoes of the past* □ *verb* **1** to send back sound **2** to repeat (a thing said) **3** to imitate

éclair (*pronounced* ei-**kleir**) *noun* an oblong sweet pastry filled with cream

eclipse *noun* **1** the covering of the whole or part of the sun or moon, *eg* when the moon comes between the sun and the earth **2** loss of position or prestige □ *verb* **1** to throw into the shade **2** to blot out (someone's achievement) by doing better

eco- *prefix* relating to the environment: *ecofriendly/ eco-summit*

This prefix has been created by taking the start of 'ecology' and adding different endings

ecological *adjective* **1** having to do

with plants, animals *etc* and their natural surroundings **2** concerned with protecting and preserving plants, animals and the natural environment □ **ecologically** *adverb*: *make society more ecologically aware*

ecologist *noun* **1** someone who studies, or is an expert in, ecology **2** someone who believes that our world will not survive if all its plants and animals are not properly cared for and preserved

ecology *noun* the study of plants, animals *etc* in relation to their natural surroundings

ⓘ Comes from Greek *oikos* meaning 'house', and *logos* meaning 'discourse'

economic *adjective* **1** concerning economy **2** making a profit

economical *adjective* thrifty, not wasteful

economics *noun singular* the study of how money is created and spent

economist *noun* someone who studies or is an expert on economics

economize *verb* to be careful in spending or using

economy *noun* (*plural* **economies**) **1** the management of a country's finances **2** the careful use of something, especially money

ecstasy *noun* (*plural* **ecstasies**) **1** very great joy or pleasure **2** Ecstasy a hallucinogenic drug □ **ecstatic** *adjective* (meaning 1) □ **ecstatically** *adverb* (meaning 1)

ECT *abbreviation* electro-convulsive therapy

ecu *abbreviation* European currency unit, a reserve currency with a rate based on a range of European currencies

ecumenical *adjective* concerned with the unity of the whole Christian church

eczema (*pronounced* ek-sim-*a*) *noun* a skin disease causing red swollen patches on the skin □ **eczematic** *adjective*

eddy *noun* (*plural* **eddies**) a circling current of water or air running against the main stream □ *verb* to flow in circles

edelweiss (*pronounced* eid-*el*-vais) *noun* an Alpine plant with white flowers

ⓘ Comes from German *edel* meaning 'noble', and *weiss* meaning 'white'

edge *noun* **1** the border of anything, farthest from the middle **2** the cutting side of a blade **3** sharpness: *put an edge on my appetite* **4** advantage: *Brazil had the edge at half-time* □ *verb* **1** to put a border on **2** to move little by little: *edging forward* □ **on edge** nervous, edgy □ **set someone's teeth on edge** to grate on their nerves, make them wince

edgeways *adverb* sideways

edging *noun* a border, a fringe

edgy *adjective* unable to relax, irritable

edible *adjective* fit to be eaten

edict *noun* an order, a command

edification *noun* mental and spiritual improvement

edifice *noun* a large building

edify *verb* to improve the mind, enlighten □ **edifying** *adjective*

edify ⇨ **edifies, edifying, edified**

edit *verb* to prepare (a text, film *etc*) for publication or broadcasting

edition *noun* **1** the form in which a book *etc* is published after being edited **2** the copies of a book, newspaper *etc* printed at one time **3** a special issue of a newspaper, *eg* for a local area

editor *noun* **1** someone who edits a book, film *etc* **2** the chief journalist of a newspaper or section of a newspaper: *the sports editor*

editorial *adjective* of editing □ *noun* a newspaper column written by the chief editor

educate *verb* to teach (people), especially in a school or college

educated *adjective* knowledgeable and cultured, as a result of receiving a good education

educated guess a guess based on knowledge of the subject involved

education *noun* **1** the process or system of teaching in schools and other establishments **2** the development of a person's knowledge **3** an experience from which you think you have learnt something

educational *adjective* **1** concerned with

formal teaching **2** concerned with giving information, rather than simply entertaining or amusing **3** interesting from the point of view of teaching you something which you did not know before

EEC *abbreviation* European Economic Community

eel *noun* a long, ribbon-shaped fish

eerie *adjective* causing fear of the unknown

> Originally a Scots word meaning 'afraid' or 'cowardly'

efface *verb* to rub out □ **efface yourself** to keep from being noticed

effect *noun* **1** the result of an action **2** strength, power: *the pills had little effect* **3** an impression produced: *the effect of the sunset* **4** general meaning **5** use, operation: *that law is not yet in effect* **6** **effects** goods, property □ *verb* to bring about

○ Comes from Latin *effectus* meaning 'finished'

> **♦** Do not confuse with: **affect**. **Effect** is usually a noun. **Affect** is usually a verb. 'To AFFECT' means 'to have an EFFECT on'

effective *adjective* **1** producing the desired effect **2** actual

effectual *adjective* able to do what is required □ **effectually** *adverb*

effeminate *adjective* unmanly, womanish

effervesce *verb* **1** to froth up **2** to be very lively, excited *etc* □ **effervescence** *noun* □ **effervescent** *adjective*

effete *adjective* weak, feeble

efficacious *adjective* effective □ **efficacy** *noun*

efficient *adjective* able to do things well; capable □ **efficiency** *noun* □ **efficiently** *adverb*

effigy *noun* (*plural* **effigies**) a likeness of a person carved in stone, wood *etc*

effluent *noun* **1** a stream flowing from another stream or lake **2** liquid industrial waste; sewage

effort *noun* **1** an attempt using a lot of strength or ability **2** hard work

■ **Alternative words**: (meaning 1) attempt

effrontery *noun* impudence

effusive *adjective* speaking freely, gushing □ **effusively** *adverb*

EFL *abbreviation* English as a foreign language

eg *abbreviation* for example (from Latin *exempli gratia*)

egg *noun* **1** an oval shell containing the embryo of a bird, insect or reptile **2** (*also called* **ovum**) a human reproductive cell **3** a hen's egg used for eating □ **egg on** to urge, encourage

eggplant *noun, US* an aubergine

ego *noun* **1** the conscious self **2** self-conceit, egotism

egoism or **egotism** *noun* the habit of considering only your own interests, selfishness □ **egoist** or **egotist** *noun* □ **egoistic** or **egotistic** *adjective*

eiderdown *noun* **1** soft feathers from the eider, a type of northern sea-duck **2** a feather quilt

eight *noun* the number 8 □ *adjective* 8 in number

eighteen *noun* the number 18 □ *adjective* 18 in number

eighteenth *adjective* the last of a series of eighteen □ *noun* one of eighteen equal parts

eighth *adjective* the last of a series of eight □ *noun* one of eight equal parts

eightieth *adjective* the last of a series of eighty □ *noun* one of eighty equal parts

eighty *noun* the number 80 □ *adjective* 80 in number

either *adjective & pronoun* **1** one or other of two: *either bus will go there/ either of the dates would suit me* **2** each of two, both: *there is a crossing on either side of the road* □ *conjunction* used with **or** to show alternatives: *either he goes or I do* □ *adverb* any more than another: *that won't work either*

ejaculate *verb* **1** to emit semen **2** to shout out, exclaim □ **ejaculation** *noun*

eject *verb* **1** to throw out **2** to force to leave a house, job *etc* □ **ejection** *noun*

eke *verb*: **eke out** to make last longer by adding to: *eked out the stew with more vegetables*

elaborate *verb* (*pronounced* i-**lab**-*o*-reit) **1** to work out in detail: *you must elaborate your escape plan* **2** (often **elaborate on**) to explain fully □ *adjective* (*pronounced* i-**lab**-*o*-rat) highly detailed or decorated □ **elaboration** *noun*

elapse *verb* of time: to pass

elastic *adjective* able to stretch and spring back again, springy □ *noun* a piece of cotton *etc* interwoven with rubber to make it springy □ **elasticity** *noun*

elated *adjective* in high spirits, very pleased □ **elation** *noun*

elbow *noun* the joint where the arm bends □ *verb* to push with the elbow, jostle

elbow grease 1 vigorous rubbing **2** hard work, effort

elbow-room *noun* plenty of room to move

elder¹ *adjective* older □ *noun* **1** someone who is older **2** an office-bearer in the Presbyterian church

elder² *noun* a type of tree with purple-black berries

elderberry *noun* (*plural* **elderberries**) a berry from the elder tree

elderly *adjective* nearing old age

eldest *adjective* oldest

elect *verb* **1** to choose by voting **2** to choose (to) *adjective* **1** chosen **2** chosen for a post but not yet in it: *president elect*

election *noun* the choosing by vote of people to sit in parliament *etc*

electorate *noun* all those who have the right to vote

electric or **electrical** *adjective* produced or worked by electricity

electrician *noun* someone skilled in working with electricity

electricity *noun* a form of energy used to give light, heat and power

electrify *verb* **1** to supply with electricity **2** to excite greatly

electrify ⇨ electrif*ies*, electrif*ying*, electrif*ied*

electro- *prefix* electric, of or by electricity
  🕐 Comes from Greek *elektro-*, a form of *elektron* meaning 'amber'

electrocute *verb* to kill by an electric current

electrode *noun* a conductor through which an electric current enters or leaves a battery *etc*

electron *noun* a very light particle within an atom, having the smallest possible charge of electricity

electronic *adjective* of or using electrons or electronics

electronics *noun singular* a branch of physics dealing with electrons and their use in machines *etc*

elegant *adj* **1** graceful, well-dressed, fashionable **2** of clothes *etc*: well-made and tasteful □ **elegance** *noun* □ **elegantly** *adverb*

elegy *noun* (*plural* **elegies**) a poem written on someone's death

element *noun* **1** a part of anything **2** a substance that cannot be split chemically into simpler substances, *eg* oxygen, iron **3** circumstances which suit someone best: *she is in her element when singing* **4** a heating wire carrying the current in an electric heater **5 elements** first steps in learning **6 elements** the powers of nature, the weather

elemental *adjective* of the elements

elementary *adjective* **1** at the first stage **2** simple

elephant *noun* a very large animal with a thick skin, a trunk and two ivory tusks

elephantine (*pronounced* el-i-**fan**-tain) *adjective* big and clumsy

elevate *verb* **1** to raise to a higher position **2** to cheer up **3** to improve (the mind)

elevation *noun* **1** the act of raising up **2** rising ground **3** height **4** a drawing of a building as seen from the side **5** an angle measuring height: *the sun's elevation*

elevator *noun, US* a lift in a building

eleven *noun* **1** the number 11 **2** a team of eleven players, *eg* for cricket □ *adjective* 11 in number

elevenses *noun plural* coffee, biscuits *etc* taken around eleven o'clock in the morning

eleventh *adjective* the last of a series of eleven □ *noun* one of eleven equal parts

elf *noun* (*plural* **elves**) a tiny, mischievous supernatural creature

elfin, elfish or **elvish** *adjective* like an elf

elicit *verb* to draw out (information *etc*)
Ⓛ Comes from Latin *elicit-*, a form of *elicere* meaning 'to lure out'
🖢 Do not confuse with: **illicit**

eligible *adjective* fit or worthy to be chosen, especially for marriage
□ **eligibility** *noun*

eliminate *verb* **1** to get rid of **2** to exclude, omit □ **elimination** *noun*

élite or **elite** (*pronounced* ei-**leet**) *noun* a part of a group selected as, or believed to be, the best

elixir (*pronounced* e-**liks**-eer) *noun* a liquid believed to give eternal life, or to be able to turn iron *etc* into gold

elk *noun* a very large deer found in N Europe and Asia, related to the moose

ellipse *noun* (*plural* **ellipses**) an oval shape

elliptic or **elliptical** *adjective* **1** oval **2** having part of the words or meaning left out

elm *noun* a tree with a rough bark and leaves with saw-like edges

elocution *noun* **1** the art of what is thought to be correct speech **2** style of speaking

elongate *verb* to stretch out lengthwise, make longer □ **elongation** *noun*

elope *verb* to run away from home to get married □ **elopement** *noun*

eloquent *adjective* **1** good at expressing thoughts in words **2** persuasive
□ **eloquence** *noun*

else *adverb* otherwise: *come inside or else you will catch cold* □ *adjective* other than the person or thing mentioned: *someone else has taken her place*

elsewhere *adverb* in or to another place

elucidate *verb* to make (something) easy to understand

elude *verb* **1** to escape by a trick **2** to be too difficult to remember or understand
Ⓛ Comes from Latin *eludere* meaning 'to outplay'
🖢 Do not confuse with: **allude**

elusive *adjective* hard to catch
🖢 Do not confuse with: **allusive** and **illusive. Elusive** comes from the verb **elude**

elves *see* **elf**

elvish *see* **elfin**

em- *see* **in-**

emaciated *adjective* very thin, like a skeleton

E-mail *noun* electronic mail

emanate *verb* to flow, come out from
□ **emanation** *noun*

emancipate *verb* to set free, *eg* from slavery or repressive social conditions
□ **emancipation** *noun*

embalm *verb* to preserve (a dead body) from decay by treating it with spices or drugs

embankment *noun* a bank of earth or stone to keep back water, or carry a railway over low-lying places

embargo *noun* (*plural* **embargoes**) an official order forbidding something, especially trade with another country

embark *verb* **1** to go on board ship **2** **embark on** to start (a new career *etc*)
□ **embarkation** *noun* (meaning 1)

embarrass *verb* to make to feel uncomfortable and self-conscious
□ **embarrassing** *adjective*
□ **embarrassed** *adjective*

▦ **Alternative words:** disconcert, mortify, discompose, humiliate

embarrassment *noun* **1** the state of being embarrassed **2** something which makes you embarrassed

embassy *noun* (*plural* **embassies**) the offices and staff of an ambassador in a foreign country

embellish *verb* **1** to decorate **2** to add details to (a story *etc*) □ **embellishment** *noun*

ember *noun* a piece of wood or coal glowing in a fire

embezzle *verb* to use for yourself money entrusted to you □ **embezzlement** *noun*

emblazon *verb* **1** to decorate, adorn **2** to show in bright colours or conspicuously

emblem *noun* **1** an image which represents something: *the dove is the emblem of peace/ the leek is the emblem of Wales* **2** a badge

embodiment *noun* a person or thing that perfectly symbolizes some idea or quality

embody *verb* **1** to include **2** to express, give form to: *embodying the spirit of the age*

> **embody** ⇨ embod**ies**, embody**ing**, embod**ied**

emboss *verb* to make a pattern in leather, metal *etc*, which stands out from a flat surface □ **embossed** *adjective*

embrace *verb* **1** to throw your arms round in affection **2** to include **3** to accept, adopt eagerly □ *noun* an affectionate hug

embrocation *noun* an ointment for rubbing on the body, *eg* to relieve stiffness

embroider *verb* **1** to decorate with designs in needlework **2** to add false details to (a story)

embroidery *noun* **1** the art or practice of sewing designs on to cloth **2** the designs sewn on to cloth

embroil *verb* **1** to get (someone) into a quarrel, or into a difficult situation **2** to throw into confusion

embryo *noun* (*plural* **embryos**) **1** the young of an animal or plant in its earliest stage **2** the beginning of anything

embryonic *adjective* in an early stage of development

emend *verb* a rather formal word meaning 'to remove faults or errors from' □ **emendation** *noun*

> 🖋 Do not confuse with: **amend**. **Emending** consists simply of deleting errors. **Amending** involves making changes or improvements

emerald *noun* a bright green precious stone

emerge *verb* **1** to come out **2** to become known or clear □ **emergence** *noun*

emergency *noun* (*plural* **emergencies**) an unexpected event requiring very quick action

emergency exit a way out of a building for use in an emergency

emergent *adjective* **1** arising **2** newly formed or newly independent: *emergent nation*

emery *noun* a very hard mineral, used for smoothing and polishing

emetic *adjective* causing vomiting □ *noun* an emetic medicine

emigrant *noun* someone who emigrates

emigrate *verb* to leave your country to settle in another □ **emigration** *noun*
🕐 Comes from Latin *e* meaning 'from', and *migrare* meaning 'to remove'

> 🖋 Do not confuse with: **immigrate**. You are **Emigrating** when you leave your home country (the E comes from the Latin meaning 'from'). You **IMmigrate** to the country where you plan to start living (the IM comes from the Latin meaning 'into')

émigré (*pronounced* ei-mee-**grei**) *noun* someone who is forced to emigrate for political reasons

eminence *noun* **1** distinction, fame **2** a title of honour **3** a hill

eminent *adjective* famous, notable
🕐 Comes from Latin *eminens* meaning 'standing out'

> 🖋 Do not confuse with: **imminent**

eminently *adverb* very, obviously: *eminently suitable*

emit *verb* to send or give out (light, sound *etc*) □ **emission** *noun*

emit ⇨ emit*s*, emit*ting*, emit*ted*

emolument *noun, formal* wages, salary

emotion *noun* a feeling that disturbs or excites the mind, *eg* fear, love, hatred

emotional *adjective* 1 moving the feelings 2 of a person: having feelings easily excited

emotionally *adverb* in a way which relates to the emotions

emotive *adjective* causing emotion rather than thought

empathize *verb* to share another person's feelings *etc*

empathy *noun* the ability to share another person's feelings *etc*

emperor *noun* the ruler of an empire

emphasis *noun* 1 stress placed on a word or words in speaking 2 greater attention or importance: *the emphasis is on playing, not winning*

emphasize *verb* to put emphasis on; call attention to

emphatic *adjective* spoken strongly: *an emphatic 'no'* □ **emphatically** *adverb*

emphysema (*pronounced* em-fi-seem-a) *noun* a lung disease causing breathing difficulties

empire *noun* 1 a group of nations *etc* under the same ruling power 2 a large business organization including several companies

empirical *adjective* 1 based on experiment and experience, not on theory alone □ **empiricism** *noun*

employ *verb* 1 to give work to 2 to use 3 to occupy the time of □ *noun* employment

employee *noun* someone who works for an employer

employer *noun* someone who gives work to employees

employment *noun* work, occupation

emporium *noun* (*plural* **emporia** or **emporiums**) a large shop; a market

empower *verb* 1 to authorize 2 to give self-confidence to

empress *noun* the female ruler of an empire

empty *adjective* 1 containing nothing or no one 2 unlikely to result in anything: *empty threats* □ *verb* to make or become empty □ *noun* (*plural* **empties**) an empty bottle *etc* □ **emptiness** *noun*

empty ⇨ empt*ies*, empt*ying*, empt*ied*

empty-handed *adjective* bringing or gaining nothing

empty-headed *adjective* flighty, irresponsible

EMU *abbreviation* European Monetary Union

emu *noun* a type of Australian bird which cannot fly

emulate *verb* to try to do as well as, or better than □ **emulation** *noun*

emulsion *noun* a milky liquid, especially that made by mixing oil and water

en- see **in-**

enable *verb* to make it possible for, allow: *the money enabled him to retire*

enact *verb* 1 to act, perform 2 to make a law

enamel *noun* 1 a glassy coating fired on to metal 2 a paint with a glossy finish 3 the smooth white coating of the teeth □ *verb* to coat or paint with enamel □ **enamelling** *noun*

enamel *verb* ⇨ enamel*s*, enamel*ling*, enamel*led*

enamoured *adjective*: **enamoured of** fond of

encampment *noun* a military camp

encapsulate *verb* to capture the essence of; describe briefly and accurately

encephalitis *noun* inflammation of the brain

enchant *verb* 1 to delight, please greatly 2 to put a spell or charm on □ **enchanter, enchantress** *noun* (meaning 2)

enchanting *adjective* delightful, charming

enchantment *noun* 1 a feeling of delight and wonder 2 a spell or charm

enclave *noun* an area enclosed within foreign territory

enclose *verb* **1** to put inside an envelope with a letter *etc* **2** to put (*eg* a wall) around

enclosure *noun* **1** the act of enclosing **2** something enclosed *eg* a small field with a high fence or wall round it

encompass *verb* to surround; to include

encore (*pronounced* ong-kawr) *noun* **1** an extra performance of a song *etc* in reply to audience applause **2** a call for an encore

encounter *verb* **1** to meet by chance **2** to come up against (a difficulty, enemy *etc*) *noun* a meeting, a fight

encourage *verb* **1** to give hope or confidence to **2** to urge (to do) □ **encouragement** *noun* □ **encouraging** *adjective* (meaning 1)

encroach *verb* to go beyond your rights or land and interfere with someone else's □ **encroachment** *noun*

encumber *verb* to burden, load down

encumbrance *noun* a heavy burden, a hindrance

encyclopedia or **encyclopaedia** *noun* a reference book containing information on many subjects, or on a particular subject

encyclopedic or **encyclopaedic** *adjective* giving complete information

end *noun* **1** the last point or part **2** death **3** the farthest point of the length of something: *at the end of the road* **4** a result aimed at **5** a small piece left over □ *verb* to bring or come to an end □ **on end 1** standing on one end **2** in a series, without a stop: *go for days on end without eating*
① Comes from Old English *ende*

endanger *verb* to put in danger or at risk

■ **Alternative words**: jeopardize

endear *verb* to make dear or more dear

endearing *adjective* appealing

endearment *noun* an expression of love

endeavour *verb* to try hard (to) □ *noun* a determined attempt

endemic *adjective* of a disease: found regularly in a certain area

ending *noun* the last part

endorse *verb* **1** to give your support to something said or written **2** to sign the back of a cheque to confirm receiving money for it **3** to indicate on a motor licence that the owner has broken a driving law □ **endorsement** *noun*

endow *verb* **1** to give money for the buying and upkeep of: *he endowed a bed in the hospital* **2** to give a talent, quality *etc* to: *nature endowed her with a good brain* □ **endowment** *noun*

endurable *adjective* bearable

endurance *noun* the power of enduring

endure *verb* to bear without giving way; last

enema (*pronounced* en-im-*a*) *noun* the injection of fluid into the bowels

enemy *noun* (*plural* **enemies**) **1** someone hostile to another; a foe **2** someone armed to fight against another **3** someone who is against something: *an enemy of socialism*

energetic *adjective* active, lively □ **energetically** *adverb*

■ **Alternative words**: vigorous, animated, dynamic, tireless, zestful, potent

energy *noun* (*plural* **energies**) **1** strength to act, vigour **2** a form of power, *eg* electricity, heat *etc*

enfold *verb* to enclose, embrace

enforce *verb* to cause (a law *etc*) to be carried out

enfranchise *verb* **1** to set free **2** to give the right to vote to

engage *verb* **1** to begin to employ (workers *etc*) **2** to book in advance **3** to take or keep hold of (someone's attention *etc*) **4** to be busy with, occupied (in) **5** of machine parts: to fit together **6** to begin fighting

engaged *adjective* **1** bound by a promise of marriage **2** busy with something **3** of a telephone: in use

engagement *noun* **1** a promise of

marriage **2** an appointment to meet **3** a fight: *naval engagement*

engaging *adjective* pleasant, charming

engine *noun* **1** a machine which converts heat or other energy into motion **2** the part of a train which pulls the coaches

engineer *noun* **1** someone who works with, or designs, engines or machines **2** someone who designs or makes bridges, roads *etc* □ *verb* to bring about by clever planning

engineering *noun* the science of designing machines, roadmaking *etc*

engrave *verb* **1** to draw with a special tool on glass, metal *etc* **2** to make a deep impression on: *engraved on his memory*

engraving *noun* a print made from a cut-out drawing in metal or wood

engross *verb* to take up the whole interest or attention

engulf *verb* to swallow up wholly

enhance *verb* to improve, make greater or better

enigma *noun* something or someone difficult to understand, a mystery □ **enigmatic** *adjective*

enjoy *verb* **1** to take pleasure in **2** to experience, have (something beneficial): *enjoying good health* □ **enjoy yourself** to have a pleasant time

enjoyable *adjective* pleasant and satisfying

enjoyment *noun* **1** pleasure and satisfaction **2** the experiencing or having (of something beneficial)

enlarge *verb* **1** to make larger **2 enlarge on** to say much or more about something

enlargement *noun* **1** an increase in size **2** a larger photograph made from a smaller one

enlighten *verb* **1** to give more knowledge or information to **2** to correct the false beliefs of

enlightenment *noun* **1** new understanding or awareness □ **The Enlightenment** a French philosophical movement of the 18th century

enlist *verb* **1** to join an army *etc* **2** to obtain the support and help of

enliven *verb* to make more active or cheerful

en masse (*pronounced* on **mas**) *adverb* all together, in a body

enmity (from **enemy**) *noun* hostility

enormity *noun* **1** hugeness **2** extreme badness

enormous *adjective* very large

enormously *adverb* **1** very greatly, a great deal: *enjoy yourself enormously* **2** extremely: *enormously confident*

enough *adjective & pronoun* (in) the number or amount wanted or needed: *I have enough coins/ do you have enough money?* □ *adverb* as much as is wanted or necessary: *she's been there often enough to know the way*

enquire *see* **inquire**

enquiring *see* **inquiring**

enquiry *see* **inquiry**

enrage *verb* to make angry

enrol or **enroll** *verb* to enter (a name) in a register or list □ **enrolment** *noun*

enrol ⇨ enrol*s*, enrol*ling*, enrol*led*

en route (*pronounced* on **root**) *adverb* on the way

ensconce *verb*: **ensconce yourself** to settle comfortably

ensemble *noun* **1** the parts of a thing taken together **2** an outfit of clothes **3** a group of musicians

enshrine *verb* to treat as sacred, cherish

ensign *noun* **1** the flag of a nation, regiment *etc* **2** *historical* a young officer who carried the flag

enslave *verb* to make a slave of

ensue *verb* **1** to follow, come after **2** to result (from)

ensure *verb* to make sure

  ☛ Do not confuse with: **insure**

entail *verb* **1** to leave land so that the heir cannot sell any part of it **2** to bring as a result, involve: *the job entailed extra work*

entangle *verb* **1** to make tangled or complicated **2** to involve (in difficulties)

entente (*pronounced* on-**tont**) *noun* a treaty

enter *verb* 1 to go or come in or into 2 to put (a name *etc*) on to a list 3 to take part (in) 4 to begin (on)

enterprise *noun* 1 an undertaking, especially if risky or difficult 2 boldness in trying new things 3 a business concern

enterprising *adjective* inventive, clever, original, go-ahead

entertain *verb* 1 to amuse 2 to receive as a guest 3 to give a party 4 to consider (*eg* a suggestion) 5 to hold in the mind: *entertain a belief*

entertainer *noun* someone who entertains professionally

entertaining *adjective* amusing

entertainment *noun* 1 performances and activities that amuse and interest people 2 a performance or activity organized for the public

enthral *verb* to give great delight to

enthral ⇨ enthral**s**, enthral**ling**, enthral**led**

enthuse *verb* to be enthusiastic (about)

enthusiasm *noun* great interest and keenness

enthusiast *noun* someone who is very keen on a certain activity

enthusiastic *adjective* greatly interested, very keen ◻ **enthusiastically** *adverb*

entice *verb* to attract with promises, rewards *etc*

enticement *noun* a bribe, an attractive promise

enticing *adjective* very attractive and tempting

entire *adjective* whole, complete

entirely *adverb* utterly, wholly, fully, absolutely

entirety *noun* whole and complete state

entitle *verb* 1 to give a name to (a book *etc*) 2 to give (someone) a right to

entity *noun* (*plural* **entities**) something which exists; a being

entomology *noun* the study of insects ◻ **entomologist** *noun*

entrails *noun plural* the inner parts of an animal's body, the bowels

entrance[1] (*pronounced* **en**-trans) *noun* 1 a place for entering, *eg* a door 2 the act of coming in 3 the right to enter

entrance[2] (*pronounced* in-**trahns**) *verb* 1 to delight, charm 2 to bewitch ◻ **entrancing** *adjective*

entrant *noun* someone who goes in for a race, competition *etc*

entreat *verb* to ask earnestly

entreaty *noun* (*plural* **entreaties**) earnest request or plea

entrenched *adjective* 1 firmly established 2 unmoving, inflexible

entrepreneur (*pronounced* on-tre-pre-**ner**) *noun* someone who undertakes an enterprise, often with financial involvement

entrepreneurial (*pronounced* on-tre-pre-**ner**-ri-*al* or on-tre-pre-**nyoo**-ri-*al*) *adjective* of an entrepreneur

entrust or **intrust** *verb* to place in someone else's care

entry *noun* (*plural* **entries**) 1 the act of entering 2 a place for entering, a doorway 3 a name or item in a record book

E-number *noun* an identification code for food additives, *eg* E102 for tartrazine

enumerate *verb* 1 to count 2 to mention individually ◻ **enumeration** *noun*

enunciate *verb* 1 to pronounce distinctly 2 to state formally ◻ **enunciation** *noun*

envelop (*pronounced* in-**vel**-*op*) *verb* 1 to cover by wrapping 2 to surround entirely: *enveloped in mist*

envelope *noun* a wrapping or cover, especially for a letter

enviable *adjective* worth envying, worth having

envious *adjective* feeling envy ◻ **enviously** *adverb*

environment *noun* surroundings, circumstances in which someone or an animal lives

environs (*pronounced* in-**vai**-ronz) *noun*

plural surrounding area, neighbourhood

envisage *verb* **1** to visualize, picture in the mind **2** to consider, contemplate

envoy (*pronounced* en-voi) *noun* a messenger, especially one sent to deal with a foreign government

envy *noun* (*plural* **envies**) greedy desire for someone else's property, qualities *etc verb* to feel envy for

envy *verb* ⇨ envi*es*, envy*ing*, envi*ed*

enzyme *noun* a substance produced in a living body which affects the speed of chemical changes

eon *another spelling of* **aeon**

epaulet or **epaulette** *noun* a shoulder ornament on a uniform

ephemeral *adjective* very short-lived, fleeting □ **ephemerality** *noun*

epi- or **ep-** *prefix* upon or over: *epidermis*
① Comes from Greek *epi* meaning 'on' or 'over'

epic *noun* a long poem, story, film *etc* about heroic deeds □ *adjective* **1** of an epic; heroic **2** large-scale, impressive

epicene *noun* common to both sexes

epicentre or *US* **epicenter** *noun* the centre of an earthquake

epicure *noun* a gourmet □ **epicurean** *adjective*

epidemic *noun* a widespread outbreak of a disease *etc*

epidermis *noun* the top covering of the skin □ **epidermal** or **epidermic** *adjective*

epidural *noun* (short for **epidural anaesthetic**) the injection of anaesthetic into the spine to ease pain in the lower half of the body

epiglottis *noun* a piece of skin at the back of the tongue which closes the windpipe during swallowing

epigram *noun* a short, witty saying □ **epigrammatic** *adjective*

epilepsy *noun* an illness causing attacks of unconsciousness and convulsions

epileptic *adjective* **1** suffering from epilepsy **2** of epilepsy: *an epileptic fit* □ *noun* someone suffering from epilepsy

epilogue or *US* **epilog** *noun* **1** the very end part of a book, programme *etc* **2** a speech at the end of a play

epiphany *noun* **1** a Christian festival celebrated on 6 January **2** a sudden revelation or insight

episcopacy *noun* church government by bishops

episcopal *adjective* of or ruled by bishops

episcopalian *adjective* belonging to a church ruled by bishops

episode *noun* **1** one of several parts of a story *etc* **2** an interesting event

episodic *adjective* happening at irregular intervals

epistle *noun* a formal letter, especially one from an apostle of Christ in the Bible

epistolary *adjective* written in the form of letters

epitaph *noun* words on a gravestone about a dead person

epithet *noun* a word used to describe someone; an adjective

epitome (*pronounced* i-pit-om-i) *noun* **1** a perfect example or representative of something: *the epitome of good taste* **2** a summary of a book *etc*

epitomize *verb* to be the epitome of something

epoch (*pronounced* eep-ok) *noun* an extended period of time, often marked by a series of important events □ **epochal** (*pronounced* ep-ok-*a*l) *adjective*

epochmaking *adjective* marking an important point in history

EPROM (*pronounced* eep-rom) *abbreviation, computing* electrically programmable read-only memory

equ- *prefix* of or relating to horses: *equine/ equestrian*
① Comes from Latin *equus* meaning 'horse'

equable *adjective* **1** of calm temper **2** of climate: neither very hot nor very cold

equal *adjective* **1** of the same size, value, quantity *etc* **2** evenly balanced **3** **equal to** able, fit for: *not equal to the job*

□ *noun* someone of the same rank, cleverness *etc* as another □ *verb* **1** to be or make equal to **2** to be the same as □ **equally** *adverb*

equal *verb* ⇨ equals, equall**ing**, equall**ed**

equality *noun* equal treatment for all the people in a group or society

equalize *verb* to make equal

equalizer *noun* a goal *etc* which draws the score in a game

equanimity *noun* evenness of temper, calmness

equate *verb* **1** to regard or treat as the same **2** to state as being equal

equation *noun* a statement, especially in mathematics, that two things are equal

equator *noun* an imaginary line around the earth, halfway between the North and South Poles

equatorial *adjective* on or near the equator

equerry *noun* (*plural* **equerries**) *noun* a royal attendant

equestrian *adjective* **1** of horse-riding **2** on horseback □ *noun* a horse-rider

equi- *prefix* equal: *equidistant/ equilateral*
① Comes from Latin *aequus* meaning 'equal'

equidistant *adjective* equally distant

equilateral *adjective* of a triangle: with all sides equal (*compare with*: **isosceles**)

equilibrium *noun* **1** equal balance between weights, forces *etc* **2** a balanced state of mind or feelings

equine *adjective* of or like a horse

equinox *noun* either of the times (about 21 March and 23 September) when the sun crosses the equator, making night and day equal in length □ **equinoctial** *adjective*

equip *verb* to supply with everything needed for a task

equip ⇨ equips, equipp**ing**, equipp**ed**

equipage (*pronounced* **ek**-wip-eij) *noun* attendants, retinue

equipment *noun* a set of tools *etc* needed for a task; an outfit

equipoise *noun* balance

equitable *adjective* fair, just

equity *noun* **1** fairness, just dealing **2** **Equity** the trade union for the British acting profession □ **negative equity** *see* **negative**

equivalent *adjective* equal in value, power, meaning *etc* □ *noun* something that is the equal of another

equivocal *adjective* having more than one meaning; ambiguous, uncertain □ **equivocally** *adverb*

equivocate *verb* to use ambiguous words in order to mislead □ **equivocation** *noun*

era *noun* a period in history: *the Jacobean era/ the era of steam*

eradicate *verb* to get rid of completely □ **eradication** *noun*

erase *verb* **1** to rub out **2** to remove

eraser *noun* something which erases, a rubber

erasure *noun* **1** a letter or word that has been rubbed out **2** the complete removal or destruction of something

ere *preposition* & *conjunction* before: *ere long*

erect *verb* **1** to build **2** to set upright □ *adjective* standing straight up

erection *noun* **1** the act of erecting **2** something erected or erect

ERM *abbreviation* exchange rate mechanism

ermine (*pronounced* **er**-min) *noun* **1** a stoat **2** its white fur

erode *verb* to wear away, destroy gradually □ **erosion** *noun*

erotic *adjective* of or arousing sexual desire

erotica *noun plural* erotic art or literature

eroticism *noun* **1** use of erotic ideas and images **2** sexual excitement

eroticize *verb* to make erotic

err *verb* **1** to make a mistake **2** to sin

errand *noun* a short journey to carry a message, buy something *etc*

errant *adjective* **1** doing wrong **2** wandering in search of adventure: *knight errant*

erratic *adjective* **1** irregular, not following a fixed course **2** not steady or reliable in behaviour □ **erratically** *adverb*

erroneous *adjective* wrong, mistaken □ **erroneously** *adverb*

error *noun* **1** a mistake **2** wrongdoing

erudite *adjective* well-educated or well-read, learned □ **erudition** *noun*

erupt *verb* to break out or through

eruption *noun* **1** an outburst from a volcano **2** a rash or spot on the skin

escalate *verb* to increase in amount, intensity *etc* □ **escalation** *noun*

escalator *noun* a moving stairway

escapade *noun* an adventure

escape *verb* **1** to get away safe or free **2** of gas *etc*: to leak **3** to slip from memory: *his name escapes me* □ *noun* the act of escaping

escapism *noun* the tendency to escape from reality by daydreaming *etc* □ **escapist** *noun & adjective*

escarpment *noun* a steep side of a hill or rock

escort *noun* someone who accompanies others for protection, courtesy *etc* □ *verb* to act as escort to

Eskimo *noun* (*plural* **Eskimos**) Inuit

ESP *abbreviation* extrasensory perception

especial *adjective* **1** special, extraordinary **2** particular

especially *adverb* particularly

Esperanto *noun* an international language created in the 19th century

espionage *noun* spying, especially by one country to find out the secrets of another

esplanade *noun* a level roadway, especially along a seafront

espouse *verb* to adopt, embrace (a cause)

espresso *noun* strong coffee made by extraction under high pressure

espy (*pronounced* es-**pai**) *verb, old* to watch, observe

Esq *abbreviation* or **Esquire** *noun* a courtesy title written after a man's name: *Robert Brown, Esq*

essay *noun* (*pronounced* **es**-ei) **1** a written composition **2** an attempt □ *verb* (*pronounced* es-**ei**) to try

essence *noun* **1** the most important part or quality of something **2** a concentrated extract from a plant *etc*: *vanilla essence*

essential *adjective* absolutely necessary □ *noun* an absolute requirement

essentially *adverb* **1** basically **2** necessarily

establish *verb* **1** to settle in position **2** to found, set up **3** to show to be true, prove (that)

established *adjective* **1** firmly set up **2** accepted, recognized **3** of a church: officially recognized as national

establishment *noun* **1** a place of business, residence *etc* □ **The Establishment** the people holding influential positions in a community

estate *noun* **1** a large piece of private land **2** someone's total possessions **3** land built on with houses, factories *etc*: *housing estate/ industrial estate*

estate agent someone who sells and leases property for clients

estate car a car with an inside luggage compartment and a rear door

esteem *verb* to think highly of; value □ *noun* high value or opinion

esteemed *adjective* respected, valued

estimate *verb* (*pronounced* es-tim-eit) to judge roughly the size, amount or value of something □ *noun* (*pronounced* es-tim-*at*) a rough judgement of size *etc*

estimation *noun* opinion, judgement

estranged *adjective* no longer friendly; separated

estuary *noun* (*plural* **estuaries**) the wide lower part of a river, up which the tide travels

etc or **&c** *abbreviation* and other things of the same sort (from Latin *et cetera*)

etch *verb* to draw on metal or glass by eating out the lines with acid

etching *noun* a picture printed from an etched metal plate

eternal *adjective* 1 lasting for ever 2 seemingly endless

eternally *adverb* for ever

eternity *noun* 1 time without end 2 the time or state after death

ether *noun* a colourless liquid used as an anaesthetic, or to dissolve fats

ethereal (*pronounced* i-**theer**-ri-*al*) *adjective* delicate, airy, spirit-like □ **ethereally** *adverb* □ **ethereality** *noun*

ethical *adjective* having to do with right behaviour, justice, duty; right, just, honourable □ **ethically** *adverb*

ethics *noun singular* 1 the study of right and wrong 2 (belief in) standards leading to right, ethical behaviour

ethnic *adjective* 1 of race or culture 2 of the culture of a particular race or group □ **ethnically** *adverb*

ethnic cleansing the removal of the members of less powerful ethnic groups by the most powerful ethnic group living in an area

ethnicity *noun* racial or cultural character

ethnocentric *adjective* believing in the superiority of your own culture □ **ethnocentrism** *noun*

ethnocide *noun* the extermination of a racial or cultural group

ethnology *noun* the study of human cultures and civilizations □ **ethnological** *adjective* □ **ethnologist** *noun*

etiquette *noun* rules governing correct social behaviour

etymology *noun* (*plural* **etymologies**) 1 the study of the history of words 2 the history of a word □ **etymological** *adjective*

eucalyptus *noun* (*plural* **eucalyptuses** or **eucalypti**) a large Australian evergreen tree whose leaves produce a pungent oil

eucharist *noun* 1 the Christian sacrament of the Lord's Supper 2 bread and wine *etc* taken as a sacrament

eulogize *verb* to praise greatly

eulogy *noun* (*plural* **eulogies**) a speech, poem *etc* in praise of someone

eunuch (*pronounced* **yoo**-nuk) *noun* a castrated man

euphemism (*pronounced* **yoof**-e-mizm) *noun* a vague word or phrase used to refer to an unpleasant subject, *eg* 'passed on' for 'died' □ **euphemistic** *adjective*

euphonium *noun* a brass musical instrument with a low tone

euphoria *noun* a feeling of great happiness, joy □ **euphoric** *adjective*

Euro- *prefix* of Europe or the European community: *Euro-budget/ Eurocrat*

Eurosceptic *noun & adjective, Brit* (someone) opposed to strengthening the powers of the European community

euthanasia *noun* the killing of someone painlessly, especially to end suffering

evacuate *verb* to (cause to) leave especially because of danger; make empty □ **evacuation** *noun*

evacuee *noun* someone who has been evacuated (from danger)

evade *verb* to avoid or escape, especially by cleverness or trickery

evaluate *verb* to find or state the value of

evangelical *adjective* 1 spreading Christian teaching 2 strongly supporting and speaking for some cause

evangelist *noun* 1 a person who spreads Christian teaching or supports and speaks for some cause 2 **Evangelist** an author of a Gospel, especially Matthew, Mark, Luke or John □ **evangelistic** *adjective*

evaporate *verb* 1 to change into vapour 2 to vanish □ **evaporation** *noun*

evasion *noun* 1 the act of evading 2 an attempt to avoid the point of an argument or accusation

evasive *adjective* with the purpose of evading; not straightforward: *an evasive answer*

eve *noun* 1 the evening or day before a festival: *New Year's Eve* 2 the time just before an event: *the eve of the revolution*

even *adjective* 1 level, smooth 2 equal 3 of a number: able to be divided by 2 without a remainder (*contrasted with*: **odd**) 4 calm □ *adverb* 1 used to emphasize another word: *even harder than before/ even a child would understand* 2 exactly, just □ *verb* to make even or smooth □ **even out** to become equal □ **get even with** to get revenge on

even-handed *adverb* fair, unbiased

evening *noun* the last part of the day and early part of the night

evenly *adverb* 1 levelly, smoothly 2 equally 3 calmly

evenness *noun* the quality of being even

evensong *noun* an evening service in the Anglican church

event *noun* 1 an important happening 2 an item in a sports programme *etc*

eventful *adjective* exciting

eventual *adjective* 1 final 2 happening as a result

eventuality *noun* (*plural* **eventualities**) a possible happening

eventually *adverb* at last, finally

ever *adverb* 1 always, for ever 2 at any time, at all: *I won't ever see her again* 3 that has existed, on record: *the best ever*

evergreen *noun* a tree with green leaves all the year round

everlasting *adjective* lasting for ever, eternal

evermore *adverb, old* forever

every *adjective* each of several things without exception □ **every other** one out of every two, alternate

everybody or **everyone** *pronoun* each person without exception

everyday *adjective* 1 daily 2 common, usual

everything *pronoun* all things

everywhere *adverb* in every place

evict *verb* to force (someone) out of their house, especially by law □ **eviction** *noun*

evidence *noun* 1 a clear sign; proof 2 information given in a law case

evident *adjective* easily seen or understood

evidently *adverb* seemingly, obviously

evil *adjective* wicked, very bad; malicious □ *noun* wickedness □ **evilly** *adverb*

evocative *adjective* evoking memories or atmosphere

evoke *verb* to draw out, produce: *evoking memories of their childhood*

evolution *noun* 1 gradual development 2 the belief that the higher forms of life have gradually developed out of the lower □ **evolutionary** *adjective*

evolve *verb* 1 to develop gradually 2 to work out (a plan *etc*)

ewe *noun* a female sheep

ewer *noun* a large jug with a wide spout

ex *noun, informal* a former husband, wife or lover

ex- *prefix* 1 no longer, former: *ex-husband/ ex-president* 2 outside, not in: *ex-directory number*
ⓘ Comes from Latin *ex* meaning 'out of' or 'from'

exacerbate *verb* to make worse or more severe
ⓘ Comes from Latin *acerbare* meaning 'to embitter'

❗ Do not confuse with:
exasperate

exact *adjective* 1 accurate, precise 2 punctual 3 careful □ *verb* to compel to pay, give *etc*: *exacting revenge*

exacting *adjective* 1 asking too much 2 wearying, tiring

exactly *adverb* 1 precisely 2 as a reply to something someone has said: 'that's right' or 'I agree'

exactness *noun* accuracy, correctness

exaggerate *verb* to make to seem larger or greater than reality □ **exaggeration** *noun*

exalt *verb* 1 to raise in rank 2 to praise 3 to make joyful

exaltation *noun* 1 joy 2 the act of praising and glorifying someone or something

exam *noun* an examination

examination *noun* **1** a formal test of knowledge or skill: *driving examination* **2** a close inspection or inquiry **3** formal questioning

examine *verb* **1** to put questions to (pupils *etc*) to test knowledge **2** to question (a witness) **3** to look at closely, inquire into **4** to look over (someone's body) for signs of illness □ **examiner** *noun* (meaning 1)

example *noun* **1** something taken as a representative of its kind: *an example of early French glass* **2** a warning

exasperate *verb* to make very angry □ **exasperation** *noun*
ⓘ Comes from Latin *asperare* meaning 'to make rough'

> ◆ Do not confuse with: **exacerbate**

excavate *verb* **1** to dig, scoop out **2** to uncover by digging

excavation *noun* **1** the act of digging out **2** a hollow made by digging

excavator *noun* a machine used for excavating

exceed *verb* to go beyond, be greater than
ⓘ Comes from Latin *ex-*meaning 'beyond', and *cedere* meaning 'to go'

exceedingly *adverb* very

excel *verb* **1** to do very well **2** to be better than

> **excel** ⇨ excel*s*, excel*ling*, excel*led*

excellence *noun* the fact of being excellent, very high quality

Excellency *noun* (*plural* **Excellencies**) a title of ambassadors *etc*

excellent *adjective* unusually or extremely good

except *preposition* leaving out, not counting □ *conjunction* with the exception (that) □ *verb* to leave out, not to count □ **except for** with the exception of

excepting *preposition* except

exception *noun* **1** something left out **2** something unlike the rest: *an exception to the rule* □ **take exception to** to object to, be offended by
ⓘ Comes from Latin *exceptio* meaning 'an exception, restriction or objection'

exceptional *adjective* standing out from the rest

exceptionally *adverb* very, extremely

excerpt (*pronounced* **ek**-sert) *noun* a part chosen from a whole work: *excerpt from a play*
ⓘ Comes from Latin *excerptum* meaning 'picked out'

> ◆ Do not confuse with: **exert**

excess *noun* (*pronounced* ik-**ses**) **1** a going beyond what is usual or proper **2** the amount by which one thing is greater than another **3 excesses** very bad behaviour □ *adjective* (*pronounced* **ek**-ses) beyond the amount allowed
ⓘ (for origin, see **exceed**)

> ◆ Do not confuse with: **access**

excessive *adjective* too much, too great *etc* □ **excessively** *adverb*

exchange *verb* to give (one thing) and get another in return □ *noun* **1** the act of exchanging **2** exchanging money of one country for that of another **3** the difference between the value of money in different places: *rate of exchange* **4** a central office or building: *telephone exchange* **5** a place where business shares are bought and sold

exchequer *noun* a government office concerned with a country's finances □ **Chancellor of the Exchequer** *see* **chancellor**

> From the chequered cloth used to aid calculation in medieval revenue offices

excise[1] *verb* to cut off or out □ **excision** *noun*

excise[2] *noun* tax on goods *etc* made and sold within a country and on certain licences *etc*

excitable *adjective* easily excited

excite *verb* **1** to rouse the feelings of **2** to move to action

excited *adjective* unable to be calm because of extreme feelings of happiness, impatience or arousal

> ▤ **Alternative words**: stirred, thrilled, elated, restless, wild

excitement *noun* the state of being excited

exciting *adjective* creating feelings of excitement

exclaim *verb* to cry or shout out

exclamation *noun* a sudden shout

exclamation mark a punctuation mark (!) used for emphasis, or to indicate surpise *etc*

exclamatory (*pronounced* iks-**klam**-at-ri) *adjective* exclaiming, emphatic

exclude *verb* 1 to shut out 2 to prevent from sharing 3 to leave out of consideration □ **exclusion** *noun*

exclusive *adjective* 1 only open to certain people, select: *an exclusive club* 2 not obtainable elsewhere: *exclusive offer* □ **exclusive of** not including

excommunicate *verb* to expel from membership of a church □ **excommunication** *noun*

excrement *noun* the waste matter cast out by humans or animals

excrescence *noun* an unwelcome growth, *eg* a wart

excreta *noun plural* discharged waste products

excrete *verb* to discharge (waste matter) from the body

excruciating *adjective* 1 of pain *etc*: very severe 2 painfully bad: *an excruciating performance*

exculpate *verb* to absolve from a crime; vindicate □ **exculpation** *noun* □ **exculpatory** *adjective*

excursion *noun* an outing for pleasure, *eg* a picnic

excusable *adjective* pardonable

excuse *verb* (*pronounced* eks-**kyooz**) 1 to forgive, pardon 2 to set free from a duty or task □ *noun* (*pronounced* eks-**kyoos**) an explanation for having done something wrong

execrable *adjective* very bad

execrate *verb* to curse, denounce

execute *verb* 1 to perform: *execute a dance step* 2 to carry out: *execute commands* 3 to put to death legally

execution *noun* 1 a doing or performing 2 killing by order of the law

executioner *noun* someone with the job of putting condemned prisoners to death

executive *adjective* having power to act or carry out laws □ *noun* 1 the part of a government with such power 2 a business manager

executor *noun* someone who sees that the requests stated in a will are carried out

exemplary *adjective* 1 worth following as an example: *exemplary conduct* 2 acting as a warning: *exemplary punishment*

exemplify *verb* 1 to be an example of 2 to demonstrate by example

exemplify ⇨ exemplifies, exemplifying, exemplified

exempt *verb* to grant freedom from an unwelcome task, payment *etc* □ *adjective* free (from), not liable for payment *etc* □ **exemption** *noun*

exercise *noun* 1 a task for practice 2 a physical routine for training muscles *etc* □ *verb* 1 to give exercise to 2 to use: *exercise great care*
ⓘ Comes from Latin *exercere* meaning 'to make thoroughly effective'
🖝 Do not confuse with: **exorcize**

exert *verb* to bring into action, use: *exerting great influence* □ **exert yourself** to make a great effort
ⓘ Comes from Latin *exsert-*, a form of *exserere* meaning 'to thrust out'
🖝 Do not confuse with: **excerpt**

exertion *noun* or **exertions** *noun plural* effort(s); hard work

exeunt *verb* leave the stage (a direction printed in a playscript): *exeunt Rosencrantz and Guildenstern*

exhale *verb* to breathe out □ **exhalation** *noun*

exhaust *verb* 1 to tire out 2 to use up completely: *we've exhausted our supplies* 3 to say all that can be said about (a subject *etc*) □ *noun* a device for expelling waste fumes from fuel engines

exhausted *adjective* 1 tired out 2 emptied; used up □ **exhaustion** *noun*

exhaustive *adjective* extremely

exhibit 177 **expel**

thorough: *exhaustive research*
□ **exhaustively** *adverb*

exhibit *verb* to show; put on public display □ *noun* something on display in a gallery *etc*

exhibition *noun* a public show, an open display

exhibitionism *noun* a tendency to try to attract people's attention

exhibitionist *noun* someone who tries to get people's attention all the time, a show-off

exhibitor *noun* a person who has presented something belonging to them for display at an exhibition

exhilarate *verb* to make joyful or lively, refresh □ **exhilarating** *adjective*
□ **exhilaration** *noun*

exhort *verb* to urge (to do)
□ **exhortation** *noun*

exhume *verb* to dig out (a buried body)
□ **exhumation** *noun*

exile *noun* 1 someone who lives outside their own country, by choice or unwillingly 2 a period of living in a foreign country □ *verb* to drive (someone) away from their own country; banish

exist *verb* 1 to be, have life; live 2 to live in poor circumstances

existence *noun* life, being

existent *adjective* existing at the moment

exit *noun* 1 a way out 2 the act of going out: *a hasty exit*

exodus *noun* a going away of many people (especially those leaving a country for ever)

exonerate *verb* to free from blame
□ **exoneration** *noun*

exorbitant *adjective* going beyond what is usual or reasonable: *exorbitant price* □ **exorbitance** *noun*

exorcize *verb* 1 to drive out (an evil spirit) 2 to free from possession by an evil spirit
⊕ Comes from Greek *ex* meaning 'out', and *horkos* meaning 'an oath'
☞ Do not confuse with: **exercise**

exorcism *noun* the act of driving away evil spirits

exorcist *noun* a person who drives evil spirits away

exotic *adjective* 1 coming from a foreign country 2 unusual, colourful

expand *verb* 1 to grow wider or bigger 2 to open out

expanse *noun* a wide stretch of land *etc*

expansion *noun* a growing, stretching or spreading

expansive *adjective* 1 spreading out 2 talkative, telling much □ **expansively** *adverb*

expat *noun, informal* an expatriate

expatriate *adjective* living outside your native country □ *noun* someone living abroad

expect *verb* 1 to think of as likely to happen or arrive soon: *what did you expect her to say?* 2 to think, assume: *I expect he's too busy*

expectancy *noun* the feeling of excitement that you get when you know something good is about to happen

expectant *adjective* 1 hopeful, expecting 2 waiting to become: *expectant mother*

expectation *noun* a firm belief or hope that something will happen

expecting *adjective, informal* pregnant

expedience or **expediency** *noun* speed or convenience in a particular situation, rather than fairness or truth

expedient *adjective* done for speed or convenience rather than fairness or truth □ *noun* something done to get round a difficulty

expedite *verb* to hasten, hurry on

expedition *noun* 1 a journey with a purpose, often for exploration 2 people making such a journey

expeditionary *adjective* of or forming an expedition

expeditious *adjective* swift, speedy
□ **expeditiously** *adverb*

expel *verb* 1 to drive or force out 2 to send away in disgrace, *eg* from a school

expel ⇨ expels, expelling, expelled

expend *verb* to spend, use up

expenditure *noun* an amount spent or used up, especially money

expense *noun* 1 cost 2 a cause of spending: *the house was a continual expense* 3 **expenses** money spent in carrying out a job *etc*

expensive *adjective* costing a lot of money □ **expensively** *adverb*

▤ Alternative words: costly, exorbitant, extortionate, extravagant

experience *noun* 1 an event in which you are involved: *a horrific experience* 2 knowledge gained from events, practice *etc* □ *verb* to go through, undergo

experienced *adjective* skilled, knowledgeable

experiment *noun* a trial, a test (of an idea, machine *etc*) □ *verb* to carry out experiments

experimental *adjective* of something new: being done for the first time, to see how successful it will be □ **experimentally** *adverb*

expert *adjective* highly skilful or knowledgeable (in a particular subject) □ *noun* someone who is highly skilled or knowledgeable

▤ Alternative words: (adjective) adroit

expertise (*pronounced* eks-per-**teez**) *noun* skill

expiate (*pronounced* **ek**-spi-eit) *verb* to make up for (a crime *etc*) □ **expiation** *noun*

expire *verb* 1 to die 2 to come to an end, become invalid: *your visa has expired*

expiry *noun* the end or finish

explain *verb* 1 to make clear 2 to give reasons for: *please explain your behaviour*

▤ Alternative words: (meaning 2) justify

explanation *noun* a statement which makes clear something difficult or puzzling; a reason (*eg* for your behaviour)

explanatory (*pronounced* eks-**plan**-at-ri) *adjective* intended to make clear

expletive *noun* an exclamation, especially a swear word

explicable *adjective* able to be explained

explicit *adjective* plainly stated or shown; outspoken, frank □ **explicitly** *adverb*: *I explicitly told you not to touch that!*

explode *verb* 1 to blow up like a bomb with loud noise 2 to prove to be wrong or unfounded: *that explodes your theory*

exploit *noun* (*pronounced* **eks**-ploit) a daring deed; a feat □ *verb* (*pronounced* eks-**ploit**) 1 to make use of selfishly 2 to make good use of (resources *etc*) □ **exploitation** *noun*

exploration *noun* 1 travel for the sake of discovery 2 the act of searching or searching for something thoroughly

exploratory (*pronounced* eks-**plo**-rat-ri) *adjective* having the purpose of discovering things

explore *verb* 1 to make a journey of discovery 2 to think about very carefully, research □ **explorer** *noun* (meaning 1)

explosion *noun* a sudden violent burst or blow-up

explosive *adjective* 1 liable to explode 2 hot-tempered □ *noun* something that will explode, *eg* gunpowder

exponent *noun* someone who shows skill in a particular art or craft: *an exponent of karate*

exponential *adjective* 1 relating to exponents 2 having an increasingly steep rate of increase

export *verb* (*pronounced* eks-**pawt**) to sell goods *etc* in a foreign country □ *noun* (*pronounced* **eks**-pawt) 1 an act of exporting 2 something exported □ **exportation** *noun*

expose *verb* 1 to place in full view 2 to show up (a hidden crime *etc*) 3 to lay open to the sun or wind 4 to allow light to reach and act on (a film)

expostulate (*pronounced* eks-**pos**-chuwl-eit) *verb* to protest □ **expostulation** *noun*

exposure (from **expose**) *noun* **1** the state of being allowed to experience something or be affected by something **2** appearance or mention in public, *eg* on television or in newspapers **3** the extremely harmful effects of severe cold on a person's body **4** the fact of revealing something about someone, usually something unpleasant, that has been kept secret **5** a single photograph or frame on a film

expound *verb* to explain fully

express *verb* **1** to show by action **2** to put into words **3** to press or squeeze out □ *adjective* **1** clearly stated: *express instructions* **2** sent in haste: *express messenger* □ *noun* a fast train, bus *etc*

expression *noun* **1** the look on someone's face: *expression of horror* **2** showing meaning or emotion through language, art *etc* **3** a show of emotion in an artistic performance *etc* **4** a word or phrase: *idiomatic expression* **5** pressing or squeezing out

expressive *adjective* expressing meaning or feeling clearly

expulsion (from **expel**) *noun* **1** the act of driving or forcing a person or thing out **2** the sending away of someone in disgrace, *eg* from a school

expunge *verb* to rub out, remove

exquisite (*pronounced* **eks**-kwiz-it or iks-**kwiz**-it) *adjective* **1** extremely beautiful **2** excellent **3** very great, utter: *exquisite pleasure*

extemporize (*pronounced* iks-**tem**-po-raiz) *verb* to make up on the spot, improvise

extend *verb* **1** to stretch, make longer **2** to hold out: *extended a hand* **3** to last, carry over: *my holiday extends into next week*

extension *noun* **1** a part added to a building **2** an additional amount of time on a schedule, holiday *etc* **3** a telephone connected with a main one

extensive *adjective* **1** wide; covering a large space **2** happening in many places **3** wide-ranging, sweeping: *extensive changes* □ **extensively** *adverb*

extent *noun* **1** the space something covers **2** degree: *to a great extent*

extenuate *verb* **1** to lessen **2** to make

to seem less bad: *extenuating circumstances* □ **extenuation** *noun*

exterior *adjective* on the outside; outer: *exterior wall* □ *noun* the outside of a building *etc*

exterminate *verb* to kill off completely (a race, a type of animal *etc*), wipe out □ **extermination** *noun*

external *adjective* **1** outside; on the outside **2** not central: *external considerations*

extinct *adjective* **1** of an old volcano: no longer erupting **2** no longer found alive: *the dodo is now extinct*

■ **Opposite**: (meaning 1) active

extinction *noun* making or becoming extinct

extinguish *verb* **1** to put out (fire *etc*) **2** to put an end to

extinguisher *noun* a spray containing chemicals for putting out fires

extirpate *verb* to destroy completely, exterminate
⊕ Comes from Latin *exstirpare* meaning 'to pluck up by the root'

◆ Do not confuse with: **extricate** and **extrapolate**

extol *verb* to praise greatly

extol ⇨ extol*s*, extoll*ing*, extoll*ed*

extort *verb* to take by force or threats □ **extortion** *noun*

extortionate *adjective* of a price: much too high

extra *adjective* more than is usual or necessary; additional □ *adverb* unusually; more than is average: *extra large* □ *noun* **1** something extra **2** someone employed to be one of a crowd in a film

extra- *prefix* outside, beyond
⊕ Comes from Latin *extra* meaning 'outside'

extract *verb* (*pronounced* eks-**trakt**) **1** to draw or pull out, especially by force: *extract a tooth* **2** to remove selected parts of a book *etc* **3** to draw out by pressure or chemical action □ *noun* (*pronounced* **eks**-trakt) **1** an excerpt from a book *etc* **2** a substance obtained by extraction: *vanilla extract*

extraction *noun* **1** the act of extracting **2** someone's descent or lineage: *of Irish extraction*

extracurricular *adjective* done outside school or college hours

extradite *verb* to hand over (someone wanted for trial) to the police of another country □ **extradition** *noun*

extramarital *adjective* happening outside a marriage: *extramarital affair*

extramural *adjective* of a university department: teaching courses which are not part of the regular degree courses

extraneous *adjective* having nothing to do with the subject: *extraneous information*

extraordinary *adjective* **1** not usual, exceptional **2** very surprising **3** specially employed: *ambassador extraordinary* □ **extraordinarily** *adverb* (meanings 1 and 2)

extrapolate *verb* to take known facts and use them to infer or predict things which are beyond what is known

Extrapolate was created by replacing the 'inter-' beginning of the word 'interpolate' (= to fill in additional details between known facts) with the prefix 'extra-'

☛ Do not confuse with: **extirpate** and **extricate**

extrasensory *adjective* beyond the range of the ordinary senses: *extrasensory perception*

extraterrestrial *adjective* from outside the earth □ *noun* a being from another planet

extravagant *adjective* **1** spending too freely; wasteful **2** too great, overblown: *extravagant praise* □ **extravagantly** *adverb* □ **extravagance** *noun*

extravaganza *noun* an extravagant creation or production

extravert or **extrovert** *noun* an outgoing, sociable person

extreme *adjective* **1** far from the centre **2** far from the ordinary or usual **3** very great: *extreme sadness* □ *noun* an extreme point

extremely *adverb* very, exceptionally

extremist *noun* someone who carries ideas foolishly far □ **extremism** *noun*

extremity (*pronounced* eks-**trem**-it-i) *noun* (*plural* **extremities**) **1** a part or place furthest from the centre **2** great distress or pain **3 extremities** the hands and feet

extricate *verb* to free from (difficulties *etc*)
🕓 Comes from Latin *extricare* meaning 'to disentangle'

☛ Do not confuse with: **extirpate** and **extrapolate**

extrovert *another spelling of* **extravert**

extrude *verb* to protrude, stick out

exuberant *adjective* in very high spirits □ **exuberantly** *adverb* □ **exuberance** *noun*

exude *verb* to give off in large amounts: *exuding sweat/ exuded happiness*

exult *verb* to be very glad, rejoice greatly: *exulting in their victory* □ **exultant** *adjective* □ **exultation** *noun*

eye *noun* **1** the part of the body with which you see **2** the ability to notice: *an eye for detail* **3** sight **4** something the shape of an eye, *eg* the hole in a needle □ *verb* to look at with interest: *eyeing the last slice of cake*

eye *verb* ⇨ eyes, eyeing, eyed

eyeball *noun* the round part of the eye; the eye itself (the part between the eyelids)

eyebrow *noun* the hairy ridge above the eye

eyeglass *noun* a lens to correct faulty eyesight

eyelash *noun* one of the hairs on the edge of the eyelid

eyelet *noun* a small hole for a shoelace *etc*

eyelid *noun* the skin covering of the eye

eye-opener *noun* that which shows up something unexpected

eyesore *noun* anything that is ugly (especially a building)

eye-wash *noun* a lotion for the eye

eyewitness *noun* someone who sees a thing done (*eg* a crime committed)

Ff

If you can't find the word you're looking for under letter **F**, it could be that it starts with a different letter. Try looking under **PH** for words like *pharmacy*, *photograph* and *physical*.

°F *abbreviation* degree(s) Fahrenheit

FA *abbreviation*, *Brit* Football Association

fable *noun* a story about animals *etc*, including a lesson or moral

fabric *noun* **1** cloth **2** framework; the external parts of a building *etc*

fabricate *verb* to make up (lies) □ **fabrication** *noun*

fabulous *adjective* **1** *informal* very good, excellent **2** imaginary, mythological

fabulously *adverb* extremely, unbelievably: *fabulously rich*

fabulousness *noun* the quality of being fabulous

façade (*pronounced* fa-**sahd**) *noun* **1** the front of a building **2** a deceptive appearance or act; a mask

face *noun* **1** the front part of the head **2** the front of anything **3** appearance □ *verb* **1** to turn or stand in the direction of **2** to stand opposite to **3** to put an additional surface on □ **face up to** to meet or accept boldly: *facing up to responsibilities*

face-lift 1 a surgical operation to smooth and firm the tissues of the face **2** a renovating process, especially one applied to the outside of a building

face pack a cosmetic paste applied to the face and left to dry before being peeled or washed off

facepowder *noun* cosmetic powder for the face

facet *noun* **1** a side of a many-sided object, *eg* a cut gem **2** an aspect; a characteristic

facetious (*pronounced* fa-**see**-sh*u*s) *adjective* not meant seriously; joking □ **facetiously** *adverb*

facial *adjective* of the face

facile (*pronounced* **fas**-ail) *adjective* **1** not deep or thorough; superficial, glib **2** fluent □ **facilely** *adverb*

facilitate *verb* to make easy

facility *noun* **1** ease **2** skill, ability **3 facilities** buildings, equipment *etc* provided for a purpose: *sports facilities*

facsimile *noun* an exact copy

fact *noun* **1** something known or held to be true **2** reality **3** *law* a deed □ **in fact** actually, really
- ① Comes from Latin *factum* meaning 'something done or accomplished'
- ■ **Alternative words**: **in fact** actually, really, indeed

faction *noun* a group that is part of a larger group: *rival factions*

factor *noun* **1** something affecting the course of events **2** someone who does business for another **3** a number which exactly divides into another (*eg* 3 is a factor of 6)

factory *noun* (*plural* **factories**) a workshop producing goods in large quantities

factotum *noun* someone employed to do all kinds of work

factual *adjective* consisting of facts; real, not fictional: *factual account*

faculty *noun* (*plural* **faculties**) **1** power of the mind, *eg* reason **2** a natural power of the body, *eg* hearing **3** ability, aptitude **4** a department of study in a university: *Faculty of Arts*

fad *noun* 1 an odd like or dislike 2 a temporary fashion

faddy *adjective* having odd likes and dislikes

fade *verb* 1 to (make to) lose colour or strength 2 to disappear gradually, *eg* from sight or hearing

faeces (*pronounced* fees-eez) *noun plural* solid excrement

faff *verb*, *informal* to dither, fumble: *don't faff about*

fag *noun* 1 tiring work 2 *slang* a cigarette 3 *informal* a young schoolboy forced to do jobs for an older one

fag end *informal* 1 a cigarette butt 2 the very end, the tail end

fagged out *informal* exhausted, tired out

faggot or *US* **fagot** *noun* 1 a bundle of sticks 2 a meatball

Fahrenheit *noun* a temperature scale on which water freezes at 32° and boils at 212° □ *adjective* measured on this scale: *70° Fahrenheit*

fail *verb* 1 to (declare to) be unsuccessful 2 to break down, stop 3 to lose strength 4 to be lacking or insufficient 5 to disappoint □ **without fail** certainly, for sure

failing *noun* a fault; a weakness

fail-safe *adjective* made to correct automatically, or be safe, if a fault occurs

failure *noun* 1 the act of failing 2 someone or something which fails

fain *adverb*, *old* willingly: *I would fain go with you*

faint *adjective* 1 lacking in strength, brightness *etc* 2 about to lose consciousness: *feel faint* □ *verb* 1 to become faint 2 to fall down unconscious □ *noun* a loss of consciousness

🖋 Do not confuse with: **feint**

faintly *adverb* dimly, not clearly

faintness *noun* 1 lack of strength, brightness *etc* 2 a feeling of weakness, as if you were about to lose consciousness

fair[1] *adjective* 1 of a light colour: *fair hair* 2 of weather: clear and dry 3 unbiased, just: *fair assessment* 4 good enough but not excellent 5 beautiful

■ **Alternative words**: (meaning 3) just, equitable, dispassionate, impartial, disinterested; (meaning 4) average, moderate, adequate, mediocre

fair[2] *noun* 1 a large market held at fixed times 2 an exhibition of goods from different producers *etc*: *craft fair* 3 a travelling collection of merry-go-rounds, stalls *etc*
🕔 Comes from Late Latin *feria* meaning 'market'

🖋 Do not confuse with: **fare**

fair-haired *adjective* having light-coloured hair; blond

fairly *adverb* 1 in a just and reasonable way 2 rather, reasonably 3 only moderately, to a limited extent 4 absolutely: *She fairly flung herself at me*

fairness *noun* the quality of being reasonable or just in your treatment of people

fairway *noun* 1 the mown part on a golf course, between the tee and the green 2 the deep-water part of a river

fair-weather friend someone who is a friend only when things are going well

fairy *noun* (*plural* **fairies**) a small imaginary creature, human in shape, with magical powers

fairy light a small coloured light for decorating Christmas trees *etc*

fairy story or **fairy tale** 1 a traditional story of fairies, giants *etc* 2 *informal* a lie

faith *noun* 1 trust 2 belief in a religion or creed 3 loyalty to a promise: *kept faith with them*

faithful *adjective* 1 loyal; keeping your promises 2 true, accurate: *faithful account of events* 3 believing in a particular religion or creed □ **faithfully** *adverb* (meanings 1 and 2)

faithless *adjective* 1 untrustworthy, inconstant 2 without faith or belief, especially in God or Christianity

fake *adjective* not genuine, forged □ *noun* 1 someone who is not what they pretend to be 2 a forgery □ *verb* to make an imitation or forgery of

fakir *noun* an Islamic or Hindu holy man

falcon *noun* a kind of bird of prey

falconry *noun* the training of falcons for hunting

fall *verb* 1 to drop down 2 to become less 3 of a fortress *etc*: to be captured 4 to die in battle 5 to happen, occur: *Christmas falls on a Monday this year* □ *noun* 1 a dropping down 2 something that falls: *a fall of snow* 3 lowering in value *etc* 4 *US* autumn 5 an accident involving falling 6 ruin, downfall, surrender 7 (**falls**) a waterfall □ **fall flat** to fail to have the intended effect □ **fall in love** to begin to be in love □ **fall out with** to quarrel with □ **fall through** of a plan: to fail, come to nothing

fall *verb* ⇨ fall*s*, fall*ing*, fall*en*, fell

fallacious *adjective* wrong, because based on false information or on faulty reasoning

fallacy *noun* (*plural* **fallacies**) a false belief; something believed to be true but really false

fall guy a scapegoat

fallible *adjective* liable to make a mistake or to be wrong □ **fallibility** *noun*

fallopian tubes two tubes along which egg cells pass from a woman's ovaries to her uterus

fallout *noun* radioactive dust resulting from the explosion of an atomic bomb *etc*

fallow[1] *adjective* of land: left unsown for a time after being ploughed

fallow[2] *adjective* of a yellowish-brown colour

fallow deer a type of yellowish-brown deer

false *adjective* 1 untrue 2 not real, fake 3 not natural: *false teeth*

Alternative words: (meaning 2) counterfeit, sham, bogus, assumed; (meaning 3) artificial, synthetic, imitation, mock

falsehood *noun* a lie, an untruth

falseness or **falsity** *noun* quality of being false

falsetto *noun* a singing voice forced higher than its natural range

falsify *verb* to make false, alter for a dishonest purpose: *falsified his tax forms*

falsify ⇨ falsifi*es*, falsify*ing*, falsifi*ed*

falsity *see* **falseness**

falter *verb* to stumble or hesitate

fame *noun* the quality of being well-known, renown

famed *adjective* famous

familiar *adjective* 1 well-known 2 seen, known *etc* before 3 well-acquainted (with) 4 over-friendly, cheeky □ **familiarity** *noun*

familiarize *verb* to make quite accustomed or acquainted (with)

family *noun* (*plural* **families**) 1 a couple and their children 2 the children alone 3 a group of people related to one another 4 a group of animals, languages, *etc* with common characteristics ⓛ Comes from Latin *familia* meaning 'the slaves in a household'

famine *noun* a great shortage of food

famished *adjective* very hungry

famous *adjective* well-known, having fame

Alternative words: renowned, celebrated, illustrious, eminent, prominent, signal

famously *adverb*, *informal* very well: *get along famously*

fan[1] *noun* 1 a device or appliance for making a rush of air 2 a small hand-held device for cooling the face □ *verb* 1 to cause a rush of air with a fan 2 to increase the strength of: *fanning her anger* □ **fan out** to spread out in the shape of a fan

fan *verb* ⇨ fan*s*, fan*ning*, fan*ned*

fan[2] *noun* an admirer, a devoted follower: *a fan of traditional music*

fanatic *noun* someone who is over-enthusiastic about something □ *adjective* fanatical

fanatical *adjective* wildly or excessively enthusiastic □ **fanatically** *adverb*

fancier *noun* someone whose hobby is

to keep prize animals, birds *etc*: *a pigeon fancier*

fanciful *adjective* **1** inclined to have fancies **2** imaginary, not real

fancy *noun* (*plural* **fancies**) **1** a sudden liking or desire: *he had a fancy for ice-cream* **2** imagination **3** something imagined □ *adjective* not plain, elaborate □ *verb* **1** to picture, imagine **2** to have a liking or a sudden wish for **3** to think without being sure

fancy *verb* ⇨ fanc**ies**, fancy**ing**, fanc**ied**

fancy dress an elaborate costume worn *eg* for a party, often representing a famous character

fanfare *noun* a loud flourish from a trumpet or bugle

fang *noun* **1** a long tooth of a wild animal **2** the poison-tooth of a snake

fankle *noun, Scottish* a muddle, a tangle

fanlight *noun* a window above a door, usually semi-circular

fantastic *adjective* **1** very unusual, strange **2** *informal* very great **3** *informal* excellent

fantasy *noun* (*plural* **fantasies**) **1** an imaginary scene, story *etc* **2** an idea not based on reality

fanzine *noun, informal* **1** a magazine for a particular group of fans **2** a small-circulation magazine

FAO *abbreviation* for the attention of

far *adverb* **1** at or to a long way: *far off* **2** very much: *far better* □ *adjective* **1** a long way off, distant: *a far country* **2** more distant: *the far side* □ *See* also *further*

far *adjective* ⇨ farth**er**, farth**est**

farce *noun* **1** a play with far-fetched characters and plot **2** a ridiculous situation

farcical *adjective* absurd, ridiculous

fardel *noun* a burden, a pack

fare *verb* to get on (either well or badly): *they fared well in the competition* □ *noun* **1** the price of a journey **2** a paying passenger in a taxi *etc* **3** food
Ⓞ Comes from Old English *faran*

🖝 Do not confuse with: **fair**

farewell *exclamation* & *noun* goodbye

far-fetched *adjective* very unlikely: *a far-fetched story*

far-flung *adjective* extending over a great distance

farm *noun* **1** an area of land for growing crops, breeding and feeding animals *etc* **2** a place where certain animals, fish *etc* are reared: *a salmon farm* □ *verb* to work on a farm □ **farm out** to give (work) to others to do for payment

farmer *noun* the owner or tenant of a farm

farmhouse *noun* the house attached to a farm

farmstead *noun* a farm and farmhouse

farmyard *noun* the yard surrounded by farm buildings

farrow *noun* a litter of baby pigs □ *verb* to give birth to a litter of pigs

far-sighted *adjective* foreseeing what is likely to happen and preparing for it

farther and **farthest** *see* **far**

farthing *noun, historical* an old coin, worth $\frac{1}{4}$ of an old penny

fascinate *verb* **1** to charm, attract irresistibly **2** to hypnotize

fascinating *adjective* extremely interesting

fascination *noun* an intense and deep interest

fascism *noun* a form of authoritarian government characterized by extreme nationalism and suppression of individual freedom

From Italian word, *fascio* meaning 'bundle' or 'group'

fascist *noun* **1** a supporter of fascism **2** a right-wing extremist

fashion *noun* **1** the style in which something is made, especially clothes **2** a way of behaving or dressing which is popular for a time **3** a manner, a way: *acting in a strange fashion* □ *verb* to shape, form □ **after a fashion** to some extent, in a way □ **in fashion** fashionable

fashionable *adjective* up-to-date, agreeing with the latest style

fast *adjective* **1** quick-moving **2** of a clock: showing a time in advance of the correct time **3** of dyed colour: fixed, not likely to wash out □ *adverb* **1** quickly **2** firmly: *stand fast* **3** soundly, completely: *fast asleep* □ *verb* to go without food voluntarily, *eg* for religious reasons or as a protest □ *noun* abstinence from food □ **in the fast lane** having an exciting but stressful lifestyle

---

■ **Alternative words**: (adjective, meaning 1) quick, swift, accelerated, speedy

---

fasten *verb* to fix; make firm by tying, nailing *etc*

fastidious *adjective* difficult to please, liking things properly done in every detail

fastidiously *adverb* extremely thoroughly, taking much care

fastidiousness *noun* the quality of being fastidious

fast-track *adjective* of a career: liable for quick promotion

fat *noun* an oily substance made by the bodies of animals and by plants □ *adjective* **1** having a lot of fat; plump **2** thick, wide

---

■ **Alternative words**: (adjective, meaning 1) plump, obese, tubby, stout, corpulent, portly, round, rotund, paunchy, pot-bellied, overweight, heavy, beefy, solid, chubby, podgy, fleshy, flabby, gross

---

fatal *adjective* causing death or disaster

fatality *noun* (*plural* **fatalities**) a death, especially caused by accident or disaster

fate *noun* **1** what the future holds; fortune, luck **2** end, death: *met his fate bravely*

fated *adjective* doomed

fateful *adjective* with important consequences; crucial, significant

father *noun* **1** a male parent **2** a priest **3** the creator or inventor of something: *Poe is the father of crime fiction* □ *verb* to be the father of

father-in-law *noun* the father of someone's husband or wife

fatherland *noun* someone's native country

fathom *noun* a measure of depth of water (6 feet, 1.83 metres) □ *verb* to understand, get to the bottom of

fatigue (*pronounced* fa-**teeg**) *noun* **1** great tiredness **2** weakness or strain caused by use: *metal fatigue* □ *verb* to tire out

fatten *verb* to make or become fat

fatty *adjective* containing a lot of fat

fatuous (*pronounced* **fat**-yoo-*us*) *adjective* very foolish □ **fatuously** *adverb*

fault *noun* **1** a mistake **2** a flaw, something bad or wrong, *eg* with a machine **3** a long crack in the earth's surface where a section of the rock layer has slipped

faultless *adjective* perfect □ **faultlessly** *adverb*

faulty *adjective* having a fault or faults

faun *noun* a mythological creature, half human and half animal

fauna *noun* the animals of a district or country as a whole

faux pas (*pronounced* foh pah) an embarrassing mistake, a blunder

favour *noun* **1** a kind action **2** goodwill, approval **3** a gift, a token □ *verb* **1** to show preference for **2** to be an advantage to: *the darkness favoured our escape* □ **in favour of 1** in support of **2** for the benefit of

favourable *adjective* **1** showing approval **2** advantageous, helpful (to)

favourably *adverb* in a positive or advantageous way □ **compare favourably with** to be better than, or at least as good as, the other thing or things mentioned

favourite *adjective* best liked □ *noun* **1** a liked or best-loved person or thing **2** a competitor, horse, *etc* expected to win a race

favouritism *noun* showing favour towards one person *etc* more than another

fawn[1] *noun* **1** a young deer **2** a light yellowish-brown colour □ *adjective* of this colour

fawn[2] *verb* **1** to show affection as a dog does **2** **fawn on** to flatter in a grovelling fashion

fax *noun* 1 a machine that scans a document electronically and transfers the information by a telephone line to a receiving machine that produces a corresponding copy 2 a document copied and sent in this way □ *verb* 1 to send by fax 2 to send a fax message to

FBI *abbreviation*, *US* Federal Bureau of Investigation

FE *abbreviation* Further Education

fear *noun* an unpleasant feeling caused by danger, evil *etc*

fearful *adjective* 1 timid, afraid 2 terrible 3 *informal* very bad: *a fearful headache*

fearfully *adverb* 1 timidly, showing fear 2 extremely, dreadfully

fearless *adjective* brave, daring □ **fearlessly** *adverb*

feasible *adjective* able to be done, likely □ **feasibility** *noun* □ **feasibly** *adverb*

feast *noun* 1 a rich and plentiful meal 2 a festival day commemorating some event □ *verb* to eat or hold a feast

feat *noun* a deed requiring some effort

feather *noun* one of the growths which form the outer covering of a bird

feathery *adjective* 1 covered in feathers 2 soft 3 light

feature *noun* 1 an identifying mark, a characteristic 2 a special article in a newspaper *etc* 3 the main film in a cinema programme 4 a special attraction 5 **features** the various parts of someone's face, *eg* eyes, nose *etc* □ *verb* 1 to have as a feature 2 to take part (in) 3 to be prominent in

February *noun* the second month of the year

fed *past form* of **feed**

federal *adjective* joined by treaty or agreement

federated *adjective* joined after an agreement is made

federation *noun* a group of states *etc* joined together for a common purpose, a league

fee *noun* a price paid for work done, or for a special service

feeble *adjective* weak □ **feebly** *adverb*

feed *verb* 1 to give food to 2 to eat food 3 to supply with necessary materials □ *noun* food for animals: *cattle feed* □ **fed up** *adjective* tired, bored and disgusted

feed *verb* ⇨ feeds, feeding, fed

feel *verb* 1 to explore by touch 2 to experience, be aware of: *he felt no pain* 3 to believe, consider 4 to think (yourself) to be: *I feel ill* 5 to be sorry (for): *we felt for her in her grief* □ *noun* an act of touching □ **feel like** to want, have an inclination for: *do you feel like going out tonight?*

feel *verb* ⇨ feels, feeling, felt

feeler *noun* one of two thread-like parts on an insect's head for sensing danger *etc*

feelgood *adjective* causing a feeling of comfort or security: *feelgood movie*

feeling *noun* 1 sense of touch 2 emotion: *spoken with great feeling* 3 affection 4 an impression, belief

feelings *noun plural* what someone feels inside; emotions

feet *plural* of **foot**

feign (*pronounced* fein) *verb* to pretend to feel or be: *feigning illness*

feint (*pronounced* feint) *noun* 1 a pretence 2 a move to put an enemy off guard □ *adjective* of paper: ruled with faint lines: *narrow feint* (= having lines which are close together) □ *verb* to make a feint (noun, meanings 1 and 2)

◆ Do not confuse with: **faint**

felicitous *adjective* 1 lucky 2 well-chosen, suiting well

felicity *noun* happiness

feline *adjective* 1 of or relating to cats 2 like a cat

fell¹ *noun* a barren hill

fell² *verb* to cut down (a tree)

fell³ *adjective*, *old* cruel, ruthless

fell⁴ *past form* of **fall**

fellow *noun* 1 an equal 2 one of a pair 3 a member of an academic society, college *etc* 4 a man, a boy

fellowship *noun* 1 comradeship, friendship 2 an award to a university graduate

felon *noun* a committer of a serious crime

felony *noun* (*plural* **felonies**) a serious crime

felt[1] *noun* a type of rough cloth made of rolled and pressed wool

felt[2] *past form of* **feel**

female *adjective* of the sex which produces children □ *noun* a human or animal of this sex

feminine *adjective* 1 of or relating to women 2 characteristic of women

femininity *noun* 1 the circumstance of being a woman 2 the quality of being feminine, or of having physical and mental characteristics traditionally thought suitable and essential for women

feminism *noun* a social and cultural movement aiming to win equal rights for women

feminist *noun* a supporter of feminism □ *adjective* relating to this movement: *feminist literature*

femme fatale an irresistibly attractive woman who brings disaster on men

femur *noun* the thigh bone

fen *noun* low marshy land, often covered with water

fence *noun* 1 a railing, hedge *etc* for closing in animals or land 2 *slang* a receiver of stolen goods □ *verb* 1 to close in with a fence 2 to fight with swords 3 to give evasive answers when questioned

fencing *noun* 1 material for fences 2 the sport of fighting with swords, using blunted weapons

fend *verb*: **fend for yourself** to look after and provide for yourself

fender *noun* 1 a low guard round a fireplace to keep in coal *etc* 2 a piece of matting over a ship's side acting as a buffer against the quay 3 *US* the bumper of a car

ferment *verb* (*pronounced* fe-**ment**) 1 to change by fermentation 2 to stir up (trouble *etc*) □ *noun* (*pronounced* **ferm**-ent)

ⓘ Comes from Latin *fermentum* meaning 'yeast'

◆ Do not confuse with: **foment**

fermentation *noun* 1 a reaction caused by bringing certain substances together, *eg* by adding yeast to dough in bread-making 2 great excitement or agitation

fern *noun* a plant with no flowers and feather-like leaves

ferocious *adjective* fierce, savage □ **ferociously** *adverb* □ **ferocity** *noun*

ferret *noun* a small weasel-like animal used to chase rabbits out of their warrens □ *verb* to search busily and persistently

ferry *verb* to carry over water by boat, or overland by aeroplane □ *noun* (*plural* **ferries**) 1 a crossing place for boats 2 a boat which carries passengers and cars *etc* across a channel

ferry *verb* ⇨ ferries, ferrying, ferried

fertile *adjective* 1 able to produce children or young 2 full of ideas, creative, productive □ **fertility** *noun*

fertilize *verb* 1 to make (soil *etc*) fertile 2 to start the process of reproduction in an egg or plant by combining them with sperm or pollen □ **fertilization** *noun*

fertilizer *noun* manure or chemicals used to make soil more fertile

fervent *adjective* very eager; intense □ **fervently** *adverb*

fervour *noun* ardour, zeal

fest *noun or* -**fest** *suffix* a gathering or festival around some subject: *news-fest/trade fest*

ⓘ Comes from German *Fest* meaning 'a festival'

fester *verb* of a wound: to produce pus because of infection

festival *noun* 1 a celebration; a feast 2 a season of musical, theatrical or other performances

festive *adjective* 1 of a feast 2 in a happy, celebrating mood

festivity *noun* (*plural* **festivities**) a celebration, a feast

festoon *verb* to decorate with chains of ribbons, flowers *etc*

fetch *verb* 1 to go and get 2 to bring in (a price): *fetched £100 at auction*

fete or **fête** *noun* a public event with stalls, competitions *etc* to raise money □ *verb* to entertain lavishly, make much of

fetish *noun* (*plural* **fetishes**) **1** a sacred object believed to carry supernatural power **2** an object of excessive fixation or (especially sexual) obsession □ **fetishist** *noun* □ **fetishistic** *adjective*

fetlock *noun* the part of a horse's leg just above the foot

fetters *noun plural, formal* chains for imprisonment

fettle *noun*: **in fine fettle** in good health or condition

feu (*pronounced* fyoo) *noun, Scottish* a right to use land, a house *etc* indefinitely in return for an annual payment

feud (*pronounced* fyood) *noun* a private, drawn-out war between families, clans *etc*

feudal (*pronounced* **fyood**-al) *adjective, historical* of a social system under which tenants were bound to give certain services to the overlord in return for their tenancies □ **feudalism** *noun* □ **feudalist** *adjective*

fever *noun* an above-normal body temperature and quickened pulse

fevered *adjective* **1** having a fever **2** very excited

feverish *adjective* **1** having a slight fever **2** excited **3** too eager, frantic: *feverish pace*

few *adjective* not many: *only a few tickets left* □ **a good few** or **quite a few** several, a considerable number

few ⇨ fewer, fewest

fez *noun* (*plural* **fezzes**) a brimless flowerpot-shaped hat, usually with a top tassel

fiancé (*pronounced* fi-**on**-sei) *noun* the man a woman is engaged to marry

fiancée (*pronounced* fi-**on**-sei) *noun* the woman a man is engaged to marry

fiasco *noun* (*plural* **fiascos**) a complete failure

Based on an Italian phrase *far fiasco* 'make a bottle', meaning forget your lines on stage

fib *verb* to lie about something unimportant □ *noun* an unimportant lie

fib *verb* ⇨ fibs, fibbing, fibbed

fibre *noun* **1** a thread or string **2** the essence or material of something: *the fibre of her being* **3** roughage in foods

fibreglass *noun* a lightweight material made of very fine threads of glass, used for building boats *etc*

fibre-optic *adjective* of a cable: made of glass or plastic filaments which transmit light signals

fibrous *adjective* thread-like, stringy

fickle *adjective* changeable; not stable or loyal

fiction *noun* **1** stories about imaginary characters and events **2** a lie
ⓘ Comes from Latin *fictio* meaning 'a forming'

fictional *adjective* imagined, created for a story: *fictional character*
ⓘ for origin, see **fiction**

● Do not confuse: **fictional** and **fictitious**

fictitious *adjective* **1** not real, imaginary **2** untrue
ⓘ Comes from Latin *ficticius* meaning 'counterfeit'

fiddle *noun, informal* **1** a violin **2** a tricky or delicate operation **3** a cheat, a swindle □ *verb* **1** to play the violin **2** to play aimlessly (with) **3** to interfere, tamper (with) **4** *informal* to falsify (accounts *etc*) with the intention of cheating

fiddly *adjective* needing delicate or careful handling

fidelity *noun* **1** faithfulness **2** truth, accuracy

fidget *verb* to move about restlessly

field *noun* **1** a piece of enclosed ground for pasture, crops, sports *etc* **2** an area of land containing a natural resource: *goldfield/ coalfield* **3** a branch of interest or knowledge **4** those taking part in a race □ *verb, cricket* to catch the ball and return it

field-day *noun* a day of unusual activity or success

fieldglasses *noun plural* binoculars

field-gun *noun* a light, mobile cannon

field-marshal *noun* the highest ranking army officer

fiend *noun* **1** an evil spirit **2** a wicked person **3** an extreme enthusiast: *a crossword fiend*

fiendish *adjective* **1** evil or wicked **2** extremely bad **3** very complicated or clever

fierce *adjective* **1** very angry-looking, hostile, likely to attack **2** intense, strong: *fierce competition* □ **fiercely** *adverb*

fiery *adjective* **1** like fire **2** quick-tempered, volatile

fife *noun* a small flute

fifteen *noun* the number 15 □ *adjective* 15 in number

fifteenth *adjective* the last of a series of fifteen □ *noun* one of fifteen equal parts

fifth *adjective* the last of a series of five □ *noun* one of five equal parts

fiftieth *adjective* the last of a series of fifty □ *noun* one of fifty equal parts

fifty *noun* the number 50 □ *adjective* 50 in number

fig *noun* **1** a soft roundish fruit with thin, dark skin and red pulp containing many seeds **2** the tree which bears it

fight *verb* **1** to struggle with fists, weapons *etc* **2** to quarrel **3** to go to war with □ *noun* a struggle; a battle

fight *verb* ⇨ fights, fight*ing*, fought

fighter *noun* **1** someone who fights **2** a fast military aircraft armed with guns

figment *noun* an imaginary story or idea

figurative *adjective* of a word: used not in its ordinary meaning but to show likenesses, *eg* 'she was a tiger' for 'she was as ferocious as a tiger'; metaphorical (*contrasted with*: **literal**) □ **figuratively** *adverb*

figure *noun* **1** outward form or shape **2** a number **3** a geometrical shape **4** an unidentified person: *a shadowy figure approached* **5** a diagram or drawing on a page **6** a set of movements in skating *etc* □ *verb* to appear, take part: *he figures in the story* □ **figure out** to work out, understand

figured *adjective* marked with a design: *figured silk*

figurehead *noun* **1** a carved wooden figure fixed to the prow of a ship **2** a leader who has little real power

filament *noun* a slender thread, *eg* of wire in a light bulb

filch *verb, informal* to steal

file *noun* **1** a loose-leaf book *etc* to hold papers **2** an amount of computer data held under a single name **3** a line of soldiers *etc* walking one behind another **4** a steel tool with a roughened surface for smoothing wood, metal *etc* □ *verb* **1** to put (papers *etc*) in a file **2** to rub with a file **3** to walk in a file

filial *adjective* of or characteristic of a son or daughter

filibuster *noun* a long speech given in parliament to delay the passing of a law

filigree *noun* very fine gold or silver work in lace or metal

fill *verb* **1** to put (something) into until there is no room for more: *fill the bucket with water* **2** to become full: *her eyes filled with tears* **3** to satisfy, fulfil (a requirement *etc*) **4** to occupy: *fill a post* **5** to appoint someone to (a job *etc*): *have you filled the vacancy?* **6** to put something in a hole to stop it up □ *noun* as much as is needed to fill: *we ate our fill* □ **fill in 1** to fill (a hole) **2** to complete (a form *etc*) **3** to do another person's job while they are absent: *I'm filling in for Anne* □ **fill up** to fill completely

filler *noun* **1** a funnel for pouring liquids through **2** a substance used to increase bulk **3** a material used to fill up holes in wood, plaster *etc*

fillet *noun* a piece of meat or fish with bones removed □ *verb* to remove the bones from

fillet *verb* ⇨ fillets, fillet*ing*, fillet*ed*

filling *noun* something used to fill a hole or gap □ *adjective* of food: satisfying

filling-station *noun* a garage which sells petrol

filly *noun* (*plural* **fillies**) a young female horse

film *noun* **1** a thin skin or coating **2** a

chemically-coated strip of celluloid on which photographs are taken **3** a narrative photographed on celluloid and shown in a cinema, on television *etc* □ *verb* **1** to photograph on celluloid **2** to develop a thin coating: *his eyes filmed over*

filmstar *noun* a famous actor or actress in films

Filofax *noun, trademark* a personal organizer

filter *noun* **1** a strainer for removing solid material from liquids **2** a green arrow on a traffic light signalling one lane of traffic to move while the main stream is held up □ *verb* **1** to strain through a filter **2** to move or arrive gradually: *the news filtered through* **3** of cars *etc*: to join gradually a stream of traffic **4** of a lane of traffic: to move in the direction shown by a filter

filter *verb* ⇨ filter*s*, filter*ing*, filter*ed*

filth *noun* **1** dirt **2** obscene words or pictures

filthily *adverb* dirtily or obscenely

filthiness *noun* extreme dirtiness or obscenity

filthy *adjective* **1** very dirty **2** obscene, lewd

fin *noun* a flexible projecting part of a fish's body used for balance and swimming

final *adjective* **1** last **2** allowing of no argument: *the judge's decision is final* □ *noun* the last contest in a competition: *World Cup final*

finale (*pronounced* fi-**nah**-lei) *noun* the last part of anything (*eg* a concert)

finality *noun* the quality of being final and decisive

finalize *verb* to put (*eg* plans) in a final or finished form

finally *adverb* in the end, at last, eventually, lastly

finance *noun* **1** money affairs **2** the study or management of these **3** **finances** the money someone has to spend □ *verb* to supply with sums of money □ **financial** *adjective* (noun, meaning 1) □ **financially** *adverb* (noun, meaning 1)

financier *noun* someone who manages (public) money

finch *noun* (*plural* **finches**) a small bird

find *verb* **1** to come upon accidentally or after searching: *I found an earring in the street* **2** to discover **3** to judge to be: *finds it hard to live on her pension* □ *noun* something found, especially something of interest or value □ **find out** to discover, detect

find *verb* ⇨ find*s*, find*ing*, found

① Comes from Old English *findan*

■ **Alternative words**: (verb, meaning 1) retrieve, recover, trace; (verb, meaning 2) locate, unearth, expose, detect □ **find out** learn, ascertain

fine¹ *adjective* **1** made up of very small pieces, drops *etc* **2** not coarse: *fine linen* **3** thin, delicate **4** slight: *a fine distinction* **5** beautiful, handsome **6** of good quality; pure **7** bright, not rainy **8** well, healthy

fine² *noun* money to be paid as a punishment □ *verb* to compel to pay (money) as punishment

finery *noun* splendid clothes *etc*

finesse (*pronounced* fi-**nes**) *noun* cleverness and subtlety in handling situations *etc*

finger *noun* one of the five branching parts of the hand □ *verb* to touch with the fingers

fingering *noun* **1** the positioning of the fingers in playing a musical instrument **2** the showing of this by numbers

fingerprint *noun* the mark made by the tip of a finger, used by the police as a means of identification

finish *verb* **1** to end or complete the making of **2** to stop: *when do you finish work today?* □ *noun* **1** the end (*eg* of a race) **2** the last coating of paint, polish *etc*

finished *adjective* **1** ended, complete **2** of a person: ruined, not likely to achieve further success *etc*

finite *adjective* having an end or limit

fiord or **fjord** *noun* a long narrow inlet between steep hills, especially in Norway

fir *noun* a kind of cone-bearing tree

fir-cone *noun* one of the small, woody cones which grow on a fir tree and hold its seeds

fire *noun* **1** the heat and light given off by something burning **2** a mass of burning material, objects *etc* **3** a heating device: *electric fire* **4** eagerness, keenness □ *verb* **1** to set on fire **2** to make eager: *fired by his enthusiasm* **3** to make (a gun) explode, shoot

> **fire** *verb* ⇨ fires, firing, fired

fire alarm a device to sound a bell *etc* as a warning of fire

firearm *noun* a gun *eg* a pistol

fire brigade a company of firemen

fire-damp *noun* a dangerous gas found in coal mines

fire engine a vehicle carrying firefighters and their equipment

fire escape a means of escape from a building in case of fire

firefly *noun* a type of insect which glows in the dark

fire-guard *noun* a framework of iron placed in front of a fireplace for safety

fireman *noun* a man whose job it is to put out fires

fireplace *noun* a recess in a room below a chimney for a fire

firewoman *noun* a woman whose job it is to put out fires

firewood *noun* wood for burning on a fire

fireworks *noun plural* **1** squibs, rockets *etc* sent up at night for show **2** *informal* angry behaviour

firm *adjective* **1** not easily moved or shaken **2** with mind made up □ *noun* a business company

firmament *noun, formal* the heavens, the sky

first *adjective & adverb* before all others in place, time or rank □ *adjective* before doing anything else

first-aid *noun* treatment of a wounded or sick person before the doctor's arrival

first-born *noun* the eldest child

first-class *adjective* of the highest standard, best kind *etc*

first-hand *adjective* direct

first name a person's name that is not their surname

first-rate *adjective* first-class

firth *noun* a narrow arm of the sea, especially at a river mouth

fiscal *adjective* **1** of the public revenue **2** of financial matters

fish *noun* (*plural* **fish** or **fishes**) a kind of animal that lives in water, and breathes through gills □ *verb* **1** to try to catch fish with rod, nets *etc* **2** to search (for): *fishing for a handkerchief in her bag* **3** to try to obtain: *fish for compliments*

fisherman *noun* a man who fishes, especially for a living

fishmonger *noun* someone who sells fish for eating

fishy *adjective* **1** like a fish **2** doubtful, arousing suspicion

fission *noun* splitting

fissure *noun* a crack

fist *noun* a tightly-shut hand

fisticuffs *noun plural, old* a fight with the fists

fit *adjective* **1** suited to a purpose; proper **2** in good training or health □ *noun* a sudden attack or spasm of laughter, illness *etc* □ *verb* **1** to be of the right size or shape **2** to be suitable

fitful *adjective* coming or doing in bursts or spasms □ **fitfully** *adverb*

fitness *noun* good physical health and strength

fitting *adjective* suitable □ *noun* something fixed or fitted in a room, house *etc*

> **fit** *verb* ⇨ fits, fitting, fitted

five *noun* the number 5 □ *adjective* 5 in number
  ① Comes from Old English *fif*

fives *noun plural* a handball game played in a walled court

fix *verb* **1** to make firm; fasten **2** to mend, repair

fixed *adjective* settled; set in position

fixedly adverb steadily, intently: staring fixedly

fixture noun 1 a piece of furniture etc fixed in position 2 an arranged sports match or race

fizz verb to make a hissing sound □ noun a hissing sound

fizzle or **fizzle out** verb to fail, coming to nothing

fizzy adjective of a drink: forming bubbles on the surface

fjord another spelling of **fiord**

flabbergasted adjective very surprised

flabby adjective not firm, soft, limp; weak, feeble □ **flabbily** adverb

flaccid (pronounced fla-sid) adjective 1 hanging loosely 2 limp, not firm

flag noun 1 a banner, standard, or ensign 2 a flat paving-stone □ verb to become tired or weak

  flag verb ⇨ flags, flagging, flagged

flagon noun a large container for liquid

flagrant adjective 1 conspicuous 2 openly wicked □ **flagrancy** noun □ **flagrantly** adverb

flail verb to wave or swing in the air □ noun, old a tool for threshing corn

flair noun talent, skill: a flair for languages

flak noun 1 anti-aircraft fire 2 strong criticism

flake noun 1 a thin slice or chip of anything 2 a very small piece of snow etc □ verb to form into flakes □ **flake off** to break off in flakes

flaky adjective 1 forming flakes, crumbly: flaky pastry 2 US informal eccentric

flamboyant adjective 1 splendidly coloured 2 too showy, gaudy

flame noun the bright leaping light of a fire □ verb 1 to burn brightly 2 computing slang to send abusive electronic mail (to)

flaming adjective 1 burning 2 red 3 violent: a flaming temper

flamingo noun (plural **flamingoes**) a type of long-legged bird of pink or bright-red colour

flammable adjective easily set on fire

flan noun a flat, open tart

flank noun the side of an animal's body, of an army etc □ verb 1 to go by the side of 2 to be situated at the side of

flannel noun 1 loosely woven woollen fabric 2 a small towel or face cloth

flap noun 1 anything broad and loose-hanging: tent flap 2 the sound of a wing etc moving through air 3 a panic: getting in a flap over nothing □ verb 1 to hang down loosely 2 to move with a flapping noise 3 to get into a panic

  flap verb ⇨ flaps, flapping, flapped

flapjack noun 1 Brit a biscuit made with rolled oats, butter and sugar 2 US a pancake

flare verb to blaze up □ noun a bright light, especially one used at night as a signal, to show the position of a boat in distress etc

  flare verb ⇨ flares, flaring, flared

flash noun (plural **flashes**) 1 a quick burst of light 2 a moment, an instant 3 a distinctive mark on a uniform □ verb 1 to shine out suddenly 2 to pass quickly □ **in a flash** very quickly or suddenly

flashlight noun 1 a burst of light in which a photograph is taken 2 an electric torch

flashy adjective showy, gaudy

flask noun 1 a narrow-necked bottle 2 a small flat bottle 3 an insulated bottle or vacuum flask

flat adjective 1 level: a flat surface 2 of a drink: no longer fizzy 3 leaving no doubt, downright: a flat denial 4 below the right musical pitch 5 of a tyre: punctured 6 dull, uninteresting □ adverb stretched out: lying flat on her back □ noun 1 an apartment on one storey of a building 2 music a sign (♭) which lowers a note by a semitone 3 a punctured tyre □ **flat out** adverb as fast as possible, with as much effort as possible

flatly adverb in a definite or emphatic way

flatness noun the quality of being flat

flat race a race over level ground without hurdles

flat rate a rate which is the same in all cases

flatten *verb* to make or become flat

flatter *verb* to praise insincerely □ **flattery** *noun*

flatulence *noun* wind in the stomach □ **flatulent** *adjective*

flaunt (*pronounced* flawnt) *verb* to display in an obvious way: *flaunted his wealth*

● Do not confuse with: **flout**. Remember that the use of **flaunt** is perfectly illustrated in the well-known phrase 'if you've got it, **flaunt** it'. On the other hand, when you **flout** something, you treat it with contempt instead of showing it off, *eg* you might **flout the rules** or **flout tradition**

flautist *noun* (*pronounced* flawt-ist) a flute player

flavour *noun* **1** taste: *lemon flavour* **2** quality or atmosphere: *an exotic flavour* □ *verb* to give a taste to

flavouring *noun* an ingredient used to give a particular taste: *chocolate flavouring*

flaw *noun* a fault, an imperfection

flawless *adjective* with no faults or blemishes □ **flawlessly** *adverb*

flax *noun* a plant whose fibres are woven into linen cloth

flaxen *adjective* **1** made of or looking like flax **2** of hair: fair

flay *verb* to strip the skin off

flea *noun* a small, wingless, blood-sucking insect with great jumping power

fleck *noun* a spot, a speck

flecked *adjective* marked with spots or patches

fled *past form* of **flee**

fledgling *noun* a young bird with fully-grown feathers

flee *verb* to run away from danger *etc*

flee ⇨ flees, fleeing, fled

fleece *noun* a sheep's coat of wool

□ *verb* **1** to clip wool from **2** *informal* to rob by cheating

fleecy *adjective* soft and fluffy like wool

fleet *noun* **1** a number of ships **2** a number of cars or taxis □ *adjective* swift; nimble, quick in movement

fleeting *adjective* passing quickly: *fleeting glimpse*

fleetingly *adverb* very briefly

fleetness *noun* swiftness

flesh *noun* **1** the soft tissue which covers the bones of humans and animals **2** meat **3** the body **4** the soft eatable part of fruit □ **flesh and blood 1** relations, family **2** human, mortal

fleshy *adjective* fat, plump

flew *past form* of **fly**

flex *verb* to bend □ *noun* a length of covered wire attached to electrical devices

flexible *adjective* **1** easily bent **2** willing to adapt to new or different conditions □ **flexibility** *noun*

flexitime *noun* a system in which an agreed number of hours' work is done at times chosen by the worker

flick *verb* **1** to strike lightly with a quick movement **2** to remove (dust *etc*) with a movement of this kind □ *noun* a quick, sharp movement: *a flick of the wrist*

flicker¹ *verb* **1** to flutter **2** to burn unsteadily □ *noun*: *a flicker of hope*

flicker² *noun*, *US* a woodpecker

flick-knife *noun* a knife with a blade which springs out at the press of a button

flight *noun* **1** the act of flying **2** a journey by plane **3** the act of fleeing or escaping **4** a flock (of birds) **5** a number (of steps)

flighty *adjective* changeable, impulsive

flimsy *adjective* **1** thin; easily torn or broken *etc* **2** weak: *a flimsy excuse*

flinch *verb* to move or shrink back in fear, pain *etc*

fling *verb* to throw □ *noun* **1** a throw **2** a casual attempt **3** a period of time devoted to pleasure **4** a brief romantic affair

fling verb ⇨ flings, flinging, flung

flint noun a kind of hard stone □ adjective made of flint

flip verb to toss lightly □ noun a light toss or stroke

flip verb ⇨ flips, flipping, flipped

flippant adjective joking, not serious □ **flippancy** noun □ **flippantly** adverb

flipper noun 1 a limb of a seal, walrus etc 2 a webbed rubber shoe worn by divers

flip side 1 the reverse side of a record etc 2 the converse of anything

flirt verb 1 to play at courtship without any serious intentions 2 **flirt with something** to take an interest in something without committing yourself seriously to it □ noun someone who flirts □ **flirt with danger** to take unnecessary risks □ **flirtation** noun

flirtatious adjective fond of flirting

flit verb 1 to move quickly and lightly from place to place 2 Scottish to move house

flit ⇨ flits, flitting, flitted

float verb 1 to keep on the surface of a liquid without sinking 2 to set going: float a fund □ noun 1 a cork etc on a fishing line 2 a raft 3 a van delivering milk etc 4 a large lorry for transporting cattle 5 a platform on wheels, used in processions 6 a sum of money set aside for giving change

flock[1] noun 1 a number of animals or birds together 2 a large number of people 3 the congregation of a church □ verb 1 **flock to** to go to in large numbers or in a large crowd 2 **flock together** to gather in a crowd

flock[2] noun 1 a shred or tuft of wool 2 wool or cotton waste

floe (pronounced floh) noun a sheet of floating ice

flog verb 1 to beat, lash 2 slang to sell □ **flogging** noun (meaning 1)

flog ⇨ flogs, flogging, flogged

flood noun 1 a great flow, especially of water 2 the rise or flow of the tide 3 a great quantity: a flood of letters □ verb

1 to (cause to) overflow 2 to cover or fill with water

floodlight verb to illuminate with floodlighting □ noun a light used to floodlight

floodlight verb ⇨ floodlights, floodlighting, floodlit

floodlighting noun strong artificial lighting to illuminate an exterior or stage

floor noun 1 the base level of a room on which people walk 2 a storey of a building: a third-floor flat □ verb 1 to make a floor 2 informal to knock flat 3 informal to puzzle: floored by the question

flop verb 1 to sway or swing about loosely 2 to fall or sit down suddenly and heavily 3 to move about clumsily 4 to fail badly □ noun 1 an act of flopping 2 a complete failure

flop ⇨ flops, flopping, flopped

floppy adjective flopping, soft and flexible

floppy disk a flexible computer disk, often in a harder case, used to store data

flora noun the plants of a district or country as a whole

floral adjective (made) of flowers

florist noun a seller or grower of flowers

floss noun 1 fine silk thread 2 thin, often waxed thread for passing between the teeth to clean them □ verb to clean (teeth) with dental floss

flotilla noun a fleet of small ships

flotsam noun floating objects washed from a ship or wreck

flounce[1] verb to walk away suddenly and impatiently, eg in anger

flounce[2] noun a gathered decorative strip sewn on to the hem of a dress

flounder[1] verb 1 to struggle to move your legs and arms in water, mud etc 2 to have difficulty speaking or thinking clearly, or in acting efficiently

Flounder was probably formed by a gradual blending of 'blunder' and 'founder'

♦ Do not confuse with: **founder**

flounder² *noun* a small flatfish

flour *noun* **1** finely-ground wheat **2** any grain crushed to powder: *rice flour*

flourish *verb* **1** to be successful, especially financially **2** to grow well, thrive **3** to be healthy **4** to wave or brandish as a show or threat □ *noun* (*plural* **flourishes**) **1** fancy strokes in writing **2** a sweeping movement with the hand, sword *etc* **3** showy splendour **4** an ornamental passage in music

floury *adjective* **1** covered with flour **2** powdery

♦ Do not confuse with: **flowery**

flout *verb* to treat with contempt, defy openly: *flouted the speed limit*
🕐 Probably comes from *floute*, a form found in Middle English meaning 'to play the flute'

♦ Do not confuse with: **flaunt**

flow *verb* **1** to run, as water **2** to move or come out in an unbroken run **3** of the tide: to rise □ *noun* a smooth or unbroken run: *flow of ideas*

flower *noun* **1** the part of a plant or tree from which fruit or seeds grow **2** the best of anything □ *verb* **1** of plants *etc*: to produce a flower **2** to be at your best, flourish

flowering *noun* of plants: producing flowers

flowery *adjective* **1** full of or decorated with flowers **2** using fine-sounding, fancy language: *flowery prose style*

♦ Do not confuse with: **floury**

flown *see* **fly**

flu *noun, informal* influenza

fluctuate *verb* **1** to vary in number, price *etc* **2** to be always changing □ **fluctuation** *noun*

flue *noun* a passage for air and smoke in a stove or chimney

fluent *adjective* finding words easily in speaking or writing without any awkward pauses □ **fluency** *noun*

fluff *noun* soft, downy material □ *verb* **1** to spoil something by doing it badly or making a mistake **2 fluff up** or **fluff**

out to shake or arrange into a soft mass □ **fluffy** *adjective*

fluid *noun* a substance whose particles can move about freely, a liquid or gas □ *adjective* **1** flowing **2** not settled or fixed: *my plans for the weekend are fluid*

fluke¹ *noun* a small worm which harms sheep

fluke² *noun* the part of an anchor which holds fast in sand

fluke³ *noun* an accidental or unplanned success

flume *noun* a water chute

flummox *verb* to bewilder, confuse totally

flung *past form of* **fling**

flunk *verb, slang* to fail

fluoride *noun* a chemical added to water or toothpaste to prevent tooth decay

fluoridize or **fluoridate** *verb* to add fluoride to

flurry *noun* (*plural* **flurries**) a sudden rush of wind *etc* □ *verb* to excite

flurry *verb* ⇨ flurries, flurry*ing*, flurri*ed*

flush *noun* (*plural* **flushes**) **1** a reddening of the face **2** freshness, glow □ *verb* **1** to become red in the face **2** to clean by a rush of water □ *adjective* **1 flush with** having the surface level with the surface around **2** *informal* well supplied with money

fluster *noun* excitement caused by hurry □ *verb* to harass, confuse

flute *noun* **1** a high-pitched musical wind instrument **2** a tall narrow wine glass

fluted *adjective* decorated with grooves

flutter *verb* to move (eyelids, wings *etc*) back and forth quickly □ *noun* **1** a quick beating of pulse *etc* **2** nervous excitement: *in a flutter*

flux *noun* an ever-changing flow: *in a state of flux*

fly *noun* (*plural* **flies**) **1** a small winged insect **2** a fish-hook made to look like a fly to catch fish **3** a flap of material with buttons or a zip, especially at the front of trousers □ *verb* **1** to move through the air on wings or in an aeroplane **2** to run away

fly *verb* ⇨ flies, flying, flew, flown

flyer *noun* a small poster or advertising sheet

flying saucer a disc-shaped object believed to be an alien spacecraft

flying squad a group of police officers organized for fast action or movement

flyover *noun* a road built on pillars to cross over another

flysheet *noun* the outer covering of a tent

flywheel *noun* a heavy wheel which enables a machine to run at a steady speed

FM *abbreviation* frequency modulation (*compare with*: **AM**)

foal *noun* a young horse □ *verb* to give birth to a foal

foam *noun* a mass of small bubbles on liquids □ *verb* to produce foam

foam rubber sponge-like form of rubber for stuffing chairs, mattresses *etc*

fob[1] *noun* **1** a small watch pocket **2** an ornamental chain hanging from such a pocket

fob[2] *verb* to force to accept (something worthless): *I won't be fobbed off with a silly excuse*

focal *adjective* central, pivotal: *focal point*

fo'c'sle *another spelling of* **forecastle**

focus *noun* (*plural* **focuses** or **foci**) **1** the meeting point for rays of light **2** the point to which light, a look, or someone's attention is directed □ *verb* **1** to get the right length of ray of light for a clear picture **2** to direct (one's attention *etc*) to one point

focus *verb* ⇨ focuses, focusing, focused

fodder *noun* dried food, *eg* hay or oats, for farm animals

foe *noun, formal* an enemy

foetal *adjective* relating to a foetus □ **foetal alcohol syndrome** a range of birth defects caused by an excessive alcohol intake during pregnancy

foetus *noun* a young human being or animal in the womb or egg

fog *noun* thick mist □ *verb* **1** to cover in fog **2** to bewilder, confuse □ **foggy** *adjective*

foghorn *noun* a horn used as a warning to or by ships in fog

fogy or **fogey** *noun* someone with old-fashioned views

foil *verb* to defeat, disappoint □ *noun* **1** metal in the form of paper-thin sheets **2** a dull person against which someone else seems brighter **3** a blunt sword with a button at the end, used in fencing practice

foist *verb* **1** to pass off as genuine **2** to palm off (something undesirable) on someone

fold *noun* **1** a part laid on top of another **2** an enclosure for sheep *etc* □ *verb* to lay one part on top of another

folder *noun* a cover to hold papers

foliage *noun* leaves

folio *noun* (*plural* **folios**) **1** a leaf (two pages back to back) of a book **2** a page number **3** a sheet of paper folded once

folk *noun* **1** people **2** a nation, race **3 folks** family or relations

folklore *noun* the study of the customs, beliefs, stories *etc* of a people

folk music traditional music of a particular culture

folksong *noun* a traditional song passed on orally

follicle *noun* the pit surrounding a root of hair

follow *verb* **1** to go or come after **2** to happen as a result **3** to act according to: *follow your instincts* **4** to understand: *I don't follow you* **5** to work at (a trade)

follower *noun* **1** someone who follows **2** a supporter, disciple: *a follower of Jung*

following *noun* supporters: *the team has a large following* □ *adjective* next in time: *we left the following day* □ *preposition* after, as a result of: *following the fire, the house collapsed*

folly *noun* (*plural* **follies**) **1** foolishness **2** a purposeless building

foment *verb* to stir up, encourage growth of (a rebellion *etc*)
🕐 Comes from Latin *fomentum* meaning 'a warm lotion' or 'a poultice'
🔹 Do not confuse with: **ferment**

fond *adjective* **1** loving; tender **2** *old* foolish □ **fond of** having a liking for

fondle *verb* to caress

fondly *adverb* **1** with fondness **2** foolishly

fondness *noun* **1** affection, love, tenderness **2** liking

font *noun* **1** a basin holding water for baptism **2** a main source: *a font of knowledge*

food *noun* that which living beings eat

food processor an electrical appliance for chopping, blending *etc* food

foodstuff *noun* something used for food

fool *noun* **1** a silly person **2** *historical* a court jester **3** a dessert made of fruit, sugar and whipped cream □ *verb* to deceive; play the fool □ **fool about** to behave in a playful or silly manner

foolery *noun* silliness, foolish behaviour

foolhardy *adjective* rash, taking foolish risks

foolish *adjective* unwise, ill-considered □ **foolishly** *adverb*

foolproof *adjective* unable to go wrong

foolscap *noun* paper for writing or printing, 17 x 13 in (43 x 34 cm)
Referring to the original watermark used on this size of paper, showing a jester's cap and bells

foot *noun* (*plural* **feet**) **1** the part of the leg below the ankle **2** the lower part of anything **3** twelve inches, 30 cm □ *verb* to pay (a bill *etc*) □ **foot the bill** to pay up □ **my foot!** *exclamation* used to express disbelief □ **put a foot wrong** to make a mistake, act inappropriately

football *noun* **1** a game played by two teams of 11 on a field with a round ball **2** *US* a game played with an oval ball which can be handled or kicked **3** a ball used in football

football coupon a form on which people guess the results of football matches in the hope of winning money

foothill *noun* a smaller hill at the foot of a mountain

foothold *noun* **1** a place to put the foot in climbing **2** a firm position from which to begin something

footing *noun* balance; degree of friendship, seniority *etc*

footlight *noun* a light at the front of a stage, which shines on the actors

footloose *adjective* unattached, with no responsibilities

footnote *noun* a note at the bottom of a page

footplate *noun* a driver's platform on a railway engine

footprint *noun* a mark of a foot

footsie *noun, informal* the rubbing of a foot against someone's leg *etc* in sexual play

footsore *adjective* tired out from too much walking

footstep *noun* the sound of someone's foot when walking

footwear *noun* shoes *etc*

fop *noun* a man who is vain about the way he dresses □ **foppish** *adjective*

for *preposition* **1** sent to or to be given to: *there is letter for you* **2** towards: *headed for home* **3** during (an amount of time): *waited for three hours* **4** on behalf of: *for me* **5** because of: *for no good reason* **6** as the price of: *£5 for a ticket* **7** in order to obtain: *only doing it for the money*

for- *prefix* forms words containing a notion of 'loss' or of 'not having or not doing something': *forbid/ forget*
🕐 Comes from Latin *foris* meaning 'outside'
🔹 Note that **for-** has a different meaning from the prefix **fore-** (which is connected with 'before', 'in front of' or 'beforehand'). There are a few words which do not fit this general rule of thumb: note the spelling of 'foreclose' and 'forward'. See also the note at 'forgo'

forage *noun* food for horses and cattle

□ *verb* to search for food, fuel *etc*

foray *noun* **1** a sudden raid **2** a brief journey

forbade *past form of* **forbid**

forbearance *noun* control of temper

forbid *verb* to order not to

> **forbid** ⇨ forbids, forbidding, forbade, forbidden

forbidden *adjective* not allowed

forbidding *adjective* rather frightening

force *noun* **1** strength, violence **2** the police **3** a group of workers, soldiers *etc* **4 forces** those in the army, navy and airforce □ *verb* **1** to make, compel: *forced him to go* **2** to get by violence: *force an entry* **3** to break open **4** to hurry on **5** to make vegetables *etc* grow more quickly

forced *adjective* done unwillingly, with effort: *a forced laugh*

forceful *adjective* **1** acting with power **2** persuasive, convincing, powerful □ **forcefully** *adverb*

forceps *noun* surgical pincers for holding or lifting

forcible *adjective* **1** done by force **2** strong and effective **3** powerful □ **forcibly** *adverb*

ford *noun* a shallow crossing-place in a river □ *verb* to cross (water) on foot

fore- *prefix* **1** before **2** beforehand **3** in front

> Fore- is a prefix coming from Old English

> ✏ Note that fore- has a different meaning from the prefix for- (which usually indicates some notion of 'loss' or 'not having or not doing something'). There are a few words which do not fit this general rule of thumb: note the spelling of 'foreclose' and 'forward'. See also the note at 'forgo'

forearm¹ (*pronounced* faw-rahm) *noun* the part of the arm between elbow and wrist

forearm² (*pronounced* faw-**rahm**) *verb* to prepare beforehand

foreboding *noun* a feeling of coming evil

forecast *verb* to tell about beforehand, predict □ *noun* a prediction

forecastle or **fo'c'sle** (*both pronounced* fohk-sl) **1** a raised deck at the front of a ship **2** the part of a ship under the deck containing the crew's quarters

foreclose *verb* **1** to prevent, preclude **2** to bar from redeeming (a mortgage)

forefather *noun, formal* an ancestor

forefinger *noun* the finger next to the thumb

forefront *noun* the very front

foregoing *adjective* preceding, going before

foregone *adjective*: **a foregone conclusion** a result that can be guessed rightly in advance □ *see also* **forgo**

foreground *noun* the part of a view or picture nearest the person looking at it

forehead *noun* the part of the face above the eyebrows

foreign *adjective* **1** belonging to another country **2** not belonging naturally in a place *etc*: *a foreign body in an eye* **3** not familiar

■ **Alternative words:** (meaning 1) alien

foreigner *noun* **1** someone from another country **2** somebody unfamiliar

foreleg *noun* an animal's front leg

forelock *noun* the lock of hair next to the forehead

foreman *noun* (*plural* **foremen**) **1** an overseer of a group of workers **2** the leader of a jury

foremast *noun* a ship's mast nearest the bow

foremost *adjective* the most famous or important

forensic *adjective* relating to courts of law or criminal investigation: *forensic medicine*

forerunner *noun* an earlier example or sign of what is to follow: *the forerunner of cinema*

foresee *verb* to see or know beforehand

foresee ⇨ foresees, foreseeing, foreseen, foresaw

foreshore *noun* the part of the shore between high and low tide-marks

foresight *noun* 1 ability to see what will happen later 2 a fitting on the front of the barrel of a gun to help the aim

forest *noun* 1 a large piece of land covered with trees 2 a stretch of country kept for game

forestall *verb* to upset someone's plan by acting earlier than they expect

forester *noun* a worker in a forest

forestry *noun* the science of forest-growing

foretaste *noun* a sample of what is to come

foretell *verb* to tell in advance, prophesy

foretell ⇨ foretells, foretelling, foretold

forethought *noun* thought or care for the future

foretold *past form of* foretell

forewarn *verb* to warn beforehand □ **forewarning** *noun*

forewoman *noun* 1 a woman overseer 2 a head woman in a shop or factory

foreword (*pronounced* **faw**-werd) *noun* a piece of writing at the beginning of a book

🖝 Do not confuse with: **forward**. It is helpful to remember that the foreWORD in a book is made up of WORDs

forfeit *verb* to lose (a right) as a result of doing something: *forfeit the right to appeal* □ *noun* something given in compensation or punishment for an action, *eg* a fine

forfeiture *noun* the loss of something as a punishment

forge *noun* 1 a blacksmith's workshop 2 a furnace in which metal is heated □ *verb* 1 to hammer (metal) into shape 2 to imitate for criminal purposes 3 to move steadily on: *forged ahead with the plan* □ **forger** *noun* (verb, meaning 2)

forge *verb* ⇨ forges, forging, forged

forgery *noun* (*plural* **forgeries**) 1 something imitated for criminal purposes 2 the act of criminal forging

forget *verb* to lose or put away from the memory

forget ⇨ forgets, forgetting, forgot, forgotten

forgetful *adjective* likely to forget, having a tendency to forget things □ **forgetfully** *adverb*

forgive *verb* 1 to be no longer angry with 2 to overlook (a fault, debt *etc*)

forgive ⇨ forgives, forgiving, forgave, forgiven

forgiveness *noun* pardon

forgiving *adjective* merciful, willing to forgive other people for their faults

forgo *verb* to give up, do without

forgo ⇨ forgoes, forgoing, forwent, forgone

🖝 It is possible to spell **forgo** and many of its forms with an 'e' – 'forego', 'forewent' *etc*. However, it is probably less confusing to stick to the basic spellings shown above when you are writing, and to keep the 'e' spelling for **forego** meaning 'to go before' (most commonly used in the expression 'a foregone conclusion'). See also prefix entries **for-** and **fore-**

forgot and **forgotten** *see* forget

fork *noun* 1 a pronged tool for piercing and lifting things 2 the point where a road, tree *etc* divides into two branches □ *verb* to divide into two branches *etc*

fork-lift truck a power-driven truck with steel prongs that can lift and carry heavy packages

forlorn *adjective* pitiful, unhappy

forlorn hope a wish which seems to have no chance of being granted

form *noun* 1 shape or appearance 2 kind, type 3 a paper with printed questions and space for answers 4 a long seat 5 a school class 6 the nest of a hare □ *verb* 1 to give shape to 2 to make

formal *adjective* 1 of manner: cold, business-like 2 done according to custom or convention □ **formally** *adverb*

formal dress clothes required to be worn on formal social occasions, *eg* balls and banquets

formality *noun* (*plural* **formalities**) 1 something which must be done but has little meaning: *the nomination was only a formality* 2 cold correctness of manner

format *noun* 1 the size, shape *etc* of a printed book 2 the design or arrangement of an event, *eg* a television programme 3 *computing* the description of the way data is arranged on a disk □ *verb* 1 to arrange into a specific format 2 *computing* to arrange data for use on a disk 3 *computing* to prepare (a disk) for use by dividing it into sectors

format ⇨ forma**ts**, format**ting**, format**ted**

formation *noun* 1 the act of forming 2 arrangement, *eg* of aeroplanes in flight

former *adjective* 1 of an earlier time 2 of the first-mentioned of two (*contrasted with*: **latter**)

formerly *adverb* in earlier times; previously

formic *adjective* relating to ants

formica *noun*, *trademark* a tough, heat-resistant material used for covering work surfaces

formic acid an acid found in ants

formidable *adjective* 1 fearsome, frightening 2 difficult to overcome

formula *noun* (*plural* **formulae** or **formulas**) 1 a set of rules to be followed 2 an arrangement of signs or letters used in chemistry, arithmetic *etc* to express an idea briefly, *eg* H_2O = water

formulate *verb* 1 to set down clearly: *formulate the rules* 2 to make into a formula

forsake *verb* to desert

forsake ⇨ forsa**kes**, forsa**king**, forsook, forsa**ken**

forsaken *adjective* deserted; miserable

forswear *verb*, *formal* to give up

fort *noun* a place of defence against an enemy

forte (*pronounced* **for**-tei) *noun* someone's particular talent or specialty

forth *adverb* forward, onward

forthcoming *adjective* 1 happening soon 2 willing to share knowledge; friendly and open

forthright *adjective* outspoken, straightforward

forthwith *adverb* immediately

fortieth *adjective* the last of a series of forty □ *noun* one of forty equal parts

fortifications *noun plural* walls *etc* built to strengthen a position

fortify *verb* to strengthen against attack

fortify ⇨ forti**fies**, forti**fying**, forti**fied**

fortitude *noun* courage in meeting danger or bearing pain

fortnight *noun* two weeks

fortnightly *adjective* or *adverb* once a fortnight

FORTRAN *noun* a computer language

fortress *noun* (*plural* **fortresses**) a fortified place

fortuitous *adjective* happening by chance □ **fortuitously** *adverb*

fortunate *adjective* lucky □ **fortunately** *adverb*

fortune *noun* 1 luck (good or bad) 2 large sum of money

forty *noun* the number 40 □ *adjective* 40 in number

forum *noun* 1 a public place where speeches are made 2 a meeting to talk about a particular subject 3 *historical* a market-place in ancient Rome

forward *adjective* 1 advancing: *a forward movement* 2 near or at the front 3 of fruit: ripe earlier than usual 4 too quick to speak or act, pert □ *verb* 1 to help towards success: *forwarded his plans* 2 to send on (letters) □ *adverb* forwards

🖝 Do not confuse with: **foreword**. It is helpful to remember that for**WARD** is an indication of direction, similar to back**WARD**s and home**WARD**s

forwards *adverb* onward, towards the front

forwent *past form of* **forgo**

fossil *noun* the hardened remains of the shape of a plant or animal found in rock

fossilize *verb* to change into a fossil

foster *verb* **1** to bring up or nurse (a child not your own) **2** to help on, encourage

foster-child *noun* a child fostered by a family

foster-parent *noun* someone who brings up a fostered child

fought *past form of* **fight**

foul *adjective* **1** very dirty **2** smelling or tasting bad **3** stormy: *foul weather/ in a foul temper* □ *verb* **1** to become entangled with **2** to dirty **3** to play unfairly □ *noun* a breaking of the rules of a game

foul play a criminal act

found[1] *verb* **1** to establish, set up **2** to shape by pouring melted metal into a mould

found[2] *past form of* **find**

foundation *noun* **1** that on which anything rests **2** a sum of money left or set aside for a special purpose **3** an organization *etc* supported in this way

founder[1] *verb* **1** of a ship: to sink **2** of a horse: to stumble, go lame
Ⓒ Comes from Old French *fondrer* meaning 'to fall in'

☛ Do not confuse with: **flounder**

founder[2] (from **found**[1]) *noun* someone who founds

foundling *noun* a child abandoned by its parents

foundry *noun* (*plural* **foundries**) a workshop where metal founding is done

fountain *noun* **1** a rising jet of water **2** the pipe or structure from which it comes **3** the beginning of anything

four *noun* the number 4 □ *adjective* 4 in number
Ⓒ Comes from Old English *feower*

fourteen *noun* the number 14 □ *adjective* 14 in number

fourteenth *adjective* the last of a series of fourteen □ *noun* one of fourteen equal parts

fourth *adjective* the last of a series of four □ *noun* **1** one of four equal parts **2** *music* an interval of four notes

fowl *noun* a bird, especially a domestic cock or hen

fox *noun* (*plural* **foxes**) a wild animal related to the dog, with reddish-brown fur and a long bushy tail □ *verb* **1** to trick by cleverness **2** to puzzle, baffle

foxglove *noun* a tall wild flower

foxhound *noun* a breed of dog trained to chase foxes

foxtrot *noun* a ballroom dance made up of walking steps and turns

foxy *adjective* **1** cunning **2** *US, informal* sexually attractive

foyer (*pronounced* **foi**-ei) *noun* an entrance hall to a theatre, hotel *etc*

FP *abbreviation* Former Pupil(s)

fracas (*pronounced* **frak**-ah) *noun* **1** uproar **2** a noisy quarrel

fraction *noun* **1** a part, not a whole number, *eg* 4/5 **2** a small part

fractious *adjective* cross, quarrelsome

fracture *noun* a break in something hard, especially in a bone of the body

fragile *adjective* easily broken □ **fragility** *noun*

fragment *noun* (*pronounced* **frag**-ment) a part broken off; something not complete □ *verb* (*pronounced* frag-**ment**) to break into pieces

fragmentary *adjective* consisting of small pieces, not amounting to a connected whole

fragmentation *noun* breaking up, division into fragments

fragrance *noun* sweet scent

fragrant *adjective* sweet-smelling

frail *adjective* weak; easily tempted to do wrong

frailty *noun* (*plural* **frailties**) weakness

frame *verb* **1** to put a frame round **2** to put together, construct **3** *slang* to make (someone) appear to be guilty of a crime □ *noun* **1** a case or border round anything **2** build of human body **3** state (of mind)

frame *verb* ⇨ frame*s*, fram*ing*, fram*ed*

framework *noun* the outline or skeleton of something

franc *noun* the standard unit of French, Belgian and Swiss money

franchise *noun* 1 the right to vote in a general election 2 a right to sell the goods of a particular company □ *verb* to give a business franchise to

Franco- *prefix* of France, French: *Francophile*

franglais *noun* French sprinkled with words borrowed from English

frank *adjective* open, speaking your mind □ *verb* to mark a letter by machine to show that postage has been paid

frankincense *noun* a sweet-smelling resin used as incense

frankly *adverb* 1 openly 2 to be honest, I tell you

frankness *noun* the quality of being frank

frantic *adjective* wildly excited or anxious □ **frantically** *adverb*

frater- or **fratri-** *prefix* brother: *fraternize with someone* (= to behave towards them with brotherly friendliness)/ *fratricide*
ⓒ Comes from Latin *frater* meaning 'brother'

fraternal *adjective* brotherly; of a brother □ **fraternally** *adverb*

fraternity *noun* (*plural* **fraternities**) 1 a society, a brotherhood 2 a North American male college society (*compare with*: **sorority**)

fraternize *verb* to make friends with

fratricide *noun* 1 the murder of a brother 2 someone who murders their brother

fraud *noun* 1 deceit, dishonesty 2 an impostor; a fake

fraudulence or **fraudulency** *noun* deceitful or dishonest nature

fraudulent *adjective* deceitful, dishonest □ **fraudulently** *adverb*

fraught *adjective* 1 anxious, tense 2 **fraught with** filled with

fray *verb* to wear away □ *noun* a fight, a brawl

freak *noun* 1 an unusual event 2 an odd or eccentric person 3 *informal* a keen fan: *film freak*

freckle *noun* a small brown spot on the skin

free *adjective* 1 not bound or shut in 2 generous 3 frank, open 4 costing nothing □ *verb* 1 to make or set free 2 **free someone from something** or **free someone of something** to get rid of it for them
ⓒ Comes from Old English *freo*

freebie *noun, informal* a free event, performance *etc*

freedom *noun* liberty

freehand *adjective* of drawing: done without the help of rulers, tracing *etc*

freehold *adjective* of an estate: belonging to the holder or their heirs for all time

freelance or **freelancer** *noun* someone working independently (such as a writer who is not employed by any one newspaper)

Freemason *noun* a member of a certain men's society, sworn to secrecy

free-range *adjective* 1 of poultry: allowed to move about freely and feed out of doors 2 of eggs: laid by poultry of this kind

free speech the right to express opinions of any kind

freestyle *adjective* of swimming, skating *etc*: in which any style may be used

freeze *verb* 1 to turn into ice 2 to make (food) very cold in order to preserve 3 to go stiff with cold, fear *etc* 4 to fix (prices or wages) at a certain level

freeze *verb* ⇨ freeze*s*, freez*ing*, froze, froz*en*

freezer *noun* a type of cabinet in which food is made, or kept, frozen

freezing-point *noun* the point at which liquid becomes a solid (of water, 0°C)

freight *noun* 1 load, cargo 2 a charge for carrying a load □ *verb* to load with goods

freighter *noun* a ship or aircraft that carries cargo

freight train a goods train

French fries *US* fried potatoes

French leave: take French leave to go or stay away without permission

French polish a kind of varnish for furniture

French toast bread dipped in egg and fried

French window a long window also used as a door

frenetic *adjective* frantic

frenzied *adjective* mad □ **frenziedly** *adverb*

frenzy *noun* 1 a fit of madness 2 wild excitement

frequency *noun* (*plural* **frequencies**) 1 the rate at which something happens 2 the number per second of vibrations, waves *etc*

frequent *adjective* (*pronounced* **freek-**went) happening often □ *verb* (*pronounced* frik-**went**) to visit often

fresco *noun* (*plural* **frescoes** or **frescos**) a picture painted on a wall while the plaster is still damp

fresh *adjective* 1 new, unused: *fresh sheet of paper* 2 newly made or picked; not preserved: *fresh fruit* 3 cool, refreshing: *fresh breeze* 4 not tired 5 cheeky, impertinent □ *adverb* newly: *fresh-laid eggs*

freshen *verb* to make fresh; to grow strong

freshly *adverb* newly, recently

freshwater *adjective* of inland rivers, lakes *etc*, not of the sea

fret¹ *verb* to worry or show discontent

> **fret** *verb* ⇨ frets, fretting, fretted

fret² *noun* one of the ridges on the fingerboard of a guitar

fretful *adjective* showing feelings of worry or discontent

fretsaw *noun* a narrow-bladed, fine-toothed saw for fretwork

fretwork *noun* decorated cut-out work in wood

friar *noun* a member of one of the Roman Catholic brotherhoods, especially someone who has vowed to live in poverty

friary *noun* (*plural* **friaries**) the friars' house

friction *noun* 1 rubbing of two things together 2 the wear caused by rubbing 3 quarrelling, bad feeling

Friday *noun* the sixth day of the week

fridge *noun, informal* refrigerator

fried *see* **fry**

friend *noun* 1 someone who likes and knows well another person 2 sympathizer, helper
Ⓛ Comes from Old English *freon* meaning 'to love'

━━ **Alternative words:** (meaning 2) ally

friendly *adjective* 1 kind 2 **friendly with** on good terms with □ *noun* (*plural* **friendlies**) a sports match that is not part of a competition □ **friendliness** *noun*

━━ **Alternative words:** (meaning 1) amiable, affable, genial; (meaning 2) intimate, close

friendship *noun* the state of being friends; mutual affection

frieze *noun* 1 a part of a wall below the ceiling, often ornamented with designs 2 a picture on a long strip of paper *etc*, often displayed on a wall

frigate *noun* a small warship

fright *noun* sudden fear: *gave me a fright/ took fright and ran away*

frighten *verb* to make afraid □ **frightening** *adjective*

frightful *adjective* 1 causing terror 2 *informal* very bad

frightfully *adverb* 1 very badly 2 extremely

frigid *adjective* 1 frozen, cold 2 cold in manner 3 sexually unresponsive □ **frigidity** *noun* □ **frigidly** *adverb*

frill *noun* 1 an ornamental edging 2 an unnecessary ornament

fringe *noun* 1 a border of loose threads 2 hair cut to hang over the forehead 3 a border of soft material, paper *etc* □ *verb* to edge round

Frisbee *noun, trademark* a plastic plate-like object skimmed through the air as a game

frisk *verb* 1 to skip about playfully 2 *informal* to search someone closely for concealed weapons *etc*

frisky *adjective* lively, playful and keen to have fun □ **friskily** *adverb*

fritter *noun* a piece of fried batter containing fruit *etc*

fritter away *verb* to waste, squander

frivolity *noun* (*plural* **frivolities**) levity, lack of seriousness

frivolous *adjective* playful, not serious □ **frivolously** *adverb*

frizzy *adjective* of hair: massed in small curls

fro *adverb*: **to and fro** forwards and backwards

frock *noun* 1 a woman's or girl's dress 2 a monk's wide-sleeved garment

frock-coat *noun* a man's long coat

frog *noun* a small greenish jumping animal living on land and in water

frogman *noun, informal* an underwater diver with flippers and breathing apparatus

frogmarch *verb* to seize (someone) from behind and push them forward while holding their arms tight behind their back

frolic *noun* a merry, lighthearted playing □ *verb* to play lightheartedly

> **frolic** *verb* ⟹ frolic**s**, frolic**k**ing, frolic**k**ed

frolicsome *adjective* in the mood for, or fond of, frolicking

from *preposition* 1 used before the place, person *etc* that is the starting point of an action *etc*: *sailing from England to France/ the office is closed from Friday to Monday* 2 used to show separation: *warn them to keep away from there*

frond *noun* a leaf-like growth, especially a branch of a fern or palm

front *noun* 1 the part of anything nearest the person who sees it 2 the part which faces the direction in which something moves 3 the fighting line in a war □ *adjective* at or in the front □ **in front of** at the head of, before

frontage *noun* the front part of a building

frontier *noun* a boundary between countries

frontispiece *noun* a picture at the very beginning of a book

frost *noun* 1 frozen dew 2 the coldness of weather needed to form ice □ *verb* 1 to cover with frost 2 *US* to ice (a cake)

frosted *adjective* having an appearance as if covered in frost, *eg* glass with a specially roughened surface

frosting *noun, US* icing on a cake *etc*

frosty *adjective* 1 of weather: cold enough for frost to form 2 cold, unwelcoming: *gave me a frosty look*

froth *noun* foam on liquids □ *verb* to throw up foam □ **frothy** *adjective*

frown *verb* to wrinkle the brows in deep thought, disapproval *etc* □ *noun* 1 a wrinkling of the brows 2 a disapproving look □ **frown on** to look upon with disapproval

froze and **frozen** *see* **freeze**

frugal *adjective* 1 careful in spending, thrifty 2 costing little, small: *a frugal meal* □ **frugality** *noun*

frugally *adverb* in a way which reduces spending to a minimum

fruit *noun* 1 the part of a plant containing the seed 2 result: *all their hard work bore fruit* □ **fruit machine** a gambling machine into which coins are put

fruitarian *noun* someone who eats only fruit

fruiterer *noun* someone who sells fruit

fruitful *adjective* 1 producing plenty of fruit 2 producing good results: *a fruitful meeting*

fruition (*pronounced* froo-**ish**-*u*n) *noun* 1 ripeness 2 a good result

fruitless *adjective* useless, done in vain

frump *noun* a plain, badly or unfashionably dressed woman □ **frumpish** *adjective*

frustrate *verb* 1 to make to feel

powerless **2** to bring to nothing:
frustrated his wishes

frustration *noun* **1** a feeling of irritation
and annoyance as a result of being
powerless or unable to do something **2**
the bringing to nothing or spoiling of
something

fry[1] *verb* to cook in hot fat □ *noun* food
cooked in hot fat

fry *verb* ⇨ fries, frying, fried

fry[2] *noun* a young fish □ **small fry**
unimportant people or things

fuchsia (*pronounced* **fyoo**-sha) *noun* a
plant with long hanging flowers

fuddle *verb* to confuse, muddle

fudge[1] *noun* a soft, sugary sweet

fudge[2] *verb* to cheat □ *noun* a cheat

fuel *noun* a substance such as coal, gas
or petrol, used to keep a fire or engine
going

fugitive *adjective* running away, on the
run □ *noun* someone who is running
away from the police *etc*: *a fugitive from
justice*

fugue (*pronounced* fyoog) *noun* a piece
of music with several interwoven tunes

fulcrum *noun* (*plural* **fulcrums** or
fulcra) the point on which a lever turns,
or a balanced object rests

fulfil *verb* to carry out (a task, promise
etc)

fulfil ⇨ fulfils, fulfilling, fulfilled

fulfilment *noun* **1** successful
completion, accomplishment **2**
satisfaction with things achieved

full *adjective* **1** holding as much as can
be held **2** plump: *full face* **3** **full of**
having a great deal or plenty of □ *adverb*
(used with *adjectives*) fully: *full-grown*

fullback *noun* a defensive player in
football *etc*, the nearest to their team's
goal-line

full moon the moon when it appears at
its largest

full stop a punctuation mark (.) placed
at the end of a sentence

fully *adverb* **1** entirely, completely **2** at
least

fulmar *noun* a white sea bird

fulsome *adjective*, *formal* overdone:
fulsome praise

fumble *verb* **1** to use the hands
awkwardly **2** to drop (a thrown ball
etc)

fume *verb* **1** to give off smoke or vapour
2 to be in a silent rage

fume *verb* ⇨ fumes, fuming, fumed

fumes *noun plural* smoke, vapour

fumigate *verb* to kill germs by means
of strong fumes □ **fumigation** *noun*

fun *noun* enjoyment, a good time: *are
you having fun?* □ **make fun of** to tease,
make others laugh at

■ **Alternative words: make fun of** rag,
jeer at, ridicule, laugh at, mock,
taunt, tease

function *noun* **1** a special job, use or
duty of a machine, person, part of the
body *etc* **2** an arranged public gathering
□ *verb* **1** to work, operate: *the engine
isn't functioning properly* **2** to carry out
usual duties: *I can't function at this time
in the morning*

fund *noun* **1** a sum of money for a
special purpose: *charity fund* **2** a store
or supply

fundamental *adjective* **1** of great or
far-reaching importance **2** basic,
essential: *fundamental to her happiness*
□ *noun* **1** a necessary part **2**
fundamentals the groundwork, the first
stages

funeral *noun* the ceremony of burial or
cremation

funereal *adjective* mournful

funfair *noun* an amusement park

fungus *noun* (*plural* **fungi** – *pronounced*
fungg-i) **1** a soft, spongy plant growth,
eg a mushroom **2** disease-growth on
animals and plants

funk *noun* **1** funky music **2** *informal*
fear, panic

funky *adjective*, *informal* **1** of jazz and
pop music: unsophisticated, earthy and
soulful, like early blues **2** fashionable,
trendy **3** odd, eccentric

funnel *noun* **1** a cone ending in a tube,
for pouring liquids into bottles **2** a tube
or passage for escape of smoke, air *etc*

□ *verb* to pass through a funnel; channel

funnel *verb* ⇨ funnels, funnelling, funnelled

funny *adjective* **1** amusing **2** odd □ **funnily** *adverb* □ **funny bone** part of the elbow which gives a prickly feeling when knocked

■ **Alternative words**: (meaning 1) humorous, entertaining, comical, hilarious, witty, facetious, droll, farcical, laughable, ridiculous, absurd, silly; (meaning 2) strange, curious, puzzling, mysterious

fur *noun* **1** the short fine hair of certain animals **2** their skins covered with fur **3** a coating on the tongue, on the inside of kettles *etc* □ *verb* to line or cover with fur

fur *verb* ⇨ furs, furring, furred

furbish *verb* to rub until bright; burnish

furious *adjective* **1** extremely angry **2** stormy **3** fast, energetic and rather disorganized □ **furiously** *adverb*

furlong *noun* one-eighth of a mile (220 yards, 201.17 metres)

furnace *noun* a very hot oven for melting iron ore, making steam for heating *etc*

furnish *verb* **1** to fit up (a room or house) completely **2** to supply: *furnished with enough food for a week*

furnishings *noun plural* fittings, furniture

furniture *noun* movable articles in a house, *eg* tables, chairs

furore (*pronounced* fyoo-**raw**-rei) *noun* uproar; excitement

furrier (*pronounced* **fu**-ri-er) *noun* someone who trades in or works with furs

furrow *noun* **1** a groove made by a plough **2** a deep groove **3** a deep wrinkle □ *verb* **1** to cut deep grooves in **2** to wrinkle: *furrowed brow*

furry *adjective* covered with fur

further *adverb* & *adjective* to a greater

distance or degree; in addition □ *verb* to help on or forward

furthermore *adverb* in addition to what has been said

furthest *adverb* to the greatest distance or degree

furtive *adjective* stealthy, sly: *furtive glance* □ **furtively** *adverb*

fury *noun* violent anger

furze *another name* for **gorse**

fuse *verb* **1** to melt **2** to join together **3** to put a fuse in (a plug *etc*) **4** of a circuit *etc*: to stop working because of the melting of a fuse □ *noun* **1** easily-melted wire put in an electric circuit for safety **2** any device for causing an explosion to take place automatically

fuse *verb* ⇨ fuses, fusing, fused

fuselage *noun* the body of an aeroplane

fusion *noun* **1** melting **2** a merging: *a fusion of musical traditions*

fuss *noun* **1** unnecessary activity, excitement or attention, often about something unimportant: *making a fuss about nothing* **2** strong complaint □ *verb* **1** to be unnecessarily concerned about details **2** to worry too much

fussy *adjective* **1** over-elaborate **2** choosy, finicky **3** partial, in favour of one thing over another: *either will do; I'm not fussy* □ **fussily** *adverb* (meanings 1 and 2) □ **fussiness** *noun* (meanings 1 and 2)

fusty *adjective* mouldy; stale-smelling

futile *adjective* useless; having no effect

futility *noun* uselessness

futon (*pronounced* foo-ton) *noun* a sofa bed with a low frame and detachable mattress

future *adjective* happening later in time □ *noun* **1** the time to come: *foretell the future* **2** the part of your life still to come: *planning for their future* **3** *grammar* the future tense in verbs

fuzz *noun* **1** fine, light hair or feathers **2** *Brit slang* the police

fuzzy *adjective* **1** covered with fuzz, fluffy **2** tightly curled: *fuzzy hairdo*

Gg

If the word you're looking for sounds like it begins with a straightforward **G** but you can't find it, try looking under **GH** for words like *ghastly* and *ghost*, and **GU** for words like *guard* and *guide*.

g *abbreviation* gramme; gram

gabble *verb* to talk fast, chatter □ *noun* fast talk

gaberdine *noun* **1** a heavy overcoat **2** a heavy fabric

gable *noun* the triangular area of wall at the end of a building with a ridged roof

gadabout *noun* someone who loves going out or travelling

gadget *noun* a small simple machine or tool

Gaelic *noun* **1** the language of the Scottish Highlands **2** the Irish language; Erse □ *adjective* written or spoken in Gaelic

gaff *noun* **1** a large hook used for landing fish, such as salmon **2** a spar made from a mast, for raising the top of a sail □ **blow the gaff** *informal* to let out a secret

gag *verb* to silence by stopping the mouth □ *noun* **1** a piece of cloth *etc* put in or over someone's mouth to silence them **2** *informal* a joke

> **gag** *verb* ⇨ gag**s**, gag**ging**, gag**ged**

gaggle *noun* a flock of geese

gaiety and **gaily** *see* **gay**

gain *verb* **1** to win; earn **2** to reach **3** to get closer, especially in a race: *gaining on the leader* **4** of a clock: to go ahead of correct time **5** to take on (*eg* weight) □ *noun* **1** something gained **2** profit

gait *noun* way or manner of walking

> ☞ Do not confuse with: **gate**

gaiter *noun* a cloth ankle-covering,

fitting over the shoe, sometimes reaching to the knee

gala *noun* **1** a public festival **2** a sports meeting: *swimming gala*

galaxy *noun* (*plural* **galaxies**) **1** a system of stars **2** an impressive gathering □ **the Galaxy** the Milky Way

gale *noun* a strong wind

gall (*pronounced* gawl) *noun* **1** bile, a bitter fluid produced by the liver and stored in the **gallbladder 2** bitterness of feeling **3** a growth caused by insects on trees and plants □ *verb* to annoy

gallant *adjective* **1** brave; noble **2** polite or attentive towards women □ *noun* a gallant man

gallantry *noun* gallant behaviour

galleon *noun, historical* a large Spanish sailing ship

gallery *noun* (*plural* **galleries**) **1** a long passage **2** the top floor of seats in a theatre **3** a room or building for showing artworks

galley *noun* (*plural* **galleys**) **1** *historical* a long, low-built ship driven by oars **2** a ship's kitchen

galley-slave *noun, historical* a prisoner condemned to row in a galley

galling *adjective* annoying, frustrating

gallivant *verb* to travel or go out for pleasure

gallon *noun* a measure for liquids (8 pints, 4.546 litres)

gallop *verb* **1** to move by leaps **2** to (cause to) move very fast □ *noun* a fast pace

gallows *noun singular* a wooden

framework on which criminals were hanged

gallus (*pronounced* **gal-***us*) *adjective, Scottish* spirited, perky; bold

galore *adverb* in plenty: *whisky galore*

Based on an Irish Gaelic phrase *go leor*, meaning 'sufficient'

galosh or **golosh** *noun* (*plural* **galoshes** or **goloshes**) a rubber shoe worn over ordinary shoes in wet weather

galvanic *adjective* relating to electricity produced by the action of acids or other chemicals on metal □ **galvanism** *noun*

Named after the Italian physicist, Luigi *Galvani*

galvanize *verb* **1** to stir into activity **2** to stimulate by electricity **3** to coat (iron *etc*) with zinc

gambit *noun* **1** *chess* a first move involving sacrificing a piece to make the player's position stronger **2** an opening move in a transaction, or an opening remark in a conversation

gamble *verb* **1** to play games for money **2** to risk money on the result of a game, race *etc* **3** to take a wild chance □ *noun* a risk; a bet on a result

gambol *verb* to leap playfully

gambol ⇨ gambol*s*, gamboll*ing*, gamboll*ed*

game *noun* **1** a contest played according to rules **2** **games** athletic competition **3** wild animals and birds hunted for sport □ *adjective* **1** plucky **2** of a limb: lame

gamekeeper *noun* someone who looks after game birds, animals, fish *etc*

gaming *noun & adjective* gambling

gammon *noun* leg of a pig, salted and smoked

gamut *noun* **1** the whole range or extent of anything **2** the range of notes of an individual voice or musical instrument

From the name of a medieval 6-note musical scale, two notes of which were *gamma* and *ut*

gander *noun* a male goose

gang *noun* **1** a group of people who meet regularly **2** a team of criminals **3** a number of labourers

gangrene *noun* the rotting of some part of the body □ **gangrenous** *adjective*

gangsta *noun* **1** a style of rap music with violent lyrics **2** a singer of this kind of music

gangster *noun* a member of a gang of criminals

gangway *noun* **1** a passage between rows of seats **2** a movable bridge leading from a quay to a ship

gannet *noun* a large white sea bird

gantry *noun* (*plural* **gantries**) a platform or structure for supporting a travelling crane *etc*

gaol *another spelling of* **jail**

gaoler *another spelling of* **jailer**

gap *noun* an opening or space between things

gape *verb* **1** to open the mouth wide (as in surprise) **2** to be wide open

garage *noun* **1** a building for storing a car (or cars) **2** a shop which carries out car repairs and sells petrol, oil *etc*

garb *noun, formal* dress □ *verb* to clothe

garbage *noun* rubbish

garble *verb* to mix up, muddle: *garbled account of events*

Originally meaning 'sift', which gradually developed into the sense of confusing by leaving out too much

garden *noun* a piece of ground on which flowers or vegetables are grown □ *verb* to work in a garden □ **garden party** a large tea party, held out of doors

gardener *noun* someone who tends a garden

gargantuan *adjective* extremely large, huge

Named after *Gargantua*, a giant with an enormous appetite in a 16th-century French novel by Rabelais

gargle *verb* to rinse the throat with a liquid, without swallowing

gargoyle *noun* a grotesque carving of

a human or animal head, jutting out from a roof

garish *adjective* tastelessly over-bright: *garish book cover*

garland *noun* flowers or leaves tied or woven into a circle

garlic *noun* an onion-like plant with a strong smell and taste, used in cooking

garment *noun* an article of clothing

garner *verb*, *formal* to gather; collect and store

garnet *noun* a semi-precious stone, usually red in colour

garnish *verb* to decorate (a dish of food) □ *noun* (*plural* **garnishes**) a decoration on food □ **garnishing** *noun*

garret *noun* an attic room

garrison *noun* a body of troops for guarding a fortress

garrotte *verb* to strangle someone by tightening a noose *etc* round their neck (originally by tightening an iron collar, also called a **garrotte**)

garrulous *adjective* fond of talking □ **garrulity** *noun*

garter *noun* a broad elastic band to keep a stocking up

gas *noun* (*plural* **gases**) **1** a substance like air (though you can smell some gases) **2** natural or manufactured form of this which will burn and is used as a fuel **3** *US* petrol □ *verb* to poison with gas

gas *verb* ⇨ gases, gassing, gassed

gaseous *adjective* in gas form

gash *noun* (*plural* **gashes**) a deep, open cut □ *verb* to cut deeply into

gasket *noun* a layer of padding used to make air-tight or gas-tight joints

gas mask a covering for the face to prevent breathing in poisonous gas

gasoline *noun*, *US* petrol

gasometer *noun* a tank for storing gas

gasp *noun* the sound made by a sudden intake of breath □ *verb* **1** to breathe with difficulty **2** to say breathlessly **3** *informal* to want badly: *gasping for a cup of tea*

gastric *adjective* relating to the stomach: *gastric ulcer*

gasworks *noun* place where gas is made

gate *noun* **1** a door across an opening in a wall, fence *etc* **2** the number of people at a football match **3** the total entrance money paid by those at a football match

 ☛ Do not confuse with: **gait**

gateau (*pronounced* **gat**-oh) *noun* (*plural* **gateaus** or **gateaux**) a rich cake, usually layered and filled with cream

gatecrash *verb* to go to a party uninvited □ **gatecrasher** *noun*

gateway *noun* **1** an opening containing a gate **2** an entrance **3** *computing* a connection between networks

gather *verb* **1** to bring together, or meet, in one place **2** to pick (flowers *etc*) **3** to increase in: *gather speed* **4** to learn, come to the conclusion (that): *I gather you don't want to go*

gathering *noun* a crowd

GATT (*pronounced* gat) *abbreviation* General Agreement on Tariffs and Trade (now **WTO**)

gauche (*pronounced* gohsh) *adjective* awkward and clumsy in people's company

Taken from the French word for 'left', because of the supposed awkwardness of using the left hand

gaudy *adjective* showy; vulgarly bright in colour □ **gaudily** *adverb*

gauge (*pronounced* geij) *verb* **1** to measure **2** to make a guess □ *noun* a measuring device

gaunt *adjective* thin, haggard

gauntlet[1] *noun* **1** a long glove (often of leather) with a guard for the wrist, used by motor-cyclists *etc* **2** *historical* an iron glove worn with armour □ **take up the gauntlet** to accept a challenge □ **throw down the gauntlet** to offer a challenge

gauntlet[2] *noun*: **run the gauntlet** to expose yourself to criticism, hostility *etc*

The *gauntlet* was an old military punishment of being made to run past a line of soldiers armed with sticks; the word is of Swedish origin and unrelated to **gauntlet**[1]

gauze *noun* thin cloth that can be seen through

gawky *adjective* awkward

gay *adjective* 1 homosexual 2 lively; merry, full of fun 3 brightly coloured □ *noun* a homosexual □ **gaiety** *noun* (sense 2) □ **gaily** *adverb* (senses 2 and 3)

gaze *verb* to look steadily □ *noun* a fixed look

gazelle *noun* a small deer

gazette *noun* a newspaper, especially one having lists of government notices

gazetteer *noun* a geographical dictionary

GBH or **gbh** *abbreviation* grievous bodily harm

GDP *abbreviation* gross domestic product

gear *noun* 1 clothing and equipment needed for a particular job, sport *etc* 2 a connection by means of a set of toothed wheels between a car engine and the wheels □ *verb* **gear to** to adapt to, design for what is needed

geese *plural* of **goose**

gelatine *noun* a jelly-like substance made from hooves, animal bones *etc*, and used in food

gelatinous (*pronounced* jel-**at**-in-*u*s) *adjective* jelly-like

geld *verb* to castrate (an animal)

gelding *noun* a castrated horse

gem *noun* 1 a precious stone, especially when cut 2 something greatly valued

gender *noun* (in grammar, especially in languages other than English) any of three types of noun, masculine, feminine or neuter

gene *noun* the basic unit of heredity responsible for passing on specific characteristics from parents to offspring

genealogical *adjective* relating to genealogy

genealogy *noun* (*plural* **genealogies**) 1 the history of families from generation to generation 2 a personal family history

general *adjective* 1 not detailed, broad: *a general idea of the person's interests* 2 involving everyone: *a general election* 3 to do with several different things: *general knowledge* 4 of most people: *the general opinion* □ *noun* a high-ranking army officer □ **in general** generally

generalization *noun* a too general view, statement *etc*

generalize *verb* to make a broad general statement, meant to cover all individual cases

generally *adverb* 1 usually, in most cases 2 by most people: *generally known*

general practitioner a doctor who treats most ordinary illnesses

generate *verb* to produce, bring into being: *generate electricity/ generate good will*

generation *noun* 1 creation, making 2 a step in family descent 3 people born at about the same time: *90s generation*

generator *noun* a machine for making electricity *etc*

generic *adjective* general, applicable to any member of a group or class

generous *adjective* giving plentifully; kind □ **generosity** *noun* □ **generously** *adverb*

■ **Alternative words**: liberal, unstinting, magnanimous, philanthropic, benevolent

genesis *noun* beginning, origin

genetic *adjective* 1 relating to genes 2 inherited through genes: *genetic disease* □ **genetically** *adverb*

genial *adjective* good-natured □ **geniality** *noun* □ **genially** *adverb*

genie *noun* (*plural* **genii** – *pronounced* jeen-i-ai) a guardian spirit

genitals *noun plural* the organs of sexual reproduction

genius *noun* (*plural* **geniuses**) 1 unusual cleverness 2 someone who is unusually clever

genocide *noun* the deliberate extermination of a race of people
□ **genocidal** *adjective*

gent *noun, informal* a man

genteel *adjective* good-mannered, especially excessively

gentile (*pronounced* **jen**-tail) *noun* a non-Jew

gentility *noun* 1 aristocracy 2 good manners, refinement, often in excess

gentle *adjective* 1 mild-mannered, not brutal 2 mild, not extreme: *gentle breeze* 3 having a pleasant light or soft quality, not harsh or forceful □ **gentleness** *noun* □ **gently** *adverb*

gentleman *noun* (*plural* **gentlemen**) 1 a man, especially one of noble birth 2 a well-mannered man

gentlemanly *adjective* behaving in a polite manner

gentry *noun* a wealthy, land-owning class of people

the gents *informal* a men's public toilet

genuine *adjective* 1 real, not fake or pretended: *genuine antique/ She may have been lying, but her distress was genuine* 2 honest and straightforward □ **genuinely** *adverb* (meaning 1) □ **genuineness** *noun*

genus *noun* (*plural* **genera**) a group of living things made up of a number of kinds

geo- *prefix* of or relating to the earth: *geography/ geometry* (= a branch of mathematics originally concerned with measuring the earth)
Ⓞ Comes from Greek *ge* meaning 'earth'

geographer *noun* someone who studies geography

geography *noun* the study of the surface of the earth and its inhabitants □ **geographic** or **geographical** *adjective*

geologist *noun* someone who studies geology

geology *noun* the study of the earth's history as shown in its rocks and soils □ **geological** *adjective*

geometric or **geometrical** *adjective* of a shape or pattern: made up of angles and straight lines

geometry *noun* the branch of mathematics which deals with the study of lines, angles, and figures

Geordie *noun, Brit informal* someone who was born or lives in Newcastle

geranium *noun* a plant with thick leaves and bright red or pink flowers

gerbil (*pronounced* **jerb**-il) *noun* a small, rat-like desert animal, often kept as a pet

germ *noun* 1 a small living organism which can cause disease 2 the earliest or initial form of something, *eg* a fertilized egg 3 that from which anything grows: *germ of an idea*

German shepherd (*also called* **alsatian**) a breed of large wolf-like dog

germicide *noun* a germ-killing substance

germinate *verb* to begin to grow; sprout □ **germination** *noun*

gerrymander *verb* to rearrange (voting districts *etc*) to suit a political purpose □ **gerrymandering** *noun*

After US governor, Elbridge *Gerry*, who rearranged the map of Massachusetts in 1811 to a shape resembling that of a sala*mander*

gerund *noun* an action noun with the ending -*ing*, *eg* watch*ing*, wait*ing*

gesticulate *verb* to wave hands and arms about in excitement *etc* □ **gesticulation** *noun*

gesture *noun* 1 a meaningful action with the hands, head *etc* 2 an action expressing your feelings or intent: *gesture of good will*

get *verb* 1 to go and find, take hold of, obtain: *get a carton of milk on the way home/ I'll get you, you rascal!/ I'm at the station. Can you come and get me?* 2 to go or move 3 to cause to be done: *get your hair cut* 4 to receive: *get a letter* 5 to cause to be in some condition: *get the car started* 6 to arrive: *what time did you get home?* 7 to catch or have (a disease): *I think I've got flu* 8 to become: *get rich* □ **get at** 1 to reach 2 to hint at: *what are you getting at?* 3 to criticize continually: *stop getting at me* 4 to affect badly, distress: *the pressure is getting to him* 5 *slang* to try to influence by bribes or threats □ **get away with** to escape punishment for □ **get on with** to be on friendly terms with □ **get over** to recover from □ **get up 1** to stand up **2** to get out of bed

get ⇨ gets, getting, got
US gets, getting, got, gotten

① Comes from Old Norse *geta*

☛ **Get** is one of the most overused words in the English language. Make sure **you** don't use it too much!

■ **Alternative words**: (meaning 1) fetch, catch, seize, acquire, procure, secure, realize; (meaning 6) reach; (meaning 7) develop; (meaning 8) grow

geyser (*pronounced* **geez**-er) *noun* **1** a natural hot spring **2** a device which heats domestic water when the tap is turned on

ghastly *adjective* **1** very ill: *feeling ghastly* **2** horrible, ugly **3** very pale, death-like **4** very bad □ **ghastliness** *noun*

gherkin *noun* a small pickled cucumber

ghetto *noun* (*plural* **ghettos**) a poor residential part of a city in which a certain group (especially of immigrants) lives

ghost *noun* the spirit of a dead person

ghostly *adjective* like a ghost

ghoul (*pronounced* gool) *noun* **1** an evil spirit which robs dead bodies **2** someone unnaturally interested in death and disaster □ **ghoulish** *adjective*

GHQ *abbreviation* general headquarters

giant *noun* **1** an imaginary being, like a human but enormous **2** a very tall or large person □ *adjective* huge

giantess *noun* a female giant

gibber *verb* **1** to speak nonsense **2** to make meaningless noises; babble

gibberish *noun* words without meaning; rubbish

gibbet *noun*, *historical* a gallows where criminals were executed, or hung up after execution

gibbon *noun* a large, tailless ape

gibe *another spelling of* **jibe**

giblets *noun plural* eatable organs from the inside of a chicken *etc*

giddy *adjective* **1** unsteady, dizzy **2** causing dizziness: *from a giddy height* □ **giddiness** *noun* (meaning 1)

gift 1 something freely given, *eg* a present **2** a natural talent: *a gift for music* **3** *informal* something easily done: *the exam paper was a gift* □ **look a gift horse in the mouth** to find fault with a gift

gifted *adjective* having special natural power or ability

gigantic *adjective* huge, of giant size

giggle *verb* to laugh in a nervous or silly manner □ *noun* a nervous or silly laugh

gild (*pronounced* gild) *verb* **1** to cover with beaten gold **2** to make bright □ **gild the lily** to try to improve something already beautiful enough
① Comes from Old English *gyldan* which is related to *gold*

☛ Do not confuse with: **guild**

gill (*pronounced* gil) *noun* one of the openings on the side of a fish's head through which it breathes

gillie (*pronounced* gil-i) *noun* an assistant and guide to someone fishing or shooting on a Scottish estate

gilt (*pronounced* gilt) *noun* beaten gold used for gilding □ *adjective* **1** covered with thin gold **2** gold in colour

☛ Do not confuse with: **guilt**. Gilt is a past participle of the verb 'gild'

gilt-edged *adjective* not risky, safe to invest in: *gilt-edged stocks*

gimlet (*pronounced* **gim**-lit) *noun* a small tool for boring holes by hand

gimmick *noun* something meant to attract attention

gin¹ *noun* an alcoholic drink made from grain, flavoured with juniper berries

gin² *noun* a trap or snare

ginger *noun* a hot-tasting root, used as a seasoning in food □ *adjective* **1** flavoured with ginger **2** reddish-brown in colour: *ginger hair*

gingerbread *noun* cake flavoured with ginger

gingerly *adverb* very carefully and gently: *opened the door gingerly*

gipsy *another spelling of* **gypsy**

giraffe *noun* an African animal with very long legs and neck

Called a *camelopard* until the 17th century

gird *verb, formal* to bind round

girder *noun* a beam of iron, steel or wood used in building

girdle *noun* **1** a belt for the waist **2** a tight-fitting piece of underwear to slim the waist

girl *noun* a female child or young woman

girlhood *noun* the state or time of being a girl

girlie *adjective* **1** girlish **2** pornographic: *girlie magazines*

girlish *adjective* of a woman's appearance or behaviour: attractively youthful, like that of a girl

giro (*pronounced* **jai**-roh) *noun* (*plural* **giros**) **1** a system by which payment may be made through banks, post offices *etc* **2** (*also called* **girocheque**) a form like a cheque by which such payment is made **3** *informal* social security paid by girocheque

girth *noun* **1** measurement round the middle **2** a strap tying a saddle on a horse

gist (*pronounced* jist) *noun* the main points or ideas of a story, argument *etc*: *give me the gist of the story*

give *verb* **1** to hand over freely or in exchange **2** to utter (a shout or cry) **3** to break, crack: *the bridge gave under the weight of the train* **4** to produce: *this lamp gives a good light* □ **giver** *noun* (meaning 1) □ **give away 1** to hand over (something) to someone without payment **2** to betray □ **give in** to yield □ **give over** *informal* to stop (doing something) □ **give rise to** to cause □ **give up 1** to hand over **2** to yield **3** to stop, abandon (a habit *etc*) □ **give way 1** to yield **2** to collapse **3** to let traffic crossing your path go before you

give ⇨ **gives, giving, gave, given**

ⓛ Comes from Old English *gefan*

■ **Alternative words**: (meaning 1) present, confer, grant, bestow, endow, furnish, devote; (meaning 4) make, cause, occasion □ **give up** (meaning 2) surrender, capitulate; (meaning 3) abandon, renounce, relinquish

give-away *noun* (*plural* **give-aways**) something that you say or do which reveals a secret to other people

glacé *adjective* iced or sugared: *glacé cherries*

glacial *adjective* **1** of ice or glaciers **2** icy, cold: *glacial expression*

glacier *noun* a slowly-moving river of ice in valleys between high mountains

glad *adjective* **1** pleased: *I'm glad you were able to come* **2** giving pleasure: *glad tidings* **3 glad to** perfectly willing and happy to **gladly** *adverb* (meanings 1 and 3) □ **gladness** *noun* (meanings 1 and 2)

gladden *verb* to make glad

glade *noun* an open space in a wood

gladiator *noun, historical* in ancient Rome, a man trained to fight with other men or with animals for the amusement of spectators □ **gladiatorial** *adjective*

glad rags best clothes

glaikit *adjective, Scottish* stupid, daft

glam *adjective, slang* glamorous

glamorous *adjective* **1** dressing and behaving in a way which people find fascinating and attractive **2** fashionable and extravagant

glamour *noun* fascination, charm, beauty, especially artificial

glance *noun* a quick look □ *verb* to take a quick look at □ **glance off** to hit and fly off sideways

gland *noun* a part of the body which takes substances from the blood and stores them for later use or elimination by the body

glandular *adjective* of, or affecting, the glands

glandular fever an infectious disease with symptoms including a slight fever and an enlargement of the glands

glare *noun* 1 an unpleasantly bright light 2 an angry or fierce look □ *verb* 1 to shine with an unpleasantly bright light 2 to look angrily

glaring *adjective* 1 dazzling 2 very clear, obvious: *glaring mistake*

glaringly *adverb* extremely, unmissably: *glaringly obvious*

glasnost *noun* a political policy of openness and forthrightness, originally in the Soviet Union in the 1980s

glass *noun* (*plural* **glasses**) 1 a hard transparent substance made from metal and other oxides 2 (**glasses**) spectacles 3 a drinking vessel made of glass 4 *old* a mirror □ *adjective* made of glass

glass ceiling a barrier to promotion at work experienced by some women but not officially recognized

glasshouse *noun* a greenhouse

glassy *adjective* 1 of eyes: without expression 2 of surfaces, especially water: smooth and shiny with no ripples

glaucoma *noun* an eye disease causing dimness in sight

glaze *verb* 1 to cover with a thin coating of glass or other shiny stuff 2 to ice (a cake *etc*) 3 to put panes of glass in a window 4 of eyes: to become glassy □ *noun* 1 a shiny surface 2 sugar icing

glazier *noun* someone who sets glass in window-frames

gleam *verb* 1 to glow 2 to flash □ *noun* 1 a beam of light 2 brightness

glean *verb* 1 to collect, gather 2 *old* to gather corn in handfuls after the reapers

glee *noun* 1 joy 2 a song in parts

gleeful *adjective* merry, usually in a mischievous way □ **gleefully** *adverb*

glen *noun* in Scotland, a long narrow valley

glib *adjective* 1 speaking smoothly and fluently (often insincerely and superficially) 2 quick and ready, but showing little thought: *glib reply* □ **glibly** *adverb*

glide *verb* 1 to move smoothly and

easily 2 to travel by glider □ *noun* the act of gliding

glider *noun* an aeroplane without an engine

glimmer *noun* 1 a faint light 2 a faint indication: *a glimmer of hope* □ *verb* to burn or shine faintly

glimpse *noun* a brief view □ *verb* to get a brief look at

glint *verb* to sparkle, gleam □ *noun* a sparkle, a gleam

glisten *verb* to sparkle

glitter *verb* to sparkle □ *noun* 1 sparkling 2 shiny granules used for decorating paper *etc*

glittery *adjective* shiny, sparkly

glitz *noun* showiness, garishness □ **glitzy** *adjective*

Originally a Yiddish word meaning 'glitter'

gloaming *noun* twilight, dusk

gloat *verb* to look at or think about with malicious joy: *gloating over their rivals' defeat*

global *adjective* 1 of or affecting the whole world: *global warming* 2 applying generally: *global increase in earnings*

globe *noun* 1 the earth 2 a ball with a map of the world drawn on it 3 a ball, a sphere 4 a glass covering for a lamp

globular *adjective* ball-shaped

globule *noun* 1 a droplet 2 a small ball-shaped piece

gloom *noun* dullness, darkness; sadness

gloomy *adjective* 1 sad, depressed 2 miserable, depressing 3 dimly lighted □ **gloomily** *adverb*

■ **Alternative words**: (meanings 1 and 2) joyless

glorify *verb* 1 to make glorious 2 to praise highly

glorify ⇨ glorifies, glorifying, glorified

glorious *adjective* 1 spendid 2 deserving great praise 3 delightful □ **gloriously** *adverb*

glory *noun* (*plural* **glories**) 1 fame,

honour **2** great show, splendour □ *verb* to rejoice, take great pleasure (in)

gloss *noun* brightness on the surface □ *verb* **1** to make bright **2** to explain **3 gloss over** to try to hide (a fault *etc*) by treating it quickly or superficially

glossary *noun* (*plural* **glossaries**) a list of words with their meanings

glossy *adjective* shiny, highly polished

glove *noun* **1** a covering for the hand with a separate covering for each finger **2** a boxing glove

glow *verb* **1** to burn without flame **2** to give out a steady light **3** to be flushed from heat, cold *etc* **4** to be radiant with emotion: *glow with pride* □ *noun* **1** a glowing state **2** great heat **3** bright light

glower *verb* to stare (at) with a frown

glowering *adjective* **1** scowling **2** threatening

glowing *adjective* **1** giving out a steady light **2** flushed **3** radiant **4** full of praise: *glowing report*

glow-worm *noun* a kind of beetle which glows in the dark

glucose *noun* a sugar found in fruits *etc*

glue *noun* a substance for sticking things together □ *verb* to join with glue

gluey *adjective* sticky

glum *adjective* sad, gloomy □ **glumly** *adverb*

glut *verb* **1** to feed greedily till full **2** to supply too much to (a market) □ *noun* an over-supply: *a glut of fish on the market*

> **glut** *verb* ⇨ **gluts**, **glut**t*ing*, **glut**t*ed*

gluten *noun* a sticky protein found in wheat and certain other cereals

glutinous *adjective* sticky, gluey

glutton *noun* **1** someone who eats too much **2** someone who is eager for anything: *a glutton for punishment*

gluttonous *adjective* **1** fond of overeating **2** eating greedily

gluttony *noun* greediness in eating

glycerine *noun* a colourless, sticky, sweet-tasting liquid

GMT *abbreviation* Greenwich Mean Time

gnarled (*pronounced* narld) *adjective* knotty, twisted

gnash (*pronounced* nash) *verb* to grind (the teeth)

gnat (*pronounced* nat) *noun* a small blood-sucking fly, a midge

gnaw (*pronounced* naw) *verb* to bite at with a scraping action

gnome (*pronounced* nohm) *noun* a small, imaginary, human-like creature who lives underground, often guarding treasure

GNP *abbreviation* gross national product

gnu (*pronounced* noo or nyoo) *noun* a type of African antelope

GNVQ *abbreviation* General National Vocational Qualification

go *verb* **1** to move: *I want to go home/when are you going to Paris?* **2** to leave: *time to go* **3** to lead: *that road goes north* **4** to become: *go mad* **5** to work: *the car is going at last* **6** to intend (to do): *I'm going to have a bath* **7** to be removed or taken: *the best seats have all gone now* **8** to be given, awarded *etc*: *the first prize went to Janet* □ *noun* **1** the act or process of going **2** energy, spirit **3** *informal* an attempt, a try: *have a go* **4** *informal* fashion, style: *all the go* □ **from the word go** from the start □ **go about** to try, set about □ **go ahead** to proceed (with), begin on □ **go along with** to agree with □ **go back on** to fail to keep (a promise *etc*) □ **go for 1** to aim to get **2** to attack □ **go off 1** to explode **2** to become rotten **3** to come to dislike □ **go on 1** to continue **2** to talk too much □ **go round** to be enough for everyone: *will the trifle go round?* □ **go steady with** to court, go out with □ **go the whole hog** to do something thoroughly □ **go under** to be ruined □ **on the go** very active

> **go** *verb* ⇨ **goes**, **going**, **went**, **gone**

⊕ Comes from Old English *gan* meaning 'to go'

goad *noun* **1** a sharp-pointed stick for driving animals **2** something used to urge action □ *verb* to urge on by annoying

go-ahead *adjective* eager to succeed □ *noun* permission to act

goal *noun* **1** the upright posts between which the ball is to be driven in football and other games **2** a score in football and other games **3** anything aimed at or wished for: *my goal is to pass this exam*

goat *noun* an animal of the sheep family with horns and a long-haired coat

gob *slang* the mouth

gobble *verb* **1** to eat quickly **2** to make a noise like a turkey

go-between *noun* someone who helps two people to communicate with each other

goblet *noun, historical* **1** a large cup without handles **2** a drinking glass with a stem

goblin *noun* a mischievous, ugly spirit in folklore

gobsmacked *adjective, slang* shocked, astonished

gobstopper *noun* a hard round sweet for sucking

god *noun* a male supernatural being who is worshipped □ **God** *noun* the creator and ruler of the world in the Christian, Jewish *etc* religions

goddess *noun* a female supernatural being who is worshipped

godfather *noun* a man who agrees to see that a child is brought up according to the beliefs of the Christian Church

godly *adjective* holy, good living

godmother *noun* a woman who agrees to see that a child is brought up according to the beliefs of the Christian Church

godsend *noun* a very welcome piece of unexpected good fortune

goggle-eyed *adjective* with staring eyes

goggles *noun plural* spectacles for protecting the eyes from dust, sparks *etc*

go-kart *noun* a small low-powered racing car

gold *noun* **1** a precious yellow metal **2** riches □ *adjective* **1** made of gold **2** golden in colour

golden *adjective* **1** of or like gold **2** very fine

golden handshake money given by a firm to a retiring employee

golden rule a guiding principle

golden wedding the 50th anniversary of a wedding

goldfinch *noun* a small colourful bird

goldfish *noun* a golden-yellow Chinese carp, often kept as a pet

gold-leaf *noun* gold beaten to a thin sheet

goldsmith *noun* a maker of gold articles

golf *noun* a game in which a ball is struck with a club and aimed at a series of holes on a large open course

golf club **1** a club used in golf **2** a society of golf players **3** the place where they meet

golfer *noun* someone who plays golf

golosh *another spelling* of **galosh**

gondola *noun* **1** a canal boat used in Venice **2** a car suspended from an airship, cable railway *etc* **3** a shelved display unit in a supermarket

gondolier *noun* a boatman who rows a gondola

gone *past participle* of **go**

gong *noun* a metal plate which makes a booming sound when struck, used to summon people to meals *etc*

gonorrhoea *noun* a common sexually transmitted disease

good *adjective* **1** having desired or positive qualities: *a good butcher will bone it for you/ a good restaurant* **2** having a positive effect: *fruit is good for you* **3** virtuous: *a good person* **4** kind: *she was good to me* **5** pleasant, enjoyable: *a good time* **6** substantial, sufficiently large: *a good income* ◷ Comes from Old English *god*

■ **Alternative words**: (meaning 1) competent, proficient, accomplished, skilful, excellent, commendable; (meaning 2) beneficial, advantageous; (meaning 3) moral, exemplary, righteous; (meaning 5) agreeable; (meaning 6) thorough, considerable, satisfactory

good afternoon a common formal greeting used when meeting or leaving people in the afternoon

good-bye noun (plural **good-byes**) what you say when leaving people

good-day noun an old-fashioned greeting used when meeting or leaving people

good evening a common formal greeting used when meeting or leaving people in the evening

good-for-nothing adjective useless, lazy

goodly adjective 1 large 2 ample, plentiful

good morning a common formal greeting used when meeting or leaving people in the morning

good name good reputation

good-natured adjective kind, cheerful

goodness noun the quality of being good □ exclamation an exclamation of surprise

good night a phrase used when leaving people at night

goods noun plural 1 personal belongings 2 things to be bought and sold

good taste good judgement for what is aesthetically pleasing or socially acceptable

goodwill noun 1 kind wishes 2 a good reputation in business

goofy adjective, US stupid, silly

goose noun (plural **geese**) a web-footed bird larger than a duck

gooseberry noun a sour-tasting, pale green berry

goosebumps or **goosepimples** noun plural small bumps on the skin caused by cold or fear

gopher noun a piece of software used to search or index services on the Internet

gore¹ noun a mass of blood □ verb to run through with horns, tusks etc: gored by an elephant

gore² noun a triangular-shaped piece of cloth in a garment etc

Gore-Tex noun, trademark a fabric which is water-repellent, but which has tiny pores to allow air and water vapour to escape from inside

gorge noun 1 the throat 2 a narrow valley between hills □ verb to eat greedily till full: gorging himself on chocolate biscuits

gorge verb ⇨ gorges, gorging, gorged

gorgeous adjective 1 beautiful, very attractive 2 showy, splendid 3 informal excellent, very enjoyable

gorilla noun the largest kind of ape

🖝 Do not confuse with: **guerrilla**

The *Gorillai* were a tribe of hairy women in ancient times

gormless adjective, Brit stupid, senseless

gorse noun a prickly bush with yellow flowers

gory adj full of gore; bloody: a very gory film

gosling noun a young goose

go-slow noun a slowing of speed at work as a form of protest

gospel noun 1 the teaching of Christ 2 informal the absolute truth

gossamer noun 1 fine spider-threads floating in the air or lying on bushes 2 a very thin material

gossip noun 1 talk, not necessarily true, about other people's personal affairs etc 2 someone who listens to and passes on gossip □ verb 1 to engage in gossip 2 to chatter

gossip verb ⇨ gossips, gossiping, gossiped

Originally *godsibb*, meaning 'godparent'

got *past form of* **get**

gouge (*pronounced* gowj) *noun* a chisel with a hollow blade for cutting grooves □ *verb* to scoop (out)

> **gouge** *verb* ⇨ gouge*s*, goug*ing*, goug*ed*

goulash *noun* (*plural* **goulashes**) a stew of meat and vegetables, flavoured with paprika

gourd (*pronounced* goord) *noun* **1** a large fleshy fruit **2** the skin of a gourd used to carry water *etc*

gourmand (*pronounced* goor-**mond**) *noun* a glutton

gourmet (*pronounced* **goor**-mei) *noun* someone with a taste for good wines or food

gout *noun* a painful swelling of the smaller joints, especially of the big toe

gouty *adjective* suffering from gout

govern *verb* **1** to rule, control **2** to put into action the laws *etc* of a country ◷ Comes from Latin *gubernare* meaning 'to steer a ship'

governess *noun* a woman who teaches young children at their home

government *noun* **1** rule; control **2** those who rule and administer the laws of a country

governor *noun* someone who rules a state or country *etc*

gown *noun* **1** a woman's formal dress **2** a loose robe worn by members of the clergy, lawyers, teachers *etc*

GP *abbreviation* general practitioner

GPO *abbreviation* General Post Office

grab *verb* **1** to seize or grasp suddenly: *grabbed me by the arm* **2** to secure possession of quickly: *grab a seat* **3** to get in a hurry: *grab a bite to eat* □ *noun* a sudden grasp or catch

> **grab** *verb* ⇨ grab*s*, grab*bing*, grab*bed*

grab-bag *noun* a miscellaneous collection: *grab-bag of ideas*

grace *noun* **1** beauty of form or movement **2** a short prayer at a meal **3** the title of a duke or archbishop: *Your Grace* **4** favour, mercy: *by God's grace*

□ **with bad grace** unwillingly □ **with good grace** willingly

graceful *adjective* **1** beautiful in appearance or movement **2** done in a neat way **3** polite □ **gracefully** *adverb*

grace-note *noun*, *music* a short note played before the main note in a melody

gracious *adjective* kind, polite □ *exclamation* an exclamation of surprise or shock □ **graciously** *adverb*

gradation *noun* arrangement in order of rank, difficulty *etc*

grade *noun* a step or placing according to quality or rank; class □ *verb* to arrange in order, *eg* from easy to difficult □ **make the grade** to do as well as is necessary

gradient *noun* a slope on a road, railway *etc*

gradual *adjective* step by step; going slowly but steadily □ **gradually** *adverb*

graduate *verb* (*pronounced* grad-yoo-eit) **1** to divide into regular spaces **2** to pass university examinations and receive a degree □ *noun* (*pronounced* grad-yoo-*a*t) someone who has done so

graduation *noun* the act of getting a degree from a university, or the ceremony to celebrate this

graffiti *noun plural* words or drawings scratched or painted on a wall *etc*

graft *verb* **1** to fix a shoot or twig of one plant on to another for growing **2** to fix (skin) from one part of the body on to another part **3** to transfer (a part of the body) from one person to another **4** to get illegal profit □ *noun* **1** living tissue (*eg* skin) which is grafted **2** a shoot grafted **3** hard work **4** profit gained by illegal or unfair means

Grail *noun* the plate or cup believed to have been used by Christ at the Last Supper

grain *noun* **1** a seed *eg* of wheat, oats **2** corn in general **3** a very small quantity **4** a very small measure of weight **5** the run of the lines of fibre in wood, leather *etc* □ **against the grain** against your natural feelings or instincts

gram *another spelling of* **gramme**

grammar *noun* **1** the correct use of

words in speaking or writing: *his grammar is very bad* **2** the rules applying to a particular language: *French grammar*

grammar school a kind of secondary school

grammatical *adjective* correct according to rules of grammar □ **grammatically** *adverb*

gramme or **gram** *noun* the basic unit of weight in the metric system

gramophone *noun, old* a record-player

granary *noun* (*plural* **granaries**) a storehouse for grain

grand *adjective* great; noble; fine ① Comes from French *grand* meaning 'big'

grandchild *noun* a son's or daughter's child

grand-daughter *noun* a son's or daughter's daughter

grand duke a duke of specially high rank

grandeur (*pronounced* **grand**-yer) *noun* greatness

grandfather *noun* a father's or mother's father

grandiose *adjective* planned on a large scale

grand master a chess-player of the greatest ability

grandmother *noun* a father's or mother's mother

grand piano a piano with a large flat top

grandson *noun* a son's or daughter's son

grandstand *noun* rows of raised seats at a sports ground giving a good view

granite *noun* a hard rock of greyish or reddish colour

granny *noun* (*plural* **grannies**) *informal* a grandmother

grant *verb* **1** to give, allow (something asked for) **2** to admit as true □ *noun* money awarded for a special purpose

granted or **granting** *conjunction* (often with *that*) even if, assuming: *granted that you are right* □ **take for granted 1**

to assume that something will happen without checking **2** to treat (someone) casually, without respect or kindness

gran turismo (a car) designed for touring in luxury and at high speed

granular *adjective* made up of grains

granulated *adjective* broken into grains

granule *noun* a tiny grain or part

grape *noun* the green or black smooth-skinned berry from which wine is made

grapefruit *noun* a sharp-tasting fruit like a large yellow orange

graph *noun* lines drawn on squared paper to show changes in quantity, *eg* in temperature, money spent

graphic *adjective* **1** relating to writing, drawing or painting **2** vivid, well told **3** explicit: *graphic violence* □ *noun* a painting, print, illustration or diagram □ **graphically** *adverb*

graphite *noun* a form of carbon used in making pencils

grapple *verb*: **grapple with 1** to struggle with **2** to try to deal with (a problem *etc*)

grasp *verb* **1** to clasp and grip with the fingers or arms **2** to understand □ *noun* **1** a grip with the hand or arms **2** someone's power of understanding

grasping *adjective* greedy, mean

grass *noun* (*plural* **grasses**) **1** the plant covering fields of pasture **2** a kind of plant with long narrow leaves, *eg* wheat, reeds, bamboo **3** *slang* the drug marijuana

grasshopper *noun* a type of jumping insect

grass-snake *noun* a type of harmless snake

grass-widow *noun* a woman whose husband is temporarily away

grass-widower *noun* a man whose wife is temporarily away

grassy *adjective* covered with grass

grate *noun* a framework of iron bars for holding a fire □ *verb* **1** to rub down into small pieces **2** to make a harsh, grinding sound **3** to irritate

grateful *adjective* **1** feeling thankful **2**

showing or giving thanks □ **gratefully** *adverb*

grater *noun* an instrument with a rough surface for rubbing cheese *etc* into small pieces

gratification *noun* pleasure; satisfaction

gratify *verb* to please; satisfy

gratify ⇨ gratif*ies*, gratify*ing*, gratif*ied*

grating *noun* a frame of iron bars

gratis *adverb* for nothing, without payment

gratitude *noun* thankfulness; desire to repay kindness

gratuitous *adjective* uncalled-for, done without good reason: *gratuitous violence* □ **gratuitously** *adverb*

gratuity *noun* (*plural* **gratuities**) a money gift in return for a service; a tip

grave *noun* a pit in which a dead person is buried □ *adjective* **1** serious, important: *grave error* **2** not cheerful, solemn □ **gravely** *adverb* □ **gravity** *noun*

grave accent (*pronounced* grahv) a backward-leaning stroke (`) placed over letters in some languages to show their pronunciation

gravel *noun* small stones or pebbles

graven *adjective*, *old* carved: *graven images*

gravestone *noun* a stone placed to mark a grave

graveyard *noun* a place where the dead are buried, a cemetery

gravitate *verb* to move towards as if strongly attracted (to) □ **gravitation** *noun*

gravity *noun* **1** seriousness, importance: *gravity of the situation* **2** lack of levity, solemnity **3** weight **4** the force which attracts things towards earth and causes them to fall to the ground

gravy *noun* (*plural* **gravies**) a sauce made from juices of meat that is cooking

gravy train a situation producing large, easy profits

gray *US spelling of* **grey**

graze *verb* **1** to feed on (growing grass) **2** to scrape the skin of **3** to touch lightly in passing □ *noun* **1** a scraping of the skin **2** a light touch

grazing *noun* grass land for animals to graze on

grease *noun* **1** thick animal fat **2** an oily substance □ *verb* to smear with grease, apply grease to

grease-paint *noun* theatrical make-up

greasy *adjective* **1** full of, or covered in, grease **2** of skin: having a slightly moist appearance because the body releases a lot of natural oils into it **3** wet and slippery

great *adjective* **1** very large **2** powerful **3** very important, distinguished **4** very talented: *a great singer* **5** of high rank, noble **6** *informal* excellent, very good □ **greatness** *noun* (meanings 1, 2, 3, 4 and 5)
⊙ Comes from Old English

great-grandchild *noun* the son or daughter of a grandson or grand-daughter

great-grandfather *noun* the father of a grandfather or grandmother

great-grandmother *noun* the mother of a grandfather or grandmother

greatly *adverb* very much

grebe *noun* a fresh-water diving bird

greed *noun* great and selfish desire for food, money *etc*

greedy *adjective* full of greed □ **greedily** *adverb*

green *adjective* **1** of the colour of growing grass *etc* **2** inexperienced, naive **3** concerned with care of the environment □ *noun* **1** the colour of growing grass **2** a piece of ground covered with grass **3** **Green** a member of the Green Party, an environmentalist **4** **greens** green vegetables for food

green belt open land surrounding a city

greenery *noun* green plants

green fingers: **have green fingers** to be a skilful gardener

greenfly *noun* (*plural* **greenfly**) a bright green, small insect which attacks plants

greengage *noun* a kind of plum, green but sweet

greengrocer *noun* someone who sells fresh vegetables

greenhouse *noun* a building with large glass panes in which plants are grown

greenhouse effect the warming-up of the earth's surface due to excess carbon dioxide and certain other gases in the atmosphere

the green light permission to go ahead with a plan

Green Party a political party concerned with conserving natural resources and decentralizing political and economic power

greet *verb* 1 to meet someone with kind words 2 to say hello *etc* to 3 to react to, respond to: *greeted the news with relief* 4 to become evident to

greeting *noun* 1 words of welcome or kindness 2 reaction, response

gregarious *adjective* 1 sociable, liking the company of others 2 living in flocks and herds

grenade *noun* a small bomb thrown by hand

From a French word for 'pomegranate', because of its shape

grew *past form* of **grow**

grey or *US* **gray** *adjective* 1 of a colour between black and white 2 grey-haired, old □ *noun* 1 grey colour 2 a grey horse

greyhound *noun* a breed of fast-running dog

grey matter *informal* brains

grid *noun* 1 a grating of bars 2 a network of lines, *eg* for helping to find a place on a map 3 a network of wires carrying electricity over a wide area

grid-iron *noun* 1 a frame of iron bars for cooking food over a fire 2 *US* a football field

grief *noun* deep sorrow, especially after bereavement □ **come to grief** to meet with misfortune

grievance *noun* a cause for complaining

grieve *verb* to feel grief or sorrow

grievous *adjective* 1 painful; serious 2 causing grief

griffin or **griffon** *noun* a mythological animal with the body and legs of a lion and the beak and wings of an eagle

grill *verb* 1 to cook directly under heat (provided by an electric or gas cooker) 2 to cook on a grid-iron over a fire 3 to question closely □ *noun* 1 a frame of bars for grilling food on 2 grilled food 3 the part of a cooker used for grilling 4 a restaurant serving grilled food

grille *noun* a metal grating over a door, window *etc*

grim *adjective* 1 stern, fierce-looking 2 terrible; very unpleasant: *a grim sight* 3 unyielding, stubborn: *grim determination* □ **grimly** *adverb*

grimace *noun* a twisting of the face in fun or pain □ *verb* to make a grimace

grime *noun* dirt

grimy *adjective* covered with a layer of ground-in dirt

grin *verb* to smile broadly □ *noun* a broad smile □ **grin and bear it** to suffer something without complaining

grin *verb* ⇨ grins, grinning, grinned

grind *verb* 1 to crush to powder 2 to sharpen by rubbing 3 to rub together: *grinding his teeth* □ *noun* hard or unpleasant work

grind *verb* ⇨ grinds, grinding, ground

grinder *noun* someone or something that grinds

grindstone *noun* a revolving stone for grinding or sharpening tools □ **back to the grindstone** back to work □ **keep your nose to the grindstone** to work hard without stopping

grip *noun* 1 a firm hold, a grasp: *these shoes have a good grip* 2 a way of holding or grasping; control: *a loose grip* 3 a handle or part for holding 4 a travelling bag, a holdall □ *verb* to take a firm hold of

grip *verb* ⇨ grips, gripping, gripped

gripe *noun* 1 a sharp stomach pain 2 *informal* a complaint □ *verb* to complain

gripping *adjective* commanding attention, compelling

grisly *adjective* frightful, hideous
⊕ Comes from Old English *grislic* which is related to *agrisan* meaning 'to terrify'
☛ Do not confuse with: **grizzly**

grist *noun* corn for grinding □ **grist to the mill** something which brings profit or advantage

gristle *noun* a tough elastic substance in meat □ **gristly** *adjective*

grit *noun* **1** a mixture of rough sand and gravel, spread on icy surfaces **2** courage □ *verb* **1** to apply grit to (an icy surface): *has the road been gritted?* **2** to clench: *grit your teeth*

  grit *verb* ⇨ grits, gritting, gritted

gritty *adjective* **1** covered in grit or having a texture like grit **2** courageous **3** honest in the portrayal of harsh realities □ **grittiness** *noun*

grizzled *adjective* grey; mixed with grey

grizzly *adjective* grey in colour □ *noun* (*plural* **grizzlies**) *informal* a grizzly bear
⊕ Comes from French *gris* meaning 'grey'
☛ Do not confuse with: **grisly**

grizzly bear a type of large bear of North America

groan *verb* **1** to moan in pain, disapproval *etc* **2** to be full or loaded: *a table groaning with food*

grocer *noun* a dealer in certain kinds of food and household supplies

groceries *noun plural* food *etc* sold by grocers

groggy *adjective* weak and light-headed after illness or blows

  Originally meaning 'drunk', from *grog*, a mixture of rum and water

groin *noun* the part of the body where the inner thigh joins the torso

groom *noun* **1** a bridegroom **2** someone in charge of horses □ *verb* **1** to look after (a horse) **2** to make smart and tidy

groove *noun* a furrow, a long hollow □ *verb* to cut a groove (in)

grope *verb* to search (for) by feeling as if blind: *groping for his socks in the dark*

gross *adjective* **1** coarse **2** very fat **3** great, obvious: *gross error* **4** of money: total, before any deductions for tax *etc*: *gross profit* **5** *US informal* disgusting, revolting □ *noun* **1** the whole taken together **2** twelve dozen

grossly *adverb* extremely

grossness *noun* coarseness

grotesque *adjective* very odd or unnatural-looking

grotto *noun* (*plural* **grottoes** or **grottos**) a cave

ground[1] *noun* **1** the surface of the earth **2** (also **grounds**) a good reason: *ground for complaint* **3** **grounds** lands surrounding a large house *etc* **4** **grounds** dregs: *coffee grounds* □ *verb* **1** of a ship: to strike the sea-bed and become stuck **2** to prevent (aeroplanes) from flying **3** to prevent (someone in your charge) from going out

ground[2] *past form* of **grind**

ground floor the storey of a building at street level

grounding *noun* the first steps in learning something

groundless *adjective* without reason

groundnut same as **peanut**

groundwork *noun* the first stages of a task

group *noun* a number of people or things together □ *verb* **1** to form or gather into a group **2** to classify
⊕ Comes from French *groupe* meaning 'group'

grouse[1] *noun* (*plural* **grouse**) a game bird hunted on moors and hills

grouse[2] *noun* (*plural* **grouses**) a grumble, a complaint □ *verb* to grumble, complain

grove *noun* a small group of trees

grovel *verb* **1** to crawl or lie on the ground **2** to be overly humble

  grovel ⇨ grovels, grovelling, grovelled

grow *verb* **1** to become bigger or stronger: *the local population is growing* **2** to become: *grow old* **3** to rear, cause to grow (plants, trees *etc*): *grow from seed*

  grow ⇨ grows, growing, grew, grown

growl *verb* to utter a deep sound like a

harmony *noun* (*plural* **harmonies**) **1** agreement of one part, colour or sound with another **2** agreement between people: *living in harmony* **3** *music* a part intended to agree in sound with the melody

harness *noun* **1** the leather and other fittings for a workhorse **2** an arrangement of straps *etc* attaching something to the body: *parachute harness* □ *verb* **1** to put a harness on a horse **2** to use as a resource: *harnessing the power of the wind* □ **in harness** working, not on holiday or retired

harp *noun* a triangular, stringed musical instrument played upright by plucking with the fingers □ *verb* to play the harp □ **harp on about** to talk too much about

harper or **harpist** *noun* a harp player

harpoon *noun* a spear tied to rope, used for killing whales □ *verb* to strike with a harpoon

harpsichord *noun* an early musical instrument with keys, played like a piano

harrow *noun* a frame with iron spikes for breaking up lumps of earth □ *verb* **1** to drag a harrow over **2** to distress greatly

harrowing *adjective* very distressing

harry *verb* **1** to plunder, lay waste **2** to harass, worry

     harry ⇨ harri*es*, harry*ing*, harri*ed*

harsh *adjective* rough, bitter; cruel □ **harshly** *adverb*

hart *noun* the stag or male deer, especially from the age of six years

harvest *noun* **1** the time of the year when ripened crops are gathered in **2** the crops gathered at this time □ *verb* to gather in (a crop)

harvester *noun* **1** a farm worker who helps with the harvest **2** (*also called* **combine harvester**) a large machine that cuts and threshes grain **3** a creature like a spider

harvest home a feast held after a harvest is gathered in

has *see* **have**

has-been *noun* someone no longer important or popular

hash *noun* a dish of chopped meat *etc* □ **make a hash of** to spoil completely

hashish *noun* the strongest form of the drug made from hemp (*see also* **cannabis**)

hassle *verb* to cause problems for □ *noun* difficulty, trouble

hassock *noun* a thick cushion used as a footstool or for kneeling on

haste *noun* speed, hurry □ **make haste** to hurry

hasten *verb* **1** to hurry (on) **2** to drive forward

hasty *adjective* hurried; done without thinking □ **hastily** *adverb*

hat *noun* a covering for the head □ **keep something under your hat** to keep it secret

hatch *noun* (*plural* **hatches**) a door or cover over an opening in a floor, wall *etc* □ *verb* **1** to produce young from eggs **2** to form and set working: *hatch (a plan/ evil)* **3** to shade (part of a picture *etc*) with fine lines

hatchback *noun* a car with a sloping rear door which opens upwards

hatchery *noun* (*plural* **hatcheries**) a place for hatching eggs (especially of fish)

hatchet *noun* a small axe □ **bury the hatchet** to put an end to a quarrel

hate *verb* to dislike very much □ *noun* great dislike

■ **Alternative words**: (verb) abhor, loathe, detest, abominate
---

hateful *adjective* horrible, causing hatred

hatred *noun* extreme dislike

hatter *noun* someone who makes or sells hats

hat-trick *noun* **1** *cricket* the putting out of three batsmen by three balls in a row **2** *football* three goals scored by the same player **3** any action performed three times in a row

haughty *adjective* proud, looking on others with scorn □ **haughtily** *adverb*

haul *verb* to drag, pull with force □ *noun* **1** a strong pull **2** *informal* a difficult or tiring job: *a long haul* **3** an amount gathered at one time: *a haul of fish* **4** a rich find, booty

haulage *noun* **1** the carrying of goods **2** money charged for this

haulier *noun* a transporter of goods

haunch *noun* (*plural* **haunches**) **1** the fleshy part of the hip **2** a leg and loin of meat, especially venison

haunt *verb* **1** to visit often **2** of a ghost: to inhabit, linger in (a place) □ *noun* a place often visited

haunted *adjective* inhabited by ghosts

have *verb* **1** used with another verb to show that an action is in the past and completed: *we have decided to move house* **2** to own, possess: *do you have a cat?* **3** to hold, contain: *the hotel has a swimming pool* **4** to give birth to: *have a baby* **5** to suffer from: *have a cold* **6** to cause to be done: *have your hair cut* **7** to put up with: *I won't have him being so rude* □ **have done with** to finish □ **have it out** to settle by argument

> **have** ⇨ ha*s*, hav*ing*, ha*d*

🕐 Comes from Old English *habban*

📰 Opposite: (meanings 2 and 3) lack

haven *noun* a place of safety

haver *verb*, *Scottish* **1** to speak nonsense **2** to dawdle, potter

haversack *noun* a bag made of canvas *etc* with shoulder-straps, for carrying on the back

havoc *noun* great destruction

haw *noun* a berry of the hawthorn tree

hawk *noun* a bird of prey like a falcon □ *verb* **1** to hunt birds with trained hawks **2** to carry goods about for sale

hawker *noun* a door-to-door salesman

hawthorn *noun* a prickly tree with white flowers and small red berries

hay *noun* cut and dried grass, used as cattle food

hay-fever *noun* an illness with effects like a bad cold, caused by pollen *etc*

hayrick or **haystack** *noun* hay built up into a mound

haywire *adjective* tangled, in a state of disorder

hazard *noun* **1** chance **2** risk of harm or danger □ *verb* **1** to risk **2** to put forward (a guess) at the risk of being wrong

hazardous *adjective* dangerous, risky

haze *noun* a thin mist

hazel *noun* a nut-producing tree of the birch family □ *adjective* light greenish-brown in colour

hazelnut *noun* a light brown nut produced by the hazel tree

hazy *adjective* **1** misty **2** not clear, vague □ **hazily** *adverb*

H-bomb *noun* a hydrogen bomb

he *pronoun* a male person or animal already spoken about (used only as the subject of a verb): *he ate a banana*

head *noun* **1** the uppermost part of the body, containing the brain, skull *etc* **2** someone's mind: *can't get that tune out of my head* **3** a person in charge, a chief □ *verb* **1** to lead **2** to go in front of **3** to go in the direction of: *heading for home* **4** to hit (a ball) with the head **5** **head off** to turn aside, deflect: *head off an attack* □ **head over heels** completely, thoroughly □ **off your head** mad, crazy □ **per head** per person

headache *noun* **1** a pain in the head **2** a worrying problem

headband *noun* a band worn round the head

headboard *noun* a board across the top end of a bed

headdress *noun* a covering for the head

header *noun*, *football* a shot at goal striking the ball with the head

headfirst *adverb* **1** with the head first: *fall headfirst down the stairs* **2** rashly, without thinking

heading *noun* the title of a book or chapter

headland *noun* a point of land running out into the sea, a cape

headlight *noun* a strong light on the front of a car *etc*

headline *noun* a line in large letters at the top of a newspaper page

headlong *adjective* & *adverb* headfirst

headmaster *noun* a man who is the principal teacher of a school

headmistress *noun* a woman who is the principal teacher of a school

head-on *adjective & adverb* with the head or front first

headphones *noun plural* a listening device that fits over the ears

headquarters *noun singular* and *noun plural* place from which the chief officers of an army *etc* control their operations; the chief office (of a business *etc*)

headrest *noun* a support for the head in a vehicle *etc*

headstone *noun* a gravestone

headstrong *adjective* determined, stubborn

headteacher *noun* the principal teacher of a school

headway *noun* forward movement

headwind *noun* a wind blowing straight in your face

heady *adjective* exciting

heal *verb* to make or become healthy or sound; cure

health *noun* 1 someone's physical condition: *how's your health?* 2 good or natural physical condition □ **your** *etc* **health!** (as a toast) a wish that someone may have good health

healthy *adjective* 1 in good health or condition 2 encouraging good health

heap *noun* 1 a pile of things thrown one on top of another 2 a great many (of) □ *verb* to throw in a pile

hear *verb* 1 to receive (sounds) by the ear 2 to listen to 3 to be told, understand: *I hear you want to speak to me* □ **hear! hear!** *exclamation* a cry to show agreement with a speaker □ **will not hear of** will not allow: *he wouldn't hear of her going there alone*

  hear ⇨ hears, hearing, heard

■ **Alternative words**: (verb, meaning 1) catch, overhear; (verb, meaning 3) learn, gather

hearing *noun* 1 the act or power of listening 2 a court case

hearsay *noun* gossip, rumour

hearse *noun* a car for carrying a dead body to the grave *etc*

heart *noun* 1 the part of the body which acts as a blood pump 2 the inner or chief part of anything: *the heart of the problem* 3 courage: *take heart* 4 will, enthusiasm: *his heart isn't in it* 5 love, affection: *with all my heart* 6 a sign (♥) representing a heart, or often love 7 this sign used in one of the suits on playing-cards

heartache *noun* sorrow, grief

heartbroken *adjective* very upset, very sad

heartburn *noun* a burning feeling in the chest after eating, indigestion

hearten *verb* to cheer on, encourage

heart-failure *noun* the sudden stopping of the heart's beating

heartfelt *adjective* felt deeply, sincere

hearth *noun* a fireplace

heartily *adverb* 1 cheerfully and with great enthusiasm 2 thoroughly, absolutely: *I'm heartily sick of his moaning*

heartless *adjective* cruel

heart-rending *adjective* very moving, very upsetting

heartstrings *noun plural* inmost feelings of love

heart-throb *noun* a sexually attractive person, with whom others fall in love

heart-to-heart *noun* a frank, intimate discussion

hearty *adjective* 1 strong, healthy 2 of a meal: large, satisfying 3 eager, over-cheerful

heat *noun* 1 high temperature 2 anger 3 a round in a competition, race *etc* □ *verb* to make or become hot □ **in heat** of a female animal: ready for mating in the breeding season

heath *noun* 1 barren, open country 2 heather

heathen *noun* someone who does not believe in an established religion, especially someone who worships idols □ *adjective* of heathens, pagan

heather *noun* a plant with small purple

or white flowers growing on moorland □ *adjective* of the colour of purple heather

heat wave *noun* a period of hot weather

heave *verb* 1 to lift by force 2 to throw 3 to rise and fall 4 to produce, let out (especially a sigh)

heaven *noun* 1 the sky (often **the heavens**) 2 the dwelling place of God; paradise 3 any place of great happiness

heavenly *adjective* 1 living in heaven 2 *informal* delightful

heavenly bodies the sun, moon and stars

heavily *adverb* 1 with great force, in great amount: *It was raining heavily* 2 to a serious or great extent, intensely: *heavily in debt/ heavily pregnant* (= at an advanced stage of pregnancy) 3 loudly and deeply: *He sighed heavily/ breathing heavily* 4 in a thick, solid-looking way: *He was short, but heavily built* 5 in a slow, sleepy, or sad way: *'I can't help you,' he said heavily*

heavy *adjective* 1 of great weight 2 great in amount, force *etc*: *heavy rainfall* 3 not easy to bear 4 slow; sleepy 5 loud and deep: *heavy breathing* 6 having a thick, solid appearance: *heavy eyebrows/ a heavy oak table* □ **heaviness** *noun*

heavyhanded *adjective* clumsy, awkward

heavy metal a very loud repetitive form of rock music

heavyweight *noun* 1 a boxer in the highest weight category 2 someone very important or powerful

heckle *verb* to shout insults at, or ask awkward questions of, a public speaker

heckler *noun* someone who heckles

hectare *noun* 10 000 square metres

hectic *adjective* rushed; feverish

hecto- or **hect-** *prefix* forms words of measurement equal to one hundred times the basic unit: *hectare* (= 100 ares, each equivalent to 100 square metres) ℚ Comes from Greek *hekaton* meaning 'one hundred'

hector *verb* to bully

After *Hector*, the Trojan hero in the *Iliad*

hedge *noun* a fence of bushes, shrubs *etc verb* 1 to make a hedge 2 to shut in with a hedge 3 to avoid giving a straight answer □ **hedge your bets** to keep open two or more possible courses of action

hedgehog *noun* a small animal with prickly spines on its back

hedgerow *noun* a row of bushes forming a hedge

heed *verb* to give attention to, listen to □ **pay heed to** to take notice of

heedless *adjective* careless

heel *noun* the back part of the foot □ *verb* 1 to hit (especially a ball) with the heel 2 to put a heel on (a shoe) 3 of a ship: to lean over □ **take to your heels** or **show a clean pair of heels** to run away

hefty *adjective* 1 powerful, muscular 2 heavy

Hegira *noun* the Islamic era, dating from AD 622

heifer (*pronounced* **hef-**er) *noun* a young cow

height *noun* 1 the state of being high 2 distance from bottom to top 3 the highest point 4 (often **heights**) a high place

heighten *verb* to make more intense

heinous (*pronounced* **heen-**us) *adjective* extremely bad, atrocious: *heinous crime*

heir *noun* the legal inheritor of a title or property on the death of the owner

heir-apparent *noun* someone expected to receive a title or property when the present holder dies

heiress *noun* a woman or girl who is the legal inheritor of a large amount of property or money on the death of the owner

heirloom *noun* something that has been handed down in a family from generation to generation

held *past form of* **hold**

helicopter *noun* a flying machine kept in the air by propellers rotating on a vertical axis

A coinage based on Greek words meaning 'spiral wing'

helio- *prefix* of or relating to the sun: *heliograph/ heliotrope* (= a plant that turns its flowers towards the sun)/ *helium* (= a gas first discovered in the atmosphere of the sun)
Ⓘ Comes from Greek *helios* meaning 'the sun'

heliograph *noun* a means of signalling, using the sun's rays

heliotrope *noun* **1** a plant with small, sweet-smelling, lilac-blue flowers **2** a light purple colour

helium *noun* a very light gas

helix *noun* a screw-shaped coil

hell *noun* **1** a place of punishment of the wicked after death **2** the dwelling place of the Devil **3** any place of great misery or pain

hellbent on determined to

hellish *adjective* very bad, unpleasant, horrible or difficult

hellishly *adverb* extremely, horribly

hello or **hallo** or **hullo** *noun* (*plural* **hellos** or **helloes** *etc*) a greeting used between people: *I said hello to him/ Hello! How are you?*

helm *noun* the wheel or handle by which a ship is steered

helmet *noun* an armoured or protective covering for the head

helmsman *noun* the person who steers a ship

help *verb* **1** to aid, do something useful for **2** to give the means for doing something to **3** to stop yourself from (doing): *I can't help liking him* □ *noun* **1** aid, assistance **2** someone who assists □ **help yourself** serve yourself, take what you want
Ⓘ Comes from Old English *helpan*

■ **Alternative words:** (verb, meaning 1) assist

helpful *adjective* useful, giving help □ **helpfully** *adverb*

helping *noun* a share, especially of food

helpless *adjective* useless; powerless □ **helplessly** *adverb*

helpmate *noun* a partner

helter-skelter *adverb* in a great hurry, in confusion □ *noun* a spiral slide in a fairground *etc*

hem *noun* the border of a garment doubled down and stitched □ *verb* to put or form a hem on □ **hem in** to surround

hem *verb* ⇨ hem*s*, hem*ming*, hem*med*

hemi- *prefix* half
Hemi- is a Greek prefix

hemisphere *noun* **1** a half of a sphere or ball-shape **2** half of the earth: *western hemisphere/ southern hemisphere*

hemispherical *adjective* like half a ball in shape

hemlock *noun* a poisonous plant with spotted leaves

hemo- *US spelling of* **haemo-**

hemp *noun* a plant used for making ropes, bags, sails *etc* and the drug cannabis

hen *noun* **1** a female bird **2** a female domestic fowl

hence *adverb* **1** from this place or time: *ten years hence* **2** for this reason: *hence, I am unable to go*

henceforth or **henceforward** *adverb* from now on

henchman *noun* a follower; a servant

henna *noun* a reddish plant dye used for colouring the hair *etc*

henpecked *adjective* of a husband: dominated by his wife

hepatitis *noun* inflammation of the liver caused by one of several viruses

hepta- *prefix* seven
Ⓘ Comes from Greek *hepta* meaning 'seven'

heptagon *noun* a seven-sided figure □ **heptagonal** *adjective*

her *pronoun* a female person already spoken about (used only as the object in a sentence): *have you seen her?* □ *adjective* belonging to such a person: *her house*

herald *noun* **1** something that is a sign

of future things **2** *historical* someone who carries and reads important notices □ *verb* **1** to announce loudly **2** to be a sign of

heraldic *adjective* of heraldry

heraldry *noun* the study of coats of arms, crests *etc*

herb *noun* a plant used in the making of medicines or in cooking
⏱ Comes from French *herbe* meaning 'grass'

herbaceous *adjective* **1** of a plant: with a stem which dies every year **2** of a flower-bed: filled with such plants

herbal *adjective* of or using herbs: *herbal remedy*

herbalism *noun* the study and use of plants in medicine

herbivore *noun* an animal which feeds on plants □ **herbivorous** *adjective*

Herculean *adjective* requiring tremendous strength or effort: *a Herculean task*

After the Greek hero, *Hercules*, who was given twelve seemingly impossible tasks to do by the gods

herd *noun* **1** a group of animals of one kind **2** (**the herd**) most people □ *verb* to group together like a herd of animals

here *adverb* at, in or to this place: *he's here already/ come here!*

hereabouts *adverb* approximately in this place

hereafter *adverb* after this □ **the hereafter** life after death

hereby *adverb* by this means

hereditary *adjective* passed on from parents to children

heredity *noun* the passing on of physical qualities from parents to children

heresy (*pronounced* he-re-si) *noun* (*plural* **heresies**) an opinion which goes against the official (especially religious) view

heretic (*pronounced* he-re-tik) *noun* someone who holds or teaches an opinion which goes against the official (especially religious) view □ **heretical** *adjective*

heritage *noun* something passed on by or inherited from an earlier generation

hermaphrodite (*pronounced* her-**maf**-ro-dait) *noun* an animal which has the qualities of both male and female sexes

hermetically *adverb*: **hermetically sealed** closed completely and airtight

hermit *noun* someone who lives alone, often for religious reasons

hermitage *noun* the dwelling of a hermit

hermit crab a kind of crab which lives in the abandoned shell of a shellfish

hernia *noun* the bursting out of part of an internal organ through a weak spot in surrounding body tissue

hero *noun* (*plural* **heroes**) **1** someone much admired for their bravery **2** the chief male character in a story, film *etc*

heroic *adjective* **1** brave as a hero **2** of heroes □ **heroically** *adverb*

heroin *noun* a very addictive drug derived from morphine

heroine *noun* **1** a woman much admired for her bravery **2** the chief female character in a story, film *etc*

heroism *noun* bravery

heron *noun* a large water bird, with long legs and neck

herpes *noun* a name for various types of a skin disease

herring *noun* (*plural* **herring** or **herrings**) an edible sea fish with silvery colouring, which moves in large shoals

hers *pronoun* something belonging to such a person: *the idea was hers*

herself *pronoun* **1** used reflexively: *she washed herself* **2** used for emphasis: *she herself won't be there but her brother will*

hertz *noun* a unit of frequency for radio waves *etc*

hesitant *adjective* undecided about whether to do something or not, because of anxiety or worry about the possible results □ **hesitancy** *noun*

hesitate *verb* **1** to pause because of uncertainty **2** to be unwilling (to do something): *I hesitate to ask* □ **hesitation** *noun*

hessian *noun* a type of coarse cloth

hetero- *prefix* forms words containing the idea of 'other' or 'different'
ⓘ Comes from Greek *heteros* meaning 'other'

heterodox *noun* heretical, having an opinion other than the accepted one (*contrasted with*: **orthodox**)
□ **heterodoxy** *noun*

heterogeneous (*pronounced* het-e-ro-jeen-i-us) *adjective* composed of many different kinds (*contrasted with*: **homogeneous**)

heterosexual *noun* someone who is sexually attracted to the opposite sex
□ *adjective* attracted to the opposite sex (*contrasted with*: **homosexual**)
□ **heterosexuality** *noun*

hew *verb* to cut or shape with an axe *etc*

hew ⇨ hews, hewing, hewed, hewn or hewed

hex *noun* a spell to bring bad luck; a curse

hexa- *prefix* six
ⓘ Comes from Greek *hex* meaning 'six'

hexagon *noun* a six-sided figure
□ **hexagonal** *adjective*

heyday *noun* the time of greatest strength, the prime
From an old English expression *heyda*, meaning 'hurrah'. The -*day* ending and current sense developed much later

HGV *abbreviation* heavy goods vehicle

hi *exclamation, informal* 1 hello 2 hey

hiatus (*pronounced* hai-**eit**-us) *noun* a gap, a rift

hibernate *verb* of an animal: to pass the winter in a sleep-like state
□ **hibernation** *noun* □ **hibernator** *noun*

hiccup *noun* 1 a sharp gasp, caused by laughing, eating, drinking 2 **hiccups** a fit of such gasping 3 a minor setback or difficulty □ *verb* to make a hiccuping sound

hickory *noun* (*plural* **hickories**) a N American tree

hidden *adjective* 1 concealed, out of sight 2 unknown: *hidden meaning*

hide[1] *verb* to put or keep out of sight
□ *noun* a concealed place from which to watch birds *etc*

hide *verb* ⇨ hides, hiding, hid, hidden

■ **Alternative words:** (verb) conceal, shroud, obscure, eclipse, secrete, withhold

hide[2] *noun* the skin of an animal

hidebound *adjective* not open to new ideas

hideous *adjective* 1 horrible, ghastly 2 very ugly

hideously *adverb* 1 of something horrible, ghastly or very ugly: extremely: *a hideously deformed body* 2 of something unpleasant or unreasonable: extremely: *hideously expensive*

hiding *noun* a beating

hie (*pronounced* hai) *verb, old* to hurry, hasten

hierarchy *noun* a number of people or things arranged in order of rank
□ **hierarchical** *adjective*

hieroglyphics (*pronounced* hai-e-ro-**glif**-iks) *noun plural* ancient Egyptian writing, in which pictures are used as letters

hi-fi *adjective* short for **high-fidelity** *noun, informal* high-quality equipment for reproducing recorded sound

higgledy-piggledy *adverb & adjective* in a complete muddle

high *adjective* 1 raised far above 2 extending far upwards, tall 3 well up on any scale of measurement, rank *etc* 4 great, large: *high hopes/ high prices* 5 of sound: shrill, acute in pitch 6 of meat: beginning to go bad □ *adverb* 1 far above in the air 2 well up on any scale 3 to a high degree □ **for the high jump** expecting trouble or punishment □ **on your high horse** behaving with exaggerated pride or superiority
ⓘ Comes from Old English *heah*

■ **Alternative words:** (adjective, meaning 1) lofty, elevated, soaring; (adjective, meaning 2) towering

highball *noun, US* an alcoholic drink and mixer (*eg* whisky and soda) with ice in a tall glass

highbrow *adjective* intellectual, very literary (*contrasted with*: **lowbrow**)

High Court a supreme court

Higher *noun* an examination in Scottish secondary schools, usually taken at the end of the 5th year

high-fidelity *adjective* reproducing sound very clearly

high-five *noun* a sign of greeting made by slapping together one another's raised palms

high-flier *noun* a highly ambitious and successful person

high-flown *adjective* (of language, style) using words that sound too grand or pompous

high-handed *adjective* thoughtless, overbearing

high jinks lively games or play

Highlander *noun* someone who comes from the Highlands

the Highlands a mountainous region, especially the north of Scotland

highlight *noun* 1 a bright spot or area in a picture 2 a lighter patch in hair *etc* made obvious by bright light 3 the most memorable part or experience: *the highlight of the week* □ *verb* to emphasize, make the focus of attention

highlighter *noun* a coloured felt-tip pen used to mark but not obscure lines of text

highly *adverb* 1 very: *highly delighted* 2 to or at a high level 3 in an approving way: *I've always thought highly of him*

highly-strung *adjective* nervous, easily excited

high-minded *adjective* having strong principles and high moral standards

Highness *noun* a title of a monarch

highroad *noun* a main road

the high seas the open seas

high-spirited *adjective* bold, lively

high tea a cooked meal in the late afternoon

high tech short for **high-technology**, referring to the use of advanced, especially electronic, equipment and devices □ *adjective* (**high-tech**) modern and sophisticated

high tide or **high water** the time when the tide is farthest up the shore

high treason the crime of acting against the safety of your own country

highway *noun* the public road

Highway Code a set of official rules for road users in Britain

highwayman *noun* a robber who attacked people on the public road

hijack *verb* to steal (a car, aeroplane *etc*) while it is moving, forcing the driver or pilot to take a new route □ *noun* the action of hijacking a vehicle *etc* □ **hijacker** *noun*

hike *verb* to travel on foot through countryside □ *noun* a country walk □ **hiker** *noun*

hilarious *adjective* extremely funny

hilariously *adverb* of something funny: extremely

hilarity *noun* great amusement and laughter

hill *noun* a mound of high land, less high than a mountain

hillock *noun* a small hill

hilly *adjective* covered with hills

hilt *noun* the handle of a sword □ **up to the hilt** thoroughly, completely

him *pronoun* a male person already spoken about (used only as the object in a sentence): *I saw him yesterday/ what did you say to him?*

himself *pronoun* 1 used reflexively: *he cut himself shaving* 2 used for emphasis: *he wrote it himself*

hind *noun* a female deer □ *adjective* placed behind

hinder *verb* to keep back, delay, prevent

hindmost *adjective* farthest behind

hindrance *noun* something that hinders

hinge *noun* a joint on which a door, lid *etc* turns □ *verb* 1 to move on a hinge 2 to depend (on): *everything hinges on the weather*

hint *noun* 1 a remark which suggests a meaning without stating it clearly: *I'll* *give you a hint* **2** a slight impression, a suggestion: *a hint of panic in her voice* □ *verb* to suggest without stating clearly: *he hinted that he might be there*

hinterland *noun* an area lying inland from the coast

hip¹ *noun* the part of the side of the body just below the waist

hip² *noun* the fruit of the wild rose

hip³ *adjective* very fashionable, trendy

hip-flask *noun* a small pocket flask for alcohol

hip-hop *noun* a popular culture movement which started in the US in the early 1980's and is associated with rap music, breakdancing, graffiti and baggy sports clothes

hippie *noun* a member of a youth movement rebelling against conventional society, dress codes *etc*

Hippocratic oath an oath taken by a doctor agreeing to observe a code of medical ethics

hippodrome *noun* **1** an arena for horse-racing **2** a large theatre

hippopotamus *noun* (*plural* **hippopotami** or **hippopotamuses**) a large African animal living in and near rivers

> Based on a Greek word which translates as 'river horse'

hire *noun* money paid for work done, or for the use of something belonging to another person □ *verb* to give or get the use of by paying money

hire-purchase *noun* a way of buying an article by paying for it in instalments

hirsute *adjective* hairy, shaggy

his *adjective* belonging to him: *his book* □ *pronoun*: *that jacket is his*

Hispanic *adjective* **1** Spanish **2** Spanish-American

hiss *verb* to make a sound like a snake □ *noun* (*plural* **hisses**) such a sound, made to show anger or displeasure

histamine *noun* a chemical present in pollen *etc* which can cause an allergic reaction

historian *noun* someone who studies or writes history

historic *adjective* important, likely to be remembered

historical *adjective* **1** of history **2** true of something in the past

history *noun* (*plural* **histories**) **1** the study of the past **2** a description of past events, society *etc*

histrionic *adjective* relating to stage-acting or actors

histrionics *noun plural* an exaggerated show of strong feeling

hit *verb* **1** to strike with a blow **2** to occur suddenly to: *it finally hit me* □ *noun* **1** a blow, a stroke **2** a shot which hits a target **3** a success **4** a successful song, recording *etc* **5** *slang* a murder by criminals □ **hit the ceiling** or **hit the roof** to explode with anger □ **hit the ground running** to react immediately and efficiently □ **hit the nail on the head** to identify the important point, be exactly right □ **hit upon** to come upon, discover

> **hit** *verb* ⇨ **hits, hitting, hit**

hit-and-miss *adjective* haphazard, sometimes working and sometimes not

hit-and-run *adjective* of a driver: driving away after causing injury without reporting the accident

hitch *verb* **1** to fasten with a hook *etc* **2** to lift with a jerk **3** to hitch-hike □ *noun* (*plural* **hitches**) **1** a jerk **2** an unexpected stop or delay **3** a type of knot

hitchhike *verb* to travel by getting lifts in other people's vehicles □ **hitchhiker** *noun*

hi tech another spelling of **high tech**

hither *adverb* to this place □ **hither and thither** back and forwards

hitherto *adverb* up till now

hitman *noun, slang* someone employed to kill or attack others

HIV *abbreviation* human immuno-deficiency virus

hive *noun* **1** place where bees live **2** a busy place: *hive of industry*

HIV-positive *adjective* carrying HIV

HM *abbreviation* Her or His Majesty

HMS *abbreviation* **1** Her or His

Majesty's Service **2** Her or His Majesty's Ship

hoard *noun* a hidden store of treasure, food *etc* □ *verb* to store up secretly
℗ Comes from Old English *hord* meaning 'treasure' or 'secret place'

🖈 Do not confuse with: **horde**

hoarding *noun* a fence of boards

hoar-frost *noun* white frost

hoarse *adjective* having a harsh voice, *eg* from a cold or cough

hoary *adjective* **1** white with age **2** very old

hoax *noun* (*plural* **hoaxes**) a trick played to deceive □ *verb* to play a hoax on

hob *noun* **1** the top of a cooker, with rings for heating *etc* **2** a small shelf next to a fireplace for keeping pans *etc* hot

hobble *verb* **1** to walk with short unsteady steps **2** to tie the legs of (a horse *etc*) loosely **3** to impede, hamper

hobby *noun* (*plural* **hobbies**) a favourite way of passing your spare time

Originally *hobby-horse*, a horse used in morris dances and therefore for amusement or pleasure

hobby-horse *noun* **1** a toy wooden horse **2** a favourite subject of discussion

hobgoblin *noun* a mischievous fairy

hobnail *noun* a large nail used for horseshoes and in the soles of heavy boots

hobnob *verb* to be on friendly terms (with); socialize (with)

hobnob ⇨ hobnobs, hobnobbing, hobnobbed

Hobson's choice the choice of having something as offered, or nothing at all

Named after *Hobson*, a Cambridge horsekeeper who reputedly gave customers the choice of the horse nearest the door or none at all

hock¹ *noun* a joint on the hind leg of an animal, below the knee

hock² *noun* a white German wine

hock³ *verb, slang* to pawn □ **in hock** pawned

hockey *noun* an eleven-a-side ball-game played with clubs curved at one end

hoe *noun* a tool used for weeding, loosening earth *etc* □ *verb* to use a hoe

hog *noun* a pig □ *verb, informal* to take or use selfishly

hog *verb* ⇨ hogs, hogging, hogged

Hogmanay *noun* the name in Scotland for 31 December and the celebrations held that night

From an old French word *aguillanneuf*, a gift given at New Year

hogwash *noun* nonsense, rubbish

hoi polloi the masses, the rabble

Taken from a Greek phrase for 'the people'

hoist *verb* to lift, raise □ *noun* a lift, an elevator for goods

hoity-toity *adjective* haughty, superior

hold *verb* **1** to keep in your possession or power; have **2** to contain **3** to occupy (a position *etc*) **4** to think, believe **5** to put on, organize: *hold a meeting* **6** to apply: *that rule doesn't hold any longer* **7** to celebrate: *hold Christmas* □ *noun* **1** grip, grasp **2** influence: *a hold over the others* **3** a large space for carrying a ship's cargo □ **hold forth** to speak at length □ **hold good** to be true □ **hold out** to refuse to give in □ **hold over** to keep till later □ **hold up 1** to support **2** to hinder **3** to attack and demand money from

hold *verb* ⇨ holds, holding, held

℗ Comes from Old English *haldan*

■ **Alternative words**: (verb, meaning 2) accommodate

holdall *noun* a large carrying bag with a zip

holder *noun* **1** container **2** someone who holds (a position *etc*)

holding *noun* an amount of land, shares *etc* held

hold-up *noun* **1** an armed attempt at robbery **2** a delay, or something that causes it

hole *noun* 1 an opening in something solid 2 a pit, a burrow 3 a miserable place □ **in a hole** in a difficult situation

holiday *noun* 1 a day when businesses *etc* are closed 2 a period away from work for rest

holiness *noun* 1 the quality of being holy or sacred 2 **Your Holiness** the official form of address used for the leader of a religion *eg* the Pope

hollow *adjective* 1 having empty space inside, not solid 2 false, unreal: *hollow victory/ hollow smile* □ *noun* 1 a sunken place 2 a dip in the land □ *verb* to scoop (out)

holly *noun* (*plural* **hollies**) an evergreen shrub with scarlet berries and prickly leaves

hollyhock *noun* a tall garden plant

holocaust *noun* a great destruction (by fire)

hologram *noun* a 3-D image created by laser beams

holograph *noun* a document written entirely by one person

holster *noun* a case for a pistol

holy *adjective* 1 of or like God 2 religious, righteous 3 for religious use; sacred □ **holy of holies** an inner sanctum □ **holier than thou** superior and smug

holy ⇨ holier, holiest

homage *noun* a show of respect; an acknowledgement of debt: *paying homage to the pioneers of cinema*

home *noun* 1 the place where someone lives 2 the house of someone's family 3 a centre or place of origin: *Nashville is the home of country music* 4 a place where children, the elderly *etc* live and are looked after □ *adjective* 1 of someone's house or family: *home comforts* 2 domestic, not foreign: *home affairs* □ *adverb* 1 towards home 2 to the full length: *drive the nail home* □ **bring home to** to make (someone) realize
ⓘ Comes from Old English *ham*

home economics the study of how to run a home

homely *adjective* 1 plain but pleasant 2 *US* plain, not attractive

home-made *adjective* made at home

homeo- or **homoeo-** (*both pronounced* hom-i-o *or* hoh-mi-o) *prefix* like, similar
ⓘ Comes from Greek *homoios* meaning 'similar'

homeopath or **homoeopath** *noun* a practitioner of homeopathy

homeopathic or **homoeopathic** *adjective* of or using homeopathy (*contrasted with*: **allopathic**)

homeopathy or **homoeopathy** *noun* the treatment of illness by small quantities of substances that produce symptoms similar to those of the illness

homeostasis or **homoeostasis** *noun* a tendency towards health or stable condition □ **homeostatic** *adjective*

home rule government of a country *etc* by its own parliament

Home Secretary *Brit* the government minister who deals with domestic issues, *eg* law and order, immigration *etc*

homesick *adjective* longing for home

homestead *noun* a farmhouse

home truth a frank statement of something true but unpleasant

homewards *adverb* towards home

homework *noun* work for school *etc* done at home

homi- *prefix* of or relating to men or people: *homicide*
ⓘ Comes from Latin *homo* meaning 'man'

homicidal *adjective* likely to commit murder

homicide *noun* 1 the killing of a human being 2 someone who kills a person

homily *noun* 1 a plain, practical sermon 2 a talk giving advice

homing *adjective* of a pigeon: having the habit of making for home

homo- *prefix* 1 same: *homosexual/ homonym* 2 of or relating to homosexuality: *homoerotic*
ⓘ Comes from Greek *homos* meaning 'same'

homoeopathy *another spelling of* homeopathy

homoeostasis *another spelling of* homeostasis

homoerotic *adjective* relating to homosexual desire □ **homoeroticism** *noun*

homogeneous (*pronounced* hom-oh-jeen-i-*us*) *adjective* composed of parts of the same kind (*contrasted with*: **heterogeneous**) □ **homogeneity** *noun*

homogenize (*pronounced* ho-**moj**-en-aiz) *verb* to treat (milk) so that the cream does not separate and rise to the surface □ **homogenization** *noun*

homograph *noun* a word which has the same spelling as, but a different meaning from, another, *eg keen* meaning 'eager' is a homograph of *keen* meaning 'lament'

homonym *noun* a word which has the same sound as, but a different meaning from another, *eg pair* is a homonym of *pear*

homo sapiens a human being

homosexual *noun* someone who is sexually attracted to the same sex □ *adjective* sexually attracted to the same sex □ **homosexuality** *noun*

hone *verb* to sharpen (a knife *etc*)

honest *adjective* truthful; not inclined to steal, cheat *etc*

honestly *adverb* 1 truthfully 2 without cheating or stealing *etc* 3 when you are trying to convince someone of something: really 4 an expression of annoyance: *Honestly, I don't know why I bother!*

honesty *noun* the quality of being honest, truthful or trustworthy

honey *noun* 1 a sweet, thick fluid made by bees from the nectar of flowers 2 *informal* sweetheart, dear

honeycomb *noun* a network of wax cells in which bees store honey

honeycombed *adjective* patterned with holes like honey cells

honeymoon *noun* a holiday spent immediately after marriage □ *verb* to spend a honeymoon

honeysuckle *noun* a climbing shrub with sweet-smelling flowers

honk *noun* a noise like the cry of the wild goose or the sound of a motor horn □ *verb* to make this sound

honorary *adjective* 1 done to give honour 2 without payment

honour or *US* **honor** *noun* 1 respect for truth, honesty *etc* 2 fame, glory 3 reputation, good name 4 a title of respect, especially to a judge: *Your Honour* 5 a privilege 6 **honours** recognition given for exceptional achievements □ *verb* 1 to give respect to 2 to give high rank to 3 to pay money when due: *honour a debt* □ **do the honours** to perform a ceremonial task

honourable *adjective* worthy of honour □ **honourably** *adverb*

hood *noun* 1 a covering for the head 2 a protective cover for anything 3 *US* the bonnet of a car

hoodwink *verb* to deceive

hoof *noun* (*plural* **hoofs** or **hooves**) the horny part on the feet of certain animals (*eg* horses) □ **on the hoof** *informal* on the move, while moving

hook *noun* 1 a bent piece of metal *etc* for hanging things on 2 a piece of metal on the end of a line for catching fish □ *verb* to hang or catch with a hook □ **by hook or by crook** by one means or another, whatever the cost

hookah or **hooka** *noun* a tobacco pipe in which the smoke is drawn through water

hooked *adjective* 1 curved, bent 2 caught by a hook 3 *slang* addicted to, fascinated by

hooligan *noun* a wild, unruly person

hooliganism *noun* unruly behaviour

hoop *noun* a thin ring of wood or metal

hooray *another spelling of* **hurrah**

hoot *verb* 1 to sound (a siren, car horn *etc*) 2 of an owl: to call, cry 3 to laugh loudly □ *noun* 1 the sound made by a car horn, siren or owl 2 a shout of scorn or disgust 3 *informal* someone or something extremely funny

hooter *noun* 1 a siren or horn which makes a hooting sound 2 *slang* a large nose

hoover *verb* to vacuum (a floor *etc*)

Hoover *noun, trademark* a vacuum cleaner

hop[1] *verb* to leap on one leg □ *noun* a short jump on one leg

> **hop** *verb* ⇨ hops, hopping, hopped

hop[2] *noun* a climbing plant with bitter-tasting fruits which are used in brewing beer

hope *noun* 1 the state of expecting or wishing something good to happen 2 something desired □ *verb* to expect or wish good to happen

hopeful *adjective* 1 confident or optimistic about something 2 promising, encouraging

hopefully *adverb* 1 with hope 2 used when expressing hopes: 'I hope that . . .'

hopeless *adjective* 1 without hope 2 very bad □ **hopelessly** *adverb*

hopper *noun* a funnel for shaking down corn to a grinding machine

hopscotch *noun* a hopping game over lines drawn on the ground

horde *noun* a large crowd or group
🕑 Comes from Turkish *ordu* meaning 'camp'

> 🖝 Do not confuse with: **hoard**

horizon *noun* 1 the imaginary line formed where the earth meets the sky 2 the limit of someone's experience or understanding

horizontal *adjective* lying level or flat □ **horizontally** *adverb*

hormone *noun* a substance produced by certain glands of the body, which acts on a particular organ □ **hormonal** *adjective*

horn *noun* 1 a hard growth on the heads of certain animals, *eg* deer, sheep 2 something curved or sticking out like an animal's horn 3 part of a car which gives a warning sound 4 a brass wind instrument (originally made of horn)

horned *adjective* having horns

hornet *noun* a kind of large wasp □ **stir up a hornet's nest** to cause a commotion or violent reaction

hornpipe *noun* a lively sailor's dance

horny *adjective* hard like horn

horoscope *noun* a prediction of someone's future based on the position of the stars at their birth

horrendous *adjective, informal* awful, terrible

horrible *adjective* 1 very unpleasant 2 very bad, awful □ **horribly** *adverb*

horrid *adjective* hateful; very unpleasant

horrific *adjective* 1 terrifying 2 awful, very bad □ **horrifically** *adverb*

horrify *verb* to frighten greatly, shock: *we were horrified by his behaviour* □ **horrifying** *adjective*

> **horrify** ⇨ horrifies, horrifying, horrified

horror *noun* 1 great fear, terror 2 something which causes fear 3 an unruly or demanding child

horse *noun* 1 a four-footed animal with hooves and a mane 2 a wooden frame for drying clothes on 3 a piece of gymnastic equipment for vaulting □ **from the horse's mouth** directly from the source, first-hand □ **horses for courses** people will do best in situations that suit them individually

horse-chestnut *noun* a tree which produces a shiny, inedible nut (a conker)

horsefly *noun* a large fly which bites

horse laugh a loud, harsh laugh

horseplay *noun* rough play, fooling around

horsepower *noun* a unit of mechanical power for car engines (*short form* **hp**)

horseradish *noun* a plant with a sharp-tasting root which is used in sauces

horseshoe *noun* 1 a shoe for horses, made of a curved piece of iron 2 a horseshoe-shaped thing

horticulture *noun* the study and art of gardening □ **horticultural** *adjective*

hosanna *noun* an exclamation of praise to God

hose *noun* 1 (*plural* **hose**) an old-fashioned word meaning 'a covering for the legs or feet', *eg* stockings 2 (*plural* **hoses**) a rubber tube for carrying water

hosiery *noun* stockings, tights *etc*

hospice *noun* a home providing special nursing care for incurable invalids

hospitable *adjective* showing kindness to guests or strangers □ **hospitably** *adverb*

hospital *noun* a building for the treatment of the sick and injured

hospitality *noun* the quality of being hospitable, or of being friendly and welcoming to guests and strangers, entertaining them with food or drink, or providing them with accommodation

host[1] *noun* **1** someone who welcomes and entertains guests **2** an innkeeper or hotel-keeper **3** the person on a television or radio show who introduces guests and performers to the audience, or interviews them **4** *medicine* or *zoology* the person or animal on which an insect or other organism is living or feeding as a parasite

host[2] *noun* a very large number

hostage *noun* someone held prisoner by an enemy to make sure that an agreement will be kept to

hostel *noun* a building providing rooms for students *etc*

hostelry *noun* (*plural* **hostelries**), *old* an inn

hostess *noun* **1** a woman who welcomes and entertains guests **2** an air hostess

hostile *adjective* **1** of an enemy **2** not friendly **3** showing dislike or opposition (to)

hostility *noun* **1** unfriendliness, dislike **2** (*plural* **hostilities**) acts of warfare

hot *adjective* **1** very warm **2** spicy **3** passionate **4** radioactive **5** *slang* stolen **6** *slang* not safe □ **hot on someone's heels** following them closely □ **hot under the collar** indignant, enraged □ **in hot water** in trouble □ **sell like hot cakes** to sell very quickly

hot ⇨ **hot**t*er*, **hot**t*est*

■ **Alternative words**: (adjective, meaning 1) scalding, blistering, scorching, sweltering, sultry; (adjective, meanings 1 and 3) torrid; (adjective, meaning 2) spicy, peppery, piquant

hot air meaningless talk

hotbed *noun* a centre or breeding ground for anything: *a hotbed of rebellion*

hot-blooded *adjective* passionate, easily angered

hotdog *noun* a hot sausage in a long roll

hotel *noun* a building with several rooms which people can pay to stay in for a number of nights

hotfoot *adverb* in great haste

hot-headed *adjective* inclined to act rashly without thinking

hothouse *noun* a heated glasshouse for plants □ *verb* to give (a child) intensive schooling at an early age

hotline *noun* a direct telephone line between heads of government

hot potato a touchy subject

hot seat a position of responsibility

hound *noun* a dog used in hunting □ *verb* to hunt, pursue

hour *noun* **1** sixty minutes, the 24th part of a day **2** a time or occasion: *the hour of reckoning*

hour-glass *noun* an instrument which measures the hours by the running of sand from one glass into another

hourly *adjective* happening or done every hour □ *adverb* every hour

house *noun* **1** a building in which people live **2** a household **3** a business firm **4** a building where school boarders stay □ *verb* to provide a house for; accommodate □ **like a house on fire** very successfully, extremely well □ **on the house** free, complimentary ⓘ Comes from Old English *hus*

house arrest confinement under guard in a private house, hospital *etc*

houseboat *noun* a river barge with a cabin for living in

housebreaker *noun* someone who breaks into a house to steal

household *noun* the people who live together in a house

householder *noun* someone who owns or pays the rent of a house

a household name or **a household word** a person or thing that is well known and often mentioned by people

housekeeper *noun* someone employed to look after the running of a house

house-proud *adjective* proud of keeping your house clean and tidy

house-trained *adjective* of a pet: trained to go outdoors to pass urine and faeces

housewarming *noun* a party held when someone moves into a new house

housewife *noun* a woman who looks after a house and her family

housing *noun* 1 accommodation, *eg* houses, flats *etc* 2 a casing for a machine *etc*

hovel *noun* a small squalid dwelling

hover *verb* 1 to stay in the air in the same spot 2 to stay near, linger (about) 3 to be undecided or uncertain

hovercraft *noun* a craft able to travel over land or sea supported on a cushion of air

how *adverb* 1 in what manner: *how are they getting there?* 2 to what extent: *how old are you?/ how cold is it outside?* 3 to a great extent: *how young he seems/ how well you play* 4 by what means: *how do you switch this on?* 5 in what condition: *how is she?*

however *adverb* 1 no matter how 2 in spite of that

howk *verb, Scottish* to dig out

howl *verb* 1 to make a long, loud sound like that of a dog or wolf 2 to yell in pain, anger *etc* 3 to laugh loudly □ *noun* a howling sound

howler *noun, informal* a ridiculous mistake

HP or **hp** *abbreviation* 1 hire-purchase 2 horsepower

HQ *abbreviation* headquarters

hub *noun* 1 the centre part of a wheel through which the axle passes 2 a thriving centre of anything: *the hub of the entertainment industry*

hubbub *noun* a confused sound of many voices

Originally meaning 'battle' or 'war cry', based on an Irish Gaelic word

huddle *verb* to crowd together □ *noun* a close group

hue *noun* colour, shade

hue and cry a commotion, a fuss

huff *noun* a fit of bad temper and sulking

huffy *adjective* inclined to sulk; peevish

hug *verb* 1 to hold tightly with the arms 2 to keep close to: *hugging the kerb* □ *noun* a tight embrace

hug *verb* ⇨ hug**s**, hug**ging**, hug**ged**

huge *adjective* extremely big

hula-hoop *noun* a light hoop for spinning round the waist

hulk *noun* 1 an old ship unfit for use 2 something big and clumsy

hulking *adjective* big and clumsy

hull *noun* the body or framework of a ship

hullabaloo *noun* a noisy disturbance

hullo *another spelling of* **hello**

hum *verb* 1 to make a buzzing sound like that of bees 2 to sing with the lips shut 3 of a place: to be noisily busy □ *noun* 1 the noise of bees 2 any buzzing, droning sound

hum *verb* ⇨ hum**s**, hum**ming**, hum**med**

human *adjective* 1 relating to people as opposed to animals or gods 2 having natural qualities, feelings *etc* □ *noun* a man, woman or child

humane *adjective* kind, showing mercy, gentle □ **humanely** *adverb*

humanism *noun* a set of ideas about or interest in ethics and mankind, not including religious belief □ **humanist** *noun*

humanitarian *adjective* kind to fellow human beings

humanity *noun* 1 people in general 2 kindness, gentleness

humble *adjective* 1 modest, meek 2 not of high rank, unimportant □ *verb* to make to feel low and unimportant □ **eat humble pie** to admit a mistake openly

■ **Alternative words**: (verb) abase

humbug *noun* **1** nonsense, rubbish **2** a kind of hard minty sweet

humdrum *adjective* dull, not exciting

humdudgeon *noun, Scottish* an unnecessary fuss

humid *adjective* of air *etc*: moist, damp

humidifier *noun* a device which controls the amount of humidity in the air

humidity *noun* dampness

humiliate *noun* make to feel humble or ashamed, hurt someone's pride □ **humiliating** *adjective* □ **humiliation** *noun*

humility *noun* humble state of mind, meekness

humming-bird *noun* a small brightly-coloured bird which beats its wings rapidly making a humming noise

humongous or **humungous** *adjective, informal* enormous, huge

humorist *noun* a comedian, a comic writer

humorous *adjective* funny, amusing

humour or *US* **humor** *noun* **1** the ability to see things as amusing or ridiculous **2** funniness; the amusing side of anything: *failed to see the humour of the situation* **3** state of mind; temper, mood □ *verb* to do as someone else wishes in order to please them

hump *noun* **1** a lump, a mound **2** a lump on the back

humpback *noun* **1** a back with a hump **2** someone with a hump on their back

humpbacked *adjective* **1** with a hump on the back **2** of a bridge: rising and falling so as to form a hump shape

humungous *another spelling* of **humongous**

humus (*pronounced* **hyoom**-*u*s) *noun* soil made of rotted leaves *etc*

hunch *noun* (*plural* **hunches**) a suspicion that something is untrue or is going to happen *etc* □ *verb* to draw (your shoulders) up towards your ears and forward towards your chest, giving

your body a rounded, stooping appearance

hunchback *noun* humpback

hunchbacked *adjective* humpbacked

hundred *noun* the number 100 □ *adjective* 100 in number

hundredth *adjective* the last of a hundred (things *etc*) □ *noun* one of a hundred equal parts

hundredweight *noun* 112 lb, 50.8 kilogrammes (often written **cwt**)

hunger *noun* **1** a desire for food **2** a strong desire for anything □ *verb* **1** to go without food **2** to long (for)

hunger-strike *noun* a refusal to eat as a protest

hungover *adjective* suffering from a hangover

hungry *adjective* wanting or needing food □ **hungrily** *adverb*

hunk *noun, informal* a muscular, sexually attractive man

hunker *verb*: **hunker down** to squat

hunt *verb* **1** to chase animals or birds for food or sport **2** to search (for) □ *noun* **1** chasing wild animals **2** a search

huntsman *noun* a man who hunts

huntswoman *noun* a woman who hunts

hurdle *noun* **1** a light frame to be jumped over in a race **2** a difficulty which must be overcome

hurdygurdy *noun* a barrel organ

hurl *verb* to throw with force

hurlyburly *noun* a great stir, uproar

hurrah or **hurray** *exclamation* a shout of joy, approval *etc*

hurricane *noun* a violent storm of wind blowing at a speed of over 75 miles (120 kilometres) per hour

hurricane lamp a lamp specially made to keep alight in strong wind

hurried *adjective* done in a hurry □ **hurriedly** *adverb*

hurry *verb* **1** to act or move quickly **2** to make (someone) act quickly □ *noun* eagerness to act quickly, haste

hurry *verb* ⇨ **hurries, hurrying, hurried**

hurt *verb* **1** to cause pain or distress to **2** to injure physically, wound **3** to damage, spoil □ *noun* **1** pain, distress **2** damage

■ **Alternative words**: (verb, meaning 1) ache, upset, afflict, offend, annoy; (verb, meaning 2) wound, maim

hurtful *adjective* causing pain, distress or damage

hurtle *verb* to rush at great speed

husband *noun* a married man (the partner of a **wife**) □ *verb* to spend or use (*eg* money, strength) carefully

husbandry *noun* **1** farming **2** management **3** care with money, thrift

hush *exclamation* be quiet! □ *noun*, *informal* silence, quiet □ *verb* to make quiet □ **hush up** to stop (a scandal *etc*) becoming public

hush-hush *adjective*, *informal* top secret

husk *noun* the dry thin covering of certain fruits and seeds

husky[1] *adjective* **1** of a voice: deep and rough **2** big and strong □ **huskily** *adverb* (meaning 1)

husky[2] *noun* (*plural* **huskies**) a Canadian sledge-dog

hussar (*pronounced* hu-**zahr**) *noun* a light-armed horse soldier

hussy *noun* (*plural* **hussies**) a forward, cheeky girl

hustings *noun plural* political campaigning just before an election

hustle *verb* **1** to push rudely **2** to hurry

hut *noun* a small wooden building

hutch *noun* (*plural* **hutches**) a box in which pet rabbits are housed

hyacinth *noun* a sweet-smelling flower which grows from a bulb

hyaena *another spelling of* **hyena**

hybrid *noun* **1** an animal or plant bred from two different kinds, *eg* a mule, which is a hybrid from a horse and an ass **2** a word formed of parts from different languages

hydra *noun* **1** a mythological many-headed snake that grew two heads for each one cut off **2** a sea creature that can divide and redivide itself

hydrant *noun* a connection to which a hose can be attached to draw water off the main water supply

hydraulic *adjective* **1** carrying water **2** worked by water or other fluid

hydro *noun* (*plural* **hydros**) a hotel with a swimming pool and gymnasium *etc*

hydro- or **hydr-** *prefix* water: *hydroelectricity/ hydraulic*
Ⓞ Comes from Greek *hydor* meaning 'water'

hydroelectricity *noun* electricity obtained from water-power □ **hydroelectric** *adjective*

hydrogen *noun* the lightest gas, which with oxygen makes up water

hydrogen bomb an extremely powerful bomb using hydrogen

hydrophobia *noun* **1** a fear of water, a symptom of rabies **2** rabies □ **hydrophobic** *adjective*

hyena or **hyaena** *noun* a dog-like wild animal with a howl sounding like laughter

hygiene (*pronounced* **hai**-jeen) *noun* the maintaining of cleanliness as a means to health □ **hygienic** *adjective*

hymn *noun* a religious song of praise

hymnal or **hymnary** (*plural* **hymnaries**) *noun* a book of hymns

hype (*pronounced* haip) *noun*, *informal* extravagant advertisement or publicity □ *verb* to promote extravagantly

hyper- *prefix* to a greater extent than usual, excessive: *hypersensitive*
Ⓞ Comes from Greek *hyper* meaning 'over'

hyperbole (*pronounced* hai-**perb**-*o*-li) *noun* exaggeration □ **hyperbolical** *adjective*

hypermarket *noun* a large self-service store stocking a wide range of goods

hypernym *noun* a general word whose meaning contains several specific words, *eg dance* is a hypernym of *waltz* and *reel* (*contrasted with*: **hyponym**)

hypertension *noun* high blood pressure

hypertext *noun* electronic text containing cross-references which can be accessed by keystrokes *etc*

hyphen *noun* a short stroke (-) used to link or separate parts of a word or phrase: *touch-and-go/ re-elect*

hypnosis *noun* **1** a sleep-like state in which suggestions are obeyed **2** hypnotism

hypnotic *adjective* **1** of hypnosis or hypnotism **2** causing a sleep-like state

hypnotism *noun* the putting of someone into hypnosis □ **hypnotist** *noun*

hypnotize *verb* to put someone into hypnosis

hypo- *prefix* below, under: *hypodermic/ hypothermia*
🕐 Comes from Greek *hypo* meaning 'under'

hypoallergenic *adjective* specially formulated in order to reduce the risk of allergy

hypochondria *noun* over-anxiety about your own health

hypochondriac *noun* someone who is over-anxious about their health, and who is inclined to think they are ill when they are perfectly healthy □ *adjective* relating to or affected with hypochondria

hypocorism (*pronounced* hai-**pok**-*o*-rizm) *noun* a pet-name □ **hypocoristic** *adjective*

hypocrite (*pronounced* **hip**-*o*-krit) *noun* someone who pretends to be something they are not, or to believe something they do not □ **hypocrisy** *noun* □ **hypocritical** *adjective*

hypodermic *adjective* used for injecting drugs just below the skin:

hypodermic syringe/ hypodermic needle □ *noun* a hypodermic syringe

hypoglycaemia or **hypoglycemia** (*both pronounced* hai-po-gli-**seem**-i-*a*) *noun* an abnormally low amount of sugar in the blood □ **hypoglycaemic** or **hypoglycemic** *adjective*

hyponym *noun* one of a group of words whose meanings are included in a more general term, *eg guitar* and *piano* are hyponyms of *musical instrument* (*contrasted with*: **hypernym**)

hypostyle *adjective* of a roof: supported by pillars

hypotenuse (*pronounced* hai-**pot**-*e*-nyooz) *noun* the longest side of a right-angled triangle

hypothermia *noun* an abnormally low body temperature caused by exposure to cold

hypothesis (*pronounced* hai-**poth**-*e*-sis) *noun* (*plural* **hypotheses**) something taken as true for the sake of argument

hypothetical *adjective* supposed, based on an idea or a possibility rather than on facts

hysterectomy *noun* (*plural* **hysterectomies**) surgical removal of the womb

hysteria *noun* **1** a nervous excitement causing uncontrollable laughter, crying *etc* **2** a nervous illness

Based on a Greek word for 'womb', because originally thought to be caused by womb disease or abnormalities

hysterical *adjective* **1** suffering from a severe emotional disturbance, often as a result of shock **2** wild with panic, excitement or anger **3** very funny □ **hysterically** *adverb*

hysterics *noun plural* a fit of hysteria □ **in hysterics** laughing uncontrollably

I *pronoun* the word used by a speaker or writer in mentioning themselves (as the subject of a verb): *you and I/ I, myself*

ibex *noun* (*plural* **ibexes**) a wild mountain goat

ibid *adverb* in the same book, article *etc*

ice *noun* **1** frozen water **2** ice-cream □ *verb* **1** to cover with icing **2** to freeze

ice age an age when the earth was mostly covered with ice

iceberg *noun* a huge mass of floating ice

icebox *noun*, *US* refrigerator

ice-cap *noun* a permanent covering of ice, as at the north and south poles

ice-cream *noun* a sweet creamy mixture, flavoured and frozen

ice floe a piece of floating ice

ice hockey hockey played with a rubber disc (called a **puck**) on an ice rink

ice-skate *noun* a skate for moving on ice

ice-skating *noun* the sport of moving about on ice wearing ice-skates

icicle *noun* a hanging, pointed piece of ice formed by the freezing of dropping water

icing *noun* powdered sugar, mixed with water or egg-white, spread on cakes or biscuits □ **icing on the cake** an unnecessary extra detail, added to something which is already satisfactory

icky *adjective*, *informal* disgusting, repulsive

icon *noun* **1** a painted or mosaic image

of Christ or a saint (*also* **ikon**) **2** *computing* a small graphic image which is clicked to access a particular program

icy *adjective* **1** covered with ice **2** very cold **3** unfriendly □ **icily** *adverb*

ID *abbreviation* identification □ *noun*, *US* a means of identification, *eg* a driving licence

I'd *short for* I would, I should or I had: *I'd sooner go than stay*

id *noun* the unconscious part of the personality, the source of instincts and dreams

idea *noun* **1** a thought, a notion **2** a plan

ideal *adjective* **1** perfect **2** existing in imagination only (*contrasted with*: **real**) □ *noun* the highest and best; a standard of perfection

idealism *noun* the belief that perfection can be reached

idealist *noun* someone who thinks that perfection can be reached □ **idealistic** *adjective*

idealize *verb* to think of as perfect □ **idealization** *noun*

ideally *adverb* in ideal circumstances: *ideally all children should have a place in nursery school*

identical *adjective* the same in all details □ **identically** *adverb*

identification *noun* **1** an official document, such as a passport or driving licence, that proves who you are **2** the process of finding out who someone is or what something is

identify *verb* to claim to recognize, prove to be the same: *he identified the man as his attacker* □ **identify with 1** to feel close to or involved with **2** to think of as the same, equate: *identifying money with happiness*

> **identify** ⇨ identif*ies*, identify*ing*, identifi*ed*

Identikit (picture) *trademark* a rough picture of a wanted person which police put together from descriptions

identity *noun* (*plural* **identities**) **1** who or what someone or something is **2** the state of being the same

ideological *adjective* **1** of or relating to an ideology **2** resulting from a clash between different ideologies

ideology *noun* (*plural* **ideologies**) a set of ideas, often political or philosophical

idiocy (from **idiot**) *noun* feeble-mindedness, foolishness

idiom *noun* a common expression whose meaning cannot be guessed from the individual words, *eg* 'I'm feeling *under the weather*' □ **idiomatic** *adjective* □ **idiomatically** *adverb*

idiosyncrasy *noun* (*plural* **idiosyncrasies**) a personal oddness of behaviour □ **idiosyncratic** *adjective*

idiot *noun* a feeble-minded person; a fool

idiotic *adjective* extremely foolish, ridiculous □ **idiotically** *adverb*

idle *adjective* **1** not working **2** lazy **3** meaningless, without a useful purpose: *idle chatter* □ *verb* **1** to spend time in doing nothing **2** of an engine: to run without doing any work □ **idly** *adverb* (adjective, meanings 2 and 3)

idler *noun* a person who wastes time or is reluctant to work

idol *noun* **1** an image worshipped as a god **2** someone much loved or honoured

idolatry *noun* **1** the worship of an image as if it were a god **2** the excessive loving or honouring of someone or something □ **idolatrous** *adjective*

idolize *verb* to adore, worship

idyll *noun* **1** a poem on a pastoral theme **2** a time of pleasure and contentment

idyllic *adjective* very happy and content, blissful

ie *abbreviation* that is, that means (from Latin *id est*)

if *conjunction* **1** on condition that, supposing that: *If you go, I'll go* **2** whether: *do you know if she'll be there?*

iffy *adjective*, *informal* dubious, uncertain

ig- *see* **in-**

igloo *noun* an Inuit snow hut

igneous *adjective* **1** relating to fire **2** of rock: formed by the action of great heat within the earth

ignite *verb* **1** to set on fire **2** to catch fire

ignition *noun* **1** the act of setting on fire or catching fire **2** the sparking part of a motor engine

ignoble *adjective* dishonourable; of low birth

ignominious *adjective* bringing disgrace or dishonour

ignominy (*pronounced* ig-nom-in-i) *noun* disgrace, dishonour

ignoramus (*pronounced* ig-no-**rei**-mus) *noun* an ignorant person

ignorant *adjective* knowing very little □ **ignorant of** unaware of □ **ignorance** *noun*

ignore *verb* to take no notice of

iguana (*pronounced* ig-**wah**-na) *noun* a type of tree lizard

ikon *another spelling of* **icon**

il- *see* **in-**

I'll *short for* I shall, I will

ill *adjective* **1** unwell, sick **2** evil, bad **3** unlucky □ *adverb* badly □ *noun* **1** evil **2** **ills** misfortunes, troubles

■ **Alternative words**: (adjective, meaning 1) indisposed, ailing, infirm, seedy

ill-at-ease *adjective* uncomfortable

illegal *adjective* against the law □ **illegality** *noun* (*plural* **illegalities**)

illegible *adjective* impossible to read, indistinct □ **illegibility** *noun* □ **illegibly** *adverb*

illegitimate *adjective* born of parents not married to each other

ill-feeling *noun* dislike, resentment

ill-gotten *adjective* got in a dishonest or unethical way

ill-humoured *adjective* bad-tempered

illicit *adjective* unlawful, forbidden
- Comes from Latin *il-* meaning 'not', and *licitus* meaning 'allowed'

  ● Do not confuse with: **elicit**

illiterate *adjective* not able to read or write □ **illiteracy** *noun*

ill-natured *adjective* bad-tempered

illness *noun* disease, sickness

illogical *adjective* not logical, not showing sound reasoning □ **illogicality** *noun* □ **illogically** *adverb*

ill-starred *adjective* unlucky

ill-treat *verb* to treat badly

illuminate *verb* **1** to light up **2** to make more clear

illuminated *adjective* of a manuscript: decorated with ornamental lettering

illuminations *noun plural* a decorative display of lights

ill-use *verb* to treat badly

illusion *noun* **1** something which deceives the mind or eye **2** a mistaken belief
- Comes from Latin *illudere* meaning 'to make sport of'

  ● Do not confuse with: **allusion** and **delusion**

illusive *adjective* misleading, deceptive

  ● Do not confuse with: **allusive** and **elusive**. Illusive is related to the noun **illusion**.

illusory *adjective* mistaken or untrue, despite seeming believable

illustrate *verb* **1** to draw pictures for (a book *etc*) **2** to explain, show by example □ **illustrative** *adjective*

illustration *noun* **1** a picture in a book *etc* **2** an example which illustrates

illustrator *noun* someone who illustrates books *etc*

illustrious *adjective* famous, distinguished

ill-will *noun* dislike, resentment

I'm *short for* I am

im- *see* **in-**

image *noun* **1** a likeness made of someone or something **2** a striking likeness: *she is the image of her mother* **3** a picture in the mind **4** public reputation

imagery *noun* words that suggest images, used to make a piece of writing more vivid

imaginary *adjective* existing only in the imagination, not real
- Comes from Latin word-beginning *imagin-*, a form of the word for 'image', and Latin word-ending *-arius* meaning 'connected with'

  ● Do not confuse with: **imaginative**

imagination *noun* the power of forming pictures in the mind of things not present or experienced

imaginative *adjective* **1** having a lively imagination **2** done with imagination: *an imaginative piece of writing*
- Comes from Latin word-beginning *imaginat-*, a form of a verb meaning 'to imagine', and French word-ending *-ive* meaning 'tending to'

  ● Do not confuse with: **imaginary**

imagine *verb* **1** to form a picture in the mind, especially of something that does not exist **2** to think, suppose

imam *noun* **1** the priest who leads the prayers in a mosque **2 Imam** an Islamic leader

imbecile *noun* a feeble-minded person; a fool

imbecility *noun* feeble-mindedness, stupidity

imbibe *verb* to drink (in)

imbue *verb* to fill or affect (with): *imbued her staff with enthusiasm*

imitate *verb* to try to be the same as, copy

imitation *noun* a copy □ *adjective* made to look like: *imitation leather*

imitator *noun* someone who copies, or tries to do the same things as, someone else

immaculate *adjective* spotless; very

clean and neat □ **immaculately** *adverb*

immaterial *adjective* of little importance

immature *adjective* not mature □ **immaturity** *noun*

immediacy *noun* of paintings, photographs, writing *etc*: a striking quality, giving the observer a strong sense of involvement

immediate *adjective* 1 happening straight away: *immediate reaction* 2 close: *immediate family* 3 direct: *my immediate successor*

immediately *adverb* without delay

immemorial *adjective* going further back in time than can be remembered

immense *adjective* very large □ **immensity** *noun*

immensely *adverb* greatly

immerse *verb* to plunge something into liquid so that it is completely covered □ **immerse yourself in** to give your whole attention to

immersion *noun* 1 the plunging of something into liquid so that it is completely covered 2 deep involvement in a certain subject or situation □ **immersion heater** an electric water-heater inside a hot-water tank

immigrant *noun* someone who immigrates

immigrate *verb* to come into a country and settle there □ **immigration** *noun*
Ⓒ Comes from Latin *in* meaning 'into', and *migrare* meaning 'to remove'
🖝 Do not confuse with: **emigrate**. You **IM**migrate to a new country where you plan to start living (the IM comes from the Latin meaning 'into'). You are **E**migrating when you leave your original or home country (the E comes from the Latin meaning 'from')

imminent *adjective* about to happen: *imminent danger*
Ⓒ Comes from Latin *imminens* meaning 'overhanging'
🖝 Do not confuse with: **eminent**

immobile *adjective* 1 without moving 2 not easily moved □ **immobility** *noun*

immobilize *verb* to put out of action

immoral *adjective* 1 wrong, unscrupulous 2 sexually improper □ **immorally** *adverb* □ **immorality** *noun*
Ⓒ Comes from prefix *im-* meaning 'not', and Latin *moralis* meaning 'moral'

🖝 Do not confuse with: **amoral**. An **immoral** person behaves badly in the full knowledge that what they are doing is wrong. An **amoral** person behaves badly because they do not understand the difference between right and wrong

immortal *adjective* 1 living forever 2 famous forever

immortality *noun* unending life or fame

immortalize *verb* to make immortal or famous forever

immovable *adjective* not able to be moved or changed □ **immovably** *adverb*

immune *adjective* 1 not likely to catch a particular disease: *immune to measles* 2 not able to be affected by: *she is immune to his charm* □ **immunity** *noun*

immune system the natural defensive system of an organism that identifies and neutralizes harmful matter within itself

immunize *verb* to make someone immune to (a disease), especially by inoculation

immunodeficiency *noun* weakened ability to produce antibodies

immunology *noun* the study of the human immune system

imp *noun* 1 a small malignant spirit 2 a mischievous child □ **impish** *adjective*

impact *noun* (*pronounced* im-pakt) 1 the blow of one thing striking another; a collision 2 strong effect: *made an impact on the audience* □ *verb* (*pronounced* im-pakt or im-**pakt**) to press firmly together □ **impact on** to affect strongly

impair *verb* to damage, weaken □ **impairment** *noun*

impala *noun* a large African antelope

impale *verb* to pierce through with a spear *etc*

impart verb to tell (information, news etc) to others

impartial adjective not favouring one side over another; unbiased □ **impartiality** noun □ **impartially** adverb

impassable adjective of a road: not able to be driven through

impasse (pronounced **am**-pas) noun a situation from which there seems to be no way out

impassioned adjective moved by strong feeling

impassive adjective not easily moved by strong feeling □ **impassively** adverb

impatient adjective 1 restlessly eager 2 irritable, short-tempered □ **impatience** noun □ **impatiently** adverb

impeach verb to accuse publicly of, or charge with, misconduct □ **impeachment** noun

impeccable adjective faultless, perfect □ **impeccably** adverb

impede verb to hinder, keep back

impediment noun 1 a hindrance 2 a speech defect, eg a stutter or stammer

impel verb 1 to urge 2 to drive on

impel ⇨ impel**s**, impell**ing**, impell**ed**

impending adjective about to happen: an impending storm

impenetrable adjective 1 not allowing light etc through 2 incomprehensible, inscrutable

impenitent adjective not sorry for wrongdoing, unrepentant

imperative adjective 1 necessary, urgent 2 grammar expressing command, eg look! or read this

imperceptible adjective so small as not to be noticed

imperfect adjective having a fault or flaw, not perfect □ noun, grammar the **imperfect** the tense used to describe continuing or incomplete actions or states in the past: The sun was shining and the birds were singing

imperfection noun a fault or a flaw

imperfectly adverb not perfectly or thoroughly

imperial adjective 1 of an emperor or empire 2 commanding, superior

imperialism noun the policy of annexing the territory of, and ruling, other nations and people □ **imperialist** adjective: imperialist policies

imperious adjective having an air of authority, haughty

impermanence noun lack of permanence, transitoriness □ **impermanent** adjective

impermeable adjective not able to be passed through: impermeable by water

impersonal adjective 1 not influenced by personal feelings 2 not connected with any person □ **impersonally** adverb

impersonate verb to dress up as, or act the part of, someone □ **impersonation** noun

impersonator noun someone who impersonates others

impertinent adjective 1 cheeky, impudent 2 old not pertinent, irrelevant □ **impertinence** noun (meaning 1) □ **impertinently** adverb (meaning 1)

imperturbable adjective not easily worried, calm □ **imperturbably** adverb

impervious to not able to be affected by: impervious to suggestions

impetuous adjective rushing into action, rash □ **impetuosity** noun

impetus (pronounced **im**-pet-us) noun 1 moving force, motivation 2 impulse

impiety noun lack of respect for holy things

impinge verb: **impinge on** or **impinge upon** 1 to come in contact with 2 to trespass on, interfere with

impious (from **impiety**, pronounced im-pi-us) adjective lacking the proper respect, especially for holy things

implacable adjective not able to be soothed or calmed □ **implacably** adverb

implant verb (pronounced im-**plant**) to fix in, plant firmly □ noun (pronounced **im**-plant) an artificial organ, graft etc inserted into the body

implement noun a tool □ verb to carry out, fulfil (eg a promise) □ **implementation** noun

implicate verb to bring in, involve: the

statement implicates you in the crime

implication *noun* something meant though not actually said

implicit *adjective* **1** understood, meant though not actually said **2** unquestioning: *implicit obedience*

implicitly *adverb* without questioning or doubting: *trust someone implicitly*

implode *verb* to collapse inwards suddenly □ **implosion** *noun*

implore *verb* to beg, entreat

imply *verb* to suggest: *her silence implies disapproval*
ⓘ Comes from Latin *implicare* meaning 'to involve'

●ᵉ Do not confuse with: **infer**. **Implying** is an action of expression – you **imply** something by dropping subtle hints about it. **Inferring** is an action of understanding – you **infer** something by drawing conclusions from what you have seen or heard

impolite *adjective* not polite, rude

imponderable *adjective* not able to be judged or evaluated

import *verb* (*pronounced* im-**poht** or im-poht) to bring in (goods) from abroad for sale □ *noun* (*pronounced* **im**-poht) **1** the act of importing **2** goods imported **3** meaning, significance □ **importation** *noun*

important *adjective* worthy of attention; special □ **importance** *noun* □ **importantly** *adverb*
ⓘ Comes from Latin *importare* meaning 'to bring in'

Alternative words: momentous, salient, seminal, leading, influential, eminent, prominent

importune *verb*: **importune someone** to keep asking them for something which they are unwilling to give

impose *verb* **1** to place (a tax *etc*) on **2 impose on** to take advantage of, inconvenience

imposing *adjective* impressive, commanding attention

imposition *noun* a burden, an inconvenience

impossible *adjective* **1** not able to be done or to happen **2** extremely difficult to deal with, intolerable □ **impossibility** *noun* (meaning 1) □ **impossibly** *adverb*

Alternative words: (adjective, meaning 1) hopeless, impracticable, infeasible, inconceivable, preposterous

impostor *noun* someone who pretends to be someone else in order to deceive

imposture *noun* deceit consisting of pretending to be someone else

impotent (*pronounced* **im**-pot-ent) *adjective* without power or effectiveness □ **impotence** *noun* □ **impotently** *adverb*

impound *verb* to seize possession of (something) by law

impoverish *verb* **1** to make financially poor **2** to lessen in quality: *an impoverished culture* □ **impoverishment** *noun*

impracticable *adjective* not able to be done □ **impracticability** *noun*
ⓘ Comes from prefix *im-* meaning 'not', and *practicable*

●ᵉ Do not confuse: **impracticable** and **impractical**

impractical *adjective* lacking common sense □ **impracticality** *noun*
ⓘ Comes from prefix *im-* meaning 'not', and *practical*

imprecise *adjective* not precise, vague

impregnable *adjective* too strong to be taken by attack

impregnate *verb* **1** to make pregnant **2** to saturate: *impregnated with perfume*

impresario *noun* (*plural* **impresarios**) the organizer of an entertainment

impress *verb* **1** to arouse the interest or admiration of **2** to mark by pressing upon **3** to fix deeply in the mind

impression *noun* **1** someone's thoughts or feelings about something: *my impression is that it's likely to rain* **2** a deep or strong effect: *the film left a lasting impression on me* **3** a mark made by impressing **4** a quantity of copies of a book printed at one time

impressionable *adjective* easily influenced or affected

impressionism *noun* an artistic or literary style aiming to reproduce personal impressions of things or events

impressionist *noun* **1** a follower of impressionism **2** an entertainer who impersonates people

impressive *adjective* having a strong effect on the mind

imprint *verb* (*pronounced* im-**print**) **1** to stamp, press **2** to fix in the mind □ *noun* (*pronounced* **im**-print) **1** the printer's or publisher's name *etc* on a book **2** a common title for a series of related books from one publisher

imprison *verb* to shut up as in a prison □ **imprisonment** *noun*

improbable *adjective* not likely to happen □ **improbability** *noun*

impromptu *adjective* & *adverb* without preparation or rehearsal

improper *adjective* **1** not suitable; wrong **2** indecent

improper fraction a fraction greater than 1 (as $\frac{5}{4}$, $\frac{11}{8}$)

impropriety *noun* (*plural* **improprieties**) something improper

improve *verb* to make or become better □ **improvement** *noun*

■ **Alternative words:** ameliorate, enhance, recuperate

improvident *adjective* giving no thought to future needs □ **improvidence** *noun*

improvise *verb* **1** to put together from available materials: *we improvised a stretcher* **2** to create (a tune, script *etc*) spontaneously: *the actors had to improvise their lines* □ **improvisation** *noun*

impudent *adjective* cheeky, insolent □ **impudence** *noun* □ **impudently** *adverb*

impulse *noun* **1** a sudden force or push **2** a sudden urge resulting in sudden action

impulsive *adjective* acting on impulse, without taking time to consider □ **impulsively** *adverb*

impunity *noun* freedom from punishment, injury or loss

impure *adjective* mixed with other substances; not clean

impurity *noun* (*plural* **impurities**) **1** a small amount of something which is present in, and spoils the quality of, another substance **2** the state of being impure

imputation *noun* suggestion of fault; blame

impute *verb* to think of as being caused, done *etc* by someone: *imputing the blame to others*

in *preposition* **1** showing position in space or time: *sitting in the garden/ born in the 60s* **2** showing state, manner *etc*: *in part/ in cold blood* □ *adverb* **1** towards the inside, not out **2** in power **3** *informal* in fashion □ *adjective* **1** that is in, inside or coming in **2** *informal* fashionable □ **be in for 1** to be trying to get (a prize *etc*) **2** to be about to receive (trouble, punishment)

in- *prefix* **1** (also **il-**, **im-**, **ir-**, **em-**, **en-**) into, on, towards: *inshore/ illusion/ impulse/ embrace* (= to take in the arms)/ *endure* **2** (also **il-**, **im-**, **ir-**) not: *inaccurate/ ignoble* (= not noble)/ *illiterate/ improper/ irregular* (= not regular)

inability *noun* (*plural* **inabilities**) lack of power, means *etc* (to do something)

inaccessible *adjective* not able to be easily reached or obtained

inaccurate *adjective* **1** not correct **2** not exact □ **inaccuracy** *noun* (*plural* **inaccuracies**)

inaction *noun* lack of action

inactive *adjective* **1** not active **2** not working, doing nothing

inactivity *noun* idleness; rest

inadequate *adjective* **1** not enough **2** unable to cope with a situation

inadmissible *adjective* not allowable: *inadmissible evidence*

inadvertent *adjective* unintentional

inadvisable *adjective* not advisable, unwise

inalienable *adjective* not able to be removed or transferred: *inalienable rights*

inalterable *adjective* not able to be altered

inane *adjective* silly, foolish, mindless

inanimate *adjective* without life

inanity *noun* (*plural* **inanities**) 1 an empty, meaningless remark 2 silliness, foolishness, mindlessness

inapplicable *adjective* not applicable

inappropriate *adjective* not suitable

inapt *adjective* unsuitable, unfit
ⓘ Comes from prefix *in-* meaning 'not', + *apt*

📌 Do not confuse with: **inept**

inaptitude or **inaptness** *noun* unfitness, awkwardness

inarticulate *adjective* 1 unable to express yourself clearly 2 said indistinctly

inasmuch as *conjunction* because, since

inattentive *adjective* not paying attention □ **inattention** *noun*

inaudible *adjective* not loud enough to be heard

inaugural *adjective* relating to, or performed at, an inauguration

inaugurate *verb* to mark the beginning of (*eg* a presidency) with a ceremony

inauguration *noun* the ceremony to mark the beginning of something (*eg* a presidency)

inauspicious *adjective* unlucky, unlikely to end in success

inborn *adjective* innate, natural: *inborn talent*

inbred *adjective* 1 inborn 2 resulting from inbreeding

inbreeding *noun* repeated mating and producing of offspring within the same family

inc *abbreviation* 1 incorporated 2 inclusive 3 including

Inca *noun* a member of a complex pre-Columbian civilization in Peru □ **Incan** *adjective*

incalculable *adjective* not able to be counted or estimated

incandescent *adjective* white-hot

incantation *noun* a spell

incapable *adjective* 1 unable (to do what is expected) 2 helpless (through drink *etc*)

incapacitate *verb* 1 to take away power, strength or rights 2 to disable

incapacity *noun* 1 inability 2 disability

incarcerate *verb* to imprison □ **incarceration** *noun*

incarnate *adjective* having human form

incarnation *noun* 1 a person whose appearance or behaviour are the perfect example of a particular quality *eg* beauty or honour 2 of a spirit: appearance in a physical form

incendiary *adjective* meant for setting (buildings *etc*) on fire: *an incendiary bomb*

incense *verb* (*pronounced* in-**sens**) to make angry □ *noun* (*pronounced* **in**-sens) a mixture of resins, gums *etc* burned to give off fumes, especially in religious ceremonies

incentive *noun* something which encourages someone to do something

inception *noun* beginning

incessant *adjective* going on without pause

incest *noun* illegal sexual intercourse between close relatives

incestuous *adjective* 1 involving incest 2 done within a closely-knit group

inch *noun* (*plural* **inches**) one twelfth of a foot (about 2.5 centimetres) □ *verb* to move very gradually

incidence *noun* 1 the frequency of something occurring 2 a falling of a ray of light *etc*

incident *noun* a happening

incidental *adjective* 1 happening in connection with something: *an incidental expense* 2 casual

incidentally *adverb* by the way

incinerate *verb* to burn to ashes □ **incineration** *noun*

incinerator *noun* an apparatus for burning rubbish *etc*

incipient *adjective* beginning to exist: *an incipient dislike*

incise *verb* to cut into, engrave

incision *noun* 1 cutting into something 2 a cut, a gash

incisive *adjective* sharp, clear, firm

incisor *noun* a front tooth

incite *verb* to move to action; urge on □ **incitement** *noun*

incivility *noun* (*plural* **incivilities**) impoliteness

inclement *adjective* of weather: stormy □ **inclemency** *noun*

inclination *noun* 1 liking, tendency 2 a slope, an angle

incline *verb* (*pronounced* in-**klain**) 1 to lean, slope (towards) 2 to bend, bow 3 to have a liking for □ *noun* (*pronounced* **in**-klain) a slope

inclined *adjective* 1 talented or gifted 2 **inclined to** having a tendency, or a hesitant desire to

include *verb* to count in, along with others

inclusion *noun* the act of including something, or the fact that it is included

inclusive *adjective* including everything mentioned: *from Tuesday to Thursday inclusive is 3 days*

incognito (*pronounced* in-cog-**neet**-oh) *adjective & adverb* in disguise, with identity concealed □ *noun* (*plural* **incognitos**) a disguise

incoherent *adjective* 1 unconnected, rambling 2 speaking in an unconnected, rambling way □ **incoherence** *noun*

incombustible *adjective* not able to be burned by fire

income *noun* 1 personal earnings 2 gain, profit

incoming *adjective* approaching, next

incomparable *adjective* without equal

incompatible *adjective* 1 of statements: contradicting each other 2 of people: not suited, bound to disagree □ **incompatibility** *noun*

incompetent *adjective* not good enough at doing a job □ **incompetence** *noun*

■ Opposite: able

incomplete *adjective* not finished

incomprehensible *adjective* not able to be understood, puzzling

incomprehension *noun* the state of not understanding something

inconceivable *adjective* not able to be imagined or believed

inconclusive *adjective* not leading to a definite decision or conclusion

incongruous *adjective* 1 not matching well 2 out of place, unsuitable □ **incongruity** (*plural* **incongruities**)

inconsequential *adjective* unimportant □ **inconsequence** *noun*

inconsiderable *adjective* slight, unimportant

inconsiderate *adjective* not thinking of others

inconsistent *adjective* not consistent, contradicting

inconsolable *adjective* not able to be comforted

inconspicuous *adjective* not noticeable

inconstant *adjective* often changing □ **inconstancy** *noun*

incontinent *adjective* 1 unable to control the bladder or bowels 2 uncontrolled, unrestrained □ **incontinence** *noun*

incontrovertible *adjective* not to be doubted

inconvenience *noun* minor trouble or difficulty: *I don't want you to go to any inconvenience on my behalf*

inconvenient *adjective* causing awkwardness or difficulty

incorporate *verb* 1 to contain as parts of a whole: *the new building incorporates a theatre, cinema and restaurant* 2 to include, take account of: *the new text incorporates the author's changes*

incorporated *adjective* (*short form* **inc**) formed into a company or society

incorrect *adjective* wrong

incorrigible *adjective* too bad to be put right or reformed

incorruptible *adjective* **1** not able to be bribed **2** not likely to decay

increase *verb* (*pronounced* in-**krees**) to grow, make greater or more numerous □ *noun* (*pronounced* **in**-krees) **1** growth **2** the amount added by growth

increasingly *adverb* more and more

incredible *adjective* impossible to believe □ **incredibility** *noun*
ⓘ Comes from Latin *incredibilis* meaning 'beyond belief'

> ☛ Do not confuse: **incredible** and **incredulous**. IncredIBLE means unbelievABLE. IncredULOUS means unbelievING. You might, for example, be **incredulous** at (= unable to believe) another person's **incredible** (= unbelievable) stupidity

incredibly *adverb* extremely, unbelievably

incredulity (*pronounced* in-kred-**yool**-it-i) *noun* disbelief

incredulous (*pronounced* in-**kred**-yul-us) *adjective* not believing what is said □ **incredulously** *adverb*
ⓘ Comes from Latin *incredulus* meaning 'unbelieving'

increment *noun* an annual increase in a salary

incriminate *verb* to show that (someone) has taken part in a crime

incubate *verb* to brood, hatch

incubation period the time that it takes for a disease to develop from infection to the first symptoms

incubator *noun* **1** a large heated box for hatching eggs **2** a hospital crib for rearing premature babies

incumbent *adjective* resting on (someone) as a duty: *it is incumbent upon me to warn you* □ *noun* someone who holds an official position

incur *verb* to bring (blame, debt *etc*) upon yourself

> **incur** ⇨ incur*s*, incur*ring*, incur*red*

incurable *adjective* unable to be cured

incurious *adjective* not curious, uninterested

incursion *noun* an invasion, a raid

indebted *adjective* having cause to be grateful: *we are indebted to you for your kindness*

indecent *adjective* offending against normal or usual standards of (especially sexual) behaviour □ **indecency** *noun*

■ **Alternative words**: obscene

indecent assault an assault involving indecency but not rape

indecipherable *adjective* **1** illegible **2** incomprehensible

indecision *noun* slowness in making up your mind, hesitation

indecisive *adjective* **1** not coming to a definite result **2** unable to make up your mind

indecorous *adjective* unseemly, inappropriate □ **indecorum** *noun*

indeed *adverb* **1** in fact: *she is indeed a splendid cook* **2** (used for emphasis) really: *did he indeed?* □ *exclamation* expressing surprise

indefatigable *adjective* untiring

indefensible *adjective* **1** unable to be defended **2** inexcusable

indefinable *adjective* not able to be stated or described clearly

indefinite *adjective* **1** not fixed, uncertain **2** without definite limits

indefinite article the name given to the adjectives *a* and *an*

indefinitely *adverb* for an indefinite period of time

indelible *adjective* unable to be rubbed out or removed

indelicate *adjective* impolite, rude □ **indelicacy** *noun*

indemnify *verb* **1** to compensate for loss **2** to exempt (from)

> **indemnify** ⇨ indemnif*ies*, indemnif*ying*, indemnif*ied*

indemnity *noun* **1** security from damage or loss **2** compensation for loss

indemonstrable *adjective* not proveable

indent *verb* 1 to begin a new paragraph by going in from the margin 2 **indent for** to apply for (stores, equipment *etc*)

indentation *noun* 1 a hollow, a dent 2 an inward curve in an outline, coastline *etc*

indenture *noun* a written agreement □ *verb* to bind by a written agreement

independent *adjective* 1 free to think or act for yourself 2 not relying on someone else for support, guidance *etc* 3 of a country: self-governing □ **independence** *noun*

indescribable *adjective* not able to be described

indestructible *adjective* not able to be destroyed

indetectable *adjective* not able to be detected

indeterminate *adjective* not fixed, indefinite

index *noun* (*plural* **indexes**) 1 an alphabetical list giving the page number of subjects mentioned in a book 2 an indication 3 (*plural* **indices**) *maths* an upper number which shows how many times a number is multiplied by itself (*eg* 4^3 means 4 x 4 x 4) 4 a numerical scale showing changes in the cost of living, wages *etc*

index-linked *adjective* of pensions *etc*: directly related to the cost-of-living index

Indian corn maize

Indian ink a very black ink used by artists

Indian summer a period of summer warmth in autumn

indiarubber *noun* a rubber eraser

indicate *verb* to point out, show

indication *noun* a sign

indicative *adjective* pointing out, being a sign of: *indicative of his attitude*

indicator *noun* 1 something which indicates; a pointer 2 a flashing light on either side of a vehicle for signalling to other drivers

indices *plural* of **index** (meaning 3)

indict (*pronounced* in-**dait**) *verb* to accuse formally of a crime

indictment (*pronounced* in-**dait**-ment) *noun* something which shows or proves how bad something else is

indie (*pronounced* **in**-di) *noun, informal* an independent record, film or television company □ *adjective* of a band: using an independent company to record their music

indifferent *adjective* 1 neither very good nor very bad 2 **indifferent to** showing no interest in □ **indifference** *noun* (meaning 2)

indigenous *adjective* native to a country or area

indigent *adjective* poor, impoverished □ **indigence** *noun*

indigestible *adjective* difficult to digest

indigestion *noun* discomfort or pain experienced in digesting food

indignant *adjective* angry, especially because of wrong done to yourself or others) □ **indignation** *noun*

indignity *noun* (*plural* **indignities**) 1 loss of dignity 2 insult

indigo *noun* a purplish-blue colour □ *adjective* purplish-blue

indirect *adjective* 1 not straight or direct 2 not affecting or affected directly

indirect speech speech reported not in the speaker's actual words, *eg they said **that they'd leave the next day*** (rather than: *they said, 'We'll leave tomorrow.'*) (*contrasted with*: **direct speech**)

indirect tax a tax on particular goods, paid by the customer in the form of a higher price

indiscreet *adjective* 1 rash, not cautious 2 giving away too much information

indiscretion *noun* a rash or unwise remark or act, rash or unwise behaviour

indiscriminate *adjective* making no distinction between one person (or thing) and another: *indiscriminate buying/ indiscriminate killing*

indispensable *adjective* not able to be done without, necessary

indisposed *adjective* unwell □ **indisposition** *noun*

indisputable *adjective* not able to be denied

indistinct *adjective* not clear

indistinguishable *adjective* 1 difficult to make out 2 too alike to tell apart

individual *adjective* 1 relating to a single person or thing 2 distinctive, unusual □ *noun* a single person or thing

individualist *noun* someone with an independent or distinctive lifestyle □ **individualistic** *adjective*

individuality *noun* 1 separate existence 2 the quality of standing out from others

indivisible *adjective* not able to be divided

indoctrinate *verb* to fill with a certain teaching or set of ideas

indolent *adjective* lazy □ **indolence** *noun*

indomitable *adjective* unconquerable, unyielding

indoor *adjective* done *etc* inside a building

indoors *adverb* in or into a building *etc*

indubitable *adjective* not to be doubted

induce *verb* 1 to persuade 2 to bring on, cause

inducement *noun* something which encourages or persuades: *money is an inducement to work*

induct *verb* to introduce, install

induction *noun* 1 the formal installation of someone in a new post 2 the production of electricity in something by placing it near an electric source 3 the drawing of conclusions from particular cases □ **inductive** *adjective* (meaning 3)

indulge *verb* 1 to be inclined to give into the wishes of; spoil: *she indulges that child too much* 2 to give way to, not restrain: *indulging his sweet tooth*

indulgence *noun* 1 the act of indulging 2 a pardon for a sin

indulgent *adjective* not strict, kind

industrial *adjective* 1 related to or used in trade or manufacture 2 of a country: having highly developed industry

industrialist *noun* someone involved in organizing an industry

industrious *adjective* hard-working

industry *noun* (*plural* **industries**) 1 a branch of trade or manufacture: *the clothing industry* 2 steady attention to work

inebriated *adjective* drunk

inedible *adjective* not eatable

ineffective *adjective* useless, having no effect

ineffectual *adjective* achieving nothing

inefficient *adjective* 1 not efficient, not capable 2 wasting time, energy *etc* □ **inefficiency** *noun* (*plural* **inefficiencies**)

inelegant *adjective* not graceful □ **inelegance** *noun*

ineligible *adjective* not qualified, not suitable to be chosen

inept *adjective* clumsy, badly done □ **ineptitude** *noun*

① Comes from Latin *ineptus* meaning 'useless'

☛ Do not confuse with: **inapt**

inequality *noun* (*plural* **inequalities**) 1 lack of equality, unfairness 2 unevenness

inert *adjective* 1 not moving or able to move 2 disinclined to move or act 3 not lively 4 chemically inactive

inertia *noun* 1 lack of energy or the will to move or act 2 *physics* the resistance of an object to a change in its state of motion *eg* when you try to stop a moving object, or to set a stationary object in motion

inescapable *adjective* unable to be avoided

inessential *adjective* not essential, unnecessary

inestimable *adjective* too great to be estimated

inevitable *adjective* not able to be avoided □ **inevitability** *noun*

inexact *adjective* not exact, approximate

inexcusable *adjective* not to be excused

inexhaustible *adjective* very plentiful; not likely to be used up

inexorable *adjective* not able to be persuaded; relentless

inexpensive *adjective* cheap in price

inexperience *noun* lack of (skilled) knowledge or experience
□ **inexperienced** *adjective*

inexpert *adjective* unskilled, amateurish

inexplicable *adjective* not able to be explained

inexplicit *adjective* not clear

inexpressible *adjective* not able to be described in words

inextricable *adjective* not able to be disentangled

infallible *adjective* 1 never making an error 2 certain to produce the desired result: *infallible cure* □ **infallibility** *noun*

infamous *adjective* having a very bad reputation; notorious, disgraceful

infamy *noun* public disgrace, notoriety

infancy *noun* 1 early childhood, babyhood 2 the beginning of anything: *when psychiatry was in its infancy*

infant *noun* a baby

infanticide *noun* 1 the murder of a child 2 a child murderer

infantile *adjective* 1 of babies 2 childish

infantry *noun* foot-soldiers

infatuated *adjective* filled with foolish love □ **infatuation** *noun*

infect *verb* 1 to fill with disease-causing germs 2 to pass on disease to 3 to pass on, spread (*eg* enthusiasm)

infection *noun* 1 a disease which can be spread to others 2 something that spreads widely and affects many people

infectious *adjective* likely to spread from person to person

infelicitous *adjective* unfortunate, inappropriate: *an infelicitous remark*

infer *verb* to reach a conclusion from facts or reasoning: *Am I to infer from what you say that you wish to resign?*

infer ➩ infers, inferring, inferred

🕓 Comes from Latin *inferre* meaning 'to bring in'

🖋 **Infer** is sometimes used to mean 'imply' or 'suggest': *'Are you inferring that I'm a liar?'*, but this use is considered incorrect by some people

inference *noun* a conclusion that you reach, based on information which you have been given

inferior *adjective* 1 lower in any way 2 not of best quality □ *noun* someone lower in rank *etc* □ **inferiority** *noun*

inferiority complex a constant feeling that you are less good in some way than other people

infernal *adjective* 1 of hell 2 *informal* annoying, blasted

inferno *noun* 1 hell 2 (*plural* **infernos**) a raging fire

infertile *adjective* 1 of soil: not producing much 2 not able to bear children or young □ **infertility** *noun*

infest *verb* to swarm over: *infested with lice*

infidel *adjective* someone who does not believe in a particular religion (especially Christianity)

infidelity *noun* unfaithfulness, disloyalty

infighting *noun* rivalry or quarrelling between members of the same group

infiltrate *verb* to enter (an organization *etc*) secretly to spy or cause damage □ **infiltration** *noun*

infinite *adjective* without end or limit

infinitesimal *adjective* absolutely tiny

infinitive *noun*, *grammar* the part of a verb which expresses the action but has no subject, *eg* I hate *to lose*

infinity *noun* space or time without end

infirm *adjective* feeble, weak

infirmary *noun* (*plural* **infirmaries**) a hospital

infirmity *noun* (*plural* **infirmities**) 1 a physical weakness 2 a character flaw

inflame *verb* 1 to make hot or red 2 to arouse passion in □ **inflamed** *adjective*

inflammable *adjective* **1** easily set on fire **2** easily excited

inflammation *noun* heat in a part of the body, with pain, redness and swelling

inflammatory *adjective* arousing passion (especially anger)

inflate *verb* **1** to blow up (a balloon, tyre *etc*) **2** to puff up (with pride), exaggerate: *an inflated sense of her own importance* **3** to increase to a great extent

inflation *noun* **1** the act of inflating **2** an economic situation in which prices and wages keep forcing each other to increase

inflect *verb* **1** to change the tone of (your voice) **2** to vary the endings of (a verb) to show tense, number *etc*

inflection *noun* **1** change in the tone of your voice **2** a change in the basic form of a word to show tense, number *etc* **3** the new form of a word which has been changed in this way: *The inflections of the verb 'find' are: 'finds', 'finding' and 'found'.* □ **inflectional** *adjective*

inflexible *adjective* not yielding, unbending □ **inflexibility** *noun*

inflict *verb* to bring down (blows, punishment *etc*) on □ **infliction** *noun*

in-flight *adjective* happening or used during an air flight: *in-flight movie*

inflow *noun* a flowing in, influx

influence *noun* the power to affect other persons or things □ *verb* to have power over □ **influential** *adjective*

influenza *noun* an infectious illness with fever, headache, muscle pains *etc*

influx *noun* **1** a flowing in **2** the arrival of large numbers of people

info *noun, informal* information

inform *verb* **1** to give knowledge to **2 inform on** to tell on, betray

informal *adjective* not formal; relaxed, friendly □ **informality** *noun*

informant *noun* someone who informs

information *noun* knowledge, news

informative *adjective* giving information

informer *noun* someone who gives information to the police or authorities

infra- *prefix* below, beneath
Ⓛ Comes from Latin *infra* meaning 'below' or 'underneath'

infraction *noun* a violation, a breach

infra-red *adjective* of rays of heat: with wavelengths longer than visible light

infrastructure *noun* inner structure, framework

infrequent *adjective* rare, happening seldom

infringe *verb* to break (a rule or law) □ **infringement** *noun*

infuriate *verb* to drive into a rage

infuriating *adjective* extremely annoying

infuse *verb* **1** to pour on or over **2** to fill the mind (with a desire *etc*)

infusion *noun* **1** the act of infusing **2** a tea formed by steeping a herb *etc* in water

ingenious (*pronounced* in-**jeen**-i-*us*) *adjective* **1** skilful in inventing **2** cleverly thought out

☛ Do not confuse with: **ingenuous**. It may help you remember which is which if you link the adjective **ingenuous** with the noun **ingénue** (= a naive young girl)

ingénue (*pronounced* an-szei-**noo**) *noun* a naive young girl

ingenuity *from* **ingenious** *noun* cleverness; quickness of ideas

ingenuous (*pronounced* in-**jen**-yoo-*us*) *adjective* frank; without cunning

☛ Do not confuse with: **ingenious**.

ingot *noun* a block of metal (especially gold or silver) cast in a mould

ingrained *adjective* deeply fixed: *ingrained laziness*

ingratiate *verb* to work your way into someone's favour by flattery *etc* □ **ingratiating** *adjective*

ingratitude *noun* lack of gratitude or thankfulness

ingredient *noun* one of the things of which a mixture is made

ingrown *adjective* of a nail: growing into the flesh

inhabit *verb* to live in

inhabitant *noun* someone who lives permanently in a place

inhalant *noun* a medicine which is inhaled

inhalation *noun* 1 the act of inhaling 2 a medicine which is inhaled

inhale *verb* to breathe in

inhaler *noun* a device for breathing in medicine, steam *etc*

inhere *verb* to stick, be fixed (in)

inherent *adjective* inborn, belonging naturally

inherit *verb* 1 to receive property *etc* as an heir 2 to get (a characteristic) from your parents *etc*: *she inherits her sense of humour from her father*

inheritance *noun* something received by will when someone dies

inheritor *noun* an heir

inhibit *verb* to hold back, prevent

inhibited *adjective* unable to let yourself go

inhibition *noun* a holding back of natural impulses *etc*, restraint

inhospitable *adjective* unwelcoming, unfriendly

inhuman *adjective* not human; brutal □ **inhumanity** *noun*

inhumane *adjective* cruel

inimitable *adjective* impossible to imitate

iniquitous *adjective* unjust; wicked

iniquity *noun* (*plural* **iniquities**) wickedness; a sin

initial *adjective* of or at the beginning: *initial difficulties* □ *noun* the letter beginning a word, especially someone's name □ *verb* to sign with the initials of your name

initial *verb* ⇨ initials, initialling, initialled

initiate *verb* 1 to begin, start: *initiate the reforms* 2 to give first lessons to 3 to formally make someone a member of a society *etc* □ **initiation** *noun* (meanings 1 and 3)

initiative *noun* 1 the right to take the first step 2 readiness to take a lead

inject *verb* 1 to force (a fluid *etc*) into the veins or muscles with a syringe 2 to put (*eg* enthusiasm) into □ **injection** *noun*

in-joke *noun* a joke only understood by a particular group

injudicious *adjective* unwise

injunction *noun* an official order or command

injure *verb* to harm, damage, wrong

■ **Alternative words**: disfigure, mutilate, wound, offend

injured *adjective* hurt; offended

injury *noun* (*plural* **injuries**) 1 hurt, damage, harm 2 a wrong

injustice *noun* 1 unfairness 2 a wrong

ink *noun* a coloured liquid used in writing, printing *etc* □ *verb* to mark with ink

inkling *noun* a hint or slight sign

inky *adjective* 1 of or covered in ink 2 very dark

inlaid *past form of* **inlay**

inland *adjective* 1 not beside the sea 2 happening inside a country □ *adverb* towards the inner part of a country

inland revenue taxes *etc* collected within a country

inlay *noun* decoration made by fitting pieces of different shapes and colours into a background □ *verb* to fit into a background as decoration □ **inlaid** *adjective*

inlay *verb* ⇨ inlays, inlaying, inlaid

inlet *noun* a small bay

inmate *noun* a resident, an occupant (especially of an institution): *the inmates of the prison*

inmost *adjective* the most inward, the farthest in

inn *noun* a small country hotel

innards *noun plural* 1 internal parts 2 entrails

innate *adjective* inborn, natural

inner *adjective* 1 farther in 2 of feelings *etc*: hidden

innermost *adjective* farthest in; most secret

innings *noun singular* **1** a team's turn for batting in cricket **2** a turn, a go at something

innkeeper *noun* someone who keeps an inn

innocent *adjective* **1** not guilty, blameless **2** having no experience of how unpleasant people, and life in general, can be, and therefore tending to trust everyone **3** harmless **4** innocent of lacking, without □ **innocence** *noun* (meanings 1 and 2)

innocuous *adjective* not harmful

innovation *noun* something new

innuendo *noun* (*plural* **innuendoes**) an indirect reference, a hint

innumerable *adjective* too many to be counted

innumerate *adjective* not understanding arithmetic or mathematics □ **innumeracy** *noun*

inoculate *verb* to inject (someone) with a mild form of a disease to prevent them later catching it □ **inoculation** *noun*

inoffensive *adjective* harmless, giving no offence

inoperative *adjective* not active, not working

inopportune *adjective* at a bad or inconvenient time

inordinate *adjective* going beyond the limit, unreasonably great

inorganic *adjective* not of animal or vegetable origin

in-patient *noun* a patient who stays in a hospital during their treatment (*contrasted with*: **out-patient**)

input *noun* **1** an amount (of energy, labour *etc*) put into something **2** data fed into a computer (*contrasted with*: **output**)

inquest *noun* a legal inquiry into a case of sudden death

inquire or **enquire** *verb* to ask

inquiring or **enquiring** *adjective* questioning, curious: *inquiring mind*

inquiry or **enquiry** *noun* (*plural* **inquiries** or **enquiries**) **1** a question; a search for information **2** an official investigation

inquisition *noun* a careful questioning or investigation

inquisitive *adjective* **1** very curious **2** fond of prying, nosy □ **inquisitively** *adverb*

inquisitor *noun* an official investigator

inroad *noun* a raid, an advance □ **make inroads into** to use up large amounts of: *the holiday made inroads into their savings*

insane *adjective* mad, not sane □ **insanity** *noun*

insanitary *adjective* not sanitary; encouraging the spread of disease

insatiable *adjective* not able to be satisfied: *insatiable appetite*

inscribe *verb* to write or engrave (*eg* a name) on a book, monument *etc*

inscription *noun* the writing on a book, monument *etc*

inscrutable *adjective* not able to be understood, mysterious

insect *noun* a small six-legged creature with wings and a body divided into sections

insecticide *noun* powder or liquid for killing insects

insectivorous *adjective* feeding on insects

insecure *adjective* **1** not safe; not firm **2** lacking confidence, not feeling settled □ **insecurity** *noun*

inseminate *verb* **1** to plant, introduce (into) **2** to impregnate, especially artificially □ **insemination** *noun*

insensible *adjective* **1** unconscious, unaware (of) **2** not having feeling

insensitive *adjective* **1** **insensitive to** not feeling: *insensitive to cold* **2** unsympathetic (to): *insensitive to her grief* **3** unappreciative, crass □ **insensitivity** *noun*

inseparable *adjective* not able to be separated or kept apart □ **inseparably** *adverb*

insert *verb* (*pronounced* in-**sert**) to put in or among □ *noun* (*pronounced* **in**-sert) **1** a special feature added to a television programme *etc* **2** a separate leaflet or pullout section in a magazine *etc* □ **insertion** *noun*

in-service *adjective* happening as part of someone's work: *in-service training*

inset *noun* **1** an insert **2** a small picture, map *etc* in a corner of a larger one

inshore *adjective & adverb* in or on the water but near or towards the shore

inside *noun* **1** the side, space or part within **2** indoors □ *adjective* **1** being on or in the inside **2** indoor **3** coming from or done by someone within an organization: *inside information* □ *adverb* to, in or on the inside □ *preposition* to the inside of; within

insidious *adjective* **1** likely to trap those who are not careful, treacherous **2** of a disease: coming on gradually and unnoticed

insight *noun* ability to consider a matter and understand it clearly

insignia *noun plural* signs or badges showing that someone holds an office, award *etc*

insignificant *adjective* of little importance □ **insignificance** *noun*

insincere *adjective* not sincere □ **insincerity** *noun*

insinuate *verb* **1** to hint (at a fault) **2** to put in gradually and secretly **3** to work yourself into (someone's favour *etc*)

insinuation *noun* a sly hint

insipid *adjective* **1** dull, without liveliness **2** tasteless, bland

insist *verb* **1** to urge something strongly: *insist on punctuality* **2** to refuse to give way, hold firmly to your intentions: *he insists on walking there* **3** to go on saying (that): *she insists that she saw a UFO*

insistent *adjective* **1** insisting on having or doing something **2** forcing you to pay attention □ **insistence** *noun* (meaning 1) □ **insistently** *adverb* (meaning 1)

in situ *adverb* in position, in place

insolent *adjective* rude, impertinent, insulting □ **insolence** *noun*

insoluble *adjective* **1** not able to be

dissolved **2** of a problem: not able to be solved

insolvent *adjective* not able to pay your debts, impoverished □ **insolvency** *noun*

insomnia *noun* sleeplessness

insomniac *noun* someone who suffers from insomnia

inspect *verb* **1** to look carefully into, examine **2** to look over (troops *etc*) ceremonially

inspection *noun* careful examination

inspector *noun* **1** an official who inspects **2** a police officer below a superintendent and above a sergeant in rank

inspiration *noun* **1** something or someone that influences or encourages others **2** a brilliant idea **3** breathing in

inspirational *adjective* inspiring, brilliant

inspire *verb* **1** to encourage, rouse **2** to be the source of creative ideas **3** to breathe in

inspired *adjective* **1** seeming to be aided by higher powers **2** brilliantly good

instability *noun* lack of steadiness or stability (especially in the personality)

install or **instal** *verb* **1** to place in position, ready for use: *has the telephone been installed?* **2** to introduce formally to a new job *etc* □ **installation** *noun*

install ⇨ install*s* or instal*s*, install*ing*, install*ed*

instalment *noun* **1** a part of a sum of money paid at fixed times until the whole amount is paid **2** one part of a serial story

instance *noun* an example, a particular case □ *verb* to mention as an example □ **at the instance of** at the request of □ **for instance** for example

instant *adjective* **1** immediate, urgent **2** able to be prepared almost immediately: *instant coffee* □ *noun* **1** a very short time, a moment **2** point or moment of time: *I need it this instant*

instantaneous *adjective* done or happening very quickly

instantly *adverb* immediately

instead *adverb* in place of someone or something: *you can go instead* □ **instead of** in place of

instep *noun* the arching, upper part of the foot

instigate *verb* to stir up, encourage

instigation *noun*: **at someone's instigation** following that person's instructions or wishes

instil or **instill** *verb* to put in little by little (especially ideas into the mind)

instil ⇨ **instil**s or **instill**s, **instil**l*ing*, **instil**l*ed*

instinct *noun* a natural feeling or knowledge which someone has without thinking and without being taught

instinctive *adjective* due to instinct

institute *verb* to set up, establish, start □ *noun* a society, organization *etc* or the building it uses

institution *noun* 1 an organization, building *etc* established for a particular purpose (especially care or education) 2 an established custom □ **institutional** *adjective*

institutionalize *verb* 1 to confine in an institution 2 to make an established custom of

institutionalized *adjective* unable to think and act as an individual, and over-dependent on routine, as a result of living in an institution for too long

instruct *verb* 1 to teach 2 to direct, command □ **instructor** *noun*

instruction *noun* 1 teaching 2 a command 3 **instructions** rules showing how something is to be used

instructive *adjective* containing or giving information or knowledge

instrument *noun* 1 something used for a particular purpose, a tool 2 a device for producing musical sounds, *eg* a piano, a harp

instrumental *adjective* 1 helpful in bringing (something) about 2 written for or played by musical instruments, without voice accompaniment

instrumentalist *noun* someone who plays on a musical instrument

insubordinate *adjective* rebellious, disobedient □ **insubordination** *noun*

insufferable *adjective* not able to be endured

insufficient *adjective* not enough □ **insufficiency** *noun*

insular *adjective* 1 of an island or islands 2 narrow-minded, prejudiced □ **insularity** *noun*

insulate *verb* 1 to cover with a material that will not let through electrical currents, heat, frost *etc* 2 to cut off, isolate □ **insulation** *noun*

insulin *noun* a substance used in the treatment of diabetes

Based on the Latin word for 'island', because insulin is secreted by cells called the *islets* of Langerhans

insult *verb* to treat with scorn or rudeness □ *noun* a rude or scornful remark

insulting *adjective* scornful, rude

insuperable *adjective* that cannot be overcome

insure *verb* to arrange for payment of a sum of money on (something) if it should be lost, damaged, stolen *etc* □ **insurance** *noun*

☞ Do not confuse with: **ensure**

insurgent *adjective* rising up in rebellion □ *noun* a rebel □ **insurgency** *noun*

insurmountable *adjective* not able to be got over

insurrection *noun* a rising up in rebellion

intact *adjective* whole, unbroken

intake *noun* an amount of people or things taken in: *this year's intake of students*

intangible *adjective* 1 not able to be felt by touch 2 difficult to define or describe, not clear

integer *noun* a whole number, not a fraction

integral *adjective* 1 of or essential to a whole: *an integral part of the machine* 2 made up of parts forming a whole

integrate *verb* 1 to fit parts together to form a whole 2 to enable (racial groups) to mix freely and live on equal terms □ **integration** *noun*

integrity *noun* **1** honesty **2** wholeness, completeness

intellect *noun* the thinking power of the mind

intellectual *adjective* showing or requiring intellect □ *noun* someone of natural ability or with academic interests

intelligence *noun* **1** mental ability **2** information sent, news

intelligent *adjective* clever, quick at understanding

■ **Alternative words**: clever, alert, acute, rational

intelligentsia *noun* the intellectuals within a particular society

intelligible *adjective* able to be understood

intemperate *adjective* **1** going beyond reasonable limits, uncontrolled **2** tending to drink too much alcohol □ **intemperance** *noun*

intend *verb* to mean or plan to (do something)

intense *adjective* **1** very great **2** tending to feel strongly, deeply emotional □ **intensely** *adverb*

intensify *verb* to increase, make more concentrated

intensify ⇨ intensif*ies*, intensif*ying*, intensif*ied*

intensity *noun* (*plural* **intensities**) strength, *eg* of feeling, colour *etc*

intensive *adjective* very thorough, concentrated

intensive care a unit in a hospital where a patient's condition is carefully monitored

intent *noun* purpose □ *adjective* **1** with all your concentration (on), attentive **2** determined (to)

intention *noun* **1** what someone means to do, an aim **2** meaning

intentional *adjective* done on purpose □ **intentionally** *adverb*

inter (*pronounced* in-**ter**) *verb* to bury

inter ⇨ inter*s*, inter*ring*, inter*red*

Ⓛ Comes from Latin *in* meaning 'into', and *terra* meaning 'the earth'

inter- *prefix* between, among, together: *intermingle/ interplanetary*

Ⓛ Comes from Latin *inter* meaning 'between', 'among' or 'mutually'

interact *verb* to act on one another

interactive *adjective* allowing two-way communication, *eg* between a computer and its user

intercede *verb* to act as peacemaker between two people, nations *etc* □ **intercession** *noun*

intercept *verb* **1** to stop or seize on the way **2** to cut off, interrupt (a view, the light *etc*)

interchange *verb* **1** to put each in the place of the other **2** to alternate □ *noun* **1** the act of interchanging **2** a junction of two or more major roads on separate levels

interchangeable *adjective* able to be used one for the other

intercom *noun* a telephone system within a building, aeroplane *etc*

intercourse *noun* **1** communication **2** dealings between people *etc* **3** sexual intercourse

interdict *noun* an order forbidding something

interest *noun* **1** special attention, curiosity **2** someone's personal concern or field of study **3** advantage, benefit **4** a sum paid for the loan of money □ *verb* to catch or hold the attention of

interested *adjective* having or taking an interest

■ **Alternative words**: attentive, absorbed, engrossed, fascinated, keen, affected

interesting *adjective* holding the attention

■ **Alternative words**: engaging, absorbing, engrossing, fascinating, intriguing, compelling, stimulating, curious, unusual

interface *noun*, *computing* a connection between two parts of the same system

interfere *verb* **1 interfere in** to take part in what is not your business, meddle in

2 interfere with to get in the way of, hinder, have a harmful effect on: *interfering with her work*

interference *noun* **1** the act of interfering **2** the spoiling of radio or television reception by another station or disturbance from traffic *etc*

interim *noun* time between; the meantime □ *adjective* temporary

interior *adjective* **1** inner **2** inside a building **3** inland □ *noun* **1** the inside of anything **2** the inland part of a country

interject *verb* **1** to make a sudden remark in a conversation **2** to exclaim

interjection *noun* a word or phrase of exclamation, *eg* Ah! Oh dear!

interlock *verb* **1** to lock or clasp together **2** to fit into each other

interloper *noun* someone who enters without permission, an intruder

interlude *noun* **1** an interval **2** a short piece of music played between the parts of a play, film *etc*

intermarry *verb* **1** to marry with members of another race *etc* **2** to marry with members of the same group, race *etc*

intermediary *noun* (*plural* **intermediaries**) someone who acts between two people in trying to settle a quarrel

intermediate *adjective* in the middle; coming between

interment (from **inter**) *noun* a burial
   ✐ Do not confuse with: **internment**

interminable *adjective* never-ending, boringly long

intermission *noun* an interval, a pause

intermittent *adjective* stopping every now and then and starting again

intern *verb* to keep (someone from an enemy country) prisoner during a war

internal *adjective* **1** of the inner part, especially of the body **2** inside, within a country, organization *etc*: *internal affairs*

international *adjective* **1** happening between nations **2** concerning more than one nation **3** world-wide □ *noun* a sports match between teams of two countries

internee *noun* someone from an enemy country who is confined as a prisoner during a war

Internet *noun* an international computer network linking users through telephone lines

internment (from **intern**) *noun* confinement within a country or prison, especially during a war
   ✐ Do not confuse with: **interment**
   ⏱ Comes from French *interne* meaning 'internal'

interplanetary *adjective* between planets

interplay *noun* the action of one thing on another

interpose *verb* **1** to place or come between **2** to make (a remark *etc*) which interrupts someone

interpret *verb* **1** to explain the meaning of something **2** to translate **3** to bring out the meaning of (music, a part in a play *etc*) in performance **4** to take the meaning of something to be
   □ **interpretation** *noun*

interpreter *noun* someone who translates (on the spot) the words of a speaker into another language

interregnum *noun* the time between the end of one reign and the beginning of the next

interrogate *verb* to examine by asking questions □ **interrogation** *noun*
   □ **interrogator** *noun*

interrogative *noun* a word used in asking a question, *eg* who? where?
   □ *adjective* questioning

interrupt *verb* **1** to stop (someone) while they are saying or doing something **2** to stop doing (something) **3** to get in the way of, cut off (a view *etc*) □ **interruption** *noun*

intersect *verb* of lines: to meet and cross

intersection *noun* **1** the point where two lines cross **2** a crossroads

intersperse *verb* to scatter here and there in □ **interspersion** *noun*

intertwine *verb* to twine or twist together

interval *noun* **1** a time or space between two things **2** a short pause in a programme *etc*

intervene *verb* **1** to come or be between, or in the way **2** to join in (in order to stop) a fight or quarrel between other persons or nations □ **intervention** *noun*

interview *noun* a formal meeting of one person with others to apply for a job, give information to the media *etc* □ *verb* **1** to ask questions *etc* of in an interview **2** to conduct an interview

intestines *noun plural* the inside parts of the body, especially the bowels and passages leading to them □ **intestinal** *adjective*

intifada *noun* the uprising in 1987 and continued resistance by Palestinians to Israeli occupation of the Gaza Strip and West Bank of Jordan
ⓘ In Arabic, *intifada* means 'shaking off'

intimacy *noun* (*plural* **intimacies**) **1** close friendship **2** familiarity **3** sexual intercourse

intimate *adjective* (*pronounced* **in**-tim-at) **1** knowing a lot about, familiar (with) **2** of friends: very close **3** private, personal: *intimate details* **4** having a sexual relationship (with) □ *noun* (*pronounced* **in**-tim-at) a close friend □ *verb* (*pronounced* **in**-tim-eit) **1** to hint **2** to announce □ **intimately** *adverb*

intimation *noun* **1** a hint **2** announcement

intimidate *verb* to frighten or threaten into submission □ **intimidating** *adjective* □ **intimidation** *noun*

into *preposition* **1** to the inside: *into the room* **2** towards: *into the millennium* **3** to a different state: *a tadpole changes into a frog* **4** *maths* expressing the idea of division: *2 into 4 goes twice*

intolerable *adjective* not able to be endured

intolerant *adjective* not willing to put up with (people of different ideas, religion *etc*) □ **intolerance** *noun*

intonation *noun* the rise and fall of the voice

intone *verb* to speak in a singing manner, chant

intoxicant *noun* a strong drink

intoxicate *verb* **1** to make drunk **2** to enthuse, excite
Literally, to affect with arrow-poison

intoxication *noun* drunkenness

intra- *prefix* within
ⓘ Comes from Latin *intra* meaning 'within'

intractable *adjective* difficult, stubborn □ **intractability** *noun*

intransigent *adjective* refusing to come to an agreement □ **intransigence** *noun*

intransitive *adjective*, *grammar* of a verb: not needing an object, *eg* to *go*, to *fall*

in-tray *noun* an office tray for letters and work still to be dealt with (*contrasted with*: **out-tray**)

intrepid *adjective* without fear, brave □ **intrepidity** *noun*

intricate *adjective* complicated, having many twists and turns □ **intricacy** *noun* (*plural* **intricacies**)

intrigue *noun* **1** a secret plot **2** a secret love affair □ *verb* **1** to plot, scheme **2** to rouse the curiosity of, fascinate □ **intriguing** *adjective*

intrinsic *adjective* belonging to something as part of its nature

introduce *verb* **1** to bring in or put in **2** to make (someone) known to another person

introduction *noun* **1** the introducing of someone or something **2** an essay at the beginning of a book *etc* briefly explaining its contents

introductory *adjective* coming at the beginning

introspective *adjective* inward-looking, fond of examining your own thoughts and feelings □ **introspection** *noun*

intrude *verb* to thrust yourself into somewhere uninvited □ **intrusion** *noun* □ **intrusive** *adjective*

intruder *noun* someone who breaks in or intrudes

intuition *noun* **1** ability to understand

something without thinking it out **2** an instinctive feeling or belief

Inuit *noun* **1** the Eskimo people, especially those in Greenland, Canada and N Alaska **2** their language

inundate *verb* **1** to flood **2** to overwhelm: *inundated with work* □ **inundation** *noun*

inure *verb* to make accustomed (to): *inured to pain*

invade *verb* **1** to enter (a country *etc*) as an enemy to take possession **2** to interfere with (someone's rights, privacy *etc*) □ **invader** *noun* □ **invasion** *noun*

invalid¹ (*pronounced* in-**val**-id) *adjective* not valid, not legally effective □ **invalidity** *noun*

invalid² (*pronounced* **in**-val-id) *noun* someone who is ill or disabled □ *adjective* **1** ill or disabled **2** suitable for people who are ill or disabled □ *verb* **1** to make an invalid of **2 invalid out** to discharge from the army as an invalid

invalidate *verb* to prove to be wrong, or make legally ineffective

invaluable *adjective* priceless, essential

invariable *adjective* unchanging

invariably *adverb* always

invasion *see* **invade**

invective *noun* abusive words; scorn

inveigle *verb* to coax, entice □ **inveiglement** *noun*

invent *verb* **1** to make or think up for the first time **2** to make up (a story, an excuse) □ **inventor** *noun*

invention *noun* something invented

inventive *adjective* good at inventing, resourceful

inventory *noun* (*plural* **inventories**) a detailed list of contents

inverse *adjective* opposite, reverse □ *noun* the opposite □ **inversely** *adverb*

inversion *noun* **1** a turning upside-down **2** a reversal

invert *verb* **1** to turn upside down **2** to reverse the order of

invertebrate *adjective* of an animal: not having a backbone □ *noun* an

animal with no backbone, *eg* a worm or insect

inverted commas *noun plural* commas written or printed upside down (' ' or " ") to show where direct speech begins and ends

invest *verb* **1** to put money in a firm, property *etc* to make a profit **2** to give a particular quality to **3** *old* to besiege

investigate *verb* to search into with care □ **investigator** *noun*

investigation *noun* a careful search

investiture *noun* a ceremony before taking on an important office

investment *noun* **1** money invested **2** something in which money is invested **3** *old* a siege

investor *noun* someone who invests

inveterate *adjective* **1** firmly fixed in a habit: *an inveterate gambler* **2** deep-rooted □ **inveteracy** *noun*

invidious *adjective* likely to cause ill-will or envy

invigilate *verb* to supervise (an examination *etc*) □ **invigilator** *noun*

invigorate *verb* to strengthen, refresh □ **invigorating** *adjective*

invincible *adjective* not able to be defeated or overcome □ **invincibility** *noun*

inviolable *adjective* sacred, not to be disregarded or harmed □ **inviolability** *noun*

inviolate *adjective* not violated, free from harm *etc*

invisible *adjective* not able to be seen □ **invisibility** *noun*

invitation *noun* a request to do something

invite *verb* **1** to ask (someone) to do something, especially to come for a meal *etc* **2** to seem to ask for: *inviting punishment*

inviting *adjective* tempting, attractive

invoice *noun* a letter sent with goods with details of price and quantity □ *verb* to make such a list

invoke *verb* **1** to call upon in prayer **2** to ask for (*eg* help) □ **invocation** *noun*

involuntary *adjective* not done willingly or intentionally □ **involuntarily** *adverb*

involve *verb* **1** to have as a consequence, require **2** to take part (in), be concerned (in): *involved in publishing/involved in the scandal* □ **involvement** *noun*

involved *adjective* complicated

invulnerable *adjective* not vulnerable, not able to be hurt □ **invulnerability** *noun*

inward *adjective* **1** placed within **2** situated in the mind or soul □ *adverb* (also **inwards**) towards the inside

inwardly *adverb* **1** within **2** in your heart, privately

in-your-face *adjective, slang* aggressive, demanding attention

iodine *noun* a liquid chemical used to kill germs

ion *noun* an electrically-charged atom or group of atoms

ionizer *noun* a device which sends out negative ions to improve the quality of the air

iota *noun* a little bit, a jot

IOU *short for* I owe you, a note given as a receipt for money borrowed

IQ *abbreviation* intelligence quotient

ir- *see* **in-**

IRA *abbreviation* Irish Republican Army

irascible *adjective* easily made angry □ **irascibility** *noun*

irate *adjective* angry

ire *noun, formal* anger

iridescent *adjective* **1** coloured like a rainbow **2** shimmering with changing colours □ **iridescence** *noun*

iris *noun* (*plural* **irises**) **1** the coloured part of the eye around the pupil **2** a lily-like flower which grows from a bulb

irk *verb* to weary, annoy

irksome *adjective* tiresome

iron (*pronounced* **ai**-on or *Scottish* **ai**-ron) *noun* **1** a common metal, widely used to make tools *etc* **2** an iron instrument: *a branding iron* **3** a golf club (originally with an iron head) **4** an appliance for pressing clothes **5 irons** a prisoner's chains □ *adjective* **1** made of iron **2** stern, resolute: *iron will* **3** of a rule: not to be broken □ *verb* **1** to press (clothes) with an iron **2 iron out** to smooth out (difficulties)

Iron Age human culture at the stage of using iron for tools *etc*

Iron Curtain *historical* the border separating the West from the countries of the former Soviet bloc

ironic or **ironical** *adjective* **1** containing or expressing irony **2** of a person: frequently using irony

ironically *adverb* **1** strangely enough (used to draw attention to a strange and perhaps amusing contradiction or paradox) **2** in such a way as to make clear that you are saying the opposite of what is obviously true

ironmonger *noun* a shopkeeper selling household tools, gardening equipment *etc*

ironmongery *noun* goods sold by an ironmonger

irony *noun* (*plural* **ironies**) **1** a form of humour in which someone says the opposite of what is obviously true **2** an absurd contradiction or paradox: *the irony of it was that she would have given him the money if he hadn't stolen it*

irrational *adjective* against logic or common sense □ **irrationality** *noun*

irregular *adjective* **1** uneven, variable **2** against the rules □ **irregularity** *noun* (*plural* **irregularities**)

■ **Alternative words**: (meaning 2) anomalous

irrelevant *adjective* not having to do with what is being spoken about □ **irrelevancy** *noun* (*plural* **irrelevancies**)

irreparable *adjective* not able to be repaired

irreplaceable *adjective* too good or rare to be replaced

irrepressible *adjective* not restrainable or controllable

irreproachable *adjective* not able to be criticized or blamed

irresistible *adjective* too strong or too charming to be resisted

irresolute *adjective* not able to make up your mind or keep to a decision

irrespective *adjective* taking no account of: *irrespective of the weather*

irresponsible *adjective* having no sense of responsibility, thoughtless

irreverent *adjective* having no respect, *eg* for holy things □ **irreverence** *noun*

irrevocable (*pronounced* i-**rev**-ok-a-bl) *adjective* not to be changed

irrigate *verb* to supply (land) with water by canals *etc* □ **irrigation** *noun*

irritable *adjective* cross, easily annoyed

irritate *verb* **1** to annoy **2** to cause discomfort to (the skin, eyes *etc*) □ **irritation** *noun*

■ **Alternative words:** (meaning 1) aggravate

Islam *noun* **1** the Muslim religion, founded by the prophet Mohammed **2** the Muslim world □ **Islamic** *adjective*

island *noun* **1** an area of land surrounded by water **2** an isolated place, a haven □ **traffic island** a platform in the middle of a road for pedestrians to stand on while waiting to cross

islander *noun* an inhabitant of an island

isle *noun, formal* an island

ISO *abbreviation* International Standards Organization

iso- *prefix* equal: *isobar/ isotherm* ○ Comes from Greek *isos* meaning 'equal'

isobar *noun* a line on the map connecting places where atmospheric pressure is the same

isolate *verb* **1** to place or keep separate from other people or things **2** to consider (something) by itself: *isolate the problem* □ **isolation** *noun*

isolationism *noun* the political policy of avoiding as much as possible any dealings with other countries □ **isolationist** *adjective*

isomer *noun* a chemical substance with the same molecular weight as another, but with its atoms in a different

arrangement □ **isomeric** *adjective*

isosceles *adjective* of a triangle: having two sides equal (*compare with:* **equilateral**)

isotherm *noun* a line on the map connecting places which have the same temperature

isotope *noun* an atom with the same atomic number as, but different mass number from, another

issue *verb* **1** to go or come out **2** to give out (orders *etc*) **3** to publish □ *noun* **1** a flowing out **2** *formal* children: *he died without issue* **3** the copies of a book published at one time **4** one number in a series of magazines *etc* **5** result, consequence **6** the matter which is being discussed □ **take issue with** to disagree with

it *pronoun* **1** the thing spoken of: *I meant to bring the book, but I left it at home* **2** used in sentences with no definite subject: *it snowed today/ it is too late now* **3** used in phrases as a kind of object: *go it alone/ brave it out*

italicize *verb* to print in italics

italics *noun plural* a kind of type which *slopes to the right*

itch *noun* **1** an irritating feeling in the skin, made better by scratching **2** a strong desire □ *verb* **1** to have an itch **2** to be impatient (to do), long (to): *itching to open his presents* □ **itchy** *adjective*

item *noun* a separate article or detail in a list

itemize *verb* to list item by item, detail

itinerant *adjective* travelling from place to place, especially on business □ *noun* someone who travels around, especially a tramp, pedlar *etc*

itinerary *noun* (*plural* **itineraries**) a route or plan of a journey

its *adjective* belonging to it: *keep the hat in its box*

> ✎ Do not confuse: **its** and **it's**. **Its**, meaning 'belonging to it', is spelt with no apostrophe ('). **It's** means 'it is' or 'it has'

it's *short for* it is *or* it has

itself *pronoun* **1** used reflexively: *the cat*

licked itself **2** used for emphasis or contrast: *after I've read the introduction, I'll begin the book itself*

ITV *abbreviation* Independent Television

IU or **IUD** *abbreviation* intra-uterine (contraceptive) device

ivory *noun* (*plural* **ivories**) the hard white substance which forms the tusks of the elephant, walrus *etc*

ivy *noun* (*plural* **ivies**) a creeping evergreen plant

Jj

If you can't find the word you're looking for under letter J, it could be that it starts with a different letter. Try looking under **G** for words like *gem*, *gin* and *gymnast*.

jabber *verb* to talk rapidly and indistinctly

jack *noun* **1** a device with a lever for raising heavy weights **2** (*also called* **knave**) the playing-card between ten and queen □ **jack up 1** to raise with a jack **2** to raise (prices *etc*) steeply

jackal *noun* a dog-like wild animal

jackass *noun* **1** a male ass **2** *informal* an idiot

jackboots *noun plural* large boots reaching above the knee

jackdaw *noun* a type of small crow

jacket *noun* **1** a short coat **2** a loose paper cover for a book

jacket potato a baked potato

jack-in-the-box *noun* a doll fixed to a spring inside a box that leaps out when the lid is opened

jack-knife *noun* **1** a large folding knife **2** a dive forming a sharp angle and then straightening □ *verb* of a vehicle and its trailer: to swing together to form a sharp angle

jackpot *noun* a fund of prize money which increases until someone wins it

Jacobean *noun, historical* relating to the period of James VI of Scotland, I of England (1603–1625)

Jacobite *noun, historical* a supporter of James VII of Scotland, II of England and his descendants

Jacuzzi *noun, trademark* a bath fitted with a device that agitates the water

jade *noun* a hard green mineral substance used for ornaments

jaded *adjective* tired

jagged *adjective* rough-edged, uneven

jaguar *noun* a S American animal like a leopard

jail *noun* a prison

jailbird *noun* a convict or ex-convict

jailer *noun* someone in charge of a jail or prisoners

Jain *noun* a member of an ascetic Indian religion similar to Buddhism

jam *noun* **1** fruit boiled with sugar till it is set **2** a crush **3** a blockage caused by crowding **4** *informal* a difficult situation □ *verb* **1** to press or squeeze tight **2** to crowd full **3** to stick and so be unable to move: *the back wheel has jammed* **4** to cause interference with another radio station's broadcast **5** *music* to play with other musicians in an improvised style

> **jam** *verb* ⇨ jam*s*, jamm*ing*, jamm*ed*

> ■ **Alternative words**: (verb, meaning 2) block

jamb *noun* the side post of a door

jamboree *noun* **1** a large, lively gathering **2** a rally of Scouts

jam-packed *adjective* packed tightly, congested

jam session an informal gathering to play improvised music

jangle *verb* **1** to make a harsh ringing noise **2** to irritate

janitor *noun* **1** a caretaker **2** a doorkeeper
① Comes from Latin *janua* meaning 'a door'

January *noun* the first month of the year

jape *noun, informal* a trick, a practical joke

jar *noun* a glass or earthenware bottle with a wide mouth □ *verb* **1** to have a harsh, startling effect **2** to be discordant, not agree

> **jar** *verb* ⇨ **jar**s, **jar**r**ing**, **jar**r**ed**

jargon *noun* special words used within a particular trade, profession *etc*

jarring *adjective* harsh, startling

jasmine *noun* a shrub with white or yellow sweet-smelling flowers

jaundice *noun* a disease which causes the skin and eyes to turn yellow

jaundiced *adjective* **1** having jaundice **2** discontented, bitter

jaunt *noun* a short journey for pleasure

jaunty *adjective* cheerful □ **jauntily** *adverb*

> ■ **Alternative words**: sprightly

javelin *noun* a long spear for throwing

jaw *noun* **1** the lower part of the face, including the mouth and chin **2 jaws** an animal's mouth

jay *noun* a brightly-coloured bird like a crow

jaywalker *noun* someone who walks carelessly among traffic

jazz *noun* a style of music with a strong rhythm, based on African-American folk music □ **jazz something up** to make it more lively or colourful

jazzy *adjective* **1** resembling or containing certain elements of jazz **2** colourful, flamboyant

JCB *noun* a type of mobile digger used in the construction industry

> **JCB** is an abbreviation of *J C Bamford*, the manufacturer's name

jealous *adjective* **1** wanting to have what someone else has; envious **2** guarding closely (possessions *etc*) □ **jealousy** *noun*

jeans *noun plural* denim trousers

Jeep *noun, trademark* a small army motor vehicle

jeer *verb* to make fun of, scoff □ *noun* a scoff

> ■ **Alternative words**: (verb) heckle, taunt

Jehovah *noun* the Hebrew God of the Old Testament

jejune (*pronounced* je-**joon**) *adjective* naive, inexperienced

> From a Latin word meaning 'hungry' or 'fasting'

jelly *noun* (*plural* **jellies**) **1** fruit juice boiled with sugar till it becomes firm **2** a transparent wobbly food, often fruit-flavoured **3** an extremely nervous person **4 jellies** *slang* the drug Temazepam

jellyfish *noun* a sea animal with a jelly-like body

jemmy *noun* (*plural* **jemmies**) a burglar's iron tool

jeopardize *verb* to put in danger or at risk

jeopardy *noun* danger

> Originally a gambling term, based on French *jeu parti* meaning 'even chance'

jerk *verb* to give a sudden sharp movement □ *noun* a sudden sharp movement

jerkin *noun* a type of short coat

jerky *adjective* moving or coming in jerks □ **jerkily** *adverb*

jerry-built *adjective* hastily and badly built

jersey *noun* (*plural* **jerseys**) a sweater, pullover

jest *noun* a joke □ *verb* to joke

jester *noun, historical* a fool employed to amuse a royal court *etc*

jet *noun* **1** a hard black mineral, used for ornaments and jewellery **2** a spout of flame, air or liquid **3** a jet plane

jet-black *adjective* very black

jet lag tiredness caused by the body's inability to cope with being in a new time zone

jet plane an aeroplane driven by jet propulsion

jet propulsion high-speed forward motion produced by sucking in air or liquid and forcing it out from behind

jetsam *noun* goods thrown overboard and washed ashore

jet set rich people who enjoy frequent expensive holidays

jet stream 1 a band of high-speed winds far above the earth 2 the exhaust of a jet engine

jettison *verb* 1 to throw overboard 2 to abandon

jetty *noun* (*plural* **jetties**) a small pier

Jew *noun* someone who is of the race or religion of the Israelites

jewel *noun* 1 a precious stone 2 someone or something highly valued

jewelled or *US* **jeweled** *adjective* set with jewels

jeweller or *US* **jeweler** *noun* someone who makes or sells articles made of precious jewels and metals

jewellery or *US* **jewelry** *noun* articles made or sold by a jeweller

Jewish *adjective* of the Jews

Jew's harp a small harp-shaped musical instrument played between the teeth

Jezebel *noun* a wicked, scheming woman

jib *noun* 1 a three-cornered sail in front of a ship's foremast 2 the jutting-out arm of a crane □ **jib at** to refuse to do, object to

  jib *verb* ⇨ jib**s**, jib**bing**, jib**bed**

jibe or **gibe** *verb* to jeer, scoff □ *noun* a jeer

Jiffy bag *trademark* a padded envelope

jig *noun* a lively dance or tune □ *verb* to jump about

  jig *verb* ⇨ jig**s**, jig**ging**, jig**ged**

jigsaw *noun* or **jigsaw puzzle** a puzzle consisting of many different-shaped pieces that fit together to form a picture

jihad (*pronounced* jee-**had**) *noun* an Islamic holy war

jilt *verb* to cast aside (a lover) after previously encouraging them

jingle *noun* 1 a clinking sound like that of coins 2 a simple rhyme

jingoism (*pronounced* **jing**-goh-i-zm) *noun* chauvinism, narrow-minded nationalism □ **jingoistic** *adjective*

jinx *noun* someone or something thought to bring bad luck

  Probably from the *Jynx* bird which was once invoked in spells and charms

jitterbug *noun* a dance to rock music

jitters *noun plural*: **have the jitters** to be very nervous

jittery *adjective* very nervous, shaking with nerves

■ **Alternative words**: edgy

jive *noun* a style of fast dancing to jazz or rock-and-roll music

jo *noun, Scottish* sweetheart, dear

job *noun* 1 someone's daily work 2 any piece of work

job centre a government office where information about available jobs is shown

job-lot *noun* a collection of odds and ends

job-share *noun* the division of one job between two people, each working part-time

jockey *noun* (*plural* **jockeys**) someone who rides a horse in a race □ *verb* to push your way into a good position

jockstrap *noun* a genital support for men while playing sports

jocular *adjective* joking, merry □ **jocularity** *noun* □ **jocularly** *adverb*

jocund *adjective* merry, cheerful

jodhpurs *noun plural* riding breeches, fitting tightly from knee to ankle

joey *noun* (*plural* **joeys**) *Australian, informal* a young kangaroo

jog *verb* 1 to nudge, push slightly 2 to run at a gentle pace □ *noun* a gentle run □ **jogging** *noun* (meaning 2)

  jog *verb* ⇨ jog**s**, jog**ging**, jog**ged**

jogger *noun* someone who runs gently to keep fit

joggle *verb* to shake slightly

joie de vivre (*pronounced* szwah de **vee**-vre) enthusiasm for life; sparkle, spirit

join *verb* 1 to put or come together 2 to connect, fasten 3 to become a member of 4 to come and meet □ *noun* the place where two or more things join □ **join battle** to begin fighting in battle

■ **Alternative words:** (verb, meanings 1 and 2) attach, connect, link; (verb, meaning 4) meet, converge

joiner *noun* someone who makes wooden fittings, furniture *etc*

joint *noun* 1 the place where two or more things join 2 the place where two bones are joined, *eg* an elbow or knee 3 meat containing a bone 4 *slang* a cannabis cigarette □ *adjective* 1 united 2 shared among more than one

jointly *adverb* together

joist *noun* the beam to which the boards of a floor or the laths of a ceiling are nailed

joke *noun* something said or done to cause laughter □ *verb* to make a joke, tease

joker *noun* 1 someone who jokes 2 an extra playing-card in a pack

jollification *noun* noisy festivity or celebration

jolliness or **jollity** *noun* merriment

jolly *adjective* merry

■ **Alternative words:** jovial

jolt *verb* 1 to shake suddenly 2 to go forward with sudden jerks □ *noun* a sudden jerk

■ **Alternative words:** (verb, meaning 1) jog, knock

joss-stick *noun* a stick of gum which gives off a sweet smell when burned

jostle *verb* to push or knock against

jot *noun* a very small amount □ *verb* to write down hurriedly or briefly

   jot *verb* ⇨ jot*s*, jott*ing*, jott*ed*

jotter *noun* a book for taking notes

joule *noun* a unit of energy

journal *noun* 1 a personal account of each day's events; a diary 2 a newspaper, a magazine

journalism *noun* the business of

recording daily events for the media □ **journalist** *noun* □ **journalistic** *adjective*

journey *noun* (*plural* **journeys**) a distance travelled □ *verb* to travel

journeyman *noun* someone whose apprenticeship is finished

joust *noun, historical* the armed contest between two knights on horseback at a tournament □ *verb* to fight on horseback at a tournament

jovial *adjective* cheerful, good-humoured □ **joviality** *noun*

jowl *noun* the lower part of the jaw or cheek

joy *noun* gladness

joyful or **joyous** *adjective* full of joy

joyless *adjective* dismal

■ **Alternative words:** cheerless

joyride *noun* a reckless trip for amusement in a stolen car □ **joyrider**

joy-stick *noun* a control-lever for something *eg* an aeroplane, an invalid car or a video game

JP *abbreviation* Justice of the Peace

Jr *abbreviation* Junior: *John Brown Jr*

jubilant *adjective* full of rejoicing, triumphant □ **jubilation** *noun*

jubilee *noun* celebrations arranged for the anniversary of a wedding, coronation *etc*

   From a Hebrew word for 'ram's horn', which was blown to announce the start of a celebratory Jewish year

Judaism *noun* the Jewish religion or way of life □ **Judaic** *adjective*

judder *noun* a strong vibration or jerky movement

judge *verb* 1 to make a decision on (a law case) after hearing all the evidence 2 to form an opinion 3 to decide the winners in a competition *etc* □ *noun* 1 an official who hears cases in the law-courts and decides on them according to the country's or state's laws 2 someone skilled in evaluating anything: *a good judge of character*

■ **Alternative words:** (verb, meaning 2) ascertain, determine, estimate; (verb, meaning 3) adjudicate, arbitrate

judgement or **judgment** *noun* **1** a decision in a law case **2** an opinion **3** good sense in forming opinions

judicial *adjective* of a judge or court of justice □ **judicially** *adverb*

judiciary *noun* the judges of a country or state

judicious *adjective* wise □ **judiciously** *adverb*

judo *noun* a Japanese form of wrestling for self-defence

jug *noun* a dish for liquids with a handle and a shaped lip for pouring

juggernaut *noun* a large articulated lorry

From a Hindi word for a large wagon used to carry the image of the god Krishna in religious processions

juggle *verb* **1** to toss a number of things (balls, clubs *etc*) into the air and catch them in order **2** to handle or present in a deceitful way □ **juggler** *noun* (meaning 1)

■ **Alternative words:** (meaning 2) manipulate

jugular vein the large vein at the side of the neck

juice *noun* the liquid in vegetables, fruits *etc*

juicy *adjective* **1** full of juice **2** sensational, scandalous

jujitsu *noun* a Japanese martial art similar to judo

jukebox *noun* a coin-operated machine which plays selected records automatically

July *noun* the seventh month of the year

jumble *verb* to throw together without order, muddle □ *noun* **1** a confused mixture **2** second-hand goods to be sold in a jumble sale

jumble sale a sale of odds and ends, cast-off clothing *etc*

jumbo *noun* (*plural* **jumbos**) **1** a child's name for an elephant **2** a jumbo jet □ *adjective* very large

jumbo jet a large jet aircraft

jump *verb* **1** to leap **2** to make a sudden startled movement **3** to pass over without spending time on: *She read the book in an afternoon, jumping all the boring bits* □ *noun* **1** a leap **2** a sudden start

■ **Alternative words:** (verb, meaning 1) spring, bound, vault, bounce; (verb, meaning 3) omit, skip

jumper *noun* a sweater, a jersey

jump-suit *noun* a one-piece garment combining trousers and top

jumpy *adjective* easily startled

■ **Alternative words:** edgy

junction *noun* a place or point of joining, especially of roads or railway lines

juncture *noun* point: *it's too early to decide at this juncture*

June *noun* the sixth month of the year

jungle *noun* a dense growth of trees and plants in tropical areas

junior *adjective* **1** younger **2** in a lower class or rank □ *noun* someone younger: *he is my junior*

juniper *noun* an evergreen shrub with berries and prickly leaves

junk[1] *noun* worthless articles, rubbish

junk[2] *noun* a Chinese flat-bottomed sailing ship, high in the bow and stern

junket *noun* **1** a dish made of curdled milk sweetened and flavoured **2** a trip made by a government official and paid for out of public funds

junk food convenience food with little nutritional value

junkie or **junky** *noun* (*plural* **junkies**) an insulting name for a drug addict

junk mail unsolicited mail, especially advertising material

jurisdiction *noun* **1** a legal authority or power **2** the district over which a judge, court *etc* has power

jurisprudence *noun* the study or knowledge of law

juror *noun* someone who serves on a jury

jury *noun* (*plural* **juries**) **1** a group of people selected to reach a decision on whether an accused prisoner is guilty or not **2** a group of judges for a competition *etc*

juryman *noun* a man who serves on a jury

jurywoman *noun* a woman who serves on a jury

just *adjective* **1** fair in judgement; unbiased **2** correct □ *adverb* **1** exactly: *just right* **2** not long since: *only just arrived* **3** merely, only **4** really: *just beautiful* □ **justly** *adverb* (from adjective)

justice *noun* **1** fairness in making judgements **2** what is right or rightly deserved **3** a judge

Justice of the Peace (*short form* **JP**) a citizen who acts as a judge for certain matters

justifiable *adjective* able to be justified or defended

justifiably *adverb* with good reason

justification *noun* **1** good reason **2** the arrangement of text so that it forms an even margin down the page

justify *verb* **1** to prove or show to be right or desirable **2** *printing* to make (text) form an even margin down the page

justify ⇨ justifi*es*, justify*ing*, justifi*ed*

■ **Alternative words**: (meaning 1) defend

jut *verb* to stand or stick out

jut ⇨ jut*s*, jut*ting*, jut*ted*

jute *noun* fibre from certain plants for making sacking, canvas *etc*

juvenile *adjective* **1** young; of young people **2** childish □ *noun* a young person

juxtapose *verb* to place side by side □ **juxtaposition** *noun*

Kk

If you can't find the word you're looking for under letter **K**, it could be that it starts with a different letter. Try looking under **C** for words like *can*, **CH** for words like *character*, and **Q** for words like *quite*. Also, don't forget **KH** for words like *khaki*.

kaftan *another spelling of* **caftan**

kaiser (*pronounced* **kaiz**-er) *noun, historical* a German emperor

kale *noun* a cabbage with open curled leaves

kaleidoscope *noun* a tube held to the eye and turned, so that loose, coloured shapes reflected in two mirrors change patterns

kaleidoscopic *adjective* **1** with changing colours **2** changing quickly

kamikaze *noun, historical* a Japanese pilot trained to make a suicidal attack □ *adjective* suicidal, self-destructive

kangaroo *noun* a large Australian animal with long hindlegs and great jumping power, the female carrying its young in a pouch on the front of her body

kaolin (*pronounced* **kei**-oh-lin) *noun* China clay

kaput (*pronounced* ka-**poot**) *adjective, slang* broken, not working

karaoke *noun* an entertainment of singing well-known songs against pre-recorded backing music

karate *noun* a Japanese form of unarmed fighting using blows and kicks

karma *noun* in Buddhist belief, someone's destiny as determined by their actions in a previous life

kayak *noun* **1** an Inuit sealskin canoe **2** a lightweight canoe for one person, manoeuvred with a single paddle

KB *abbreviation, computing* kilobyte

kebab *noun* small pieces of meat or vegetables cooked on a skewer

kedgeree *noun* a dish made with rice, fish and hard-boiled eggs

keek *verb, Scottish* to look, peep

keel *noun* the piece of a ship's frame that lies lengthways along the bottom □ **keel over** to overturn, fall over

keelhaul *verb, historical* to punish by hauling under the keel of a ship with ropes

keelson *noun* a ship's inner keel

keen¹ *adjective* **1** eager, enthusiastic **2** very sharp; bitingly cold □ **keenness** *noun*

Alternative words: (meaning 1) anxious

keen² *verb* to wail in grief; lament □ **keening** *noun*

keenly *adverb* intensely, passionately, alertly

keep *verb* **1** to hold on to, not give or throw away **2** to look after; feed and clothe **3** to have or use **4** to fulfil (a promise) **5** to remain in a position or state **6** (also **keep on**) to continue (doing something): *keep taking the tablets* **7** of food: to stay in good condition **8** to celebrate: *keep Christmas* □ *noun* **1** food, board **2** a castle stronghold □ **in keeping with** suited to □ **keep out 1** to exclude **2** to stay outside □ **keep up** to go on with, continue □ **keep up with** to go as fast *etc* as

keep *verb* ⇨ keeps, keeping, kept

ⓘ Comes from Old English *cepan*

keeper *noun* someone who looks after something: *zookeeper*

keeping *noun* care, charge □ **in keeping with** suitable for or fitting in with

keepsake *noun* a gift in memory of an occasion *etc*

keg *noun* a small cask or barrel

kelp *noun* a type of large brown seaweed

kelvin *noun* a measure of temperature

ken *noun* the extent of someone's knowledge or understanding: *beyond the ken of the average person* □ *verb*, *Scottish* to know

kendo *noun* a Japanese martial art using bamboo staves

kennel *noun* **1** a hut for a dog **2 kennels** a place where dogs can be looked after

kept *past form of* **keep**

kerb *noun* the edge of something, especially a pavement

☛ Do not confuse with: **curb**

kerb-crawling *noun* driving a car slowly in order to pick up prostitutes

kerchief *noun* a square of cloth used as a headscarf

kernel *noun* **1** a soft substance in the shell of a nut, or inside the stone of a fruit **2** the important part of anything

kerosine *noun* paraffin oil

kestrel *noun* a type of small falcon which hovers

ketchup *noun* a flavouring sauce made from tomatoes *etc*

Originally spelt *catsup*, as it still is in US English; based on a Chinese word for 'fish brine'

kettle *noun* a pot with a spout for heating liquids

kettledrum *noun* a drum made of a metal bowl covered with stretched skin *etc*

key *noun* **1** a device which is turned in a corresponding hole to lock or unlock, tighten, tune *etc* **2** a lever pressed on a piano *etc* to produce a note **3** a button on a typewriter or computer keyboard which is pressed to type letters **4** the chief note of a piece of music **5** something which explains a mystery or deciphers a code **6** a book containing answers to exercises □ *verb* to type on a typewriter or computer □ *adjective* important, essential

keyboard *noun* **1** the keys in a piano or organ arranged along a flat board **2** the keys of a typewriter or computer **3** an electronic musical instrument with keys arranged as on a piano *etc*

keyed-up *adjective* excited

keyhole *noun* the hole in which a key of a door is placed □ **keyhole surgery** surgery using miniature instruments, performed through tiny holes instead of large openings in the patient's flesh

keynote *noun* **1** the chief note of a piece of music **2** the chief point about anything

keypad *noun* a device with buttons that can be pushed to operate a television, telephone *etc*

keystone *noun* the stone at the highest point of an arch holding the rest in position

KGB *abbreviation*, *historical* Committee of State Security (in Russian, *Komitet Gosudarstvennoi Bezopasnosti*)

khaki *adjective* greenish-brown in colour □ *noun* **1** greenish-brown **2** cloth of this colour used for military uniforms

From an Urdu word meaning 'dusty'

kibbutz *noun* (*plural* **kibbutzim**) a farming settlement in Israel in which all share the work

kick *verb* **1** to hit or strike out with the foot **2** of a gun: to spring back violently when fired □ *noun* **1** a blow with the foot **2** the springing-back of a gun when fired □ **for kicks** *informal* for fun

kick-off *noun* the start (of a football game)

kid *noun* **1** *informal* a child **2** a young goat **3** the skin of a young goat □ *adjective* made of kid leather □ **with kid gloves** very carefully or tactfully

kidnap *verb* to carry (someone) off by force, often demanding money in exchange □ **kidnapper** *noun* □ **kidnapping** *noun*

kidnap ⇨ kidnaps, kidnapping, kidnapped

▪ **Alternative words**: abduct

kidney *noun* (*plural* **kidneys**) either of

a pair of organs in the lower back which filter waste from the blood and produce urine

kidney bean a bean with a curved shape like a kidney

kids' stuff *informal* something very easy or tame

kill *verb* 1 to put to death 2 to put an end to □ *noun* 1 the act of killing 2 the animals killed by a hunter □ **be in at the kill** to be there at the most exciting moment □ **killer** *noun*

■ **Alternative words**: (verb, meaning 1) slaughter, slay, exterminate, dispatch, annihilate

killing *noun*: **make a killing** to make a lot of money quickly

kiln *noun* a large oven or furnace for baking pottery, bricks *etc* or for drying grain, hops *etc*

kilo- *prefix* a thousand: *kilogramme/kilometre*
Ⓞ Comes from Greek *chilioi* meaning 'a thousand'

◆ In computing terminology **kilo-** does not mean exactly 1000, but 1024 (= 2^{10})

kilobyte *noun, computing* a measure of capacity equal to 1024 bytes

◆ See note at entry for prefix 'kilo-'

kilocalorie *noun* a measure of energy equal to 1000 calories

kilogramme *noun* a measure of weight equal to 1000 grammes (about 2 lb)

kilometre *noun* a measure of length equal to 1000 metres (about $\frac{5}{8}$ of a mile)

kilowatt *noun* a measure of electrical power equal to 1000 watts

kilt *noun* a pleated tartan skirt reaching to the knee, part of traditional Scottish dress

kilter *noun*: **out of kilter** out of sequence, off balance

kimono *noun* (*plural* **kimonos**) a loose Japanese robe, fastened with a sash

kin *noun* members of the same family, relations □ **kith and kin** *see* kith □ **next of kin** your nearest relative

kind *noun* 1 a sort, type 2 goods, not money: *paid in kind* □ *adjective* having good feelings towards others; generous, gentle

kindergarten *noun* a nursery school

kindhearted *adjective* kind

kindle *verb* 1 to light a fire 2 to catch fire 3 to stir up (feelings)

kindling *noun* material for starting a fire

kindly *adverb* in a kind way □ *adjective* kind, warm-hearted □ **kindliness** *noun*

kindred *noun* relatives, relations □ *adjective* of the same sort; related: *a kindred spirit*

kinetic *adjective* of or expressing motion: *kinetic sculpture* (= sculpture which moves)

king *noun* 1 the inherited male ruler of a nation 2 a playing-card with a picture of a king 3 the most important chess piece

kingdom *noun* 1 the area ruled by a king 2 any of the three major divisions of natural objects, *ie* animal, vegetable or mineral

kingfisher *noun* a type of fish-eating bird with brightly-coloured feathers

kingly *adjective* like a king; royal

kingpin *noun* the most important person in an organization

kink *noun* 1 a bend or curl in a rope, hair *etc* 2 a peculiarity of the mind

kinky *adjective* twisted, contorted

kinsfolk *noun plural* relations, relatives

kinsman *noun* a close male relation

kinswoman *noun* a close female relation

kiosk *noun* 1 a small stall for the sale of papers, sweets *etc* 2 a telephone box

kip *noun slang* a bed □ *verb* to go to bed, sleep

kipper *noun* a smoked and dried herring

kirk *noun, Scottish* a church

kiss *verb* 1 to touch lovingly with the lips 2 to touch gently □ *noun* (*plural* **kisses**) □ **kiss of life** a mouth-to-mouth method of restoring breathing

kit *noun* an outfit of clothes, tools *etc* necessary for a particular job

kitchen *noun* a room where food is cooked

kitchenette *noun* a small kitchen

kitchen-garden *noun* a vegetable garden

kite *noun* **1** a light frame, covered with paper or other material, for flying in the air **2** a kind of hawk

kith *noun*: **kith and kin** friends and relatives

kitsch *noun* vulgarly tasteless art *etc*

kitten *noun* a young cat □ **have kittens** *informal* to make a great fuss

kittenish *adjective* behaving like a kitten, playful

kitty¹ *noun* (*plural* **kitties**) a sum of money set aside for a purpose

kitty² *noun* (*plural* **kitties**) *informal* a cat or kitten

kiwi *noun* **1** a fast-running almost wingless bird of New Zealand **2** a kiwi fruit

kiwi fruit an edible fruit with a thin hairy skin and bright green flesh

kleptomania *noun* an uncontrollable desire to steal □ **kleptomaniac** *noun* & *adjective*

klondyker *noun* a factory ship processing fish for sale in a foreign country

After the famous *Klondyke* gold rush in Canada, because these ships originally traded in the lucrative herring market

knack (*pronounced* nak) *noun* a special talent

knacker (*pronounced* nak-er) *noun* a buyer of old horses for slaughter □ *verb, informal* to exhaust, tire out

knapsack (*pronounced* nap-sak) *noun* a bag for food, clothes *etc* slung on the back

knave (*pronounced* neiv) *noun* **1** a cheating rogue **2** in playing-cards, the jack

knavery (*pronounced* neiv-e-ri) *noun* dishonesty

knavish (*pronounced* neiv-ish) *adjective* cheating, wicked

knead (*pronounced* need) *verb* **1** to work (dough *etc*) by pressing with the fingers **2** to massage

knee (*pronounced* nee) *noun* the joint at the bend of the leg

kneecap (*pronounced* nee-kap) *noun* the flat round bone on the front of the knee joint □ *verb* to cause to suffer

kneecapping (*pronounced* nee-kap-ing) *noun* a form of torture or punishment in which the victim is shot or otherwise injured in the kneecap

kneel (*pronounced* neel) *verb* to go down on one or both knees

kneel ⇨ kneels, kneeling, knelt

knell (*pronounced* nel) *noun* **1** the tolling of a bell for a death or funeral **2** a warning of a sad end or failure

knickerbockers (*pronounced* nik-e-bok-ez) *noun plural* loose breeches tucked in at the knee

Named after Diedrich *Knickerbocker*, a fictional Dutchman invented by US author Washington Irving in the 19th century

knickers (*pronounced* nik-ez) *noun plural* women's or girls' underpants

knick-knack (*pronounced* nik-nak) *noun* a small, ornamental article

knife (*pronounced* naif) *noun* (*plural* **knives**) a tool for cutting □ *verb* to stab □ **at knife point** under threat of injury

knight (*pronounced* nait) *noun* **1** *historical* an aristocrat trained to use arms **2** a rank, with the title *Sir*, which is not inherited by a son **3** a piece used in chess □ *verb* to raise to the rank of knight

knighthood (*pronounced* nait-huwd) *noun* the rank of a knight

knightly (*pronounced* nait-li) *adjective* **1** of knights **2** gallant, courageous

knit (*pronounced* nit) *verb* **1** to form a garment from yarn or thread by making a series of knots using knitting needles **2** to join closely

knit ⇨ knits, knitting, knitted

knitting (*pronounced* **nit**-ing) *noun* work done by knitting

knitting needles *noun plural* a pair of thin pointed rods used in knitting

knob (*pronounced* nob) *noun* 1 a small rounded projection 2 a round door-handle

knock (*pronounced* nok) *verb* 1 to strike, hit 2 to drive or be driven against 3 to tap on a door to have it opened □ *noun* 1 a sudden stroke 2 a tap (on a door) □ **knock back** *informal* to eat or drink greedily □ **knock down** 1 to demolish 2 *informal* to reduce in price □ **knock off** *informal* 1 to stop work for the day 2 to plagiarize, copy illegally □ **knock out** to hit (someone) hard enough to make them unconscious □ **knock up** 1 to put together hastily 2 to knock on someone's door to wake them up

■ **Alternative words**: (verb, meaning 1) jog, jolt

knocker (*pronounced* **nok**-er) *noun* a hinged weight on a door for knocking with

knock-kneed (*pronounced* nok-**need**) *adjective* having knees that touch in walking

knoll (*pronounced* nohl) *noun* a small rounded hill

knot (*pronounced* not) *noun* 1 a hard lump, *eg* one made by tying string, or found in wood at the join between trunk and branch 2 a tangle 3 a small gathering, a cluster of people 4 a measure of speed for ships (about 1.85 kilometre per hour) □ *verb* to tie in a knot

knot *verb* ⇨ knots, knotting, knotted

knotted (*pronounced* **not**-id) *adjective* full of knots □ **get knotted!** *exclamation, informal* expressing anger or defiance towards someone

knotty (*pronounced* **not**-i) *adjective* 1 having knots 2 difficult, complicated: *knotty problem*

know (*pronounced* noh) *verb* 1 to be aware or sure of 2 to recognize

know ⇨ knows, knowing, known, knew

ⓘ Comes from Old English *cnawan*

knowing (*pronounced* **noh**-ing) *adjective* clever; cunning

knowingly (*pronounced* **noh**-ing-li) *adverb* 1 intentionally 2 in a way which shows you understand something which is secret or which has not been directly expressed

knowledge (*pronounced* **nol**-ij) *noun* 1 that which is known 2 information 3 ability, skill

knowledgeable (*pronounced* **nol**-ij-*a*-bl) *adjective* showing or having knowledge

knuckle (*pronounced* **nu**-kl) *noun* a joint of the fingers □ **knuckle under** to give in, yield

knuckleduster *noun* a metal covering worn on the knuckles as a weapon

knucklehead *noun, informal* an idiot

koala bear an Australian tree-climbing animal resembling a small bear

kohl *noun* a black powder used as an eyeliner

kookaburra *another word* for **laughing jackass**

Koran *noun* the sacred book of Islam

kosher *adjective* 1 pure and clean according to Jewish law 2 *informal* acceptable, all right

kowtow to *verb* to treat with too much respect

Based on a Chinese phrase meaning to prostrate yourself before the emperor

krill *noun* a small shrimplike creature eaten by whales *etc*

Krugerrand *noun* a South African coin used only for investment

krypton *noun* an inert gas present in the air, used in fluorescent lighting

kudos (*pronounced* **kyood**-os) *noun* fame, glory

kung-fu *noun* a Chinese form of self-defence

kyrie (*pronounced* **kee**-ri-ei) *noun* 1 a prayer in the Roman Catholic mass following the opening anthem 2 a musical setting for this

lab *noun, informal* a laboratory

label *noun* a small written note fixed onto something listing its contents, price *etc* □ *verb* 1 to fix a label to 2 to call something by a certain name

> **label** *verb* ⇨ labels, labelling, labelled

labial *adjective* of the lips

laboratory *noun* (*plural* **laboratories**) a scientist's workroom

laborious *adjective* requiring hard work; wearisome

labour or *US* **labor** *noun* 1 hard work 2 workers on a job 3 the process of childbirth □ *verb* 1 to work hard to move slowly or with difficulty 2 to emphasize (a point) too greatly

laboured *adjective* showing signs of effort

labourer *noun* someone who does heavy unskilled work

Labour Party one of the chief political parties of Great Britain, which has the aim of representing the working people and achieving greater social equality

labrador *noun* a large black or fawn-coloured dog, often used for retrieving game after it has been shot

laburnum *noun* a tree with large clusters of yellow flowers and poisonous seeds

labyrinth *noun* a maze

lace *noun* 1 a cord for fastening shoes *etc* 2 decorative openwork fabric made with fine thread □ *verb* 1 to fasten with a lace 2 to add alcohol to (a drink)

lacerate *verb* 1 to tear, rip 2 to wound □ **laceration** *noun*

lachrymal *adjective* of tears

lack *verb* 1 to be in want 2 to be without □ *noun* want, need

lackadaisical *adjective* bored, half-hearted

lackey *noun* (*plural* **lackeys**) 1 a manservant 2 someone who acts like a slave

lacklustre or *US* **lackluster** *adjective* dull, insipid

laconic *adjective* using few words to express meaning □ **laconically** *adverb*

lacquer *noun* a varnish □ *verb* to varnish

lacrosse *noun* a twelve-a-side ball-game played with sticks having a shallow net at the end

lactate *verb* to produce or secrete milk

lactic *adjective* of milk

lactose *noun* (*also called* **milk sugar**) a sugar obtained by evaporating whey

lad *noun* a boy, a youth

ladder *noun* 1 a set of rungs or steps between two supports, for climbing up or down 2 a run from a broken stitch, in a stocking *etc*

laden *adjective* loaded, burdened

lading *noun* a load; cargo

ladle *noun* a large spoon for lifting out liquid □ *verb* to lift with a ladle

lady *noun* *plural* **ladies** 1 a woman of good manners 2 a title for the wife of a knight, lord or baronet, or a daughter of a member of the aristocracy 3 **ladies** a public lavatory for women

ladybird *noun* a small beetle, usually red with black spots

ladyship *noun*: **Her Ladyship** the title used in addressing a titled lady

lag *verb* **1** to move slowly and fall behind **2** to cover (a boiler or pipes) with a warm covering □ *noun* a delay

lag ⇨ lags, lagging, lagged

lager *noun* a light beer

lager lout a person who frequently drinks too much, and whose behaviour becomes vulgar, antisocial and probably violent when they do so

laggard *noun* someone who lags behind □ *adjective* lagging behind

lagging *noun* material for covering pipes *etc*

lagoon *noun* a shallow stretch of water separated from the sea by low sandbanks, rocks *etc*

laid *past form of* **lay¹**

laid-back *adjective*, *informal* relaxed, easy-going

laid-up *adjective* ill in bed

lain *past participle of* **lie²**

lair (*pronounced* leir) *noun* the den of a wild beast

🕐 Comes from Old English *leger* meaning 'a couch'

🖝 Do not confuse with: **layer**

laird *noun* in Scotland, a landowner

laissez-faire (*pronounced* les-ei-**feir**) *noun* a general principle of not interfering

laity (from **lay²**) (*pronounced* **lei**-*i*-ti) *noun* ordinary people, not clergymen

lake *noun* a large stretch of water surrounded by land

lama *noun* a Buddhist priest of Tibet

lamb *noun* **1** a young sheep **2** the meat of this animal **3** a gentle person

lambast *verb* to beat or reprimand severely

lame *adjective* **1** unable to walk, crippled **2** not good enough, not very convincing or impressive: *a lame excuse* □ *verb* to make lame □ **lamely** *adverb* (adjective, meaning 2)

lame duck an inefficient, useless person or organization

lament (*pronounced* la-**ment**) *verb* **1** to mourn, feel or express grief for **2** to regret □ *noun* **1** a show of grief **2** a mournful poem or piece of music □ **lamentation** *noun*

lamentable (*pronounced* **lam**-en-tab-l) *adjective* **1** pitiful **2** very bad

laminated *adjective* made by putting layers together: *laminated glass*

Lammas *noun* 1 August, an old feast day celebrating the beginning of the harvest

lamp *noun* a device to give out light, containing an electric bulb, candle *etc*

lampoon *noun* a piece of ridicule or satire directed at someone □ *verb* to ridicule, satirize

lamppost *noun* a pillar supporting a street lamp

lamprey (*pronounced* **lamp**-ri) *noun* (*plural* **lampreys**) a type of fish like an eel

LAN (*pronounced* lan) *abbreviation*, *computing* local area network

lance *noun* a long shaft of wood, with a spearhead □ *verb* to cut open (a boil *etc*) with a knife

lance-corporal *noun* a soldier with rank just below a corporal

lancet *noun* a sharp surgical instrument

land *noun* **1** the solid portion of the earth's surface **2** ground **3** soil **4** a part of a country □ *verb* **1** to arrive on land or on shore **2** to set (an aircraft, ship *etc*) on land or on shore

landed *adjective* owning lands and estates: *landed gentry*

landing *noun* **1** a coming ashore or to ground **2** a place for getting on shore **3** the level part of a staircase between the flights of steps

landlocked *adjective* almost or completely shut in by land

landlord, landlady *noun* **1** the owner of land or accommodation for rent **2** the owner or manager of an inn *etc*

landlubber *noun* someone who works on land and knows little about the sea

landmark *noun* **1** an object on land that serves as a guide **2** an important event

land mine *noun* a bomb laid on or near the surface of the ground which explodes when someone passes over it

landscape *noun* a painting, photograph *etc* of inland scenery

landscape gardening the art of laying out grounds so as to produce the effect of a picturesque landscape

landslide *noun* a mass of land that slips down from the side of a hill

landslide victory a win in an election in which a great mass of votes goes to one side

lane *noun* **1** a narrow street or passage **2** a part of the road, sea or air to which cars, ships, aircraft *etc* must keep

lang syne (*pronounced* lang **sain**) *adverb, Scottish* long since, long ago

language *noun* **1** human speech **2** the speech of a particular people or nation

languid *adjective* lacking liveliness and spirit

languish *verb* **1** to grow weak, droop **2** to pine: *the dog was languishing for its master* □ **languishing** *adjective*

languor *noun* a languid state, listlessness

laniard another spelling of **lanyard**

lank *adjective* **1** tall and thin **2** of hair: straight and limp

lanky *adjective* tall and thin

lanolin *noun* a fat extracted from sheep's wool

lantern *noun* a case for holding or carrying a light

lantern-jawed *adjective* hollow-cheeked, long-jawed

lanyard or **laniard** *noun* **1** a short rope used for fastening rigging *etc* on a ship **2** a cord for hanging a whistle *etc* round the neck

lap *verb* **1** to lick up with the tongue **2** to wash or flow against **3 lap up** to accept (praise *etc*) greedily **4** to wrap round, surround **5** to get a lap ahead of other competitors in a race □ *noun* **1** the front part, from waist to knees, of someone seated **2** a fold **3** one round of a racetrack or competition course

lap *verb* ➪ lap**s**, lap**ping**, lap**ped**

lapdog *noun* a small pet dog

lapel *noun* the part of a coat joined to the collar and folded back on the chest

lapse *verb* **1** to fall into bad habits **2** to cease, be no longer valid □ *noun* **1** a mistake, a failure **2** a period of time passing

laptop *noun* a compact portable computer combining screen, keyboard and processor in one unit

lapwing *noun* (*also called* **peewit**) a type of bird of the plover family

larceny *noun* stealing, theft

larch *noun* (*plural* **larches**) a cone-bearing deciduous tree

lard *noun* the melted fat of a pig □ *verb* **1** to put strips of bacon in meat before cooking **2** to smear, lay on thickly

larder *noun* **1** a room or place where food is kept **2** a stock of food

large *adjective* great in size, amount *etc* □ **at large 1** at liberty, free **2** in general: *the public at large*
♦ Comes from French *large* meaning 'broad' or 'wide'

largely *adverb* mainly, to a great extent

largesse (*pronounced* lah-**szes**) *noun* a generous giving away of money *etc*

lark *noun* **1** a general name for several kinds of singing bird **2** a piece of fun or mischief □ *verb* to fool about, behave mischievously

larva *noun* (*plural* **larvae**) an insect in its first stage after coming out of the egg, a grub

laryngitis *noun* inflammation of the larynx

larynx *noun* (*plural* **larynxes** or **larynges**) the upper part of the windpipe containing the cords that produce the voice

lasagne *noun plural* flat sheets of pasta □ *noun singular* (or **lasagna**) a baked dish made with this

lascivious *adjective* lustful; indecent, lewd

laser *noun* **1** a very narrow powerful beam of light **2** an instrument that concentrates light into such a beam

An acronym of '*l*ight *a*mplification by *s*timulated *e*mission of *r*adiation'

lash *noun* (*plural* **lashes**) **1** a thong or cord of a whip **2** a stroke with a whip **3** an eyelash □ *verb* **1** to strike with a whip **2** to fasten tightly with a rope *etc* **3** to attack with bitter words □ **lash out 1** to kick or swing out without thinking **2** to speak angrily **3** to spend extravagantly

lass *noun* (*plural* **lasses**) a girl

lassitude *noun* lack of energy, weariness

lasso *noun* (*plural* **lassoes** or **lassos**) a long rope with a loop that tightens when the rope is pulled, used for catching wild horses *etc* □ *verb* to catch with a lasso

lasso *verb* ⇨ lasso*es*, lasso*ing*, lasso*ed*

last *adjective* **1** coming after all the others: *last person to arrive* **2** the final one remaining: *last ticket* **3** most recent: *my last employer* □ *adverb* **1** after all others **2** most recently **3** lastly □ *verb* **1** to continue, go on **2** to remain in good condition □ *noun* a foot-shaped tool on which shoes are made or repaired □ **at last** in the end □ **on your last legs** completely worn out, about to collapse □ **to the last** to the end

lastly *adverb* finally

last rites religious ceremonies performed for the dying

last straw the last in a series of unpleasant events, which makes a situation unbearable

last word the final comment or decision about something

latch *noun* (*plural* **latches**) **1** a wooden or metal catch used to fasten a door **2** a light door-lock □ *verb* to fasten with a latch

latchkey *noun* a key to raise the latch of a door

latchkey child a child who regularly returns home to an empty house

late *adjective* & *adverb* **1** coming after the expected time: *his train was late* **2** far on in time: *it's getting late* **3** recent: *our late disagreement* **4** recently dead: *the late author* **5** recently, but no longer,

holding an office or position: *the late chairman* □ **of late** recently □ **lateness** *noun* (meanings 1 and 2)

lately *adverb* recently

latent *adjective* hidden, undeveloped as yet: *latent ability/ latent hostility*

lateral *adjective* of, at, to or from the side

lateral thinking thinking which seeks new ways of looking at a problem and does not merely proceed in logical stages

latex *noun* the milky juice of plants, especially of the rubber tree

lath (*pronounced* lahth) *noun* a thin narrow strip of wood
ⓘ Comes from Old English *læt*

　　✎ Do not confuse: **lath** and **lathe**

lathe (*pronounced* leidh) *noun* a machine for turning and shaping articles of wood, metal *etc*
ⓘ Probably comes from Old Danish *lad* meaning 'a supporting framework'

lather *noun* **1** a foam or froth, *eg* from soap and water **2** *informal* a state of agitation □ *verb* to cover with lather

Latin *noun* the language of ancient Rome

latitude *noun* **1** the distance, measured in degrees, of a place north or south of the equator (*compare with*: **longitude**) **2** freedom of action or choice: *the new job allows him far more latitude than his previous one*

latrine *noun* a toilet in a camp, barracks *etc*

latter *adjective* **1** the last of two things mentioned (*contrasted with*: **former**): *between working and sleeping, I prefer the latter* **2** recent

latter-day *adjective* of recent times

latterly *adverb* recently

lattice *noun* **1** a network of crossed wooden *etc* strips **2** a window constructed this way

laud *verb, formal* to praise

laudable *adjective* worthy of being praised □ **laudably** *adverb*

laudanum (*pronounced* lawd-*a*n-*u*m) *noun* an alcoholic solution of opium,

taken as a popular medicine in
Victorian times

laudatory *adjective* expressing praise

laugh *verb* to make sounds with the
voice in showing amusement, scorn *etc*
□ *noun* the sound of laughing

■ **Alternative words**: (verb) chuckle,
giggle, guffaw, snigger, titter,
chortle

laughable *adjective* comical, ridiculous

laughing jackass (*also called*
kookaburra) the Australian giant
kingfisher

laughing stock an object of scornful
laughter

laughter *noun* the act or noise of
laughing

launch *verb* 1 to slide a boat or ship
into water, especially on its first voyage
2 to fire off (a rocket *etc*) 3 to start off
on a course 4 to put (a product) on the
market with publicity 5 to throw, hurl
□ *noun* (*plural* **launches**) 1 the act of
launching 2 a large motor boat

launder *verb* to wash and iron clothes
etc

launderette *noun* a shop where
customers may wash clothes *etc* in
washing machines

laundry *noun* (*plural* **laundries**) 1 a
place where clothes are washed 2 clothes
to be washed

laurel *noun* 1 the bay tree, from which
ceremonial wreaths were made 2
laurels honours or victories gained
□ **rest on your laurels** to be content
with past successes and not try for any
more

lava *noun* molten rock *etc* thrown out
by a volcano, becoming solid as it cools

lavatory *noun* (*plural* **lavatories**) a
toilet

lavender *noun* 1 a sweet-smelling plant
with small pale purple flowers 2 a pale-
purple colour

lavish *verb* to spend or give very freely
□ *adjective* very generous

law *noun* 1 the official rules that apply
in a country or state 2 one such rule 3
a scientific rule stating the conditions

under which certain things always
happen

law-abiding *adjective* obeying the law

law court a place where people accused
of crimes are tried

lawful *adjective* allowed by law
□ **lawfully** *adverb*

lawless *adjective* paying no attention
to, and not observing, the laws

lawn *noun* 1 an area of smooth grass,
eg as part of a garden 2 a kind of fine
linen

lawnmower *noun* a machine for cutting
grass

lawn tennis tennis played on a hard or
grass court

lawsuit *noun* a quarrel or dispute to be
settled by a court of law

lawyer *noun* someone whose work it is
to give advice in matters of law

lax *adjective* 1 not strict 2 careless,
negligent □ **laxity** *noun*

laxative *noun* a medicine which loosens
the bowels

lay¹ *verb* 1 to place or set down: *lay the
book on the table* 2 to put (*eg* a burden,
duty) on (someone): *new laws laying a
heavy burden of responsibility on
teachers/ try to lay the blame on someone
else* 3 to beat down: *All the barley in
the field had been laid flat by the storm*
4 to make to leave or subside: *lay a
ghost* 5 to set in order, arrange: *lay a
trap/ lay the table* 6 of a hen: to produce
eggs: *Young hens quite often lay double-
yolkers* 7 to bet, wager: *He's sure to be
late – I'd lay money on it* □ **lay about
someone** to beat them all over □ **lay
down** 1 to assert: *laying down the law* 2
to store (*eg* wine) □ **lay off** 1 to dismiss
(workers) temporarily 2 *informal* to
stop: *lay off arguing* □ **lay up** to store
for future use □ **lay waste** to ruin,
destroy

lay *verb* ⇨ lays, lay*ing*, laid

● Do not confuse with: **lie**. It may
help to remember that the verb
lay always takes an object, while
an object is not used with the verb
lie

lay² *adjective* 1 not of the clergy 2

without special training in a particular subject

lay³ *noun, old* a short poem or song

layabout *noun* a lazy idle person

layby *noun* a parking area at the side of a road

layer *noun* a thickness forming a covering or level

☛ Do not confuse with: **lair**. Layer comes from the verb 'to lay'

layered *adjective* having a number of distinct layers: *layered cake*

lay-figure *noun* a jointed model of a human figure used by artists

layman *noun* a man without special training in a subject

laywoman *noun* a woman without special training in a subject

laze *verb* to be lazy; idle

lazy *adjective* not inclined to work; idle □ **lazily** *adverb*

lazy *adjective* ⇨ laz*ier*, laz*iest*

■ **Alternative words**: idle, slothful, lethargic

lazy-bones *noun, informal* an idler

lea *noun, old* a meadow

leach *verb* to seep slowly through or out of something
Ⓒ Comes from Old English *leccan* meaning 'to water' or 'to moisten'
☛ Do not confuse with: **leech**

lead¹ *verb* **1** to show the way by going first **2** to direct, guide **3** to persuade **4** to live (a busy, quiet *etc* life) **5** of a road: to go (to) □ *noun* **1** the first or front place **2** guidance, direction **3** a leash for a dog *etc*

lead *verb* ⇨ leads, lead*ing*, led

lead² *noun* **1** a soft bluish-grey metal **2** the part of a pencil that writes, really made of graphite **3** a weight used for sounding depths at sea *etc*

leaden *adjective* **1** made of lead **2** lead-coloured **3** dull, heavy

leader *noun* **1** someone who leads or goes first; a chief **2** a column in a newspaper expressing the editor's opinions

leadership *noun* **1** the state of being a leader **2** the ability to lead

lead-free *adjective* of petrol: containing no lead

leading question one asked in such a way as to suggest the desired answer

leaf *noun* (*plural* **leaves**) **1** a part of a plant growing from the side of a stem **2** a page of a book **3** a hinged flap on a table *etc* □ **turn over a new leaf** to begin again and do better

leaflet *noun* a small printed sheet

leafy *adjective* **1** of a plant or tree: having a lot of leaves **2** of a place: having a lot of trees and plants

league *noun* **1** a union of people, nations *etc* for the benefit of each other **2** an association of clubs for games **3** *old* a measure of distance, approximately 3 miles (about 4.8 kilometres) □ **in league with** allied with

leak *noun* **1** a hole through which liquid passes **2** an escape of gas *etc* **3** a release of secret information □ *verb* **1** to escape, pass out **2** to give (secret information) to the media *etc*

leakage *noun* a leaking

lean *verb* **1** to slope over to one side **2** to rest (against) **3** to rely (on) □ *adjective* **1** thin **2** poor, scanty **3** of meat: not fat

lean *verb* ⇨ leans, lean*ing*, leant

lean-burn *adjective* of an engine: able to run on a reduced amount of fuel

leaning *noun* a liking for, or interest in, something

lean-to *noun* a shed *etc* built against another building or wall

leap *verb* **1** to move with jumps **2** to jump (over) □ *noun* a jump

leap *verb* ⇨ leaps, leap*ing*, leapt

leapfrog *noun* a game in which one player leaps over another's bent back

leap year a year which has 366 days (February having 29), occurring every fourth year

learn *verb* **1** to get to know (something) **2** to gain skill

learn ⇨ learns, learn*ing*, learnt or learn*ed*

learned (*pronounced* ler-nid) *adjective* having or showing great knowledge

learner *noun* someone who is learning something

learning *noun* knowledge

lease *noun* 1 an agreement giving the use of a house *etc* in return for payment of rent 2 the period of this agreement □ *verb* to let or rent

lease-back *noun* an arrangement in which the buyer of a property leases it back to the seller

leasehold *noun* property or land held by lease

leash *noun* (*plural* **leashes**) a lead by which a dog *etc* is held □ *verb* to put (a dog *etc*) on a leash

least *adjective* the smallest amount of anything: *he had the least money* □ *adverb* (often **the least**) the smallest or lowest degree: *I like her least* □ **at least** at any rate, anyway □ **not in the least** not at all

leather *noun* the skin of an animal, prepared by tanning for use □ *verb* to beat

leathering *noun* a thrashing

leathery *adjective* like leather; tough

leave *noun* 1 permission to do something (*eg* to be absent) 2 a holiday □ *verb* 1 to allow to remain 2 to abandon, forsake 3 to depart (from) 4 to hand down to someone in a will 5 to give over to someone's responsibility, care *etc*: *leave the choice to her* □ **take your leave of** 1 to part from 2 to say goodbye to

leave *verb* ⇨ leaves, leaving, left

leaven *noun* yeast

leavened *adjective* raised with yeast

leavings *noun plural* things left over

lecher *noun* a lustful man

lecherous *adjective* lustful in a sexual way □ **lechery** *noun*

lectern *noun* a stand for a book to be read from

lecture *noun* 1 a formal talk on a certain subject given to an audience 2 a scolding □ *verb* 1 to deliver a lecture 2 to scold

lecturer *noun* someone who lectures, especially to students

LED *abbreviation* light-emitting diode

led *past form* of **lead**[1]

ledge *noun* 1 a shelf or projecting rim: *window-ledge* 2 an underwater ridge

ledger *noun* the accounts book of an office or shop

lee *noun* the side away from the wind, the sheltered side

leech *noun* (*plural* **leeches**) a kind of blood-sucking worm
⏱ Comes from Old English *lœce*
🖝 Do not confuse with: **leach**

leek *noun* a long green and white vegetable of the onion family

leer *noun* a sly, sidelong or lustful look □ *verb* to look sideways or lustfully (at)

leeward *adjective* & *adverb* in the direction towards which the wind blows

leeway *noun* 1 a ship's drift off course 2 lost time, ground *etc*: *a lot of leeway to make up* 3 room to manoeuvre, latitude

left[1] *adjective* on or of the side of the body that in most people has the less skilful hand (*contrasted with*: **right**) □ *adverb* on or towards the left side □ *noun* 1 the left side 2 a political grouping with left-wing ideas *etc*

left[2] *past form* of **leave**

left-field *adjective, informal* odd, eccentric

left-handed *adjective* 1 using the left hand rather than the right 2 awkward

left-wing *adjective* of or holding socialist or radical political views, ideas *etc*

leg *noun* 1 one of the limbs by which humans and animals walk 2 a long slender support for a table *etc* 3 one stage in a journey, contest *etc*

legacy *noun* (*plural* **legacies**) 1 something which is left by will 2 something left behind by the previous occupant of a house, job *etc*

legal *adjective* 1 allowed by law, lawful 2 of law

legalistic *adjective* sticking rigidly to the law or rules

legality *noun* (*plural* **legalities**) the state of being legal

legalize *verb* to make lawful

legate *noun* an ambassador, especially from the Pope

legend *noun* 1 a traditional story handed down, a myth 2 a caption

legendary *adjective* 1 of legend; famous 2 not to be believed

leggings (from **leg**) *noun plural* 1 outer coverings for the lower legs 2 close-fitting trousers for women

leggy (from **leg**) *adjective* having long legs

legible *adjective* able to be read easily □ **legibility** *noun*

legion *noun* 1 *historical* a body of from three to six thousand Roman soldiers 2 a very great number

legionary *noun* (*plural* **legionaries**) a soldier of a legion

Legionnaires' disease a serious disease similar to pneumonia caused by a bacterium

So called after an outbreak of the disease at an American *Legion* convention in 1976

legislate *verb* to make laws □ **legislation** *noun*

legislative *adjective* law-making

legislator *noun* someone who makes laws

legislature *noun* the part of the government which has the powers of making laws

legitimate *adjective* 1 lawful 2 of a child: born of parents married to each other 3 correct, reasonable □ **legitimacy** *noun*

legless *adjective*, *informal* drunk

legroom *noun* room to move the legs

leisure *noun* time free from work, spare time

leisured *adjective* not occupied with business

leisurely *adjective* unhurried: *leisurely pace*

leitmotiv (*pronounced* **lait**-moh-teef) *noun* 1 a musical theme in an opera associated with a particular character *etc* 2 a recurring theme

lemming *noun* 1 a small rat-like animal of the arctic regions, reputed to follow others of its kind over sea-cliffs *etc* when migrating 2 someone who follows others unquestioningly

lemon *noun* 1 an oval fruit with pale yellow rind and sour juice 2 the tree that bears this fruit

lemonade *noun* a soft drink flavoured with lemons

lemur *noun* an animal related to the monkey but with a pointed nose

lend *verb* 1 to give use of (something) for a time 2 to give, add (a quality) to someone or something: *his presence lent an air of respectability to the occasion* □ **lend itself to** to be suitable for, adapt easily to

lend ⇨ lend*s*, lend*ing*, **lent**

length *noun* 1 extent from end to end in space or time 2 the quality of being long 3 a great extent 4 a piece of cloth *etc* □ **at length** 1 in detail 2 at last

lengthen *verb* to make or grow longer

lengthways or **lengthwise** *adverb* in the direction of the length

lengthy *adjective* 1 long 2 tiresomely long

lenient *adjective* merciful, punishing only lightly □ **lenience** or **leniency** *noun*

lens *noun* (*plural* **lenses**) 1 a piece of glass curved on one or both sides, used in spectacles, cameras *etc* 2 a part of the eye

Lent *noun* in the Christian church, a period of fasting before Easter lasting forty days

lent *past form of* **lend**

lentil *noun* the seed of a pod-bearing plant, used in soups *etc*

leonine *adjective* like a lion

leopard *noun* an animal of the cat family with a spotted skin

leopardess *noun* a female leopard

leotard *noun* a tight-fitting, stretchy

garment worn for dancing, gymnastics *etc*

leper *noun* 1 someone with leprosy 2 an outcast

lepidopterology *noun* the study of butterflies and moths

leprechaun *noun* a creature in Irish folklore

leprosy *noun* a contagious skin disease causing thickening or numbness in the skin

lesbian *noun* a female homosexual □ *adjective* of a woman: homosexual

lesion *noun* a wound

less *adjective* 1 not as much: *take less time* 2 smaller: *think of a number less than 40* □ *adverb* not as much, to a smaller extent: *he goes less often than he should* □ *noun* a smaller amount: *he has less than I have* □ *preposition* minus: *5 less 2 equals 3*

lessen *verb* to make smaller

lesser *adjective* smaller

lesson *noun* 1 something which is learned or taught 2 a part of the Bible read in church 3 a period of teaching

lest *conjunction* for fear that, in case

let *verb* 1 to allow 2 to grant use of (*eg* a house, shop, farm) in return for payment □ **let down** to fail to act as expected, disappoint □ **let off** to excuse, not punish □ **let up** to become less

let *verb* ⇨ let*s*, lett*ing*, let

■ **Alternative words**: (verb, meaning 1) permit, authorize, give leave □ **let up** subside, abate

lethal *adjective* causing death

lethargy *noun* a lack of energy or interest; sleepiness □ **lethargic** *adjective*

letter *noun* 1 a mark expressing a sound 2 a written message 3 **letters** learning: *a woman of letters* □ **to the letter** according to the exact meaning of the words: *following instructions to the letter*

lettering *noun* letters which have been drawn or painted, usually in a particular style

lettuce *noun* a kind of green plant whose leaves are used in a salad

leucocyte *noun* a white blood corpuscle

leukaemia *noun* a cancerous disease of the white blood cells in the body

level *noun* 1 a flat, smooth surface 2 a height, position *etc* in comparison with some standard: *water level* 3 an instrument for showing whether a surface is level: *spirit level* 4 personal rank or degree of understanding: *a bit above my level* □ *adjective* 1 flat, even, smooth 2 horizontal □ *verb* 1 to make flat, smooth or horizontal 2 to make equal 3 to aim (a gun *etc*) 4 to pull down (a building *etc*)

level *verb* ⇨ level*s*, level*ling*, level*led*

level crossing a place where a road crosses a railway track

level-headed *adjective* having good sense

level playing-field a position of equality from which to compete fairly

lever *noun* 1 a bar of metal, wood *etc* used to raise or shift something heavy 2 a handle for operating a machine 3 a method of gaining advantage

leverage *noun* 1 the use of a lever 2 power, influence

leveret *noun* a young hare

levitate *verb* to float in the air

levitation *noun* the illusion of raising a heavy body in the air without support

levity *noun* lack of seriousness, frivolity

levy *verb* to collect by order (*eg* a tax, army conscripts) □ *noun* (*plural* **levies**) money, troops *etc* collected by order

levy ⇨ levi*es*, levy*ing*, levi*ed*

lewd *adjective* taking delight in indecent thoughts or acts

lexical *adjective* of words

lexicographer *noun* someone who compiles or edits a dictionary □ **lexicography** *noun*

lexicon *noun* 1 a dictionary 2 a glossary of terms

liability *noun* (*plural* **liabilities**) 1 legal responsibility 2 a debt 3 a disadvantage

liable *adjective* 1 legally responsible (for) 2 likely or apt (to do something or happen) **3 liable to** likely to have, suffer from: *liable to colds*

liaise (*pronounced* lee-**eiz**) *verb* to make a connection (with), be in touch (with)

liaison (*pronounced* lee-**eiz**-on) *noun* **1** contact, communication **2** a sexual affair

liar (from **lie¹**) *noun* someone who tells lies

lib *noun*, *informal* liberation: *women's lib*

libation *noun* wine poured to honour a god

Lib Dem *short for* Liberal Democrat

libel *noun* something written to hurt another's reputation □ *verb* to write something libellous about

  libel *verb* ⇨ libels, libelling, libelled

libellous *adjective* containing a written false statement which hurts a person's reputation

liberal *adjective* generous; broad-minded, tolerant □ *noun* (**Liberal**) a member of the former Liberal Party, which supported social and political reform □ **liberality** *noun*

Liberal Democrats one of the chief political parties of Great Britain, formed in 1988 from the Liberal Party and the Social Democratic Party

liberate *verb* to set free □ **liberation** *noun*

libertine *noun* someone who lives a wicked, immoral life

liberty *noun* (*plural* **liberties**) **1** freedom, especially of speech or action **2 liberties** rights, privileges □ **take liberties** to behave rudely or impertinently

libido *noun* sexual drive or urge

librarian *noun* a person employed in or in charge of a library

library *noun* (*plural* **libraries**) **1** a collection of books, records *etc* **2** a building or room housing these

libretto *noun* (*plural* **libretti** or **librettos**) the words of an opera, musical show *etc*

lice *plural* of **louse**

licence *noun* **1** a form giving

permission to do something, *eg* to keep a television set, drive a car *etc* **2** too great freedom of action

  ☛ Do not confuse: **licence** and **license**. **Licence/license** and **practice/practise** follow the same pattern: you spell the verbs with an S (**licenSe**, **practiSe**), and the nouns with a C (**licenCe**, **practiCe**)

license *verb* to permit

licensee *noun* someone to whom a licence is given

licentious *adjective* given to behaving immorally or improperly

lichen (*pronounced* **laik**-en) *noun* a large group of moss-like plants that grow on rocks *etc*

lick *verb* **1** to pass the tongue over **2** of flames: to reach up, touch □ *noun* **1** the act of licking **2** a tiny amount □ **lick into shape** to make vigorous improvements on

licorice *another spelling of* **liquorice**

lid *noun* **1** a cover for a box, pot *etc* **2** the cover of the eye

lido (*pronounced* **lee**-doh) *noun* **1** a bathing beach **2** an open-air swimming pool

lie¹ *noun* a false statement meant to deceive □ *verb* to tell a lie

  lie¹ *verb* ⇨ lies, lying, lied

  ▤ **Alternative words**: (verb) fib, fabricate, perjure yourself, prevaricate, equivocate

lie² *verb* **1** to rest in a flat position: *lie flat on your back* **2** to be or remain in a state or position: *lie dormant* □ *noun* the position or situation in which something lies □ **lie in wait** to keep hidden in order to surprise someone □ **lie low** to keep quiet or hidden □ **the lie of the land** the present state of affairs

  lie² *verb* ⇨ lies, lying, lay, lain

  ☛ Do not confuse with: **lay**. It may help to remember that an object is not used with the verb **lie**, while the verb **lay** always takes an object

liege (*pronounced* leesz) *noun* **1** a loyal subject **2** a lord or superior

lieu (*pronounced* lyoo or loo) *noun*: **in lieu of** instead of

lieutenant (*pronounced* lef-ten-ant or *US* loo-ten-ant) *noun* **1** an army officer next below captain **2** in the navy, an officer below a lieutenant-commander **3** a rank below a higher officer: *lieutenant-colonel*

life *noun* (*plural* lives) **1** the period between birth and death **2** the state of being alive **3** liveliness **4** manner of living **5** the story of someone's life **6** living things: *animal life*
Ⓞ Comes from Old English *lif*

lifebelt *noun* a ring made of cork or filled with air for keeping someone afloat

lifeboat *noun* a boat for rescuing people in difficulties at sea

life-blood *noun* a source of necessary strength or life

lifebuoy *noun* a float to support someone awaiting rescue at sea

life-cycle *noun* the various stages through which a living thing passes

life drawing drawing from a live human model

life-jacket *noun* a buoyant jacket for keeping someone afloat in water

lifeless *adjective* **1** dead **2** not lively, spiritless

life-like *adjective* like a living person

lifeline *noun* a vital means of communication

lifelong *adjective* lasting the length of a life

life-size *adjective* full size, as in life

lifespan *noun* the length of someone's life

lifestyle *noun* the way in which someone lives

life-support machine a device for keeping a human being alive during severe illness, space travel *etc*

lifetime *noun* the period during which someone is alive

lift *verb* **1** to raise, take up **2** *informal* to steal **3** of fog: to disappear, disperse
□ *noun* **1** a moving platform carrying goods or people between floors in a large building **2** a ride in someone's car *etc* **3** a boost

lift-off *noun* the take-off of a rocket, spacecraft *etc*

ligament *noun* a tough substance that connects the bones of the body

ligature *noun* **1** something which binds **2** a printed character formed from two or more letters joined together, *eg* æ or ffi

light¹ *noun* **1** the brightness given by the sun, moon, lamps *etc* that makes things visible **2** a source of light, *eg* a lamp **3** a flame on a cigarette lighter **4** knowledge □ *adjective* **1** bright **2** of a colour: pale **3** having light, not dark □ *verb* **1** to give light to **2** to set fire to □ **bring to light** to reveal, cause to be noticed □ **come to light** to be revealed or discovered □ **in the light of** taking into consideration (information *etc*)

> **light** *verb* ⇨ lights, lighting, lit or lighted

light² *adjective* **1** not heavy **2** easy to bear or do: *light work* **3** easy to digest **4** nimble **5** lively **6** not grave, cheerful **7** not serious: *light reading* **8** of rain *etc*: little in quantity

light³ *verb, old*: **light on 1** to land, settle on **2** to come upon by chance

> **light** ⇨ lights, lighting, lit or lighted

lighten *verb* **1** to make less heavy **2** to make or become brighter **3** of lightning: to flash

lightening (*pronounced* lait-en-ing) (from **lighten**) *noun* a making or becoming lighter or brighter

> ♠ Do not confuse with: **lightning**

lighter *noun* **1** a device with a flame *etc* for lighting **2** a large open boat used in unloading and loading ships

light-fingered *adjective* apt to steal

light-headed *adjective* dizzy

light-hearted *adjective* cheerful

lighthouse *noun* a tower-like building with a flashing light to warn or guide ships

lighting *noun* **1** a means of providing

light **2** the combination of lights used, *eg* in a theatre or a disco

lightly *adverb* **1** gently **2** not seriously

lightning *noun* an electric flash in the clouds

☛ Do not confuse with: **lightening**

lightning conductor a metal rod on a building *etc* which conducts electricity down to earth

lightweight *noun* a weight category in boxing □ *adjective* not serious enough to demand much concentration

light-year *noun* the distance light travels in a year (6 billion miles)

like¹ *adjective* the same as or similar to □ *adverb* in the same way as: *he sings like an angel* □ *noun* something or someone that is the equal of another: *you won't see her like again*

like² *verb* **1** to be pleased with **2** to be fond of
ⓞ Comes from Old English *lician* meaning 'to please' or 'to be suitable'

⊞ **Opposite:** dislike

likeable or **likable** *adjective* attractive, lovable

likelihood *noun* probability

likely *adjective* **1** probable **2** liable (to do something) □ *adverb* probably

liken *verb* to think of as similar, compare

likeness *noun* **1** similarity, resemblance **2** a portrait, photograph *etc* of someone

likewise *adverb* **1** in the same way **2** also

liking *noun* **1** fondness **2** satisfaction: *to my liking*

lilac *noun* a small tree with hanging clusters of pale purple or white flowers □ *adjective* of pale purple colour

lilliputian *adjective* tiny, minuscule

After *Lilliput*, a country on a tiny scale in Jonathan Swift's 18th-century satirical novel, *Gulliver's Travels*

lilt *noun* a striking rhythm or swing □ *verb* to have this rhythm

lily *noun* (*plural* **lilies**) a tall plant grown from a bulb with large white or coloured flowers

lily-of-the-valley *noun* a plant with small white bell-shaped flowers

limb *noun* **1** a leg or arm **2** a branch

limber *adjective* easily bent, supple □ **limber up** to exercise so as to become supple

limbo¹ *noun* the borderland of Hell, reserved for those unbaptized before death □ **in limbo** forgotten, neglected

limbo² *noun* a W Indian dance in which the dancer passes under a low bar

lime *noun* **1** (*also called* **quicklime**) a white substance left after heating limestone, used in making cement **2** a tree related to the lemon **3** the greenish-yellow fruit of this tree **4** another name for **linden**

limelight *noun* the glare of publicity □ **in the limelight** attracting publicity or attention

limerick *noun* a type of humorous poetry in five-line verses

After *Limerick* in Ireland, the name of which was repeated in nonsense songs in an old Victorian parlour game

Limericks are funny poems with five lines and a strict rhyme scheme. Maybe you know this one:
There was a young lady from Tottenham
Whose manners, she quite had forgotten 'em,
At tea at the vicar's
She took off her knickers
Because, she explained, she felt hot in 'em.
🔑 **Can you make up some more?**

limit *noun* **1** the farthest point or place **2** a boundary **3** the largest (or smallest) extent, degree *etc* **4** a restriction □ *verb* to set or keep to a limit

limitation *noun* **1** something which limits **2** a weak point, a flaw

limo *noun, informal* a limousine

limousine *noun* a kind of large car, especially one with a separate compartment for the driver

Named after a type of cloak worn in *Limousin* in France, because the car's roof was supposedly similar in shape

limp *adjective* 1 not stiff, floppy 2 weak □ *verb* 1 to walk lamely 2 of a damaged ship *etc*: to move with difficulty □ *noun* 1 the act of limping 2 a limping walk

limpet *noun* 1 a small cone-shaped shellfish that clings to rocks 2 someone who is difficult to get rid of

limpid *adjective* clear, transparent

linchpin *noun* a pin-shaped rod used to keep a wheel on an axle

line *noun* 1 a cord, rope *etc* 2 a long thin stroke or mark 3 a wrinkle 4 a row of people, printed words *etc* 5 a service of ships or aircraft 6 a railway 7 a telephone connection 8 a short letter 9 a family from generation to generation 10 course, direction 11 a subject of interest, activity *etc* 12 **lines** army trenches 13 **lines** a written school punishment exercise □ *verb* 1 to mark out with lines 2 (often **line up**) to place in a row or alongside of 3 to form lines along (a street) 4 to cover on the inside: *line a dress*

lineage *noun* descent, traced back to your ancestors

lineal *adjective* directly descended through the father, grandfather *etc*

linear *adjective* 1 made of lines 2 in one dimension (length, breadth or height) only 3 capable of being represented on a graph by a straight line

linen *noun* 1 cloth made of flax 2 articles made of linen: *tablelinen/ bedlinen*

liner *noun* a ship or aeroplane working on a regular service

linesman *noun* a male umpire at a boundary line

lineswoman *noun* a female umpire at a boundary line

linger *verb* 1 to stay for a long time or for longer than expected 2 to loiter, delay

lingerie *noun plural* women's underwear

lingo *noun* (*plural* **lingoes**) a language, a dialect

linguist *noun* 1 someone skilled in languages 2 someone who studies language

linguistic *adjective* to do with language

linguistics *noun singular* the scientific study of languages and of language in general

liniment *noun* an oil or ointment rubbed into the skin to cure stiffness in the muscles, joints *etc*

lining *noun* a covering on the inside

link *noun* 1 a ring of a chain 2 a single part of a series 3 anything connecting two things □ *verb* 1 to connect with a link 2 to join closely 3 to be connected □ **linkage** *noun*

links *noun plural* 1 a stretch of flat or slightly hilly ground near the seashore 2 a golf course

linnet *noun* a small songbird of the finch family

lino *noun, informal* linoleum

lino-cut *noun* a design for printing cut into a block of linoleum

linoleum *noun* a type of smooth, hard-wearing covering for floors

linseed *noun* flax seed

linseed oil oil from flax seed

lint *noun* 1 a soft woolly material for putting over wounds 2 fine pieces of fluff

lintel *noun* a timber or stone over a doorway or window

lion *noun* a powerful animal of the cat family, the male of which has a shaggy mane □ **the lion's share** the largest share

lioness *noun* a female lion

lip *noun* 1 either of the two fleshy flaps in front of the teeth forming the rim of the mouth 2 the edge of a container *etc*

liposuction *noun* a surgical operation to remove unwanted body fat

lip-reading *noun* reading what someone says from the movement of their lips

lip-service *noun* saying one thing but believing another: *paying lip-service to the rules*

lipstick *noun* a stick of red, pink *etc* colouring for the lips

liquefy *verb* to make or become liquid □ **liquefaction** *noun*

> **liquefy** ▷ liquefies, liquefying, liquefied

liqueur (*pronounced* lik-**yoor**) *noun* a strong alcoholic drink, strongly flavoured and sweet

> 🖤 Do not confuse with: **liquor**

liquid *noun* a flowing, water-like substance □ *adjective* 1 flowing 2 looking like water 3 soft and clear

liquidate *verb* 1 to close down, wind up the affairs of (a bankrupt business company) 2 *slang* to kill, murder □ **liquidation** *noun* □ **liquidator** *noun*

liquidize *verb* 1 to make liquid 2 to make into a purée

liquidizer *noun* a machine for liquidizing

liquor (*pronounced* lik-er) *noun* an alcoholic drink, especially a spirit (*eg* whisky)

> 🖤 Do not confuse with: **liqueur**

liquorice or **licorice** *noun* 1 a plant with a sweet-tasting root 2 a black, sticky sweet flavoured with this root

lisp *verb* 1 to say *th* for *s* or *z* because of being unable to pronounce these letters correctly 2 to speak imperfectly, like a child □ *noun* a speech disorder of this kind

list¹ *noun* a series of names, numbers, prices *etc* written down one after the other □ *verb* to write (something) down in this way

list² *verb* of a ship: to lean over to one side □ *noun* a slope to one side

listed building one protected from being changed, knocked down *etc* because it is of architectural or historical interest

listen *verb* to hear, pay attention to □ **listener** *noun*

> ■ **Alternative words**: hark, attend, heed

listeria *noun* a bacterium found in certain foods which can damage the nervous system if not killed during cooking

listless *adjective* weary, without energy or interest

lit *past form of* **light¹** and **light³**

litany *noun* (*plural* **litanies**) 1 a set form of prayer 2 a long list or catalogue

liter *US spelling of* **litre**

literacy *noun* ability to read and write

literal *adjective* following the exact or most obvious meaning (*contrasted with*: **figurative**)

literally *adverb* exactly as stated, not just as a figure of speech: *he was literally blinded by the flash*

literary *adjective* 1 relating to books, authors *etc* 2 knowledgeable about books

literate *adjective* able to read and write

literature *noun* 1 the books *etc* that are written in any language 2 anything in written form on a subject

lithe *adjective* bending easily, supple, flexible

lithium *noun* a metallic element whose salts are used in treating some mental illnesses

lithograph *noun* a picture made from a drawing done on stone or metal □ **lithography** *noun* printing done by this method

litigation *noun* a law case

litmus paper treated paper which changes colour when dipped in an acid or alkaline solution

litmus test something which indicates underlying attitudes *etc*

litre *noun* a metric measure of liquids (1.76 pint)

litter *noun* 1 an untidy mess of paper, rubbish *etc* 2 a heap of straw as bedding for animals 3 a number of animals born at one birth 4 *historical* a bed for carrying the sick and injured □ *verb* 1 to scatter rubbish carelessly about 2 to produce a litter of young

little *adjective* small in quantity or size □ *adverb* 1 **a little** to a small extent or degree 2 not much 3 not at all: *little does she know* □ *pronoun* a small amount, distance *etc*: *have a little more/ move a little to the right*
Ⓞ Comes from Old English *lytel*

liturgy (*pronounced* lit-*u*-ji) *noun* (*plural* **liturgies**) the form of service of a church □ **liturgical** *adjective*

live¹ (*pronounced* liv) *verb* **1** to have life **2** to dwell **3** to pass your life **4** to continue to be alive **5** to survive **6** to be lifelike or vivid □ **live and let live** to allow others to live as they please □ **live down** to live until (an embarrassment *etc*) is forgotten by others □ **live on 1** to keep yourself alive **2** to be supported by □ **live up to** to be as good as expected from
Ⓛ Comes from Old English *lifian*

live² (*pronounced* laiv) *adjective* **1** having life, not dead **2** full of energy **3** of a television broadcast *etc*: seen as the event takes place, not recorded **4** charged with electricity and apt to give an electric shock

livelihood (*pronounced* laiv-li-huwd) *noun* someone's means of living, *eg* their daily work

livelong (*pronounced* liv-long or laiv-long) *adjective, old* whole: *the livelong day*

lively *adjective* full of life, high spirits □ **liveliness** *noun*

liven *verb* to make lively

liver *noun* a large gland in the body that carries out several important functions including purifying the blood

livery *noun* (*plural* **liveries**) the uniform of a manservant *etc* □ **at livery** of a horse: being kept at a livery stable in exchange for payment by its owner

livery stable a stable where horses may be kept at livery or hired

livestock *noun* farm animals

livewire *noun* a very lively, energetic person

livid *adjective* **1** of a bluish lead-like colour **2** very angry

living *adjective* **1** having life **2** active, lively **3** of a likeness: exact □ *noun* means of living

living-room *noun* an informal sitting-room

living wage a wage on which it is possible to live comfortably

lizard *noun* a four-footed reptile

llama *noun* a S American animal of the camel family without a hump

lo *exclamation, old* look

load *verb* **1** to put on what is to be carried **2** to put the ammunition in (a gun) **3** to put a film in (a camera) **4** to weight for some purpose: *loaded dice* □ *noun* **1** as much as can be carried at once **2** cargo **3** a heavy weight or task **4** the power carried by an electric circuit

loaded question one meant to trap someone into making a damaging admission

loaf *noun* (*plural* **loaves**) a shaped mass of bread □ *verb* to pass time idly or lazily

loafer *noun* **1** an idler **2 loafers** casual shoes

loam *noun* a rich soil □ **loamy** *adjective*

loan *noun* something lent, especially a sum of money □ *verb* to lend

loath or **loth** (*pronounced* lohth) *adjective* unwilling (to)

> 🖝 Do not confuse: **loath** and **loathe**. Remember that loaTHE has an ending common to quite a few other verbs *eg* cloTHE and baTHE

loathe (*pronounced* lohdh) *verb* to dislike greatly

loathing (*pronounced* lohdh-ing) *noun* great hate or disgust

loathsome (*pronounced* lohdh-som) *adjective* causing loathing or disgust, horrible

loaves *plural* of **loaf**

lob *noun* **1** *cricket* a slow, high ball bowled underhand **2** *tennis* a ball high overhead dropping near the back of the court □ *verb* **1** to send such a ball **2** *informal* to throw

> **lob** *verb* ⇨ lobs, lobb*ing*, lobb*ed*

lobby *noun* (*plural* **lobbies**) **1** a small entrance hall **2** a passage off which rooms open **3** a group of people who try to influence the government or another authority □ *verb* **1** to try to influence (public officials) **2** to conduct a campaign to influence public officials

lobby *verb* ⇨ lobbies, lobbying, lobbied

lobe *noun* 1 the hanging-down part of an ear 2 a division of the brain, lungs *etc*

lobotomize *verb* 1 to perform a lobotomy on 2 to make bland or spiritless

lobotomy *noun* 1 the surgical operation of cutting into a lobe or gland 2 a surgical operation on the front lobes of the brain which has the effect of changing the patient's character

lobster *noun* a kind of shellfish with large claws, used for food

lobster pot a basket in which lobsters are caught

local *adjective* of or confined to a certain place □ *noun, informal* 1 the public house nearest someone's home 2 **locals** the people living in a particular place or area
🕔 Comes from Latin *locus* meaning 'a place'

local colour details in a story which make it more interesting and realistic

locale *noun* scene, location

local government administration of the local affairs of a district *etc* by elected inhabitants

locality *noun* a particular place and the area round about

localize *verb* to confine to one area, keep from spreading

locate *verb* 1 to find 2 to set in a particular place: *a house located in the Highlands*

location *noun* 1 the act of locating 2 position, situation □ **on location** of filming *etc*: in natural surroundings, not in a studio

loch *noun* 1 in Scotland, a lake 2 an arm of the sea

lock *noun* 1 a fastening for doors *etc* needing a key to open it 2 a part of a canal for raising or lowering boats 3 the part of a gun which explodes the charge 4 a tight hold 5 a section of hair 6 **locks** hair □ *verb* 1 to fasten with a lock 2 to become fastened 3 **lock up** to

shut in with a lock □ **lock, stock and barrel** completely

locker *noun* a small cupboard

locker-room *noun* a room for changing clothes and storing personal belongings

locket *noun* a little ornamental case hung round the neck

lockjaw *noun* a form of tetanus which stiffens the jaw muscles

lockout *noun* the locking out of workers by their employer during wage disputes

locksmith *noun* a person who makes locks

lock-up *noun* a lockable garage

locomotion *noun* movement from place to place

locomotive *noun* a railway engine □ *adjective* of or capable of locomotion

locum *noun* (*plural* **locums**) a doctor, dentist *etc* taking another's place for a time

locus *noun* (*plural* **loci**) a place, a locality

locust *noun* a large insect of the grasshopper family which destroys growing plants

lode *noun* a vein containing metallic ore

lodestar *noun* the Pole star

lodestone *noun* 1 a form of the mineral magnetite with magnetic properties 2 a magnet

lodge *noun* 1 a small house, often at the entrance to a larger building 2 a beaver's dwelling 3 a house occupied during the shooting or hunting season 4 a branch of a society □ *verb* 1 to live in rented rooms 2 to become fixed (in) 3 to put in a safe place 4 to make (a complaint, appeal *etc*) officially

lodger *noun* someone who stays in rented rooms

lodging *noun* 1 a place to stay, sleep *etc* 2 **lodgings** a room or rooms rented in someone else's house

loft *noun* 1 a room just under a roof 2 a gallery in a hall, church *etc*

lofty *adjective* 1 of great height 2 noble,

proud □ **loftily** *adverb* (meaning 2)

log *noun* 1 a thick, rough piece of wood, part of a felled tree 2 a device for measuring a ship's speed 3 a logbook □ *verb* to write down (events) in a logbook

log *verb* ⇨ logs, logging, logged

loganberry *noun* a kind of fruit like a large raspberry

logbook *noun* 1 an official record of a ship's or aeroplane's progress 2 a record of progress, attendance *etc* 3 the registration documents of a motor vehicle

loggerhead *noun*: **at loggerheads** quarrelling

logic *noun* 1 the study of reasoning correctly 2 correctness of reasoning

logical *adjective* according to the rules of logic or sound reasoning □ **logically** *adverb*

logo *noun* (*plural* **logos**) a symbol of a business firm *etc* consisting of a simple picture or lettering

loin *noun* 1 the back of an animal cut for food 2 **loins** the lower part of the back

loincloth *noun* a piece of cloth worn round the hips, especially in India and south-east Asia

loiter *verb* 1 to proceed, move slowly 2 to linger 3 to stand around

loll *verb* 1 to lie lazily about 2 of the tongue: to hang down or out

lollipop *noun* a large boiled sweet on a stick

lollipop man, lollipop woman *Brit* a person employed to stop cars to allow schoolchildren to cross the street, who carries a pole with a disc at the top

lollop *verb* 1 to bound clumsily 2 to lounge, idle

lolly *noun, informal* 1 a lollipop 2 money

lone *adjective* alone; standing by itself

lonely *adjective* 1 lone 2 lacking or needing companionship 3 of a place: having few people □ **loneliness** *noun*

lonesome *adjective* 1 lone 2 feeling lonely

long *adjective* 1 not short, measuring a lot from end to end 2 measuring a certain amount: *cut a strip 2 cm long/ the film is 3 hours long* 3 far-reaching 4 slow to do something □ *adverb* 1 for a great time 2 through the whole time: *all day long* □ *verb* to wish very much (for): *longing to see him again* □ **before long** soon □ **in the long run** in the end □ **so long** *informal* goodbye

Ⓛ Adjective: comes from Old English *lang/long*; adverb: comes from Old English *lange/longe*; verb: comes from Old English *langian*

▦ **Alternative words:** (verb) ache

longevity *noun* great length of life

longhand *noun* writing in full (*contrasted with*: **shorthand**)

longing *noun* a strong desire

longitude *noun* the distance, measured in degrees, of a place east or west of the Greenwich meridian (*compare with*: **latitude**)

long johns men's under-trousers reaching to the ankles

long jump an athletics contest in which competitors jump as far as possible along the ground from a running start

long-range *adjective* 1 able to reach a great distance 2 looking a long way into the future

longship *noun, historical* a Viking sailing ship

long-sighted *adjective* able to see things at a distance but not those close at hand

long-standing *adjective* begun a long time ago, having lasted a long time

long-suffering *adjective* putting up with troubles without complaining

long-term *adjective* 1 extending over a long time 2 taking the future, not just the present, into account

long-wave *adjective* of radio: using wavelengths over 1000 metres (*compare with*: **short wave**)

long-winded *adjective* using too many words

loo *noun, informal* a toilet

loofah *noun* the fibrous fruit of a tropical plant, used as a rough sponge

look *verb* **1** to turn the eyes towards so as to see **2** to appear, seem: *you look tired/ it looks as if I can go after all* **3** to face: *his room looks south* □ *noun* **1** the act of looking **2** the expression on someone's face **3** appearance **4 looks** personal appearance □ **look after** to take care of, take responsibility for □ **look alive** *informal* to rouse yourself, get ready for action □ **look down on** to think of as being inferior □ **look for** to search for □ **look forward to** to anticipate with pleasure □ **look into** to investigate □ **look on 1** to stand by and watch **2** to think of (as): *he looks on her as his mother* □ **look out!** be careful! □ **look over** to examine briefly □ **look sharp** *informal* to be quick, hurry up ① Comes from Old English *locian* meaning 'to look'

■ **Alternative words**: (verb, meaning 1) observe, view, survey, regard, gaze, study, stare, examine, inspect, scrutinize, glance, contemplate, scan, peep □ **look after** mind, attend to, tend, keep an eye on, supervise, guard

look-alike *noun* someone who looks physically like someone else

look-in *noun* a chance of doing something

looking-glass *noun* a mirror

lookout *noun* **1** (someone who keeps) a careful watch **2** a high place for watching from **3** concern, responsibility

loom *noun* a machine for weaving cloth □ *verb* to appear indistinctly, often threateningly

loony *noun, informal* a lunatic, an insane person □ *adjective* mad, insane

loop *noun* **1** a doubled-over part in a piece of string *etc* **2** a U-shaped bend □ **loop the loop** to fly (an aircraft) upwards, back and down as if going round a circle

loophole *noun* **1** a narrow slit in a wall **2** a way of avoiding a difficulty

loose (*pronounced* loos) *adjective* **1** not tight, slack **2** not tied, free **3** not closely packed **4** vague, not exact **5** careless □ *verb* **1** to make loose, slacken **2** to untie □ **break loose** to escape □ **on the**

loose free □ **loosely** *adverb* (adjective, meanings 1, 3, 4 and 5)

◆ Do not confuse with: **lose**

loose-leaf *adjective* having a cover that allows pages to be inserted or removed

loosen *verb* to make loose or looser

loot *noun* goods stolen or plundered □ *verb* to plunder, ransack

lop *verb* to cut off the top or ends of

lop ⇨ lop*s*, lop*ping*, lop*ped*

lope *verb* to run with a long stride

lop-eared *adjective* of an animal: having ears hanging down

lop-sided *adjective* leaning to one side, not symmetrical

loquacious (*pronounced* lok-**wei**-sh*u*s) *adjective* talkative □ **loquacity** (*pronounced* lok-**was**-*i*t-i) *noun*

lord *noun* **1** the owner of an estate **2** a title for a male member of the aristocracy, bishop, judge *etc* **3** *old* a master, a ruler **4 the Lord** God or Christ □ **drunk as a lord** extremely drunk □ **House of Lords** the upper (non-elected) house of the British parliament □ **lord it over someone** to act in a domineering manner towards them

Lord Chancellor the head of the English legal system

lordly *adjective* **1** relating to a lord **2** noble, proud

lordship *noun* **1** power, rule **2** used in addressing a lord: *his lordship*

lore *noun* knowledge, beliefs *etc* handed down

lorelei (*pronounced* lo-rel-ai) *noun* a mythological siren in the Rhine who lured sailors to their death

lorgnette (*pronounced* lawn-**yet**) *noun* eyeglasses with a handle

lorry *noun* (*plural* **lorries**) a motor vehicle for carrying heavy loads

lose (*pronounced* looz) *verb* **1** to cease to have, have no longer **2** to have (something) taken away from **3** to put (something) where it cannot be found **4** to waste (time) **5** to miss (a train, chance *etc*) **6** to not win (a game)

lose ⇨ lose*s*, los*ing*, lost

✒ Do not confuse with: **loose**

loser noun 1 someone unlikely to succeed at anything 2 someone who loses a game or contest 3 someone who is put in a disadvantageous situation as the result of a certain event

loss noun (plural **losses**) 1 the act of losing 2 something which is lost 3 waste, harm, destruction □ **at a loss** uncertain what to do or say

lost adjective 1 not able to be found 2 no longer possessed; thrown away 3 not won 4 ruined □ **lost in** completely taken up by, engrossed in: lost in thought

lot noun 1 a large number or quantity 2 someone's fortune or fate 3 a separate portion □ **draw lots** to decide who is to do something by drawing names out of a hat etc

loth another spelling of **loath**

lotion noun a liquid for treating or cleaning the skin or hair

lottery noun (plural **lotteries**) an event in which money or prizes are won through drawing lots

lotus noun (plural **lotuses**) 1 a kind of water-lily 2 a mythical tree whose fruit caused forgetfulness

louche (pronounced loosh) adjective shady, disreputable

loud adjective 1 making a great sound; noisy 2 showy, over-bright □ adverb in a way that makes a great sound; noisily □ **loudly** adverb (adjective, meaning 1) □ **loudness** noun (adjective, meaning 1)

loudhailer noun a megaphone with microphone and amplifier

loudmouth noun, informal someone who talks offensively and too much

loudspeaker noun a device for converting electrical signals into sound

lounge verb 1 to lie back in a relaxed way 2 to move about lazily □ noun a sitting-room

lounge lizard someone who spends a lot of time aimlessly at social events

lounger noun 1 a lazy person 2 an extending chair or light couch for relaxing on

lounge suit a man's suit for everyday (but not casual) wear

lour see **lower²**

louse noun (plural **lice**) a small blood-sucking insect sometimes found on the bodies of animals and people

lousy adjective 1 swarming with lice 2 informal inferior, of poor quality

lout noun a clumsy or boorish man

louvre or US **louver** noun a slat set at an angle

louvre door a slatted door allowing air and light to pass through

louvre window 1 a window covered with sloping slats 2 a window with narrow panes that can be set open at an angle

lovable adjective worthy of love

love noun 1 a great liking or affection 2 a loved person 3 tennis no score, zero □ verb to be very fond of; like very much □ **in love (with)** 1 feeling love and desire (for) 2 having a great liking (for): in love with his own voice □ **make love to 1** to have sexual intercourse with 2 old to make sexual advances to, court

■ **Alternative words**: (verb) adore, cherish, dote on, idolize, enjoy, delight in

love affair a relationship between people in love but not married

lovebite noun a mark on the skin caused by the sucking bites of a lover

love-child noun an illegitimate child

lovely adjective beautiful; delightful □ **loveliness** noun

lovemaking noun 1 old courtship 2 sexual play and intercourse

lover noun 1 someone who loves another 2 an admirer, an enthusiast: an art lover 3 someone who is having a love affair

lovesick adjective languishing with love

loving adjective full of love □ **lovingly** adverb

low adjective 1 not high; not lying or reaching far up 2 of a voice: not loud 3 cheap: low air-fare 4 feeling sad, depressed 5 humble 6 mean, unworthy

□ *verb* to make the noise of cattle; bellow, moo □ *adverb* **1** in or to a low position **2** not loudly **3** cheaply □ **lowbrow** *adjective* populist, not intellectual (*contrasted with:* **highbrow**) □ **lowdown** *noun* damaging information □ **lowkey** *adjective* not elaborate, unpretentious □ **lowland** *noun* flattish country, without high hills □ **keep a low profile** to not make your feelings or presence known

lower[1] (*pronounced* **loh**-er) *adjective* less high □ *verb* **1** to make less high: *lower the price* **2** to let or come down: *lower the blinds*

lower[2] or **lour** (*pronounced* **low**-er) *verb* **1** of the sky: to become dark and cloudy **2** to frown □ **lowering** *adjective*

lower-case *adjective* of a letter: not a capital, *eg a* not *A* (*contrasted with:* **upper-case**)

lowly *adjective* low in rank, humble □ **lowliness** *noun*

loyal *adjective* faithful, true □ **loyally** *adverb*

loyalist *noun* someone loyal to their sovereign or country

loyalty *noun* (*plural* **loyalties**) **1** faithful support of *eg* your friends **2 loyalties** feelings of faithful friendship and support, especially for a particular person or thing

lozenge *noun* **1** a diamond-shaped figure **2** a small sweet for sucking

LP *noun* a long-playing record

LSD *abbreviation* **1** lysergic acid diethylamide, a hallucinogenic drug **2** pounds, shillings and pence (British coinage before decimalization)

Ltd *abbreviation* limited liability

lubricant *noun* something which lubricates; an oil

lubricate *verb* **1** to apply oil *etc* to (something) to overcome friction and make movement easier **2** *informal* to ply with alcohol □ **lubrication** *noun*

lucid *adjective* **1** easily understood **2** clear in mind; not confused □ **lucidity** *noun* □ **lucidly** *adverb*

Lucifer *noun* Satan, the Devil

luck *noun* **1** fortune, either good or bad

2 chance: *as luck would have it* **3** good fortune: *have any luck?*

luckless *adjective* unfortunate, unhappy

lucky *adjective* **1** fortunate, having good luck **2** bringing good luck: *lucky charm* **3** happening as a result of good luck: *a lucky coincidence* □ **luckily** *adverb*

lucky ⇨ luck**i**er, luck**i**est

■ **Alternative words**: (meaning 1) fortunate, favoured, successful, prosperous; (meaning 2) auspicious; (meaning 3) timely, happy, serendipitous

lucrative *adjective* profitable

lucre (*pronounced* **loo**-ker) *noun* gain; money

Luddite *noun* an opponent of technological innovation

Originally a group of protesters against the Industrial Revolution in the early 19th century, who based their name on Ned *Ludd*, an earlier opponent of machines for weaving stockings

ludicrous *adjective* ridiculous □ **ludicrously** *adverb*

ludo *noun* a game played with counters on a board

lug[1] *verb* to pull or drag with effort

lug ⇨ lug**s**, lug**ging**, lug**ged**

lug[2] *noun, informal* the ear

luge *noun* a light toboggan □ *verb* to glide on such a sledge as a sport

luggage *noun* suitcases and other travelling baggage

lugger *noun* a small sailing vessel

lugubrious (*pronounced* lu-**goo**-bri-us) *adjective* mournful, dismal □ **lugubriously** *adverb*

lukewarm *adjective* **1** neither hot nor cold **2** not very keen, unenthusiastic

lull *verb* to soothe or calm □ *noun* a period of calm

lullaby *noun* (*plural* **lullabies**) a song to lull children to sleep

lumbago *noun* a pain in the lower part of the back

lumbar *adjective* of or in the lower part of the back

lumber *noun* 1 sawn-up timber 2 discarded old furniture *etc* □ *verb* to move about clumsily

lumberjack *noun* someone who fells, saws and shifts trees

luminescent *adjective* giving out light □ **luminescence** *noun*

luminous *adjective* 1 giving light 2 shining; clear □ **luminosity** *noun*

lump *noun* 1 a small, solid mass of indefinite shape 2 a swelling 3 the whole taken together: *considered in a lump* 4 a heavy, dull person □ *verb* 1 to form into lumps 2 to treat as being alike: *lumped all of us together*

lumpectomy *noun* surgery to remove a lump in the breast

lumpish *adjective* heavy, dull

lump sum an amount of money given all at once

lumpy *adjective* full of lumps

lunacy *noun* madness, insanity

lunar *adjective* of the moon: *lunar eclipse*

lunatic *noun* someone who is insane or crazy □ *adjective* insane, mad

lunch *noun* (*plural* **lunches**) a midday meal □ *verb* to eat lunch

luncheon *noun* lunch

lung *noun* either of the two bag-like organs which fill with and expel air in the course of breathing

lunge *noun* a sudden thrust or push □ *verb* to thrust or plunge forward suddenly

lupin *noun* a type of plant with flowers on long spikes

lurch *verb* to roll or pitch suddenly to one side; stagger □ *noun* a pitch to one side □ **leave in the lurch** to leave in a difficult position without help

lure *noun* something which entices; a bait □ *verb* to attract, entice away

lurid *adjective* 1 glaring, garish: *lurid book cover* 2 horrifying, sensational: *lurid story* 3 pale, ghostly

lurk *verb* 1 to keep out of sight; be hidden 2 to move or act secretly and slyly □ **lurker** *noun*

lurking *adjective* vague, hidden

luscious *adjective* sweet, delicious, juicy

lush *adjective* of grass *etc*: thick and plentiful

lust *noun* 1 a greedy desire for power, riches *etc* 2 a strong sexual desire □ *verb* to have a strong desire (for)

luster *US spelling of* **lustre**

lustful *adjective* full of, or showing, strong sexual desire

lustre or *US* **luster** *noun* brightness, shine, gloss

> ☛ This is one of a large number of words which is spelled with an **-re** ending in British English, but with an **-er** in American English, *eg* centre/center, calibre/caliber, metre/meter

lustrous *adjective* bright, shining

lusty *adjective* lively, strong □ **lustily** *adverb*

lute *noun* a stringed musical instrument with a pear-shaped, round-backed body and fretted fingerboard

luxuriant *adjective* 1 thick with leaves, flowers *etc*: *ornamental gardens full of fountains and luxuriant plants* 2 richly ornamented

> ☛ Do not confuse with: **luxurious**

luxuriate *verb* 1 to be luxuriant 2 to enjoy; take delight (in)

luxurious *adjective* full of luxuries; very comfortable: *a luxurious new home* □ **luxuriously** *adverb*

> ☛ Do not confuse with: **luxuriant**

luxury *noun* (*plural* **luxuries**) 1 something very pleasant or expensive but not necessary: *having a car is a luxury* 2 the use or enjoyment of such things

lychgate (*pronounced* lich-geit) *noun* a churchyard gate with a porch

Lycra *noun, trademark* a lightweight synthetic elastic fabric

lying *see* **lie**

lymph *noun* a colourless fluid in the body

lymph gland one of the glands carrying lymph

lynch *verb* to condemn and put to death without legal trial

Named after William *Lynch*, 19th-century Virginian planter who organized unofficial trials of suspected criminals

lynx *noun* (*plural* **lynxes**) a wild animal of the cat family, noted for its keen sight

lyre *noun* an ancient stringed musical instrument, played like a harp

lyrebird *noun* an Australian bird with a lyre-shaped tail

lyric *noun* 1 a short poem, often expressing the poet's feelings 2 **lyrics** the words of a song □ *adjective* 1 of a lyric 2 full of joy

lyrical *adjective* 1 lyric 2 song-like 3 full of enthusiastic praise □ **lyrically** *adverb*

Mm

MA *abbreviation* Master of Arts

macabre *adjective* gruesome, horrible

macadamize *verb* to surface (a road) with small broken stones
> Named after the 19th-century Scottish engineer John *McAdam* who invented the process

macaroni *noun* pasta shaped into short hollow tubes

macaroon *noun* a sweet cake or biscuit made with ground almonds and sugar

macaw *noun* a long-tailed brightly-coloured parrot

mace¹ *noun* a heavy staff with an ornamental head, carried as a sign of office

mace² *noun* a spice made from the covering of a nutmeg

macerate *verb* **1** to make into pulp by steeping **2** to emaciate

machair (*pronounced* **makh**-ar) *noun*, *Gaelic* a low-lying sandy beach used for grazing

machete (*pronounced* ma-**shet**-i) *noun* a heavy knife used to cut through foliage *etc*

machinations *noun plural* a crafty scheme, a plot

machine *noun* **1** a working arrangement of wheels, levers *etc* **2** a (motor) bicycle **3** a political party organization □ *verb* to sew *etc* with a machine

machine code a system of symbols that can be understood by a computer

machinegun *noun* an automatic rapid-firing gun

machinery *noun* **1** machines in general **2** the working parts of a machine **3** organization: *machinery of local government*

machinist *noun* a machine maker or operator

machismo (*pronounced* ma-**kiz**-moh or ma-**chiz**-moh) *noun* overt or aggressive masculinity

Mach number (*pronounced* makh or mahkh) the ratio of the speed of an aircraft to the velocity of sound (*eg* Mach 5 = 5 times the speed of sound)

macho (*pronounced* **mach**-oh) *adjective* overtly or aggressively masculine

mackerel *noun* an edible seafish with wavy markings

mackintosh *noun* (*plural* **mackintoshes**) a waterproof overcoat

macro *noun*, *computing* a single instruction that prompts a computer to carry out a series of short instructions embedded in it

macro- *prefix* forms words for things which are long, large or great: *macrobiotic* (= of diet: intended to prolong life)
> Comes from Greek *makros* meaning 'long' or 'great'

macrobiotic *adjective* of diet: consisting of organic unprocessed food, especially vegetables

mad *adjective* **1** out of your mind, insane **2** wildly foolish **3** furious with anger □ **like mad** very quickly or energetically □ **madness** *noun* (meanings 1 and 2)

madam *noun* a polite form of address to a woman

madcap *noun* a rash, hot-headed person □ *adjective* foolishly rash: *madcap scheme*

madden *verb* to make angry or mad

maddening *adjective* extremely annoying

made *past form of* **make**

madhouse *noun* 1 a place of confusion and noise 2 *historical* an insane asylum

madly *adverb* 1 insanely 2 extremely: *madly in love*

madman *noun* a man who is mad

Madonna *noun* the Virgin Mary as depicted in art

madrigal *noun* a part-song for several voices

madwoman *noun* a woman who is mad

maelstrom (*pronounced* **meil**-strom) *noun* 1 a whirlpool 2 any place of great confusion

maestro (*pronounced* **mais**-troh) *noun* (*plural* **maestros**) someone highly skilled in an art, especially music

MAFF (*pronounced* maf) *abbreviation* Ministry of Agriculture, Fisheries and Food

magazine *noun* 1 a periodical paper containing articles, stories and pictures 2 a storage place for military equipment 3 a place for extra cartridges in a rifle

The sense of *magazine* as a periodical developed from the military use, being intended as a storehouse or treasury of information

magenta *noun* a reddish-purple colour □ *adjective* of this colour

maggot *noun* a small worm-like creature, the grub of a bluebottle *etc*

maggoty *adjective* full of maggots

Magi *see* magus

magic *noun* 1 a process which produces results which cannot be explained or which are remarkable 2 conjuring tricks □ *adjective* 1 using magic 2 used in magic 3 magical

■ **Alternative words**: (adjective) charming, enchanting, bewitching, fascinating, spellbinding

magical *adjective* 1 of or produced by magic 2 very wonderful or mysterious □ **magically** *adverb*

magician *noun* someone skilled in magic

magisterial *adjective* 1 of magistrates 2 having an air of authority

magistrate *noun* someone with the power to enforce the law, *eg* a provost or justice of the peace

magma *noun* molten rock

magnanimity (*pronounced* mag-na-**nim**-it-i) *noun* generosity

magnanimous (*pronounced* mag-**nan**-im-*us*) *adjective* very generous □ **magnanimously** *adverb*

magnate *noun* someone with great power or wealth

magnesia *noun* a white powder formed from magnesium

magnesium *noun* a white metal which burns with an intense white light

magnet *noun* 1 a piece of iron, steel *etc* which has the power to attract other pieces of metal 2 someone or something that attracts strongly

magnetic *adjective* 1 having the powers of a magnet 2 strongly attractive: *magnetic personality*

magnetic north the direction in which the magnetized needle of a compass points

magnetic tape tape on which sound, pictures, computer material *etc* can be recorded

magnetism *noun* 1 the attractive power of a magnet 2 attraction, great charm

magnetize *verb* 1 to make magnetic 2 to attract, influence

magneto *noun* (*plural* **magnetos**) a device producing electric sparks, *eg* for lighting the fuel in a car engine

magnification *noun* 1 the process of making objects appear larger or closer, or the power that instruments such as microscopes and binoculars have to do this 2 a measure of how much larger or closer an object is made to appear than it is in reality

magnificent *adjective* **1** splendid in appearance or action **2** excellent, very fine □ **magnificence** *noun* □ **magnificently** *adverb*

magnify *verb* **1** to make to appear larger by using special lenses **2** to exaggerate

magnify ⇨ magnif*ies*, magnify*ing*, magnif*ied*

magnitude *noun* great size

magnolia *noun* a tree which produces large white or purplish sweet-scented flowers

magnum *noun* a bottle of wine or champagne equal to two ordinary bottles

magnum opus a great work, a masterpiece

magpie *noun* a black-and-white bird of the crow family, known for its habit of collecting objects

Originally *maggot pie*, meaning 'pied Margaret'

magus *noun* (*plural* **magi**) an ancient Persian priest or astrologer □ **the Magi** the three wise men who brought gifts to the infant Christ

Maharajah *noun* an important Indian prince, especially the ruler of a state

mah-jong *noun* a Chinese table game played with small painted bricks

The name **mah-jong** means *sparrows* in Chinese, and is thought to refer to the chattering sound which the little bricks make while the game is being played

mahogany *noun* **1** a tropical American hardwood tree **2** its hard reddish-brown wood, often used for furniture

maid *noun* **1** a female servant **2** *old* an unmarried woman; a young girl

maiden *noun, old* an unmarried girl; a virgin □ *adjective* **1** of a maiden **2** unmarried: *maiden aunt* **3** first, initial: *maiden speech/ maiden voyage*

maiden name the surname of a married woman before her marriage

maiden over *cricket* an over in which no runs are made

mail[1] *noun* letters, parcels *etc* carried by post □ *verb* to post

mail[2] *noun* body armour of steel rings or plates

mail order an order for goods to be sent by post

mail shot unsolicited advertising material sent by post

maim *verb* to cripple, disable

main *adjective* chief, most important □ *noun, old* **1** the ocean **2** (**the mains**) a chief pipe, wire *etc* supplying gas, water or electricity □ **in the main** for the most part

mainframe *noun* the central processing unit and storage unit of a computer □ *adjective* of a computer: of the large, powerful type rather than the small-scale kind

mainland *noun* a large piece of land off whose coast smaller islands lie

mainly *adverb* chiefly, mostly

mainstay *noun* the chief support

maintain *verb* **1** to keep (something) as it is **2** to continue to keep in good working order **3** to support (a family *etc*) **4** to state (an opinion) firmly

maintenance *noun* **1** the act of maintaining; upkeep, repair **2** means of support, especially money for food, clothing *etc*

■ **Alternative words**: (meaning 2) alimony

maize *noun* a cereal crop grown in N and S America

majestic *adjective* stately, regal

majesty *noun* (*plural* **majesties**) **1** a title used in addressing a king or queen: *Your Majesty* **2** greatness of rank or manner

major *adjective* great in size, importance *etc* (*contrasted with*: **minor**) □ *noun* a senior army officer

majority *noun* (*plural* **majorities**) **1** the greater number or quantity **2** the difference in amount between the greater and the lesser number **3** the age when someone becomes legally an adult (18 in the UK)

make *verb* **1** to form, construct **2** to cause to be: *he makes me mad at times* **3** to bring about: *make trouble* **4** to amount to: *2 and 2 make 4* **5** to earn: *she made £300 last week* **6** to force: *I made him do it* **7** to undergo (a journey *etc*) **8** to prepare (a meal *etc*): *I'll make some tea* □ *noun* **1** kind, shape, form **2** brand □ **make believe** to pretend □ **make good 1** to do well **2** to carry out (a promise) **3** to make up for (a loss) □ **make light of** to treat as unimportant □ **make much of** to fuss over, treat as important □ **make nothing of 1** to be unable to understand, do *etc* **2** to make light of □ **make off** to run away □ **make out 1** to see in the distance or indistinctly **2** to declare, prove **3** to write out (a bill *etc*) formally □ **make up 1** to form a whole: *eleven players make up the side* **2** to put together, invent (a false story) **3** to put make-up on the face **4** to be friendly again after a quarrel □ **make up for** to give or do something in return for damage done □ **on the make** *informal* **1** looking for personal gain **2** looking for a sexual partner

make *verb* ➪ makes, making, made
Ⓞ Comes from Old English *macian*

make-believe *noun* fantasy

maker *noun* the person or organization that has made something □ **meet your maker** to die

makeshift *adjective* used for a time for want of something better

make-up *noun* cosmetics

maladjusted *adjective* unable to fit in happily in your environment, society *etc*

maladministration *noun* bad management, especially of public affairs

malady *noun* (*plural* **maladies**) illness, disease

malaise *noun* a feeling or general air of depression or despondency

malapropism *noun* the use of a wrong word which sounds similar to the one intended, *eg contemptuous* for *contemporary*

After Mrs *Malaprop* in Sheridan's play, *The Rivals* (1775), who habitually used the wrong word. One of the most famous is her exclamation: 'She's as headstrong as an allegory on the banks of the Nile.'

🖉 Everybody makes malapropisms sometimes. **Have you heard any funny ones lately?**

malaria *noun* a fever caused by the bite of a particular mosquito □ **malarial** *adjective*

From an Italian phrase meaning 'bad air', malarial fever being originally thought to be caused by poisonous marsh gases

male *adjective* of the sex that is able to father children or young, masculine □ *noun* a member of this sex

malediction *noun* a curse; cursing □ **maledictory** *adjective*

malefactor *noun* an evildoer

malevolent *adjective* wishing ill to others; spiteful □ **malevolence** *noun* □ **malevolently** *adverb*

malformation *noun* faulty or wrong shape

malfunction *verb* to fail to work or operate properly □ *noun* failure to operate

malice *noun* ill will; spite

malicious *adjective* intending harm; spiteful □ **maliciously** *adverb*

malign (*pronounced* ma-lain) *verb* to speak ill of

malignant (*pronounced* ma-lig-nant) *adjective* **1** wishing harm, spiteful **2** of a disease: likely to cause death (*contrasted with*: **benign**) □ **malignantly** *adverb*

malinger *verb* to pretend to be ill to avoid work *etc* □ **malingerer** *noun*

mall (*pronounced* mol) *noun*, *US* a shopping centre

malleable *adjective* **1** of metal: able to be beaten out by hammering **2** of people: easy to influence □ **malleability** *noun*

mallet *noun* a heavy wooden hammer

malnutrition *noun* lack of sufficient or proper food; under-nourishment

malpractice *noun* **1** wrongdoing **2** professional misconduct

malt *noun* **1** barley or other grain prepared for making beer or whisky **2** a malt whisky

maltreat *verb* to treat roughly or unkindly □ **maltreatment** *noun*

mama or **mamma** *noun, informal* mother

mammal *noun* a member of the class of animals of which the female parent feeds the young with her own milk □ **mammalian** *adjective*

mammary *adjective* of a female breast or breasts: *mammary gland*

mammogram *noun* an X-ray taken of a woman's breast to detect early signs of cancer

mammoth *noun* a very large elephant, now extinct □ *adjective* enormous, huge: *mammoth savings*

man *noun* (*plural* **men**) **1** a grown-up human male **2** a human being **3** the human race **4** *informal* a husband **5** a piece in chess or draughts □ *verb* to supply with workers, crew *etc*: *man the boats* □ **the man in the street** the ordinary person □ **to a man** every single one

man *verb* ⇨ **mans, manning, manned**

ⓘ Comes from Old English *mann*

manacle *noun, formal* a handcuff □ *verb* to handcuff

manage *verb* **1** to have control or charge of **2** to deal with, cope: *can't manage on his own* **3** to succeed: *managed to finish on time*

manageable *adjective* easily managed or controlled

management *noun* **1** those in charge of a business *etc* **2** the art of managing a business *etc*

manager *noun* someone in charge of a business *etc*

manageress *noun, old* a woman manager

mañana (*pronounced* man-**yah**-na) *noun* tomorrow; sometime in the future

Mancunian (*pronounced* man-**kyoo**-ni-an) *noun* someone born or living in Manchester

mandarin *noun* **1** a small orange-like citrus fruit **2** *historical* a senior Chinese official

mandate *noun* **1** power to act on someone else's behalf **2** a command

mandatory *adjective* compulsory

mandible *noun* the jaw or lower jawbone

mandolin or **mandoline** *noun* a round-backed stringed instrument similar to a lute

mane *noun* **1** long hair on the head and neck of a horse or male lion **2** a long or thick head of hair

maneuver *US spelling of* **manoeuvre**

manful *adjective* courageous and noble-minded □ **manfully** *adverb*

manganese *noun* a hard easily-broken metal of a greyish-white colour

mange (*pronounced* meinj) *noun* a skin disease of dogs, cats *etc*

mangel-wurzel (*pronounced* mang-gel-**wer**-zel) *noun* a kind of beetroot used as cattle food

manger *noun* a box or trough holding dry food for horses and cattle

mangle *noun* a machine for squeezing water out of clothes or for smoothing them □ *verb* **2** to squeeze (clothes) through a mangle **2** to crush, tear, damage badly

mango *noun* (*plural* **mangoes**) **1** the fruit of a tropical Indian tree, with juicy orange flesh **2** the tree which produces mangoes

mangrove *noun* a type of tree which grows in swamps in hot countries

mangy *adjective* **1** shabby, squalid **2** of an animal: suffering from mange

manhandle *verb* to handle roughly

manhole *noun* a hole (into a drain, sewer *etc*) large enough to let a man through

manhood *noun* the state of being a man

mania *noun* **1** a form of mental illness in which the sufferer is over-active, over-excited and unreasonably happy **2** extreme fondness or enthusiasm: *a mania for stamp-collecting*

maniac *noun* **1** a mad person **2** a very rash or over-enthusiastic person

manic *adjective* **1** suffering from mania **2** very energetic or excited

manicure *noun* **1** the care of hands and nails **2** professional treatment for the hands and nails □ *verb* to perform a manicure on

manicurist *noun* someone who performs manicures

manifest *adjective* easily seen or understood □ *verb* to show plainly

manifestation *noun* behaviour, actions or events which reveal or display something

manifestly *adverb* obviously, clearly

manifesto *noun* (*plural* **manifestoes** or **manifestos**) a public announcement of intentions, *eg* by a political party

manifold *adjective* many and various

manioc *noun* tapioca

manipulate *verb* to handle so as to turn to your own advantage

mankind *noun* the human race

manly *adjective* brave, strong □ **manliness** *noun*

manna *noun* an unexpected or delicious treat

The name given in the Bible to the food miraculously provided for the Israelites in the wilderness

mannequin *noun* **1** someone who models clothes for prospective buyers **2** a display dummy

manner *noun* **1** the way in which something is done **2** the way in which someone behaves **3** **manners** polite behaviour towards others □ **all manner of** all kinds of

mannerism *noun* an odd and obvious habit or characteristic

mannerly *adjective* polite

mannish *adjective* of a woman: behaving, looking like a man

manoeuvre or *US* **maneuver** *noun* **1** a planned movement of troops, ships

or aircraft **2** a trick, a cunning plan □ *verb* **1** to perform a manoeuvre **2** to manipulate

man-of-war *noun* a warship

manor *noun* **1** a large house, usually attached to a country estate **2** *historical* the land belonging to a lord or squire □ **manorial** *adjective*

manpower *noun* the number of people available for work

manse *noun* the house of a minister in certain Christian churches, *eg* the Church of Scotland

mansion *noun* a large house

manslaughter *noun* killing someone without deliberate intent

mantelpiece *noun* a shelf over a fireplace

mantis *noun* an insect of the cockroach family, with large spiny forelegs (*also called*: **praying mantis**)

mantle *noun* **1** a cloak or loose outer garment **2** a covering: *mantle of snow* **3** a thin, transparent shade around the flame of a gas or paraffin lamp

mantra *noun* a word or phrase, chanted or repeated inwardly in meditation

manual *adjective* **1** of the hand or hands **2** worked by hand **3** working with the hands: *manual worker* □ *noun* a handbook giving instructions on how to use something: *a car manual* □ **manually** *adverb* (adjective, meaning 2)

manufacture *verb* to make (articles or materials) in large quantities, usually by machine □ *noun* **1** the process of manufacturing **2** a manufactured article □ **manufacturer** *noun*

manure *noun* a substance, especially animal dung, spread on soil to make it more fertile □ *verb* to treat with manure

manuscript *noun* **1** the prepared material for a book *etc* before it is printed **2** a book or paper written by hand

Manx cat a tailless breed of cat

many *adjective* a large number of: *many people were present* □ *pronoun* a large number: *many survived* ■ **many a** a large number of: *many a voice was raised*

map 313 **mark**

map *noun* a flat drawing of all or part of the earth's surface, showing geographical features □ *verb* **1** to make a map of **2 map something out** to plan it

map *verb* ⇨ map*s*, map*ping*, map*ped*

maple *noun* **1** a tree related to the sycamore, one variety of which produces sugar **2** its hard light-coloured wood used for furniture *etc*

mar *verb* to spoil, deface

mar ⇨ mar*s*, mar*ring*, mar*red*

maracas *noun plural* a pair of filled gourds shaken as a percussion instrument

marathon *noun* a long-distance foot-race, usually covering 26 miles 385 yards

After the distance run by a Greek soldier from *Marathon* to Athens with news of the victory over the Persians

maraud *verb* to plunder, raid

marauder *noun* a plundering robber

marauding *adjective* roaming about with the intention of plundering, raiding or killing

marble *noun* **1** limestone that takes a high polish, used for sculpture, decorating buildings *etc* **2** a small glass ball used in a children's game

March *noun* the third month of the year

march¹ *verb* **1** to (cause) to walk in time with regular step **2** to go on steadily □ *noun* (*plural* **marches**) **1** a marching movement **2** a piece of music for marching to **3** the distance covered by marching **4** a steady progression of events: *the march of time*

march² *noun* a boundary or border □ **riding the marches** the traditional ceremony of riding around the boundaries of a town *etc*

marchioness *noun* (*plural* **marchionesses**) a woman marquess

Mardi Gras a carnival held on Shrove Tuesday in certain countries

mare *noun* a female horse

margarine *noun* an edible spread similar to butter, made mainly of vegetable fats

margin *noun* **1** an edge, a border **2** the blank edge on the page of a book **3** additional space or room; allowance: *margin for error*

marginal *adjective* **1** of or in a margin **2** borderline, close to a limit **3** of a political constituency: without a clear majority for any one candidate or party **4** of little effect or importance: *marginal improvement* □ *noun* a marginal political constituency

marginalize *verb* to make less important or central

marginally *adverb* very slightly, to a very small degree

marigold *noun* a kind of plant with a yellow flower

marijuana *noun* a drug made from the plant hemp

marina *noun* a place with moorings for yachts, dinghies *etc*

marinade *noun* a mixture of oil, wine, herbs, spices *etc* in which food is steeped for flavour □ *verb* to marinate

marinate *verb* to steep in a marinade

marine *adjective* of the sea □ *noun* a soldier serving on board a ship

mariner (*pronounced* **ma**-rin-er) *noun*, *old* a sailor

marionette *noun* a puppet moved by strings

marital *adjective* of marriage

maritime *adjective* **1** of the sea or ships **2** lying near the sea

marjoram *noun* a sweet-smelling herb used in cooking

Mark *noun* a Deutschmark, the standard unit of German money

mark *noun* **1** a sign that can be seen **2** a stain, spot *etc* **3** a target aimed at **4** a trace **5** a point used to assess the merit of a piece of schoolwork *etc* **6** the starting-line in a race: *on your marks!* □ *verb* **1** to make a mark on; stain **2** to observe, watch **3** to stay close to (an opponent in football *etc*) **4** to award marks to (a piece of schoolwork *etc*) **5 mark off** to separate, distinguish

□ **mark time 1** to move the feet up and down, as if marching, but without going forward **2** to keep things going without progressing □ **up to the mark** coming up to the required standard

marked *adjective* easily noticed: *marked improvement*

markedly *adverb* noticeably

marker *noun* **1** someone who marks the score at games **2** a counter *etc* used to mark a score

market *noun* **1** a public place for buying and selling **2** (a country, place *etc* where there is) a need or demand (for certain types of goods) □ *verb* to put on sale □ **on the market** for sale

market forces commerce not restricted by government intervention

market garden a garden in which fruit and vegetables are grown to be sold

marketing *noun* the act or practice of advertising and selling

market leader a company, or brand of goods, that outsells its competitors

marksman *noun* a man who shoots well

markswoman *noun* a woman who shoots well

marmalade *noun* a jam made from citrus fruit, especially oranges

marmite *noun, trademark* a savoury spread made from yeast and vegetable extracts

marmoset *noun* a type of small monkey found in America

maroon[1] *noun* **1** a brownish-red colour **2** a firework used as a distress signal □ *adjective* brownish-red

maroon[2] *verb* **1** to abandon on an island *etc* without means of escape **2** to leave in a helpless or uncomfortable position

marquee (*pronounced* mah-**kee**) *noun* a large tent used for large gatherings, *eg* a wedding reception or circus

marquess or **marquis** (*both pronounced* mah-kwis) *noun* (*plural* **marquesses** or **marquises**) a nobleman below a duke in rank

marriage *noun* **1** the ceremony by which two people become husband and wife **2** a joining together: *marriage of minds*

marriageable *adjective* suitable or old enough for marriage

marrow *noun* **1** the soft substance in the hollow part of bones **2** a long thick-skinned vegetable

marry *verb* to join, or be joined, together in marriage

marry ⇨ marr*ies*, marry*ing*, marr*ied*

marsh *noun* (*plural* **marshes**) a piece of low-lying wet ground

marshal *noun* **1** a high-ranking officer in the army or air force **2** someone who directs processions *etc* **3** *US* a law-court official **4** *US* the head of a police force □ *verb* **1** to arrange (troops, facts, arguments *etc*) in order **2** to show the way, conduct, lead

marshal *verb* ⇨ marshal*s*, marshal*ling*, marshal*led*

marsh-gas *see* **methane**

marshmallow *noun* **1** a spongy jellylike sweet made from sugar and egg-whites *etc* **2** a marsh plant with pink flowers, similar to the hollyhock

marsh marigold a marsh plant with yellow flowers (*also called*: **kingcup**)

marshy *adjective* wet underfoot; boggy

marsupial *noun* an animal which carries its young in a pouch, *eg* the kangaroo

marten *noun* an animal related to the weasel

martial *adjective* **1** of war or battle **2** warlike

martial art a combative sport or method of self-defence

martial law the government of a country by its army

Martian *noun* a potential or imaginary being from the planet Mars

martin *noun* a bird of the swallow family

martinet *noun* someone who keeps strict order; a disciplinarian

Named after Jean *Martinet*, a 17th-century French officer who invented a type of military drill

Martinmas *noun* 11 November, the feast of St Martin

martyr *noun* someone who suffers death or hardship for their beliefs □ *verb* to execute or make suffer for beliefs

martyrdom *noun* the death or suffering of a martyr

marvel *noun* something astonishing or wonderful □ *verb* to feel amazement (at)

> **marvel** *verb* ⇨ marvel*s*, marvel*ling*, marvel*led*

marvellous *adjective* 1 astonishing, extraordinary 2 *informal* excellent, very good

Marxist *noun* a follower of the theories of Karl Marx; a communist □ **Marxism** *noun*

marzipan *noun* a mixture of ground almonds, sugar *etc*, used in cake-making and confectionery

mascara *noun* a cosmetic paint used to colour the eyelashes

mascot *noun* a person, animal or thing believed to bring good luck

masculine *adjective* 1 of the male sex 2 manly □ **masculinity** *noun*

mash *verb* to beat or crush into a pulp □ *noun* 1 mashed potato 2 a mixture of bran, meal *etc*, used as animal food

mask *noun* 1 a cover for the face for disguise or protection 2 a pretence, a disguise □ *verb* 1 to hide, disguise 2 to cover the face with a mask

masochism *noun* an unnatural pleasure taken in being dominated, treated cruelly, or made to suffer in any way

> After Leopold von Sacher-*Masoch*, 19th-century Austrian novelist

masochist *noun* someone who takes an unnatural pleasure in being dominated, treated cruelly, or made to suffer in any way

masochistic *adjective* involving an unnatural eagerness to experience suffering or pain

mason *noun* 1 someone who carves stone 2 a Freemason □ **masonic** *adjective* (meaning 2)

masonry *noun* stonework

masquerade *noun* 1 a dance at which masks are worn 2 pretence □ *verb* to pretend to be someone else: *masquerading as a journalist*

mass *noun* (*plural* **masses**) 1 a lump or quantity gathered together 2 a large quantity 3 the main part or body 4 **Mass** a measure of quantity of matter in an object 5 **Mass** (in some Christian churches) the celebration of Christ's last supper with his disciples 6 music for a Mass □ *adjective* 1 of a mass 2 of or consisting of large numbers or quantities □ *verb* to form into a mass □ **the masses** ordinary people

massacre *noun* the merciless killing of a large number of people □ *verb* to kill (a large number) in a cruel way

massage *noun* the rubbing of parts of the body to remove pain or tension □ *verb* to perform massage on

masseur *noun* someone who performs massage

masseuse *noun* a female masseur

massif *noun* a central mountain mass

massive *adjective* bulky, heavy, huge

massively *adverb* enormously, heavily

mass media means of communicating information to a large number of people, *eg* television

mass production production in large quantities of articles all exactly the same

mast *noun* a long upright pole holding up the sails *etc* in a ship, or holding an aerial, flag *etc*

mastectomy *noun* the surgical removal of a woman's breast or breasts

master *noun* 1 someone who controls or commands 2 an owner of a dog *etc* 3 an employer 4 a male teacher 5 the commander of a merchant ship 6 someone who is very skilled in something, an expert 7 a degree awarded by universities: *Master of Arts* □ *adjective* chief, controlling: *master switch* □ *verb* 1 to overcome, defeat 2 to become able to do or use properly: *I've finally mastered this computer program* □ **master of ceremonies** someone who directs the form and order of events at a public occasion; a compère

masterful *adjective* strong-willed and expecting to be obeyed

masterkey *noun* a key which is so made that it opens a number of different locks

masterly *adjective* showing the skill of an expert or master, clever

mastermind *verb* to plan, work out the details of (a scheme *etc*) □ *noun*: *he is the mastermind of the scheme*

masterpiece *noun* the best example of someone's work, especially a very fine picture, book, piece of music *etc*

mastery *noun* 1 victory (over) 2 control (of) 3 great skill (in)

mastic *noun* a gum resin from Mediterranean trees, used as a varnish or glue

masticate *verb, formal* to chew □ **mastication** *noun*

mastiff *noun* a breed of large, powerful dog

masturbate *verb* to stimulate the sexual organs to a state of orgasm □ **masturbation** *noun*

mat *noun* 1 piece of material (coarse plaited plant fibre, carpet *etc*) for wiping shoes on, covering the floor *etc* 2 a piece of material, wood *etc* put below dishes at table □ *adjective, another spelling* of **matt**

matador *noun* the person who kills the bull in bullfights

match[1] *noun* (*plural* **matches**) a small stick of wood *etc* tipped with a substance which catches fire when rubbed against an abrasive surface

match[2] *noun* (*plural* **matches**) 1 a person or thing similar to or the same as another 2 a person or thing agreeing with or suiting another 3 an equal 4 someone suitable for marriage 5 a contest or game □ *verb* 1 to be of the same make, size, colour *etc* 2 to set (two things, teams *etc*) against each other 3 to hold your own with, be equal to

matchbox *noun* a box for holding matches

matchless *adjective* having no equal

matchmaker *noun* someone who tries to arrange marriages or partnerships

matchstick *noun* a single match

mate *noun* 1 a friend, a companion 2 an assistant worker: *plumber's mate* 3 a husband or wife 4 the sexual partner of an animal, bird *etc* 5 a merchant ship's officer, next in rank to the captain □ *verb* 1 to marry 2 to bring or come together to breed

mater- or **matri-** *prefix* mother: *maternal/ matricide*
○ Comes from Latin *mater* meaning 'mother'

material *adjective* 1 made of matter, able to be seen and felt 2 not spiritual, concerned with physical comfort, money *etc*: *a material outlook on life* 3 important, essential: *material difference* □ *noun* 1 something out of which anything is, or may be, made 2 cloth, fabric

materialism *noun* 1 a tendency to attach too much importance to material things (*eg* physical comfort, money) 2 the belief that only things we can see or feel really exist or are important □ **materialist** *noun* □ **materialistic** *adjective*

materialize *verb* 1 to appear in bodily form 2 to happen, come about

materially *adverb* 1 to a large extent, greatly 2 relating to objects, possessions or physical comfort, rather than to emotional or spiritual well-being

maternal *adjective* 1 of a mother 2 like a mother, motherly 3 related through your mother: *maternal grandmother* □ **maternally** *adverb*

maternity *noun* the state of being a mother, motherhood □ *adjective* of or for a woman having or about to have a baby: *maternity clothes*

math *noun, US informal* mathematics

mathematical *adjective* 1 of or done by mathematics 2 very exact

mathematician *noun* an expert in mathematics

mathematics *noun singular* the study of measurements, numbers and quantities

maths *noun singular, informal* mathematics

matinée (*pronounced* mat-in-ei) *noun* an afternoon performance in a theatre or cinema

matinée coat a baby's short jacket

matins *noun plural* the morning service in certain churches

matri- *see* mater-

matriarch (*pronounced* meit-ri-ahk) *noun* a woman who controls a family or community

matriarchal (*pronounced* meit-ri-**ahk**-al) *adjective* of a family, community or social system: controlled by women

matrices *plural of* matrix

matricide *noun* 1 the killing of your own mother 2 someone who kills their own mother

matriculate *verb* to admit, or be admitted, to a university □ **matriculation** *noun*

matrilineal *adjective* of family descent: progressing through the female line

matrimonial *adjective* relating to marriage

matrimony *noun, formal* marriage

matrix *noun* (*plural* **matrices**) 1 a mould in which metals *etc* are shaped 2 a mass of rock in which gems *etc* are found 3 a rectangular table of data

matron (*pronounced* meit-ron) *noun* 1 a married woman 2 a senior nurse in charge of a hospital 3 *old* a woman in charge of housekeeping or nursing in a school, hostel *etc*

matronly (*pronounced* meit-ron-li) *adjective* 1 of a woman: dignified, staid 2 rather plump

matt or **mat** *adjective* having a dull surface; not shiny or glossy

matted *adjective* thickly tangled

matter *noun* 1 anything that takes up space, can be seen, felt *etc*; material, substance 2 a subject written or spoken about 3 **matters** affairs, business 4 trouble, difficulty: *what is the matter?* 5 importance: *of no great matter* 6 pus □ *verb* 1 to be of importance: *it doesn't matter* 2 *medical* to give out pus □ **a matter of course** something that is to

be expected □ **a matter of opinion** a subject on which different opinions are held □ **as a matter of fact** in fact

matter-of-fact *adjective* keeping to the actual facts; unimaginative, uninteresting

matting *noun* material from which mats are made

mattress *noun* (*plural* **mattresses**) a thick layer of padding covered in cloth, usually as part of a bed

mature *adjective* 1 fully grown or developed 2 ripe, ready for use □ *verb* 1 to (cause to) become mature 2 of an insurance policy *etc*: to be due to be paid out □ **maturely** *adverb*

maturity *noun* ripeness

maudlin *adjective* silly, sentimental

From Mary *Magdalene*, who was frequently depicted crying in paintings

maul *verb* to hurt badly by rough or savage treatment

Maundy Thursday the day before Good Friday in the Christian calendar

mausoleum *noun* a large or elaborate tomb

mauve *adjective* of a purple colour

maverick *noun* someone who refuses to conform; a determined individualist

After Samuel *Maverick*, Texas rancher who never branded his cattle

maw *noun* 1 an animal's jaws or gullet 2 a wide or gaping cavity

mawkish *adjective* weak and sentimental

maxi- *prefix* very large or long: *maxi-skirt*

The prefix *maxi-* has been formed by taking the start of '**maxi**mum' and adding on various words or parts of words

maxim *noun* a general truth or rule about behaviour *etc*

maximum *adjective* greatest, most □ *noun* (*plural* **maxima**) 1 the greatest number or quantity 2 the highest point or degree

May *noun* the fifth month of the year

may *verb* **1** used with another verb to express permission or possibility: *you may watch the film/ I thought I might find him there* **2** used to express a wish: *may your wishes come true*

> **may** ⇨ may, might

maybe *adverb* perhaps

Mayday *noun* the first day of May

mayday *noun* an international distress signal

mayfly *noun* a short-lived insect that appears in May

mayhem *noun* widespread chaos or confusion

mayonnaise (*pronounced* mei-*o*-**neiz**) *noun* a sauce made of eggs, oil and vinegar or lemon juice

mayor *noun* the chief elected public official of a city or town

> *Note*: *mayor* is used for a woman mayor, never *mayoress*

mayoress *noun* a mayor's wife

maypole *noun* a decorated pole traditionally danced around on Mayday

maze *noun* **1** a series of winding paths in a park *etc*, planned to make exit difficult **2** something complicated and confusing: *maze of regulations*

MB *abbreviation* Bachelor of Medicine (in Latin, *Medicinae Baccalaureus*)

Mb *abbreviation* megabyte(s)

MBE *abbreviation* Member of the Order of the British Empire

MC *abbreviation* **1** Master of Ceremonies **2** Military Cross

MD *abbreviation* **1** Doctor of Medicine (from Latin *Medicinae Doctor*) **2** Managing Director

MDMA *abbreviation* methylene-dioxymethamphetamine, the drug Ecstasy

ME *abbreviation* myalgic encephalomyelitis, a condition of chronic fatigue and muscle pain following a viral infection

me *pronoun* the word used by a speaker or writer in mentioning themselves: *she kissed me/ give it to me*

mead *noun* an alcoholic drink made with honey

meadow *noun* a field of grass

meadowsweet *noun* a wild flower with sweet-smelling cream-coloured flowers

meagre or *US* **meager** *adjective* **1** thin **2** poor in quality **3** scanty, not enough

meal¹ *noun* the food taken at one time, *eg* breakfast or dinner

meal² *noun* grain ground to a coarse powder

mealy-mouthed *adjective* not frank and straightforward in speech

mean¹ *adjective* **1** not generous with money *etc* **2** unkind, selfish **3** lowly, humble □ **meanness** *noun*

mean² *adjective* **1** midway between two other points, quantities *etc*; middle **2** average □ *noun* □ **in the meantime** meanwhile

mean³ *verb* **1** to intend to express; indicate: *what do you mean?/ when I say no, I mean no* **2** to intend: *how do you mean to do that?* □ **mean well** to have good intentions

> **mean** ⇨ means, meaning, meant

meander *verb* **1** of a river: to flow in a winding course **2** to wander about slowly and aimlessly

> After the winding *Maeander* river in Turkey

meaning *noun* **1** what is intended to be expressed or conveyed **2** purpose, intention

meaningful *adjective* full of significance; expressive

meaningless *adjective* **1** pointless **2** having no meaning

means *noun plural* **1** an action or instrument by which something is brought about **2** money, property *etc*: *a woman of means* □ **by all means 1** certainly, of course **2** in every way possible □ **by no means** certainly not; not at all

meanwhile *adverb* in the time between two happenings

measles *noun* an infectious disease causing red spots

measly *adjective, informal* mean, stingy

measure *noun* **1** size or amount (found by measuring) **2** an instrument or container for measuring **3** musical time **4 measures** a plan of action: *measures to prevent crime* **5** a law brought before parliament to be considered □ *verb* **1** to find out the size, quantity *etc* by using some form of measure **2** to be of a certain length, amount *etc* **3** to indicate the measurement of **4** to mark (off) or weigh (out) in portions □ **for good measure** as a bonus

measured *adjective* steady, unhurried

measurement *noun* **1** the act of measuring **2** the size, amount *etc* found by measuring

meat *noun* animal flesh used as food

meaty *adjective* **1** full of meat; tasting of meat **2** of a book *etc*: full of information

Mecca *noun* **1** the birthplace of Mohammed **2** a place of pilgrimage

mechanic *noun* a skilled worker with tools or machines

mechanical *adjective* **1** of machinery: *mechanical engineering* **2** worked by machinery **3** done without thinking □ **mechanically** *adverb*

mechanics *noun* **1** *singular* the study and art of constructing machinery **2** *plural* the actual details of how something works: *the mechanics of the plan are beyond me*

mechanism *noun* **1** a piece of machinery **2** the way a piece of machinery works **3** an action by which a result is produced

mechanize *verb* **1** to equip (a factory *etc*) with machinery **2** to supply (troops) with armoured vehicles □ **mechanization** *noun*

medal *noun* a metal disc stamped with a design, inscription *etc*, made to commemorate an event or given as a prize

medallion *noun* a large medal or piece of jewellery like one

medallist *noun* someone who has gained a medal

meddle *verb* **1** to concern yourself with things that are not your business **2** to

interfere or tamper (with) □ **meddler** *noun*

meddlesome *adjective* fond of meddling

media *noun*: **the media** television, newspapers *etc* as a form of communication

mediaeval another spelling of **medieval**

median *noun* **1** a straight line from an angle of a triangle to the centre of the opposite side **2** the middle value or point of a series □ *adjective* mid, middle

mediate *verb* to act as a peacemaker (between) □ **mediation** *noun*

mediator *noun* someone who tries to make peace between people who are quarrelling

medic *noun*, *informal* a medical student

medical *adjective* of doctors or their work □ *noun* a health check, a physical examination

medicate *verb* to give medicine to

medicated *adjective* including medicine or disinfectant

medication *noun* **1** medical treatment **2** a medicine

medicinal *adjective* **1** used in medicine **2** used as a medicine □ **medicinally** *adverb*

medicine *noun* **1** something given to a sick person to make them better **2** the science of the treatment of illness

medicine man a tribal healer or shaman

medieval *adjective* of or in the Middle Ages

mediocre *adjective* not very good, ordinary □ **mediocrity** *noun*

meditate *verb* **1** to think deeply and in quietness **2** to contemplate religious or spiritual matters **3** to consider, think about

meditation *noun* **1** deep, quiet thought **2** contemplation on a religious or spiritual theme

meditative *adjective* thinking deeply

medium *noun* (*plural* **media** or **mediums**) **1** a means or substance through which an effect is produced **2**

(*plural* **mediums**) someone through whom spirits (of dead people) are said to speak □ *adjective* middle or average in size, quality *etc* □ **the media** *see* **media**

medley *noun* (*plural* **medleys**) **1** a mixture **2** a piece of music put together from a number of other pieces

meek *adjective* gentle, uncomplaining □ **meekly** *adverb*

meet *verb* **1** to come face to face (with) **2** to come together, join **3** to make the acquaintance of **4** to pay (bills *etc*) fully **5** to be suitable for, satisfy: *able to meet the demand* □ *noun* a gathering for a sports event □ *adjective* proper, suitable

meet *verb* ⇨ meet**s**, meet**ing**, **met**

meeting *noun* a gathering of people for a particular purpose

mega *adjective*, *slang* **1** huge **2** excellent, very good

mega- *prefix* **1** great, huge: *megaphone* **2** a million: *megaton* ① Comes from Greek *megas* meaning 'big'

megalith *noun* a huge stone erected in prehistoric times

megalomania *noun* an exaggerated idea of your own importance or abilities

megalomaniac *noun* someone suffering from megalomania

megaphone *noun* a portable cone-shaped device with microphone and amplifier to increase sound

megaton *adjective* of a bomb: having an explosive force equal to a million tons of TNT

melancholy *noun* lowness of spirits, sadness □ *adjective* sad, depressed □ **melancholic** *adjective*

melanin *noun* the dark pigment in human skin or hair

melanoma *noun* a skin tumour which usually develops from a mole

mêlée (*pronounced* mel-ei) *noun* a confused fight between two groups of people

mellifluous *adjective* sweet-sounding

mellow *adjective* **1** of fruit: ripe, juicy, sweet **2** having become pleasant or

agreeable with age **3** of light, colour *etc*: soft, not harsh □ *verb* to make or become mellow

melodic *adjective* of melody

melodious *adjective* pleasant sounding; tuneful

melodrama *noun* a type of play with a sensational or exaggerated plot

melodramatic *adjective* exaggerated, sensational, over-dramatic

melody *noun* (*plural* **melodies**) **1** a tune **2** pleasant music

melon *noun* a large round fruit with soft juicy flesh

melt *verb* **1** to make or become liquid, eg by heating **2** to disappear gradually: *the crowd melted away* **3** to soften in feeling: *his heart melted at the sight*

meltdown *noun* the process in which the radioactive fuel in a nuclear reactor overheats and melts through the insulation into the environment

member *noun* **1** someone who belongs to a group or society **2** a limb or organ of the body

Member of Parliament (shortened to **MP**) someone elected to the House of Commons

membership *noun* **1** the group of people who are members, or the number of members, in a club *etc* **2** the state of being a member

membrane *noun* a thin skin or covering, especially as part of a human or animal body, plant *etc*

memento *noun* (*plural* **mementos**) something by which an event is remembered

memento mori an object used as a reminder of human mortality

memo *noun* (*plural* **memos**) *short for* **memorandum**

memoirs *noun plural* a personal account of someone's life; an autobiography

memorable *adjective* worthy of being remembered; famous □ **memorably** *adverb*

memorandum *noun* (*plural* **memoranda**) **1** a note which acts as a reminder **2** a written statement of something under discussion **3** a brief note sent to colleagues in an office *etc*

memorial *noun* a monument commemorating an historical event or people □ *adjective* commemorating an event or person

memorize *verb* to learn by heart

memory *noun* (*plural* **memories**) **1** the power to remember **2** the mind's store of remembered things **3** something remembered **4** *computing* a store of information **5** what is remembered about someone □ **in memory of** in remembrance of, as a memorial of

menace *noun* **1** potential harm or danger **2** someone persistently threatening or annoying □ *verb* to be a danger to; threaten

menacing *adjective* looking evil or threatening

menagerie (*pronounced* me-**naj**-*e*-ri) *noun* **1** a collection of wild animals **2** a place where these are kept

mend *verb* to repair; make or grow better □ *noun* a repaired part □ **on the mend** getting better, recovering

mendacious *adjective* not true; lying □ **mendaciously** *adverb* □ **mendacity** *noun*

mendicant *noun* a beggar □ *adjective* begging

menial (*pronounced* **meen**-i-al) *adjective* of work: unskilled, unchallenging

meningitis *noun* an illness caused by inflammation of the covering of the brain

menopause *noun* the ending of menstruation in middle age

menses (*pronounced* **men**-seez) *noun plural* the discharge of blood *etc* during menstruation

menstrual *adjective* of menstruation

menstruate *verb* to experience menstruation

menstruation *noun* the monthly discharge of blood from a woman's womb

mental *adjective* **1** of the mind **2** done, made, happening *etc* in the mind: *mental arithmetic* **3** of illness: affecting the mind □ **mentally** *adverb*

mental hospital a hospital for people suffering from mental illness

mentality *noun* (*plural* **mentalities**) **1** mental power **2** type of mind; way of thinking

menthol *noun* a sharp-smelling substance obtained from peppermint oil

mention *verb* **1** to speak of briefly **2** to remark (that) □ *noun* a mentioning, a remark

mentor *noun* someone who gives advice as a tutor or supervisor

After *Mentor*, a friend of Odysseus, who guides Telemachus in his search for his father

menu *noun* (*plural* **menus**) **1** (a card with) a list of dishes to be served at a meal **2** *computing* a list of options

MEP *abbreviation* Member of the European Parliament

mercantile *adjective* of buying and selling; trading

Mercator's projection a map of the globe in the form of a rectangle evenly marked with lines of latitude and longitude

mercenary *adjective* **1** working for money **2** influenced by the desire for money □ *noun* (*plural* **mercenaries**) a soldier paid by a foreign country to fight in its army

merchandise *noun* goods to be bought and sold

merchant *noun* someone who carries on a business in the buying and selling of goods, a trader □ *adjective* of trade

merchant bank a bank providing especially commercial banking services

merchant navy ships and crews employed in trading

merciful *adjective* **1** willing to forgive or be lenient **2** easing or relieving pain, trouble or difficulty

mercifully *adverb* fortunately, to one's great relief

merciless *adjective* showing no mercy; cruel □ **mercilessly** *adverb*

mercurial *adjective* changeable, volatile

mercury *noun* an element, a heavy, silvery liquid metal (also **quicksilver**)

mercy *noun* (*plural* **mercies**) lenience or forgiveness towards an enemy *etc*; pity □ **at someone's mercy** in their power

mere *adjective* nothing more than: *mere nonsense*

merely *adverb* only, simply

meretricious *adjective*, *formal* superficially attractive, flashy
ⓘ Comes from Latin *meretrix* meaning 'a prostitute'

☛ Do not confuse with: **meritorious**

merge *verb* **1** to combine or join together **2** to blend, come together gradually

▓ **Alternative words**: (meaning 1) amalgamate

merger *noun* a joining together, eg of business companies

meridian (*pronounced* me-**rid**-i-*a*n) *noun* **1** an imaginary line around the globe passing through the north and south poles **2** the highest point of the sun's path **3** in Chinese medicine: a main energy channel in the body

meringue (*pronounced* me-**rang**) *noun* a baked cake or shell made of sugar and egg-white

merino *noun* (*plural* **merinos**) **1** a sheep with very fine soft wool **2** its wool, or a soft fabric made from it

merit *noun* **1** positive worth or value **2** a commendable quality □ *verb* to deserve

meritorious *adjective*, *formal* deserving honour or reward
ⓘ Comes from Latin *meritum* meaning 'an act deserving praise (or blame)'

☛ Do not confuse with: **meretricious**

mermaid *noun* an imaginary sea creature with a woman's upper body and a fish's tail

merry *adjective* **1** full of fun; cheerful and lively **2** slightly drunk □ **merrily** *adverb* (meaning 1)

merry-go-round *noun*, *Brit* a fairground roundabout with wooden horses *etc* for riding on

mesh *noun* (*plural* **meshes**) **1** network, netting **2** the opening between the threads of a net □ *verb* of gears *etc*: to interconnect, engage

mesmeric *adjective* **1** hypnotic **2** commanding complete attention, fascinating

mesmerize *verb* **1** to hypnotize **2** to hold the attention of completely; fascinate

An earlier term than *hypnotize*, the word comes from the name of the 18th-century Austrian doctor, Franz Anton Mesmer, who claimed to be able to cure disease through the influence of his will on patients

mess (*plural* **messes**) **1** an untidy or disgusting sight **2** disorder, confusion **3** a group of soldiers *etc* who take their meals together, or the place where they eat □ **mess up** to make untidy, dirty or muddled □ **mess with** *US informal* to interfere with, fool with

message *noun* **1** a piece of news or information sent from one person to another **2** a lesson, a moral □ **get the message** *informal* to understand, get the point

messenger *noun* someone who carries a message

messiah *noun* a saviour, a deliverer

messy *adjective* **1** dirty **2** untidy, disordered □ **messily** *adverb*

metabolic *adjective* of metabolism

metabolism *noun* **1** the combined chemical changes in the cells of a living organism that provide energy for living processes and activity **2** the conversion of nourishment into energy

metal *noun* any of a group of substances (eg gold, silver, iron *etc*) able to conduct heat and electricity

☛ Do not confuse with: **mettle**

metallic *adjective* **1** made of metal **2** shining like metal: *metallic thread*

metallurgy *noun* the study of metals □ **metallurgic** or **metallurgical** *adjective* □ **metallurgist** *noun*

metamorphose (*pronounced* met-*a*-

maw-fohz) *verb* to change completely in appearance or character

metamorphosis (*pronounced* met-*a*-maw-fos-is) *noun* (*plural* **metamorphoses**) **1** a complete change in appearance or character; a transformation **2** a physical change that occurs during the growth of some creatures, *eg* from a tadpole into a frog

metaphor *noun* a way of describing something by suggesting that it is, or has the qualities of, something else, *eg the camel is the ship of the desert*

metaphorical *adjective* using a metaphor or metaphors

metaphorically *adverb* not in real terms, but as an imaginitive way of describing something

metaphysics *noun* **1** the study of being and knowledge **2** any abstruse or abstract philosophy □ **metaphysical** *adjective* □ **metaphysician** *noun*

meteor *noun* a small piece of matter moving rapidly through space, becoming bright as it enters the earth's atmosphere

meteoric *adjective* **1** of a meteor **2** extremely rapid: *meteoric rise to fame*

meteorite *noun* a meteor which falls to the earth as a piece of rock

meteorologist *noun* someone who studies or forecasts the weather

meteorology *noun* the study of weather and climate □ **meteorological** *adjective*

mete out *verb, formal* to deal out (punishment *etc*)

meter¹ *noun* an instrument for measuring the amount of gas, electricity, *etc* used □ *verb* to measure with a meter

meter² *US* spelling of **metre**

meth *noun, slang* the drug methadone

methadone *noun* a synthetic drug similar to morphine, used to treat addiction

methane *noun* a colourless gas produced by rotting vegetable matter (*also called*: **marsh-gas**)

methanol *noun* methyl alcohol (*also called*: **wood spirit**)

method *noun* **1** a planned or regular way of doing something **2** orderly arrangement

methodical *adjective* orderly, done or acting according to some plan □ **methodically** *adverb*

meths *noun, informal* methylated spirits

methyl *noun* a poisonous alcohol found in nature

methylated spirits an alcohol with added violet dye, used as a solvent or fuel

meticulous *adjective* careful and accurate about small details □ **meticulously** *adverb*

métier (*pronounced* mei-ti-ei) *noun, formal* occupation, profession

metre or *US* **meter** *noun* **1** the chief unit of length in the metric system (about 1.1 yards) **2** the arrangement of syllables in poetry, or of musical notes, in a regular rhythm

> 🖋 This is one of a large number of words which is spelled with an **-re** ending in British English, but with an **-er** in American English, *eg* centre/center, calibre/caliber, lustre/luster

ⓘ Comes from Greek *metron* meaning 'measure'

metric *adjective* **1** of the metric system **2** metrical

metrical *adjective* **1** of poetry: of or in metre **2** arranged in the form of verse

metrication *noun* the change-over of a country's units of measurements to the metric system

metric system the system of weights and measures based on tens (1 metre = 10 decimetres = 100 centimetres *etc*)

metronome *noun* an instrument that keeps a regular beat, used for music practice

metropolis *noun* (*plural* **metropolises**) a large city, usually the capital city of a country □ **metropolitan** *adjective*

mettle *formal* courage, pluck □ **on your mettle** out to do your best

> 🖋 Do not confuse with: **metal**

mew *noun* a whining cry made by a cat *etc* □ *verb* to cry in this way

mews *noun* buildings (originally stables) built around a yard or in a lane

> Originally a cage for hawks, *mews* took on its present meaning after royal stables were built in the 17th century on a site formerly used to house the King's hawks

mezzanine *noun* **1** a low storey between two main storeys **2** *US* a balcony in a theatre

MI5 *informal* a British government counter-espionage agency

MI6 *informal* a British espionage and intelligence agency

miaow *noun* the sound made by a cat □ *verb* to make the sound of a cat

miasma (*pronounced* mai-**az**-ma) *noun* an unhealthy or depressing atmosphere

mica *noun* a mineral which glitters and divides easily into thin transparent layers

mice *plural* of **mouse**

Michaelmas *noun* the festival of St Michael, 29 September

mickey *noun*: **take the mickey** *informal* to tease, make fun of someone

micro *noun, informal* (*plural* **micros**) **1** a microwave oven **2** a microcomputer

micro- *prefix* **1** very small: *microchip/microphone* (= an instrument which picks up and can amplify small sounds) **2** using a microscope: *microsurgery* ① Comes from Greek *mikros* meaning 'small'

microbe *noun* a tiny living organism

microchip *noun* a tiny piece of silicon designed to act as a complex electronic circuit

microcomputer *noun* a small desktop computer containing a microprocessor

microcosm *noun* a version on a small scale: *a microcosm of society*

microfiche (*pronounced* **maik**-roh-feesh) *noun* a sheet of microfilm suitable for filing

microfilm *noun* narrow photographic film on which books, newspapers, *etc*

are recorded in miniaturized form □ *verb* to record on microfilm

microphone *noun* an instrument which picks up sound waves for broadcasting, recording or amplifying

microprocessor *noun* a computer processor consisting of one or more microchips

microscope *noun* a scientific instrument which magnifies very small objects placed under its lens

microscopic *adjective* tiny, minuscule

microsecond *noun* a millionth of a second

microsurgeon *noun* a surgeon who performs microsurgery

microsurgery *noun* delicate surgery carried out under a microscope

microwave *noun* **1** a microwave oven **2** a very short radio wave

microwave oven an oven which cooks food by passing microwaves through it

mid- *prefix* placed or occurring in the middle: *mid-morning* ① Comes from Old English *midd*

midday *noun* noon

midden *noun* a rubbish or dung heap

middle *noun* the point or part of anything equally distant from its ends or edges; the centre □ *adjective* **1** occurring in the middle or centre **2** coming between extreme positions *etc*: *trying to find a middle way* □ **in the middle of** in the midst of doing, busy doing

middle-aged *adjective* between youth and old age

Middle Ages the time roughly between AD 500 and AD 1500

middle class the class of people between the working and upper classes

middle-of-the-road *adjective* bland, unadventurous

middling *adjective* **1** of middle size or quality **2** neither good nor bad; mediocre

midge *noun* a small biting insect

midget *noun* an abnormally small person or thing □ *adjective* very small

midnight *noun* twelve o'clock at night □ *adjective* occurring at midnight

midriff *noun* the middle of the body, just below the ribs

midst *noun* the middle □ **in our midst** among us

midsummer *noun* the time around 21 June, which is the longest day in the year

midway *adverb* half-way

midwife *noun* (*plural* **midwives**) a nurse trained to assist women during childbirth

Meaning literally 'with woman'

midwifery (*pronounced* mid-wif-e-ri or mid-**waif**-ri) *noun* the practice or occupation of being a midwife

midwinter *noun* the time around 21 December, the winter solstice and shortest day in the year

mien (*pronounced* meen) *noun, formal* look, appearance, aspect

might¹ *noun* power, strength

might² *past tense* of **may** ① Comes from Old English *mihte*

mightily *adverb* 1 extremely, greatly 2 with great strength or force

mighty *adjective* very great or powerful □ *adverb, US informal* very □ **mightiness** *noun*

mighty ⇨ might**ier**, might**iest**

migraine (*pronounced* **mee**-grein) *noun* a severe form of headache

migrant *noun* 1 someone migrating, or recently migrated, from another country 2 a bird that migrates annually

migrate *verb* 1 to change your home or move to another area or country 2 of birds: to fly to a warmer region for the winter □ **migration** *noun*

migratory *adjective* 1 migrating 2 wandering

mike *noun, informal* a microphone

milch cow (*pronounced* milch or milsh) 1 a cow kept for milk production 2 a ready source of money

mild *adjective* 1 not harsh or severe; gentle 2 of taste: not sharp or bitter 3 of weather: not cold 4 of an illness: not serious

Opposite: (meaning 4) acute

mildew *noun* a whitish mark on plants, fabric *etc* caused by fungus □ **mildewed** *adjective*

mildly *adverb* 1 in a mild or calm manner 2 slightly □ **to put it mildly** expressing oneself much less strongly than would be possible in the circumstances

mile *noun* a measure of length (1.61 kilometre or 1760 yards)

mileage *noun* 1 distance in miles 2 travel expenses (counted by the mile) 3 the amount of use or benefit you can get out of something

milestone *noun* 1 a stone beside the road showing the number of miles to a certain place 2 something which marks an important event

milieu (*pronounced* meel-**yer**) *noun* surroundings

militant *adjective* 1 fighting, warlike 2 aggressive, favouring or taking part in forceful action □ *noun* someone who is militant

military *adjective* of soldiers or warfare □ *noun* (**the military**) the army

militate *verb* 1 to fight or work (against): *Her age will certainly militate against her finding employment* 2 to act to your disadvantage ① Comes from Latin *militare* meaning 'to serve as a soldier'

◆ Do not confuse with: **mitigate**. It may be helpful to remember that the idea of fighting is contained in the word **MILIT**ate (in common with 'military' and 'militia') but not in **mitigate**

militia *noun* a group of fighters, not regular soldiers, trained for emergencies

milk *noun* 1 a white liquid produced by female animals as food for their young 2 this liquid, especially from cows, used as a drink □ *verb* 1 to draw milk from 2 to take (money *etc*) from

milk float a vehicle that makes deliveries of milk to homes

milkmaid *noun, old* a woman who milks cows

milkman *noun* a man who sells or delivers milk

milk-tooth *noun* a tooth from the first set of teeth in humans and other mammals

milky *adjective* 1 like milk, creamy 2 white

Milky Way a bright band of stars seen in the night sky

mill *noun* 1 a machine for grinding or crushing grain, coffee *etc* 2 a building where grain is ground 3 a factory □ *verb* 1 to grind 2 to cut grooves round the edge of (a coin) 3 to move round and round in a crowd

millennium *noun* (*plural* **millennia**) a period of a thousand years

miller *noun* someone who grinds grain

millet *noun* a type of grain used for food

milli- or **mill-** *prefix* thousand; a thousandth part of: *millimetre/ millennium/ millipede* (= an insect with many – although not actually a thousand – legs)
Ⓛ Comes from Latin *mille* meaning 'thousand'

milligramme *noun* a thousandth of a gramme

millilitre *noun* a thousandth of a litre

millimetre *noun* a thousandth of a metre

milliner *noun* someone who makes and sells women's hats

millinery *noun* the goods sold by a milliner

million *noun* a thousand thousands (1 000 000)

millionaire *noun* someone who has a million pounds (or dollars) or more

millipede *noun* a small crawling insect with a long body and many pairs of legs

millisecond *noun* a thousandth of a second

millrace *noun* the stream of water which turns a millwheel

millstone *noun* 1 one of two heavy stones used to grind grain 2 something felt as a burden or hindrance

millwheel *noun* a water-wheel which drives the machinery of a mill

mime *noun* 1 a theatrical art using body movements and facial expressions in place of speech 2 a play performed through mime □ *verb* 1 to perform a mime 2 to express through mime

mimic *verb* to imitate, especially in a mocking way □ *noun* someone who mimics □ **mimicry** *noun*

> **mimic** *verb* ⇨ mimics, mimick**ing**, mimick**ed**

mimosa *noun* a tree producing bunches of yellow, scented flowers

minaret *noun* a slender tower on an Islamic mosque

mince *verb* 1 to cut or chop into small pieces 2 to walk primly with short steps □ *noun* meat chopped finely □ **not mince matters** to not try to soften an unpleasant fact or statement

mincemeat *noun* a chopped-up mixture of dried fruit, suet *etc* □ **make mincemeat of** to pulverize, destroy

mince-pie *noun* a pie filled with mincemeat

mincer *noun* a machine for mincing food

mind *noun* 1 consciousness, intelligence, understanding 2 intention: *I've a good mind to tell him so* □ *verb* 1 to see to, look after: *mind the children* 2 to watch out for, be careful of: *mind the step* 3 to object to: *do you mind if I open the window?* □ **change your mind** to change your opinion or intention □ **in two minds** undecided □ **make up your mind** to decide □ **out of your mind** mad, crazy □ **presence of mind** ability to act calmly and sensibly □ **speak your mind** to speak frankly

minder *noun* 1 someone who looks after a child *etc* 2 an aide or adviser to a public figure

mindful *adjective*: **mindful of** paying attention to

mindless *adjective* foolish, unthinking; pointless

mine¹ *noun* 1 an underground pit or system of tunnels from which metals, coal *etc* are dug **2** a heavy charge of explosive material □ *verb* **1** to dig or work a mine **2** to lay explosive mines in

mine² *pronoun* a thing or things belonging to me: *that drink is mine*

minefield *noun* an area covered with explosive mines

minelayer *noun* a ship which lays explosive mines

miner *noun* someone who works in a mine

mineral *noun* a natural substance mined from the earth, *eg* coal, metals, gems *etc* □ *adjective* of or containing minerals

mineralogy *noun* the study of minerals □ **mineralogist** *noun*

mineral water 1 water containing small amounts of minerals **2** *informal* carbonated water

minestrone (*pronounced* min-is-**troh**-ni) *noun* a thick Italian vegetable soup containing rice or pasta

minesweeper *noun* a ship which removes explosive mines

mingle *verb* to mix

mingy (*pronounced* **min**-ji) *adjective*, *informal* stingy, mean

Mini *noun, trademark* a small, two-doored British car

mini- *prefix* smaller than average; compact: *minibus/ minicab*

The prefix **mini-** is an abbreviation of 'miniature'

miniature *noun* **1** a small-scale painting **2** a small bottle of spirits □ *adjective* on a small scale

minibus *noun* (*plural* **minibuses**) a type of small bus

minim *music* a note (♩) equal to two crotchets, or half a semibreve, in length

minimize *verb* **1** to make to seem small or unimportant **2** to make as small as possible

minimum *noun* (*plural* **minima**) the smallest possible quantity □ *adjective* the least possible

minimum wage the lowest wage per

hour which can legally be paid for a particular type of work

minion *noun* a slave-like follower

miniscule *noun another spelling* of **minuscule**

The **miniscule** spelling is not yet standard

minister *noun* **1** the head of a government department: *minister of trade* **2** a member of the clergy **3** an agent, a representative □ *verb* **minister to** to help, supply the needs of

ministerial *adjective* of a minister

ministry *noun* (*plural* **ministries**) **1** a government department or its headquarters **2** the work of a member of the clergy

mink *noun* a small weasel-like kind of animal or its fur

minnow *noun* a type of very small river or pond fish

minor *adjective* **1** of less importance, size *etc* **2** small, unimportant (*contrasted with*: **major**) □ *noun* someone not yet legally an adult (*ie* in the UK, under 18)

minority *noun* (*plural* **minorities**) **1** the smaller number or part **2** the state of being a minor

Minotaur *noun* a mythological creature with a bull's head, living in the Cretan labyrinth

minster *noun* a large church or cathedral

minstrel *noun* **1** *historical* a medieval travelling musician **2** a singer, an entertainer

mint¹ *noun* a plant with strong-smelling leaves, used as flavouring

mint² *noun* **1** a place where coins are made **2** *informal* a large sum of money: *cost a mint* □ *verb* to make coins □ **in mint condition** in perfect condition

minuet *noun* **1** a kind of slow, graceful dance **2** the music for this

minus *preposition* **1** used to show subtraction, represented by the sign (−): *five minus two equals three or 5−2= 3* **2** *informal* without: *I'm minus my car today* □ *adjective* of a quantity less than zero

minuscule (*pronounced* **min**-is-kyool) *noun* a small cursive script originally used by monks for manuscripts □ *adjective* 1 written in minuscule 2 tiny, minute

minute¹ (*pronounced* **min**-it) *noun* 1 a sixtieth part of an hour 2 in measuring an angle, the sixtieth part of a degree 3 a very short time 4 **minutes** notes taken of what is said at a meeting

minute² (*pronounced* mai-**nyoot**) *adjective* 1 very small 2 very exact

minx *noun* (*plural* **minxes**) a cheeky young girl

miracle *noun* 1 a wonderful act beyond normal human powers 2 a fortunate happening with no natural cause or explanation □ **miraculous** *adjective* □ **miraculously** *adverb*

mirage *noun* something imagined but not really there, *eg* an oasis seen by travellers in the desert

mire *noun* deep mud □ **miry** *adjective*

mirror *noun* a backed piece of glass which shows the image of someone looking into it □ *verb* 1 to reflect like a mirror 2 to copy exactly

mirth *noun* merriment, laughter □ **mirthful** *adjective*

mirthless *adjective* of a laugh or smile: not showing genuine amusement

mis- *prefix* wrong(ly), bad(ly): *mispronounce/ misapply*

    mis- is an Old English prefix

misadventure *noun* an unlucky happening

misandry *noun* hatred of men

misanthropist *noun* someone who hates humanity □ **misanthropic** *adjective* □ **misanthropy** *noun*

misappropriate (*pronounced* mis-ap-roh-pri-eit) *verb* to put to a wrong use, *eg* use (someone else's money) for yourself

misbehave *verb* to behave badly □ **misbehaviour** *noun*

miscarriage *noun* 1 a going wrong, failure: *miscarriage of justice* 2 the accidental loss of a foetus during pregnancy

miscarry *verb* 1 to go wrong or astray 2 to be unsuccessful 3 to have a miscarriage in pregnancy

    miscarry ⇨ miscarries, miscarrying, miscarried

miscellaneous *adjective* assorted, made up of several kinds

miscellany *noun* (*plural* **miscellanies**) a mixture or collection of things, *eg* pieces of writing

mischance *noun* an unlucky accident

mischief *noun* 1 naughtiness 2 *old* harm, damage

mischievous *adjective* naughty, teasing; causing trouble □ **mischievously** *adverb*

misconceive *verb* to misunderstand

misconception *noun* a wrong idea, a misunderstanding

misconduct *noun* bad or immoral behaviour

misconstruction *noun* a wrong interpretation

misconstrue *verb* to misunderstand

miscreant *noun* a wicked person

misdeed *noun* a bad deed; a crime

misdemeanour *noun* a minor offence

miser *noun* someone who hoards money and spends very little

miserable *adjective* 1 very unhappy; wretched 2 having a tendency to be bad-tempered and grumpy 3 depressing

  ▤ **Alternative words**: (meaning 1) abject

miserly *adjective* stingy, mean

misery *noun* (*plural* **miseries**) 1 great unhappiness, pain, poverty *etc* 2 a person who is always sad or bad-tempered

misfire *verb* 1 of a gun: to fail to go off 2 of a plan: to go wrong

misfit *noun* 1 someone who cannot fit in happily in society *etc* 2 something that fits badly

misfortune *noun* 1 bad luck 2 an unlucky accident

misgiving *noun* fear or doubt, *eg* about the result of an action

misguided *adjective* led astray, mistaken, unwise

mishandle *verb* to treat badly or roughly

mishap *noun* an unlucky accident

misinform *verb* to inform wrongly

misinterpret *verb* to interpret wrongly

misjudge *verb* to judge unfairly or wrongly

mislay *verb* to put (something) aside and forget where it is; lose

> **mislay** ⇨ mislay*s*, mislay*ing*, mislaid

mislead *verb* to give a false idea (to); deceive □ **misleading** *adjective*

> **mislead** ⇨ mislead*s*, mislead*ing*, misled

mismatch *noun* an unsuitable match

misnomer *noun* a wrong or unsuitable name

misogynist (*pronounced* mi-**so**-jin-ist) *noun* a man who hates women

misplace *verb* to put in the wrong place; mislay

misprint *noun* a mistake in printing

misquote *verb* to make a mistake in repeating something written or said

misrepresent *verb* to give a wrong idea of (someone's words, actions *etc*)

Miss *noun* (*plural* **Misses**) **1** a form of address used before the surname of an unmarried woman **2 miss** a young woman or girl

miss *verb* **1** to fail to hit, see, hear, understand *etc* **2** to discover the loss or absence of **3** to feel the lack of: *missing old friends* □ *noun* (*plural* **misses**) **1** the act of missing **2** a failure to hit a target **3** a loss □ **miss out 1** to leave out **2** to be left out of something worthwhile or advantageous

missal *noun* the Mass book of the Roman Catholic Church

misshapen *adjective* badly or abnormally shaped

missile *noun* a weapon or other object that is thrown or fired

missing *adjective* lost

mission *noun* **1** a task that someone is sent to do **2** a group of representatives sent to another country **3** a group sent to spread a religion **4** the headquarters of such groups **5** someone's chosen task or purpose: *his only mission is to make money*

missionary *noun* (*plural* **missionaries**) someone sent abroad *etc* to spread a religion

missive *noun* something sent, *eg* a letter

misspell *verb* to spell wrongly □ **misspelling** *noun*

> **misspell** ⇨ misspell*s*, misspell*ing*, misspell*ed* or misspelt

misspent *adjective* spent unwisely, wasted: *misspent youth*

mist *noun* a cloud of moisture in the air; thin fog or drizzle □ **mist up** or **mist over** to cover or become covered with mist □ **misty** *adjective*

mistake *verb* **1** to misunderstand, be wrong or make an error about **2** to take (one thing or person) for another □ *noun* a wrong action or statement; an error

> **mistake** *verb* ⇨ mistake*s*, mistak*ing*, mistaken, mistook

mistaken *adjective* making an error, unwise: *mistaken belief*

mistletoe *noun* a plant with white berries, used as a Christmas decoration

mistreat *verb* to treat badly; abuse

mistress *noun* (*plural* **mistresses**) **1** a female teacher **2** a female owner of a dog *etc* **3** a woman skilled in an art **4** a woman who is the lover though not the legal wife of a man **5** *full form of* **Mrs**

mistrust *noun* a lack of trust or confidence in □ *verb* to have no trust or confidence in

misunderstand *verb* to take a wrong meaning from what is said or done

misunderstanding *noun* **1** a mistake about a meaning **2** a slight disagreement

misuse *noun* bad or wrong use □ *verb* **1** to use wrongly **2** to treat badly

mite *noun* **1** something very small, *eg* a tiny child **2** a very small spider **3** *historical* a very small coin

mithridate an antidote to poison

Named after *Mithridates*, king of Pontus, who acquired immunity to poison by taking gradual doses

mitigate *verb* to make (punishment, anger *etc*) less great or severe: *Reasonable efforts must be made to mitigate the risks to society* □ **mitigation** *noun*

Ⓛ Comes from Latin *mitigare* meaning 'to make mild or soft'

🖝 Do not confuse with: **militate**. It may be helpful to remember that the idea of fighting is contained in the word **MILITate** (in common with 'military' and 'militia') but not in **mitigate**

mitre *noun* **1** the pointed head-dress worn by archbishops and bishops **2** a slanting joint between two pieces of wood

mitt or **mitten** *noun* a glove without separate divisions for the four fingers

mix *verb* **1** to unite or blend two or more things together **2 mix up** to confuse, muddle **3** to have social contact with other people □ *noun* a mixture, a blending

■ **Alternative words**: (verb, meaning 2) jumble; (verb, meaning 3) associate

mixed *adjective* **1** jumbled together **2** confused, muddled **3** consisting of different kinds **4** for both sexes: *mixed doubles*

mixed-up *adjective* confused, bewildered, emotionally unstable

mixer *noun* **1** a machine that mixes food **2** someone who mixes socially **3** a soft drink added to alcohol

mixture *noun* **1** a number of things mixed together **2** a medicine

mizzen-mast *noun* the mast nearest the stern of a ship

MLitt *abbreviation* Master of Letters or Literature (from Latin *Magister Litterarum*)

mnemonic (*pronounced* ni-**mon**-ik) *noun* a rhyme *etc* which helps you to remember something

🖉 Some people use this mnemonic to help them remember the colours of the rainbow: **R**ichard **o**f **Y**ork gave **b**attle **i**n vain (red orange yellow green blue indigo violet). **Can you think of any more?**

moan *noun* a low sound of grief or pain □ *verb* to make this sound

moat *noun* a deep trench round a castle *etc*, often filled with water

mob *noun* a noisy crowd □ *verb* to crowd round, or attack, in disorder

mob ⇨ mob*s*, mob*bing*, mob*bed*

mobile *adjective* **1** able to move or be moved easily **2** not fixed, changing quickly **3** portable, not relying on fixed cables *etc*: *mobile phone* □ *noun* **1** a decoration or toy hung so that it moves slightly in the air **2** *informal* a mobile phone

mobility *noun* freedom or ease of movement, either in physical or career terms

mobilize *verb* to gather (troops *etc*) together ready for active service □ **mobilization** *noun*

Möbius strip (*pronounced* **mer**-bi-*us*) *maths* a one-sided surface made by twisting and joining together the ends of a rectangular strip

moccasin *noun* a soft leather shoe of the type originally worn by Native Americans

mocha (*pronounced* **mok**-*a* or **mohk**-*a*) *noun* **1** a fine coffee **2** coffee and chocolate mixed together **3** a deep brown colour

mock *verb* to laugh at, make fun of □ *adjective* false, pretended, imitation: *mock battle*

mockery *noun* **1** the act of mocking **2** a ridiculous imitation

MOD *abbreviation* Ministry of Defence

modal verb *grammar* a verb which modifies the sense of a main verb, *eg* can, may, must *etc*

mode *noun* **1** a manner of doing or acting **2** kind, sort; fashion

model *noun* **1** a design or pattern to be

copied **2** a small-scale copy of something: *model railway* **3** a living person who poses for an artist **4** someone employed to wear and display new clothes □ *adjective* **1** acting as a model **2** fit to be copied, perfect: *model behaviour* □ *verb* **1** to make a model of **2** to shape according to a particular pattern **3** to wear and display (clothes)

model *verb* ⇨ model**s**, model**ling**, model**led**

modem *noun* a device which transmits information from a computer along telephone cables

moderate *verb* (*pronounced* **mod**-*e*-reit) to make or become less great or severe □ *adjective* (*pronounced* **mod**-*e*-rat) **1** keeping within reason, not going to extremes **2** of medium or average quality, ability *etc*

moderately *adverb* slightly, quite, fairly

moderation *noun* **1** a lessening or calming down **2** the practice of not going to extremes

modern *adjective* belonging to the present or to recent times; not old □ **modernity** *noun*

■ **Alternative words**: current, contemporary, advanced, avant-garde, progressive, modernistic, state-of-the-art

modernize *verb* to bring up to date

modest *adjective* **1** not exaggerating achievements; not boastful **2** not very large: *modest salary* **3** behaving decently; not shocking □ **modesty** *noun*

modicum *noun* (*plural* **modicums**) a small quantity or amount: *a modicum of kindness*

modify *verb* **1** to make a change in: *modified my design* **2** to make less extreme: *modified his demands* □ **modification** *noun*

modify ⇨ modif**ies**, modif**ying**, modif**ied**

modish *adjective* fashionable, smart

modular *adjective* of or composed of modules

modulate *verb* **1** to vary or soften in

tone or pitch **2** *music* to change key □ **modulation** *noun*

module *noun* **1** a set course forming a unit in an educational scheme **2** a separate, self-contained section of a spacecraft **3** *architecture* a standard unit of size

mogul *noun* **1** a mound of hard snow forming an obstacle on a ski-slope **2** an influential person; a magnate

mohair *noun* **1** the long silky hair of an Angora goat **2** fabric made from this

Mohammed *noun* a prophet, the founder of Islam

moist *adjective* damp, very slightly wet

moisten *verb* to make slightly wet or damp

moisture *noun* slight wetness; water or other liquid in tiny drops in the atmosphere or on a surface

moisturize *verb* to add moisture to

moisturizer *noun* a cosmetic cream that restores moisture to the skin

molar *noun* a back tooth used for grinding food

molasses *noun singular* a thick dark syrup left when sugar is refined

mole[1] *noun* **1** a small burrowing animal, with tiny eyes and soft fur **2** a spy who successfully infiltrates a rival organization

mole[2] *noun* a small dark spot on the skin, often raised

molecule *noun* the smallest part of a substance that has the same qualities as the substance itself

molehill *noun* a small heap of earth created by a burrowing mole

molest *verb* **1** to annoy or torment **2** to injure or abuse sexually

mollify *verb* to calm down; lessen the anger of

mollify ⇨ mollif**ies**, mollif**ying**, mollif**ied**

mollusc *noun* one of a group of boneless animals, usually with hard shells, *eg* shellfish and snails

mollycoddle *verb* to pamper, over-protect

molten *adjective* of metal *etc*: melted

moment *noun* **1** a very short space of time; an instant **2** importance, consequence

momentary *adjective* lasting for a moment □ **momentarily** *adverb*

momentous *adjective* of great importance: *a momentous discovery*

momentum *noun* (*plural* **momenta**) the force of a moving body

mon- *see* **mono-**

monarch *noun* a king, queen, emperor or empress

monarchist *noun* someone who believes in government by a monarch

monarchy *noun* (*plural* **monarchies**) **1** government by a monarch **2** an area governed by a monarch **3** the royal family

monastery *noun* (*plural* **monasteries**) a building housing a group of monks

monastic *adjective* of or like monasteries or monks

monasticism *noun* the way of life in a monastery

Monday *noun* the second day of the week

monetarism (*pronounced* **mun**-it-ar-i-zm) *noun* an economic policy based on control of a country's money supply

monetary (*pronounced* **mun**-*i*-tri) *adjective* of money or coinage

money *noun* **1** coins and banknotes used for payment **2** wealth

> The Roman goddess Juno was known in ancient times as Juno *Moneta* (= Juno the Reminder), and it was in her temple in Rome that money was coined. This resulted in the word *moneta* being used first to mean 'a mint', and then the money which was made there; this meaning survives today in the English words **money** and **mint²**.

moneyed or **monied** *adjective* wealthy

mongoose *noun* (*plural* **mongooses**) a small weasel-like animal which kills snakes

mongrel *noun* an animal of mixed breed

monitor *noun* **1** an instrument used to check the operation of a system or apparatus **2** a screen in a television studio showing the picture being transmitted **3** a computer screen **4** a school pupil given certain responsibilities □ *verb* **1** to keep a check on **2** to listen to and report on foreign broadcasts *etc*

monk *noun* a member of a male religious group living secluded in a monastery

monkey *noun* (*plural* **monkeys**) **1** a long-tailed mammal which walks on four legs **2** a mischievous child □ **monkey about** to fool about

monkey-nut *noun* a peanut

monkey-puzzle *noun* a pine tree with prickly spines along its branches

monkey-wrench *noun* an adjustable spanner

monkfish *noun* a type of sea-fish, used as food

mono- or **mon-** *prefix* one, single: *monarch* (= a person who is the sole ruler of a country)/ *carbon monoxide* (= a gas with only one oxygen atom in its molecule)
  ① Comes from Greek *monos* meaning 'single' or 'alone'

monoboard *noun* a wide single ski, controlled with both feet

monochrome *adjective* **1** in one colour **2** black and white

monocle *noun* a single eyeglass

monogamy *noun* marriage to one spouse at a time □ **monogamous** *adjective*

monogram *noun* two or more letters, usually initials, made into a single design

monolith *noun* **1** an upright block of stone **2** something unmovable or intractable

monolithic *adjective* intractable, obstinate

monologue *noun* a long speech by one person

monoplane *noun* an aeroplane with a single pair of wings

monopolize *verb* **1** to have exclusive

rights to **2** to take up the whole of: *monopolizing the conversation*

monopoly *noun* (*plural* **monopolies**) **1** an exclusive right to make or sell something **2** complete unshared possession, control *etc*

monorail *noun* a railway on which the trains run along a single rail

mono-ski *noun* one large ski on which both feet are placed □ *verb* to ski using a mono-ski

monosyllable *noun* a word of one syllable □ **monosyllabic** *adjective*

monotone *noun* a single, unchanging tone

monotonous 1 in a single tone **2** unchanging, dull □ **monotonously** *adverb*

monotony *noun* lack of variety

monsoon *noun* **1** a wind that blows in the Indian Ocean **2** the rainy season caused by the south-west monsoon in summer

monster *noun* **1** something of unusual size or appearance **2** a huge terrifying creature **3** an evil person □ *adjective* huge

monstrosity *noun* (*plural* **monstrosities**) **1** something unnatural **2** something very ugly

monstrous *adjective* huge, horrible

montage (*pronounced* mon-**tahsz**) *noun* **1** a composite picture **2** a film made up of parts of other films

month *noun* a twelfth part of a year, approximately four weeks

monthly *adjective & adverb* happening once a month □ *noun* (*plural* **monthlies**) a magazine *etc* published once a month

monument *noun* a building, pillar, tomb *etc* built in memory of someone or an event

monumental *adjective* **1** of a monument **2** huge, enormous □ **monumentally** *adverb* (meaning 2)

moo *noun* the sound made by a cow

mood *noun* the state of a person's feelings or temper

moody *adjective* **1** often changing in

mood **2** ill-tempered, cross □ **moodily** *adverb* (meaning 2)

moon *noun* the heavenly body which travels round the earth once each month and reflects light from the sun □ *verb* **1** to wander (about) **2** to gaze dreamily (at)

moonbeam *noun* a beam of light from the moon

moonlight *noun* the light of the moon □ *verb* to work secretly at a second job, usually avoiding paying tax on the money earned

moonshine *noun* **1** the shining of the moon **2** rubbish, foolish ideas or talk **3** alcoholic spirits which have been illegally distilled or smuggled

moor *noun* a large stretch of open ground, often covered with heather □ *verb* to tie up or anchor (a ship *etc*)

moorhen *noun* a kind of water bird

moorings *noun plural* **1** the place where a ship is moored **2** the anchor, rope *etc* holding it

moorland *noun* a stretch of moor

moose *noun* (*plural* **moose**) a large deer-like animal, found in N America

moot point a debatable point; a question with no obvious solution

mop *noun* **1** a pad of sponge or a bunch of short pieces of coarse yarn *etc* on a handle for washing or cleaning **2** a thick head of hair □ *verb* **1** to clean with a mop **2** to clean or wipe: *mopped his brow* □ **mop up** to clean up

mop *verb* ⇨ mops, mopp*ing*, mopp*ed*

mope *verb* to be unhappy and gloomy

moped *noun* a pedal bicycle with a motor

moquette *noun* fabric with a velvety pile and canvas backing, used for upholstery

moraine *noun* a line of rocks and gravel left by a glacier

moral *adjective* **1** relating to standards of behaviour and character **2** of correct or acceptable behaviour or character □ *noun* **1** the lesson of a story **2** **morals** principles and standards of (especially sexual) behaviour

morale (*pronounced* mo-**rahl**) *noun* spirit and confidence

morality *noun* moral standards

moralize *verb* to draw a lesson from a story or event

moral support encouragement without active help

moral victory a failure that can really be seen as a success

morass *noun* (*plural* **morasses**) 1 a marsh or bog 2 a bewildering mass of something: *a morass of regulations*

moratorium *noun* (*plural* **moratoria**) an official suspension or temporary ban

morbid *adjective* 1 too concerned with gloomy, unpleasant things, especially death 2 diseased, unhealthy □ **morbidity** *noun* □ **morbidly** *adverb*

more *adjective* a greater number or amount of: *more money* □ *adverb* to a greater extent: *more beautiful/ more than I can say* □ *noun* 1 a greater proportion or amount 2 a further or additional number: *there are more where this came from*

moreish *adjective* of food *etc*: enjoyable, making you want more

moreover *adverb* besides

morganatic *adjective* of a marriage: in which the woman has no claim to the title or property of her husband

From early German *morgengabe* 'morning gift', a present given to a spouse on the morning after the wedding

morgue (*pronounced* mawg) *noun* a place where dead bodies are laid, awaiting identification *etc*

MORI *abbreviation* Market and Opinion Research Institute

moribund *adjective* 1 dying 2 stagnant

morn *noun, formal* morning

morning *noun* the part of the day before noon □ *adjective* of or in the morning

morning star Venus when it rises before the sun

morocco *noun* a fine goatskin leather first brought from Morocco

moron *noun* someone of low mental ability; an idiot □ **moronic** *adjective*

morose *adjective* bad-tempered, gloomy □ **morosely** *adverb* □ **morosity** *noun*

morphia *noun* morphine

morphine *noun* a drug which causes sleep or deadens pain (*also called* **morphia**)

morris dance a traditional English country dance in which male dancers carry sticks and wear bells

Originally a *Moorish* dance brought from Spain

morrow *noun, old*: **the morrow** tomorrow, the day after

morse *noun* a signalling code of signals made up of dots and dashes

morsel *noun* a small piece, *eg* of food

mort- *prefix* forms words related to death: *immortal/ mortuary*
Ⓛ Comes from Latin *mort-*, a form of *mori* meaning 'to die'

mortal *adjective* 1 liable to die 2 causing death; deadly: *mortal injury* □ *noun* a human being

mortality *noun* (*plural* **mortalities**) 1 the state of being mortal 2 death 3 frequency of death; death-rate: *infant mortality*

mortally *adverb* 1 fatally: *mortally wounded* 2 very much, dreadfully: *mortally offended*

mortar *noun* 1 a heavy bowl for crushing and grinding substances with a pestle 2 a short gun for throwing shells 3 a mixture of lime, sand and water, used for fixing stones *etc*

mortarboard *noun* a university or college cap with a square flat top

mortgage *noun* a sum of money lent through a legal agreement for buying buildings, land *etc* □ *verb* to offer (buildings *etc*) as security for money borrowed

mortice *another spelling of* **mortise**

mortician *noun, US* an undertaker

mortify *verb* 1 to make to feel ashamed or humble: *I was mortified* 2 of a part of the flesh: to die □ **mortification** *noun* □ **mortifying** *adjective*

mortify ⇨ mortifi*es*, mortifi*ing*, mortifi*ed*

mortise or **mortice** *noun* a hole in a piece of wood to receive the shaped end (**tenon**) of another piece

mortise-lock or **mortice-lock** *noun* a lock whose mechanism is sunk into the edge of a door

mortuary *noun* (*plural* **mortuaries**) a place where dead bodies are kept before burial or cremation

mosaic *noun* a picture or design made up of many small pieces of coloured glass, stone *etc*

Moses basket a portable cot for babies

Moslem *another spelling* of **Muslim**

mosque *noun* an Islamic place of worship

mosquito *noun* (*plural* **mosquitoes** or **mosquitos**) a biting or blood-sucking insect, often carrying disease

moss *noun* (*plural* **mosses**) a very small flowerless plant, found in moist places

mossy *adjective* covered with moss

most *adjective* the greatest number or amount of: *most children attend school regularly* □ *adverb* **1** very, extremely: *most grateful* **2** to the greatest extent: *the most severely injured* □ *noun* the greatest number or amount: *he got most* □ **at most** not more than □ **for the most part** mostly

mostly *adverb* mainly, chiefly

MOT *noun* a compulsory annual check on behalf of the *M*inistry *o*f *T*ransport on vehicles over a certain age

motel *noun* a hotel built to accommodate motorists and their vehicles

moth *noun* **1** a flying insect, seen mostly at night **2** the cloth-eating grub of the clothes-moth

mothball *noun* a small ball of chemical used to protect clothes from moths □ *verb* (*also* **put in mothballs**) to put aside for later use *etc*

moth-eaten *adjective* **1** full of holes made by moths **2** tatty, shabby

mother *noun* **1** a female parent **2** the female head of a convent □ *verb* **1** to be the mother of **2** to care for like a mother

motherboard *noun, computing* a printed circuit board into which other boards can be slotted

motherhood *noun* the state of being a mother

mother-in-law *noun* the mother of your husband or wife

motherland *noun* the country of your birth

motherly *adjective* of or like a mother

mother-of-pearl *noun* a hard shiny substance which forms inside certain shells

mother tongue a native language

motif (*pronounced* moh-**teef**) *noun* (*plural* **motifs**) a distinctive feature or idea in a piece of music, a play *etc*

☛ Do not confuse with: **motive**

motion *noun* **1** the act or state of moving **2** a single movement **3** a suggestion put before a meeting for discussion □ *verb* **1** to make a signal by a movement or gesture **2** to direct (someone) in this way: *the policeman motioned us forward*

motionless *adjective* not moving

motivate *verb* to cause (someone) to act in a certain way

motive *noun* the cause of someone's actions; a reason

☛ Do not confuse with: **motif**

motley *adjective* made up of different colours or kinds

motocross *noun* the sport of motorcycle racing across rough terrain

motor *noun* **1** an engine which causes motion **2** a car □ *verb* to travel by motor vehicle

motorbike or **motorcycle** *noun* a bicycle with a petrol-driven engine □ **motorbiker** *noun* □ **motorcyclist** *noun*

motorcade *noun* a procession of cars carrying a head of state *etc*

motorist *noun* someone who drives a car

motorize *verb* to supply with an engine

motorway *noun* a dual carriageway on which traffic is allowed to drive faster than on other roads

mottled *adjective* marked with spots or blotches

motto *noun* (*plural* **mottoes**) a phrase which acts as a guiding principle or rule

mould[1] *noun* a shape into which a liquid is poured to take on that shape when it cools or sets: *jelly mould* □ *verb* 1 to form in a mould 2 to shape

mould[2] *noun* 1 a fluffy growth on stale food *etc* 2 soil containing rotted leaves *etc*

moulder *verb* to crumble away to dust

moulding *noun* a decorated border of moulded plaster round a ceiling *etc*

mouldy *adjective* affected by mould; stale

moult *verb* of a bird: to shed its feathers

mound *noun* 1 a bank of earth or stones 2 a hill; a heap

mount *verb* 1 to go up, ascend 2 to climb on to (a horse, bicycle *etc*) 3 to fix (a picture *etc*) on to a backing or support 4 to fix (a gemstone) in a casing 5 to organize (an exhibition) *noun* 1 a support or backing for display 2 a horse, bicycle *etc* to ride on 3 *old* a mountain

mountain *noun* 1 a large hill 2 a large quantity

mountain-ash *noun* the rowan tree

mountaineer *noun* a mountain climber

mountainous *adjective* 1 having many mountains 2 huge

mountebank *noun* a charlatan, a quack

> Originally a street pedlar who climbed on a mound or bench to sell his goods

Mounties *informal*: **the Mounties** the Canadian horseback police

mourn *verb* 1 to grieve for 2 to be sorrowful □ **mourner** *noun*

mournful *adjective* sad

mourning *noun* 1 the showing of grief 2 the period during which someone grieves 3 dark-coloured clothes traditionally worn by mourners

mouse *noun* (*plural* **mice**) 1 a small gnawing animal, found in houses and fields 2 a shy, timid, uninteresting person 3 *computing* a device moved by hand which causes corresponding cursor movements on a screen

mousse *noun* a frothy set dish including eggs, cream *etc*, either sweet or savoury

moustache *noun* unshaved hair above a man's upper lip

mousy *adjective* 1 of a light-brown colour 2 shy, timid, uninteresting

mouth *noun* (*pronounced* mowth) 1 the opening in the head through which an animal or person eats and makes sounds 2 the point of a river where it flows into the sea 3 an opening, an entrance □ *verb* (*pronounced* mowdh) 1 to speak 2 to shape (words) in an exaggerated way

mouthful *noun* (*plural* **mouthfuls**) as much as fills the mouth

mouth-organ *noun* a small wind instrument, moved across the lips

mouthpiece *noun* 1 the part of a musical instrument, tobacco-pipe *etc* held in the mouth 2 someone who speaks for others

movable *adjective* able to be moved, changed *etc*

move *verb* 1 to (cause to) change place or position 2 to change your house 3 to rouse or affect the feelings of 4 to rouse into action 5 propose, suggest □ *noun* 1 an act of moving 2 a step, an action 3 a shifting of pieces in a game of chess *etc*

movement *noun* 1 the act or manner of moving 2 a change of position 3 a division of a piece of music 4 a group of people united in a common aim: *the peace movement* 5 an organized attempt to achieve an aim: *the movement to reform the divorce laws*

movie *noun* a cinema film □ **the movies** the cinema

moving *adjective* 1 in motion 2 causing emotion □ **movingly** *adverb* (meaning 2)

■ **Opposite:** (meaning 1) immobile

mow *verb* 1 to cut (grass, hay *etc*) with a scythe or machine 2 **mow someone** or **something down** to destroy them in great numbers

mower *noun* a machine for mowing

MP *abbreviation* 1 Member of Parliament 2 Military Police

MPhil *abbreviation* Master of Philosophy

Mr *noun* (*short* for **mister**) the form of address used before a man's surname

Mrs *noun* (*short* for **mistress**) the form of address used before a married woman's surname

MS *abbreviation* 1 multiple sclerosis 2 manuscript

Ms *noun* a form of address used before the surname of a married or unmarried woman

MSc *abbreviation* Master of Science

MSG *abbreviation* monosodium glutamate

much *adjective* a great amount of □ *adverb* to or by a great extent: *much loved/ much faster* □ *pronoun* 1 a great amount 2 something important: *made much of it* □ **much the same** nearly the same

muck *noun* dung, dirt, filth

muck-raking *noun* looking for scandals to expose

mucous *adjective* like or covered by mucus

◆ Do not confuse: **mucous** and **mucus**

mucus *noun* slimy fluid secreted from the nose *etc*

mud *noun* wet, soft earth

muddle *verb* 1 to confuse, bewilder 2 to mix up 3 to make a mess of □ *noun* 1 a mess 2 a state of confusion

muddy *adjective* 1 covered with mud 2 unclear, confused □ *verb* to make or become muddy

mudguard *noun* a shield or guard over wheels to catch mud splashes

muesli *noun* a mixture of grains, nuts and fruit eaten with milk

muff[1] *noun* a tube of warm fabric to cover and keep the hands warm

muff[2] *verb* to fail in an opportunity, *eg* to catch a ball

muffin *noun* 1 a round, flat spongy cake, toasted and eaten hot with butter 2 *US* a small sweet cake made of flour, cornmeal *etc*

muffle *verb* 1 to wrap up for warmth *etc* 2 to deaden (a sound)

muffler *noun* 1 a scarf 2 *US* a silencer for a car

mufti *noun* clothes worn by soldiers *etc* when off duty

mug[1] *noun* 1 a straight-sided cup 2 *informal* a stupid person 3 *informal* the face

mug[2] *verb* to attack and rob (someone) in the street □ **mugger** *noun*

   mug ⇨ mug**s**, mug**ging**, mug**ged**

mug[3] *verb*: **mug up** *informal* to study hard; swot up

muggy *adjective* of weather: close and damp □ **mugginess** *noun*

mulberry *noun* 1 a tree on whose leaves silkworms are fed 2 its purple berry

mulch *noun* loose straw *etc* laid down to protect plant roots □ *verb* to cover with mulch

mule[1] *noun* an animal bred from a horse and an ass

mule[2] *noun* a backless slipper

mulish *adjective* stubborn

mulled *adjective* of wine, *etc*: mixed with spices and served warm

mullet *noun* an edible small sea-fish

mull over *verb* to think over, ponder over

multi- *prefix* many
Ⓛ Comes from Latin *multus* meaning 'many'

multi-coloured *adjective* many-coloured

multifarious *adjective* of many kinds

multimedia *adjective* of a computer: able to run various sound and visual applications

multimillionaire *noun* someone who

has property worth several million pounds (or dollars)

multinational *adjective* of a company: having branches in several different countries

multiple *adjective* 1 affecting many parts: *multiple injuries* 2 involving many things of the same sort, *eg* vehicles in a *multiple crash* □ *noun* a number or quantity which contains another an exact number of times

multiple sclerosis a progressive nerve disease resulting in paralysis (shortened to **MS**)

multiplex *adjective* of a cinema: including several screens and theatres in one building

multiplication *noun* the act of multiplying

multiplicity *noun*: **a multiplicity of** a great number of

multiplier *noun* the number by which another is to be multiplied

multiply *verb* 1 to increase 2 to increase a number by adding it to itself a certain number of times: *2 multiplied by 3 is 6*

multiply ⇨ multipli*es*, multiply*ing*, multipli*ed*

multitasking *noun*, *computing* the action of running several processes simultaneously

multitude *noun* a great number; a crowd

multitudinous *adjective* very many

mum¹ *noun*, *informal* mother

mum² *adjective* silent

mumble *verb* to speak indistinctly

mummify *verb* to make into a mummy (meaning 2)

mummify ⇨ mummifi*es*, mummify*ing*, mummifi*ed*

mummy¹ *noun* (*plural* **mummies**) *informal* mother

mummy² *noun* (*plural* **mummies**) a dead body preserved by wrapping in bandages and treating with wax, spices *etc*

mumps *noun singular* an infectious disease affecting glands at the side of the neck, causing swelling

munch *verb* to chew noisily

munchies: **the munchies** hunger pangs

mundane *adjective* dull, ordinary

municipal *adjective* of or owned by a city or town

municipality *noun* a city or town; an area covered by local government

munificent *adjective* very generous □ **munificence** *noun*

munitions *noun plural* weapons and ammunition used in war

Munro *noun* (*plural* **Munros**) a British or Irish mountain above 3000 feet

Originally applied only to mountains in Scotland, from a list prepared by the Scottish mountaineer, Hugh *Munro*

mural *adjective* of or on a wall □ *noun* a painting or design on a wall

murder *verb* to kill someone unlawfully and on purpose □ *noun* the act of murdering

murderer *noun* someone who commits murder

murderess *noun*, *old* a woman murderer

murderous *adjective* capable or guilty of murder; wicked

murky *adjective* dark, gloomy □ **murkiness** *noun*

murmur *noun* 1 a low indistinct continuous sound 2 a hushed speech or tone □ *verb* 1 to make a murmur 2 to complain, grumble

Murphy's Law the law that if something can go wrong, it will

muscle *noun* 1 fleshy tissue which contracts and stretches to cause body movements 2 an area of this in the body 3 physical strength or power

muscular *adjective* 1 of muscles 2 strong

muscular dystrophy a hereditary disease in which the muscles gradually deteriorate

Muse *noun* one of the nine goddesses of poetry, music, dancing *etc* in classical mythology

muse *verb* to think (over) in a quiet, leisurely way

museum *noun* (*plural* **museums**) a building for housing and displaying objects of artistic, scientific or historic interest

mush *noun* 1 something soft and pulpy 2 an overly sentimental film, song *etc*

mushroom *noun* an edible fungus, usually umbrella-shaped □ *verb* to grow very quickly: *buildings mushroomed all over town*

mushy *adjective* 1 soft and pulpy 2 overly sentimental

music *noun* 1 the art of arranging, combining *etc* certain sounds able to be produced by the voice, or by instruments 2 an arrangement of such sounds or its written form 3 a sweet or pleasant sound

musical *adjective* 1 of music 2 sounding sweet or pleasant 3 having a talent for music □ *noun* a light play or film with a lot of songs and dancing in it □ **musically** *adverb*

musician *noun* 1 a specialist in music 2 someone who plays a musical instrument

musk *noun* a strong perfume, obtained from the male musk deer or artificially

musket *noun* a kind of gun once used by soldiers

musketeer *noun* a soldier armed with a musket

musky *adjective* smelling like musk

Muslim *noun* a follower of the Islamic religion □ *adjective* Islamic

muslin *noun* a fine, soft cotton cloth

mussel *noun* an edible shellfish with two separate halves to its shell

must *verb* 1 used with another verb to express necessity: *I must finish this today* 2 expressing compulsion: *you must do as you're told* 3 expressing certainty or probability: *that must be the right answer* □ *noun* something that must be done; a necessity

Ⓒ Comes from Old English *moste*

mustache *US spelling of* **moustache**

mustang *noun* a North American wild horse

mustard *noun* 1 a plant with sharp-tasting seeds 2 a hot yellow paste made from its seeds

muster *verb* to gather up or together (*eg* troops, courage) □ **pass muster** to be accepted as satisfactory

musty *adjective* smelling old and stale □ **mustiness** *noun*

mutable *adjective* changeable

mute *adjective* 1 not able to speak; dumb 2 silent 3 of a letter in a word: not pronounced □ *noun* a mute person

muted *adjective* 1 of a sound: made quieter, hushed 2 of a colour: not bright

mutilate *verb* 1 to inflict great physical damage on; maim 2 to damage greatly □ **mutilation** *noun*

mutineer *noun* someone who takes part in a mutiny

mutinous *adjective* rebellious; refusing to obey orders

mutiny *verb* 1 to rise against those in power 2 to refuse to obey the commands of military officers □ *noun* (*plural* **mutinies**) refusal to obey commands; rebellion

mutiny *verb* ⇨ mutin*ies*, mutiny*ing*, mutin*ied*

mutt *noun, informal* an idiot

mutter *verb* to speak in a low voice; mumble

mutton *noun* meat from a sheep, used as food

mutual *adjective* 1 given by each to the other(s): *mutual help* 2 shared by two or more: *mutual friend*

mutually *adverb* of a relationship between two people or things: each to the other, in both directions

Muzak *noun, trademark* recorded music played in shops *etc*

muzzle *noun* 1 an animal's nose and mouth 2 a fastening placed over an animal's mouth to prevent it biting 3 the open end of a gun □ *verb* 1 to put a muzzle on (a dog *etc*) 2 to prevent from speaking freely

muzzy *adjective* cloudy, confused

my *adjective* belonging to me: *this is my book*

myopia *noun* short-sightedness

myopic *adjective* short-sighted

myriad *noun* a very great number □ *adjective* very many, countless

myrmidon *noun* someone who carries out orders ruthlessly or fearlessly

After the *Myrmidons*, Greek warriors who accompanied Achilles to Troy

myrrh *noun* a bitter-tasting resin used in medicines, perfumes *etc*

myrtle *noun* a type of evergreen shrub

myself *pronoun* 1 used reflexively: *I can see myself in the mirror* 2 used for emphasis: *I wrote this myself*

mysterious *adjective* 1 puzzling, difficult to understand 2 secret, hidden, intriguing □ **mysteriously** *adverb*

mystery *noun* (*plural* **mysteries**) 1 something that cannot be or has not been explained; something puzzling 2 a deep secret

mystic *noun* someone who seeks knowledge of sacred or mystical things by going into a state of spiritual ecstasy

mystical *adjective* having a secret or sacred meaning beyond ordinary human understanding

mystify *verb* 1 to puzzle greatly 2 to confuse, bewilder

mystify ⇨ mystif*ies*, mystify*ing*, mystif*ied*

mystique (*pronounced* mis-**teek**) *noun* an atmosphere of mystery about someone or something

myth *noun* 1 a story about gods, heroes *etc* of ancient times; a fable 2 something imagined or untrue

mythical *adjective* 1 of a myth 2 invented, imagined

mythological *adjective* of myth or mythology; mythical

mythology *noun* 1 the study of myths 2 a collection of myths

myxomatosis *noun* a contagious disease of rabbits

Nn

If you can't find the word you're looking for under letter **N**, it could be that it starts with a different letter. Try looking under **KN** for words like *knot* and *know*, **GN** for words like *gnat*, **PN** for words like *pneumonia*, and **MN** for words like *mnemonic*.

N *abbreviation* **1** north **2** northern

nab *verb, informal* **1** to snatch, seize **2** to arrest

nab ⇨ nab**s**, nab**b**ing, nab**b**ed

nadir *noun* **1** the point of the heavens opposite the zenith **2** the lowest point of anything

naevus or *US* **nevus** (*both* pronounced **neev**-*us*) *noun* a birthmark
ⓘ Comes from Latin *naevus* meaning 'a mole on the body'

naff *adjective, slang* inferior, crass, tasteless

nag *verb* to find fault with constantly □ *noun* a horse

nag *verb* ⇨ nag**s**, nag**g**ing, nag**g**ed

naiad *noun* a mythological river nymph

nail *noun* **1** a horny covering protecting the tips of the fingers and toes **2** a thin pointed piece of metal for fastening wood *etc* □ *verb* **1** to fasten with nails **2** to enclose in a box *etc* with nails **3** *informal* to catch, trap

naive or **naïve** (*both* pronounced nai-**eev**) *adjective* **1** simple in thought, manner or speech **2** inexperienced and lacking knowledge of the world
□ **naiveté** or **naïveté** (*both* pronounced nai-**eev**-i-tei) *noun*

naked *adjective* **1** without clothes **2** having no covering **3** bald, blatant: *naked lie* **4** of feelings: bad or unpleasant, and neither hidden nor controlled □ **nakedly** *adverb* (meaning 4)

NALGO (*pronounced* **nal**-goh) *abbreviation* National and Local Government Officers' Association

namby-pamby *adjective* childish, feeble
Originally a nickname of the 18th-century sentimental English poet, *Ambrose* Philips

name *noun* **1** a word by which a person, place or thing is known **2** fame, reputation: *making a name for himself* **3** an offensive description: *don't call people names* **4** authority: *I arrest you in the name of the king* □ *verb* **1** to give a name to **2** to speak of by name, mention **3** to appoint

nameless *adjective* without a name, not named

namely *adverb* that is to say

namesake *noun* someone with the same name as another

nanny *noun* (*plural* **nannies**) a children's nurse

nanny-goat *noun* a female goat

nano- *prefix* **1** a thousand millionth: *nanosecond* **2** microscopic in size
ⓘ Comes from Greek *nanos* meaning 'a dwarf'

nap *noun* **1** a short sleep **2** a woolly or fluffy surface on cloth **3** a kind of card game □ *verb* to take a short sleep
□ **caught napping** taken unawares

nap *verb* ⇨ nap**s**, nap**p**ing, nap**p**ed

napalm *noun* petroleum jelly, used to make bombs

nape *noun* the back of the neck

napkin *noun* a small piece of cloth or paper for wiping the lips at meals

nappy *noun* (*plural* **nappies**) a piece of cloth, or thick pad, put between a baby's legs to absorb urine and faeces

narcissus *noun* (*plural* **narcissi** or **narcissuses**) a plant like a daffodil with a white, star-shaped flower

narcotic *noun* a type of drug that brings on sleep or stops pain

nark *noun* a persistent complainer □ *verb* to grumble

narky *adjective* irritable, complaining

narrate *verb* to tell a story □ **narrator** *noun*

narration *noun* the telling of a story

narrative *noun* a story □ *adjective* telling a story

narrow *adjective* 1 of small extent from side to side, not wide: *a narrow road* 2 with little to spare: *a narrow escape* 3 lacking wide interests or experience: *narrow views* □ *verb* to make or become narrow

narrow-gauge *adjective* of a railway: having the distance between rails less than the **standard gauge** (4ft 8in, or 1.435 metre)

narrowly *adverb* closely; barely

narrow-minded *adjective* unwilling to accept or tolerate new ideas

narrows *noun plural* a narrow sea passage, a strait

NASA *abbreviation, US* National Aeronautics and Space Administration

nasal *adjective* 1 of the nose 2 sounded through the nose

nascent *adjective* beginning to develop, in an early stage □ **nascency** *noun*

nasturtium *noun* a climbing plant with brightly-coloured flowers

nasty *adjective* 1 very disagreeable or unpleasant 2 of a problem *etc*: difficult to deal with 3 of an injury: serious □ **nastily** *adverb* (meaning 1)

nat- *prefix* forms words related to being born: *natal/ nature* (= the basic qualities or features that a person or thing is born with)
Ⓛ Comes from Latin *nat-*, a form of *nasci* meaning 'to be born'

natal *adjective* of birth

nation *noun* 1 the people living in the same country, or under the same

government 2 a race of people: *the Jewish nation*

national *adjective* of, relating to or belonging to a nation or race □ *noun* someone belonging to a nation: *a British national* □ **nationally** *adverb*

national anthem a nation's official song or hymn

national call a long-distance, but not international, telephone call

nationalism *noun* the desire to bring the people of a nation together under their own government □ **nationalist** *noun & adjective* □ **nationalistic** *adjective*

nationality *noun* membership of a particular nation

nationalize *verb* to place (industries *etc*) under the control of the government □ **nationalization** *noun*

native *adjective* 1 born in a person: *native intelligence* 2 of someone's birth: *my native land* □ *noun* 1 someone born in a certain place: *a native of Scotland* 2 an inhabitant of a country from earliest times before the discovery by explorers, settlers *etc*

Nativity: **the Nativity** the birth of Christ

NATO *abbreviation* North Atlantic Treaty Organization

natty *adjective* trim, tidy, smart □ **nattily** *adverb*

natural *adjective* 1 of nature 2 produced by nature, not artificial 3 of a quality *etc*: present at birth, not learned afterwards 4 unpretentious, simple 5 of a result *etc*: expected, normal □ *noun* 1 an idiot 2 someone with a natural ability 3 *music* a note which is neither a sharp nor a flat, shown by the sign (♮)

natural gas gas suitable for burning found in the earth or under the sea

natural history the study of animals and plants

naturalist *noun* someone who studies animal and plant life

naturalize *verb* to give the rights of a citizen to (someone born in another country)

naturally *adverb* 1 by nature 2 simply 3 of course

natural resources the natural wealth of a country in its forests, minerals, water *etc*

natural selection evolution by survival of the fittest, who pass their characteristics on to the next generation

nature *noun* 1 the things which make up the physical world, *eg* animals, trees, rivers, mountains *etc* 2 the qualities which characterize someone or something: *a kindly nature*

-natured *adjective* (added to another word) having a certain temper or personality: *good-natured*

naturism *noun* the belief in nudity practised openly □ **naturist** *noun*

naught *noun* nothing: *plans came to naught*

💣 Do not confuse with: **nought**

naughty *adjective* bad, misbehaving □ **naughtily** *adverb*

nausea *noun* a feeling of sickness

nauseate *verb* to make sick, fill with disgust

nauseated *adjective* sickened, disgusted

nauseous *adjective* sickening; disgusting

naut- *prefix* of or related to ships and sailing, or to spaceships and their crews: *nautical*
ⓒ Comes from Greek *nautes* meaning 'a sailor'

nautical *adjective* of ships or sailors

nautical mile 1.85 kilometre (6080 ft)

nautilus *noun* (*plural* **nautiluses** or **nautili**) a small sea creature related to the octopus

naval (from **navy**) *adjective* of the navy

nave *noun* the middle or main part of a church

navel *noun* the small hollow in the centre of the front of the belly

navigable *adjective* able to be used by ships

navigate *verb* 1 to steer or pilot a ship,

aircraft *etc* on its course 2 to sail on, over or through

navigation *noun* the art of navigating

navigator *noun* someone who steers or sails a ship *etc*

navvy *noun* (*plural* **navvies**) a labourer working on roads *etc*

navy *noun* (*plural* **navies**) 1 a nation's fighting ships 2 the men and women serving on these

navy blue dark blue

nay *adverb*, *old* no

Nazi (*pronounced* **naht**-si) *noun*, *historical* a member of the German National Socialist Party, a fascist party ruling Germany in 1933–45 □ **Nazism** *noun*

NB or **nb** *abbreviation* note well (from Latin *nota bene*)

NCO *abbreviation* non-commissioned officer

NE *abbreviation* north-east; north-eastern

neap *adjective* of the tide: at its smallest extent between low and high level

near *adjective* 1 not far away in place or time 2 close in relationship, friendship *etc* 3 barely avoiding or almost reaching (something): *a near disaster* □ *adverb* to or at a short distance; nearby □ *preposition* close to □ *verb* to approach

nearby *adverb* to or at a short distance: *do you live nearby?*

nearly *adverb* 1 almost: *nearly four o'clock* 2 closely: *nearly related*

nearside *adjective* of the side of a vehicle: furthest from the centre of the road (*contrasted with*: **offside**)

near-sighted *adjective* short-sighted

neat *adjective* 1 trim, tidy 2 skilfully done 3 of an alcoholic drink: not diluted with water *etc*

neb *noun*, *Scottish* a nose

nebula *noun* (*plural* **nebulae**) a shining cloud-like appearance in the night sky, produced by very distant stars or by a mass of gas and dust

nebulous *adjective* hazy, vague

necessarily *adverb* for certain, definitely, inevitably

necessary *adjective* not able to be done without □ *noun* (*plural* **necessaries**) something that cannot be done without, such as food, clothing *etc*

necessitate *verb* to make necessary; force □ **necessity** (*plural* **necessities**) **1** something necessary **2** great need; want, poverty

neck *noun* **1** the part between the head and body **2** a narrow passage or area: *neck of a bottle/ neck of land* □ **neck and neck** running side by side, staying exactly equal

necklace *noun* a string of beads or precious stones *etc* worn round the neck

necktie *noun, US* a man's tie

necromancer *noun* someone who works with black magic □ **necromancy** *noun*

nectar *noun* **1** the sweet liquid collected from flowers by bees to make honey **2** the drink of the ancient Greek gods **3** a delicious drink

nectarine *noun* a kind of peach with a smooth skin

née (*pronounced* nei) *adjective* born (in stating a woman's surname before her marriage): *Mrs Janet Brown, née Phillips*

need *verb* **1** to be without, be in want of **2** to require □ *noun* **1** necessity, needfulness **2** difficulty, want, poverty
ⓘ Comes from Old English *ned, nied, nyd*

■ **Alternative words:** (verb, meaning 1) miss, lack, want; (verb, meaning 2) demand, necessitate, crave

needful *adjective* necessary

needle *noun* **1** a small, sharp piece of steel used in sewing, with a small hole (**eye**) at the top for thread **2** a long thin piece of metal, wood *etc* used *eg* in knitting **3** a thin hollowed-out piece of steel attached to a hypodermic syringe *etc* **4** the moving pointer in a compass **5** the long, sharp-pointed leaf of a pine, fir *etc* **6** a stylus on a record-player

needle bank a place where drug-users can exchange used hypodermic needles for new ones, to help prevent the spread of disease

needless *adjective* unnecessary

needy *adjective* poor

neep *noun, Scottish* a turnip

ne'er *adjective, formal* never

ne'er-do-well or *Scottish* **ne'er-do-weel** *noun* a lazy, worthless person who makes no effort

nefarious *adjective* very wicked; villainous, shady

neg- *prefix* forms words containing the meaning 'not': *neglect* (= not to trouble oneself about)/ *negotiate* (= an activity which is not leisure)
  neg- is a Latin prefix meaning 'not'

negate *verb* **1** to prove the opposite **2** to refuse to accept, reject (a proposal *etc*)

negative *adjective* **1** meaning or saying 'no', as an answer (*contrasted with*: **positive**) **2** of a person, attitude *etc*: timid, lacking spirit or ideas □ *noun* **1** a word or statement by which something is denied **2** the photographic film, from which prints are made, in which light objects appear dark and dark objects appear light □ **negative equity** a situation where the value of a property falls below the value of the mortgage held on it

neglect *verb* **1** to treat carelessly **2** to fail to give proper attention to **3** to fail to do □ *noun* lack of care and attention

neglectful *adjective* careless, having a habit of not bothering to do things

negligée *noun* a women's loose dressing-gown made of thin material

negligent *adjective* careless □ **negligence** *noun* □ **negligently** *adverb*
ⓘ Comes from Latin *negligens* meaning 'neglecting'
  ☞ Do not confuse: **negligent** and **negligible**

negligible *adjective* not worth thinking about, very small: *a negligible amount*
ⓘ Comes from an old spelling of French *négligeable* meaning 'able to be neglected'

■ Opposite: appreciable

negotiable *adjective* able to be negotiated

negotiate *verb* **1** to discuss a subject (with) in order to reach agreement **2** to arrange (a treaty, payment *etc*) **3** to get past (an obstacle or difficulty)
□ **negotiation** *noun* (meanings 1 and 2)
□ **negotiator** *noun* (meanings 1 and 2)

Negress *noun* a Black woman

Negro *noun* (*plural* **Negroes**) a Black African, or Black person of African descent

neigh *verb* to cry like a horse □ *noun* a horse's cry

neighbour or *US* **neighbor** *noun* someone who lives near another

neighbourhood *noun* surrounding district or area: *in the neighbourhood of Paris/ a poor neighbourhood* □ **in the neighbourhood of** approximately, nearly

neighbouring *adjective* near or next in position

neighbourly *adjective* friendly

neither *adjective & pronoun* not either: *neither bus goes that way/ neither of us can afford it* □ *conjunction* (sometimes with **nor**) used to show alternatives in the negative: *neither Bill or David knew the answer/ she is neither eating nor sleeping*

nemesis *noun* fate, punishment that is bound to follow wrongdoing

neo- *prefix* new, recently
ⓘ Comes from Greek *neos* meaning 'new'

Neolithic *adjective* relating to the later Stone Age

neologism *noun* a new word or expression □ **neologistic** *adjective*

neonatal *adjective* of newborn babies

neon lighting a form of lighting in which an electric current is passed through a small quantity of gas

neophyte *noun* **1** a new convert **2** a novice, a beginner

nephew *noun* the son of a brother or sister, or of a brother-in-law or sister-in-law

nerd *noun* a socially inept, irritating person

nerve *noun* **1** one of the fibres which carry feeling from all parts of the body to the brain **2** courage, coolness **3** *informal* impudence, cheek □ *verb* to strengthen the nerve or will of

nervous *adjective* **1** of the nerves **2** easily excited or frightened; timid **3** worried, frightened or uneasy
□ **nervously** *adverb* (meaning 3)
□ **nervousness** *noun* (meanings 2 and 3)

■ Alternative words: (meaning 2) highly-strung, excitable; (meaning 3) anxious, agitated, on edge, edgy, jumpy, jittery, tense, apprehensive, uneasy, worried

nervous system the brain, spinal cord and nerves of an animal or human being

nervy *adjective* excitable, jumpy

nest *noun* **1** a structure in which birds (and some animals and insects) live and rear their young **2** a shelter, a den □ *verb* to build a nest and live in it

nestle (*pronounced* ne-sl) *verb* **1** to lie close together as in a nest **2** to settle comfortably

nestling (*pronounced* **nest**-ling) *noun* a young newly hatched bird

Net *noun*: **the Net** *informal* the Internet

net *noun* **1** a loose arrangement of crossed and knotted cord, string or thread, used for catching fish, wearing over the hair *etc* **2** fine meshed material, used to make curtains, petticoats *etc*
□ *adjective* (*also* **nett**) **1** of profit: remaining after expenses and taxes have been paid **2** of weight: not including packaging □ *verb* **1** to catch or cover with a net **2** to put (a ball) into a net **3** to make by way of profit

  net *verb* ⇨ nets, netting, netted

netball *noun* a team game in which a ball is thrown into a high net

nether *adjective* lower

nethermost *adjective* lowest

nett *see* **net**

netting *noun* fabric of netted string, wire *etc*

nettle *noun* a plant covered with hairs

which sting sharply □ *verb* to make angry, provoke

nettlerash *noun* a skin rash, like that caused by a sting from a nettle

network *noun* 1 an arrangement of lines crossing one another 2 a widespread organization 3 a system of linked computers, radio stations *etc*

neur- or **neuro-** *prefix* of the nerves: *neuralgia*
◑ Comes from Greek *neuron* meaning 'nerve'

neuralgia *noun* a pain in the nerves, especially in those of the head and face

neurosis *noun* a type of mental illness in which the patient suffers from extreme anxiety

neurotic *adjective* 1 suffering from neurosis 2 in a bad nervous state □ *noun* someone suffering from neurosis □ **neurotically** *adverb*

neuter *adjective* 1 *grammar* neither masculine nor feminine 2 of an animal: neither male nor female 3 of an animal: infertile, sterile □ *verb* to sterilize (an animal)

neutral *adjective* 1 taking no side in a quarrel or war 2 of a colour: not strong or definite □ *noun* 1 someone or a nation that takes no side in a war *etc* 2 the gear position used when a vehicle is remaining still □ **neutrality** *noun* (adjective, meaning 1)

neutralize *verb* 1 to make neutral 2 to make useless or harmless

neutron *noun* one of the uncharged particles which, together with protons, make up the nucleus of an atom

neutron bomb a nuclear bomb that kills people by intense radiation but leaves buildings intact

never *adverb* 1 not ever; at no time 2 under no circumstances

nevertheless *adverb* in spite of that: *I hate opera, but I shall come with you nevertheless*

nevus *US spelling of* **naevus**

new *adjective* 1 recent; not seen or known before 2 not used or worn; fresh
◑ Comes from Old English *niwe, neowe*

newcomer *noun* someone lately arrived

newfangled *adjective* new and not thought very good

newly *adverb* (used before past participles) only recently

news *noun singular* 1 report of a recent event 2 new information

newsagent *noun* a shopkeeper who sells newspapers

newspaper *noun* a paper printed daily or weekly containing news

newt *noun* a small lizard-like animal, living on land and in water

next *adjective* nearest, closest in place, time *etc*: *the next page* □ *adverb* in the nearest place or at the nearest time: *she won and I came next/ do that sum next*
◑ Comes from Old English *nehst* meaning 'nearest'

NHS *abbreviation* National Health Service

nib *noun* a pen point

nibble *verb* to take little bites (of) □ *noun* a little bite

nice *adjective* 1 agreeable, pleasant 2 careful, precise, exact: *a nice distinction*

■ **Alternative words**: (meaning 1) pleasant, agreeable, delightful, charming, likable, attractive, good, kind, friendly, well-mannered, polite, respectable

nicely *adverb* pleasantly; very well

nicety (*pronounced* **nais**-*e*-ti) *noun* (*plural* **niceties**) a small fine detail □ **to a nicety** with great exactness

niche (*pronounced* neesh) *noun* 1 a hollow in a wall for a statue, vase *etc* 2 a suitable place in life: *she hasn't yet found her niche* 3 a gap in a market for a type of product

nick *noun* 1 a little cut, a notch 2 *slang* prison, jail □ *verb* 1 to cut notches in 2 *slang* to steal

nickel *noun* 1 a greyish-white metal used for mixing with other metals and for plating 2 *US* a 5-cent coin

nickname *noun* an informal name used instead of someone's real name, *eg* for fun or as an insult

nicky-tams *noun plural, Scottish* ties to keep trouser legs from getting dirty, flapping *etc*

nicotine *noun* a poisonous substance contained in tobacco

Named after Jean *Nicot*, 16th-century French ambassador who sent tobacco samples back from Portugal

niece *noun* the daughter of a brother or sister, or of a brother-in-law or sister-in-law

niff *noun, slang* a bad smell

nifty *adjective, slang* 1 fine, smart, neat 2 speedy, agile

niggardly *adjective* mean, stingy

niggle *verb* to irritate, rankle □ *noun* 1 an irritation 2 a minor criticism

niggling *adjective* 1 unimportant, trivial, fussy 2 of a worry or fear: small but always present

nigh *adjective, old* near

night *noun* 1 the period of darkness between sunset and sunrise 2 darkness □ *adjective* 1 of or for night 2 happening, active *etc* at night ℗ Comes from Old English *niht*

nightdress or **nightgown** *noun* a garment worn in bed

nightfall *noun* the beginning of night

nightingale *noun* a small bird, the male of which sings beautifully by night and day

nightly *adjective & adverb* 1 by night 2 every night

nightmare *noun* a frightening dream

The *-mare* ending comes from an old English word meaning 'evil spirit', nightmares being thought to be caused by an evil spirit pressing on the body

night-watchman *noun* someone who looks after a building during the night

nihilism *noun* belief in nothing, extreme scepticism □ **nihilist** *noun* □ **nihilistic** *adjective*

nil *noun* nothing

nimble *adjective* quick and neat, agile □ **nimbly** *adverb*

nimbus *noun* a rain cloud

nincompoop *noun* a weak, foolish person

nine *noun* the number 9 □ *adjective* 9 in number

ninepins *noun* a game in which nine bottle-shaped objects are set up, and knocked down by a ball

nineteen *noun* the number 19 □ *adjective* 19 in number

nineteenth *adjective* the last of a series of nineteen □ *noun* one of nineteen equal parts

ninetieth *adjective* the last of a series of ninety □ *noun* one of ninety equal parts

ninety *noun* the number 90 □ *adjective* 90 in number

ninja *noun, historical* an assassin in feudal Japan, trained in martial arts

ninny *noun* (*plural* **ninnies**) a fool

ninth *adjective* the last of a series of nine □ *noun* one of nine equal parts

nip *verb* 1 to pinch, squeeze tightly 2 to be stingingly painful 3 to bite, cut (off) 4 to halt the growth of, damage (plants *etc*) 5 *informal* to go nimbly or quickly □ *noun* 1 a pinch 2 a sharp coldness in the weather: *a nip in the air* 3 a small amount: *nip of whisky*

nip *verb* ➪ **nips, nipping, nipped**

nipper *noun, informal* 1 a child, a youngster 2 **nippers** pincers, pliers

nipple *noun* the pointed part of the breast from which a baby sucks milk

nippy *adjective, informal* 1 speedy, nimble 2 frosty, very cold

Nirvana *noun* 1 the state to which a Buddhist or Hindu aspires as the best attainable 2 **nirvana** a blissful state

nit *noun* 1 the egg of a louse or other small insect 2 *informal* an idiot, a nitwit

nitrate *noun* a substance formed from nitric acid, often used as a soil fertilizer

nitric acid a strong acid containing nitrogen

nitrogen *noun* a gas forming nearly four-fifths of ordinary air

nitro-glycerine *noun* a powerful kind of explosive

nitwit *noun* a very stupid person

No or **no** *abbreviation* number

no *adjective* **1** not any: *they have no money* **2** not a: *she is no beauty* □ *adverb* not at all: *the patient is no better* □ *exclamation* expressing a negative: *are you feeling better today? No* □ *noun* (*plural* **noes**) **1** a refusal **2** a vote against □ **no dice** no answer, no success □ **no doubt** surely □ **no go** not possible, futile □ **no joke** not something to laugh about or dismiss □ **no way** *informal* under no circumstances

no-ball *noun, cricket* a bowled ball disallowed by the rules

nobble *verb, slang* **1** get hold of **2** persuade, coerce **3** seize, arrest

Nobel prize an annual international prize awarded for achievements in arts, science, politics *etc*

noble *adjective* **1** great and good, fine **2** of aristocratic birth □ *noun* an aristocrat □ **nobility** *noun* **1** the aristocracy **2** goodness, greatness of mind or character □ **nobleman, noblewoman** *noun* □ **nobly** *adverb*

nobody *pronoun* not any person □ *noun* someone of no importance: *just a nobody*

nocturnal *adjective* happening or active at night

nocturne *noun* a piece of music intended to have an atmosphere of night-time

nod *verb* **1** to bend the head forward quickly, often as a sign of agreement **2** to let the head drop in weariness □ *noun* an action of nodding □ **nodding acquaintance with** a slight knowledge of □ **nod off** to fall asleep

  nod *verb* ⇨ nod*s*, nodd*ing*, nodd*ed*

node *noun* **1** the swollen part of a branch or twig where leaf-stalks join it **2** a swelling

nodule *noun* a small rounded lump

Noël *noun* Christmas

noise *noun* a sound, often one which is loud or harsh □ *verb, old* to spread (a rumour *etc*) □ **noiseless** *adjective*

noisy *adjective* making a loud sound

  noisy ⇨ nois*ier*, nois*iest*

nomad *noun* **1** one of a group of people without a fixed home who wander with their animals in search of pasture **2** someone who wanders from place to place □ **nomadic** *adjective*

no-man's-land *noun* land owned by no one, especially that lying between two opposing armies

nom de plume *noun* (*plural* **noms de plume**) a pen-name

nomenclature *noun* **1** a system of naming **2** names

nominal *adjective* **1** in name only **2** very small: *a nominal fee*

nominate *verb* to propose (someone) for a post or for election; appoint □ **nomination** *noun*

nominee *noun* someone whose name is put forward for a post

non- *prefix* not (used with many words to change their meaning to the opposite): *non-aggression/ non-event/ non-smoking*
  ⓘ Comes from Latin *non* meaning 'not'

nonagenarian *noun* someone from ninety to ninety-nine years old

nonchalant *adjective* not easily roused or upset, cool □ **nonchalance** *noun* □ **nonchalantly** *adverb*

non-commissioned *adjective* belonging to the lower ranks of army officers, below second-lieutenant

non-committal *adjective* unwilling to express, or not expressing, an opinion

nonconformist *noun* someone who does not agree with those in authority, especially in church matters □ *adjective* not agreeing with authority

nondescript *adjective* not easily described, lacking anything noticeable or interesting

none *adverb* not at all: *none the worse* □ *pronoun* not one, not any

nonentity *noun* (*plural* **nonentities**) someone of no importance

non-existent *adjective* not existing, not real

nonplussed *adjective* taken aback, confused

nonsense *noun* 1 words that have no sense or meaning 2 foolishness □ **nonsensical** *adjective*

non sequitur a remark unconnected with what has gone before

non-stop *adjective* going on without a stop

noodle *noun* a long thin strip of pasta, eaten in soup or served with a sauce

nook *noun* 1 a corner 2 a small recess □ **every nook and cranny** *informal* everywhere

noon *noun* twelve o'clock midday

no one or **no-one** *pronoun* not any person, nobody

noose *noun* a loop in a rope *etc* that tightens when pulled

nor *conjunction* used (often with **neither**) to show alternatives in the negative: *neither James nor I can speak Japanese*

Nordic *adjective* 1 relating to Finland or Scandinavia 2 of skiing: involving cross-country and jumping events

norm *noun* a pattern or standard to judge other things from

normal *adjective* ordinary, usual according to a standard □ **normality** *noun* □ **normally** *adverb*

Opposite: abnormal

north *noun* 1 one of the four chief directions, that to the left of someone facing the rising sun □ *adjective & adverb* in or to the north □ **northerly** *adjective* of, from or towards the north □ **northern** *adjective* of the north □ **north-east** *noun* the point of the compass midway between north and east □ **north pole** *see* **pole** □ **northward** or **northwards** *adjective & adverb* towards the north □ **north-west** *noun* the point of the compass midway between north and west

nose *noun* 1 the part of the face by which people and animals smell and breathe 2 a jutting-out part, *eg* the front of an aeroplane □ *verb* 1 to track by smelling 2 *informal* to interfere in other people's affairs, pry (into) 3 to push a

way through: *the ship nosed through the ice* 4 to move forward cautiously

nosedive *noun* a headfirst dive by an aeroplane □ *verb* to dive headfirst

nosegay *noun, old* a bunch of flowers

nosey or **nosy** *adjective* inquisitive, fond of prying

no-show *noun* someone expected who does not arrive

nostalgia *noun* 1 a longing for past times 2 a longing for home □ **nostalgic** *adjective* □ **nostalgically** *adverb*

nostril *noun* either of the two openings of the nose

not *adverb* expressing a negative, refusal or denial: *I am not going/ give it to me, not to him/ I did not break the window*

notability *noun* (*plural* **notabilities**) a well-known person

notable *adjective* worth taking notice of; important, remarkable □ *noun* an important person

notably *adverb* 1 in a notable or noticeable way 2 particularly

notary *noun* (*plural* **notaries**) an official who sees that written documents are drawn up in a way required by law

notation *noun* 1 the showing of numbers, musical sounds *etc* by signs: *sol-fa notation* 2 a set of such signs

notch *noun* (*plural* **notches**) a small V-shaped cut □ *verb* to make a notch □ **notched** *adjective*

note *noun* 1 a sign or piece of writing to draw someone's attention 2 **notes** details for a speech, from a talk *etc* set down in a short form 3 a short explanation 4 a short letter 5 a piece of paper used as money: *£5 note* 6 a single sound or the sign standing for it in music 7 a key on the piano *etc* □ *verb* 1 to make a note of 2 to notice □ **of note** well-known, distinguished □ **take note of** to notice particularly

notebook *noun* 1 a small book for taking notes 2 a small laptop computer

noted *adjective* well-known

notepaper *noun* writing paper

noteworthy *adjective* notable, remarkable

nothing *noun* 1 no thing, not anything 2 nought, zero 3 something of no importance □ *adverb* not at all: *he's nothing like his father*

nothingness *noun* 1 non-existence 2 space, emptiness

notice *noun* 1 a public announcement 2 attention: *the colour attracted my notice* 3 a period of warning given before leaving, or before dismissing someone from, a job □ *verb* to see, observe, take note of

noticeable *adjective* easily noticed, standing out

Alternative words: appreciable

notifiable *adjective* that must be reported: *a notifiable disease*

notify *verb* 1 to inform 2 to give notice of □ **notification** *noun*

notify ➪ noti*fies*, notif*ying*, notif*ied*

notion *noun* 1 an idea 2 a vague belief or opinion

notorious *adjective* well known because of badness: *a notorious criminal* □ **notoriety** *noun*

notwithstanding *preposition* in spite of: *notwithstanding his poverty, he refused all help*

nougat (*pronounced* **noo**-gah or **nug**-et) *noun* a sticky kind of sweet containing nuts *etc*

nought *noun* the figure 0, zero

♦° Do not confuse with: **naught**

noun *noun, grammar* the word used as the name of someone or something, *eg John* and *tickets* in the sentence *John bought the tickets*

nourish *verb* 1 to feed 2 to encourage the growth of

nourishing *adjective* giving the body what is necessary for health and growth

nourishment *noun* 1 food 2 an act of nourishing

nouveau riche (*pronounced* noo-voh **reesh**) someone who has recently acquired wealth but not good taste

nova *noun* (*plural* **novae** – *pronounced* **noh**-vee – or **novas**) a star that suddenly increases in brightness for a period

novel (*pronounced* **nov**-el) *adjective* new and strange □ *noun* a book telling a long story

novelist (*pronounced* **nov**-el-ist) *noun* a writer of novels

novelty (*pronounced* **nov**-el-ti) *noun* (*plural* **novelties**) 1 something new and strange 2 newness 3 a small, cheap souvenir or toy

November *noun* the eleventh month of the year

novice *noun* a beginner

now *adverb* 1 at the present time: *I can see him now* 2 immediately before the present time: *I thought of her just now* 3 in the present circumstances: *I can't go now because my mother is ill* □ *conjunction* (often **now that**) because, since: *you can't go out now that it's raining* □ **now and then** or **now and again** sometimes, from time to time

nowadays *adverb* in present times, these days

nowhere *adverb* not in, or to, any place

no-win *adjective* of a situation: in which you are bound to lose or fail

noxious *adjective* harmful: *noxious fumes*
Ⓛ Comes from Latin *noxius* meaning 'hurtful'

♦° Do not confuse with: **obnoxious**

nozzle *noun* a spout fitted to the end of a pipe, tube *etc*

NSPCC *abbreviation* National Society for the Prevention of Cruelty to Children

nuance (*pronounced* **nyoo**-ons) *noun* a slight difference in meaning or colour *etc*

nub *noun* a small lump, a knob

nubile *adjective* of a young woman: attractive, and old enough to be sexually mature □ **nubility** *noun*

nuclear *adjective* 1 of a nucleus, especially that of an atom produced by the splitting of the nuclei of atoms

Alternative words: (meaning 2) atomic

nuclear energy energy released or

absorbed during reactions taking place in atomic nuclei

nuclear family the family unit made up of the mother and father with their children

nuclear fission the splitting of atomic nuclei

nuclear fusion the creation of a new nucleus by merging two lighter ones, with release of energy

nuclear missile a missile whose warhead is an atomic bomb

nuclear reactor apparatus for producing nuclear energy

nucleus *noun* (*plural* **nuclei**) 1 the central part of an atom 2 the central part round which something collects or from which it grows: *the nucleus of my book collection* 3 the part of a plant or animal cell that controls its development

nude *adjective* without clothes, naked □ *noun* 1 an unclothed human figure 2 a painting or statue of such a figure □ **in the nude** naked

nudge *noun* a gentle push, *eg* with the elbow or shoulder □ *verb*: *I nudged him*

nudist *noun* someone who is in favour of going without clothes in public □ **nudism** *noun*

nudity *noun* the state of being nude

nugget *noun* a lump, especially of gold

nuisance *noun* someone or something annoying or troublesome

null *adjective*: **null and void** having no legal force

nullify *verb* 1 to make useless or of no effect 2 to declare to be null and void

nullify ⇨ nullifies, nullifying, nullified

numb *adjective* having lost the power to feel or move □ *verb* to make numb

number *noun* 1 a word or figure showing how many, or showing a position in a series 2 a collection of people or things 3 a single issue of a newspaper or magazine 4 a popular song or piece of music □ *verb* 1 to count 2 to give numbers to 3 to amount to in number

ⓛ Comes from French *nombre* meaning 'number'

numberless *adjective* more than can be counted

numeral *noun* a figure (*eg* 1, 2 *etc*) used to express a number

numerate (*pronounced* **nyoom**-*e*-rat) *adjective* having some understanding of mathematics and science

numerator *noun* the number above the line in vulgar fractions, *eg* 2 in $\frac{2}{3}$ (*compare with*: **denominator**)

numerical *adjective* of, in, using or consisting of numbers

numerous *adjective* many

numismatics *noun singular* the study of coins

numismatist *noun* someone who collects and studies coins

numskull *noun* a stupid person

nun *noun* a member of a female religious group living in a convent

nunnery *noun* (*plural* **nunneries**) a house where a group of nuns live, a convent

nuptial *adjective* of marriage

nuptials *noun plural*, *formal* a wedding ceremony

nurse *noun* someone who looks after sick or injured people, or small children □ *verb* 1 to look after sick people *etc* 2 to give (a baby) milk from the breast 3 to hold or look after with care: *he nurses his tomato plants* 4 to encourage (feelings) in yourself: *nursing her wrath*

nursery (*plural* **nurseries**) 1 a room for young children 2 a place where young plants are reared 3 a nursery school

nursery school a school for very young children

nursing home a small private hospital

nurture *verb* to bring up, rear; to nourish: *nurture tenderness* □ *noun* care, upbringing; food, nourishment

NUT *abbreviation* National Union of Teachers

nut *noun* 1 a fruit with a hard shell which contains a kernel 2 a small metal block with a hole in it for screwing on the end of a bolt □ **in a nutshell** expressed very briefly

nutcrackers *noun plural* an instrument for cracking nuts open

nutmeg *noun* a hard aromatic seed used as a spice in cooking

nutrient *noun* a substance which provides nourishment

nutriment *noun* nourishment, food

nutrition *noun* nourishment, food

nutritious or **nutritive** *adjective* valuable as food, nourishing

nutty *adjective* 1 containing, or having the flavour of nuts 2 *informal* mad, insane

nuzzle *verb* 1 to press, rub or caress with the nose 2 to lie close to, snuggle, nestle

NVQ *abbreviation, Brit* National Vocational Qualification

NW *abbreviation* north-west; north-western

nylon *noun* 1 a synthetic material made from chemicals 2 **nylons** stockings made of nylon

nymph *noun* 1 a mythological female river or tree spirit 2 a beautiful girl 3 an insect not yet fully developed

nymphomania *noun* excessively strong sexual desire in women

nymphomaniac *noun* someone suffering from nymphomania

NZ *abbreviation* New Zealand

O! or **Oh!** *exclamation* expressing surprise, admiration, pain *etc*

oaf *noun* (*plural* **oafs**) a stupid or clumsy person

oak *noun* **1** a tree which produces acorns as fruit **2** its hard wood □ **oak** or **oaken** *adjective* made of oak

OAP *abbreviation* **1** Old Age Pension **2** Old Age Pensioner

oar *noun* a pole for rowing, with a flat blade on the end □ *verb* to row □ **put your oar in** to interfere in

oarsman *noun* a man who rows

oarswoman *noun* a woman who rows

oasis *noun* (*plural* **oases**) a place in a desert where water is found and trees *etc* grow

oatcake *noun* a thin flat cake made of oatmeal

oath *noun* (*plural* **oaths**) **1** a solemn promise to speak the truth, keep your word, be loyal *etc* **2** a swear word

oatmeal *noun* meal made by grinding down oat grains

oats *noun plural* a type of grassy plant or its grain, used as food

OBE *abbreviation* Officer of the Order of the British Empire

obedience *noun* **1** the act of obeying **2** willingness to obey

obedient *adjective* obeying, ready to obey □ **obediently** *adverb*

obeisance *noun* a bow or curtsy showing respect

obelisk *noun* a tall four-sided pillar with a pointed top

obese *adjective* very fat

obesity *noun* the condition of someone who is overweight as a result of the accumulation of excess fat in the body

obey *verb* to do what you are told to do: *obey the instructions*

obituary *noun* (*plural* **obituaries**) a notice in a newspaper *etc* of someone's death, sometimes with a brief biography

object *noun* (*pronounced* ob-jekt) **1** something that can be seen or felt **2** an aim, a purpose: *our main object is not to make money* **3** *grammar* the word in a sentence which stands for the person or thing on which the action of the verb is done, *eg* me in the sentence *he gave me some good advice* □ *verb* (*pronounced* ob-**jekt**) (often **object to something**) to feel or show disapproval of it

objection *noun* **1** the act of objecting **2** a reason for objecting

objectionable *adjective* nasty, disagreeable

objective *adjective* not influenced by personal interests, fair (*contrasted with*: **subjective**) □ *noun* aim, purpose, goal

obligation *noun* **1** a promise or duty by which someone is bound: *under an obligation to help* **2** a debt of gratitude for a favour received

obligatory (*pronounced* ob-**lig**-at-o-ri) *adjective* required to be done with no exceptions by law, rule or custom

▤ **Alternative words:** compulsory
▨ **Opposite:** optional, voluntary

oblige *verb* **1** to force, compel: *we were obliged to go home* **2** to do a favour or service to: *oblige me by shutting the door*

353

obliged *adjective* owing or feeling gratitude

obliging *adjective* ready to help others

oblique *adjective* **1** slanting **2** indirect, not straight or straightforward: *an oblique reference* □ **obliquely** *adverb*

obliterate *verb* **1** to blot out (writing *etc*), efface **2** to destroy completely

obliteration *noun* being obliterated, extinction

oblivion *noun* **1** forgetfulness **2** the state of being forgotten

oblivious *adjective* **1** unaware (of), not paying attention (to) **2** forgetful

oblong *noun* a rectangle which is longer than it is wide, *eg* ▇ □ *adjective* of the shape of an oblong

obnoxious *adjective* offensive, causing dislike □ **obnoxiously** *adverb*
ⓘ Comes from Latin *obnoxious* meaning 'liable to punishment' or 'guilty of'
🖝 Do not confuse with: **noxious**

oboe *noun* (*plural* **oboes**) a high-pitched woodwind instrument

oboist *noun* someone who plays the oboe

obscene *adjective* **1** sexually indecent, lewd **2** disgusting, repellent

▤ **Alternative words**: (meaning 1) indecent

obscenity *noun* (*plural* **obscenities**) **1** the state or quality of being obscene: *the obscenity of war* **2** an obscene act or word: *the youths shouted obscenities at the police*

obscure *adjective* **1** dark **2** not clear or easily understood **3** unknown, not famous: *an obscure poet* □ *verb* **1** to darken **2** to make less clear

obscurity *noun* **1** the state of being difficult to see or understand **2** the state of being unknown or forgotten

obsequious *adjective* trying to win favour by flattery, willingness to agree *etc*

observance *noun* the act of keeping (a law, tradition *etc*)

observant *adjective* good at noticing

observation *noun* **1** the act of seeing and noting; attention **2** a remark

observatory *noun* (*plural* **observatories**) a place for making observations of the stars, weather *etc*

observe *verb* **1** to notice **2** to watch with attention **3** to remark (that) **4** to obey (a law *etc*) **5** to keep, preserve: *observe a tradition*

observer *noun* someone sent to listen to, but not take part in, a discussion *etc*

obsess *verb* to fill the mind completely

obsession *noun* **1** a feeling or idea which someone cannot stop thinking about **2** the state of being obsessed

obsessive *adjective* **1** forming an obsession **2** having or likely to have an obsession

obsolescence *noun* being obsolescent

obsolescent *adjective* going out of date
ⓘ Comes from Latin *obsolescere* meaning 'to grow old'

obsolete *adjective* gone out of use
ⓘ Comes from Latin *obsoletus* meaning 'grown old'
🖝 Do not confuse: **obsolete** and **obsolescent**

obstacle *noun* something which stands in the way and hinders

obstacle race a race in which obstacles have to be passed, climbed *etc*

obstetric or **obstetrical** *adjective* of obstetrics

obstetrician *noun* a doctor trained in obstetrics

obstetrics *noun singular* the study of helping women before, during and after childbirth

obstinacy *noun* stubbornness

obstinate *adjective* **1** of a person: rigidly sticking to decisions or opinions and unwilling to be influenced by persuasion **2** difficult to deal with, defeat or remove

▤ **Alternative words**: stubborn

obstreperous *adjective* noisy, unruly

obstruct *verb* **1** to block up, keep from passing **2** to hold back

obstruction *noun* 1 a hindrance 2 something which blocks up

obtain *verb* 1 to get, gain 2 to be in use, be valid: *that rule still obtains*

obtainable *adjective* able to be got

obtrude *verb* 1 to thrust (something unwanted) on someone 2 to thrust (yourself) forward when not wanted

obtrusion *noun* an act of obtruding

obtrusive *adjective* 1 too noticeable 2 pushy, impudent

obtuse *adjective* 1 of an angle: greater than a right angle (*contrasted with*: **acute**) 2 blunt, not pointed 3 stupid, not quick to understand

obverse *noun* the side of a coin showing the head or main design

obvious *adjective* easily seen or understood; plain, evident

obviously *adverb* in an obvious way; as is obvious, clearly

occasion *noun* 1 a particular time: *on that occasion* 2 a special event: *a great occasion* 3 a cause, a reason 4 opportunity □ *verb* to cause

occasional *adjective* happening or used now and then

occasionally *adverb* on occasions; now and then

Occident *noun* the West

occidental *adjective* from or relating to the Occident; western

occult *adjective* 1 secret, mysterious 2 supernatural

occupancy *noun* (*plural* **occupancies**) the act, fact or period of occupying

occupant *noun* a person who occupies, has, or takes possession of something, not always the owner

occupation *noun* 1 the state of being occupied 2 something which occupies 3 someone's trade or job 4 possession of a house *etc*

occupier *noun* someone who has possession of a house *etc*

occupy *verb* 1 to dwell in 2 to keep busy 3 to take up, fill (space, time *etc*) 4 to seize, capture (a town, fort *etc*)

occupy ⇨ occupies, occupying, occupied

occur *verb* 1 to happen 2 to appear, be found 3 **occur to someone** to come into their mind: *that never occurred to me*

occur ⇨ occurs, occurring, occurred

occurrence *noun* 1 a happening, an event 2 the act or fact of occurring

ocean *noun* 1 the stretch of salt water surrounding the land of the earth 2 one of five main divisions of this, *ie* the Atlantic, Pacific, Indian, Arctic or Antarctic

ocelot *noun* a wild American cat like a small leopard

ochre (*pronounced* **oh**-ker) *noun* a fine pale-yellow or red clay, used for colouring

octa- also **octo-**, **oct-** *prefix* eight: *octave/ octopus/ October* (which was the eighth month in the Roman calendar)
ⓘ Comes from Latin and Greek *octo* meaning 'eight'

octagon *noun* an eight-sided figure

octagonal *adjective* having eight sides

octane *noun* a colourless liquid found in petroleum and used in petrol

octave *noun*, *music* a range of eight notes, *eg* from one C to the C next above or below it

octavo *noun* (*plural* **octavos**) a book folded to give eight leaves to each sheet of paper

octet *noun* a group of eight things which go together *eg* the first eight lines of a sonnet, or a group of eight singers

octo- *see* **octa-**

October *noun* the tenth month of the year

octogenarian *noun* someone from eighty to eighty-nine years old

octopus *noun* (*plural* **octopuses**) a deep-sea creature with eight arms

ocular *adjective* of the eye

oculist *noun* someone who specializes in diseases and defects of the eye

odd *adjective* 1 of a number: leaving a remainder of one when divided by two, *eg* the numbers 3, 17, 31 (*contrasted with*: **even**) **2** unusual, strange **3** not one of a matching pair or group, left over: *an odd glove* □ *noun* **1 odds** chances or probability: *the odds are that they will win* **2 odds** difference: *it makes no odds* □ **at odds** quarrelling □ **odds and ends** objects, scraps *etc* of different kinds

oddity *noun* (*plural* **oddities**) **1** queerness, strangeness **2** a strange person or thing

odd jobs jobs of different kinds, not part of regular employment

oddments *noun plural* scraps

ode *noun* a type of poem, often written to someone or something: *ode to autumn*

odious *adjective* hateful □ **odiously** *adverb*

odium *noun* dislike, hatred

odour *noun* smell, either pleasant or unpleasant

odourless *adjective* without smell

oesophagus (*pronounced* ee-**sof**-*ag*-*u*s) or *US* **esophagus** (*pronounced* i-**sof**-*ag*-*u*s) *noun* the gullet

oestrogen (*pronounced* ees-tro-jen) or *US* **estrogen** (*pronounced* es-tro-jen) *noun* a female sex hormone which regulates the menstrual cycle, prepares the body for pregnancy *etc*

oestrus (*pronounced* ees-tr*u*s) or *US* **estrus** (*pronounced* es-tr*u*s) *noun* the period during which a female mammal is ready for conceiving; heat

oeuvre (*pronounced* er-vre) *noun* the complete works of an artist, writer *etc*

of *preposition* **1** belonging to: *the house of my parents* **2** from (a place, person *etc*): *within two miles of his home* **3** from among: *one of my pupils* **4** made from, made up of: *a house of bricks* **5** indicating an amount, measurement *etc*: *a gallon of petrol* **6** about, concerning: *talk of old friends* **7** with, containing: *a class of twenty children/ a cup of coffee* **8** as a result of: *die of hunger* **9** indicating removal or taking away: *robbed her of her jewels* **10** indicating a connection between an action and its object: *the joining of the pieces* **11** indicating character, qualities

etc: *a man of good taste/ it was good of you to come* **12** *US* (in telling the time) before, to: *ten of eight*

off *adverb* **1** away from a place, or from a particular state, position *etc*: *he walked off rudely/ switch the light off* **2** entirely, completely: *finish off your work* □ *adjective* **1** cancelled: *the holiday is off* **2** rotten, bad: *the meat is off* **3** not working, not on: *the control is in the off position* **4** not quite pure in colour: *off-white* □ *preposition* **1** not on, away from: *fell off the table* **2** taken away: *10% off the usual price* **3** below the normal standard: *off his game* □ **badly off** poor □ **be off** to go away, leave quickly □ **off and on** occasionally □ **off the cuff** *see* **cuff** □ **off the wall** *see* **wall** □ **well off** rich

offal *noun* **1** the parts of an animal unfit for use as food **2** certain internal organs of an animal (heart, liver *etc*) that are eaten

off-beam *adjective* mistaken, misguided

off-beat *adjective* not standard, eccentric

off-chance *noun* a slight chance □ **on the off-chance** just in case

off-colour *adjective* not feeling well

offence or *US* **offense** **1** displeasure, hurt feelings **2** a crime, a sin □ **take offence at** to be angry or feel hurt at

offend *verb* **1** to hurt the feelings of; insult, displease **2** to do wrong

offender *noun* a person who has committed an offence

offensive *noun* **1** the position of someone who attacks **2** an attack □ *adjective* **1** insulting, disgusting **2** used for attack or assault: *an offensive weapon*

offer *verb* **1** to put forward (a gift, payment *etc*) for acceptance or refusal **2** to lay (a choice, chance *etc*) before **3** to say that you are willing to do something □ *noun* **1** an act of offering **2** a bid of money **3** something proposed

offering *noun* **1** a gift **2** a collection of money in church

offhand *adjective* **1** said or done without thinking or preparation **2** rude, curt □ *adverb* without preparation; impromptu

office *noun* 1 a place where business is carried on 2 the people working in such a place 3 a duty, a job 4 a position of authority, especially in the government 5 (**offices**) services, helpful acts

officer *noun* 1 someone who carries out a public duty 2 someone holding a commission in the armed forces

official *adjective* 1 done or given out by those in power: *official announcement/ official action* 2 forming part of the tasks of a job or office: *official duties* 3 having full and proper authority □ *noun* someone who holds an office in the service of the government *etc*

> ☛ Do not confuse with: **officious**. **Official** is a neutral adjective showing neither approval nor disapproval, and it is used most often with reference to position or authority rather than people's characters

officially *adverb* 1 as an official, formally 2 as announced or said in public (though not necessarily truthfully)

officiate *verb* to perform a duty or service, especially as a clergyman at a wedding *etc*

officious *adjective* fond of interfering, especially in a pompous way □ **officiously** *adverb*

> ☛ Do not confuse with: **official**. **Officious** is a negative adjective showing disapproval, and it is used to describe people and their characters

offing *noun*: **in the offing** expected to happen soon, forthcoming

off-licence *noun* a shop selling alcohol which must not be drunk on the premises

offload *verb* 1 to unload 2 to get rid of (something) by passing on to someone else

offpeak *adjective* not at the time of highest use or demand

off-putting *adjective* causing aversion

offset *verb* to weigh against, make up

for: *the cost of the project was partly offset by a government grant*

offshoot *noun* 1 a shoot growing out of the main stem 2 a small business, project *etc* created out of a larger one: *an offshoot of an international firm*

offshore *adjective & adverb* 1 in or on the sea close to the coast 2 at a distance from the shore 3 from the shore: *offshore winds*

offside *adjective & adverb, sport* 1 illegally ahead of the ball, *eg* in football, in a position between the ball and the opponent's goal 2 of the side of a vehicle: nearest to the centre of the road (*contrasted with*: **nearside**)

offspring *noun* 1 someone's child or children 2 the young of animals *etc*

oft *adverb, formal* often

often *adverb* many times

ogle *verb* to eye (someone) impudently in order to show admiration

ogre *noun* 1 a mythological man-eating giant 2 someone extremely frightening or threatening

Oh! *another spelling of* **O!**

ohm *noun* a unit of electrical resistance

OHMS *abbreviation* On Her (or His) Majesty's Service

oil *noun* 1 a greasy liquid obtained from plants (*eg* olive oil), from animals (*eg* whale oil), and from minerals (*eg* petroleum) 2 (**oils**) oil colours for painting □ *verb* to smear with oil, put oil on or in

oil colour paint made by mixing a colouring substance with oil

oilfield *noun* an area where mineral oil is found

oil painting a picture painted in oil colours

oilrig *noun* a structure set up for drilling an oil-well

oilskin *noun* 1 cloth made waterproof with oil 2 a heavy coat made of this

oil-well *noun* a hole drilled into the earth's surface or into the sea bed to extract petroleum

oily *adjective* 1 of or like oil 2 obsequious, too friendly or flattering

oink *noun* the noise of a pig □ *verb* to make this noise

ointment *noun* a greasy substance rubbed on the skin to soothe, heal *etc*

OK or **okay** *exclamation, adjective & adverb* all right □ **okay** *verb* to mark or pass as being all right

> **okay** *verb* ⇨ okay*s*, okay*ing*, okay*ed*

old *adjective* 1 advanced in age, aged 2 having a certain age: *ten years old* 3 not new, having existed a long time: *an old joke* 4 belonging to far-off times 5 worn, worn-out 6 out-of-date, old-fashioned 7 of a person's past, replaced by something different in the present: *I preferred my old school to the one I'm at now* □ **of old** long ago
Ⓘ Comes from Old English *ald*

▪ **Alternative words**: (meaning 1) aged, elderly, grey, senile; (meaning 3) long-standing, time-honoured, traditional; (meaning 4) ancient, primitive, antiquated; (meaning 7) former, previous, ex-

old age the later part of life

old-fashioned *adjective* in a style common in the past, out-of-date

▪ **Alternative words**: obsolete, archaic, passé, obsolescent, quaint

old guard the conservative element in an organization *etc*

old hand someone with long experience in a job *etc*

old maid 1 *derogatory* a spinster 2 a game played by passing and matching playing cards

old timer 1 an old person 2 a veteran, someone with experience

olfactory *adjective* of or used for smelling: *olfactory glands*

oligarch (*pronounced* **ol**-ig-ahk) *noun* a member of an oligarchy

oligarchic (*pronounced* ol-ig-**ahk**-ik) or **oligarchical** (*pronounced* ol-ig-**ahk**-ik-al) *adjective* relating to or characteristic of an oligarchy

oligarchy (*pronounced* **ol**-ig-ahk-i) *noun* government by a small exclusive group

olive *noun* 1 a small oval fruit with a hard stone, which is pressed to produce a cooking oil 2 the Mediterranean tree that bears this fruit □ *adjective* of a yellowish-green colour

olive branch a sign of a wish for peace

ombudsman *noun* an official appointed to look into complaints against the government

> From a Swedish word meaning 'administration man', introduced into English in the 1960s

omega *noun* the last letter of the Greek alphabet

omelette or **omelet** *noun* beaten eggs fried in a single layer in a pan

omen *noun* a sign of future events

ominous *adjective* suggesting future trouble

omission *noun* 1 something omitted 2 the act of omitting

omit *verb* 1 to leave out 2 to fail to do

> **omit** ⇨ omit*s*, omit*ting*, omit*ted*

omni- *prefix* all: *omniscient* (= all-knowing)/ *omnipotent* (= all-powerful)
Ⓘ Comes from Latin *omnis* meaning 'all'

omnibus *noun* (*plural* **omnibuses**) *old* a bus □ *adjective* 1 widely comprehensive 2 of miscellaneous contents

omnibus edition a radio or TV programme made up of material from preceding editions of the series

omnipotence *noun* unlimited power

omnipotent *adjective* having absolute, unlimited power: *omnipotent ruler*

omnipresence *noun* being present everywhere at the same time

omnipresent *adjective* present everywhere at the same time

omniscience *noun* knowledge of all things

omniscient *adjective* knowing everything

omnivorous *adjective* feeding on all kinds of food

on *preposition* 1 touching or fixed to the outer or upper side: *on the table* 2 supported by: *standing on one foot* 3 receiving, taking *etc*: *suspended on half-*

pay/ on antibiotics **4** occurring in the course of a specified time: *on the following day* **5** about: *a book on Scottish history* **6** with: *do you have your cheque book on you?* **7** next to, near: *a city on the Rhine* **8** indicating membership of: *on the committee* **9** in the process or state of: *on sale/ on show* **10** by means of: *can you play that on the piano?* **11** followed by: *disaster on disaster* □ *adverb* **1** so as to be touching or fixed to the outer or upper side: *put your coat on* **2** onwards, further: *they carried on towards home* **3** at a further point: *later on* □ *adjective* **1** working, performing: *the television is on* **2** arranged, planned: *do you have anything on this afternoon?* □ **from now on** after this time, henceforth □ **on and off** occasionally, intermittently □ **you're on!** I agree, accept the challenge *etc*

once *adverb* **1** at an earlier time in the past: *people once lived in caves* **2** for one time only: *I've been to Paris once in the last two years* □ *noun* one time only: *do it just this once* □ *conjunction* when: *once you've finished, you can go* □ **all at once 1** immediately: *come here at once!* **2** (sometimes **all at once**) at the same time, together: *trying to do several things all at once* □ **once and for all** for the last time □ **once upon a time** at some time in the past

oncoming *adjective* approaching from the front: *oncoming traffic*

one *noun* **1** the number 1 **2** a particular member of a group: *she's the one I want to meet* □ *pronoun* **1** a single person or thing: *one of my cats* **2** in formal or pompous English used instead of **you**, meaning anyone: *one must do what one can* □ *adjective* **1** 1 in number, a single: *we had only one reply* **2** identical, the same: *we are all of one mind* **3** some, an unnamed (*time etc*): *one day soon* □ **one another** used when an action takes place between two or more people: *they looked at one another*
Ⓞ Comes from Old English *an*

onerous *adjective* heavy, hard to bear or do: *onerous task*

oneself *pronoun* **1** used reflexively: *wash oneself* **2** used for emphasis: *one usually has to finish the job oneself*

one-sided *adjective* with one person, side *etc* having a great advantage over the other

one-way *adjective* meant for traffic moving in one direction only

ongoing *adjective* continuing: *ongoing talks*

onion *noun* a bulb vegetable with a strong taste and smell □ **know your onions** *informal* to know your subject or job well

oniony *adjective* tasting of onions

onlooker *noun* someone who watches an event, but does not take part in it

only *adverb* **1** not more than: *only two weeks left* **2** alone, solely: *only you are invited* **3** not longer ago than: *I saw her only yesterday* **4** indicating an unavoidable result: *he'll only be offended if you ask* **5** **only too** extremely: *only too pleased to help* □ *adjective* single, solitary: *an only child* □ *conjunction, informal* but, except that: *I'd like to go, only I have to work*

ono *abbreviation* or nearest offer

onomatopoeia *noun* the forming of a word which sounds like the thing it refers to, *eg* moo, swish

onomatopoeic *adjective* relating to or characterized by onomatopoeia

onrush *noun* a rush forward

onset *noun* **1** beginning **2** a fierce attack

onslaught *noun* a fierce attack

onus *noun* burden; responsibility

onward *adjective* going forward in place or time: *the onward march of science* □ **onward** or **onwards** *adverb*: *from four o'clock onwards/ we stumbled onward, close to exhaustion*

onyx *noun* a precious stone with layers of different colours

oodles *noun plural, informal* lots (of), many

ooze *verb* to flow gently or slowly □ *noun* **1** soft mud **2** a gentle flow

opacity *noun* opaqueness

opal *noun* a bluish-white precious stone, with flecks of various colours

opalescent *noun* milky and iridescent

opaque *adjective* not able to be seen through

OPEC *abbreviation* Organization of Petroleum-Exporting Countries

open *adjective* 1 not shut, allowing entry or exit 2 not enclosed or fenced 3 showing the inside or inner part; uncovered 4 not blocked 5 free for all to enter 6 honest, frank 7 of land: without many trees □ *verb* 1 to make open; unlock 2 to begin □ **in the open** 1 out-of-doors, in the open air 2 widely known, not secret □ **open to** likely or willing to receive: *open to attack/ open to suggestions* □ **with open arms** warmly, enthusiastically

open air any place not indoors or underground

open-air *adjective* happening outside

open book something that can be easily seen or understood

open-cast *adjective* of a mine: excavating in the open, above ground

open-ended *adjective* without definite limits

opener *noun* something that opens: *tin opener*

open-heart *adjective* of surgery: performed on a heart which has been temporarily stopped, with blood being circulated by a heart-lung machine

opening *noun* 1 a hole, a gap 2 an opportunity 3 a vacant job

openly *adverb* without trying to hide or conceal anything

open-minded *adjective* ready to take up new ideas

open-plan *adjective* of an office: with desks *etc* in the same room, not divided by walls or partitions

opera¹ *noun* a play in which the characters sing accompanied by an orchestra

opera² *plural of* **opus**

operate *verb* 1 to act, work 2 to bring about an effect 3 to perform an operation

operatic *adjective* of or for opera: *an operatic voice*

operating *adjective* of or for an operation on someone's body

operation *noun* 1 action 2 method or way of working 3 the cutting of a part of the human body to examine or treat disease 4 **operations** movements of armies, troops

operative *adjective* 1 working, in action 2 of a rule *etc*: in force, having effect □ *noun* a workman in a factory *etc*

operator *noun* 1 someone who works a machine 2 someone who connects telephone calls

operetta *noun* a play with music and singing

ophthalmic *adjective* relating to the eye: *an ophthalmic surgeon*

ophthalmologist *noun* a doctor who specializes in eye diseases and injuries

opiate *noun* 1 a drug containing opium used to make someone sleep 2 anything that calms or dulls the mind or feelings

opinion *noun* 1 what someone thinks or believes 2 professional judgement or point of view: *he wanted another opinion on his son's case* 3 judgement of the value of someone or something: *I have a low opinion of her*

opinionated *adjective* having and expressing strong opinions

opium *noun* a drug made from the dried juice of a type of poppy

opossum *noun* a small American animal that carries its young in a pouch

opponent *noun* someone who opposes; an enemy, a rival

opportune *adjective* coming at the right or convenient time

opportunism *noun* the practice of regulating actions by favourable opportunities rather than by consistent principles

opportunist *noun* someone who takes advantage of a favourable situation □ **opportunistic** *adjective*

opportunity *noun* (*plural* **opportunities**) a chance (to do something)

oppose *verb* 1 to struggle against, resist 2 to stand against, compete against

opposite *adjective* 1 facing, across from 2 lying on the other side (of) 3 as different as possible □ *preposition* 1 facing, across from: *he lives opposite the post office* **2** acting a role in a play, opera *etc* in relation to another: *she played Ophelia opposite his Hamlet* □ *noun* something as different as possible (from something else): *black is the opposite of white*

opposition *noun* **1** resistance **2** those who resist **3** the political party which is against the governing party

oppress *verb* **1** to govern harshly like a tyrant **2** to treat cruelly **3** to distress, worry greatly

oppression *noun* **1** the state of suffering cruelty and injustice **2** worry or mental distress

oppressive *adjective* **1** oppressing **2** cruel, harsh **3** of weather: close, tiring

opt *verb* **1** (**opt for something**) to choose it **2** to decide (to do) □ **opt out** to decide not to (do something)

optic or **optical** *adjective* relating to the eyes or sight

optical illusion an impression that something seen is different from what it is

optician *noun* someone who makes and sells spectacles

optics *noun singular* the science of light

optimal *adjective* very best, optimum

optimism *noun* the habit of taking a bright, hopeful view of things (*contrasted with*: **pessimism**)

optimist *noun* someone who tends to take a positive view of things

optimistic *adjective* relating to or characterized by optimism

optimum *adjective* best, most favourable: *optimum conditions*

option *noun* **1** choice; the right or power to choose **2** something chosen

optional *adjective* left to choice, not compulsory

opulence *noun* riches

opulent *adjective* wealthy; luxurious

opus *noun* (*plural* **opera**) an artistic work, especially a musical composition

or *conjunction* **1** used (often with **either**) to show alternatives: *would you prefer tea or coffee?* **2** because if not: *you'd*

better go or you'll miss your bus

oracle *noun* **1** someone thought to be very wise or knowledgeable **2** *historical* a sacred place where a god answered questions **3** someone through whom such answers were made known

oracular *adjective* **1** of or like an oracle **2** difficult to interpret; mysterious and ambiguous **3** prophetic

oral *adjective* **1** spoken, not written: *oral literature* **2** relating to the mouth □ *noun* an oral examination or test
🕓 Comes from Latin *or-*, a form of *os* meaning 'mouth'

> 🖋 Do not confuse with: **aural**. Aural means 'relating to the ear'. It may help to think of the 'O' as looking like an open mouth

orally *adverb* by mouth

orange *noun* **1** a juicy citrus fruit, with a thick reddish-yellow skin **2** the colour of this fruit

orang-utan *noun* a large man-like ape

> Based on a Malay phrase which translates as 'wild man'

oration *noun* a public speech, especially one in fine formal language

orator *noun* a public speaker

oratorio *noun* (*plural* **oratorios**) a sacred story set to music, performed by soloists, choir and often orchestra

oratory *noun* the art of speaking well in public

orb *noun* anything in the shape of a ball, a sphere

orbit *noun* **1** the path of a planet or moon round a sun, or of a space capsule round the earth **2** range or area of influence: *within his orbit* □ *verb* to go round the earth *etc* in space

orchard *noun* a large garden of fruit trees

orchestra *noun* a group of musicians playing together under a conductor

orchestrate *verb* **1** to arrange (a piece of music) for an orchestra **2** to organize so as to produce the best effect

orchid *noun* a plant with unusually shaped, often brightly coloured, flowers

ordain *verb* **1** to declare something to

ordeal noun 1 a hard trial or test 2 suffering, painful experience

order noun 1 an instruction to act made by someone in authority 2 a request or list of requests: *put an order in with the grocer* 3 an arrangement according to a system 4 an accepted way of doing things 5 a tidy or efficient state 6 peaceful conditions: *law and order* 7 rank, position, class 8 a society or brotherhood, *eg* of monks □ verb 1 to give an order to, tell to do 2 to put in an order for: *I've ordered another copy of the book* 3 to arrange □ **in order 1** correct according to what is regularly done 2 in a tidy arrangement □ **in order to** for the purpose of: *in order to live you must eat* □ **out of order 1** not working 2 not the correct way of doing things 3 not in a tidy arrangement

orderly adjective 1 in proper order 2 well-behaved, quiet □ noun (plural **orderlies**) 1 a soldier who carries the orders and messages of an officer 2 a hospital attendant who does routine jobs

ordinal adjective of or in an order

ordinal number a number which shows order in a series, *eg* first, second, third (*compare with*: **cardinal number**)

ordinance noun a command; a law

ordinarily adverb usually, normally

ordinariness noun being ordinary

ordinary adjective 1 common, usual 2 normal; not exceptional □ **out of the ordinary** unusual

ordination noun the act or ceremony of ordaining a priest or minister of the church

Ordnance Survey a government office which produces official detailed maps

ore noun a mineral from which a metal is obtained: *iron ore*

oregano (*pronounced* o-ri-**gah**-noh *or US* o-**reg**-an-oh) noun a Mediterranean herb used in cooking

organ noun 1 an internal part of the body, *eg* the liver 2 a large musical wind instrument with a keyboard 3 a means of spreading information or propaganda, *eg* a newspaper: *an organ of conservatism*

organdie (*pronounced* **aw**-gan-di) noun a fine, thin, stiff muslin

organic adjective 1 of or produced by the bodily organs 2 of living things 3 made up of parts each with its separate function 4 of food: grown without the use of artificial fertilizers *etc* □ **organically** adverb

organism noun any living thing

organist noun someone who plays the organ

organization noun 1 the act of organizing 2 a group of people working together for a purpose

organize verb 1 to arrange, set up (an event *etc*) 2 to form into a whole

orgasm noun the climax of sexual excitement □ verb to experience an orgasm

orgy noun (plural **orgies**) a drunken or other unrestrained celebration

Orient noun, old the countries of the East

oriental adjective eastern; from the East

orientate verb 1 to find your position and sense of direction 2 to set or put facing a particular direction

orientation noun 1 the act or an instance of orientating or being orientated 2 a position relative to a fixed point

orienteering noun the sport of finding your way across country with the help of map and compass

orifice noun, formal an opening

origami noun the Japanese art of folding paper

origin noun 1 the starting point 2 the place from which someone or something comes 3 cause

original adjective 1 first in time 2 not copied 3 able to think or do something new □ noun 1 the earliest version 2 a model from which other things are made

originally adverb 1 in or from the beginning: *his family is from Ireland originally* 2 in a new and different way: *she dresses very originally*

originate *verb* 1 to bring or come into being 2 to produce

Orion *noun* a constellation containing seven bright stars, forming the shape of a hunter

ornament *noun* something added to give or enhance beauty □ *verb* to adorn, decorate

ornamental *adjective* used for ornament; decorative

ornamentation *noun* decorating or the state of being decorated

ornate *adjective* richly decorated □ **ornately** *adverb*

ornithological *adjective* relating to or involving ornithology

ornithologist *noun* someone who studies or is an expert on birds

ornithology *noun* the scientific study of birds and their behaviour

orphan *noun* a child who has lost one or both parents

orphanage *noun* a home for orphans

ortho- or **orth-** *prefix* forms words containing the idea of 'straightness' or 'correctness': *orthography* (= originally the art of spelling words correctly)/ *orthopaedics* (= the correction of bone diseases and injuries)
ⓘ Comes from Greek *orthos* meaning 'straight', 'upright' or 'correct'

orthodox *adjective* 1 agreeing with the prevailing or established religious, political *etc* views (*contrasted with*: **heterodox**) 2 normal, generally practised and accepted

orthodoxy *noun* 1 the state of being orthodox or of having orthodox beliefs 2 an orthodox belief or practice

orthographic or **orthographical** *adjective* relating to spelling

orthography *noun* an established system of spelling

orthopaedic or *US* **orthopedic** *adjective* relating to orthopaedics

orthopaedics or *US* **orthopedics** *noun singular* the branch of medicine which deals with bone diseases and injuries

oscillate *verb* 1 to swing to and fro like the pendulum of a clock 2 to keep changing your mind

From Latin *oscillum*, literally 'small face', a mask of the god Bacchus which hung in Roman vineyards and swayed in the wind

oscillation *noun* 1 oscillating 2 a regular movement or change, such as the movement of a pendulum

osier *noun* 1 a type of willow tree whose twigs are used for weaving baskets *etc* 2 a twig from this tree

osmosis *noun* 1 diffusion of liquids through a membrane 2 gradual absorption or assimilation

osprey *noun* (*plural* **ospreys**) a type of eagle which eats fish

ostensible *adjective* of a reason *etc*: apparent, but not always real or true

ostentation *noun* pretentious display of wealth, knowledge *etc*, especially to attract attention or admiration

ostentatious *adjective* showy, meant to catch the eye

osteopath *noun* someone who practises osteopathy

osteopathy *noun* a system of healing or treatment, mainly involving manipulation of the bones and joints and massage of the muscles, that provides relief for many bone and joint disorders

osteoporosis *noun* a disease which makes bones porous and brittle, caused by lack of calcium

ostracism *noun* social exclusion

Based on *ostrakon*, a piece of pottery used in ancient Greece to cast votes to decide if someone was to be exiled

ostracize *verb* to banish (someone) from the company of a group of people

ostrich *noun* (*plural* **ostriches**) a large African bird with showy plumage, which cannot fly but runs very fast

ostrich-like *adjective* avoiding facing up to difficulties (after the ostrich's supposed habit of burying its head in the sand when chased)

other *adjective* 1 the second of two: *where is the other sock?* 2 remaining, not previously mentioned: *these are for the other children* 3 different, additional: *there must be some other reason* **4 every other** second: *every other day* **5** recently past: *the other day* □ *pronoun* **1** the second of two **2** those remaining, those not previously mentioned: *the others arrived the next day* **3** the previous one: *one after the other* □ **other than** except: *no hope other than to retreat* □ **someone or other** or **something or other** someone or something not named or specified: *there's always someone or other here*

OTT *abbreviation* over-the-top, extravagant

otter *noun* a type of river animal living on fish

Ottoman *adjective, historical* relating to the Turkish empire from the 14th to the 19th centuries

ottoman *noun* a low, cushioned seat without a back

ought *verb* **1** used with other verbs to indicate duty or need: *we ought to set an example/ I ought to practise more* **2** to indicate what can be reasonably expected: *the weather ought to be fine*

ounce *noun* a unit of weight, one-sixteenth of a pound, 28.35 grammes

our *adjective* belonging to us: *our house*

ours *pronoun* something belonging to us: *the green car is ours*

ourselves *pronoun* **1** used reflexively: *we exhausted ourselves swimming* **2** used for emphasis: *we ourselves don't like it, but other people may*

oust *verb* **1** to drive out (from) **2** to take the place of: *she ousted him as leader of the party*

out *adverb* **1** into or towards the open air: *go out for a walk* **2** from within: *take out a handkerchief* **3** not inside: *out of prison* **4** far from here: *out in the Far East* **5** not at home, not in the office *etc*: *she's out at the moment* **6** aloud: *shouted out* **7** to or at an end: *hear me out* **8** inaccurate: *the total was five pounds out* **9** *informal* on strike **10** published: *is the book not out yet?* **11** no longer hidden: *the secret is out* **12** openly admitting to being homosexual **13** dismissed from a game of cricket, baseball *etc* **14** finished, having won at

cards *etc* **15** no longer in power or office **16** determined: *out to win*

out-and-out *adjective* complete, total, thorough

outback *noun* the wild interior parts of Australia

outbid *verb* to offer a higher price than (somebody else)

> **outbid** ➪ outbid*s*, outbidd*ing*, outbid

outboard *adjective* on the outside of a ship or boat: *an outboard motor*

outbreak *noun* a beginning, a breaking out, *eg* of war or disease

outbuilding *noun* a building that is separate from the main buildings

outburst *noun* a bursting out, especially of angry feelings

outcast *noun* someone driven away from friends and home

outcome *noun* result

outcrop *noun* the part of a rock formation that can be seen at the surface of the ground

outcry *noun* (*plural* **outcries**) a widespread show of anger, disapproval *etc*

outdo *verb* to do better than

> **outdo** ➪ outdo*es*, outdo*ing*, outdid, outdone

outdoor *adjective* of or in the open air

outdoors *adverb* **1** outside the house **2** in or into the open air

outer *adjective* nearer the edge, surface *etc*; further away

outermost *adjective* nearest the edge; furthest away

outfit *noun* a set of clothes worn together, often for a special occasion *etc*

outfitter *noun* a seller of outfits, especially men's clothes

outgoings *noun plural* money spent or being spent

outgrow *verb* to get too big or old for (clothes, toys *etc*)

> **outgrow** ➪ outgrow*s*, outgrow*ing*, outgrew, outgrown

out-house *noun* a shed

outing *noun* a trip, excursion

outlandish *adjective* looking or sounding very strange

outlaw *noun* someone put outside the protection of the law; a robber or bandit □ *verb* 1 to place beyond the protection of the law 2 to ban, forbid

outlay *noun* money paid out

outlet *noun* 1 a passage to the outside, *eg* for a water-pipe 2 a means of expressing or getting rid of (a feeling, energy *etc*) 3 a market for goods

outline *noun* 1 the outer line of a figure in a drawing *etc* 2 a sketch showing only the main lines 3 a rough sketch 4 a brief description □ *verb* to draw or describe an outline of

outlive *verb* to live longer than

outlook *noun* 1 a view from a window *etc* 2 what is thought likely to happen: *the weather outlook*

outlying *adjective* far from the centre, distant

outnumber *verb* to be greater in number than: *their team outnumbered ours*

out-of-date *adjective* or **out of date** 1 old-fashioned 2 no longer valid: *this voucher is out of date/ an out-of-date ticket*

out-patient *noun* a patient who does not stay in a hospital while receiving treatment (*contrasted with*: **in-patient**)

outpost *noun* a military station in front of or far from the main army; an outlying settlement

output *noun* the goods produced by a machine, factory *etc*; the amount of work done by a person 2 data produced by a computer program (*contrasted with*: **input**)

outrage *noun* 1 an act of great violence 2 an act which shocks or causes offence □ *verb* 1 to injure, hurt by violence 2 to insult, shock

outrageous *adjective* 1 violent, very wrong 2 not moderate, extravagant

outright *adverb* completely □ *adjective* complete, thorough

outset *noun* start, beginning

outside *noun* the outer surface or place: *the outside of the box* □ *adjective* 1 in, on or of the outer surface or place: *the outside seat* 2 relating to leisure rather than your full-time job: *outside interests* 3 slight: *an outside chance of winning* □ *adverb* 1 beyond the limits of: *go outside the building/ locked outside working hours* 2 out-of-doors; in or into the open air: *let's eat outside* □ *preposition* beyond the range of, not within □ **at the outside** at the most: *ten miles at the outside*

outsider *noun* 1 someone not included in a particular social group 2 a runner *etc* whom no one expects to win

outsize *adjective* of a very large size

outskirts *noun plural* the outer borders of a city *etc*

outspoken *adjective* bold and frank in speech

outstanding *adjective* 1 well-known 2 excellent 3 of a debt: unpaid

outstretched *adjective* reaching out

out-tray *noun* an office tray for letters and work already dealt with (*contrasted with*: **in-tray**)

outvote *verb* to defeat by a greater number of votes

outward *adjective* 1 towards or on the outside 2 of a journey: away from home, not towards it

outwardly or **outwards** *adverb* on the outside, externally

outweigh *verb* to be more important than: *the advantages outweigh the disadvantages*

outwit *verb* to defeat by cunning

> **outwit** ⇨ outwit**s**, outwitt**ing**, outwitt**ed**

outwith *preposition, Scottish* outside of

ova *plural* of **ovum**

oval *adjective* having the shape of an egg □ *noun* an egg shape

ovary *noun* (*plural* **ovaries**) one of two organs in the female body in which eggs are formed

ovation *noun* an outburst of cheering, hand-clapping *etc*

oven *noun* a covered place for baking; a small furnace

over *preposition* **1** higher than, above: *the number is over the door/ she won over £200/ we've lived here for over thirty years* **2** across: *going over the bridge* **3** on the other side of: *the house over the road* **4** on top of: *threw his coat over the body* **5** here and there on: *paper scattered over the carpet* **6** about: *they quarrelled over their money* **7** by means of: *over the telephone* **8** during, throughout: *fell asleep over his dinner* □ *adverb* **1** above, higher up: *two birds flew over our heads* **2** across a distance: *he walked over and spoke* **3** downwards: *did you fall over?* **4** above in number *etc*: *aged four and over* **5** as a remainder: *three left over* **6** through: *read the passage over* □ *adjective* finished: *the sale is over* □ *noun, cricket* a fixed number of balls bowled from one end of the wicket □ **over again** once more

over- *prefix* too much, to too great an extent: *overcook/ over-excited*

overall *noun* **1** a garment worn over ordinary clothes to protect them against dirt **2** hard-wearing trousers with a bib worn as work clothes □ *adjective* **1** from one end to the other: *overall length* **2** including everything: *overall cost* □ **over all** altogether

overawe *verb* to frighten or astonish into silence

overbalance *verb* to lose your balance and fall

overbearing *adjective* over-confident, domineering

overboard *adverb* out of a ship into the water: *man overboard*

overcast *adjective* of the sky: cloudy

overcoat *noun* an outdoor coat worn over all other clothes

overcome *verb* to get the better of, defeat □ *adjective* helpless from exhaustion, emotion *etc*

overdo *verb* **1** to do too much **2** to exaggerate: *they rather overdid the sympathy* **3** to cook (food) too long

overdose *noun* too great an amount (of medicine, a drug *etc*) □ *verb* to give or take too much medicine *etc*

overdraft *noun* the amount of money overdrawn from a bank

overdraw *verb* to draw more money from the bank than you have in your account

overdue *adjective* **1** later than the stated time: *the train is overdue* **2** of a bill *etc*: still unpaid although the time for payment has passed

overflow *verb* **1** to flow or spill over: *the river overflowed its banks/ the crowd overflowed into the next room* **2** to be so full as to flow over □ *noun* **1** a running-over of liquid **2** a pipe or channel for getting rid of excess water *etc*

overgrown *adjective* **1** covered with wild plant growth **2** grown too large

overhang *verb* to jut out over

overhaul *verb* to examine carefully and carry out repairs □ *noun* a thorough examination and repair

overhead *adverb* directly above: *the aeroplane flew overhead* □ *adjective* placed high above the ground: *overhead cables* □ *noun* (**overheads**) the general expenses of a business *etc*

overhear *verb* to hear what you were not meant to hear

overjoyed *adjective* filled with great joy

overland *adverb & adjective* on or by land, not sea

overlap *verb* **1** to extend over and partly cover: *the two pieces of cloth overlapped* **2** to cover a part of the same area or subject as another; partly coincide □ *noun* the amount by which something overlaps

overleaf *adjective* on the other side of a leaf of a book

overload *verb* to load or fill too much

overlook *verb* **1** to look down on from a higher point; have or give a view of: *the house overlooked the village* **2** to fail to see, miss **3** to pardon, not punish

overlord *noun, historical* a lord with power over other lords

overly *adverb* too, excessively

overmuch *adverb* too much

overnight *adverb* **1** during the night: *staying overnight with a friend* **2** in a very short time: *he changed completely* *overnight* □ *adjective* **1** for the night: *an overnight bag* **2** got or made in a very short time: *an overnight success*

overpass *noun* a road going over above another road, railway, canal *etc*

overpower *verb* **1** to defeat through greater strength **2** to overwhelm, make helpless

overpowering *adjective* **1** unable to be resisted **2** overwhelming, very strong: *overpowering smell*

overrate *verb* to value more highly than is deserved: *his new film is overrated*

overreach *verb*: **overreach yourself** to try to do or get more than you can and so fail

override *verb* to ignore, set aside: *overriding the teacher's authority*

overrule *verb* to go against or cancel an earlier judgement or request

overrun *verb* **1** to grow or spread over: *overrun with weeds* **2** to take possession of (a country)

overseas *adjective* & *adverb* abroad; beyond the sea

oversee *verb* to watch over, supervise

overseer *noun* a person who oversees workers, a supervisor

overshadow *verb* to lessen the importance of by doing better than

oversight *noun* **1** something left out or forgotten by mistake **2** failure to notice

overstep *verb* to go further than (a set limit, rules *etc*)

overt *adjective* not hidden or secret; openly done

overtake *verb* to catch up with and pass

overthrow *verb* to defeat

overtime *noun* **1** time spent working beyond the agreed normal hours **2** payment for this, usually at a higher rate

overtone *noun* an additional meaning or association, not directly stated

overture *noun* **1** a proposal intended to open discussions: *overtures of peace* **2** a piece of music played as an introduction to an opera

overwhelm *verb* **1** to defeat completely **2** to load with too great an amount: *overwhelmed with work* **3** to overcome, make helpless: *overwhelmed with grief*

overwhelming *adjective* physically or mentally crushing; intensely powerful

overwork *verb* to work more than is good for you

overworked *adjective* having too much work to do

overwrought *adjective* excessively nervous or excited, agitated

ovoid *adjective* egg-shaped □ *noun* an egg-shaped form or object

ovum *noun* (*plural* **ova**) the egg from which the young of animals and people develop

owe *verb* **1** to be in debt to: *I owe Peter three pounds* **2** to have (a person or thing) to thank for: *he owes his success to his family* □ **owing to** because of

owl *noun* a bird of prey which comes out at night

owlet *noun* a young owl

own *verb* **1** to have as a possession **2** to admit, confess to be true □ *adjective* belonging to the person mentioned: *is this all your own work?* □ **hold your own** to keep your place or position, not weaken □ **on your own 1** by your own efforts **2** alone

owner *noun* someone who possesses anything

ownership *noun* possession

own goal a goal scored by mistake against your own side

ox *noun* (*plural* **oxen**) a male cow, usually castrated, used for drawing loads *etc*

oxide *noun* a compound of oxygen and another element

oxidize *verb* **1** to combine with oxygen **2** to become rusty

oxygen *noun* a gas with no taste, colour or smell, forming part of the air and of water

oxygenate *verb* to supply (*eg* the blood) with oxygen

oyster *noun* a type of eatable shellfish

ozone *noun* a form of oxygen, O_3

ozone layer a layer of the upper atmosphere which protects the earth from the sun's ultraviolet rays

Pp

p *abbreviation* **1** page **2** pence

pace *noun* **1** a step **2** rate of walking, running *etc* □ *verb* **1** to measure by steps **2** to walk backwards and forwards

pacemaker *noun* **1** someone who sets the pace in a race **2** a device used to correct weak or irregular heart rhythms

pachyderm (*pronounced* **pak**-id-erm) *noun* a thick-skinned animal such as an elephant

pacifist *noun* someone who is against war and works for peace

pacify *verb* **1** to make peaceful **2** to calm, soothe

pacify ⇨ pacifies, pacifying, pacified

pack *noun* **1** a bundle, especially one carried on the back **2** a set of playing-cards **3** a group of animals, especially dogs or wolves □ *verb* **1** to place (clothes *etc*) in a case or trunk for a journey **2** to press or crowd together closely
□ **pack in** to cram in tightly

package *noun* a bundle, a parcel □ *verb* **1** to put into a container **2** to wrap

package holiday or **package tour** a holiday or tour arranged by an organizer with all travel and accommodation included in the price

packet *noun* **1** a small parcel **2** a container made of paper, cardboard *etc*

pack-ice *noun* a mass of large pieces of floating ice driven together by wind, currents *etc*

packing *noun* **1** the act of putting things in cases, parcels *etc* **2** material for wrapping goods to pack **3** something used to fill an empty space

□ **send someone packing** to send them away forcefully

pact *noun* **1** an agreement **2** a treaty, a contract

pad *noun* **1** a soft cushion-like object to prevent jarring or rubbing *etc* **2** a bundle of sheets of paper fixed together **3** the paw of certain animals **4** a rocket-launching platform □ *verb* **1** to stuff or protect with a soft material **2** (often **pad something out**) to fill it up with unnecessary material **3** to walk making a dull, soft noise

pad *verb* ⇨ pads, padding, padded

padding *noun* **1** stuffing material **2** words included in a speech, book *etc* just to fill space or time

paddle *verb* **1** to move forward by the use of paddles; row **2** to wade in shallow water □ *noun* a short, broad, spoon-shaped oar

paddle-steamer *noun* a steamer driven by two large wheels made up of paddles

paddock *noun* a small closed-in field used for pasture

paddy-field *noun* a muddy field in which rice is grown

padlock *noun* a removable lock with a hinged hook

paean (*pronounced* pee-an) *noun* a song of praise or thanksgiving

paediatrician or *US* **pediatrician** *noun* a doctor specializing in studying and treating children's illnesses

paediatrics or *US* **pediatrics** *noun singular* the treatment of children's diseases

paedo- (*pronounced* pee-doh) also **paed-** (*pronounced* peed), **ped-** *prefix*

of or relating to children: *paedophile/ pedagogical* (relating to the education of children)
Ⓛ Comes from Greek *paidos* meaning 'of a boy'

paedophile or *US* **pedophile** *noun* an adult who has sexual desire for children

pagan *noun* someone who does not believe in any religion; a heathen □ *adjective* heathen

paganism *noun* pagan beliefs and practices

page *noun* 1 one side of a blank, written or printed sheet of paper 2 a boy servant 3 a boy who carries the train of the bride's dress in a marriage service

pageant *noun* 1 a show or procession made up of scenes from history 2 an elaborate parade or display

pageantry *noun* elaborate show or display

pagoda *noun* an Eastern temple, especially in China or India

paid *past form of* **pay**

pail *noun* an open vessel of tin, zinc, plastic *etc* for carrying liquids; a bucket

pain *noun* 1 feeling caused by hurt to mind or body 2 threat of punishment: *under pain of death* 3 **pains** care: *takes great pains with his work* □ *verb* to cause suffering to, distress

pained *adjective* showing pain or distress

painful *adjective* 1 causing pain: *a painful injury* 2 affected by something which causes pain: *a painful finger* 3 causing distress: *a painful duty* 4 laborious: *painful progress* □ **painfully** *adverb*

painkiller *noun* a medicine taken to lessen pain

painless *adjective* without pain □ **painlessly** *adverb*

painstaking *adjective* very careful □ **painstakingly** *adverb*

paint *verb* 1 to apply colour to in the form of liquid or paste 2 to describe in words □ *noun* a liquid substance used for colouring and applied with a brush, a spray *etc*

paintball *noun* a type of war game in which the participants fire paint-pellets at one another

painter *noun* 1 someone whose trade is painting 2 an artist who works in paint 3 a rope used to fasten a boat

painting *noun* 1 the act or art of creating pictures with paint 2 a painted picture

pair *noun* 1 two of the same kind 2 a set of two □ *verb* 1 to join to form a pair 2 to go in twos 3 to mate

pajamas *another spelling of* **pyjamas**

pal *noun, informal* a friend

palace *noun* the house of a king, queen, archbishop or aristocrat

palaeolithic or **paleolithic** *adjective* relating to the early Stone Age when people used stone tools

palatable *adjective* 1 pleasant to the taste
2 acceptable, pleasing: *the truth is often not palatable*

palate (*pronounced* **pal**-at) *noun* 1 the roof of the mouth 2 taste
Ⓛ Comes from Latin *palatum* meaning 'the roof of the mouth'
 🖝 Do not confuse with: **palette** and **pallet**

palatial *adjective* like a palace, magnificent

pale¹ *noun* a wooden stake used in making a fence to enclose ground

pale² *adjective* 1 light or whitish in colour 2 not bright □ *verb* to make or turn pale

palette (*pronounced* **pal**-et) *noun* a board or plate on which an artist mixes paints
Ⓛ Comes from Italian *paletta* meaning 'a small shovel'
 🖝 Do not confuse with: **pallet** and **palate**

palindrome *noun* a word or phrase that reads the same backwards as forwards, *eg* 'level'
Ⓛ From Greek *palindromos*, meaning 'running back'

What is the longest palindrome you can make up? Remember your palindrome can have several words, so long as it is the same when you read it backwards, like the sentence: 'Able was I ere I saw Elba'

paling *noun* a row of wooden stakes forming a fence

palisade *noun* a fence of pointed wooden stakes

pall (*pronounced* pawl) *noun* **1** the cloth over a coffin at a funeral **2** a dark covering or cloud: *a pall of smoke* □ *verb* to become dull or uninteresting

pallbearer *noun* one of those carrying or walking beside the coffin at a funeral

pallet (*pronounced* **pal**-et) *noun* **1** a straw bed or mattress **2** a platform that can be lifted by a fork-lift truck for stacking goods

① Meaning 1: comes from French *paille* meaning 'straw'; meaning 2: shares the same origin as 'palette'

☛ Do not confuse with: **palette** and **palate**

palliative *adjective* making less severe or harsh □ *noun* something which lessens pain, *eg* a drug

pallid *adjective* pale

pallor *noun* paleness

palm *noun* **1** a tall tree with broad fan-shaped leaves, which grows in hot countries **2** the inner surface of the hand between the wrist and the start of the fingers □ **palm off** to give with the intention of cheating: *that shopkeeper palmed off a foreign coin on me*

palmist *noun* someone who claims to tell fortunes by the lines and markings of the hand

palmistry *noun* the telling of fortunes from the lines and markings of the hand

palpable *adjective* **1** able to be touched or felt **2** easily noticed, obvious

palpate *verb* to examine by touch

palpation *noun* examining by touch

palpitate *verb* of the heart: to beat rapidly, throb

palpitations *noun plural* uncomfortable rapid beating of the heart

palsied *adjective* affected with palsy; paralysed

palsy *noun* a loss of power and feeling in the muscles

paltry *adjective* of little value

pampas *noun plural* the vast treeless plains of South America

pamper *verb* to spoil (a child *etc*) by giving too much attention to

pamphlet *noun* a small book, stitched or stapled, often with a light paper cover

pan *noun* **1** a broad shallow pot used in cooking, a saucepan **2** a shallow dent in the ground **3** the bowl of a toilet □ *verb* to move a television or film camera so as to follow an object or give a wide view □ **pan out 1** to turn out (well or badly) **2** to come to an end

pan *verb* ⇨ pan*s*, pan*ning*, pan*ned*

pan- *prefix* all, whole: *pandemonium/panoply*

① Comes from Greek *pan*, a form of *pas* meaning 'all'

panacea (*pronounced* pan-*a*-**see**-*a*) *noun* a cure for all things

panache (*pronounced* pa-**nash**) *noun* a sense of style, swagger

Pan American including all America or Americans, North and South

pancake *noun* a thin cake of flour, eggs, sugar and milk, fried in a pan

panda *noun* **1** a large black-and-white bear-like animal found in Tibet *etc* **2** a raccoon-like animal found in the Himalayas

panda car *Brit, informal* a police patrol car

pandemic *adjective* of a disease *etc*: occurring over a wide area and affecting a large number of people

pandemonium *noun* a state of confusion and uproar

The name of the capital of Hell in Milton's *Paradise Lost* (1667)

pander *noun* a pimp □ **pander to** to indulge, easily comply with

After *Pandarus*, who acts as a go-between in the story of Troilus and Cressida

Pandora's box something which causes unexpected havoc

After the story of *Pandora*, who disobeyed the Greek gods and opened a box containing all the troubles of the world

pane *noun* a sheet of glass

panegyric (*pronounced* pan-i-**ji**-rik) *noun* a speech praising highly someone, an achievement *etc*

panel *noun* **1** a flat rectangular piece of wood such as is set into a door or wall **2** a group of people chosen to judge a contest, take part in a television quiz *etc*

pang *noun* a sudden sharp pain; a twinge

panic *noun* **1** a sudden and great fright **2** fear that spreads from person to person □ *verb* **1** to throw into panic **2** to act wildly through fear

panic *verb* ⇨ panics, panic*king*, panic*ked*

pannier *noun* **1** a basket slung on a horse's back **2** a light container attached to a bicycle *etc*

panoply *noun* (*plural* **panoplies**) **1** the ceremonial dress, equipment *etc* associated with a particular event: *the panoply of a military funeral* **2** *historical* a full suit of armour

panorama *noun* a wide view of a landscape, scene *etc*

pansy *noun* (*plural* **pansies**) a flower like the violet but larger

pant *verb* **1** to gasp for breath **2** to say breathlessly **3** to wish eagerly (for)

pantechnicon *noun* a large van for transporting furniture

pantheism *noun* **1** the belief that all things in the physical universe are part of God **2** belief in many gods

pantheist *noun* a believer in pantheism

pantheistic or **pantheistical** *adjective* relating to pantheism or pantheists

panther *noun* **1** a large leopard **2** *US* a puma

panties *noun plural* women's or children's knickers with short legs

pantomime *noun* a Christmas play, with songs, jokes *etc*, based on a popular fairy tale *eg* Cinderella

pantry *noun* (*plural* **pantries**) a room for storing food

pants *noun plural* **1** underpants **2** women's short-legged knickers **3** *US* trousers

papa *noun* a child's name for **father**

papacy *noun* the position or power of the Pope

papal *adjective* of, or relating to, the pope or the papacy

paparazzo *noun* (*plural* **paparazzi**) a press photographer who hounds celebrities *etc*

papaya *noun* (*also called*: **pawpaw**) a green-skinned edible fruit from S America

paper *noun* **1** a material made from rags, wood *etc* used for writing or wrapping **2** a single sheet of this **3** a newspaper **4** an essay on a learned subject **5** a set of examination questions **6 papers** documents proving someone's identity, nationality *etc* □ *verb* to cover up (especially walls) with paper

paperback *noun* a book bound in a flexible paper cover

paper-chase *noun* a game in which one runner leaves a trail of paper so that others may track them

paper-tiger *noun* someone who appears to be powerful but really is not

paperweight *noun* a heavy glass, metal *etc* object used to keep a pile of papers in place

papier-mâché (*pronounced* pap-yei-**mash**-ei) *noun* a substance consisting of paper pulp and some sticky liquid or glue, shaped into models, bowls *etc*

paprika *noun* a type of ground red pepper

papyrus *noun* (*plural* **papyri** — *pronounced* pa-**pai**-rai — or **papyruses**) a reed used by the ancient Egyptians *etc* to make paper

par *noun* **1** an accepted standard, value *etc* **2** *golf* the number of strokes allowed for each hole if the play is perfect □ **below par 1** not up to standard **2** not feeling very well □ **on a par with** equal to or comparable with

parable *noun* a story (*eg* in the Bible) which teaches a moral lesson

parabola *noun* **1** a curve **2** the intersection of a cone with a plane parallel to its side

paracetamol *noun* a pain-relieving drug which causes kidney failure if taken in excessive quantities

parachute *noun* an umbrella-shaped device made of light material and rope which supports someone or something dropping slowly to the ground from an aeroplane □ *verb* to drop by parachute

parachutist *noun* someone dropped by parachute from an aeroplane

parade *noun* **1** an orderly arrangement of troops for inspection or exercise **2** a procession of people, vehicles *etc* in celebration of some event □ *verb* **1** to arrange (troops) in order **2** to march in a procession **3** to display in an obvious way

paradise *noun* **1** heaven **2** a place or state of great happiness

paradox *noun* (*plural* **paradoxes**) a saying which seems to contradict itself but which may be true

paradoxical *adjective* combining two apparently contradictory elements: *it is paradoxical that so many should be homeless when there are many empty houses in the area* □ **paradoxically** *adverb*

paraffin *noun* an oil which burns and is used as a fuel (for heaters, lamps *etc*)

paragliding *noun* the sport of gliding, supported by a modified type of parachute

paragon *noun* a model of perfection or excellence: *a paragon of good manners*

paragraph *noun* **1** a division of a piece of writing shown by beginning the first sentence on a new line **2** a short item in a newspaper

parakeet *noun* a type of small parrot

parallel *adjective* **1** of lines: going in the same direction and never meeting, always remaining the same distance apart **2** similar or alike in some way: *parallel cases* □ *noun* **1** a parallel line **2** something comparable in some way with something else **3** a line to mark latitude, drawn east and west across a map or round a globe at a set distance from the equator

parallelogram *noun* a four-sided figure, the opposite sides of which are parallel and equal in length

paralyse or *US* **paralyze** *verb* **1** to affect with paralysis **2** to make helpless or ineffective **3** to bring to a halt

paralysis *noun* loss of the power to move and feel in part of the body

paralytic *adjective* **1** suffering from paralysis **2** *informal* helplessly drunk □ *noun* a paralysed person

paramedic *noun* someone helping doctors and nurses, *eg* a member of an ambulance crew

paramedical *adjective* denoting personnel or services that are supplementary to and support the work of the medical profession

parameter *noun* (often **parameters**) the limiting factors or characteristics which affect the way in which something can be done or made
ⓘ Comes from Greek *para* meaning 'beside' or 'beyond', and *metron* meaning 'measure'

✎ Do not confuse with: **perimeter**. Notice that words starting with **peri-** often relate to the idea of 'going around' – and the **perimeter** of a figure or shape is the line that goes around it

paramilitary *adjective* **1** on military lines and intended to supplement the military **2** organized illegally as a military force □ *noun* a member of a paramilitary force

paramount *adjective* **1** above all others in rank or power **2** very greatest: *of paramount importance*

paranoia *noun* **1** a form of mental disorder characterized by delusions of grandeur, persecution *etc* **2** intense, irrational fear or suspicion

paranormal *adjective* beyond what is

normal in nature; supernatural, occult

parapet *noun* a low wall on a bridge or balcony to prevent people falling over the side

paraphernalia *noun plural* belongings; gear, equipment

Originally a woman's property which was not part of her dowry, and which therefore remained her own after marriage

paraphrase *verb* to express (a piece of writing) in other words □ *noun* an expression in different words

paraplegia *noun* paralysis of the lower part of the body and legs

paraplegic *adjective* of paraplegia □ *noun* someone who suffers from paraplegia

parasailing *noun* a sport similar to paragliding, in which the participant wears water-skis and is towed into the air by a motorboat

parascending *noun* a sport similar to paragliding, in which the participant is towed into the wind behind a motor vehicle

parasite *noun* an animal, plant or person living on another without being any use in return

parasitic *adjective* 1 of an animal or plant: living on another 2 of a person: depending on others

parasol *noun* a light umbrella used as a sunshade

paratrooper *noun* a soldier who is specially trained to drop from an aeroplane using a parachute

paratroops *noun plural* soldiers carried by air to be dropped by parachute into enemy country

parboil *verb* to boil (food) slightly

parcel *noun* a wrapped and tied package to be sent by post □ *verb* 1 **parcel something out** to divide it into portions 2 **parcel something up** to wrap it up as a package □ **part and parcel** an absolutely necessary part

parcel *verb* ⇨ parcel**s**, parcel**ling**, parcel**led**

parch *verb* 1 to make hot and very dry 2 to make thirsty

parched *adjective* 1 very dry 2 very thirsty

parchment *noun* 1 the dried skin of a goat or sheep used for writing on 2 paper resembling this

pardon *verb* 1 to forgive 2 to free from punishment 3 to allow to go unpunished □ *noun* 1 forgiveness 2 the act of pardoning

pardonable *adjective* able to be forgiven

pare *verb* 1 to peel or cut off the edge or outer surface of 2 to make smaller gradually

parent *noun* a father or mother

parentage *noun* descent from parents or ancestors

parental *adjective* 1 of parents 2 with the manner or attitude of a parent

parenthesis *noun* (*plural* **parentheses**) 1 a word or group of words in a sentence forming an explanation or comment, often separated by brackets or dashes, *eg* he and his wife (*so he said*) were separated 2 **parentheses** brackets

parenthetical *adjective* 1 of the nature of a parenthesis 2 using parenthesis

par excellence *adjective* superior to all others of the kind

pariah *noun* someone driven out from a community or group; an outcast

Originally a member of a low caste in southern India

parings *noun plural* small pieces cut away or peeled off

parish *noun* (*plural* **parishes**) a district with its own church and minister or priest

parishioner (*pronounced* pa-**rish**-*o*n-er) *noun* a member of a parish

parity *noun* equality

park *noun* 1 a public place for walking, with grass and trees 2 an enclosed piece of land surrounding a country house □ *verb* to stop and leave (a car *etc*) in a place for a time

parka *noun* a type of thick jacket with a hood

Parkinson's disease a disease causing

trembling in the hands *etc* and rigid muscles

parley *verb* to hold a conference, especially with an enemy □ *noun* (*plural* **parleys**) a meeting between enemies to settle terms of peace *etc*

> **parley** *verb* ⇨ parley*s*, parley*ing*, parley*ed*

parliament *noun* **1** the chief law-making council of a nation **2** *Brit* the House of Commons and the House of Lords

parliamentary *adjective* **1** of, for or concerned with parliament: *a parliamentary candidate* **2** used in or suitable for parliament: *parliamentary procedures*

parlour *noun* a sitting room in a house

parlourmaid *noun* a woman or girl whose job is to wait at table

parochial *adjective* **1** relating to a parish **2** interested only in local affairs; narrow-minded □ **parochially** *adverb*

parody *noun* (*plural* **parodies**) an amusing imitation of someone's writing style, subject matter *etc* □ *verb* to make a parody of

> **parody** *verb* ⇨ parodi*es*, parody*ing*, parodi*ed*

parole *noun* the release of a prisoner before the end of a sentence on condition that they will have to return if they break the law □ *verb* to release on parole

> From French *parole* meaning 'word' because prisoners are released on their word of honour

paroxysm *noun* a fit of pain, rage, laughter *etc*

paroxysmal *adjective* relating to or of the nature of a paroxysm

parquet *noun* a floor covering of wooden blocks arranged in a pattern

parrot *noun* a bird found in warm countries with a hooked bill and often brightly coloured feathers

parry *verb* to deflect, turn aside (a blow, question *etc*)

> **parry** ⇨ parri*es*, parry*ing*, parri*ed*

parse *verb* to name the parts of speech

of (words in a sentence) and say how the words are connected with each other

Parsee or **Parsi** *noun* a member of an Indian religious sect descended from the Persian Zoroastrians

parsimonious *adjective* too careful in spending money; stingy

parsimony *noun* great care in spending money, meanness

parsley *noun* a bright green leafy herb, used in cookery

parsnip *noun* a plant with an edible yellowish root shaped like a carrot

parson *noun* a member of the clergy, especially one in charge of a parish

parsonage *noun* a parson's house

part *noun* **1** a portion, a share **2** a piece forming part of a whole: *the various parts of a car engine* **3** a character taken by an actor in a play **4** a role in an action or event: *played a vital part in the campaign* **5** *music* the notes to be played or sung by a particular instrument or voice **6 parts** talents: *a man of many parts* □ *verb* **1** to divide **2** to separate, send or go in different ways **3** to put or keep apart □ **in good part** without being hurt or taking offence □ **part of speech** one of the grammatical groups into which words are divided, *eg* noun, verb, adjective, preposition □ **part with** to let go, be separated from □ **take someone's part** to support them in an argument *etc* ⏰ Comes from Latin *pars* meaning 'a part', 'a section' or 'a share'

partake *verb*: **partake of 1** to eat or drink some of something **2** to take a part in

> **partake** ⇨ partake*s*, partak*ing*, partook, partak*en*

partial *adjective* **1** in part only, not total or complete: *partial payment* **2** having a liking for (someone or something): *partial to cheese*

partiality *noun* **1** the favouring of one thing more than another, bias **2** a particular liking (for something)

partially *adverb* not completely or wholly; not yet to the point of completion: *the house is only partially built*

participant or **participator** *noun* someone who takes part in anything

participate *verb* **1** to take part (in) **2** to have a share in

participation *noun* participating; involvement

participatory *adjective* capable of being participated in or shared

participle *noun* **1** a form of a verb which can be used with other verbs to form tenses, *eg* 'he was *eating*' or 'she has *arrived*' **2** used as an adjective, *eg* '*stolen* jewels' **3** used as a noun, *eg* '*running* makes me tired'

particle *noun* a very small piece: *a particle of sand*

particular *adjective* **1** relating to a single definite person, thing *etc* considered separately from others: *I want this particular colour* **2** special: *take particular care of the china* **3** fussy, difficult to please: *particular about her food* □ *noun* (**particulars**) the facts or details about someone or something

parting *noun* **1** the act of separating or dividing **2** a place of separation **3** a going away (from each other), a leave-taking **4** a line dividing hair on the head brushed in opposite directions

partisan *adjective* giving strong support or loyalty to a particular cause, theory *etc*, often without considering other points of view □ *noun* someone with partisan views

partition *noun* **1** a division **2** something which divides, *eg* a wall between rooms □ *verb* **1** to divide into parts **2** to divide by making a wall *etc*

partly *adverb* in part, or in some parts; not wholly or completely: *the house is built partly of stone and partly of wood*

partner *noun* **1** someone who shares the ownership of a business *etc* with another or others **2** one of a pair in games, dancing *etc* **3** a husband, wife or lover □ *verb* to act as someone's partner

partnership *noun* **1** a relationship in which two or more people or groups operate together as partners **2** the status of a partner: *she was offered a partnership at the age of 30* **3** a business or other enterprise jointly owned or run by two or more people *etc*

partridge *noun* a type of bird which is shot as game

party *noun* (*plural* **parties**) **1** a gathering of guests: *birthday party/ dinner party* **2** a group of people travelling together: *party of tourists* **3** a number of people with the same plans or ideas: *a political party* **4** someone taking part in, or approving, an action

party line **1** a shared telephone line **2** policy laid down by the leaders of a political party

PASCAL *noun* a high-level computer programming language

pass *verb* **1** to go, move, travel *etc*: *he passed out of sight over the hill* **2** to move on or along: *pass the salt* **3** to go by: *I saw the bus pass our house* **4** to overtake **5** of parliament: to put (a law) into force **6** to be successful in an examination **7** to be declared healthy or in good condition after an inspection **8** to come to an end: *the feeling of dizziness soon passed* **9** to hand on, give: *he passed the story on to his son* **10** to spend (time): *passing a pleasant hour by the river* **11** to make, utter (*eg* a remark) □ *noun* **1** a narrow passage over or through a range of mountains **2** a ticket or card allowing someone to go somewhere **3** success in an examination **4** a sexual advance □ **pass off** to present (a forgery *etc*) as genuine □ **pass on 1** to go forward, proceed **2** to hand on **3** to die □ **pass out** to faint □ **pass up** to fail to take up (an opportunity)

pass *verb* ⇨ **passes, passing, passed**

passable *adjective* **1** fairly good **2** of a river *etc*: able to be crossed □ **passably** *adverb* (meaning 1)

passage *noun* **1** the act of passing: *passage of time* **2** a journey in a ship **3** a corridor **4** a way through **5** a part of the text of a book

passageway *noun* a passage, a way through

passenger *noun* a traveller, not a member of the crew, in a train, ship, aeroplane *etc*

passer-by *noun* (*plural* **passers-by**) someone who happens to pass by when something happens

passing *adjective* 1 going by: *a passing car* 2 not lasting long: *passing interest* 3 casual: *passing remark* □ *noun* 1 the act of someone or something which passes 2 a going away, a coming to an end 3 death

passion *noun* strong feeling, especially anger or love □ **the Passion** the sufferings and death of Christ

passionate *adjective* 1 easily moved to passion 2 full of passion □ **passionately** *adverb*

passionfruit *noun* the edible, oblong fruit of the passionflower

passive *adjective* 1 making no resistance 2 acted upon, not acting □ **passively** *adverb* □ **passivity** *noun*

passive smoking the involuntary inhaling of smoke from cigarettes smoked by others

Passover *noun* a Jewish festival celebrating the exodus of the Israelites from Egypt

passport *noun* a card or booklet which gives someone's name and description, and which is needed to travel in another country

password *noun* 1 a secret word which allows those who know it to pass 2 a word typed into a computer to allow access to restricted data

past *noun* 1 (**the past**) the time gone by 2 someone's previous life or career 3 *grammar* the past tense □ *adjective* 1 of an earlier time: *past kindnesses* 2 just over, recently ended: *the past year* 3 gone, finished: *the time for argument is past* □ *preposition* 1 after: *it's past midday* 2 up to and beyond, further than: *go past the traffic lights* □ *adverb* by: *she walked past, looking at no one*

pasta *noun* 1 a dough used in making spaghetti, macaroni *etc* 2 the prepared shapes of this, *eg* spaghetti

paste *noun* 1 pastry dough 2 a gluey liquid for sticking paper *etc* together 3 any soft, kneadable mixture: *almond paste* 4 fine glass used to make imitation gems

pastel *adjective* of a colour: soft, pale □ *noun* 1 a chalk-like crayon used for drawing 2 a drawing made with this

pasteurize *verb* to heat food (especially milk) in order to kill harmful germs in it

Named after Louis *Pasteur*, the 19th-century French chemist who invented the process

pastiche (*pronounced* pas-**teesh**) *noun* a humorous imitation, a parody

pastille *noun* a small sweet, sometimes sucked as a medicine

pastime *noun* a hobby, a spare-time interest

pastor *noun* a member of the clergy

pastoral *adjective* 1 relating to country life 2 of a pastor or the work of the clergy

pastry *noun* (*plural* **pastries**) 1 a flour paste used to make the bases and crusts of pies, tarts *etc* 2 a small cake

pasturage *noun* grazing land

pasture *noun* ground covered with grass on which cattle graze

pasty¹ (*pronounced* **peis**-ti) *adjective* 1 like paste 2 pale

pasty² (*pronounced* **pas**-ti) *noun* a pie containing meat and vegetables in a covering of pastry

pat *noun* 1 a light, quick blow or tap with the hand 2 a small lump of butter *etc* 3 a cake of animal dung □ *verb* to strike gently, tap □ **off pat** memorized thoroughly, ready to be said when necessary

pat *verb* ⇨ pats, patt*ing*, patt*ed*

patch *verb* 1 to mend (clothes) by putting in a new piece of material to cover a hole 2 **patch something up** to mend it, especially hastily or clumsily 3 **patch something up** to settle (a quarrel) □ *noun* (*plural* **patches**) 1 a piece of material sewn on to mend a hole 2 a small piece of ground

patchwork *noun* fabric formed of small patches or pieces of material sewn together

patchy *adjective* uneven, mixed in quality □ **patchily** *adverb*

pate (*pronounced* peit) *noun*, *formal* the head: *a bald pate*

pâté *noun* a paste made of finely minced

meat, fish or vegetables, flavoured with herbs, spices *etc*

patent *noun* an official written statement granting someone the sole right to make or sell something that they have invented □ *adjective* **1** protected from copying by a patent **2** open, easily seen □ *verb* to obtain a patent for

patent leather leather with a very glossy surface

patently *adverb* openly, clearly: *patently obvious*

pater- or **patri-** *prefix* father: *paternal/patricide*
Ⓞ Comes from Latin *pater* meaning 'father'

paternal *adjective* **1** of a father **2** like a father, fatherly **3** on the father's side of the family: *my paternal grandfather*

paternalism *noun* governmental or managerial benevolence taken to the extreme of over-protectiveness and authoritarianism

paternalistic *adjective* characterized by or involving paternalism

paternity *noun* the state or fact of being a father

paternity leave leave of absence from work for a father after the birth of a child

path *noun* **1** a way made by people or animals walking on it, a track **2** the route to be taken by a person or vehicle: *in the lorry's path* **3** a course of action, a way of life

pathetic *adjective* **1** causing pity **2** causing contempt; feeble, inadequate: *a pathetic attempt* □ **pathetically** *adverb*

patho- (*pronounced* path-o) *prefix* of or relating to diseases or other disorders: *pathology*
Ⓞ Comes from Greek *patheia* meaning 'suffering'

pathological *adjective* **1** relating to disease **2** *informal* compulsive, obsessive: *pathological liar*

pathologist *noun* **1** a doctor who studies the causes and effects of disease **2** a doctor who makes post-mortem examinations

pathology *noun* the study of diseases

pathos (*pronounced* pei-thos) *noun* a quality that arouses pity: *the pathos of the situation made me weep*

pathway *noun* a path

patience *noun* **1** the ability or willingness to be patient **2** (*also called*: **solitaire**) a card game played by one person

patient *adjective* suffering delay, discomfort *etc* without complaint or anger □ *noun* someone under the care of a doctor *etc* □ **patiently** *adverb*

patio (*pronounced* pat-i-oh) *noun* (*plural* **patios**) a paved open yard attached to a house

patri- *see* **pater-**

patriarch (*pronounced* pei-tri-ahk) *noun* **1** the male head of a family or tribe **2** the head of the Greek Orthodox Church

patriarchal (*pronounced* pei-tri-**ahk**-*al*) *adjective* ruled or controlled by men or patriarchs

patriarchy (*pronounced* pei-tri-ahk-i) *noun* a society in which a man is head of the family and descent is traced through the male line

patrician *adjective* aristocratic

patricidal *adjective* relating to or involving patricide

patricide *noun* **1** the murder of your own father **2** someone who commits such a murder

patrimony *noun* property handed down from a father or ancestors

patriot *noun* someone who loves and is loyal to their country

patriotic *adjective* loyal or devoted to one's country □ **patriotically** *adverb*

patriotism *noun* love of and loyalty to your country

patrol *verb* to keep guard or watch by moving regularly around an area *etc* □ *noun* **1** the act of keeping guard in this way **2** the people keeping watch **3** a small group of Scouts or Guides

patrol *verb* ⇨ patrol*s*, patrol*ling*, patrol*led*

patrol car a police car used to patrol an area

patron (*pronounced* peit-ron) *noun* **1**

someone who protects or supports (an artist, a form of art *etc*) **2** a customer of a shop *etc*

patronage *noun* the support given by a patron

patronize *verb* **1** to be a patron towards: *patronize your local shops* **2** to treat (someone) as an inferior, look down on: *don't patronize me*

patron saint a saint chosen as the protector of a country *etc*

patter¹ *verb* of rain, footsteps *etc*: to make a quick tapping sound ▫ *noun* the sound of falling rain, of footsteps *etc*

patter² *noun* **1** chatter, rapid talk, especially that used by salesmen to encourage people to buy their goods **2** the jargon of a particular group

pattern *noun* **1** an example suitable to be copied **2** a model or guide for making something **3** a decorative design **4** a sample: *a book of tweed patterns*

patterned *adjective* having a design, not self-coloured

patty *noun* (*plural* **patties**) a small flat cake of chopped meat *etc*

paucity *noun* smallness of number or quantity

paunch *noun* (*plural* **paunches**) a fat stomach

pauper *noun* a very poor person

pause *noun* **1** a short stop, an interval **2** a break or hesitation in speaking or writing **3** *music* a symbol (⌒) showing the holding of a note or rest ▫ *verb* to stop for a short time

pave *verb* to lay (a street) with stone or concrete to form a level surface for walking on ▫ **pave the way for** to prepare or make the way easy for

pavement *noun* a paved footway at the side of a road for pedestrians

pavilion *noun* **1** a building in a sports ground with facilities for changing clothes **2** a large ornamental building **3** a large tent

paw *noun* the foot of an animal ▫ *verb* **1** of an animal: to scrape with one of the front feet **2** to handle or touch roughly or rudely **3** to strike out wildly with the hand: *paw the air*

pawn *verb* to put (an article of some value) in someone's keeping in exchange for a sum of money which, when repaid, buys back the article ▫ *noun* **1** *chess* a small piece of the lowest rank **2** someone who lets themselves be used by another for some purpose ▫ **in pawn** having been pawned

pawnbroker *noun* someone who lends money in exchange for pawned articles

pawnshop *noun* a pawnbroker's place of business

pawpaw *another word* for **papaya**

pay *verb* **1** to give (money) in exchange for (goods *etc*): *I paid £30 for it* **2** to suffer the punishment (for) **3** to be advantageous or profitable: *it pays to be prepared* **4** to give (*eg* attention) ▫ *noun* money given or received for work; wages ▫ **pay off 1** to pay in full and discharge (workers) owing to lack of work **2** to have good results: *his hard work paid off* ▫ **pay out 1** to spend **2** to give out (a length of rope *etc*)

pay *verb* ⇨ pays, paying, paid

■ **Alternative words**: (verb, meaning 1) remit, discharge, remunerate, recompense, reimburse; (verb, meaning 2) atone, compensate, answer

payable *adjective* requiring to be paid

pay-as-you-earn *adjective* of income tax: deducted from a salary before it is given to the worker

PAYE *abbreviation* pay as you earn

payee *noun* someone to whom money is paid

payment *noun* **1** the act of paying **2** money paid for goods *etc*

payphone *noun* a coin-or card-operated public telephone

pay-roll *noun* a list of people entitled to receive pay

payroll *noun* the money for paying wages

PC *abbreviation* **1** police constable **2** privy councillor **3** political correctness

pc *abbreviation* **1** personal computer **2** postcard **3** percent

PE *abbreviation* physical education

pea noun 1 a climbing plant which produces round green seeds in pods 2 the seed itself, eaten as a vegetable

peace noun 1 quietness, calm 2 freedom from war or disturbance 3 a treaty bringing this about

peaceable adjective of a quiet nature, fond of peace

peaceful adjective quiet; calm
□ **peacefully** adverb

■ **Alternative words:** tranquil, serene, placid

peach noun (plural **peaches**) 1 a juicy, velvet-skinned fruit 2 the tree that bears it 3 an orangey-pink colour

peacock noun a large bird, the male of which has brightly coloured, patterned tail feathers

peahen noun a female peacock

peak noun 1 the pointed top of a mountain or hill 2 the highest point 3 the jutting-out part of the brim of a cap □ verb 1 to rise to a peak 2 to reach the highest point: *prices peaked in July and then fell steadily*

peaked adjective 1 pointed 2 of a cap: having a peak

peaky adjective looking pale and unhealthy

peal noun 1 a set of bells tuned to each other 2 the changes rung on such bells 3 a succession of loud sounds: *peals of laughter* □ verb to sound loudly

The noun 'appeal' is said to have gradually lost its inital 'a-' to form the word **peal**

☛ Do not confuse with: **peel**

peanut noun a type of nut similar to a pea in shape (*also called* **groundnut, monkey-nut**)

peanut butter a paste of ground roasted peanuts, spread on bread *etc*

pearl noun 1 a gem formed in the shell of the oyster and several other shellfish 2 a valuable remark *etc*: *pearls of wisdom*

pearly gates the entrance to heaven

pear-shaped adjective in the shape of a pear

peasant noun someone who works and lives on the land, especially in an underdeveloped area

peat noun turf cut out of boggy places, dried and used as fuel

pebble noun a small, roundish stone

pebble dash a coating for outside walls with small stones set into the mortar

pebbly adjective 1 full of pebbles 2 rough, knobbly

peccadillo noun (plural **peccadilloes** or **peccadillos**) a slight misdemeanour or wrong

peck verb 1 to strike with the beak 2 to pick up with the beak 3 to eat little, nibble (at) 4 to kiss someone quickly and briefly □ noun 1 a sharp blow with the beak 2 a brief kiss

peckish adjective slightly hungry

pectoral adjective of the breast or chest: *pectoral muscles*

peculiar adjective 1 belonging to one person or thing only: *a custom peculiar to England* 2 strange, odd: *he is a very peculiar person*

peculiarity noun (plural **peculiarities**) that which marks someone or something off from others in some way; something odd

peculiarly adverb in a peculiar way

pecuniary adjective of money

pedagogic or **pedagogical** adjective of a teacher or of education

pedagogue noun a teacher

pedal noun 1 a lever worked by the foot on a bicycle, piano, harp *etc* 2 a key worked by the foot on an organ □ verb 1 to work the pedals of 2 to ride on a bicycle

pedal verb ⇨ pedals, pedalling, pedalled

pedant noun 1 someone who makes a great show of their knowledge 2 someone overly fussy about minor details

pedantic adjective over-concerned with correctness

pedantry noun 1 fussiness about

unimportant details **2** a display of knowledge

peddle *verb* to travel from door to door selling goods

pedestal *noun* the foot or support of a pillar, statue *etc*

pedestrian *adjective* **1** going on foot **2** for those on foot **3** unexciting, dull: *a pedestrian account* □ *noun* someone who goes or travels on foot

pedestrian crossing a place where pedestrians may cross the road when the traffic stops

pediatrics, pediatrician *US spelling* of **paediatrics, paediatrician**

pedicure *noun* a treatment for the feet including treating corns, cutting nails *etc*

pedicurist *noun* someone who gives a pedicure

pedigree *noun* **1** a list of someone's ancestors **2** the ancestry of a pure-bred animal **3** a distinguished descent or ancestry □ *adjective* of an animal: pure-bred, from a long line of ancestors of the same breed

Literally 'crane's foot', because the forked feet of the bird were thought to resemble the lines of a family tree

pediment *noun* a triangular structure over the front of an ancient Greek building

pedlar *noun* someone who peddles, a hawker

pedo- *see* **paedo-**

pee *verb, informal* to urinate □ *noun* **1** the act of urinating **2** urine
  pee *verb* ⇨ pee**s**, pee**ing**, pee**d**

peek *verb* to peep, glance, especially secretively □ *noun* a secret look

peel *verb* **1** to strip off the outer covering or skin of: *peel an apple* **2** of skin, paint *etc*: to come off in small pieces **3** to lose skin in small flakes, *eg* as a result of sunburn □ *noun* skin, rind
Ⓛ Comes from Latin *pelare* meaning 'to deprive of hair'

  ◆ Do not confuse with: **peal**

peelie-wally *adjective, Scottish* pale-looking, off-colour

peep *verb* **1** to look through a narrow opening, round a corner *etc* **2** to look slyly or quickly (at) **3** to begin to appear: *the sun peeped out* **4** to make a high, small sound □ *noun* **1** a quick look, a glimpse, often from hiding **2** a high, small sound

peeping Tom someone who spies secretly on people, especially when they are undressing

peer *verb* to look at with half-closed eyes, as if with difficulty □ *noun* **1** someone's equal in rank, merit or age **2** a nobleman of the rank of baron upwards **3** a member of the House of Lords

peerage *noun* **1** a peer's title **2** the peers as a group

peerless *adjective* without any equal, better than all others

peeve *verb, informal* to irritate

peeved *adjective* annoyed

peevish *adjective* cross, bad-tempered, irritable

peewit *noun* the lapwing

peg *noun* **1** a pin or stake of wood, metal *etc* **2** a hook fixed to a wall for hanging clothes *etc* □ *verb* **1** to fasten with a peg **2** to fix (prices *etc*) at a certain level
  peg *verb* ⇨ pegs, pegging, pegged

pejorative *adjective* showing disapproval, scorn *etc*: *a pejorative remark*

Pekinese or **Pekingese** *noun* a breed of small dog with a long coat and flat face

pelican *noun* a large waterbird with a pouched bill for storing fish

pelican crossing a street-crossing where the lights are operated by pedestrians
Taken from the phrase '*pe*destrian *li*ght *con*trolled crossing'

pellet **1** a small ball of shot *etc* **2** a small pill

pell-mell *adverb* in great confusion; headlong

Pelmanism *noun* a card-game in which cards are spread out face down and must be picked up in matching pairs

Named after a form of memory training devised by the *Pelman* Institute

pelmet *noun* a strip or band hiding a curtain rail

pelt *noun* the untreated skin of an animal □ *verb* **1** to throw (things) at **2** to run fast **3** of rain: to fall heavily □ **at full pelt** at top speed

pelvis *noun* the frame of bone which circles the body below the waist

pen[1] *noun* an instrument with a nib for writing in ink □ *verb* to write (*eg* a letter)

pen ⇨ pen*s*, penn*ing*, penn*ed*

pen[2] *noun* a small enclosure for sheep, cattle *etc* □ *verb* to enclose in a pen

pen[3] *noun* a female swan

penalize *verb* **1** to punish **2** to put under a disadvantage

penal servitude imprisonment with hard labour as an added punishment

penalty *noun* (*plural* **penalties**) **1** punishment **2** a disadvantage put on a player or team for having broken a rule of a game

penance *noun* punishment willingly suffered by someone to make up for a wrong

pence *plural* of **penny**

penchant *noun* an inclination (for), a bias

pencil *noun* an instrument containing a length of graphite or other substance for writing, drawing *etc* □ *verb* to draw, mark *etc* with a pencil

pencil *verb* ⇨ pencil*s*, pencill*ing*, pencill*ed*

pendant *noun* **1** an ornament hung from a necklace *etc* **2** a necklace with such an ornament

pendent *adjective* hanging

pending *adjective* awaiting a decision or attention: *this matter is pending* □ *preposition* awaiting, until the coming of: *pending confirmation*

pendulous *adjective* hanging down, drooping

pendulum *noun* a swinging weight which drives the mechanism of a clock

penetrate *verb* **1** to pierce or pass into or through **2** to enter by force

penetrating *adjective* **1** of a sound: piercing **2** keen, probing: *penetrating question*

penetration *noun* **1** the process of penetrating or being penetrated: *penetration of the Japanese market* **2** the ability to understand quickly and clearly

pen-friend *noun* someone you have never seen (usually living abroad) with whom you exchange letters

penguin *noun* a large sea bird of Antarctic regions, which cannot fly

penicillin *noun* a medicine obtained from mould, which kills many bacteria

peninsula *noun* a piece of land almost surrounded by water

peninsular *adjective* relating to or of the nature of a peninsula

penis *noun* the part of the body which a male human or animal uses in sexual intercourse and for urinating

penitence *noun* being penitent and wishing to improve

penitent *adjective* sorry for your sins □ *noun* a penitent person

penitential *adjective* relating to penitence or penance

penitentiary *noun*, *US* a prison

penknife *noun* a pocket knife with folding blades

pen-name *noun* a name adopted by a writer instead of their own name

pennant *noun* a long flag coming to a point at the end

penniless *adjective* having no money

penny *noun* **1** a coin worth $\frac{1}{100}$ of £1 **2** (*plural* **pence**) used to show an amount in pennies: *the newspaper costs forty-two pence* **3** (*plural* **pennies**) used for a number of coins: *I need five pennies for the coffee machine*

penny-farthing *noun* a old type of bicycle with a large front wheel and small rear wheel

penny-pinching *adjective* mean, stingy

pension *noun* a sum of money paid regularly to a retired person, a widow, someone wounded in war *etc* □ **pension off** to dismiss or allow to retire with a pension

pensionable *adjective* having or giving the right to a pension: *pensionable age*

pensioner *noun* someone who receives a pension

pensive *adjective* thoughtful □ **pensively** *adverb*

pent or **pent-up** *adjective* **1** shut up, not allowed to go free **2** of emotions: not freely expressed

penta- *prefix* five
Ⓛ Comes from Greek *pente* meaning 'five'

pentagon *noun* a five-sided figure □ **the Pentagon** the headquarters of the US armed forces in Washington, DC

pentagonal *adjective* having five sides and angles

pentathlete *noun* an athlete who takes part in the pentathlon

pentathlon *noun* a five-event contest in the Olympic Games *etc*

pentatonic *adjective, music* of a scale: consisting of five notes, *ie* a major scale omitting the fourth and seventh

Pentecost *noun* **1** a Jewish festival held fifty days after Passover **2** a Christian festival held seven weeks after Easter

penthouse *noun* a luxurious flat at the top of a building

penultimate *adjective* last but one

penumbra *noun* a light shadow surrounding the main shadow of an eclipse

penurious *adjective* impoverished, penniless

penury *noun* poverty, want

peony *noun* (*plural* **peonies**) a type of garden plant with large red, white or pink flowers

people *noun plural* **1** the men, women and children of a country or nation **2** persons generally □ *verb* **1** to fill with people **2** to inhabit, make up the population of
Ⓛ Comes from Latin *populus* meaning 'a people' or 'a nation'

pep *noun, informal* spirit, verve □ **pep up** to invigorate, enliven

pepper *noun* **1** a plant whose berries are dried, powdered and used as seasoning **2** the spicy powder it produces **3** a hot-tasting hollow fruit containing many seeds, eaten raw, cooked or pickled □ *verb* **1** to sprinkle with pepper **2** **pepper with** to throw at or hit: *peppered with bullets*

peppercorn *noun* the dried berry of the pepper plant

pepper mill a small device for grinding peppercorns over food

peppermint *noun* **1** a type of plant with a powerful taste and smell **2** a flavouring taken from this and used in sweets *etc*

peppery *adjective* **1** containing much pepper **2** inclined to be hot-tempered

pep pill a pill containing a stimulating drug

pep talk a talk meant to encourage or arouse enthusiasm

peptic *adjective* of the digestive system: *peptic ulcer*

per *preposition* **1** in, out of **2** for each: *£2 per dozen* **3** in each: *six times per week* □ **per annum** in each year □ **per capita** or **per head** for each person □ **per cent** out of every hundred: *five per cent* (= 5 out of every hundred)

perambulator *full form of* **pram**

perceive *verb* **1** to become aware of through the senses **2** to see **3** to understand

percentage *noun* the rate per hundred

perceptible *adjective* able to be seen or understood

perception *noun* the ability to perceive; understanding

perceptive *adjective* able or quick to perceive or understand

perch[1] *noun* (*plural* **perches**) **1** a rod on which birds roost **2** a high seat or position □ *verb* to roost

perch[2] *noun* (*plural* **perches**) a type of freshwater fish

perchance *adverb, old* by chance; perhaps

percolate *verb* **1** of a liquid: to drip or drain through small holes **2** to cause (a liquid) to do this **3** of news *etc*: to pass slowly down or through

percolator *noun* a device for percolating: *a coffee percolator*

percussion *noun* **1** a striking of one object against another **2** musical instruments played by striking, *eg* drums, cymbals *etc*

percussive *adjective* making the noise of percussion; loud, striking

perdition *noun* **1** utter loss or ruin **2** everlasting punishment

peregrinations *noun plural* wanderings

peregrine *noun* a type of falcon used in hawking

peremptory *adjective* **1** urgent **2** of a command: to be obeyed at once **3** domineering, dictatorial

perennial *adjective* **1** lasting through the year **2** everlasting, perpetual **3** of a plant: growing from year to year without replanting or sowing □ *noun* a perennial plant

perestroika (*pronounced* pe-ris-**troi**-ka) *noun* reconstruction, restructuring of the state (originally in the former Soviet Union)

perfect *adjective* (*pronounced* **per**-fikt) **1** complete, finished **2** faultless **3** exact □ *verb* (*pronounced* pe-**fekt**) **1** to make perfect **2** to finish

■ **Alternative words**: (adjective, meaning 2) impeccable, flawless, immaculate; (adjective, meaning 3) precise, accurate, true

perfection *noun* **1** the state of being perfect **2** the highest state or degree

perfectionist *noun* someone who is satisfied only by perfection

perfidious (*pronounced* pe-**fid**-i-*us*) *adjective* treacherous, unfaithful

perfidy (*pronounced* **per**-fi-di) *noun* perfidious behaviour or an instance of this

perforate *verb* to make a hole or holes through

perforated *adjective* pierced with holes

perforce *adverb*, *old* of necessity, unavoidably

perform *verb* **1** to do, act **2** to act (a part) on the stage **3** to provide entertainment for an audience **4** to play (a piece of music)

performance *noun* **1** an entertainment in a theatre *etc* **2** the act of doing something **3** the level of success of a machine, car *etc*

performer *noun* someone who acts or performs

perfume *noun* **1** smell, fragrance **2** a fragrant liquid put on the skin, scent □ *verb* **1** to put scent on or in **2** to give a sweet smell to

perfumery *noun* a shop or factory where perfume is sold or made

perfunctory *adjective* done carelessly or half-heartedly: *perfunctory inspection* □ **perfunctorily** *adverb*

perhaps *adverb* it may be (that), possibly: *perhaps she'll resign*

peri- *prefix* around: *perimeter* (= the outside line around a figure or shape)/ *perinatal* (= around the time of birth) ① Comes from Greek *peri* meaning 'around'

peril *noun* a great danger □ **at your peril** at your own risk

perilous *adjective* very dangerous □ **perilously** *adverb*

perimeter *noun* **1** the outside line enclosing a figure or shape **2** the outer edge of any area ① Comes from Greek *peri* meaning 'around', and *metron* meaning 'measure'

🖝 Do not confuse with: **parameter**. Notice that words starting with **peri-** often relate to the idea of 'going around' – and the **perimeter** of a figure or shape is the line that goes around it

perinatal *adjective* relating to the period between the seventh month of pregnancy and the first week of the baby's life

perineal *adjective* relating to the perineum

perineum *noun* the part of the body between the genitals and the anus

period *noun* **1** a stretch of time **2** a stage in the earth's development or in history **3** a full stop after a sentence **4** a time of menstruation

periodic *adjective* **1** of a period **2** happening at regular intervals, *eg* every month or year **3** happening every now and then: *a periodic clearing out of rubbish*

periodical *adjective* issued or done at regular intervals; periodic □ *noun* a magazine which appears at regular intervals

peripatetic *adjective* moving from place to place; travelling

peripheral *adjective* **1** of or on a periphery; away from the centre **2** not essential, of little importance

periphery *noun* (*plural* **peripheries**) **1** the line surrounding something **2** an outer boundary or edge

periphrastic *adjective* of speech: roundabout, using more words than necessary

periscope *noun* a tube with mirrors by which a viewer in a submarine *etc* is able to see objects on the surface

perish *verb* **1** to be destroyed, pass away completely; die **2** to decay, rot

perishable *adjective* liable to go bad quickly

peristyle *noun* a group of columns surrounding a building

peritoneum *noun* a membrane in the stomach and pelvis

peritonitis *noun* inflammation of the peritoneum

periwinkle *noun* **1** a small shellfish, shaped like a small snail, eaten as food when boiled **2** a creeping evergreen plant with a small blue flower

perjure *verb* (**perjure yourself** *etc*) to tell a lie when you have sworn to tell the truth, especially in a court of law

perjurer *noun* a person who commits perjury

perjury *noun* the crime of lying while under oath in a court of law

perk¹ *noun* something of value allowed in addition to payment for work; a side benefit

perk² *verb*: **perk up** to recover energy or spirits

perky *adjective* jaunty, in good spirits □ **perkily** *adverb*

perm *noun* short for **permanent wave** □ *verb* to give a permanent wave to (hair)

permaculture *noun* farming without using artificial fertilizers and with minimal weeding

permafrost *noun* permanently frozen subsoil

permanence or **permanency** *noun* the state of continuing or remaining for a long time or for ever

permanent *adjective* lasting, not temporary □ **permanently** *adverb*

permanent wave a wave or curl put into the hair by a special process and usually lasting for some months

permeable *adjective* able to be permeated by liquids, gases *etc*

permeate *verb* **1** to pass into through small holes, soak into **2** to fill every part of

permissible *adjective* allowable

permission *noun* freedom given to do something

permissive *adjective* **1** allowing something to be done **2** too tolerant □ **permissiveness** *noun*: *the permissiveness of the 1960s*

permit *verb* (*pronounced* pe-**mit**) **1** to agree to an action, allow **2** to make possible □ *noun* (*pronounced* **per**-mit) a written order, allowing someone to do something: *a fishing permit*

permutation *noun* **1** the arrangement of numbers, letters *etc* in a certain order **2** the act of changing the order of things

pernicious *adjective* destructive

pernickety *adjective* fussy about small details

peroration *noun* **1** the closing part of a speech **2** a speech

peroxide a chemical (hydrogen peroxide) used for bleaching hair *etc*

perpendicular *adjective* **1** standing upright, vertical **2** at right angles (to) □ *noun* a line at right angles to another

perpetrate *verb* to commit (a sin, error *etc*)
Ⓛ Comes from Latin *perpetrare* meaning 'to achieve'

☛ Do not confuse with: **perpetuate**

perpetration *noun* 1 perpetrating 2 something that is perpetrated

perpetrator *noun* a person who perpetrates; the one who is guilty

perpetual *adjective* everlasting, unending □ **perpetually** *adverb*

perpetuate *verb* to make to last for ever or for a long time
Ⓛ Comes from Latin *perpetuare* meaning 'to cause to continue uninterruptedly'

☛ Do not confuse with: **perpetrate**

perpetuity *noun* □ **in perpetuity** 1 for ever 2 for the length of someone's life

perplex *verb* 1 to puzzle, bewilder 2 to make more complicated

perplexity *noun* 1 a puzzled state of mind 2 something which puzzles

perquisite *noun* a perk

per se *adverb* in itself, essentially

persecute *verb* 1 to harass over a period of time 2 to cause to suffer, especially because of religious beliefs
Ⓛ Comes from Latin *persequi* meaning 'to follow persistently'

☛ Do not confuse with: **prosecute**

persecution *noun* persecuting or being persecuted

persecutor *noun* a person who persecutes

perseverance *noun* the act of persevering

persevere *verb* to keep trying to do a thing (in spite of difficulties)

persist *verb* 1 to hold fast to (*eg* an idea) 2 to continue to do something in spite of difficulties 3 to survive, last

persistence *noun* 1 persisting 2 being persistent

persistent *adjective* 1 obstinate, refusing to be discouraged 2 lasting, not dying out □ **persistently** *adverb*

person *noun* 1 a human being 2 someone's body: *jewels hidden on his person* 3 form, shape: *trouble arrived in*

the person of Gordon □ **in person** personally, not represented by someone else

persona *noun* the outward part of the personality presented to others; social image

personable *adjective* good-looking

personage *noun* a well-known person

personal *adjective* 1 your own; private: *personal belongings* 2 of a remark: insulting, offensive to the person it is aimed at
Ⓛ Comes from Latin *persona* meaning 'an actor's mask'

☛ Do not confuse with: **personnel**

personality *noun* (*plural* **personalities**) 1 all of a person's characteristics as seen by others 2 a well-known person

personally *adverb* 1 speaking from your own point of view 2 by your own action, not using an agent or representative: *he thanked me personally*

personal organizer a small loose-leaf filing system containing a diary and an address book, maps, indexes *etc*

personal stereo a small portable cassette player with earphones

persona non grata someone disliked or out of favour

personification *noun* 1 giving human qualities to things or ideas 2 in art or literature, representing an idea or quality as a person 3 a person or thing that is seen as a perfect example of a quality: *the personification of patience*

personify *verb* 1 to talk about things, ideas *etc* as if they were living persons (*eg* 'Time marches on') 2 to typify, be a perfect example of

personify ⇨ personifies, personifying, personified

personnel (*pronounced* pers-*o*-nel) *noun* the people employed in a firm *etc*

☛ Do not confuse with: **personal**.

Personnel is a noun coming from French company terminology, used to describe the 'person-assets' of a company (= the people who work for it) in contrast to its 'material-assets' (= all its non-human items of value)

perspective *noun* 1 a point of view 2 the giving of a sense of depth, distance *etc* in a painting like that in real life □ **in perspective** 1 of an object in a painting *etc*: of a size in relation to other things that it would have in real life 2 of an event: in its true degree of importance when considered in relation to other events: *keep things in perspective*

Perspex *noun, trademark* a transparent plastic which looks like glass

perspicacious *adjective* of clear or sharp understanding

perspicacity *noun* keenness of understanding

perspicuity *noun* clearness in expressing thoughts

perspiration *noun* sweat

perspire *verb* to sweat

persuade *verb* to bring someone to do or think something, by arguing with them or advising them

persuasion *noun* 1 the act of persuading 2 a firm belief, especially a religious belief

persuasive *adjective* having the power to convince

pert *adjective* saucy, cheeky

pertain to *verb* to belong, have to do with: *duties pertaining to the job*

pertinacious *adjective* holding strongly to an idea, obstinate

pertinacity *noun* obstinacy

pertinent *adjective* connected with the subject spoken about, to the point

perturb *verb* to disturb greatly; to make anxious or uneasy

perturbation *noun* great worry, anxiety

perusal *noun* perusing; careful reading

peruse *verb* to read (with care)

pervade *verb* to spread through: *silence pervaded the room*

perverse *adjective* obstinate in holding to the wrong point of view; unreasonable

perverseness or **perversity** *noun* stubbornness

perversion *noun* 1 the act of perverting 2 an unnatural or perverted act

pervert *verb* 1 to turn away from what is normal or right: *pervert the course of justice* 2 to turn (someone) to crime or evil; corrupt □ *noun* someone who commits unnatural or perverted acts

pessimism *noun* the habit of thinking that things will always turn out badly (*contrasted with*: **optimism**)

pessimist *noun* someone who tends to think that things will always turn out badly

pessimistic *adjective* relating to or characterized by pessimism □ **pessimistically** *adverb*

pest *noun* 1 a troublesome person or thing 2 a creature that is harmful or destructive, *eg* a mosquito

pester *verb* to annoy continually

pesticide *noun* any substance which kills animal pests

pestilence *noun* a deadly, spreading disease

pestilent or **pestilential** *adjective* 1 very unhealthy 2 troublesome

pestle *noun* a tool for pounding things to powder

pet *noun* 1 a tame animal kept in the home, such as a cat 2 a favourite 3 a fit of sulks □ *adjective* 1 kept as a pet 2 favourite 3 chief: *my pet hate* □ *verb* to fondle

pet *verb* ⇨ pet**s**, pet**ting**, pet**ted**

petal *noun* one of the leaf-like parts of a flower

petard *noun*: **hoist with your own petard** caught in a trap of your own making

peter *verb*: **peter out** to fade or dwindle away to nothing

petite *adjective* small and neat in appearance

petition *noun* a request or note of protest signed by many people and sent to a government or authority □ *verb* to send a petition to

petitioner *noun* 1 a person who petitions 2 a person who applies for a divorce

petrel *noun* a small, long-winged sea-bird

petrifaction *noun* the process whereby something is turned into stone

petrify *verb* 1 to turn into stone 2 to turn (someone) stiff with fear

> **petrify** ⇨ petrif*ies*, petrify*ing*, petrif*ied*

petrol *noun* petroleum when refined as fuel for use in cars *etc*

petroleum *noun* oil in its raw, unrefined form, extracted from natural wells below the earth's surface

petticoat *noun* an underskirt worn by women

pettifogger *noun* a lawyer who deals in trivial cases

pettish *adjective* sulky

petty *adjective* of little importance, trivial □ **pettiness** *noun*

petty cash money paid or received in small sums

petty officer a rank of officer in the navy (equal to a non-commissioned officer in the army)

petulance *noun* being petulant

petulant *adjective* 1 cross, irritable 2 unreasonably impatient

petunia *noun* a S American flowering plant related to tobacco

pew *noun* a seat or bench in a church

pewter *noun* a mixture of tin and lead

PG *abbreviation* parental guidance (certificate awarded to a film denoting possible unsuitability for young children)

phagocyte *noun* a white blood corpuscle that surrounds and destroys bacteria

phalanx *noun* (*plural* **phalanxes**) 1 a company of foot soldiers in an oblong-shaped formation 2 a group of supporters

phallic *adjective* relating to or resembling a phallus

phallus *noun* a representation of a penis

phantasm *noun* a vision, an illusion

phantasmagoria *noun* a dream-like series of visions or hallucinations

phantom *noun* a ghost

Pharaoh *noun, historical* a ruler of ancient Egypt

pharmaceutical *adjective* relating to the making up of medicines and drugs

pharmacist *noun* someone who prepares and sells medicines

pharmacy *noun* (*plural* **pharmacies**) 1 the art of preparing medicines 2 a chemist's shop

pharmacological *adjective* relating to or involving pharmacology

pharmacologist *noun* an expert in pharmacology

pharmacology *noun* the scientific study of drugs and their effects

pharynx *noun* the back part of the throat behind the tonsils

phase *noun* 1 one in a series of changes in the shape or appearance of something (*eg* the moon) 2 a stage in the development of something (*eg* a war, a scheme *etc*)

PhD *abbreviation* Doctor of Philosophy

pheasant *noun* a bird with brightly-coloured feathers which is shot as game

phenomenal *adjective* very unusual, remarkable

phenomenally *adverb* extremely: *phenomenally successful*

phenomenon *noun* (*plural* **phenomena**) 1 an event (especially in nature) that is observed by the senses: *the phenomenon of lightning* 2 something remarkable or very unusual, a wonder

phial *noun* a small glass bottle

phil- *see* philo-

philander *verb* to flirt, or have casual love affairs, with women

philanderer *noun* a womanizer

philanthropic *adjective* kind and generous

philanthropist *noun* someone who does good to others

philanthropy *noun* love of mankind, often shown by giving money for the benefit of others

philatelist *noun* a stamp-collector

philately *noun* the study and collecting of stamps

philharmonic *adjective* (in names of orchestras *etc*) music-loving

philistine *noun* someone ignorant of, or hostile to, culture and the arts

After a people of ancient Palestine, enemies of the Israelites

philo-, phil- *prefix* forms words related to the love of a particular thing: *philharmonic/ philosopher* (= a friend or lover of wisdom)
Ⓛ Comes from Greek *philos* meaning 'friend', and *phileein* meaning 'to love'

philologist *noun* a person who studies or is expert in philology

philology *noun* the study of words and their history

philosopher *noun* someone who studies philosophy

philosophic or **philosophical** *adjective* **1** of philosophy **2** calm, not easily upset

philosophy *noun* (*plural* **philosophies**) **1** the study of the nature of the universe, or of human behaviour **2** someone's personal view of life

philtre *noun* a love potion

phlegm (*pronounced* flem) *noun* **1** thick slimy matter brought up from the throat by coughing **2** coolness of temper, calmness

phlegmatic (*pronounced* fleg-**mat**-ik) *adjective* not easily excited

phobia *noun* an intense, often irrational, fear or dislike
Ⓛ Comes from Greek *phobos* meaning 'fear'

phoenix (*pronounced* fee-niks) *noun* a mythological bird believed to burn itself and to rise again from its ashes

phon- *prefix* forms words relating to sound or speech: *phonetics*
Ⓛ Comes from Greek *phone* meaning 'sound' or 'voice'

phone *noun* short for **telephone**

phonecard *noun* a card that can be used instead of cash to operate certain public telephones

phoneme *noun* the smallest meaningful unit of sound in a language

phonetic *adjective* **1** relating to the sounds of language **2** of a word: spelt according to sound, *eg* flem for 'phlegm'

phonetics *noun singular* **1** the study of the sounds of language **2** a system of writing according to sound

phoney or **phony** *adjective, informal* fake, not genuine

phosphate *noun* a soil fertilizer containing phosphorus

phosphorescence *noun* faint glow of light in the dark

phosphorescent *adjective* glowing in the dark

phosphorus *noun* a wax-like, poisonous substance that gives out light in the dark

photo *noun* (*plural* **photos**) *informal* a photograph

photo- *prefix* **1** of or relating to light: *photosensitive/ photograph* **2** forms words relating to photography: *photocopy/ photogenic*
Ⓛ Comes from Greek *photos* meaning 'of light'

photocopy *noun* a copy of a document made by a device which photographs and develops images of the document □ *verb* to make a photocopy of

photofit *noun, trademark* a method of making identification pictures by combining photographs of individual features

photogenic *adjective* being a good subject for a photograph; photographing well

photograph *noun* a picture taken with a camera □ *verb* to take a picture with a camera

photographer *noun* a person who takes photographs, especially professionally

photography *noun* the art of taking pictures with a camera

photosensitive *adjective* affected by light

photosynthesis *noun* the conversion of light into complex compounds by plants

phrase *noun* **1** a small group of words

expressing a single idea, eg 'after dinner', 'on the water' **2** a short saying or expression **3** *music* a short group of bars forming a distinct unit □ *verb* to express in words: *he could have phrased it more tactfully*

phraseology (*pronounced* freiz-i-**ol**-oj-i) *noun* someone's personal choice of words and phrases

phrenology *noun* the study of the surface of the skull as a sign of personality *etc*

physical *adjective* **1** relating to the body: *physical strength/ physical exercises* **2** relating to things that can be seen or felt □ **physically** *adverb*: *he is physically fit*

physician *noun* a doctor specializing in medical rather than surgical treatment

physicist *noun* someone who specializes in physics

physics *noun singular* the science which includes the study of heat, light, sound, electricity, magnetism *etc*

physio- *prefix* **1** of or relating to body or the natural processes of life: *physiology* **2** forms words describing the treatment of disease by physical rather than medicinal means: *physiotherapy* ⊙ Comes from Greek *physis* meaning 'nature'

physiognomy *noun* the features or expression of the face

physiological *adjective* relating to or involving physiology

physiologist *noun* a person skilled in physiology

physiology *noun* the study of the way in which living bodies work, including blood circulation, food digestion *etc*

physiotherapist *noun* a person skilled in treatment by physiotherapy

physiotherapy *noun* the treatment of disease by bodily exercise, massage *etc* rather than by drugs

physique *noun* **1** the build of someone's body **2** bodily strength

pianist *noun* someone who plays the piano

piano *noun* (*plural* **pianos**) a large

musical instrument played by striking keys

piazza *noun* a market-place or town square surrounded by buildings

piccolo *noun* (*plural* **piccolos**) a small, high-pitched flute

pick *verb* **1** to choose **2** to pluck, gather (flowers, fruit *etc*) **3** to peck, bite, nibble (at) **4** to poke, probe (teeth *etc*) **5** to open (a lock) with a tool other than a key □ *noun* **1** choice: *take your pick* **2** the best or best part **3** a pickaxe **4** an instrument for picking, eg a toothpick □ **pick a quarrel** to start a quarrel deliberately □ **pick on 1** to single out for criticism *etc* **2** to nag at □ **pick up 1** to lift up **2** to learn (a language, habit *etc*) **3** to give (someone) a lift in a car **4** to find or get by chance **5** to improve, gain strength

pickaxe *noun* a heavy tool for breaking ground, pointed at one end or both ends

picket *noun* **1** a pointed stake **2** a small sentry-post or guard **3** a number of workers on strike who prevent others from going into work □ *verb* **1** to fasten (a horse *etc*) to a stake **2** to place a guard or a group of strikers at (a place)

pickle *noun* **1** a liquid in which food is preserved **2** vegetables preserved in vinegar **3** *informal* an awkward, unpleasant situation □ *verb* to preserve with salt, vinegar *etc*

pickpocket *noun* someone who robs people's pockets or handbags

picky *adjective* choosy, fussy

picnic *noun* a meal eaten out-of-doors, often during an outing *etc* □ *verb* to have a picnic

picnic *verb* ⊳ picnic**s**, picnick**ing**, picnick**ed**

pictorial *adjective* **1** having pictures **2** consisting of pictures **3** calling up pictures in the mind

picture *noun* **1** a painting or drawing **2** a portrait **3** a photograph **4** a film **5** **the pictures** the cinema **6** a vivid description □ *verb* **1** to make a picture of **2** to see in the mind, imagine

picturesque *adjective* such as would make a good or striking picture; pretty, colourful

PID *abbreviation* pelvic inflammatory disease

pidgin *noun* a distorted form of a language arising because of its combination with a different language

Pidgin is a distorted form of the word 'business', originally used in Chinese

💣 Do not confuse with: **pigeon**

pie *noun* meat, fruit or other food baked in a casing or covering of pastry

piebald *adjective* white and black in patches

piece *noun* 1 a part or portion of anything 2 a single article or example: *a piece of paper* 3 an artistic work: *a piece of popular music* 4 a coin 5 a man in chess, draughts *etc* □ *verb* to put (together)

pièce de résistance (*pronounced* pyes de rei-zis-**tons**) the best item or work

piecemeal *adverb* by pieces, little by little

piecework *noun* work paid according to how much is done, not to the time spent on it

pied *adjective* with two or more colours in patches

pier *noun* 1 a platform stretching from the shore into the sea as a landing place for ships 2 a pillar supporting an arch, bridge *etc*

pierce *verb* to make a hole through; force a way into; move (the feelings) deeply

piercing *adjective* shrill, loud; sharp

piety *noun* the quality of being pious

piffle *noun* nonsense

pig *noun* 1 a farm animal, from whose flesh ham and bacon are made 2 an oblong moulded piece of metal (*eg* pig-iron)

pigeon *noun* a bird of the dove family ⓘ Comes from Latin *pipire* meaning 'to cheep'

💣 Do not confuse with: **pidgin**

pigeon-hole *noun* a small division in a case or desk for papers *etc* □ *verb* 1 to lay aside 2 to classify, put into a category

piggery *noun* (*plural* **piggeries**) or **pigsty** *noun* (*plural* **pigsties**) a place where pigs are kept

piggy-back *noun* a ride on someone's back with your arms round their neck

piggy-bank *noun* a china pig with a slit along its back to insert coins for saving

pig-headed *adjective* stubborn

pigment *noun* 1 paint or other substance used for colouring 2 a substance in animals and plants that gives colour to the skin *etc*

pigmentation *noun* colouring of skin *etc*

pigmy *another spelling of* **pygmy**

pigtail *noun* hair formed into a plait

pike *noun* 1 a freshwater fish 2 a weapon like a spear, with a long shaft and a sharp head

pilchard *noun* a small sea-fish like a herring, often tinned

pile *noun* 1 a number of things lying one on top of another, a heap 2 a great quantity 3 a large building 4 a large stake or pillar driven into the earth as a foundation for a building, bridge *etc* 5 the thick, soft surface on carpets and on cloth such as velvet □ *verb* (often **pile up** or **pile something up**) to make or form a pile or heap

piles *noun plural* haemorrhoids

pilfer *verb* to steal small things

pilgrim *noun* a traveller to a holy place

pilgrimage *noun* a journey to a holy place

pill *noun* 1 a tablet of medicine 2 (often **the pill**) a contraceptive in the form of a small tablet taken by mouth

pillage *verb* to seize goods and money, especially as loot in war □ *noun* the act of plundering in this way

pillar *noun* 1 an upright support for roofs, arches *etc* 2 an upright post or column as a monument 3 someone or something that gives support: *a pillar of the community*

pillarbox *noun* a tall box with a slot through which letters *etc* are posted

pillion *noun* 1 a seat for a passenger on

a motor-cycle **2** *old* a light saddle for a passenger on horseback, behind the main saddle

pillory *noun* (*plural* **pillories**) *historical* a wooden frame fitted over the head and hands of wrongdoers as a punishment □ *verb* to mock in public

> **pillory** *verb* ⇨ pillories, pillorying, pilloried

pillow *noun* a soft cushion for the head □ *verb* to rest or support on a pillow

pillowcase or **pillowslip** *noun* a cover for a pillow

pilot *noun* **1** someone who steers a ship in or out of a harbour **2** someone who flies an aeroplane **3** a guide, a leader □ *verb* to steer, guide

pilot-light *noun* **1** a small gas-light from which larger jets are lit **2** an electric light showing that a current is switched on

pilot scheme a scheme introduced on a small scale to act as a guide to a full-scale one

pimp *noun* a man who manages prostitutes and takes money from them

pimpernel *noun* a plant of the primrose family, with small pink or scarlet flowers

pimple *noun* a small round infected swelling on the skin

pimpled or **pimply** *adjective* having pimples

PIN (*pronounced* pin) *abbreviation* personal identification number (for automatic teller machines *etc*)

pin *noun* **1** a short pointed piece of metal with a small round head, used for fastening fabric **2** a wooden or metal peg **3** a skittle □ *verb* **1** to fasten with a pin **2** to hold fast, pressed against something: *the bloodhound pinned him to the ground*

> **pin** *verb* ⇨ pins, pinning, pinned

pinafore *noun* **1** an apron to protect the front of a dress **2** a sleeveless dress worn over a jersey, blouse *etc*

pinball *noun* a game played on a slot-machine in which a ball runs down a sloping board between obstacles

pincers *noun plural* **1** a tool like pliers,

but with sharp points for gripping, pulling out nails *etc* **2** the claw of a crab or lobster

pinch *verb* **1** to squeeze (especially flesh) between the thumb and forefinger, nip **2** to grip tightly, hurt by tightness **3** *informal* to steal □ *noun* (*plural* **pinches**) **1** a squeeze, a nip **2** a small amount (*eg* of salt) □ **at a pinch** if really necessary or urgent □ **feel the pinch** to suffer from lack of money

pinchbeck *adjective* sham, in poor imitation

> From Christopher *Pinchbeck*, a 17th-century watchmaker who invented a copper alloy to imitate gold

pinched *adjective* of a face: looking cold, pale or thin

pine *noun* **1** an evergreen tree with needle-like leaves which produces cones **2** the soft wood of such a tree used for furniture *etc* □ *verb* **1** to waste away, lose strength **2** to long (for something)

pineapple *noun* a large tropical fruit shaped like a pine-cone

ping *noun* a whistling sound such as that of a bullet □ *verb* to make a brief high-pitched sound

ping-pong *noun*, *trademark* table-tennis

pinion *noun* **1** a bird's wing **2** a small toothed wheel □ *verb* **1** to hold (someone) fast by binding or holding their arms **2** to cut or fasten the wings of (a bird)

pink *noun* **1** a pale red colour **2** a sweet-scented garden flower like a carnation **3** a healthy or good state: *feeling in the pink* □ *verb* **1** of an engine: to make a faint clinking noise **2** to cut (cloth *etc*) with pinking scissors

pinkie *noun*, *informal* the little finger

pinking scissors or **pinking shears** scissors with blades which give cloth a zig-zag edge

pinnacle *noun* **1** a slender spire or turret **2** a high pointed rock or mountain **3** the highest point

pinnie *noun*, *informal* an apron or overall

pint *noun* a liquid measure equal to just over ½ litre

pioneer *noun* **1** an explorer **2** an inventor, or an early exponent of something: *pioneers of the cinema* □ *verb* to act as a pioneer

pious *adjective* respectful in religious matters

pip *noun* **1** a seed of a fruit **2** a spot or symbol on dice or cards **3** a star on an army officer's tunic **4** a short bleep as part of a time signal *etc* on the radio or telephone

pipe *noun* **1** a tube for carrying water, gas *etc* **2** a tube with a bowl at the end, for smoking tobacco **3 pipes** a musical instrument made of several small pipes joined together **4 pipes** bagpipes □ *verb* **1** to play (notes, a tune) on a pipe or pipes **2** to whistle, chirp **3** to speak in a shrill high voice **4** to convey (*eg* water) by pipe □ **pipe down** to become silent, stop talking □ **pipe up** to speak up, express an opinion

pipeline *noun* a long line of pipes, *eg* to carry oil from an oil-field □ **in the pipeline** in preparation, soon to become available

piper *noun* someone who plays a pipe, especially the bagpipes

pipette *noun* a small glass tube used in laboratories

piping *adjective* high-pitched, shrill □ *noun* **1** a length of tubing **2** a system of pipes **3** a narrow ornamental cord for trimming clothes **4** a strip of decorative icing round a cake □ **piping hot** very hot

pippin *noun* a kind of apple

pipsqueak *noun, informal* an insignificant, or very small, person

piquant (*pronounced* **peek**-*a*nt) *adjective* **1** sharp-tasting, spicy **2** arousing interest

pique (*pronounced* peek) *noun* anger caused by wounded pride, spite, resentment □ *verb* **1** to wound the pride of **2** to arouse (curiosity)

piracy *noun* **1** the activity of pirates **2** unauthorized publication or reproduction of copyright material

piranha *noun* a S American river-fish which eats flesh

pirate *noun* **1** someone who robs ships at sea **2** someone who steals or plagiarizes another's work

piratical *adjective* **1** relating to pirates **2** practising piracy

pirouette *noun* a rapid whirling on the toes in dancing □ *verb* to twirl in a pirouette

pistachio *noun* (*plural* **pistachios**) a greenish nut, often used as a flavouring

pistil *noun* the seed-bearing part of a flower

pistol *noun* a small gun held in the hand

piston *noun* a round piece of metal that moves up and down inside a cylinder, *eg* in an engine

pit *noun* **1** a hole in the ground **2** a place from which coal and other minerals are dug **3** the ground floor of a theatre behind the stalls **4** (often **pits**) a place beside the racecourse for repairing and refuelling racing cars *etc* □ *verb* to set one thing or person against another: *pitting my wits against his*

> **pit** *verb* ⇨ pits, pit*ting*, pit*ted*

pitch *verb* **1** to fix a tent *etc* in the ground **2** to throw **3** to fall heavily; lurch: *pitch forward* **4** to set the level or key of a tune □ *noun* (*plural* **pitches**) **1** a thick dark substance obtained by boiling down tar **2** a throw **3** an attempt at selling or persuading: *sales pitch* **4** the height or depth of a note **5** a peak, an extreme point: *reach fever pitch* **6** the field for certain sports **7** *cricket* the ground between wickets **8** the slope of a roof *etc* **9** the spot reserved for a street seller or street-entertainer

pitchblende *noun* a black mineral made up of uranium oxides

pitch-dark *adjective* very dark

pitched battle a battle on chosen ground between sides arranged in position beforehand

pitcher *noun* a kind of large jug

pitchfork *noun* a fork for lifting and throwing hay □ *verb* to throw suddenly and violently

piteous or **pitiable** *adjective* deserving pity; wretched

pitfall *noun* a trap, a possible danger

pith *noun* **1** the soft substance in the centre of plant stems **2** the white substance under the rind of an orange, lemon *etc* **3** the important part of anything

pithy *adjective* **1** full of pith **2** full of meaning, to the point: *a pithy saying*

pitiable *see* **piteous**

pitiful *adjective* poor, wretched

pittance *noun* a very small wage or allowance

pitted *adjective* marked with small holes

pituitary gland a gland in the brain affecting growth

pity *noun* **1** feeling for the sufferings of others, sympathy **2** a cause of grief **3** a regrettable fact □ *verb* to feel sorry for

pity *verb* ⇨ pit**ies**, pit**ying**, pit**ied**

pivot *noun* **1** the pin or centre on which anything turns **2** something or someone greatly depended on □ *verb* **1** to turn on a pivot **2** to depend (on)

pivotal *adjective* **1** acting as a pivot **2** crucially important; critical

pixy or **pixie** *noun* (*plural* **pixies**) a kind of fairy

pizza *noun* a flat piece of dough spread with tomato, cheese *etc* and baked

pizzicato *adverb, music* played by plucking the strings rather than bowing

placard *noun* a printed notice (as an advertisement *etc*) placed on a wall *etc*

placate *verb* to calm, soothe, make less angry *etc*

place *noun* **1** a physical location; any area or building **2** a particular spot **3** an open space in a town: *market place* **4** a seat in a theatre, train, at a table *etc* **5** a position in football *etc* **6** a position on a course, in a job *etc* **7** rank □ *verb* **1** to put in a particular place **2** to find a place for **3** to give (an order for goods *etc*) **4** to remember who someone is: *I can't place him at all* □ **in place 1** in the proper position **2** suitable □ **in place of** instead of □ **out of place**

1 not in the proper position **2** unsuitable

place *verb* ⇨ plac**es**, plac**ing**, plac**ed**

○ Comes from Latin *platea* meaning 'a street'

placed *adjective* **1** having a place **2** among the first three in a competition

placenta *noun* a part of the womb that connects an unborn mammal to its mother, shed at birth

placid *adjective* calm, not easily disturbed

placidity *noun* being placid

plagiarism *noun* plagiarizing

plagiarist *noun* a person who plagiarizes

plagiarize *verb* to steal or borrow from the writings or ideas of someone else without permission

plague *noun* **1** a fatal infectious disease carried by rat fleas **2** a great and troublesome quantity: *a plague of flies* □ *verb* to pester or annoy continually

plaice *noun* a type of edible flatfish

plaid *noun* a long piece of cloth (especially tartan) worn over the shoulder

plain *adjective* **1** flat, level **2** simple, ordinary **3** without ornament or decoration **4** clear, easy to see or understand **5** not good-looking, not attractive □ *noun* a level stretch of land

plain-clothes *adjective* of a police detective: wearing ordinary clothes, not uniform

plaintiff *noun* someone who takes action against another in the law courts

plaintive *adjective* sad, sorrowful

plait *noun* **1** a length of hair arranged by intertwining three or more separate pieces **2** threads *etc* intertwined in this way □ *verb* to form into a plait

plan *noun* **1** a diagram of a building, town *etc* as if seen from above **2** a scheme or arrangement to do something □ *verb* **1** to make a sketch or plan of **2** to decide or arrange to do (something)

plan *verb* ⇨ plan**s**, plan**ning**, plan**ned**

plane[1] *short for* **aeroplane**

plane² *noun* 1 a level surface 2 a carpentry tool for smoothing wood 3 a standard (of achievement *etc*) □ *adjective* flat, level □ *verb* 1 to smooth with a plane 2 to glide over water *etc*

plane³ *noun* a type of tree with broad leaves

planet *noun* any of the bodies (*eg* the earth, Venus) which move round the sun or round another fixed star

planetary *adjective* relating to, consisting of or produced by planets

plank *noun* a long, flat piece of timber

plankton *noun* tiny living creatures floating in seas, lakes *etc*

plant *noun* 1 a living growth from the ground, with a stem, root and leaves 2 a factory or machinery □ *verb* 1 to put (something) into the ground so that it will grow 2 to put (an idea) into the mind 3 to put in position: *plant a bomb* 4 to set down firmly: *plant your feet on the floor* 5 *informal* to place (something) as false evidence

plantation *noun* 1 an area planted with trees 2 an estate for growing cotton, sugar, rubber, tobacco *etc*

planter *noun* the owner of a plantation

plaque *noun* 1 a decorative plate of metal, china *etc* for fixing to a wall 2 a film of saliva and bacteria which forms on the teeth

plasma *noun* the liquid part of blood and certain other fluids

plaster *noun* 1 a mixture of lime, water and sand which sets hard, for covering walls *etc* 2 (*also called* **plaster of Paris**) a fine mixture containing gypsum used for moulding, making casts for broken limbs *etc* 3 a small dressing which can be stuck over a wound □ *adjective* made of plaster □ *verb* 1 to apply plaster to 2 to cover too thickly (with)

plasterer *noun* someone who plasters walls

plastic *adjective* 1 easily moulded or shaped 2 made of plastic □ *noun* a chemically manufactured substance that can be moulded when soft, formed into fibres *etc*

plastic bullet a cylinder of PVC fired from a gun

Plasticine *noun, trademark* a soft clay-like substance used for modelling

plasticity *noun* the quality of being easily moulded

plastic surgery an operation to repair or replace damaged areas of skin, or to improve the appearance of a facial feature

plate *noun* 1 a shallow dish for holding food 2 a flat piece of metal, glass, china *etc* 3 gold and silver articles 4 a sheet of metal used in printing 5 a book illustration 6 the part of false teeth that fits to the mouth □ *verb* to cover with a coating of metal

plateau *noun* (*plural* **plateaus** or **plateaux**) 1 a broad level stretch of high land 2 a steady, unchanging state: *prices have now reached a plateau*

plate-glass *noun* glass in thick sheets, used for shop windows, mirrors *etc*

platform *noun* 1 a raised level surface for passengers at a railway station 2 a raised floor for speakers, entertainers *etc*

plating *noun* a thin covering of metal

platinum *noun* a heavy and very valuable steel-grey metal

platitude *noun* a dull, ordinary remark made as if it were important

platonic *adjective* of a relationship: not sexual

Although originally an adjective describing anything related to the Greek philosopher Plato, **platonic** is now most commonly used with the above meaning based on a Renaissance interpretation of his theory

platoon *noun* a section of a company of soldiers

platter *noun* a large, flat plate

platypus *noun* (*plural* **platypuses**) a small water animal of Australia that has webbed feet and lays eggs (*also called* **duck-billed platypus**)

plaudits *noun plural* applause, praise

plausibility *noun* a plausible quality

plausible *adjective* 1 seeming to be truthful or honest 2 seeming probable or reasonable

play *verb* **1** to amuse yourself **2** to take part in a game **3** to gamble **4** to act (on a stage *etc*) **5** to perform on (a musical instrument) **6** to carry out (a trick) **7** to trifle or fiddle (with): *don't play with your food* **8** to move over lightly: *the firelight played on his face* □ *noun* **1** amusement, recreation **2** gambling **3** a story for acting, a drama **4** a way of behaving: *foul play* **5** freedom of movement □ **play at** to treat in a light-hearted, not serious way: *he only plays at being a businessman* □ **play off** to set off (one person) against another to gain some advantage for yourself □ **play on** to make use of (someone's feelings) to turn to your own advantage □ **a play on words** a pun □ **play the game** to act fairly and honestly
🕔 Comes from Old English verb *plegian*, and noun *plega*

player *noun* **1** an actor **2** someone who plays a game, musical instrument *etc*: *a lute player*

playful *adjective* **1** wanting to play: *a playful kitten* **2** fond of joking, not serious □ **playfully** *adverb*

playground *noun* an open area for playing at school, in a park *etc*

playgroup *noun* a group of young children who play together supervised by adults

playing-card *noun* one of a pack of cards used in playing card games

playmate *noun* a friend with whom you play

play-off *noun* **1** a game to decide a tie **2** a game between the winners of other competitions

playschool *noun* a nursery school or playgroup

plaything *noun* a toy

playwright *noun* a writer of plays

PLC *abbreviation* public limited company

plea *noun* **1** an excuse **2** an accused person's answer to a charge in a law-court **3** an urgent request

plead *verb* **1** to state your case in a lawcourt **2** **plead with someone** to beg earnestly **3** to give as an excuse □ **plead**

guilty or **not guilty** to admit or deny guilt in a law court

pleasant *adjective* giving pleasure; agreeable

pleasantry *noun* (*plural* **pleasantries**) a good-humoured joke

please *verb* **1** to give pleasure or delight to **2** to satisfy **3** to choose, like (to do): *do as you please* □ *exclamation* added for politeness to a command or request: *please keep off the grass* □ **if you please** please

pleasurable *adjective* delightful, pleasant

pleasure *noun* **1** enjoyment, joy, delight **2** what you wish: *what is your pleasure?* □ **at your pleasure** when or if you please

pleat *noun* a fold in cloth, which has been pressed or stitched down □ *verb* to put pleats in

pleated *adjective* having pleats

pleb *noun, informal* someone of no taste or culture, a boor

plebeian *adjective* **1** of the ordinary or common people **2** vulgar, lacking culture or taste

plebiscite *noun* a vote by everyone in an area on a special issue, for or against

plectrum *noun* a small piece of horn, metal *etc* used for plucking the strings of a guitar

pledge *noun* **1** something handed over as security for a loan **2** a solemn promise □ *verb* **1** to give as security, pawn **2** to promise solemnly: *pledged himself to carry out the plan* **3** to drink to the health of, toast

plenary *adjective* full, complete

plenteous or **plentiful** *adjective* not scarce, abundant

plenty *noun* **1** a full supply, as much as is needed **2** a large number or quantity (of)

plethora *noun* too large a quantity of anything: *a plethora of politicians*

pleurisy *noun* an illness in which the covering of the lungs becomes inflamed

pliable *adjective* **1** easily bent or folded **2** easily persuaded

pliant *adjective* pliable

pliers *noun plural* a tool used for gripping, bending and cutting wire *etc*

plight *noun* a bad state or situation □ *verb, old* to promise solemnly, pledge

plimsoll *noun* a light rubber-soled canvas shoe for sports

Plimsoll line a ship's loadline

plinth *noun* **1** the square slab at the foot of a column **2** the base or pedestal of a statue, vase *etc*

PLO *abbreviation* Palestine Liberation Organization

plod *verb* **1** to travel slowly and steadily **2** to work on steadily

plod ⇨ plods, plodding, plodded

plodder *noun* a dull but hard-working person

plop *noun* the sound made by a small object falling into water □ *verb* to make this sound

plop *verb* ⇨ plops, plopping, plopped

plot *noun* **1** a small piece of ground **2** a plan for an illegal or malicious action **3** the story of a play, novel *etc* □ *verb* **1** to plan secretly **2** to make a chart, graph *etc* of **3** to mark points on one of these

plot *verb* ⇨ plots, plotting, plotted

plough *noun* a farm tool for turning up the soil □ *verb* **1** to turn up the ground in furrows **2** to work through slowly: *ploughing through the ironing* □ **the Plough** a group of seven stars forming a shape like an old plough

ploughshare *noun* the blade of a plough

plover (*pronounced* pluv-er) *noun* any of several kinds of bird that nest on the ground in open country

ploy *noun* an activity, an escapade

pluck *verb* **1** to pull out or off **2** to pick (flowers, fruit *etc*) **3** to strip off the feathers of (a bird) before cooking □ *noun* courage, spirit □ **pluck up courage** to prepare yourself to face a danger or difficulty

plucky *adjective* brave, determined

plug *noun* **1** an object fitted into a hole to stop it up **2** a fitting on an appliance put into a socket to connect with an electric current **3** *informal* a brief advertisement □ *verb* **1** to stop up with a plug **2** *informal* to advertise, publicize

plug ⇨ plugs, plugging, plugged

plum *noun* **1** a soft fruit, often dark red or purple, with a stone in the centre **2** the tree that produces this fruit □ *adjective* very good, very profitable *etc*: *a plum job*

plum cake or **plum pudding** a rich cake or pudding containing dried fruit

plumage (*pronounced* ploo-mij) *noun* the feathers of a bird
ⓘ Comes from French *plume* meaning 'feather'

plumb *noun* a lead weight hung on a string (**plumbline**), used to test if a wall has been built straight up □ *adjective* & *adverb* standing straight up, vertical □ *verb* to test the depth of (the sea *etc*)

plumber *noun* someone who fits and mends water, gas and sewage pipes

plumbing *noun* **1** the work of a plumber **2** the drainage and water systems of a building *etc*

plume *noun* **1** a feather, especially an ornamental one **2** something looking like a feather: *a plume of smoke*

plummet *noun* a weight of lead hung on a line, for taking depths at sea □ *verb* to plunge

plump *adjective* fat, rounded, well filled out □ *verb* **1** to grow fat, swell **2** to beat or shake (cushions *etc*) back into shape **3** to sit or sink down heavily **4** **plump for something** to choose, vote for it

plunder *verb* to carry off goods by force, loot, rob □ *noun* goods seized by force

plunge *verb* **1** to dive (into water *etc*) **2** to rush or lurch forward **3** to thrust suddenly (into): *he plunged the knife into its neck* □ *noun* a thrust; a dive

pluperfect *noun, grammar* showing an action which took place before the main past actions being described, *eg* 'he *had* already *left*, when you phoned'

plural *adjective* more than one □ *noun, grammar* the form which shows more than one, *eg* mice is the plural of *mouse*

plurality *noun* **1** the fact of being plural

or more than one **2** a large number or variety **3** a majority that is not absolute, ie a winning number of votes that represents less than half of the votes cast

plus *preposition* used to show addition and represented by the sign (+): *five plus two equals seven* □ *adjective* of a quantity more than zero □ *adverb*, *informal* and a bit extra: *she earns £20 000 plus*

plus fours *noun plural* baggy trousers reaching to just below the knees

So called from the four additional inches of cloth needed for their length

plush *noun* cloth with a soft velvety surface on one side □ *adjective* luxurious

plutocrat *noun* someone who is powerful because of their wealth

ply *verb* **1** to work at steadily **2** to make regular journeys: *the ferry plies between Oban and Mull* **3** to use (a tool) energetically **4** to keep supplying with (food, questions to answer *etc*) □ **two-** or **three-** *etc* **ply** having two or three *etc* layers or strands

ply ⇨ plies, plying, plied

plywood *noun* a board made up of thin sheets of wood glued together

PM *abbreviation* prime minister

pm *abbreviation* after noon (from Latin *post meridiem*)

PMS *abbreviation* premenstrual syndrome

PMT *abbreviation* premenstrual tension

pneumatic (*pronounced* nyoo-**mat**-ik) *adjective* **1** filled with air **2** worked by air: *pneumatic drill*
Ⓛ Comes from Greek *pneuma* meaning 'breath'

pneumonia (*pronounced* nyoo-**moh**-ni-a) *noun* a disease in which the lungs become inflamed
Ⓛ Comes from Greek *pneumon* meaning 'lung'

PO *abbreviation* **1** post office **2** postal order

poach *verb* **1** to cook gently in boiling water or stock **2** to catch fish or hunt game illegally

poacher *noun* someone who hunts or fishes illegally

pocket *noun* **1** a small pouch or bag, especially as part of a garment **2** a personal supply of money: *well beyond my pocket* **3** a small isolated area: *a pocket of unemployment* □ *verb* **1** to put in a pocket **2** to steal □ **in** or **out of pocket** having gained or lost money on a deal *etc*

pocket-book *noun* a wallet

pocket money an allowance of money for personal spending

pockmark *noun* a scar or small hole in the skin left by disease

pod *noun* a long seed-case of the pea, bean *etc* □ *verb* **1** to remove from a pod **2** to form pods

pod *verb* ⇨ pods, podding, podded

podgy *adjective* short and fat

podium *noun* a low pedestal, a platform

poem *noun* a piece of imaginative writing set out in lines which often have a regular rhythm or rhyme

poet *noun* someone who writes poetry

poetic *adjective* of or like poetry □ **poetically** *adverb*

poetic justice a fitting reward or punishment

poetic licence a departure from truth, logic *etc* for the sake of effect

poetry *noun* **1** the art of writing poems **2** poems

po-faced *adjective* stupidly solemn, humourless

pogrom *noun* an organized killing or massacre of a group of people

poignancy *noun* a poignant quality

poignant *adjective* **1** sharp, keen **2** very painful or moving; pathetic

point *noun* **1** a sharp end of anything **2** a headland **3** a dot: *decimal point* **4** a full stop in punctuation **5** an exact place or spot **6** an exact moment of time **7** the chief matter of an argument **8** the meaning of a joke **9** a mark in a competition **10** a purpose, an advantage: *there is no point in going* **11**

a movable rail to direct a railway engine from one line to another **12** an electrical wall socket **13** a mark of character: *he has many good points* □ *verb* **1** to make pointed: *point your toes* **2** to direct, aim **3** to indicate with a gesture: *pointing to the building* **4** to fill (wall joints) with mortar

○ Comes from French *point* meaning 'dot' or 'stitch', and *pointe* meaning 'sharp point'

point-blank *adjective* **1** of a shot: fired from very close range **2** of a question: direct

pointed *adjective* **1** having a point, sharp **2** of a remark: obviously aimed at someone

pointer *noun* **1** a rod for pointing **2** a type of dog used to show where game has fallen after it has been shot

pointless *adjective* having no meaning or purpose

poise *verb* **1** to balance, keep steady **2** to hover in the air □ *noun* **1** a state of balance **2** dignity, self-confidence

poised *adjective* **1** balanced, having poise **2** prepared, ready: *poised for action*

poison *noun* **1** a substance which, when taken into the body, kills or harms **2** anything harmful □ *verb* **1** to kill or harm with poison **2** to add poison to **3** to make bitter or bad: *poisoned her mind*

poison ivy a N American plant whose juice causes a skin rash

poisonous *adjective* **1** harmful because of containing poison **2** causing evil

poison pen a writer of malicious anonymous letters

poke *verb* **1** to push (*eg* a finger or stick) into something **2** to prod, thrust at **3** to search about inquisitively □ *noun* **1** a nudge, a prod **2** a prying search

poker *noun* **1** a rod for stirring up a fire **2** a card game in which players bet on their chance of winning

poky *adjective* cramped and shabby

polar *adjective* of the regions round the north or south poles

polarity *noun* the state of having two opposite poles

polarize *verb* **1** to give polarity to **2** to split into opposing sides

polaroid *noun, trademark* **1** a plastic through which light is seen less brightly **2 polaroids** sunglasses **3** a camera that develops individual pictures in a few seconds

pole *noun* **1** a long rounded rod or post **2** the north or south end of the earth's axis (**the north** or **south pole**) **3** either of the opposing points of a magnet or electric battery

polecat *noun* **1** a large kind of weasel **2** *US* a skunk

pole-star *noun* the star most directly above the north pole

pole vault a sport in which an athlete jumps over a bar with the aid of a flexible pole

police *noun* the body of men and women whose work it is to see that laws are obeyed *etc* □ *verb* to keep law and order in (a place) by use of police

policeman *noun* a male police officer

police station *noun* the headquarters of the police in a district

policewoman *noun* a female police officer

policy *noun* (*plural* **policies**) **1** an agreed course of action **2** a written agreement with an insurance company

polio *short for* **poliomyelitis**

poliomyelitis *noun* a disease of the spinal cord, causing weakness or paralysis of the muscles

polish *verb* **1** to make smooth and shiny by rubbing **2** to improve (a piece of writing *etc*) **3** to make more polite □ *noun* **1** a gloss on a surface **2** a substance used for polishing **3** fine manners, style *etc*

polite *adjective* having good manners, courteous □ **politely** *adverb*

politic *adjective* wise, cautious

political *adjective* of government, politicians or politics

politician *noun* someone involved in politics, especially a member of parliament

politicize *verb* to make aware of political issues

politics *noun singular* the art or study of government

polka *noun* a lively dance or the music for it

poll *noun* **1** a counting of voters at an election **2** total number of votes **3** (*also called* **opinion poll**) a test of public opinion by questioning □ *verb* **1** to cut or clip off (hair, branches *etc*) **2** to receive (votes): *they polled 5000 votes*

pollard *noun* a tree with its top cut off to allow new growth □ *verb* to cut the top off (a tree)

pollen *noun* the fertilizing powder of flowers

pollinate *verb* to fertilize with pollen

pollination *noun* fertilization with pollen

polling station a place where voting is done

poll tax *Brit* the community charge

pollutant *noun* something that pollutes

pollute *verb* **1** to make dirty or impure **2** to make (the environment) harmful to life

pollution *noun* **1** the act of polluting **2** dirt

polo *noun* a game like hockey played on horseback

polo neck **1** a close-fitting neck with a part turned over at the top **2** a jumper with a neck like this

poltergeist *noun* a kind of ghost believed to move furniture and throw objects around a room (literally, 'a ghost which makes a racket')

poly- *prefix* **1** many, much: *polyglot/ polygon* **2** *chemistry* a polymer of: *polystyrene* (= a polymer of styrene)/ *polythene* (= the name of a number of polymers of ethylene)
Ⓒ Comes from Greek *polys* meaning 'much'

polyanthus *noun* a hybrid plant which produces many flowers

polycarpous *noun* of a tree: producing fruit year after year

polyester *noun* a synthetic material often used in clothing

polygamist *noun* a person who has more than one husband or wife at the same time

polygamous *adjective* having more than one husband or wife at the same time

polygamy *noun* the fact of having more than one wife or husband at the same time

polyglot *adjective* speaking, or written in, many languages □ *noun* someone fluent in many languages

polygon *noun* a figure with many angles and sides

polygonal *adjective* having many angles and many sides

polygraph *noun* an instrument which measures pulse rate *etc*, used as a lie-detector

polymath *noun* someone with knowledge of a wide range of subjects

polymer *noun* a chemical compound with large molecules

polymorphous *noun* occurring in several different forms

polyp *noun* **1** a small sea-animal with arms or tentacles **2** a kind of tumour

polyphonic (*pronounced* pol-i-**fon**-ik) *adjective* relating to polyphony

polyphony (*pronounced* po-**lif**-on-i) *noun* musical composition in parts, each with a separate melody

polystyrene *noun* a synthetic material which resists moisture, used for packing and disposable cups *etc*

polysyllabic *adjective* of a word: having three or more syllables

polysyllable *noun* a word of three or more syllables

polytechnic *noun* a college which teaches technical and vocational subjects

polythene *noun* a type of plastic that can be moulded when hot

polyunsaturated *adjective* of oil: containing no cholesterol

polyurethane *noun* a resin used to produce foam materials

pomegranate *noun* a fruit with a thick skin, many seeds and pulpy edible flesh

① Comes from Old French *pome grenate* meaning 'grainy apple'

pommel *noun* 1 the knob on the hilt of a sword 2 the high part of a saddle

pomp *noun* solemn and splendid ceremony, magnificence

pomposity *noun* a pompous quality or manner

pompous *adjective* self-important, excessively dignified

poncho *noun* (*plural* **ponchos**) a S American cloak made of a blanket with a hole for the head

pond *noun* a small lake or pool

ponder *verb* to think over, consider

ponderous *adjective* 1 weighty 2 clumsy 3 sounding very important

pontiff *noun* 1 a Roman Catholic bishop 2 the Pope

pontifical *adjective* 1 of a pontiff 2 pompous in speech

pontificate *verb* to speak in a pompous manner

pontoon[1] *noun* a flat-bottomed boat used to support a temporary bridge (a **pontoon bridge**)

pontoon[2] *noun* a card-game in which players try to collect 21 points

pony *noun* (*plural* **ponies**) a small horse

pony-trekking *noun* riding cross-country in small parties

poodle *noun* a breed of dog, with curly hair often clipped in a fancy way

pool *noun* 1 a small area of still water 2 a deep part of a river 3 a joint fund or stock (of money, typists *etc*) 4 the money played for in a gambling game □ *verb* to put (money *etc*) into a joint fund □ **football pools** organized betting on football match results

poop *noun* 1 a ship's stern, or back part 2 a high deck in the stern

poor *adjective* 1 having little money or property 2 not good: *this work is poor* 3 lacking (in): *poor in sports facilities* 4 deserving pity: *poor Tom has broken his leg* □ **the poor** those with little money

■ **Alternative words**: (meaning 1) impoverished, destitute, straitened, needy; (meaning 4) unfortunate, pitiable

poorly *adjective* in bad health, ill

pop *noun* 1 a sharp quick noise, *eg* that made by a cork coming out of a bottle 2 a fizzy soft drink 3 popular music □ *verb* 1 to make a pop 2 to move quickly, dash: *pop in/ pop along the road* □ *adjective* of music: popular

pop *verb* ⇨ pop*s*, pop*ping*, pop*ped*

popadom or **popadum** *noun* a thin circle of dough fried in oil until crisp

popcorn *noun* a kind of maize that bursts open when heated

Pope or **pope** *noun* the bishop of Rome, head of the Roman Catholic Church

poplar *noun* a tall, narrow quick-growing tree

poplin *noun* strong cotton cloth

poppy *noun* (*plural* **poppies**) a plant growing wild in fields *etc* with large scarlet flowers

populace *noun* the people of a country or area

popular *adjective* 1 of the people: *popular vote* 2 liked by most people 3 widely held or believed: *popular belief*

popularity *noun* the state of being generally liked

popularize *verb* to make popular or widely known

popularly *adverb* in a popular way; in terms of most people: *a popularly held belief*

populate *verb* to fill (an area) with people

population *noun* the number of people living in a place

populous *adjective* full of people

porcelain *noun* a kind of fine china

porch *noun* (*plural* **porches**) a covered entrance to a building

porcupine *noun* a large gnawing animal, covered with sharp quills

pore *noun* 1 a tiny hole 2 the hole of a sweat gland in the skin

🕓 Comes from Greek *poros* meaning 'a passage'

💢 Do not confuse with: **pour**

pore over study closely or eagerly

pork *noun* the flesh of the pig, prepared for eating

porn *noun, informal* pornography

pornographic *adjective* relating to pornography

pornography *noun* literature or art that is sexually explicit and often offensive

porosity *noun* being porous

porous *adjective* 1 having pores 2 allowing fluid to pass through

porpoise *noun* a blunt-nosed sea animal of the dolphin family

porridge *noun* a food made from oatmeal boiled in water or milk

porringer *noun* a small bowl for soup, porridge *etc*

port *noun* 1 a harbour 2 a town with a harbour 3 the left side of a ship as you face the front 4 a strong, dark-red sweet wine

portability *noun* the quality of being portable

portable *adjective* able to be lifted and carried □ *noun* a computer, telephone *etc* that can be carried around

portal *noun* a grand entrance or doorway

portcullis *noun* (*plural* **portcullises**) a grating which is let down quickly to close a gateway

portend *verb* to give warning of, foretell

portent *noun* a warning sign

portentous *adjective* 1 strange, wonderful 2 important, weighty

porter *noun* 1 someone employed to carry luggage, push hospital trolleys *etc* 2 a doorkeeper 3 a kind of dark brown beer

portfolio *noun* (*plural* **portfolios**) 1 a case for carrying papers, drawings *etc* 2 the job of a government minister

port-hole *noun* a small round window in a ship's side

portico *noun* (*plural* **porticoes** or **porticos**) a row of columns in front of a building forming a porch or covered walk

portion *noun* 1 a part 2 a share, a helping □ *verb* to divide into parts

portly *adjective* stout and dignified

portmanteau *noun* a large leather travelling bag

portrait *noun* 1 a drawing, painting, or photograph of a person 2 a description of a person, place *etc*

portray *verb* 1 to make a painting or drawing of 2 to describe in words 3 to act the part of

portray ⇨ portrays, portray*ing*, portray*ed*

portrayal *noun* 1 representation in a picture or pictures 2 portraying

Portuguese man-of-war a stinging jellyfish

pose *noun* 1 a position of the body: *a relaxed pose* 2 behaviour put on to impress others, a pretence □ *verb* 1 to position yourself for a photograph *etc* 2 **pose as someone** or **something** to pretend or claim to be what you are not: *posing as an expert* 3 to put forward (a problem, question *etc*)

poser *noun* 1 someone who poses to impress others 2 a difficult question

posh *adjective, informal* high-class; smart

position *noun* 1 place, situation 2 manner of standing, sitting *etc*, posture: *in a crouching position* 3 a rank or job: *a high position in a bank* □ *verb* to place

positive *adjective* 1 meaning or saying 'yes': *a positive answer* (*contrasted with*: **negative**) 2 not able to be doubted: *positive proof* 3 certain, convinced: *I am positive that she did it* 4 definite: *a positive improvement* 5 greater than zero 6 *grammar* of an adjective or adverb: of the first degree of comparison, *eg big*, not *bigger* or *biggest*

positron *noun* a particle with a positive electrical charge

posse (*pronounced* **pos**-i) *noun* a body of police *etc*

possess *verb* 1 to own, have 2 to take

hold of your mind: *anger possessed her*

possessed *adjective* **1** in the power of an evil spirit **2** obsessed **3** self-possessed, calm

possession *noun* the state of possessing; the state of being possessed; something owned

possessive *adjective* **1** *grammar* of an adjective: showing possession, *eg* the adjectives *my, mine, your, their etc* **2** over-protective and jealous in attitude

possibility *noun* (*plural* **possibilities**) something that may happen or that may be done

possible *adjective* **1** able to happen or to be done **2** not unlikely
Ⓛ Comes from Latin *possibilis* meaning 'which may exist' or 'which may be done'

possibly *adverb* perhaps

possum *noun*: **play possum** to pretend to be asleep or dead

post *noun* **1** an upright pole or stake **2** the service which delivers letters and other mail **3** a job: *teaching post* **4** a place of duty: *the soldier remained at his post* **5** a settlement, a camp: *military post/ trading post* □ *verb* **1** to put (a letter) in a postbox for collection **2** to send or station somewhere: *posted abroad* **3** to put up, stick up (a notice etc)

post- *prefix* after: *postgraduate/ postmortem*
Ⓛ Comes from Latin *post* meaning 'after' or 'behind'

postage *noun* money paid for sending a letter *etc* by post

postage stamp a small printed label to show that postage has been paid

postal *adjective* of or by post

postal order a document bought at a post office which can be exchanged for a stated amount of money

postbox *noun* a box with an opening in which to post letters *etc*

postcard *noun* a card for sending a message by post

post code a short series of letters and numbers, used for sorting mail by machine

post-date *verb* to mark (a cheque) with a date in the future, so that it cannot be cashed immediately

poster *noun* **1** a large notice or placard **2** a large printed picture

posterior *adjective* situated behind, coming after □ *noun* the buttocks

posterity *noun* **1** all future generations **2** someone's descendants

postern *noun* a back door or gate to a castle *etc*

postgraduate *adjective* of study *etc*: following on from a first university degree □ *noun* someone continuing to study after a first degree

post-haste *adverb* with great speed

posthumous (*pronounced* **pos**-tyu-mus) *adjective* **1** of a book: published after the author's death **2** of a child: born after the father's death

postilion or **postillion** *noun, old* a carriage driver who rides on one of the horses

Post-it *noun, trademark* a small sticky label for writing messages on

postman *noun* a man who delivers letters

postmark *noun* a date stamp put on a letter at a post office

postmaster *noun* a male official in charge of a post office

postmistress *noun* a female official in charge of a post office

postmortem *noun* an examination of a dead body to find out the cause of death

post office an office for receiving and sending off letters by post *etc*

postpone *verb* to put off to a future time, delay

postponement *noun* postponing

postscript *noun* an added remark at the end of a letter, after the sender's name

postulant *noun* someone applying to enter a religious order

postulate *verb* to assume or take for granted (that)

posture *noun* **1** the manner in which

someone holds themselves in standing or walking **2** a position, a pose

postwar *adjective* relating to the time after a war

postwoman *noun* a woman who delivers letters

posy *noun* (*plural* **posies**) a small bunch of flowers

pot *noun* **1** a deep vessel used in cooking, as a container, or for growing plants **2** *slang* the drug marijuana **3 pots** *informal* a great deal: *pots of money* □ *verb* **1** to plant in a pot **2** to make articles of baked clay □ **take pot-luck** to take whatever is available or offered

pot *verb* ⇨ pots, pott*ing*, pott*ed*

potash *noun* potassium carbonate, obtained from the ashes of wood

potassium *noun* a type of silvery-white metal

potato *noun* (*plural* **potatoes**) **1** a plant with round starchy roots which are eaten as a vegetable **2** the vegetable itself □ **couch potato** *see* couch

pot belly a protruding stomach

pot-boiler *noun* a book with a sensational plot, written to sell

potency *noun* power

potent *adjective* powerful, strong

potentate *noun* a powerful ruler

potential *adjective* that may develop, possible □ *noun* the possibility of further development

potentiality *noun* (*plural* **potentialities**) a possibility

pothole *noun* **1** a deep cave **2** a hole worn in a road surface

potholer *noun* someone who explores caves

potion *noun* a drink, often containing medicine or poison

pot plant a household plant kept in a pot

potpourri (*pronounced* poh-**poo**-ri) *noun* **1** a scented mixture of dried petals *etc* **2** a mixture or medley

pot shot a casual or random shot

potted *adjective* **1** of meat: pressed down and preserved in a jar **2** condensed and simplified: *potted history*

potter *noun* someone who makes articles of baked clay □ *verb* to do small odd jobs, dawdle

pottery *noun* **1** articles made of baked clay **2** (*plural* **potteries**) a place where such things are made **3** the art of making them

potty[1] *adjective, informal* mad, eccentric

potty[2] *noun, informal* a child's chamberpot

pouch *noun* (*plural* **pouches**) **1** a pocket or small bag **2** a bag-like fold on the front of a kangaroo, for carrying its young

pouffe *noun* a low, stuffed seat without back or arms

poultice *noun* a wet dressing spread on a bandage and put on inflamed skin □ *verb* to put a poultice on

poultry *noun* farmyard fowls, *eg* hens, ducks, geese, turkeys

pounce *verb*: **pounce on something** or **someone** to seize, attack them □ *noun* **1** a sudden attack them **2** a bird's claw

pound *noun* **1** the standard unit of money in Britain, shown by the sign (£), equal to 100 new pence **2** a measure of weight, written 'lb', equal to 16 ounces (about $\frac{1}{2}$ kilogramme) **3** an enclosure for animals □ *verb* **1** to beat into powder **2** to beat heavily **3** to walk or run with heavy steps

pour *verb* **1** to flow in a stream: *the blood poured out* **2** to make flow: *pour the tea* **3** to rain heavily
ⓒ Comes from Middle English *pouren*

🖝 Do not confuse with: **pore**

pout *verb* to push out the lips sulkily to show displeasure □ *noun* a sulky look

poverty *noun* **1** the state of being poor **2** lack, want: *poverty of ideas*

POW *abbreviation* prisoner of war

powder *noun* **1** a substance made up of very fine particles **2** gunpowder **3** cosmetic facepowder □ *verb* **1** to sprinkle or dab with powder **2** to grind down to powder

powdered *adjective* **1** in fine particles **2** covered with powder

powdery *adjective* 1 covered with powder 2 like powder: *powdery snow*

power *noun* 1 strength, force 2 ability to do things 3 authority or legal right 4 a strong nation 5 someone in authority 6 the force used for driving machines: *electric power/ steam power* 7 *maths* the product obtained by multiplying a number by itself a given number of times (*eg* 2 x 2 x 2 or 2³ is the third power of 2)

power-driven or **powered** *adjective* worked by electricity, not by hand

powerful *adjective* having great power, strength, vigour, authority, influence, force or effectiveness

powerless *adjective* without power or ability

power station a building where electricity is produced

pp *abbreviation* pages

practicable *adjective* able to be used or done
Ⓛ Comes from an old spelling of French *praticable* meaning 'able to be put into practice'

practical *adjective* 1 preferring action to thought 2 efficient 3 learned by practice, rather than from books: *practical knowledge*
Ⓛ Comes from an old spelling of French *pratique* meaning 'handy', + word-ending -al

practical joke a joke consisting of action, not words

practically *adverb* 1 in a practical way 2 in effect, in reality 3 almost: *practically empty*

practice *noun* 1 habit: *it is my practice to get up early* 2 the actual doing of something: *I always intend to get up early but in practice I stay in bed* 3 repeated performance to improve skill: *piano practice/ in practice for the race* 4 the business of a doctor, lawyer *etc*
🖝 Do not confuse: **practice** and **practise**. To help you remember – 'ice' is a noun, 'ise' is not!

practise or *US* **practice** *verb* 1 to perform or exercise repeatedly to improve a skill: *he practises judo nightly* 2 to make a habit of: *practise self-control* 3 to follow (a profession): *practise dentistry*

practitioner *noun* someone engaged in a profession: *a medical practitioner*

pragmatic or **pragmatical** *adjective* practical; matter-of-fact; realistic

pragmatism *noun* a practical, matter-of-fact approach to dealing with problems *etc*

pragmatist *noun* a pragmatic person

prairie *noun* a stretch of level grassland in N America

praise *verb* 1 to speak highly of 2 to glorify (God) by singing hymns *etc* □ *noun* an expression of approval

praiseworthy *adjective* deserving to be praised

pram *noun* a small wheeled carriage for a baby, pushed by hand (*short for* **perambulator**)

prance *verb* 1 to strut or swagger about 2 to dance about 3 of a horse: to spring from the hind legs

prank *noun* a trick played for mischief

prat *noun, informal* an idiot

prattle *verb* to talk or chatter meaninglessly □ *noun* meaningless talk

prawn *noun* a type of shellfish like the shrimp

pray *verb* 1 to ask earnestly, beg 2 to speak to God in prayer
Ⓛ Comes from Latin *precarius* meaning 'obtained by prayer'
🖝 Do not confuse with: **prey**

prayer *noun* 1 an earnest request for something 2 a request, or thanks, given to God

praying mantis *see* **mantis**

pre- *prefix* 1 before: *prehistoric* 2 to the highest degree: *pre-eminent*
Ⓛ Comes from Latin *prae* meaning 'in front of' or 'before'

preach *verb* 1 to give a sermon 2 to teach, speak in favour of: *preach caution*

preacher *noun* a religious teacher

preamble *noun* something said as an introduction

prearrange *verb* to arrange beforehand

precarious *adjective* uncertain, risky, dangerous

precaution *noun* care taken beforehand to avoid an accident *etc*

precautionary *adjective* suggesting precaution

precede *verb* to go before in time, rank or importance
ⓘ Comes from Latin *praecedere* meaning 'to go before'

☛ Do not confuse with: **proceed**

precedence *noun* the right to go before; priority

precedent *noun* a past action which serves as an example or rule for the future

preceding *adjective* going before; previous

precept *noun* a guiding rule, a commandment

precinct *noun* 1 an area enclosed by the boundary walls of a building 2 **precincts** the area closely surrounding any place 3 *US* an administrative district □ **shopping precinct** a shopping centre, often closed to traffic

precious *adjective* 1 highly valued or valuable 2 over-fussy or precise

precipice *noun* a steep cliff

precipitate *verb* (*pronounced* pri-**sip**-it-eit) 1 to throw head foremost 2 to force into (hasty action *etc*) 3 to hasten (death, illness *etc*) □ *adjective* (*pronounced* pri-**sip**-it-*a*t) 1 headlong 2 hasty, rash □ *noun* (*pronounced* pri-**sip**-it-*a*t) sediment at the bottom of a liquid

precipitation *noun* 1 great hurry 2 rainfall

precipitous *adjective* very steep

précis (*pronounced* **prei**-see) *noun* (*plural* **précis** — *pronounced* **prei**-seez) a summary of a piece of writing

precise *adjective* 1 definite 2 exact, accurate □ **precisely** *adverb*
ⓘ Comes from Latin *praecisus* meaning 'cut short'

☛ Do not confuse with: **concise**

precision *noun* 1 preciseness 2 exactness, accuracy

preclude *verb* to prevent, make impossible

preclusion *noun* precluding

precocious *adjective* of a child: unusually advanced or well-developed

precocity *noun* being precocious

precognitive *adjective* knowing beforehand, foretelling

preconceive *verb* to form (ideas *etc*) before having actual knowledge or experience

preconception *noun* an idea formed without actual knowledge

precursor *noun* a person or thing which goes before, an early form of something: *the precursor of jazz*

predate *verb* to happen before in time

predator *noun* a bird or animal that kills others for food

predatory *adjective* 1 of a predator 2 using other people for your own advantage

predecessor *noun* the previous holder of a job or office

predestine *verb* to destine beforehand, preordain

predetermine *verb* to settle beforehand

predicament *noun* an unfortunate or difficult situation

predicate *noun, grammar* something said about the subject of a sentence, *eg has green eyes* in the sentence *Anne has green eyes*

predict *verb* to foretell, forecast

predictable *adjective* able to be foretold

prediction *noun* an act of predicting; something predicted

predilection *noun* a preference, a liking for something

predispose *verb* 1 to make (someone) in favour of something beforehand: *we were predisposed to believe her* 2 to make liable (to): *predisposed to colds*

predisposition *noun* the condition of being predisposed

predominance *noun* being predominant

predominant *adjective* **1** ruling **2** most noticeable or outstanding

predominantly *adverb* mostly, mainly: *her books are predominantly about life in Africa*

predominate *verb* **1** to be the strongest or most numerous **2** to have control (over)

pre-eminence *noun* a pre-eminent quality: *everybody recognizes his pre-eminence in the field of family law*

pre-eminent *adjective* outstanding, excelling all others ▫ **pre-eminently** *adverb*

pre-empt *verb* to block or stop by making a first move

pre-emptive *adjective* having the effect of pre-empting

preen *verb* **1** of a bird: to arrange its feathers **2** to smarten your appearance in a conceited way ▫ **preen yourself** to show obvious pride in your achievements

prefabricated *adjective* made of parts made beforehand, ready to be fitted together

preface (*pronounced* **pref**-is) *noun* an introduction to a book *etc* ▫ *verb* to precede or introduce (with)

prefect *noun* **1** the head of an administrative district in France *etc* **2** a senior pupil in some schools with certain powers

prefer *verb* **1** to like better: *I prefer tea to coffee* **2** to put forward (a claim or request)

prefer ⇨ prefer*s*, prefer*ring*, prefer*red*

preferable (*pronounced* **pref**-ra-bl) *adjective* more desirable

preference *noun* **1** greater liking **2** something preferred: *what is your preference?*

preferential *adjective* giving preference

preferment *noun* promotion

prefix *noun* (*plural* **prefixes**) a syllable or word at the beginning of a word which adds to its meaning, *eg* dis-, un-, re-, in *dis*like, *un*happy, *re*gain

pregnancy *noun* (*plural* **pregnancies**) the state of being pregnant or the time during which a female is pregnant

pregnant *adjective* **1** carrying a foetus in the womb **2** full of meaning: *pregnant pause*

prehensile *adjective* able to grasp or hold: *prehensile tail*

prehistoric *adjective* relating to the time before history was written down

prehistory *noun* the period before historical records

prejudge *verb* to decide (something) before hearing the facts of a case

prejudice *noun* **1** an unfair feeling for or against anything **2** an opinion formed without careful thought **3** harm, injury ▫ *verb* **1** to fill with prejudice **2** to do harm to, damage: *his late arrival prejudiced his chances of success*

prejudiced *adjective* showing prejudice

prejudicial *adjective* damaging, harmful

prelate (*pronounced* **prel**-it) *noun* a bishop or archbishop

preliminary *adjective* going before, preparatory: *preliminary investigation* ▫ *noun* (*plural* **preliminaries**) something that goes before

prelude *noun* **1** a piece of music played as an introduction to the main piece **2** a preceding event: *a prelude to a brilliant career*

premature *adjective* coming, born *etc* before the right, proper or expected time

premeditate *verb* to think out beforehand, plan: *premeditated murder*

premeditation *noun* planning beforehand

premenstrual *adjective* before menstruation

premier (*pronounced* **prem**-i-er) *adjective* first, leading, foremost ▫ *noun* a prime minister

❧ Do not confuse: **premier** and **première**

première (*pronounced* **prem**-i-eir) *noun* a first performance of a play, film *etc*

premise or **premiss** *noun* (*plural* **premises** or **premisses**) something assumed from which a conclusion is drawn

premises *noun plural* a building and its grounds

premium *noun* (*plural* **premiums**) **1** a reward **2** a payment on an insurance policy □ **at a premium** very desirable and therefore difficult to obtain

premonition *noun* a feeling that something is going to happen; a forewarning

prenatal *adjective* before birth, or before giving birth

preoccupation *noun* **1** being preoccupied **2** something that preoccupies: *she has a preoccupation with death*

preoccupied *adjective* deep in thought

preoccupy *verb* to completely engross the attention of (someone)

preordain *verb* to determine beforehand

prep *noun, informal* preparation

prepaid *past form of* **prepay**

preparation *noun* **1** an act of preparing **2** study for a lesson **3** something prepared for use, *eg* a medicine

preparatory *adjective* **1** acting as an introduction or first step **2 preparatory to something** before it, in preparation for it

preparatory school a private school educating children of primary-school age

prepare *verb* **1** to make or get ready **2** to train, equip

prepared *adjective* **1** ready **2** willing

prepay *verb* to pay beforehand
   prepay ⇨ prepays, prepaying, prepaid

prepayment *noun* payment in advance

preponderance *noun* greater amount or number: *a preponderance of young people in the audience*

preposition *noun, grammar* a word placed before a noun or pronoun to show its relation to another word, *eg* '*through* the door', '*in* the town', 'written *by* me'

   ☛ Do not confuse with: **proposition**

prepossessing *adjective* pleasant, making a good impression

preposterous *adjective* very foolish, absurd

prep school a preparatory school

pre-Raphaelite *noun* one of a group of 19th-century British artists who painted in a naturalistic style

prerequisite *noun* something necessary before another thing can happen

prerogative *noun* a right enjoyed by someone because of rank or position

presbyter *noun* a minister or elder in a Presbyterian church

Presbyterian *adjective* **1** of a church: managed by ministers and elders **2** belonging to such a church □ *noun* a member of a Presbyterian church

presbytery *noun* (*plural* **presbyteries**) **1** a body of presbyters **2** the house of a Roman Catholic priest

prescribe *verb* **1** to lay down as a rule **2** to order the use of (a medicine)
   ℗ Comes from Latin *praescribere* meaning 'to write before'

   ☛ Do not confuse with: **proscribe**. It may help to remember that the **pre-** in **prescribe** means 'before', and that the whole verb refers to the process by which a doctor has to write down an order for medication before it can be obtained by a patient

prescription *noun* **1** a doctor's written instructions for preparing a medicine **2** something prescribed

   ☛ Do not confuse with: **proscription**. **Prescription** is related to the verb **prescribe**

prescriptive *adjective* laying down rules

presence *noun* **1** the state of being present (*contrasted with:* **absence**) **2** someone's personal appearance, manner *etc* □ **in your presence** while you are present □ **presence of mind** calmness, ability to act sensibly in an emergency, difficulty *etc*

present¹ *adjective* **1** here, in this place **2** happening or existing now: *present rates of pay/ the present situation* □ *noun* **1** the time now **2** *grammar* the tense describing events happening now, *eg* 'we *are* on holiday'

present² *noun* (pronounced **prez**-ent) a gift □ *verb* (pronounced pri-**zent**) **1** to hand over (a gift) formally **2** to offer, put forward **3** to introduce (someone) to another □ **present yourself 1** to introduce yourself **2** to arrive

presentation *noun* **1** the giving of a present **2** something presented **3** a formal talk or demonstration **4** a showing of a play *etc*

presentiment *noun* a feeling that something bad is about to happen, a foreboding

presently *adverb* soon

preservation *noun* preserving or being preserved

preservative *noun* a substance added to food to prevent it from going bad

preserve *verb* **1** to keep safe from harm **2** to keep in existence, maintain **3** to treat (food) so that it will not go bad □ *noun* **1** a place where game animals, birds *etc* are protected **2** jam

preside *verb* to be in charge at a meeting *etc*

presidency *noun* (*plural* **presidencies**) the position of president

president *noun* **1** the leading member of a society *etc* **2** the head of a republic

press *verb* **1** to push on, against or down **2** to urge, force **3** to iron (clothes *etc*) □ *noun* **1** a crowd **2** a printing machine **3** the news media, journalists

pressgang *noun, historical* a group of men employed to carry off people by force into the army or navy □ *verb* **1** *historical* to carry off in a pressgang **2** to force (someone) to do something: *pressganged into joining the committee*

pressing *adjective* requiring immediate action, insistent

pressure *noun* **1** force on or against a surface **2** strong persuasion, compulsion **3** stress, strain **4** urgency

pressure cooker a pan in which food is cooked quickly by steam under pressure

pressure group a group of people who

try to influence the authorities on a particular issue

pressurize *verb* **1** to fit (an aeroplane *etc*) with a device that maintains normal air pressure **2** to force (someone) to do something

prestige *noun* reputation, influence due to rank, success *etc*

prestigious *adjective* having or giving prestige

presumably *adverb* I suppose

presume *verb* **1** to take for granted, assume (that) **2 presume on something** to take advantage of (someone's kindness *etc*)

presumption *noun* **1** a strong likelihood **2** impertinent behaviour

presumptuous *adjective* unsuitably bold

presuppose *verb* to take for granted

pretence *noun* **1** the act of pretending **2** a false claim

pretend *verb* **1** to make believe, fantasize **2** to make a false claim: *pretending to be ill*

pretender *noun* someone who lays claim to something (especially to the crown)

pretension *noun* **1** a claim (whether true or not) **2** self-importance

pretentious *adjective* self-important; showy, ostentatious

preterite *noun, grammar* the past tense in verbs

pretext *noun* an excuse

pretty *adjective* pleasing or attractive to see, listen to *etc* □ *adverb* fairly, quite: *pretty good* □ **prettiness** *noun*

prevail *verb* **1 prevail against** or **over someone** or **something** to gain control over them **2** to win, succeed **3 prevail on someone** to persuade them: *she prevailed on me to stay* **4** to be most usual or common

prevailing *adjective* **1** controlling **2** most common: *the prevailing mood*

prevalence *noun* being prevalent: *the prevalence of the rose in English gardens*

prevalent *adjective* common, widespread

prevaricate *verb* to avoid telling the truth

prevarication *noun* prevaricating

prevaricator *noun* a person who prevaricates

prevent *verb* to hinder, stop happening □ *noun* the act of preventing

preventive *adjective* of medicine: helping to prevent illness

preview *noun* a view of a performance, exhibition *etc* before its official opening

previous *adjective* going before in time; former

previously *adverb* before, earlier

prey *noun* 1 an animal killed by others for food 2 a victim □ *verb* **prey on someone** or **something** 1 to seize and eat them: *preying on smaller birds* 2 to stalk and harass them
① Comes from Latin *praeda* meaning 'booty'

🖝 Do not confuse with: **pray**

price *noun* 1 the money for which something is bought or sold, the cost 2 something that must be given up in order to gain something: *the price of fame*

priceless *adjective* 1 very valuable 2 *informal* very funny

prick *verb* 1 to pierce slightly 2 to give a sharp pain to 3 to stick up (the ears) □ *noun* a pricking feeling on the skin

prickle *noun* a sharp point on a plant or animal □ *verb* 1 to be prickly 2 to feel prickly

prickly *adjective* 1 full of prickles 2 stinging, pricking

pride *noun* 1 too great an opinion of yourself 2 pleasure in having done something well 3 dignity 4 a group of lions □ **pride yourself on** to feel or show pride in

priest *noun* 1 a member of the clergy in the Roman Catholic and Anglican churches 2 an official in a non-Christian religion

priestess *noun* a female, non-Christian priest

priesthood *noun* those who are priests

prig *noun* a smug, self-righteous person

priggish *adjective* self-righteously smug

prim *adjective* unnecessarily formal and correct

prima ballerina the leading female dancer of a ballet company

prima donna 1 a leading female opera singer 2 a woman who is over-sensitive and temperamental

primaeval *another spelling of* **primeval**

primary *adjective* 1 first 2 most important, chief

primary colours those from which all others can be made, *eg* red, blue and yellow

primary school a school for the early stages of education

primate *noun* 1 a member of the highest order of mammals including humans, monkeys and apes 2 an archbishop

prime *adjective* 1 first in time or importance 2 best quality, excellent □ *noun* the time of greatest health and strength: *the prime of life* □ *verb* 1 to prepare the surface of for painting: *prime a canvas* 2 to supply with detailed information: *she was well primed before the meeting*

prime minister the head of a government

primer *noun* 1 a simple introductory book on a subject 2 a substance for preparing a surface for painting

primeval or **primaeval** *adjective* 1 relating to the beginning of the world 2 primitive, instinctive

primitive *adjective* 1 belonging to very early times 2 old-fashioned 3 not skilfully made, rough

primogeniture *noun* 1 the fact of being born first 2 the rights of a first-born child

primrose *noun* a pale-yellow spring flower common in woods and hedges

prince *noun* 1 the son of a king or queen 2 a ruler of certain states

princely *adjective* splendid, impressive: *a princely reward*

princess *noun* (*plural* **princesses**) the daughter of a king or queen

principal *adjective* most important,

chief □ *noun* **1** the head of a school or university **2** a leading part in a play *etc* **3** money in a bank on which interest is paid

🕔 Comes from Latin *principalis* meaning 'first'

🖛 Do not confuse: **principal** and **principle**. It may help to remember that the adjective **principAL** means 'first or most important', and that it also contains an A – the first letter of the alphabet

principality *noun* (*plural* **principalities**) a state ruled by a prince

principally *adverb* chiefly, mostly

principle *noun* **1** a general truth or law **2** the theory on which the working of a machine is based **3 principles** someone's personal rules of behaviour, sense of right and wrong *etc*

🕔 Comes from Latin *principium* meaning 'beginning'

print *verb* **1** to mark letters on paper with type **2** to write in capital letters **3** to publish in printed form **4** to stamp patterns on (cloth *etc*) **5** to make a finished photograph □ *noun* **1** a mark made by pressure: *footprint* **2** printed lettering **3** a photograph made from a negative **4** a printed reproduction of a painting *etc* **5** cloth printed with a design □ **in print** of a book: published and available to buy

printed circuit a wiring circuit, formed by printing a design on copper foil bonded to a flat base

printer *noun* **1** someone who prints books, newspapers *etc* **2** a machine that prints, attached to a computer system

print-out *noun* the printed information produced by a computer

prior[1] *adjective* **1** earlier **2** previous (to)

prior[2] *noun* the head of a priory

priority *noun* (*plural* **priorities**) **1** first position **2** the right to be first: *ambulances must have priority in traffic* **3** something that must be done first: *our priority is to get him into hospital*

priory *noun* (*plural* **priories**) a building where a community of monks or nuns live

prise *verb* to force open or off with a lever: *prised off the lid*

prism *noun* a glass tube with triangular ends that breaks light into different colours

prison *noun* **1** a building for holding criminals **2** a place where someone is confined against their will

prisoner *noun* someone held under arrest or locked up

prisoner of war someone captured by the enemy forces during war

pristine *adjective* in the original or unspoilt state

privacy *noun* freedom from observation; secrecy

private *adjective* **1** relating to an individual, not to the general public; personal **2** not open to the public **3** secret, not generally known □ *noun* the lowest rank of ordinary soldier (not an officer)

private eye *informal* a detective

privately *adverb* in a private way

private parts *euphemism* the external sexual organs

privation *noun* **1** want, poverty, hardship **2** taking away, loss

privatize *verb* to transfer from state to private ownership, denationalize

privet *noun* a type of shrub used for hedges

privilege *noun* a right available to one person or to only a few people

privileged *adjective* having privileges

privy *adjective*: **privy to** knowing about (something secret)

privy council an appointed group of advisers to a king or queen

prize *noun* **1** a reward **2** something won in a competition **3** something captured **4** something highly valued □ *adjective* very fine, worthy of a prize □ *verb* to value highly

pro *short for* **professional**

pro- *prefix* **1** before, forward, front **2** in favour of: *pro-devolution* □ **pros and cons** the arguments for and against anything

🕘 Comes from Latin and Greek *pro* meaning 'before' or 'for'

probability *noun* (*plural* **probabilities**) 1 likelihood 2 something likely to happen

probable *adjective* 1 likely to happen 2 likely to be true

probably *adverb* very likely

probation *noun* 1 a trial period in a new job *etc* 2 a system of releasing prisoners on condition that they commit no more offences and report regularly to the authorities

probationer *noun* someone who is training to be a member of a profession

probe *noun* 1 a long, thin instrument used to examine a wound 2 a thorough investigation 3 a spacecraft for exploring space □ *verb* 1 to examine very carefully 2 to investigate thoroughly to find out information

probity *noun* honesty, goodness of character

problem *noun* a question to be solved; a matter which is difficult to deal with

problematic or **problematical** *adjective* doubtful, uncertain

proboscis (*pronounced* pro-**boh**-sis or pro-**bos**-is or pro-**bos**-kis) *noun* (*plural* **proboscises**) 1 an animal's nose, especially an elephant trunk 2 an insect's mouth

procedure *noun* 1 method of doing business 2 a course of action

proceed *verb* 1 to go on with, continue 2 to begin (to do something) 3 to take legal action (against)
🕘 Comes from Latin *procedere* meaning 'to go forward'

◆ Do not confuse with: **precede**

proceeding *noun* 1 a step forward 2 **proceedings** a record of the meetings of a society *etc* 3 a law action

proceeds (*pronounced* **proh**-seedz) *noun plural* profit made from a sale *etc*

process *noun* (*plural* **processes**) 1 a series of operations in manufacturing goods 2 a series of events producing change or development 3 a law-court case □ **in the process of** in the course of

procession *noun* a line of people or vehicles moving forward in order

proclaim *verb* to announce publicly, declare openly

proclamation *noun* an official announcement made to the public

procrastinate *verb* to put things off, delay doing something till a later time

procrastination *noun* procrastinating

proctitis *noun* inflammation of the rectum

procure *verb* to obtain; to bring about

prod *verb* to poke; urge on
prod ⇨ prods, prodding, prodded

prodigal *adjective* spending money recklessly, wasteful

prodigality *noun* being prodigal or extravagant

prodigious *adjective* 1 strange, astonishing 2 enormous

prodigy *noun* (*plural* **prodigies**) 1 a wonder 2 someone astonishingly clever: *child prodigy*

produce *verb* (*pronounced* pro-**dyoos**) 1 to bring into being 2 to bring about, cause 3 to prepare (a play *etc*) for the stage 4 to make, manufacture □ *noun* (*pronounced* **prod**-yoos) food grown or produced on a farm or in a garden

producer *noun* someone who produces a play, film *etc*

product *noun* 1 something produced 2 a result 3 *maths* the number that results from the multiplication of two or more numbers

production *noun* 1 the act of producing; the process of producing or being produced: *the new model goes into production next year* 2 the quantity produced or rate of producing it: *an increase in oil production* 3 a particular presentation of a play, opera, ballet *etc*: *a new production of 'The Marriage of Figaro'*

productive *adjective* fruitful, producing results

productivity *noun* the rate of work done

Prof *abbreviation* Professor

profane *adjective* 1 not sacred 2

treating holy things without respect

profanity (*pronounced* pro-**fan**-*i*t-i) *noun* (*plural* **profanities**) 1 swearing 2 lack of respect for sacred things

profess *verb* 1 to declare (a belief *etc*) openly 2 to pretend, claim: *he professes to be an expert on Scott*

professed *adjective* 1 declared 2 pretended

profession *noun* 1 an occupation requiring special training, *eg* that of a doctor, lawyer, teacher *etc* 2 an open declaration

professional *adjective* 1 of a profession 2 earning a living from a game or an art (*contrasted with*: **amateur**) 3 skilful, competent □ *noun* 1 someone who works in a profession 2 someone who earns money from a game or art

professionalism *noun* 1 a professional status 2 professional expertise or competence

professionally *adverb* in a professional way; in terms of one's profession: *professionally qualified*

professor *noun* 1 a teacher of the highest rank in a university 2 *US* a university teacher

proffer *verb* to offer

proficiency *noun* skill

proficient *adjective* skilled, expert

profile *noun* 1 an outline 2 a side view of a face, head *etc* 3 a short description of someone's life, achievements *etc*

profit *noun* 1 gain, benefit 2 money got by selling an article for a higher price than was paid for it □ *verb* to gain (from), benefit

profitable *adjective* bringing profit or gain

profiteer *noun* someone who makes large profits unfairly □ *verb* to make large profits

profligacy *noun* being profligate

profligate *adjective* 1 living an immoral life 2 very extravagant □ *noun* a profligate person

profound *adjective* 1 very deep 2 deeply felt 3 showing great knowledge or understanding: *a profound comment*

profundity *noun* 1 being profound 2 depth

profuse *adjective* abundant, lavish, extravagant

profusion *noun* 1 being profuse 2 extravagance

progenitor *noun* an ancestor

progeny *noun* children

progesterone *noun* a female sex hormone that maintains pregnancy

prognosis *noun* a prediction of the course of a disease

prognosticate *verb* to foretell

prognostication *noun* prognosticating

program *noun* a set of instructions telling a computer to carry out certain actions □ *verb* 1 to give instructions to 2 to prepare instructions to be carried out by a computer

> **program** *verb* ⇨ programs, programming, programmed

programme or *US* **program** *noun* 1 a booklet with details of an entertainment, ceremony *etc* 2 a scheme, a plan 3 a TV or radio broadcast

progress *noun* 1 advance, forward movement 2 improvement □ *verb* 1 to go forward 2 to improve

progression *noun* 1 the process of moving forwards or advancing in stages 2 *music* a succession of chords, the advance from one to the next being determined on a fixed pattern 3 *maths* a sequence of numbers, each of which bears a specific relationship to the preceding one

progressive *adjective* 1 going forward 2 favouring reforms

prohibit *verb* 1 to forbid 2 to prevent

prohibition *noun* the forbidding by law of making and selling alcoholic drinks

prohibitive *adjective* 1 prohibiting 2 of price: too expensive, discouraging

project *noun* (*pronounced* **proj**-ekt) 1 a plan, a scheme 2 a task 3 a piece of study or research □ *verb* (*pronounced* pro-**jekt**) 1 to throw out or up 2 to jut out 3 to cast (an image, a light *etc*) on to a surface 4 to plan, propose

projectile *noun* a missile

projection *noun* an act of projecting; something projected; something which juts out

projectionist *noun* someone who operates a film projector

projector *noun* a machine for projecting cinema pictures on a screen

proletarian *noun* a member of the proletariat

proletariat *noun* the ordinary working people

proliferate *verb* to grow or increase rapidly

prolific *adjective* producing a lot, fruitful

prologue *noun* a preface or introduction to a play *etc*

prolong *verb* to make longer

prom *informal, short for* 1 promenade 2 promenade concert

promenade *noun* 1 a level roadway or walk, especially by the seaside 2 a walk, a stroll □ *verb* to walk for pleasure

promenade concert a concert at which a large part of the audience stands instead of being seated

prominence *noun* being prominent

prominent *adjective* 1 standing out, easily seen 2 famous, distinguished

promiscuity *noun* being promiscuous

promiscuous *adjective* 1 having many sexual relationships 2 mixed in kind 3 not making distinctions between people or things

promise *verb* 1 to give your word (to do or not do something) 2 to show signs for the future: *the weather promises to improve* □ *noun* 1 a statement of something promised 2 a sign of something to come 3 a sign of future success: *his painting shows great promise*

■ **Alternative words**: (verb, meaning 1) vow, pledge, contract, undertake, warrant, guarantee

promising *adjective* showing signs of being successful

promontory *noun* (*plural*

promontories) a headland jutting out into the sea

promote *verb* 1 to raise to a higher rank 2 to help onwards, encourage 3 to advertise, encourage the sales of

promotion *noun* 1 advancement in rank or honour 2 encouragement 3 advertising, or an effort to publicize and increase sales of a particular brand

promotional *adjective* relating to or involving promotion

prompt *adjective* 1 quick, immediate 2 punctual □ *verb* 1 to move to action 2 to supply words to an actor who has forgotten their lines

prompter *noun* a person positioned offstage to prompt actors when they forget their lines

promptly *adverb* 1 without delay 2 punctually

promptness *noun* being prompt

promulgate *verb* to make widely known

promulgation *noun* promulgating or being promulgated

prone *adjective* 1 lying face downward 2 inclined (to): *prone to laziness*

prong *noun* the spike of a fork

pronged *adjective* having prongs

pronoun *noun* a word used instead of a noun, *eg* I, you, who

pronounce *verb* 1 to speak (words, sounds) 2 to announce (an opinion), declare

pronounced *adjective* noticeable, marked

pronouncement *noun* a statement, an announcement

pronto *adverb, informal* quickly

pronunciation *noun* the way a word is said

proof *noun* 1 evidence that makes something clear beyond doubt 2 the standard strength of whisky *etc* 3 a copy of a printed sheet for correction before publication □ *adjective* able to keep out or withstand: *proof against attack/ waterproof*

proofread *verb* to read and correct printed page proofs of a text

proofreader *noun* a person who reads and corrects printed proofs of a text

prop *noun* **1** a support **2** *short for* propeller **3** *short for* stage property (= an item needed on stage for a play) □ *verb* to hold up, support

prop *verb* ⇨ prop*s*, prop*ping*, prop*ped*

propaganda *noun* **1** the spreading of ideas to influence public opinion **2** material used for this, *eg* posters, leaflets

propagandist *noun* someone who spreads propaganda

propagate *verb* **1** to spread **2** to produce seedlings or young

propagator *noun* **1** a person or thing that propagates **2** a heated box with a cover in which plants may be grown from cuttings or seeds

propane *noun* a gas used as fuel

propel *verb* to drive forward

propel ⇨ propel*s*, propel*ling*, propel*led*

propellant *noun* **1** an explosive for firing a rocket **2** the gas in an aerosol spray

propeller *noun* a shaft with revolving blades which drives forward a ship, aircraft *etc*

propensity *noun* (*plural* **propensities**) a natural inclination: *a propensity for bumping into things*

proper *adjective* **1** right, correct: *the proper way to do it* **2** full, thorough: *a proper search* **3** prim, well-behaved

properly *adverb* **1** in the right way **2** thoroughly

proper noun or **proper name** *grammar* a name for a particular person, place or thing, *eg* Shakespeare, the Parthenon (*contrasted with*: **common noun**)

property *noun* (*plural* **properties**) **1** land or buildings owned **2** a quality **3 properties** the furniture *etc* required by actors in a play

prophecy (*pronounced* prof-*es*-i) *noun* (*plural* **prophecies**) **1** foretelling the future **2** something prophesied

⚫ Do not confuse: **prophecy** and **prophesy**. The spelling with the 'c' is the noun, the spelling with the 's' the verb. It may help to remember that this is a common pattern, seen also in such pairs as practice/practise, licence/license and advice/advise

prophesy (*pronounced* prof-*es*-ai) *verb* to foretell the future, predict

prophesy ⇨ prophesi*es*, prophesy*ing*, prophesi*ed*

prophet *noun* **1** someone who claims to foretell events **2** someone who tells what they believe to be the will of God

propinquity *noun* nearness

propitiate *verb* to calm the anger of

propitious *adjective* favourable: *propitious circumstances*

proponent *noun* someone in favour of a thing

proportion *noun* **1** a part of a total amount: *a large proportion of income is taxed* **2** relation in size, number *etc* compared with something else: *the proportion of girls to boys is small* □ **in** or **out of proportion** appropriate or inappropriate in size or degree when compared with other things

proportional or **proportionate** *adjective* in proportion

proportional representation a voting system in which parties are represented in proportion to their voting strength

proposal *noun* **1** an act of proposing **2** anything proposed **3** an offer of marriage

propose *verb* **1** to put forward for consideration, suggest **2** to intend **3** to make an offer of marriage (to)

proposition *noun* **1** a proposal, a suggestion **2** a statement **3** a situation that must be dealt with: *a tough proposition*

⚫ Do not confuse with: **preposition**

propound *verb* to state, put forward for consideration

proprietor, proprietress *noun* an owner, especially of a hotel

propriety *noun* (*plural* **proprieties**) **1** fitness, suitability **2** correct behaviour, decency

propulsion *noun* an act of driving forward

prorogation *noun* proroguing

prorogue *verb* to discontinue meetings of (parliament *etc*) for a period

prosaic *adjective* dull, not interesting □ **prosaically** *adverb*

proscenium (*pronounced* proh-**see**-ni-um) *noun* the front part of a stage

proscribe *verb* to ban, prohibit
ⓘ Comes from Latin *proscribere* meaning 'to publish in writing'

> 🖝 Do not confuse with: **prescribe**.
> It may help to remember that
> **PROscribe** and **PROhibit** share
> the same three first letters

proscription *noun* proscribing or being proscribed

> 🖝 Do not confuse with:
> **prescription**. **Proscription** is
> related to the verb **proscribe**

proscriptive *adjective* tending to proscribe

prose *noun* **1** writing which is not in verse **2** ordinary written or spoken language

prosecute *verb* **1** to bring a law-court action against **2** to carry on (studies, an investigation *etc*)
ⓘ Comes from Latin *prosequi* meaning 'to accompany someone on their way forth'

> 🖝 Do not confuse with: **persecute**

prosecution *noun* **1** an act of prosecuting **2** *law* those bringing the case in a trial (*contrasted with*: **defence**)

proselyte *noun* a convert

prosody *noun* study of the rhythms and construction of poetry

prospect *noun* (*pronounced* **pros**-pekt) **1** a view, a scene **2** a future outlook or expectation: *the prospect of a free weekend/ a job with good prospects* □ *verb* (*pronounced* pros-**pekt**) to search for gold or other minerals

prospective *adjective* soon to be, likely to be: *the prospective election*

prospector *noun* someone who prospects for minerals

prospectus *noun* (*plural* **prospectuses**) a booklet giving information about a school, organization *etc*

prosper *verb* to get on well, succeed

prosperity *noun* success, good fortune

prosperous *adjective* successful, wealthy

prostate *noun* a gland in a man's bladder which releases a fluid used in semen

prostitute *noun* someone who offers sexual intercourse for payment

prostrate *adjective* **1** lying flat face downwards **2** worn out, exhausted □ *verb* **1** to lie on the ground as a sign of respect: *prostrated themselves before the emperor* **2** to exhaust, tire out completely

prostrated *adjective* worn out by grief, tiredness *etc*

prostration *noun* the act of prostrating

protagonist *noun* a chief character in a play *etc*

protect *verb* to shield from danger, keep safe

protection *noun* **1** the act of protecting **2** safety, shelter

protectionism *noun* the policy of protecting home industry from foreign competition

protectionist *noun* a person who favours protectionism

protective *adjective* giving protection; intended to protect

protector *noun* a guardian, a defender

protectorate *noun* a country which is partly governed and defended by another country

protégé *noun* a male pupil or employee who is taught or helped in their career by someone important or powerful

protégée *noun* a female pupil or employee who is taught or helped in their career by someone important or powerful

protein *noun* a substance present in milk, eggs, meat *etc* which is a necessary part of a human or animal diet

protest *verb* 1 to object strongly 2 to declare solemnly: *protesting his innocence* □ *noun* a strong objection

Protestant *noun* a member of one of the Christian churches that broke away from the Roman Catholic Church at the time of the Reformation

protestation *noun* 1 a solemn declaration 2 a protest

protocol *noun* correct procedure

proton *noun* a particle with a positive electrical charge, forming part of the nucleus of an atom (*compare with:* **electron**)

prototype *noun* the original model from which something is copied

protract *verb* to lengthen in time

protractor *noun* an instrument for drawing and measuring angles on paper

protrude *verb* to stick out, thrust forward □ **protrusion** *noun*

protuberance *noun* a swelling, a bulge □ **protuberant** *adjective*

proud *adjective* 1 thinking too highly of yourself, conceited 2 feeling pleased at an achievement *etc* 3 dignified, self-respecting: *too proud to accept the money* □ **do someone proud** to treat them grandly

prove *verb* 1 to show to be true or correct 2 to try out, test 3 to turn out (to be): *his prediction proved correct*

provenance *noun* source, origin

provender *noun* food, especially for horses and cattle

proverb *noun* a well-known wise saying, *eg* 'nothing ventured, nothing gained'

In what sort of situation might you say, 'A stitch in time saves nine', or 'Too many cooks spoil the broth'? What would someone mean if they said, 'It's an ill wind that blows nobody any good', or 'Little strokes fell great oaks'?

✏ **Try writing a short story where the last line takes the form of a proverb**

proverbial *adjective* well-known, widely spoken of

provide *verb* to supply □ **providing that** on condition that

providence *noun* 1 foresight; thrift 2 **Providence** God

provident *adjective* thinking of the future; thrifty

providential *adjective* fortunate, coming as if by divine help

province *noun* 1 a division of a country 2 the extent of someone's duties or knowledge 3 **provinces** all parts of a country outside the capital

provincial *adjective* 1 of a province or provinces 2 narrow-minded, parochial

provision *noun* 1 an agreed arrangement 2 a rule or condition 3 **provisions** a supply of food

provisional *adjective* used for the time being; temporary

proviso (*pronounced* pro-**vai**-zoh) *noun* (*plural* **provisos**) a condition laid down beforehand

provocative (*pronounced* pro-**vok**-at-iv) *adjective* 1 tending to rouse anger 2 likely to arouse sexual interest

provoke *verb* 1 to cause, result in 2 to rouse to anger or action: *don't let him provoke you* □ **provocation** *noun* (meaning 2)

provoking *adjective* annoying

provost *noun* the chief magistrate of a burgh in Scotland

prow *noun* the front part of a ship

prowess *noun* skill, ability

prowl *verb* to go about stealthily

proximity *noun* nearness

proxy *noun* (*plural* **proxies**) someone who acts or votes on behalf of another

prude *noun* an over-modest, priggish person □ **prudery** *noun* □ **prudish** *adjective*

prudent *adjective* wise and cautious □ **prudently** *adverb* □ **prudence** *noun*

prune¹ *verb* 1 to trim (a tree) by cutting off unneeded twigs 2 to shorten, reduce

prune² *noun* a dried plum

prurient *adjective* excessively concerned with sexual matters □ **prurience** *noun*

pry verb to look closely into things that are not your business □ **prying** adjective

pry ⇨ pries, prying, pried

PS abbreviation postscript

psalm noun a sacred song

psalmist noun a writer of psalms

psalter noun a book of psalms

p's and q's correct social manners

psephologist (pronounced se-**fol**-oj-ist) noun someone who studies elections and voting trends

Coined in the 1950s, based on Greek psephos, a pebble used in the ancient Greek system of casting votes

pseud (pronounced sood) adjective, informal pseudo □ noun, informal a fraud

pseud- (pronounced sood) or **pseudo-** prefix false: pseudonym
ⓘ Comes from Greek pseudes meaning 'false'

pseudo (pronounced **sood**-oh) adjective, informal false, fake, pretended: his Spanish accent is pseudo

pseudonym (pronounced **sood**-o-nim) noun a false name used by an author

psych- see psycho-

psychedelic adjective bright and multi-coloured

psychiatrist noun someone who treats mental illness

psychiatry noun the treatment of mental illness □ **psychiatric** (pronounced sai-ki-**at**-rik) adjective

psychic (pronounced **sai**-kik) or **psychical** adjective 1 relating to the mind 2 able to read other people's minds, or tell the future

psycho- (pronounced **sai**-koh) or **psych-** prefix relating to the mind: psychology/ psychoanalysis
ⓘ Comes from Greek psyche meaning 'soul'

psychoanalyse verb to treat by psychoanalysis

psychoanalysis noun a method of treating mental illness by discussing with the patient its possible causes in their past □ **psychoanalyst** noun

psychological adjective of psychology or the mind

psychology noun the science which studies the human mind □ **psychologist** noun

psychosis noun, medicine a mental illness

psychosomatic adjective of an illness: having a psychological cause

psychotherapy noun treatment of mental illness by psychoanalysis etc □ **psychotherapist** noun

psychotic adjective, medicine affected by mental illness, mad

PT abbreviation physical training

PTA abbreviation parent teacher association

ptarmigan (pronounced **tah**-mig-an) noun a mountain-dwelling bird of the grouse family, which turns white in winter

pterodactyl (pronounced te-ro-**dak**-til) noun an extinct flying reptile

PTO abbreviation please turn over

pub short for public house

puberty (pronounced **pyoob**-et-i) noun the time during youth when the body becomes sexually mature

pubic (pronounced **pyoob**-ik) adjective of the lowest part of the abdomen: pubic hair

public adjective 1 relating to or shared by the people of a community or nation in general: public opinion/ public library 2 generally or widely known: a public figure □ noun people in general □ **in public** in front of or among other people □ **public address system** a system of microphones, amplifiers and loudspeakers used to enable an audience to hear voices, music etc

publican noun the keeper of an inn or public house

publication noun 1 the act of making news etc public 2 the act of publishing a book, newspaper etc 3 a published book, magazine etc

public house a building where alcoholic drinks are sold and consumed, a pub

publicity *noun* advertising; bringing to public notice or attention

publicize *verb* to make public, advertise

public relations 1 the relations between a business *etc* and the public **2** a department of a business *etc* dealing with this

publish *verb* **1** to make generally known **2** to prepare and put out (a book *etc*) for sale

publisher *noun* someone who publishes books

puce *adjective* of a brownish-purple colour

pucker *verb* to wrinkle □ *noun* a wrinkle, a fold

pudding *noun* **1** the sweet course of a meal **2** a sweet dish made with eggs, flour, milk *etc* **3** a type of sausage: *mealy pudding*

puddle *noun* a small, often muddy, pool

puerile (*pronounced* **pyoor**-ral) *adjective* childish, silly □ **puerility** *noun*
Ⓒ Comes from Latin *pueriis* meaning 'childish'

puerperal (*pronounced* pyoo-**er**-pe-ral) *adjective, formal* relating to childbirth
Ⓒ Comes from Latin *puerpera* meaning 'a woman in labour'

puff *verb* **1** to blow out in small gusts **2** to breathe heavily, *eg* after running **3** to blow up, inflate **4** to swell (up or out) □ *noun* **1** a short, sudden gust of wind, breath *etc* **2** a powder puff **3** a piece of advertising

puffin *noun* a type of sea bird, with a short, thick, brightly-coloured beak

puff pastry a light, flaky kind of pastry

puffy *adjective* **1** swollen, flabby **2** breathing heavily

pug *noun* a breed of small dog with a snub nose

pugilism (*pronounced* **pyoo**-jil-i-zm) *noun* boxing
Ⓒ Comes from Latin *pugil* meaning 'a boxer'

pugilist (*pronounced* **pyoo**-jil-ist) *noun* a boxer
Ⓒ For origin, see **pugilism**

pugnacious *adjective* quarrelsome, fond of fighting □ **pugnacity** *noun*
Ⓒ Comes from Latin *pugnax* meaning 'warlike'

puke *noun & verb, slang* (to) vomit

pulchritude (*pronounced* **pulk**-rit-yood) *noun, formal* beauty □ **pulchritudinous** *adjective*
Ⓒ Comes from Latin *pulchritudo* meaning 'beauty'

pull *verb* **1** to move or try to move (something) towards yourself by force **2** to drag, tug **3** to stretch, strain: *pull a muscle* **4** to tear: *pull to pieces* □ *noun* **1** the act of pulling **2** a pulling force, *eg* of a magnet **3** a handle for pulling **4** *informal* advantage, influence □ **pull yourself together** to regain self-control or self-possession □ **pull through** to get safely to the end of a difficult or dangerous experience □ **pull up** to stop, halt

pullet *noun* a young hen

pulley *noun* (*plural* **pulleys**) a grooved wheel fitted with a cord and set in a block, used for lifting weights *etc*

Pullman *noun* luxurious or superior seating on a train, in a cinema *etc*

Named after George M *Pullman*, an American who made the first luxury sleeping car for railways in the 19th century

pullover *noun* a knitted garment for the top half of the body, a jersey

pulmonary *adjective* relating to the lungs

pulp *noun* **1** the soft fleshy part of a fruit **2** a soft mass of wood *etc* which is made into paper **3** any soft mass □ *verb* to reduce to pulp

pulpit *noun* an enclosed platform in a church for the minister or priest

pulsate *verb* to beat, throb

pulse *noun* the beating or throbbing of the heart and blood vessels as blood flows through them □ *verb* to throb, pulsate

pulses *noun plural* beans, peas, lentils and other edible seeds of this family

pulverize *verb* to make or crush into powder

puma *noun* an American wild animal like a large cat

pumice *noun* or **pumice stone** a piece of light solidified lava used for smoothing skin and for rubbing away stains

pummel *verb* to beat with the fists

pummel ⇨ pummel*s*, pummel*ling*, pummel*led*

pump *noun* 1 a machine used for making water rise to the surface 2 a machine for drawing out or forcing in air, gas *etc*: *bicycle pump* 3 a kind of thin- or soft-soled shoe for dancing, gymnastics *etc* □ *verb* 1 to raise or force with a pump 2 *informal* to draw out information from by clever questioning

pumpkin *noun* a large, roundish, thick-skinned, yellow fruit, with stringy edible flesh

pun *noun* a play upon words which sound similar but have different meanings, *eg* 'two *pears* make a *pair*' □ *verb* to make a pun

pun *verb* ⇨ pun*s*, pun*ning*, pun*ned*

punch[1] *verb* 1 to hit with the fist 2 to make a hole in with a tool: *punch a ticket* □ *noun* (*plural* **punches**) 1 a blow with the fist 2 a tool for punching holes

punch[2] *noun* a drink made of spirits or wine, water, sugar *etc*

punch-drunk *adjective* dizzy from being hit

punch line the words that give the main point to a joke

punchy *adjective* having a powerful effect, striking

punctilious *adjective* paying attention to details, especially in behaviour; fastidious

punctual *adjective* 1 on time, not late 2 strict in keeping the time of appointments □ **punctuality** *noun*

punctuate *verb* 1 to divide up sentences by commas, full stops *etc* 2 to interrupt at intervals: *the silence was punctuated by occasional coughing*

punctuation *noun* the use of punctuation marks

punctuation marks the symbols used in punctuating sentences, *eg* full stop,

comma, colon, question mark *etc*

puncture *noun* 1 an act of pricking or piercing 2 a small hole made with a sharp point 3 a hole in a tyre

pundit *noun* an expert

pungent *adjective* 1 sharp-tasting or sharp-smelling 2 of a remark: strongly sarcastic

punish *verb* 1 to make (someone) suffer for a fault or crime 2 to inflict suffering on 3 to treat roughly or harshly

punishable *adjective* likely to bring punishment

punishment *noun* pain or constraints inflicted for a fault or crime

punitive (*pronounced* **pyoo**-n*i*t-iv) *adjective* inflicting punishment or suffering

punnet *noun* a small basket for holding fruit

punt *noun* a flat-bottomed boat with square ends □ *verb* to move (a punt) by pushing a pole against the bottom of a river

punter *noun* 1 a professional gambler 2 a customer, a client 3 an ordinary person

puny *adjective* little and weak

pup *noun* 1 a young dog (also **puppy**) 2 the young of certain other animals, *eg* a seal

pupa (*pronounced* **pyoo**-p*a*) *noun* (*plural* **pupae** – *pronounced* **pyoo**-pee) the stage in the growth of an insect in which it changes from a larva to its mature form, *eg* from a caterpillar into a butterfly

pupate (*pronounced* pyoo-**peit**) *verb* to become a pupa

pupil *noun* 1 someone who is being taught by a teacher 2 the round opening in the middle of the eye through which light passes

puppet *noun* 1 a doll which is moved by strings or wires 2 a doll that fits over the hand and is moved by the fingers 3 someone who acts exactly as they are told to

puppy *see* pup

puppy fat temporary fat in childhood or adolescence

puppy love immature love when very young

purchaser *noun* someone who buys

purchase *verb* to buy □ *noun* **1** the act of buying **2** something which is bought **3** the power to lift by using a lever *etc* **4** firm grip or hold

purdah *noun, historical* the seclusion of Hindu or Islamic women from strangers, behind a screen or under a veil

pure *adjective* **1** clean, spotless **2** free from dust, dirt *etc* **3** not mixed with other substances **4** free from faults or sin, innocent **5** utter, absolute, nothing but: *pure nonsense*

purée *noun* food made into a pulp by being put through a sieve or liquidizing machine □ *verb* to make into a purée, pulp

purely *adverb* **1** in a pure way **2** wholly, entirely: *purely on merit* **3** merely, only: *purely for the sake of appearance*

purgative *noun* a medicine which clears waste matter out of the body □ *adjective*

purgatory *noun* **1** in the Roman Catholic Church, a place where souls are made pure before entering heaven **2** a state of suffering for a time

purge *verb* **1** to make clean, purify **2** to clear (something) of anything unwanted: *the new president purged the party of those who disagreed with her*

purify *verb* to make pure □ **purification** *noun*

purify ⇨ purifies, purifying, purified

purist *noun* someone who insists on correctness

puritan *noun* **1** someone of strict, often narrow-minded, morals **2** **Puritan** *historical* one of a group believing in strict simplicity in worship and daily life □ **puritanical** *adjective* □ **puritanism** *noun*

purity (*from* **pure**) *noun* the state of being pure

purl *verb* to knit in stitches made with the wool in front of the work

purloin *verb* to steal

purple *noun* a dark colour formed by the mixture of blue and red

purport *noun* meaning □ *verb* **1** to mean **2** to seem, pretend: *he purports to be a film expert*

purpose *noun* **1** aim, intention **2** use, function (of a tool *etc*) □ *verb* to intend □ **on purpose** intentionally □ **to the purpose** to the point

purposely *adverb* intentionally

purr *noun* the low, murmuring sound made by a cat when pleased □ *verb* of a cat: to make this sound

purse *noun* **1** a small bag for carrying money **2** *US* a handbag □ *verb* to close (the lips) tightly

purser *noun* the officer who looks after a ship's money

pursue *verb* **1** to follow after (in order to overtake or capture), chase **2** to be engaged in, carry on (studies, an enquiry *etc*) **3** to follow (a route, path *etc*)

pursuer *noun* someone who pursues

pursuit *noun* **1** the act of pursuing **2** an occupation or hobby

purvey *verb* to supply (food *etc*) as a business □ **purveyor** *noun*

pus *noun* a thick yellowish liquid produced from infected wounds

push *verb* **1** to press hard against **2** to thrust (something) away with force, shove **3** to urge on **4** to make a big effort □ *noun* **1** a thrust **2** effort **3** *informal* energy and determination

push-chair *noun* a folding chair on wheels for a young child

pushy *adjective* aggressively assertive

pusillanimous (*pronounced* pyoo-si-lan-im-*us*) *adjective* cowardly □ **pusillanimity** *noun*

pussy *noun, informal* a cat, a kitten

pussy-foot *verb* to act timidly or non-committally

pussy-willow *noun* an American willow tree with silky catkins

pustule *noun* a small pimple containing pus

put *verb* **1** to place, lay, set: *put the book on the table* **2** to bring to a certain

position or state: *put the light on/ put it out of your mind* **3** to express: *put the question more clearly* □ **put about 1** to change course at sea **2** to spread (news) □ **put by** to set aside, save up □ **put down** to defeat □ **put in for** to make a claim for, apply for □ **put off 1** to delay **2** to turn (someone) away from their plan or intention □ **put out 1** to extinguish (a fire, light *etc*) **2** to annoy, embarrass □ **put up 1** to build **2** to propose, suggest (a plan, candidate *etc*) **3** to let (someone) stay in your house *etc* **4** to stay as a guest in someone's house
□ **put up with** to bear patiently, tolerate

put ⇨ put*s*, putt*ing*, put
Ⓛ Comes from Late Old English *putian*

■ **Alternative words**: (verb, meaning 1) deposit, dispose, situate

putative *adjective* supposed, commonly accepted
Ⓛ Comes from Latin *putare* meaning 'to suppose'

putrefy *verb* to go bad, rot
□ **putrefaction** *noun*

putrefy ⇨ putrefi*es*, putrefy*ing*, putrefi*ed*

putrid *adjective* rotten; stinking

putsch *noun* a sudden move to seize political power; a coup d'état

putt *verb, golf* to send a ball gently forward □ **putter** *noun* a golf club used for this

putty *noun* a cement made from ground chalk, used in putting glass in windows *etc*

puzzle *verb* **1** to present with a difficult problem or situation *etc* **2** to be difficult (for someone) to understand: *her moods puzzled him* **3 puzzle something out** to consider long and carefully in order to

solve (a problem) □ *noun* **1** a difficulty which needs a lot of thought **2** a toy or riddle to test knowledge or skill: *crossword puzzle/ jigsaw puzzle*

PVC *abbreviation* polyvinyl chloride

pygmy or **pigmy** (*plural* pygmies or pigmies) *noun* one of a race of very small human beings

pyjamas or **pajamas** *noun plural* a sleeping suit consisting of trousers and a jacket

pylon *noun* **1** a high, steel tower supporting electric power cables **2** a guiding mark at an airfield

pyramid *noun* **1** a solid shape with flat sides which come to a point at the top **2** *historical* a building of this shape used as a tomb in ancient Egypt

pyre *noun* a pile of wood on which a dead body is burned

Pyrex *noun, trademark* a type of glassware for cooking that will withstand heat

pyro- (*pronounced* pai-roh) *prefix* relating to fire, heat or fever
Ⓛ Comes from Greek *pyr* meaning 'fire'

pyromania *noun* an obsessive fascination with fire

pyromaniac *noun* someone who gets pleasure from starting fires

pyrotechnics *noun plural* a display of fireworks

Pyrrhic victory (*pronounced* pi-rik) a victory gained at so great a cost that it is equal to a defeat

After the costly defeat of the Romans by *Pyrrhus*, king of Epirus, in 280 BC

python *noun* a large, non-poisonous snake which crushes its victims

Qq

QC *abbreviation* Queen's Counsel

qed (*pronounced* kyoo ee **dee**) *abbreviation quod erat demonstrandum*, which was to be demonstrated (from Latin)

quack *noun* **1** the cry of a duck **2** someone who falsely claims to have medical knowledge or training □ *verb* to make the noise of a duck

quad *short for* **1** quadruplet **2** quadrangle

quadrangle *noun* **1** *maths* a figure with four equal sides and angles **2** a four-sided courtyard surrounded by buildings in a school, college *etc*

quadrangular *adjective* having the shape of a quadrangle

quadrant *noun* **1** one quarter of the circumference or area of a circle **2** an instrument used in astronomy, navigation *etc* for measuring heights

quadri- or **quadru-** *prefix* four: *quadrilateral/ quadruped*
ⓘ Comes from Latin *quattuor* meaning 'four'

quadrilateral *noun* a four-sided figure or area □ *adjective* four-sided

quadrille *noun* a dance for four couples arranged to form a square

quadriplegia *noun* paralysis of both arms and both legs

quadriplegic *noun* someone suffering from quadriplegia

quadruped *noun* a four-footed animal

quadruple *adjective* **1** four times as much or many **2** made up of four parts □ *verb* to make or become four times greater: *quadrupled the price*

quadruplet *noun* one of four children born to the same mother at one birth

quaff (*pronounced* kwahf or kwof) *verb* to drink up eagerly

quagmire *noun* wet, boggy ground

quaich (*pronounced* kweikh) *noun, Scottish* a shallow ornamental cup with two handles

quail *verb* to shrink back in fear □ *noun* a type of small bird like a partridge

quaint *adjective* pleasantly odd, especially because of being old-fashioned

quake *verb* to shake, tremble with fear □ *noun, informal* an earthquake

quake *verb* ⟹ quakes, quak*ing*, quak*ed*

Quaker *noun* a member of a religious group opposed to violence and war, founded in the 17th century

Originally a nickname given to the group because their founder, George Fox, told them to *quake* at the word of God

qualification *noun* **1** a qualifying statement **2** a skill that makes someone suitable for a job

qualified *adjective* having the necessary qualifications for a job

qualify *verb* **1** to be suitable for a job or position **2** to pass a test **3** to lessen the force of (a statement) by adding or changing words

qualitative *adjective* relating to quality rather than quantity

quality *noun* (*plural* **qualities**) **1** an outstanding feature of someone or thing: *kindness is a quality admired by* *all* **2** degree of worth: *cloth of poor quality*

qualm *noun* doubt about whether something is right

quandary *noun* (*plural* **quandaries**) **1** a state of uncertainty **2** a situation in which it is difficult to decide what to do

quango *noun* (*plural* **quangos**) an official body, funded and appointed by government, that supervises some national activity *etc*

quantifiable *adjective* capable of being quanitified

quantify *verb* to state the quantity of

> **quantify** ⇨ quanti*fies*, quanti*fying*, quanti*fied*

quantitative *adjective* relating to quantity, not quality

quantity *noun* (*plural* **quantities**) **1** amount: *a large quantity of paper* **2** a symbol which represents an amount: *x is the unknown quantity*

quantum leap a huge, dramatic jump

quarantine *noun* the isolation of people or animals who might be carrying an infectious disease ▫ *verb* to put in quarantine

quark *noun*, *physics* a sub-atomic particle

> A word invented by James Joyce in *Finnegans Wake* (1939)

quarrel *noun* an angry disagreement or argument ▫ *verb* **1** to disagree violently or argue angrily (with) **2** to find fault (with)

> **quarrel** *verb* ⇨ quarrel*s*, quarrel*ling*, quarrel*led*

quarrelsome *adjective* fond of quarrelling, inclined to quarrel

quarry *noun* (*plural* **quarries**) **1** a pit from which stone is taken for building **2** a hunted animal **3** someone or something eagerly looked for ▫ *verb* to dig (stone *etc*) from a quarry

> **quarry** *verb* ⇨ quarri*es*, quarry*ing*, quarri*ed*

quart *noun* a measure of liquids, 1.136 litre (2 pints)

quarter *noun* **1** one of four equal parts

of something **2** a fourth part of a year, three months **3** direction: *no help came from any quarter* **4** a district **5** mercy shown to an enemy: *no quarter was given by either side* **6** **quarters** lodgings, accommodation ▫ *verb* **1** to divide into four equal parts **2** to accommodate

quarter-deck *noun* the upper deck of a ship between the stern and the mast nearest it

quarter-final *noun* a match in a competition immediately before a semi-final

quarterly *adjective* happening every three months ▫ *adverb* every three months ▫ *noun* (*plural* **quarterlies**) a magazine *etc* published every three months

quartet *noun* **1** a group of four players or singers **2** a piece of music written for such a group

quartz *noun* a hard substance often in crystal form, found in rocks

quash *verb* **1** to crush, put down (*eg* a rebellion) **2** to wipe out, annul (*eg* a judge's decision)

quasi- *prefix* to some extent, but not completely: *quasi-historical*

> ⓘ Comes from Latin *quasi* meaning 'as if'

quatrain *noun* a poetic stanza of four lines

quaver *verb* **1** to shake, tremble **2** to speak in a shaking voice ▫ *noun* **1** a trembling of the voice **2** *music* a note (♪) equal to half a crotchet in length

quay (*pronounced* kee) *noun* a solid landing place for loading and unloading boats

queasy *adjective* **1** feeling nauseous **2** easily shocked or disgusted ▫ **queasiness** *noun*

queen *noun* **1** a female monarch **2** the wife of a king **3** the most powerful piece in chess **4** a high value playing-card with a picture of a queen **5** an egg-laying female bee, ant or wasp

queen bee 1 an egg-laying female bee **2** a woman who is the centre of attention

queenly *adjective* of or like a queen

queen mother the mother of the

reigning king or queen who was once herself queen

queer *adjective* 1 odd, strange 2 *informal* (sometimes *derogatory*) homosexual □ *noun*, *informal* (sometimes *derogatory*) a homosexual

quell *verb* 1 to crush (a rebellion *etc*) 2 to remove (fears, suspicions *etc*)

quench *verb* 1 to drink and so satisfy (thirst) 2 to put out (*eg* a fire)

querulous *adjective* complaining

query *noun* (*plural* **queries**) 1 a question 2 a question mark (?) □ *verb* to question (*eg* a statement)

> **query** *verb* ⇨ queries, querying, queried

quest *noun* a search

question *noun* 1 something requiring an answer, *eg* 'where do you live?' 2 a subject, matter *etc*: *the energy question/ a question of ability* 3 a matter for dispute or doubt: *there's no question of him leaving* □ *verb* 1 to ask questions of (someone) 2 to express doubt about □ **out of the question** not even to be considered, unthinkable

questionable *adjective* doubtful

question mark a symbol (?) put after a question in writing

questionnaire *noun* a written list of questions to be answered by several people to provide information for a survey

queue *noun* a line of people waiting, *eg* for a bus □ *verb* to stand in, or form, a queue

quibble *verb* to avoid an important part of an argument by quarrelling over details □ *noun* a petty argument or complaint

quiche (*pronounced* keesh) *noun* an open pastry case filled with beaten eggs, cheese *etc* and baked

quick *adjective* 1 done or happening in a short time 2 acting without delay, fast-moving: *a quick brain* □ *noun* a tender area of skin under the nails □ *adverb*, *informal* quickly □ **the quick** *old* the living

quicken *verb* to speed up, become or make faster

quicklime *noun* lime (= calcium oxide, a white, caustic substance) which has not been mixed with water

quickly *adverb* without delay, rapidly

quicksand *noun* sand that sucks in anyone who stands on it

quicksilver *noun* mercury

quickstep *noun* a ballroom dance like a fast foxtrot

quick-tempered *adjective* easily made angry

quid *noun*, *slang* a pound (£1)

quiddity *noun* 1 the essence or nature of something 2 a quibble

quiescence *noun* a quiescent state

quiescent *adjective* not active

quiet *adjective* 1 making little or no noise 2 calm: *a quiet life* □ *noun* 1 the state of being quiet 2 lack of noise, peace □ *verb* to make or become quiet

> ♠ Do not confuse with: **quite**

■ **Alternative words**: (adjective, meaning 1) silent, noiseless, inaudible, hushed, soft, low

quieten *verb* to make or become quiet

quietly *adverb* in a quiet way; with little or no sound

quietness *noun* being quiet

quiff *noun* a tuft of hair brushed up and back from the forehead

quill *noun* 1 a large feather of a goose or other bird made into a pen 2 one of the sharp spines of a porcupine

quilt *noun* a bedcover filled with down, feathers *etc*

quilted *adjective* made of two layers of material with padding between them

quin *short for* **quintuplet**

quince *noun* a pear-like fruit with a sharp taste, used to make jams *etc*

quinine *noun* a bitter drug taken from the bark of a S American tree, used to treat malaria

quint- *prefix* fifth
ⓘ Comes from Latin *quintus* meaning 'fifth'

quintessence *noun* 1 the most

important part of anything **2** the purest part or form of something

> Literally 'fifth essence', sought after by medieval alchemists as the highest essence or ether

quintessential *adjective* central, essential

quintet *noun* **1** a group of five players or singers **2** a piece of music written for such a group

quintuplet *noun* one of five children born to a mother at the same time

quip *noun* a witty remark or reply □ *verb* to make a witty remark

> **quip** *verb* ⇨ quips, quipp*ing*, quipp*ed*

quire *noun* a set of 24 sheets of paper
🕐 Probably comes from Late Latin *quaternum* meaning 'a set of four sheets'

> 👆 Do not confuse with: **choir**

quirk *noun* **1** an odd feature of someone's behaviour **2** a trick, a sudden turn: *quirk of fate*

quirky *adjective* full of sudden twists; unpredictable, inconsistent

quisling *noun* someone who collaborates with an enemy, especially a puppet ruler

> After Vidkun *Quisling*, head of the Norwegian fascist party during the German occupation

quit *verb* **1** to give up, stop: *I'm going to quit smoking* **2** *informal* to leave, resign from (a job) □ **be quits** to be even with each other

> **quit** ⇨ quits, quitt*ing*, quit or quitt*ed*

quite *adverb* **1** completely, entirely: *quite empty* **2** fairly, moderately: *quite good*

> 👆 Do not confuse with: **quiet**

quiver[1] *noun* a tremble, a shake □ *verb* to tremble, shake

quiver[2] *noun* a carrying case for arrows

quixotic *adjective* having noble but foolish and unrealistic aims
□ **quixotically** *adverb*

> After Don *Quixote*, the knight in Cervantes's 16th-century Spanish romance

quiz *verb* to question □ *noun* (*plural* **quizzes**) a competition to test knowledge

> **quiz** *verb* ⇨ quizz*es*, quizz*ing*, quizz*ed*

quizzical *adjective* of a look: as if asking a question, especially mockingly

quoits *noun singular* a game in which heavy flat rings (**quoits**) are thrown on to small rods

quorum *noun* the least number of people
who must be present at a meeting before any business can be done

> From Latin phrase *quorum vos .. esse volumus* 'of whom we wish that you be (one, two etc)', used in legal commissions

quota *noun* a part or share to be given or received by each member of a group

quotation *noun* **1** the act of repeating something said or written **2** the words repeated **3** a price stated

quotation marks marks used in writing to show that someone's words are being repeated exactly, *eg* 'he said, "I'm going out"'

quote *verb* **1** to repeat the words of (someone) exactly as said or written **2** to state (a price for something)

quoth *verb, old* said

quotient *noun, maths* the result obtained by dividing one number by another, *eg* 4 is the quotient when 12 is divided by 3

Rr

If you can't find the word you're looking for under letter **R**, it could be that it starts with a different letter. Try looking under **WR** for words like *wrap*, *wrist* and *wrong*. Also, don't forget **RH** for words like *rhetoric*, *rhyme* and *rhinoceros*.

rabbi *noun* (*plural* **rabbis**) a Jewish priest or teacher of the law

rabbit *noun* a small, burrowing, long-eared animal

rabble *noun* a disorderly, noisy crowd

rabid *adjective* **1** of a dog: suffering from rabies **2** violently enthusiastic or extreme: *a rabid nationalist*

rabies *noun* (*also called*: **hydrophobia**) a disease transmitted by the bite of an infected animal, causing fear of water and madness

raccoon or **racoon** *noun* a small furry animal of N America

race¹ *noun* **1** a group of people with the same ancestors and physical characteristics **2** descent: *of noble race*

race² *noun* a competition to find the fastest person, animal, vehicle *etc* □ *verb* **1** to run fast **2** to take part in a race

racecourse or **racetrack** *noun* a course over which races are run

racehorse *noun* a horse bred and used for racing

racial *adjective* of or according to race

racism or **racialism** *noun* **1** the belief that some races of people are superior to others **2** prejudice on the grounds of race

racist or **racialist** *noun* someone who believes in, or practises, racism □ *adjective* involving racism

rack *noun* **1** a framework for holding letters, plates, coats *etc* **2** *historical* an instrument for torturing victims by stretching their joints **3** a bar with teeth which fits into and moves a toothed wheel □ **rack and ruin** a state of neglect and decay □ **rack your brains** to think hard about something

racket¹ or **racquet** *noun* a bat made up of a strong frame strung with gut or nylon for playing tennis, badminton *etc*

racket² *noun* **1** a great noise, a din **2** *informal* a dishonest way of making a profit

racketeer *noun* someone who makes money dishonestly

racoon *another spelling of* **raccoon**

racquet *another spelling of* **racket**

racy *adjective* of a story: full of action, and often involving sexual exploits

radar *noun* a method of detecting solid objects using radio waves which bounce back off the object and form a picture of it on a screen

radiance *noun* brightness, splendour

radiant *adjective* **1** sending out rays of light, heat *etc* **2** showing joy and happiness: *a radiant smile*

radiate *verb* **1** to send out rays of light, heat *etc* **2** to spread or send out from a centre

radiation *noun* **1** the giving off of rays of light, heat *etc* or of those from radioactive substances **2** radioactivity

radiator *noun* **1** a device (especially a series of connected hot-water pipes) which sends out heat **2** the part of a car which cools the engine

radical *adjective* **1** thorough: *a radical change* **2** basic, deep-seated: *radical differences* **3** proposing dramatic changes in the method of government □ *noun* someone who has radical political views

radio noun (plural **radios**) a device for sending and receiving signals by means of electromagnetic waves □ verb to send a message to (someone) in this way

radio verb ⇨ radios, radioing, radioed

radioactive adjective giving off rays which are often dangerous but which can be used in medicine

radioactivity noun the spontaneous disintegration of the atomic nuclei of some elements, eg uranium, resulting in the giving off of radiation

radiographer noun a technician involved in radiology, eg in taking X-rays or giving radiotherapy

radiography noun photography of the interior of the body by X-rays

radiologist noun a specialist in the use of X-rays

radiology noun 1 the study of radioactive substances and radiation 2 the branch of medicine involving the use of X-rays and radium

radiotherapy noun the treatment of certain diseases by X-rays or radioactive substances

radish noun (plural **radishes**) a plant with a sharp-tasting root, eaten raw in salads

radium noun a radioactive metal used in radiotherapy

radius noun (plural **radii**) 1 a straight line from the centre to the circumference of a circle 2 an area within a certain distance from a central point

RAF abbreviation Royal Air Force

raffia noun strips of fibre from the leaves of a palm tree, used in weaving mats etc

raffish adjective flashy, dashing

raffle noun a way of raising money by selling numbered tickets, one or more of which wins a prize □ verb to give as a prize in a raffle

raft noun a number of logs etc fastened together and used as a boat

rafter noun one of the sloping beams supporting a roof

rag noun 1 a torn or worn piece of cloth 2 **rags** worn-out, shabby clothes □ adjective made of rags: a rag doll □ verb to tease, play tricks on

rag verb ⇨ rags, ragging, ragged

ragamuffin noun a ragged, dirty child

rag-doll noun a floppy doll made of scrap material

rage noun great anger, fury □ verb 1 to be violently angry 2 of a storm, battle etc: to be violent □ **all the rage** very fashionable or popular

ragged adjective 1 in torn, shabby clothes 2 torn and tattered

raglan noun a cardigan or coat with the sleeves in one piece with the shoulders

Named after Lord *Raglan*, British commander in the Crimean war

ragtime noun a style of jazz music with highly syncopated melody

raid noun 1 a short, sudden attack 2 an unexpected visit by the police to catch a criminal, recover stolen goods etc □ verb to make a raid on

raider noun a person who raids

rail noun 1 a bar of metal used in fences 2 **rails** strips of steel which form the track on which trains run 3 the railway: I came here by rail □ verb **rail against** or **at something** or **someone** to complain about or criticize them angrily or bitterly

railing noun a fence or barrier of rails

railway or US **railroad** noun a track laid with steel rails on which trains run

raiment noun, old clothing

rain noun 1 water falling from the clouds in drops 2 a great number of things falling □ verb to pour or fall in drops: It's raining today

rainbow noun 1 the brilliant coloured bow or arch sometimes to be seen in the sky opposite the sun when rain is falling 2 a member of the most junior branch of the Guides

raincheck noun, US an arrangement to keep an appointment etc at a later, postponed date

raincoat noun a waterproof coat to keep out the rain

rainfall *noun* the amount of rain that falls in a certain time

rain-forest *noun* a tropical forest with very heavy rainfall

rainy *adjective* 1 full of rain: *rainy skies* 2 showery, wet: *a rainy day*

raise *verb* 1 to lift up: *raise the flag* 2 to make higher: *raise the price* 3 to bring up (a subject) for consideration 4 to bring up (a child, family *etc*) 5 to breed or grow (*eg* pigs, crops) 6 to collect, get together (a sum of money)
🕐 Comes from Old Norse *reisa* meaning 'to cause to rise'

💠 Do not confuse with: **raze**

raisin *noun* a dried grape

Raj *noun, historical* the time of British rule in India, 1858–1947

rajah *noun, historical* an Indian prince

rake¹ *noun* a tool, like a large comb with a long handle, for smoothing earth, gathering hay *etc* □ *verb* 1 to draw a rake over 2 to scrape (together) 3 to aim gunfire at (*eg* a ship) from one end to the other

rake² *noun, old* someone who lives an immoral life

rakish *adjective* at a slanting, jaunty angle

rally *verb* 1 to gather again: *rally troops* 2 to come together for a joint action or effort: *the club's supporters rallied to save it* 3 to recover from an illness □ *noun* (*plural* **rallies**) 1 a gathering 2 a political mass meeting 3 an improvement in health after an illness 4 *tennis* a long series of shots before a point is won or lost 5 a competition to test driving skills over an unknown route

rally *verb* ⇨ rallies, rallying, rallied

RAM *abbreviation, computing* random access memory

ram *noun* 1 a male sheep 2 something heavy, especially as part of a machine, for ramming □ *verb* 1 to press or push down hard 2 of a ship, car *etc*: to run into and cause damage to

ram *verb* ⇨ rams, ramming, rammed

Ramadan *noun* 1 the ninth month of the Islamic calendar, a period of fasting by day 2 the fast itself

ramble *verb* 1 to walk about for pleasure, especially in the countryside 2 to speak in an aimless or confused way □ *noun* a country walk for pleasure

rambler *noun* 1 someone who goes walking in the country for pleasure 2 a climbing rose or other plant

rambunctious *adjective* boisterous, exuberant

ramekin *noun* 1 a baked mixture of cheese and eggs 2 a baking dish for a single portion

ramification *noun* 1 a branch or part of a subject, plot *etc* 2 a consequence, usually indirect and one of several

ramp *noun* a sloping surface (*eg* of a road)

rampage *verb* to rush about angrily or violently □ **on the rampage** rampaging

rampant *adjective* 1 widespread and uncontrolled 2 *heraldry* standing on the left hind leg: *lion rampant*

rampart *noun* a mound or wall built as a defence

ram-raid *noun* a raid in which thieves gain access to a shop by smashing into its display window with a stolen car

ramrod *noun* 1 a rod for pushing the charge down a gun barrel 2 someone strict or inflexible in their views

ramshackle *adjective* badly made, falling to pieces

ran *past form* of **run**

ranch *noun* (*plural* **ranches**) a large farm in North America for rearing cattle or horses

rancid *adjective* of butter: smelling or tasting stale

rancorous *adjective* resentful, bitter

rancour *noun* ill-will, hatred

random *adjective* done without any aim or plan; chance: *a random sample* □ **at random** without any plan or purpose

random access memory a computer memory in which data can be directly located

range *noun* 1 a line or row: *a range of mountains* 2 extent, number: *a wide* *range of goods* **3** a piece of ground with targets for shooting or archery practice **4** the distance which an object can be thrown, or across which a sound can be heard **5** the distance between the top and bottom notes of a singing voice **6** a large kitchen stove with a flat top □ *verb* **1** to set in a row or in order **2** to wander (over) **3** to stretch, extend

ranger *noun* a keeper who looks after a forest or park

Ranger Guide an older member of the Guide movement

rank *noun* **1** a row or line (*eg* of soldiers) **2** class, order: *the upper ranks of society/ the rank of captain* **3 ranks** ordinary soldiers, not officers □ *verb* **1** to place in order of importance, merit *etc* **2** to have a place in an order: *apes rank above dogs in intelligence* □ *adjective* **1** of a plant: growing too plentifully **2** having a strong, unpleasant taste or smell **3** absolute: *rank nonsense* □ **rank and file 1** soldiers of the rank of private **2** ordinary people, the majority

rankle *verb* to cause lasting annoyance, bitterness *etc*

ransack *verb* to search thoroughly; plunder

ransom *noun* the price paid for the freeing of a captive □ *verb* to pay money to free (a captive)

rant *verb* to talk foolishly and angrily for a long time

rap¹ *noun* **1** a sharp blow or knock **2** *slang* a criminal charge □ *verb* **1** (often **rap on something**) to strike it with a quick, sharp blow **2 rap something out** to say it sharply

> **rap** *verb* ⇨ raps, rapping, rapped

rap² *noun* **1** *informal* an informal talk or discussion **2** a style of music accompanied by a rhythmic monologue

rapacious *adjective* greedy, eager to seize as much as possible

rape¹ *verb* to have sexual intercourse with (someone) against their will, usually by force □ *noun* **1** the act of raping **2** the act of seizing and carrying off by force

rape² *noun* a type of plant like the turnip whose seeds give oil

rapid *adjective* quick, fast: *a rapid rise to fame*

rapidity *noun* swiftness

rapidly *adverb* quickly

rapids *noun plural* a part in a river where the current flows swiftly

rapier *noun* a type of light sword with a narrow blade

rapist *noun* someone who commits rape

rapport (*pronounced* ra-**pawr**) *noun* a good relationship, sympathy

rapt *adjective* having the mind fully occupied, engrossed: *rapt attention*

rapture *noun* great delight

rapturous *adjective* experiencing or demonstrating rapture

rare *adjective* **1** seldom found, uncommon **2** of meat: lightly cooked

> ☛ Do not confuse with: **unique**.
> You can talk about something being **rare**, quite **rare**, very **rare** *etc*. It would be incorrect, however, to describe something as very **unique**, since things either are or are not **unique** – there are no levels of this quality

rarefy or **rarify** *verb* to make thin or less dense

> **rarefy** or **rarify** ⇨ rarefies or rarifies, rarefying or rarifying, rarefied or rarified

raring *adjective*: **raring to go** very keen to go, start *etc*

rarity *noun* (*plural* **rarities**) **1** something uncommon **2** uncommonness

rascal *noun* a naughty or wicked person

rash *adjective* acting, or done, without thought □ *noun* redness or outbreak of spots on the skin

rasher *noun* a thin slice (of bacon or ham)

rashness *noun* the state of being rash

rasp *noun* **1** a coarse file **2** a rough, grating sound □ *verb* **1** to rub with a file **2** to make a rough, grating noise **3** to say in a rough voice

raspberry *noun* **1** a type of red berry

similar to a blackberry **2** the bush which bears this fruit

rasping *adjective* of a sound: rough and unpleasant

rat *noun* a gnawing animal, larger than a mouse □ *verb* to hunt or kill rats □ **rat on** to inform against

> **rat** *verb* ⇨ rat**s**, rat**ting**, rat**ted**

ratchet *noun* a toothed wheel, *eg* in a watch

rate *noun* **1** the frequency with which something happens or is done: *a high rate of road accidents* **2** speed: *speak at a tremendous rate* **3** level of cost, price *etc*: *paid at a higher rate* **4 rates** the sum of money to be paid by the owner of a shop *etc* to pay for local public services □ *verb* **1** to work out the value of for taxation *etc* **2** to value: *I don't rate his work very highly*

rateable value a value of a shop *etc* used to work out the rates to be paid on it

rather *adverb* **1** somewhat, fairly: *it's rather cold today* **2** more willingly: *I'd rather talk about it now than later* **3** more correctly speaking: *he agreed, or rather he didn't say no*

ratification *noun* ratifying or being ratified

ratify *verb* to approve officially and formally: *ratified the treaty*

> **ratify** ⇨ ratif**ies**, ratify**ing**, ratif**ied**

rating *noun* a sailor below the rank of an officer

ratio *noun* (*plural* **ratios**) the proportion of one thing to another: *a ratio of two parts flour to one of sugar*

ration *noun* **1** a measured amount of food given out at intervals **2** an allowance □ *verb* **1** to deal out (*eg* food) in measured amounts **2** to allow only a certain amount to (someone)

rational *adjective* **1** able to reason **2** sensible; based on reason: *rational arguments*

rationality *noun* being rational

rationalization *noun* rationalizing or being rationalized

rationalize *verb* **1** to think up a good reason for (an action or feeling) so as

not to feel guilty about it **2** to make (an industry or organization) more efficient and profitable by reorganizing it to get rid of unnecessary costs and labour

rationally *adverb* in a rational way

rat-race *noun* a fierce, unending competition for success or wealth

rattle *verb* **1** to give out short, sharp, repeated sounds: *the coins rattled in the tin* **2** to fluster or irritate (someone) □ *noun* **1** a sharp noise, quickly repeated **2** a toy or instrument which makes such a sound □ **rattle off** to go through (a list of names *etc*) quickly

rattlesnake *noun* a poisonous snake with bony rings on its tail which rattle when shaken

ratty *adjective* irritable

raucous *adjective* hoarse, harsh: *a raucous voice*

raunchy *adjective* sexually suggestive, lewd

ravage *verb* to cause destruction or damage to; plunder □ *noun plural* damaging effects: *the ravages of time*

rave *verb* **1** to talk wildly, as if mad **2** *informal* to talk very enthusiastically (about) □ *noun* a large party held in a warehouse *etc* with electronic music

raven *noun* a type of large black bird of the crow family □ *adjective* of hair: black and glossy

ravenous *adjective* very hungry

ravine *noun* a deep, narrow valley between hills

raving *adjective* mad, crazy

ravish *verb* **1** to plunder **2** to rape **3** to delight

ravishing *adjective* filling with delight

raw *adjective* **1** not cooked **2** not prepared or refined, in its natural state: *raw cotton/ raw text* **3** of weather: cold **4** sore □ **a raw deal** unjust treatment

ray *noun* **1** a line of light, heat *etc* **2** a small degree or amount: *a ray of hope* **3** one of several lines going outwards from a centre **4** a kind of flat-bodied fish

rayon *noun* a type of artificial silk

raze *verb* to destroy, knock flat (a town, house *etc*)
⏰ Comes from French *raser* meaning 'to shave'
☛ Do not confuse with: **raise**

razor *noun* a sharp-edged instrument for shaving

razzmatazz *noun* showiness, glamorous or extravagant show

RC *abbreviation* Roman Catholic

re *preposition* concerning, about

re- *prefix* 1 again, once more: *recreate* 2 back: *reclaim*
re- is a Latin prefix

reach *verb* 1 to arrive at: *reach the summit/ your message never reached me* 2 to stretch out (the hand) so as to touch: *I couldn't reach the top shelf* 3 to extend □ *noun* 1 a distance that can be travelled easily: *within reach of home* 2 the distance someone can stretch their arm 3 a straight part of a stream or river between bends

react *verb* 1 to act or behave in response to something done or said 2 to undergo a chemical change: *metals react with sulphuric acid*

reaction *noun* 1 behaviour as a result of action 2 a chemical change 3 a movement against a situation or belief: *a reaction against Victorian morality*

reactionary *adjective* favouring a return to old ways, laws *etc* □ *noun* (*plural* **reactionaries**) someone who holds reactionary views

read *verb* 1 to look at and understand, or say aloud written or printed words 2 to study a subject in a university or college: *reading law*
read ⇨ read**s**, read**ing**, read

readable *adjective* quite interesting to read

reader *noun* 1 someone who reads books *etc* 2 someone who reads manuscripts for a publisher 3 a senior university lecturer 4 a reading book for children

readily *adverb* easily; willingly

readiness *noun* 1 the state of being ready and prepared 2 willingness: *the readiness of the troops to fight*

read only memory *computing* a memory device that can only be read, not written to

read-out *noun* 1 data from a computer; output 2 data from a radio transmitter

ready *adjective* 1 prepared: *packed and ready to go* 2 willing: *always ready to help* 3 quick: *too ready to find fault* 4 available for use: *your coat is ready for collection*

readymade *adjective* of clothes: made for general sale, not made specially for one person

real *adjective* 1 actually existing, not imagined 2 not imitation, genuine: *real leather* 3 sincere: *a real love of music* □ **the real Mackay** *or* **the real McCoy** the genuine article, the real thing
■ **Alternative words**: (meaning 1) actual, material, tangible, veritable; (meaning 2) authentic, bona fide, valid; (meaning 3) honest, unfeigned, unaffected

realism *noun* the showing or viewing of things as they really are

realist *noun* someone who claims to see life as it really is

realistic *adjective* 1 life-like 2 viewing things as they really are □ **realistically** *adverb*

reality *noun* (*plural* **realities**) that which is real and not imaginary; truth

realization *noun* realizing or being realized

realize *verb* 1 to come to understand, know: *I never realized you could sing* 2 to make real, accomplish: *realize an ambition* 3 to get (money) for: *realized £16 000 on the sale of the house*
■ **Alternative words**: (meaning 1) appreciate

really *adverb* 1 in fact 2 very: *really dark hair*
■ **Alternative words**: (meaning 1) actually, truly, honestly, sincerely, genuinely, positively, certainly, absolutely, categorically, indeed; (meaning 2) extremely, most

realm *noun* 1 a kingdom, a country 2 an area of activity or interest

ream *noun* 1 a measure for paper, 20 quires 2 **reams** a large quantity, especially of paper: *she wrote reams in her English exam*

reap *verb* 1 to cut and gather (corn *etc*) 2 to gain: *reap the benefits of hard work*

reaper *noun* 1 someone who reaps 2 a machine for reaping

rear *noun* 1 the back part of anything 2 the last part of an army or fleet □ *verb* 1 to bring up (children) 2 to breed (animals) 3 of an animal: to stand on its hindlegs □ **bring up the rear** to come or be last in a series

rearguard *noun* troops which protect the rear of an army

reason *noun* 1 cause, excuse: *what is the reason for this noise?* 2 purpose: *what is your reason for visiting America?* 3 the power of the mind to form opinions, judge right and truth *etc* 4 common sense □ *verb* 1 to think out (opinions *etc*) 2 **reason with someone** to try to persuade them by arguing

reasonable *adjective* 1 sensible 2 fair

reassurance *noun* something which reassures, or the feeling of being reassured

reassure *verb* to take away (someone's) doubts or fears

reassuring *adjective* that reassures

rebarbative *adjective* repellent

rebate *noun* a part of a payment or tax which is given back to the payer

rebel *noun* (*pronounced* **reb**-el) someone who opposes or fights against those in power □ *verb* (*pronounced* ri-**bel**) to take up arms against or oppose those in power

    rebel *verb* ⟹ rebel*s*, rebell*ing*, rebell*ed*

rebellion *noun* 1 an open or armed fight against those in power 2 a refusal to obey

rebellious *adjective* rebelling or likely to rebel

rebelliousness *noun* being rebellious

reboot *verb* to restart (a computer) using its start-up programs

rebound *verb* (*pronounced* ri-**bownd**) to bounce back: *the ball rebounded off the wall* □ *noun* (*pronounced* **ree**-bownd) 1 the act of rebounding 2 a reaction following an emotional situation or crisis

rebuff *noun* a blunt refusal or rejection □ *verb* to reject bluntly

rebuke *verb* to scold, blame □ *noun* a scolding

rebut *verb* to deny (what has been said)

    rebut ⟹ rebut*s*, rebutt*ing*, rebutt*ed*

rebuttal *noun* a rejection or contradiction

recalcitrance *noun* stubbornness; disobedience

recalcitrant *adjective* stubborn; disobedient

recall *verb* 1 to call back: *recalled to headquarters* 2 to remember □ *noun* 1 a signal or message to return 2 the act of recalling or remembering

recant *verb* 1 to take back what you have said 2 to reject publicly your beliefs

recantation *noun* recanting

recap *short for* 1 recapitulation 2 recapitulate

    recap ⟹ recap*s*, recapp*ing*, recapp*ed*

recapitulate *verb* to go over again quickly the chief points of anything (*eg* a discussion)

recapitulation *noun* an act or instance of recapitulating or summing up

recapture *verb* to capture (what has escaped or been lost)

recast *verb* to shape in a new form

    recast ⟹ recast*s*, recast*ing*, recast

recede *verb* 1 to go back 2 to become more distant 3 to slope backwards

receding *adjective* 1 going or sloping backwards 2 becoming more distant

receipt *noun* 1 the act of receiving (especially money or goods) 2 a written note saying that money has been received

receive *verb* 1 to have something given or brought to you: *receive a gift/ receive a letter* 2 to meet and welcome: *receiving visitors* 3 to take goods, knowing them to be stolen

receiver *noun* **1** someone who receives stolen goods **2** the part of a telephone through which words are heard and into which they are spoken **3** an apparatus through which television or radio broadcasts are received

recent *adjective* happening, done or made only a short time ago

recently *adverb* a short time ago

receptacle *noun* an object to receive or hold things, a container

reception *noun* **1** a welcome: *a warm reception* **2** a large meeting to welcome guests **3** the quality of radio or television signals

receptionist *noun* someone employed in an office or hotel to answer the telephone *etc*

receptive *adjective* quick to take in or accept ideas *etc*

recess *noun* (*plural* **recesses**) **1** part of a room set back from the rest, an alcove **2** the time during which parliament or the law courts do not work **3** remote parts: *in the recesses of my memory*

recession *noun* **1** the act of moving back **2** a temporary fall in a country's or world business activities

recessive *adjective* tending to recede

recipe *noun* instructions on how to prepare or cook a certain kind of food

recipient *noun* someone who receives

reciprocal *adjective* both given and received: *reciprocal affection*

reciprocate *verb* to feel or do the same in return: *I reciprocate his dislike of me*

recital *noun* **1** the act of reciting **2** a musical performance **3** the facts of a story told one after the other

recitation *noun* a poem *etc* recited

recite *verb* to repeat aloud from memory

reckless *adjective* rash, careless □ **recklessly** *adjective*

reckon *verb* **1** to count **2** to consider, believe

reckoning *noun* **1** the settling of debts, grievances *etc* **2** payment for sins **3** a bill **4** a sum, calculation

reclaim *verb* **1** to claim back **2** to win back (land from the sea) by draining, building banks *etc* **3** to make waste land fit for use

reclamation *noun* reclaiming or being reclaimed

recline *verb* to lean or lie on your back or side

recluse *noun* someone who lives alone and avoids other people

reclusive *adjective* solitary

recognition *noun* the act of recognizing someone or something

recognizable *adjective* capable of being recognized

recognize *verb* **1** to know from a previous meeting *etc* **2** to admit, acknowledge: *everyone recognized his talent* **3** to show appreciation of: *they recognized his courage by giving him a medal*

■ **Alternative words**: (meaning 2) appreciate

recoil *verb* **1** to shrink back in horror or fear **2** of a gun: to jump back after a shot is fired □ *noun* a shrinking back

recollect *verb* to remember

recollection *noun* **1** the act or power of remembering **2** a memory, something remembered

recommend *verb* **1** to urge, advise: *I recommend that you take a long holiday* **2** to speak highly of

■ **Alternative words**: (meaning 1) advocate

recommendation *noun* **1** the act of recommending **2** a point in favour of someone or something

recompense *verb* to pay money to or reward (a person) to make up for loss, inconvenience *etc* □ *noun* payment in compensation

reconcile *verb* **1** to bring together in friendship, after a quarrel **2** to show that two statements, facts *etc* do not contradict each other **3** **be reconciled to** or **reconcile oneself to something** to agree to accept an unwelcome fact or situation patiently: *I became reconciled to her absence*

reconciliation *noun* the fact of being friendly with someone again, after an argument, dispute or conflict: *there seems little hope of reconciliation*

reconnaissance (*pronounced* ri-**kon**-is-ens) *noun* a survey to obtain information, especially before a battle

reconnoitre (*pronounced* rek-*o*-**noi**-ter) *verb* to make a reconnaissance of

reconstitute *verb* 1 to put back into its original form: *reconstitute the milk* 2 to make up, form in a different way

record *verb* (*pronounced* ri-**kawd**) 1 to write down for future reference 2 to put (music, speech *etc*) on tape or disc so that it can be listened to later 3 to show in writing (*eg* a vote) 4 to show, register: *the thermometer recorded 30°C yesterday* □ *noun* (*pronounced* **rek**-awd) 1 a written report of facts 2 a round, flat piece of plastic on which sounds are recorded for playing on a record-player 3 the best known performance: *John holds the school record for the mile* □ **break** or **beat the record** to do better than any previous performance □ **off the record** of a remark *etc*: not to be made public

recorder *noun* 1 someone who records 2 a type of simple musical wind instrument 3 a judge in certain courts

recording *noun* 1 the act of recording 2 recorded music, speech *etc*

record-player *noun* a machine for playing records

recount *verb* 1 (*pronounced* ree-**kownt**) to count again 2 (*pronounced* ri-**kownt**) to tell (the story of) □ *noun* (*pronounced* **ree**-kownt) a second count, especially of votes in an election

recoup (*pronounced* ri-**koop**) *verb* to make good, recover (expenses, losses *etc*)
① Comes from French *recouper* meaning 'to cut back'
♠ Do not confuse with: **recuperate**

recourse *noun*: **have recourse to** to make use of in an emergency

recover *verb* 1 to get possession of again 2 to become well again after an illness

recoverable *adjective* able to be recovered

recovery *noun* (*plural* **recoveries**) 1 a return to health 2 the regaining of something lost *etc*

recreation *noun* a sport, hobby *etc* done in your spare time

recriminate *verb* to accuse your accuser in return

recriminations *noun plural* accusations made by someone who is themselves accused

recriminatory *adjective* involving recrimination

recruit *noun* a newly-enlisted soldier, member *etc* □ *verb* to enlist (someone) in an army, political party *etc*

recruitment *noun* recruiting

rectangle *noun* a four-sided figure with all its angles right angles and its opposite sides equal in length, an oblong

rectangular *adjective* of or like a rectangle

recti- or **rect-** *prefix* forms words containing the meaning 'straight' or 'correct': *rectilineal/ rectangle*
① Comes from Latin *rectus* meaning 'straight' or 'right'

rectifiable *adjective* capable of being rectified

rectify *verb* to put right
rectify ⇨ rectifies, rectifying, rectified

rectilineal or **rectilinear** *adjective* in a straight line or lines

rectitude *noun* honesty; correctness of behaviour

recto *noun* the right-hand page of an open book (*compare with*: **verso**)

rector *noun* 1 a member of the Anglican clergy in charge of a parish 2 the headmaster of some Scottish secondary schools 3 a Scottish university official elected by the students

rectory *noun* (*plural* **rectories**) the house of an Anglican rector

rectum *noun* the lower part of the alimentary canal

recumbent *adjective* lying down

recuperate *verb* to recover strength or health

ⓘ Comes from Latin *recuperare* meaning 'to recover'

✦ Do not confuse with: **recoup**

recuperation *noun* recovery

recur *verb* to happen again

recur ⇨ recurs, recurring, recurred

recurrence *noun* the process of recurring

recurrent *adjective* happening often or regularly

recycle *verb* 1 to remake into something different 2 to treat (material) by some process in order to use it again

red *adjective* 1 of the colour of blood □ *noun* this colour □ **see red** to become very angry

red deer a type of reddish-brown deer

redden *verb* to make or grow red

redeem *verb* 1 to buy back (*eg* articles from a pawnbroker) 2 to save from sin or condemnation 3 to make amends for

redeemer *noun* 1 a person who redeems 2 **the Redeemer** Jesus Christ

redeeming *adjective* making up for other faults: *a redeeming feature*

redemption *noun* the act of redeeming or state of being redeemed, especially the freeing of humanity from sin by Christ

redeploy *verb* to move (*eg* soldiers, workers) to a different place where they will be more useful

red-handed *adverb* in the act of doing wrong: *caught red-handed*

red herring something mentioned to lead a discussion away from the main subject; a false clue

Red Indian *offensive* a Native American

red-letter *adjective* of a day: especially important or happy for some reason

red light 1 a danger signal 2 a signal to stop

redolent *adjective* 1 sweet-smelling 2 smelling (of) 3 suggestive, making one think (of): *redolent of earlier times*

redouble *verb* to make twice as great: *redouble your efforts*

redoubtable *adjective* brave, bold

redress *verb* to set right, make up for (a wrong *etc*) □ *noun* something done or given to make up for a loss or wrong, compensation

red tape unnecessary and troublesome rules about how things are to be done

reduce *verb* 1 to make smaller 2 to lessen 3 to bring to the point of by force of circumstances: *reduced to begging in the streets* 4 to bring to a lower rank or state 5 to change into other terms: *reduce pounds to pence*

reducible *adjective* capable of being reduced

reduction *noun* 1 an act or instance of reducing; the state of being reduced 2 the amount by which something is reduced 3 a reduced copy of a picture, document *etc*

redundance or **redundancy** (*plural* **redundancies**) *noun* 1 being redundant, or an instance of this 2 a dismissal or a person dismissed because they are no longer needed

redundant *adjective* 1 more than what is needed 2 of a worker: no longer needed because of the lack of a suitable job

reed *noun* 1 a tall stiff grass growing in moist or marshy places 2 a part (originally made of reed) of certain wind instruments which vibrates when the instrument is played

reedy *adjective* 1 full of reeds 2 like a reed 3 sounding like a reed instrument: *a reedy voice*

reef *noun* a chain of rocks lying at or near the surface of the sea

reefer *noun* 1 a short coat, as worn by sailors 2 *slang* a marijuana cigarette

reef knot a square, very secure knot

reek *noun* 1 a strong, unpleasant smell 2 smoke □ *verb* 1 to send out smoke 2 to smell strongly

reel *noun* 1 a cylinder of plastic, metal or wood on which thread, film, fishing lines *etc* may be wound 2 a length of cinema film 3 a lively Scottish or Irish dance □ *verb* 1 to wind on a reel 2 **reel**

something in to draw, pull in (a fish on a line) **3** to stagger □ **reel off** to repeat or recite quickly, without pausing

ref *abbreviation* **1** referee **2** reference

refectory *noun* (*plural* **refectories**) a communal dining hall for monks, students *etc*

refer *verb*: **refer to 1** to mention **2** to turn to for information **3** to relate to, apply to **4** to direct to for information, consideration *etc*: *I refer you to the managing director*

refer ⇨ refer**s**, refer**ring**, refer**red**

■ **Alternative words**: (meaning 1) allude to

referee *noun* **1** someone to whom a matter is taken for settlement **2** a judge in a sports match **3** someone willing to provide a note about someone's character, work record *etc*

reference *noun* **1** the act of referring **2** a mention **3** a note about a person's character, work *etc*

reference book a book to be consulted for information, *eg* an encyclopedia

reference library a library of books to be looked at for information but not taken away

referendum *noun* (*plural* **referenda** or **referendums**) a vote given by the people of a country about some important matter

refine *verb* **1** to purify **2** to improve, make more exact *etc*

refined *adjective* **1** purified **2** polite in manners, free of vulgarity

refinement *noun* **1** good manners, taste, learning **2** an improvement

refinery *noun* (*plural* **refineries**) a place where sugar, oil *etc* are refined

refit *verb* to repair damages (especially to a ship)

refit ⇨ refit**s**, refit**ting**, refit**ted**

reflect *verb* **1** to throw back (light or heat): *reflecting the sun's heat* **2** to give an image of: *reflected in the mirror* **3** **reflect on someone** to throw blame on them: *her behaviour reflects on her*

mother **4 reflect on something** to think it over carefully

reflection *noun* **1** the act of throwing back **2** the image of someone *etc* reflected in a mirror **3** blame, unfavourable criticism

reflective *adjective* thoughtful

reflector *noun* something (*eg* a piece of shiny metal) which throws back light

reflex *noun* (*plural* **reflexes**) an action which is automatic, not intended, *eg* jerking the leg when the kneecap is struck □ *adjective* done as an automatic response, unthinking

reflexive *adjective, grammar* showing that the object (**reflexive pronoun**) of the verb (**reflexive verb**) is the same as its subject, *eg* in 'he cut himself', *himself* is a *reflexive pronoun* and *cut* a *reflexive verb*

reform *verb* **1** to improve, remove faults from **2** to give up bad habits, evil *etc* □ *noun* an improvement

reformation *noun* **1** a change for the better **2 the Reformation** the religious movement in the Christian Church in the 16th century from which the Protestant Church arose

reformer *noun* someone who wishes to bring about improvements

refract *verb* to change the direction of (a wave of light, sound, *etc*)

refraction *noun* a change in the direction of (a wave of light, sound *etc*)

refractory *adjective* unruly, not easily controlled

refrain *noun* a chorus coming at the end of each verse of a song □ *verb* to keep yourself back (from doing something): *please refrain from smoking*

refresh *verb* to give new strength, power or life to □ **refresh your memory** to go over facts again so that they are clear in your mind

refresher course a course of study intended to keep up or increase existing knowledge of a subject

refreshing *adjective* **1** bringing back strength **2** cooling

refreshments *noun plural* food and drink

refrigerate *verb* to make or keep (food) cold or frozen to prevent it from going bad

refrigeration *noun* the process whereby a cabinet or room and its contents are kept at a low temperature, especially in order to prevent food from going bad

refrigerator *noun* a storage machine which keeps food cold and so prevents it from going bad

refuel *verb* to supply with, or take in, fresh fuel

refuel ⇨ refuel*s*, refuel*ling*, refuel*led*

refuge *noun* a place of safety (from attack, danger *etc*)

refugee *noun* someone who seeks shelter from persecution in another country

refund *verb* (*pronounced* ri-**fund**) to pay back ◻ *noun* (*pronounced* **ree**-fund or ri-**fund**) a payment returned, *eg* for unsatisfactory goods

refusal *noun* **1** an act of refusing **2** the option of accepting or refusing something: *I promised to give him first refusal on my car* (= offer to sell it to him before advertising it generally)

refuse[1] (*pronounced* ri-**fyooz**) *verb* **1** to say that you will not do something: *he refused to leave the room* **2** to withhold, not give (*eg* permission)

refuse[2] (*pronounced* **ref**-yoos) *noun* something which is thrown aside as worthless, rubbish

refutation *noun* **1** refuting **2** an argument, *etc* that refutes

refute *verb* to prove wrong (something that has been said or written)

reg- *prefix* forms words connected to the activity of ruling: *regent* (= a ruler)/*regular* (= governed by or according to rules)
ⓘ Comes from Latin *regere* meaning 'to rule'

regain *verb* **1** to win back again **2** to get back to: *regain the shore*

regal *adjective* kingly, royal

regale (*pronounced* ri-**geil**) *verb* to entertain lavishly

regalia *noun plural* symbols of royalty, *eg* a crown and sceptre

regard *verb* **1** to look upon, consider: *I regard you as a nuisance* **2** to look at carefully **3** to pay attention to ◻ *noun* **1** concern **2** affection **3** respect **4** *regards* good wishes ◻ **with regard to** or **in regard to** concerning

regarding *preposition* concerning, to do with: *a reply regarding his application*

regardless *adverb* not thinking or caring about costs, problems, dangers *etc*; in spite of everything: *carry on regardless* ◻ **regardless of** paying no care or attention to

regatta *noun* a meeting for yacht or boat races

From the name of a gondola race held on the Grand Canal in Venice

regency *noun* (*plural* **regencies**) **1** rule by a regent **2** the period of a regent's rule **3** *Brit history* the period during which George IV was regent, 1811–1820

regenerate *verb* to make new and good again

regeneration *noun* regenerating or being regenerated

regent *noun* someone who governs in place of a king or queen

reggae *noun* a strongly rhythmic type of rock music, originally from the West Indies

regicide *noun* **1** the killing of a monarch **2** someone who kills a monarch

régime or **regime** (*both pronounced* rei-**szeem**) *noun* method or system of government or administration

regiment *noun* a body of soldiers, commanded by a colonel ◻ *verb* to organize or control too strictly

regimental *adjective* of a regiment

regimentation *noun* too strict control

region *noun* an area, a district ◻ **in the region of** somewhere near: *in the region of £10*

regional *adjective* of a region

register *noun* **1** a written list (*eg* of attendances at school, of those eligible to vote *etc*) **2** the distance between the highest and lowest notes of a voice or instrument ◻ *verb* **1** to write down in a register **2** to record, cast (a vote *etc*) **3** to show, record: *a thermometer registers temperature*

registered letter one insured against loss by the post office

registrar *noun* a public official who keeps a register of births, deaths and marriages

registry *noun* (*plural* **registries**) an office where a register is kept

registry office one where records of births, marriages and deaths are kept and where marriages may be performed

regress *verb* to go back to an earlier state

regret *verb* **1** to be sorry about: *I regret any inconvenience you have suffered* **2** to be sorry (to have to say something): *we regret to inform you* □ *noun* sorrow for anything

   regret *verb* ⇨ regret*s*, regret*ting*, regret*ted*

regretful *adjective* feeling or showing regret □ **regretfully** *adverb*

regrettable *adjective* to be regretted, unwelcome □ **regrettably** *adverb*

regular *adjective* **1** done according to rule or habit; usual **2** arranged in order; even: *regular teeth* **3** happening at certain fixed times **4** having normal bowel movements □ *noun* a soldier of the regular army

regular army the part of the army which is kept always in training, even in peacetime

regularity *noun* being regular

regularly *adverb* in a regular way or at a regular time

regulate *verb* **1** to control by rules **2** to adjust to a certain order or rate

regulation *noun* a rule, an order

regulator *noun* someone or something that regulates

regurgitate *verb* to bring back into the mouth after swallowing

regurgitation *noun* regurgitating

rehabilitate *verb* **1** to give back rights, powers or health to **2** to train or accustom (a disabled person *etc*) to live a normal life

rehabilitation *noun* rehabilitating or being rehabilitated

rehash *verb* to express in different words, do again

rehearsal *noun* **1** a private practice of a play, concert *etc* before performance in public **2** a practice for a future event or action

rehearse *verb* **1** to practise beforehand **2** to recount (facts, events *etc*) in order

reign *noun* **1** rule **2** the time during which a king or queen rules □ *verb* **1** to rule **2** to prevail: *silence reigned at last*

reimburse *verb* to pay (someone) an amount to cover expenses

reimbursement *noun* **1** reimbursing **2** repayment

rein *noun* **1** one of two straps attached to a bridle for guiding a horse **2 reins** a simple device for controlling a child when walking □ *verb* to control with reins

reincarnation *noun* the rebirth of the soul in another body after death

reindeer *noun* (*plural* **reindeer**) a type of deer found in the far North

reinforce *verb* to strengthen (*eg* an army with men, concrete with iron)

reinforcement *noun* **1** the act of reinforcing **2** something which strengthens **3 reinforcements** additional troops

reinstate *verb* to put back in a former position

reinstatement *noun* **1** reinstating **2** re-establishment

reiterate *verb* to repeat several times

reiteration *noun* reiterating

reject *verb* (*pronounced* ri-**jekt**) **1** to throw away, cast aside **2** to refuse to take: *she rejected his offer of help* **3** to turn down (*eg* an application, request) □ *noun* (*pronounced* **ree**-jekt) something discarded or refused

rejection *noun* **1** rejecting or being rejected **2** something that is rejected

rejig *verb* to rearrange, especially in an unexpected way

   rejig ⇨ rejig*s*, rejig*ging*, rejig*ged*

rejoice *verb* to feel or show joy

rejoicing *noun* **1** being joyful **2** festivities, celebrations, merrymaking

rejoinder *noun* an answer to a reply

rejuvenate *verb* to make young again

rejuvenation *noun* rejuvenating

relapse *verb* to fall back (*eg* into ill health, bad habits) □ *noun* a falling back

relate *verb* **1** to show a connection between (two or more things) **2** to tell (a story)

related *adjective* **1** (often **related to someone**) of the same family (as): *I'm related to him/ we are not related* **2** connected

relation *noun* **1** someone who is of the same family, either by birth or marriage **2** a connection between two or more things

relationship *noun* **1** a connection between things or people **2** an emotional or sexual partnership or affair: *she isn't married, but she's in a steady relationship*

relative *noun* someone who is of the same family *etc* □ *adjective* comparative: *relative merits*

relatively *adverb* more or less: *relatively happy*

relativity *noun* **1** the state of being relative **2** (also **special theory of relativity**) Einstein's theory that the mass of a body varies with its speed, based on the fundamental assumptions that all motion is relative and that the speed of light relative to an observer is constant **3** (also **general theory of relativity**) this same theory extended to include gravitation and accelerated motion

relax *verb* **1** to become or make less tense **2** to slacken (*eg* your grip or control) **3** to make (laws or rules) less severe

relaxation *noun* **1** a slackening **2** rest from work, leisure

relay *verb* to receive and pass on (*eg* a message, a television programme) □ *noun* **1** the sending out of a radio or television broadcast received from another station **2** a fresh set of people

to replace others at a job *etc* □ **in relays** in groups which take over from one another in series

> **relay** *verb* ⇨ relay**s**, relay**ing**, relay**ed**

relay race a race in which members of each team take over from each other, each running a set distance

release *verb* **1** to set free; let go **2** to allow (news *etc*) to be made public □ *noun* a setting free

relegate *verb* **1** to put down (to a lower position, group *etc*) **2** to leave (a task *etc*) to someone else

relegation *noun* relegating or being relegated

relent *verb* to treat (someone) less severely or strictly

relentless *adjective* **1** without pity **2** refusing to be turned from a purpose □ **relentlessly** *adverb*

relevance *noun* being relevant

relevant *adjective* having to do with what is being spoken about

reliability or **reliance** *noun* trust

reliable *adjective* able to be trusted or counted on

reliant *adjective* relying on or having confidence in, trusting

relic *noun* something left over from a past time; an antiquity

relief *noun* **1** a lessening of pain or anxiety **2** release from a post or duty **3** people taking over someone's duty *etc* **4** help given to those in need: *famine relief* **5** the act of freeing (a town *etc*) from a siege **6** a way of carving or moulding in which the design stands out from its background

relieve *verb* **1** to lessen (pain or anxiety) **2** to take over a duty from (someone else) **3** to come to the help of (a town *etc* under attack)

■ **Alternative words**: (meaning 1) alleviate

---

religion *noun* belief in, or worship of, a god

religious *adjective* **1** of or relating to religion: *religious beliefs* **2** following the rules of worship of a particular religion very closely

relinquish *verb* to give up, abandon: *relinquish control*

relish *verb* 1 to enjoy 2 to like the taste of □ *noun* (*plural* **relishes**) 1 enjoyment 2 flavour 3 something which adds flavour

relocate *verb* to move to another position, residence *etc*

reluctance *noun* unwillingness; lack of enthusiasm

reluctant *adjective* unwilling

rely *verb* to have full trust in, depend (on)

> **rely** ⇨ relies, relying, relied

remain *verb* 1 to stay, not leave 2 to be left: *only two tins of soup remained* 3 to be still the same: *the problem remains unsolved*

remainder *noun* 1 something which is left behind after removal of the rest 2 *maths* the number left after subtraction or division

remains *noun plural* 1 that which is left 2 a dead body

remake *noun* (*pronounced* **ree**-meik) a second making of a film *etc* □ *verb* (*pronounced* ree-**meik**) to make again

remand *verb* to put (someone) back in prison until more evidence is found □ **on remand** having been remanded

remark *verb* 1 to say 2 to comment (on) 3 to notice □ *noun* something said

remarkable *adjective* deserving notice, unusual □ **remarkably** *adverb*: *she prepared it remarkably quickly*

remedial *adjective* 1 remedying 2 relating to the teaching of slow-learning children

remedy *noun* (*plural* **remedies**) a cure for an illness, evil *etc* □ *verb* 1 to cure 2 to put right

remember *verb* 1 to keep in mind 2 to recall after having forgotten 3 to send your best wishes (to): *remember me to your mother* 4 to reward, give a present to: *he remembered her in his will*

remembrance *noun* 1 the act of remembering 2 memory 3 something given to remind someone of a person

or event, a keepsake 4 **remembrances** a friendly greeting

remind *verb* 1 to bring (something) back to a person's mind: *remind me to post that letter* 2 to cause (someone) to think about (someone or something) by resemblance: *she reminds me of her sister*

reminder *noun* something which reminds

reminisce *verb* to think and talk about things remembered from the past

reminiscence *noun* 1 something remembered from the past 2 **reminiscences** memories, especially told or written

reminiscent *adjective* 1 reminding (of): *reminiscent of Paris* 2 in a mood to remember and think about past events *etc*

remiss *adjective* careless, unthinking

remission *noun* 1 a shortening of a prison sentence 2 a lessening of a disease or illness

remit *verb* 1 to pardon, excuse (a crime *etc*) 2 to wipe out, cancel (a debt *etc*) 3 to lessen, become less intense 4 to send (money) 5 to hand over (*eg* a prisoner to a higher court)

> **remit** ⇨ remits, remitting, remitted

remittance *noun* 1 the sending of money in payment 2 the money sent

remnant *noun* a small piece or number left over

remonstrate *verb* to protest (about)

remorse *noun* regret about something done in the past

remorseful *adjective* full of remorse, sorrowful

remorseless *adjective* having no remorse; cruel

remote *adjective* 1 far away in time or place 2 isolated, far from other people 3 slight: *a remote chance*

removal *noun* the act of removing, especially of moving furniture to a new home

remove *verb* 1 to take (something) from its place 2 to dismiss from a job 3 to take off (clothes *etc*) 4 to get rid of: *remove a stain* □ *noun* a stage away (from): *one remove from anarchy*

removed *adjective* 1 distant (from) 2 of cousins: separated by a generation: *first cousin once removed* (a cousin's child)

remunerate *verb* to pay (someone) for something done

remuneration *noun* pay, salary

remunerative *adjective* profitable

renaissance *noun* 1 a rebirth 2 a period of cultural revival and growth

renal *adjective* of the kidneys

rend *verb* to tear (apart), divide

   rend ⟹ rend*s*, rend*ing*, rent

render *verb* 1 to give (*eg* thanks) 2 to translate into another language 3 to perform (music *etc*) 4 to cause to be: *his words rendered me speechless*

rendering *noun* 1 a translation 2 a performance

rendezvous (*pronounced* ron-dei-voo) *noun* (*plural* **rendezvous** – *pronounced* ron-dei-vooz) 1 a meeting place fixed beforehand 2 an arranged meeting

renegade *noun* someone who deserts their own side, religion or beliefs

renew *verb* 1 to make as if new again 2 to begin again: *renew your efforts* 3 to make valid for a further period (*eg* a driving licence) 4 to replace: *renew the water in the tank*

renewal *noun* renewing or being renewed: *my contract is due for renewal*

rennet *noun* a substance used in curdling milk for making cheeses *etc*

renounce *verb* to give up publicly or formally

renovate *verb* to make (something) like new again, mend

renovation *noun* renovating or being renovated

renown *noun* fame

renowned *adjective* famous

rent[1] *noun* payment made for the use of property or land □ *verb* 1 to pay rent for (a house *etc*) 2 (also **rent something out**) to receive rent for (a house *etc*)

rent[2] *noun* a tear, a split □ *verb*, *past form* of **rend**

rental *noun* money paid as rent

renunciation *noun* an act of renouncing: *their renunciation of trade links with Japan*

reorganization *noun* reorganizing or being reorganized

reorganize *verb* to put in a different order

rep *noun*, *short for* 1 representative: *sales rep* 2 repertory

repair *verb* 1 to mend 2 to make up for (a wrong) 3 *old* to go, move: *repair to the drawing room* □ *noun* 1 state, condition: *in bad repair* 2 mending: *in need of repair* 3 a mend, a patch

  ■ **Alternative words**: (meaning 1) fix, overhaul, service, restore, renovate

reparation *noun* compensation for a wrong

repartee *noun* 1 an exchange of witty remarks 2 skill in witty conversation

repast *noun*, *old* a meal

repatriate *verb* to send (someone) back to their own country

repatriation *noun* repatriating or being repatriated

repay *verb* 1 to pay back 2 to give or do something in return: *he repaid her kindness with a gift*

   repay ⟹ repay*s*, repay*ing*, repaid

repayment *noun* repaying

repeal *verb* to do away with, cancel (especially a law) □ *noun* a cancellation of a law *etc*

repeat *verb* 1 to say or do over again 2 to say from memory 3 to pass on (someone's words) □ *noun* a musical passage, television programme *etc* played or shown for a second time

repeatedly *adverb* again and again

repel *verb* 1 to drive back or away 2 to disgust

   repel ⟹ repel*s*, repel*ling*, repel*led*

repellent *adjective* disgusting □ *noun* something that repels: *insect repellent*

repent *verb* 1 to be sorry for your actions 2 **repent of something** to regret it

repentance *noun* sorrow and regret for your actions

repentant *adjective* feeling or showing sorrow and regret for your actions

repercussion *noun* an indirect or resultant effect of something which has happened

repertoire *noun* the range of works performed by a musician, theatre company *etc*

repertory *noun* (*plural* **repertories**) repertoire

repertory theatre a theatre with a permanent company which performs a series of plays

repetition *noun* 1 the act of repeating or being repeated 2 a thing that is repeated

repetitive *adjective* repeating too often, predictable

replace *verb* 1 to put (something) back where it was 2 to put in place of another

replenish *verb* to refill (a stock, supply)

replete *adjective* full

replica *noun* an exact copy of a work of art

reply *verb* to speak or act in answer to something □ *noun* (*plural* **replies**) an answer

> **reply** *verb* ⇨ repli*es*, reply*ing*, repli*ed*

report *verb* 1 to pass on news 2 to give a description of (an event) 3 to give information about events for a newspaper 4 to make a formal complaint against □ *noun* 1 a statement of facts 2 an account, a description 3 a news article 4 a rumour 5 a written description of a school pupil's work 6 a loud noise

reporter *noun* a news journalist

repose *noun, formal* sleep, rest □ *verb* 1 to rest 2 to place (*eg* trust in a person)

repository *noun* (*plural* **repositories**) a storage place for safe keeping

repossess *verb* to take back (goods, property), especially because of non-payment

reprehensible *adjective* deserving blame

represent *verb* 1 to speak or act on behalf of others: *representing the tenants' association* 2 to stand for, be a symbol of: *each letter represents a sound* 3 to claim to be 4 to explain, point out

representation *noun* 1 an image, a picture 2 a strong claim or appeal

representative *adjective* 1 typical, characteristic: *a representative specimen* 2 standing or acting for others □ *noun* 1 someone who acts or speaks on behalf of others 2 a travelling salesman for a company

repress *verb* 1 to keep down by force 2 to keep under control

repression *noun* 1 the strict controlling of people, not allowing them to do things such as vote in elections or attend religious worship 2 the defence mechanism whereby an unpleasant or unacceptable thought, memory or wish is deliberately excluded from conscious thought

repressive *adjective* severe; harsh

reprieve *verb* 1 to pardon (a criminal) 2 to relieve from trouble or difficulty □ *noun* a pardon, a relief

reprimand *verb* to scold severely, censure □ *noun* scolding, censure

reprint *verb* to print more copies of (a book *etc*) □ *noun* another printing of a book

reprisal *noun* a return of wrong for wrong, a repayment in kind

reproach *verb* to scold, blame □ *noun* 1 blame, discredit 2 a cause of blame or censure

reproachful *adjective* expressing or full of reproach

reprobate *noun* someone of evil or immoral habits □ *adjective* immoral

reproduce *verb* 1 to produce a copy of 2 to produce (children or young)

reproduction *noun* 1 a copy or imitation (especially of a work of art) 2 the act or process of producing (children or young)

reproof *noun* a scolding, criticism for a fault

reprove *verb* to scold, blame

reproving *adjective* disapproving

reptile *noun* a creeping, cold-blooded animal, such as a snake, lizard *etc*

reptilian *adjective* of or like reptiles

republic *noun* a form of government in which power is in the hands of elected representatives with a president at its head

Republican *adjective* belonging to the more conservative of the two chief political parties in the United States

repudiate *verb* to refuse to acknowledge or accept: *repudiate a suggestion*

repudiation *noun* repudiating

repugnance *noun* aversion

repugnant *adjective* hateful, distasteful

■ **Alternative words**: abhorrent

repulse *verb* **1** to drive back **2** to reject, snub

repulsion *noun* disgust

repulsive *adjective* causing disgust, loathsome

reputable (*pronounced* rep-yut-*a*-bl) *adjective* having a good reputation, well thought of

reputation *noun* **1** opinion held by people in general of a particular person **2** good name

repute *noun* reputation

reputed *adjective* **1** considered, thought (to be something): *reputed to be dangerous* **2** supposed: *the reputed author of the book*

reputedly *adverb* in the opinion of most people

request *verb* to ask for □ *noun* **1** an asking for something **2** something asked for

requiem *noun* a hymn or mass sung for the dead

require *verb* **1** to need **2** to demand, order

requirement *noun* **1** something needed **2** a demand

requisite *adjective* required; necessary □ *noun* something needed or necessary

requisition *noun* a formal request for supplies, *eg* for a school or army □ *verb* to put in a formal request for

requite *verb* **1** to repay, give back in return **2** to avenge (one action) by another

rerun *verb* to run again □ *noun* a repeated television programme

rescue *verb* **1** to save from danger **2** to free from capture □ *noun* an act of saving from danger or capture

research *noun* (*plural* **researches**) close and careful scientific study to try to find out new facts: *cancer research* □ *verb* to study carefully

researcher *noun* someone who does research

resemblance *noun* likeness

resemble *verb* to look like or be like: *he doesn't resemble his sister*

resent *verb* to feel injured, annoyed or insulted by

resentful *adjective* full of or caused by resentment

resentment *noun* annoyance, bitterness

reservation *noun* **1** the act of reserving, booking **2** an exception or condition: *she agreed to the plan, but with certain reservations* **3** doubt, objection: *I had reservations about their marriage* **4** an area of land set aside by treaty for Native American people in the United States

reserve *verb* **1** to set aside for future use **2** to book, have kept for you (*eg* a seat, a table) □ *noun* **1** something reserved **2 reserves** troops outside the regular army kept ready to help those already fighting **3** a piece of land set apart for some reason: *nature reserve* **4** shyness, reluctance to speak or act openly

reserved *adjective* **1** shy, reluctant to speak openly **2** kept back for a particular person or purpose

reservoir *noun* an artificial lake where water is kept in store

reshuffle *verb* to rearrange ministerial posts within (a government cabinet) □ *noun* a rearrangement of a cabinet

reside *verb* **1** to live, stay (in) **2** of authority *etc*: to be placed (in)

residence *noun* **1** the building where

someone lives **2** living, or time of living, in a place

resident *noun* someone who lives in a particular place: *a resident of Dublin* □ *adjective* **1** living in (a place) **2** living in a place of work: *resident caretaker*

residential *adjective* **1** of an area: containing houses rather than shops, offices *etc* **2** providing accommodation: *a residential course*

residual *adjective* remaining; left over

residue *noun* what is left over

resign *verb* to give up (a job, position *etc*) □ **resign yourself to** to accept (a situation) patiently and calmly

resignation *noun* **1** the act of resigning **2** a letter to say you are resigning **3** patient, calm acceptance of a situation

resigned *adjective* patient, not actively complaining

resilience *noun* being resilient

resilient *adjective* **1** able to recover easily from misfortune, hurt *etc* **2** of an object: readily recovering its original shape after being bent, twisted *etc*

resin *noun* a sticky substance produced by certain plants (*eg* firs, pines)

resinous *adjective* like or containing resin

resist *verb* **1** to struggle against, oppose **2** to stop yourself from (doing something)

resistance *noun* **1** the act of resisting **2** an organized opposition, especially to an occupying force **3** ability to turn a passing electrical current into heat

resistant *adjective* able to resist or remain unaffected or undamaged by something

resit *verb* to sit (an examination) again □ *noun* a retaking of an examination

resit *verb* ⇨ resits, resitting, resat

resolute *adjective* determined, with mind made up □ **resolutely** *adverb*

resolution *noun* **1** determination of mind or purpose **2** a firm decision (to do something) **3** a proposal put before a meeting **4** a decision expressed by a public meeting

resolve *verb* **1** to decide firmly (to do

something) **2** to solve (a difficulty) **3** to break up into parts □ *noun* a firm purpose

resonance *noun* a deep, echoing tone

resonant *adjective* echoing, resounding

resonate *verb* to echo

resort *verb* **1** to begin to use **2** to turn (to) in a difficulty: *resorting to bribery* □ *noun* a popular holiday destination □ **in the last resort** when all else fails

resound *verb* **1** to sound loudly **2** to echo

resounding *adjective* **1** echoing **2** thorough: *a resounding victory*

resourceful *adjective* good at finding ways out of difficulties

resources *noun plural* **1** a source of supplying what is required **2** the natural sources of wealth in a country *etc* **3** money or other property **4** an ability to handle situations skilfully and cleverly

respect *verb* **1** to feel a high regard for **2** to treat with consideration: *respect his wishes* □ *noun* **1** high regard, esteem **2** consideration **3** a detail, a way: *alike in some respects* **4** **respects** good wishes □ **in respect of** concerning, as regards □ **with respect to** with reference to

respectability *noun* being respectable

respectable *adjective* **1** worthy of respect **2** having a good reputation **3** considerable, fairly good: *a respectable score*

respectful *adjective* showing respect

respective *adjective* belonging to each (person or thing mentioned) separately: *my brother and his friends went to their respective homes* (that is, each went to their own home)

respectively *adverb* in the order given: *James, Andrew and Ian were first, second and third respectively*

respiration *noun* breathing

respirator *noun* **1** a mask worn over the mouth and nose to purify the air taken in **2** a device to help people breathe when they are too ill to do so naturally

respire *verb* to breathe

respite (*pronounced* **res**-pait *or* **res**-pit)

noun a pause, a rest: *no respite from work*

resplendent *adjective* very bright or splendid in appearance

respond *verb* **1** to answer **2** to react in response to: *I waved but he didn't respond* **3** to show a positive reaction to: *responding to treatment*

respondent *see* **corespondent**

response *noun* **1** a reply **2** an action, feeling *etc* in answer to another **3** an answer made during a church service

responsibility *noun* (*plural* **responsibilities**) **1** something or someone for which one is responsible **2** the state of being responsible or having important duties for which one is responsible

responsible *adjective* **1** (sometimes **responsible for something**) being the cause of: *responsible for this mess* **2** liable to be blamed (for): *responsible for the conduct of his staff* **3** involving making important decisions *etc*: *a responsible post* **4** trustworthy

---

■ **Alternative words:** (meaning 2) accountable

---

responsive *adjective* quick to react, to show sympathy *etc*

rest *noun* **1** a break in work **2** a sleep **3** *music* a pause in playing or singing for a given number of beats **4** a support, a prop: *book rest* **5** what is left, the remainder **6** the others, those not mentioned: *I went home but the rest went to the cinema* □ *verb* **1** to stop working for a time **2** to be still **3** to sleep **4** to depend (on), be based on: *the case rests on your evidence* **5** to stop, develop no further: *I can't let the matter rest there* **6** to lean or place on a support □ **rest with** to be the responsibility of: *the choice rests with you*

restaurant *noun* a place where meals may be bought and eaten

restaurateur *noun* the owner or manager of a restaurant

restful *adjective* **1** relaxing **2** relaxed

restitution *noun* **1** the return of what has been lost or taken away **2** compensation for harm or injury done

restive *adjective* restless, impatient

restless *adjective* **1** unable to keep still **2** agitated

restoration *noun* **1** the act of giving back something lost or stolen **2** a model or reconstruction (*eg* of a ruin)

restorative *adjective* curing, giving strength

restore *verb* **1** to put or give back **2** to repair (a building, a painting *etc*) so that it looks as it used to **3** to cure (a person)

restrain *verb* **1** to hold back (from) **2** to keep under control

restraint *noun* **1** the act of restraining **2** self-control **3** a tie or bond used to restrain

restrict *verb* **1** to limit, keep within certain bounds: *restricted space for parking* **2** to open only to certain people: *restricted area*

restriction *noun* **1** an act or instance of restricting **2** a regulation or rule which restricts or limits

restrictive *adjective* restricting

result *noun* **1** a consequence of something already done or said **2** the answer to a sum **3** a score in a game □ *verb* **1** **result from something** to be the result or effect of it **2** **result in something** to have it as a result: *result in a draw*

■ **Alternative words:** (verb, meaning 1) arise

---

resultant *adjective* happening as a result

resume *verb* **1** to begin again after an interruption: *resume a discussion* **2** to take again: *he resumed his seat*

résumé (*pronounced* **rez**-yoo-mei) *noun* **1** a summary **2** *US* a curriculum vitae

resumption *noun* the act of resuming

resurgence *noun* the act of returning to life, to a state of activity *etc* after a period of decline

resurgent *adjective* rising again, becoming prominent again

resurrect *verb* to bring back to life or into use

resurrection *noun* **1** a rising from the dead **2** **Resurrection** the rising of

Christ from the dead **3** the act of bringing back into use

resuscitate *verb* to bring back to consciousness, revive

resuscitation *noun* resuscitating or being resuscitated

retail *verb* **1** to sell goods to someone who is going to use them (not to another seller) **2** to tell (*eg* a story) fully and in detail □ *noun* the sale of goods to the actual user

retailer *noun* a shopkeeper, a trader

retain *verb* **1** to keep possession of **2** to keep (something) in mind **3** to reserve (someone's services) by paying a fee in advance **4** to hold back, keep in place

retainer *noun* **1** a fee for services paid in advance **2** *old* a servant (to a family)

retake *verb* to take or capture again □ *noun* the filming of part of a film again

retaliate *verb* to return like for like, hit back

retaliation *noun* an act of retaliating; revenge

retard *verb* **1** to keep back, hinder **2** to make slow or late

retardation *noun* retarding or being retarded

retarded *adjective* slow in mental or physical growth

retch *verb* to make the actions and sound of vomiting, without actually vomiting

retention *noun* **1** the act of holding in or keeping **2** the act of retaining the services of (*eg* a lawyer)

retentive *adjective* able to hold or retain well: *retentive memory*

reticence *noun* being reticent

reticent *adjective* unwilling to speak openly and freely, reserved

retina *noun* (*plural* **retinas** or **retinae**) the part of the back of the eye that receives the image of what is seen

retinue *noun* the attendants of someone important

retire *verb* **1** to give up work permanently, usually because of age **2** to go to bed **3** to draw back, retreat

retired *adjective* **1** having given up work **2** out-of-the-way, quiet

retirement *noun* **1** the act of retiring from work **2** someone's life after they have given up work

retiring *adjective* shy, avoiding being noticed

retort *verb* to make a quick and witty reply □ *noun* **1** a quick, witty reply **2** a bottle of thin glass used for distilling liquids

retrace *verb* to go over again: *retrace your steps*

retract *verb* **1** to take back (something said or given) **2** to draw back: *the cat retracted its claws*

retractable *adjective* able to be retracted

retraction *noun* a retracting (especially of something one has said, agreed or promised)

retreat *verb* **1** to draw back, withdraw **2** to go away □ *noun* **1** a movement backwards corresponding to the advance of an enemy **2** a withdrawal **3** a quiet, peaceful place

retrenchment *noun* economizing in spending

retribution *noun* punishment

retrieve *verb* **1** to get back, recover (something lost) **2** to search for and fetch

retriever *noun* a breed of dog trained to find and fetch shot birds

retro *adjective* recreating the past for effect

retro- *prefix* forms words containing the meaning 'backwards' or 'behind'
🕔 Comes from Latin *retro* meaning 'back' or 'behind'

retroflex *adjective* bent backwards

retrograde *adjective* **1** going backward **2** going from a better to a worse stage

retrospect *noun*: **in restrospect** considering or looking back on the past

retrospective *adjective* **1** looking back on past events **2** of a law: applying to the past as well as the present and the future

return *verb* **1** to go or come back **2** to

give, send, pay *etc* back **3** to elect to parliament □ *noun* **1** the act of returning **2** a profit: *return on your investment* **3** a statement of income for calculating income tax □ **by return** sent by the first post back

return match a second match played between the same team or players

return ticket a ticket which covers a journey both to and from a place

reunion *noun* a meeting of people who have been apart for some time

reunite *verb* to join after having been separated

Rev or **Revd** *abbreviation* Reverend

rev *noun* a revolution of an engine □ *verb* (often **rev up**) to increase the speed of (an engine)

> **rev** *verb* ⇨ revs, revving, revved

revamp *verb* to renovate, renew the appearance of

reveal *verb* **1** to make known **2** to show

reveille (*pronounced* ri-**val**-i) *noun* a bugle call at daybreak to waken soldiers

revel *verb* **1** to take great delight (in) **2** to celebrate □ *noun* (**revels**) festivities

> **revel** *verb* ⇨ revels, revelling, revelled

revelation *noun* **1** the act of revealing **2** something unexpected which is made known

reveller *noun* a merrymaker, a partygoer

revelry *noun* noisy lively enjoyment, festivities, or merrymaking

revenge *noun* **1** harm done to someone in return for harm they themselves have committed **2** the desire to do such harm □ *verb* **1** to inflict punishment in return for harm done: *revenging his father's murder* **2** **revenge oneself** to take revenge: *he revenged himself on his enemies*

revenue *noun* **1** money received as payment **2** a country's total income

reverberate *verb* to echo and re-echo, resound

reverberation *noun* reverberating

revere *verb* to look upon with great respect

reverence *noun* great respect

reverend *adjective* **1** worthy of respect **2 Reverend** a title given to a member of the clergy (*short form*: **Rev** or **Revd**)
ⓘ Comes from Latin *reverendus* meaning 'who must be respected'

> 🖝 Do not confuse: **reverend** and **reverent**

reverent or **reverential** *adjective* showing respect
ⓘ Comes from Latin *reverent-*, a form of *reverens* meaning 'respecting'

reverie (*pronounced* rev-e-ri) *noun* a daydream

reversal *noun* the act of reversing or being reversed

reverse *verb* **1** to turn upside down or the other way round **2** to move backwards **3** to undo (a decision, policy *etc*) □ *noun* **1** the opposite (of) **2** the other side (of a coin *etc*) **3** a defeat

reversible *adjective* of clothes: able to be worn with either side out

revert *verb* **1** to go back to an earlier topic **2** to return to a previous owner

review *verb* **1** to give an opinion or criticism of (an artistic work) **2** to consider again: *review the facts* **3** to inspect (*eg* troops) □ *noun* **1** a critical opinion of a book *etc* **2** a magazine consisting of reviews **3** a second look, a reconsideration **4** an inspection of troops *etc*

> 🖝 Do not confuse with: **revue**

reviewer *noun* someone who reviews, a critic

revile *verb* to say harsh things about

revise *verb* **1** to correct faults in and make improvements **2** to study notes *etc* in preparation for an examination **3** to change (*eg* an opinion)

revision *noun* **1** the act of revising **2** a revised version of a book *etc*

revival *noun* **1** a return to life, use *etc* **2** a fresh show of interest: *a religious revival*

revive *verb* to bring or come back to life, use or fame

revoke *verb* **1** to cancel (a decision *etc*) **2** to fail to follow suit in a card-game

revolt *verb* **1** to rise up (against), rebel **2** to feel disgust (at) **3** to disgust □ *noun* a rising, a rebellion

revolting *adjective* causing disgust

revolution *noun* **1** a full turn round a centre **2** the act of turning round a centre **3** a general uprising against those in power **4** a complete change in ideas, way of doing things *etc*

revolutionary *adjective* **1** relating to a revolution **2** bringing about great changes **3** turning □ *noun* (*plural* **revolutionaries**) someone who is involved in, or is in favour of, revolution

revolutionize *verb* to bring about a complete change in

revolve *verb* to roll or turn round

revolver *noun* a kind of pistol

revue *noun* a light theatre show, with short topical plays or sketches
♠ Do not confuse with: **review**

revulsion *noun* **1** disgust **2** a sudden change of feeling

reward *noun* **1** something given in return for work done or for good behaviour *etc* **2** a sum of money offered for helping to find a criminal, lost property *etc* □ *verb* **1** to give a reward to **2** to give a reward for (a service)

rewarding *adjective* giving pleasure or satisfaction

rewind *verb* to wind back (a spool, cassette *etc*) to the beginning

rewrite *verb* to write again

rhapsodize *verb* to talk or write enthusiastically (about)

rhapsody *noun* music or poetry which expresses strong feeling □ **go into rhapsodies over** to show wild enthusiasm for

rhesus factor a substance normally present in human blood

rhesus-negative *adjective* having blood which does not contain the rhesus factor

rhesus-positive *adjective* having blood which contains the rhesus factor

rhetoric *noun* **1** the art of good speaking or writing **2** language which is too showy, consisting of unnecessarily long or difficult words *etc*

rhetorical *adjective* **1** relating to or using rhetoric **2** of language: over-elaborate □ **rhetorical question** one which the asker answers, or which does not need an answer

rheumatic *adjective* relating to or caused by rheumatism

rheumatism *noun* a disease which causes stiffness and pain in the joints

rhinestone *noun* an artificial paste diamond

rhino (*plural* **rhinos**) *short for* rhinoceros

rhino- or **rhin-** *prefix* of or relating to the nose
Ⓘ Comes from Greek *rhis* meaning 'nose'

rhinoceros (*plural* **rhinoceros** or **rhinoceroses**) a large, thick-skinned animal, with a horn (or two) on its nose

rhinoplasty *noun* plastic surgery on the nose

rhododendron *noun* a flowering shrub with thick evergreen leaves and large flowers

rhombus *noun* (*plural* **rhombi** or **rhombuses**) a geometrical figure with four equal straight sides

rhubarb *noun* a plant with long red-skinned stalks, edible when cooked

rhyme *noun* **1** a similarity in sounds between words or their endings, *eg humble* and *crumble,* or *convention* and *prevention* **2** a word which sounds like another **3** a short poem □ *verb* (sometimes **rhyme with**) to sound like, be rhymes: *harp rhymes with carp*

rhythm *noun* **1** a regular repeated pattern of sounds or beats in music or poetry **2** a regularly repeated pattern of movements □ **rhythm and blues** a type of music combining the styles of rock-and-roll and the blues

rhythmic or **rhythmical** *adjective* of or with rhythm

rhythm method a method of contraception by abstaining from intercourse when a woman is most fertile

rib noun 1 any of the bones which curve round and forward from the backbone, enclosing the heart and lungs 2 a spar of wood in the framework of a boat, curving up from the keel 3 a ridged knitting pattern

ribald adjective of a joke etc: coarse, vulgar

ribbed adjective arranged in ridges and furrows

ribbon noun a narrow strip of silk or other material, used for decoration, tying hair etc

rice noun the seeds of a plant, grown for food in well-watered ground in tropical countries

rice paper thin edible paper often put under baking to prevent it sticking

rich adjective 1 having a lot of money or valuables, wealthy 2 valuable: a rich reward 3 rich in something having a lot of it: rich in natural resources 4 of food: containing a lot of fat, eggs etc 5 of material: heavily decorated or textured, lavish 6 of a colour: deep in tone

■ **Alternative words**: (meaning 1) wealthy, affluent, moneyed, prosperous, well-to-do, well-off

riches noun plural wealth

richly adverb 1 in a rich or elaborate way: richly decorated 2 fully and suitably: richly deserved

richness noun being rich

Richter scale (pronounced **rikh**-ter) a scale for measuring the intensity of earthquakes

rickets noun singular a children's disease caused by lack of calcium, with softening and bending of the bones

rickety adjective 1 suffering from rickets 2 unsteady: a rickety table

rickshaw noun a two-wheeled carriage pulled by a man, used in Japan etc

ricochet (pronounced **rik**-osh-ei) verb of a bullet: to rebound at an angle from a surface

ricochet ➪ ricochets, ricocheting, ricocheted

rid verb to free from, clear of: rid the city of rats □ **get rid of** to free yourself of

rid ➪ rids, ridding, rid

riddance noun: **good riddance to** I am happy to have got rid of

riddle[1] noun 1 a puzzle in the form of a question which describes something in a misleading way 2 something difficult to understand 3 a tray with holes for separating large objects from smaller ones

riddle[2] verb: **riddled with** covered with small holes made by: riddled with woodworm

ride verb 1 to travel on a horse or bicycle, or in a vehicle 2 to travel on and control (a horse) 3 of a ship: to float at anchor □ noun 1 a journey on horseback, bicycle etc 2 a path through a wood, for riding horses □ **ride up** of a skirt etc: to work itself up out of position

ride verb ➪ rides, riding, rode, ridden

rider noun 1 someone who rides 2 something added to what has already been said

ridge noun 1 a raised part between furrows 2 a long crest on high ground

ridicule verb to laugh at, mock □ noun mockery

ridiculous adjective deserving to be laughed at, very silly

rife adjective very common: disease was rife in the country

riff-raff noun worthless people

rifle[1] verb 1 to search through and rob 2 to steal

rifle[2] noun a gun fired from the shoulder

rift noun 1 a crack 2 a disagreement between friends

rift valley a long valley formed by the fall of part of the earth's crust

rig verb 1 **rig someone out** to clothe or dress them 2 to fix (an election result) illegally or dishonestly □ **rig up 1** to fit (a ship) with sails and ropes 2 to make or build hastily

rig ⇨ rigs, rigging, rigged

rigging noun ship's spars, ropes etc

right adjective 1 on or belonging to the side of the body which in most people has the more skilful hand (contrasted with: **left**) 2 correct, true 3 just, good 4 straight □ adverb 1 to or on the right side 2 correctly 3 straight 4 all the way: right along the pier and back □ noun 1 something good which ought to be done 2 something you are entitled to: a right to a fair trial 3 the right-hand side, direction etc 4 the conservative side in politics □ verb to mend, set in order □ **by right** because you have the right □ **in your own right** not because of anyone else, independently

right angle an angle like one of those in a square, an angle of 90°

righteous adjective living a good life; just

rightful adjective by right, proper: the rightful owner

right-handed adjective using the right hand more easily than the left

right-of-way noun a road or path over private land along which people may go as a right

right-wing adjective of conservative views in politics

rigid adjective 1 not easily bent, stiff 2 strict

rigidity noun a rigid state or quality

rigmarole noun a long, rambling speech

Originally ragman roll, a Scots term for a long list or catalogue

rigor mortis stiffening of the body after death

rigorous adjective very strict

rigour noun strictness; harshness

rill noun a small stream

rim noun an edge or border, eg the top edge of a cup

rind noun a thick firm covering, eg fruit peel, bacon skin, the outer covering of cheese

ring noun 1 a small hoop worn on the finger, on the ear etc 2 a hollow circle 3 an enclosed space for boxing, circus performances etc 4 the sound of a bell being struck 5 a small group of people formed for business or criminal purposes: a drug ring □ verb¹ (past ringed) 1 to encircle, go round 2 to mark (a bird etc) by putting on a ring □ verb² (past rang) 1 to make the sound of a bell 2 to strike (a bell etc) 3 to telephone

ring ⇨ rings, ringing, rang or ringed, rung or ringed

ringleader noun someone who takes the lead in mischief etc

ringlet noun a long curl of hair

ringmaster noun someone who is in charge of the performance in a circus ring

ring road a road that circles a town etc avoiding the centre

rink noun a sheet of ice, often artificial, for skating or curling

rinse verb 1 to wash lightly to remove soap etc 2 to clean (a cup, your mouth etc) by swilling with water □ noun 1 the act of rinsing 2 liquid colour for the hair

riot noun 1 a noisy disturbance by a crowd 2 a striking display: a riot of colour 3 a hilarious event □ verb to take part in a riot

riotous adjective noisy, uncontrolled

RIP abbreviation may he or she rest in peace

rip verb 1 to tear apart or off 2 to come apart □ noun a tear □ **let rip** to express yourself fully, without restraint

rip ⇨ rips, ripping, ripped

ripe adjective 1 of fruit etc: ready to be picked or eaten 2 fully developed, mature

ripen verb to make or become ripe

ripeness noun being ripe

rip-off noun, slang a cheat, a swindle

riposte noun a quick return or reply

ripple noun 1 a little wave or movement on the surface of water 2 a soft sound etc that rises and falls quickly and gently: a ripple of laughter

rise verb 1 to get up from bed 2 to stand up 3 to move upwards 4 of a river: to have its source (in): *the Rhone rises in the Alps* **5** to rebel (against) □ *noun* **1** a slope upwards **2** an increase in wages, prices *etc* □ **give rise to** to cause

rise *verb* ⇨ rises, rising, rose, risen

risible *adjective* laughable

rising *noun* **1** an act of rising **2** a rebellion

risk *noun* a chance of loss or injury; a danger □ *verb* **1** to take the chance of: *risk death* **2** to take the chance of losing: *risk one's life, health etc*

risky *adjective* possibly resulting in loss or injury

rissole *noun* a fried cake or ball of minced meat, fish *etc*

rite *noun* a solemn ceremony, especially a religious one

ritual *noun* a traditional way of carrying out religious worship *etc* □ *adjective* relating to a rite or ceremony

ritualistic *adjective* done in a set, unchanging way

rival *noun* someone who tries to equal or beat another □ *verb* to try to equal

rival *verb* ⇨ rivals, rivalling, rivalled

rivalry *noun* (*plural* **rivalries**) the state of being a rival or rivals

riven *adjective*, *old* split

river *noun* a large stream of water flowing across land

rivet *noun* a bolt for fastening plates of metal together □ *verb* **1** to fasten with a rivet **2** to fix firmly (someone's attention *etc*): *riveted to the spot*

rivulet *noun* a small stream

roach *noun* (*plural* **roaches**) a type of freshwater fish

road *noun* **1** a hard, level surface for vehicles and people **2** a way of getting to (somewhere), a route **3 roads** a place where ships may lie at anchor (*also called*: **roadstead**)

road hog a reckless or selfish driver

road movie a film showing the travels of a character or characters

roadway *noun* the part of a road used by cars *etc*

roadworthy *adjective* (of a vehicle) fit to be used on the road

roam *verb* to wander about

roan *noun* a horse with a dark coat spotted with grey or white

roar *verb* **1** to give a loud, deep sound **2** to laugh loudly **3** to say (something) loudly □ *noun* a loud, deep sound or laugh

roast *verb* to cook or be cooked in an oven or over a fire □ *adjective* roasted: *roast beef* □ *noun* **1** meat roasted **2** meat for roasting

rob *verb* to steal from

rob ⇨ robs, robbing, robbed

robber *noun* a person who robs; a thief

robbery *noun* (*plural* **robberies**) the act of stealing

robe *noun* **1** a long loose garment **2** *US* a dressing-gown **3 robes** the official dress of a judge *etc* □ *verb*, *formal* to dress

robin *noun* a type of small bird, known by its red breast

robot *noun* **1** a mechanical man or woman **2** a machine that can do the work of a person

robotic *adjective* relating to or characteristic of robots

robust *adjective* strong, healthy

rock *noun* **1** a large lump of stone **2** a hard sweet made in sticks **3** *music* with a heavy beat and simple melody (*also called*: **rock music**) □ *verb* to sway backwards and forwards or from side to side

rock-and-roll or **rock'n'roll** *noun* a simpler, earlier form of rock music

rock cake a small rough-textured cake

rocker *noun* a curved support on which a chair, cradle *etc* rocks

rockery *noun* (*plural* **rockeries**) a collection of stones amongst which small plants are grown

rocket *noun* **1** a tube containing inflammable materials, used for launching a spacecraft, signalling and as a firework **2** a spacecraft □ *verb* to move upwards rapidly: *prices are rocketing*

rocking-chair *noun* a chair which rocks backwards and forwards on rockers

rocking-horse *noun* a toy horse which rocks backwards and forwards on rockers

rocky *adjective* 1 full of rocks 2 inclined to rock, unsteady

rod *noun* 1 a long thin stick 2 a fishing rod 3 *historical* a measure of distance, about 5 metres

rode *past form of* **ride**

rodent *noun* a gnawing animal, such as a rat, beaver *etc*

rodeo *noun* (*plural* **rodeos**) 1 a round-up of cattle for marking 2 a show of riding by cowboys

roe *noun* 1 the eggs of fishes 2 (also **roe deer**) a small kind of deer 3 a female red deer

roebuck *noun* the male roe deer

rogue *noun* a dishonest or mischievous person, a rascal

roguery *noun* dishonesty; mischief

roguish *adjective* characteristic of a rogue; mischievous, dishonest

rôle *noun* a part played by an actor

roll *verb* 1 to move along by turning over like a wheel 2 of a ship: to rock from side to side 3 of thunder *etc*: to rumble 4 to wrap round and round: *roll up a carpet* 5 to flatten with a roller: *roll the lawn* □ *noun* 1 a sheet of paper, length of cloth *etc* rolled into a cylinder 2 a very small loaf of bread 3 a rocking movement 4 a list of names 5 a long, rumbling sound

rollcall *noun* the calling of names from a list

roller *noun* 1 a cylindrical tool for flattening 2 a tube over which hair is rolled and styled 3 a small solid wheel 4 a long heavy wave on the sea

rollerblades *noun plural* rollerskates with the wheels in a single line

rollerskates *noun plural* skates with wheels at each corner of the shoe

rollicking *adjective* noisy and full of fun

rolling pin a roller for flattening dough

rolling stock the stock of engines, carriages *etc* that run on a railway

ROM *abbreviation, computing* read-only memory

Roman *adjective* of a number: written in letters, as I, II, III, IV *etc* for 1, 2, 3, 4 *etc* □ **Roman Catholic Church** the Church whose head is the Pope, the Bishop of Rome

romance *noun* 1 a story about heroic events not likely to happen in real life 2 a love story 3 a love affair □ *verb* to write or tell imaginative stories

romantic *adjective* 1 of romance 2 full of feeling and imagination 3 relating to love

romanticism *noun* (often **Romanticism**) the late 18th-and early 19th-century movement in art, literature and music, characterized by an emphasis on feelings and emotions

Romany *noun* 1 a gypsy 2 the gypsy language

romp *verb* 1 to play in a lively way 2 to move quickly and easily □ *noun* a lively game

rompers *noun plural* a short suit for a baby

rondo *noun* (*plural* **rondos**) a musical composition with a recurring section

rood *noun, old* 1 a measure of area, equal to a quarter of an acre 2 a cross carrying an image of Christ

roof *noun* (*plural* **roofs**) 1 the top covering of a building, car *etc* 2 the upper part of the mouth □ *verb* to cover with a roof

rook *noun* 1 a kind of crow 2 *chess* the castle

rookery *noun* (*plural* **rookeries**) 1 a nesting place of rooks 2 a breeding place of penguins or seals

room *noun* 1 an inside compartment in a house 2 space: *room for everybody* 3 **rooms** lodgings

roomy *adjective* having plenty of space

roost *noun* a perch on which a bird rests at night □ *verb* to sit or sleep on a roost

rooster *noun* a farmyard cock

root *noun* 1 the underground part of a

plant **2** the base of anything, *eg* a tooth **3** a cause, a source **4** a word from which other words have developed □ *verb* **1** to form roots and begin to grow **2** to be fixed **3** of an animal: to turn up ground in a search for food **4** to search (about) □ **root out** or **root up 1** to tear up by the roots **2** to get rid of completely □ **take root 1** to form roots and grow firmly **2** to become firmly fixed

rooted *adjective* firmly planted

rope *noun* **1** a thick cord, made by twisting strands together **2** anything resembling a thick cord □ *verb* **1** to fasten or catch with a rope **2** to enclose, mark off with a rope

ropy *adjective* **1** like ropes, stringy **2** *informal* bad, not well

rosary *noun* (*plural* **rosaries**) **1** a set of prayers **2** a string of beads used in saying prayers **3** a rose garden

rose¹ *see* **rise**

rose² *noun* **1** a type of flower, often scented, usually growing on a prickly bush **2** a deep pink colour

rosé *noun* a pink-coloured wine produced by removing red grape-skins during fermentation

rosehip *noun* the fruit of the rose

rosemary *noun* an evergreen sweet-smelling shrub, used as a cooking herb

rosette *noun* a badge shaped like a rose, made of ribbons

rosewood *noun* a dark Brazilian or Indian wood, which smells of roses when cut

roster *noun* a list showing a repeated order of duties *etc*

rostrum *noun* (*plural* **rostrums** or **rostra**) a platform for public speaking

rosy *adjective* **1** red, pink **2** (of the future *etc*) bright, hopeful

rot *verb* to go bad, decay □ *noun* **1** decay **2** *informal* nonsense

rot *verb* ⇨ **rots, rotting, rotted**

rota *noun* a list of duties *etc* to be repeated in a set order

rotary *adjective* turning round like a wheel

rotate *verb* **1** to turn round like a wheel **2** to go through a repeating series of changes

rotation *noun* **1** an act of rotating or state of being rotated **2** one complete turn around an axis **3** a regular and recurring sequence **4** (also **crop rotation**) the growing of different crops on a field, usually in an ordered sequence, to help keep the land fertile

rote *noun*: **by rote** off by heart, automatically

rotor a turning part of a motor, dynamo *etc*

rotten *adjective* **1** decayed, bad **2** worthless, disgraceful

rotter *noun*, *informal* a very bad, worthless person

rotund *adjective* round; plump

rotundity *noun* roundness

rouble or **ruble** *noun* a standard unit of Russian coinage

rouge *noun* a powder or cream used to add colour to the cheeks

rough *adjective* **1** not smooth **2** uneven **3** coarse, harsh **4** boisterous, wild **5** not exact: *a rough guess* **6** stormy □ *noun* **1** a hooligan, a bully **2** rough ground □ **rough and ready** not fine or carefully made, but effective □ **rough out** to sketch or shape roughly

▦ **Alternative words**: (adjective, meaning 5) approximate

roughage *noun* bran or fibre in food

roughcast *noun* plaster mixed with fine gravel, for coating outside walls □ *verb* to cover with roughcast

roughen *verb* to make rough

roulette *noun* a gambling game, played with a ball which is placed on a wheel

round *adjective* **1** shaped like a circle **2** plump **3** even, exact: *a round dozen* □ *adverb* & *preposition* **1** on all sides (of), around: *look round the room* **2** in a circle (about): *the earth moves round the sun* **3** from one (person, place *etc*) to another: *the news went round* □ *noun* **1** a circle, something round in shape **2** a single bullet or shell **3** a burst of firing, cheering *etc* **4** a song in which the singers take up the tune in turn **5** a usual route: *a postman's round* **6** a series of calls or deliveries **7** each stage of a contest □ *verb* **1** to make or become round **2** of a ship: to go round (*eg* a headland) □ **round on** to make a sudden attack on □ **round up** to gather or drive together

roundabout *noun* **1** a revolving machine for children to ride on in a park *etc* **2** a meeting place of roads, where traffic must move in a circle □ *adjective* not straight or direct: *a roundabout route*

rounders *noun singular* a ball game played with a bat in which players run around a series of stations

Roundhead *noun* a supporter of Parliament during the English Civil War

roundly *adverb* boldly, plainly

round trip *US* a journey to a place and back

rouse *verb* **1** to awaken **2** to stir up, excite

rousing *adjective* stirring, exciting

rout *noun* a complete defeat □ *verb* to defeat utterly

route *noun* the course to be followed, a way of getting to somewhere □ *verb* to fix the route of

routine *noun* a fixed, unchanging order of doing things □ *adjective* regular, usual: *routine enquiries*

rove *verb* to wander or roam

rover 1 a wanderer; an unsettled person **2** *history* a pirate

Rover Scout an older member of the Scout Association

row¹ *noun* **1** a line of people or things **2** a trip in a rowing boat □ *verb* to drive (a boat) by oars

row² *noun* **1** a noisy quarrel **2** a noise **3** *informal* a scolding

rowan *noun* (*also called*: **mountain ash**) a tree with clusters of bright red berries

rowdy *adjective* noisy, disorderly

rower *noun* someone who rows

rowing boat a boat rowed by oars

rowlock *noun* a place to rest an oar on the side of a rowing boat

royal *adjective* **1** relating to a king or queen **2** splendid, magnificent: *royal welcome*

royal blue a deep, bright blue

royal icing stiff cake icing made with egg-white

royal jelly a jelly secreted by worker bees to feed developing larvae

royalty *noun* (*plural* **royalties**) **1** the state of being royal **2** royal people as a whole **3** a sum paid to the author of a book for each copy sold

RSA *abbreviation* **1** Royal Society of Arts **2** Royal Scottish Academy

RSPB *abbreviation* Royal Society for the Protection of Birds

RSPCA *abbreviation* Royal Society for the Prevention of Cruelty to Animals

RSSPCC *abbreviation* Royal Scottish Society for Prevention of Cruelty to Children

RSVP *abbreviation* please reply (from French *répondez, s'il vous plaît*)

rub *verb* **1** to move one thing against the surface of another **2** to clean, polish (something) **3 rub something out** or **away** to remove (a mark) □ *noun* **1** the act of rubbing **2** a wipe □ **rub in 1** to work into (a surface) by rubbing **2** to keep reminding someone of (something unpleasant)

rub *verb* ⇨ rubs, rub*b*ing, rub*b*ed

rubber *noun* **1** a tough elastic substance made from plant juices **2** a piece of rubber used for erasing pencil marks **3** an odd number (three or five) of games in cards, cricket *etc*

rubber bullet a hard rubber pellet fired by police in riot control

rubber stamp an instrument with rubber figures or letters for stamping dates *etc* on paper

rubber-stamp *verb* to authorize, approve

rubbish *noun* **1** waste material, litter **2** nonsense

rubble *noun* small rough stones, bricks *etc* left from a building

rubella *noun* German measles

Rubicon *noun*: **cross the Rubicon** to take a decisive step

> After Caesar's crossing of the *Rubicon* river which meant declaring war on his neighbouring province

rubicund *adjective* red or rosy-faced

ruble *another spelling of* **rouble**

rubric *noun* **1** a heading **2** a guiding rule

> From a Latin word for red ink, originally an entry in a Biblical text written in red ink

ruby *noun* (*plural* **rubies**) a type of red, precious stone

ruck *noun* a wrinkle, a crease

rucksack *noun* a bag carried on the back by walkers, climbers *etc*

ruckus *noun, US* an uproar, a rumpus

ructions *noun plural* a row, a disturbance

rudder *noun* a device fixed to the stern of a boat, or tail of an aeroplane, for steering

ruddy *adjective* **1** red **2** of the face: rosy, in good health

rude *adjective* **1** showing bad manners, not polite **2** roughly made: *a rude shelter* **3** rough, not refined **4** startling and sudden: *a rude awakening* **5** coarse, vulgar, lewd □ **rudely** *adverb*

rudimentary *adjective* in an early stage of development

rudiments *noun plural* the first simple rules or facts of anything

rue *noun* a shrub with bitter-tasting leaves □ *verb* to be sorry for, regret

rueful *adjective* sorrowful, regretful

ruff *noun* **1** *historical* a pleated frill worn round the neck **2** a band of feathers round a bird's neck

ruffian *noun* a rough, brutal person

ruffianly *adjective* characteristic or typical of a ruffian

ruffle *verb* **1** to make unsmooth, crumple (*eg* hair, a bird's feathers) **2** to annoy, offend

rug *noun* **1** a floor mat **2** a blanket

Rugby or **rugby** *noun* a form of football using an oval ball which can be handled

> Named after *Rugby* School in Warwickshire, where the game was supposedly invented

rugged (*pronounced* **rug**-id) *adjective* **1** having a rough, uneven appearance **2** strong, robust **3** stern, harsh

ruin *noun* **1** complete loss of money *etc* **2** a downfall **3** **ruins** broken-down remains of buildings □ *verb* **1** to destroy **2** to spoil completely: *ruin your chances* **3** to make very poor

ruination *noun* the act of ruining or state of being ruined

ruined *adjective* in ruins, destroyed

ruinous *adjective* **1** ruined **2** likely to cause ruin

rule *noun* **1** government: *under military rule* **2** a regulation: *school rules* **3** what usually happens **4** a guiding principle **5** a measuring ruler □ *verb* **1** to govern, be in power **2** to decide (that) **3** to draw (a line) **4** to mark with lines □ **as a rule** usually □ **rule out** to leave out, not consider

ruler *noun* **1** someone who rules **2** a marked tool for measuring length and drawing straight lines

ruling *adjective* governing; most important □ *noun* a decision, a rule

rum¹ *noun* an alcoholic spirit made from sugar-cane

rum² *adjective, informal* strange, odd

rumble *verb* to make a low rolling noise like that of thunder *etc* □ *noun* a low rolling noise

ruminant *noun* an animal, such as a cow, that chews the cud

ruminate *verb* **1** to chew the cud **2** to be deep in thought

rumination *noun* deep thought

rummage *verb* to turn things over in search □ *noun* a thorough search

rummy *noun* a card game played with hands of seven cards

rumour *noun* **1** general talk **2** a story passed from person to person which may not be true □ *verb* **1** to spread a rumour of **2** to tell widely

rump *noun* 1 the hind part of an animal 2 the meat from this part

rumple *verb* 1 to make untidy 2 to crease

rumpus *noun* an uproar, a clamour

run *verb* 1 to move swiftly, hurry 2 to race 3 to travel: *the train runs every day* 4 of water: to flow 5 to follow a certain route: *the main road running between Glasgow and Edinburgh* 6 of a machine: to work 7 to spread (rapidly): *this colour is running* 8 to continue, extend: *the programme runs for two hours* 9 to operate (machinery *etc*) 10 to organize, conduct (a business *etc*) 11 to compete with other candidates in an election □ *noun* 1 a trip 2 a distance run 3 a spell of running 4 a continuous period: *a run of good luck* 5 a ladder in a stocking *etc* 6 free use of: *the run of the house* 7 a single score in cricket 8 an enclosure for hens *etc* □ **run a risk** to take a chance of loss, failure *etc* □ **run down** 1 to knock (someone) down 2 to speak ill of □ **run into** 1 to bump into, collide with 2 to meet accidentally □ **run out of** to become short of □ **run over** to knock down or pass over with a car

run *verb* ⇨ runs, running, ran, run

Ⓘ Comes from Old English *rinnan* meaning 'to run'

▇ **Alternative words**: (verb, meanings 1 and 2) sprint, jog, career, tear, dash, rush, speed, bolt, dart, scoot, scuttle

runaway *noun* a person that runs away □ *adjective* of an animal or vehicle: out of control and moving very fast

run-down *adjective* in poor health or condition

rune *noun* a letter of an early alphabet used in ancient writings

rung¹ *noun* a step of a ladder

rung² *see* ring

runic *adjective* written in runes

runner *noun* 1 someone who runs 2 a messenger 3 a rooting stem of a plant 4 a blade of a skate or sledge □ **do a runner** *slang* to leave without paying a bill

runner-up *noun* (*plural* **runners-up**)

someone who comes second in a race or competition

running *noun* 1 the act of moving fast 2 management, control □ *adjective* 1 for use in running 2 giving out fluid: *running sore* 3 carried on continuously: *running commentary* □ *adverb* one after another: *three days running* □ **in (or out of) the running** having (or not having) a chance of success

run-of-the-mill *adjective* ordinary

runrig *noun, Scottish* a system of dividing land into strips for leasing to tenants

runway *noun* a path for aircraft to take off from or land on

rupee *noun* the standard currency of India, Pakistan and Sri Lanka

rupture *noun* 1 a breaking, *eg* of a friendship 2 a tear in a part of the body □ *verb* to break, burst

rural *adjective* of the country (*contrasted with*: **urban**)

ruse *noun* a trick, a cunning plan

rush¹ *verb* 1 to move quickly, hurry 2 to make (someone) hurry 3 to take (a fort *etc*) by a sudden attack □ *noun* (*plural* **rushes**) 1 a quick, forward movement 2 a hurry

rush² *noun* (*plural* **rushes**) a tall grasslike plant growing near water

rusk *noun* a hard dry biscuit like toast

russet *adjective* reddish-brown □ *noun* a type of apple of russet colour

rust *noun* a reddish-brown coating on metal, caused by air and moisture □ *verb* to form rust

rustic *adjective* 1 relating to the country 2 roughly made 3 simple, unsophisticated □ *noun* someone who lives in the country

rusticate *verb* to live in the country

rusticity *noun* 1 country living 2 simplicity

rustle *verb* 1 of silk *etc*: to make a soft, whispering sound 2 to steal (cattle) 3 **rustle something up** *informal* to prepare quickly: *rustle up a meal* □ *noun* a soft, whispering sound

rustler *noun* someone who steals cattle

rusty *adjective* **1** covered with rust **2** *informal* showing lack of practice: *my French is rusty*

rut *noun* a deep track made by a wheel *etc* □ **in a rut** having a dull, routine way of life

ruthless *adjective* without pity, cruel

rutted *adjective* full of ruts

rye *noun* a kind of grain

rye-grass *noun* a grass grown for cattle-feeding

Ss

If you can't find the word you're looking for under letter **S**, perhaps it starts with a different letter. Try looking under **C** for words like *century, city* and *cycle*, and **PS** for words like *psychology*. Also, don't forget **SC** for words like *scent*, **SCH** for words like *schism*, and **SW** for words like *sword*.

If the word you're looking for sounds like it begins **SH** but you can't find it there, remember that **CH** is sometimes pronounced *sh* (as in *chivalry*), as is **SCH** (*schist*).

s *abbreviation* **1** south **2** southern

Sabbath *noun* the day of the week regularly set aside for religious services and rest (among Muslims, Friday; Jews, Saturday; and Christians, Sunday)

sabbatical *noun* a period of paid leave from work

sable *noun* a small weasel-like animal with dark brown or blackish fur □ *adjective* black or dark brown in colour

sabotage (*pronounced* **sab**-ot-ahsz) *noun* deliberate destruction of machinery, an organization *etc* by enemies or dissatisfied workers □ *verb* to destroy or damage deliberately

Originally meaning the destruction of machinery by factory workers, from French *sabot* 'clog'

saboteur *noun* someone who carries out sabotage

sabre *noun, historical* a curved sword used by cavalry

sac *noun* any bag-like part in a plant or animal, especially containing liquid

saccharine *noun* a very sweet substance used as a sugar substitute

sachet (*pronounced* **sash**-ei) *noun* **1** a small bag to hold handkerchiefs *etc* **2** a small sealed packet containing powder or liquid, *eg* shampoo

sack¹ *noun* **1** a large bag of coarse cloth for holding flour *etc* **2 the sack** *informal* dismissal from your job □ *verb*, *informal* to dismiss from a job □ **get the sack** *informal* to be dismissed from your job

sack² *noun* the plundering of a captured town □ *verb* to plunder

sackcloth *noun* **1** coarse cloth for making sacks **2** a garment made of this, worn as a sign of repentance

sacking *noun* sackcloth

sacral (*pronounced* **seik**-ral) *adjective* of the sacrum
🕐 Comes from Latin *sacrum* meaning 'a sacred object' + word-ending -*al*
☛ Do not confuse with: **sacred**

sacrament *noun* a religious ceremony, *eg* baptism or communion

sacred *adjective* **1** holy **2** dedicated to some purpose or person: *sacred to her memory* **3** religious: *sacred music*
🕐 Comes from Middle English *sacre* meaning 'make holy', combined with the word-ending -*ed* to give the sense of 'made holy'
☛ Do not confuse with: **sacral**

sacrifice *noun* **1** the offering of an animal killed for the purpose to a god **2** an animal *etc* offered to a god **3** the giving up of something for the benefit of another person, or to gain something more important **4** something given up for this purpose □ *verb* **1** to offer (an animal *etc*) as a sacrifice to a god **2** to give up (something) for someone or something else

sacrificial *adjective* of or for sacrifice

sacrilege *noun* the use of something holy in a blasphemous way

sacrilegious *adjective* committing or involving sacrilege

sacrosanct *adjective* **1** very sacred **2** not to be harmed or touched

sacrum (*pronounced* sei-krum) *noun* a triangular bone forming part of the human pelvis

sad *adjective* **1** sorrowful, unhappy **2** showing sorrow **3** causing sorrow: *sad story* **4** *informal* pitiful, feeble

■ **Alternative words**: (meanings 1 and 2) tearful, upset, distressed, miserable, downcast, glum, crestfallen, dejected, downhearted, despondent, melancholy, depressed, low, gloomy, dismal

sadden *verb* to make or become sad

saddle *noun* **1** a seat for a rider on the back of a horse or bicycle **2** a cut or joint of meat from the back of an animal □ *verb* to put a saddle on (an animal) □ **saddle with** to burden with: *saddled with debts*

saddler *noun* a maker of saddles and harnesses

sadism (*pronounced* seid-i-zm) *noun* taking pleasure in cruelty to others

Sadism is a word which was invented to describe the particular type of sexual cruelty which the 18th-century French author Marquis de Sade wrote about in his novels

sadist (*pronounced* seid-ist) *noun* someone who gets pleasure from inflicting pain and suffering on others

sadistic (*pronounced* sa-**dis**-tik) *adjective* getting, or seeming to get, pleasure from inflicting pain and suffering on others

SAE or **sae** *abbreviation* stamped addressed envelope

safari *noun* an expedition for observing or hunting wild animals

safari park an enclosed area where wild animals are kept outdoors and on view to visitors

safe *adjective* **1** unharmed **2** free from harm or danger **3** reliable, trustworthy □ *noun* **1** a lockable box for keeping money and valuables **2** a storage place for meat *etc* □ **safe and sound** unharmed

safeguard *noun* anything that gives protection or security □ *verb* to protect

safety *noun* freedom from harm or danger □ *adjective* giving protection or safety: *safety belt*

safety belt a seat belt

safety-pin *noun* a curved pin in the shape of a clasp, with a guard covering its point

saffron *noun* a type of crocus from which is obtained a yellow food dye and flavouring agent

sag *verb* to droop or sink in the middle

sag ⇨ sag*s*, sag*ging*, sag*ged*

saga *noun* **1** an ancient story about heroes *etc* **2** a novel or series of novels about several generations of a family **3** a long detailed story

sagacious *adjective* very wise, quick at understanding □ **sagaciously** *adverb*

sagacity *noun* good judgement

sage *noun* **1** a type of herb with grey-green leaves which are used for flavouring **2** a wise man □ *adjective* wise □ **sagely** *adverb*

sago *noun* a white starchy substance obtained from a palm-tree, often used in puddings

said *adjective* mentioned before: *the said shopkeeper* □ *past form* of **say**

sail *noun* **1** a sheet of canvas spread out to catch the wind and drive forward a ship or boat **2** a journey in a ship or boat **3** an arm of a windmill □ *verb* **1** to travel in a ship or boat (with or without sails) **2** to navigate or steer a ship or boat **3** to begin a sea voyage **4** to glide along easily □ **set sail** to set out on a sea voyage

sailboard *noun* a surfboard fitted with a mast and sail

sailor *noun* **1** someone who sails **2** a member of a ship's crew

saint *noun* **1** a very good or holy person **2** a title conferred after death on a holy person by the Roman Catholic Church (*short form*: **St**)

Saint Bernard or **St Bernard** a breed of large dog, famous for its use in mountain rescues

sainted or **saintly** *adjective* very holy or very good

sake *noun* 1 cause, purpose: *for the sake of making money* 2 benefit, advantage: *for my sake*

salaam *noun* a low bow with the right palm on the forehead, a form of Eastern greeting □ *verb* to perform this greeting

salad *noun* a dish of raw vegetables, *eg* lettuce, cucumber *etc*

salamander *noun* a kind of small lizard-like animal

salami *noun* a type of highly seasoned sausage

salary *noun* (*plural* **salaries**) fixed wages regularly paid for work

Based on Latin *salarium*, ration money given to Roman legionaries for buying salt

sale *noun* 1 the exchange of anything for money 2 a selling of goods at reduced prices 3 an auction

salesman *noun* a man who sells or shows goods to customers

saleswoman *noun* a woman who sells or shows goods to customers

salient *adjective* 1 pointing outwards: *salient angle* 2 outstanding, chief: *salient points of the speech*

saline *adjective* containing salt, salty: *saline solution*

saliva *noun* the liquid that forms in the mouth to help digestion; spittle

salivary *adjective* of or producing saliva

salivate *verb* 1 to produce saliva 2 to anticipate keenly

sallow *adjective* of complexion: pale, yellowish

sally *noun* (*plural* **sallies**) 1 a sudden rush forward 2 a trip, an excursion 3 a witty remark or retort □ *verb* to rush out suddenly □ **sally forth** to go out, emerge

sally *verb* ⇨ sall**ies**, sally**ing**, sall**ied**

salmon *noun* a large fish with yellowish-pink flesh

salmonella *noun* a bacterium which causes food poisoning

salon *noun* 1 a shop in which hairdressing *etc* is done 2 a large room

for receiving important guests 3 a gathering of such people

saloon *noun* 1 a passengers' dining-room in a ship 2 a covered-in car 3 a public house, a bar

salt *noun* 1 a substance used for seasoning, either mined from the earth or obtained from sea water 2 a substance formed from a metal and an acid 3 *informal* a sailor □ *adjective* 1 containing salt: *salt water* 2 tasting of salt 3 preserved in salt: *salt herring* □ *verb* 1 to sprinkle with salt 2 to preserve with salt

salt cellar a small container for salt

salty *adjective* 1 tasting of salt 2 piquant, racy

salubrious *adjective* 1 health-giving 2 pleasant, respectable

salutary *adjective* 1 giving health or safety 2 beneficial, useful: *salutary lesson*

salutation *noun* an act of greeting

salute *verb* 1 to greet with words, an embrace *etc* 2 *military* to raise the hand to the forehead to show respect to 3 to honour someone by a firing of guns *etc* □ *noun* an act or way of saluting

salvage *noun* 1 goods saved from destruction or waste 2 the act of saving a ship's cargo, goods from a fire *etc* 3 payment made for this act □ *verb* to save from loss or ruin

salvation *noun* 1 an act, means or cause of saving: *the arrival of the police was his salvation* 2 the saving of humanity from sin

salve *noun* an ointment for healing or soothing □ *verb* to soothe (pride, conscience *etc*)

salver *noun* a small tray, often of silver

salvo *noun* (*plural* **salvos**) a great burst of gunfire, clapping *etc*

same *adjective* 1 exactly alike, identical: *we both had the same feeling* 2 not different, unchanged: *he still looks the same* 3 mentioned before: *the same person came again* □ *pronoun* the thing just mentioned □ **all the same** or **just the same** in spite of that □ **at the same time** still, nevertheless
ℚ Comes from Old Norse *same*

sameness *noun* lack of change or variety

samovar *noun* a Russian tea-urn

sampan *noun* a kind of small boat used in Far Eastern countries

sample *noun* a small part extracted to show what the whole is like □ *verb* to test a sample of: *sample a cake*

sampler *noun* **1** someone who samples **2** a piece of needlework *etc* showing skill in different techniques

sanatorium *noun* **1** a hospital, especially for people suffering from respiratory diseases **2** a sick-room in a school *etc*

sanctification *noun* making holy or sacred

sanctify *verb* to make holy or sacred

   sanctify ⇨ sanctif*ies*, sanctify*ing*, sanctif*ied*

sanctimonious *adjective* self-righteous, priggish

sanction *noun* **1** permission, approval **2** a penalty for breaking a law or rule **3** **sanctions** measures applied to force another country *etc* to stop a course of action

sanctity *noun* holiness; sacredness

sanctuary *noun* (*plural* **sanctuaries**) **1** a sacred place **2** the most sacred part of a temple or church **3** a place of safety from arrest or violence **4** a protected reserve for birds or animals

sanctum *noun*: **inner sanctum** a very sacred or private room *etc*

sand *noun* **1** a mass of tiny particles of crushed rocks *etc* **2** **sands** a stretch of sand on the seashore □ *verb* **1** to sprinkle with sand **2** to add sand to **3** to smooth or polish with sandpaper

sandal *noun* a shoe with straps to hold the sole onto the foot

sandalwood *noun* a fragrant E Indian wood

sandbag *noun* a bag filled with sand, used as a protective barrier

sand dune a ridge of sand blown up by the wind

sandpaper *noun* paper with a layer of

sand glued to it for smoothing and polishing

sandshoe *noun* a light shoe with a rubber sole

sandstone *noun* a soft rock made of layers of sand pressed together

sandwich *noun* (*plural* **sandwiches**) two slices of bread, or a split roll, stuffed with a filling □ *verb* to fit between two other objects

   After the 18th-century Earl of *Sandwich*, said to have invented it to allow him to gamble without interruption for meals

sandy *adjective* **1** covered with sand **2** like sand **3** of hair: yellowish-red in colour

sane *adjective* **1** of sound mind, not mad **2** sensible □ **sanely** *adverb*

sang *past form* of **sing**

sangui- *prefix* of or relating to blood
  ⓘ Comes from Latin *sanguis* meaning 'blood'

sanguinary *adjective* bloodthirsty, bloody
  ⓘ Comes from Latin *sanguinarius* meaning 'for blood' or 'blood-thirsty'

   ♦ Do not confuse: **sanguinary** and **sanguine**

sanguine *adjective* **1** hopeful, cheerful **2** of a complexion: red, ruddy
  ⓘ Comes from Latin *sanguineus* meaning 'blood-stained'

sanitary *adjective* **1** promoting good health, especially by having good drainage and sewage disposal **2** free from dirt, infection *etc*

sanitary towel a pad of absorbent material worn to soak up menstrual blood

sanitation *noun* arrangements for protecting health, especially drainage and sewage disposal

sanity *noun* **1** soundness of mind **2** mental health **3** good sense or judgement

sank *past form* of **sink**

Sanskrit *noun* the ancient literary language of India

sap *noun* **1** the juice in plants, trees *etc*

2 *informal* a weakling, a fool □ *verb* to weaken (someone's strength *etc*)

sap *verb* ⇨ sap**s**, sap**ping**, sap**ped**

sapling *noun* a young tree

sapphire *noun* a precious stone of a deep blue colour

Saracen *noun, historical* an Islamic opponent of the Crusaders; a Moor

sarcasm *noun* **1** scornful humour, characterized by the use of a mocking tone to say the exact opposite of what you really think **2** a hurtful remark made in scorn

sarcastic *adjective* **1** of a remark: containing sarcasm **2** often using sarcasm, scornful □ **sarcastically** *adverb*

■ **Alternative words**: (meaning 1) acid

sarcophagus *noun* a stone coffin

sardine *noun* a young pilchard, often tinned in oil □ **like sardines** crowded closely together

sardonic *adjective* bitter, mocking, scornful

sari *noun* a long cloth wrapped round the waist and brought over the shoulder, traditionally worn by Indian women

sarong *noun* a skirt traditionally worn by Malay men and women

sartorial *adjective* relating to dress or clothes: *sartorial elegance*

sash[1] *noun* (*plural* **sashes**) a decorative band worn round the waist or over the shoulder

sash[2] *noun* (*plural* **sashes**) a sliding frame for window panes

Sassenach *noun, Scottish derogatory* an English person

sat *past form* of **sit**

Satan *noun* the Devil

Satanic *adjective* of Satan, devilish

satanism *noun* devil worship

satchel *noun* a small bag for carrying schoolbooks *etc*

sate *verb, old* to satisfy fully; give more than enough to

satellite *noun* **1** a moon orbiting a larger planet **2** a man-made object launched into space to orbit a planet **3** a state controlled by a more powerful neighbour

satellite television the broadcasting of television programmes via satellite

satiate *verb* to satisfy fully; to give more than enough to

satiety *noun* the state of being satisfied fully or to excess

satin *noun* a closely woven silk with a glossy surface

satire *noun* **1** a piece of writing *etc* which makes fun of particular people or events **2** ridicule, scorn

satirical *adjective* containing or using satire to attack or criticize someone or something

satirist *noun* a writer of satire

satisfaction *noun* **1** the act of satisfying or being satisfied **2** a feeling of pleasure or comfort **3** something that satisfies **4** compensation for damage *etc*

satisfactory *adjective* **1** satisfying **2** fulfilling the necessary requirements □ **satisfactorily** *adverb*: *he completed the test satisfactorily*

satisfy *verb* **1** to give enough (of something) to **2** to please, make content **3** to give enough to lessen or quieten: *satisfied her curiosity* **4** to convince: *satisfied that he was innocent* **5** to fulfil: *satisfy all our requirements*

satisfy ⇨ satisf**ies**, satisf**ying**, satisf**ied**

satsuma *noun* a small seedless orange

saturate *verb* **1** to soak or immerse in water **2** to cover or fill completely (with): *saturated with information*

saturation *noun* saturating or being saturated: *the market has reached saturation point*

Saturday *noun* the seventh day of the week

saturnine *adjective* gloomy, sullen

satyr (*pronounced* **sat**-er) *noun* a mythological creature, half man, half goat, living in the woods

sauce *noun* **1** a liquid seasoning added to food to improve flavour **2** *informal* cheek, impudence

saucepan *noun* a deep-sided cooking pan with a long handle

saucer *noun* a small, shallow dish for placing under a cup

saucy *adjective* impudent, cheeky

sauna *noun* a room filled with dry steam to induce sweating

saunter *verb* to stroll about without hurrying □ *noun* a leisurely stroll

sausage *noun* minced meat seasoned and stuffed into a tube of animal gut *etc*

savage *adjective* 1 wild, untamed 2 fierce and cruel 3 uncivilized 4 very angry □ *noun* 1 an uncivilized person 2 someone fierce or cruel □ *verb* to attack very fiercely □ **savagely** *adverb*

savagery *noun* extreme cruelty or fierceness

savanna or **savannah** *noun* a grassy, treeless plain

save *verb* 1 to bring out of danger, rescue 2 to protect from harm, damage or loss 3 to keep from spending or using: *saving money/ saves time* 4 to put money aside for the future □ *preposition* except (for): *all the CDs were damaged save this one* □ **save up** to put money aside for future use

savings *noun plural* money put aside for the future

saviour *noun* 1 someone who saves others from harm or evil 2 **Saviour** Christ

savour *noun* 1 characteristic taste or flavour 2 an interesting quality □ *verb* 1 to taste or smell of 2 to taste with enjoyment 3 to have a trace or suggestion (of): *his reaction savours of jealousy* 4 to experience

savoury *adjective* 1 having a pleasant taste or smell 2 salt or sharp in flavour; not sweet □ *noun* (*plural* **savouries**) a savoury dish or snack

savoy *noun* a type of winter cabbage

saw[1] *noun* 1 a tool with a toothed edge for cutting wood *etc* 2 *old* a wise saying □ *verb* to cut with a saw

saw *verb* ⇨ **saw**s, **saw**ing, **sawn**, **saw**ed

saw[2] *past form* of **see**

sawdust *noun* a dust of fine fragments of wood, made in sawing

sawmill *noun* a mill where wood is sawn up

Saxon *noun, historical* one of a Germanic people who invaded Britain in the 5th century

saxophone *noun* a wind instrument with a curved metal tube and keys for the fingers

So called because it was invented by a man whose name was Sax

saxophonist *noun* a player of the saxophone

say *verb* 1 to speak, utter: *why don't you say 'Yes'?* 2 to express in words, state: *they said they knew him* □ *noun* 1 the right to speak: *no say in the matter* 2 the opportunity to speak: *I've had my say* □ **I say!** *interjection* 1 expressing surprise or protest 2 used to try to attract attention □ **that is to say** in other words

say *verb* ⇨ **say**s, **say**ing, **said**

⏱ Comes from Old English *secgan*

■ **Alternative words**: (verb, meaning 1) pronounce, deliver, exclaim, ejaculate, drawl, mutter, grunt; (verb, meaning 2) tell, declare, assert, affirm, maintain, claim, allege, imply, disclose, divulge

saying *noun* something often said; a proverb

scab *noun* 1 a crust formed over a sore 2 any of several diseases of animals or plants 3 *informal* a blackleg

scabbard *noun* the sheath in which the blade of a sword is kept

scabby *adjective* 1 covered in scabs 2 *informal* disgusting, revolting

scabies *noun* an itchy skin disease

scaffold *noun* a platform on which people are put to death

scaffolding *noun* a framework of poles and platforms used by people doing repairs on a building *etc*

scald *verb* 1 to burn with hot liquid or steam 2 to heat (milk *etc*) just short of boiling point □ *noun* a burn caused by hot liquid or steam

scale *noun* **1** a set of regularly spaced marks for measurement on a thermometer *etc* **2** a series or system of increasing values: *salary scale* **3** *music* a group of notes going up or down in order **4** the measurements of a map compared with the actual size of the area shown: *drawn to the scale 1:50000* **5** the size of a business *etc*: *manufacture on a small scale* **6** a small thin flake on the skin of a fish or snake **7 scales** a weighing machine □ *verb* **1** to climb up **2** to remove the scales from (*eg* a fish) **3** to remove in thin layers

scallop *noun* a shellfish with a pair of hinged fan-shaped shells

scalloped *adjective* of an edge: cut into curves or notches

scallywag *noun* a rogue

scalp *noun* **1** the outer covering of the skull **2** the skin and hair on top of the head □ *verb* to cut the scalp from

scalpel *noun* a small, thin-bladed knife, used in surgery

scaly *adjective* having scales; flaky

scamp *noun* a rascal

scamper *verb* **1** to run about playfully **2** to run off in haste

scampi *noun plural* Norway lobsters (large prawns) cooked for eating

scan *verb* **1** to count the beats in a line of poetry **2** of poetry: to have the correct number of beats **3** to examine carefully **4** *informal* to read quickly, skim over **5** to pass an X-ray, ultrasonic wave *etc* over □ *noun* an act of scanning

scan *verb* ⇨ scan*s*, scan*ning*, scan*ned*

scandal *noun* **1** something disgraceful or shocking **2** talk or gossip about people's (supposed) misdeeds

scandalize *verb* to shock, horrify

scandalmonger *noun* someone who spreads gossip or scandal

scandalous *adjective* **1** shameful, disgraceful **2** containing scandal □ **scandalously** *adverb*: *it is scandalously expensive*

scanner *noun* a machine which scans

scansion *noun* scanning of poetry

scant *adjective* not plentiful, hardly enough: *pay scant attention*

scanty *adjective* little or not enough in amount: *scanty clothing* □ **scantily** *adverb*: *pictures of scantily-clad young women*

scapegoat *noun* someone who bears the blame for the wrongdoing of others

Literally 'escape goat', after an ancient Jewish ritual of transferring the people's sins to a goat which was afterwards let free in the wilderness

scar *noun* **1** the mark left by a wound or sore **2** a mark, a blemish □ *verb* to mark with a scar

scar *verb* ⇨ scar*s*, scar*ring*, scar*red*

scarab *noun* a beetle regarded as sacred by the ancient Egyptians

scarce *adjective* **1** not plentiful, not enough **2** rare, seldom found □ **make yourself scarce** to go, run away

scarcely *adverb* **1** only just, barely: *could scarcely hear* **2** surely not: *you can scarcely expect me to eat that*

scarcity *noun* (*plural* **scarcities**) want, shortage

scare *verb* **1** to drive away with fear **2** to startle, frighten □ *noun* a sudden fright or alarm

scarecrow *noun* a figure set up to scare birds away from crops

scarey *adjective another spelling of* **scary**

scarf *noun* (*plural* **scarves** or **scarfs**) a strip of material worn round the neck, shoulders or head

scarlet *noun* a bright red colour □ *adjective* bright red

scarlet fever an infectious illness, causing a rash

scarper *verb, slang* to run away

scary or **scarey** *adjective* frightening

scathing *adjective* cruel, hurtful: *scathing remark*

scatter *verb* **1** to throw loosely about; sprinkle **2** to spread widely **3** to flee in all directions

scatterbrain *noun* someone who frequently forgets things

scattered *adjective* thrown or spread about widely

scattering *noun* a small amount thinly spread or scattered

scavenger *noun* an animal which feeds on dead flesh

scenario (*pronounced* si-**nah**-ri-oh) *noun* **1** a scene-by-scene outline of a play, film *etc* **2** an outline of a plan or project
Ⓞ Comes from Italian *scenario* meaning 'scenery'

  ● Do not confuse with: **scene**

scene *noun* **1** the place where something happens: *scene of the accident* **2** a view, a landscape **3** a division of a play or opera **4** an area of activity: *the music scene* **5** a show of bad temper: *don't make a scene*
Ⓞ Comes from Latin *scaena* meaning 'the scene presented' or 'the stage'

  ● Do not confuse with: **scenario**

scenery *noun* **1** the painted background on a theatre stage **2** the general appearance of a stretch of country

scenic *adjective* **1** of scenery **2** picturesque

scent *verb* **1** to discover by the smell **2** to give a suspicion of, sense: *scent danger* **3** to give a pleasant smell to: *roses scented the air* □ *noun* **1** perfume **2** an odour, a smell **3** the trail of smell used to track an animal *etc*

sceptic (*pronounced* **skep**-tik) *noun* someone who doubts what they are told
Ⓞ Comes from Greek *skeptikos* meaning 'thoughtful'

  ● Do not confuse with: **septic**

sceptical (*pronounced* **skep**-tik-al) *adjective* unwilling to believe, doubtful □ **sceptically** *adverb*

scepticism (*pronounced* **skep**-tis-i-zm) *noun* a doubting state or attitude

sceptre (*pronounced* **sep**-ter) *noun* an ornamental rod carried by a monarch on ceremonial occasions

schedule (*pronounced* **shed**-yool or **sked**-yool) *noun* **1** the time set for doing something: *I'm two weeks behind*

schedule **2** a written statement of details **3** a form for filling in information □ *verb* **1** to form into a schedule **2** to plan, arrange

schematic *adjective* according to a plan

scheme (*pronounced* skeem) *noun* **1** a plan, a systematic arrangement **2** a dishonest or crafty plan □ *verb* to make schemes, plot

scheming *adjective* crafty, cunning

scherzo (*pronounced* **sker**-tsoh) *noun* (*plural* **scherzos**), *music* a lively movement in triple time

schism (*pronounced* **si**-zm or **ski**-zm) *noun* a breaking away from the main group

schizo- (*pronounced* **skit**-so) *prefix* forms words containing the idea of a split or division: *schizophrenia* (= literally, 'a split mind')
Ⓞ Comes from Greek *schizein* meaning 'to split'

schizophrenia (*pronounced* skit-sof-**ree**-ni-a) *noun* a mental illness involving a distorted perception of reality

schizophrenic (*pronounced* skit-sof-**ren**-ik) *noun & adjective* (someone) suffering from schizophrenia

scholar *noun* **1** someone of great learning **2** someone who has been awarded a scholarship **3** a pupil, a student

scholarly *adjective* showing or having knowledge, high intelligence and love of accuracy □ **scholarliness** *noun*

scholarship *noun* **1** learning **2** a sum of money given to help a clever student to carry on further studies

scholastic *adjective* of schools or scholars

school *noun* **1** a place for teaching, especially children **2** a group of artists *etc* who share the same ideas **3** a large number of fish, whales *etc* □ *verb* **1** to educate in a school **2** to train by practice

schooling *noun* **1** education in a school **2** training

schoolmaster *noun* a male teacher at a school

schoolmistress *noun* a female teacher at a school

schooner *noun* 1 a two-masted sailing ship 2 a large sherry glass 3 *US & Austral* a large beer glass

sci- forms words containing the concept of knowledge: *science/prescient* (= having foreknowledge) ① Comes from Latin *scire* meaning 'to know', and *scientia* meaning 'knowledge'

sciatic (*pronounced* sai-**at**-ik) *adjective* relating to the hip

sciatica (*pronounced* sai-**at**-ik-*a*) *noun* severe pain in the upper part of the leg

science *noun* 1 knowledge obtained by observation and experiment 2 a branch of this knowledge, *eg* chemistry, physics, biology *etc* 3 these sciences considered together

science fiction stories dealing with future life on earth, space travel, other planets *etc*

scientific *adjective* 1 of science 2 done according to the methods of science □ **scientifically** *adverb*

scientist *noun* someone who studies one or more branches of science

sci fi *abbreviation* science fiction

scimitar *noun* a sword with a short curved blade

scintillate *verb* 1 to sparkle 2 to show brilliant wit *etc*

scion (*pronounced* **sai**-*on*) *noun* 1 a young member of a family 2 a descendant 3 a cutting for grafting on another plant

scissors *noun plural* a cutting instrument with two hinged blades

scoff *verb* 1 to express scorn 2 **scoff at someone** or **something** to make fun of, mock them

scold *verb* to tell off; blame or rebuke with angry words □ *noun* a bad-tempered person

■ **Alternative words**: (verb) admonish, reprimand

scolding *noun* a telling-off

scone *noun* a small plain cake made with flour, milk and a little fat

scoop *noun* 1 a hollow instrument used for lifting loose material, water *etc* 2 an exclusive news story □ *verb* to lift or dig out with a scoop

scooter *noun* 1 a two-wheeled toy vehicle pushed along by foot 2 a low-powered motor-cycle

scope *noun* 1 opportunity or room to do something: *scope for improvement* 2 extent, range: *outside the scope of this dictionary*

scorch *verb* 1 to burn slightly, singe 2 to dry up with heat

scorching *adjective* 1 burning, singeing 2 very hot 3 harsh, severe: *scorching criticism*

score *noun* 1 a gash, a notch 2 an account, a debt: *settle old scores* 3 the total number of points gained in a game 4 a written piece of music showing separate parts for voices and instruments 5 a set of twenty 6 **scores** a great many: *scores of people* 7 a reason, account: *don't worry on that score* □ *verb* 1 to mark with lines or notches 2 to gain (points) 3 to keep a note of points gained in a game □ **score out** to cross out

scorn *verb* 1 to look down on, despise 2 to refuse (help *etc*) because of pride □ *noun* mocking contempt

scornful *adjective* full of scorn □ **scornfully** *adverb*

scorpion *noun* a spider-like creature with a poisonous sting in its tail

scotch *verb* to stamp out, suppress

scot-free *adjective* unhurt; unpunished

SCOTVEC *abbreviation* Scottish Vocational Education Council

scoundrel *noun* a rascal

scour *verb* 1 to clean by hard rubbing; scrub 2 to search thoroughly

scourge *noun* 1 a whip 2 a cause of great suffering □ *verb* 1 to whip, lash 2 to afflict, cause to suffer

Scouse *noun*, *Brit* a native or inhabitant of Liverpool

scout *noun* 1 a guide or spy sent ahead to bring back information 2 **Scout** a member of the Scout Association

scowl *verb* to wrinkle the brows in

displeasure or anger □ *noun* a frown

Scrabble *noun, trademark* a word-building game

scrabble *verb* to scratch or grope about

scraggy *adjective* 1 long and thin 2 uneven, rugged

scram *exclamation* go away!

scramble *verb* 1 to struggle to seize something before others 2 to wriggle along on hands and knees 3 to mix or toss together: *scrambled eggs* 4 to jumble up (a message) to make it unintelligible without decoding □ *noun* 1 a rush and struggle to get something 2 a motor-cycle race over rough country

scrap *noun* 1 a small piece, a fragment 2 a picture for pasting in a scrapbook 3 *informal* a fight 4 parts of a car *etc* no longer required: *sold as scrap* 5 **scraps** small pieces, odds and ends □ *verb* 1 to abandon as useless 2 *informal* to fight, quarrel

> **scrap** *verb* ⇨ scrap**s**, scrap**ping**, scrap**ped**

scrapbook *noun* a blank book in which to stick pictures *etc*

scrape *verb* 1 to rub and mark with something sharp 2 to drag or rub against or across a surface with a harsh grating sound 3 **scrape something up** or **together** to collect (money *etc*) with difficulty □ *noun* 1 an act of scraping 2 a mark or sound made by scraping 3 *informal* a difficult situation □ **scrape through** to only just avoid failure

scrap-heap *noun* a heap of old metal *etc*, a rubbish heap □ **on the scrap-heap** no longer needed

scrapie *noun* a disease of sheep

scrap metal metal for melting and re-using

scrappy *adjective* made up of odd scraps, not well put together □ **scrappily** *adverb*

scratch *verb* 1 to draw a sharp point across the surface of 2 to mark by doing this 3 to tear or dig with claws, nails *etc* 4 to rub with the nails to relieve or stop itching 5 to withdraw from a competition □ *noun* (*plural* scratches) 1 a mark or sound made by scratching 2 a slight wound □ *adjective* 1 *golf* too good to be allowed a handicap 2 of a team: made up of players hastily got together □ **come up to scratch** to be satisfactory □ **start from scratch** to start from nothing, right at the beginning

scrawl *verb* to write or draw untidily or hastily □ *noun* 1 untidy, hasty or bad writing 2 something scrawled

scrawny *adjective* thin, skinny

scream *verb* to utter a shrill, piercing cry as in pain, fear *etc*; shriek □ *noun* a shrill cry

scree *noun* loose stones covering a steep mountain side

screech *verb* to utter a harsh, shrill and sudden cry □ *noun* a harsh shrill cry

screed *noun* a long boring speech or letter

screen *noun* 1 a flat covered framework to shelter from view or protect from heat, cold *etc* 2 something that shelters from wind, danger, difficulties *etc* 3 the surface on which cinema films are projected 4 the surface on which a television picture, or computer data, appears □ *verb* 1 to shelter, hide 2 to make a film of 3 to show on a screen 4 to sift, sieve 5 to sort out (the good from the bad) by testing 6 to conduct examinations on someone to test for disease □ **screen off** to hide behind, or separate by, a screen

screw *noun* 1 a nail with a slotted head and a winding groove or ridge (called the **thread**) on its surface 2 a kind of propeller (a **screw-propeller**) with spiral blades, used in ships and aircraft 3 a turn or twist (of a screw *etc*) □ *verb* 1 to fasten or tighten with a screw 2 to fix (*eg* a stopper) in place with a twisting movement 3 to twist, turn round (your head *etc*) 4 to twist up, crumple, pucker

screwdriver *noun* a tool for turning screws

scribble *verb* 1 to write carelessly 2 to make untidy or meaningless marks with a pencil *etc* □ *noun* 1 careless writing 2 meaningless marks, a doodle

scribe *noun, historical* 1 a clerk who

copied out manuscripts **2** a Jewish teacher of law

scrimp *verb* to be sparing or stingy with money: *scrimping and saving for a holiday*

script *noun* **1** the text of a play, talk *etc* **2** handwriting like print

scripture *noun* **1** sacred writings **2** **Scripture** the Christian Bible

scroll *noun* **1** a piece of paper rolled up **2** an ornament shaped like this

scrotum *noun* the bag of skin enclosing the testicles

scrounge *verb, slang* **1** to cadge **2** to get by begging □ *noun* an attempt to beg or cadge: *on the scrounge*

scrounger *noun* a person who scrounges

scrub *verb* to rub hard in order to clean □ *noun* countryside covered with low bushes

   scrub *verb* ⇨ scrubs, scrubbing, scrubbed

scruff *noun* the back of the neck

scruffy *adjective* untidy

scrum *noun, Rugby* a struggle for the ball by the forwards of the opposing sides bunched together

scrumptious *adjective, informal* delicious

scrunch *verb* to crumple

scruple *noun* doubt over what is right or wrong that keeps someone from doing something □ *verb* to hesitate because of a scruple

scrupulous *adjective* careful over the smallest details

scrutinize *verb* to examine very closely

scrutiny *noun* (*plural* **scrutinies**) careful examination, a close look

scuba *noun* breathing apparatus used by skin-divers

scud *verb* to move or sweep along quickly: *scudding clouds*

   scud ⇨ scuds, scudding, scudded

Scud missile *noun* a kind of missile made in the former Soviet Union

scuffle *noun* a confused fight

scull *noun* a short oar □ *verb* to move (a boat) with a pair of these or with one oar worked at the back of the boat

scullery *noun* (*plural* **sculleries**) a room for rough kitchen work

sculptor *noun* a male artist who carves or models figures in wood, stone, clay *etc*

sculptress *noun* a female artist who carves or models figures in wood, stone, clay *etc*

sculpture *noun* **1** the art of the sculptor or sculptress **2** a piece of their work

scum *noun* **1** foam that rises to the surface of liquids **2** the most worthless part of anything: *the scum of the earth*

scunner *noun, Scottish* a nuisance, a pest

scupper *noun* a hole in the side of a ship to drain water from the deck □ *verb* to put an end to, ruin: *scupper his chances*

scurf *noun* small flakes of dead skin (especially on the scalp)

scurrilous *adjective* insulting, abusive: *a scurrilous attack*

scurry *verb* to hurry along, scamper

   scurry ⇨ scurries, scurrying, scurried

scurvy *noun* a type of disease caused by a lack of fresh fruit and vegetables

scuttle *noun* **1** a fireside container for coal **2** an opening with a lid in a ship's deck or side □ *verb* **1** to make a hole in (a ship) in order to sink it **2** to hurry along, scamper

scythe (*pronounced* saidh) *noun* a large curved blade, on a long handle, for cutting grass *etc* by hand □ *verb* to cut with a scythe

SE *abbreviation* south-east; south-eastern

sea *noun* **1** the mass of salt water covering most of the earth's surface **2** a great stretch of water of less size than an ocean **3** a great expanse or number: *a sea of faces* □ **at sea 1** on the sea **2** completely puzzled

sea anemone a type of small plant-like animal found on rocks at the seashore

seaboard *noun* land along the edge of the sea

seafarer *noun* a traveller by sea, a sailor

seafaring *adjective* travelling by or working at sea

seafront *noun* a promenade with its buildings facing the sea

seagull *noun* a type of web-footed sea bird

sea-horse *noun* a type of small fish with a horse-like head and neck

seal[1] *noun* a furry sea animal living partly on land

seal[2] *noun* 1 a piece of wax with a design pressed into it, attached to a document to show that it is legal or official 2 a piece of wax used to keep a parcel closed 3 anything that closes tightly 4 a piece of sticky paper with a picture on it: *a Christmas seal* □ *verb* 1 to mark or fasten with a seal 2 to close up completely 3 to make (legally) binding and definite: *seal a bargain*

sea level the level of the surface of the sea

sealing wax a hard kind of wax for sealing letters, documents *etc*

sea lion a large kind of seal, the male of which has a mane

seam *noun* 1 the line formed by the sewing together of two pieces of cloth 2 a line or layer of metal, coal *etc* in the earth

seaman *noun* (*plural* **seamen**) a sailor, especially a member of a ship's crew who is not an officer

seamanship *noun* the art of steering and looking after ships at sea

seamstress *noun* a woman who sews for a living

seamy *adjective* sordid; disreputable □ **the seamy side** the more unpleasant side (*eg* of life)

séance (*pronounced* **sei**-ons) *noun* a meeting of people to receive messages from the spirits of the dead

seaplane *noun* an aeroplane which can take off from and land on the water

sear *verb* 1 to scorch, burn 2 to hurt severely

search *verb* 1 to look over in order to find something 2 **search for something** to look for it □ *noun* (*plural* **searches**) 1 an act of searching 2 an attempt to find

searching *adjective* examining closely and carefully: *searching question*

searchlight *noun* a strong beam of light used for picking out objects at night

seascape *noun* a picture of a scene at sea

seashore *noun* the land next to the sea

seasick *adjective* made ill by the rocking movement of a ship

seaside *noun* the land beside the sea

season *noun* 1 one of the four divisions of the year (spring, summer, autumn, winter) 2 the proper time for anything 3 a time associated with a particular activity: *football season* □ *verb* 1 to add (salt *etc*) to improve the flavour of (food) 2 to dry (wood) till it is ready for use

seasonable *adjective* 1 happening at the proper time 2 of weather: suitable for the season

seasonal *adjective* 1 of the seasons or a season 2 of work *etc*: taking place in one particular season only

seasoned *adjective* 1 of food: flavoured 2 of wood: ready to be used 3 trained, experienced: *a seasoned traveller*

seasoning *noun* something (*eg* salt, pepper) added to food to give it more taste

season ticket a ticket that can be used repeatedly for a certain period of time

seat *noun* 1 a piece of furniture for sitting on 2 the part of a chair on which you sit 3 the buttocks 4 a mansion 5 a place in parliament, on a council *etc* 6 the centre of some activity: *the seat of government* □ *verb* 1 to make to sit down 2 to have seats for (a certain number): *the room seats forty*

seat belt *noun* a belt fixed to a seat in a car *etc* to prevent an occupant from being thrown violently forward in the event of a crash

sea urchin a type of small sea creature with a spiny shell

seaward *adjective & adverb* towards the sea

seaweed *noun* any of many kinds of plants growing in the sea

seaworthy *adjective* in a good enough condition to go to sea

secateurs *noun plural* a tool like scissors, for trimming bushes *etc*

secede *verb* to break away from a group, society *etc*

secession *noun* 1 seceding 2 a group of seceders

seclude *verb* to keep (yourself) apart from people's notice or company

seclusion *noun* the state of being secluded; peacefulness and privacy

second *adjective* 1 next after the first in time, place *etc* 2 other, alternate: *every second week* 3 another of the same kind as: *they thought him a second Mozart* □ *noun* 1 someone or something that is second 2 an attendant to someone who boxes or fights a duel 3 the 60th part of a minute of time, or of a degree (in measuring angles) 4 an article not quite perfectly made: *these gloves are seconds* □ *verb* 1 to support, back up 2 (*pronounced* se-**kond**) to transfer temporarily to a special job ⓞ Comes from Latin *secundus* meaning 'following'

secondary *adjective* second in position or importance

secondary school a school between primary school and university *etc*

second-hand *adjective* 1 not new; having been used by another: *second-hand clothes* 2 of a shop: dealing in second-hand goods

secondly *adverb* in the second place

second nature a firmly fixed habit: *organizing people is second nature to her*

second-rate *adjective* not of the best quality, inferior

secrecy *noun* the state of being secret, mystery

secret *adjective* 1 hidden from, or not known by, others 2 secretive □ *noun* a fact, plan *etc* that is not told or known

secretarial *adjective* of a secretary or their work

secretary *noun* (*plural* **secretaries**) 1 someone employed to write letters, keep records *etc* in an office 2 someone elected to deal with the written business of a club *etc* □ **Secretary of State** 1 a government minister in charge of an administrative department 2 *US* the person in charge of foreign affairs

secrete *verb* 1 to hide, conceal in a secret place 2 of a part of the body: to store up and give out (a fluid)

secretion *noun* 1 a substance secreted 2 the process of secreting

secretive *adjective* inclined to hide or conceal your feelings, activities *etc*

secret service a government department dealing with spying

sect *noun* a group of people who hold certain views, especially in religious matters

sectarian *adjective* 1 of a sect 2 loyal to a sect 3 narrow-minded 4 of a crime, especially a murder: committed as a result of hatred between rival religious groups

section *noun* 1 a part, a division: *a section of the community* 2 a thin slice of a specimen for examination under a microscope 3 the view of the inside of anything when it is cut right through or across: *a section of a plant*

sector *noun* 1 a three-sided part of a circle whose sides are two radii and a part of the circumference 2 a part, a section

secular *adjective* 1 of worldly, not spiritual or religious things 2 of music *etc*: not sacred or religious

secure *adjective* 1 safe, free from danger or fear 2 confident: *secure in the knowledge that she had no rivals* 3 firmly fixed or fastened: *the lock is secure* □ *verb* 1 to make safe, firm or established: *secure your position* 2 to seize, get hold of: *secure the diamonds* 3 to fasten: *secure the lock*

security *noun* 1 safety 2 **securities** property or goods which a lender may keep until the loan is paid back

sedan *noun* 1 an enclosed chair for one person, carried on two poles by two bearers (*also called*: **sedan chair**) 2 *US* a saloon car

sedate *adjective* calm, serious, dignified

sedation *noun* the use of sedatives to calm a patient

sedative *adjective* calming, soothing □ *noun* a medicine with this effect

sedentary *adjective* of a job *etc*: requiring much sitting

sedge *noun* a type of coarse grass growing in swamps and rivers

sediment *noun* the grains or solid parts which settle at the bottom of a liquid

sedition *noun* the stirring up of rebellion against the government

seditious *adjective* encouraging rebellion, rebellious

seduce *verb* 1 to tempt (someone) away from right or moral behaviour 2 to persuade (someone) to have sexual intercourse 3 to attract

seducer *noun* a person who seduces someone else

seduction *noun* seducing or being seduced

seductive *adjective* attractive, tempting

sedulous *adjective* diligent, painstaking

see *verb* 1 to have sight 2 to be aware of, notice by means of the eye: *he can see us coming* 3 to form a picture of in the mind 4 to understand: *I see what you mean* 5 to find out: *I'll see what is happening* 6 to make sure: *see that he finishes his homework* 7 to accompany: *I'll see you home* 8 to meet: *I'll see you at the usual time* □ *noun* the district over which a bishop or archbishop has authority
□ **seeing that** since, because
□ **see through** 1 to take part in to the end 2 to not be deceived by (a person, trick *etc*) □ **see to** to take charge of (the preparation of): *see to a meal*

see *verb* ⇨ sees, seeing, saw, seen

🕐 Comes from Old English *seon*

■ **Alternative words**: (verb, meaning 2) perceive, glimpse, discern, distinguish, observe, mark, note □ **see to** attend to, deal with, organize

seed *noun* 1 the part of a tree, plant *etc* from which a new plant may grow 2 a seed-like part of a grain or a nut 3 the beginning from which anything grows: *the seeds of rebellion* 4 a seeded player in a tournament 5 *old* children, descendants □ *verb* 1 of a plant: to produce seed 2 to sow 3 to remove the seeds from (*eg* a fruit) 4 to arrange (good players) in a tournament so that they do not compete against each other till the later rounds □ **go to seed** or **run to seed** 1 of a plant: to develop seeds 2 of a person, area *etc*: to deteriorate, become run down

seedling *noun* a young plant just sprung from a seed

seedy *adjective* 1 full of seeds 2 shabby 3 sickly, not very well

seek *verb* 1 to look or search for 2 to try (to do something): *seek to establish proof* 3 to try to get (advice *etc*) □ **sought after** popular, much in demand

seek ⇨ seeks, seeking, sought

seem *verb* 1 to appear to be: *he seems kind* 2 to appear: *she seems to like it*

seeming *adjective* apparent but not actual or real: *a seeming success*

seemly *adjective* suitable; decent

seen *see* see

seep *verb* to flow slowly through a small opening, leak

seer *noun* a prophet

seersucker *noun* a lightweight ribbed cotton fabric

seesaw *noun* 1 a plank balanced across a stand so that one end of it goes up when the other goes down 2 an up-and-down movement like that of a seesaw □ *verb* 1 to go up and down on a seesaw 2 to move with a seesaw-like movement

seethe *verb* 1 to boil 2 to be very angry

seething *adjective* 1 boiling 2 furious

segment *noun* 1 a part cut off 2 a part of a circle cut off by a straight line

segregate *verb* to separate (someone or a group) from others

segregation *noun* 1 enforced separation into groups 2 the systematic isolation of one group, especially a racial or ethnic minority, from the rest of society

seismic (*pronounced* **saiz**-mik) *adjective* of earthquakes

seismograph (*pronounced* **saiz**-mo-grahf) *noun* an instrument that records earthquake shocks and measures their force

seize *verb* 1 to take suddenly by force 2 to overcome: *seized with fury* 3 **seize up** of machinery: to become stuck, break down

seizure *noun* 1 sudden capture 2 a sudden attack of illness, rage *etc*

seldom *adverb* not often, rarely: *you seldom see an owl during the day*

select *verb* to pick out from several according to your preference, choose □ *adjective* 1 picked out, chosen 2 very good 3 exclusive, allowing only certain people in

selection *noun* 1 the act of choosing 2 things chosen 3 a number of things from which to choose

selective *adjective* 1 selecting carefully 2 of weedkiller: harmless to garden plants

selector *noun* someone who chooses (*eg* members for a national team)

self *noun* (*plural* **selves**) 1 someone's own person 2 someone's personality, character

self-assured *adjective* trusting in your own power or ability, confident

self-centred *adjective* concerned with your own affairs, selfish

self-confident *adjective* believing in your own powers or abilities

self-conscious *adjective* too aware of your faults *etc* and therefore embarrassed in the company of others

self-contained *adjective* 1 of a house: complete in itself, not sharing any part with other houses 2 of a person: self-reliant

self-control *noun* control over yourself, your feelings *etc*

self-defence *noun* the defence of your own person, property *etc*

self-denial *noun* doing without

something, especially in order to give to others

self-effacing *adjective* keeping yourself from being noticed, modest

self-esteem *noun* respect for yourself; conceit

self-evident *adjective* clear enough to need no proof

self-expression *noun* expressing your own personality in your activities

self-important *adjective* having a mistakenly high sense of your own importance

self-indulgent *adjective* too ready to satisfy your own inclinations and desires

self-interest *noun* a selfish desire to consider only your own interests or advantage

selfish *adjective* caring only for your own pleasure or advantage □ **selfishly** *adverb*

selfless *adjective* thinking of others before yourself, unselfish

self-made *adjective* owing success *etc* to your own efforts: *a self-made man*

self-portrait *noun* an artist's portrait of themselves

self-possessed *adjective* calm in mind or manner, quietly confident

self-raising flour flour already containing an ingredient to make it rise

self-reliant *adjective* trusting in your own abilities *etc*

self-respect *noun* respect for yourself and concern for your own character and reputation

self-righteous *adjective* thinking highly of your own goodness and virtue

self-sacrifice *noun* the act of giving up your own life, possessions *etc* in order to do good to others

selfsame *adjective* the very same

self-satisfied *adjective* pleased, smug, satisfied with yourself

self-service *adjective* of a restaurant: where customers help or serve themselves

self-sufficient *adjective* needing no help or support from anyone else

self-willed *adjective* determined to have your own way, obstinate

sell *verb* 1 to give or hand over for money 2 to have or keep for sale: *he sells newspapers* 3 to be sold for, cost: *this book sells for £20*

> **sell** ⇨ sell*s*, sell*ing*, sold

seller *noun* someone who sells

Sellotape *noun, trademark* transparent adhesive tape, especially for use on paper

selvage *noun* the firm edge of a piece of cloth, that does not fray

semantic *adjective* relating to the meaning of words *etc*

semaphore *noun* a form of signalling using the arms to form different positions for each letter

semblance *noun* an outward, often false, appearance: *a semblance of listening*

semen *noun* the liquid that carries sperm

semester *noun, US* a term at a university *etc*

semi- *prefix* 1 half: *semicircle* 2 *informal* partly
① Comes from Latin prefix *semi-* meaning 'half'

semibreve *noun, music* a whole-note (𝅝), equal to four crotchets in length

semicircle *noun* half of a circle

semicolon *noun* the punctuation mark (;)

semi-detached *adjective* of a house: joined to another house on one side but not on the other

semi-final *noun* the stage or match of a contest immediately before the final

seminal *adjective* influential, important

seminar *noun* a group of students working on, or meeting to discuss, a particular subject

seminary *noun* (*plural* **seminaries**) a school or college

semi-precious *adjective* of a stone: having some value, but not considered a gem

Semitic *adjective* Jewish

semolina *noun* the hard particles of wheat sifted from flour, used for puddings *etc*

Semtex *noun, trademark* a material used to make explosives

senate *noun* 1 the upper house of parliament in the USA, Australia *etc* 2 the governing council of some universities 3 *historical* the law-making body in ancient Rome

senator *noun* a member of a senate

send *verb* 1 to make (someone) go 2 to have (something) carried or delivered to a place □ **send for** to order to be brought

> **send** ⇨ send*s*, send*ing*, sent

sender *noun* a person who sends something, especially by post

senile *adjective* 1 of old age 2 showing the mental feebleness of old age

senility *noun* 1 old age 2 mental deterioration in old age

senior *adjective* older in age or higher in rank □ *noun* someone older or in a senior position

seniority *noun* the state of being senior

senna *noun* the dried leaves of certain plants, used as a laxative

sensation *noun* 1 a feeling through any of the five senses 2 a vague effect: *a floating sensation* 3 a state of excitement: *causing a sensation*

sensational *adjective* causing great excitement, horror *etc*

sense *noun* 1 one of the five powers by which humans feel or notice (hearing, taste, sight, smell, touch) 2 a feeling: *a sense of loss* 3 an ability to understand or appreciate: *a sense of humour* 4 **senses** right mind, common sense: *to take leave of your senses* 5 wisdom, ability to act in a reasonable way 6 ability to be understood: *your sentence does not make sense* 7 meaning: *to what sense of this word are your referring?* □ *verb* to feel, realize: *sense disapproval*

senseless *adjective* stunned, unconscious; foolish

sensibility *noun* (*plural* **sensibilities**) ability to feel, sensitivity

sensible *adjective* 1 wise 2 able to be felt or noticed 3 **sensible of** aware of

■ **Alternative words**: (meaning 1) prudent, judicious, well-advised, shrewd

sensitive *adjective* 1 feeling, especially strongly or painfully 2 strongly affected by light, movements *etc*

sensitivity *noun* the quality or condition of being sensitive

sensitize *verb* to make sensitive (especially to light)

sensor *noun* a device that detects and measures physical changes

sensory *adjective* of the senses

sensual *adjective* 1 driven by, or affecting, the senses rather than the mind: *discover the sensual pleasures of aromatherapy* 2 indulging too much in bodily pleasures: *a sensual and extremely promiscuous woman*

☛ Do not confuse: **sensual** and **sensuous**

sensuality *noun* 1 the quality of being sensual 2 indulgence in physical pleasures

sensuous *adjective* pleasing to the senses, particularly by being beautiful or luxurious: *car designs favouring smooth edges and sensuous curves*

sent *see* **send**

sentence *noun* 1 a number of words which together make a complete statement 2 a judgement announced by a judge or court □ *verb* to condemn to a particular punishment

sentiment *noun* 1 a thought expressed in words 2 a show of feeling or emotion, often excessive

sentimental *adjective* having or showing too much feeling or emotion

sentimentality *noun* a sentimental quality or inclination

sentinel *noun* a soldier on guard

sepal *noun* one of the green leaves beneath the petals of a flower

separate *verb* (*pronounced* sep-*a*-reit) 1 to set or keep apart 2 to divide into parts 3 to disconnect 4 to go different ways 5 to live apart by choice □ *adjective* (*pronounced* sep-*a*-rat) 1 placed, kept *etc* apart 2 divided 3 not connected 4 different

separation *noun* a dividing or putting apart

separatism *noun* 1 a tendency to separate or to be separate 2 support for separation 3 the practices and principles of separatists

separatist *noun* someone who withdraws or urges separation from an established church, state *etc*

sepia *noun* a brown colour

sept- *prefix* seven: *septet/ September* (which was the seventh month in the Roman calendar)
ⓘ Comes from Latin *septem* meaning 'seven'

September *noun* the ninth month of the year

septet *noun* a group of seven musicians *etc*

septic *adjective* of a wound: full of germs that are poisoning the blood
ⓘ Comes from Greek *sepein* meaning 'to putrefy'

☛ Do not confuse with: **sceptic**

septuagenarian (*pronounced* sep-tyoo-*a*-ji-**neir**-ri-*an*) *noun* someone from seventy to seventy-nine years old

sepulchral (*pronounced* sip-**ul**-kr*a*l) *adjective* 1 of sepulchres 2 dismal, gloomy 3 of a voice: deep, hollow in tone

sepulchre (*pronounced* **sep**-*u*l-ker) *noun* a tomb

sequel *noun* 1 a result, a consequence 2 a story that is a continuation of an earlier story

sequence *noun* 1 the order (of events) in time 2 a number of things following in order, a connected series

sequestrate *verb* to keep apart, isolate

sequin *noun* a small round sparkling ornament sewn on a dress *etc*

seraph *noun* (*plural* **seraphs** or **seraphim**) an angel of the highest rank

seraphic *adjective* like an angel

serenade noun music played or sung in the open air at night, especially under a woman's window □ verb to sing or play a serenade (to)

serendipitous adjective discovered by luck or chance

serendipity noun happy chance, luck

serene adjective 1 calm 2 not worried, happy, peaceful

serenity noun calmness, peacefulness

serf noun, historical a slave bought and sold with the land on which he worked

serfdom noun slavery

serge noun a strong type of cloth

sergeant noun 1 an army rank above corporal 2 a rank in the police force above a constable

sergeant-major noun an army rank above sergeant

serial noun a story which is published, broadcast or televised in instalments

series noun (plural series) 1 a number of things following each other in order 2 a set of things of the same kind: a series of books on art

serious adjective 1 grave, thoughtful: serious expression on her face 2 not joking, in earnest: serious remark 3 important, needing careful thought: a serious matter 4 likely to have dangerous results: serious accident □ seriously adverb

sermon noun a serious talk, especially one given in church

serpent noun, old a snake

serpentine adjective like a serpent; winding, full of twists

serrated adjective having notches or teeth like a saw

serried adjective crowded together: serried ranks

serum noun 1 a clear watery fluid in blood that helps fight disease 2 a fluid injected into the body to help fight disease

servant noun 1 someone paid to work for another, especially in helping to run a house 2 a government employee: civil servant/ public servant

serve verb 1 to work for and obey 2 to attend or wait upon at table 3 to give out food, goods etc 4 to be able to be used (as): the cave will serve as a shelter 5 to be suitable for: serve a purpose 6 to carry out duties as a member of the armed forces 7 to undergo (a sentence in prison etc) 8 tennis to throw up the ball and hit it with the racket to start play □ **serve someone right** to be deserved by them

service noun 1 an act of serving 2 the duty required of a servant or other employee 3 a performance of (public) worship 4 use: bring the new machine into service 5 time spent in the armed forces 6 **services** the armed forces 7 **services** help: services to refugees 8 a regular supply: bus service 9 **services** public supply of water, gas, electricity etc 10 a set of dishes: dinner service □ verb to keep (a car, machine etc) in good working order by regular checks and repairs □ **active service** service in battle □ **at your service** ready to help or be of use

serviceable adjective useful; lasting a long time: serviceable clothes

serviette noun a table napkin

servile adjective slave-like; showing lack of spirit: a servile attitude to his employer

servility noun being servile

servitude noun slavery; the state of being under strict control

sesame (pronounced ses-am-i) noun a SE Asian plant whose seeds produce an edible oil

session noun 1 a meeting of a court, council etc 2 the period of the year when classes are held in a school etc 3 a period of time spent on a particular activity

sestet noun a group of six musicians etc

set verb 1 to place or put 2 to fix in the proper place (eg broken bones) 3 to arrange (a table for a meal, jewels in a necklace etc) 4 to fix (a date, a price etc) 5 to fix hair (in waves or curls) 6 to adjust (a clock or a machine etc) so that it is ready to work or perform some function 7 to give (a task etc): set him three problems 8 to put in a certain state or condition: set free 9 **set off** or

out or **forth** to start (on a journey *etc*) **10** of a jelly *etc*: to become firm or solid **11** to compose music for: *he set the poem to music* **12** of the sun: to go out of sight below the horizon □ *adjective* **1** fixed or arranged beforehand; ready: *all set* **2** fixed, stiff: *a set expression on his face* □ *noun* **1** a group of people **2** a number of things of a similar kind, or used together: *set of carving tools* **3** an apparatus: *a television set* **4** scenery made ready for a play *etc* **5** pose, position: *the set of his head* **6** a series of six or more games in tennis **7** a fixing of hair in waves or curls **8** a badger's burrow (*also called*: **sett**) **9** a street paving-block (*also called*: **sett**) □ **set about 1** to begin (doing something) **2** to attack □ **set in** to begin: *winter has set in* □ **set on** to attack

> **set** *verb* ⇨ **sets, setting, set**

🕘 Comes from Old English verb *settan* and noun *set* meaning 'a seat'

setback *noun* a movement in the wrong direction, a failure

set-square *noun* a triangular drawing instrument, with one right angle

sett *another spelling of* **set** (senses 8 and 9)

settee *noun* a sofa

setter *noun* a dog trained to point out game in hunting

setting *noun* **1** the act of someone who or something that sets **2** an arrangement **3** a background: *against a setting of hills and lochs*

settle *verb* **1** to place in a position or at rest **2** to come to rest **3** to agree over (a matter): *settle the price* **4** (sometimes **settle down**) to become calm or quiet **5** (sometimes **settle down**) to make your home in a place **6** to pay (a bill) **7** to fix, decide (on) **8** to bring (a quarrel *etc*) to an end **9** to sink to the bottom □ *noun* a long high-backed bench

settlement *noun* **1** the act of settling **2** a decision, an agreement **3** payment of a bill **4** money given to a woman on her marriage **5** a number of people who have come to live in a country

settler *noun* someone who goes to live in a new country

seven *noun* the number 7 □ *adjective* 7 in number

seventeen *noun* the number 17 □ *adjective* 17 in number

seventeenth *adjective* the last of a series of seventeen □ *noun* one of seventeen equal parts

seventh *adjective* the last of a series of seven □ *noun* one of seven equal parts

seventieth *adjective* the last of a series of seventy □ *noun* one of seventy equal parts

seventy *noun* the number 70 □ *adjective* 70 in number

sever *verb* **1** to cut apart or away, break off **2** to separate, part

several *adjective* **1** more than one or two, but not many **2** various **3** different: *going their several ways* □ *pronoun* more than one or two people, things *etc*, but not a great many

severance *noun* **1** severing or being severed **2** separation

severe *adjective* **1** serious: *a severe illness* **2** harsh, strict **3** very plain and simple, not fancy

severity *noun* strictness, harshness

sew *verb* **1** to join together with a needle and thread **2** to make or mend in this way

> **sew** ⇨ **sews, sewing, sewed, sewn**

sewage *noun* water and waste matter

sewer *noun* an underground drain for carrying off water and waste matter

sex *noun* **1** either of the two classes (male or female) into which animals are divided according to the part they play in producing children or young **2** sexual intercourse

sex- *prefix* six
🕘 Comes from Latin *sex* meaning 'six'

sexagenarian *noun* someone from sixty to sixty-nine years old

sexism *noun* discrimination against someone on the grounds of their sex

sexist *noun* someone who treats the opposite sex unfairly or thinks that they are inferior □ *adjective* relating to or characteristic of sexism: *a sexist attitude*

sextant *noun* an instrument used for calculating distances by means of measuring angles, *eg* the distance between two stars

sextet *noun* a group of six musicians *etc*

sexton *noun* someone who has various responsibilities in a church, *eg* bellringing, gravedigging *etc*

sexual *adjective* **1** of sex or gender **2** relating to sexual intercourse □ **sexually** *adverb*

sexual intercourse physical union between a man and a woman involving the insertion of the penis into the vagina

sexuality *noun* the way in which a person expresses, or their ability to experience, sexual feelings

sexy *adjective* sexually attractive or sexually exciting

SF *abbreviation* science fiction

shabby *adjective* **1** worn-looking **2** poorly dressed **3** of behaviour: mean, unfair □ **shabbily** *adverb*

shack *noun* a roughly-built hut

shackle *verb* **1** to fasten with a chain **2** to hold back, prevent, hinder

shackles *noun plural* chains fastening a prisoner's legs or arms

shade *noun* **1** slight darkness caused by cutting off some light **2** a place not in full sunlight **3** a screen from the heat or light **4** **shades** *informal* sunglasses **5** the deepness or a variation of a colour **6** the dark parts in a picture **7** a very small amount or difference: *a shade larger* **8** a ghost □ *verb* **1** to shelter from the sun or light **2** to make parts of a picture darker **3** to change gradually, *eg* from one colour into another

shading *noun* the marking of the darker places in a picture

shadow *noun* **1** shade caused by some object coming in the way of a light **2** the dark shape of that object on the ground **3** a dark part in a picture **4** a very small amount: *a shadow of doubt* □ *verb* **1** to shade, darken **2** to follow someone about secretly and watch them closely

shadow cabinet leading members of the opposition in parliament

shady *adjective* **1** sheltered from light or heat **2** *informal* dishonest, underhand: *a shady character*

shaft *noun* **1** anything long and straight **2** the rod on which the head of an axe, arrow *etc* is fixed **3** an arrow **4** a revolving rod which turns a machine or engine **5** the pole of a cart to which the horses are tied **6** the deep, narrow passageway leading to a mine **7** a deep vertical hole for a lift **8** a ray (of light)

shaggy *adjective* rough, hairy, or woolly

shake *verb* **1** to move backwards and forwards or up and down with quick, jerky movements **2** to make or be made unsteady **3** to shock, disturb: *his parting words shook me* □ *noun* **1** the act of shaking or trembling **2** a shock **3** a drink mixed by shaking or stirring quickly: *milk shake*

> **shake** *verb* ⇨ shake*s*, shak*ing*, shak*en*, shook

shaky *adjective* unsteady; trembling □ **shakily** *adverb*

shale *noun* a kind of rock from which oil can be obtained

shall *verb* **1** used to form future tenses of other verbs when the subject is *I* or *we*: *I shall tell you later* **2** used for emphasis, or to express a promise, when the subject is *you, he, she, it* or *they*: *you shall go if I say you must/ you shall go if you want to* □ *see also* **should**

shallot *noun* a kind of onion

shallow *adjective* **1** not deep **2** not capable of thinking or feeling deeply □ *noun* (often **shallows**) a place where the water is not deep

sham *noun* something which is not what it appears to be, a pretence □ *adjective* false, imitation, pretended: *a sham fight* □ *verb* to pretend, feign: *shamming sleep*

> **sham** *verb* ⇨ sham*s*, shamm*ing*, shamm*ed*

shaman *noun* a tribal healer or medicine man

shamble *verb* to walk in a shuffling or awkward manner

shambles *noun singular*, *informal* a mess, confused disorder

shambolic *adjective, slang* chaotic, messy

shame *noun* **1** an uncomfortable feeling caused by realization of guilt or failure **2** disgrace, dishonour **3** *informal* bad luck, a pity: *it's a shame that you can't go* □ *verb* **1** to make to feel shame or ashamed **2 shame into** to cause (someone to do something) by making them ashamed: *they shamed him into paying his share* □ **put to shame** to cause to feel ashamed

shamefaced *adjective* showing shame or embarrassment

shameful *adjective* disgraceful

shameless *adjective* feeling or showing no shame

shammy *another spelling of* **chamois**

shampoo *verb* to wash (the hair and scalp) □ *noun* **1** an act of shampooing **2** a soapy liquid used for cleaning the hair **3** a similar liquid used for cleaning carpets or upholstery

shamrock *noun* a plant like clover with leaves divided in three

shank *noun* **1** the part of the leg between the knee and the foot **2** a long straight part (of a tool *etc*)

shank's pony walking, on foot

shan't *short for* shall not

shanty *noun* (*plural* **shanties**) **1** a roughly-made hut **2** a sailors' song

shantytown *noun* an area of makeshift, squalid housing

shape *noun* **1** the form or outline of anything **2** a mould for a jelly *etc* **3** a jelly *etc* turned out of a mould **4** condition: *in good shape* □ *verb* **1** to make into a certain form **2** to model, mould **3** to develop (in a particular way): *our plans are shaping well*

shapeless *adjective* having no shape or regular form

shapely *adjective* having an attractive shape

share *noun* **1** one part of something that is divided among several people **2** one of the parts into which the money of a business firm is divided □ *verb* **1** to divide out among a number of people **2** to allow others to use (your possessions *etc*) **3** to have or use in common with someone else: *we share a liking for music*

shareholder *noun* someone who owns shares in a business company

shark *noun* **1** a large, very fierce, flesh-eating fish **2** *informal* a swindler

sharp *adjective* **1** cutting, piercing **2** having a thin edge or fine point **3** hurting, stinging, biting: *sharp wind/ sharp words* **4** alert, quick-witted **5** sensitive, perceptive, able to pick up faint signals **6** severe, inclined to scold **7** *music* of a note: raised half a tone in pitch **8** of a voice: shrill **9** of an outline: clear □ *adverb* punctually: *come at ten o'clock sharp* □ *noun, music* a sign (♯) showing that a note is to be raised half a tone □ **look sharp** to hurry

■ **Alternative words**: (adjective, meanings 4 and 5) acute

sharpen *verb* to make or grow sharp

sharpener *noun* an instrument for sharpening: *pencil sharpener*

sharper *noun* a cheat, especially at cards

sharp practice cheating

shatter *verb* to break in pieces; to upset, ruin (hopes, health *etc*)

shave *verb* **1** to cut away hair with a razor **2** to scrape away the surface of (wood *etc*) **3** to touch lightly, or just avoid touching, in passing □ *noun* **1** the act of shaving **2** a narrow escape: *a close shave*

shaven *adjective* shaved

shavings *noun plural* very thin slices of wood *etc*

shawl *noun* a loose covering for the shoulders

she *pronoun* a woman, girl or female animal *etc* already spoken about (used only as the subject of a verb): *when the girl saw us, she waved*

sheaf *noun* (*plural* **sheaves**) a bundle (*eg* of corn, papers) tied together

shear *verb* **1** to clip, cut (especially wool from a sheep) **2** to cut through, cut off

shear ➪ shear*s*, shear*ing*, shorn, shear*ed*

ⓘ Comes from Old English *sceran*, from a Germanic base meaning 'cut', 'divide', 'shear' or 'shave'

☛ Do not confuse with: **sheer**

shears *noun plural* large scissors

sheath *noun* 1 a case for a sword or dagger 2 a long close-fitting covering 3 a condom

sheathe *verb* to put into a sheath

shed *noun* 1 a building for storage or shelter: *coalshed/ bicycle shed* 2 an out-house □ *verb* 1 to throw or cast off (leaves, a skin, clothing) 2 to pour out (tears, blood) 3 to give out (light *etc*)

sheen *noun* brightness, gloss

sheep *noun* 1 an animal whose flesh is used as food and whose fleece is used for wool 2 a very meek person who lacks confidence

sheep-dip *noun* a liquid for disinfecting sheep

sheepdog *noun* a dog trained to look after sheep

sheepish *adjective* shy; embarrassed, shamefaced

sheepshank *noun* a kind of knot, used for shortening a rope

sheepskin *noun* 1 the skin of a sheep 2 a kind of leather made from this

sheer *adjective* 1 very steep: *sheer drop from the cliff* 2 pure, not mixed: *sheer delight/ sheer nonsense* 3 of cloth: very thin or fine □ *adverb* straight up and down, very steeply: *rock face rising sheer* □ *verb* to turn aside from a straight line, swerve

ⓘ Adjective and adverb: come perhaps from the Old English equivalent of Old Norse *skærr* meaning 'bright'; verb: formed from a combination of Late German or Dutch *scheren* meaning 'to cut', and an alternative spelling of English *shear*

☛ Do not confuse with: **shear**

sheet *noun* 1 a large piece of linen, cotton, nylon *etc* for a bed 2 a large thin piece of metal, glass, ice *etc* 3 a piece of paper 4 a sail 5 the rope fastened to the lower corner of a sail

sheikh *noun* an Arab chief

shelf *noun* (*plural* **shelves**) 1 a board fixed on a wall, for laying things on 2 a flat layer of rock, a ledge 3 a sandbank

shell *noun* 1 a hard outer covering (of a shellfish, egg, nut *etc*) 2 a husk or pod (*eg* of peas) 3 a metal case filled with explosive fired from a gun 4 a framework, *eg* of a building not yet completed or burnt out: *only the shell of the warehouse was left* □ *verb* 1 to take the shell from (a nut, egg *etc*) 2 to fire shells at

shellfish *noun* a water creature covered with a shell, *eg* an oyster, limpet or mussel

shelter *noun* 1 a building which acts as a protection from harm, rain, wind *etc* 2 the state of being protected from any of these □ *verb* 1 to give protection to 2 to put in a place of safety or protection 3 to go to, or stay in, a place of safety □ **take shelter** to go to a place of safety

shelve *verb* 1 to put up shelves in 2 to put aside (a problem *etc*) for later consideration 3 of land: to slope gently

shepherd *noun* a man who looks after sheep □ *verb* to watch over carefully, guide

shepherdess *noun* a woman who looks after sheep

shepherd's pie a dish of minced meat covered with mashed potatoes

sherbet *noun* 1 a fizzy drink 2 powder for making this

sheriff *noun* 1 the chief representative of a monarch in a county, whose duties include keeping the peace 2 in Scotland, the chief judge of a county 3 *US* the chief law-enforcement officer of a county

sherry *noun* a strong kind of wine, often drunk before a meal

shibboleth *noun* a word or attribute which identifies members of a group

Originally a word giving membership to a group, after a Biblical story in which its correct pronunciation was used as a password

shied *past form* of **shy**

shield *noun* 1 anything that protects

from harm **2** a broad piece of metal carried by a soldier *etc* as a defence against weapons **3** a shield-shaped trophy won in a competition **4** a shield-shaped plaque bearing a coat-of-arms □ *verb* to protect, defend, shelter

shift *verb* **1** to move, change the position of: *shift the furniture/ trying to shift the blame* **2** to change position or direction: *the wind shifted* **3** to get rid of □ *noun* **1** a change: *shift of emphasis* **2** a change of position, transfer **3** a group of workers on duty at the same time: *day shift/ night shift* **4** a specified period of work or duty **5** a loose-fitting lightweight dress □ **shift for yourself** to manage to get on by your own efforts

shifty *adjective* not to be trusted, looking dishonest

shilling *noun, Brit historical* a silver-coloured coin in use before decimalization, worth $\frac{1}{20}$ of £1 (now the 5 pence piece)

shillyshally *verb* to hesitate in making up your mind, waver

    shillyshally ⇨ shillyshall*ies*, shillyshally*ing*, shillyshall*ied*

shimmer *verb* to shine with a quivering or unsteady light □ *noun* a quivering light

shin *noun* the front part of the leg below the knee □ **shin up** to climb

shindy *noun* (*plural* **shindies**) *informal* a noise, uproar

shine *verb* **1** to give out or reflect light **2** to be bright **3** to polish (shoes etc) **4** to be very good at: *he shines at arithmetic* □ *noun* **1** brightness **2** an act of polishing

    shine *verb* ⇨ shin*es*, shin*ing*, shone

shingle *noun* coarse gravel of rounded stones on the shores of rivers or of the sea

shingles *noun plural* an infectious disease causing a painful rash

shining *adjective* **1** very bright and clear **2** admired, distinguished: *a shining example*

shiny *adjective* glossy, polished

■ **Alternative words**: burnished, lustrous, glossy, sleek, bright, gleaming, glistening

ship *noun* a large vessel for journeys across water □ *verb* **1** to take onto a ship **2** to send by ship **3** to go by ship

    ship *verb* ⇨ ship*s*, ship*ping*, ship*ped*

shipment *noun* **1** an act of putting on board ship **2** a load of goods sent by ship

shipping *noun* **1** ships as traffic: *a gale warning to shipping* **2** the business of transporting goods and freight, especially by ship

shipshape *adjective* in good order, neat, trim

shipwreck *noun* **1** the sinking or destruction of a ship (especially by accident) **2** a wrecked ship **3** ruin

shipwrecked *adjective* involved in a shipwreck

shipyard *noun* the yard in which ships are built or repaired

shire *noun* a county

shirk *verb* to avoid or evade (doing your duty *etc*)

shirker *noun* a person who avoids work or responsibilities

shirt *noun* **1** a garment worn by men on the upper part of the body, having a collar, sleeves and buttons down the front **2** a similar garment for a woman

shiver *verb* **1** to tremble with cold or fear **2** to break into small pieces, shatter □ *noun* **1** the act of shivering **2** a small broken piece: *shivers of glass*

shoal *noun* **1** a group of fishes, moving and feeding together **2** a shallow place, a sandbank

shock *noun* **1** a sudden forceful blow **2** a feeling of fright, horror, dismay *etc* **3** a state of weakness or illness following such feelings **4** the effect on the body of an electric current passing through it **5** an earthquake **6** a bushy mass (of hair) □ *verb* **1** to give a shock to **2** to upset or horrify

shock-absorber *noun* a device in an aircraft, car *etc* for lessening the impact or force of bumps

shocking *adjective* causing horror or dismay; disgusting

shod *adjective* wearing shoes □ *verb, past form of* **shoe**

shoddy *adjective* **1** of poor material or quality: *shoddy goods* **2** mean, low: *a shoddy trick*

shoe *noun* **1** a stiff outer covering for the foot, not reaching above the ankle **2** a rim of iron nailed to the hoof of a horse □ *verb* to put shoes on (a horse)

> **shoe** *verb* ⇨ shoes, shoeing, shod

shoehorn *noun* a curved piece of horn, metal *etc* for making a shoe slip easily over your heel

shoelace *noun* a cord or string used for fastening a shoe

shoemaker *noun* someone who makes and mends shoes

shoestring *noun, US* a shoelace □ **on a shoestring** with very little money

shone *past form of* **shine**

shoo *exclamation* used to scare away birds, animals *etc* □ *verb* to drive or scare away

> **shoo** *verb* ⇨ shoos, shooing, shooed

shoogle *verb, Scottish* to shake

shook *see* **shake**

shoot *verb* **1** to send a bullet from a gun, or an arrow from a bow **2** to hit or kill with an arrow, bullet *etc* **3** to let fly swiftly and with force **4** to kick for a goal **5** to score (a goal) **6** of a plant: to grow new buds **7** to photograph, film **8** to move very swiftly or suddenly **9** to slide (a bolt) □ *noun* **1** a new sprout on a plant **2** an expedition to shoot game **3** land where game is shot

> **shoot** *verb* ⇨ shoots, shot

shooting-brake *noun, old* an estate car

shooting star a meteor

shop *noun* **1** a place where goods are sold **2** a workshop □ *verb* **1** to visit shops and buy goods **2** *slang* to betray (someone) to the police □ **talk shop** *informal* to talk about work when off duty

> **shop** *verb* ⇨ shops, shopping, shopped

shopkeeper *noun* someone who owns and keeps a shop

shoplifter *noun* someone who steals goods from a shop

shopper *noun* someone who shops, a customer

shop steward a worker elected by the other workers as their representative

shore *noun* the land bordering on a sea or lake □ *verb* to prop (up), support: *shoring up an unprofitable organization*

shorn *see* **shear**

short *adjective* **1** not long: *short skirt* **2** not tall **3** brief, not lasting long: *short talk* **4** not enough, less than it should be **5** rude, sharp, abrupt **6** of pastry: crisp and crumbling easily □ *adverb* **1** suddenly, abruptly: *stop short* **2** not as far as intended: *the shot fell short* □ *noun* **1** a short film **2** a short-circuit **3** a drink of an alcoholic spirit **4** **shorts** short trousers □ *verb* to short-circuit □ **give short shrift to** to waste little time or consideration on □ **in short** in a few words □ **short of 1** not having enough: *short of money* **2** less than, not as much or as far as: *5 miles short of Inverness/ £5 short of the price* **3** without going as far as: *he didn't know how to get the money, short of stealing it*

shortage *noun* a lack

shortbread *noun* a thick biscuit made of butter and flour *etc*

short-circuit *noun* the missing out of a major part of an intended electric circuit, sometimes causing blowing of fuses □ *verb* **1** of an electrical appliance: to have a short-circuit **2** to bypass (a difficulty *etc*)

shortcoming *noun* a fault, a defect

short cut a short way of going somewhere or doing something

shorten *verb* to make less in length

shorthand *noun* a method of swift writing using strokes and dots to show sounds (*contrasted with*: **longhand**)

short list a list of candidates selected from the total number of applicants or contestants

shortlived *adjective* living or lasting only a short time

shortly *adverb* 1 soon 2 curtly, abruptly 3 briefly

short-sighted *adjective* 1 seeing clearly only things which are near 2 taking no account of what may happen in the future

short-tempered *adjective* easily made angry

short-term *adjective* intended to last only a short time

short wave a radio wave with a wavelength of between 10 and 100 metres

shot *noun* 1 something which is shot or fired 2 small lead bullets, used in cartridges 3 a single act of shooting 4 the sound of a gun being fired 5 the distance covered by a bullet, arrow *etc* 6 a marksman 7 a throw or turn in a game 8 an attempt at doing something, guessing *etc* 9 a photograph 10 a scene in a motion picture □ *adjective* 1 of silk: showing changing colours 2 streaked or mixed with (a colour *etc*) □ *verb, past form* of **shoot** □ **a shot in the dark** a guess

shotgun *noun* a light type of gun which fires shot

should *verb* 1 the form of the verb **shall** used to express a condition: *I should go if I had time* 2 used to mean 'ought to': *you should know that already*

shoulder *noun* 1 the part of the body between the neck and upper arm 2 the upper part of an animal's foreleg 3 a hump, a ridge: *the shoulder of the hill* □ *verb* 1 to carry on the shoulders 2 to bear the full weight of (a burden *etc*) 3 to push with the shoulder

shoulderblade *noun* the broad flat bone of the shoulder

shout *noun* 1 a loud cry or call 2 a loud burst (of laughter *etc*) □ *verb* to make a loud cry

■ **Alternative words**: call, cry, scream, shriek, yell, roar, bellow, bawl, howl, bay, cheer

shove *verb* to push roughly, thrust, push aside □ *noun* a rough push

shovel *noun* a spade-like tool used for lifting coal, gravel *etc* □ *verb* to lift or move with a shovel

show *verb* 1 to allow, or cause, to be seen: *show me your new dress* 2 to be able to be seen: *your underskirt is showing* 3 to exhibit, display (an art collection *etc*) 4 to point out (the way *etc*) 5 to direct, guide: *show her to a seat* 6 to make clear, demonstrate: *that shows that I was right* □ *noun* 1 the act of showing 2 a display, an exhibition 3 a performance, an entertainment □ **show off** 1 to show or display (something) 2 to try to impress others with your talents *etc* □ **show up** 1 to make to stand out clearly 2 to expose, make obvious (especially someone's faults)

show *verb* ⇨ shows, show*ing*, shown, show*ed*

■ **Alternative words**: show off (meaning 1) flaunt, exhibit, enhance; (meaning 2) parade, strut, swagger, brag, boast

show business the branch of the theatre concerned with variety entertainments

shower *noun* 1 a short fall of rain 2 a large quantity: *a shower of questions* 3 a bath in which water is sprayed from above 4 the apparatus which sprays water for this 5 *US* a party at which gifts are given to someone about to be married □ *verb* 1 to pour (something) down on 2 to bathe under a shower

showerproof *adjective* of material, a coat *etc*: able to withstand light rain

showery *adjective* raining from time to time

shown *see* show

showroom *noun* a room where goods are laid out for people to see

showy *adjective* bright, gaudy; (too) obvious, striking

shrank *see* shrink

shrapnel *noun* 1 a shell containing bullets *etc* which scatter on explosion 2 splinters of metal, a bomb *etc*

After Henry *Shrapnel*, 18th-century British general who invented the shell

shred *noun* 1 a long, narrow piece, cut or torn off 2 a scrap, a very small amount: *not a shred of evidence* □ *verb* to cut or tear into shreds

shred *verb* ➪ shred*s*, shred*ding*, shred*ded*

shrew *noun* **1** a small mouse-like type of animal with a long nose **2** a quarrelsome or scolding woman

shrewd *adjective* clever, cunning

shrewish *adjective* quarrelsome, ill-tempered

shriek *verb* to make a shrill scream or laugh □ *noun* a shrill scream or laugh

shrift *noun*: **give someone short shrift** to dismiss them quickly

Originally a short confession made before being executed

shrill *adjective* of a sound or voice: high in tone, piercing □ **shrilly** *adverb*

shrimp *noun* **1** a small, long-tailed edible shellfish **2** *informal* a small person

shrine *noun* a holy or sacred place

shrink *verb* **1** to make or become smaller **2** to draw back in fear and disgust (from) □ *noun, informal* a psychiatrist

shrink ➪ shrink*s*, shrink*ing*, shrank, shrunk

shrinkage *noun* the amount by which something grows smaller

shrive *verb, old* **1** to hear a confession **2** to confess

shrive ➪ shrive*s*, shriv*ing*, shrove, shriv*en*

shrivel *verb* to dry up, wrinkle, wither

shrivel ➪ shrivel*s*, shrivel*ling*, shrivel*led*

shroud *noun* **1** a cloth covering a dead body **2** something which covers: *a shroud of mist* **3 shrouds** the ropes from the mast-head to a ship's sides □ *verb* to wrap up, cover

Shrove Tuesday sometimes called Pancake Day: the day before Ash Wednesday

shrub *noun* a small bush or plant

shrubbery *noun* (*plural* **shrubberies**) a place where shrubs grow

shrug *verb* to show doubt, lack of

interest *etc* by drawing up the shoulders □ *noun* a movement of the shoulders to show doubt, lack of interest *etc* □ **shrug off** to dismiss, treat as being unimportant

shrug *verb* ➪ shrug*s*, shrug*ging*, shrug*ged*

shrunk *see* **shrink**

shrunken *adjective* shrunk

shudder *verb* to tremble from fear, cold, disgust □ *noun* a trembling

shuffle *verb* **1** to mix, rearrange (*eg* playing-cards) **2** to move by dragging or sliding the feet along the ground without lifting them **3** to move (the feet) in this way □ *noun* **1** a rearranging **2** a dragging movement of the feet

shun *verb* to avoid, keep clear of

shun ➪ shun*s*, shun*ning*, shun*ned*

shunt *verb* to move (railway trains, engines *etc*) onto a side track

shut *verb* **1** to move (a door, window, lid *etc*) so that it covers an opening **2** to close, lock (a building *etc*) **3** to become closed: *the door shut with a bang* **4** to confine, restrain in a building *etc*: *shut the dog in his kennel* □ **shut down** to close (a factory *etc*) □ **shut up** **1** to close completely **2** *informal* to stop speaking or making other noise

shut ➪ shut*s*, shut*ting*, shut

shutter *noun* **1** a cover for a window **2** a cover which closes over a camera lens as it takes a picture

shuttle *noun* the part of a weaving loom which carries the cross thread from side to side □ *adjective* of a transport service: going to and fro between two places

shuttlecock *noun* a rounded cork stuck with feathers, used in the game of badminton

shy *adjective* **1** of a wild animal: easily frightened, timid **2** lacking confidence in the presence of others **3** not wanting to attract attention □ *verb* **1** to jump or turn suddenly aside in fear **2** to throw, toss □ *noun* a try, an attempt □ **shyly** *adverb* □ **fight shy of** to avoid, keep away from

shy *verb* ➪ shies, shy*ing*, shied

■ **Alternative words**: (meaning 2) timid, reticent, diffident, self-conscious; (meaning 3) bashful, coy, effacing

Siamese *adjective*: **Siamese cat** a fawn-coloured domestic cat □ **Siamese twins** twins joined by their flesh at birth

sibilant *adjective* of a sound: hissing

sibling *noun* a brother or sister

sibyl *noun* a prophetess

sick *adjective* **1** wanting to vomit **2** vomiting **3** not well, ill **4 sick of something** or **someone** tired of them □ **be sick** to vomit

■ **Alternative words**: be sick vomit, heave, retch, puke, spew

sick bed or **sick room** a bed or room for people to rest in when ill

sicken *verb* to make or become sick

sickening *adjective* **1** causing sickness **2** disgusting, revolting

sickle *noun* a hooked knife for cutting or reaping grain, hay *etc*

sick leave time off work for illness

sickly *adjective* **1** unhealthy **2** feeble

sickness *noun* **1** an illness: *a mysterious sickness* **2** vomiting or nausea: *have you been having any sickness or diarrhoea?*

side *noun* **1** an edge, border or boundary line **2** a surface that is not the top, bottom, front or back **3** either surface of a piece of paper, cloth *etc* **4** the right or left part of the body **5** a division, a part: *the north side of the town* **6** an aspect, point of view: *all sides of the problem* **7** a slope (of a hill) **8** a team or party which is opposing another □ *adjective* **1** on or towards the side: *side door* **2** indirect, additional but less important: *side issue* □ *verb* **side with** to support (one person, group *etc* against another) □ **take sides** to choose to support (a party, person) against another

sideboard *noun* a piece of furniture in a dining-room for holding dishes *etc*

sidecar *noun* a small car for a passenger, attached to a motor-cycle

side effect an additional (often bad) effect of a drug

sideline *noun* an extra bit of business outside regular work

sidelong *adjective* & *adverb* from or to the side: *sidelong glance*

sidereal *adjective* relating to the stars

sideshow *noun* a less important show that is part of a larger one

sidestep *verb* to avoid by stepping to one side

sidetrack *verb* to turn (someone) away from what they were going to do or say

sidewalk *noun*, *US* a pavement

sideways *adverb* **1** with the side foremost **2** towards the side

siding *noun* a short line of rails on which trucks are shunted off the main line

sidle *verb* **1** to go or move sideways **2** to move stealthily, sneak

siege (*pronounced* seej) *noun* **1** an attempt to capture a town *etc* by keeping it surrounded by an armed force **2** a constant attempt to gain control □ **lay siege to** to besiege

sienna *noun* a reddish-brown, or yellowish-brown, pigment used in paints

sierra *noun* a range of mountains with jagged peaks

siesta *noun* a short sleep or rest taken in the afternoon

sieve (*pronounced* siv) *noun* a container with a mesh used to separate liquids from solids, or fine pieces from coarse pieces *etc* □ *verb* to put through a sieve

sift *verb* **1** to separate by passing through a sieve **2** to consider and examine closely: *sifting all the evidence*

sigh *noun* a long, deep-sounding breath, showing tiredness, longing *etc* □ *verb* to give out a sigh

sight *noun* **1** the act or power of seeing **2** a view, a glimpse: *catch sight of her* **3** (often **sights**) something worth seeing: *the sights of London* **4** something or someone unusual, ridiculous, shocking *etc*: *she's quite a sight in that hat* **5** a guide on a gun for taking aim □ *verb* **1** to get a view of, see suddenly **2** to look at through the sight of a gun

🕐 Comes from Old English *sihth* meaning 'vision' or 'appearance'

🔷 Do not confuse with: **site** and **cite**

sight-reading *noun* playing or singing from music that has not been seen previously

sightseeing *noun* visiting the chief buildings, monuments *etc* of a place

sign *noun* 1 a mark with a special meaning, a symbol 2 a gesture (*eg* a nod, wave of the hand) to show your meaning 3 an advertisement or notice giving information 4 something which shows what is happening or is going to happen: *signs of irritation/ a sign of good weather* □ *verb* 1 to write your name on (a document, cheque *etc*) 2 to make a sign or gesture to 3 to show (your meaning) by a sign or gesture □ **sign on** to enter your name on a list for work, the army *etc*

signal *noun* 1 a gesture, light or sound giving a command, warning etc: *air-raid signal* 2 something used for this purpose: *railway signals* 3 the wave of sound received or sent out by a radio *etc* set □ *verb* 1 to make signals (to) 2 to send (information) by signal □ *adjective* remarkable: *a signal success*

signal *verb* ⇨ signals, signalling, signalled

signalman *noun* someone who works railway signals, or who sends signals

signatory *noun* (*plural* **signatories**) someone who has signed an agreement *etc*

signature *noun* 1 a signed name 2 an act of signing 3 *music* the flats or sharps at the beginning of a piece which show its key, or figures showing its timing

signature tune a tune used to identify a particular radio or television series *etc* played at the beginning or end of the programme

signet *noun* a small seal, usually bearing someone's initials
🕐 Comes from Medieval Latin *signetum* meaning 'a small seal'

🔷 Do not confuse with: **cygnet**

signet ring a ring imprinted with a signet

significance *noun* 1 meaning 2 importance

significant *adjective* meaning much; important: *no significant change* □ **significantly** *adverb*

signify *verb* 1 to mean, be a sign of 2 to show, make known by a gesture: *signifying disapproval* 3 to have meaning or importance

signify ⇨ signifies, signifying, signified

signpost *noun* a post with a sign, especially one showing direction and distances to certain places

silage *noun* green fodder preserved in a silo

silence *noun* 1 absence of sound or speech 2 a time of quietness □ *verb* to cause to be silent

silencer *noun* a device (on a car engine, gun *etc*) for making noise less

silent *adjective* 1 free from noise 2 not speaking □ **silently** *adverb*

silhouette *noun* 1 an outline drawing of someone, often in profile, filled in with black 2 a dark outline seen against the light

After the 18th-century French finance minister, Etienne de *Silhouette*, possibly because of his notorious stinginess

silk *noun* 1 very fine, soft fibres spun by silkworms 2 thread or cloth made from this □ *adjective* 1 made of silk 2 soft, smooth

silken *adjective* 1 made of silk 2 smooth like silk

silkworm *noun* the caterpillar of certain moths which spins silk

silky *adjective* like silk

sill *noun* a ledge of wood, stone *etc* below a window or a door

silly *adjective* foolish, not sensible

silo *noun* (*plural* **silos**) 1 a tower for storing grain *etc* 2 a pit or airtight chamber for holding silage 3 an underground chamber built to contain a guided missile

silt *noun* sand or mud left behind by

flowing water □ **silt up** to become blocked by mud

silver *noun* **1** a white precious metal, able to take on a high polish **2** money made of silver or of a metal alloy resembling it **3** objects (especially cutlery) made of, or plated with, silver □ *adjective* made of, or looking like, silver □ *verb* **1** to cover with silver **2** to become like silver

silversmith *noun* someone who makes or sells articles of silver

silver wedding the 25th anniversary of a wedding

silvery *adjective* **1** like silver **2** of sound: ringing and musical

simian *adjective* ape-like

simil- or **simul-** *prefix* forms words containing the notion 'like': *simile/ simulate*
Ⓒ Comes from Latin *similis* meaning 'like'

similar *adjective* alike, almost the same

🔲 **Alternative words**: analogous

similarity *noun* (*plural* **similarities**) **1** being similar, likeness **2** resemblance

similarly *adverb* **1** in the same, or a similar, way **2** likewise, also

simile *noun* an expression using 'like' or 'as', in which one thing is likened to another that is well-known for a particular quality (*eg* 'as black as night', 'to swim like a fish')

simmer *verb* to cook gently just below or at boiling-point

simper *verb* **1** to smile in a silly manner **2** to say with a simper □ *noun* a silly smile

simple *adjective* **1** easy, not difficult or complicated **2** plain, not fancy: *simple hairstyle* **3** ordinary: *simple, everyday objects* **4** of humble rank: *a simple peasant* **5** mere, nothing but: *the simple truth* **6** too trusting, easily cheated **7** foolish, half-witted

simpleton *noun* a foolish person

simplicity *noun* the state of being simple

simplification *noun* **1** an act of making simpler **2** a simple form of anything

simplify *verb* to make simpler

simplify ⇨ simpli*fies*, simpli*fying*, simpli*fied*

simply *adverb* **1** in a simple manner **2** merely: *I do it simply for the money* **3** absolutely: *simply beautiful*

simulacrum *noun* (*plural* **simulacra**) a resemblance, an image

simulate *verb* **1** to pretend, feign: *she simulated illness* **2** to have the appearance of, look like

simulated *adjective* **1** pretended **2** having the appearance of: *simulated leather*

simulation *noun* **1** the act of simulating something or the methods used to simulate something **2** something that has been created artificially to reproduce a real event or real set of conditions

simulcast *noun* a simultaneous television and radio broadcast of the same event

simultaneous *adjective* happening, or done, at the same time
□ **simultaneously** *adverb*: *a submarine capable of firing two missiles simultaneously*

sin *noun* **1** a wicked act, especially one which breaks religious laws **2** wrongdoing **3** *informal* a shame, pity □ *verb* to commit a sin, do wrong □ **original sin** the supposed sinful nature of all human beings since the time of Adam's sin

sin *verb* ⇨ sin*s*, sin*ning*, sin*ned*

since *adverb* **1** (often **ever since**) from that time onwards: *I have avoided him ever since* **2** at a later time: *we have since become friends* **3** ago: *long since* **4** from the time of: *since his arrival* □ *conjunction* **1** after the time when: *I have been at home since I returned from Italy* **2** because: *since you are going, I will go too*

sincere *adjective* **1** honest in word and deed, meaning what you say or do, true: *a sincere friend* **2** truly felt: *a sincere desire* □ **sincerely** *adverb*

sincerity *noun* the state or quality of being truthful and genuine in what you believe and say

sinecure (*pronounced* **sin**-ik-yoor) *noun*

a job for which someone receives money but has little or no work to do
🕐 Comes from Latin *sine* meaning 'without', and *cura* meaning 'care'

sinew *noun* **1** a tough cord that joins a muscle to a bone **2 sinews** equipment and resources necessary for something: *sinews of war*

sinewy *adjective* having strong sinews, tough

sinful *adjective* wicked

sing *verb* **1** to make musical sounds with your voice **2** to utter (words, a song *etc*) by doing this

sing ⇨ sing**s**, sing**ing**, s**a**ng, s**u**ng

singe *verb* to burn slightly on the surface, scorch □ *noun* a surface burn

singer *noun* someone who sings or whose voice has been specially trained for singing

single *adjective* **1** one only **2** not double **3** not married **4** for one person: *a single bed* **5** between two people: *single combat* **6** for one direction of a journey: *a single ticket* □ **single out** to pick out, treat differently in some way

single-handed *adjective* working *etc* by yourself

single-minded *adjective* having one aim only

singlet *noun* a vest, an undershirt

singly *adverb* one by one, separately

sing-song *noun* a gathering of people singing informally together □ *adjective* of a speaking voice *etc*: having a fluctuating rhythm

singular *adjective* **1** *grammar* the opposite of **plural**, showing one person, thing *etc* **2** exceptional: *singular success* **3** unusual, strange: *a singular sight*

singularly *adverb* strangely, exceptionally: *singularly ugly*

sinister *adjective* suggesting evil, evil-looking

sink *verb* **1** to go down below the surface of the water *etc* **2** to go down or become less: *my hopes sank* **3** of a very ill person: to become weaker **4** to lower yourself (into): *sink into a chair* **5** to make by digging (a well *etc*) **6** to push (your teeth *etc*) deep into

(something) **7** to invest (money *etc*) in a business □ *noun* a basin in a kitchen, bathroom *etc*, with a water supply connected to it and a drain for carrying off dirty water *etc*

sink *verb* ⇨ sink**s**, sink**ing**, s**a**nk, s**u**nk

sinner *noun* a person who has committed a sin or sins

Sino- *prefix* relating to China or the Chinese
🕐 Comes from Greek *Sinai* meaning 'Chinese'

sinuous *adjective* bending in and out, winding

sinus *noun* (*plural* **sinuses**) an air cavity in the head connected with the nose

sinusitis *noun* inflammation of (one of) the sinuses

sip *verb* to drink in very small quantities □ *noun* a taste of a drink, a swallow

sip *verb* ⇨ sip**s**, sip**ping**, sip**ped**

siphon or **syphon** *noun* **1** a bent tube for drawing off liquids from one container into another **2** a glass bottle, for soda water *etc*, containing such a tube □ *verb* **1** to draw (off) through a siphon **2 siphon off** to take (part of something) away gradually: *he siphoned off some of the club's funds*

sir *noun* **1** a polite form of address used to a man **2 Sir** the title of a knight or baronet

sire *noun* **1** a male parent, especially of a horse **2** *historical* a title used in speaking to a king □ *verb* of an animal: to be the male parent of

siren *noun* **1** an instrument that gives out a loud hooting noise as a warning **2** a mythical sea nymph whose singing enchanted sailors and tempted them into danger **3** an attractive but dangerous woman

sirloin *noun* the upper part of the loin of beef

sirocco *noun* a hot dry wind blowing from N Africa to the Mediterranean coast

sirrah *noun, old* sir

sisal *noun* a fibre from a W Indian plant, used for making ropes

sister *noun* **1** a female born of the same parents as yourself **2** a senior nurse, often in charge of a hospital ward **3** a nun □ *adjective* **1** closely related **2** of similar design or structure: *a sister ship*

sisterhood *noun* **1** the state of being a sister **2** a religious community of women

sister-in-law *noun* **1** the sister of your husband or wife **2** the wife of your brother or of your brother-in-law

sisterly *adjective* like a sister

sit *verb* **1** to rest on the buttocks, be seated **2** of a bird: to perch **3** to rest on eggs in order to hatch them **4** to be an official member: *sit in parliament/ sit on a committee* **5** of a court *etc*: to meet officially **6** to pose (for) a photographer, painter *etc* **7** to take (an examination *etc*) □ **sit tight** to be unwilling to move □ **sit up 1** to sit with your back straight **2** to stay up instead of going to bed

sit *verb* ⇨ sits, sitting, sat

sitcom *noun* a television comedy series with a running theme

site *noun* a place where a building, town *etc* is or is to be placed □ *verb* to select a place for (a building *etc*)
① Comes from Latin *situs* meaning 'situation'

● Do not confuse with: **sight** and **cite**

sitter *noun* **1** someone who poses for a portrait *etc* **2** a babysitter **3** a bird sitting on eggs

sitting *noun* the state or time of sitting □ *adjective* **1** seated **2** for sitting in or on **3** in office: *sitting member of parliament* **4** in possession: *sitting tenant*

sitting-room *noun* a room chiefly for sitting in

situated *adjective* placed

situation *noun* **1** the place where anything stands **2** a job, employment **3** a state of affairs, circumstances: *in an awkward situation*

six *noun* the number 6 □ *adjective* 6 in number □ **at sixes and sevens** in confusion

sixpence *noun, old* a silver-coloured coin worth $\frac{1}{40}$ of £1

sixteen *noun* the number 16 □ *adjective* 16 in number

sixteenth *adjective* the last of a series of sixteen □ *noun* one of sixteen equal parts

sixth *adjective* the last of a series of six □ *noun* one of six equal parts

sixtieth *adjective* the last of a series of sixty □ *noun* one of sixty equal parts

sixty *noun* the number 60 □ *adjective* 60 in number

size *noun* **1** space taken up by anything **2** measurements, dimensions **3** largeness **4** a class into which shoes and clothes are grouped according to size: *she takes size 4 in shoes* **5** a weak kind of glue □ **size up** to form an opinion of a person, situation *etc*

sizeable or **sizable** *adjective* fairly large

sizzle *verb* **1** to make a hissing sound **2** to fry, scorch

skate *noun* **1** a steel blade attached to a boot for gliding on ice **2** a rollerskate **3** a type of large flatfish □ *verb* to move on skates

skateboard *noun* a narrow board on four rollerskate wheels

skateboarding *noun* the sport of riding on a skateboard

skein (*pronounced* skein) *noun* a coil of thread or yarn, loosely tied in a knot

skeletal *adjective* of or like a skeleton

skeleton *noun* **1** the bony framework of an animal or person, without the flesh **2** any framework or outline □ *adjective* of staff *etc*: reduced to a very small or minimum number

skeleton key a key from which the inner part has been cut away so that it can open many different locks

skerry *noun* a reef of rock

sketch *noun* (*plural* **sketches**) **1** a rough plan or drawing **2** a short or rough account **3** a short play, dramatic scene *etc* □ *verb* **1** to draw roughly **2** to give the chief points of **3** to draw in pencil or ink

sketchy *adjective* **1** roughly done **2** not

thorough, incomplete: *my knowledge of geography is rather sketchy*

skew *adjective & adverb* off the straight, slanting □ *verb* to set at a slant

skewer *noun* a long pin of wood or metal for holding meat together while roasting *etc* □ *verb* to fix with a skewer or with something sharp

ski *noun* (*plural* **skis**) one of a pair of long narrow strips of wood or metal that are attached to boots for gliding over snow □ *verb* to move or travel on skis

ski *verb* ⇨ skis, skiing, skied

skid *noun* 1 a slide sideways: *the car went into a skid* 2 a wedge put under a wheel to check it on a steep place 3 **skids** logs *etc* on which things can be moved by sliding □ *verb* 1 of a wheel: to slide along without turning 2 to slip sideways □ **on the skids** on the way down □ **put the skids under** to hurry along

ski-jump *noun* 1 a steep, snow-covered track ending in a platform from which a skier jumps 2 a jump made by a skier from such a platform

ski-jumping *noun* the sport of jumping from a ski-jump

skilful *adjective* having or showing skill □ **skilfully** *adverb*

Alternative words: adroit, adept

skill *noun* cleverness at doing a thing, either from practice or as a natural gift

skilled *adjective* 1 having skill, especially through training 2 of a job: requiring skill

skim *verb* 1 to remove cream, scum *etc* from the surface of (something) 2 to move lightly and quickly over (a surface) 3 to read quickly, missing parts

skim ⇨ skims, skimming, skimmed

skimp *verb* 1 to give (someone) hardly enough 2 to do (a job) imperfectly 3 to spend too little money (on): *skimping on clothes*

skimpy *adjective* 1 too small 2 of clothes: too short or tight

skin *noun* 1 the natural outer covering of an animal or person 2 a thin outer layer on a fruit 3 a thin film that forms on a liquid □ *verb* to strip the skin from □ **by the skin of your teeth** very narrowly

skin *verb* ⇨ skins, skinning, skinned

skin-deep *adjective* as deep as the skin only, on the surface

skin-diver *noun* a diver who wears simple equipment (originally someone who dived naked for pearls)

skinflint *noun* a very mean person

skinny *adjective* very thin

skint *adjective*, *Brit informal* broke, without much money

skip *verb* 1 to go along with a rhythmic step and hop 2 to jump over a turning rope 3 to leap, especially lightly or joyfully 4 to leave out (parts of a book, a meal *etc*) □ *noun* 1 an act of skipping 2 the captain of a side at bowls *etc* 3 a large metal container for transporting refuse

skip *verb* ⇨ skips, skipping, skipped

Alternative words: (verb, meaning 4) jump

skipper *noun* the captain of a ship, aeroplane or team □ *verb* to act as captain for (a ship, team *etc*)

skipping rope a rope used in skipping

skirmish *noun* (*plural* **skirmishes**) 1 a fight between small parties of soldiers 2 a short sharp contest or disagreement □ *verb* to fight briefly or informally

skirt *noun* 1 a garment, worn by women, that hangs from the waist 2 the lower part of a dress 3 **skirts** the outer edge or border □ *verb* to pass along, or lie along, the edge of

skirting or **skirting-board** *noun* the narrow board next to the floor round the walls of a room (*also called*: **wainscot**)

skit *noun* a piece of writing, a short play *etc* that makes fun of a person, event *etc*

skittish *adjective* frivolous, light-headed

skittle *noun* 1 a bottle-shaped object used as a target in bowling, a ninepin

2 skittles a game in which skittles are knocked over by a ball

skive *verb, informal* (often **skive off**) to avoid doing a duty

skiver *noun* a shirker

skivvy *noun, informal* a domestic servant, a cleaner

skulduggery or *US* **skullduggery** *noun* trickery, underhand practices

skulk *verb* **1** to wait about, stay hidden **2** to move stealthily away, sneak

skull *noun* **1** the bony case which encloses the brain **2** the head □ **skull and crossbones** the sign on a pirate's flag

skullcap *noun* a cap which fits closely to the head

skunk *noun* **1** a small American animal which defends itself by giving off a bad smell **2** a contemptible person

sky *noun* (*plural* **skies**) **1** the upper atmosphere, the heavens **2** the weather, the climate

sky-diving *noun* jumping with a parachute as a sport

skylark *noun* the common lark which sings while hovering far overhead

skylight *noun* a window in a roof or ceiling

skyline *noun* the horizon

skyscraper *noun* a high building of very many storeys

slab *noun* a thick flat slice or piece of anything: *stone slab/ cut a slab of cake*

slack *adjective* **1** not firmly stretched **2** not firmly in position **3** not strict **4** lazy and careless **5** not busy: *slack holiday season* □ *noun* **1** the loose part of a rope **2** small coal and coal-dust **3** **slacks** loose, casual trousers □ *verb* **1** to do less work than you should, be lazy **2** to slacken

slacken *verb* **1** to make or become looser **2** to make or become less active, less busy or less fast *etc*

slag *noun* waste left from metal-smelting □ *verb, slang* to criticize, make fun of cruelly

slag *verb* ➪ slag**s**, slag**ging**, slag**ged**

slain *see* **slay**

slake *verb* **1** to quench, satisfy (thirst, longing *etc*) **2** to put out (fire) **3** to mix (lime) with water

slalom *noun* **1** a downhill, zigzag ski run among posts or trees **2** an obstacle race in canoes

slam *verb* **1** to shut (a door, lid *etc*) with a loud noise **2** to put down with a loud noise □ *noun* **1** the act of slamming **2** (also **grand slam**) a winning of every trick in cards or every contest in a competition *etc*

slam *verb* ➪ slam**s**, slam**ming**, slam**med**

slander *noun* an untrue statement (in England, a spoken one) aimed at harming someone's reputation □ *verb* to speak slander against (someone)

slanderous *adjective* of a statement: untrue and therefore unfairly damaging someone's reputation

slang *noun* **1** popular words and phrases that are used in informal, everyday speech or writing **2** the special language of a particular group: *Cockney slang* □ *verb* to scold, abuse

slant *verb* **1** to slope **2** to lie or move diagonally or in a sloping position **3** to give or present (facts or information) in a distorted way that suits your own purpose □ *noun* **1** a slope **2** a diagonal direction **3** a point of view

slap *noun* a blow with the palm of the hand or anything flat □ *verb* to give a slap to

slap *verb* ➪ slap**s**, slap**ping**, slap**ped**

slapdash *adjective* hasty, careless

slapstick *adjective* of comedy: boisterous, funny in a very obvious way □ *noun* comedy in this style

slash *verb* **1** to make long cuts in **2** to strike at violently □ *noun* (*plural* **slashes**) **1** a long cut **2** a sweeping blow

slat *noun* a thin strip of wood, metal or other material

slate *noun* an easily split blue-grey rock, used for roofing, or at one time for writing upon □ *adjective* **1** made of slate **2** slate-coloured □ *verb* **1** to cover with slate **2** to say or write harsh things to or about: *the play was slated*

slatted *adjective* having slats

slattern *noun* a woman of untidy appearance or habits

slaughter *noun* **1** the killing of animals, especially for food **2** cruel killing of great numbers of people □ *verb* **1** to kill (an animal) for food **2** to kill brutally

slaughterhouse *noun* a place where animals are killed in order to be sold for food

📇 **Alternative words**: abattoir

slave *noun, historical* **1** someone forced to work for a master and owner **2** someone who serves another devotedly **3** someone who works very hard **4** someone who is addicted to something: *a slave to fashion* □ *verb* to work like a slave

slaver *noun* saliva running from the mouth □ *verb* to let saliva run out of the mouth

slavery *noun* **1** the state of being a slave **2** the system of owning slaves

Slavic *adjective* relating to a group of E European people or their languages, including Russian, Polish *etc*

slavish *adjective* thinking or acting exactly according to rules or instructions

slay *verb, formal* to kill

slay ⇨ slays, slaying, slew, slain

sleaze *noun, informal* corrupt or illicit practices, especially in public life

sleaziness *noun* a sleazy quality

sleazy *adjective* squalid, disreputable

sled or **sledge** *noun* a vehicle with runners, made for sliding upon snow □ *verb* to ride on a sledge

sledgehammer *noun* a large, heavy hammer

sleek *adjective* **1** smooth, glossy **2** of an animal: well-fed and well-cared for **3** elegant, well-groomed

sleep *verb* to rest with your eyes closed in a state of natural unconsciousness □ **go to sleep 1** to pass into the state of being asleep **2** of a limb: to become numb, tingle □ **put to sleep 1** to make to go to sleep, make unconscious **2** to put (an animal) to death painlessly, *eg* by an injection of a drug □ **sleep with** *informal* to have sexual intercourse with

sleep *verb* ⇨ sleeps, sleeping, slept

📇 **Alternative words**: doze, snooze, slumber, hibernate, rest, repose

sleeper *noun* **1** someone who sleeps **2** a beam of wood or metal supporting railway lines **3** a sleeping car or sleeping berth on a railway train **4** **sleepers** *slang* the drug barbiturate

sleeping bag a large warm bag for sleeping in, used by campers *etc*

sleepless *adjective* unable to sleep, without sleep

sleepwalker *noun* someone who walks *etc* while asleep

sleepy *adjective* **1** drowsy, wanting to sleep **2** looking as if needing sleep **3** quiet, not bustling: *sleepy town* □ **sleepily** *adverb*

sleet *noun* rain mixed with snow or hail

sleeve *noun* **1** the part of a garment which covers the arm **2** a cover for a gramophone record **3** a cover for an arm-like piece of machinery

sleeveless *adjective* without sleeves

sleigh *noun* a large horse-drawn sledge

sleight-of-hand *noun* skill and quickness of hand movement in performing card tricks *etc*

slender *adjective* **1** thin, narrow **2** slim **3** small in amount: *by a slender margin*

sleuth *noun* someone who tracks down criminals, a detective

slew *past form of* **slay**

slice *noun* **1** a thin, broad piece of something: *slice of toast* **2** a broad-bladed utensil for serving fish *etc* □ *verb* **1** to cut into slices **2** to cut through **3** to cut (off from *etc*) **4** *golf* to hit (a ball) in such a way that it curves away to the right

slick *adjective* **1** smart, clever, often too much so **2** smooth □ *noun* a thin layer of spilt oil

slide *verb* **1** to move smoothly over a surface **2** to slip **3** to pass quietly or secretly □ *noun* **1** an act of sliding **2** a smooth, slippery slope or track **3** a chute **4** a groove or rail on which a thing slides **5** a fastening for the hair **6** a

picture for showing on a screen **7** a piece of glass on which to place objects to be examined under a microscope
slide *verb* ⇨ slide**s**, slid**ing**, slid

slide-rule *noun* an instrument used for calculating, made up of one ruler sliding against another

slight *adjective* **1** of little amount or importance: *slight breeze/ slight quarrel* **2** small, slender □ *verb* to treat as unimportant, insult by ignoring □ *noun* an insult, an offence

slim *adjective* **1** slender, thin **2** small, slight: *slim chance* □ *verb* **1** to make slender **2** to use means (such as eating less) to become slender
slim *verb* ⇨ slim**s**, slim**ming**, slim**med**

slime *noun* sticky, half-liquid material, especially thin, slippery mud

slimy *adjective* **1** covered with slime **2** oily, greasy

sling *noun* **1** a bandage hanging from the neck or shoulders to support an injured arm **2** a strap with a string attached to each end, for flinging stones **3** a net of ropes *etc* for hoisting and carrying heavy objects □ *verb* **1** to throw with a sling **2** to move or swing by means of a sling **3** *informal* to throw
sling *verb* ⇨ sling**s**, sling**ing**, slung

slink *verb* to sneak away, move stealthily
slink ⇨ slink**s**, slink**ing**, slunk

slip *verb* **1** to slide accidentally and lose footing or balance: *slip on the ice* **2** to fall out of place, or out of your control: *the plate slipped from my grasp* **3** to move quickly and easily **4** to move quietly, quickly and secretly **5** to escape from: *slip your mind* □ *noun* **1** the act of slipping **2** an error, a slight mistake **3** a cutting from a plant **4** a strip or narrow piece of anything (*eg* paper) **5** a slim, slight person: *a slip of a girl* **6** a slipway **7** a thin undergarment worn under a dress, an underskirt **8** a cover for a pillow **9** *cricket* a fielding position □ **slip up** to make a mistake
slip *verb* ⇨ slip**s**, slip**ping**, slip**ped**

slipknot *noun* a knot made with a loop so that it can slip

slipper *noun* a loose indoor shoe

slippery *adjective* **1** causing skidding or slipping **2** not trustworthy

slip road a road by which vehicles join or leave a motorway

slipshod *adjective* untidy, careless

slipstream *noun* the stream of air driven back by an aircraft propeller *etc*

slip-up *noun* a mistake

slipway *noun* a smooth slope on which a ship is built

slit *verb* **1** to make a long narrow cut in **2** to cut into strips □ *noun* a long narrow cut or opening
slit *verb* ⇨ slit**s**, slit**ting**, slit

slither *verb* **1** to slide or slip about (*eg* on mud) **2** to move with a gliding motion

slithery *adjective* slippery

sliver *noun* a thin strip or slice

slobber *verb* to let saliva dribble from the mouth, slaver

sloe *noun* the small black fruit of a blackthorn shrub, often used to flavour gin

slog *verb* to work or plod on steadily, especially against difficulty □ *noun* a difficult spell of work
slog *verb* ⇨ slog**s**, slog**ging**, slog**ged**

slogan *noun* an easily remembered and frequently repeated phrase, used in advertising *etc*

sloop *noun* a one-masted sailing ship

slop *verb* **1** to flow over, spill **2** to splash □ *noun* **1** spilt liquid **2** **slops** dirty water **3** **slops** thin, tasteless food
slop *verb* ⇨ slop**s**, slop**ping**, slop**ped**

slope *noun* **1** a position or direction that is neither level nor upright, a slant **2** a surface with one end higher than the other, *eg* a hillside □ *verb* to be in a slanting, sloping position

sloppy *adjective* **1** wet, muddy **2** careless, untidy **3** silly, sentimental

slosh *verb* **1** to splash **2** *informal* to hit

slot *noun* **1** a small, narrow opening, *eg* to insert coins **2** a position □ *verb* **1** to make a slot in **2** (sometimes **slot into**)

to find a position or place for
slot *verb* ⇨ slo**ts**, slo**tting**, slo**tted**

sloth *noun* **1** laziness **2** a slow-moving
S American animal that lives in trees

slothful *adjective* lazy

slot machine a vending machine
worked by putting a coin in a slot

slouch *noun* a hunched-up body
position □ *verb* to walk with shoulders
rounded and head hanging

slough[1] (*pronounced* slow) *noun* a bog,
a marsh

slough[2] (*pronounced* sluf) *noun* the
cast-off skin of a snake □ *verb* **1** to cast
off (*eg* a skin) **2** of skin: to come (off)

slovenly *adjective noun* untidy, careless,
dirty

slow *adjective* **1** not fast **2** not hasty or
hurrying **3** of a clock: behind in time **4**
not quick in learning, dull □ *verb* (often
slow down) to make or become slower
□ **slowly** *adverb*

slowcoach *noun* someone who moves,
works *etc* slowly

slow-motion *adjective* **1** slower than
normal movement **2** of a film: slower
than actual motion

sludge *noun* soft, slimy mud

slug *noun* **1** a snail-like animal with no
shell **2** a small piece of metal used as a
bullet **3** a heavy blow

sluggard *noun* someone who has slow
and lazy habits

sluggish *adjective* moving slowly

sluice *noun* **1** a sliding gate for
controlling a flow of water in an
artificial channel (*also called*:
sluicegate) **2** the stream which flows
through this □ *verb* to clean out with a
strong flow of water

slum *noun* **1** an overcrowded part of a
town where the houses are dirty and
unhealthy **2** a house in a slum

slumber *verb* to sleep □ *noun* sleep

slump *verb* **1** to fall or sink suddenly
and heavily **2** to lose value suddenly
□ *noun* a sudden fall in values, prices
etc

slung *past form of* **sling**

slunk *past form of* **slink**

slur *verb* **1** to pronounce indistinctly **2**
to damage (a reputation *etc*), speak evil
of □ *noun* **1** a blot or stain (on someone's
reputation) **2** a criticism, an insult
slur *verb* ⇨ slu**rs**, slu**rring**, slu**rred**

slurp *verb* to drink or gulp noisily
□ *noun* a noisy gulp

slurry *noun* **1** thin, liquid cement **2**
liquid waste

slush *noun* **1** watery mud **2** melting
snow **3** something very sentimental **4**
sentimentality

slushy *adjective* **1** covered with, or like,
slush **2** sentimental

slut *noun* **1** a woman who regularly
engages in casual sex **2** a prostitute **3** a
dirty, untidy woman

sly *adjective* cunning; wily; deceitful
□ **slyly** *adverb* □ **on the sly** secretly,
surreptitiously

smack *verb* **1** to strike smartly, slap **2**
to have a trace or suggestion (of): *this
smacks of treason* □ *noun* **1** an act of
smacking **2** the sound made by
smacking **3** a boisterous kiss **4** a taste,
a flavour **5** a trace, a suggestion **6** a
small fishing vessel **7** *slang* the drug
heroin □ *adverb* with sudden violence:
run smack into the door

small *adjective* **1** little, not big or much
2 not important: *a small matter* **3** not
having a large or successful business: *a
small businessman* **4** of a voice: soft
□ *noun* the most slender or narrow part:
the small of the back □ *adverb* into small
pieces: *cut up small*

🔲 **Alternative words**: (adjective,
meaning 1) little, tiny, minute,
minuscule, short, slight, puny,
petite, diminutive, miniature, mini,
young, inadequate, insufficient,
scanty, meagre, paltry, mean,
limited

small beer something trivial or
unimportant

small hours *noun plural* the hours just
after midnight

small-minded *adjective* having narrow
opinions, ungenerous

smallpox *noun* a serious infectious

illness, causing a rash of large pimples (**pocks**)

small talk polite conversation about nothing very important

smarmy *adjective* smooth in manner, unctuous, ingratiating

■ **Alternative words**: obsequious

smart *adjective* **1** clever and quick in thought or action **2** well-dressed **3** brisk **4** sharp, stinging □ *noun* a sharp, stinging pain □ *verb* **1** to feel a sharp, stinging pain **2** to feel annoyed, resentful *etc* after being insulted

smash *verb* **1** to break in pieces, shatter **2** to strike with force: *smash a ball with a racket* **3** to crash (into *etc*): *the car smashed into the wall* □ *noun* (*plural* **smashes**) **1** an act of smashing **2** a crash, a collision (of vehicles) **3** the ruin of a business *etc*

smattering *noun* a very slight knowledge of a subject

smear *verb* **1** to spread (something sticky or oily) **2** to spread, smudge with (something sticky *etc*) **3** to become smeared **4** to slander, insult □ *noun* a smudge of something sticky

smear test the taking of a sample of cells from a woman's cervix for examination

smell *noun* **1** the sense or power of being aware of things through your nose **2** an act of using this sense **3** something sensed through the nose, a scent □ *verb* **1** to notice by the sense of smell: *I smell gas* **2** to use your sense of smell on: *smell this fish* **3** to give off a smell: *this room smells* □ **smell out** to find out by prying or inquiring closely

smell *verb* ⇨ smell**s**, smell**ing**, smell**t** or smell**ed**

■ **Alternative words**: (noun, meaning 3) aroma

smelling-salts *noun plural* strong-smelling chemicals in a bottle, used to revive fainting people

smelly *adjective* having a bad smell

smelt *verb* **1** to melt (ore) in order to separate the metal from other material **2** *past form* of **smell**

smile *verb* **1** to show pleasure by drawing up the corners of the lips **2** (sometimes **smile on**) to be favourable to: *fortune smiled on him* □ *noun* an act of smiling

■ **Alternative words**: (verb, meaning 1) grin, beam, simper, smirk, leer

smirch *verb* to stain, soil □ *noun* a stain

smirk *verb* to smile in a self-satisfied or foolish manner □ *noun* a self-satisfied smile

smite *verb* to strike, hit hard

smite ⇨ smite**s**, smit**ing**, smitten, smote

smith *noun* a worker in metals; a blacksmith

smithereens *noun plural* fragments

smithy *noun* (*plural* **smithies**) the workshop of a smith

smitten *past participle* of **smite**: **smitten with** affected by; strongly attracted by

smock *noun* a loose shirt-like garment, sometimes worn over other clothes as a protection

smog *noun* thick, smoky fog

smoke *noun* **1** the cloud-like gases and particles of soot given off by anything burning **2** an act of smoking (a cigarette *etc*) □ *verb* **1** to give off smoke **2** to inhale and exhale tobacco smoke from a cigarette, pipe *etc* **3** to cure or preserve (ham, fish *etc*) by applying smoke **4** to darken (*eg* glass) by applying smoke

smokeless *adjective* **1** burning without smoke **2** where the emission of smoke is prohibited: *a smokeless zone*

smoker *noun* **1** someone who smokes **2** a railway compartment in which smoking is allowed

smokescreen *noun* anything (originally smoke) meant to confuse or mislead

smoky *adjective* **1** full of smoke **2** tasting of smoke

smooch *verb, informal* to kiss, pet

smooth *adjective* **1** not rough **2** having an even surface **3** without lumps: *a smooth sauce* **4** hairless **5** without breaks, stops or jolts: *smooth journey* **6** too agreeable in manner □ *verb* **1** to make smooth **2** to calm, soothe **3** to free from difficulty

smote *past form of* **smite**

smother *verb* **1** to kill by keeping air from, *eg* by covering over the nose and mouth **2** to die by this means **3** to cover up, conceal (feelings *etc*) **4** to put down, suppress (a rebellion *etc*)

smoulder *verb* **1** to burn slowly without bursting into flame **2** to exist in a hidden state **3** to show otherwise hidden emotion, *eg* anger, hate: *her eyes smouldered with hate*

smudge *noun* a smear □ *verb* to make dirty with spots or smears

smug *adjective* well-satisfied, too obviously pleased with yourself

smuggle *verb* **1** to take (goods) into, or out of, a country without paying the required taxes **2** to send or take secretly

smuggler *noun* someone who smuggles goods

smut *noun* **1** a spot of dirt or soot **2** vulgar or indecent talk *etc*

smutty *adjective* **1** dirty, grimy **2** indecent, vulgar

snack *noun* a light, hasty meal

snaffle *verb, slang* to steal

snag *noun* a difficulty, an obstacle □ *verb* to catch or tear on something sharp

snag *verb* ⇨ snag**s**, snag**ging**, snag**ged**

snail *noun* **1** a soft-bodied, small, crawling animal with a shell **2** someone who is very slow

snake *noun* **1** a legless reptile with a long body, which moves along the ground with a winding movement **2** anything snake-like in form or movement **3** a cunning, deceitful person

snap *verb* **1** to make a sudden bite **2** **snap something up** to eat it up, or grab it, eagerly **3** to break or shut suddenly with a sharp noise **4** to cause (the fingers) to make a sharp noise **5** to speak sharply **6** to take a photograph of □ *noun* **1** the noise made by snapping **2** a sudden spell (*eg* of cold weather) **3**

a card-game in which players try to match cards **4** a photograph

snap *verb* ⇨ snap**s**, snap**ping**, snap**ped**

snapdragon *noun* a garden plant whose flower, when pinched, opens and shuts like a mouth

snappy *adjective* irritable, inclined to speak sharply □ **snappily** *adverb*

snapshot *noun* a quickly taken photograph

snare *noun* **1** a noose or loop that draws tight when pulled, for catching an animal **2** a trap **3** a hidden danger or temptation □ *verb* to catch in or with a snare

snarl *verb* **1** to growl, showing the teeth **2** to speak in a furious, spiteful tone **3** to become tangled □ *noun* **1** a growl, a furious noise **2** a tangle, a knot **3** a muddled or confused state

snatch *verb* **1** to seize or grab suddenly **2** to take quickly when you have time: *snatch an hour's sleep* □ *noun* (*plural* **snatches**) **1** an attempt to seize **2** a small piece or quantity: *a snatch of music*

sneak *verb* **1** to creep or move in a stealthy, secretive way **2** to tell tales, tell on others □ *noun* **1** someone who tells tales **2** a deceitful, underhand person

sneaky *adjective* underhand, deceitful □ **sneakily** *adverb*

sneer *verb* to show contempt by a scornful expression, words *etc* □ *noun* a scornful expression or remark

sneeze *verb* to make a sudden, unintentional and violent blowing noise through the nose and mouth □ *noun* an involuntary blow through the nose

snicker *verb* **1** to snigger **2** of a horse: to neigh

snide *adjective* mean, malicious: *snide remark*

sniff *verb* **1** to draw in air through the nose with a slight noise, *eg* when having a cold, or showing disapproval **2** to smell (a scent *etc*) **3** **sniff at something** to treat it with scorn or suspicion □ *noun* a quick drawing in of air through the nose

sniffle *noun* a light sniff, a snuffle □ *verb* to sniff lightly

snigger *verb* to laugh in a quiet, sly manner □ *noun* a quiet, sly laugh

snip *verb* to cut off sharply, especially with a single cut □ *noun* 1 a cut with scissors 2 a small piece snipped off 3 *informal* a bargain: *a snip at the price*

snip *verb* ⇨ snip*s*, snipp*ing*, snipp*ed*

snipe *noun* a bird with a long straight beak, found in marshy places □ *verb* 1 **snipe at someone** to shoot at them from a place of hiding 2 **snipe at someone** to attack them with critical remarks

sniper *noun* someone who shoots at a single person from cover

snippet *noun* a little piece, especially of information or gossip

snitch *noun, informal* an informer, a tell-tale □ *verb* to inform (on)

snivel *verb* 1 to have a running nose, eg because of a cold 2 to whine or complain tearfully □ *noun* 1 a running nose 2 a whine

snivel *verb* ⇨ snivel*s*, snivell*ing*, snivell*ed*

snob *noun* someone who looks down on those in a lower social class

Originally a slang term for 'shoemaker' which changed its meaning to someone of low social class, and later to someone who enjoys showing off their wealth and social standing

snobbery *noun* the behaviour that is typical of a snob or snobs

snobbish *adjective* admiring things associated with the higher social classes and despising things associated with the lower classes

snooker *noun* a game like billiards, using twenty-two coloured balls

snoop *verb* to spy or pry in a sneaking secretive way □ *noun* someone who pries

snooty *adjective* haughty, snobbish

snooze *verb* to sleep lightly, doze □ *noun* a light sleep

snore *verb* to make a snorting noise in your sleep while breathing □ *noun* a snorting sound made in sleep

snorkel *noun* 1 a tube with one end above the water, to enable an underwater swimmer to breathe 2 a similar device for bringing air into a submarine

snort *verb* 1 to force air noisily through the nostrils 2 to make such a noise to express disapproval, anger, laughter *etc* □ *noun* a loud noise made through the nostrils

snot *noun* mucus of the nose

snotty *adjective* supercilious

snout *noun* the projecting nose and mouth of an animal, *eg* of a pig

snow *noun* 1 frozen water vapour which falls in light white flakes 2 *slang* the drug cocaine □ *verb* to fall down in, or like, flakes of snow □ **snowed under** overwhelmed

snowball *noun* a ball made of snow pressed hard together □ *verb* 1 to throw snowballs 2 to grow increasingly quickly: *unemployment has snowballed recently*

snowboard *noun* a single board used as a ski on snow

snowdrift *noun* a bank of snow blown together by the wind

snowdrop *noun* a small white flower growing from a bulb in early spring

snowflake *noun* a flake of snow

snowman *noun* a figure shaped like a human being, made of snow

snowplough *noun* a large vehicle for clearing snow from roads *etc*

snowshoe *noun* a long broad frame with a mesh, one of a pair for walking on top of snow

snowy *adjective* 1 covered with snow 2 white, pure

snub *verb* to treat or speak to in an abrupt, scornful way, insult □ *noun* an act of snubbing □ *adjective* of a nose: short and turned up at the end

snub *verb* ⇨ snub*s*, snubb*ing*, snubb*ed*

snuff *verb* to put out or trim the wick of (a candle) □ *noun* powdered tobacco for drawing up into the nose

snuffbox *noun* a box for holding snuff

snuffle *verb* to make a sniffing noise through the nose, *eg* because of a cold □ *noun* a sniffling through the nose

snug *adjective* 1 lying close and warm 2 cosy, comfortable 3 closely fitting; neat and trim

snuggle *verb* 1 to curl up comfortably 2 to draw close to for warmth, affection *etc*

so *adverb* 1 as shown, *eg* by a hand gesture: *so high* 2 to such an extent, to a great extent: *so heavy/ you look so happy* 3 in this or that way: *point your toes so* 4 correct: *is that so?* 5 (used in contradicting) indeed: *It's not true. It is so* □ *conjunction* therefore: *you don't need it, so don't buy it* □ **so as to** in order to □ **so far** up to this or that point □ **so forth** more of the same sort of thing: *pots, pans and so forth* □ **so much for** that is the end of: *so much for that idea!* □ **so that** with the purpose or result that □ **so what?** what difference does it make? does it matter?

soak *verb* 1 to let stand in a liquid until wet through 2 to drench (with) 3 **soak something up** to suck it up, absorb it

soaking *adjective* wet through □ *noun* a wetting, drenching □ **soaking wet** thoroughly wet, drenched

so-and-so *noun, informal* 1 this or that person or thing 2 *euphemistic* used instead of a stronger insult: *she's a real so-and-so, saying that to you!*

soap *noun* 1 a mixture containing oils or fats and other substances, used in washing 2 *informal* a soap opera □ *verb* to use soap on

soap-box *noun* 1 a small box for holding soap 2 a makeshift platform for standing on when speaking to a crowd out of doors

soap opera a television series about a group of characters and their daily lives

soapsuds *noun plural* soapy water worked into a froth

soapy *adjective* 1 like soap 2 full of soap

soar *verb* 1 to fly high into the air 2 of prices: to rise high and quickly

sob *verb* to weep noisily □ *noun* a noisy weeping

> **sob** *verb* ⇨ sobs, sobbing, sobbed

sober *adjective* 1 not drunk 2 serious, staid 3 not florid, unelaborate □ *verb* (sometimes **sober up**) to make or become sober □ **soberly** *adverb*

soberness or **sobriety** *noun* the state of being sober

sobriquet *noun* a nickname

> From a French phrase meaning literally an affectionate chuck under the chin

sob story a story told to arouse sympathy

so-called *adjective* called by such a name, often mistakenly: *a so-called expert*

soccer *noun* football

sociability or **sociableness** *noun* being sociable

sociable *adjective* fond of the company of others, friendly

social *adjective* 1 relating to society, or to a community: *social history* 2 living in communities: *social insects* 3 of companionship: *social gathering* 4 of rank or level in society: *social class*

socialism *noun* the belief that a country's wealth should belong to the people as a whole, not to private owners

socialist *noun* someone who believes in socialism □ *adjective* relating to or characteristic of socialism

social security the system, paid for by taxes, of providing insurance against old age, illness, unemployment *etc*

social work work which deals with the care of the people in a community, especially of the poor or underprivileged

social worker a person working for a private or government organization whose job it is to provide help for people in need

society *noun* 1 humanity considered as a whole 2 a community of people 3 a social club, an association 4 the class of people who are wealthy, fashionable *etc* **5** company, companionship: *I enjoy his society*

socio- *prefix* of or relating to society or social behaviour
🕲 Comes from Latin *socius* meaning 'a companion'

sociological *adjective* dealing or concerned with social questions and problems of human society

sociologist *noun* someone who studies the structure and organization of human societies and human behaviour in society

sociology *noun* the study of human society

sociopath *noun* someone who hates the company of others

sock *noun* a short stocking

socket *noun* a hollow into which something is fitted: *an electric socket*

sod *noun* a piece of earth with grass growing on it, a turf

soda *noun* **1** the name of several substances formed from sodium **2** soda-water □ **baking soda** sodium bicarbonate, a powder used as a raising agent in baking

soda-water *noun* water through which gas has been passed, making it fizzy

sodden *adjective* soaked through and through

sodium *noun* a metallic element from which many substances are formed, including common salt

sofa *noun* a kind of long, stuffed seat with back and arms

sofa bed a sofa incorporating a fold-away bed

soft *adjective* **1** easily put out of shape when pressed **2** not hard or firm **3** not loud **4** of a colour: not bright or glaring **5** not strict enough **6** lacking strength or courage **7** lacking common sense, weak in the mind **8** of a drink: not alcoholic **9** of water: containing little calcium *etc* □ *adverb* gently, quietly

■ **Alternative words**: (adjective, meanings 1 and 2) yielding, elastic, malleable, spongy, squashy, pulpy, downy, velvety; (adjective, meaning 3) quiet, faint, mellow, dulcet; (adjective, meaning 4) pale, pastel, delicate, muted; (adjective, meaning 5) lenient, lax, permissive

soften *verb* to make or grow soft

soft-hearted *adjective* kind and generous

software *noun*, *computing* programs *etc* as opposed to the machines (*contrasted with:* **hardware**)

soggy *adjective* **1** soaked **2** soft and wet

soil *noun* **1** the upper layer of the earth in which plants grow **2** loose earth; dirt □ *verb* to make dirty

sojourn *verb* to stay for a time □ *noun* a short stay

solace *noun* something which makes pain or sorrow easier to bear, comfort □ *verb* to comfort

solar *adjective* **1** relating to the sun **2** influenced by the sun **3** powered by energy from the sun's rays

solar system the sun with the planets (including the earth) going round it

sold *past form of* **sell**

solder *noun* melted metal used for joining metal surfaces □ *verb* to join (with solder)

soldering-iron *noun* an electric tool for soldering joints

soldier *noun* someone in military service, especially someone who is not an officer

sole[1] *noun* **1** the underside of the foot **2** the underside of a shoe *etc* □ *verb* to put a sole on (a shoe etc)

sole[2] *adjective* **1** only: *the sole survivor* **2** belonging to one person or group only: *the sole right*

sole[3] *noun* a small type of flatfish

solely *adverb* only, alone

solemn *adjective* **1** serious, earnest **2** of an occasion: celebrated with special ceremonies

solemnity *noun* being solemn

solemnize *verb* to carry out (a wedding *etc*) with religious ceremonies

sol-fa *noun*, *music* a system of syllables (do, ray, me *etc*) to be sung to the notes of a scale

solicit *verb* **1** to ask earnestly for: *solicit advice* **2** to ask (someone for something) **3** to offer yourself as a prostitute

solicitor noun a lawyer who advises people about legal matters

solicitous adjective **1** anxious **2** considerate, careful □ **solicitously** adverb

solicitude noun care or anxiety about someone or something

solid adjective **1** fixed in shape, not in the form of gas or liquid **2** in three dimensions, with length, breadth and height **3** not hollow **4** firm, strongly made **5** made or formed completely of one substance: *solid silver* **6** reliable, sound: *solid business* **7** informal without a break: *three solid hours' work* □ noun **1** a substance that is solid **2** a figure that has three dimensions

solidarity noun unity of interests etc

solidify verb to make or become firm or solid

> **solidify** ⇨ solidi**fies**, solidi**fying**, solidi**fied**

solidity noun the state of being solid

soliloquize verb to speak to yourself, especially on the stage

soliloquy noun (plural **soliloquies**) a speech made by an actor etc to themselves

solitaire noun a card-game for one player (also called: **patience**)

solitary adjective **1** lone, alone **2** single: *not a solitary crumb remained*

solitude noun the state of being alone; lack of company

solo noun (plural **solos**) a musical piece for one singer or player □ adjective performed by one person alone: *solo flight*

soloist noun someone who plays or sings a solo

solstice noun the time of longest daylight (**summer solstice** about 21 June) or longest dark (**winter solstice** about 21 December)

solubility noun the ability of a substance to dissolve

soluble adjective **1** able to be dissolved or made liquid **2** of a problem etc: able to be solved

solution noun **1** a liquid with something dissolved in it **2** the act of solving a problem etc **3** an answer to a problem, puzzle etc

solve verb **1** to clear up or explain (a mystery) **2** to discover the answer or solution to

solvency noun the state of being able to pay all debts

solvent adjective able to pay all debts □ noun anything that dissolves another substance

sombre adjective gloomy, dark, dismal

sombrero noun (plural **sombreros**) a broad-brimmed Mexican hat

some adjective **1** several **2** a few: *some oranges, but not many* **3** a little: *some bread, but not much* **4** certain: *some people are rich* □ pronoun **1** a number or part out of a quantity: *please try some* **2** certain people: *some won't be happy*

somebody or **someone** noun **1** an unknown or unnamed person: *somebody I'd never seen before* **2** an important person: *he really is somebody now*

somehow adverb in some way or other

somersault noun a forward or backward roll in which the heels go over the head □ verb to perform a somersault

something pronoun **1** a thing not known or not stated **2** a thing of importance **3** a slight amount, a degree: *he has something of his father's looks*

sometime adverb at a time not known or stated definitely

sometimes adverb at times, now and then

somewhat adverb rather: *somewhat boring*

somewhere adverb in some place

somn- of or relating to sleep: *somnambulist/ insomnia*
  ① Comes from Latin *somnus* meaning 'sleep'

somnambulist noun a sleepwalker

somnolence noun sleepiness

somnolent adjective sleepy; causing sleepiness

son *noun* a male child

sonata *noun* a piece of music with three or more movements, usually for one instrument

song *noun* **1** singing **2** a piece of music to be sung □ **for a song** (bought, sold *etc*) very cheaply

songbird *noun* a bird that sings

songster *noun*, *old* a talented (especially male) singer

sonic *adjective* of sound waves

son-in-law *noun* a daughter's husband

sonnet *noun* a type of poem in fourteen lines

sonorous *adjective* giving a clear, loud sound

soon *adverb* **1** in a short time from now or from the time mentioned: *he will come soon* **2** early: *too soon to tell* **3 as soon** as readily, as willingly: *I would as soon stand as sit*

sooner *adverb* more willingly, rather: *I would sooner stand than sit* □ **sooner or later** at some time in the future

soot *noun* the black powder left by smoke

soothe *verb* **1** to calm or comfort (a person, feelings *etc*) **2** to help or ease (a pain *etc*)

soothing *adjective* that soothes

soothsayer *noun* someone who predicts the future

sooty *adjective* like, or covered with, soot

sop *noun* **1** bread dipped in soup *etc* **2** a bribe to keep someone quiet □ *verb* to soak (up)

soph- *prefix* forms words connected with the idea of wisdom
ⓘ Comes from Greek *sophos* meaning 'wise', and *sophia* meaning 'wisdom'

sophism *noun* a plausible fallacy

sophist *noun* a person who uses clever arguments that are fundamentally unsound

sophistic *adjective* of or relating to sophists

sophisticated *adjective* **1** of a person: full of experience, accustomed to an elegant, cultured way of life **2** of ways of thought, or machinery *etc*: highly developed, complicated, elaborate

sophomore *noun*, *US* a second-year college student

soporific *adjective* causing sleep □ *noun* something which causes sleep

sopping *adjective* wet through

soppy *adjective* overly sentimental

soprano *noun* (*plural* **sopranos**) **1** a singing voice of high pitch **2** a singer with this voice

sorcerer *noun* someone who works magic spells; a witch or wizard

sorceress *noun* a woman who works magic spells; a witch

sorcery *noun* magic, witchcraft

sordid *adjective* **1** dirty, filthy **2** mean, selfish **3** contemptible

sore *adjective* painful □ *noun* a painful, inflamed spot on the skin

sorely *adverb* very greatly: *sorely in need*

sorority *noun* (*plural* **sororities**) a society of female students (*compare with*: **fraternity**)

sorrel *noun* a type of plant with sour-tasting leaves

sorrow *noun* sadness caused by a loss, disappointment *etc* □ *verb* to be sad

sorrowful *adjective* full of sadness

sorry *adjective* **1** feeling regret for something you have done: *I'm sorry I mentioned it* **2** feeling sympathy or pity (for): *sorry for you* **3** miserable: *in a sorry state*

sort *noun* a kind of (person or thing): *the sort of sweets I like* □ *verb* to separate things, putting each in its place: *sort letters* □ **a sort of** used of something which is like something else, but not exactly: *he wore a sort of crown* □ **of a sort** or **of sorts** of a kind, usually inadequate: *a party of sorts* □ **out of sorts** not feeling very well

sortie *noun* a sudden attack made by the defenders of a place on those who are trying to capture it

SOS *noun* **1** a code signal calling for help **2** any call for help

so-so *adjective* not particularly good

sotto voce (*pronounced* sot-oh **vo**-chei) *adverb* in a low voice, so as not to be overheard

sought *past form of* **seek**

soul *noun* 1 the spirit, the part of someone which is not the body 2 a person: *a dear old soul* 3 a perfect example (of): *the soul of kindness*

soulful *adjective* full of feeling

sound *noun* 1 anything that can be heard, a noise 2 a distance from which something may be heard: *within the sound of Bow Bells* 3 a narrow passage of water □ *verb* 1 to strike you as being: *that sounds awful* 2 **sound like** to resemble in sound: *that sounds like Henry's voice* 3 to make a noise with: *sound a horn* 4 to examine by listening carefully to: *sound a patient's chest* 5 to measure (the depths of water) 6 to try to find out someone's opinions: *I'll sound him out tomorrow* □ *adjective* 1 healthy, strong 2 of sleep: deep 3 thorough: *a sound beating* 4 reliable: *sound opinions*

soundproof *adjective* built or made so that sound cannot pass in or out □ *verb* to make soundproof

soundtrack *noun* the strip on a film where the speech and music are recorded

soup *noun* a liquid food made from meat, vegetables *etc*

sour *adjective* 1 having an acid or bitter taste, often as a stage in going bad: *sour milk* 2 bad-tempered □ *verb* to make sour

source *noun* 1 the place where something has its beginning or is found 2 a spring, especially one from which a river flows

souse *verb* to soak (*eg* herrings) in salted water

south *noun* one of the four chief directions, that to one's left as one faces the setting sun □ *adjective & adverb* to or in the south

south-east *noun* the point of the compass midway between south and east □ *adjective* in the south-east

southerly *adjective* 1 towards the south 2 of wind: from the south

southern *adjective* of, from or in the south

southerner *noun* someone living in a southern region or country

south pole the southern end of the imaginary axis on which the earth turns

southward or **southwards** *adverb* towards the south

south-west *noun* the point of the compass midway between south and west □ *adjective* in the south-west

souvenir *noun* something bought or given as a reminder of a person, place or occasion

sou'wester *noun* a kind of waterproof hat

sovereign *noun* 1 a king or queen 2 *historical* a British gold coin worth £1 □ *adjective* 1 supreme, highest: *sovereign lord* 2 having its own government: *sovereign state*

sovereignty *noun* highest power

sow[1] (*pronounced* sow) *noun* a female pig

sow[2] (*pronounced* soh) *verb* 1 to scatter (seeds) so that they may grow 2 to cover (an area) with seeds

> **sow** ⇨ sow*s*, sow*ing*, sow*n* or sow*ed*, sow*ed*

sower *noun* a person who sows something

soya bean or **soy bean** a kind of bean, rich in protein, used as a substitute for meat

soya sauce or **soy sauce** a sauce made from soya beans used in Chinese cooking

spa *noun* a place where people go to drink or bathe in the water from a natural spring

space *noun* 1 a gap, an empty place 2 the distance between objects 3 an uncovered part on a sheet of paper 4 length of time: *in the space of a day* 5 the empty region in which all stars, planets *etc* are situated □ *verb* to put things apart from each other, leaving room between them

spacecraft *noun* a machine for travelling in space

spaceman *noun* a male traveller in space

space-ship *noun* a manned spacecraft

spacewoman *noun* a female traveller in space

spacious *adjective* having plenty of room

spade *noun* 1 a tool with a broad blade for digging in the earth 2 one of the four suits of playing-cards □ **call a spade a spade** to say plainly and clearly what you mean

spaghetti *noun* a type of pasta made into long sticks

spake *verb, old* spoke

span *noun* 1 the distance between the tips of the little finger and the thumb when the hand is spread out (about 23 centimetres, 9 inches) 2 the full time anything lasts 3 an arch of a bridge □ *verb* to stretch across: *the bridge spans the river*

> **span** *verb* ⇨ span*s*, span*ning*, span*ned*

spangle *noun* a thin sparkling piece of metal used as an ornament □ *verb* to sprinkle with spangles *etc*

spaniel *noun* a breed of dog with large, hanging ears

spank *verb* to strike with the flat of the hand □ *noun* a slap with the hand, especially on the buttocks

spanking *noun* a beating with the hand □ *adjective* fast: *a spanking pace*

spanner *noun* a tool used to tighten or loosen nuts, screws *etc*

spar *noun* a long piece of wood or metal used as a ship's mast or its crosspiece □ *verb* 1 to fight with the fists 2 to engage in an argument

> **spar** *verb* ⇨ spar*s*, spar*ring*, spar*red*

spare *verb* 1 to do without: *I can't spare you today* 2 to afford, set aside: *I can't spare the time to do it* 3 to treat with mercy, hold back from injuring 4 to avoid causing (trouble *etc*) to □ *adjective* 1 extra, not yet in use: *spare tyre* 2 thin, small: *spare but strong* □ *noun* another of the same kind (*eg* a tyre, part of a machine) kept for emergencies □ **to spare** over and above what is needed

sparing *adjective* careful, economical

spark *noun* 1 a small red-hot part thrown off from something burning 2 a trace: *a spark of humanity* 3 a lively person □ *verb* to make sparks

sparking-plug or **spark-plug** *noun* a device in a car engine that produces a spark to set on fire explosive gases

sparkle *noun* 1 a little spark 2 brightness, liveliness 3 bubbles, as in wine □ *verb* 1 to shine in a glittering way 2 to be lively or witty 3 to bubble

sparkling *adjective* 1 glittering 2 witty 3 of a drink: bubbling, fizzy

sparrow *noun* a type of small dull-coloured bird

sparse *adjective* 1 thinly scattered 2 not much, not enough

spartan *adjective* of conditions *etc:* hard, without luxury

spasm *noun* 1 a sudden involuntary jerk of the muscles 2 a strong, short burst (*eg* of anger, work)

spasmodic *adjective* 1 occurring in spasms 2 coming now and again, not regularly □ **spasmodically** *adverb*

spastic *adjective* suffering from brain damage which has resulted in extreme muscle spasm and paralysis

spat *past form of* **spit**

spate *noun* 1 flood: *the river is in spate* 2 a sudden rush: *a spate of new books*

spatial *adjective* of or relating to space

spats *noun plural* short gaiters reaching just above the ankle

spatter *verb* to splash (*eg* with mud)

spatula *noun* a tool with a broad, blunt blade

spawn *noun* a mass of eggs of fish, frogs *etc* □ *verb* 1 of fish *etc*: to lay eggs 2 to cause, produce

spay *verb* to remove the ovaries of (a female animal)

speak *verb* 1 to say words, talk 2 to hold a conversation (with) 3 to make a speech 4 to be able to talk (a certain language) □ **speak your mind** to give your opinion openly □ **speak up 1** to speak more loudly or clearly **2** to give your opinion openly

speak ⇨ speak*s*, speak*ing*, spoke, spoken

spear *noun* **1** a long weapon, with an iron or steel point **2** a long, pointed shoot or leaf (especially of grass) □ *verb* to pierce with a spear

special *adjective* **1** not ordinary, exceptional: *special occasion/ special friend* **2** put on for a particular purpose: *special train* **3** belonging to one person or thing and not to others: *special skills/ a special tool for drilling holes in tiles*

specialist *noun* someone who studies one branch of a subject or field: *heart specialist*

speciality *noun* (*plural* **specialities**) something for which a person is well-known

specialization *noun* specializing: *more and more need for specialization in the fields of science and engineering*

specialize *verb* to work in, or study, a particular job, subject *etc*

specialized *adjective* of knowledge: obtained by specializing

specie (*pronounced* **spee**-shi) *noun* gold and silver coins

species *noun* (*plural* **species**) **1** a group of plants or animals which are alike in most ways **2** a kind (of anything)

specific *adjective* giving all the details clearly; particular, exactly stated: *a specific purpose*

specifically *adverb* **1** particularly or for the purpose stated and no other: *the house was designed specifically for the elderly* **2** exactly and clearly: *I specifically told you not to leave the gate open*

specification *noun* **1** the act of specifying **2** a full description of details (*eg* in a plan or contract)

specify *verb* **1** to set down or say clearly (what is wanted) **2** to make particular mention of

specify ⇨ specif*ies*, specify*ing*, specif*ied*

specimen *noun* something used as a sample of a group or kind of anything, especially for study or for putting in a collection

specious *adjective* looking or seeming good but really not so good

speck *noun* **1** a small spot **2** a tiny piece (*eg* of dust)

speckle *noun* a spot on a different-coloured background

speckled *adjective* dotted with speckles

-spect- or **-spec-** forms words connected with looking or seeing: *spectacle/ inspect* (= to look into)
⊙ Comes from Latin *specere* meaning 'to look at'

spectacle *noun* **1** a striking or wonderful sight **2 spectacles** glasses which someone wears to improve eyesight

spectacular *adjective* **1** very impressive to see or watch: *spectacular scenery* **2** remarkable or dramatic: *a spectacular success* □ **spectacularly** *adverb* (meaning 2): *the value of the shares has increased spectacularly*

spectator *noun* someone who watches (an event *eg* a football match)

spectral *adjective* ghostly

spectre *noun* a ghost

spectrum *noun* (*plural* **spectra** or **spectrums**) **1** the band of colours as seen in a rainbow, sometimes formed when light passes through water or glass **2** the range or extent of anything

speculate *verb* **1** to guess **2** to wonder (about) **3** to buy goods, shares *etc* in order to sell them again at a profit

speculation *noun* the act or process of speculating

speculative *adjective* speculating

speculator *noun* a person who buys things in the hope of making a profit when they sell them, without knowing for sure what the future selling price will be: *a property speculator*

sped *past form of* **speed**

speech *noun* **1** the power of making sounds which have meaning for other people **2** a way of speaking: *his speech is always clear* **3** (*plural* **speeches**) a (formal) talk given to an audience

speechless *adjective* so surprised *etc* that you cannot speak

speed *noun* 1 quickness of, or rate of, movement or action 2 *slang* the drug amphetamine □ *verb* 1 (*past* **sped**) to (cause to) move along quickly, hurry 2 (*past* **speeded**) to drive very fast in a car *etc* (especially faster than is allowed by law)

  speed *verb* ⇨ speed*s*, speed*ing*, sped or speed*ed*

speeding *noun* driving at (an illegally) high speed

speed limit the greatest speed permitted on a particular road

speedometer *noun* an instrument that shows how fast you are travelling

speedway *noun* a motor-cycle racing track

speedwell *noun* a type of small plant with blue flowers

speedy *adjective* going quickly

speleology *noun* the study or exploration of caves

spell *noun* 1 words which, when spoken, are supposed to have magic power 2 magic or other powerful influence 3 a (short) space of time 4 a turn (at work, rest, play) □ *verb* 1 to give or write correctly the letters which make up a word 2 to mean, imply: *this defeat spells disaster for us all* □ **spell out** to say (something) very frankly or clearly

  spell *verb* ⇨ spell*s*, spell*ing*, spelt or spell*ed*

spellbound *adjective* charmed, held by a spell

spelling *noun* 1 the ability to spell words 2 the study of spelling words correctly

spelt see **spell**

spend *verb* 1 to use (money) for buying 2 to use (energy *etc*) 3 to pass (time): *I spent a week there* 4 to use up energy, force: *the storm spent itself and the sun shone*

  spend ⇨ spend*s*, spend*ing*, spent

spendthrift *noun* someone who spends money freely and carelessly

spent *adjective* exhausted; having lost force or power: *a spent bullet*

sperm *noun* (the fluid in a male carrying) the male sex-cell that fertilizes the female egg

spermatozoon *noun* (*plural* **spermatozoa**) a male sex cell contained in sperm

spermicide *noun* a substance which kills spermatozoa

sperm-whale *noun* a kind of whale from the head of which **spermaceti**, a waxy substance, is obtained

spew *verb* to vomit

sphere *noun* 1 a ball or similar perfectly round object 2 a position or level in society: *he moves in the highest spheres* 3 range (of influence or action)

spherical *adjective* having the shape of a sphere

Sphinx *noun* 1 a mythological monster with the head of a woman and the body of a lioness 2 the large stone model of the Sphinx in Egypt 3 **sphinx** someone whose real thoughts you cannot guess

spice *noun* 1 any substance used for flavouring, *eg* pepper, nutmeg 2 anything that adds liveliness, interest □ *verb* to flavour with spice

spick-and-span *adjective* neat, clean and tidy

spicy *adjective* 1 full of spices 2 lively and sometimes slightly indecent: *a spicy tale* □ **spiciness** *noun*

spider *noun* a kind of small, insect-like creature with eight legs, that spins a web

spidery *adjective* 1 like a spider 2 of handwriting: having fine, sprawling strokes

spiel (*pronounced* speel or shpeel) *noun*, *informal* a (long or often repeated) story or speech
ⓘ Comes from German *spielen* meaning 'to play'

spike *noun* 1 a pointed piece of rod (of wood, metal *etc*) 2 a type of large nail 3 an ear of corn 4 a head of flowers □ *verb* 1 to pierce with a spike 2 to make useless 3 *informal* to add an alcoholic drink, especially to a soft drink

spiky *adjective* having spikes or a sharp point

spill *verb* to (allow liquid to) run out or overflow □ *noun* **1** a fall **2** a thin strip of wood or twisted paper for lighting a candle, a pipe *etc* □ **spill the beans** *informal* to give away a secret, especially unintentionally

spill *verb* ⇨ spill*s*, spill*ing*, spilt or spill*ed*

spillage *noun* an act of spilling or what is spilt

spin *verb* **1** to draw out (cotton, wood, silk *etc*) and twist into threads **2** to (cause to) whirl round quickly **3** to travel quickly, especially on wheels **4** to produce a fine thread as a spider does □ *noun* **1** a whirling motion **2** a ride (especially on wheels) □ **spin a yarn** to tell a long story □ **spin out** to make to last a long or longer time

spin *verb* ⇨ spin*s*, spin*ning*, spun

spina bifida a birth defect which leaves part of the spinal cord exposed

spinach *noun* a type of plant whose leaves are eaten as vegetables

spinal *see* spine

spinal cord a cord of nerve cells in the spine

spindle *noun* **1** the pin from which the thread is twisted in spinning wool or cotton **2** a pin on which anything turns round (*eg* that in the centre of the turntable of a record-player)

spindly *adjective* long and thin

spindrier *noun* a machine for taking water out of clothes by whirling them round

spindrift *noun* the spray blown from the tops of waves

spine *noun* **1** the line of linked bones running down the back in animals and humans, the backbone **2** a ridge **3** a stiff, pointed spike which is part of an animal's body (*eg* a porcupine) **4** a thorn

spineless *adjective* having no spine; weak

spinet *noun* a kind of small harpsichord

spinney *noun* (*plural* **spinneys**) a small clump of trees

spinning wheel a machine for spinning thread, consisting of a wheel which drives spindles

spinster *noun* a woman who is not married

spiral *adjective* **1** coiled round like a spring **2** winding round and round, getting further and further away from the centre □ *noun* **1** anything with a spiral shape **2** a spiral movement **3** an increase which gets ever more rapid □ *verb* **1** to move in a spiral **2** to increase ever more rapidly

spiral *verb* ⇨ spiral*s*, spiral*ling*, spiral*led*

spire *noun* a tall, sharp-pointed tower (especially on the roof of a church)

spirit *noun* **1** the soul **2** a being without a body, a ghost: *an evil spirit* **3** liveliness, boldness: *he acted with spirit* **4** a feeling or attitude: *a spirit of kindness* **5** the intended meaning: *the spirit of the laws* **6** a distilled liquid, especially alcohol **7 spirits** strong alcoholic drinks in general (*eg* whisky) **8 spirits** state of mind, mood: *in high spirits* □ *verb* (*especially* **spirit away**) to remove, as if by magic

spirited *adjective* lively

spiritual *adjective* having to do with the soul or with ghosts □ *noun* an emotional, religious song of a kind originally developed by the African American slaves

spiritualism *noun* the belief that living people can communicate with the souls of dead people

spiritualist *noun* someone who holds this belief

spit *noun* **1** the liquid which forms in a person's mouth **2** a metal bar on which meat is roasted **3** a long piece of land running into the sea □ *verb* (*past form* **spat**) **1** to throw liquid out from the mouth **2** to rain slightly **3** (*past form* **spitted**) to pierce with something sharp

spit *verb* ⇨ spit*s*, spit*ting*, spat or spit*ted*

spite *noun* the wish to hurt (especially feelings) □ *verb* to annoy out of spite □ **in spite of 1** taking no notice of: *he left in spite of his father's command* **2** although something has happened or is a fact: *the ground was dry in spite of all the rain*

spiteful *adjective* motivated by spit; malicious

spitting image an exact likeness

spittle *noun* spit

spittoon *noun* a kind of dish into which you may spit

splash *verb* 1 to spatter with water, mud *etc* 2 to move or fall with a splash or splashes □ *noun* (*plural* **splashes**) 1 the sound made by, or the scattering of liquid caused by, something hitting water *etc* 2 a mark made by splashing (*eg* on your clothes) 3 a bright patch: *a splash of colour* □ **make a splash** to attract a lot of attention

splay *verb* to turn out at an angle

spleen *noun* 1 a spongy, blood-filled organ inside the body, near the stomach 2 bad temper

splendid *adjective* 1 magnificent, brilliant 2 *informal* excellent □ **splendidly** *adverb*

splendour *noun* the state or quality of being very grand and beautiful in appearance or style

splice *verb* to join (two ends of a rope) by twining the threads together □ *noun* a joint so made

spliff *noun, slang* a cannabis cigarette

splint *noun* a piece of wood *etc* tied to a broken limb to keep it in a fixed position

splinter *noun* a sharp, thin, broken piece of wood, glass *etc* □ *verb* to split into splinters

split *verb* 1 to cut or break lengthways 2 to crack, break 3 to divide into pieces or groups *etc* □ *noun* a crack, a break □ **the splits** the feat of going down on the floor with one leg stretched forward and the other back □ **a split second** a fraction of a second □ **split your sides** to laugh heartily

splitting *adjective* of a headache: severe, intense

splutter *verb* 1 to make spitting noises 2 to speak hastily and unclearly

spoil *verb* 1 to make useless; damage, ruin 2 to give in to the wishes of (a

child *etc*) and so ruin its character 3 of food: to become bad or useless 4 (*past form* **spoiled**) to rob, plunder □ *noun* (often **spoils**) plunder □ **spoiling for** eager for (especially a fight)

spoil *verb* ⇨ spoils, spoil*ing*, spoil*ed*

spoil-sport *noun* someone who won't join in other people's fun

spoke *noun* one of the ribs or bars from the centre to the rim of a wheel □ *verb*, *past form* of **speak**

spoken *see* **speak**

spokesman, spokeswoman *noun* someone who speaks on behalf of others

spoliation *noun* plundering

sponge *noun* 1 a sea animal 2 its soft, elastic skeleton which can soak up water and is used for washing 3 an artificial object like this used for washing 4 a light cake or pudding □ *verb* 1 to wipe with a sponge 2 *informal* to live off money *etc* given by others □ **throw in the sponge** to give up a fight or struggle

sponger *noun, informal* someone who lives at others' expense

spongy *adjective* soft like a sponge

sponsor *noun* 1 someone who takes responsibility for introducing something, a promoter 2 someone who promises to pay a sum of money if another person completes a set task (*eg* a walk, swim *etc*) 3 a business firm which pays for a radio or television programme and advertises its products during it □ *verb* to act as a sponsor to

sponsorship *noun* the act of sponsoring

spontaneity *noun* being spontaneous

spontaneous *adjective* 1 not planned beforehand 2 natural, not forced

spoof *noun* a trick played as a joke, a hoax

spook *noun* a ghost

spooky *adjective* frightening

spool *noun* a reel for thread, film *etc*

spoon *noun* a piece of metal *etc* with a hollow bowl at one end, used for lifting food to the mouth □ *verb* to lift with a spoon

spoonerism *noun* a mistake in speaking in which the first sounds of words change position, as in *every crook and nanny* for *every nook and cranny*

spoonfeed *verb* to teach without encouraging independent thought

spoor *noun* the footmarks or trail left by an animal

sporadic *adjective* happening here and there, or now and again □ **sporadically** *adverb*: *fighting broke out sporadically*

spore *noun* the seed of certain plants (*eg* ferns, fungi)

sporran *noun* a small pouch worn hanging in front of a kilt

sport *noun* **1** games such as football, tennis, skiing *etc* in general **2** any one game of this type **3** a good-natured, obliging person □ *verb* **1** to have fun, play **2** to wear: *sporting a pink tie*

sporting *adjective* **1** fond of sport **2** believing in fair play, good-natured

sporting chance a reasonably good chance

sports car a small, fast car with only two seats

sportsman *noun* **1** a man who plays sports **2** someone who shows fair play in sports

sportsmanlike *adjective* fair, sporting

sportswoman *noun* a woman who plays sport

spot *noun* **1** a small mark or stain (of mud, paint *etc*) **2** a round mark as part of a pattern on material *etc* **3** a pimple **4** a place □ *verb* **1** to mark with spots **2** to catch sight of □ **in a spot** in trouble □ **on the spot 1** in the place where someone is most needed **2** right away, immediately **3** in an embarrassing or difficult position

spot *verb* ⇨ spot*s*, spot*ting*, spot*ted*

spotless *adjective* very clean

spotlight *noun* a bright light that is shone on an actor on the stage □ *verb* **1** to show up clearly **2** to draw attention to

spotted or **spotty** *adjective* covered with spots

spouse *noun* a husband or wife

spout *noun* **1** the part of a kettle, teapot *etc* through which liquid is poured out **2** a strong jet of liquid □ *verb* to pour or spurt out

sprain *noun* a painful twisting (*eg* of an ankle) □ *verb* to twist painfully

sprang *past form* of **spring**

sprat *noun* a small fish similar to a herring

sprawl *verb* **1** to sit, lie or fall with the limbs spread out widely **2** of a town *etc*: to spread out in an untidy, irregular way

spray *noun* **1** a fine mist of liquid like that made by a waterfall **2** a device with many small holes (*eg* on a watering-can or shower) for producing spray **3** a liquid for spraying **4** a shoot spreading out in flowers □ *verb* to cover with a mist or fine jets of liquid

spread *verb* **1** to put more widely or thinly over an area: *spread the butter on the bread* **2** to cover: *spread the bread with jam* **3** to open out (*eg* your arms, a map) **4** to scatter or distribute over a wide area, length of time *etc* □ *noun* **1** the act of spreading **2** the extent or range (of something) **3** a food which is spread on bread: *sandwich spread* **4** *informal* a large meal laid out on a table

spread *verb* ⇨ spread*s*, spread*ing*, spread

spread-eagled *adjective* with limbs spread out

spreadsheet *noun* a computer program with which data can be viewed on screen and manipulated

spree *noun* a careless spell of some activity: *a spending spree*

sprig *noun* a small twig or shoot

sprightly *adjective* lively, brisk

spring *verb* **1** to jump, leap **2** to move swiftly **3** **spring back** to return suddenly to an earlier position when released **4** to set off (a trap *etc*) **5** to give, reveal unexpectedly: *he sprang the news on me* **6** to come from: *his bravery springs from his love of adventure* □ *noun* **1** a leap **2** a coil of wire used in a mattress **3** the ability to stretch and spring back **4** bounce, energy **5** a small stream flowing out from the ground **6** the season which follows winter, when plants begin to grow again □ **spring a leak** to begin to leak □ **spring up** to appear suddenly

spring *verb* ⇨ springs, springing, sprang, sprung

springboard *noun* a springy board from which swimmers may dive

springbok *noun* a type of deer found in S Africa

spring-cleaning *noun* a thorough cleaning of a house, especially in the spring

springy *adjective* able to spring back into its former position *etc*, elastic

sprinkle *verb* to scatter or cover in small drops or pieces

sprinkler *noun* something which sprinkles water

sprinkling *noun* a few, a small amount: *we had a sprinkling of snow in the night*

sprint *verb* to run at full speed □ *noun* a short running race

sprinter *noun* someone who is good at running fast over short distances

sprite *noun* **1** a supernatural spirit **2** *computing* an icon which can be moved about a screen

sprocket *noun* one of a set of teeth on the rim of a wheel

sprout *verb* **1** to begin to grow **2** to put out new shoots □ *noun* **1** a young bud **2** **sprouts** Brussels sprouts

spruce *adjective* neat, smart □ *noun* a kind of fir-tree

sprung *see* **spring**

spry *adjective* lively, active

spud *noun, informal* a potato

spume *noun* froth, foam

spun *past form of* **spin**

spur *noun* **1** a sharp point worn by a horse-rider on the heel and used to urge on a horse **2** a claw-like point at the back of a bird's leg **3** anything that urges someone on **4** a small line of mountains running off from a larger range □ *verb* **1** to use spurs on (a horse) **2** to urge on □ **on the spur of the moment** without thinking beforehand

spur *verb* ⇨ spurs, spurring, spurred

spurious *adjective* not genuine, false

spurn *verb* to cast aside, reject with scorn

spurt *verb* to pour out in a sudden stream □ *noun* **1** a sudden stream pouring or squirting out **2** a sudden increase of effort: *put a spurt on*

sputnik *noun* a small spacecraft orbiting the earth, originally Russian

sputter *verb* to make a noise as of spitting and throw out moisture in drops

spy *noun* (*plural* **spies**) someone who secretly collects (and reports) information about another person, country, firm *etc* □ *verb* **1** to catch sight of **2** **spy on someone** to watch them secretly

spy *verb* ⇨ spies, spying, spied

squabble *verb* to quarrel noisily □ *noun* a noisy quarrel

squad *noun* **1** a group of soldiers, workmen *etc* doing a particular job **2** a group of people

squaddie *noun, informal* a private, an ordinary soldier

squadron *noun* a division of a regiment, section of a fleet or group of aeroplanes

squalid *adjective* **1** very dirty, filthy **2** contemptible

squall *noun* **1** a sudden violent storm **2** a squeal, a scream

squally *adjective* stormy

squalor *noun* dirty or squalid living conditions

squander *verb* to waste (money, goods, strength *etc*)

square **1** a figure with four equal sides and four right angles, of this shape: □ **2** an open space enclosed by buildings in a town **3** the answer when a number is multiplied by itself (*eg* the square of 3 is 9) □ *adjective* **1** shaped like a square **2** equal in scores in a game **3** of two or more people: not owing one another anything **4** straight, level □ *verb* **1** to make like a square **2** to straighten (the shoulders) **3** to multiply a number by itself **4** to fit, agree: *that doesn't square with what you said earlier* **5 square up** or **square something up** to settle a debt □ *adverb* **1** in a straight or level position **2** directly; exactly: *hit square on the nose* □ **square foot** or **square metre** *etc* an area equal to that of a square each side of which is one foot or one metre *etc* long

square deal fair treatment

square meal a large, satisfying meal

square root the number which, multiplied by itself, gives a certain other number (*eg* 3 is the square root of 9)

squash *verb* **1** to crush flat or to a pulp **2** to put down, defeat (rebellion *etc*) □ *noun* **1** a crushing or crowding **2** a mass of people crowded together **3** a drink made from the juice of crushed fruit **4** a game with rackets and a rubber ball played in a walled court

squat *verb* **1** to sit down on the heels **2** to settle without permission in property which you do not pay rent for □ *adjective* short and thick

squat *verb* ⇨ squat*s*, squatt*ing*, squatt*ed*

squatter *noun* someone who squats in a building, on land *etc*

squaw *noun, derogatory* **1** a Native American woman or wife **2** a woman

squawk *verb* to give a harsh cry □ *noun* a harsh cry

squeak *verb* to give a short, high-pitched sound □ *noun* a high-pitched noise

squeaky *adjective* **1** high-pitched: *a squeaky voice* **2** tending to squeak: *a squeaky floorboard*

squeal *verb* **1** to give a loud, shrill cry **2** *informal* to inform on

squeamish *adjective* **1** easily sickened or shocked **2** feeling sick

squeegee *noun* a sponge for washing windows *etc*

squeeze *verb* **1** to press together **2** to grasp tightly **3** to force out (liquid or juice from) by pressing **4** to force a way: *squeeze through the hole in the wall* □ *noun* **1** a squeezing or pressing **2** a few drops got by squeezing: *a squeeze of lemon juice* **3** a crowd of people crushed together

squelch *noun* a sound made, *eg* by walking through marshy ground □ *verb* to make this sound

squib *noun* a type of small firework

squid *noun* a sea animal with tentacles, related to the cuttlefish

squiggle *noun* a curly or wavy mark

squint *verb* **1** to screw up the eyes in looking at something **2** to have the eyes looking in different directions □ *noun* **1** a fault in eyesight which causes squinting **2** *informal* a quick, close glance

squire *noun, historical* **1** a country landowner **2** a knight's servant

squirm *verb* to wriggle or twist the body, especially in pain or embarrassment

squirrel *noun* a small gnawing animal, either reddish-brown or grey, with a bushy tail

squirt *verb* to shoot out a narrow jet of liquid □ *noun* a narrow jet of liquid

St *abbreviation* **1** saint **2** street **3** strait

stab *verb* **1** to wound or pierce with a pointed weapon **2** to poke (at) □ *noun* **1** the act of stabbing **2** a wound made by stabbing **3** a sharp pain □ **have a stab at** to make an attempt at

stab *verb* ⇨ stab*s*, stabb*ing*, stabb*ed*

stability *noun* steadiness

stabilize *verb* to make steady

stable *noun* a building for keeping horses □ *verb* to put or keep (horses) in a stable □ *adjective* firm, steady

staccato *adjective* **1** of sounds: sharp and separate, like the sound of tapping **2** *also adverb, music* (with each note) sounded separately and clearly

stack *noun* a large pile (of straw, hay, wood *etc*) □ *verb* to pile in a stack

stadium *noun* (*plural* **stadiums** or **stadia**) a large sports-ground or race-course with seats for spectators

staff *noun* **1** a stick or pole carried in the hand **2** *music* a stave **3** workers employed in a business, school *etc* **4** a group of army officers who assist a commanding officer □ *verb* to supply (a school *etc*) with staff

stag *noun* a male deer

stage *noun* **1** a platform for performing or acting on **2 the stage** the theatre; the job of working as an actor **3** a step in development: *the first stage of the plan* **4** a landing place (*eg* for boats) **5** a part of a journey **6** a stopping place on a journey □ *verb* **1** to prepare and put on a performance of (a play *etc*) **2** to arrange (an event, *eg* an exhibition) □ **on the stage** in the theatre-world

stagecoach *noun, historical* a coach running every day with passengers

stage fright an actor's fear when acting in public, especially for the first time

stage whisper a loud whisper

stagger *verb* **1** to walk unsteadily, totter **2** to astonish **3** to arrange (people's hours of work *etc*) so that they do not begin or end together

staggered *adjective* of two or more things: arranged to begin and end at different times

staggering *adjective* astonishing

staging *noun* **1** scaffolding **2** putting on the stage

stagnant *adjective* of water: standing still, not flowing and therefore not pure

stagnate *verb* **1** of water: to remain still and so become impure **2** to remain for a long time in the same situation and so become bored, inactive *etc*

stagnation *noun* **1** stagnating **2** being stagnant

stag party a party for men only held the night before one of them gets married

staid *adjective* set in your ways, sedate

stain *verb* **1** to give a different colour to (wood *etc*) **2** to mark or make dirty by accident □ *noun* **1** a liquid which dyes or colours something **2** a mark which is not easily removed **3** something shameful in someone's character or reputation

stained glass coloured glass cut in shapes and leaded together

stainless steel a mixture of steel and chromium which does not rust

stair *noun* **1** one or all of a number of steps one after the other **2 stairs** a series or flight of steps

staircase *noun* a stretch of stairs with rails on one or both sides

stake *noun* **1** a strong stick pointed at one end **2** money put down as a bet **3** *historical* a post to which people were tied to be burned □ *verb* **1** to mark the limits or boundaries (of a field *etc*) with stakes **2** to bet (money) **3** to risk □ **at stake 1** be won or lost **2** in great danger: *his life is at stake* □ **have a stake in** to be concerned in (because you have something to gain or lose) □ **stake a claim** to establish ownership or right (to something)

stalactite *noun* a spike of limestone hanging from the roof of a cave, formed by the dripping of water containing lime

stalagmite *noun* a spike of limestone, like a stalactite, rising from the floor of a cave

stale *adjective* **1** of food: no longer fresh **2** no longer interesting because heard, done *etc* too often before **3** not able to do your best (because of overworking, boredom *etc*)

stalemate *noun* **1** *chess* a position in which a player cannot move without putting their king in danger **2** a position in an argument in which neither side can win

stalk *noun* the stem of a plant or of a leaf or flower □ *verb* **1** to walk stiffly or proudly **2** to go quietly up to animals being hunted to shoot at close range

stall *noun* **1** a division for one animal in a cowshed *etc* **2** a table on which things are laid out for sale **3** an open-fronted shop **4** a seat in a church (especially for choir or clergy) **5 stalls** theatre seats on the ground floor □ *verb* **1** of a car engine: to come to a halt without the driver intending it to do so **2** of an aircraft: to lose flying speed and so fall out of control **3** *informal* to avoid action or decision for the time being

stallion *noun* a male horse, especially one kept for breeding purposes

stalwart *adjective* brave, stout-hearted □ *noun*

stamen *noun* one of the thread-like spikes in the middle of a flower which bear the pollen

stamina *noun* strength, power to keep going

stammer *verb* 1 to have difficulty in saying the first letter of words in speaking 2 to stumble over words □ *noun* a speech difficulty of this kind

stamp *verb* 1 to bring the foot down firmly on the ground 2 to stick a (postage stamp) on 3 to mark with a design cut into a mould and inked 4 to fix or mark deeply: *forever stamped in my memory* □ *noun* 1 the act of stamping 2 a design *etc* made by stamping 3 a cut or moulded design for stamping 4 kind, sort: *of a different stamp* 5 a postage stamp □ **stamp out** 1 to put out (a fire) by stamping 2 to suppress, crush

stampede *noun* 1 a wild rush of frightened animals 2 a sudden, wild rush of people □ *verb* to rush wildly

stance *noun* someone's manner of standing

stanchion *noun* an upright iron bar used as a support (*eg* in windows, ships)

stand *verb* 1 to be on your feet (not lying or sitting down) 2 to rise to your feet 3 of an object: to (cause to) be in a particular place: *it stood by the door/ stood the case in the corner* 4 to bear: *I cannot stand this heat* 5 to treat (someone) to: *stand you tea* 6 to remain: *this law still stands* 7 to be a candidate (for): *he stood for parliament* 8 to be short (for): *PO stands for Post Office* □ *noun* 1 something on which anything is placed 2 an object made to hold, or for hanging, things: *a hat-stand* 3 lines of raised seats from which people may watch games *etc* 4 an effort made to support, defend, resist *etc*: *a stand against violence* 5 (*US*) a witness box in a law court □ **stand by** to be ready or available to be used or help in an emergency *etc* (**standby** *noun*) □ **stand down** to withdraw (from a contest) or resign (from a job) □ **stand fast** to refuse to give in □ **stand in (for)** to take another's place, job *etc* for a time (**stand-in** *noun*) □ **stand out** to stick out, be noticeable □ **stand to reason** to be likely or reasonable □ **stand up for**

to defend strongly □ **stand up to** to face or oppose bravely

stand *verb* ⇨ stand*s*, stand*ing*, stood

■ **Alternative words**: (verb, meaning 4) abide

stand-alone *noun* & *adjective*, *computing* (of) a system, device *etc* that can operate unconnected to any other

standard *noun* 1 a level against which things may be judged 2 a level of excellence aimed at: *artistic standards* 3 a large flag *etc* on a pole □ *adjective* 1 normal, usual: *standard charge* 2 ordinary, without extras: *standard model* □ **standard of living** a level of material comfort considered necessary by a particular group of society *etc*

standardization *noun* standardizing or being standardized

standardize *verb* to make all of one kind or size

standard lamp a kind of tall lamp which stands on the floor of a room *etc*

standby *noun* 1 something that is kept ready for use, especially in an emergency 2 (*usually* **standby ticket**) a ticket for a journey by air that is offered at a reduced price because you must wait until just before the flight takes off to see if there is a seat available

standing *noun* social position or reputation □ *adjective* 1 on your feet 2 placed on end 3 not moving 4 lasting, permanent: *a standing joke*

stand-offish *adjective* unfriendly

■ **Alternative words**: aloof

standpoint *noun* the position from which you look at something (*eg* a question, problem), point of view

standstill *noun* a complete stop

stank *past form of* **stink**

stanza *noun* a group of lines making up a part of a poem, a verse

staple *noun* 1 a U-shaped iron nail 2 a piece of wire driven through sheets of paper to fasten them together 3 the main item in a country's production, a person's diet *etc* 4 a fibre of wool, cotton *etc* □ *verb* to fasten with a staple □ *adjective* chief, main

star *noun* **1** any of the bodies in the sky appearing as points of light **2** the fixed bodies which are really distant suns, not the planets **3** an object, shape or figure with a number of pointed rays (often five) **4** a leading actor or actress or other well-known performer □ *adjective* for or of a star (in a film *etc*) □ *verb* **1** to act the chief part (in a play or film) □ **2** of a play *etc*: to have as its star □ **Stars and Stripes** the flag of the United States of America

star *verb* ➪ stars, starring, starred

starboard *noun* the right side of a ship, as you look towards the bow (or front) *adjective*

starch *noun* (*plural* **starches**) **1** a white carbohydrate (found in flour, potatoes, bread, biscuits *etc*) **2** a form of this used for stiffening clothes

starchy *adjective* **1** of food: containing starch **2** stiff and unfriendly

stardom *noun* the state of being a leading performer

stare *verb* to look with a fixed gaze □ *noun* a fixed gaze

starfish *noun* a type of small sea creature with five points or arms

stark *adjective* **1** barren, bare **2** harsh, severe **3** sheer: *stark idiocy* □ *adverb* completely: *stark naked*

starling *noun* a common bird with dark, glossy feathers

starry *adjective* full of stars; shining like stars

start *verb* **1** to begin (an action): *he started to walk home* **2** to get (a machine *etc*) working: *he started the car* **3** to jump or jerk (*eg* in surprise) □ *noun* **1** the act of starting (*eg* on a task, journey) **2** a sudden movement of the body **3** a sudden shock: *you gave me a start* **4** in a race *etc* the advantage of beginning before, or farther forward than, others, or the amount of this: *a start of five metres*

startle *verb* to give a shock or fright to

startling *adjective* that startles, surprising

starvation *noun* a potentially fatal form of malnutrition caused by eating insufficient quantities of food over a long period, or by total lack of food

starve *verb* **1** to die for want of food **2** to suffer greatly from hunger **3** to deprive (of something needed or wanted badly): *starved of company here*

Star Wars the informal name for a defence system (officially the *Strategic Defence Initiative*) proposed by the US, in which laser-equipped satellites in space would destroy enemy missiles

state *noun* **1** the condition (of something): *the bad state of the roads* **2** the people of a country under a government **3** (*US*) an area and its people with its own laws forming part of the whole country **4** a government and its officials **5** great show, pomp: *the king drove by in state* □ *adjective* **1** of the government **2** national and ceremonial: *state occasions* **3** (*US*) of a certain state of America: *the state capital of Texas is Austin* □ *verb* to tell, say or write (especially clearly and fully)

stately *adjective* noble-looking; dignified □ **stateliness** *noun*

statement *noun* that which is said or written

state-of-the-art *adjective* most up-to-date

statesman *noun* someone skilled in government

statesmanlike *adjective* diplomatic

static *adjective* not moving □ *noun* **1** atmospheric disturbances causing poor reception of radio or television programmes **2** electricity on the surface of objects which will not conduct it *eg* hair, nylons *etc* (*also called*: **static electricity**)

station *noun* **1** a building with a ticket office, waiting rooms *etc* where trains, buses or coaches stop to pick up or set down passengers **2** a place which is the centre for work or duty of any kind: *fire station/ police station* **3** rank, position: *lowly station* □ *verb* **1** to assign to a position or place **2** to take up a position: *stationed himself by the door*

stationary *adjective* standing still, not moving

① Comes from Latin *stationarius* meaning 'belonging to a military station'

◆ Do not confuse: **stationary** and **stationery**. Remember that a stationER's shop sells **stationERy**

stationer *noun* someone who sells writing paper, envelopes, pens *etc*

In Medieval Latin, a *stationarius* was a tradesman – usually a bookseller – who did not travel from place to place, but had a regular station or a permanent shop

stationery *noun* writing paper, envelopes, pens *etc*
① For origin, see **stationer**

statistical *adjective* of or shown by statistics: *the report includes a lot of statistical information* □ **statistically** *adverb*: *statistically, a man is unlikely to live as long as a woman*

statistician *noun* someone who produces or studies statistics

statistics 1 *noun plural* figures and facts set out in order: *statistics of road accidents for last year* 2 *noun singular* the study of these: *statistics is not an easy subject*

statue *noun* a likeness of someone or an animal carved in stone, metal *etc*

statuesque *adjective* like a statue in dignity *etc*

statuette *noun* a small statue

stature *noun* 1 height 2 importance, reputation

status *noun* position, rank (of a person) in the eyes of others

status quo the state of affairs now existing, or existing before a certain time or event

status symbol a possession which is thought to show the high status of the owner (*eg* a powerful car)

statute *noun* a written law of a country

statutory *adjective* according to law

staunch *adjective* firm, loyal; trustworthy

stave *noun* 1 a set of spaced lines on which music is written 2 one of the strips making the side of a barrel □ *verb* 1 **stave something in** to crush it 2 **stave something off** to keep it away, delay it

stave *verb* ⇨ stave*s*, stav*ing*, stove or stav*ed*

stay *verb* 1 to continue to be: *stayed calm/ stay here while I go for help* 2 to live (for a time): *staying in a hotel* 3 *old* to stop □ *noun* 1 time spent in a place 2 a rope running from the side of a ship to the mast-head 3 **stays** *old* corsets □ **stay put** to remain in the same place

St Bernard see **Saint Bernard**

STD *abbreviation* sexually transmitted disease

stead *noun* place: *she went in my stead* □ **stand you in good stead** to turn out to be helpful to you: *his German stood him in good stead*

steadfast *adjective* 1 steady, fixed 2 faithful, loyal

steading *noun* farm buildings

steady *adjective* 1 firm, not moving or changing 2 not easily upset or put off 3 even, regular, unchanging: *moving at a steady pace* □ *verb* to make or become steady □ **steadily** *adjective*

steady *verb* ⇨ steadi*es*, steady*ing*, steadi*ed*

steak *noun* a thick slice of meat *etc* for cooking

steal *verb* 1 to take (something not belonging to you) without permission 2 to move quietly 3 to take quickly or secretly: *stole a look at him*

steal ⇨ steal*s*, steal*ing*, stole, stolen

■ **Alternative words**: (meaning 1) thieve, pilfer, filch, take, appropriate, snatch, embezzle, lift

stealth *noun* a secret way of doing, acting *etc*

stealthy *adjective* of movement: slow, quiet and secretive □ **stealthily** *adverb*

steam *noun* 1 vapour from hot liquid, especially from boiling water 2 power produced by steam: *in the days of steam* □ *verb* 1 to give off steam 2 to cook by steam 3 to open or loosen by putting into steam: *steam open the envelope* 4 to move or travel by steam □ **steam up**

of glass: to become covered with condensed steam in the form of small drops of water

steam-engine *noun* an engine (especially a railway engine) worked by steam

steamer *noun* a ship driven by steam

steamroller *noun* a steam-driven engine with large and very heavy wheels, used for flattening the surfaces of roads

steamship *noun* a steamer

steamy *adjective* **1** full of steam: *steamy atmosphere* **2** *informal* passionate, erotic

steed *noun, old* a horse

steel *noun* **1** a very hard mixture of iron and carbon **2** a bar of steel for sharpening knife blades □ **of steel** hard, strong: *a grip of steel* □ **steel yourself** to get up courage (to)

steely *adjective* hard, cold, strong *etc* like steel: *a steely gaze*

steep *adjective* **1** of a slope: rising nearly straight up **2** *informal* of a price: too great □ *verb* to soak in a liquid □ **be steeped in something** to be very familiar with something (eg a subject of knowledge): *steeped in French literature*

steeple *noun* a tower of a church *etc* rising to a point, a spire

steeplechase *noun* **1** a race run across open country, over hedges *etc* **2** a race over a course on which obstacles (eg walls) have been made

steeplejack *noun* someone who climbs steeples or other high buildings to make repairs

steer *noun* a young ox raised for its beef □ *verb* **1** to control the course of (a car, ship, discussion *etc*) **2** to follow (a course) □ **steer clear of** to keep away from

steering *noun* the parts of a ship, car *etc* which have to do with controlling its course

steering-wheel *noun* the wheel in a car used by the driver to steer it

stellar *adjective* of the stars

stem *noun* **1** the part of a plant from which the leaves and flowers grow **2** the thin support of a wine-glass □ *verb*

1 to stop, halt: *stem the bleeding* **2** to start, spring (from): *hate stems from envy*

> **stem** *verb* ⇨ stem*s*, stem*ming*, stem*med*

stench *noun* a strong unpleasant smell

stencil *noun* **1** a sheet of metal, cardboard *etc* with a pattern cut out **2** the drawing or design made by rubbing ink or brushing paint *etc* over a cut-out pattern **3** a piece of waxed paper on which words are cut with a typewriter, and which is then used to make copies □ *verb* to make a design or copy in one of these ways

> **stencil** *verb* ⇨ stencil*s*, stencil*ling*, stencil*led*

stentorian *adjective* **1** of the voice: loud **2** loud-voiced

> Named after *Stentor*, a loud-voiced Greek herald in the *Iliad*

> 🖝 Do not confuse with: **stertorous**

Step *noun, trademark* a form of exercise involving stepping on and off a small platform

step *noun* **1** a movement of the leg in walking, running *etc* **2** the distance covered by this **3** a particular movement of the feet, as in dancing: **4** the sound made by the foot in walking *etc*: *heard a step outside* **5** a riser on a stair, or rung on a ladder **6** one of a series of moves in a plan, career *etc*: *take the first step* **7** a way of walking: *springy step* **8 steps** a flight of stairs **9 steps** a step-ladder □ *verb* **1** to take a step **2** to walk, move: *step this way, please* □ **in step 1** of two or more people walking: with the same foot going forward at the same time **2** acting *etc* in agreement (with) □ **out of step** not in step (with) □ **step up** to increase (eg production) □ **take steps** to begin to do something for a certain purpose

> **step** *verb* ⇨ step*s*, step*ping*, step*ped*

step- *prefix* related as the result of a second marriage: *stepfather/ stepdaughter*
○ Comes from Old English prefix *steop-* meaning 'orphan'

step-ladder *noun* a ladder with a support on which it rests

steppe *noun* a dry, grassy treeless plain in SE Europe and Asia

stepping-stone *noun* **1** a stone rising above water or mud, used to cross on **2** anything that helps you to advance

stereo *adjective*, *short for* **stereophonic** □ *noun* (*plural* **stereos**) stereophonic equipment, especially a record-player and/or tape recorder, with amplifier and loudspeakers

stereo- *prefix* solid, three-dimensional: *stereophonic* (= with sounds coming from different directions in three-dimensional space)/ *stereotype* (= a solid metal plate for printing)
① Comes from Greek *stereos* meaning 'solid'

stereophonic *adjective* of sound: giving a life-like effect, with different instruments, voices *etc* coming from different directions

stereotype *noun* **1** a fixed metal plate for printing, with letters *etc* moulded onto its surface **2** something fixed and unchanging **3** a characteristic type of person

Originally a printing term for a fixed block of type

stereotyped or **stereotypical** *adjective* fixed, not changing: *stereotyped ideas*

sterile *adjective* **1** unable to have children or reproduce **2** producing no ideas *etc*: *sterile imagination* **3** free from germs

sterility *noun* the state of being sterile

sterilization *noun* **1** a surgical operation that is performed on humans or animals so that offspring can no longer be produced **2** the treatment of food *etc* in order to destroy germs

sterilize *verb* **1** to make sterile **2** to free from germs by boiling *etc*

sterling *noun* British money, when used in international trading: *one pound sterling* □ *adjective* **1** of silver: of a certain standard of purity **2** worthy, good: *sterling qualities*

So called after the image of a small star that was impressed on medieval silver pennies

stern¹ *adjective* **1** looking or sounding angry or displeased **2** severe, strict,

harsh: *stern prison sentence* □ **sternly** *adverb*

stern² *noun* the back part of a ship

sternness *noun* the state or quality of being stern

steroid *noun* any of a number of substances, including certain hormones (*see also* **anabolic steroids**)

stertorous *adjective* making a snoring noise
① Comes from Latin *stertere* meaning 'to snore'

🖝 Do not confuse with: **stentorian**

stethoscope *noun* an instrument by means of which a doctor listens to someone's heartbeats, breathing *etc*

stevedore *noun* someone employed to load and unload ships

stew *verb* to cook by boiling slowly □ *noun* **1** a dish of stewed food, often containing meat and vegetables **2** *informal* a state of worry; a flap

steward *noun* **1** a flight attendant on an aircraft **2** someone who shows people to their seats at a meeting *etc* **3** an official at a race meeting *etc* **4** someone who manages an estate or farm for someone else

stewardess *noun* a female flight attendant (*also called:* **air hostess**)

stick *noun* **1** a long thin piece of wood; a branch or twig from a tree **2** a piece of wood shaped for a special purpose: *hockey-stick/ drumstick* **3** a long piece (*eg* of rhubarb) □ *verb* **1** to push or thrust (something): *stick the knife in your belt* **2** to fix with glue *etc*: *I'll stick the pieces back together* **3** to be or become caught, fixed or held back: *stuck in the ditch* **4** to hold fast to, keep to (*eg* a decision)
□ **stick up for** to speak in defence of

stick *verb* ⇨ sticks, sticking, stuck

■ **Alternative words**: (verb, meanings 1 and 3) jam; (verb, meanings 2 and 4) adhere

sticking-plaster *noun* a kind of tape with a sticky surface, used to protect slight cuts *etc*

stick-in-the-mud *noun* someone who is against new ideas, change *etc*

stickleback *noun* a type of small river-fish with prickles on its back

stickler *noun* someone who attaches great importance to a particular (often small) matter: *stickler for punctuation*

sticky *adjective* 1 clinging closely (like glue, treacle *etc*) 2 covered with something sticky 3 difficult: *a sticky problem* □ **stickiness** *noun*

■ **Alternative words**: (meanings 1 and 2) adhesive

stiff *adjective* 1 not easily bent or moved 2 of a mixture, dough *etc*: thick, not easily stirred 3 cold and distant in manner 4 hard, difficult: *stiff examination* 5 severe: *stiff penalty* 6 strong: *stiff drink*

stiffen *verb* to make or become stiff

stifle *verb* 1 to suffocate 2 to put out (flames) 3 to keep back (tears, a yawn *etc*)

stifling *adjective* very hot and stuffy

stigma *noun* 1 (*plural* **stigmata**) a mark of disgrace 2 (*plural* **stigmas**) in a flower, the top of the pistil

stigmatize *verb* to mark, describe as something bad: *stigmatized for life*

stile *noun* a step or set of steps for climbing over a wall or fence

stiletto *noun* (*plural* **stilettos**) 1 a dagger, or a type of instrument, with a narrow blade 2 (a shoe with) a stiletto heel

stiletto heel a high, thin heel on a shoe

still *adjective* 1 not moving 2 calm, without wind; quiet 3 of drinks: not fizzy □ *verb* to make calm or quiet □ *adverb* 1 up to the present time or the time spoken of: *it was still there* 2 even so, nevertheless: *it's difficult but we must still try* 3 even: *still more people* □ *noun* an apparatus for distilling spirits (*eg* whisky)

stillborn *adjective* of a child: dead at birth

still life a picture of something that is not living (as a bowl of fruit *etc*)

stillness *noun* the state of being still

stilted *adjective* stiff, not natural

stilts *noun plural* 1 long poles with footrests on which someone may walk clear of the ground 2 tall poles (*eg* to support a house built above water)

stimulant *noun* something which makes a part of the body more active or which makes you feel livelier

stimulate *verb* 1 to make more active 2 to encourage 3 to excite

stimulus *noun* (*plural* **stimuli**) 1 something that brings on a reaction in a living thing 2 something that rouses (someone *etc*) to action or greater effort

sting *noun* 1 the part of some animals and plants (*eg* the wasp, the nettle) which can prick the skin and cause pain or irritation 2 the act of piercing with a sting 3 the wound, swelling or pain caused by a sting □ *verb* 1 to pierce with a sting or ... cause pain like that of a sting 2 to be painful, smart: *made his eyes sting* 3 to hurt the feelings of: *stung by his words*

sting *verb* ⇨ stings, stinging, stung

stingy (pronounced **stin**-ji) *adjective* mean, not generous □ **stinginess** *noun*

stink *noun* a bad smell □ *verb* to give out a bad smell

stink *verb* ⇨ stinks, stinking, stank or stunk, stunk

stint *verb* to allow (someone) very little: *don't stint on ...* □ *noun* 1 limit: *praise without stint* 2 a fixed amount of work: *my daily stint*

stipend *noun* pay, salary, especially of a parish minister

stipple *verb* to paint or mark with tiny dots from a brush

stipulate *verb* to state as a condition (of doing something)

stipulation *noun* something stipulated, a condition

stir *verb* 1 to set (liquid) in motion, especially with a spoon *etc* moved circularly 2 to move slightly: *he stirred in his sleep* 3 to arouse (a person, a feeling *etc*) □ *noun* disturbance, fuss □ **stir up** to rouse, cause (*eg* trouble)

stir *verb* ⇨ stirs, stirring, stirred

stirring *adjective* exciting

stirrup *noun* a metal loop hung from a

horse's saddle as a support for the rider's foot

stitch *noun* (*plural* **stitches**) **1** the loop made in a thread, wool *etc* by a needle in sewing or knitting **2** a sharp, sudden pain in your side □ *verb* to put stitches in, sew

stoat *noun* a type of small fierce animal similar to a weasel, sometimes called an ermine when in its white winter fur

stock *noun* **1** family, race: *of ancient stock* **2** goods in a shop, warehouse *etc* **3** the capital of a business company divided into shares **4** the animals of a farm (*also called*: **livestock**) **5** liquid (used for soup) obtained by boiling meat, bones *etc* **6** a type of scented garden flower **7** the handle of a whip, rifle *etc* **8** **stocks** *historical* a wooden frame, with holes for the ankles and wrists, in which criminals *etc* were fastened as a punishment **9** **stocks** the wooden framework upon which a ship is supported when being built □ *verb* **1** to keep a supply of (for sale) **2** to supply (a farm with animals *etc*) □ *adjective* **1** usual, known by everyone: *a stock joke* **2** usually stocked (by a shop *etc*) □ **take stock of** to form an opinion or estimation about (a situation *etc*)

stockade *noun* a fence of strong posts set up round an area or building for defence

stockbroker *noun* someone who buys and sell shares in business companies on behalf of others

stock exchange 1 a place where stocks and shares are bought and sold **2** an association of people who do this

stocking *noun* a close-fitting covering in a knitted fabric (wool, nylon *etc*) for the leg and foot

stock market the stock exchange; dealings in stocks and shares

stockpile *noun* a store, a reserve supply □ *verb* to build up a store

stock-still *adjective* perfectly still

stocktaking *noun* a regular check of the goods in a shop or warehouse

stocky *adjective* short and stout □ **stockiness** *noun*

stodgy *adjective* **1** of food: heavy, not easily digested **2** of a person, book *etc*: dull □ **stodginess** *noun*

stoic *noun* someone who bears pain, hardship *etc* without showing any sign of feeling it

stoical *adjective* accepting pain, hardship *etc* without showing any sign of feeling it

stoicism *noun* the bearing of pain *etc* patiently

stoke *verb* to put coal, wood, or other fuel on (a fire)

stole[1] *noun* a length of silk, linen or fur worn over the shoulders

stole[2] *and* **stolen** *see* **steal**

stolid *adjective* of someone *etc*: dull; not easily excited □ **stolidly** *adverb*

stolidity *noun* being stolid

stomach *noun* **1** the bag-like part of the body into which the food passes when swallowed **2** desire or courage (for something): *no stomach for a fight* □ *verb* to put up with, bear: *can't stomach her rudeness*

stomp *verb* to stamp the feet, especially noisily

stone *noun* **1** the material of which rocks are composed **2** a (small) loose piece of this **3** a piece of this shaped for a certain purpose: *tombstone* **4** a precious stone (*eg* a diamond) **5** the hard shell around the seed of some fruits (*eg* peach, cherry) **6** a measure of weight (14lb, 6.35 kilogrammes) **7** a piece of hard material that forms in the kidney, bladder *etc*, causing pain □ *verb* **1** to throw stones at **2** to take the stones out of fruit □ *adjective* made of stone □ **a stone's throw** a very short distance □ **leave no stone unturned** to do everything possible

Stone Age human culture before the use of metal

stone-cold *adjective* very cold

stone-dead *adjective* completely dead

stone-deaf *adjective* completely deaf

stony *adjective* **1** like stone **2** covered with stones **3** hard, cold in manner: *stony look*

stood *past form of* **stand**

stooge *noun* someone who is used by

another to do a (usually humble or unpleasant) job

stookie *noun, Scottish* a plaster-cast for a broken limb

stool *noun* a seat without a back

stoop *verb* 1 to bend the body forward and downward 2 to be low or wicked enough to do a certain thing: *I wouldn't stoop to stealing* □ *noun* 1 the act of stooping 2 a forward bend of the body

stop *verb* 1 to bring to a halt: *stop the car* 2 to prevent from doing: *stop him from working* 3 to put an end to: *stop this nonsense* 4 to come to an end: *the rain has stopped* 5 **stop something up** to block (a hole *etc*) □ *noun* 1 the state of being stopped 2 a place where something stops 3 a full stop 4 a knob on an organ which brings certain pipes into use

stop *verb* ⇨ stops, stopping, stopped

stopcock *noun* a tap for controlling the flow of liquid through a pipe

stopgap *noun* something which is used in an emergency until something better is found

stoppage *noun* 1 something which blocks up (*eg* a tube or a passage in the body) 2 a halt (*eg* in work in a factory)

stopper *noun* something that stops up an opening (especially in the neck of a bottle, jar *etc*)

stop press a space in a newspaper for news put in at the last minute

stopwatch *noun* a watch that can be stopped and started, used in timing races

storage *noun* 1 the act of storing 2 the state of being stored: *our furniture is in storage*

store *noun* 1 a supply (*eg* of goods) from which things are taken when needed 2 a place where goods are kept 3 a shop 4 a collected amount or number □ *verb* to put aside for future use □ **in store for** awaiting: *trouble in store* □ **set (great) store by** to value highly

storey *noun* (*plural* **storeys**) all that part of a building on the same floor

☛ Do not confuse with: **story**

stork *noun* a wading bird with a long bill, neck and legs

storm *noun* 1 a sudden burst of bad weather (especially with heavy rain, lightning, thunder, high wind) 2 a violent outbreak (*eg* of anger) □ *verb* 1 to be in a fury 2 to rain, blow *etc* violently 3 to attack (a stronghold *etc*) violently □ **go down a storm** to be popular or well received □ **storm in a teacup** a great fuss over nothing

story *noun* (*plural* **stories**) an account of an event or events, real or imaginary

☛ Do not confuse with: **storey**

stout *adjective* 1 fat, stocky 2 brave: *stout resistance* 3 strong: *stout walking-stick* □ *noun* a strong, dark-coloured beer

stout-hearted *adjective* having a brave heart

stoutness *noun* being stout

stove *noun* an apparatus using coal, gas or electricity *etc*, used for heating, cooking *etc* □ *verb, past form of* **stave**

stow *verb* 1 to pack or put away 2 to fill, pack

stowaway *noun* someone who hides in a ship in order to travel without paying a fare

straddle *verb* 1 to stand or walk with legs apart 2 to sit with one leg on each side of (*eg* a chair or horse)

straggle *verb* 1 to wander from the line of a march *etc* 2 to lag behind 3 to grow or spread beyond the intended limits: *his long beard straggled over his chest*

straggler *noun* someone who straggles

straggly *adjective* spread out untidily

straight *adjective* 1 not bent or curved: *a straight line* 2 direct, frank, honest: *a straight answer* 3 in the proper position or order: *your tie isn't straight* 4 of a hanging picture *etc*: placed level with ceiling or floor 5 without anything added: *a straight vodka* 6 expressionless: *he kept a straight face* □ *adverb* 1 by the shortest way, directly: *straight across the desert* 2 at once, without

delay: *I came straight here after work* **3** fairly, frankly: *he's not playing straight with you* □ *noun* (**the straight**) the straight part of a racecourse *etc* □ **straight away** immediately
Ⓛ Comes from Old English *streht*

☛ Do not confuse with: **strait**

straighten *verb* to make straight

straightforward *adjective* **1** without any difficulties **2** honest, frank

strain *verb* **1** to hurt (a muscle or other part of the body) by overworking or misusing it **2** to work or use to the fullest: *he strained his ears to hear the whisper* **3** to make a great effort: *he strained to reach the rope* **4** to stretch too far, to the point of breaking (a person's patience *etc*) **5** to separate liquid from a mixture of liquids and solids by passing it through a sieve □ *noun* **1** the act of straining **2** a hurt to a muscle *etc* caused by straining it **3** (the effect of) too much work, worry *etc*: *suffering from strain* **4** too great a demand: *a strain on my patience* **5** manner: *they grumbled on in the same strain for hours* **6** a streak: *a strain of selfishness* **7** a tune **8** a kind, breed: *a strain of fowls*

strained *adjective* **1** not natural, done with effort: *a strained conversation* **2** unfriendly: *strained relations*

strainer *noun* a sieve

strait *noun* **1** a narrow strip of sea between two pieces of land **2 straits** difficulties, hardships: *dire straits*
Ⓛ Comes from Latin *strictus* meaning 'straight' or 'narrow'

☛ Do not confuse with: **straight**

straitened *adjective* poor and needy

straitjacket *noun* a jacket with long sleeves tied behind to prevent a violent or insane person from using their arms

straitlaced *adjective* strict in attitude and behaviour

stramash *noun, Scottish* a fuss, a commotion

strand *noun* **1** a length of something soft and fine (*eg* hair, thread) **2** *old* the shore of a sea or lake

stranded *adjective* **1** of a ship: run aground on the shore **2** left helpless without money or friends

strange *adjective* **1** unusual, odd: *a strange look on his face* **2** not known, seen, heard *etc* before, unfamiliar: *the method was strange to me* **3** not accustomed (to) **4** foreign: *a strange country* □ **strangely** *adverb*

■ Alternative words: (meaning 1) peculiar, curious, bizarre, funny, perplexing, unexplained; (meaning 2) new, unknown, alien

stranger *noun* **1** someone who is unknown to you **2** a visitor □ **a stranger to** someone who is quite unfamiliar with: *a stranger to hard work*

strangle *verb* **1** to kill by gripping or squeezing the throat tightly **2** to keep in, prevent oneself from giving (*eg* a scream, a sigh) **3** to stop the growth of

stranglehold *noun* a tight control over something which prevents it from escaping, growing *etc*

strangulate *verb* to strangle, constrict

strangulation *noun* being strangled

strap *noun* a narrow strip of leather, cloth *etc* used to hold things in place or together *etc* □ *verb* **1** to bind or fasten with a strap *etc* **2** to beat with a strap

strap *verb* ⇨ strap**s**, strap**ping**, strap**ped**

strapping *adjective* tall and strong: *strapping young man*

stratagem *noun* a cunning act, meant to deceive and outwit an enemy

strategic *adjective* **1** of strategy **2** done according to a strategy: *a strategic retreat* **3** giving an advantage: *a strategic position*

strategist *noun* someone who plans military operations

strategy *noun* (*plural* **strategies**) the art of guiding, forming or carrying out a plan

stratification *noun* **1** the formation of strata **2** a stratified condition

stratosphere *noun* the layer of the earth's atmosphere between 10 and 60 kilometres above the earth

stratum *noun* (*plural* **strata**) **1** a layer of rock or soil **2** a level of society

straw *noun* **1** the stalk on which corn grows **2** a paper or plastic tube for sucking up a drink

strawberry *noun* a type of small, juicy, red fruit or the low creeping plant which bears it

strawberry blonde a woman with reddish blond hair

stray *verb* **1** to wander **2** to lose your way, become separated (from companions *etc*) □ *adjective* **1** wandering, lost **2** happening *etc* here and there: *a stray example* □ *noun* a wandering animal which has been abandoned or lost

streak *noun* **1** a line or strip different in colour from that which surrounds it **2** a smear of dirt, polish *etc* **3** a flash (*eg* of lightning) **4** a trace of some quality in one's character: *a streak of selfishness* □ *verb* **1** to mark with streaks **2** *informal* to move very fast

streaked *adjective* having streaks

streaky *adjective* marked with streaks □ **streakiness** *noun*

stream *noun* **1** a flow (of water, air, light *etc*) **2** a small river, a brook **3** any steady flow of people or things: *a stream of traffic* □ *verb* to flow or pour out

streamer *noun* **1** a long strip, usually of paper, used for decorating rooms *etc* (especially at Christmas) **2** a narrow flag blowing in the wind

streamline *verb* **1** to shape (a vehicle *etc*) so that it may cut through the air or water as easily as possible **2** to make more efficient: *we've streamlined our methods of paying*

street *noun* a road lined with houses *etc* □ **streets ahead of** much better *etc* than □ **up someone's street** relating to their interests or abilities

street cred knowledge of current fashion, speech *etc*

strength *noun* **1** the state of being strong **2** an available number or force (of soldiers, volunteers *etc*) **3** an area of high performance or particular ability: *her greatest strength is her ability to listen to people* □ **on the strength of** encouraged by or counting on

■ **Alternative words**: (meaning 3) asset

strengthen *verb* to make, or become, strong or stronger

strenuous *adjective* performed with or needing great effort: *the plans met strenuous resistance/ squash is a strenuous game*

stress *noun* (*plural* **stresses**) **1** force, pressure, pull *etc* of one thing on another **2** physical or nervous pressure or strain: *the stress of modern life* **3** emphasis, importance **4** extra weight laid on a part of a word (as in **butter**) □ *verb* to put stress, pressure, emphasis or strain on

stretch *verb* **1** to draw out to greater length, or too far, or from one point to another: *don't stretch that elastic too far/ stretch a rope from post to post* **2** to be able to be drawn out to a greater length or width: *that material stretches* **3** to (cause to) exert (yourself): *the work stretched him to the full* **4** to hold (out) **5** to make (something, *eg* words, the law) appear to mean more than it does □ *noun* (*plural* **stretches**) **1** the act of stretching **2** the state of being stretched **3** a length in distance or time: *a stretch of bad road* □ **at a stretch** continuously: *working three hours at a stretch* □ **at full stretch** at the limit, using all resources

stretcher *noun* a light folding bed with handles for carrying the sick or wounded

strew *verb* **1** to scatter: *papers strewn over the floor* **2** to cover, sprinkle (with): *the floor was strewn with papers*

strew ⇨ strews, strewing, strewed, strewn or strewed

striated *adjective* streaked

stricken *adjective* **1** wounded **2** deeply affected (*eg* by illness) **3** struck

strict *adjective* **1** insisting on exact obedience to rules **2** exact: *the strict meaning of a word* **3** allowing no exception: *strict orders* **4** severe □ **strictly** *adverb*

stricture *noun* criticism, blame

stride *verb* **1** to walk with long steps **2** to take a long step **3** to walk over, along *etc* □ *noun* **1** a long step **2** the distance covered by a step **3** a step forward □ **take in your stride** to manage to do it easily

stride *verb* ⇨ strides, striding, strode, stridden

stridency *noun* a strident quality

strident *adjective* **1** of a sound: harsh, grating **2** forceful; assertive: *their demands for reform became more and more strident*

strife *noun* quarrelling; fighting

strike *verb* **1** to hit with force **2** to give, deliver **3** to knock: *to strike your head on the beam* **4** to attack: *the enemy struck at dawn* **5** to light (a match) **6** to make (a musical note) sound **7** of a clock: to sound (*eg* at ten o'clock with ten chimes) **8** (often **strike something off** or **out**) to cross it out, cancel it **9** to hit or discover suddenly: *strike oil* **10** to take a course: *he struck out across the fields* **11** to stop working (in support of a claim for more pay *etc*) **12** to give (someone) the impression of being: *did he strike you as lazy?* **13** to affect, impress: *I am struck by her beauty* **14** to make (an agreement *etc*) □ **strike camp** to take down tents □ **strike home 1** of a blow: to hit the point aimed at **2** of a remark: to have the intended effect □ **strike up 1** to begin to play or sing (a tune) **2** to begin (a friendship, conversation *etc*)

strike *verb* ⇨ strikes, striking, struck

striking *adjective* **1** noticeable: *a striking resemblance* **2** impressive

■ **Alternative words**: (meaning 2) arresting

string *noun* **1** a long narrow cord for binding, tying *etc* made of threads twisted together **2** a piece of wire or gut producing a note on a musical instrument **3 strings** the stringed instruments in an orchestra **4** a line of objects threaded together: *string of pearls* **5** a number of things coming one after another: *string of abuse* □ *verb* **1** to put on a string **2** to stretch out in a line □ **string along** to give false expectations to, deceive □ **string up** to hang

string ⇨ strings, stringing, strung

stringed *adjective* having strings

stringency *noun* strictness

stringent *adjective* strictly enforced: *stringent rules*

stringy *adjective* **1** like string **2** of meat: tough and fibrous

strip *noun* a long narrow piece (*eg* of paper) □ *verb* **1** to pull (off) in strips **2** to remove (*eg* leaves, fruit) from **3** to remove the clothes from **4** to deprive: *stripped of his disguise* **5** to make bare or empty: *strip the bed*

strip *verb* ⇨ strips, stripping, stripped

strip-cartoon *noun* a line of drawings which tell a story

stripe *noun* **1** a band of colour different from the background on which it lies **2** a blow with a whip or rod □ *verb* to make stripes on

stripling *noun* a growing youth

striptease *noun* an act in which a performer strips naked

stripy *adjective* patterned with stripes

strive *verb* **1** to try hard **2** *old* to fight

strive ⇨ strives, striving, strove, striven

strobe *noun* a light which produces a flickering beam

strode *past form of* **stride**

stroke *noun* **1** the act of striking **2** a blow (*eg* with a sword, whip) **3** something unexpected: *a stroke of good luck* **4** one movement (of a pen, an oar) **5** one chime of a clock **6** one complete movement of the arms and legs in swimming **7** a particular style of swimming: *breast stroke* **8** a way of striking the ball (*eg* in tennis, cricket) **9** an achievement **10** a sudden attack of illness causing paralysis □ *verb* to rub gently, especially as a sign of affection □ **at a stroke** in a single action or effort

stroll *verb* to walk slowly in a leisurely way □ *noun* a leisurely walk; an amble

strong *adjective* **1** not easily worn away: *strong cloth* **2** not easily defeated *etc* **3** forceful, not easily resisted: *strong wind* **4** very healthy and robust, with great muscular strength **5** forceful, commanding respect or obedience **6** of a smell, colour *etc*: striking, very noticeable **7** of a feeling: intense: *strong* dislike **8** in number: *a workforce 500 strong*

■ **Alternative words**: (meaning 1) tough, resilient, durable, robust, sturdy, stout; (meaning 4) muscular, lusty, strapping, burly, beefy, brawny, sinewy; (meaning 6) intense, deep, vivid, pungent; (meaning 7) intense, keen, ardent, vehement

stronghold *noun* a place built to withstand attack, a fortress

strongly *adverb* **1** in a strong way **2** to a strong degree: *strongly flavoured*

strong point something in which a person excels

■ **Alternative words**: asset

strop *noun* a strip of leather on which a razor is sharpened □ *verb* to sharpen a razor

strop *verb* ⇨ strop*s*, stropp*ing*, stropp*ed*

stroppy *adjective*, *informal* quarrelsome, disobedient, rowdy

strove *past form of* **strive**

struck *past form of* **strike**

structural *adjective* of or relating to structure, or a basic structure or framework □ **structurally** *adverb*

structure *noun* **1** a building; a framework **2** the way the parts of anything are arranged: *the structure of the story*

struggle *verb* **1** to try hard (to do something) **2** to twist and fight to escape **3** to fight (with or against someone) **4** to move with difficulty: *struggling through the mud* □ *noun* **1** a great effort **2** a fight

strum *verb* to play (a guitar *etc*) in a relaxed way

strum ⇨ strum*s*, strumm*ing*, strumm*ed*

strung *past form of* **string** □ **highly strung** easily excited or agitated

strut *verb* to walk in a proud manner □ *noun* **1** a proud way of walking **2** a bar *etc* which supports something

strut *verb* ⇨ strut*s*, strutt*ing*, strutt*ed*

strychnine *noun* a bitter, poisonous drug

stub *noun* a small stump (*eg* of a pencil, cigarette) □ *verb* **1** to put out, (*eg* a cigarette) by pressure against something **2** to knock (your toe) painfully against something

stub *verb* ⇨ stub*s*, stubb*ing*, stubb*ed*

stubble *noun* **1** the short ends of the stalks of corn left after it is cut **2** a short growth of beard

stubborn *adjective* **1** unwilling to give way, obstinate **2** of resistance *etc*: strong, determined **3** difficult to manage or deal with □ **stubbornly** *adverb* □ **stubbornness** *noun*

■ **Alternative words**: obstinate; (meanings 1 and 2) obdurate

stubby *adjective* short, thick and strong: *stubby fingers*

stucco *noun* (*plural* **stuccos**) **1** a kind of plaster used for covering walls, moulding ornaments *etc* **2** work done in stucco

stuck *past form of* **stick**

stud *noun* **1** a nail with a large head **2** a decorative knob on a surface **3** a button with two heads for fastening a collar **4** a collection of horses kept for breeding □ *verb* **1** to cover or fit with studs **2** to sprinkle thickly (with): *the meadow is studded with flowers*

student *noun* someone who studies, especially at college, university *etc*

studied *adjective* **1** done on purpose, intentional: *a studied insult* **2** too careful, not natural: *a studied smile*

studio *noun* (*plural* **studios**) **1** the workshop of an artist or photographer **2** a building or place in which cinema films are made **3** a room from which television or radio programmes are broadcast

studious *adjective* **1** studying carefully and much **2** careful: *his studious avoidance of quarrels* □ **studiously** *adverb*

study *verb* **1** to gain knowledge of (a subject) by reading, experiment *etc* **2** to look carefully at **3** to consider carefully (*eg* a problem) □ *noun* (*plural*

studies) 1 the gaining of knowledge of a subject: *the study of history* **2** a room where someone reads and writes **3** a piece of music which is meant to develop the skill of the player **4** a work of art done as an exercise, or to try out ideas for a later work

study *verb* ⇨ stud*ies*, study*ing*, stud*ied*

stuff *noun* **1** the material of which anything is made **2** cloth, fabric **3** substance or material of any kind: *what is that stuff all over the wall?* □ *verb* **1** to pack full **2** to fill the skin of (a dead animal) to preserve it **3** to fill (a prepared bird) with stuffing before cooking □ **stuffed shirt** an inflexible, old-fashioned person □ **get stuffed** *slang* get lost, go away

stuffing *noun* **1** feathers, scraps of material *etc* used to stuff a cushion, chair *etc* **2** breadcrumbs, onions *etc* packed inside a fowl or other meat and cooked with it

stuffy *adjective* **1** full of stale air, badly ventilated **2** *informal* dull, having old-fashioned ideas □ **stuffily** *adverb*

stultify *verb* to dull the mind, make stupid

stultify ⇨ stultif*ies*, stultify*ing*, stultif*ied*

stumble *verb* **1** to trip in walking **2** to walk unsteadily, as if blind **3** to make mistakes or hesitate in speaking **4 stumble on something** to find it by chance □ *noun* the act of stumbling

stumbling block a difficulty in the way of a plan or of progress

stump *noun* **1** the part of a tree, leg, tooth *etc* left after the main part has been cut away **2** *cricket* one of the three wooden stakes which make up a wicket □ *verb*, *cricket* **1** to put out (a batsman) by touching the stumps with the ball **2** to puzzle completely **3** to walk stiffly or heavily □ **stump up** *informal* to pay up

stumpy *adjective* short and thick

stun *verb* **1** to knock senseless (by a blow *etc*) **2** to surprise or shock very greatly: *stunned by the news*

stun *verb* ⇨ stun*s*, stun*ning*, stun*ned*

stung *past form of* **sting**

stunk *past form & past participle of* **stink**

stunt *noun* **1** a daring trick **2** something done to attract attention: *a publicity stunt* □ *verb* to stop the growth of

stunted *adjective* small and badly shaped

stup- *prefix* forms words related to the idea of being knocked senseless
ⓞ Comes from Latin *stupere* meaning 'to be stunned'

stupefaction *noun* stupefying or being stupefied

stupefy *verb* **1** to make stupid, deaden the feelings of **2** to astonish

stupefy ⇨ stupef*ies*, stupefy*ing*, stupef*ied*

stupendous *adjective* wonderful, amazing (*eg* because of size and power)

stupid *adjective* **1** foolish: *a stupid thing to do* **2** dull, slow at learning **3** stupefied (*eg* from lack of sleep)

■ **Alternative words**: (meaning 1) silly, ill-advised, foolhardy, inane, puerile, mindless

stupidity *noun* the quality or condition of being stupid

stupor *noun* the state of being only partly conscious

sturdy *adjective* strong, well built; healthy □ **sturdily** *adverb*

sturgeon *noun* a type of large fish from which caviare is taken

stutter *verb* to speak in a halting, jerky way; stammer □ *noun* a stammer

sty¹ *noun* (*plural* **sties**) a pen in which pigs are kept

sty² or **stye** *noun* (*plural* **sties** or **styes**) an inflamed swelling on the eyelid

style *noun* **1** manner of acting, writing, speaking *etc* **2** fashion: *in the style of the late 19th century* **3** an air of elegance **4** the middle part of the pistil of a flower □ *verb* to call, name: *styling himself 'Lord John'* □ **in style** with no expense or effort spared

stylish *adjective* smart, elegant, fashionable

stylized *adjective* elaborate, especially creating an impression of unnaturalness

stylus *noun* (*plural* **styluses**) a needle for a record-player

stymie (*pronounced* stai-mi) *verb, Scottish* to block, impede

> Originally a golfing term for an opponent's ball in the way of your own

suave (*pronounced* swahv) *adjective* of a person: superficially polite and sophisticated, smooth

sub- *prefix* **1** under, below **2** less than **3** lower in rank or importance
  Ⓠ Comes from Latin *sub* meaning 'under' or 'near'

subaltern (*pronounced* sub-al-ten) *noun* an officer in the army under the rank of captain

subconscious *noun* the contents of the mind of which someone is not themselves aware □ *adjective* of the subconscious, not conscious or aware: *a subconscious desire for fame*

subcontract *verb* to give a contract for (work forming part of a larger contract) to another company

subculture *noun* an identifiable group within a larger culture or group

subcutaneous *adjective* beneath the skin

subdivide *verb* to divide into smaller parts

subdivision *noun* a part made by subdividing

subdue *verb* **1** to conquer (an enemy *etc*) **2** to keep under control (*eg* a desire) **3** to make less bright (*eg* a colour, a light) **4** to make quieter: *he seemed subdued after the fight*

subject *adjective* (*pronounced* sub-jekt) **1** under the power of another: *a subject nation* **2 subject to something** liable to suffer from it (*eg* colds) **3 subject to something** depending on it: *subject to your approval* □ *noun* (*pronounced* sub-jekt) **1** someone under the power of another: *the king's subjects* **2** a member of a nation with a monarchy: *a British subject* **3** something or someone spoken about, studied *etc* **4** *grammar* the word

in a sentence or clause which stands for the person or thing doing the action of the verb (*eg cat* is the subject in 'the *cat* drank the milk') □ *verb* (*pronounced* sub-**jekt** – often **subject someone to something**) to force them to submit to it

subjection *noun* the act of subjecting or the state of being subjected

subjective *adjective* based on personal feelings, thoughts *etc*, not impartial (*contrasted with*: **objective**)

subjectivity *noun* being subjective

subjugate *verb* to bring under your power; make obedient

subjunctive *adjective, grammar* of a verb: in a form which indicates possibility *etc, eg* 'were' in: *If I were you* □ *noun* a subjunctive form of a verb

sublet *verb* to let out (rented property) to another person, *eg* while the original tenant is away

sublime *adjective* very noble, great or grand

subliminal *adjective* working below the level of consciousness: *subliminal messages*

submachine-gun *noun* a light machine-gun fired from the hip or shoulder

submarine *noun* a type of ship which can travel under water □ *adjective* under the surface of the sea

submerge *verb* to cover with water; sink

submergence or **submersion** *noun* submerging or being submerged

submersible *noun* a boat that can operate under water

submission *noun* **1** the act of submitting **2** readiness to yield, meekness **3** an idea, statement *etc* offered for consideration

submissive *adjective* meek, yielding easily

submit *verb* **1** to give in, yield **2** to place (a matter) before someone for making a judgement

> **submit** ⇨ **submit**s, **submit**t*ing*, **submit**t*ed*

subordinate *adjective* (*pronounced* su-baw-din-*at* – often **subordinate to someone**) lower in rank or importance than them □ *noun* (*pronounced* su-**baw**-din-*at*) someone who is subordinate □ *verb* (*pronounced* su-**baw**-din-eit – **subordinate one person** or **thing to another**) to consider them as being of less importance

subordination *noun* subordinating or being subordinated

suborn *verb* to persuade (someone) to do something illegal, especially by bribery

subpoena (*pronounced* su-**pee**-na) *noun* an order for someone to appear in court □ *verb* to order to appear in court

subscribe *verb* **1** to make a contribution (especially of money) towards a charity **2** to promise to take and pay for a number of issues of a magazine *etc* **3 subscribe to something** to agree with (an idea, statement *etc*)

subscription *noun* a payment for *eg* a club membership fee or a number of issues of a magazine for a given period

subsequent *adjective* following, coming after

subservience *noun* a subservient state

subservient *adjective* weak-willed, ready to do as you are told

subside *verb* **1** to settle down, sink lower **2** of noise *etc*: to get less and less

subsidence *noun* a sinking down, especially into the ground

subsidiarity *noun* **1** the state of being subsidiary **2** the concept of a central governing body permitting its member states or branches to make their own decisions on certain local issues

subsidiary *adjective* **1** acting as a help **2** of less importance **3** of a company: controlled by another company

subsidize *verb* to give money as a help

subsidy *noun* (*plural* **subsidies**) money paid by a government *etc* to help an industry

subsist *verb* **1** to exist **2 subsist on something** to live on (a kind of food *etc*)

subsistence *noun* **1** existence **2** means or necessities for survival

subsoil *noun* the layer of the earth just below the surface soil

substance *noun* **1** a material that can be seen and felt: *glue is a sticky substance* **2** general meaning (of a talk, essay *etc*) **3** thickness, solidity **4** wealth, property: *a woman of substance*

substantial *adjective* **1** solid, strong **2** large: *a substantial building* **3** able to be seen and felt **4** in the main, but not in detail: *substantial agreement*

substantially *adverb* for the most part: *substantially the same*

substantiate *verb* to give proof of, or evidence for

substitute *verb*: **substitute something** or **substitute one thing for another** to put in place or instead of □ *noun* someone or thing used instead of another

substitution *noun* **1** the process of substituting or being substituted **2** something that is substituted

subterfuge *noun* a cunning trick to get out of a difficulty *etc*

subterranean *adjective* found under the ground

subtitle *noun* **1** a second additional title of a book *etc* **2** a translation of a foreign-language film, appearing at the bottom of the screen

subtle (*pronounced* **su**-tl) *adjective* **1** difficult to describe or explain: *a subtle difference* **2** cunning: *by a subtle means* □ **subtly** *adverb*

subtlety (pronounced **su**-tl-ti) *noun* (*plural* **subtleties**) the quality of being subtle

subtotal *noun* a total of one set of figures within a larger group

subtract *verb* **1** to take away (a part from) **2** to take away (one number from another)

subtraction *noun* the process of subtracting

suburb *noun* a residential area on the outskirts of a town

suburban *adjective* of suburbs

suburbia *noun* the suburbs

subversive *adjective* likely to overthrow (government, discipline *etc*)

subway *noun* **1** an underground crossing for pedestrians *etc* **2** an underground railway

succeed *verb* **1** succeed in something to manage to do what you have been trying to do **2** to get on well **3** to take the place of, follow **4** (often **succeed to**) to follow in order (to the throne *etc*)

success *noun* (*plural* **successes**) **1** the achievement of something you have been trying to do **2** someone who succeeds **3** something that turns out well

successful *adjective* **1** having achieved what was aimed at **2** having achieved wealth, importance *etc* **3** turning out as planned

succession *noun* **1** the act of following after **2** the right of becoming the next holder (of a throne *etc*) **3** a number of things coming one after the other: *a succession of failures* □ **in succession** one after another

successive *adjective* following one after the other

successor *noun* someone who comes after, follows in a post *etc*

succinct *adjective* in a few words, brief, concise: *a succinct reply*

succour *verb* to help in time of distress □ *noun* help

succulent *adjective* **1** juicy **2** of a plant: having thick, juicy leaves or stems

succumb *verb* to yield (to): *succumbed to temptation*

such *adjective* **1** of a kind previously mentioned: *such things are difficult to find* **2** similar: *doctors, nurses and such people* **3** so great: *his excitement was such that he shouted out loud* **4** used for emphasis: *it's such a disappointment!* □ *pronoun* thing, people *etc* of a kind already mentioned: *such as these are not to be trusted* □ **as such** by itself □ **such as** of the same kind as

such-and-such *adjective* & *pronoun* any given (person or thing): *such-and-such a book*

suck *verb* **1** to draw into the mouth **2** to draw milk from with the mouth **3** to hold in the mouth and lick hard (*eg* a sweet) **4** (often **suck up** or **in**) to draw in, absorb □ *noun* **1** a sucking action **2** the act of sucking

sucker *noun* **1** a side shoot rising from the root of a plant **2** a part of an animal's body by which it sticks to objects **3** a pad (of rubber *etc*) which can stick to a surface **4** *informal* someone easily fooled

suckle *verb* of a woman or female animal: to give milk from the breast or teat

suckling *noun* a baby or young animal which still sucks its mother's milk

suction *noun* **1** the act of sucking **2** the process of reducing the air pressure, and so producing a vacuum, on the surface or between surfaces

sudden *adjective* happening all at once without being expected: *a sudden attack* □ **suddenly** *adverb* □ **suddenness** *noun*

suds *noun plural* frothy, soapy water

sue *verb* to start a law case against

suede (*pronounced* sweid) *noun* a kind of leather with a soft, dull surface

suet *noun* a kind of hard animal fat

suffer *verb* **1** to feel pain or punishment **2** to bear, endure **3** *old* to allow **4** to go through, undergo (a change *etc*)

sufferance *noun*: **on sufferance** allowed or tolerated but not really wanted

suffering *noun* pain or distress

suffice *verb* to be enough, or good enough

sufficient *adjective* enough □ **sufficiently** *adverb*

■ **Alternative words**: adequate

suffix *noun* (*plural* **suffixes**) a small part added to the end of a word to make another word, such as *-ness* to *good* to make *goodness, -ly* to *quick* to make *quickly etc*

suffocate *verb* **1** to kill by preventing the breathing of **2** to die from lack of air **3** to feel unable to breathe freely: *suffocating in this heat*

■ **Alternative words**: (meanings 1 and 2) asphyxiate

suffocation *noun* suffocating or being suffocated

suffrage *noun* **1** a vote **2** the right to vote

suffuse *verb* to spread over

sugar *noun* a sweet substance obtained mostly from sugar-cane and sugar-beet □ *verb* to mix or sprinkle with sugar

sugar-beet *noun* a vegetable whose root yields sugar

sugar-cane *noun* a tall grass from whose juice sugar is obtained

sugar daddy an older man who lavishes money on a younger woman in exchange for companionship and, often, sex

sugary *adjective* **1** tasting of sugar **2** too sweet

suggest *verb* **1** to put forward, propose (an idea *etc*) **2** to put into the mind, hint

suggestible *adjective* easily influenced by suggestions

suggestion *noun* **1** an act of suggesting **2** an idea put forward **3** a slight trace: *a suggestion of anger in her voice*

suggestive *adjective* **1** that suggests something particular, especially sexually improper: *suggestive remarks* **2** **suggestive of something** giving the idea of it: *suggestive of mental illness*

suicidal *adjective* **1** of or considering suicide **2** likely to cause your death or ruin: *suicidal action*

suicide *noun* **1** the taking of your own life **2** someone who kills themselves

suit *noun* **1** a set of clothes to be worn together **2** a case in a law court **3** *old* a request for permission to court a woman **4** one of the four divisions (spades, hearts, diamonds, clubs) of playing-cards □ *verb* **1** to be convenient or suitable for: *the climate suits me* **2** to look well on: *that dress suits you* **3** **suit to** to make fitting or suitable for: *suited his words to the occasion* □ **follow suit** to do just as someone else has done

suitability *noun* being suitable

suitable *adjective* **1** fitting the purpose **2** just what is wanted, convenient

suitcase *noun* a travelling case for carrying clothes *etc*

suite (*pronounced* sweet) *noun* **1** a number of things in a set, *eg* rooms, furniture, pieces of music **2** a group of attendants for an important person

suitor *noun* a man who tries to gain the love of a woman

sulk *verb* to keep silent because of being displeased □ **the sulks** a fit of sulking

sulky *adjective* sulking; inclined to sulk

sullen *adjective* angry and silent, sulky □ **sullenness** *noun*

sully *verb* to make less pure, dirty
sully ⇨ sullies, sullying, sullied

sulphur *noun* a yellow substance found in the ground which gives off a choking smell when burnt, used in matches, gunpowder *etc*

sulphuric acid a powerful acid much used in industry

sultan *noun* **1** *historical* the head of the Turkish Ottoman empire **2** an Islamic ruler

sultana *noun* **1** a sultan's wife **2** a light-coloured raisin

sultry *adjective* **1** of weather: very hot and close **2** passionate, steamy

sum *noun* **1** the amount made by two or more things added together **2** a quantity of money **3** a problem in arithmetic **4** the general meaning (of something said or written) □ **sum up** to give the main points of (a discussion, evidence in a trial *etc*)

summarize *verb* to state briefly, make a summary of

summary *noun* (*plural* **summaries**) a shortened form (of a story, statement *etc*) giving only the main points □ *adjective* **1** short, brief **2** done without wasting time or words □ **summarily** *adverb*: *he was summarily dismissed*

summer *noun* the warmest season of the year □ *adjective* of or in summer

summerhouse *noun* a small house in a garden for sitting in

summit *noun* the highest point of a hill *etc*

summit conference a conference between heads of governments

summon *verb* **1** to order (someone) to come to you, appear in a court of law *etc* **2 summon up** to gather up (courage, strength *etc*)

summons *noun* (*plural* **summonses**) an order to appear in court

sumo *noun* a Japanese form of wrestling

sump *noun* **1** part of a motor-engine which contains the oil **2** a small drainage pit

sumptuous *adjective* costly, splendid

sun *noun* **1** the round body in the sky which gives light and heat to the earth **2** sunshine □ *verb* **sun yourself** to lie in the sunshine, sunbathe

> **sun** *verb* ⇨ sun*s*, sun*ning*, sun*ned*

sunbathe *verb* to lie or sit in the sun to acquire a suntan

sunbeam *noun* a ray of light from the sun

sunburn *noun* a burning or redness caused by over-exposure to the sun

sunburned or **sunburnt** *adjective* affected by sunburn

sundae *noun* a sweet dish of ice-cream served with fruit, syrup *etc*

Sunday *noun* the first day of the week, the Christian Sabbath

sunder *verb*, *old* to separate, part

sundial *noun* an instrument for telling the time from the shadow of a rod on its surface cast by the sun

sundries *noun plural* odds and ends

sundry *adjective* several, various: *sundry articles for sale*

sunflower *noun* a large yellow flower with petals like rays of the sun

sung *past participle* of **sing**

sunglasses *noun plural* spectacles with tinted lenses that shield the eyes from sunlight

sunk *adjective* **1** on a lower level than the surroundings; sunken **2** *informal* defeated, done for

sunken *adjective* **1** that has been sunk **2** of cheeks *etc*: hollow

sunlight *noun* the light from the sun

sunlit *adjective* lighted up by the sun

sunny *adjective* **1** full of sunshine **2** cheerful: *sunny nature*

sunrise *noun* the rising of the sun in the morning

sunset *noun* the setting of the sun in the evening

sunshine *noun* **1** bright sunlight **2** cheerfulness

sunstroke *noun* a serious illness caused by over-exposure to very hot sunshine

suntan *noun* a browning of the skin caused by exposure to the sun

sup *verb* to eat or drink in small mouthfuls

> **sup** ⇨ sup*s*, sup*ping*, sup*ped*

super *adjective*, *informal* extremely good

super- *prefix* above, beyond, very, too: *superannuate* (= make someone retire because they are 'beyond the years')/ *superhuman* (= beyond what a normal person is capable of)
ⓘ Comes from Latin *super* meaning 'above'

superannuate *verb* to make (someone) retire from their job because of old age

superannuation *noun* a pension given to someone retired

superb *adjective* magnificent, very fine, excellent: *a superb view*

supercilious *adjective* looking down on others, haughty

superficial *adjective* **1** of a wound: affecting the surface of the skin only, not deep **2** not thorough or detailed: *superficial interest* **3** apparent at first glance, not actual: *superficial likeness* **4** of a person: not capable of deep thoughts or feelings □ **superficially** *adverb*
ⓘ Comes from Latin *superficies* meaning 'surface'

> ◆ Do not confuse: **superficial** and **superfluous**

superficiality *noun* a superficial quality

superfluity (*pronounced* soo-pe-**floo**-it-

i) *noun* **1** being superfluous **2** a thing that is superfluous

superfluous (*pronounced* soo-**per**-floo-us) *adjective* beyond what is enough or necessary

&#9percaps; Comes from Latin *superfluus* meaning 'overflowing'

superhuman *adjective* **1** divine, godly **2** greater than would be expected of an ordinary person: *superhuman effort*

superimpose *verb* to lay or place (one thing on another)

superintend *verb* to be in charge or control, manage

superintendent *noun* **1** someone who is in charge of an institution, building *etc* **2** a police officer above a chief inspector

superior *adjective* **1** higher in place or rank **2** better or greater than others: *superior forces/ superior goods* **3** having an air of being better than others □ *noun* someone better than, or higher in rank than, others

superiority *noun* **1** a superior state **2** pre-eminence **3** advantage

superlative *adjective* **1** better than, or going beyond, all others: *superlative skill* **2** *grammar* an adjective or adverb of the highest degree of comparison, *eg* kindest, worst, most quickly

supermarket *noun* a large self-service store selling food *etc*

supernatural *adjective* not happening in the ordinary course of nature, miraculous

supernova *noun* an exploding star surrounded by a bright cloud of gas

supersede *verb* **1** to take the place of: *he superseded his brother as headmaster* **2** to replace (something with something else)

supersonic *adjective* faster than the speed of sound: *supersonic flight*

superstition *noun* **1** belief in magic and in things which cannot be explained by reason **2** an example of such belief (*eg* not walking under ladders)

superstitious *adjective* having superstitions

supervene *verb* to come after or in addition

supervise *verb* to be in charge of work and see that it is properly done

supervision *noun* the act of supervising; control, inspection

supervisor *noun* a person who is responsible for making sure that other people's work is done correctly

supine *adjective* **1** lying on the back **2** not showing any interest or energy

supper *noun* a meal taken in the evening

supplant *verb* to take the place of somebody or of something: *the baby supplanted the dog in her affections*

supple *adjective* **1** bending easily, flexible **2** of an object: bending easily without breaking □ **supply** (*pronounced* sup-li) *adverb*

supplement *noun* **1** something added to supply a need or lack **2** a special section added to the main part of a newspaper or magazine □ *verb* to make or be an addition to: *her earnings supplemented his income*

supplementary *adjective* added to supply a need; additional

suppliant *adjective* asking earnestly and humbly □ *noun* someone who asks in this way

supplicate *verb* to ask earnestly, beg

supplication *noun* a humble, earnest request

supply *verb* **1** to provide (what is wanted or needed) **2** to provide (someone with something) □ *noun* (*plural* **supplies**) **1** an act of supplying **2** something supplied **3** a stock or store **4 supplies** a stock of essentials, *eg* food, equipment, money *etc* □ *adjective* of a teacher: filling another's place or position for a time

supply *verb* ⇨ suppl*ies*, supply*ing*, suppl*ied*

support *verb* **1** to hold up, take part of the weight of **2** to help, encourage **3** to supply with a means of living: *support a family* **4** to bear, put up with: *I can't support lies* □ *noun* **1** an act of supporting **2** something that supports

supporter *noun* someone who supports (especially a football club)

suppose *verb* **1** to take as true, assume for the sake of argument: *suppose that we have £100 to spend* **2** to believe, think probable: *I suppose you know* **3** used to give a polite order: *suppose you leave now* □ **be supposed to** to be required or expected to (do) □ **supposing** in the event that: *supposing it rains*

supposed *adjective* believed (often mistakenly) to be so: *her supposed generosity*

supposedly *adverb* according to what is supposed

supposition *noun* **1** the act of supposing **2** something supposed

suppress *verb* **1** to crush, put down (a rebellion *etc*) **2** to keep back (a yawn, a piece of news *etc*)

suppression *noun* the act of suppressing

supra- *prefix* above
ⓒ Comes from Latin *supra* meaning 'above'

supremacist *noun* someone who believes in the supremacy of their own race *etc*: *white supremacist*

supremacy *noun* highest power or authority

supreme *adjective* **1** highest, most powerful: *supreme ruler* **2** greatest: *supreme courage*

■ **Alternative words**: (meaning 1) absolute

surcharge *noun* an extra charge or tax

sure *adjective* **1** having no doubt: *I'm sure that I can come* **2** certain (to do, happen *etc*): *he is sure to be there* **3** reliable, dependable: *a sure method* □ **be sure** to see to it that: *be sure that he does it* □ **make sure** to act so that, or check that, something is sure □ **sure of yourself** confident □ **to be sure 1** certainly! **2** undoubtedly: *to be sure, you are correct*

sure-footed *adjective* unlikely to slip or stumble

surely *adverb* **1** certainly, without doubt **2** sometimes expressing a little doubt: *surely you won't tell him?* **3** without hesitation, mistake *etc*

surety *noun* (*plural* **sureties**) **1** someone who promises that another person will do something (especially appear in court) **2** a pledge, a guarantee

surf *noun* the foam made by the breaking of waves

surface *noun* the outside or top part of anything (*eg* of the earth, of a road *etc*) □ *verb* **1** to come up to the surface of (water *etc*) **2** to put a (smooth) surface on □ *adjective* **1** on the surface **2** travelling on the surface of land or water: *surface mail*

surfboard *noun* a long, narrow board on which someone can ride over the surf

surfeit *noun* too much of anything

surfer *noun* someone who surfs

surfing *noun* the sport of riding on a surfboard

surge *verb* **1** to move (forward) like waves **2** to rise suddenly or excessively □ *noun* **1** the swelling of a large wave **2** a swelling or rising movement like this **3** a sudden rise or increase (of pain *etc*)

surgeon *noun* a doctor who performs operations, often cutting the body open to examine or remove a diseased part

surgery *noun* (*plural* **surgeries**) **1** treatment of diseases *etc* by operation **2** a doctor's or dentist's consulting room

surgical *adjective* of, for use in, or by means of surgery: *a surgical operation/ a surgical mask/ surgical equipment* □ **surgically** *adverb*: *the lump will have to be surgically removed*

surly *adjective* gruff, rude, ill-mannered □ **surliness** *noun*

surmise *verb* to suppose, guess □ *noun* a supposition

surmount *verb* **1** to overcome (a difficulty *etc*) **2** to climb over, get over

surmountable *adjective* capable of being overcome or dealt with successfully

surname *noun* a person's last name or family name

surpass *verb* to go beyond, be more

or better than: *his work surpassed my expectations*

surplice (*pronounced* ser-plis) *noun* a loose white gown worn by members of the clergy

⏱ Comes from Late Latin *superpellicium* meaning 'an overgarment'

◆ Do not confuse: **surplice** and **surplus**

surplus (*pronounced* ser-plus) *noun* the amount left over after what is needed has been used up □ *adjective* left over, extra

⏱ Comes from French word-beginning *sur-* meaning 'over', and *plus* meaning 'more'

surprise *noun* **1** the feeling caused by an unexpected happening **2** an unexpected happening □ *verb* **1** to cause someone to feel surprise **2** to come upon (someone) suddenly and without warning □ **take by surprise** to come upon, or capture, without warning

surprised *adjective* experiencing feelings of surprise

■ **Alternative words**: amazed, astonished, astounded, staggered, flabbergasted, dumbfounded

surreal *adjective* dreamlike, using images from the subconscious

surrealism *noun* the use of surreal images in art

surrealist *noun* an adherent of surrealism □ *adjective* relating to or characteristic of surrealism: *a surrealist painting*

surrender *verb* **1** to give up, give in, yield: *surrender to the enemy* **2** to hand over: *she surrendered the note to the teacher* □ *noun* an act of surrender, especially in a war

surreptitious *adjective* done in a secret, underhand way

surrogate *adjective* used or acting as a substitute for another person or thing: *a surrogate mother* □ *noun* a substitute

surround *verb* **1** to be all round (someone or something) **2** to enclose, put round □ *noun* a border

surroundings *noun plural* **1** the country lying round a place **2** the

people and places with which you have to deal in daily life

surveillance *noun* a close watch or constant guard

survey *verb* **1** to look over **2** to inspect, examine **3** to make careful measurements of (a piece of land *etc*) □ *noun* (*plural* **surveys**) **1** a general view **2** a detailed examination or inspection **3** a piece of writing giving results of this **4** a careful measuring of land *etc* **5** a map made with the measurements obtained

survey *verb* ⇨ surveys, surveying, surveyed

surveyor *noun* someone who makes surveys of land, buildings *etc*

survival *noun* **1** the state of surviving **2** a custom, relic *etc* that remains from earlier times

survive *verb* **1** to remain alive, continue to exist (after an event *etc*) **2** to live longer than: *he survived his wife*

survivor *noun* someone who remains alive: *the only survivor of the crash*

susceptibility *noun* (*plural* **susceptibilities**) **1** the state or degree of being susceptible to something **2** **susceptibilities** strong feelings or sensibilities

susceptible *adjective* **1** **susceptible to something** liable to be affected by: *susceptible to colds* **2** easily affected or moved

suspect *verb* (*pronounced* sus-pekt) **1** to be inclined to think (someone) guilty: *I suspect her of the crime* **2** to distrust, have doubts about: *I suspected his air of frankness* **3** to guess: *I suspect that we're wrong* □ *noun* (*pronounced* sus-pekt) someone thought to be guilty of a crime *etc* □ *adjective* (*pronounced* sus-pekt) arousing doubt, suspected

suspend *verb* **1** to hang **2** to keep from falling or sinking: *particles suspended in a liquid* **3** to stop for a time: *suspend business* **4** to take away a job, privilege *etc* from for a time: *they suspended the student from classes*

suspender *noun* **1** an elastic strap to keep up socks or stockings **2** **suspenders** *US* braces

suspense *noun* **1** a state of being

undecided **2** a state of uncertainty or worry

suspension *noun* **1** the act of suspending **2** the state of being suspended **3** the state of a solid which is mixed with a liquid or gas and does not sink or dissolve in it

suspension bridge a bridge which is suspended from cables hanging from towers

suspicion *noun* **1** a feeling of doubt or mistrust **2** an opinion, a guess

suspicious *adjective* **1** inclined to suspect or distrust **2** arousing suspicion □ **suspiciously** *adverb*

sustain *verb* **1** to hold up, support **2** to bear (an attack *etc*) without giving way **3** to suffer (an injury *etc*) **4** to give strength to: *the food will sustain you* **5** to keep up, keep going: *sustain a conversation*

sustenance *noun* food, nourishment

suzerain *noun* **1** a feudal lord **2** a supreme ruler

svelte *adjective* slender, trim

SW *abbreviation* south-west; south-western

swab *noun* **1** a mop for cleaning a ship's deck **2** a piece of cottonwool used for cleaning, absorbing blood *etc* □ *verb* to clean with a swab

> **swab** *verb* ⇨ swab*s*, swab*bing*, swab*bed*

swaddle *verb* to wrap up (a young baby) tightly

swaddling clothes *old* strips of cloth used to wrap up a young baby

swag *noun, Austral informal* a bundle of possessions

swagger *verb* **1** to walk proudly, swinging the arms and body **2** to boast □ *noun* a proud walk or attitude

swain *noun, old* a young man

swallow¹ *verb* **1** to pass (food or drink) down the throat into the stomach **2** **swallow something up** to make it disappear **3** to receive (an insult *etc*) without objection **4** to keep back (tears, a laugh *etc*) □ *noun* an act of swallowing

swallow² *noun* a bird with pointed wings and a forked tail

swamp *noun* wet, marshy ground □ *verb* **1** to fill (a boat) with water **2** to overwhelm: *swamped with work*

swan *noun* a large, stately water bird, with white feathers and a long neck

swank *verb, informal* to show off

swan song the last work of a musician, writer *etc*

swap or **swop** *verb* to give one thing in exchange for another: *swap addresses*

> **swap** or **swop** *verb* ⇨ swap*s* or swop*s*, swap*ping* or swop*ping*, swap*ped* or swop*ped*

swarm *noun* **1** a large number of insects flying or moving together **2** a dense moving crowd □ *verb* **1** of insects: to gather together in great numbers **2** to move in crowds **3** to be crowded with: *swarming with tourists* **4** **swarm up something** to climb up (a wall *etc*)

swarthy *adjective* dark-skinned

swashbuckling *adjective* bold, swaggering

swastika *noun* an ancient design of a cross with bent arms, taken up as a symbol of Nazism

swat *verb* to squash (a fly *etc*) □ *noun* an instrument for squashing insects

> **swat** *verb* ⇨ swat*s*, swat*ting*, swat*ted*

swath or **swathe** *noun* **1** a line of corn or grass cut by a scythe **2** a strip

swathe¹ *verb* to wrap round with clothes or bandages

swathe² *another spelling of* **swath**

sway *verb* **1** to swing or rock to and fro **2** to bend in one direction or to one side **3** to influence: *sway opinion* □ *noun* **1** a swaying movement **2** rule, power: *hold sway over*

swear *verb* **1** to promise or declare solemnly **2** to vow **3** to curse, using the name of God or other sacred things without respect **4** to make (someone) take an oath: *to swear someone to secrecy* □ **swear by** to rely on, have complete faith in

swear ⇨ swears, swearing, swore, sworn

swear word a word used in swearing or cursing

sweat *noun* moisture secreted by the skin, perspiration □ *verb* 1 to give out sweat 2 *informal* to work hard

sweater *noun* a jersey, a pullover

sweaty *adjective* wet, or stained with, sweat

swede *noun* a kind of large yellow turnip

sweep *verb* 1 to clean (a floor *etc*) with a brush or broom 2 (often **sweep up** or **sweep something up**) to gather up (dust *etc*) by sweeping 3 to carry (away, along, off) with a long brushing movement 4 to travel over quickly, move with speed: *a new fad which is sweeping the country* 5 to move quickly in a proud manner (*eg* from a room) 6 **sweep something of something** to clear it of: *sweep the sea of enemy mines* 7 to curve widely or stretch far □ *noun* 1 a sweeping movement 2 a curve, a stretch 3 a chimney sweeper 4 a sweepstake

sweep *verb* ⇨ sweeps, sweeping, swept

sweeping *adjective* 1 that sweeps 2 of a victory *etc*: great, overwhelming 3 of a statement *etc*: too general, allowing no exceptions, rash

sweepstake *noun* a gambling system in which those who take part stake money which goes to the holder of the winning ticket

sweet *adjective* 1 having the taste of sugar, not salty, sour or bitter 2 pleasing to the taste 3 pleasant to hear or smell 4 kindly, agreeable, charming □ *noun* 1 a small piece of sweet substance, *eg* chocolate, toffee *etc* 2 something sweet served towards the end of a meal, a pudding

sweetbreads *noun plural* an animal's pancreas used for food

sweetcorn *noun* maize

sweeten *verb* to make or become sweet

sweetener *noun* 1 an artificial

substance used to sweeten food or drinks 2 *informal* a bribe

sweetheart *noun* a lover

sweetly *adverb* in a sweet way

sweetmeat *noun*, *old* a sweet, a confection

sweetness *noun* a sweet quality

sweet pea a sweet-smelling climbing flower grown in gardens

sweet talk flattery, persuasion

sweet tooth a liking for sweet-tasting things

swell *verb* 1 to grow in size or volume 2 of the sea: to rise into waves □ *noun* 1 an increase in size or volume 2 large, heaving waves 3 a gradual rise in the height of the ground 4 a dandy □ *adjective*, *US informal* fine, splendid

swell *verb* ⇨ swells, swelling, swelled, swollen

swelling *noun* a swollen part of the body, a lump

swelter *verb* to be too hot

sweltering *adjective* very hot

swept *past form* of **sweep**

swerve *verb* to turn quickly to one side □ *noun* a quick turn aside

swift *adjective* moving quickly; rapid □ *noun* a bird rather like the swallow □ **swiftly** *adverb*

swig *noun*, *informal* a mouthful of liquid, a large drink □ *verb*, *informal* to gulp down

swig *verb* ⇨ swigs, swigging, swigged

swill *verb* 1 to wash out 2 *informal* to drink a great deal □ *noun* 1 partly liquid food given to pigs 2 *informal* a big drink

swim *verb* 1 to move on or in water, using arms, legs, fins *etc* 2 to cross by swimming: *swim the Channel* 3 to float, not sink 4 to move with a gliding motion 5 to be dizzy 6 to be covered (with liquid): *meat swimming in grease* □ *noun* an act of swimming

swim *verb* ⇨ swims, swimming, swam, swum

swimmer *noun* someone or something that swims: *he's not a very strong* *swimmer/ penguins are excellent swimmers*

swimming bath or **swimming pool** a large water-filled tank designed for swimming, diving in *etc*

swimming costume or **swimsuit** *noun* a brief close-fitting garment for swimming in

swimmingly *adverb* smoothly, easily, successfully

swindle *verb* **1** to cheat, defraud **2** to get (money *etc* from someone) by cheating ▢ *noun* a fraud, a deception

swindler *noun* a person who swindles others

swine *noun* (*plural* **swine**) **1** *old* a pig **2** *informal* a contemptible person

swineherd *noun, old* someone who looks after pigs

swing *verb* **1** to move to and fro, sway **2** to move backwards and forwards on a swinging seat **3** to turn or whirl round **4** to walk quickly, moving the arms to and fro ▢ *noun* **1** a swinging movement **2** a seat for swinging, hung on ropes *etc* from a support ▢ **in full swing** going on busily

     swing *verb* ⇨ swing**s**, swing**ing**, swung

     ① Comes from Old English *swingan*

swingeing (*pronounced* swin-jing) *adjective* very great: *swingeing cuts in taxation*

     ① Comes from Old English *swengan* meaning 'to shake'

     ☛ Do not confuse with: **swinging**

swipe *verb* to strike with a sweeping blow ▢ *noun* a sweeping blow

swirl *verb* to sweep along with a whirling motion ▢ *noun* a whirling movement

swish *verb* **1** to strike or brush against with a rustling sound **2** to move making such a noise: *swishing out of the room in her long dress* ▢ *noun* a rustling sound or movement

switch *noun* (*plural* **switches**) **1** a small lever or handle, *eg* for turning an electric current on and off **2** an act of switching **3** a change: *a switch of loyalty* **4** a thin stick ▢ *verb* **1** to strike with a switch **2** to turn (off or on) by means

of a switch **3** to change, turn: *switch jobs/ hastily switching the conversation*

switchback *noun* a road or railway with steep ups and downs or sharp turns

switchblade *noun* a flick-knife

switchboard *noun* a board with equipment for making telephone connections

swivel *noun* a joint that turns on a pin or pivot ▢ *verb* to turn on a swivel, pivot

     swivel *verb* ⇨ swivel**s**, swivel**ling**, swivel**led**

swollen *adjective* increased in size by swelling ▢ *verb, past form of* **swell**

swoon *verb, old* to faint ▢ *noun* a fainting fit

swoop *verb* to come down with a sweep, like a bird of prey ▢ *noun* a sudden downward rush ▢ **at one fell swoop** all at one time, at a stroke

swop *another spelling of* **swap**

sword *noun* a type of weapon with a long blade for cutting or piercing

swordfish *noun* a large type of fish with a long pointed upper jaw like a sword

swore *past form of* **swear**

sworn *past participle of* **swear** ▢ *adjective* holding steadily to an attitude *etc*: *they had been sworn friends since childhood/ the two rivals became sworn enemies*

swot *verb, informal* to study hard ▢ *noun* someone who studies hard

sybaritic *adjective* **1** luxurious **2** fond of luxury

     After the ancient Greek city of *Sybaris* in Italy, noted for its luxury

sycamore *noun* a name given to several different types of tree, the maple, plane, and a kind of fig tree

sycophant *noun* someone who flatters others in order to gain favour or personal advantage

sycophantic *adjective* characteristic of a sycophant

syl- *see* **syn-**

syllabic *adjective* of or relating to syllables, or the division of words into syllables

syllable *noun* a word or part of a word spoken with one breath (*cheese* has one syllable, *but-ter* two, *mar-gar-ine* three)

syllabus *noun* (*plural* **syllabuses** or **syllabi**) a programme or list of lectures, classes *etc*

syllogism *noun* a combination of two propositions which lead to a third conclusion, as in *All dogs are animals, foxhounds are dogs, therefore foxhounds are animals*

sylph *noun* 1 a type of fairy supposed to inhabit the air 2 a slender, graceful woman

sylphlike *adjective* like a sylph, slim

sym- *see* **syn-**

symbol *noun* 1 something that stands for or represents another thing, *eg* the red cross, which stands for first aid 2 a character used as a short form of something, *eg* the signs + meaning plus, and O meaning oxygen

symbolic or **symbolical** *adjective* standing as a symbol of

symbolism *noun* the use of symbols to express ideas especially in art and literature

symbolize *verb* to be a symbol of

symmetrical *adjective* having symmetry; not lopsided in appearance □ **symmetrically** *adverb*: *coloured squares arranged symmetrically on the canvas*

Opposite: asymmetric

symmetry *noun* the equality in size, shape and position of two halves on either side of a dividing line: *spoiling the symmetry of the building*

sympathetic *adjective* feeling or showing sympathy □ **sympathetic to** or **towards** inclined to be in favour of: *sympathetic to the scheme* □ **sympathetically** *adverb*: *she patted his hand sympathetically*

sympathize *verb*: **sympathize with** to express or feel sympathy (for)

sympathy *noun* (*plural* **sympathies**) 1 a feeling of pity or sorrow for someone in trouble 2 agreement with, or understanding of, the feelings, attitudes *etc* of others

symphony *noun* (*plural* **symphonies**) a long piece of music written for an orchestra of many different instruments

symptom *noun* an outward sign indicating the presence of a disease *etc*: *symptoms of measles*

symptomatic *adjective* serving as a symptom

syn- also **sym-**, **syl-** *prefix* with, together: *synthesis*/ *sympathize* (= have so much pity for someone that you feel sorrow with them)/ *syllable* (= sounds which are pronounced together in one breath)
Ⓞ Comes from Greek *syn* meaning 'with'

synagogue *noun* a Jewish place of worship

synchronize *verb* 1 to cause to happen at the same time 2 to set to the same time: *synchronize watches*

syncopate *verb*, *music* to change the beat by accenting beats not usually accented

syncopation *noun* 1 syncopating 2 the beat or rhythm produced by syncopating

syndicate *noun* a number of persons who join together to manage some piece of business

syndrome *noun* a pattern of behaviour, events *etc* characteristic of some problem or condition

synod *noun* a meeting of members of the clergy

synonym *noun* a word which has the same, or nearly the same, meaning as another, *eg* 'ass' and 'donkey', or 'brave' and 'courageous' □ **synonymous (with)** *adjective* having the same meaning (as)

synopsis *noun* (*plural* **synopses**) a short summary of the main points of a book, speech *etc*

syntactic or **syntactical** *adjective* relating or belonging to syntax

syntax *noun* rules for the correct combination of words to form sentences

synthesis *noun* **1** the act of making a whole by putting together its separate parts **2** the making of a substance by combining chemical elements

synthesize *verb* to make (*eg* a drug) by synthesis

synthesizer *noun* a computerized instrument which creates electronic musical sounds

synthetic *adjective* **1** made artificially to look like a natural product: *synthetic leather* **2** not natural, pretended: *synthetic charm* □ **synthetically** *adverb*

syphilis *noun* an infectious disease, transmitted sexually

syphon *another spelling* of **siphon**

syringe *noun* a tubular instrument with a needle and plunger, used to extract blood, inject drugs *etc* □ *verb* to clean out with a syringe: *needing his ears syringed*

syrup *noun* **1** a thick sticky liquid made by boiling water or fruit juice with sugar **2** a purified form of treacle

system *noun* **1** an arrangement of several parts which work together: *railway system/ solar system* **2** a way of organizing: *democratic system of government* **3** a regular method of doing something **4** the body, or its parts, considered as a whole: *my system is run down*

① Comes from Greek *sy-* meaning 'together', and the root of *histanai* meaning 'to set'

systematic *adjective* following a system; methodical □ **systematically** *adverb*

Tt

If you can't find the word you're looking for under letter **T**, it could be that it starts with a different letter. Try looking under **PT** for words like *pterodactyl*. Also, don't forget **TH** for words like *thyme*.

tab *noun* **1** a small tag or flap attached to something **2** a running total, a tally

tabard *noun* a short sleeveless tunic

tabby *noun* (*plural* **tabbies**) or **tabby-cat** a striped (usually female) cat

tabernacle *noun* a place of worship

table *noun* **1** a flat-topped piece of furniture, supported by legs **2** a flat surface, a plateau **3** facts or figures set out in columns: *multiplication tables* □ *verb* **1** to make into a list or table **2** to put forward for discussion: *table a motion*

tableau *noun* (*plural* **tableaux**) a striking group or scene

tablecloth *noun* a cloth for covering a table

tablespoon *noun* a large size of spoon

tablespoonful *noun* (*plural* **tablespoonfuls**) the amount held in a tablespoon

tablet *noun* **1** a small flat plate on which to write, paint *etc* **2** a small flat piece, *eg* of soap or chocolate **3** a pill **4** a brittle sweet made with sugar and condensed milk

table tennis a form of tennis played across a table with small bats and a light ball

tabloid *noun* a small-sized newspaper giving news in shortened and often simplified form

Originally a trademark for a medicine in tablet form, and then, by association, the name for a small-sized newspaper giving information in concentrated form

taboo *adjective* forbidden by common consent; not approved by social custom □ *noun* a taboo subject or behaviour

tabular *adjective* set in the form of a table

tabulate *verb* to set out (information *etc*) in columns or rows

tachograph *noun* an instrument showing a vehicle's mileage, number of stops *etc*

tacit (*pronounced* **tas**-it) *adjective* understood but not spoken aloud, silent: *tacit agreement*

taciturn (*pronounced* **tas**-it-ern) *adjective* not inclined to talk

taciturnity (*pronounced* tas-it-**ern**-*i*t-i) *noun* an unwillingness to talk

tack *noun* **1** a short sharp nail with a broad head **2** a sideways movement allowing a yacht *etc* to sail against the wind **3** a direction, a course **4** a rough stitch to keep material in place while sewing □ *verb* **1** to fasten with tacks **2** to sew with tacks **3** of a yacht *etc*: to move from side to side across the face of the wind □ **change tack** to change course or direction □ **on the wrong tack** following the wrong train of thought

tackle *verb* **1** to come to grips with, deal with **2** *football etc* to try to stop, or take the ball from, another player □ *noun* **1** the ropes and rigging of a ship **2** equipment, gear: *fishing tackle* **3** ropes and pulleys for raising heavy weights **4** an act of tackling

tacky[1] *adjective* sticky, gluey

tacky[2] *adjective*, *informal* shabby; vulgar, in bad taste

tact *noun* skill in dealing with people so as to avoid giving offence

tactful *adjective* using tact; avoiding giving offence □ **tactfully** *adverb*

tactical *adjective* **1** involving clever and successful planning **2** diplomatic, politic: *tactical withdrawal*

tactics *noun plural* **1** a way of acting in order to gain advantage **2** the art of coordinating military forces in action

tactile *adjective* of or perceived through touch

tactless *adjective* giving offence through lack of thought □ **tactlessly** *adverb*

tadpole *noun* a young frog or toad in its first stage of life

tae kwon do (*pronounced* tei kwon doh) a Korean martial art similar to karate

taffeta *noun* a thin, glossy fabric made mainly of silk

tag *noun* **1** a label: *price tag* **2** a familiar saying or quotation **3** a chasing game played by children (*also called* **tig**) □ *verb* to put a tag or tags on □ **tag on to** or **tag after** to follow closely and continually

t'ai chi (*pronounced* tai **chee**) a Chinese system of exercise and self-defence stressing the importance of balance and coordination

tail *noun* **1** an appendage sticking out from the end of the spine on an animal, bird or fish **2** an appendage on a machine *etc*: *tail of an aeroplane* **3** the stalk on a piece of fruit **4** **tails** the side of a coin opposite to the head **5** **tails** a tail-coat □ *verb* **1** *informal* to follow closely **2** to remove the tails from (fruit *etc*) □ **tail off** to become less, fewer or worse □ **turn tail** to run away

tailcoat *noun* a coat with a divided tail, part of a man's evening dress

tail-end *noun* the very end of a procession *etc*

tailor *noun* someone who cuts out and makes clothes □ *verb* **1** to make and fit (clothes) **2** to make to fit the circumstances, adapt: *tailored to your needs*

tailor-made *adjective* exactly suited to requirements

taint *verb* **1** to spoil by contact with something bad or rotten **2** to corrupt □ *noun* a trace of decay or evil

take *verb* **1** to lay hold of, grasp **2** to choose: *take a card!* **3** to accept, agree to have: *do you take credit cards?/ please take a biscuit* **4** to have room for: *my car only takes four people* **5** to eat, swallow **6** to get or have regularly: *doesn't take sugar* **7** to capture (a fort *etc*) **8** to subtract: *take two from eight* **9** to lead, carry, drive: *take the children to school* **10** to use, make use of: *take care!* **11** to require: *it'll take too much time* **12** to travel by: *took the afternoon train* **13** to experience, feel: *takes great pride in his work* **14** to photograph: *took some shots inside the house* **15** to understand: *took what I said the wrong way* **16** of a plant: to root successfully **17** to become popular, please □ **take account of** to consider, remember □ **take advantage of 1** to make use of (an opportunity) **2** to treat or use unfairly □ **take after** to be like in appearance or behaviour □ **take care of** to look after □ **take down** to write, note down □ **take for** to believe (mistakenly) to be: *I took him for his brother* □ **take heed** to pay careful attention □ **take ill** to become ill □ **take in 1** to include **2** to receive **3** to understand: *didn't take in what you said* **4** to make smaller: *take in a dress* **5** to cheat, deceive □ **take leave of** to say goodbye to □ **take someone's life** to kill them □ **taken with** attracted to □ **take off 1** to remove (clothes *etc*) **2** to imitate unkindly **3** of an aircraft: to leave the ground □ **take on 1** to undertake (work *etc*) **2** to accept (as an opponent): *take you on at tennis* □ **take over** to take control of □ **take part in** to share or help in □ **take pity on** to show pity for □ **take place** to happen □ **take to 1** to be attracted to **2** to begin to do or use regularly: *took to rising early* □ **take to heart** to be deeply affected or upset by □ **take to your heels** to run away, flee □ **take up 1** to lift, raise **2** to occupy (space, time *etc*) **3** to begin to learn, show interest in: *take up playing the harp*

> **take** ⇨ take*s*, tak*ing*, tak*en*, took

Ⓛ Comes from Late Old English *tacan* meaning 'to touch' or 'to take'

■ **Alternative words**: (verb, meaning 1) seize, grab, snatch, steal; (verb, meaning 2) pick, select; (verb, meaning 6) accommodate; (verb, meaning 7) seize, capture; (verb, meaning 8) subtract, deduct; (verb, meaning 9) transport, escort, bring; (verb, meaning 11) need, necessitate, demand □ **take in** (meaning 3) absorb, assimilate □ **take off** (meaning 1) remove, doff, shed

take-away *noun* **1** a meal prepared and bought in a restaurant or shop but taken away and eaten somewhere else **2** a restaurant or shop providing such meals

take-off *noun* **1** the act of an aircraft leaving the ground **2** an act of imitating or mimicking

takeover *noun* the act of taking control of something, especially a company by buying the majority of its shares

taking *adjective* pleasing, attractive □ *noun* **1** an act of taking **2 takings** money received from things sold

talc *noun* **1** a soft mineral, soapy to the touch **2** *informal* talcum powder

talcum powder a fine powder made from talc, used for rubbing on the body

tale *noun* **1** a story **2** an untrue story, a lie

talent *noun* **1** a special ability or skill: *a talent for music* **2** *historical* a measure of weight for gold or silver

talented *adjective* skilled, gifted

talisman *noun* (*plural* **talismans**) an object believed to have magic powers; a charm

talk *verb* **1** to speak **2** to gossip **3** to give information □ *noun* **1** conversation **2** gossip **3** the subject of conversation: *the talk is of revolution* **4** a discussion or lecture: *gave a talk on stained glass* □ **talk over 1** to discuss **2** to persuade □ **talk round 1** to discuss without coming to the main point **2** to persuade □ **talk shop** *see* **shop**

■ **Alternative words**: (verb, meaning 1) speak, utter; (verb, meaning 2) chat, chatter, natter; (verb, meaning 3) communicate, converse, confer

talkative *adjective* inclined to chatter

tall *adjective* **1** high or higher than average **2** hard to believe: *tall story*

tall order a request to do something awkward or unreasonable

tallow *noun* animal fat melted down to make soap, candles *etc*

tally *noun* (*plural* **tallies**) **1** an account **2** a ticket, a label **3** *old* a notched stick for keeping a score □ *verb* to agree (with): *his story doesn't tally with yours*

tally *verb* ⇨ tallies, tallying, tallied

tambourine *noun* a small one-sided drum with tinkling metal discs set into the sides

tame *adjective* **1** of an animal: not wild, used to living with humans **2** dull, not exciting □ *verb* to make tame, subdue

tamper *verb*: **tamper with** to meddle with so as to damage or alter

tampon *noun* a plug of cotton-wool inserted into the vagina to absorb blood during menstruation

tan *verb* **1** to make (animal skin) into leather by treating with tannin **2** to make or become brown, *eg* by exposure to the sun □ *noun* **1** a yellowish-brown colour **2** a suntan

tan *verb* ⇨ tans, tanning, tanned

tandem *noun* a long bicycle with two seats and two sets of pedals one behind the other □ *adverb* one behind the other □ **in tandem** together, in conjunction

tandoori *noun* a style of Indian cookery in which food is baked over charcoal in a clay oven

tang *noun* a strong taste, flavour or smell: *the tang of lemons*

tangent *noun* a straight line which touches a circle or curve without crossing it □ **go off at a tangent** to go off suddenly in another direction or line of thought

tangerine *noun* a small type of orange

Originally meaning 'from Tangiers', from where the fruit was exported in the 19th century

tangible *adjective* **1** able to be felt by touching **2** real, definite: *tangible profits* □ **tangibly** *adverb*

tangle *verb* **1** to twist together in knots **2** to make or become difficult or confusing ▫ *noun* **1** a twisted mass of knots **2** a confused situation

tango *noun* (*plural* **tangos**) a ballroom dance with long steps and pauses, originally from South America

tank *noun* **1** a large container for water, petrol *etc* **2** a heavy armoured vehicle which moves on caterpillar wheels

tankard *noun* a large drinking mug

tanker *noun* **1** a ship or large lorry for carrying liquids, *eg* oil **2** an aircraft carrying fuel

tanner *noun* someone who works at tanning leather

tannery *noun* (*plural* **tanneries**) a place where leather is made

tannin *noun* a bitter-tasting substance found in tea, red wine *etc*, also used in tanning and dyeing

tantalize *verb* to torment by offering something and keeping it out of reach

tantalizing *adjective* teasing; tormenting: *tantalizing smells were coming from the kitchen*

tantamount *adjective*: **tantamount to** coming to the same thing as, equivalent to: *tantamount to stealing*

tantrum *noun* a fit of rage or bad temper

tap *noun* **1** a light touch or knock **2** a device with a valve for controlling the flow of liquid, gas *etc* ▫ *verb* **1** to knock or strike lightly **2** to draw on, start using **3** to attach a listening device secretly to (a telephone) ▫ **on tap** ready, available for use

tap *verb* ⇨ tap**s**, tap**ping**, tap**ped**

tapdance *noun* a dance done with special shoes that make a tapping sound ▫ *verb* to perform a tapdance

tape *noun* **1** a narrow band or strip used for tying **2** a piece of string stretched over the finishing line on a racetrack **3** a tape-measure **4** a strip of magnetic material for recording sound or pictures ▫ *verb* **1** to fasten with tape **2** to record on tape ▫ **have someone taped** to have a good understanding of their character or worth

tape-measure *noun* a narrow strip of paper, plastic *etc* used for measuring distance

taper *noun* **1** a long, thin kind of candle **2** a long waxed wick used for lighting oil lamps *etc* ▫ *verb* to make or become thinner at one end

tape-recorder *noun* a kind of instrument for recording sound *etc* on magnetic tape

tapering *adjective* becoming gradually thinner at one end

tapestry *noun* (*plural* **tapestries**) a cloth with designs or figures woven into it, used to decorate walls or cover furniture

tapeworm *noun* a type of long worm sometimes found in the intestines of humans and animals

tapioca *noun* a starchy food obtained from the root of the cassava plant

tapir *noun* a kind of wild animal something like a large pig

tar *noun* **1** a thick, black, sticky liquid derived from wood or coal, used in roadmaking *etc* **2** *informal* a sailor ▫ *verb* to smear with tar ▫ **tarred with the same brush (as)** having the same faults (as)

tar *verb* ⇨ tar**s**, tar**ring**, tar**red**

tarantula *noun* a type of large, poisonous spider

tardiness *noun* being late or delayed

tardy *adjective* slow; late

target *noun* **1** a mark to aim at in shooting, darts *etc* **2** a result or sum that is aimed at: *a target of £3000* **3** someone at whom unfriendly remarks are aimed: *the target of her criticism*

tariff *noun* **1** a list of prices **2** a list of taxes payable on goods brought into a country

tarmac *noun* the surface of a road or airport runway, made of tarmacadam ▫ *verb* to surface with tarmacadam

tarmacadam *noun* a mixture of small stones and tar used to make road surfaces *etc*

tarnish *verb* **1** of metal: to (cause to) become dull or discoloured **2** to spoil (a reputation *etc*)

tarot (*pronounced* **ta**-roh) *noun* a system of fortune-telling using special cards divided into suits

tarpaulin *noun* **1** strong waterproof cloth **2** a sheet of this material

tarragon *noun* a herb used in cooking

tarry[1] (*pronounced* **ta**-ri) *verb* **1** to stay behind, linger **2** to be slow or late

tarry[2] (*pronounced* **tah**-ri) *adjective* like or covered with tar; sticky

tart *noun* a small pie containing fruit, vegetables *etc* □ *adjective* sharp, sour

tartan *noun* **1** fabric patterned with squares of different colours, traditionally used by Scottish Highland clans **2** one of these patterns: *Macdonald tartan* □ *adjective* with a pattern of tartan

tartar *noun* **1** a substance that gathers on the teeth **2** a difficult or demanding person **3** a substance that forms inside wine casks □ **cream of tartar** a white powder obtained from the tartar from wine casks, used in baking

task *noun* a set piece of work to be done □ **take to task** to scold, find fault with

task force a group of people gathered together with the purpose of performing a special or specific task

taskmaster *noun* someone who sets and supervises tasks

tassel *noun* a hanging bunch of threads, used to decorate a hat *etc*

taste *verb* **1** to try by eating or drinking a sample **2** to eat or drink some of: *taste this soup* **3** to recognize (a flavour): *can you taste the chilli in it?* **4** to have a particular flavour: *tasting of garlic* **5** to experience: *taste success* □ *noun* **1** the act or sense of tasting **2** a flavour **3** a small quantity of something **4** a liking: *taste for literature* **5** ability to judge what is suitable in behaviour, dress *etc*, or what is fine or beautiful

tasteful *adjective* showing good taste and judgement □ **tastefully** *adverb* □ **tastefulness** *noun*

tasteless *adjective* **1** without flavour **2** not tasteful; vulgar □ **tastelessly** *adverb*

tasty *adjective* having a good flavour

tattered *adjective* ragged

tatters *noun plural* torn, ragged pieces

tattie *noun, Scottish* a potato

tattle *noun* gossip

tattoo *noun* **1** a coloured design on the skin, made by pricking with needles **2** a drumbeat **3** an outdoor military display with music *etc* □ *verb* to prick coloured designs into the skin

> From a Dutch term meaning to shut off beer taps at closing time, later applied to a military drumbeat at the end of the day

tattooed *adjective* marked with tattoos

tatty *adjective* shabby, tawdry

taught *past form of* **teach**

taunt *verb* to tease or jeer at unkindly □ *noun* a jeer

> Originally a phrase *taunt for taunt*, based on the French *tant pour tant* meaning 'tit for tat'

taut *adjective* **1** pulled tight **2** tense, strained

tauten *verb* to make or become tight

tautology *noun* a form of repetition in which the same thing is said in different ways, *eg* 'he looked *anxious and worried*'

tavern *noun, old* a public house, an inn

tawdry *adjective* cheap-looking and gaudy

> From *St Audrey's lace*, once used to make cheap lace neckties

tawny *adjective* yellowish-brown

tax *noun* (*plural* **taxes**) **1** a charge made by the government on income, certain types of goods *etc* **2** a strain, a burden: *severe tax on my patience* □ *verb* **1** to make to pay a tax **2** to put a strain on: *taxing her strength* □ **tax with** to accuse of

taxation 1 the act or system of taxing **2** taxes

taxi *noun* (*plural* **taxis**) a vehicle which may be hired, with a driver (*also called*: **taxi-cab**) □ *verb* **1** to travel in a taxi **2** of an aeroplane: to travel on the runway before or after take-off

> **taxi** *verb* ⇨ taxi*es*, taxi*ing*, taxi*ed*

taxidermist *noun* someone who prepares and stuffs the skins of dead animals

taxidermy *noun* the art of preparing and stuffing the skins of animals to make them lifelike

taxpayer *noun* someone who pays taxes

TB *abbreviation* tuberculosis

tea *noun* 1 a plant grown in India, China *etc*, or its dried and prepared leaves 2 a drink made by infusing its dried leaves 3 a hot drink, an infusion: *beef tea/ camomile tea* 4 an afternoon or early evening meal

teacake *noun* a light, flat bun

teach *verb* 1 to give (someone) skill or knowledge 2 to give knowledge of, or training in (a subject): *she teaches French* 3 to be a teacher: *decide to teach*

> **teach** ⇨ teaches, teaching, taught

teacher *noun* someone employed to teach others in a school, or in a particular subject: *guitar teacher*

tea chest a tall box of thin wood used to pack tea for export, often used as a packing case when empty

teaching *noun* 1 the work of a teacher 2 guidance, instruction 3 **teachings** beliefs or rules of conduct that are preached or taught

teacup *noun* a medium-sized cup for drinking tea □ **storm in a teacup** *see* **storm**

teak *noun* 1 a hardwood tree from the East Indies 2 its very hard wood 3 a type of African tree

teal *noun* a small water-bird like a duck

team 1 a group of people working together 2 a side in a game: *a football team* 3 two or more animals working together: *team of oxen* □ **team up with** to join together with, join forces with
ⓘ Comes from Old English *team* meaning 'child-bearing', 'brood' or 'team'

> 🖝 Do not confuse with: **teem**

teapot *noun* a pot with a spout, for making and pouring tea

tear¹ (*pronounced* teer) *noun* 1 a drop of liquid from the eye 2 **tears** grief □ **in tears** weeping

tear² (*pronounced* teir) *verb* 1 to pull with force: *tear apart/ tear down* 2 to make a hole or split in (material *etc*) 3 to hurt deeply 4 *informal* to rush: *tearing off down the road* □ *noun* a hole or split made by tearing

> **tear** *verb* ⇨ tears, tearing, torn, tore

tearful *adjective* 1 inclined to weep 2 in tears, crying □ **tearfully** *adverb*

tear gas gas which causes the eyes to stream with tears

tease *verb* 1 to annoy, irritate on purpose 2 to pretend to upset or annoy for fun: *I'm only teasing* 3 to untangle (wool *etc*) with a comb 4 to sort out (a problem or puzzle) □ *noun* someone who teases

teasel *noun* a type of prickly plant

teaser *noun* a problem, a puzzle

teaspoon *noun* a small spoon

teat *noun* 1 the part of an animal through which milk passes to its young 2 a rubber object shaped like this attached to a baby's feeding bottle

tea-towel *noun* a cloth for drying dishes

techn- *see* **techno-**

technical *adjective* 1 relating to a particular art or skill, especially a mechanical or industrial one: *what is the technical term for this?/ a technical expert* 2 according to strict laws or rules: *technical defeat*

technicality *noun* (*plural* **technicalities**) a technical detail or point

technically *adverb* according to the rules, strictly speaking

technician *noun* someone trained in the practical side of an art

technique *noun* the way in which a process is carried out; a method

techno *noun, short for* **technomusic**

techno- or **techn-** *prefix* 1 forms words relating to the art or craft involved in doing something: *technical* 2 of or relating to technology
ⓘ Comes from Greek *techne* meaning 'skill'

technological *adjective* relating to or involving technology □ **technologically**

adverb: *a technologically advanced country*

technologist *noun* a person skilled in technology and its applications

technology *noun* **1** science applied to practical (especially industrial) purposes **2** the practical skills of a particular civilization, period *etc*

technomusic *noun* a style of popular music which uses electronic effects

teddy or **teddybear** *noun* (*plural* **teddies** or **teddybears**) **1** a stuffed toy bear **2 teddy** a one-piece woman's undergarment

tedious *adjective* long and tiresome □ **tediously** *adverb*

tedium *noun* boredom: *the endless tedium of dinner with his boring relations*

tee *noun* **1** the square of level ground from which a golfball is driven **2** the peg or sand heap on which the ball is placed for driving □ **tee up** to place (a ball) on a tee

teem *verb* **1** to be full: *teeming with people* **2** to rain heavily
ⓘ Meaning 1: comes from Old English *tieman*, related to the word *team*; meaning 2: comes from Old Norse *tema* meaning 'to empty'

☛ Do not confuse with: **team**

teenage *adjective* suitable for, or typical of, those in their teens

teenager *noun* someone in their teens

teens *noun plural* the years of age from thir*teen* to nine*teen*

teeny *adjective, informal* tiny, minute

tee-shirt or **T-shirt** *noun* a short-sleeved shirt pulled on over the head

teeth *plural* of **tooth**

teethe *verb* of a baby: to grow its first teeth

teetotal *adjective* never drinking alcohol

teetotaller *noun* a person who never drinks alcohol

tele- *prefix* at a distance: *television/telegram* (= a message sent over a long distance)
ⓘ Comes from Greek *tele* meaning 'far'

telecommunications *noun plural* the sending of information by telephone, radio, television *etc*

telecottage *noun* an office building in a rural area equipped with computers *etc*

telegram *noun* a message sent by telegraph

telegraph *noun* an instrument for sending messages to a distance using electrical impulses □ *verb* to send (a message) by telegraph

telegraphic *adjective* **1** of a telegraph **2** short, brief, concise

telekinesis *noun* the movement of objects from a distance through will-power not touch

telepathic *adjective* relating to or involving telepathy

telepathy *noun* communication between people without using sight, hearing *etc*

telephone *noun* an instrument for speaking over distances, which uses an electric current travelling along a wire, or radio waves □ *verb* to send (a message) by telephone

telephonist *noun* an operator on a telephone switchboard

telephoto *adjective* of a lens: used to photograph enlarged images of distant objects

teleprinter *noun* a typewriter which receives and prints out messages sent by telegraph

telescope *noun* a tubular instrument fitted with lenses which magnify distant objects □ *verb* **1** to push or fit together so that one thing slides inside another **2** to force together, compress

teletex *noun* a high-speed means of transmitting data, similar to telex

teletext *noun* news and general information transmitted by television companies, viewable only on special television sets

televise *verb* to broadcast on television: *are they televising the football match?*

television *noun* **1** the reproduction on a small screen of pictures sent from a distance **2** an apparatus for receiving these pictures

eleworker *noun* someone who works rom home and communicates with heir employer by computer, fax *etc*

elex *noun* 1 the sending of messages y means of teleprinters 2 a message ent in this way

ell *verb* 1 to say or express in words: *he's telling the truth* 2 to give the facts f (a story) 3 to inform, give nformation: *can you tell me when it's 9 'clock* 4 to order, command: *tell him o go away!* 5 to make out, distinguish: *can't tell one wine from the other* 6 to ive away a secret: *promise not to tell* 7 to be effective, produce results: *raining will tell in the end* □ **all told** lltogether, counting all □ **tell off** *nformal* to scold □ **tell on** 1 to have an ffect on 2 to give information about □ **tell tales** to give away information bout the misdeeds of others

tell ➪ tells, telling, told

Alternative words: (verb, meaning 2) narrate, recount, relate; (verb, meaning 3) notify; (verb, meaning 4) instruct □ **tell off** scold, chide, upbraid, reprove, rebuke, berate, censure

eller *noun* 1 a bank clerk who receives nd pays out money 2 someone who ounts votes at an election

elling *adjective* having a marked effect: *elling remark*

emerity *noun* rashness, boldness

emp *abbreviation* 1 temperature 2 *mporary* □ *noun, informal* a mporarily employed secretarial orker □ *verb, informal* to work as a mp

emper *noun* 1 habitual state of mind: *f an even temper* 2 a passing mood: *in good temper* 3 a tendency to get angry asily 4 a fit of anger 5 the amount of ardness in metal, glass *etc* □ *verb* 1 to ring (metal) to the right degree of ardness by heating and cooling 2 to ake less severe □ **lose your temper** to now anger

emperament *noun* someone's nature s it affects the way they feel and act; isposition

emperamental *adjective* 1 of emperament 2 excitable, emotional

temperance *noun* the habit of not drinking much (or any) alcohol

temperate *adjective* 1 moderate in temper, eating or drinking *etc* 2 of climate: neither very hot nor very cold

temperature *noun* 1 degree of heat or cold: *today's temperature* 2 a body heat higher than normal

tempest *noun* a storm, with great wind

tempestuous *adjective* 1 very stormy and windy 2 passionate, violently emotional

template *noun* a thin plate cut in a design for drawing round

temple[1] *noun* a building used for public worship; a church

temple[2] *noun* a small flat area on each side of the forehead

tempo *noun* (*plural* **tempos** or **tempi**) 1 the speed at which music is played 2 the speed or rate of an activity

temporary *adjective* lasting only for a time, not permanent

Alternative words: impermanent, temporal, transient, transitory, ephemeral, shortlived

temporize *verb* to avoid or delay taking action in order to gain time

tempt *verb* 1 to try to persuade or entice 2 to attract 3 to make inclined (to): *tempted to phone him up*

temptation *noun* 1 the act of tempting 2 the feeling of being tempted 3 something which tempts

tempting *adjective* attractive

ten *noun* the number 10 □ *adjective* 10 in number

tenable *adjective* able to be defended; justifiable

tenacious *adjective* 1 keeping a firm hold or grip 2 obstinate, persistent, determined □ **tenaciously** *adverb*

tenacity *noun* persistence, determination

tenancy *noun* (*plural* **tenancies**) 1 the holding of a house, farm *etc* by a tenant 2 the period of this holding

tenant *noun* someone who pays rent for the use of a house, land *etc*

tend *verb* **1** to be likely or inclined to do something: *these flowers tend to wilt* **2** to move or slope in a certain direction **3** to take care of, look after

tendency *noun* (*plural* **tendencies**) a leaning or inclination (towards): *tendency to daydream*

tender *adjective* **1** soft, not hard or tough **2** easily hurt or damaged **3** hurting when touched **4** loving, gentle □ *verb* **1** to offer (a resignation *etc*) formally **2** to make a formal offer for a job □ *noun* **1** an offer to take on work, supply goods *etc* for a fixed price **2** a small boat that carries stores for a large one **3** a truck for coal and water attached to a steam engine □ **legal tender** coins or notes which must be accepted when offered □ **of tender years** very young

tendon *noun* a tough cord joining a muscle to a bone

tendril *noun* **1** a thin curling stem of a climbing plant which attaches itself to a support **2** a curling strand of hair *etc*

tenement *noun* a block of flats

tenet *noun* a belief, opinion

tenner *noun*, *informal* a ten-pound note; ten pounds

tennis *noun* a game for two or four players using rackets to hit a ball to each other over a net

tennis court a place made level and prepared for tennis

tenon *noun* a projecting part at the end of a piece of wood made to fit a **mortise**

tenor *noun* **1** a singing voice of the highest normal pitch for an adult male **2** a singer with this voice **3** the general course: *the even tenor of country life* **4** general meaning: *the tenor of the speech*

tenpin bowling a game like skittles played by bowling a ball at ten pins standing at the end of a bowling lane

tense[1] *noun* the form of a verb that shows time of action, *eg* '*I was*' (**past tense**), '*I am*' (**present tense**), '*I shall be*' (**future tense**)

tense[2] *adjective* **1** tightly stretched **2** nervous, strained: *feeling tense/ tense with excitement*

tensile *adjective* relating to stretching

tension *noun* **1** the state of being stretched **2** strain, anxiety

tent *noun* a movable shelter of canvas or other material, supported by poles and pegged to the ground

tentacle *noun* a long thin flexible part of an animal used to feel or grasp, *eg* the arm of an octopus

tentative *adjective* **1** experimental, initial: *a tentative offer* **2** uncertain, hesitating: *tentative smile* □ **tentatively** *adverb*

tenterhooks *noun plural*: **on tenterhooks** uncertain and very anxious about what will happen

tenth *adjective* the last of ten items □ *noun* one of ten equal parts

tenuous *adjective* slight, weak: *tenuous connection*

tenure *noun* **1** the holding of property or a position of employment **2** the period, or terms or conditions, of this

tepee *noun* a traditional Native American tent made of animal skins

tepid *adjective* lukewarm

term *noun* **1** a length of time: *term of imprisonment* **2** a division of an academic or school year: *autumn term* **3** a word, an expression: *dictionary of computing terms* **4 terms** the rules or conditions of an agreement: *what are their terms?* **5 terms** fixed charges **6 terms** footing, relationship: *on good terms with his neighbours* □ *verb* to name, call □ **come to terms** to reach an agreement or understanding □ **come to terms with** to accept, be able to live with □ **in terms of** from the point of view of

termagant *noun* a bad-tempered, noisy woman

terminal *adjective* **1** of or growing at the end: *terminal bud* **2** of an illness: fatal, incurable □ *noun* **1** an end **2** a point of connection in an electric circuit **3** a computer monitor connected to a network **4** a terminus **5** an airport building containing arrival and departure areas **6** a bus station in a town centre running a service to a nearby airport

terminate *verb* to bring or come to an end

termination *noun* an act of ending or the state of being brought to an end

terminology *noun* the special words or expressions used in a particular art, science *etc*

terminus *noun* (*plural* **termini** or **terminuses**) 1 the end 2 an end point on a railway, bus route *etc*

termite *noun* a pale-coloured wood-eating insect, like an ant

tern *noun* a type of sea bird like a small gull

-terr- of or relating to the earth or land: *terrestrial/ subterranean* (= under the earth)
Ⓛ Comes from Latin *terra* meaning 'the earth' or 'land'

terrace *noun* 1 a raised level bank of earth 2 a raised flat place 3 a connected row of houses □ *verb* to form into a terrace or terraces

terracotta *noun* a brownish-red mixture of clay and sand used for tiles, pottery *etc*

terrain *noun* an area of land considered in terms of its physical features: *the terrain is a bit rocky*

terrapin *noun* a small turtle living in ponds or rivers

terrazzo *noun* a hard, shiny covering for concrete floors, *eg* in railway stations, consisting of marble chips set in cement and then polished

terrestrial *adjective* of or living on the earth

terrible *adjective* 1 causing great fear: *terrible sight* 2 causing great hardship or distress: *terrible disaster* 3 *informal* very bad: *a terrible writer*

■ **Alternative words**: (meanings 2 and 3) appalling

terribly *adverb, informal* 1 badly: *sang terribly* 2 extremely: *terribly tired*

terrier *noun* a breed of small dog

terrific *adjective* 1 powerful, dreadful 2 huge, amazing 3 *informal* attractive, enjoyable *etc*: *a terrific party*

terrify *verb* to frighten greatly
terrify ➪ terrif*ies*, terrif*ying*, terrif*ied*

territorial *adjective* of, belonging to a territory

territory *noun* (*plural* **territories**) 1 an area of land, a region 2 land under the control of a ruler or state 3 an area allocated to a salesman *etc* 4 a field of activity or interest

terror *noun* 1 very great fear 2 something which causes great fear 3 *informal* an uncontrollable child

terrorism *noun* the organized use of violence or intimidation for political or other ends

terrorist *noun* someone who practises terrorism

terrorize *verb* to frighten very greatly

terse *adjective* using few words; curt, brusque □ **tersely** *adverb*

tertiary *adjective* third in position or order

tertiary education education at university or college level

test *noun* 1 a short examination 2 something done to check soundness, reliability *etc*: *ran tests on the new model* 3 a means of finding the presence of: *test for radioactivity* 4 an event that shows up a good or bad quality: *a test of courage* □ *verb* to carry out tests on

testament *noun* 1 a written statement 2 a will □ **Old Testament** and **New Testament** the two main divisions of the Christian Bible

testator *noun* the writer of a will

testicle *noun* one of two sperm-producing glands enclosed in the male scrotum

testify *verb* 1 to give evidence in a law court 2 to make a solemn declaration of 3 **testify to something** to show, give evidence of it: *testifies to his ignorance*
testify ➪ testif*ies*, testif*ying*, testif*ied*

testimonial *noun* 1 a personal statement about someone's character, abilities *etc* 2 a gift given in thanks for services given

testimony *noun* (*plural* **testimonies**) 1 the statement made by someone who testifies 2 evidence

test match *cricket* one of a series of

matches between two countries

testosterone *noun* the chief male sex hormone, secreted by the testicles

test pilot a pilot who tests new aircraft

test tube a glass tube closed at one end, used in chemical tests

testy *adjective* easily angered, irritable □ **testily** *adverb* □ **testiness** *noun*

tetanus *noun* a disease, caused especially by an infected wound, causing stiffening and spasms in the jaw muscles (*also called*: **lockjaw**)

tetchy *adjective* irritable, testy □ **tetchily** *adverb*

tether *noun* a rope or chain for tying an animal to restrict its movement □ *verb* **1** to tie with a tether **2** to limit the freedom of

text *noun* **1** the written or printed part of a book, not the pictures, notes *etc* **2** a printed or written version of a speech, play *etc* **3** a Biblical passage used as the basis for a sermon **4** the subject matter of a speech, essay *etc*

textbook *noun* a book used for teaching, giving the main facts about a subject

textile *adjective* of weaving; woven □ *noun* a woven cloth or fabric

textual *adjective* of or in a text

texture *noun* **1** the quality of cloth resulting from weaving: *loose texture* **2** the quality of a substance in terms of how it looks or feels: *rough texture/ lumpy texture*

than *conjunction & preposition* used in comparisons: *easier than I expected/ better than usual*

thane *noun, historical* a noble who held land from the crown

thank *verb* to express gratitude to (someone) for a favour, gift *etc* □ **thank you** or **thanks** a polite expression used to thank someone (*see also* **thanks**)

thankful *adjective* grateful; relieved and glad □ **thankfully** *adverb*: *thankfully, no-one was badly injured in the crash*

thankless *adjective* neither worthwhile nor appreciated: *thankless task*

thanks *noun plural* gratitude; appreciation: *you'll get no thanks for it*

□ **thanks to 1** with the help of: *we arrived on time, thanks to our friends* **2** owing to: *we were late, thanks to our car breaking down*

thanksgiving *noun* **1** a church service giving thanks to God **2 Thanksgiving** *US* the fourth Thursday of November, a national holiday commemorating the first harvest of the Puritan settlers

that *adjective & pronoun* (*plural* **those**) used to point out a thing or person *etc* (*contrasted with*: **this**): *that woman over there! don't say that* □ *relative pronoun*: *those are the colours he chose/ that's the man I spoke to* □ *adverb* to such an extent or degree: *why were you that late?* □ *conjunction* **1** used in reporting speech: *she said that she was there* **2** used to connect clauses: *I heard that you were ill*

thatch *noun* straw *etc* used to make the roof of a house □ *verb* to cover with thatch

thaw *verb* **1** to melt **2** of frozen food: to defrost, become unfrozen **3** to become friendly □ *noun* **1** the melting of ice and snow by heat **2** a change in the weather that causes this

the *adjective* **1** referring to a particular person or thing: *the boy in the park/ I like the jacket I'm wearing* **2** referring to all or any of a general group: *the horse is of great use to man*

theatre or *US* **theater** *noun* **1** a place for the public performance of plays *etc* **2** a room in a hospital for surgical operations **3** the acting profession

theatrical *adjective* **1** of theatres or acting **2** over-dramatic, overdone

theatricality *noun* a theatrical quality

thee *pronoun, old* you (*singular*) as the object of a sentence

theft *noun* stealing

their *adjective* belonging to them: *their car*

◆ Do not confuse with: **there**. Remember that the 'y' in the pronoun 'they' turns into an 'i' in **their** – and that **there** is spelt the same as 'here' except for the first letter

theirs *pronoun* belonging to them: *the red car is theirs*

them *pronoun plural* **1** people or things already spoken about (as the object of a verb): *we've seen them* **2** those: *one of them over in the corner* □ *pronoun singular* used to avoid giving the gender of the person being referred to: *if anyone phones, ask them to leave their number*

theme *noun* **1** the subject of a discussion, essay *etc* **2** *music* a main melody which is often repeated

theme park a public display in an open area, related to a single theme

theme song or **theme tune** a tune that is repeated often in a film, television series *etc*

themselves *pronoun plural* **1** used reflexively: *they tired themselves out walking* **2** used for emphasis: *they'll have to do it by themselves*

then *adverb* **1** at that time: *I didn't know you then* **2** after that: *and then where did you go?* □ *conjunction* in that case, therefore: *if you're busy, then don't come*

thence *adverb, old* from that time or place

thenceforth *adverb* from that time onward

theo- *prefix* forms words relating to God or gods: *theology*
ⓘ Comes from Greek *theos* meaning 'God' or 'a god'

theocracy *noun* government of a state according to religious laws

theocratic *adjective* relating to or involving theocracy

theologian *noun* someone who studies theology

theological *adjective* relating to or involving theology

theology *noun* the study of God and religion

theorem *noun* a proposition to be proved in mathematics *etc*

theoretical *adjective* of theory, not experience or practice □ **theoretically** *adverb*: *it is theoretically possible to travel from Glasgow to Edinburgh in one hour*

theorize *verb* to form theories

theory *noun* (*plural* **theories**) **1** an explanation that has not been proved or tested **2** the underlying ideas in an art, science *etc*, compared to practice or performance

therapeutic *adjective* **1** of therapy **2** healing, curing

therapist *noun* someone who gives therapeutic treatment: *speech therapist*

therapy *noun* (*plural* **therapies**) treatment of disease or disorders

there *adverb* at, in or to that place: *what did you do there?* □ *pronoun* used (with *be*) as a subject of a sentence or clause when the real subject follows the verb: *there is nobody at home*

   🖝 Do not confuse with: **their**. Remember that **there** is spelt the same as 'here' except for the first letter – and that the 'y' in the pronoun 'they' turns into an 'i' in **their**

thereabouts *adverb* approximately

thereafter *adverb* after that

thereby *adverb* by that means

therefore *adverb* for this or that reason

thereof *adverb* of that

thereupon *adverb* **1** because of this or that **2** immediately

therm *noun* a unit of heat used in measuring gas

thermal *adjective* **1** of heat **2** of hot springs

thermo- or **therm-** *prefix* forms words relating to heat or temperature
ⓘ Comes from Greek *therme* meaning 'heat', and *thermos* meaning 'hot'

thermodynamics *noun singular* the science of the relation between heat and mechanical energy

thermometer *noun* an instrument for measuring temperature

thermonuclear *adjective* relating to the fusion of nuclei at high temperatures

Thermos *noun, trademark* a kind of vacuum flask

thermostat *noun* a device for automatically controlling temperature in a room

thesaurus *noun* (*plural* **thesauri** or

thesauruses) 1 a reference book listing words and their synonyms 2 a dictionary or encyclopedia

these *see* **this**

thesis *noun* (*plural* **theses**) 1 a long piece of written work on a topic, often part of a university degree 2 a statement of a point of view

thespian *noun, formal* an actor

Named after *Thespis*, founder of ancient Greek tragedy

they *pronoun plural* some people or things already mentioned (used only as the subject of a verb): *they followed the others* □ *pronoun singular* used to avoid giving the gender of the person being referred to: *anyone can come if they like*

thick *adjective* 1 not thin, of reasonable width: *a thick slice/ two metres thick* 2 of a mixture: containing solid matter, stiff: *a thick soup* 3 dense, difficult to see or pass through: *thick fog/ thick woods* 4 of speech: not clear 5 *informal* stupid 6 *informal* very friendly □ *noun* the thickest, most crowded or active part: *in the thick of the fight*

■ **Alternative words**: (adjective, meaning 1) wide, broad (adjective, meaning 2) viscous

thicken *verb* to make or become thick

thicket *noun* a group of close-set trees and bushes

thickness *noun* 1 the quality of being thick 2 the distance between opposite sides 3 a layer

thickset *adjective* 1 closely set or planted 2 having a thick sturdy body

thick-skinned *adjective* not sensitive or easily hurt

thief *noun* (*plural* **thieves**) someone who steals

thieve *verb* to steal

thieving *noun* stealing □ *adjective* that thieves

thievish *adjective* inclined to stealing

thigh *noun* the thick, fleshy part of the leg between the knee and the hip

thimble *noun* a small cap worn over a fingertip, used to push a needle while sewing

thin *adjective* 1 not very wide between its two sides: *thin paper/ thin slice* 2 slim, not fat 3 not dense or crowded: *thin population* 4 poor in quality: *thin wine* 5 of a voice: weak, not resonating 6 of a mixture: not stiff, watery: *a thin soup* □ *verb* to make or become thin or thinner □ **thinness** *noun*

thin *verb* ⇨ **thin**s, **thin**ning, **thin**ned

■ **Alternative words**: (adjective, meaning 1) fine, delicate, light, flimsy, gossamer, sheer (adjective, meaning 2) lean, slim, slender, attenuated, slight, skinny, skeletal, scraggy, scrawny, lanky, gaunt, underweight, emaciated

thine *adjective, old* belonging to you (used before words beginning with a vowel or a vowel sound): *thine enemies* □ *pronoun, old* something belonging to you: *my heart is thine*

thing *noun* 1 an object that is not living 2 *informal* a person: *a nice old thing* 3 **things** belongings 4 an individual object, quality, idea *etc* that may be referred to: *several things must be taken into consideration*

Ⓘ Comes from Old English and Old Norse *thing* meaning 'parliament' or 'object'

think *verb* 1 to work things out, reason 2 to form ideas in the mind 3 to believe, judge or consider: *I think that we should go* 4 **think of doing something** to intend to do it: *she is thinking of resigning* □ **think better of** to change your mind about □ **think highly of** or **think much of** to have a good opinion of □ **think nothing of** 1 to have a poor opinion of 2 to consider as easy □ **think out** to work out in the mind

think *verb* ⇨ **think**s, **think**ing, **thought**

Ⓘ Comes from Old English *thencan*

think tank a group of people who give expert advice and come up with ideas

third *adjective* the last of a series of three □ *noun* one of three equal parts

thirl *verb, Scottish* to bind with an agreement, loyalty, love *etc*

thirst *noun* 1 a dry feeling in the mouth caused by lack of fluid 2 an eager desire (for): *thirst for knowledge* □ *verb* to feel thirsty **2 thirst for something** to desire it eagerly

thirsty *adjective* **1** having thirst **2** of earth: parched, dry **3** eager (for)

thirteen *noun* the number 13 □ *adjective* thirteen in number

thirteenth *adjective* the last of a series of thirteen □ *noun* one of thirteen equal parts

thirtieth *adjective* the last of a series of thirty □ *noun* one of thirty equal parts

thirty *noun* the number 30 □ *adjective* thirty in number

this *adjective & pronoun (plural* **these**) **1** used to point out someone or something, especially one nearby (*contrasted with:* **that**): *look at this letter/ take this instead* **2** to such an extent or degree: *this early*

thistle *noun* a prickly plant with purple flowers

thistledown *noun* the feathery bristles of the seeds of the thistle

thither *adverb* to that place

thong *noun* **1** a thin strap of leather to fasten anything **2** the lash of a whip

thorax *noun (plural* **thoraxes** or **thoraces**) **1** the chest in the human or animal body **2** the middle section of an insect's body

thorn *noun* **1** a sharp prickle sticking out from the stem of a plant **2** a bush with thorns, especially the hawthorn □ **thorn in the flesh** a cause of constant irritation

thorny *adjective* **1** full of thorns; prickly **2** difficult, causing arguments: *a thorny problem*

thorough *adjective* **1** complete, absolute: *a thorough muddle* **2** very careful, attending to every detail

thoroughbred *noun* an animal of pure breed

thoroughfare *noun* **1** a public street **2** a passage or way through: *no thoroughfare*

thoroughly *adverb* **1** completely, absolutely: *I thoroughly agree* **2** very carefully: *the product has been tested thoroughly*

those *see* **that**

thou *pronoun, old* you (as the subject of a sentence)

though *conjunction* although: *though he disliked it, he ate it all* □ *adverb, informal* however: *I wish I'd never said it, though*

thought *noun* **1** the act of thinking **2** something which you think, an idea **3** an opinion **4** consideration: *after much thought* □ *verb, past form* of **think**
🕐 Noun: comes from Old English *thoht/gethoht*, past participle of *thencan* meaning 'to think'; verb past form: Comes from Old English *thohte*, past tense of *thencan* meaning 'to think'

thoughtful *adjective* **1** full of thought **2** thinking of others, considerate

thoughtless *adjective* showing lack of thought; inconsiderate

thousand *noun* the number 1000 □ *adjective* a thousand in number

thousandth *adjective* the last of a series of a thousand □ *noun* one of a thousand equal parts

thrash *verb* **1** to beat severely **2** to move or toss violently (about) **3 thrash something out** to discuss a problem *etc* thoroughly **4** to thresh (grain) □ *noun* thrash metal music

thrashing *noun* a flogging, a beating

thrash metal very fast, loud rock music resembling punk rock, often with violent themes

thread *noun* **1** a very thin line of cotton, wool, silk *etc*, often twisted and drawn out **2** the ridge which goes in a spiral round a screw **3** a connected series of details in correct order in a story □ *verb* **1** to put a thread through a needle *etc* **2** to make (your way) in a narrow space

threadbare *adjective* of clothes: worn thin

threat *noun* **1** a warning that you intend to hurt or punish someone **2** a warning of something bad that may come: *a threat of war* **3** something likely to cause harm: *a threat to our plans*

threaten *verb* **1** to make a threat: *threatened to kill himself* **2** to suggest the approach of something unpleasant **3** to be a danger to

three *noun* the number 3 □ *adjective* 3 in number

🕓 Comes from Old English *threo*

3-D *short for* three-dimensional

thresh *verb* to beat out (grain) from straw

threshold *noun* **1** a piece of wood or stone under the door of a building **2** a doorway **3** an entry or beginning: *on the threshold of a new era*

threw *past form of* **throw**

thrice *adverb* three times

thrift *noun* careful management of money in order to save

thrifty *adjective* careful about spending

thrill *noun* **1** an excited feeling **2** quivering, vibration □ *verb* **1** to feel excitement **2** to make excited

thriller *noun* an exciting story, often about crime and detection

thrilling *adjective* very exciting

thrive *verb* **1** to grow strong and healthy **2** to get on well, be successful

throat *noun* **1** the back part of the mouth **2** the front part of the neck

throb *verb* **1** of a pulse *etc*: to beat, especially more strongly than normal **2** to beat or vibrate rhythmically and regularly

> **throb** *verb* ⇨ throb*s*, throb*bing*, throb*bed*

throes *noun plural* great suffering or struggle □ **in the throes of** in the middle of (a struggle, doing a task *etc*)

thrombosis *noun* the forming of a clot in a blood vessel

throne *noun* **1** the seat of a monarch or bishop **2** a monarch or their power

throng *noun* a crowd □ *verb* **1** to move in a crowd **2** to crowd, fill (a place)

throttle *noun* the part of an engine through which steam or petrol can be turned on or off □ *verb* to choke by gripping the throat

through *preposition* **1** entering from one direction and out in the other: *through the tunnel* **2** from end to end, or side to side, of: *all through the performance* **3** by way of: *related through his grandmother* **4** as a result of: *through his expertise* **5** *US* from (one date) to (another) inclusive: *Monday*

through Friday is five days □ *adverb* into and out, from beginning to end: *all the way through the tunnel* □ *adjective* **1** without break or change: *through train* **2** *informal* finished: *are you through with the newspaper?* **3** of a telephone call: connected: *I couldn't get through this morning*

through-and-through *adverb* completely, entirely: *a gentleman through-and-through*

throughout *preposition* **1** in all parts of: *throughout Europe* **2** from start to finish of: *throughout the journey*

throw *verb* **1** to send through the air with force **2** of a horse: to make (a rider) fall to the ground **3** to shape (pottery) on a wheel **4** to give (a party) □ *noun* **1** the act of throwing **2** the distance a thing is thrown: *within a stone's throw of the house* □ **throw away** to get rid of

> **throw** *verb* ⇨ throw*s*, throw*ing*, threw, thrown

■ **Alternative words**: (verb, meaning 1) hurl, heave, lob, pitch, sling, cast, fling, toss □ **throw away** discard, jettison, dump, scrap, dispose of

throwback *noun* a reversion to an earlier form

thrush (*plural* **thrushes**) **1** a type of singing bird with a speckled breast **2** an infection which can affect the mouth, throat or vagina

thrust *verb* **1** to push with force **2** to make a sudden push forward with a pointed weapon **3** **thrust something on** or **upon someone** to force them to accept it □ *noun* **1** a stab **2** a pushing force

> **thrust** *verb* ⇨ thrust*s*, thrust*ing*, thrust

thud *noun* a dull, hollow sound like that made by a heavy body falling □ *verb* to move or fall with such a sound

> **thud** *verb* ⇨ thud*s*, thud*ding*, thud*ded*

thug *noun* a violent, brutal person

thumb *noun* the short, thick finger of the hand □ *verb* to turn over (the pages of a book) with the thumb or fingers

□ **rule of thumb** a rough-and-ready practical method □ **thumbs down** or **thumbs up** showing disapproval, or approval, of something □ **under someone's thumb** under their control

thumbscrew *noun, historical* an instrument of torture which worked by squashing the thumbs

thump *noun* a heavy blow □ *verb* 1 to beat heavily 2 to move or fall with a dull, heavy noise

thunder *noun* 1 the deep rumbling sound heard after a flash of lightning 2 any loud, rumbling noise □ *verb* 1 to produce the sound of, or a sound like, thunder 2 to shout out angrily

thunderbolt *noun* 1 a flash of lightning followed by thunder 2 a very great and sudden surprise

thunderclap *noun* a sudden roar of thunder

thunderous *adjective* like thunder; very angry

thunderstruck *adjective* overcome by surprise

thundery *adjective* of weather: sultry, bringing thunder

Thursday *noun* the fifth day of the week

thus *adverb* 1 in this or that manner: *he always talks thus* 2 to this degree or extent: *thus far* 3 because of this, therefore: *thus, we must go on*

thwart *verb* 1 to hinder (someone) from carrying out a plan, intention *etc* 2 to prevent (an attempt *etc*) □ *noun* a cross seat for rowers in a boat

thy *adjective, old* belonging to you: *thy wife and children*

thyme *noun* a small sweet-smelling herb used for seasoning food

thyroid gland a large gland in the neck which influences the rate at which energy is used by the body

Based on a Greek word meaning 'door-shaped', because of the shape of the cartilage in the front of the throat

tiara *noun* a jewelled ornament for the head like a crown

tic *noun* a twitching motion of certain

muscles, especially of the face

tick[1] *noun* 1 a light mark (✓) used to mark as correct, or mark off in a list 2 a small quick noise, made regularly by a clock or watch 3 *informal* a moment: *I'll just be a tick* □ *verb* 1 to mark with a tick 2 of a clock *etc*: to produce regular ticks

tick[2] *noun* a tiny blood-sucking animal

ticking *noun* the noise made by a clock *etc*

tickle *verb* 1 to excite the surface nerves of a part of the body by touching lightly 2 to please or amuse

ticklish *adjective* 1 sensitive to tickling 2 not easy to deal with: *ticklish problem*

tickly *adjective* ticklish

tidal *adjective* of the tide

tidal wave an enormous wave in the sea often caused by an earthquake *etc*

tiddlywinks *noun singular* a game in which small plastic discs (**tiddlywinks**) are flipped into a cup

tide *noun* 1 the rise and fall of the sea which happens regularly twice each day 2 *old* time, season: *Christmastide* □ **tide over** to help to get over a difficulty for a time

tidings *noun plural* news

tidy *adjective* 1 in good order, neat 2 *informal* fairly big: *a tidy sum of money* □ *verb* to make neat □ **tidily** *adverb*

tidy *verb* ⇨ tidies, tidy*ing*, tidi*ed*

■ **Alternative words**: (adjective, meaning 1) orderly, organized, spick-and-span, spruce, ordered, uncluttered

tie *verb* 1 to fasten with a cord, string *etc* 2 to knot or put a bow in (string, shoelaces *etc*) 3 to join, unite 4 to limit, restrict: *tied to a tight schedule* 5 to score the same number of points (in a game *etc*), draw □ *noun* 1 a band of fabric worn round the neck, tied with a knot or bow 2 something that connects: *ties of friendship* 3 something that restricts or limits 4 an equal score in a competition 5 a game or match to be played

tie *verb* ⇨ ties, ty*ing*, ti*ed*

tie-breaker *noun* an extra question or part of a tied contest to decide a winner

tier (*pronounced* teer) *noun* a row of seats in a theatre *etc*, with others above or below it

tiff *noun* a slight quarrel

tig *another name* for **tag**

tiger *noun* a large animal of the cat family with a tawny coat striped with black

tight *adjective* 1 packed closely 2 firmly stretched, not loose 3 fitting too closely: *these jeans are a bit tight* 4 *informal* short of money 5 *informal* drunk

tighten *verb* to make or become tight or tighter

tight-fisted *adjective* stingy

tight-lipped *adjective* uncommunicative

tightrope *noun* a tightly stretched rope on which acrobats perform

tights *noun plural* a close-fitting garment covering the feet, legs and body as far as the waist

tigress *noun* a female tiger

tile *noun* a piece of baked clay *etc* used in covering floors or roofs □ *verb* to cover with tiles

till¹ *noun* a container or drawer for money in a shop □ *verb* to cultivate (land); plough

till² *see* **until**

tiller *noun* the handle of a boat's rudder

tilt *verb* 1 to fall into, or place in, a sloping position 2 *historical* to joust 3 *historical* **tilt at someone** or **something** to attack them on horseback, using a lance □ *noun* 1 a slant 2 a thrust, a jab □ **at full tilt** with full speed and force

timber *noun* 1 wood for building *etc* 2 trees suitable for this 3 a wooden beam in a house or ship

timbre *noun* the quality of a musical sound or voice

time *noun* 1 the hour of the day 2 the period at which something happens 3 (often **times**) a particular period: *in modern times* 4 opportunity: *no time to listen* 5 a suitable or right moment: *now is the time to ask* 6 one of a number of

occasions: *he won four times* 7 **times** multiplied by: *two times four* 8 the rhythm or rate of performance of a piece of music □ *adjective* 1 of time 2 arranged to go off at a certain time: *a time bomb* □ *verb* 1 to measure the minutes, seconds *etc* taken to do anything 2 to choose the time for (well, badly *etc*): *time your entrance well* □ **at times** occasionally □ **do time** *slang* to serve a prison sentence □ **in time** early enough □ **on time** or **up to time** punctual □ **the time being** the present time
⏱ Comes from Old English *tima*

time-honoured *adjective* respected because it has lasted a long time

timeless *adjective* 1 not belonging to any particular time 2 never ending: *timeless beauty*

timely *adjective* coming at the right moment: *a timely reminder*

time-sharing *noun* 1 a system of using a computer so that it can deal with several programs at the same time 2 a scheme by which someone buys the right to use a holiday home for a specified period each year

timetable *noun* a list showing times of classes, arrivals or departures of trains *etc*

timid *adjective* easily frightened; shy

timidity *noun* nervousness, shyness

timidly *adverb* shyly

timorous *adjective* very timid

tìmpani or **tympani** *noun plural* kettledrums

tin *noun* 1 a silvery-white kind of metal 2 a box or can made of **tinplate**, thin iron covered with tin or other metal □ *verb* 1 to cover with tin 2 to pack (food *etc*) in tins

> **tin** *verb* ⇨ tins, tinning, tinned

tincture *noun* 1 a slight tinge of colour 2 a characteristic quality 3 a medicine mixed in alcohol

tinder *noun* dry material easily set alight by a spark

tine *noun* a spike of a fork or of a deer's antler

tinfoil *noun* a very thin sheet of tin,

aluminium *etc* used for wrapping

tinge *verb* **1** to tint, colour slightly **2 tinge with something** to add a slight amount of it to □ *noun* a slight amount; a hint: *tinge of pink/ tinge of sadness*

tingle *verb* **1** to feel a sharp prickling sensation **2** to feel a thrill of excitement □ *noun* a sharp prickle

tinker *noun* a mender of kettles, pans *etc* □ *verb* **1** to work clumsily or unskilfully **2** to meddle (with)

tinkle *verb* to (cause to) make a light, ringing sound; clink, jingle, □ *noun* a light, ringing sound

tinny *adjective* **1** like tin **2** of sound: thin, high-pitched

tinsel *noun* a sparkling, glittering material used for decoration

tint *noun* a variety or shade of a colour □ *verb* to give slight colour to

tiny *adjective* very small

tip *noun* **1** the top or point of something thin or tapering **2** a piece of useful information **3** a small gift of money to a waiter *etc* **4** a rubbish dump **5** a light stroke, a tap □ *verb* **1** to slant **2 tip something over** to overturn it **3 tip something out** or **into** to empty it out or into **4** (also **tip off**) to give a hint to **5** to give a small gift of money **6** to strike lightly

> **tip** *verb* ⇨ tips, tipping, tipped

Tipp-Ex *noun, trademark* correcting fluid for covering over mistakes in typing or writing

tipple *verb, informal* to drink small amounts of alcohol regularly □ *noun* an alcoholic drink

tippler *noun* someone who regularly drinks alcohol

tipsiness *noun* being slightly drunk

tipsy *adjective* rather drunk

tiptoe *verb* **1** to walk on your toes in order to go very quietly □ **on tiptoe** standing or walking on your toes

tirade *noun* a long, bitter, scolding speech

tire[1] *verb* **1** to make or become weary **2 tire of something** to lose patience with or interest in it

tire[2] *US spelling of* tyre

tired *adjective* **1** weary **2 tired of something** or **someone** bored with them

> ◾ **Alternative words**: (meaning 1) drowsy, sleepy, flagging, fatigued, exhausted, drained, jaded

tireless *adjective* **1** never becoming weary **2** never resting

tiresome *adjective* **1** making weary **2** long and dull **3** annoying: *a tiresome child*

tiring *adjective* causing tiredness or weariness: *a tiring journey*

tiro or **tyro** *noun* (*plural* **tiros** or **tyros**) a beginner

tissue *noun* **1** the substance of which body organs are made: *muscle tissue* **2** a mass, a network (of lies, nonsense *etc*) **3** a paper handkerchief **4** finely woven cloth

tissue paper thin, soft paper used for wrapping

tit *noun* **1** a type of small bird: *blue tit/ great tit* **2** a teat □ **tit for tat** blow for blow, repayment of injury with injury

titanic *adjective* huge, enormous

titbit *noun* a tasty piece of food *etc*

tithe (*pronounced* taidh) *noun, historical* a tax paid to the church, a tenth part of someone's income or produce

titillate *verb* to gently stimulate or arouse (often sexually)
Ⓛ Comes from Latin *titillare* meaning 'to tickle'

> ☛ Do not confuse: **titillate** and **titivate**

titivate *verb* to make smarter; improve in appearance

> It is thought that **titivate** was created by taking 'tidy' and reforming it on the model of the verb 'cultivate'

title *noun* **1** the name of a book, poem *etc* **2** a word in front of a name to show rank or office (*eg Sir, Lady, Major*), or in addressing anyone formally (*eg Mr, Mrs, Ms*) **3** right or claim to money, an estate *etc*

titled *adjective* having a title which shows noble rank

title deed a document that proves a right to ownership (of a house *etc*)

title role the part in a play which is the same as the title *eg Hamlet*

titter *verb* to giggle □ *noun* a giggle

tizzy *noun* a state of confusion, a flap

TNT *abbreviation* trinitrotoluene, a high explosive

to *preposition* **1** showing the place or direction aimed for: *going to the cinema/ emigrating to New Zealand* **2** showing the indirect object in a phrase, sentence *etc*: *show it to me* **3** used before a verb to indicate the infinitive: *to err is human* **4** showing that one thing belongs with another in some way: *key to the door* **5** compared with: *nothing to what happened before* **6** about, concerning: *what did he say to that?* **7** showing a ratio, proportion *etc*: *odds are six to one against* **8** showing the purpose or result of an action: *tear it to pieces* □ *adverb* almost closed: *pull the door to* □ **to and fro** backwards and forwards

toad *noun* a type of amphibian like a frog

toadstool *noun* a mushroom-like fungus, often poisonous

toady *verb* to give way to someone's wishes, or flatter them, to gain favour □ *noun* someone who acts in this way

toast *verb* **1** to brown (bread) by heating at a fire or grill **2** to drink to the success or health of (someone) **3** to warm (your feet *etc*) at a fire □ *noun* **1** bread toasted **2** the person to whom a toast is drunk **3** the drinking of a toast

toaster *noun* an electric machine for toasting bread

toast-rack *noun* a stand with partitions for slices of toast

tobacco *noun* a type of plant whose dried leaves are used for smoking

tobacconist *noun* someone who sells tobacco, cigarettes *etc*

toboggan a long, light sledge □ *verb* to go in a toboggan

today *adverb & noun* **1** (on) this day **2** (at) the present time

toddle *verb* to walk unsteadily, with short steps

toddler *noun* a young child just able to walk

toddy *noun* (*plural* **toddies**) a hot drink of whisky and honey

to-do *noun* (*plural* **to-dos**) a bustle, commotion

toe *noun* **1** one of the five finger-like parts of the foot **2** the front part of an animal's foot **3** the front part of a shoe, golf club *etc* □ **on your toes** alert, ready for action □ **toe the line** to do as you are told

toffee *noun* a kind of sweet made of sugar and butter

toffee-nosed *adjective, informal* snobbish, conceited

toga *noun, historical* the loose outer garment worn by a citizen of ancient Rome

together *adverb* **1** with each other, in place or time: *we must stay together/ three buses arrived together* **2** in or into union or connection: *glue the pages together* **3** by joint action: *together we can afford it*

toggle *noun* a cylindrical fastening for a coat □ *verb* to switch quickly between two positions, states *etc* (especially between being on and off)

toil *verb* **1** to work hard and long **2** to walk, move *etc* with effort □ *noun* hard work

toilet *noun* **1** the act of washing yourself, doing your hair **2** a receptacle for waste matter from the body, with a water-supply for flushing this away **3** a room containing this

toiletries *noun plural* soaps, cosmetics *etc*

toilet water a lightly perfumed, spirit-based liquid for the skin

token *noun* **1** a mark, a sign: *a token of my friendship* **2** a stamped piece of plastic *etc*, or a voucher, for use in place of money: *bus token/ book token* □ *adjective* done for show only, insincere: *token gesture*

told *past form* of **tell**

tolerable *adjective* **1** bearable,

endurable **2** fairly good: *tolerable player* □ **tolerably** *adverb*

tolerance *noun* **1** putting up with and being fair to people with different beliefs, manners *etc* from your own **2** ability to resist the effects of a drug *etc*

tolerant *adjective* **1** fair towards other people and accepting their right to have different political and religious beliefs **2** able to resist the effects of a drug *etc*

tolerate *verb* **1** to bear, endure; put up with **2** to allow

toleration *noun* **1** the act of tolerating **2** the practice of allowing people to practise religions which are different to the established religion of the country

toll¹ *noun* **1** a tax charged for crossing a bridge *etc* **2** loss, damage □ **take toll** to cause damage or loss

toll² *verb* **1** to sound (a large bell) slowly, as for a funeral **2** of a bell: to be sounded slowly

tomahawk *noun, historical* a Native American light axe used as a weapon and tool

tomato *noun* (*plural* **tomatoes**) a juicy red-skinned fruit, used in salads, sauces *etc*

tomb *noun* **1** a grave **2** a burial vault or chamber

tombola *noun* a kind of lottery

tomboy *noun* a high-spirited active girl who enjoys the rough, boisterous activities which people tend to associate with boys

tombstone *noun* a stone placed over a grave in memory of the dead person

tomcat *noun* a male cat

tome *noun* a large heavy book

tomorrow *adverb & noun* **1** (on) the day after today **2** (in) the future: *the children of tomorrow*

tomtom *noun* a type of drum beaten with the hands

ton *noun* **1** a measure of weight equal to 2240 pounds, about 1016 kilogrammes **2** a unit (100 cubic feet) of space in a ship □ **metric ton** or **metric tonne** 1000 kilogrammes

tone *noun* **1** sound **2** quality of sound: *harsh tone* **3** *music* one of the larger

intervals in a scale, *eg* between C and D **4** the quality of a voice expressing the mood of the speaker: *a gentle tone* **5** a shade of colour **6** muscle firmness or strength □ *verb* **1** (sometimes **tone in**) to blend, fit in well **2 tone down** to make or become softer **3 tone up** to give strength to (muscles *etc*)

tongs *noun plural* an instrument for lifting and grasping coals, sugar lumps *etc*

tongue *noun* **1** the fleshy organ inside the mouth, used in tasting, speaking, and swallowing **2** a flap in a shoe **3** a long, thin strip of land **4** the tongue of an animal served as food **5** a language: *his mother tongue*

tongue-tied *adjective* not able to speak freely

tongue-twister *noun* a phrase, sentence *etc* not easy to say quickly, *eg* 'she sells sea shells'

tonic *noun* **1** a medicine which gives strength and energy **2** *music* the keynote of a scale **3** tonic water □ *adjective* **1** of tones or sounds **2** of a tonic

tonic water aerated water with quinine

tonight *adverb & noun* (on) the night of the present day

tonnage *noun* the space available in a ship, measured in tons

tonne *another spelling of* **ton**

tonsil *noun* one of a pair of soft, fleshy lumps at the back of the throat

tonsillitis *noun* reddening and painfulness of the tonsils

too *adverb* **1** to a greater extent, in a greater quantity *etc* than is wanted: *too hot to go outside/ too many people in the room* **2** (with a negative) very, particularly: *not feeling too well* (ie not feeling very well) **3** also, as well: *I'm feeling quite cold, too*

took *past form of* **take**

tool *noun* an instrument for doing work, especially by hand

toot *noun* the sound of a car horn *etc*

tooth *noun* (*plural* **teeth**) *noun* **1** any of the hard, bony objects projecting from the gums, arranged in two rows in the mouth **2** any of the points on a saw, cogwheel, comb *etc* □ **tooth and nail** fiercely, determinedly

toothache *noun* pain in a tooth

toothpaste or **tooth-powder** *noun* paste or powder for cleaning the teeth

toothpick *noun* a small sharp instrument for picking out food from between the teeth

top *noun* **1** the highest part of anything **2** the upper surface **3** the highest place or rank **4** a lid **5** a circus tent **6** a kind of spinning toy □ *adjective* highest, chief □ *verb* **1** to cover on the top **2** to rise above **3** to do better than **4** to reach the top of **5** to take off the top of

> **top** *verb* ⇨ tops, topping, topped

topaz *noun* a type of precious stone, of various colours

top dog *informal* a winner or leader

top hat a man's tall silk hat

top-heavy *adjective* having the upper part too heavy for the lower

topiary *noun* the art of trimming bushes, hedges *etc* into decorative shapes

topic *noun* a subject spoken or written about

topical *adjective* of current interest, concerned with present events

topmost *adjective* highest, uppermost

topographical *adjective* relating to or involving topography

topography *noun* the description of the features of the land in a certain region

topple *verb* to become unsteady and fall

top-secret *adjective* (of information *etc*) very secret

topsyturvy *adjective & adverb* turned upside down

torch *noun* (*plural* **torches**) **1** a small hand-held light with a switch and electric battery **2** a flaming piece of wood or coarse rope carried as a light in processions □ *verb, slang* to set fire to deliberately

tore *past form* of **tear**

toreador *noun* a bullfighter mounted on horseback

torment *verb* **1** to treat cruelly and make suffer **2** to worry greatly **3** to tease □ *noun* **1** great pain, suffering **2** a cause of these

tormentor *noun* a person who torments

torn *past participle* of **tear**

tornado *noun* (*plural* **tornadoes**) a violent whirling wind that causes great damage

torpedo *noun* (*plural* **torpedoes**) a large cigar-shaped type of missile fired by ships, planes *etc verb* to hit or sink (a ship) with a torpedo

> **torpedo** *verb* ⇨ torpedoes, torpedoing, torpedoed

torpid *adjective* slow, dull, stupid

torpidity or **torpor** *noun* dullness

torrent *noun* **1** a rushing stream **2** a heavy downpour of rain **3** a violent flow of words *etc*: *torrent of abuse*

torrential *adjective* like a torrent; rushing violently

torrid *adjective* **1** parched by heat; very hot **2** very passionate: *torrid love affair*

torsion *noun* twisting; a twist

torso *noun* (*plural* **torsos**) the body, excluding the head and limbs

tortoise *noun* a four-footed, slow-moving kind of reptile, covered with a hard shell

tortoiseshell *noun* the shell of a kind of sea turtle, used in making ornamental articles □ *adjective* **1** made of this shell **2** mottled brown, yellow and black: *a tortoiseshell cat*

tortuous *adjective* winding, roundabout, not straightforward

torture *verb* **1** to treat someone cruelly as a punishment or to force them to confess something **2** to cause to suffer □ *noun* **1** the act of torturing **2** great suffering

Tory *noun* (*plural* **Tories**) a member of the British Conservative Party

> Originally one of a group of Irish Catholics thrown off their land who waged guerrilla war on British settlers, later applied to any royalist supporter

toss *verb* **1** to throw up in the air **2** to

throw up (a coin) to see which side falls uppermost **3** to turn restlessly from side to side **4** of a ship: to be thrown about by rough water □ **toss off** to produce quickly □ **toss up** to toss a coin

toss-up *noun* an equal choice or chance

tot[1] *noun* **1** a little child **2** a small amount of alcoholic spirits

tot[2] *verb*: **tot up** to add up

total *adjective* **1** whole: *total number* **2** complete: *total wreck* □ *noun* **1** the entire amount **2** the sum of amounts added together □ *verb* **1** to add up **2** to amount to **3** *informal* to damage irreparably; wreck

> **total** *verb* ⇨ totals, totalling, totalled

totalitarian *adjective* governed by a single party that allows no rivals

totally *adverb* completely

totem *noun* an image of an animal or plant used as the badge or sign of a Native American tribe

totem pole a pole on which totems are carved and painted

totter *verb* **1** to shake as if about to fall **2** to stagger

toucan *noun* a type of S American bird with a very big beak

touch *verb* **1** to feel (with the hand) **2** to come or be in contact (with): *a leaf touched his cheek* **3** to move, affect the feelings of: *the story touched those who heard it* **4** to mark slightly with colour: *touched with gold* **5** to reach the standard of: *I can't touch him at chess* **6** to have anything to do with: *I wouldn't touch a job like that* **7** to eat or drink: *he won't touch meat* **8** to concern (someone) **9** *informal* to persuade (someone) to lend you money: *I touched him for £10* □ *noun* **1** the act of touching **2** the physical sense of touch **3** a small quantity or degree: *a touch of salt* **4** the art of an artist, pianist *etc*: skill or style **5** *football* the ground beyond the edges of the pitch marked off by **touchlines** □ **in** (or **out of**) **touch with 1** in (or not in) communication or contact with **2** aware (or unaware) of □ **touch down** of an aircraft: to land □ **touch off** to cause to happen □ **touch on** to mention briefly □ **touch up** to

improve (a drawing or photograph *etc*) by making details clearer *etc*

■ **Alternative words**: **in touch with** (meaning 2) abreast of

touch-and-go *adjective* very uncertain: *it's touch-and-go whether we'll get it done on time*

touché (*pronounced* too-**shei**) *exclamation* acknowledging a point scored in a game or argument

touching *preposition* about, concerning □ *adjective* causing emotion, moving

touchstone *noun* a test or standard of measurement of quality *etc*

touchy *adjective* **1** easily offended **2** needing to be handled with care and tact: *a touchy subject* □ **touchily** *adverb* (meaning 1)

tough *adjective* **1** strong, not easily broken **2** of meat *etc*: hard to chew **3** of strong character, able to stand hardship or strain **4** difficult to cope with or overcome: *tough opposition*

toughen *verb* to (cause to) become tough

tour *noun* a journey in which you visit various places; a pleasure trip □ *verb* to make a tour (of)

tourism *noun* the activities of tourists and of those who cater for their needs

tourist *noun* someone who travels for pleasure, and visits places of interest

tournament *noun* **1** a competition involving many contests and players **2** *historical* a meeting at which knights fought together on horseback

tourniquet (*pronounced* **toorn**-ik-ei) *noun* a bandage tied tightly round a limb to prevent loss of blood from a wound

tousled *adjective* of hair: untidy, tangled

tout *verb* to go about looking for support, votes, buyers *etc* □ *noun* **1** someone who does this **2** someone who gives tips to people who bet on horse races

tow *verb* to pull (a car etc) with a rope attached to another vehicle □ *noun* **1** the act of towing **2** the rope used for towing □ **in tow** under protection or guidance □ **on tow** being towed

towards or **toward** *preposition* **1** moving in the direction of (a place, person *etc*): *walking towards the house* **2** to (a person, thing *etc*): *his attitude towards his son* **3** as a help or contribution to: *I gave £5 towards the cost* **4** near, about (a time *etc*): *towards four o'clock*

towel *noun* a cloth for drying or wiping (*eg* the skin after washing) □ *verb* to rub dry with a towel

> **towel** *verb* ⇨ towels, towell*ing*, towell*ed*

towelling *noun* a cotton cloth often used for making towels

tower *noun* **1** a high narrow building **2** a high narrow part of a castle *etc* □ *verb* to rise high (over, above)

towering *adjective* **1** rising high **2** violent: *a towering rage*

town *noun* a place, larger than a village, which includes many buildings, houses, shops *etc*

town crier *historical* someone who made public announcements in a town

town hall the building where the official business of a town is done

towpath *noun* a path alongside a canal used by horses which tow barges

-tox- also **-toxi-**, **-toxico-** of or relating to poison: *toxaemia* (= blood poisoning)/ *intoxication*
ⓘ Comes from Greek *toxikon pharmacon* meaning 'poison for the bow'

toxaemia *noun* poisoning

toxic *adjective* **1** poisonous **2** caused by poison

toxicology *noun* the scientific study of poisons

toxic shock syndrome a condition which can be fatal, characterized by high fever, vomiting and diarrhoea, sometimes occurring in women using tampons

toxin *noun* a naturally-occurring poison

toy *noun* **1** an object for a child to play with **2** an object for amusement only □ **toy with** to play or trifle with

trace *noun* **1** a mark or sign left behind **2** a footprint **3** a small amount **4** a line drawn by an instrument recording a change (*eg* in temperature) **5 traces** the straps by which a horse pulls a cart *etc* along □ *verb* **1** to follow the tracks or course of **2** to copy (a drawing *etc*) on transparent paper placed over it

traceable *adjective* able to be traced (to)

tracery *noun* decorated stonework holding the glass in some church windows

tracing *noun* a traced copy

track *noun* **1** a mark left **2 tracks** footprints **3** a path or rough road **4** a racecourse for runners, cyclists *etc* **5** a railway line **6** an endless band on which wheels of a tank *etc* travel □ *verb* to follow (an animal) by its footprints and other marks left □ **keep** or **lose track of** to keep or fail to keep aware of the whereabouts or progress of □ **make tracks for** to set off towards □ **track down** to search for (someone or something) until caught or found

tracksuit *noun* a warm suit worn while jogging, before and after an athletic performance *etc*

tract *noun* **1** a stretch of land **2** a short pamphlet, especially on a religious subject **3** a system made up of connected parts of the body: *the digestive tract*

-tract- forms words related to the action of pulling or drawing: *tractable* (= easily pulled along)/ *subtract* (= to draw away)
ⓘ Comes from Latin *trahere* meaning 'to draw', and *tractare* meaning 'to drag about' or 'to deal with'

tractable *adjective* easily made to do what is wanted

traction *noun* **1** the act of pulling or dragging **2** the state of being pulled

traction engine a road steam-engine

tractor *noun* a motor vehicle for pulling loads, ploughs *etc*

trade *noun* **1** the buying and selling of goods **2** someone's occupation, craft, job: *a carpenter by trade* □ *verb* **1** to buy and sell **2** to have business dealings (with) **3** to deal (in) **4** to exchange, swap □ **trade in** to give as part-payment for something else (*eg* an old car for a new one) □ **trade on** to take advantage of, often unfairly

trademark *noun* a registered mark or name put on goods to show that they are made by a certain company

trader *noun* someone who buys and sells

tradesman *noun* 1 a shopkeeper 2 a workman in a skilled trade

trade union a group of workers of the same trade who join together to bargain with employers for fair wages *etc*

trade unionist a member of a trade union

trade-wind *noun* a wind which blows towards the equator (from the north-east and south-east)

tradition *noun* 1 the handing-down of customs, beliefs, stories *etc* from generation to generation 2 a custom, belief *etc* handed down in this way

traditional *adjective* of customs: having existed for a long time without changing: *the traditional English breakfast*

traditionalist *noun* someone who believes in maintaining traditions

traffic *noun* 1 the cars, buses, boats *etc* which use roads or waterways 2 trade 3 dishonest dealings (*eg* in drugs) □ *verb* 1 to trade 2 to deal (in)

traffic *verb* ➪ traffic*s*, traffic*king*, traffic*ked*

traffic lights lights of changing colours for controlling traffic at road junctions or street crossings

tragedian *noun* 1 an actor who specializes in tragic roles 2 a person who writes tragedies

tragedy *noun* (*plural* **tragedies**) 1 a very sad event 2 a play about unhappy events and with a sad ending

tragic *adjective* of tragedy; very sad □ **tragically** *adverb*: *he was tragically killed in an accident*

trail *verb* 1 to draw along, in or through: *trailing his foot through the water* 2 to hang down (from) or be dragged loosely behind 3 to hunt (animals) by following footprints *etc* 4 to walk wearily 5 of a plant: to grow over the ground or a wall □ *noun* 1 an animal's track 2 a pathway through a

wild region 3 something left stretching behind: *a trail of dust*

trailer *noun* 1 a vehicle pulled behind a car 2 a short film advertising a longer film to be shown at a later date

train *noun* 1 a railway engine with carriages or trucks 2 a part of a dress which trails behind the wearer 3 the attendants who follow an important person 4 a line (of thought, events *etc*) 5 a line of animals carrying people or baggage □ *verb* 1 to prepare yourself by practice or exercise for a sporting event, job *etc* 2 to educate 3 to exercise (animals or people) in preparation for a race *etc* 4 to tame and teach (an animal) 5 **train on** or **at something** to aim, point (a gun, telescope *etc*) at it 6 to make (a tree or plant) grow in a certain direction

trainee *noun* someone who is being trained

trainer *noun* someone who trains people or animals for a sport, circus *etc*

training *noun* 1 preparation for a sport 2 experience or learning of the practical side of a job

trait *noun* a point that stands out in a person's character: *patience is one of his good traits*

traitor *noun* 1 someone who goes over to the enemy's side, or gives away secrets to the enemy 2 someone who betrays trust

traitorous *adjective* like a traitor; treacherous

trajectory *noun* (*plural* **trajectories**) the curved path of something (*eg* a bullet) moving through the air or through space

tram *noun* a long car running on rails and driven by electric power for carrying passengers (*also called*: **tramcar**)

tramline *noun* 1 a rail of tramway 2 **tramlines** *tennis* the parallel lines marked at the sides of the court

trammel *noun* something that hinders movement □ *verb* to hinder

trammel *verb* ➪ trammel*s*, trammel*ling*, trammel*led*

tramp *verb* 1 to walk with heavy

footsteps **2** to walk along, over *etc*: *tramping the streets in search of a job* □ *noun* **1** someone with no fixed home and no job, who lives by begging **2** a journey made on foot **3** the sound of marching feet **4** a small cargo-boat with no fixed route

trample *verb* **1** to tread under foot, stamp on **2** (*usually* **trample on**) to treat roughly or unfeelingly **3** to tread heavily

trampoline *noun* a bed-like framework holding a sheet of elastic material for bouncing on, used by gymnasts *etc*

tramway *noun* a system of tracks on which trams run

trance *noun* a sleep-like or half-conscious state

tranquil *adjective* quiet, peaceful

tranquillity *noun* the state of being quiet, calm and peaceful: *she loved the tranquillity of the valley*

tranquillize *verb* to make calm

tranquillizer *noun* a drug to calm the nerves or cause sleep

trans- *prefix* across, through: *transatlantic/ translate* (= to carry across into a different language) ⓒ Comes from Latin *trans* meaning 'across' or 'beyond'

transact *verb* to do (a piece of business)

transaction *noun* a piece of business, a deal

transatlantic *adjective* **1** crossing the Atlantic Ocean: *transatlantic yacht race* **2** across or over the Atlantic: *transatlantic friends*

transcend *verb* **1** to be, or rise, above **2** to be, or do, better than

transcribe *verb* **1** to copy from one book into another or from one form of writing (*eg* shorthand) into another **2** to adapt (a piece of music) for a particular instrument

transcript *noun* a written copy

transcription *noun* **1** the act of transcribing **2** a written copy

transept *noun* the part of a church which lies across the main part

transfer *verb* **1** to remove to another

place **2** to hand over to another person □ *noun* **1** the act of transferring **2** a design or picture which can be transferred from one surface to another

transfer *verb* ⇨ transfers, transferring, transferred

transferable *adjective* able to be transferred

transference *noun* the act of moving or transferring something from one person, place or group to another: *the transference of power from central to local government*

transfiguration *noun* a change in appearance, especially to something more beautiful, glorious, or exalted

transfigure *verb* to change (greatly and for the better) the form or appearance of

transfix *verb* **1** to make unable to move or act (*eg* because of surprise): *transfixed by the sight* **2** to pierce through (as with a sword)

transform *verb* to change in shape or appearance completely and often dramatically

transformation *noun* transforming or being transformed

transformer *noun* an apparatus for changing electrical energy from one voltage to another

transfuse *verb* **1** to pass (liquid) from one thing to another **2** to transfer (blood of one person) to the body of another

transfusion *noun* (*in full* **blood transfusion**) the introduction of blood into a person's body by allowing it to drip through a needle inserted in a vein

transgress *verb* to break a rule, law *etc*

transgression *noun* the act of breaking a rule, law *etc*; a sin

transience *noun* a transient quality

transient *adjective* not lasting, passing

transistor *noun* **1** a small device, made up of a crystal enclosed in plastic or metal, which controls the flow of an electrical current **2** a portable radio set using these

transit *noun* **1** the carrying or

movement of goods, passengers *etc* from place to place **2** the passing of a planet between the sun and the earth

transition *noun* a change from one form, place, appearance *etc* to another

transitional *adjective* involving transition; temporary: *the country will pass through a transitional period between constitutions*

transitive *adjective, grammar* of a verb: having an object, *eg* the verb '*hit*' in 'he *hit* the ball')

transitory *adjective* lasting only for a short time

translate *verb* to turn (something said or written) into another language

translation *noun* **1** the act of translating **2** something translated

translator *noun* someone who translates

transliterate *verb* to write (a word) in the letters of another alphabet

translucence *noun* a translucent quality

translucent *adjective* allowing light to pass through, but not transparent

transmission *noun* **1** the act of transmitting **2** a radio or television broadcast

transmit *verb* **1** to pass on (a message, news, heat) **2** to send out signals which are received as programmes

> **transmit** ⇨ transmit*s*, transmit*ting*, transmit*ted*

transmitter *noun* an instrument for transmitting (especially radio signals)

transom *noun* a beam across a window or the top of a door

transparency *noun* (*plural* **transparencies**) **1** the state of being transparent **2** a photograph printed on transparent material and viewed by shining light through it

transparent *adjective* **1** able to be seen through **2** easily seen to be true or false: *a transparent excuse*

transpire *verb* **1** of a secret: to become known **2** to happen: *tell me what transpired* **3** to let out (moisture *etc*) through pores of the skin or through the surface of leaves

transplant *verb* **1** to lift and plant (a growing plant) in another place **2** to remove (skin) and graft it on another part of the same body **3** to remove (an organ) and graft it in another person or animal □ *noun* **1** the act of transplanting **2** a transplanted organ, plant *etc*

transplantation *noun* the transfer of an organ or tissue from one person to another, or from one part of the body to another

transport *verb* **1** to carry from one place to another **2** to overcome with strong feeling: *transported with delight* **3** *historical* to send (a prisoner) to a prison in a different country □ *noun* **1** the act of transporting **2** any means of carrying persons or goods: *rail transport* **3** strong feeling: *transports of joy*

transportation *noun* **1** the act of transporting **2** means of transport **3** *historical* punishment of prisoners by sending them to a prison in a different country

transpose *verb* **1** to cause (two things) to change places **2** to change (a piece of music) from one key to another

transposition *noun* **1** transposing or being transposed **2** something transposed

transverse *adjective* lying, placed *etc* across: *transverse beams in the roof*

transvestite *noun* someone who likes to wear clothes intended for the opposite sex

trap *noun* **1** a device for catching animals *etc* **2** a plan or trick for taking someone by surprise **3** a bend in a pipe which is kept full of water, for preventing the escape of air or gas **4** a carriage with two wheels □ *verb* to catch in a trap, or in such a way that escape is not possible

> **trap** *verb* ⇨ trap*s*, trap*ping*, trap*ped*

trapdoor *noun* a door in a floor or ceiling

trapeze *noun* a swing used in performing gymnastic exercises or feats

trapezium *noun* a figure with four sides, two of which are parallel

trapper *noun* someone who makes a

living by catching animals for their skins and fur

trappings *noun plural* **1** clothes or ornaments suitable for a particular person or occasion **2** ornaments put on horses

trash *noun* something of little worth, rubbish

trashy *adjective* worthless

trauma *noun* **1** injury to the body **2** a very violent or distressing experience which has a lasting effect **3** a condition (of a person) caused in this way

traumatic *adjective* very upsetting, unpleasant or frightening: *moving to a new house can be traumatic*

travail *noun, old* hard work

travel *verb* **1** to go on a journey **2** to move **3** to go along, across **4** to visit foreign countries □ *noun* the act of travelling

> **travel** *verb* ⇨ travel*s*, travell*ing*, travell*ed*

traveller *noun* **1** someone who travels **2** a travelling representative of a business firm who tries to obtain orders for his firm's products

traverse *verb* to go across, pass through □ *noun* **1** something that crosses or lies across **2** a going across a rock face *etc* **3** a zigzag track of a ship

travesty *noun* (*plural* **travesties**) a poor or ridiculous imitation: *a travesty of justice*

trawl *verb* to fish by dragging a trawl along the bottom of the sea □ *noun* a wide-mouthed, bag-shaped net

trawler *noun* a boat used for trawling

tray *noun* a flat piece of wood, metal *etc* with a low edge, for carrying dishes

treacherous *adjective* **1** likely to betray **2** dangerous: *treacherous road conditions* □ **treacherously** *adverb*

treachery *noun* (*plural* **treacheries**) the act of betraying those who have trusted you

treacle *noun* a thick, dark syrup produced from sugar when it is being refined

tread *verb* **1** to walk on or along **2** **tread on something** to put your foot on it **3** to crush, trample under foot □ *noun* **1** a step **2** a way of walking **3** the part of a tyre which touches the ground □ **tread on someone's toes** to offend or upset them □ **tread water** to keep yourself afloat in an upright position by moving your arms and legs

> **tread** *verb* ⇨ tread*s*, tread*ing*, trodden, trod

treadle *noun* part of a machine which is worked by the foot

treadmill *noun* **1** *historical* a mill turned by the weight of people who were made to walk on steps fixed round a big wheel **2** any tiring, routine work

treason *noun* disloyalty to your own country or its government, *eg* by giving away its secrets to an enemy

treasonable *adjective* consisting of, or involving, treason

treasure *noun* **1** a store of money, gold *etc* **2** anything of great value or highly prized □ *verb* **1** to value greatly **2** to keep carefully because of its personal value: *she treasures the mirror her mother left her*

treasurer *noun* someone who has charge of the money of a club

treasure-trove *noun* treasure or money found hidden, the owner of which is unknown

Treasury or **treasury** *noun* (*plural* **treasuries**) the part of a government which has charge of the country's money

treat *verb* **1** to deal with, handle, act towards: *I was treated very well in prison* **2** to try to cure (someone) of a disease **3** to try to cure (a disease) **4** to write or speak about **5** to buy (someone) a meal, drink *etc* **6** to try to arrange (a peace treaty *etc*) with □ *noun* something special (*eg* an outing) that gives much pleasure: *they went to the theatre as a treat*

treatise *noun* a long, detailed essay *etc* on some subject

treatment *noun* **1** the act of treating (*eg* a disease) **2** remedy, medicine: *a new treatment for cancer* **3** the way in which someone or something is dealt with: *rough treatment*

treaty *noun* (*plural* **treaties**) an

agreement made between countries

treble *adjective* **1** threefold, three times normal: *wood of treble thickness* **2** high in pitch: *treble note* □ *verb* to become three times as great □ *noun* **1** the highest part in singing **2** a child who sings the treble part of a song

tree *noun* **1** the largest kind of plant with a thick, firm wooden stem and branches **2** anything like a tree in shape

trefoil *noun* a three-part leaf or decoration

trek *noun* **1** a long or wearisome journey **2** *old* a journey by wagon □ *verb* **1** to make a long hard journey **2** *old* to make a journey by wagon

> **trek** *verb* ⇨ treks, trekking, trekked

trellis *noun* (*plural* **trellises**) a network of strips for holding up growing plants

tremble *verb* **1** to shake with cold, fear, weakness **2** to feel fear (for another person's safety *etc*) □ *noun* **1** the act of trembling **2** a fit of trembling

tremendous *adjective* **1** very great or strong **2** *informal* very good, excellent

tremendously *adverb*, *informal* very

tremor *noun* a shaking or quivering

tremulous *adjective* **1** shaking **2** showing fear: *a tremulous voice*

trench *noun* (*plural* **trenches**) a long narrow ditch dug in the ground (*eg* by soldiers as a protection against enemy fire) □ *verb* to dig a trench in

trenchant *adjective* **1** going deep, hurting: *a trenchant remark* **2** of a policy *etc*: effective, vigorous

trenchcoat *noun* a kind of waterproof overcoat with a belt

trend *noun* a general direction: *the trend of events*

trendy *adjective*, *informal* fashionable

trepidation *noun* fear, nervousness

trespass *verb* **1** to go illegally on private land *etc* **2 trespass on something** to demand too much of it: *trespassing on my time* **3** to sin □ *noun* (*plural* **trespasses**) the act of trespassing

trespasser *noun* someone who trespasses

tress *noun* (*plural* **tresses**) **1** a lock of hair **2 tresses** hair, especially long

trestle *noun* a wooden support with legs, used for holding up a table, platform *etc*

tri- *prefix* three: *triangle/ tricycle*
Ⓛ Comes from Latin *tres* and Greek *treis*, both meaning 'three'

trial *noun* **1** the act of testing or trying (*eg* something new) **2** a test **3** the judging (of a prisoner) in a court of law **4** suffering □ **on trial 1** being tried (especially in a court of law) **2** for the purpose of trying out: *goods sent on trial* **3** being tested: *I'm still on trial with the company* □ **trial and error** the trying of various methods or choices until the right one is found

triangle *noun* **1** a figure with three sides and three angles: △ **2** a triangular metal musical instrument, played by striking with a small rod

triangular *adjective* having the shape of a triangle

triathlon *noun* a sporting contest consisting of three events, often swimming, running and cycling

tribal *adjective* belonging to or done by a tribe or tribes: *tribal warfare*

tribe *noun* **1** a people who are all descended from the same ancestor **2** a group of families, especially of a wandering people ruled by a chief

tribesman *noun* a man who belongs to a particular tribe

tribeswoman *noun* a woman who belongs to a particular tribe

tribulation *noun* great hardship or sorrow

tribunal *noun* **1** a group of people appointed to give judgement, especially on an appeal **2** a court of justice

tribune *noun*, *historical* a high official elected by the people in ancient Rome

tributary *noun* (*plural* **tributaries**) **1** a stream that flows into a river or other stream **2** someone who gives money as a tribute

tribute *noun* **1** an expression, in word or deed, of praise, thanks *etc*: *a warm tribute to his courage* **2** money paid regularly by one nation or ruler to another in return for protection or peace

trice *noun*: **in a trice** in a very short time

triceps *noun* a muscle at the back of the arm that straightens the elbow

trichomoniasis (*pronounced* trik-om-o-**nai**-*a*-sis) *noun* a sexually transmitted disease caused by a small parasite which infects the vagina and urethra

trick *noun* 1 a cunning or skilful action to puzzle, amuse *etc* 2 in card games, the cards picked up by the winner when each player has played a card □ *adjective* meant to deceive: *trick photography* □ *verb* to cheat by some quick or cunning action

trickery *noun* cheating

trickle *verb* 1 to flow in small amounts 2 to arrive or leave slowly and gradually: *replies are trickling in* □ *noun* a slow, gradual flow

trickster *noun* someone who deceives by tricks

tricky *adjective* not easy to do

tricolour or *US* **tricolor** *noun* the flag of France, consisting of three upright stripes of red, white and blue

tricycle *noun* a three-wheeled bicycle

trident *noun* a three-pronged spear

tried *past form of* **try**

triennial *adjective* 1 lasting for three years 2 happening every third year

tries *see* **try**

trifle *noun* 1 anything of little value 2 a small amount 3 a pudding of whipped cream, sponge-cake, wine *etc* □ *verb* **trifle with someone** or **something** to act towards them without sufficient respect: *in no mood to be trifled with* 2 to amuse yourself in an idle way (with): *he trifled with her affections* 3 to behave in a light, thoughtless manner

trifling *adjective* very small in value or amount

trigger *noun* a small lever on a gun which, when pulled with the finger, causes the bullet to be fired □ *verb* (often **trigger off**) to start, be the cause of, an important event, chain of events *etc*

trigonometric or **trigonometrical**

adjective relating to or involving trigonometry

trigonometry *noun* the branch of mathematics which has to do chiefly with the relationship between the sides and angles of triangles

trilby *noun* a man's hat with an indented crown and narrow brim

So called because a hat of this shape was worn by an actress in the original stage version of George du Maurier's novel, *Trilby* (1894)

trill *verb* to sing, play or utter in a quivering or bird-like way □ *noun* a trilled sound; in music, a rapid repeating of two notes several times

trillion 1 a million million millions 2 (originally *US*) a million millions

trilogy (*plural* **trilogies**) a group of three related plays, novels *etc* by the same author, meant to be seen or read as a whole

trim *verb* 1 to clip the edges or ends of: *trim the hedge* 2 to arrange (sails, cargo) so that a boat is ready for sailing 3 to decorate (*eg* a hat) □ *noun* 1 the act of trimming 2 dress: *hunting trim* □ *adjective* tidy, in good order, neat □ **in good trim** 1 in good order 2 fit

trim *verb* ⇨ trim**s**, trim**ming**, trim**med**

trimming *noun* 1 a decoration added to a dress, cake *etc* 2 a piece of cloth, hair *etc* cut off while trimming

Trinity *noun* in Christianity, the union of Father, Son and Holy Ghost in one God

trinket *noun* a small ornament (especially one of little value)

trio *noun* (*plural* **trios**) 1 three performers 2 three people or things

trip *verb* 1 (often **trip up**) to stumble, fall over 2 to move with short, light steps 3 **trip up** to make a mistake □ *noun* 1 a journey for pleasure or business 2 a light short step 3 **trips** *slang* the drug LSD

trip *verb* ⇨ trip**s**, trip**ping**, trip**ped**

tripartite *adjective* 1 in or having three parts 2 of an agreement: between three countries

tripe *noun* 1 part of the stomach of the

cow or sheep used as food **2** *informal* rubbish, nonsense

triple *adjective* **1** made up of three **2** three times as large (as something else) □ *verb* to make or become three times as large

triplet *noun* **1** one of three children or animals born of the same mother at one time **2** three rhyming lines in a poem **3** *music* a group of three notes played in the time of two

triplicate *noun*: **in triplicate** in three copies

tripod *noun* a three-legged stand (especially for a camera)

tripper *noun* someone who goes on a short pleasure trip

triptych *noun* three painted panels forming a whole work of art

trisect *verb* to cut into three

trisection *noun* trisecting, dividing into three parts

trite *adjective* of a remark: used so often that it has little force or meaning

triumph *noun* **1** a great success or victory **2** celebration after a success: *ride in triumph through the streets* □ *verb* **1** to win a victory **2** to rejoice openly because of a victory

triumphal *adjective* used in celebrating a triumph

triumphant *adjective* victorious; showing joy because of, or celebrating, triumph □ **triumphantly** *adverb*

≡ Alternative words: jubilant

trivet *noun* a metal tripod for resting a teapot or kettle on

trivia *noun plural* unimportant matters or details

trivial *adjective* of very little importance

triviality *noun* (*plural* **trivialities**) **1** something unimportant **2** trivialness

trivialness *noun* the state of being trivial

trod and **trodden** *see* **tread**

troglodyte *noun* a cave-dweller

trojan *noun*, *computing* a type of computer virus

troll *noun* a mythological creature, giant or dwarf, who lives in a cave

trolley *noun* (*plural* **trolleys**) **1** a small cart (*eg* as used by porters at railway stations) **2** a supermarket basket on wheels **3** a hospital bed on wheels for transporting patients **4** a table on wheels, used for serving tea *etc*

trolley-bus *noun* a bus which gets its power from overhead wires

trombone *noun* a brass wind instrument with a sliding tube which changes the notes

troop *noun* **1** a collection of people or animals **2** **troops** soldiers **3** a unit in cavalry *etc* □ *verb* **1** to gather in numbers **2** to go in a group: *they all trooped out* □ **troop the colours** to carry a regiment's flag past the lined-up soldiers of the regiment

trooper *noun* a horse-soldier

trophy *noun* (*plural* **trophies**) **1** something taken from an enemy and kept in memory of the victory **2** a prize such as a silver cup won in a sports competition *etc*

tropic *noun* **1** either of two imaginary circles running round the earth at about 23 degrees north (**Tropic of Cancer**) or south (**Tropic of Capricorn**) of the equator **2** **tropics** the hot regions near or between these circles □ *adjective* of the tropics

tropical *adjective* **1** of the tropics **2** growing in hot countries: *tropical fruit* **3** very hot

trot *verb* **1** of a horse: to run with short, high steps **2** of a person: to run slowly with short steps **3** to make (a horse) trot □ *noun* the pace of a horse or person when trotting

     trot *verb* ⇨ trots, trotting, trotted

trotters *noun plural* the feet of pigs or sheep, especially when used as food

troubadour *noun*, *historical* a medieval travelling singer-musician, especially in France

trouble *verb* **1** to cause worry or sorrow to **2** to cause inconvenience to **3** to make an effort, bother (to): *I didn't trouble to ring him* □ *noun* **1** worry, uneasiness **2** difficulty; disturbance **3** something which causes worry, difficulty *etc* **4** a disease **5** care and effort put into doing something

■ **Alternative words**: (verb, meaning 1) agitate

troubleshooter *noun* someone whose job is to solve difficulties (*eg* in a firm's business activities)

troublesome *adjective* causing difficulty or inconvenience

trough *noun* **1** a long, open container for holding animals' food and water **2** an area of low atmospheric pressure **3** a dip between two sea waves

trounce *verb* **1** to punish or beat severely **2** to defeat heavily

troupe (*pronounced* troop) *noun* a company of actors, dancers *etc*

trouser *adjective* of a pair of trousers: *trouser leg*

trousers *noun plural* an outer garment for the lower part of the body which covers each leg separately

trousseau *noun* (*plural* **trousseaux** or **trousseaus** – *both pronounced* troos-ohz) a bride's outfit for her wedding

trout *noun* a freshwater or sea (**sea-trout**) fish, used as food

trowel *noun* **1** a small spade used in gardening **2** a similar tool with a flat blade, used for spreading mortar

troy weight a system of weights for weighing gold, gems *etc*

truancy *noun* the practice of being absent from school without permission

truant *noun* someone who stays away from school *etc* without permission □ **play truant** to stay away from school, work *etc* without permission

truce *noun* a rest from fighting or quarrelling agreed to by both sides

truck *noun* **1** a wagon for carrying goods on a railway **2** a strong lorry for carrying heavy loads □ **have no truck with** to refuse to have dealings with

trucker *noun, US* a lorry driver

truculence *noun* **1** being truculent **2** truculent behaviour

truculent *adjective* fierce and threatening, aggressive

trudge *verb* to walk with heavy steps, as if tired

true *adjective* **1** of a story *etc*: telling of something which really happened **2** correct, not invented or wrong: *it's true that the earth is round* **3** accurate **4** faithful: *a true friend* **5** real, properly so called: *the spider is not a true insect* **6** rightful: *the true heir* **7** in the correct or intended position

truffle *noun* a round fungus found underground and much valued as a flavouring for food

truism *noun* a statement which is so clearly true that it is not worth making

truly *adjective* **1** really: *Is that truly what he said?* **2** genuinely; honestly: *I'm truly sorry* **3** completely, utterly: *a truly classless society*

trump *noun* **1** a suit having a higher value than cards of other suits **2** a card of this suit □ *verb* to play a card which is a trump □ **trump up** to make up, invent □ **turn up trumps** to play your part well when things are difficult

trump card **1** a card which is a trump **2** something kept in reserve as a means of winning an argument *etc*

trumpery *noun* (*plural* **trumperies**) something showy but worthless

trumpet *noun* **1** a brass musical instrument with a clear, high-pitched tone **2** the cry of an elephant □ *verb* **1** to announce (*eg* news) so that all may hear **2** to blow a trumpet **3** of elephants: to make a long, loud cry

truncated *adjective* **1** cut off at the top or end **2** shortened: *a truncated version*

truncheon *noun* a short heavy staff or baton such as that used by police officers

trundle *verb* to wheel or roll along

trunk *noun* **1** the main stem of a tree **2** the body (not counting the head, arms or legs) of a person or animal **3** the long nose of an elephant **4** a large box or chest for clothes *etc* **5** *US* the luggage compartment of a car **6** **trunks** short pants worn by boys and men for swimming

trunkcall *noun* the former name for a **national call**

trunk road a main road

truss *noun* (*plural* **trusses**) **1** a bundle (eg of hay, straw) **2** a system of beams to support a bridge **3** a kind of supporting bandage □ *verb* **1** to bind, tie tightly (up) **2** (often **truss up**) to prepare (a bird ready for cooking) by tying up the legs and wings

trust *noun* **1** belief in the power, truth or goodness of a thing or person **2** something (eg a task or an item of value) handed over to someone in the belief that they will do it, guard it *etc* **3** charge, keeping: *the child was put in my trust* **4** arrangement by which something (eg money) is given to someone for use in a particular way **5** a number of business firms working closely together □ *verb* **1** to have faith or confidence (in) **2** to give (someone something) in the belief that they will use it well *etc*: *I can't trust your sister with my tennis racket* **3** to feel confident (that): *I trust that you can find your way here* □ **take on trust** to believe without checking or testing

■ **Alternative words**: (verb, meaning 1) rely on, depend on, count on; (verb, meaning 2) entrust, consign, assign; (verb, meaning 3) believe, surmise

trustee *noun* someone who keeps something in trust for another

trustful or **trusting** *adjective* ready to trust, not suspicious

trustworthy *adjective* able to be trusted or depended on

trusty *adjective* able to be trusted or depended on

truth *noun* **1** the state of being true **2** a true statement **3** the facts

truthful *adjective* **1** telling the truth, not lying **2** of a statement: true □ **truthfully** *adverb*

try *verb* **1** to attempt, make an effort (to do something) **2** to test by using: *try this new soap* **3** to test severely, strain: *you're trying my patience* **4** to attempt to use, open *etc*: *I tried the door but it was locked* **5** to judge (a prisoner) in a court of law □ *noun* (*plural* **tries**) **1** an effort, an attempt **2** one of the ways of scoring in Rugby football □ **try on** to put on (clothing) to see if it fits *etc* □ **try out** to test by using

try *verb* ⇨ tries, trying, tried

■ **Alternative words**: (verb, meaning 1) attempt, endeavour, venture, undertake, seek, strive; (verb, meaning 2) test, sample; (verb, meaning 5) hear, judge

trying *adjective* hard to bear; testing

tsar or **tzar** or **czar** *noun, historical* the emperor of pre-revolutionary Russia

tsarina or **tzarina** or **czarina** *noun, historical* **1** the wife of a tsar **2** an empress of Russia

tsetse (*pronounced* tset-si) *noun* or **tsetse fly** an African biting fly which spreads dangerous diseases

T-shirt *another spelling of* **tee-shirt**

TSS *abbreviation* toxic shock syndrome

tub *noun* **1** a round wooden container used for washing *etc*; a bath **2** a round container for ice-cream *etc*

tuba *noun* a large brass musical instrument giving a low note

tubby *adjective* fat and round

tube *noun* **1** a hollow, cylinder-shaped object through which liquid may pass **2** an organ of this kind in humans, animals *etc* **3** a container from which something may be squeezed **4** an underground railway system **5** a cathode ray tube

tuber *noun* a swelling on the underground stem of a plant (eg a potato)

tuberculosis *noun* an infectious disease affecting the lungs

tubing *noun* a length or lengths of tube

tubular *adjective* shaped like a tube

TUC *abbreviation* Trades Union Congress

tuck *noun* **1** a fold stitched in a piece of cloth **2** *informal* sweets, cakes *etc* □ *verb* **1** to gather (cloth) together into a fold **2** to fold or push (into or under a place) **3** **tuck someone in** or **up** to push bedclothes closely round (someone in bed) □ **tuck in** *informal* to eat with enjoyment or greedily

tuck shop a shop in a school where sweets, cakes *etc* are sold

Tuesday *noun* the third day of the week

tuft *noun* a bunch or clump of grass, hair *etc*

tug *verb* **1** to pull hard **2** to pull along □ *noun* **1** a strong pull **2** a tugboat

tug *verb* ⇨ tug**s**, tug**ging**, tug**ged**

tugboat *noun* a small but powerful ship used for towing larger ones

tug-of-war *noun* a contest in which two teams, holding the ends of a strong rope, pull against each other

tuition *noun* **1** teaching **2** private coaching or teaching

tulip *noun* a type of flower with cup-shaped flowers grown from a bulb

Based on a Persian word for 'turban', because of the similarity in shape

tulle *noun* a kind of cloth made of thin silk or rayon net

tumble *verb* **1** to fall or come down suddenly and violently **2** to roll, toss (about) **3** to do acrobatic tricks **4** to throw into disorder □ *noun* **1** a fall **2** a confused state □ **tumble to something** to understand it suddenly

tumbledown *adjective* falling to pieces

tumbler *noun* **1** a large drinking glass **2** an acrobat

tumbrel or **tumbril** *noun*, *historical* a two-wheeled cart of the kind used to take victims to the guillotine during the French Revolution

tummy *noun* (*plural* **tummies**), *informal* the stomach

tumour *noun* an abnormal growth on or in the body

tumult *noun* **1** a great noise made by a crowd **2** excitement, agitation

tumultuous *adjective* with great noise or confusion: *a tumultuous welcome*

tun *noun* a large cask, especially for wine

tuna *noun* (*plural* **tuna** or **tunas**) a large sea fish, used as food (*also called*: **tunny**)

tundra *noun* a level treeless plain in Arctic regions

tune *noun* **1** notes put together to form a melody **2** the music of a song □ *verb* **1** to put (a musical instrument) in tune **2** to adjust a radio set to a particular station **3** (sometimes **tune up**) to improve the working of an engine □ **change your tune** to change your opinions, attitudes *etc* □ **in tune 1** of a musical instrument: having each note adjusted to agree with the others or with the notes of other instruments **2** of a voice: agreeing with the notes of other voices or instruments **3** in agreement (with) □ **to the tune of** to the sum of

tuneful *adjective* having a pleasant or recognizable tune □ **tunefully** *adjective*

tungsten *noun* an element, a grey metal

tunic *noun* **1** a soldier's or police officer's jacket **2** *historical* a loose garment reaching to the knees, worn in ancient Greece and Rome **3** a similar modern garment: *gym tunic*

tuning fork a steel fork which, when struck, gives a note of a certain pitch

tunnel *noun* **1** an underground passage (*eg* for a railway train) □ *verb* **1** to make a tunnel **2** of an animal: to burrow

tunnel *verb* ⇨ tunnel**s**, tunnel**ling**, tunnel**led**

tunny *same as* **tuna**

turban *noun* **1** a long piece of cloth wound round the head, worn by Muslims **2** a kind of hat resembling this

turbid *adjective* of liquid: muddy, clouded

turbine *noun* an engine with curved blades, turned by the action of water, steam, hot air *etc*

turbo- *prefix* using a turbine engine
ⓛ Comes from Latin *turbo* meaning 'a spinning-top'

turbot *noun* a type of large flat sea fish, used as food

turbulence *noun* irregular movement of air currents, especially when affecting the flight of aircraft

turbulent *adjective* **1** disturbed, in a restless state **2** likely to cause a disturbance or riot

turd *noun* a lump of dung

tureen *noun* a large dish for holding soup at table

turf *noun* **1** grass and the soil below it **2** (**the turf**) the world of horse-racing □ *verb* to cover with turf □ **turf out** *informal* to throw out

turgid *adjective* **1** swollen **2** of language: sounding grand but meaning little, pompous

turkey *noun* (*plural* **turkeys**) a large farmyard bird, used as food

Turkish bath a type of hot air or steam bath in which someone is made to sweat heavily, is massaged and then slowly cooled

turmoil *noun* a state of wild, confused movement or disorder

turn *verb* **1** to go round: *wheels turning* **2** to face or go in the opposite direction: *turned and walked away* **3** to change direction: *the road turns sharply to the left* **4** to direct (*eg* attention) **5 turn on** to move, swing *etc*: *the door turns on its hinges* **6** to go sour **7** to become: *his hair turned white* **8** of leaves: to change colour **9** to shape in a lathe **10** to pass (the age of): *she must have turned 40* □ *noun* **1** the act of turning **2** a point where someone may change direction, *eg* a road junction: *take the first turn on the left* **3** a bend (*eg* in a road) **4** a spell of duty: *your turn to wash the dishes* **5** an act (*eg* in a circus) **6** a short stroll: *a turn along the beach* **7** a fit of dizziness, shock *etc* **8** requirement: *this will serve our turn* □ **by turns** or **in turn** one after another in a regular order □ **do someone a good** (or **bad**) **turn** to act helpfully (or unhelpfully) towards someone □ **to a turn** exactly, perfectly: *cooked to a turn* □ **turn against** to become hostile to □ **turn down 1** to say no to, refuse (*eg* an offer, a request) **2** to reduce, lessen (heat, volume of sound *etc*) □ **turn in 1** to go to bed **2** to hand over to those in authority □ **turn off 1** to stop the flow of (a tap) **2** to switch off the power for (a television *etc*) □ **turn on 1** to set running (*eg* water from a tap) **2** to switch on power for (a television *etc*) **3** to depend (on) **4** to become angry with (someone) unexpectedly **5** *slang* to arouse sexually □ **turn out 1** to make to leave, drive out **2** to make, produce **3**

to empty: *turn out your pockets* **4** of a crowd: to come out, gather for a special purpose **5** to switch off (a light) **6** to prove (to be): *he turned out to be right* □ **turn to 1** to set to work **2** to go to for help *etc* □ **turn up 1** to appear, arrive **2** to be found **3** to increase (*eg* heat, volume of sound *etc*) □ **turn someone's head** to fill them with pride or conceit

🕐 Comes from Latin *tornare* meaning 'to turn in a lathe'

📓 **Alternative words**: (verb, meaning 1) revolve, gyrate, rotate; (verb, meaning 3) veer, swerve, bend; (verb, meaning 5) pivot, hinge, swivel; (verb, meaning 6) curdle, spoil; (verb, meanings 7 and 8) go, become, grow

turncoat *noun* someone who betrays their party, principles *etc*

turning *noun* **1** the act of turning **2** a point where a road *etc* joins another **3** the act of shaping in a lathe

turning-point *noun* a crucial point of change

turnip *noun* a plant with a large round root used as a vegetable

turnover *noun* **1** rate of change or replacement (*eg* of workers in a firm *etc*) **2** the total amount of sales made by a firm during a certain time

turnpike *noun* **1** *historical* a gate across a road which opened when the user paid a toll **2** *US* a road on which a toll is paid

turnstile *noun* a gate which turns, allowing only one person to pass at a time

turntable *noun* **1** a revolving platform for turning a railway engine round **2** the revolving part of a record-player on which the record rests

turpentine *noun* an oil from certain trees used for mixing paints, cleaning paint brushes *etc*

turpitude *noun* wickedness

turquoise *noun* a greenish-blue precious stone

Literally 'Turkish stone', because first found in Turkestan

turret *noun* **1** a small tower on a castle

or other building **2** a structure for supporting guns on a warship

turreted *adjective* having turrets

turtle *noun* a kind of large tortoise which lives in water □ **turn turtle** of a boat *etc*: to turn upside down, capsize

turtledove *noun* a type of dove noted for its sweet, soft song

tusk *noun* a large tooth (one of a pair) sticking out from the mouth of certain animals (*eg* an elephant, a walrus)

tussle *noun* a struggle □ *verb* to struggle, compete

tussock *noun* a tuft of grass

tutor *noun* **1** a teacher of students in a university *etc* **2** a teacher employed privately to teach individual pupils □ *verb* to teach

tutorial *adjective* of a tutor □ *noun* a meeting for study or discussion between tutor and students

tutu *noun* a ballet dancer's short, stiff, spreading skirt

tuxedo *noun* (*plural* **tuxedos** or **tuxedoes**) *US* a dinner-jacket

TV *abbreviation* television

twaddle *noun, informal* nonsense

twain *noun, old* two □ **in twain** *old* in two, apart

twang *noun* **1** a tone of voice in which the words seem to come through the nose **2** a sound like that of a tightly-stretched string being plucked □ *verb* to make such a sound

tweak *verb* to pull with a sudden jerk, twitch □ *noun* a sudden jerk or pull

tweed *noun* **1** a woollen cloth with a rough surface **2 tweeds** clothes made of this cloth □ *adjective* made of tweed

tweezers *noun plural* small pincers for pulling out hairs, holding small things *etc*

twelfth *adjective* the last of a series of twelve □ *noun* one of twelve equal parts

twelve *noun* the number 12 □ *adjective* 12 in number

twentieth *adjective* the last of a series of twenty □ *noun* one of twenty equal parts

twenty *noun* the number 20 □ *adjective* 20 in number

twice *adverb* two times

twiddle *verb* to play with, twirl idly □ **twiddle your thumbs 1** to turn your thumbs around one another **2** to have nothing to do

twig *noun* a small branch of a tree

twilight *noun* **1** the faint light between sunset and night, or before sunrise **2** the time just before or after the peak of something: *the twilight of the dictatorship*

twill *noun* a kind of strong cloth with a ridged appearance

twin *noun* **1** one of two children or animals born of the same mother at the same birth **2** one of two things exactly the same □ *adjective* **1** born at the same birth **2** very like another **3** made up of two parts or things which are alike

twine *noun* a strong kind of string made of twisted threads □ *verb* **1** to wind or twist together **2** to wind (about or around something)

twinge *noun* a sudden, sharp pain

twinkle *verb* **1** of a star *etc*: to shine with light which seems to vary in brightness **2** of eyes: to shine with amusement *etc* □ **twinkle** or **twinkling** *noun* the act or state of twinkling □ **in a twinkling** in an instant

twirl *verb* **1** to turn or spin round quickly and lightly **2** to turn round and round with the fingers □ *noun* a spin round and round

twist *verb* **1** to wind (threads) together **2** to wind round or about something **3** to make (*eg* a rope) into a coil **4** to bend out of shape **5** to bend or wrench painfully (*eg* your ankle) **6** to make (*eg* facts) appear to have a meaning which is really false □ *noun* **1** the act of twisting **2** a painful wrench **3** something twisted: *a twist of tissue paper*

twister *noun, informal* a dishonest and unreliable person

twitch *verb* **1** to pull with a sudden light jerk **2** to jerk slightly and suddenly: *a muscle in his face twitched* □ *noun* **1** a sudden jerk **2** a muscle spasm

twitter *noun* **1** high, rapidly repeated sounds, as are made by small birds **2** slight nervous excitement □ *verb* **1** of a bird: to make a series of high quivering notes **2** of a person: to talk continuously

two *noun* the number 2 □ *adjective* 2 in number
Ⓒ Comes from Old English *twa* meaning 'two'

two-faced *adjective* deceitful, insincere

twofold *adjective* double

two-time *verb* to have a love affair with two people at the same time

tycoon *noun* a business man of great wealth and power
Based on a Japanese title for a warlord

tympani *another spelling of* **timpani**

type *noun* **1** kind **2** an example which has all the usual characteristics of its kind **3** a small metal block with a raised letter or sign, used for printing **4** a set of these **5** printed lettering □ *verb* **1** to print with a typewriter **2** to use a typewriter **3** to identify or classify as a particular type

typecast *verb* to give (an actor) parts very similar in character

typescript *noun* a typed script for a play *etc*

typewriter *noun* a machine with keys which, when struck, print letters on a sheet of paper

typist *noun* someone who works with a typewriter and does other secretarial or clerical tasks

typhoid *noun* an infectious disease caused by germs in infected food or drinking water

typhoon *noun* a violent storm of wind and rain in Eastern seas

typhus *noun* a dangerous fever carried by lice

typical *adjective* having or showing the usual characteristics: *a typical Irishman/ typical of her to be late* □ **typically** *adverb*

■ Alternative words: standard, orthodox, indicative, characteristic

typify *verb* to be a good example of: *typifying the English abroad*
typify ⇨ typif*ies*, typify*ing*, typif*ied*

typographical *adjective* relating to or involving printing or typography

typography *noun* the use of type for printing

tyrannical or **tyrannous** *adjective* like a tyrant, cruel

tyrannize *verb* to act as a tyrant; rule over harshly

tyranny *noun* (*plural* **tyrannies**) the rule of a tyrant

tyrant *noun* a ruler who governs cruelly and unjustly

tyre or *US* **tire** *noun* a thick rubber cover round a motor or cycle wheel

tyro *another spelling of* **tiro**

tzar, tzarina *another spelling of* **tsar, tsarina**

Uu

ubiquitous (*pronounced* yoo-**bik**-wit-us) *adjective* **1** being everywhere at once **2** found everywhere

ubiquity (*pronounced* yoo-**bik**-wit-i) *noun* existence everywhere

udder *noun* a bag-like part of a cow, goat *etc* with teats which supply milk

UFO (*pronounced* yoo-ef-**oh** or **yoo**-foh) *abbreviation* unidentified flying object

ugliness *noun* being ugly

ugly *adjective* **1** unpleasant to look at or hear: *ugly sound* **2** threatening, dangerous: *gave me an ugly look* □ **ugly duckling** an unattractive or disliked person who later turns into a beauty, success *etc*

■ **Alternative words:** (meaning 1) unattractive, plain, unprepossessing, hideous, monstrous, deformed, repulsive
◪ **Opposite:** (meaning 1) beautiful

UHF *abbreviation* ultra high frequency

UHT *abbreviation* **1** ultra-heat treated **2** ultra high temperature

ukelele (*pronounced* yook-*e*-**lei**-li) *noun* a small, stringed musical instrument played like a banjo

ulcer *noun* an open sore on the inside or the outside of the body

ulcerated *adjective* having an ulcer or ulcers

ulcerous *adjective* affected with ulcers

ulterior *adjective* beyond what is admitted or seen: *ulterior motive*

ultimate *adjective* last, final

ultimately *adverb* finally, in the end

ultimatum *noun* a final demand sent with a threat to break off discussion, declare war *etc* if it is not met

ultra- *prefix* **1** very: *ultra-careful* **2** beyond: *ultramicroscopic*
◔ Comes from Latin *ultra* meaning 'beyond'

ultramarine *adjective* of a deep blue colour

ultrasonic *adjective* beyond the range of human hearing

ultraviolet *adjective* having rays of slightly shorter wavelength than visible light

umber *noun* a mineral substance used to produce a brown paint

umbilical *adjective* of the navel □ **umbilical cord** a tube connecting an unborn mammal to its mother through the placenta

umbrage *noun* a feeling of offence or hurt: *took umbrage at my suggestion*

umbrella *noun* an object made up of a folding covered framework on a stick which protects against rain

Literally 'little shadow' and originally used to refer to a sunshade

umlaut (*pronounced* **oom**-lowt) *noun* a character (¨) placed over a letter to modify its pronunciation

umpire *noun* **1** a sports official who sees that a game is played according to the rules **2** a judge asked to settle a dispute □ *verb* to act as an umpire

umpteen *adjective* many, lots

Originally *umpty*, a signaller's slang term for a dash in Morse code

UN *abbreviation* United Nations

574

un- *prefix* **1** not: *unequal* **2** (with verbs) used to show the reversal of an action: *unfasten*

un- comes from a combination of two Old English prefixes: the negative prefix 'un-', and the prefix 'on-' meaning 'against'

unabashed *adjective* shameless, blatant

unable *adjective* lacking enough strength, power, skill *etc*

unaccountable *adjective* not able to be explained □ **unaccountably** *adverb*: *she was feeling unaccountably depressed*

unaccustomed *adjective* not used (to)

unadulterated *adjective* pure, not mixed with anything else

unanimity (*pronounced* yoo-na-**nim**-it-i) *noun* unanimous agreement

unanimous (*pronounced* yoo-**nan**-im-us) *adjective* **1** all of the same opinion: *we were unanimous* **2** agreed to by all: *a unanimous decision* □ **unanimously** *adjective*: *he was elected unanimously*

unapproachable *adjective* unfriendly and stiff in manner

unarmed *adjective* not armed

unassuming *adjective* modest

unattached *adjective* **1** not attached **2** single, not married or having a partner

unaware *adjective* not knowing, ignorant (of): *unaware of the danger*

unawares *adverb* **1** without warning **2** unintentionally

unbalanced *adjective* mad; lacking balance: *unbalanced view*

unbearable *adjective* too painful or bad to be endured

unbeliever *noun* someone who does not follow a certain religion

unbending *adjective* severe

unbounded *adjective* not limited, very great: *unbounded enthusiasm*

unbridled *adjective* not kept under control: *unbridled fury*

unburden *verb*: **unburden yourself** to tell your secrets or problems to someone else

uncalled *adjective*: **uncalled for** quite unnecessary: *your remarks were uncalled for*

uncanny *adjective* strange, mysterious □ **uncannily** *adverb*

uncared *adjective*: **uncared for** not looked after properly

unceremonious *adjective* informal, off-hand

uncertain *adjective* **1** not certain, doubtful **2** not definitely known **3** of weather: changeable

■ **Alternative words**: (meaning 1) unsure, dubious, ambivalent; (meaning 2) unpredictable, undetermined, unresolved; (meaning 3) variable, unsettled

uncharted *adjective* **1** not shown on a map or chart **2** little known

uncle *noun* **1** the brother of your father or mother **2** the husband of your father's or mother's sister

unclean *adjective* dirty, impure

uncoil *verb* to unwind

uncomfortable *adjective* not comfortable

uncommon *adjective* not common, strange

uncommonly *adjective* very: *uncommonly talented*

uncompromising *adjective* not willing to give in or make concessions to others

unconditional *adjective* with no conditions attached; absolute

unconscious *adjective* **1** senseless, stunned (*eg* by an accident) **2** not aware (of) **3** not recognized by the person concerned: *unconscious prejudice against women* □ *noun* the deepest level of the mind

■ **Alternative words**: (meaning 1) insensible, concussed, comatose; (meaning 2) unaware, oblivious; (meaning 3) latent, inadvertent, subliminal

uncouth *adjective* **1** clumsy, awkward **2** rude

uncover *verb* **1** to remove a cover from **2** to disclose

unction *noun* anointing; anointment

unctuous *adjective* oily, ingratiating

undaunted *adjective* fearless; not discouraged

undecided *adjective* not yet decided

undeniable *adjective* not able to be denied, clearly true

under *preposition* 1 directly below or beneath 2 less than: *costing under £5* 3 within the authority or command of: *under General Montgomery* 4 going through, suffering: *under attack* 5 having, using: *under a false name* 6 in accordance with: *under our agreement* □ *adverb* in or to a lower position, condition *etc* □ **go under** 1 to sink beneath the surface of water 2 to go bankrupt, go out of business □ **under age** younger than the legal or required age □ **under way** in motion, started

under is an Old English word

under- *prefix* 1 below, beneath: *underachieve/ underarm* 2 lower in position or rank: *underdog/ underling* 3 too little: *underdeveloped/ underrate*

underachieve *verb* to achieve less than your potential

underarm *adverb* of bowling *etc*: with the arm kept below the shoulder

undercarriage *noun* the wheels of an aeroplane and their supports

underclothes *noun plural* clothes worn next to the skin under other clothes

undercover *adjective* acting or done in secret: *an undercover agent* (ie a spy)

undercurrent *noun* 1 a flow or movement under the surface 2 a half-hidden feeling or tendency: *an undercurrent of despair in her voice*

undercut *verb* to sell at a lower price than someone else

underdeveloped *adjective* 1 not fully grown 2 of a country: lacking modern agricultural and industrial systems, and with a low standard of living

underdog *noun* the weaker side, or the loser in any conflict or fight

underdone *adjective* of food: not quite cooked

underestimate *verb* to estimate at less than the real worth, value *etc*

underfoot *adjective* under the feet

undergo *verb* 1 to suffer, endure 2 to receive (*eg* as medical treatment)

undergo ⇨ undergoes, undergoing, underwent, undergone

undergraduate *noun* a university student who has not yet passed final examinations

underground *adjective* 1 below the surface of the ground 2 secret, covert □ *noun* a railway which runs in a tunnel beneath the surface of the ground

undergrowth *noun* shrubs or low plants growing amongst trees

underhand *adjective* sly, deceitful

underlie *verb* to be the hidden cause or source of

underline *verb* 1 to draw a line under 2 to stress the importance of, emphasize

underling *noun* someone of lower rank

underlying *adjective* 1 lying under or beneath 2 fundamental, basic: *the underlying causes*

undermine *verb* to do damage to, weaken gradually (health, authority *etc*)

underneath *adjective & preposition* in a lower position (than), beneath: *look underneath the table/ wearing a jacket underneath his coat*

undernourished *adjective* not well nourished

underpants *noun plural* underwear covering the buttocks and upper legs

underpass *noun* a road passing under another one

underpay *verb* to pay too little

underpin *verb* to support from beneath, prop up

underprivileged *adjective* not having normal living standards or rights

underrate *verb* to think too little of, underestimate

undersell *verb* 1 to sell for less than the true value 2 to sell for less than someone else

undersigned *noun*: **the undersigned** the people whose names are written at the end of a letter or statement

undersized *adjective* below the usual or required size

underskirt *noun* a thin skirt worn under another skirt

understand *verb* 1 to see the meaning of 2 to appreciate the reasons for: *I don't understand your behaviour* 3 to have a thorough knowledge of: *do you understand economics?* 4 to have the impression that: *I understood that you weren't coming* 5 to take for granted as part of an agreement

> **understand** ▷ understands, understand*ing*, understood

■ **Alternative words**: (meaning 1) grasp, comprehend, discern, perceive; (meaning 2) fathom; (meaning 4) believe, gather, conclude

understandable *adjective* 1 reasonable, natural or normal: *he reacted with understandable fury* 2 capable of being understood: *his speech was barely understandable*

understanding *noun* 1 the ability to see the full meaning of something 2 an agreement 3 condition: *on the understanding that we both pay half* 4 appreciation of other people's feelings, difficulties *etc* □ *adjective* able to understand other people's feelings, sympathetic

understate *verb* to represent something as being less important or smaller than it really is

understatement *noun* a statement which does not give the whole truth, making less of certain details than is actually the case

understudy *noun* (*plural* **understudies**) an actor who learns the part of another actor and is able to take their place if necessary

undertake *verb* 1 to promise (to do something) 2 to take upon yourself (a task, duty *etc*): *I undertook responsibility for the food*

undertaker *noun* someone whose job is to organize funerals

undertaking *noun* 1 something which is being attempted or done 2 a promise 3 the business of an undertaker

under-the-counter *adjective* hidden from customers' sight; illegal

undertone *noun* 1 a soft voice 2 a partly hidden meaning, feeling *etc*: *an undertone of discontent*

undertow *noun* a current below the surface of the water which moves in a direction opposite to the surface movement

undervalue *verb* to value (something) below its real worth

underwater *adjective* under the surface of the water

underwear *noun* underclothes

underweight *adjective* under the usual or required weight

underwent *past form* of **undergo**

underworld *noun* 1 the criminal world or level of society 2 the place where spirits go after death

underwrite *verb* 1 to accept for insurance 2 to accept responsibility or liability for

underwriter *noun* someone who insures ships

undesirable *adjective* not wanted

undeveloped *adjective* not developed

undivided *adjective* not split, complete, total: *undivided attention*

undo *verb* 1 to unfasten (a coat, parcel *etc*) 2 to wipe out the effect of, reverse: *undoing all the good I did* 3 *old* to ruin, dishonour (especially a reputation): *alas, I am undone*

> **undo** ▷ undo*es*, undo*ing*, undone, undid

undoing *noun* ruin, dishonour

undoubted *adjective* not to be doubted

undoubtedly *adjective* without doubt, certainly

undreamt-of *adjective* more *etc* than could have been imagined

undress *verb* to take your clothes off

undue *adjective* too much, more than is necessary: *undue expense*

undulate *verb* 1 to move as waves do 2 to have a rolling, wavelike appearance □ **undulating** *adjective* □ **undulation** *noun*

unduly *adverb* excessively; unreasonably: *unduly worried*

undying *adjective* unending, never fading: *undying love*

unearth *verb* to bring or dig out from the earth, or from a place of hiding

unearthly *adjective* 1 strange, as if not of this world 2 *informal* absurd, especially absurdly early: *at this unearthly hour*

uneasiness *noun* an uneasy state: *feelings of uneasiness*

uneasy *adjective* anxious, worried

■ **Alternative words**: apprehensive

unemployed *adjective* 1 without a job 2 not in use □ **the unemployed** unemployed people as a group

unemployment *noun* 1 the state of being unemployed 2 the total number of unemployed people in a country

unenviable *adjective* not arousing envy: *unenviable task*

unequal *adjective* 1 not equal; unfair: *unequal distribution* 2 lacking enough strength or skill: *unequal to the job*

unequalled *adjective* without an equal, unique

unequivocal (*pronounced* un-i-kwiv-ok-al) *adjective* clear, not ambiguous: *unequivocal orders*

unerring *adjective* always right, never making a mistake: *unerring judgement*

uneven *adjective* 1 not smooth or level 2 not all of the same quality *etc*: *this work is very uneven*

unexceptionable *adjective* not causing objections or criticism

Comes from the sense of 'exception' found in the phrase 'to take exception to something' (= to object to it)

◆ Do not confuse:
  unexceptionable and
  unexceptional

unexceptional *adjective* not exceptional, ordinary

Comes from the sense of 'exception' meaning 'something unlike the rest'

unexpected *adjective* not expected, sudden

■ **Alternative words**: anomalous

unfailing *adjective* never failing, never likely to fail: *unfailing accuracy*

unfair *adjective* not just

■ **Alternative words**: unjust, biased, partisan

unfaithful *adjective* 1 not true to your marriage vows 2 failing to keep promises

■ **Alternative words**: (meaning 1) adulterous, inconstant; (meaning 2) untrue, duplicitous

unfasten *verb* to loosen, undo (*eg* a buttoned coat)

unfathomable *adjective* not understandable, not clear

unfeeling *adjective* harsh, hard-hearted

unfettered *adjective* not restrained

unfit *adjective* 1 not suitable 2 not good enough, or not in a suitable state (to, for): *unfit for drinking/ unfit to travel* 3 physically under par

unfold *verb* 1 to spread out 2 to give details of (a story, plan) 3 of details of a plot *etc*: to become known

unforgettable *adjective* unlikely to ever be forgotten; memorable

unfortunate *adjective* 1 unlucky 2 regrettable: *unfortunate turn of phrase*

unfounded *adjective* not based on fact; untrue

unfurl *verb* to unfold (*eg* a flag)

ungainly *adjective* clumsy, awkward

ungracious *adjective* rude, not polite

ungrateful *adjective* not showing thanks for kindness

unguarded *adjective* 1 without protection 2 thoughtless, careless: *unguarded remark*

unguent (*pronounced* ung-gwent) *noun* ointment

unhappy *adjective* 1 miserable, sad 2 unfortunate □ **unhappily** *adjective*

unhealthy *adjective* 1 not well, ill 2 harmful to health: *unhealthy climate* 3 showing signs of not being well: *unhealthy complexion*

unheard-of *adjective* very unusual, unprecedented

unhinged *adjective* mad, crazy

unholy *adjective* **1** evil **2** outrageous

uni- *prefix* one, a single: *unilateral/unit*
   ① Comes from Latin *unus* meaning 'one'

unicorn *noun* a mythological animal like a horse, but with one straight horn on its forehead

unification *noun* the act of unifying or the state of being unified

uniform *adjective* the same in all parts or times, never varying □ *noun* the form of clothes worn by people in the armed forces, children at a certain school *etc*

uniformity *noun* sameness: *the uniformity of modern architecture*

unify *verb* to combine into one
   unify ⇨ unifi*es*, unify*ing*, unifi*ed*

unilateral *adjective* **1** one-sided **2** involving one person or group out of several

unilateralism *noun* the abandonment of nuclear weapons by one country, without waiting for others to do likewise

uninhibited *adjective* not inhibited, unrestrained

uninitiated *adjective* not knowing, ignorant

uninterested *adjective* not interested
   ☛ Do not confuse with: **disinterested**. It is generally a negative thing to be **uninterested** (= bored). It is generally a positive thing to be **disinterested** (= fair), especially if you are trying to make an unbiased decision

uninterrupted *adjective* **1** continuing without a break **2** of a view: not blocked by anything

union *noun* **1** the act of joining together **2** partnership; marriage **3** countries or states joined together **4** a trade union □ **Union Jack** the flag of the United Kingdom

unionist *noun* **1** a member of a trade union **2** someone who supports the

union of the United Kingdom

unique *adjective* without a like or equal: *a unique sense of timing*
   ☛ Do not confuse with: **rare**. You can talk about something being **rare**, quite **rare**, very **rare** *etc*. It would be incorrect, however, to describe something as 'very **unique**', since things either are or are not **unique** – there are no levels of this quality

unisex *adjective* suitable for either men or women

unison *noun* **1** exact sameness of musical pitch **2** agreement, accord □ **in unison** all together

unit *noun* **1** a single thing, person or group, especially when considered as part of a larger whole: *army unit/ storage unit* **2** a fixed amount or length used as a standard by which others are measured (*eg* metres, litres, centimetres *etc*) **3** the number one

unitary *adjective* **1** forming a unit, not divided **2** using or based on units

unite *verb* **1** to join together; become one **2** to act together
   ▤ **Alternative words**: (meaning 1) ally, amalgamate, coalesce (meaning 2) cooperate

united *adjective* **1** in agreement about something: *united in their opposition* **2** joined together: *a united Ireland*

unity *noun* **1** complete agreement **2** the state of being one or a whole **3** the number one

universal *adjective* **1** relating to the universe **2** relating to, or coming from, all people: *universal criticism* □ **universally** *adverb* (sense 2): *universally acclaimed*

universe *noun* all known things, including the earth and planets

university *noun* (*plural* **universities**) a college which teaches a wide range of subjects to a high level, and which awards degrees to students who pass its examinations

unkempt *adjective* untidy

unkind *adjective* not kind; harsh, cruel

■ **Alternative words**: mean, callous, malevolent

unleaded *adjective* of petrol: not containing lead compounds

unleash *verb* 1 to set free (a dog *etc*) 2 to let loose (*eg* anger)

unleavened (*pronounced* un-**lev**-end) *adjective* of bread: not made to rise with yeast

unless *conjunction* if not, except in a case where: *unless he's here soon, I'm going* (*ie* if he's not here soon)

unlike *adjective* different, not similar □ *preposition* 1 different from 2 not characteristic of: *it was unlike her not to phone*

unlikely *adjective* 1 not probable: *it's unlikely that it will rain today* 2 probably not true: *an unlikely tale*

unload *verb* 1 to take the load from 2 to remove the charge from a gun

unlucky *adjective* 1 not lucky or fortunate 2 unsuccessful □ **unluckily** *adverb*

■ **Alternative words**: (meaning 1) unfortunate, ill-starred, inauspicious, ominous; (meaning 2) disastrous

unmanly *adjective* weak, cowardly

unmask *verb* 1 to take a covering off 2 to show the true character of 3 to bring to light (a plot *etc*)

unmentionable *adjective* not fit to be spoken of, scandalous, indecent

unmistakable *adjective* very clear; impossible to confuse with any other: *unmistakable handwriting*

unmitigated *adjective* complete, absolute: *unmitigated disaster*

unmoved *adjective* not affected, unsympathetic: *unmoved by my pleas*

unnatural *adjective* not natural, perverted

unnecessary *adjective* not necessary; avoidable

unnerve *verb* to disconcert, perturb

UNO *abbreviation* United Nations Organization

unobtrusive *adjective* not obvious or conspicuous; modest

unpack *verb* to open (a piece of luggage) and remove the contents

unpalatable *adjective* 1 not pleasing to the taste 2 not pleasant to have to face up to: *unpalatable facts*

unparalleled *adjective* not having an equal, unprecedented: *unparalleled success*

unpick *verb* to take out sewing stitches from

unpleasant *adjective* not pleasant, nasty

■ **Alternative words**: disagreeable, objectionable, repulsive

unprecedented *adjective* never having happened before

unprepossessing *adjective* not attractive

unprincipled *adjective* without (moral) principles

unprintable *adjective* not suitable to be printed; obscene

unquestionable *adjective* undoubted, certain

unravel *verb* 1 to unwind, take the knots out of 2 to solve (a problem or mystery)

unravel ⇨ unravels, unravelling, unravelled

unreal *adjective* 1 not real, imaginary 2 *informal* amazing, incredible

unremitting *adjective* never stopping, unending: *unremitting rain*

unrequited *adjective* of love: not given in return, one-sided

unrest *noun* a state of trouble or discontent, especially among a group of people

unrivalled *adjective* without an equal

unruly *adjective* 1 badly behaved 2 not obeying laws or rules □ **unruliness** *noun*

unsavoury *adjective* very unpleasant, causing a feeling of disgust

unscathed *adjective* not harmed

unscrew *verb* to loosen (something screwed in)

unscrupulous *adjective* having no scruples or principles

unseat *verb* 1 to remove from a political seat 2 to throw from the saddle (of a horse)

unseemly *adjective* unsuitable, improper: *unseemly haste*

unseen *adjective* not seen □ **sight unseen** (bought *etc*) without having been seen, at the buyer's risk

unsettle *verb* to disturb, upset

■ **Alternative words**: agitate

unsettled *adjective* 1 disturbed 2 of weather: changeable 3 of a bill: unpaid

unsettling *adjective* disturbing, upsetting

unsightly *adjective* ugly

unsociable *adjective* not willing to mix with other people

unsolicited *adjective* not requested: *unsolicited advice*

unsophisticated *adjective* 1 simple, uncomplicated 2 naive, inexperienced

unsound *adjective* 1 incorrect, unfounded 2 not sane

unspeakable *adjective* too bad to describe in words: *unspeakable rudeness*

unstinting *adjective* unrestrained, generous

unstoppable *adjective* not able to be stopped

unsung *adjective* not celebrated, neglected: *an unsung Scots poet*

unsuspecting *adjective* not aware of coming danger

unswerving *adjective* solid, unwavering

untenable unjustifiable: *the government's position is untenable*

unthinkable *adjective* 1 very unlikely 2 too bad to be thought of

untidy *adjective* not neat or well-organized

■ **Alternative words**: messy, unsystematic, dishevelled, unkempt, slovenly

untie *verb* 1 to release from bonds 2 to loosen (a knot)

until *preposition* up to the time of: *can you wait until Tuesday?* □ *conjunction* up to the time that: *keep walking until you come to the corner*

untimely *adjective* 1 happening too soon: *untimely arrival* 2 not suitable to the occasion: *untimely remark*

unto *preposition, old* to

untold *adjective* 1 not yet told: *the untold story* 2 too great to be counted or measured: *untold riches*

untoward *adjective* 1 unlucky, unfortunate 2 inconvenient

untrue *adjective* 1 not true, false 2 unfaithful

■ **Alternative words**: (meaning 1) fallacious, erroneous; (meaning 2) disloyal, deceitful

untruth *noun* a lie

untruthful *adjective* lying or dishonest

unusual *adjective* 1 not usual 2 rare, remarkable

■ **Alternative words**: uncommon, exceptional, anomalous

unusually *adverb* to an unusual degree: *unusually cold for the time of year*

unvarnished *adjective* 1 not varnished 2 plain, straightforward: *the unvarnished truth*

unveil *verb* 1 to remove a veil from 2 to remove a cover from (a memorial *etc*) 3 to bring to light, disclose

unwaged *adjective* unemployed

unwarranted *adjective* uncalled-for, unnecessary

unwell *adjective* not in good health

unwieldy *adjective* not easily moved or handled □ **unwieldiness** *noun*

unwind *verb* 1 to wind off from a ball or reel 2 to relax

unwitting *adjective* 1 unintended: *unwitting insult* 2 unaware □ **unwittingly** *adverb*: *you have unwittingly caused a lot of trouble*

unwonted *adjective* unaccustomed, not usual: *unwonted cheerfulness*

unworthy *adjective* 1 not worthy 2 low, worthless, despicable 3 **unworthy of something** not deserving it: *unworthy* *of attention* **4** below someone's usual standard, out of character: *that remark is unworthy of you*

up *adverb* **1** towards or in a higher or more northerly position: *walking up the hill/ they live up in the Highlands* **2** completely, so as to finish: *drink up your tea* **3** to a larger size: *blow up a balloon* **4** as far as: *he came up to me and shook hands* **5** towards a bigger city *etc*, not necessarily one further north: *going up to London from Manchester* □ *preposition* **1** towards or in the higher part of: *climbed up the ladder* **2** along: *walking up the road* □ *adjective* **1** ascending, going up: *the up escalator* **2** ahead in score: *2 goals up* **3** better off, richer: *£50 up on the deal* **4** risen: *the sun is up* **5** of a given length of time: ended: *your time is up* **6** *informal* wrong: *what's up with her today?* □ **on the up and up** progressing steadily, getting better all the time □ **up and about 1** awake **2** out of bed after an illness □ **ups and downs** times of good and bad luck □ **up front 1** at the front **2** of money: paid in advance **3** candidly, openly □ **up to 1** until: *up to the present* **2** capable of: *are you up to the job?* **3** dependent on, falling as a duty to: *it's up to you to decide* **4** doing: *up to his tricks again* □ **up to date 1** to the present time **2** containing recent facts *etc* **3** aware of recent developments □ **up to scratch** of the required standard □ **up to speed** fully competent at a new job *etc*

up ⇨ **up**per, **up**most or **up**permost

■ **Alternative words:** up to date with (meaning 3) abreast of

up-and-coming *adjective* likely to succeed

upbeat *adjective, informal* cheerful, optimistic

upbraid *verb* to scold

upbringing *noun* the rearing of, or the training given to, a child

update *verb* to bring up to date □ *noun* **1** the act of updating **2** new information: *an update on yesterday's report*

upend *verb* to turn upside down

upfront or **up-front** *adjective* **1** candid, frank **2** foremost

upgrade *verb* **1** to raise to a more

important position **2** to improve the quality of □ *noun, computing* a newer version of a software program

upheaval *noun* a violent disturbance or change

upheld *past form of* **uphold**

uphill *adjective* **1** going upwards **2** difficult: *uphill struggle* □ *adverb* upwards

uphold *verb* **1** to defend, give support to **2** to maintain, keep going (*eg* a tradition)

uphold ⇨ **up**holds, **up**holding, **up**held

upholster *verb* to fit (furniture) with springs, stuffing, covers *etc*

upholstery *noun* **1** covers, cushions *etc* **2** the skill of upholstering

upkeep *noun* **1** the act of keeping (*eg* a house or car) in a good state of repair **2** the cost of this

upland *noun* **1** high ground **2 uplands** a hilly or mountainous region

uplift *verb* to raise the spirits of, cheer up

up-market *adjective* of high quality or price, luxury

upon *preposition* **1** on the top of: *upon the table* **2** at or after the time of: *upon completion of the task*

upper *adjective* higher, further up □ *noun* **1** the part of a shoe *etc* above the sole **2** *slang* the drug amphetamine □ **upper hand** advantage; dominance, control

upper-case *adjective* of a letter: capital, *eg* A not *a* (*contrasted with*: **lower-case**)

upper-class *adjective* belonging to the highest social class, aristocratic

uppermost *adjective* highest, furthest up

upright *adjective* **1** standing up, vertical **2** honest, moral □ *noun* an upright post, piano *etc*

uprising *noun* a revolt against a government *etc*

uproar *noun* a noisy disturbance

uproarious *adjective* very noisy

uproot *verb* **1** to tear up by the roots

2 to leave your home and go to live in another place

upset *verb* (*pronounced* up-**set**) **1** to make unhappy, angry, worried *etc* **2** to overturn **3** to disturb, put out of order **4** to ruin (plans *etc*) □ *adjective* (*pronounced* up-**set**) distressed, unhappy *etc*, ill □ *noun* (*pronounced* **up**-set) **1** distress, unhappiness, worry *etc* **2** something that causes distress

upset *verb* ⇨ upset*s*, upsett*ing*, upset

■ **Alternative words**: (verb, meaning 1) distress, trouble, worry, agitate, discompose, disconcert; (verb, meaning 2) tip, spill; (verb, meanings 3 and 4) topple, overthrow, destabilize; (adjective) dismayed, troubled, disconcerted, shaken

upshot (*pronounced* **up**-shot) *noun* a result or end of a matter: *what was the upshot of all this?*

upside-down *adjective* & *adverb* **1** with the top part underneath **2** in confusion

upstage *adverb* away from the footlights on a theatre stage □ *adjective, informal* haughty, proud □ *verb* to divert attention from (someone) to yourself

upstairs *adverb* in or to the upper storey of a house *etc* □ *noun* the upper storey or storeys of a house □ *adjective* in the upper storey or storeys: *upstairs bedroom*

upstanding *adjective* **1** honest, respectable **2** strong and healthy **3** *old* standing up

upstart (*pronounced* **up**-staht) *noun* someone who has risen quickly from a low to a high position in society, work *etc*

upstream *adverb* higher up a river or stream, towards the source

upsurge (*pronounced* **up**-serj) *noun* a rising, a swelling up

uptake (*pronounced* **up**-teik) *noun*: **quick on the uptake** quick to understand

uptight *adjective* nervous, tense

up-to-date *adjective* **1** modern, in touch with recent ideas *etc* **2** belonging to the present time **3** containing all

recent facts *etc*: *an up-to-date account*

upturn *noun* a positive change, an improvement

upward *adjective* moving up, ascending □ **upwards** *adverb* from lower to higher, up □ **upwards of** more than

upwardly-mobile *adjective* moving to a higher social status

uranium (*pronounced* yoo-**rei**-ni-um) *noun* a radioactive metal

urb-*word-forming element* of or relating to a town or city: *urban/ urbane* (= cultured and sophisticated like a city-dweller)/ *suburb*
⊙ Comes from Latin *urbs* meaning 'a city'

urban *adjective* relating to a town or city (*contrasted with*: **rural**)

urbanization *noun* the process of urbanizing

urbanize *verb* to make urban

urbane *adjective* polite in a smooth way

urbanity *noun* **1** smoothness of manner **2** (*plural* **urbanities**) urbane actions

urchin *noun* a dirty, ragged child

Originally meaning 'hedgehog', the prickly sense of which survives in *sea urchin*

urethra (*pronounced* yoo-**reeth**-ra) *noun* the tube leading from the bladder down which urine travels on its way out of the body

urethritis (*pronounced* yoo-reeth-**rai**-tis) *noun* inflammation of the urethra

urge *verb* **1** to drive (on) **2** to try to persuade: *urging me to go home* **3** to advise, recommend: *urge caution* □ *noun* a strong desire or impulse

urgency *noun* an urgent state or condition

urgent *adjective* **1** requiring immediate attention **2** asking for immediate action □ **urgently** *adverb*: *medical supplies are needed urgently*

urinary *adjective* of or relating to urine or the passing of urine

urinate *verb* to pass urine from the bladder

urine *noun* the waste liquid passed out

of the body of animals and humans
from the bladder

urn *noun* **1** a vase for the ashes of the
dead **2** a metal drum with a tap, used
for heating water for tea or coffee

US or **USA** *abbreviation* United States
of America

us *pronoun* used by a speaker or writer
in referring to themselves together with
other people (as the object in a
sentence): *when would you like us to
come?*

usage *noun* **1** the act or manner of
using **2** the established way of using a
word *etc* **3** custom, habit **4** treatment:
rough usage

use *verb* **1** to put to some purpose: *use
a knife to open it* **2** to bring into action:
use your common sense **3** (often **use up**)
to spend, exhaust (*eg* patience, energy)
4 to treat: *he used his wife cruelly* □ *noun*
1 the act of using **2** value or suitability
for a purpose: *no use to anybody* **3** the
fact of being used: *it's in use at the
moment* **4** custom □ **no use** useless
□ **used to 1** accustomed to **2** was or
were in the habit of (doing something):
we used to go there every year
① Comes from Latin *uti* meaning 'to use',
and *usus* meaning 'a using'

■ **Alternative words**: (verb, meanings
1 and 2) utilize, employ, exploit
(verb, meaning 3) consume, expend

used *adjective* **1** employed, put to a
purpose **2** not new: *used cars*

useful *adjective* serving a purpose;
helpful □ **usefully** *adverb*

■ **Alternative words**: convenient,
fruitful, advantageous, beneficial

useless *adjective* having no use or
effect

■ **Alternative words**: pointless,
hopeless, worthless, futile

user *noun* someone who uses anything
(especially a computer)

user-friendly *adjective* easily
understood, easy to use

usher *noun* someone who shows people
to their seats in a theatre *etc* □ *verb*
usher someone in or **out** to lead or

convey them into or out of a room,
building *etc*

usherette *noun* a woman who shows
people to their seats in a theatre *etc*

USSR *abbreviation, historical* Union of
Soviet Socialist Republics

usual *adjective* **1** done or happening
most often: *usual method* **2** customary:
with his usual cheerfulness **3** ordinary
□ *noun* a customary event, order *etc*

usually *adverb* on most occasions

usurer (*pronounced* **yooz**-yu-rer) *noun* a
money-lender who demands an
excessively high rate of interest

usurp (*pronounced* yoo-**zerp**) *verb* to
take possession of (*eg* a throne) by
force □ **usurper** *noun*

usury (*pronounced* **yooz**-yu-ri) *noun* the
lending of money with an excessively
high rate of interest

utensil *noun* an instrument or container
used in the home (*eg* a ladle, knife, pan)

uterus *noun* (*plural* **uteri** – *pronounced*
yoo-te-rai) the womb

utilitarian *noun* concerned with
usefulness, rather than beauty, pleasure
etc

utility *noun* (*plural* **utilities**) **1** usefulness
2 a public service supplying water, gas
etc

utilization *noun* utilizing or being
utilized: *careful utilization of resources*

utilize *verb* to make use of

utmost *adjective* **1** the greatest possible:
utmost care **2** furthest □ **do your utmost**
to make the greatest possible effort

utopia (*pronounced* yoo-**toh**-pi-*a*) *noun*
a perfect place, a paradise

Literally 'no place', coined by
Thomas More for his fictional book
Utopia (1516)

utopian (*pronounced* yoo-**toh**-pi-*a*n)
adjective unrealistically ideal

utter[1] *verb* to produce with the voice
(words, a scream *etc*)

utter[2] *adjective* complete, total: *utter
darkness*

utterance *noun* something said

utterly *adverb* completely, absolutely

uttermost *adjective* most complete, utmost

U-turn *noun* a complete change in direction, policy *etc*

UVA *abbreviation* ultraviolet radiation

-vac- forms words containing the idea 'empty': *vacant/ evacuate*
🕓 Comes from Latin *vacare* meaning 'to be empty', and *vacuus* meaning 'empty'

vacancy *noun* (*plural* **vacancies**) **1** a job that has not been filled **2** a room not already booked in a hotel *etc*

vacant *adjective* **1** empty, not occupied **2** of an expression: showing no interest or intelligence □ **vacantly** *adverb* (meaning 2): *stare vacantly into space*

vacate *verb* to leave empty, cease to occupy

vacation *noun* **1** the act of vacating **2** a holiday

vaccinate *verb* to give a vaccine to, *eg* by injection into the skin

vaccination *noun* the act or process of injecting someone with a vaccine

vaccine *noun* a substance made from the germs that cause a disease, given to people and animals to try to prevent them catching that disease

vacillate *verb* to move from one opinion to another; waver

vacillation *noun* constant wavering or hesitation; indecision

vacuous *adjective* **1** empty **2** empty-headed, stupid □ **vacuously** *adverb*

vacuum *noun* a space from which all, or almost all, the air has been removed

vacuum cleaner a machine which cleans carpets *etc* by sucking up dust

vacuum flask a container with double walls enclosing a vacuum, for keeping liquids hot or cold

vagabond *noun* **1** someone with no permanent home; a wanderer **2** a rascal, a rogue

vagaries *noun plural* strange, unexpected behaviour: *vagaries of human nature*

vagina *noun* the passage connecting a woman's genitals to her womb

vaginal *adjective* of the vagina

vaginitis *noun* inflammation of the vagina

vagrancy *noun* the state of being a tramp

vagrant *adjective* unsettled, wandering □ *noun* a wanderer or tramp, with no settled home

vague *adjective* **1** not clear; not definite: *vague idea/ vague shape* **2** not practical or efficient; forgetful □ **vaguely** *adverb*

vain *adjective* **1** conceited, self-important **2** useless: *vain attempt* **3** empty, meaningless: *vain promises* □ **in vain** without success □ **vainly** *adverb*

valance *noun* a decorative frill round the edge of a bed

vale *noun, formal* a valley

valediction *noun, formal* a farewell

valedictory *adjective, formal* saying farewell: *valedictory speech*

valentine *noun* **1** a greetings card sent on St Valentine's Day, 14 February **2** a sweetheart, a lover

valet (*pronounced* **val**-*e*t or **val**-ei) *noun* a manservant □ *verb* **1** to work as a valet **2** (*pronounced* **val**-*e*t) to clean out (a car) as a service

valetudinarian (*pronounced* val-i-tyood-i-**neir**-ri-*a*n) *noun* someone who is over-anxious about their health

valiant *adjective* brave □ **valiantly** *adverb*

valid *adjective* **1** sound, acceptable: *valid reason for not going* **2** legally in force: *valid passport*

validity *noun* **1** the state of being valid or acceptable for use **2** soundness of an argument or proposition

Valium *noun, trademark* a brand name for diazepam, a tranquillizing drug

valley *noun* (*plural* **valleys**) low land between hills, often with a river flowing through it

vallies *noun plural, slang* the drug Valium

valorous *adjective* brave, courageous

valour *noun* courage, bravery

valuable *adjective* of great value

valuables *noun plural* articles of worth

valuation *noun* **1** the act of valuing **2** an estimated price or value

value *noun* **1** worth; price **2** purchasing power (of a coin *etc*) **3** importance **4** usefulness **5** *algebra* a number or quantity put as equal to an expression: *the value of x is 8* □ *verb* **1** to put a price on **2** to think highly of

value-added tax a government tax raised on the selling-price of an article, or charged on certain services

valueless *adjective* worthless

valuer or **valuator** *noun* someone trained to estimate the value of property

valve *noun* **1** a device allowing air, steam or liquid to flow in one direction only **2** a small flap controlling the flow of blood in the body **3** an electronic component found in older television sets, radios *etc*

vamp *noun* the upper part of a boot or shoe □ *verb* **1** to patch **2** to play improvised music

vampire *noun* a dead person supposed to rise at night and suck the blood of sleeping people

vampire bat a South American bat that sucks blood

van¹ *noun* a covered or closed-in vehicle

or wagon for carrying goods by road or rail

van² *noun, short for* **vanguard**

vandal *noun* someone who pointlessly destroys or damages public buildings *etc*

vandalism *noun* the activity of a vandal

vandalize *verb* to damage by vandalism

vane *noun* **1** a weathercock **2** the blade of a windmill, propeller *etc*

vanguard *noun* **1** the leading group in a movement *etc* **2** the part of an army going in front of the main body

vanilla *noun* a sweet-scented flavouring obtained from the pods of a type of orchid

vanish *verb* **1** to go out of sight **2** to fade away to nothing

vanity *noun* (*plural* **vanities**) **1** conceit **2** worthlessness **3** something vain and worthless

vanquish *verb* to defeat

vantage point a position giving an advantage or a clear view

vapid *adjective* dull, uninteresting

vaporize *verb* to change into vapour

vaporizer *noun* a device which sprays liquid very finely

vapour *noun* **1** the air-like or gas-like state of a substance that is usually liquid or solid: *water vapour* **2** mist or smoke in the air

variable *adjective* changeable; that may be varied □ *noun* something that varies *eg* in value

variance *noun* a state of differing or disagreement □ **at variance** in disagreement or conflict

variant *noun* a different form or version □ *adjective* in a different form

variation *noun* **1** a varying, a change **2** the extent of a difference or change: *variations in temperature* **3** *music* a repetition, in a slightly different form, of a main theme

varicose vein a swollen or enlarged vein, usually on the leg

variegated *adjective* marked with

different colours; multicoloured

variety noun (plural **varieties**) 1 the quality of being of many kinds, or of being different 2 a mixed collection: a variety of books 3 a sort, a type: a variety of potato 4 mixed theatrical entertainment including songs, comedy, etc

various adjective 1 of different kinds: various shades of green 2 several: various attempts

■ **Alternative words**: different, diverse, many, several, heterogeneous

variously adverb in different ways or at different times: variously described as fascinating and dull

varnish noun a sticky liquid which gives a glossy surface to paper, wood etc □ verb 1 to cover with varnish 2 to cover up (faults)

vary verb 1 to make, be, or become different 2 to make changes in (a routine etc) 3 to differ, disagree

vary ➪ varies, varying, varied

vase (pronounced vahz or US veiz) noun a jar of pottery, glass etc used as an ornament or for holding cut flowers

Vaseline noun, trademark a type of ointment made from petroleum

vassal noun, historical a tenant who held land from an overlord in return for certain services

vast adjective of very great size or amount

vastly adverb greatly or to a considerable extent: vastly different

vastness noun immensity

VAT or **vat** abbreviation value-added tax

vat noun a large tub or tank, used eg for fermenting liquors and dyeing

vaudeville noun theatrical entertainment of dances and songs, usually comic

vault noun 1 an arched roof 2 an underground room, a cellar □ verb to leap, supporting your weight on your hands, or on a pole

vaunt verb to boast

VCR abbreviation video cassette recorder

VD abbreviation venereal disease

VDU abbreviation visual display unit

veal noun the flesh of a calf, used as food

veer verb 1 to change direction or course 2 to change mood, opinions, etc

Vegan or **vegan** (pronounced vee-gan) noun a vegetarian who uses no animal products

vegetable noun a plant, especially one grown for food □ adjective 1 of plants 2 made from or consisting of plants: vegetable dye/ vegetable oil

vegetarian noun someone who eats no meat, only vegetable or dairy foods □ adjective consisting of, or eating, only vegetable or dairy foods

vegetate verb 1 to grow as a plant does 2 to lead a dull, aimless life: sitting at home vegetating

vegetation noun 1 plants in general 2 the plants growing in a particular area

vehemence noun strong and forceful feeling

vehement adjective emphatic and forceful in expressing opinions etc □ **vehemently** adverb

vehicle noun 1 a means of transport used on land, especially one with wheels: motor vehicle 2 a means of conveying information, eg television or newspapers

veil noun 1 a piece of cloth or netting worn to shade or hide the face 2 something that hides or covers up □ verb 1 to cover with a veil 2 to hide □ **take the veil** to become a nun

vein noun 1 one of the tubes which carry the blood back to the heart 2 a small rib of a leaf 3 a thin layer of mineral in a rock 4 a streak in wood, stone etc 5 a mood or personal characteristic: a vein of cheerfulness

veldt (pronounced velt) noun, South African open grass-country, with few or no trees

vellum noun 1 a fine parchment used for bookbinding, made from the skins of calves, kids or lambs **2** paper made in imitation of this

velocity *noun* rate or speed of movement

velour (*pronounced* ve-**loor**) *noun* a fabric with a soft, velvet-like surface

velvet *noun* a fabric made from silk *etc*, with a thick, soft surface □ *adjective* **1** made of velvet **2** soft or smooth as velvet; silky

velvety *adjective* soft, like velvet

venal (*pronounced* vee-nal) *adjective* **1** willing to be bribed: *the majority of the councillors are venal and corrupt* **2** done for a bribe; unworthy
ⓘ Comes from Latin *venalis* meaning 'for sale'

❧ Do not confuse with: **venial**.
Venal is related to the verb 'vend', since they both contain the concept of selling (from Latin *venum*).
Venial comes from the Latin *venia* (= forgiveness) and means 'forgivable'

vend *verb* to sell
ⓘ Comes from Latin *vendere* meaning 'to sell'

vendetta *noun* a bitter, long-lasting quarrel or feud

vending machine a machine with sweets *etc* for sale, operated by putting coins in a slot

vendor *noun* someone who sells

veneer *verb* **1** to cover a piece of wood with another thin piece of finer quality **2** to give a good appearance to what is really bad □ *noun* **1** a thin surface layer of fine wood **2** a false outward show hiding some bad quality: *a veneer of good manners*

venerable *adjective* worthy of respect because of age or wisdom

venerate *verb* to respect or honour greatly

veneration *noun* **1** the act of venerating **2** great respect

venereal disease (*pronounced* vi-**neer**-ri-al) a disease contracted through sexual intercourse

Venetian blind a window blind formed of thin movable strips of metal or plastic hung on tapes

vengeance *noun* punishment given, harm done in return for wrong or injury, revenge □ **with a vengeance** with unexpected force or enthusiasm

vengeful *adjective* seeking revenge □ **vengefully** *adverb*

venial (*pronounced* vee-ni-al) *adjective* of a sin: not very bad, pardonable (*compare with*: **cardinal**)
ⓘ Comes from Latin *venialis* meaning 'pardonable'

❧ Do not confuse with: **venal**.
Venial comes from the Latin *venia* (= forgiveness). **Venal** literally means 'willing to be bought' and is related to the verb 'vend', since they both contain the concept of selling (from the Latin *venum*)

venison *noun* the flesh of a deer, used as food

venom *noun* **1** poison **2** hatred, spite

venomous *adjective* **1** poisonous **2** spiteful □ **venomously** *adverb* (meaning 2)

vent *noun* **1** a small opening **2** a hole to allow air or smoke to pass through **3** an outlet **4** a slit at the bottom of the back of a coat *etc* □ *verb* to express (strong emotion) in some way □ **give vent to** to express, let out

ventilate *verb* **1** to allow fresh air to pass through (a room *etc*) **2** to talk about, discuss

ventilation *noun* circulation of fresh air: *this room has poor ventilation*

ventilator *noun* a grating or other device for allowing in fresh air

ventriloquism *noun* the art of speaking in a way that makes the sound appear to come from elsewhere, especially a puppet's mouth

ventriloquist *noun* someone who can speak without appearing to move their lips and can project their voice on to a puppet *etc*

Literally 'stomach speaker' and originally meaning someone possessed by a talking evil spirit

venture *noun* an undertaking which involves some risk: *business venture*

□ *verb* **1** to risk, dare **2** to do or say something at the risk of causing annoyance: *may I venture to suggest*

venturesome *adjective* **1** prepared to take risks; enterprising **2** involving danger; risky

venue *noun* the scene of an event, *eg* a sports contest or conference

ver- *see* **veri-**

veracious *adjective* truthful
Ⓛ Comes from Latin *verax* meaning 'truthful'

💣 Do not confuse with: **voracious**

veracity *noun* truthfulness

veranda or **verandah** *noun* a kind of terrace with a roof supported by pillars, extending along the side of a house

verb *noun* the word that tells what someone or something does in a sentence, *eg* 'I *sing*' / 'he *had* no idea'

-verb- forms words concerned with words: *verbose/ proverb* (= well-known wise words)
Ⓛ Comes from Latin *verbum* meaning 'a word'

verbal *adjective* **1** of words **2** spoken, not written: *verbal agreement* **3** of verbs

verbatim *adjective* in the exact words, word for word: *a verbatim account*

verbose *adjective* using more words than necessary

verbosity *noun* using or containing too many words

verdant *adjective* green with grass or leaves

verdict *noun* **1** the judge's decision at the end of a trial **2** someone's personal opinion on a matter

verdigris *noun* the greenish rust of copper, brass or bronze

verdure *noun* green vegetation

verge *noun* **1** the grassy border along the edge of a road *etc* **2** edge, brink: *on the verge of a mental breakdown* □ **verge on** to be close to: *verging on the absurd*

verger *noun* a church caretaker, or church official

veri- or **ver-** *prefix* forms words containing the concept of truth: *verify/ veracity*

Ⓛ Comes from Latin *verus* meaning 'true'

verifiable *adjective* able to be verified

verification *noun* establishing as true, confirmation

verify *verb* to prove, show to be true, confirm

verify ⇨ verif**ies**, verif**ying**, verif**ied**

verily *adjective, old* truly, really

verisimilitude *noun* realism, closeness to real life

veritable *adjective* **1** true **2** real, genuine

verity *noun* truth

vermicelli *noun* a type of food like spaghetti but in much thinner pieces

vermilion *noun* a bright red colour

vermin *noun plural* animals or insects that are considered pests, *eg* rats, mice, fleas *etc*

verminous *adjective* full of vermin

vernacular *noun* the ordinary spoken language of a country or district □ *adjective* in the vernacular

vernal *adjective* of the season of spring

verruca *noun* a wart, especially on the foot

-vers- *see* **-vert-**

versatile *adjective* **1** able to turn easily from one subject or task to another **2** useful in many different ways

versatility *noun* the ability to be adaptable

verse *noun* **1** a number of lines of poetry forming a planned unit **2** poetry as opposed to prose **3** a short division of a chapter of the Bible □ **versed in** skilled or experienced in

version *noun* **1** an account from one point of view **2** a form: *another version of the same tune* **3** a translation

verso *noun* the left-hand page of an open book (*compare with*: **recto**)

versus *preposition* against (*short form*: **v**)

-vert- or **-vers-** forms words related to the action of turning: *vertigo* (= a turning or whirling around)/ *aversion* (= a turning away from)

Ⓛ Comes from Latin *vertere* meaning 'to turn'

vertebra *noun* (*plural* **vertebrae**) one of the bones of the spine

vertebrate *noun* an animal with a backbone

vertex *noun* (*plural* **vertices**) the top or summit; the point of a cone, pyramid or angle

vertical *adjective* 1 standing upright 2 straight up and down □ **vertically** *adverb*

■ **Alternative words**: perpendicular, erect
✖ **Opposite**: horizontal

vertigo *noun* giddiness, dizziness

verve *noun* lively spirit, enthusiasm

very *adverb* 1 to a great extent or degree: *seem very happy/ walk very quietly* 2 exactly: *the very same* □ *adjective* 1 same, identical: *the very people who claimed to support him voted against him* 2 ideal, exactly what is wanted: *the very man for the job* 3 actual: *in the very act of stealing* 4 mere: *the very thought of blood*

■ **Alternative words**: (adverb, meaning 1) extremely, most, greatly, highly, deeply, truly, remarkably, excessively, exceedingly, acutely, particularly, absolutely, noticeably, unusually

vespers *noun plural* a church service in the evening

vessel *noun* 1 a ship 2 a container for liquid 3 a tube carrying fluids in the body: *blood vessels*

vest *noun* 1 an undergarment for the top half of the body 2 *US* a waistcoat

vestibule *noun* an entrance hall; a lobby

vestige *noun* a trace, an indication of something's existence

vestigial *adjective* surviving only as a trace of former existence: *vestigial wings*

vestment *noun* a ceremonial garment, worn *eg* by a religious officer during a service

vestry *noun* (*plural* **vestries**) a room in a church in which vestments are kept

vet¹ *noun*, *informal* a veterinary surgeon

vet² *verb* to examine, check

vet ⇨ vets, vetting, vetted

vetch *noun* a plant of the pea family

veteran *adjective* old, experienced □ *noun* 1 someone who has given long service 2 an old soldier 3 *US* anyone who has served in the armed forces

veterinary *adjective* relating to the treatment of animal diseases

veterinary surgeon a doctor who treats animals

veto (*pronounced* vee-toh) *noun* (*plural* **vetoes**) 1 the power to forbid or block (a proposal) 2 an act of forbidding or blocking □ *verb* to forbid, block

veto *verb* ⇨ vetos, vetoing, vetoed Latin for 'I forbid', a phrase originally used by people's tribunes in the Roman Senate when objecting to proposals

vex *verb* to annoy; cause trouble to

vexation *noun* 1 the state of being vexed 2 something that vexes

vexatious *adjective* causing trouble or annoyance

VHF *abbreviation* very high frequency

via *preposition* by way of: *travelling to Paris via London*

viable *adjective* able to be managed, practicable: *viable proposition*

viaduct *noun* a long bridge taking a railway or road over a river *etc*

viands *noun plural*, *old* food

vibrant *adjective* full of energy; lively, sparkling

vibrate *verb* 1 to shake, tremble 2 to swing to and fro rapidly 3 of sound: to resound, ring

vibration *noun* 1 the act of vibrating 2 a rapid to-and-fro movement

vicar *noun* an Anglican member of the clergy who is in charge of a parish

vicarage *noun* the house of a vicar

vicarious *adjective* 1 in place or on behalf of another person 2 not experienced personally but imagined through the experience of others: *vicarious thrill*

vice *noun* 1 a bad habit, a serious fault 2 wickedness, immorality 3 a tool with two jaws for gripping objects firmly

vice- *prefix* second in rank to: *vice-chancellor/ vice-president*
ⓒ Comes from Latin *vicis* meaning 'a turn'

vice versa *adverb* the other way round: *I needed his help and vice versa (ie he needed mine)*

vicinity *noun* 1 nearness 2 neighbourhood

vicious *adjective* wicked; spiteful □ **viciously** *adverb*

If you have trouble spelling the '-sh-' sound in **vicious**, remember the single 'c' in the related word 'vice'

vicious circle a bad situation whose results cause it to get worse

vicissitude (*pronounced* vi-sis-it-yood) *noun* 1 change from one state to another 2 **vicissitudes** changes of luck, ups and downs

victim *noun* 1 someone who is killed or harmed, intentionally or by accident: *victim of a brutal attack/ victim of the financial situation* 2 an animal for sacrifice

victimize *verb* to treat unjustly; make a victim of

victor *noun* a winner of a contest *etc*

victorious *adjective* successful in a battle or other contest

victory *noun* (*plural* **victories**) success in any battle, struggle or contest

victuals (*pronounced* vit-*a*lz) *noun plural*, *old* food

video *adjective* 1 relating to the recording and broadcasting of TV pictures and sound 2 relating to recording by video □ *noun* (*plural* **videos**) 1 a videocassette recorder 2 a recording on videotape 3 *US* television □ *verb* to make a recording by video

video *verb* ⇨ videos, videoing, videoed

videocassette *noun* a cassette containing videotape □ **videocassette recorder** a tape recorder using videocassettes for recording and playing back TV programmes

video nasty a pornographic or horror film on videotape

videotape *noun* magnetic tape for carrying pictures and sound

vie *verb*: **vie with** to compete with, try to outdo

vie ⇨ vies, vying, vied

view *noun* 1 a range or field of sight: *a good view* 2 a scene 3 an opinion □ *verb* 1 to look at 2 to watch (television) 3 to consider □ **in view** 1 in sight 2 in your mind as an aim □ **in view of** taking into consideration □ **on view** on show; ready for inspecting □ **with a view to** with the purpose or intention of

viewpoint *noun* 1 a place from which a scene is viewed 2 a personal opinion (also **point of view**)

vigil *noun* a time of watching or of keeping awake at night, often before a religious festival

vigilance *noun* watchfulness, alertness

vigilant *adjective* watchful, alert

vigilante (*pronounced* vij-i-**lan**-tei) *noun* a private citizen who assumes the task of keeping order in a community

vigorous *adjective* strong, healthy; forceful: *vigorous defence* □ **vigorously** *adverb*: *argue vigorously*

vigour *noun* strength of body or mind; energy

Viking *noun*, *historical* a Norse invader of Western Europe

vile *adjective* 1 very bad 2 disgusting, revolting □ **vilely** *adverb*

vilify *verb* to say bad things about

vilify ⇨ vilifies, vilifying, vilified

villa *noun* a house in the country *etc* used for holidays

village *noun* a collection of houses, not big enough to be called a town

villager *noun* someone who lives in a village

villain *noun* a scoundrel, a rascal

villainous *adjective* wicked

villainy *noun* (*plural* **villainies**) wickedness

villein *noun, historical* a serf

vindicate *verb* **1** to clear from blame **2** to justify

vindictive *adjective* revengeful; spiteful

vine *noun* **1** a climbing plant that produces grapes (also **grapevine**) **2** any climbing or trailing plant

vinegar *noun* a sour-tasting liquid made from wine, beer *etc*, used for seasoning or pickling

vineyard (*pronounced* **vin**-yad) *noun* an area planted with grapevines

vintage *noun* **1** the gathering of ripe grapes **2** the grapes gathered **3** wine of a particular year, especially when of very high quality **4** time of origin or manufacture □ *adjective* **1** of a vintage **2** of wine: of a particular year **3** very characteristic of an author, style *etc*: *vintage Monty Python*

vintage car one of a very early type, still able to run

viola (*pronounced* vi-**oh**-la) *noun* **1** a stringed instrument like a large violin **2** a member of the family of plants which include violets and pansies

violate *verb* **1** to break (a law, a treaty *etc*) **2** to harm sexually, especially rape **3** to treat with disrespect **4** to disturb, interrupt

violation *noun* the act or process of violating

violator *noun* a person who violates an agreement or oath

violence *noun* great roughness and force

violent *adjective* **1** acting with great force: *violent storm* **2** caused or characterized by violence: *violent death/a violent film* **3** uncontrollable: *violent temper*

■ **Alternative words**: (meaning 1) intense, devastating, tumultuous; (meaning 2) brutal, bloodthirsty; (meaning 3) impetuous, intemperate, fiery

---

violently *adverb* **1** in a violent or aggressive way **2** extremely; severely; ardently: *violently opposed to our involvement*

violet *noun* a kind of small bluish-purple flower

violin *noun* a musical instrument with four strings, held under the chin and played with a bow

violinist *noun* someone who plays the violin

violoncello *see* **cello**

VIP *abbreviation* very important person

viper *noun* **1** an adder **2** a vicious or treacherous person

virago *noun* (*plural* **viragos**) a noisy, bad-tempered woman

viral *adjective* of a virus

virgin *noun* someone who has had no sexual intercourse □ **the Virgin Mary** the mother of Christ

virginal[1] *adjective* of or like a virgin; chaste

virginal[2] or **virginals** *noun* an early type of musical instrument, with a keyboard

virile *adjective* manly; strong, vigorous

virility *noun* manhood; manliness; strength, vigour

virtual *adjective* in effect, though not in strict fact

virtually *adverb* almost, nearly: *the war is virtually over*

virtual reality a computer-created environment that the person operating the computer is able to be a part of

virtue *noun* **1** goodness of character and behaviour **2** a good quality, *eg* honesty, generosity *etc* **3** a good point: *one virtue of plastic crockery is that it doesn't break* □ **by virtue of** because of

virtuosity *noun* brilliance of technique

virtuoso *noun* (*plural* **virtuosos**) a highly skilled artist, especially a musician

virtuous *adjective* good, just, honest □ **virtuously** *adverb*

virulence *noun* **1** causing extreme harm; poisonousness **2** bitter hostility

virulent *adjective* **1** full of poison **2** bitter, spiteful **3** of a disease: dangerous

virus *noun* (*plural* **viruses**) a germ that is smaller than any bacteria, and causes diseases such as mumps, chickenpox *etc*

visa *noun* a permit given by the authorities of a country to allow someone to stay for a time in that country

visage (*pronounced* viz-ij) *noun, old* the face

viscera (*pronounced* vis-e-ra) *noun plural* the inner parts of the body

viscosity *noun* the resistance of a fluid to flow, *eg* treacle has a higher viscosity than water

viscount (*pronounced* vai-kownt) *noun* a title of nobility next below an earl

viscountess (*pronounced* vai-kownt-es) *noun* a title of nobility next below a countess

viscous (*pronounced* vis-kus) *adjective* of a liquid: sticky, not flowing easily

visibility *noun* 1 the clearness with which objects may be seen 2 the extent or range of vision as affected by fog, rain *etc*

visible *adjective* able to be seen □ **visibly** *adverb*: *visibly upset*

vision *noun* 1 the act or power of seeing 2 something seen in the imagination 3 a strange, supernatural sight 4 the ability to foresee likely future events

visionary *adjective* seen in imagination only, not real □ *noun* (*plural* **visionaries**) someone who dreams up imaginative plans

visit *verb* 1 to go to see; call on 2 to stay with as a guest □ *noun* 1 a call at a person's house or at a place of interest *etc* 2 a short stay

■ **Alternative words**: (verb) see

visitation *noun* 1 a visit of an important official 2 a great misfortune, seen as a punishment from God

visitor *noun* someone who makes a visit

visor (*pronounced* vai-zor) *noun* 1 a part of a helmet covering the face 2 a movable shade on a car's windscreen 3 a peak on a cap for shading the eyes

vista *noun* a view, especially one seen through a long, narrow opening

visual *adjective* relating to, or received

through, sight: *visual aids* □ **visual display unit** a device like a television set, on which data from a computer's memory can be displayed

visualization *noun* the act or process of visualizing

visualize *verb* to form a clear picture of in the mind

vital *adjective* 1 of the greatest importance: *vital information* 2 necessary to life 3 of life 4 vigorous, energetic: *a vital personality*

vitality *noun* life; liveliness, strength; ability to go on living

vitalize *verb* to give life or vigour to

vitally *adverb* essentially; urgently: *it is vitally important to keep copies of all documents*

vitamin *noun* one of a group of substances necessary for health, occurring in different natural foods

vitiate (*pronounced* vish-i-eit) *verb* to spoil, damage

vitreous *adjective* of or like glass

vitriol *noun* sulphuric acid

vitriolic *adjective* biting, scathing

vituperation *noun* abusive criticism or language

vivacious *adjective* lively, sprightly □ **vivaciously** *adverb*

vivacity *noun* liveliness, spark

vivi- or **viv-** forms words related to living, or to things which are alive: *vivisection/ survive*
ⓛ Comes from Latin *vivere* meaning 'to live', and *vivus* meaning 'alive'

vivid *adjective* 1 life-like 2 brilliant, striking

vividly *adverb* brightly, clearly, intensely: *I remember my grandmother vividly*

vivisection *noun* the carrying out of experiments on living animals

vixen *noun* 1 a female fox 2 an ill-tempered woman

vizier *noun, historical* a minister of state in some Eastern countries

vocabulary *noun* (*plural* **vocabularies**) 1 the range of words used by an individual or group **2** the words of a particular language **3** a list of words in alphabetical order, with their meanings

vocal *adjective* **1** of the voice **2** expressing your opinions loudly and fully

vocalist *noun* a singer

vocation *noun* **1** an occupation or profession to which someone feels called to dedicate themselves **2** a strong inclination or desire to follow a particular course of action or work

vociferous *adjective* loud in speech, noisy

vodka *noun* an alcoholic spirit made from grain or potatoes

vogue *noun* the fashion of the moment; popularity □ **in vogue** in fashion

voice *noun* **1** the sound produced from the mouth in speech or song **2** ability to sing **3** an opinion □ *verb* to express (an opinion)

void *adjective* **1** empty, vacant **2** not valid □ *noun* an empty space □ **void of** lacking completely

volatile *adjective* **1** of a liquid: quickly turning into vapour **2** of a person: changeable in mood or behaviour, fickle

volcanic *adjective* **1** relating to volcanoes **2** caused or produced by heat within the earth

volcano *noun* (*plural* **volcanoes**) a mountain with an opening through which molten rock, ashes *etc* are periodically thrown up from inside the earth

> Named after *Vulcan*, the Roman god of fire

vole *noun* any of a group of small rodents, including the water rat

volition *noun* an act of will or choice: *he did it of his own volition*

volley *noun* (*plural* **volleys**) **1** a number of shots fired or missiles thrown at the same time **2** an outburst of abuse or criticism **3** *tennis* a return of a ball before it reaches the ground □ *verb* **1** to shoot or throw in a volley **2** to return (a ball) before it reaches the ground

volt *noun* the unit used in measuring the force of electricity

voltage *noun* electrical force measured in volts

volubility *noun* the act or process of speaking insistently, fluently or at great length

voluble *adjective* speaking with a great flow of words

volume *noun* **1** a book, often one of a series **2** the amount of space taken up by anything **3** amount: *volume of trade* **4** loudness or fullness of sound

voluminous *adjective* bulky, of great volume

voluntary *adjective* **1** done or acting by choice, not under compulsion **2** working without payment □ *noun* (*plural* **voluntaries**) a piece of organ music of the organist's choice played at a church service

volunteer *noun* someone who offers to do something of their own accord, often for no payment □ *verb* **1** to act as a volunteer **2** to give (information, an opinion *etc*) unasked

voluptuous *adjective* full of, or too fond of, the pleasures of life

vomit *verb* to throw up the contents of the stomach through the mouth □ *noun* the matter thrown up by vomiting

voracious *adjective* very greedy, difficult to satisfy: *voracious appetite/ voracious reader*
① Comes from Latin *vorax* meaning 'devouring'

🖝 Do not confuse with: **veracious**

voracity *noun* extreme greed or eagerness

vortex *noun* (*plural* **vortices** or **vortexes**) **1** a whirlpool **2** a whirlwind

vote *verb* **1** to give your support to (a particular candidate, a proposal *etc*) in a ballot or show of hands **2** to decide by voting □ *noun* **1** an expression of opinion or support by voting **2** the right to vote

■ **Alternative words:** (verb) elect, ballot

voter *noun* someone who votes

vouch *verb*: **vouch for something** to say that you are sure of it or can guarantee it: *I can vouch for his courage*

voucher *noun* a paper which can be exchanged for money or goods

vouchsafe *verb* to give or grant (a reply, privilege *etc*)

vow *noun* a solemn promise or declaration, especially one made to God □ *verb* **1** to make a vow **2** to threaten (revenge *etc*)

vowel *noun* **1** a sound made by the voice that does not require the use of the tongue, teeth or lips **2** the letters *a, e, i, o, u* (or various combinations of them), and sometimes *y*, which represent those sounds

voyage *noun* a journey, usually by sea □ *verb* to make a journey

vulgar *adjective* **1** coarse, ill-mannered **2** indecent **3** of the common people

vulgar fraction a fraction not written as a decimal, *eg* $\frac{1}{3}$, $\frac{4}{5}$

vulgarity *noun* coarseness in speech or behaviour

vulgarly *adverb* in a vulgar or coarse way

vulnerability *noun* a state of being vulnerable or easily harmed

vulnerable *adjective* **1** exposed to, or in danger of, attack **2** liable to be hurt physically or emotionally

vulture *noun* a large bird that feeds mainly on the flesh of dead animals

Ww

wad 1 a lump of loose material (*eg* wool, cloth, paper) pressed together **2** a bunch of banknotes

wadding *noun* soft material (*eg* cotton wool) used for packing or padding

waddle *verb* to walk with short, unsteady steps, moving from side to side as a duck does □ *noun* the act of waddling

wade *verb* **1** to walk through deep water or mud **2** to get through with difficulty: *still wading through this book*

wader *noun* **1** a long-legged bird that wades in search of food **2 waders** high waterproof boots worn by anglers for wading

wafer *noun* **1** a very thin, light type of biscuit, as that eaten with ice-cream **2** a very thin slice of anything

waffle *noun* **1** *US* a light, crisp cake made from batter, cooked in a **waffle-iron 2** pointless, long-drawn-out talk □ *verb* to talk long and meaninglessly

waft *verb* to carry or drift lightly through the air or over water

wag *verb* to move from side to side or up and down □ *noun* **1** an act of wagging **2** someone who is always joking

wag *verb* ⇨ wag*s*, wag*ging*, wag*ged*

wage *verb* to carry on (a war *etc*) □ *noun* (often **wages**) payment for work

wager *noun* a bet □ *verb* to bet

waggle *verb* to move from side to side in an unsteady manner □ *noun* an unsteady movement from side to side

wagon or **waggon** *noun* **1** a four-wheeled vehicle for carrying loads **2** an open railway carriage for goods **3** *US* a trolley for carrying food

wagtail *noun* a small black and white bird with a long tail which it wags up and down

waif *noun* an uncared-for or homeless child or animal □ **waifs and strays** homeless children or animals

wail *verb* to cry or moan in sorrow □ *noun* a sorrowful cry

wain *noun, old* a wagon

wainscot *noun* a skirting-board

waist *noun* the narrow part of the body, between ribs and hips

waistcoat *noun* a short, sleeveless jacket, often worn under an outer jacket

wait *verb* **1** to put off or delay action **2 wait for something** to remain in expectation or readiness for it: *waiting for the bus to come* **3** to be employed as a waiter or waitress □ *noun* **1** a delay **2 waits** singers of Christmas carols □ **wait on 1** to serve (someone) at table **2** to act as a servant to

■ **Alternative words**: (verb, meaning 1) delay, linger

waiter *noun* a man whose job it is to serve people at table in a restaurant

waiting list a list of people waiting for something in order of priority

waiting room a room in which to wait at a railway station, clinic *etc*

waitress *noun* a woman whose job it is to serve people at table in a restaurant

waive *verb* to give up (a claim or right)

ⓘ Comes from Old French *guesver* meaning 'to abandon'

☛ Do not confuse with: **wave**

waiver *noun* 1 the act of waiving 2 a document indicating this
ⓘ For origin, see **waive**

☛ Do not confuse with: **waver**

wake¹ *verb* (often **wake up**) to stop sleeping □ *noun* 1 a night of watching beside a dead body 2 a feast or holiday

wake *verb* ⟹ wakes, waking, woke or waked, woken

■ **Alternative words**: (verb) rise, arise, rouse

wake² *noun* a streak of foamy water left in the track of a ship □ **in the wake of** immediately behind or after

wakeful *adjective* not sleeping, unable to sleep

waken *verb* to wake, arouse or be aroused

waking *adjective* being or becoming awake

walk *verb* 1 to move along on foot 2 to travel along (streets *etc*) on foot □ *noun* 1 an act of walking 2 a manner of walking 3 a distance to be walked over: *a short walk from here* 4 a place for walking: *a covered walk* □ **walk of life** someone's rank or occupation □ **walk the plank** *historical* to be put to death by pirates by being made to walk off the end of a plank over a ship's side

■ **Alternative words**: step, stride, pace, proceed, advance, march, plod, tramp, traipse, trek, trudge, saunter, amble, stroll, tread, hike, promenade, move

walkie-talkie *noun* a portable radio set for sending and receiving messages

walking stick a stick used for support when walking

Walkman *noun*, *trademark* a personal stereo

walk-over *noun* an easy victory

wall *noun* 1 a structure built of stone, brick *etc* used to separate or enclose 2 the side of a building □ *verb* **wall in, off** *etc* to enclose or separate with a wall □ **off the wall** unusual, eccentric

wallaby (*plural* **wallabies**) a small kind of kangaroo

wallet *noun* a small folding case for holding bank-notes, credit cards *etc*

wallflower *noun* 1 a sweet-smelling spring flower 2 someone who is continually without a partner at a dance *etc*

wallop *verb*, *informal* to beat, hit □ *noun*

wallow *verb* to roll about with enjoyment in water, mud *etc*

wallpaper *noun* paper used in house decorating for covering walls □ *verb* to cover with wallpaper

walnut *noun* 1 a tree whose wood is used for making furniture 2 the nut it produces

walrus *noun* (*plural* **walruses**) a large sea animal, like a seal, with two long tusks

waltz *noun* (*plural* **waltzes**) 1 a ballroom dance for couples with a circling movement 2 music for this dance, with three beats to each bar □ *verb* to dance a waltz

WAN *abbreviation*, *computing* wide area network

wan (*pronounced* won) *adjective* pale and sickly looking

wand *noun* a long slender rod used by a conjuror, magician *etc*

wander *verb* 1 to roam about with no definite purpose; roam 2 to go astray 3 to be mentally confused because of illness *etc*

wanderer *noun* a person or animal that wanders

wanderlust *noun* a keen desire for travel

wane *verb* 1 to become smaller (*contrasted with*: **wax**) 2 to lose power, importance *etc* □ **on the wane** becoming less

wangle *verb* to get or achieve through craftiness, skilful planning *etc*

want *verb* 1 to wish for 2 to need, lack □ *noun* 1 poverty 2 scarcity, lack
ⓘ Comes from Old Norse *vant* meaning 'lacking', and *vanta* meaning 'to lack'

■ **Alternative words**: (verb, meaning
1) desire, crave, covet, yearn for;
(verb, meaning 2) require

wanted *adjective* looked for, especially
by the police

wanting *adjective* **1** absent, missing;
without **2** not good enough **3** feeble-
minded **4 wanting in something** lacking
it: *wanting in good taste*

wanton *adjective* thoughtless,
pointless, without motive: *wanton
cruelty*

war *noun* an armed struggle, especially
between nations □ *verb* **war against** to
fight in a war, make war against

war *verb* ⇨ wars, warring, warred

warble *verb* to sing like a bird, trill

warbler *noun* a type of song-bird

ward *verb*: **ward off** to keep off, defend
yourself against (a blow *etc*) □ *noun* **1**
a hospital room containing a number
of beds **2** one of the parts into which a
town is divided for voting **3** someone
who is in the care of a guardian

warden *noun* **1** someone who guards a
game reserve **2** someone in charge of a
hostel or college

warder *noun* a prison guard

wardrobe *noun* **1** a cupboard for
clothes **2** someone's personal supply of
clothes

warehouse *noun* a building where
goods are stored

wares *noun plural* goods for sale
Ⓛ Comes from Old English *waru*

warfare *noun* the carrying on of war

warhead *noun* the part of a missile
containing the explosive

warlike *adjective* **1** fond of war **2**
threatening war

warm *adjective* **1** fairly hot **2** of clothes:
keeping the wearer warm **3** of a person:
friendly, loving □ *verb* to make or
become warm

warm-blooded *adjective* having a
blood temperature higher than that of
the surrounding atmosphere

warm-hearted *adjective* kind,
generous

warmth *noun* **1** pleasant or comfortable
heat, or the condition or quality of
being warm **2** affection, friendliness or
enthusiasm: *we were immediately won
over by her warmth and friendliness*

warn *verb* **1** to tell (someone)
beforehand about possible danger,
misfortune *etc*: *I warned him about the
icy roads* **2** to give cautionary advice
to: *I warned him not to be late*

■ **Alternative words**: caution,
admonish

warning *noun* a remark, notice *etc* that
warns

warp *verb* **1** to become twisted out of
shape **2** to distort, make unsound: *his
previous experiences had warped his
judgement* □ *noun* the threads stretched
lengthwise on a loom, which are crossed
by the weft

warpath *noun*: **on the warpath** in a
fighting or angry mood

warrant *noun* a certificate granting
someone a right or authority: *search
warrant* □ *verb* to justify, be a good
enough reason for: *the crime does not
warrant such punishment* □ **I warrant
you** or **I'll warrant** you may be sure, I
assure you

warren *noun* **1** a collection of rabbit
burrows **2** a building with many rooms
and passages; a maze

warrior *noun* a great fighter

warship *noun* a ship armed with guns
etc

wart *noun* a small hard growth on the
skin

wary *adjective* cautious, on guard
□ **warily** *adverb*

was *past form* of **be**

wash *verb* **1** to clean with water, soap
etc **2** to clean yourself with water *etc* **3**
of water: to flow over or against **4** to
sweep (away, along *etc*) by force of
water □ *noun* (*plural* **washes**) **1** a
washing **2** a streak of foamy water left
behind by a moving boat **3** a liquid
with which anything is washed **4** a thin
coat of paint *etc* □ **wash your hands of**
to have nothing further to do with
□ **wash up** to wash the dishes

■ **Alternative words**: (verb, meaning
1) cleanse, launder; (verb, meaning
2) bathe

washer *noun* 1 someone or something
that washes 2 a flat ring of metal,
rubber *etc* for keeping joints tight

washing *noun* 1 the act of cleaning by
water 2 clothes to be washed

washing machine an electric machine
for washing clothes

washing-up *noun* dishes to be washed

wasp *noun* a stinging, winged insect,
with a slender, yellow and black striped
body

wassail *verb, old* to have a convivial
drinking session

wastage *noun* 1 an amount wasted 2
loss through decay or squandering

waste *adjective* 1 thrown away,
rejected as useless: *waste paper* 2 of
land: uncultivated, barren and desolate
□ *verb* 1 to spend (money, time, energy)
extravagantly, without result or profit
2 to decay or wear away gradually
□ *noun* 1 extravagant use, squandering
2 rubbish, waste material 3
uncultivated land 4 an expanse of water,
snow *etc*

■ **Alternative words**: (verb, meaning
1) squander, dissipate; (verb,
meaning 2) consume, erode

wasteful *adjective* causing waste,
extravagant

wastepaper basket a basket for paper
rubbish

wastepipe *noun* a pipe for carrying
away dirty water or semi-liquid waste

waster or **wastrel** *noun* an idle, good-
for-nothing person

watch *verb* 1 to look at, observe closely
2 (often **watch over**) to look after,
mind 3 *old* to keep awake □ *noun* (*plural*
watches) 1 the act of keeping guard 2
someone who keeps, or those who keep,
guard 3 a sailor's period of duty on
deck 4 a small clock worn on the wrist
or kept in a pocket

■ **Alternative words**: (verb, meaning
1) observe, view, regard, mark;
(verb, meaning 2) guard,
superintend, supervise

watchdog *noun* 1 a dog which guards
a building 2 an organization which
monitors business practices *etc*

watchful *adjective* alert, cautious
□ **watchfully** *adverb*

watchman *noun* a man who guards a
building *etc* at night

watchword *noun* a motto, a slogan

water *noun* 1 a clear, tasteless liquid
which falls as rain 2 a collection of this
liquid in a lake, river *etc* 3 urine □ *verb*
1 to supply with water 2 to dilute or
mix with water 3 of the mouth: to fill
with saliva 4 of the eyes: to fill with
tears
ⓘ Comes from Old English *wæter*

water butt a large barrel for rain water

water-closet *noun* a toilet, a lavatory
(*short form*: **WC**)

water-colour *noun* 1 a paint which is
mixed with water, not oil 2 a painting
done with this paint

watercress *noun* a plant which grows
beside streams, with hot-tasting leaves
which are eaten in salads

waterfall *noun* a place where a river
falls from a height, often over a ledge
of rock

waterlily *noun* a plant which grows in
ponds *etc*, with flat floating leaves and
large flowers

waterlogged *adjective* 1 filled with
water 2 soaked with water

watermark *noun* a faint design on
writing paper showing the maker's name,
crest *etc*

watermelon *noun* a large melon with
red juicy flesh and a thick, green rind

watermill *noun* a mill driven by water

water polo a ball-game played in a
pool between teams of swimmers

waterproof *adjective* not allowing
water to pass through □ *noun* an
overcoat made of waterproof material

water rat a kind of vole

watershed *noun* a ridge separating the valleys of two rivers

water-skiing *noun* the sport of being towed very fast on skis behind a motorboat

watertight *adjective* so closely fitted that water cannot leak through

waterway *noun* a channel along which ships can sail

waterwheel *noun* a wheel moved by water

waterworks *noun plural* 1 a place which purifies and stores a town's water supply 2 *euphemistic* the urinary system 3 *informal* tears

watery *adjective* 1 full of water 2 too liquid, textureless

watt *noun* a unit of electric power

wattage *noun* electric power measured in watts

wattle *noun* 1 interwoven twigs and branches used for fences *etc* 2 an Australian acacia tree 3 a fleshy part hanging from the neck of a turkey

wave *noun* 1 a moving ridge on the surface of the water 2 a ridge or curve of hair 3 a vibration travelling through the air carrying light, sound *etc* 4 a hand gesture for attracting attention, or saying hello or goodbye 5 a rush of an emotion (*eg* despair, enthusiasm *etc*) □ *verb* 1 to make a wave with the hand 2 to move to and fro, flutter: *flags waving in the wind* 3 to curl, curve
ⓒ Comes from Old English *wafian* meaning 'to wave'

♦ Do not confuse with: **waive**

wavelength *noun* the distance from one point on a wave or vibration to the next similar point

waver *verb* 1 to be unsteady, wobble 2 to be uncertain or undecided
ⓒ Comes from Old Norse *vafra* meaning 'to flicker'

♦ Do not confuse with: **waiver**

wavy *adjective* having waves

wax 1 the sticky, fatty substance of which bees make their cells 2 a fatty substance in the ear 3 a quickly hardening substance used for sealing letters *etc* □ *adjective* made of wax □ *verb*

1 to rub with wax 2 to grow, increase (*contrasted with*: **wane**)

waxen *adjective* 1 of or like wax 2 pale

waxworks *noun plural* a museum displaying wax models of famous people

waxy *adjective* of, or like, wax

way *noun* 1 an opening, a passage: *the way out* 2 road, path 3 room to go forward or pass: *block the way* 4 direction: *he went that way* 5 route: *do you know the way?* 6 distance: *a long way* 7 condition: *in a bad way* 8 means, method: *there must be a way to do this* 9 manner: *in a clumsy way* 10 someone's own wishes or choice: *he always gets his own way* □ **by the way** incidentally, in passing □ **by way of** 1 travelling through 2 as if, with the purpose of: *by way of a favour* □ **in the way** blocking progress □ **make your way** to go
ⓒ Comes from Old English *weg*

wayfarer *noun, old* a traveller on foot

waylay *verb* to wait for and stop (someone)

wayside *noun* the edge of a road or path □ *adjective* located by the side of a road

wayward *adjective* wilful, following your own way

WC *abbreviation* water-closet

we *pronoun* used by a speaker or writer in mentioning themselves together with other people (as the subject of a verb): *we are having a party this weekend*

weak *adjective* 1 not strong, feeble 2 lacking determination, easily persuaded 3 easily overcome: *weak opposition*

■ **Alternative words**: (meaning 1) frail, infirm, debilitated, insipid; (meanings 2 and 3) impotent, ineffectual, irresolute, untenable

weaken *verb* to make or become weak

weakling *noun* a person or animal that is lacking in strength

weakly *adjective* lacking strength, sickly

weakness *noun* 1 lack of strength 2 a fault; a special fondness (for): *a weakness for chocolate*

weal *noun* a raised mark on the skin

caused by a blow from a whip

wealth *noun* 1 riches 2 a large quantity: *wealth of information*

■ **Alternative words**: (meaning 1) affluence

wealthy *adjective* rich

■ **Alternative words**: affluent

wean[1] (*pronounced* ween) *verb* 1 to make (a child or young animal) used to food other than the mother's milk 2 **wean someone from** or **off something** to make them gradually give up (a bad habit *etc*)

wean[2] (*pronounced* wein) *noun, Scottish* a child

weapon *noun* 1 an instrument used for fighting, *eg* a sword, gun *etc* 2 any means of attack

wear *verb* 1 to be dressed in, have on the body 2 to arrange in a particular way: *she wears her hair long* 3 to have (a beard, moustache) on the face 4 to damage or weaken by use, rubbing *etc* 5 to be damaged in this way 6 to last: *wear well* □ *noun* 1 use by wearing: *for my own wear* 2 damage by use 3 ability to last 4 clothes *etc*: *school wear* □ **wear and tear** damage by ordinary use □ **wear off** to pass away gradually □ **wear on** to become later: *the afternoon wore on* □ **wear out** 1 to make or become unfit for further use 2 to exhaust

> **wear** *verb* ⇨ wear*s*, wear*ing*, wore, worn

■ **Alternative words**: (verb, meaning 1) don, sport

wearable *adjective* fit to be worn

wearer *noun* a person who wears something: *wearers of contact lenses*

wearing *adjective* tiring, exhausting

wearisome *adjective* causing tiredness, boredom or impatience

weary *adjective* 1 tired, having used up your strength or patience 2 tiring, boring □ *verb* to make or become tired, bored or impatient □ **weary of** tired of, bored with

> **weary** ⇨ wear*ies*, wear*ying*, wear*ied*

■ **Alternative words**: (adjective, meaning 1) jaded

weasel *noun* a small wild animal with a long and slender body, that lives on mice, birds *etc*

weather *noun* the state of the atmosphere, *eg* heat, coldness, cloudiness *etc* □ *verb* 1 to dry or wear away through exposure to the air 2 to come safely through (a storm, difficulty *etc*)

weatherbeaten *adjective* showing signs of having been out in all weathers

weathercock or **weathervane** *noun* a flat piece of metal that swings in the wind to show its direction

weave *verb* 1 to pass threads over and under each other on a loom *etc* to form cloth 2 to plait cane *etc* for basket-making 3 to put together (a story, plan *etc*) 4 to move in and out between objects, or move from side to side: *weaving through the traffic*

> **weave** ⇨ weave*s*, weav*ing*, wove, woven

weaver *noun* someone who weaves

web *noun* 1 the net made by a spider, a cobweb 2 the skin between the toes of ducks, swans, frogs *etc* 3 something woven

webbed *adjective* of feet: having the toes joined by a web

web-footed or **web-toed** *adjective* having webbed feet or toes

wed *verb* to marry

> **wed** ⇨ wed*s*, wed*ding*, wed*ded*

we'd *short for* 1 we would; we should 2 we had

wedding *noun* 1 marriage 2 a marriage ceremony

wedge *noun* 1 a piece of wood, metal *etc* thick at one end with a thin edge at the other, used in splitting wood, forcing two surfaces apart *etc* 2 anything shaped like a wedge □ *verb* 1 to fix or become fixed with a wedge 2 to push or squeeze (in): *wedged in amongst the crowd*

wedlock *noun* the state of being married

Wednesday *noun* the fourth day of the week

wee *adjective, Scottish* small, tiny

weed *noun* 1 a useless, troublesome plant 2 a weak, worthless person 3 **weeds** a widow's mourning clothes □ *verb* to clear (a garden *etc*) of weeds

weedy *adjective* 1 full of weeds 2 like a weed 3 thin and puny, unmanly

week *noun* 1 the space of seven days from Sunday to Saturday 2 the working days of the week, not Saturday and Sunday
Ⓛ Comes from Old English *wice*

weekday *noun* any day except Saturday and Sunday

weekend *noun* Saturday and Sunday

weekly *adjective* happening, or done, once a week □ *adverb* once a week □ *noun* (*plural* **weeklies**) a newspaper, magazine *etc* coming out once a week

weep *verb* 1 to shed tears 2 to ooze, drip: *a weeping wound*

weep ⇨ weeps, weeping, wept

weeping willow a willow tree with drooping branches

weevil *noun* a small beetle that destroys grain, flour *etc*

weft *noun* the threads on a loom which cross the warp

weigh *verb* 1 to find out how heavy (something) is by putting it on a scale *etc* 2 to have a certain heaviness: *weighing 10 kilogrammes* 3 to raise (a ship's anchor) 4 of burdens *etc*: to press down, be heavy or troublesome 5 to consider (a matter, a point) carefully 6 to consider (something) important □ **weigh in** to test your weight before a boxing match □ **weigh out** to measure out a quantity by weighing it on a scale

Alternative words: (verb, meaning 4) oppress; (verb, meanings 5 and 6) contemplate, ponder, deliberate

weighbridge *noun* a large scale for weighing vehicles

weight *noun* 1 the amount that anything weighs 2 a piece of metal weighing a certain amount: *a 100 gramme weight* 3 a load, a burden 4 importance □ *verb* to make heavy by

adding or attaching a weight

weightless *adjective* 1 weighing nothing or almost nothing 2 not affected by gravity, so able to float about

weightlessness *noun* absence of the pull of gravity

weighty *adjective* 1 heavy 2 important

weir *noun* a dam across a stream

weird *adjective* 1 mysterious, supernatural 2 odd, strange

welcome *verb* 1 to receive with warmth or pleasure 2 to accept gladly: *I welcome the challenge* □ *noun* a welcoming, a warm reception □ *adjective* received with pleasure □ **welcome to** permitted to do or take □ **you're welcome!** used in reply to an expression of thanks

weld *verb* 1 to join (pieces of metal) by pressure, with or without heating 2 to join closely □ *noun* a joint made by welding

welfare *noun* comfort, good health

welfare state a country with a health service, insurance against unemployment, pensions for those who cannot work *etc*

well *noun* 1 a spring of water 2 a shaft in the earth to extract water, oil *etc* 3 an enclosed space round which a staircase winds □ *verb* (often **well up**) to rise up and gush: *tears welled up in her eyes* □ *adjective* in good health □ *adverb* 1 in a good and correct manner: *write well* 2 thoroughly: *well beaten* 3 successfully: *do well* 4 conveniently: *it fits in well with my plans* □ *exclamation* expressing surprise, or used in explaining, narrating *etc* □ **as well as** in addition to □ **it is as well** or **it is just as well** it is a good thing, it is lucky

well *adverb* ⇨ better, best

we'll *short for* we will; we shall

well-advised *adjective* wise

well-behaved *adjective* with good manners

well-being *noun* welfare; contentment

well-disposed *adjective*: **well-disposed to** inclined to favour

well-informed *adjective* having or showing knowledge

wellingtons *noun plural* high rubber boots covering the lower part of the legs

well-known *adjective* **1** familiar **2** celebrated, famous

well-meaning *adjective* having good intentions

well-meant *adjective* rightly, kindly intended

well-off *adjective* rich

well-read *adjective* having read many good books

well-to-do *adjective* rich

well-wisher *noun* someone who wishes someone success

welt *noun* **1** a firm edging or band, *eg* on the wrist or waist of a garment **2** a weal

welter *verb* to roll about, wallow □ *noun* **1** great disorder or confusion **2** a muddled mass, a jumble: *a welter of information*

wench *noun* (*plural* **wenches**) *old* a young woman, a girl

wend *verb*: **wend your way** to make your way slowly

went *past form* of **go**

wept *past form* of **weep**

were *past form* of **be**

we're *short for* we are

werewolf *noun* a mythical creature which changes periodically from a human into a wolf

west *noun* one of the four chief directions, that in which the sun sets □ *adjective* in the west □ *adverb* to or towards the west

westerly *adjective* **1** lying or moving towards the west **2** of wind: from the west

western *adjective* relating to, or in, the west □ *noun* a film or story about life among the early settlers in the western United States

westward *adjective & adverb* towards the west

westwards *adverb* towards the west

wet *adjective* **1** soaked or covered with water or other liquid **2** rainy: *a wet day* □ *noun* **1** water **2** rain □ *verb* to make wet

wet *verb* ⇨ wets, wetting, wet or wetted

■ **Alternative words**: (adjective, meaning 1) saturated, waterlogged, dank, clammy; (adjective, meaning 2) teeming, dreich

wet suit a suit that allows water to pass through but retains body heat

whack *noun* a loud, violent slap or blow □ *verb* to slap or hit violently

whale *noun* a very large mammal living in the sea □ *verb* to catch whales

whaler *noun* a ship engaged in catching whales

wharf *noun* (*plural* **wharfs** or **wharves**) a landing stage for loading and unloading ships

what *adjective & pronoun* used to indicate something about which a question is being asked: *what day is this?/ what are you doing?* □ *adjective* any that: *give me what money you have* □ *conjunction* anything that: *I'll take what you can give me* □ *adjective, adverb & pronoun* used for emphasis in exclamations: *what terrible ties he wears!/ what rubbish!* □ **what about?** used in asking whether the listener would like something: *what about a glass of milk?* □ **what if?** what will or would happen if: *what if he comes back?* □ **what with** because of: *what with having no exercise and being overweight, he had a heart attack*

whatever *adjective & pronoun* **1** anything (that): *show me whatever you have* **2** no matter what: *whatever happens*

whatsoever *adjective* at all: *nothing whatsoever to do with me*

wheat *noun* a grain from which the flour used for making bread *etc* is made

wheaten *adjective* **1** made of wheat **2** wholemeal

wheatgerm *noun* the vitamin-rich embryo of wheat

wheedle *verb* to beg or coax, often by flattery

wheel noun 1 a circular frame or disc turning on an axle, used for transporting things 2 a steering-wheel of a car etc □ verb 1 to move or push on wheels 2 to turn like a wheel or in a wide curve 3 to turn round suddenly: wheeled round in surprise

wheelbarrow noun a handcart with one wheel in front, two handles and legs behind

wheelchair noun a chair on wheels for an invalid

wheelhouse noun the shelter in which a ship's steering-wheel is placed

wheeze verb to breathe with difficulty, making a whistling or croaking sound □ noun 1 the sound of difficult breathing 2 informal a joke

whelk noun a type of small shellfish, used as food

whelp noun 1 old a young lion 2 a puppy □ verb of a lion, dog etc: to give birth to young

when adverb at what time: when did you arrive? □ adverb & conjunction the time at which: I know when you left/ I fell when I was coming in □ relative pronoun at which: at the time when I saw him □ conjunction seeing that, since: why walk when you have a car?

whence adverb, old from what place: whence did you come? □ conjunction to the place from which: he's gone back whence he came

whenever adverb & conjunction 1 at any given time: come whenever you're ready 2 at every time: I go whenever I get the chance

where adverb & conjunction to or in what place: where are you going?/ I wonder where we are □ relative pronoun & conjunction (in the place) in which, (to the place) in which: go where he tells you to go/ it's still where it was

whereabouts adverb & conjunction near or in what place: whereabouts is it?/ I don't know whereabouts it is □ noun the place where someone or something is: I don't know her whereabouts

whereas conjunction 1 when in fact: they thought I was lying, whereas I was telling the truth 2 but, on the other hand: he's tall, whereas I'm short

whereupon adverb & conjunction at or after which time, event etc

wherever adverb to what place: wherever did you go? □ conjunction to any place: wherever you may go

wherewithal noun 1 the means of doing something 2 money

whet verb 1 to sharpen (a knife etc) by rubbing 2 to make (desire, appetite etc) keener

whet ⇨ whets, whetting, whetted

whether conjunction 1 either if: whether you come or not 2 if: I don't know whether it's possible

whetstone noun a stone on which to sharpen blades

which adjective & pronoun 1 used to refer to a particular person or thing from a group: which colour do you like best? 2 the one that: show me which dress you would like □ relative pronoun referring to the person or thing just named: I bought the chair which you are sitting on □ **which is which** which is one and which is the other: they are twins and I can't tell which is which

whichever adjective & pronoun any (one), no matter which: I'll take whichever you don't want/ I saw trees whichever way I turned

whiff noun a sudden puff or scent: whiff of perfume

while or **whilst** conjunction 1 during the time that: while I'm at the office 2 although: while I sympathize, I can't really help □ **while** noun a space of time □ verb **while away** to pass (time) without boredom: he whiled away the time by reading

whim noun a sudden thought or desire

whimper verb to cry with a low, whining voice □ noun a low, whining cry

whimsical adjective 1 full of whims, fanciful 2 humorous

whine verb 1 to make a high-pitched, complaining cry 2 to complain unnecessarily □ noun an unnecessary complaint

whinge verb to whine, complain peevishly □ noun a peevish complaint

whinge verb ⇨ whinges, whingeing or whinging, whinged

whingeing or **whinging** adjective complaining

whinny verb of a horse: to neigh □ noun (plural **whinnies**) a neighing sound

whinny verb ⇨ whinnies, whinnying, whinnied

whip noun **1** a lash with a handle, for punishing, urging on animals etc **2** a member of parliament who sees that the members of their own party attend to give their vote when needed □ verb **1** to hit or drive with a lash **2** to beat (eggs, cream etc) into a froth **3** to snatch (away, off, out, up etc): whipped out a revolver **4** to move fast, like a whip

whip verb ⇨ whips, whipping, whipped

whippet noun a breed of racing dog, like a small greyhound

whipping noun a beating with a whip

whir or **whirr** noun a sound of fast, continuous whirling □ verb to move or whirl with a buzzing noise

whir verb ⇨ whirs, whirring, whirred

whirl verb **1** to turn round quickly **2** to carry (off, away etc) quickly □ noun **1** a fast circling movement **2** great excitement, confusion: in a whirl over the wedding arrangements

whirlpool noun a place in a river or sea where the current moves in a circle

whirlwind noun a violent current of wind with a whirling motion

whisk verb **1** to move quickly and lightly, sweep: their car whisked past **2** to beat or whip (a mixture) □ noun **1** a quick sweeping movement **2** a kitchen utensil for beating eggs or mixtures **3** a small bunch of twigs etc used as a brush

whisker 1 a long bristle on the upper lip of a cat etc **2** whiskers hair on the sides of a man's face, sideburns

whisky or Irish & US **whiskey** noun (plural **whiskies** or **whiskeys**) an alcoholic spirit made from grain

Based on Scottish Gaelic uisge beatha, meaning 'water of life'

whisper verb **1** to speak very softly, using the breath only, not the voice **2** to make a soft, rustling sound □ noun a soft sound made with the breath

whist noun a type of card game for four players

whistle verb **1** to make a high-pitched sound by forcing breath through the lips or teeth **2** to make such a sound with an instrument **3** to move with such a sound, like a bullet □ noun **1** the sound made by whistling **2** any instrument for whistling

whit noun a tiny bit: not a whit better

white adjective **1** of the colour of pure snow **2** pale or light-coloured: white wine **3** of a pale-coloured complexion □ noun **1** something white **2** someone with a pale-coloured complexion **3** the part of an egg surrounding the yolk

whitebait noun the young of herring or sprats

white elephant something useless and costly or troublesome to maintain

white-hot adjective having reached a degree of heat at which metals glow with a white light (hotter than **red-hot**)

whiten verb to make or become white or whiter

whiteness noun a white state or quality

whitewash noun a mixture of ground chalk and water, or lime and water, for whitening walls etc □ verb **1** to put whitewash on **2** to cover up the faults of, give a good appearance to

whither adverb & conjunction, old to what place?

whiting noun a small type of fish related to the cod

Whitsun noun the week beginning with the seventh Sunday after Easter

whittle verb **1** to pare or cut (wood etc) with a knife **2** whittle away or down to make gradually less: whittled away his savings

whiz¹ or **whizz** verb **1** to move with a hissing sound, like an arrow **2** to move very fast

whiz ⇨ whizzes, whizzing, whizzed

whiz² noun or **whizz kid** someone who

achieves rapid success while relatively young

WHO *abbreviation* World Health Organization

who *pronoun* used to refer to someone or some people unknown or unnamed (only as the subject of a verb): *who is that woman in the green hat?* □ *relative pronoun* referring to the person or people just named: *do you know who those people are?*

whoever *pronoun* any person or people

whole *adjective* **1** complete **2** all, with nothing or no one missing **3** not broken **4** in good health □ *noun* the entire thing □ **on the whole** when everything is taken into account

wholefood *noun* unprocessed food produced without the aid of artificial fertilizers

wholehearted *adjective* enthusiastic, generous

wholemeal *noun* flour made from the entire wheat grain

wholesale *noun* the sale of goods in large quantities to a shop from which they can be bought in small quantities by ordinary buyers (*compare with:* **retail**) *adjective* **1** buying or selling in large quantities **2** on a large scale: *wholesale killing*

wholesaler *noun* a person who buys goods on a large scale and sells them in smaller quantities to shopkeepers for sale to the public

wholesome *adjective* giving health, healthy

who'll *short for* who will; who shall

wholly *adverb* entirely, altogether

whom *pronoun* **1** used to refer to someone or some people unknown or unnamed (only as the object of a sentence): *whom did you see?/ to whom am I speaking?* **2** which person: *do you know to whom I gave it?* □ *relative pronoun* referring to the person or people just named: *the person whom I liked best*

whoop *noun* a loud cry, rising in pitch □ *verb* to give a whoop

whooping-cough *noun* an infectious disease in which violent bouts of coughing are followed by a whoop as the breath is drawn in

whose *adjective* & *pronoun* belonging to whom?: *whose handwriting is this?* □ *relative pronoun* of whom: *the man whose wife I know*

why *adverb* & *pronoun* for which reason?: *why did you not stay?* □ **the whys and wherefores** all the reasons, details

wick *noun* the twisted threads in a candle or lamp which draw up the oil or grease to the flame

wicked *adjective* **1** evil, sinful **2** mischievous, spiteful □ **wickedly** *adverb*

wicker *adjective* of a chair: made of woven willow twigs

wicket *noun* **1** a small gate or door, especially in or beside a larger one **2** *cricket* the set of three stumps, or one of these, at which the ball is bowled **3** the ground between the bowler and the batsman

wide *adjective* **1** broad, not narrow **2** stretching far: *a wide grin* **3** general, big: *a wide selection* **4** measuring a certain amount from side to side: *5 centimetres wide* □ *adverb* **1** off the target: *the shots went wide* **2** (often **wide apart**) far apart: *hold your arms wide* □ **wide of the mark** off the target, inaccurate

---

■ **Alternative words**: (adjective, meanings 1 and 2) broad; (adjective, meaning 2) dilated; (adjective, meaning 3) extensive, comprehensive

---

wide-awake *adjective* fully awake; alert

wide-eyed *adjective* with eyes wide open in surprise *etc*

widely *adverb* **1** over a wide area; among many: *widely believed* **2** far apart

widen *verb* to make or become wide

wideness *noun* a wide state or quality

wide-open *adjective* opened to the full extent

widespread *adjective* spread over a

large area or among many people: *a widespread belief*

widow *noun* a woman whose husband is dead

widower *noun* a man whose wife is dead

width *noun* **1** measurement across, from side to side **2** large extent

wield *verb* **1** to swing or handle (a cricket bat, sword *etc*) **2** to use (power, authority *etc*)

wife *noun* (*plural* **wives**) **1** a married woman **2** the woman to whom a man is married

wig *noun* an artificial covering of hair for the head

wiggle *verb* to move from side to side with jerky or twisting movements □ *noun* a jerky movement from side to side

wiggly *adjective* wriggly, wavy: *she drew a wiggly line*

wigwam *noun, historical* a conical tent of skins made by some Native Americans

wild *adjective* **1** of an animal: not tamed **2** of a plant: not cultivated in a garden **3** uncivilized **4** unruly, uncontrolled **5** of weather: stormy **6** frantic, mad: *wild with anxiety* **7** of a guess *etc*: rash, inaccurate □ *noun* (usually **wilds**) an uncultivated or uncivilized region

wild boar a wild type of pig

wild cat a wild type of European cat

wilderness *noun* a wild, uncultivated or desolate region

wild-goose chase a troublesome and useless errand

wildlife *noun* wild animals, birds *etc* in their natural habitats

wile *noun* a crafty trick

wilful *adjective* fond of having one's own way; intentional: *wilful damage*

will *noun* **1** the power to choose or decide **2** desire: *against my will* **3** determination: *the will to win* **4** feeling towards someone: *a sign of goodwill* **5** a written statement about what is to be done with your property after your death □ *verb* **1** to influence someone by exercising your will: *he willed her to win* **2** to hand down (property *etc*) by will

3 (*past form* **would**) also used to form future tenses of other verbs when the subject is **he, she, it, you** or **they**: *you will see me there* **4** *informal* often used for the same purpose when the subject is **I** or **we**: *I will tell you later* **5** used for emphasis, or to express a promise, when the subject is **I** or **we**: *I will do it if possible* (*see also* **shall**, **would**) □ **at will** as or when you choose □ **with a will** eagerly

will *verb* ⇨ **wills**, **will**ing, **will**ed

🕓 Noun, and verb meanings 1 and 2: come from Old English *willa* meaning 'will' or 'determination'; verb meanings 3, 4 and 5: come from Old English *wyllan* meaning 'to wish' or 'to be willing'

willing *adjective* ready to do what is asked; eager

■ **Alternative words**: disposed, compliant, agreeable, amenable

will-o'-the-wisp *noun* a pale light sometimes seen by night over marshy places

willow *noun* **1** a tree with long slender branches **2** its wood, used in cricket bats

willynilly *adverb* **1** whether you wish or not **2** notwithstanding other people's feelings

From the phrase *will I, nill I*, meaning 'whether I want or don't want'

wilt *verb* **1** of a flower or plant: to droop **2** to lose strength

wily *adjective* cunning

wimp *noun, informal* an ineffectual person

win *verb* **1** to gain by luck or in a contest **2** to gain (the love of someone *etc*) by effort **3** to come first in a contest **4** (often **win over**) to gain the support or friendship of □ *noun* an act of winning; a victory

win *verb* ⇨ **win**s, **win**ning, **won**

■ **Alternative words**: (verb, meanings 1 and 2) acquire, attain, procure, secure; (verb, meaning 3) prevail, triumph

wince *verb* to shrink or start back in

pain *etc*, flinch: *her singing made me wince*

winch *noun* (*plural* **winches**) 1 a handle or crank for turning a wheel 2 a machine for lifting things, worked by winding a rope round a revolving cylinder □ **winch up** to lift up with a winch

wind¹ *noun* 1 a current of air 2 breath 3 air carrying a scent 4 air or gas in the stomach 5 the wind instruments in an orchestra □ *verb* to put out of breath □ **get the wind up** *informal* to become afraid □ **get wind of** *informal* to hear about in an indirect way

wind² *verb* 1 to turn, twist or coil 2 (sometimes **wind up**) to screw up the spring of (a watch, clockwork toy *etc*) 3 to wrap closely □ **wind up** 1 to bring or come to an end: *wind up a meeting* 2 *informal* to annoy, tease □ **wind your way** to make your way circuitously

wind *verb* ⇨ winds, winding, wound

winder *noun* a key *etc* for winding a clock

windfall *noun* 1 a fruit blown from a tree 2 an unexpected gain, *eg* a sum of money

winding *adjective* curving, twisting

wind instrument a musical instrument sounded by the breath

windlass *noun* a machine for lifting up or hauling a winch

windmill *noun* a mill driven by sails which are moved by the wind, used for pumping water, grinding grain *etc*

window *noun* an opening in a wall, protected by glass, which lets in light and air

windpipe *noun* the tube leading from the mouth to the lungs

windscreen or *US* **windshield** *noun* a pane of glass in front of the driver of a car *etc*

windsurfer *noun* a board with a sail for riding the waves

windsurfing *noun* the sport of riding the waves on a sailboard or windsurfer

windswept *adjective* exposed to strong winds and showing the effects of it: *windswept hair*

windward *adjective* & *adverb* in the direction from which the wind blows

windy *adjective* 1 of weather: with a strong wind blowing 2 of a place: exposed to strong winds

wine *noun* 1 an alcoholic drink made from the fermented juice of grapes or other fruit 2 a rich dark red colour

wing *noun* 1 one of the arm-like limbs of a bird, bat or insect by means of which it flies 2 one of the two projections on the sides of an aeroplane 3 a part of a house built out to the side 4 the side of a stage, where actors wait to enter 5 *football etc* a player positioned at the edge of the field 6 a section of a political party: *the left wing* □ *verb* 1 to wound (a bird) in the wing 2 to soar □ **on the wing** flying, in motion □ **under someone's wing** under the protection or care of someone

winged *adjective* 1 having wings 2 swift

wink *verb* 1 to open and close an eye quickly 2 to give a hint by winking 3 of lights *etc*: to flicker, twinkle □ *noun* 1 an act of winking 2 a hint given by winking □ **forty winks** a short sleep

winkle *noun* a small edible shellfish (*also called*: **periwinkle**) □ **winkle out** to force out gradually

winning *adjective* 1 victorious, successful 2 charming, attractive: *winning smile*

winnings *noun plural* money *etc* that has been won

winnow *verb* to separate the chaff from the grain by wind

winsome *adjective* charming

winter *noun* the cold season of the year □ *adjective* of or suitable for winter □ *verb* 1 to pass the winter 2 to keep, feed (sheep *etc*) during the winter

winter sports sports on snow or ice, *eg* skiing, tobogganing *etc*

wintry *adjective* 1 cold, frosty 2 cheerless, unfriendly: *a wintry look*

wipe *verb* 1 to clean or dry by rubbing 2 **wipe something away, out, off** or **up** to clear it away □ *noun* the act of cleaning by rubbing □ **wipe something out** to totally destroy it

■ **Alternative words: wipe out**
obliterate

wiper *noun* one of a pair of moving parts which wipe the windscreen of a car

wire *noun* 1 a thread-like length of metal 2 the metal thread used in communication by telephone *etc* 3 *informal* a telegram □ *adjective* made of wire □ *verb* 1 to bind or fasten with wire 2 *informal* to send a telegram 3 to supply (a building *etc*) with wires for carrying an electric current

wireless *adjective* of communication: by radio waves □ *noun, old* a radio set

wiry *adjective* 1 made of wire 2 of a person: thin but strong

wisdom *noun* the quality of being wise □ **wisdom teeth** four large back teeth which appear after childhood

wise *adjective* 1 very knowledgeable 2 judging rightly; sensible

wish *verb* 1 to feel or express a desire: *I wish he'd leave* 2 (often **wish for**) to long for, desire: *she wished for peace and quiet* 3 to hope for on behalf of (someone): *wish someone luck* □ *noun* (*plural* **wishes**) 1 desire, longing 2 a thing desired or wanted: *her great wish was to live abroad* 3 an expression of desire: *make a wish* 4 **wishes** expression of hope for another's happiness, good fortune *etc*: *good wishes* □ **wish someone well** to feel goodwill towards them

wishbone *noun* a forked bone in the breast of fowls

wishful *adjective* wishing, eager □ **wishful thinking** basing your belief on (false) hopes rather than known facts

wishywashy *adjective* 1 of liquid: thin and weak 2 feeble, not energetic or lively 3 lacking colour

wisp *noun* a small tuft or strand: *a wisp of hair*

wispy *adjective* wisp-like; light and fine in texture: *wispy white clouds*

wistful *adjective* thoughtful and rather sad: *a wistful glance* □ **wistfully** *adverb*

wit *noun* 1 (often **wits**) intelligence, common sense 2 the ability to express ideas neatly and funnily 3 someone who can do this □ **at your wits' end** unable to solve your difficulties, desperate □ **keep your wits about you** to keep alert □ **to wit** namely, that is to say

witch *noun* (*plural* **witches**) 1 a woman with magic power obtained through evil spirits 2 an ugly old woman

witchcraft *noun* magic performed by a witch

witch doctor someone believed to have magical powers to cure illnesses *etc*

with *preposition* 1 in the company of: *I was walking with my father* 2 by means of: *cut it with a knife* 3 in the same direction as: *drifting with the current* 4 against: *fighting with his brother* 5 on the same side as 6 having: *a man with a limp* 7 in the keeping of: *leave the keys with me*

withdraw *verb* 1 to go back or away 2 to take away, remove: *withdraw cash/ withdraw troops* 3 to take back (an insult *etc*)

> **withdraw** ⇨ withdraw*s*, withdraw*ing*, withdrew, withdrawn

withdrawal *noun* an act of withdrawing

withdrawn *adjective* 1 of a place: lonely, isolated 2 of a person: unwilling to communicate with others, unsociable

wither *verb* 1 to fade, dry up or decay 2 to make to feel very unimportant or embarrassed: *she withered him with a look*

withering *adjective* 1 drying up, dying 2 of a remark *etc*: scornful, sarcastic

withers *noun plural* the ridge between the shoulder bones of a horse

withhold *verb* to keep back, refuse to give

> **withhold** ⇨ withhold*s*, withhold*ing*, withheld

within *preposition* inside the limits of: *keep within the law* □ *adverb* on the inside

without *preposition* 1 in the absence of: *we went without you* 2 not having: *without a penny* 3 outside the limits of: *without the terms of the agreement*

□ *adverb, old* **1** on the outside **2** out-of-doors

withstand *verb* to oppose or resist successfully

witness *noun* (*plural* **witnesses**) **1** someone who sees or has direct knowledge of a thing **2** someone who gives evidence in a law court **3** proof, evidence □ *verb* **1** to see, be present at **2** to sign your name to confirm the authenticity of (someone else's signature) **3** to give or be evidence □ **bear witness** to give or be evidence of: *bear witness to his character*

witticism *noun* a witty remark

wittingly *adverb* knowingly

witty *adjective* clever and amusing

■ **Alternative words**: jocular

wizard *noun* a man believed to have the power of magic

wizardry *noun* magic

wizened *adjective* dried up, shrivelled: *a wizened old man*

woad *noun* **1** a blue dye **2** the plant from which it is obtained

wobble *verb* to rock unsteadily from side to side □ *noun* an unsteady rocking

wobbly *adjective* unsteady, rocking

woe *noun* **1** grief, misery **2** a cause of sorrow, a trouble

woebegone *adjective* dismal, sad-looking

woeful *adjective* sorrowful; pitiful □ **woefully** *adverb*

wok *noun* an Asian cooking-pan shaped like a large bowl

wolf *noun* (*plural* **wolves**) a wild animal like a dog that hunts in packs □ *verb* to eat greedily: *wolfing down his food* □ **cry wolf** to give a false alarm □ **keep the wolf from the door** to keep away hunger or want

woman *noun* (*plural* **women**) **1** an adult human female **2** human females in general **3** a domestic help
Ⓞ Comes from Old English *wif* meaning 'a woman', and *man* meaning 'man' or 'human being'

womanhood *noun* the state of being a woman

womankind or **womenkind** *noun* women generally

womanly *adjective* like, or suitable for, a woman

womb *noun* the part of a female mammal's body in which the young develop and stay till birth

wombat *noun* a small, beaver-like Australian animal, with a pouch

women *plural* of **woman**

won *past form* of **win**

wonder *noun* **1** the feeling produced by something unexpected or extraordinary; surprise, awe **2** something strange, amazing or miraculous □ *verb* **1** to be curious or in doubt: *I wonder what will happen/ I wonder whether to go or not* **2** to feel surprise or amazement (at, that)

wonderful *adjective* **1** arousing wonder; strange, marvellous **2** excellent

wonderment *noun, old* amazement

wondrous *adjective, old* wonderful

wont (*pronounced* wohnt) *adjective, old* accustomed (to do something) □ *noun* habit: *as is his wont*

won't *short for* will not

woo *verb* **1** to try to win the love of (someone) **2** to try to gain (*eg* success)

woo ⇨ woos, wooing, wooed

wood *noun* **1** a group of growing trees **2** the hard part of a tree, especially when cut for use

woodcut *noun* **1** a picture engraved on wood **2** a print made from this engraving

woodcutter *noun* someone who fells trees, cuts up wood *etc*

wooded *adjective* covered with trees

wooden *adjective* **1** made of wood **2** dull, stiff, not lively: *a wooden speech* □ **woodenly** *adverb*

woodland *noun* land covered with trees

woodlouse *noun* (*plural* **woodlice**) a small beetle-like creature with a jointed shell, found under stones *etc*

woodpecker *noun* a bird that pecks

holes in the bark of trees with its beak, in search of insects

wood spirit *same as* **methanol**

woodwind *noun* wind instruments, made of wood or metal, *eg* the flute or clarinet

woodwork *noun* 1 the making of wooden articles 2 the wooden parts of a house, room *etc*

woodworm *noun* the larva of a beetle that bores holes in wood and destroys it

woody *adjective* 1 like wood 2 wooded

wooer *noun* someone who woos

wool *noun* 1 the soft hair of sheep and other animals 2 yarn or cloth made of wool

woollen *adjective* made of wool □ *noun* a knitted garment made of wool

woolly *adjective* 1 made of, or like, wool 2 vague, hazy: *a woolly argument* □ *noun* (*plural* **woollies**) a knitted woollen garment

word *noun* 1 a written or spoken sign representing a thing or an idea 2 **words** talk, remarks: *kind words* 3 news: *word of his death* 4 a promise: *break your word* □ *verb* to choose words for: *he worded his refusal carefully* □ **have words** *informal* to quarrel □ **in a word** in short, to sum up □ **take someone at their word** to treat what they say as true □ **take someone's word for something** to trust that what they say is true □ **word for word** in the exact words

wording *noun* choice or arrangement of words

word processor an electronic machine or computer program which can store, edit and print out text

wordy *adjective* using too many words

wore *past form of* **wear**

work *noun* 1 a physical or mental effort to achieve or make something 2 a job, employment: *out of work* 3 a task: *I've got work to do* 4 anything made or done 5 something produced by art, *eg* a book, musical composition, painting *etc* 6 manner of working, workmanship: *poor work* 7 **works** a factory 8 **works** the mechanism (*eg* of a watch) 9 **works**

deeds: *good works* □ *verb* 1 to be engaged in physical or mental work 2 to be employed 3 to run or operate smoothly and efficiently 4 of a plan *etc*: to be successful 5 to get into a position slowly and gradually: *the screw worked loose* 6 to organize, manage, control □ **work out** 1 to solve 2 to discover as a result of deep thought 3 of a situation: to turn out all right in the end □ **work up** to arouse, excite: *working himself up into a fury*

🕘 Comes from Old English *weorc*

■ **Alternative words**: (verb, meaning 1) toil, drudge; (verb, meaning 3) function

workable *adjective* able to be done, practical

worker *noun* someone who works at a job

working *adjective* operating properly, not broken

■ **Alternative words**: functioning, operative

working class the social class including manual workers

working day or **working hours** the hours each day that someone spends at work, on duty *etc*

workman *noun* someone who works with their hands

workmanlike *adjective* done with skill

workmanship *noun* 1 the skill of a workman 2 manner of making something

workshop *noun* a room or building where manufacturing, craftwork *etc* is done

world *noun* 1 the earth and all things on it 2 the people of the world 3 any planet or star 4 the universe 5 a state of existence: *the next world* 6 a particular area of life or activity: *the insect world/ the world of fashion* 7 a great deal: *a world of good*

🕘 Comes from Old English *world/weorold* meaning 'age or life of man'

worldly *adjective* concerned with material things such as money, possessions *etc*, not the soul or spirit

worldwide *adjective* extending

throughout the world □ *adverb* throughout the world

worm *noun* 1 a small creeping animal without a backbone, often living in soil 2 *informal* a low, contemptible person 3 something spiral-shaped, *eg* the thread of a screw 4 **worms** the condition of having threadworms *etc* in the intestines 5 *computing* a kind of virus □ *verb* 1 to move gradually and stealthily (in or into) 2 **worm out** to draw out (information) bit by bit

wormwood *noun* a plant with a bitter taste

worn *adjective* 1 damaged by use 2 tired, worn-out

worn-out *adjective* tired, exhausted

worried *adjective* in an unhappy and unrelaxed state, as a result of thinking about something bad which is happening, or which you fear may happen

■ **Alternative words**: anxious, apprehensive, overwrought, distraught

worry *verb* 1 of a dog: to shake or tear (something) with its teeth 2 to annoy 3 to make troubled and anxious 4 to be troubled and anxious □ *noun* (*plural* **worries**) 1 uneasiness, anxiety 2 a cause of unease or anxiety

worry *verb* ⇨ worri*es*, worry*ing*, worri*ed*

■ **Alternative words**: (verb, meaning 3) agitate

worse *adjective* 1 bad or evil to a greater degree 2 more ill □ *adverb* badly to a greater degree, more severely: *it's snowing worse than ever* □ **worse off** in a worse position, less wealthy *etc*

worsen *verb* to make or become worse

worship *noun* 1 a religious ceremony or service 2 deep reverence, adoration 3 a title used in addressing a mayor, provost *etc* □ *verb* 1 to pay honour to (a god) 2 to adore or admire deeply

worship ⇨ worship*s*, worship*ping*, worship*ped*

worshipful *adjective* 1 full of reverence 2 worthy of honour

worst *adjective* bad or evil to the

greatest degree □ *adverb* badly to the greatest degree □ *verb* to beat, defeat □ **at worst** under the least favourable circumstances □ **if the worst comes to the worst** if the worst possible circumstances occur

worst *verb* ⇨ worst*s*, worst*ing*, worst*ed*

worsted[1] (*pronounced* **woors**-tid) *noun* 1 a type of fine woollen yarn 2 a strong cloth made of this

worsted[2] *past form of* **worst**

worth *noun* 1 value; price 2 importance 3 excellence of character *etc* □ *adjective* 1 equal in value to 2 deserving of: *worth considering* □ **worth your while** worth the trouble spent

worthless *adjective* of no merit or value

worthwhile *adjective* deserving time and effort

worthy *adjective* 1 (often **worthy of**) deserving, suitable 2 of good character □ *noun* (*plural* **worthies**) a highly respected person: *local worthy*

would *verb* 1 the form of the verb **will** used to express a condition: *he would go if he could* 2 used for emphasis: *I tell you I would do it if possible* 3 *old* expressing a wish: *I would that he were gone*
ⓘ Comes from Old English *wolde* which is the past tense of *wyllan* meaning 'to wish'

would-be *adjective* trying to be or pretending to be: *would-be actor/ would-be socialist*

wound *noun* 1 a cut or injury caused by a weapon, in an accident *etc* 2 a hurt to someone's feelings □ *verb* 1 to make a cut or injury in 2 to hurt the feelings of

wounded *adjective* having a wound, injured, hurt

WPC *abbreviation* Woman Police Constable

wrack (*pronounced* rak) *noun* seaweed thrown on to the shore

wraith (*pronounced* reith) *noun* an apparition of a living person, often as a warning of death

wrangle (*pronounced* **rang**-gl) *verb* to

quarrel noisily □ *noun* a noisy quarrel

wrap (*pronounced* rap) *verb* 1 to fold or roll round: *wrap it in tissue paper* 2 **wrap up** to cover by folding or winding something round □ *noun* a cloak or shawl

> **wrap** *verb* ⇨ wrap*s*, wrap*ping*, wrap*ped*

wrapper (*pronounced* rap-er) *noun* a loose paper cover, *eg* round a book or sweet

wrath (*pronounced* roth or rawth or rath) *noun* violent anger

wrathful (*pronounced* roth-fuwl or rawth-fuwl or rath-fuwl) *adjective* very angry

wreak (*pronounced* reek) *verb* 1 to carry out: *wreak vengeance* 2 to cause: *wreak havoc*

wreath (*pronounced* reeth) *noun* 1 a ring of flowers or leaves 2 a curling wisp of smoke, mist *etc*

wreathe (*pronounced* reedh) *verb* to encircle

wreck (*pronounced* rek) *noun* 1 destruction, especially of a ship by the sea 2 the remains of anything destroyed, especially a ship 3 someone whose health or nerves are in bad condition □ *verb* to destroy

wreckage (*pronounced* rek-ij) *noun* the remains of something wrecked

wren (*pronounced* ren) *noun* a very small type of bird

wrench (*pronounced* rench) *verb* 1 to pull with a violent, often twisting, motion 2 to sprain (your ankle *etc*) □ *noun* (*plural* **wrenches**) 1 a violent twist 2 a tool for gripping and turning nuts, bolts *etc* 3 sadness caused by parting from someone or something

wrest (*pronounced* rest) *verb*, *formal* to twist or take by force

wrestle (*pronounced* re-sl) *verb* 1 to fight with someone, trying to bring them to the ground 2 **wrestle with something** to think deeply about (a problem *etc*)

wrestler (*pronounced* res-ler) *noun* someone who wrestles as a sport

wrestling (*pronounced* res-ling) *noun* the sport in which two people fight to throw each other to the ground

wretch (*pronounced* rech) *noun* (*plural* **wretches**) 1 a miserable, pitiable person: *a poor wretch* 2 a worthless or contemptible person

wretched (*pronounced* rech-id) *adjective* 1 very miserable 2 worthless, very bad □ **wretchedly** *adverb*

> ■ **Alternative words**: (meaning 1) abject

wriggle (*pronounced* ri-gl) *verb* 1 to twist to and fro 2 to move by doing this, as a worm does 3 to escape (out of a difficulty *etc*)

wring (*pronounced* ring) *verb* 1 to twist or squeeze (especially water out of wet clothes) 2 to clasp and unclasp (your hands) in grief, anxiety *etc* 3 to cause pain to: *the story wrung everybody's heart* 4 to force out (*eg* a promise)

> **wring** ⇨ wring*s*, wring*ing*, wrung

wringer (*pronounced* ring-er) *noun* a machine for forcing water from wet clothes

wrinkle (*pronounced* ring-kl) *noun* a small crease or fold on the skin or other surface □ *verb* to make or become wrinkled

wrinkly (*pronounced* ring-kli) *adjective* having wrinkles

wrist (*pronounced* rist) *noun* the joint by which the hand is joined to the arm

writ (*pronounced* rit) *noun* a formal document giving an order (especially to appear in a law court)

write (*pronounced* rait) *verb* 1 to form letters with a pen, pencil *etc* 2 to put into writing: *write your name* 3 to compose (a letter, a book *etc*) 4 to send a letter (to) 5 *computing* to copy (a data file) □ **write down** to record in writing □ **write off** to regard as lost for ever □ **write up** to make a written record of

> **write** ⇨ write*s*, writ*ing*, wrote, writt*en*

> ■ **Alternative words**: (verb, meanings 1 and 2) inscribe, transcribe (verb, meaning 4) correspond

writer (*pronounced* rai-ter) *noun* someone who writes, an author

writhe (*pronounced* raidh) *verb* to twist or roll about, *eg* in pain

writing (*pronounced* **rai**-ting) *noun* a written text or texts

wrong (*pronounced* rong) *adjective* **1** not correct **2** not right or just **3** evil **4** not what is intended: *take the wrong turning* **5** unsuitable: *the wrong weather for camping quite the wrong dress for the occasion* **6** mistaken: *you are wrong if you think that* □ *noun* **1** whatever is not right or just **2** an injury done to another □ *verb* to do wrong to, harm □ **wrongly** *adverb* □ **go wrong 1** to fail to work properly **2** to make a mistake or mistakes □ **in the wrong** guilty of injustice or error

---

■ **Alternative words**: (adjective, meaning 1) fallacious; (adjective, meaning 2) reprehensible; (adjective, meanings 2 and 3) iniquitous; (adjective, meaning 5) unseemly, indecorous, incongruous, inapt; (adjective, meaning 6) erroneous

---

wrongdoer (*pronounced* **rong**-doo-*e*r) *noun* someone who does wrong

wrongdoing (*pronounced* **rong**-dooing) *noun* immoral or illegal behaviour or actions

wrongful (*pronounced* **rong**-fuwl) *adjective* not lawful or just

wrote *past form* of **write**

wrought (*pronounced* rawt) *adjective, old* made, manufactured □ *verb, old, past form* of **work**

wrought iron (*pronounced* rawt **ai**-*o*n) iron hammered, rather than cast, into shape

wrung *past form* of **wring**

wry (*pronounced* rai) *adjective* **1** slightly mocking or bitter: *wry remark* **2** twisted or turned to one side □ **wryly** *adverb*

WTO *abbreviation* Warsaw Treaty Organization

WYSIWYG *abbreviation, computing* what you see (on the screen) is what you get (in the printout)

xenophobia (*pronounced* zen-*o*-**foh**-bi-*a*) *noun* hatred of foreigners or strangers

Xerox (*pronounced* **zeer**-roks) *noun, trademark* **1** a photographic process used for copying documents **2** a copy made in this way □ *verb* to copy by Xerox

Xmas *noun, informal* Christmas

X-ray *noun* a shadow picture produced by X-rays on photographic film □ *verb* to take a photographic image of with X-rays

X-rays *noun plural* rays that can pass through material impenetrable by light, and produce a photographic image of the object through which they have passed

XTC *noun, slang* the drug Ecstasy

xylophone *noun* a musical instrument consisting of a series of graded wooden bars which are struck with hammers

Yy

If you can't find the word you're looking for under letter **Y**, it could be that its starts with a different letter. Try looking under **EU** for words like *euphemism*, **EW** for words like *ewe*, and **U** for words like *use* and *usual*.

yacht *noun* a sailing or motor-driven boat for racing, cruising *etc*

yachtsman *noun* a man who sails a yacht

yachtswoman *noun* a woman who sails a yacht

yak *noun* a Tibetan long-haired ox

yam *noun* a tropical root vegetable, similar to a potato

Yank or **Yankee** *noun, Brit informal* an American

Originally a nickname for Dutch settlers in New England in the 18th century, possibly because of the Dutch forename *Jan*

yank *verb, informal* to tug or pull with a violent jerk □ *noun* a violent tug

yap *verb* to bark sharply

yap ⇨ yap**s**, yap**ping**, yap**ped**

yard *noun* **1** a measure of length (0.9144 of a metre, or 3 feet) **2** a long beam on a mast for spreading sails **3** an enclosed space used for a particular purpose: *railway yard/ shipbuilding yard* **4** *US* a garden

yard-arm *noun* half of a yard on a mast

yardstick *noun* **1** a standard for measurement **2** a yard-long measuring stick

yarn *noun* **1** wool, cotton *etc* spun into thread **2** one of several threads forming a rope **3** a long, often improbable, story

yarrow *noun* a strong-smelling plant with flat clusters of white flowers

yashmak *noun* a veil covering the lower half of the face, worn by Islamic women

yawl *noun* a small rowing boat or fishing boat

yawn *verb* **1** to take a deep breath unintentionally with an open mouth, because of boredom or sleepiness **2** of a hole: to be wide open, gape □ *noun* an open-mouthed deep breath

ye *pronoun, old* you

yea (*pronounced* yei) *interjection, old* yes

year *noun* **1** the time taken by the earth to go once round the sun, about 365 days **2** the period 1 January to 31 December **3** a period of twelve months starting at any point **4 years** age: *wise for her years*
Ⓞ Comes from Old English *gear*

yearling *noun* a year-old animal

yearly *adjective* happening every year, or once a year

yearn *verb* **1** to long (for, to do something *etc*) **2** to feel pity or tenderness (for)

yearning *noun* an eager longing

yeast *noun* a substance which causes fermentation, used to make bread dough rise and in brewing

yell *verb* to give a loud, shrill cry; scream □ *noun* a loud, shrill cry

yellow *noun* the colour of gold, egg-yolks *etc* □ *adjective* of this colour □ *verb* to become yellow, due to ageing

yelp *verb* to give a sharp bark or cry □ *noun* a sharp bark or cry

yen¹ *noun* the standard unit of Japanese currency

yen² *noun, informal* a strong desire, longing: *a yen to return to Scotland*

617

yeoman (*pronounced* **yoh**-man) *noun,
historical* a farmer with his own land
□ **Yeomen of the Guard** the company
acting as bodyguard to the British king
or queen on certain occasions

yeomanry (*pronounced* **yoh**-man-ri)
noun, historical **1** farmers **2** a troop of
cavalrymen serving voluntarily in the
British army

yes *interjection* expressing agreement
or consent □ *noun* **1** an expression of
agreement or consent **2** a vote in favour

yesterday *noun* **1** the day before today
2 the past □ *adverb*: *I bought it yesterday*

yet *adverb* **1** by now, by this time: *have
you seen that film yet?* **2** still, before the
matter is finished: *we may win yet*
□ *conjunction* but, nevertheless: *I am
defeated, yet I shall not surrender* □ **yet
another** and another one still □ **yet
more** still more

Yeti *noun, another name for the*
Abominable Snowman

yew *noun* **1** a tree with dark green
leaves and red berries **2** its wood

YHA *abbreviation* Youth Hostels
Association

yield *verb* **1** to give in, surrender **2** to
give way to pressure or persuasion **3** to
produce (a crop, results *etc*) □ *noun* an
amount produced; a crop

yielding *adjective* giving way easily

YMCA *abbreviation* Young Men's
Christian Association

yob or **yobbo** (*plural* **yobboes** or
yobbos) *noun* a lout, a hooligan

yodel *verb* to sing in a style involving
frequent changes between an ordinary
and a very high-pitched voice

   yodel ⇨ yodel*s*, yodel*ling*, yodel*led*

yoga *noun* a Hindu system of
philosophy and meditation, often
involving special physical exercises

yoghurt or **yogurt** *noun* a semi-liquid
food product made from fermented
milk

yoke *noun* **1** a wooden frame joining
oxen when pulling a plough or cart **2**
a pair of oxen or horses **3** something
that joins together **4** a frame placed
across the shoulders for carrying pails

etc **5** slavery, domination **6** a part of a
garment fitting over the neck and
shoulders **7** a part of a skirt fitting
closely over the hips □ *verb* **1** to put a
yoke on **2** to join together

yokel *noun, derogatory* an
unsophisticated country person; a
rustic

yolk *noun* the yellow part of an egg

Yom Kippur the Day of Atonement, a
Jewish fast day

yonder *adverb, old* in that place (at a
distance but within sight) □ *adjective*
that (object) over there: *by yonder tree*

yore *noun*: **of yore** *old* formerly, in times
past

you *pronoun* the person(s) spoken or
written to, used as the *singular* or *plural*
subject or object of a verb: *what did you
say?/ are you both free tomorrow?*

you'd *abbreviation* **1** you would; you
should **2** you had

you'll *abbreviation* you will; you shall

young *adjective* **1** in early life **2** in the
early part of mental or physical growth
□ *noun* **1** the offspring of animals **2** (**the
young**) young people
① Comes from Old English *geong*

━━ **Alternative words**: (adjective)
    juvenile, immature

youngster *noun* a young person

your *adjective* belonging to you: *it's
your life*

you're *short for* you are

yours *pronoun* belonging to you: *is this
pen yours?* □ **Yours**, **Yours faithfully**,
Yours sincerely or **Yours truly**
expressions used before a signature at
the end of a letter

yourself *pronoun* (*plural* **yourselves**) **1**
used reflexively: *don't trouble yourself*
2 used for emphasis: *you yourself can't
go*

youth *noun* **1** the state of being young
2 the early part of life **3** a young person
4 young people in general

youthful *adjective* **1** young **2** fresh and
vigorous

youth hostel a hostel where hikers *etc*
may spend the night

you've *abbreviation* you have

yo-yo *noun, trademark* a toy consisting of a reel which spins up and down on a string

Yule *noun, old* Christmas

Yuletide Christmas time

yuppie or **yuppy** *noun* (*plural* **yuppies**) a young well-paid urban professional

YWCA *abbreviation* Young Women's Christian Association

Zz

If you can't find the word you're looking for under letter **Z**, it could be that it starts with a different letter. Try looking under **X** for words like *xylophone* and *Xerox*.

zany *adjective, informal* crazy, madcap
> After the name of a clownish character in the Italian *commedia dell'arte*

zap *verb* **1** to strike, shoot *etc* suddenly **2** to move rapidly; zip
> **zap** ⇨ zaps, zapping, zapped

zeal *noun* **1** enthusiasm **2** keenness, determination

zealot (*pronounced* zel-ot) *noun* a fanatical enthusiast

zealous (*pronounced* zel-us) *adjective* full of zeal □ **zealously** *adverb*

zebra *noun* a striped African animal of the horse family

zebra crossing a pedestrian street crossing, painted in black and white stripes

zeitgeist (*pronounced* zait-gaist) *noun* the present cultural climate

zenith *noun* **1** the point of the heavens exactly overhead **2** the highest point, the peak

zephyr (*pronounced* zef-er) *noun, formal* a soft, gentle breeze

zero *noun* **1** nothing or the sign for it (0) **2** the point (marked 0) from which a scale (*eg* on a thermometer) begins

zero hour the exact time fixed for some action

zero option a proposal to limit or abandon the deployment of nuclear missiles if the opposing side does likewise

zero-rated *adjective* of goods: having no value-added tax

zest *noun* **1** relish, keen enjoyment **2** orange or lemon peel

zestful *adjective* keen; full of enjoyment □ **zestfully** *adverb*

zigzag *adjective* having sharp bends or angles □ *verb* move in a zigzag direction
> **zigzag** *verb* ⇨ zigzags, zigzagging, zigzagged

zimmer *noun, trademark* a hand-held metal frame used to give support in walking

zinc *noun* a bluish-white metal

zip *noun* **1** a fastening device for clothes, bags *etc*, consisting of two rows of metal or nylon teeth which interlock when a sliding tab is pulled between them **2** a whizzing sound, *eg* made by a fast-flying object **3** *informal* energy, vigour □ *verb* **1** to fasten with a zip **2** to whiz, fly past at speed
> **zip** *verb* ⇨ zips, zipping, zipped

zither *noun* a flat, stringed musical instrument, played with the fingers

zodiac *noun* an imaginary strip in space, divided into twelve equal parts □ **signs of the zodiac** the divisions of the zodiac used in astrology, each named after a group of stars

zombie *noun* **1** a corpse reanimated by witchcraft **2** a very slow or stupid person
> After the name of a voodoo snake god

zone *noun* **1** any of the five main bands into which the earth's surface is divided according to temperature: *temperate zone* **2** a section of a country, town *etc* marked off for a particular purpose: *no-*

620

parking zone/ smokeless zone □ *verb* to divide into zones

zoo *noun* a place where wild animals are kept and shown to the public

zoo- *prefix* of or relating to animals ① Comes from Greek *zoion* meaning 'animal'

zoological *adjective* 1 relating to animals 2 relating to zoos; containing a zoo: *zoological gardens*

zoologist *noun* someone who studies animal life

zoology *noun* the science of animal life

zoom *verb* 1 to move with a loud, low buzzing noise 2 to make such a noise 3 of an aircraft: to climb sharply at high speed for a short time 4 of prices: to increase sharply 5 to use a zoom lens on a camera

zoom lens *photography* a lens which makes a distant object appear gradually nearer without the camera being moved

zoon politikon a political person (literally 'animal')

Supplements

Variety and change in the language

More than 300 million people in the world speak English as their first language and many more learn it as a second language so that they can communicate with people of different nationalities. English, like all other living languages, is changing all the time. If it were possible to travel back in time over (say) 400 years, to the time when William Shakespeare was alive, we would probably find that we would have difficulty in understanding what was being said because of differences in pronunciation and vocabulary. The further back we went, the more difficult it would become. Anglo-Saxon (Old English) would be virtually unintelligible.

The earliest known inhabitants of Britain spoke a form of **Celtic**, related to modern Welsh and Gaelic. Very few Celtic words remain in use but its influence can still be seen in many place-names.

The **Angles**, **Saxons** and **Jutes** came to Britain from about AD 450 bringing with them the Germanic languages which formed the basis of **Old English**, which is one source of the English we speak today.

In the 9th and 10th centuries, the **Vikings** came to Britain from the Scandinavian countries. Their language is known as **Old Norse** and many of the words we use today come from this source.

In 1066, William the Conqueror defeated the English King Harold at the Battle of Hastings. William and his subjects came from Normandy and spoke a form of **French**, and so it was natural that the new nobility in England should be French-speaking. Most of the ordinary people still spoke English, and inevitably the two began to merge into what we now call **Middle English**.

Throughout these centuries, **Latin** had a strong and constant influence on English, largely because the Church used Latin for its rituals and services and as a form of communication. The 14th–16th centuries (**the Renaissance**) brought a renewal of interest in the culture of the ancient Greeks and Romans, and many more words from **Latin** and **Greek** were introduced into the English language.

We can date what we now call **Modern English** from about 1500 onwards. Through trade and travel, people came into contact with words from other languages which were subsequently adopted into English. The colonies of the former British Empire enriched English with words from their own languages. India, for example, has given us many words, including **bungalow**, **jodhpurs** and **khaki**.

    🖉 How many foreign words can you think of that are used in English? It may help you to think of particular areas like food, music or politics.

The English language will go on changing and developing, and if we were able to travel forward in time we could expect to have exactly the same problems of comprehension as if we went back in time. Our next section looks in more detail at the ways in which words change.

How language changes

Words change in two main ways: ● in their form
● in their meaning.

Change in form

The forms of words change over time. Often, the way people pronounce words changes, and this in turn affects the way the word is written. Old English *dæges èage* has gradually changed to become our word *daisy*. The word which began as Latin *frater* (brother) became *frere* in Old French and took on the form *friar* in English after the Norman Invasion.

In American English, words tend to be written in a way that corresponds more closely with their pronunciation. This is obvious from a comparison of a few words with different spellings in British and American English:

| **British** | cheque | draught | grey | jewellery | pyjamas | sceptic |
| **American** | check | draft | gray | jewelry | pajamas | skeptic |

🖉 How many more can you add to this list?

American English has also preserved some older English spellings which have changed in British English.

Change in meaning

Words often change in meaning over the years and there are many reasons for this process. Often, an old word is used in a new way to express a new idea or phenomenon. Think about the word **screen**. As far back as the 15th century this was used to mean a contraption to ward off heat, light etc, or a partition in a building. Of course, it can still mean these things, but the meaning that comes immediately to mind now is the part of a television set on which images are formed or the part of a computer on which information is displayed.

An example of a word which has quite recently changed in meaning is **gay**. This word used to mean 'happy' or 'carefree', with no other connotations. It took on another meaning when it started to be used to describe homosexuals who wanted to be seen as joyful about their sexuality. Nowadays, it seems old-fashioned to use the word 'gay' in its old sense — the change in meaning is almost complete.

🖉 Try keeping your own record of how the English language has changed through the years by making a list of words you come across in your reading which now mean something different. You should note the old meaning, the date the writer used it this way, and the new meaning.

🖉 Trace the change in meaning of the following words: **nice**, **clever**, **camera**, **cabaret**. You'll need a larger dictionary like *The Chambers Dictionary* to do this.

Dialects and regional variations

The principal variety of English, used widely and in teaching, is called Standard English. This is the variety that forms the basis of the language treated in this dictionary.

A dialect is a way of speaking found in a certain area or among a certain group of people. Many different dialects exist.

The *Chambers School Dictionary* includes a number of Scottish words and expressions. Look up some of the following and write down what they mean:

bairn	haver	peelie-wally
birl	howk	quaich
blether	humdudgeon	runrig
brose	jo	Sassenach
burn	keek	scunner
clachan	ken	shoogle
dreich	kirk	stookie
dry-stane	lang syne	stramash
dunt	neb	stymie
fankle	neep	tattie
feu	ne'er-do-well	thirl
flit	nicky-tams	wean
harl	outwith	wee

The dictionary also includes some words from English used outside Great Britain, eg the Irish word **colleen**, the South African word **veldt**, and the Australian word **joey**, as well as many American words and expressions.

✏ Now think about dialect words from your own region. How many can you write down? It might be useful to think of words used by older generations, eg grandparents.

✏ When you're watching TV, listening to the radio, or reading, think about the sort of English being used and the region it reflects. The language of soap operas is particularly rich in dialect words. Write down some examples from a British and a non-British soap.

Word histories in this dictionary

Some of the entries in this dictionary include a short note explaining where the word originally came from. These word histories come at the end of the entry.

We have concentrated on two main categories: (i) **Useful Word Histories** to help with understanding words and with spelling them, and (ii) **Interesting Word Histories** to give examples of how words are created, and some of the various ways in which words can change.

Useful Word Histories

Nearly every prefix and suffix (eg **un-**, **-able**, **hypo-**) included in this dictionary is accompanied by a word history. This can be a big help in understanding how words are built up from meaningful elements, and in spotting connections between words. When you understand what a word-building element means, it can help with your spelling too, eg you're less likely to confuse the prefixes **hypo-** and **hyper-** if you know that the first is Greek for 'under' and the second is Greek for 'over'.

Listed below are suffixes with their meanings. Prefixes are listed too, and you can find their meanings by looking them up at their alphabetical place in the dictionary:

Suffixes

-aholic or **-oholic** having an addiction to: *workaholic/ chocaholic* This suffix has been created by taking the end of 'alc**oholic**' and adding it on to various words or parts of words.

-algia forms nouns relating to pain: *neuralgia/ nostalgia*
① Comes from Greek *algos* meaning 'pain'

-arch chief, ruler: *monarch/ matriarch*
① Comes from Greek *arche* meaning 'rule'

-archy forms nouns describing different types of government: *monarchy/ oligarchy*
① Comes from Greek *arche* meaning 'rule'

-athon or **-thon** forms nouns describing events, usually for charity, which are long in terms of time or endurance: *telethon* (= a very long television programme)/ *talkathon* (= a long talking-session) This suffix has been created by taking the end off 'mar**athon**' and adding it on to various words or parts of words

-cide forms words describing murder or killing, or a person or thing which murders or kills: *suicide/ homicide/ insecticide*
① Comes from Latin *caedere* meaning 'to kill'

-cracy forms nouns describing different types of government, or the members of a ruling group: *democracy/ aristocracy*
① Comes from Greek *kratos* meaning 'power'

-cyte (*pronounced* sait) *medicine* forms nouns describing different types of cell in the body: *leucocyte/ phagocyte*
① Comes from Latin *kytos* meaning 'container' or 'hollow vessel'

-dox forms words related to opinions or beliefs: *orthodox/ heterodox*
① Comes from Greek *doxa* meaning 'opinion'

-ectomy *see* **-tomy**

-ferous forms adjectives related to the idea of carrying or containing: *coniferous* (= producing cones)
① Comes from Latin *ferre* meaning 'to carry'

-free not containing or involving: *additive-free/ cruelty-free*

-friendly
1 not harmful towards: *dolphin-friendly*
2 compatible with or easy to use for: *child-friendly*

-gon *mathematics* forms words related to the number of angles which certain figures have: *polygon/ hexagon*

-gram or **-gramme** forms words describing things which are written, printed or drawn: *telegram/ mammogram* (= X-ray photograph of a person's breast)/ *anagram* (= a word or sentence formed by writing the letters of another word or phrase in a different order)/ *epigram* (= a short, witty poem or saying)
Ⓛ Comes from Greek *gramma* meaning 'a letter'

-graph, -graphy
1 of or relating to writing: *biography/ autograph*
2 form words describing printed images or pictures: *photograph(y)*
Ⓛ Comes from Greek *graphein* meaning 'to write'

-ism
1 indicating a system, set of beliefs etc: *socialism/ Catholicism*
2 indicating prejudice against a particular group: *racism/ sexism*
Ⓛ Comes from Greek suffix *-ismos*, used to form nouns of action from verbs

-itis *medicine* used to describe diseases which involve inflammation: *tonsillitis* (= inflammation of the tonsils)/ *bronchitis* (= inflammation of the windpipe)
Ⓛ Comes from Greek word-ending *-itis* meaning 'belonging to'

-logy
1 forms words describing the scientific or serious study of something: *biology/ psychology*
2 forms terms related to words or discourse: *tautology* (= a form of repetition using two words or phrases that say the same thing/ *eulogy*

Ⓛ Comes from Greek *logos* meaning 'word' or 'reason'
Note that 'astrology' has taken on a special sense and has been replaced by 'astronomy' as the term for the scientific study of the stars and planets

-lysis forms words containing the idea of a splitting-up or breaking-down into smaller or simpler parts: *analysis*
Ⓛ Comes from Greek *lysis* meaning 'a loosening'

-meter forms words for measuring devices: *speedometer/ barometer*
Ⓛ Comes from Greek *metron* meaning 'measure'

-nomy forms words relating to different systems of regulation, or to the science and study of how these work: *astronomy/ autonomy* (= the power or right of a country or person to regulate themselves)
Ⓛ Comes from Greek *nomos* meaning 'law'

-nym *see* **-onym**

-oholic *see* **-aholic**

-oid forms technical terms containing the meaning 'like': *anthropoid/ android* (= a humanlike robot)/ *tabloid* (= originally a trademark for a medicine in tablet form)
Ⓛ Comes from Greek *eidos* meaning 'form'

-ology *see* **-logy**

-onym (*pronounced* on-im) forms terms containing the idea of 'word' or 'name': *synonym/ pseudonym*
Ⓛ Comes from Greek *onyma* meaning 'a name'

-osis
1 *medicine* forms terms for diseased conditions: *neurosis/ thrombosis*
2 forms words describing different processes: *metamorphosis* (= the process of changing appearance or character)/ *osmosis* (= a gradual process of absorption or assimilation)
Ⓛ Comes from Greek word-ending *-osis*, used to form nouns from verbs

-otomy *see* **-tomy**

-path
1 forms words describing people who are suffering from particular disorders

2 forms words describing people who provide therapy for particular disorders: *osteopath* (= someone who provides therapy for bone and muscle injuries)

🕔 Comes from Greek *patheia* meaning 'suffering'

-pathy
forms words describing disorders and therapies: *osteopathy*

🕔 Comes from Greek *patheia* meaning 'suffering'

-phobe
forms words describing people who suffer from particular phobias

🕔 Comes from Greek *phobos* meaning 'fear'

-scope
forms words describing devices which makes things visible, or which allow examination of something which cannot be seen: *telescope/ stethoscope*

🕔 Comes from Greek *skopeein* meaning 'to view'

-tomy
forms words relating to the surgical operation of cutting into an organ of the body: *vasectomy/ lobotomy*

🕔 Comes from Greek *tome* meaning 'a cutting'

-vore also -vorous
forms technical terms concerned with the eating habits of an animal or person: *carnivore/ herbivore* (= grass-eating)

🕔 Comes from Latin *vorare* meaning 'to devour'

-ware
manufactured material: *earthenware/ glassware*

-ways
in the direction of: *lengthways/ sideways*

-wise
1 in the manner or way of: *crabwise*

2 with reference or regard to: *careerwise*

-witted
having wits (of a certain kind): *slow-witted/ quick-witted*

-wright (*pronounced* rait)
a maker: *shipwright/ playwright*

🕔 Comes from Old English *wyrht* meaning 'a work'

Prefixes

aero-	bio-	fore-
after-	caco-	Franco-
agri-	carni- *or* carn-	frater- *or* fratri-
agro-	cata- *or* cath-	geo-
allo-	centi- *or* cent-	haemo-
ambi-	chrono- *or* chron-	hecto- *or* hect-
amphi-	circum- *or* circu-	helio-
an- *or* a-	co-	hemi-
ana- *or* an-	counter-	hepta-
andro- *or* andr-	crypto- *or* crypt-	hetero-
anemo-	cyber-	hexa-
ante-	deca- *or* dec-	homeo- *or*
antho-	deci-	homoeo-
anthropo- *or*	dermato-	homi-
anthrop-	di-	homo-
anti-	dis-	hydro- *or* hydr-
apo- *or* ap-	dys-	hyper-
aqua-	eco-	hypo-
arch-	electro-	in-
archaeo-	epi- *or* ep-	infra-
astro- *or* astr-	equi-	inter-
audio-	equi-	intra-
auto- *or* aut-	Euro-	iso-
be-	ex-	kilo-
bi-	extra-	macro-
biblio-	for-	mater- *or* matri-

maxi-	philo-	sex-
mega-	phon-	simil- *or* simul-
micro-	photo-	Sino-
mid-	physio-	socio-
milli- *or* mill-	poly-	soph-
mini-	post-	step-
mis-	pre-	stereo-
mono- *or* mon-	pro-	stup-
mort-	pseud-	sub-
multi-	*or* pseudo-	super-
nano-	psycho-	supra-
nat-	*or* psych-	syn-
naut-	pyro-	techno- *or* techn-
neg-	quadri-	tele-
neo-	*or* quadru-	theo-
neur- *or* neuro-	quasi-	thermo- *or* therm-
non-	quint-	trans-
octa-	re-	tri-
omni-	recti- *or* rect-	turbo-
ortho- *or* orth-	reg-	ultra-
over-	retro-	un-
paedo-	rhino- *or* rhin-	under-
pan-	sangui-	uni-
pater- *or* patri-	schizo-	veri- *or* ver-
patho-	sci-	vice-
penta-	semi-	zoo-.
peri-	sept-	

Other word histories are included to help you distinguish between words which might be easily confused, eg **venal** and **venial**.

Interesting Word Histories

Not all words have origins that tell a story but some do. These tell you in interesting ways how words can come into being or change over the centuries.

Here is a list of the entries in this dictionary which are accompanied by a note explaining their origin:

aftermath	Bolshevik	caprice
akimbo	bolshy	cardigan
amok/amuck	bona fide	carte blanche
ampersand	bowdlerize	castanets
antediluvian	boycott	caterpillar
archipelago	braille	chauvinist
assassin	brothel	chintz
atlas	budget	chopsticks
attic	buff	chord
badminton	bully	cipher
bain-marie	bumph/bumf	clan
barbecue	bunkum	cliché
bedlam	bureau	clove
bikini	calico	cockney
bloomers	camera	coconut
bobby	candidate	cordon bleu
boffin	canter	cravat

criss-cross	helicopter	myrmidon
cyber-	Herculean	namby-pamby
dahlia	heyday	nicotine
daisy	hippopotamus	nightmare
damask	hobby	ombudsman
dandelion	Hobson's choice	orang-utan
deadline	Hogmanay	oscillate
decimate	hoi polloi	ostracism
deed poll	hubbub	palindrome
delphinium	hysteria	pandemonium
delta	insulin	pander
denim	intoxicate	Pandora's box
dénouement	JCB	paraphernalia
derrick	jejune	pariah
derring-do	jeopardy	parole
desecrate	jinx	pasteurize
deus ex machina	jubilee	peal
diaper	juggernaut	pedigree
dinosaur	ketchup	pelican crossing
diploma	khaki	Pelmanism
dismal	klondyker	personnel
doily/doyley	knickerbockers	philistine
doldrums	kowtow to	pidgin
duck	laser	pinchbeck
duffel coat	legionnaire's	platonic
dunce	disease	plus fours
eco-	lilliputian	psephologist
eerie	limerick	Pullman
exchequer	limousine	Pyrrhic victory
extrapolate	Luddite	Quaker
fascism	lynch	quark
fiasco	macadamize	quintessence
flounder	magazine	quisling
foolscap	magpie	quixotic
galore	mah-jong	quorum
galvanic	malapropism	raglan
gamut	malaria	regatta
garble	manna	rigmarole
gargantuan	marathon	Rubicon
gauche	martinet	rubric
gauntlet[2]	masochism	Rugby/rugby
gerrymander	maudlin	sabotage
giraffe	maverick	sadism
glitz	maxi-	salary
gorilla	meander	sandwich
gossip	mentor	saxophone
grenade	mesmerize	scapegoat
groggy	mews	shibboleth
gruesome	midwife	shrapnel
guillotine	mini-	shrift
gung-ho	mithridate	silhouette
gypsy/gipsy	money	snob
haggard	morganatic	sobriquet
halcyon	morris dance	stationer
handicap	mountebank	stentorian
hector	Munro	stereotype

sterling	Tory	utopia
stymie	trilby	ventriloquist
sybaritic	tulip	veto
tabloid	turquoise	volcano
tangerine	tycoon	whisky/whiskey
tattoo	umbrella	willynilly
taunt	umpteen	Yank/Yankee
tawdry	un-	zany
thespian	unexceptionable	zombie
thyroid gland	unexceptional	
titivate	urchin	

Common Words

From our language databases, we have been able to select the 99 most frequently used nouns, verbs and adjectives (excluding *a*, *an*, *the* etc) in the English language. Each of these words is accompanied in the text by a word history:

back	hold	point
be	home	possible
best	house	put
bring	important	run
can	keep	same
case	know	say
cent	large	second
children	life	see
come	like	set
company	little	side
could	live	system
country	local	take
course	long	thing
day	look	think
do	make	thought
end	man	three
fact	men	time
family	might	turn
find	money	two
five	must	use
four	need	want
get	new	water
give	next	way
go	night	week
good	number	will
government	old	women
great	one	work
group	part	world
have	people	would
help	place	year
high	play	young

 Look up some of the words in this list. What is the source language of most of the very common words in English?

Spelling

The *Chambers School Dictionary* aims to give you help with spelling where confusion may arise, eg look at words like **practice** and **practise**. It also gives you extra guidance on finding a word you're not entirely sure how to spell, eg look at the beginning of letter **F**. Below we have listed around 200 words that are frequently misspelt. Use your dictionary to make sure you know what they mean as well as how to spell them:

abbreviation	connoisseur	gorilla (*animal*)
aberration	conscience	government
abscess	conscientious	guarantee
accelerator	conscious	guard
accommodation	correspondence	guerrilla (also
accumulate	corroborate	guerilla) (*fighter*)
accurate	courageous	guilty
achievement	courteous	haemorrhage
acknowledge	cupfuls	hangar
acquiesce	definitely	harass
aerial	deliberate	height
aeroplane	desiccate	humorous
aghast	desperate	hypocrisy
almond	detach	idiosyncrasy
annihilate	diaphragm	illegal
apparent	diarrhoea	illiterate
architecture	diphtheria	independent
Arctic	diphthong	inoculate
argument	disappoint	install
asphyxiate	discipline	instalment
assassinate	dissipate	interrogate
asthma	doubt	intrigue
attach	embarrass	jeopardy
autumn	encyclopedia (also	jeweller
bachelor	encyclopaedia)	jodhpurs
beautiful	exaggerate	journey
beauty	exceed	knowledgeable
berserk	excellent	lacquer
besiege	excerpt	languor
biscuit	exercise	languorous
breadth	exhaust	leisure
budgeted	exhibition	leopard
buses	exhilarate	liaise
business	extravagant	lieutenant
calendar	faeces	lightning
campaign	fascinate	liquefy
career	February	livelihood
caress	fluorescent	manageable
Caribbean	fulfil	manoeuvre
catarrh	gases	marriage
ceiling	gauge	martyr
cemetery	ghastly	massacre
changeable	gherkin	mayonnaise
character	ghetto	Mediterranean
chasm	ghost	messenger
commemorate	giraffe	millennium
committee	gorgeous	millionaire

miniature
miscellaneous
mortgage
neighbour
ninth
noticeable
nuisance
obscene
occasional
occurred
occurring
occurrence
outrageous
paradigm
paraffin
parallel
paralleled
paralleling
paralyse
parliament
passenger
personnel
phlegm
phlegmatic
playwright
pneumonia
privilege
professor
pronunciation
propeller
psychiatrist

publicly
pyjamas
questionnaire
quizzes
quizzed
quizzing
receipt
recommend
reconnaissance
refrigerator
reminiscent
repellent
reservoir
responsible
restaurant
rhyme
rhythm
righteous
rigorous
sapphire
satellite
scythe
secretary
seize
separate
sergeant
siege
sieve
silhouette
simultaneous
skilful

solemn
sovereign
spaghetti
species
spontaneous
stomach
subtle
succeed
success
suggest
supersede
susceptible
tariff
temperature
thorough
tranquillity
transparent
truly
turquoise
unwieldy
vacuum
valuable
vanilla
vegetable
vehicle
vigorous
visitor
Wednesday
weight
weird
wholly

✐ Everyone has their own personal spelling pitfalls. Making a list of your own as you come across them may help you avoid them in future.

Parts of Speech

noun

● a word that names things: a ***common noun*** names generally, eg *car, baby, happiness*; a ***proper noun*** names particular people, places and things, eg *Megan, Australia, Concorde*. Proper nouns are usually spelt with a capital letter.

verb

● a word that tells you what someone or something does or is: a ***transitive verb*** describes an action that affects someone or something else (the object), eg *we <u>picked</u> flowers*; *they <u>saw</u> us*; an ***intransitive verb*** has no object and often describes a state, eg *They <u>live</u> in Manchester*; *when shall we <u>go</u>?*

adjective

● a word that describes or classifies, eg *green, square, big, British*.

adverb

● a word that describes the way in which something happens or is done, eg *quickly, soon, very*.

pronoun

● a word that stands for a noun, eg *I, me, we, us, you, they*.

preposition

● a word that describes how one person or thing relates to another, eg *the book <u>on</u> the table*; *let's go <u>to</u> the zoo*.

conjunction

● a word that introduces a new part of a sentence, eg *and, because, but, although, while*.

exclamation (or interjection)

● a word that is exclaimed, eg *oh, alas, yes*. You will often find them used with an exclamation mark.

Punctuation

apostrophe (')

- used to show that one or more letters or figures have been missed out of a word or number, eg *can't* for *cannot*, *it's* for *it is*, *the '30s* for *the 1930s*.

- used with *s* to form possessive nouns, eg *the child's dog*, *James's dog*.

brackets (())

- used to separate off comments and asides from the rest of the sentence, eg *The new regulations (six copies of which are enclosed) have been issued to departmental heads.*

capital letters

- used to start the first word in a sentence.

- used to start proper nouns and words derived from proper nouns, eg *Anne, South Africa, a South African dish.*

- used to start all the important words in the titles of books, plays, people, organizations etc, eg *the Prince of Wales, the Department of Health and Social Security.*

colon (:)

- used to create a break between an introductory statement and a statement or phrase that explains or expands on it, eg *There are a great many things money can't buy: love is just one of them.*

- used to mark the beginning of a list of items, eg *Here are the things you will need: a hammer, some nails and a new pane of glass.*

- used in the same way as a comma to introduce direct speech, eg *Peter at once said: 'I want to come too.'*

comma (,)

- used in strings of adjectives and in lists, eg *a cold, wet, windy day.*

- used to mark a pause in a sentence, eg *He seems unfriendly, but I think he's just shy.*

- used to separate direct speech from the rest of the sentence, eg *Peter at once said, 'I want to come too'.*

dash (—)

- used in a similar way to a colon when introducing an explanation, eg *More time, more money and more help—these are the three things we need.*

- sometimes used with a colon to introduce a list that begins on a new line, eg

Things to do before the holiday:—
  stop milk
  cancel papers
  post Mum's birthday card.

- used as a less formal alternative to brackets to mark off an aside, eg *She told me she had inherited the money—over ten thousand pounds—from her aunt.*

- used to indicate ranges, eg *the 1914–18 War, pages 16–26.* In printing this is usually a slightly shorter dash, called an en-rule.

exclamation mark (!)

- used instead of a full stop to indicate emphasis or strong emotion such as anger or surprise, or to show that something has been shouted or exclaimed, eg *What a lovely garden!*; *Help!*; *'I can't stand working here any longer!' she screamed.*

full stop (.)

- used to mark the end of a sentence.

hyphen (-)

- used to link words, eg *an up-to-date report, his mother-in-law, a bunch of forget-me-nots.*

  used to split a word where there is not enough room to fit it into a line of writing.

inverted commas

- *see* quotation marks

question mark (?)

- used instead of a full stop to show that what comes before is a question, eg *How did he manage it?*

quotation marks ('' "")

- used to enclose direct speech (the actual words spoken by someone), eg *'You must help her,' he said.*

semicolon (;)

- used to mark a stronger and more definite break in a sentence than the break made by a comma, but less of a break than that between two separate sentences, which is indicated by a full stop, eg *I will say no more about your behaviour; the subject is closed.*

- used to separate groups of items in a list, eg *Among the area's chief industries are shipbuilding, automobile engineering and steel manufacturing; textiles and clothing; coal mining; and brewing.*

Word Games

• Call my Bluff

The class divides into two teams. Each team divides into groups of three or four. Each group then finds a difficult word in their dictionary, and the members of the team decide who will present the correct definition and who will give false ones. Groups work together to invent false definitions. When all the false definitions are ready, each team chooses a group to represent them, and the game begins. The members of one group present the word they have chosen, and give their definitions. All the members of the opposite team vote on which definition is correct. Scoring is one point for the team which guesses correctly *or* one point for the team which successfully tricks the other. A group from the opposing team now has their turn to present their word and definitions and, after the vote, each team puts forward their next group. Play continues until all teams have presented their chosen word.

• Rhyming Phrases

One person thinks of a rhyming phrase and gives a brief definition of it. For example, you might describe the phrase **fat cat** with the definition 'podgy puss'; or the phrase **wrong song** with the definition 'incorrect ditty'; or the phrase **far star** with the definition 'distant sun'. The person who correctly guesses the rhyming phrase has a turn to pose the next teaser.

• 'Fish' Game

How many words can you write down which end in the letters **-fish**, but which are not the names of different types of fish?

• Suffixes

Think about the words **gormless** and **ruthless**. They look like negatives, but neither of them now corresponds to a positive adjective **gorm** or **ruth**. Write down as many other words as you can think of which seem to be the opposite of non-existent adjectives. If you look in a bigger dictionary, you might find that some of these words did have opposites in the past.

• Snake of Words

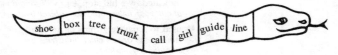

This snake is made up of words which form compounds. For example, **shoe** and **box** make **shoebox**; **box** and **tree** make **box tree** (a type of evergreen tree); **tree** and **trunk** make **tree-trunk**, and so on. What is the longest snake of words you can make? (If you get stuck, you can look in your dictionary to help you. This dictionary contains some common compounds, and larger dictionaries contain many more).

• Clockwise Game

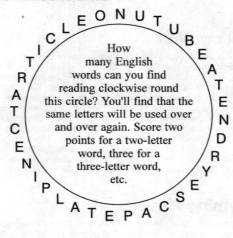

How many English words can you find reading clockwise round this circle? You'll find that the same letters will be used over and over again. Score two points for a two-letter word, three for a three-letter word, etc.